# Ethical Theory and Business

# Ethical Theory and Business

SEVENTH EDITION

Edited by

**Tom L. Beauchamp**
*Georgetown University*

**Norman E. Bowie**
*University of Minnesota*

PEARSON
Prentice Hall

Upper Saddle River, New Jersey 07458

**Library of Congress Cataloging-in-Publication Data**
Ethical theory and business/edited by Tom L. Beauchamp, Norman E. Bowie.—7th ed.
p. cm.
Include bibliographical references.
ISBN 0-13-111632-0
1. Business ethics—United States. 2. Business ethics—United States—Case studies. 3. Industries—Social aspects—United States. 4. Industries—Social aspects—United States—Case studies.
5. Commercial crimes—United States—Cases studies. 6. Consumer protection—Law and legislation—United States—Cases. I. Beauchamp, Tom L. II. Bowie, Norman E. III. Title

HF5387.E82 2004
174'.4—dc21 2003042958

**Senior Acquisitions Editor:** Ross Miller
**Editorial Director:** Charlyce Jones-Owen
**Assistant Editor:** Wendy Yurash
**Editorial Assistant:** Carla Worner
**Director of Marketing:** Beth Gilette Mejia
**Marketing Assistant:** Kimberly Daum
**Managing Editor (Production):** Joanne Riker
**Production Liaison:** Joanne Hakim
**Manufacturing Buyers:** Brian Mackey and Christina Helder
**Cover Art Director:** Jayne Conte
**Cover Design:** Joseph Sengotta
**Cover Illustration/Photo:** Linda Bleck/Stock Illustration Source
**Composition/Full-Service Project Management:** Fran Daniele/Preparé Inc.
**Printer/Binder:** R.R. Donnelly & Sons

---



Pearson Education LTD., London
Pearson Education Singapore, Pte. Ltd
Pearson Education, Canada, Ltd
Pearson Education—Japan
Pearson Education Australia PTY, Limited
Pearson Education North Asia Ltd
Pearson Educación de Mexico, S.A. de C.V.
Pearson Education Malaysia, Pte. Ltd
Pearson Education, Upper Saddle River, New Jersey

PEARSON
Prentice
Hall

10 9 8 7 6 5 4

ISBN 0-13-111632-0

# Contents

CASES

## *Chapter Ten*
## SOCIAL AND ECONOMIC JUSTICE 630

# Preface

When the sixth edition of *Ethical Theory and Business* was published, peace and prosperity reigned in America. The stock market was down from its record highs, but the gains in the various indices were still far above historical averages. Commentators referred to a new economy, and globalization was taken as a given not only in the business community but in the wider community as well. American markets were taken as the model of transparency, and many considered the American economy as the model to be followed nearly everywhere.

As the seventh edition is published the world is very different. The September 11, 2001 terrorist attack imposed huge transaction costs on the U.S. economy and on most of the economies of the industrialized world. Globalization is under attack; the wisdom of the International Monetary Fund and the World Bank is in doubt. Wave upon wave of corporate scandals have undermined trust in the integrity of American markets. Major corporations tainted by scandal now include World Com, Enron, and Global Crossing; all are bankrupt or close to it. A record number of companies have restated their financial results. The accounting firm of Arthur Andersen for all practical matters no longer exists.

The first edition of *Ethical Theory and Business* appeared in 1979. A quarter of a century separates that edition from this new edition. Those 25 years have seen their share of business scandals and ethical controversies. However, none seems to have posed the ethical challenges we see today. We have revised our anthology to take account of this very changed environment.

Chapter 3, the sixth edition chapter on regulation, now has a different focus—responsibility and accountability. Many argue that the key to ethical conduct in business is individual responsibility. If the actions of a businessperson have bad consequences, then it is argued that we should find the person responsible and hold him or her accountable. But recently emphasis has been on systems failure and organizational design. These perspectives remain in this chapter. However, that discussion has been enhanced by our addition of articles that debate whether a corporation can be held morally accountable independently and separately from individuals who work within the corporation. Even our discussion of the Federal Sentencing Guidelines is focused around this issue.

This edition includes an entirely new chapter on Ethical Issues in Information Technology. The two key issues discussed in this chapter are privacy and intellectual property in the computer age. Any student who has downloaded music for free or purchased a product in e-commerce has confronted ethical issues. We believe this chapter is a significant addition to the seventh edition.

Other changes include updated discussions of genetic testing in business, the electronic surveillance of employees, the responsibilities of international corporations to respect human rights, the place of diversity in the workforce, emerging issues in the problem of sexual harassment in the workplace, developments in responsibility for the environment, and the justification of capitalism. We believe these revisions keep *Ethical Theory and Business* in tune with the times in which we live.

In addition to the Prentice Hall reviewers: James C. Peterson, Wingate University; Robert Prevost, Wingate University; and Donald P. Casey, Felician College, several persons have played a crucial role in providing feedback for the seventh edition. Lester Myers has provided detailed feedback on all the articles in the sixth edition, and his influence has been felt as we made selections for this edition. Denis Arnold has worked closely with Norman Bowie for three editions. His experience in using the text and his insistence on the philosophical integrity of the selections has strengthened the seventh edition. In addition, Denis has contributed a number of cases. Finally, Jared Harris, a first-year PhD student in Minnesota's Carlson School of Management, has assisted with editorial work and the provision of several case studies. Able research assistants at Georgetown included Dianna Spring, Sasha Lyutse, Joseph Folio, and David Lawrence. For work with permissions and other editorial work, Norman Bowie has relied on Lois Graham, a loyal staff person at the University of Minnesota—just as Tom Beauchamp has relied on Moheba Hanif at Georgetown. Their hard work and support have been vital to getting this book to the publisher in a timely manner.

Tom L. Beauchamp
*Georgetown University*

Norman E. Bowie
*University of Minnesota*

# CHAPTER ONE

# ETHICAL THEORY AND BUSINESS PRACTICE

CAN LARGE BUSINESS organizations be just? Should the chief obligation of business be to look out for the bottom line? How far should business go to protect and preserve the environment? Is it wrong to share copyrighted music over the Internet? These are some of the many questions that permeate discussions of the role of ethics in business.

The essays and cases in this book provide an opportunity to discuss these questions by reading and reflecting on influential arguments that have been made on these subjects. The goal of this first chapter is to provide a foundation in ethical theory sufficient for reading and critically evaluating the material in the ensuing chapters. The first part of this chapter introduces basic and recurring distinctions, definitions, and issues. The second part examines influential and relevant types of normative ethical theory. The third part discusses "the case method" as an exercise in moral reflection.

## FUNDAMENTAL CONCEPTS AND PROBLEMS

### Morality and Ethical Theory

A distinction between morality and ethical theory appears in several essays in this volume. *Morality* is concerned with social practices defining right and wrong. These practices—together with other kinds of customs, rules, and mores—are transmitted within cultures and institutions from generation to generation. Similar to political constitutions and natural languages, morality exists prior to the acceptance (or rejection) of its standards by particular individuals. In this respect morality cannot be purely a personal policy or code and is certainly not confined to the rules in professional codes of conduct adopted by corporations and professional associations.

In contrast to *morality*, the terms *ethical theory* and *moral philosophy* point to reflection on the nature and justification of right actions. These words refer to attempts to introduce clarity, substance, and precision of argument into the domain of morality. Although many people go through life with an understanding of morality dictated by their culture, other persons are not satisfied to conform to the morality of society. They want difficult questions answered: Is what our society forbids wrong? Are social values the best values? What is the purpose of morality? Does religion have anything to do with morality? Do the moral rules of society fit together in a unified whole? If there are conflicts and inconsistencies in our practices and beliefs, how should they be resolved? What should people do when facing a moral problem for which society has, as yet, provided no instruction?

Moral philosophers seek to answer such questions and to put moral beliefs and social practices of morality into a unified and defensible shape. Sometimes this task involves challenging traditional moral beliefs by assessing the quality of moral arguments and suggesting modifications in existing beliefs. Morality, we might say, consists of what persons ought to do in order to conform to society's norms of behavior, whereas ethical theory concerns the philosophical reasons for and against aspects of the morality stipulated by society. Usually the latter effort centers on *justification*: Philosophers seek to justify a system of standards or some moral point of view on the basis of carefully analyzed and defended concepts and principles such as respect for autonomy, distributive justice, equal treatment, human rights, beneficence, and truthfulness.

Most moral principles are already embedded in public morality, but usually in a vague and underanalyzed form. Justice is a good example. Recurrent topics in the pages of the *Wall Street Journal*, *Fortune*, *Business Week*, and other leading business journals often discuss the justice of the present system of corporate and individual taxation as well as the salaries paid to chief executive officers. However, an extended or detailed analysis of principles of justice is virtually never provided in the media. Such matters are left at an intuitive level, where the correctness of a moral point of view is assumed, without argumentation. Yet the failure to provide anything more than a superficial justification, in terms of intuitive principles learned from parents or peers, leaves people unable to defend their principles when challenged. In a society with many diverse views of morality, one can be fairly sure that one's principles will be challenged.

## Morality and Prudence

Many students do not encounter moral philosophy as a topic of study until college or graduate school. Morality, however, is learned by virtually every young child as part of the acculturation process. The first step in this process is learning to distinguish moral rules from rules of prudence (self-interest). This task can be difficult, because the two kinds of rules are taught simultaneously, without being distinguished by the children's teachers. For example, people are constantly reminded in their early years to observe rules such as, "Don't touch the hot stove," "Don't cross the street without looking both ways," "Brush your teeth after meals," and "Eat your vegetables." Most of these "oughts" and "ought nots" are instructions in self-interest—that is, rules of prudence, but moral rules are taught at the same time. Parents, teachers, and peers teach that certain things *ought not* to be done because they are "wrong" (morally) and that certain things *ought* to be done because they are "right" (morally): "Don't pull your sister's hair." "Don't take money from your mother's pocketbook." "Share your toys." "Write a thank-you note to Grandma." These moral instructions seek to control actions that affect the interests of other people. As people mature, they learn what society expects of them in terms of taking into account the interests of other people.

One of the most common observations in business is that self-interest and good ethics generally coincide, because it is usually in one's interest to act morally. This fact makes evaluating another's conduct difficult and may tend to confuse moral reasoning with prudential reasoning. A simple example of moral and prudential reasoning run together in business is found in the decision of the Marriott Corporation to make a concerted effort to hire persons who had been on welfare. These individuals had often been considered high-risk as employees, but changes in the U.S. welfare system in the late 1990s forced many welfare recipients to seek work. Marriott was one of the few major companies to take the initiative to hire them in large numbers. Such behavior might be considered an example of moral goodwill and ethical altruism. Although corporate officials at Marriott clearly believed that their decision was ethically sound and promoted the public good, they also believed that their initiative to hire former welfare recipients was good business. J. W. Marriott Jr. said, "We're getting good employees for the long term, but we're also helping these communities. If we don't step up in these inner cities and provide work, they'll never pull out of it. But it makes bottom line sense. If it didn't, we wouldn't do it."[1]

The mixture of moral language with the language of prudence is often harmless. Many people are more concerned about the *actions* businesses take than with their *motivations* to perform those actions. These people will be indifferent as to whether businesses use the language of prudence or the language of morality to justify what they do, as long as they do the right thing. This distinction between motives and actions is very important to philosophers, however, because a business practice that might be prudentially justified may lack moral merit and may even be morally wrong. History has shown how some actions that were long accepted or at least condoned in the business community were eventually condemned as morally dubious. Examples include pollution of the air and water, plant relocation purely for economic gain, and large political contributions and lobbying directed at people of political influence.

Businesspeople often reflect on the morality of their actions not because it is prudent to do so but because it is right to do so. For example, Elo TouchSystems, Inc., a subsidiary of Raychem Corporation that manufactures computer and other monitors, decided to relocate the company from Oak Ridge, Tennessee, to Freemont, California. As a matter of fidelity to its 300 employees, the company attempted to find new jobs for them in the Oak Ridge area by placing advertisements, sponsoring job fairs, and the like. It also offered generous bonuses for those who would relocate to California. In light of the pool of talent known to the company to be available in California, none of this activity in Tennessee seemed in the company's prudential interest. It simply seemed the morally appropriate policy.

It is widely believed that acting morally is in the interest of business, and thus prudence seems to be one strong motive—perhaps the main motive—for acting ethically. However, throughout this text we will repeatedly see that prudence often dictates a different business decision than does morality.

## Morality and Law

Business ethics in the United States is currently involved in an entangled, complex, and mutually stimulating relationship with law, as is illustrated in the legal cases reprinted near the end of the following chapters. Morality and law share concerns over matters of basic social importance and often have in common certain principles, obligations, and criteria of evidence. Law is the public's agency for translating morality into explicit social guidelines and practices and for stipulating punishments for offenses. Chapter selections mention both case law (judge-made law expressed in court decisions) and statutory law (federal and state statutes and their accompanying administrative regulations). In these forms law has forced vital issues before the public and is frequently the source of emerging issues in business ethics. Case law, in particular, has established influential precedents that provide material for reflection on both legal and moral questions.

Some have said that corporate concern about business ethics can be reduced or eliminated by turning problems over to the legal department. The operative idea is, "Let the lawyers decide; if it's legal, it's moral." Although this tactic would simplify matters, moral evaluation needs to be distinguished from legal evaluation. Despite an intersection between morals and law, the law is not the sole repository of a society's moral standards and values, even when the law is directly concerned with moral problems. A law-abiding person is not necessarily morally sensitive or virtuous, and the fact that something is legally acceptable does not imply that it is morally acceptable. For example, the doctrine of employment at will permits employers to fire employees for unjust reasons and is (within certain limits) legal, yet such firings are often morally unacceptable. Many questions are raised in chapters below about the morality of business actions, such as plant relocation and mergers that cause unemployment, even though such actions are not illegal.

A typical example is the following: It was perfectly legal when Houston financier Charles E. Hurwitz doubled the rate of tree cutting in the nation's largest privately owned virgin redwood forest. He did so to reduce the debt he incurred when his company, the Maxxam Group, borrowed money to complete a hostile takeover of Pacific Lumber Company, which owned the redwoods. Before the takeover, Pacific Lumber had followed a conservative cutting policy but nonetheless had consistently operated at a profit. Despite the legality of the new clear-cutting policy initiated by the new owner, it has been criticized as immoral.[2]

A related problem involves the belief that a person found guilty under law is therefore morally guilty. Such judgments are not necessarily correct, as they depend on either the intention of the agents or the moral acceptability of the law on which the judgment has been reached. For example, if a chemical company is legally liable for polluting the environment or a pharmaceutical firm is liable for a drug that has harmed certain patients, it does not follow that any form of moral wrongdoing, culpability, or guilt is associated with the activity.

Asbestos litigation is a well-known example. Because of the strength, durability, and fire-resistance of asbestos, it was used in thousands of consumer, automotive, scientific, industrial, and maritime processes and products. Virtually no serious social attention was paid to asbestos in the United States until 1964, when a strong link was established between asbestos dust and disease. As many as 27 million workers in the United States may have been exposed to this fiber, and 100 million people may have been exposed to asbestos in buildings. Manufacturers did not know about these problems of disease until around 1964; nonetheless, beginning with the 1982 bankruptcy of the Johns-Manville Corporation, many corporations have been successfully sued. The problem continues to escalate today for companies such as Georgia-Pacific and Halliburton. From 2000 through spring 2002 there were 22 asbestos-related bankruptcies (compared to 18 for all of the 1990s). Although asbestos manufacturers and their customers originally had good intentions and good products, they paid a steep price under the law.[3]

Furthermore, the courts have often been accused, with some justification, of causing moral inequities through court judgments rendered against corporations. Here are some examples:[4] (1) Monsanto Chemical was successfully sued for $200 million, although the presiding judge asserted that there was no credible evidence linking Monsanto's Agent Orange to the severe harms that had been described in the case. (2) Chevron Oil was successfully sued for mislabeling its cans of paraquat, although the offending label conformed exactly to federal regulations, which permitted no other form of label to be used. (3) Although whooping cough vaccine indisputably reduces the risk of this disease for children who receive the vaccine, almost no manufacturer will produce it for fear of costly suits brought under product liability laws.

In each instance it is easy to understand why critics have considered various regulations, legislation, and case-law decisions to be morally unjustified. Taken together, these considerations lead to the following conclusion: If something is legal, it is not necessarily moral; if something is illegal, it is not necessarily immoral. To discharge one's legal responsibilities is not necessarily to discharge one's moral responsibilities.

## The Rule of Conscience

The slogan "Let your conscience be your guide" has long been, for many, what morality is all about. Yet, despite their admiration for persons of conscience, philosophers have typically judged appeals to conscience as alone insufficient and untrustworthy for ethical judgment. Consciences vary radically from person to person and time to time; moreover, they are often altered by circumstance, religious belief, childhood, and training. One example is found in Stanley Kresge, the son of the founder of S. S. Kresge Company—now known as the "K-Mart" Corporation—who is a teetotaler for religious reasons. When the company started selling beer and wine, Kresge sold all his stock. His conscience, he said, would not let him make a profit on alcohol. The company, though, dismissed his objection as "his own business" and said that it sees nothing wrong with earning profits on alcohol.[5] A second example is found in many individuals who believe that business has been conducted in ways that damage the environment. These feelings are particularly strong in the Pacific Northwest where the lumber industry has allegedly threatened endangered species such as the spotted owl. The consciences of members of Earth First have been so aroused that they have engaged in acts of ecoterrorism such as putting large spikes in trees that can injure loggers who are cutting them. The members of Earth First believe that they are acting as required by conscience. But whether their acts are morally acceptable is seriously in doubt.

The reliability of conscience, then, is not self-certifying. Moral justification must be based on a source external to conscience.

## Approaches to the Study of Morality

Morality and ethical theory can be studied and developed by a variety of methods, but three general approaches have dominated the literature. Two of these approaches describe and analyze morality, presumably without taking moral positions. The other approach takes a moral position and appeals to morality or ethical theory to underwrite judgments. These three approaches are: (1) Descriptive, (2) Conceptual, and (3) Prescriptive (normative). These categories do not express rigid and always clearly distinguishable approaches. Nonetheless, when understood as broad, polar, and contrasting positions, they can serve as models of inquiry and as valuable distinctions.

Social scientists often refer to the *descriptive approach* as the *scientific study* of ethics. Factual description and explanation of moral behavior and beliefs, as performed by anthropologists, sociologists, and historians, are typical of this approach. Moral attitudes, codes, and beliefs that are described include corporate policies on sexual harassment and codes of ethics in trade associations. Examples of this approach can be found in *Harvard Business Review* articles and *Forbes* magazine polls that report what business executives believe is morally acceptable and unacceptable.

The second approach involves the *conceptual study* of ethics. Here, the meanings of central terms in ethics such as *right, obligation, justice, good, virtue,* and *responsibility* are analyzed. Crucial terms in business ethics such as *liability* and *deception* can be given this same kind of careful conceptual attention. The proper analysis of the term *morality* (as defined at the beginning of this chapter) and the distinction between the moral and the nonmoral are typical examples of these conceptual problems.

The third approach, *prescriptive (normative) ethics,* is a prescriptive study attempting to formulate and defend basic moral norms. Normative moral philosophy aims at determining what *ought* to be done, which needs to be distinguished from what *is*, in fact, practiced. Ideally, an ethical theory provides reasons for adopting a whole system of moral principles or virtues. *Utilitarianism* and *Kantianism* are widely discussed theories, but they are not the only such theories. Utilitarians argue that there is but a single fundamental principle determining right action, which can be roughly stated as follows: "An action is morally right if and only if it produces at least as great a balance of value over disvalue as any available alternative action." Kantians, by contrast, have argued for principles that specify obligations rather than a balance of value. For example, one of Kant's best-known principles of obligation is "Never treat another person merely as a means to your own goals," even if doing so creates a net balance of positive value. Both forms of these theories, together with other dimensions of ethical theory, are examined in the second part of this chapter.

Principles of normative ethics are commonly used to treat specific moral problems such as famine, conflict of interest, improper disclosure of information, environmental pollution, mistreatment of animals, and racial and sexual discrimination. This use of ethical theory is often referred to, somewhat misleadingly, as *applied ethics*. Philosophical treatment of medical ethics, engineering ethics, journalistic ethics, jurisprudence, and business ethics involves distinct areas that employ general ethical principles to attempt to resolve moral problems that commonly arise in the professions.

Substantially the same general ethical principles apply to the problems across professional fields and in areas beyond professional ethics as well. One might appeal to principles of justice, for example, to illuminate and resolve issues of taxation, health care distribution, environmental responsibility, criminal punishment, and racial discrimination. Similarly, principles of veracity (truthfulness) apply to debates about secrecy and deception in international politics, misleading advertisements in business ethics, balanced reporting in journalistic ethics, and disclosure of illness to a patient in medical ethics. Increased clarity about the general conditions under which truth must be told and when it may be withheld would presumably enhance understanding of moral requirements in each of these areas.

The exercise of sound judgment in business practice together with appeals to ethical theory are central in the essays and cases in this volume. Rarely is there a straightforward "application" of principles that mechanically resolves problems. Principles are more commonly *specified*, that is, made more concrete for the context, than applied. Much of the best work in contemporary business ethics involves arguments for how to specify principles to handle particular problems.

## Relativism and Objectivity of Belief

Some writers have contended that moral views simply express the ways in which a culture accommodates the desires of its people. Cultural relativists note that moral standards vary from place to place. In the early part of the twentieth century, defenders of relativism used the discoveries of anthropologists in the South Sea Islands, Africa, and South America as evidence of a diversity of moral practices throughout the world. Their empirical discoveries about what is the case led them to the conclusion that rightness is contingent on cultural beliefs and that the concepts of rightness and wrongness are meaningless apart from the specific contexts in which they arise. The claim is that patterns of culture can only be understood as unique wholes and that moral beliefs about normal behavior are closely connected in a culture.

***Ethical Relativism.*** These *descriptive* claims about what is the case in cultures have often been used to justify a *normative* position known as ethical relativism. *Ethical relativism* asserts that whatever a culture thinks is right or wrong really is right or wrong for the members of that culture. This thesis is normative, because it makes a value judgment; it delineates *which standards or norms correctly determine right and wrong behavior.* Thus, if the Swedish tradition allows abortion, then abortion really is morally permissible in Sweden. If the Irish tradition forbids abortion, then abortion really is wrong in Ireland. If ethical relativism is correct, then there is no criterion independent of one's culture for determining whether a practice really is right or wrong.

Ethical relativism provides a theoretical basis for those who challenge what they consider to be the imposition of Western values on the rest of the world. Specifically, some spokespersons in Asia have criticized what they regard as the attempts of westerners to impose their values (as the normatively correct values) on Asian societies. Despite the influence of relativism and multiculturalism, there have been many recent attempts by both government agencies and multinational corporations to promulgate international codes of business conduct that surmount relativism (see Chapter 9). Moreover, moral philosophers have tended to reject relativism and it is important to understand why.

First, moral philosophers ask, what does the argument from the fact of cultural diversity reveal? When early anthropologists probed beneath surface "moral" disagreements, they often discovered agreement at deeper levels on more basic values. For example, one anthropologist discovered a tribe in which parents, after raising their children and when still in a relatively healthy state, would climb a high tree. Their children would then shake the tree until the parents fell to the ground and died. This cultural practice seems vastly different from Western practices. The anthropologist discovered, however, that the tribe believed that people went into the afterlife in the same bodily state in which they left this life. Their children, who wanted them to enter the afterlife in a healthy state, were no less concerned about their parents than are children in Western cultures. Although cultural disagreement exists concerning the afterlife (a disagreement about what is or is not the case), there is no ultimate *moral* disagreement over the moral principles determining how children should treat their parents.

Despite their obvious differences of practice and belief, people often actually agree about ultimate moral standards. For example, both Germany and the United States have laws to protect consumers from the adverse affects of new drugs and to bring drugs to the market as quickly as possible so that lives are saved. Yet Germany and the United States have different standards for making the tradeoff between protecting from side effects and saving lives as soon as possible. This suggests that two cultures may agree about basic principles of morality, yet disagree about how to implement those principles in particular situations.

In many "moral controversies" people may differ only because they have different factual beliefs. For instance, individuals often differ over appropriate actions to protect the environment, not because they have different sets of standards about environmental ethics but because they hold different factual views about how certain discharges of chemicals and airborne particles will or will not harm the environment. Identical sets of normative standards might be invoked in their arguments about environmental protection, yet different policies and actions might be recommended.

It is therefore essential to distinguish *relativism of judgments* from *relativism of standards*. Different judgments may rely upon the same general standards for their justification. Relativism of judgment is so pervasive in human social life that it would be foolish to deny it. People may differ in their judgments regarding whether one policy for keeping hospital information confidential is more acceptable than another, but it does not follow that they have different moral standards of confidentiality. The people may hold the same moral standard(s) on protecting confidentiality but differ over how to implement the standard(s).

However, these observations do not decide whether a relativism of standards provides the most adequate account of morality. If moral conflict did turn out to be a matter of a fundamental conflict of moral *standards*, such conflict could not be removed even if there were perfect agreement about the facts, concepts, and background beliefs of a case. Suppose, then, that disagreement does in fact exist at the deepest level of moral thinking—that is, suppose that two cultures disagree on basic or fundamental norms. It does not follow even from this *relativity of standards* that there is no ultimate norm or set of norms in which everyone *ought* to believe. To see why, consider the following analogy to religious disagreement: From the fact that people have incompatible religious or atheistic beliefs, it does not follow that there is no single correct set of religious or atheistic propositions. Nothing more than skepticism seems justified by the facts about religion that are adduced by anthropology. Similarly, nothing more than such skepticism about the moral standards would be justified if fundamental conflicts of *moral standards* were discovered in ethics.

***An Argument against Ethical Relativism.*** The evident inconsistency of ethical relativism with many of our most cherished moral beliefs is a reason to be doubtful of it. No general theory of ethical relativism is likely to convince us that a belief is acceptable merely because others believe in it strongly enough, although that is exactly the commitment of this theory. At least some moral views seem relatively more enlightened, no matter how great the variability of beliefs. The idea that practices such as slavery cannot be evaluated across cultures by some common standard seems morally unacceptable, not morally enlightened. It is one thing to suggest that such beliefs might be *excused*, still another to suggest that they are *right*.

When two parties argue about some serious, divisive, and contested moral issue—for example, conflicts of interest in business—people tend to think that some fair and justified compromise may be reached. People seldom infer from the mere fact of a conflict between beliefs that there is no way to judge one view as correct or as better argued or more reasonable than the other. The more absurd the position advanced by one party, the more convinced others become that some views are mistaken, unreasonable, or require supplementation.

## Moral Disagreements

Even if ethical relativism is unacceptable, we still must confront the indisputable fact of moral disagreement. In any pluralistic culture many conflicts of value exist. In this volume several controversies and dilemmas are examined, such as withholding pertinent information in business deals, whistleblowing in industry, advertising intended to manipulate people's feelings, practicing preferential hiring policies, and the like. Although some disagreements seem overwhelming, there are ways to resolve them or at least to reduce the level of disagreement. Several methods have been employed in the past to deal constructively with moral disagreements, each of which deserves recognition as a method of easing disagreement and conflict.

***Obtaining Objective Information.*** Many moral disagreements can be at least partially resolved by obtaining additional factual information on which moral controversies turn. Earlier it was shown how useful such information can be in trying to ascertain whether cultural variations in belief are fundamental. Unfortunately, it has often been assumed that moral disputes are by definition produced solely by differences over moral principles or their application and not by a lack of scientific or factual information. This assumption is misleading, inasmuch as moral disputes—that is, disputes over what morally ought or ought not to be done—often have nonmoral elements as their main ingredients. For example, debates over the allocation of tax dollars to prevent accidents or disease in the workplace often become bogged down in factual issues of whether particular measures such as the use of protective masks or lower levels of toxic chemicals actually function best to prevent death and disease.

Yet another example is provided by the dispute between Greenpeace and Royal Dutch Shell. After considerable investigation, Royal Dutch Shell proposed to sink a loading and storage buoy for oil in the North Sea (off England). Despite some evidence that such an operation posed no environmental danger, Greenpeace conducted protests and even used a group of small boats to thwart the attempt. Royal Dutch Shell yielded to its critics, and the buoy was cut up and made into a quay in Norway. Later, however, even Greenpeace came to the conclusion that new facts indicated that there had never been any serious environmental danger.

Controversial issues such as the following are laced with issues of both values and facts: How satisfactorily toxic substances are monitored in the workplace; how a start-up company has "appropriated" an established company's trade secrets; the effects of access to pornography through the Internet; whether an extension of current copyright laws would reduce sharing of copyrighted recordings on the Internet; and the manufacture, dissemination, and advertisement of vaccines for medical use. The arguments used by disagreeing parties may turn on a dispute about liberty, harm, or justice and therefore may be primarily moral; but they may also rest on factual disagreements over, for example, the effects of a product, service, or activity. Information may thus have only limited bearing on the resolution of some controversies, yet it may have a direct and almost overpowering influence in others.

***Definitional Clarity.*** Sometimes controversies have been settled by reaching conceptual or definitional agreement over the language used by disputing parties. Controversies discussed in Chapter 6 over the morality of affirmative action and sexual harassment, for example, are often needlessly complicated because different senses of these expressions are employed, and yet disputing parties may have much invested in their particular definitions. If there is no common point of contention in such cases, parties will be addressing entirely separate issues through their conceptual assumptions. Often these parties will not have a bona fide moral disagreement.

Although conceptual agreement provides no guarantee that a dispute will be settled, it will facilitate direct discussion of the outstanding issues. For this reason, many essays in this volume dwell at some length on problems of conceptual clarity.

***Example–Counterexample.*** Resolution of moral controversies can also be aided by posing examples and opposed counterexamples, that is, by bringing forward cases or examples that are favorable to one point of view and counterexamples that are in opposition. For instance, a famous case against AT&T involving a dispute over discriminatory hiring and promotion between the company and the Equal Employment Opportunities Commission (EEOC) was handled through the citation of statistics and examples that (allegedly) documented the claims made by each side. AT&T showed that 55 percent of the employees on its payroll were women and that 33 percent of all management positions were held by women. To sharpen its allegation of discriminatory practices in the face of this evidence, the EEOC countered by citing a government study demonstrating that 99 percent of all telephone operators were female, whereas only 1 percent of craft workers were female. Such use of example and counterexample serves to weigh the strength of conflicting considerations.

***Analysis of Arguments and Positions.*** Finally, a serviceable method of philosophical inquiry is that of exposing the inadequacies in and unexpected consequences of arguments and positions. A moral argument that leads to conclusions that a proponent is not prepared to defend and did not previously anticipate will have to be changed, and the distance between those who disagree will perhaps be reduced by this process. Inconsistencies not only in reasoning but in organizational schemes or pronouncements can be uncovered. However, in a context of controversy, sharp attacks or critiques are unlikely to eventuate in an agreement unless a climate of reason prevails. A fundamental axiom of successful negotiation is "reason and be open to reason." The axiom holds for moral discussion as well as any other disagreement.

No contention is made here that moral disagreements can always be resolved or that every reasonable person must accept the same method for approaching such problems. Many moral disagreements may not be resolvable by any of the four methods that have been discussed. A single ethical theory or method may never be developed to resolve all disagreements adequately, and the pluralism of cultural beliefs often presents a considerable barrier to the resolution of issues. Given the possibility of continual disagreement, the resolution of crosscultural conflicts such as those faced by multinational corporations may prove especially elusive. However, if something is to be done about these problems, a resolution seems more likely to occur if the methods outlined in this section are used.

## The Problem of Egoism

Attitudes in business have often been deemed fundamentally egoistic. Executives and corporations are said to act purely from prudence—that is, each business is out to promote solely its own interest. Some people say that the corporation has no other interest, because its goal is to be as successful in competition as possible.

The philosophical theory called *egoism* has familiar origins. Each person has been confronted, for example, with occasions on which a choice must be made between spending money on oneself or on some worthy charitable enterprise. When one elects to purchase new clothes for oneself rather than contribute to a university scholarship fund for poor students, self-interest is being given priority over the interests of others. Egoism generalizes beyond these occasions to all human choices. The egoist contends that all choices either involve or should involve self-promotion as their sole objective. Thus, a person's or a corporation's goal and perhaps only obligation is self-promotion. No sacrifice or obligation is owed to others.

***Psychological Egoism.*** There are two main varieties of egoism: psychological egoism and ethical egoism. Psychological egoism is the view that everyone is always motivated to act in his or her perceived self-interest. This factual theory regarding human motivation offers an *explanation* of human conduct, in contrast to a *justification* of human conduct. It claims that people always do what pleases them or what is in their interest. Popular ways of expressing this viewpoint include the following: "People are at heart selfish, even if they appear to be unselfish"; "People look out for Number One first"; "In the long run, everybody does what he or she wants to do"; and "No matter what a person says, he or she acts for the sake of personal satisfaction."

Psychological egoism presents a serious challenge to moral philosophy. If this theory is correct, there is no purely altruistic moral motivation. Yet normative ethics (with the exception of ethical egoism) appears to presuppose that people ought to behave in accordance with certain moral principles, whether or not such behavior promotes their own interests. If people *must act* in their own interest, to ask them to sacrifice for others would be absurd. Accordingly, if psychological egoism is true, the whole enterprise of normative ethics is futile.

Those who accept psychological egoism are convinced by their observation of themselves and others that people are entirely self-centered in their motivation. Conversely, those who reject the theory do so not only because they see many examples of altruistic behavior in the lives of friends, saints, heroes, and public servants, but also because contemporary anthropology, psychology, and biology offer some compelling studies of sacrificial behavior. Even if it is conceded that people are basically selfish, critics of egoism maintain that there are at least some outstanding examples of preeminently unselfish actions such as when corporations cut profits in order to provide public services (see Chapter 2) and when employees "blow the whistle" on unsafe or otherwise improper business practices even though they could lose their jobs and suffer social ostracism (see Chapter 5).

The defender of psychological egoism is not impressed by the exemplary lives of saints and heroes or by social practices of corporate sacrifice. The psychological egoist maintains that all those persons who expend effort to help others, to promote fairness in competition, to promote the general welfare, or to risk their lives for the welfare of others are, underneath it all, acting to promote themselves. By sacrificing for their children, parents seek the satisfaction that comes from their children's development or achievements. By following society's moral and legal codes, people avoid both the police and social ostracism.

Egoists maintain that no matter how self-sacrificing a person's behavior may at times seem, the desire behind the action is self-regarding. One is ultimately out for oneself, whether in the long or the short run, and whether one realizes it or not. Egoists view self-promoting actions as perfectly compatible with behavior that others categorize as altruistic. For example, many corporations have adopted "enlightened self-interest" policies through which they are responsive to community needs and promote worker satisfaction to promote their corporate image and ultimately their earnings. The clever person or corporation can appear to be unselfish, but the action's true character depends on the *motivation* behind the appearance. Apparently altruistic agents may simply believe that an unselfish appearance best promotes their long-range interests. From the egoist's point of view, the fact that some (pseudo?) sacrifices may be necessary in the short run does not count against egoism.

Consider a typical example. In mid-1985 Illinois Bell argued before the Illinois Commerce Commission that its competitors should be allowed full access to markets and that there should be no regulation to protect Illinois Bell from its competitors. Illinois Bell had long been protected by such regulation, under which it had grown to be a successful $2.7 billion company. Why, then, was it now arguing that a completely free market would be the fairest business arrangement? *Forbes* magazine asked, "Is this 'altruism' or is it 'enlightened self-interest'?" *Forbes* editors answered that, despite the appearance of altruism, what Illinois Bell wanted was "to get the state regulators off their backs" so that the company would be able to compete more successfully with fewer constraints and to avoid losing business to large companies that could set up their own telephone systems. Self-interest, not fairness, was, according to *Forbes*, the proper explanation of Illinois Bell's behavior.[6]

Even if Illinois Bell's behavior is best explained as motivated by self-interest, it need not follow that all human behavior can be best explained as motivated by self-interest. The question remains: Is psychological egoism correct? At one level this question can be answered only by empirical data—by looking at the facts. Significantly, there is a large body of evidence both from observations of daily practice and from experiments in psychological laboratories that counts against the universality of egoistic motivation. The evidence from daily practice is not limited to heroic action but includes such mundane practices as voting and leaving tips in restaurants and hotels where a person does not expect to return and has nothing to gain.

When confronted with such conflicting empirical data, the dispute often is raised from the empirical level to the conceptual. It is tempting for the psychological egoist to make the theory *necessarily* true because of the difficulties in proving it to be *empirically* true. When confronted with what look like altruistic acts, egoists may appeal to unconscious motives of self-interest or claim that every act is based on some desire of the person performing the act and that acting on that desire is what is meant by *self-interest.*

The latter explanation seems to be a conceptual or verbal trick: The egoist has changed the meaning of *self-interest.* At first, *self-interest* meant "acting exclusively on behalf of one's own self-serving interest." Now the word has been redefined to mean "acting on any interest one has." Yet the central questions remain unresolved: Are there different kinds of human motives? Do people sometimes have an interest in acting for themselves and at other times on behalf of others, or do people act only for themselves? Philosophy and psychology have yet to establish that people never act contrary to perceived self-interest; for this reason psychological egoism remains a speculative hypothesis.

***Ethical Egoism.*** Ethical egoism is a theory stating that the only valid standard of conduct is the obligation to promote one's well-being above everyone else's. Whereas psychological egoism is a descriptive, psychological theory about human motivation, ethical egoism is a normative theory about what people ought to do. According to psychological egoism, people always *do* act on the basis of perceived self-interest. According to ethical egoism, people always *ought* to act on the basis of perceived self-interest.

Ethical egoism is dramatically different from common moral beliefs. Consider maxims, such as "You're a sucker if you don't put yourself first and others second." This maxim is generally thought unacceptable, because it is believed that people must return a lost wallet to a known owner and that they must correct a bank loan officer's errors in their favor. Nevertheless, questions about why people should look out for the interests of others on such occasions have troubled many reflective persons. Some have concluded that acting against one's interest is contrary to reason. These thinkers, who regard conventional morality as tinged with irrational sentiment and indefensible constraints on the individual, are the supporters of ethical egoism. It is not their view that one should always ignore the interests of others, but rather that one should consider the interests of others only when it suits one's own interests.

What would society be like if ethical egoism were the conventional, prevailing theory of proper conduct? Some philosophers and political theorists have argued that anarchism and chaos would result unless preventive measures were adopted. A classic statement of this position was made by the philosopher Thomas Hobbes.

Imagine a world with limited resources, he said, where persons are approximately equal in their ability to harm one another and where everyone acts exclusively in his or her interest. Hobbes argued that in such a world everyone would be at everyone else's throat and society would be plagued by anxiety, violence, and constant danger. As Hobbes declared, life would be "solitary, poor, nasty, brutish, and short."[7] However, Hobbes also assumed that human beings are sufficiently rational to recognize their interests. To avoid the war of all against all, he urged his readers to form a powerful government to protect themselves.

Egoists accept Hobbes's view in the following form: Any clever person will realize that she or he has no moral obligations to others besides those obligations she or he voluntarily assumes because it is in one's own interest to agree to abide by them. Each person should accept moral rules and assume specific obligations only when doing so promotes one's self-interest. Even if one agrees to live under laws of the state that are binding on everyone, one should obey rules and laws only to protect oneself and to create a situation of communal living that is personally advantageous. One should also back out of an obligation whenever it becomes clear that it is to one's long-range disadvantage to fulfill the obligation. When confronted by a social revolution, the questionable trustworthiness of a colleague, or an incompetent administration at one's place of employment, no one is under an obligation to obey the law, fulfill contracts, or tell the truth. These obligations exist only because one assumes them, and one ought to assume them only as long as doing so promotes one's own interest.

An arrangement whereby everyone acts on more or less fixed rules such as those found in conventional moral and legal systems would produce the most desirable state of affairs from an egoistic point of view. The reason is that such rules arbitrate conflicts and make social life more agreeable. These rules would include, for example, familiar moral and legal principles of justice that are intended to make everyone's situation more secure and stable.

Only an unduly narrow conception of self-interest, the egoist might argue, leads critics to conclude that the egoist would not willingly observe conventional rules of justice. If society can be structured to resolve personal conflicts through courts and other peaceful means, egoists will view it as in their interest to accept those binding social arrangements, just as they will perceive it as prudent to treat other individuals favorably in personal contacts. Notice that the egoist is not saying that his or her interests are served by promoting the good of others but rather is claiming that his or her personal interests are served by observing impartial rules irrespective of the outcome for others. Egoists do not care about the welfare of others unless it affects their welfare, and this desire for personal well-being alone motivates acceptance of the conventional rules of morality.

***Egoistic Business Practices and Utilitarian Results.*** A different view from that of Hobbes, and one that has been extremely influential in the philosophy of the business community, is found in Adam Smith's economic and moral writings. Smith believed that the public good evolves out of a suitably restrained clash of competing individual interests. As individuals pursue their self-interest, the interactive process is guided by an "invisible hand," ensuring that the public interest is achieved. Ironically, according to Smith, egoism in commercial transactions leads not to the war of all against all, but rather to a utilitarian outcome—that is, to the largest number of benefits for the largest number of persons. The free market is, Smith thought, a better method of achieving the public good than the highly visible and authoritarian hand of Hobbes's all-powerful sovereign state.

Smith believed that government should be limited in order to protect individual freedom. At the same time, he recognized that concern with freedom and self-interest could get out of control. Hence, he proposed that minimal state regulatory activity is needed to provide and enforce the rules of the competitive game. Smith's picture of a restrained egoistic world has captivated many people in the business and economic community. They, like Smith, do not picture themselves as selfish and indifferent to the interests of others, and they recognize that a certain element of cooperation is essential if their interests are to flourish. These people recognize that when their interests conflict with the interests of others, they should pursue their interests within the established rules of the competitive game. Within the rules of business practice, they understand ethics as the maxims of a suitably restrained egoist. Their view is restrained because self-interest is kept within the bounds of the prevailing rules of business for the sake of the common good.

Many people in the business community have actively supported the view that a restrained egoism leads to commendable utilitarian outcomes. This is one form of defense of a free market economy; competition among individual firms advances the good of society as a whole. Hence, a popular view of business ethics might be captured by the phrase "Ethical egoism leads to utilitarian outcomes." As Smith said, corporations and individuals pursuing their individual interests thereby promote the public good, so long as they abide by the rules that protect the public.

An example is found in the alleviation of world hunger. Many now argue that a better life for the poor in many nations is the result of capitalistic behavior. They claim that, as a matter of historical fact, capitalistic investment and productivity increase jobs, social welfare, social cooperation, wealth in society, and morally responsible behavior. The thesis is that these benefits accrue widely across the society, affecting both poor and wealthy, even if the goal of capitalists is purely their own economic gain.[8]

## NORMATIVE ETHICAL THEORY

The central question discussed in this section is "What constitutes an acceptable ethical standard for business practice, and by what authority is the standard acceptable?" One time-honored answer is that the acceptability of a moral standard is determined by prevailing practices in business or by authoritative, profession-generated documents such as codes. Many businesspersons find this viewpoint congenial and therefore do not see the need for revisions in practices that they find already comfortable and adequate.

Professional standards do play a role in business ethics and will be discussed in this book in some detail. Ultimately, however, the internal morality of business does not supply a comprehensive framework for the many pressing questions of business ethics. Morality in the world of business evolves in the face of social change and critical philosophical argument; it cannot rely entirely on its own historical traditions. Its standards therefore need to be justified in terms of independent ethical standards such as those of public opinion, law, and philosophical ethics—just as the moral norms of a culture need to be justified by more than an appeal to those norms themselves. For this reason, the later parts in this section are devoted to a discussion of widely discussed theories and analyses of morality in the history of philosophy.

## Utilitarian Theories

Utilitarian theories hold that the moral worth of actions or practices is determined by their consequences. An action or practice is right if it leads to the best possible balance of good consequences over bad consequences for all the parties affected. In taking this perspective, utilitarians believe that the purpose or function of morality is to promote human welfare by minimizing harms and maximizing benefits.

The first developed utilitarian philosophical writings were those of David Hume (1711–1776), Jeremy Bentham (1748–1832), and John Stuart Mill (1806–1873). Mill's *Utilitarianism* (1863) is still today considered the standard exposition. Mill discusses two foundations or sources of utilitarian thinking: a *normative* foundation in the "principle of utility" and a *psychological* foundation in human nature. He proposes his principle of utility—the "greatest happiness principle"—as the foundation of normative ethical theory. Actions are right, Mill says, in proportion to their tendency to promote happiness or absence of pain, and wrong insofar as they tend to produce pain or displeasure. According to Mill, pleasure and freedom from pain are alone desirable as ends. All desirable things (which are numerous) are desirable either for the pleasure inherent in them or as means to promote pleasure and prevent pain.

Mill's second foundation derives from his belief that most persons, and perhaps all, have a basic desire for unity and harmony with their fellow human beings. Just as people feel horror at crimes, he says, they have a basic moral sensitivity to the needs of others. Mill sees the purpose of morality as tapping natural human sympathies to benefit others, while controlling unsympathetic attitudes that cause harm to others. The principle of utility is conceived as the best means to these basic human goals.

***Essential Features of Utilitarianism.*** Several essential features of utilitarianism can be extracted from the reasoning of Mill and other utilitarians. First, utilitarianism is committed to the maximization of the good and the minimization of harm and evil. It asserts that society ought always to produce the greatest possible balance of positive value or the minimum balance of disvalue for all persons affected. The means to maximization is efficiency, a goal that persons in business find congenial, because it is highly prized throughout the economic sector. Efficiency is a means to higher profits and lower prices, and the struggle to be maximally profitable seeks to obtain maximum production from limited economic resources. The utilitarian commitment to the principle of optimal productivity through efficiency is an essential part of the traditional business conception of society and a standard part of business practice.

Many businesses, as well as government agencies, have adopted specific tools such as cost-benefit analysis, risk assessment, or management by objectives—all of which are strongly influenced by a utilitarian philosophy. Other businesses do not employ such specific tools, but make utilitarian judgments about the benefits and costs of layoffs, scrapping advertising campaigns, and reducing discretionary spending. Though unpopular in the short-term, these adjustments are often welcomed because they are directed at long-term financial improvement and job security. In this respect business harbors a fundamentally utilitarian conception of the goals of its enterprise. Much the same is true of the goals of public policy in the United States.

The need both to minimize harm and to balance risks against benefits has been a perennial concern of the business community. For example, executives in the petroleum industry know that oil and gas operations exist tenuously with wetland areas, waterfowl, and fish. However, if the demands of U.S. consumers are to be met, corporate and public policies must balance possible environmental harms against the benefits of industrial productivity. Similarly, those in the nuclear power industry know that U. S. power plants are built with heavy containment structures to withstand internal failures; but they also recognize the possibility of major disasters such as that at Chernobyl, in the former USSR, in 1986. Planning for such structures requires that the planners balance public benefits, probability of failure, and the magnitude of harm in the event of failure.

A second essential feature of the utilitarian theory is a *theory of the good.* Efficiency itself is simply an instrumental good; that is, it is valuable strictly as a means to something else. In the corporation, efficiency is valuable as a means to growth and to profit maximization. Within the free enterprise system of competing firms, efficiency is valuable as a means toward maximizing the production of goods and services. Within utilitarian ethical theory, efficiency is the means for maximizing human good.

But what is "good" according to the utilitarian? An answer to this question can be formed by considering the New York stock market. Daily results on Wall Street are not intrinsically good. They are extrinsically good as a means to other ends, such as financial security and happiness. Utilitarians believe that people ought to orient their lives around conditions that are good in themselves without reference to further consequences. Health, friendship, and freedom from pain are among such values.

However, utilitarians disagree concerning what constitutes the complete range of things or states that are good. Bentham and Mill are hedonists. They believe that only pleasure or happiness (synonymous for the purposes of this discussion) can be intrinsically good. Everything besides pleasure is instrumentally good to the end of pleasure. *Hedonistic* utilitarians, then, believe that any act or practice that maximizes pleasure (when compared with any alternative act or practice) is right. Later utilitarian philosophers have argued that other values besides pleasure possess intrinsic worth, for example, friendship, knowledge, courage, health, and beauty. Utilitarians who believe in multiple intrinsic values are referred to as *pluralistic* utilitarians.

In recent philosophy, economics, and psychology, neither the approach of the hedonists nor that of the pluralists has prevailed. Both approaches have seemed relatively useless for purposes of objectively aggregating widely different interests. Another approach appeals to individual preferences. From this perspective, the concept of utility is understood not in terms of states of affairs such as happiness, but in terms of the satisfaction of individual preferences, as determined by a person's behavior. In the language of business, utility is measured by a person's purchases or pursuits. To maximize a person's utility is to provide that which he or she has chosen or would choose from among the available alternatives. To maximize the utility of all persons affected by an action or a policy is to maximize the utility of the aggregate group.

Although the preference-based utilitarian approach to value has been viewed by many as superior to its predecessors, it is not trouble-free as an ethical theory. A major problem arises over morally unacceptable preferences. For example, an airline pilot may prefer to have a few beers before going to work, or an employment officer may prefer to discriminate against women, yet such preferences are morally intolerable. Utilitarianism based purely on subjective preferences is satisfactory, then, only if a range of acceptable preferences can be formulated. This latter task has proved difficult in theory, and it may be inconsistent with a pure preference approach. Should products like cigarettes, fireworks, and semiautomatic rifles be legally prohibited because they cause harm, even though many people would prefer to purchase them? How could a preference utilitarian answer this question?

One possible utilitarian response is to ask whether society is better off as a whole when these preferences are prohibited and when the choices of those desiring them are frustrated. If these products work against the larger objectives of utilitarianism (maximal public welfare) by creating unhappiness, the utilitarian could argue that preferences for these products should not be counted in the calculus of preferences. Preferences that serve to frustrate the preferences of others would then be ruled out by the goal of utilitarianism.

A third essential feature of utilitarianism is its commitment to the measurement and comparison of goods. With the hedonistic view, people must be able to measure pleasurable and painful states and be able to compare one person's pleasures with another's to decide which is greater. Bentham, for example, worked out a measurement device that he called the *hedonic calculus*. He thought he could add the quantitative units of individual happiness, subtract the units of individual unhappiness, and thereby arrive at a total measure of happiness. By the use of this system it is allegedly possible to determine the act or practice that will provide the greatest happiness to the greatest number of people.

When Bentham's hedonic calculus turned out to be of limited practical value, Mill substituted the criterion of a panel of experts (persons of requisite experience). Because Mill believed that some pleasures were better than others, a device was needed to decide which pleasures were in fact better. The experts were designated to fill that role. Subsequently, this idea of Mill's also turned out to be of limited practical value, and the notion of *consumer choice* was substitued in some theories. Consumer behavior, in this conception, can be empirically observed as prices change in the market. If one assumes that consumers seek to rationally order and maximize their preferences, given a set of prices, an objective measurement of utility is possible.

***Act and Rule Utilitarianism.*** Utilitarian moral philosophers are conventionally divided into two types—act utilitarians and rule utilitarians. An *act utilitarian* argues that in all situations one ought to perform that act that leads to the greatest good for the greatest number. The act utilitarian regards rules such as "You ought to tell the truth in making contracts" and "You ought not to manipulate persons through advertising" as useful guidelines, but also as expendable in business and other relationships. An act utilitarian would not hesitate to break a moral rule if breaking it would lead to the greatest good for the greatest number in a particular case. *Rule utilitarians*, however, reserve a more significant place for rules, which they do not regard as expendable on grounds that utility is maximized in a particular circumstance.

There are many applications of both types of utilitarianism in business ethics.[9] Consider the following case in which U.S. business practices and standards run up against the quite different practices of the Italian business community. The case involves the tax problems encountered by the Italian subsidiary of a major U.S. bank. In Italy the practices of corporate taxation typically involve elaborate negotiations among hired company representatives and the Italian tax service, and the tax statement initially submitted by a corporation is regarded as a dramatically understated bid intended only as a starting point for the negotiating process. In the case in question, the U.S. manager of the Italian banking subsidiary decided, against the advice of locally experienced lawyers and tax consultants, to ignore the native Italian practices and file a conventional U.S.-style tax statement (that is, one in which the subsidiary's profits for the year were not dramatically understated). His reasons for this decision included his belief that the local customs violated the moral rule of truth telling.[10]

An act utilitarian might well take exception to this conclusion. Admittedly, to file an Italian-style tax statement would be to violate a moral rule of truth telling; but the act utilitarian would argue that such a rule is only a guideline and can justifiably be violated to produce the greatest good. In the present case, the greatest good would evidently be done by following the local consultants' advice to conform to the Italian practices. Only by following those practices will the appropriate amount of tax be paid. This conclusion is strengthened by the ultimate outcome of the present case: The Italian authorities forced the bank to enter into the customary negotiations, a process in which the original, truthful tax statement was treated as an understated opening bid, and a dramatically excessive tax payment was consequently exacted.

In contrast to the position of act utilitarians, rule utilitarians hold that rules have a central position in morality that cannot be compromised by the demands of particular situations. Such compromise threatens the general effectiveness of the rules, the observance of which maximizes social utility. For the rule utilitarian, then, actions are justified by appeal to abstract rules such as "Don't kill," "Don't bribe," and "Don't break promises." These rules, in turn, are justified by an appeal to the principle of utility. The rule utilitarian believes this position can escape the objections to act utilitarianism, because rules are not subject to change by the demands of individual circumstances. Utilitarian rules are in theory firm and protective of all classes of individuals, just as human rights are rigidly protective of all individuals regardless of social convenience and momentary need.

Act utilitarians have a reply to these criticisms. They argue that there is a third option beyond ignoring rules and strictly obeying them, which is that the rules should be obeyed *only sometimes.*

***Criticisms of Utilitarianism.*** A major problem for utilitarianism is whether units of happiness or some other utilitarian value can be measured and compared in order to determine the best action among the alternatives. In deciding whether to open a pristine Alaskan wildlife preserve to oil exploration and drilling, for example, how does one compare the combined value of an increase in the oil supply, jobs, and consumer purchasing power with the value of wildlife preservation and environmental protection? How does a responsible official—at, say, the William and Melinda Gates Foundation—decide how to distribute limited funds allocated for charitable contributions (for example, as this Foundation has decided, to international vaccination and children's health programs)? If a corporate social audit (an evaluation of the company's acts of social responsibility) were attempted, how could the auditor measure and compare a corporation's ethical assets and liabilities?

The utilitarian reply is that the alleged problem is either a pseudoproblem or a problem that affects all ethical theories. People make crude, rough-and-ready comparisons of values every day, including those of pleasures and dislikes. For example, workers decide to go as a group to a bar rather than have an office party, because they think the bar function will satisfy more members of the group. Utilitarians acknowledge that accurate measurements of others' goods or preferences can seldom be provided because of limited knowledge and time. In everyday affairs such as purchasing supplies, administering business, or making legislative decisions, severely limited knowledge regarding the consequences of one's actions is often all that is available.

Utilitarianism has also been criticized on the grounds that it ignores nonutilitarian factors that are needed to make moral decisions. The most prominent omission cited is a consideration of justice: The action that produces the greatest balance of value for the greatest number of people may bring about unjustified treatment of a minority. Suppose society decides that the public interest is served by denying health insurance to those testing positive for the AIDS virus. Moreover, in the interest of efficiency, suppose insurance companies are allowed to use lifestyle characteristics that are statistically associated with an enhanced risk of AIDS. Finally, suppose such policies would serve the larger public's financial interest. Utilitarianism seems to *require* that public law and insurance companies deny coverage to AIDS victims. If so, would not this denial be unjust to those who have AIDS or are at high risk for contracting AIDS?

Utilitarians insist, against such criticisms, that all entailed costs and benefits of an action or practice must be weighed, including, for example, the costs that would occur from modifying a political constitution or a statement of basic rights. In a decision that affects employee and consumer safety, for example, the costs often include protests from labor and consumer groups, public criticism from the press, further alienation of employees from executives, the loss of customers to competitors, and the like. Also, rule utilitarians deny that narrow cost-benefit determinations are acceptable. They argue that general rules of justice (which are themselves justified by broad considerations of utility) ought to constrain particular actions and uses of cost-benefit calculations. Rule utilitarians maintain that the criticisms of utilitarianism previously noted are shortsighted because they focus on injustices that might be caused through a superficial or short-term application of the principle of utility. In a long-range view, utilitarians argue, promoting utility does not eventuate in overall unjust outcomes.

## Kantian Ethics

In 1999 CNN reported that online shoppers who visited the Internet auction site eBay were surprised to find a "fully functional kidney" for sale by a man giving his home as "Sunrise, Florida." He was proposing to sell one of his two kidneys. The price had been bid up to more than $5.7 million before eBay intervened and terminated the (illegal) auction.[11] Although it was never determined whether this auction was genuine, it is known that kidneys are for sale in some parts of Asia, notably India. One study showed (after locating 305 sellers) that Indians who sold their kidneys actually worsened rather than bettered their financial position as a result of the sale; the study also showed that some men forced their wives to sell a kidney.[12] Irrespective of the consequences of a kidney sale, many people look with moral indignation on the idea of selling a kidney, whether in the United States or in India. They see it as exploitation, rather than opportunity. What is it about selling a kidney that provokes this sense of moral unfairness?

***Kantian Respect for Persons.*** Immanuel Kant's (1724–1804) ethical theory may help clarify the basis of this concern. A follower of Kant could argue that using human organs as commodities is to treat human beings as though they were merely machines or capital, and so to deny people the respect appropriate to their dignity as rational human beings. Kant argues that persons should be treated as ends and never purely as means to the ends of others. That is, failure to respect persons is to treat another as a means in accordance with one's *own* ends, and thus as if they were not independent agents. To exhibit a lack of respect for a person is to reject the person's considered judgments, to ignore the person's concerns and needs, or to deny the person the liberty to act on those judgments. For example, manipulative advertising that attempts to make sales by interfering with the potential buyer's reflective choice violates the principle of respect for persons. In the case of kidney sales, almost all sellers are in desperate poverty and desperate need. Potentially all organ "donations" will come from the poor, while the rich avoid even donating their kidneys to their relatives. In effect, the organ is treated as a commodity and the owner of the organ as a means to a purchaser's ends.

In Kantian theories respect for the human being is said to be necessary—not just as an option or at one's discretion—because human beings possess a moral dignity and therefore should not be treated as if they had merely the conditional value possessed by machinery, industrial plants, robots, and capital. This idea of "respect for persons" has sometimes been expressed in corporate contexts as "respect for the individual." An example in business ethics is found in the practices of Southwest Airlines, which has the reputation of treating its employees and customers with unusual respect. Employees report that they feel free to express themselves as individuals and that they feel a strong loyalty to the airline. Following the terrorist attacks of September 11, 2001, Southwest was the only airline that did not lay off employees or reduce its flight schedule. As a consequence, some employees offered to work overtime, without pay, to save the company money until people resumed flying.[13] The firm prides itself on a relationship with all stakeholders that is a relationship of persons, rather than simply a relationship of economic transactions.

Some have interpreted Kant to hold categorically that people can never treat other persons as a means to their ends. This interpretation fails to appreciate the subtleties of the theory. Kant did not categorically prohibit the use of persons as means to the ends of other people. He argued only that people must not treat another *exclusively* as a means to their ends. An example is found in circumstances in which employees are ordered to perform odious tasks. Clearly they are being treated as a means to an employer's or a supervisor's ends, but the employees are not exclusively used for others' purposes because they are not mere servants or objects. In an economic exchange suppose that Jones is using Smith to achieve her end, but similarly Smith is using Jones to achieve her end. So long as the exchange is freely entered into without coercion or deception by either party, neither party has used the other merely for her end. Thus even in a hierarchical organization an employer can be the boss without exploiting the employee, so long as the employee freely entered into that relationship. The key to not using others merely as a means is to respect their autonomy.

This interpretation suggests that the example of the kidney does not necessarily show any disrespect for persons. Kant seems to require only that each individual *will the acceptance* of those principles on which he or she is acting. If a person freely accepts a certain form of action and it is not intrinsically immoral, that person is a free being and has a right to so choose. Selling a kidney therefore might fall into this category.

Kant's theory finds *motives* for actions to be of the highest importance, in that it expects persons to make the right decisions *for the right reasons*. If persons are honest only because they believe that honesty pays, their "honesty" is cheapened. It seems like no honesty at all, only an action that appears to be honest. For example, when corporate executives announce that the reason they made the morally correct decision was because it was good for their business, this reason seems to have nothing to do with morality. According to Kantian thinking, if a corporation does the right thing only when (and for the reason that) it is profitable or when it will enjoy good publicity, its decision is prudential, not moral.

Consider the following three examples of three people making personal sacrifices for a sick relative. Fred makes the sacrifices only because he fears the social criticism that would result if he failed to do so. He hates doing it and secretly resents being involved. Sam, by contrast, derives no personal satisfaction from taking care of his sick relative. He would rather be doing other things and makes the sacrifice purely from a sense of obligation. Bill, by contrast, is a kind-hearted person. He does not view his actions as a sacrifice and is motivated by the satisfaction that comes from helping others. Assume in these three cases that the consequences of all the sacrificial actions are equally good and that the sick relatives are adequately cared for, as each agent intends. The question to consider is which persons are behaving in a morally praiseworthy manner. If utilitarian theory is used, this question may be hard to answer, especially if act utilitarianism is the theory in question, because the good consequences in each case are identical. The Kantian believes, however, that motives—in particular, motives of moral obligation—count substantially in moral evaluation.

It appears that Fred's motives are not moral motives but motives of prudence that spring from fear. Although his actions have good consequences, Fred does not deserve any moral credit for his acts because they are not morally motivated. To recognize the prudential basis of an action does not detract from the goodness of any consequences it may have. Given the purpose or function of the business enterprise, a motive of self-interest may be the most appropriate motive to ensure good consequences. The point, however, is that a business executive derives no special moral credit for acting in the corporate self-interest, even if society is benefited by and satisfied with the action.

If Fred's motive is not moral, what about Bill's and Sam's? Here moral philosophers disagree. Kant maintained that moral action must be motivated by moral obligation alone. From this perspective, Sam is the only individual whose actions may be appropriately described as moral. Bill deserves no more credit than Fred, because Bill is motivated by the emotions of sympathy and compassion, not by obligation. Bill is naturally kind-hearted and has been well socialized by his family, but this motivation merits no moral praise from a Kantian, who believes that actions motivated by self-interest alone or compassion alone cannot be morally praiseworthy. To be deserving of moral praise, a person must act from obligation.

To elaborate this point, Kant insisted that all persons must act for the *sake* of obligation—not merely *in accordance with* obligation. That is, the person's motive for action must involve a recognition of the duty to act. Kant tried to establish the ultimate basis for the validity of rules of obligation in pure reason, not in intuition, conscience, utility, or compassion. Morality provides a rational framework of principles and rules that constrain and guide all people, independent of their personal goals and preferences. He believed that all considerations of utility and self-interest are secondary, because the moral worth of an agent's action depends exclusively on the moral acceptability of the rule according to which the person is acting, or, as Kant preferred to say, moral acceptability depends on the rule that determines the agent's will.

An action has moral worth only if performed by an agent who possesses what Kant called a "good will." A person has a good will only if the sole motive for action is moral obligation, as determined by a universal rule of obligation. Kant developed this notion into a fundamental moral law: "I ought never to act except in such a way that I can also will that my maxim should become a universal law." Kant called this principle the *categorical imperative.* It is categorical because it admits of no exceptions and is absolutely binding. It is imperative because it gives instruction about how one must act. He gave several controversial examples of imperative moral maxims: "Do not lie," "Help others in distress," "Do not commit suicide," and "Work to develop your abilities."

***Universalizability.*** Kant's strategy was to show that the acceptance of certain kinds of action is self-defeating, because *universal* participation in such behavior undermines the action. Some of the clearest cases involve persons who make a unique exception for themselves for purely selfish reasons. Suppose a person considers breaking a promise that would be inconvenient to keep. According to Kant, the person must first formulate her or his reason as a universal rule. The rule would say, "Everyone should break a promise whenever keeping it is inconvenient." Such a rule is contradictory, Kant held, because if it were consistently recommended that all individuals should break their promises when it was convenient for them to do so, the practice of making promises would be senseless. Given the nature of a promise, a rule allowing people to break promises when it becomes convenient makes the institution of promise-making unintelligible. A rule that allows cheating on an exam similarly negates the purpose of testing.

Kant's belief is that the conduct stipulated in these rules could not be made universal without some form of contradiction emerging. If a corporation kites checks to reap a profit in the way E. F. Hutton Brokerage did in a scandal that led to the end of the firm, the corporation makes itself an exception to the system of monetary transfer, thereby cheating the system, which is established by certain rules. This conduct, if carried out by other corporations, violates the rules presupposed by the system, thereby rendering the system inconsistent. Similarly, the Russian economy has been stalled in recent years because suppliers were not being paid for the goods and services they provided. If such practices were "universalized" (in Kant's sense), suppliers would stop supplying. Russia has also had difficulty in establishing a stock market because the information on the businesses listed was so inaccurate. If deception were "universal" (that is, widely practiced), investors would not invest and a stock market would be untenable. Kant's view is that actions involving invasion of privacy, theft, line cutting, cheating, kickbacks, bribes, etc. are contradictory in that they are not consistent with the institutions or practices they presuppose.

***Criticisms of Kantianism.*** Despite Kant's contributions to moral philosophy, his theories have been criticized as narrow and inadequate to handle various problems in the moral life. He has no place for moral emotions or sentiments such as sympathy and caring. Neither does Kant have much to say about moral character and virtue other than his comments on the motive of obligation. Some people also think that Kant emphasized universal obligations (obligations common to all people) at the expense of particular obligations (obligations that fall only on those in particular relationships or who occupy certain roles such as those of a business manager). Whereas the obligation to keep a promise is a universal obligation, the obligation to grade students fairly falls only on teachers responsible for submitting grades.

Many managerial obligations result from special roles played in business. For example, businesspersons tend to treat customers according to the history of their relationship. If a person is a regular customer and the merchandise being sold is in short supply, the regular customer will be given preferential treatment because a relationship of commitment and trust has already been established. Japanese business practice has conventionally extended this notion to relations with suppliers and employees: After a trial period, the regular employee has a job for life at many firms. Also, the bidding system is used less frequently in Japan than in the West. Once a supplier has a history with a firm, the firm is loyal to its supplier, and each trusts the other not to exploit the relationship.

However, particular obligations and special relationships may not be inconsistent with Kantianism, because they may be formulable as universal. For example, the rule "Quality control inspectors have special obligations for customer safety" can be made into a "universal" law for all quality control inspectors. Although Kant wrote little about such particular duties, he would agree that a complete explanation of moral agency in terms of duty requires an account of *both* universal *and* particular duties.

A related aspect of Kant's ethical theory that has been scrutinized by philosophers is his view that moral motivation involves *impartial* principles. Impartial motivation may be distinguished from the motivation that a person might have for treating a second person in a certain way because the first person has a particular interest in the well-being of the second person (a spouse or good friend, for example). A conventional interpretation of Kant's work suggests that if conflicts arise between one's obligation and one's other motivations—such as friendship, reciprocation, or love—the motive of obligation should always prevail. In arguing against this moral view, critics maintain that persons are entitled to show favoritism to their loved ones. This criticism suggests that Kantianism (and utilitarianism as well) has too broadly cast the requirement of impartiality and does not adequately account for those parts of the moral life involving partial, intimate, and special relationships.

Special relationships with a unique history are often recognized in business. For instance, the Unocal Corporation sharply criticized its principal bank, Security Pacific Corporation, for knowingly making loans of $185 million to a group that intended to use the money to buy shares in Unocal for a hostile takeover. Fred Hartley, chairman and president of Unocal, argued that the banks and investment bankers were "playing both sides of the game." Hartley said that Security Pacific had promised him that it would not finance such takeover attempts three months before doing so and that it had acted under conditions "in which the bank [has] continually received [for the last 40 years] confidential financial, geological, and engineering information from the company."[14] A forty-year history in which the bank has stockpiled confidential information should not simply be cast aside for larger goals. Security Pacific had violated a special relationship it had with Unocal.

Nonetheless, impartiality seems at some level an irreplaceable moral concept, and ethical theory should recognize its centrality for many business relationships. For example, a major scandal occurred for some U.S. banks in 1991, because they were caught lending money to bank insiders.[15] Then, as investing became more precarious in the early years of the twenty-first century, several companies were involved in questionable insider loans to corporate executives. For example, at the height of its crisis, WorldCom loaned then-CEO Bernie Ebbers $160 million for the purpose of his personal "stock purchase/retention." The essence of federal rules governing banks—to the extent explicit rules exist—is that banks can lend money to insiders if and only if insiders are treated exactly as outsiders are treated. Here the rule of impartiality is an essential moral constraint. By contrast, 75 percent of America's 1500 largest corporations made insider loans strictly on the basis of partiality; most loans were made for stock purchases. This partiality massively backfired in 2000–2003, and many companies had to "forgive" or "pardon" the loans and charge off millions of dollars. Loans at Tyco, Lucent, Mattel, Microsoft, and Webvan became famous cases.[16]

Again, throughout much of 2002, corporate America suffered a series of business scandals, several of which ended in the bankruptcy of companies and the criminal prosecution of some corporate executives. Violations of the demand for impartiality and fair-dealing were widespread. In a notorious case, the accounting firm of Arthur Andersen had such a close and partial relationship with its client Enron that it could not perform an objective audit of the firm. Enron was treated with a deference, partiality, and favoritism that contrasted sharply with its auditing of other firms, who were treated with the conventional impartiality expected of an auditing firm. As a result of this scandal, problems of undue partiality began to be widely discussed as problems of conflict of interest. In an attempt at restoring public confidence in a fair and impartial system, the Securities and Exchange Commission (SEC) approved plans for a new oversight system that was itself independent of the accounting industry and therefore more likely to be impartial. However, political lobbying almost immediately raised questions about the impartiality of the new plans to assure impartiality.

In concluding this section on Kantian ethics, almost no moral philosopher today finds Kant's system fully satisfactory. His defenders tend to say only that Kant provides the main elements of a sound moral position. By appeal to these elements, some philosophers have attempted to construct a more encompassing theory. They use the Kantian notion of respect for persons, for example, to provide an account of human rights. Considerable controversy persists as to whether Kantian theories are adequate to this task and whether they have been more successful than utilitarian theories.

## Contemporary Challenges to the Dominant Theories

Thus far utilitarian and Kantian theories have been examined. Both meld a variety of moral considerations into a surprisingly systematized framework, centered around a single major principle. Much is attractive in these theories, and they have been the dominant models in ethical theory throughout much of the twentieth century. In fact, they have sometimes been presented as the only types of ethical theory, as if there were no available alternatives from which to choose. However, much recent philosophical writing has focused on defects in these theories and on ways in which the two theories actually affirm a similar conception of the moral life oriented around universal principles and rules.

These critics promote alternatives to the utilitarian and Kantian models. They believe that the contrast between the two types of theory has been overestimated and that they do not merit the attention they have received and the lofty position they have occupied. Four popular replacements for, or perhaps supplements to, Kantian and utilitarian theories are (1) rights theories (which are based on human rights); (2) virtue theories (which are based on character traits); (3) feminist theories and the ethics of care (which are disposition-based); and (4) common morality theories (which are generally obligation-based). These theories are the topics of the next four sections.

Each type of theory has treated some problems well and has supplied insights not found in utilitarian and Kantian theories. Although it may seem as if there is an endless array of disagreements across the theories, these theories are not in all respects competitive, and in many ways they are complementary. The reader may profitably look for convergent insights in these theories.

## Rights Theories

Terms from moral discourse such as *value, goal,* and *obligation* have thus far in this chapter dominated the discussion. *Principles* and *rules* in Kantian, utilitarian, and common morality theories have been understood as statements of obligation. Yet many assertions that will be encountered throughout this volume are claims to have rights, and public policy issues often concern rights or attempts to secure rights. Many current controversies in professional ethics, business, and public policy involve the rights to property, work, privacy, a healthy environment, and the like. This section will show that rights have a distinctive character in ethical theory and yet are connected to the obligations that have previously been examined.

In the twentieth century, public discussions about moral protections for persons vulnerable to abuse, enslavement, or neglect have typically been stated in terms of rights. Many believe that these rights transcend national boundaries and particular governments. For example, there continues to be controversy over exploitative labor conditions in factories (so-called sweatshop conditions) that manufacture products for Nike, Reebok, Abercrombie and Fitch, Target, Gap, J.C. Penney, Liz Claiborne, L. L. Bean, and many other companies. The fundamental issue is the human rights of hundreds of thousands of workers around the globe. Under discussion are the rights of workers to appropriate working conditions, a code of conduct for the industry, open-factory inspections, new monitoring systems, reduction of the illiteracy-rate among workers, and collective bargaining agreements.[17] In addition, activists have urged that American companies not do business in countries that have a record of extensive violation of human rights. China, Nigeria, and Myanmar have all come under severe criticism. (These issues, and others surrounding violations of human rights in sweatshops, are discussed in Chapter 9; see also the Nike case, set in Vietnam, in Chapter 10.)

Unlike legal rights, human rights are held independently of membership in a state or other social organization. Historically, human rights evolved from the notion of natural rights. As formulated by Locke and others in early modern philosophy, natural rights are claims that individuals have against the state. If the state does not honor these rights, its legitimacy is in question. Natural rights were thought to consist primarily of rights to be free of interference, or liberty rights. Proclamations of rights to life, liberty, property, a speedy trial, and the pursuit of happiness subsequently formed the core of major Western political and legal documents. These rights came to be understood as powerful assertions demanding respect and status.

A number of influential philosophers have maintained that ethical theory or some part of it must be "rights-based."[18] They seek to ground ethical theory in an account of rights that is not reducible to a theory of obligations or virtues. Consider a theory to be discussed in Chapter 10 that takes liberty rights to be basic. One representative of this theory, Robert Nozick, refers to his social philosophy as an "entitlement theory." The appropriateness of that description is apparent from this provocative line with which his book begins: "Individuals have rights, and there are things no person or group may do to them (without violating their rights)." Starting from this assumption, Nozick builds a political theory in which government action is justified only if it protects the fundamental rights of its citizens.

This political theory is also an ethical theory. Nozick takes the following moral rule to be basic: All persons have a right to be left free to do as they choose. The moral obligation not to interfere with a person follows from this right. That the obligation *follows* from the right is a clear indication of the priority of rights over obligations; that is, in this theory the obligation is derived from the right, not the other way around.

Rights-based theories hold that rights form the justifying basis of obligations because they best express the purpose of morality, which is the securing of liberties or other benefits for a right-holder.[19] However, few rights-based theories *deny* the importance of obligations (or duties), which they regard as central to morality. They make this point by holding that there is a correlativity between obligations and rights: "*X* has a right to do or to have *Y*" means that the moral system of rules (or the legal system, if appropriate) imposes an obligation on someone to act or to refrain from acting so that *X* is enabled to do or have *Y*.[20]

These obligations are of two types: *Negative obligations* are those that require that we not interfere with the liberty of others (thus securing liberty rights); *positive obligations* require that certain people or institutions provide benefits or services (thus securing benefit rights or welfare rights).[21] Correlatively, a *negative right* is a valid claim to liberty, that is, a right not to be interfered with, and a *positive right* is a valid claim on goods or services. The rights not to be beaten, subjected to unwanted surgery, or sold into slavery are examples of negative or liberty rights. Rights to food, medical care, and insurance are examples of positive or benefit rights.

The right to liberty is here said to be "negative" because no one has to act to honor it; presumably, all that must be done is to leave people alone. The same is not true regarding positive rights; in order to honor these rights, someone has to provide something. For example, if a starving person has a human right to well-being, someone has an obligation to provide that person with food. As has often been pointed out, positive rights place an obligation to provide something to others, who can respond that this requirement interferes with their property rights to use their resources for their chosen ends. The distinction between positive and negative rights has often led those who would include various rights to well-being (to food, housing, health care, etc.) on the list of human rights to argue that the obligation to provide for positive rights falls on the political state. This distinction has intuitive appeal to many businesspersons, because they wish to limit both the responsibilities of their firms and the number of rights conflicts they must address.

A conflict involving negative rights is illustrated by the debate surrounding attempts by employers to control the lifestyle of their employees. Some employers will not accept employees who smoke. Some will not permit employees to engage in dangerous activities such as skydiving, auto racing, or mountain climbing. By making these rules, one can argue that employers are violating the liberty rights of the employees as well as the employees' right to privacy. On the other hand, the employer can argue that he or she has a right to run the business as he or she sees fit. Thus, both sides invoke negative rights to make a moral case.

Theories of moral rights have not traditionally been a major focus of business ethics, but this situation is changing at present. For example, employees traditionally could be fired for what superiors considered disloyal conduct, and employees have had no right to "blow the whistle" on corporate misconduct. When members of minority groups complain about discriminatory hiring practices that violate their human dignity and self-respect, one plausible interpretation of these complaints is that those who register them believe that their moral rights are being infringed. Current theories of employee, consumer, and stockholder rights all provide frameworks for debates about rights within business ethics.

The language of moral rights is greeted by some with skepticism because of the apparently absurd proliferation of rights and the conflict among diverse claims to rights (especially in recent political debates). For example, some parties claim that a pregnant woman has a right to have an abortion, whereas others claim that fetuses have a right to life that precludes the right to have an abortion. As we shall see throughout this volume, rights language has been extended to include such controversial rights as the right to financial privacy, rights of workers to obtain various forms of information about their employer, the right to work in a pollution-free environment, the right to hold a job, and the right to health care.

Many writers in ethics now agree that a person can legitimately exercise a right to something only if sufficient justification exists—that is, when a right has an overriding status. Rights such as a right to equal economic opportunity, a right to do with one's property as one wishes, and a right to be saved from starvation may have to compete with other rights. The fact that rights theorists have failed to provide a hierarchy for rights claims may indicate that rights, like obligations, are not absolute moral demands, but rather ones that can be overridden in particular circumstances by more stringent competing moral claims.

### Virtue Ethics

Our discussion of utilitarian, Kantian, and rights-based theories has looked chiefly at obligations and rights. These theories do not typically emphasize the agents or actors who perform actions, have motives, and follow principles. Yet people commonly make judgments about good and evil persons, their traits of character, and their willingness to perform actions. In recent years, several philosophers have proposed that ethics should redirect its preoccupation with principles of obligation, directive rules, and judgments of right and wrong and should look to decision making by persons of good character, that is, virtuous persons.

*Virtue ethics* descends from the classical Hellenistic tradition represented by Plato and Aristotle, in which the cultivation of a virtuous character is viewed as morality's primary function. Aristotle held that virtue is neither a feeling nor an innate capacity, but a disposition bred from an innate capacity properly trained and exercised. People acquire virtues much as they do skills such as carpentry, playing a musical instrument, or cooking. They become just by performing just actions and become temperate by performing temperate actions. Virtuous character, says Aristotle, is neither natural nor unnatural; it is cultivated and made a part of the individual, much like a language or tradition.

But an ethics of virtue is more than habitual training. This approach relies even more than does Kant's theory on the importance of having a correct *motivational structure.* A just person, for example, has not only a psychological disposition to act fairly but also a morally appropriate desire to act justly. The person characteristically has a moral concern and reservation about acting in a way that would be unfair. Having only the motive to act in accordance with a rule of obligation, as Kant demands, is not morally sufficient for virtue. Imagine a Kantian who always performs his or her obligation because it is an obligation but who intensely dislikes having to allow the interests of others to be taken into account. Such a person does not cherish, feel congenial toward, or think fondly of others, and this person respects others only because obligation requires it. This person can, nonetheless, on a theory of moral obligation such as Kant's or Mill's, perform a morally right action, have an ingrained disposition to perform that action, and act with obligation as the foremost motive. The virtue theorist's criticism is that if the desire is not right, a necessary condition of virtue is lacking.

Consider an encounter with a tire salesperson. You tell the salesperson that safety is most important and that you want to be sure to get an all-weather tire. He listens carefully and then sells you exactly what you want, because he has been well trained by his manager to see his primary obligation as that of meeting the customer's needs. Acting in this way has been deeply ingrained in this salesperson by his manager's training. There is no more typical encounter in the world of retail sales than this one. However, suppose now that we go behind the salesperson's behavior to his underlying motives and desires reveals. We find that this man detests his job and hates having to spend time with every customer who comes through the door. He does not care about being of service to people or creating a better environment in the office. All he really wants is to watch the television set in the waiting lounge and to pick up his paycheck. Although this man meets his moral obligations, something in his character is morally defective.

When people engage in business or take jobs simply for the profit or wages that will result, they may meet their obligations and yet not be engaged in their work in a morally appropriate manner. On the other hand, if persons start a business because they believe in a quality product—a new, healthier yogurt, for example—and deeply desire to sell that product, their character is more in tune with our moral expectations. Entrepreneurs often exhibit this enthusiasm and commitment. For example, Microsoft and Apple Computer employees were, for many years, genuinely excited about bringing new products to market in the belief that they greatly improved the quality of life. The practice of business is morally better if it is sustained by persons whose character manifests enthusiasm, truthfulness, justice, compassion, respectfulness, and patience.

Interesting discussions in business ethics now center on the appropriate virtues of managers, employees, and other participants in business activity, as will be seen many times in this book. Among the virtues that have received discussion are integrity, courage, and compassion. However, some alleged "virtues" of business life have been sharply contested in recent years; and various of these "virtues" of the businessperson have seemed not to be *moral* virtues. Competitiveness and toughness are two examples. *Fortune* has long published a list of the toughest bosses. For many years before he was fired as CEO of Sunbeam, Al Dunlap was perennially on the list. He had earned the nickname "Chainsaw Al" for his propensity to fire people and shut down plants even when they were marginally profitable. Dunlap made stock price and profitability the only worthy goals of a business enterprise. Many would argue that in his case business toughness was a moral vice. This example suggests that some business virtues are subject to critical moral scrutiny.

There is another reason why virtue ethics may be important for business ethics. A morally good person with the right desires or motivations is more likely to understand what should be done, more likely to be motivated to perform required acts, and more likely to form and act on moral ideals than would a morally bad person. A person who is ordinarily trusted is one who has an ingrained motivation and desire to perform right actions and who characteristically cares about morally appropriate responses. A person who simply follows rules of obligation and who otherwise exhibits no special moral character may not be trustworthy. It is not the rule follower, but the person disposed by *character* to be generous, caring, compassionate, sympathetic, and fair who should be the one recommended, admired, praised, and held up as a moral model. Many experienced businesspersons say that such trust is the moral cement of the business world.

## Feminist Ethics and the Ethics of Care

Related to virtue ethics in some respects is a body of moral reflection that has come to be known as the "ethics of care." This theory develops some of the themes found in virtue ethics about the centrality of character, but the ethics of care focuses on a set of character traits that are deeply valued in close personal relationships—sympathy, compassion, fidelity, love, friendship, and the like. Noticeably absent are universal moral rules and impartial utilitarian calculations such as those espoused by Kant and Mill.

***Feminist Foundations.*** The ethics of care has grown out of the eloquent work of a group of recent philosophers that has contributed to or is indebted to feminist theory. "Feminism" is a term with several nuances of meaning; it incorporates a diverse group of female-centered reflections on moral theory and practice that augment or reconceive conventional types of moral theory. Feminist approaches to ethics will here be understood in terms of three normative tenets: First, the subordination, inequality, or oppression of women is wrong; its sources should be identified and remedied. Second, women deserve equal political and legal rights. Third, the experiences and perspectives of women are worthy of respect and should be taken seriously. Although these tenets may seem entirely noncontroversial, feminists argue that if they were acted upon, the theory and practice of ethics in business, and throughout society, would be radically transformed.

Feminist scholars are committed to pinpointing and excising forms of oppression and to reformulating ethical theory in a manner that does not subordinate the interests of women. There are different understandings among feminists of the sources of oppression and about how best to address and remedy it. These different understandings naturally result in different types or categories of "feminism." The issues are complex, and feminists take different perspectives on matters such as equality, diversity, impartiality, community, autonomy, and the objectivity of moral knowledge.

Nonetheless, several central components of feminist ethical thinking may be delineated. Feminist philosophers point out that rationality in modern ethical theory, in particular in Kantian and utilitarian theories, has most often been understood in terms of the formulation and impartial application of universally binding moral principles. Many feminist philosophers now argue that universal principles are inadequate guides to action and that abstract formulations of hypothetical moral situations separate moral agents from the particularities of their individual lives and inappropriately separate moral problems from social and historical facts. Further, they have criticized the autonomous, unified, rational beings that typify both the Kantian and the utilitarian conception of the moral self. Feminist philosophers generally agree that Kantian and utilitarian impartiality fails to recognize the moral importance of valuing the well-being of another for her or his own sake. Furthermore, they point out that although impartiality has historically been associated with respect for the individual, impartiality can undermine this very respect because it treats individuals impersonally, as anonymous and interchangeable moral agents without distinctive needs and abilities. In addition, impartial moral evaluations often pave over important differences in social, political, and economic power that are crucial to assessing the morally correct course of action in particular situations.

For example, a statistical evaluation indicating that 50 percent of a telecommunication company's workforce consists of women would suggest that the company is morally praiseworthy in this respect. However, a different assessment may be appropriate if 90 percent of the women are employed as telephone operators and clerical staff. Similarly, in evaluating a waste disposal company's competitive contract bid, feminist philosophers would urge management to look beyond the bottom line if, for example, 80 percent of the company's toxic waste disposal sites are located in poor, minority neighborhoods.

***The Voice of Care.*** Feminist philosophers have pointed out that traditional theories present a conception of morality that leaves little room for virtues such as empathy, compassion, fidelity, love, and friendship. An understanding of the context of a situation is particularly important when taking into account the distinctive "voice" that many psychologists, philosophers, and management theorists have associated with women. This distinctive moral stance was articulated in a particularly influential manner by psychologist Carol Gilligan in her influential work *In a Different Voice.*[22] The voice is one of care and compassion, and although most feminist scholars do not associate this voice or perspective with women exclusively, they argue that it does represent an important contrast to the voice of rights and justice that Gilligan associated with men.

This distinct moral perspective is characterized by a concern with relationships —especially responsiveness to the particular needs of others—and by a commitment to others' well-being. The ideas Gilligan advanced on the basis of her psychological studies have been developed by those who find the same different voice in contemporary philosophy. Contractarian models of ethics, with their emphasis on justice and rights, are firmly rejected because they omit integral virtues and place a premium on *autonomous choice* among *free* and *equal* agents. Here the ethics of care offers a fundamental rethinking of the moral universe: The terms of social cooperation, especially in families and in communal decision making, are *unchosen, intimate,* and among *unequals.* The contractarian model fails to appreciate that parents and service-oriented professionals, for example, do not perceive their responsibilities to their children and customers in terms of contracts or universal rules but see them rather in terms of care, needs, and long-term attachment. Only if every form of human relation were modeled on an exchange could these forms of caring be reduced to contract or moral law.[23]

There are additional reasons for thinking that a morality centered on virtues of care and concern cannot be squeezed into a morality of rules. Their frameworks are fundamentally dissimilar. Human warmth, friendliness, and trust in responding to others cannot be brought under rules of behavior. For example, although a lawyer may follow all the rules of good legal practice in attending to the affairs of a bankrupt businessperson, the lawyer still does not display the sensitivity and warmth that this heartsick person needs; yet such virtues of a good lawyer may be the most important part of the encounter.

Feminist theories offer a great deal to a reflective person interested in business ethics. We stand to learn how business relationships might be restructured to reflect the needs and welfare of all stakeholders. Instead of viewing relationships in the business world as fundamentally competitive, market-oriented, and contractual, business persons can more readily appreciate that many relationships are cooperative, possibly even maternalistic (here a replacement word for "paternalistic"). For example, in Chapter 7, we consider whether those involved in *sales* might reconceive their responsibilities along these lines. Again, consider a manager who is attempting to implement a mandatory drug testing program. She might come to an impasse and restructure her approach when she finds that employers, employees, and customers have legitimate concerns and sensitivities about the program. Many feminists and management experts would urge the manager to help employees to feel concern for the customers while also striving to make the workplace experience one in which the worker is less alienated and hence less likely to take drugs. Employees can in this way come to feel that they can trust their managers, and managers might more readily listen and respond to their employees.

This moral theory has the potential to transform business practice to exhibit more of the characteristics of a moral community. Traditional metaphors for business practice are often drawn from competitive arenas; they are war oriented and sports oriented. Family metaphors seem out of place, as does the language of cooperation and compassion. Yet such language is undeniably central to morality; and if some contemporary management theorists are correct, such language is central to success in business as well. Cooperation among managers and employers is no less important for success than product quality. Also, the business world is still structured in ways that make it more difficult for women to pursue their career on a level playing field with men—or even to pursue family and career at all. Supportive policies of liberal office hours, available leaves of absence, child-care facilities, and strategies to prevent sexual harassment can be championed independent of feminist ethics or the ethics of care, but these ethical theories have taken the lead in promoting such forms of restructuring in institutions.

This aspect of business has traditionally been ignored as "soft" and less important than a strong bottom line. There are signs, however, that business will in the future be more open to the contributions of the ethics of care, resulting in an improvement in both corporate morality and corporate productivity.

## Common Morality Theories

Finally, many philosophers defend the view that there is a common morality that all people share by virtue of communal life and that this morality is ultimately the source of all theories of morality. According to this approach, virtually all people in all cultures grow up with an understanding of the basic demands of morality. Its norms are familiar and unobjectionable to those committed to a moral life. They know not to lie, not to steal, to keep promises, to honor the rights of others, not to kill or cause harm to innocent persons, and the like. The *common morality* is simply the set of norms shared by all persons seriously committed to the objectives of morality. This morality is not merely *a* morality that differs from *other* moralities.[24] It is applicable to all persons in all places, and all human conduct is rightly judged by its standards. The following are examples of *standards of action* (rules of obligation) in the common morality: 1. "Don't kill"; 2. "Don't cause pain or suffering to others"; 3. "Prevent evil or harm from occurring"; and 4. "Tell the truth." There are also many examples of *moral character traits* (virtues) recognized in the common morality, including: (1) nonmalevolence; (2) honesty; (3) integrity; and (4) conscientiousness. These virtues seem to be universally admired traits of character, and a person is regarded as deficient in moral character if he or she lacks such traits.

The thesis that there are universal moral standards is rooted in (1) a theory of the objectives of the social institution of morality and (2) an hypothesis about the sorts of norms that are required to achieve those objectives. Philosophers such as Thomas Hobbes and David Hume have pointed out that centuries of experience demonstrate that the human condition tends to deteriorate into misery, confusion, violence, and distrust unless norms such as those listed earlier—the norms of the common morality—are observed. These norms prevent or minimize the threat of this deterioration. It would be an overstatement to maintain that these norms are necessary for the *survival* of a society (as various philosophers and social scientists have maintained[25]), but it is not too much to claim that these norms are necessary to *ameliorate or counteract the tendency for the quality of people's lives to worsen or for social relationships to disintegrate.*[26] In every well-functioning society norms are in place to prohibit lying, breaking promises, causing bodily harm, stealing, fraud, the taking of life, the neglect of children, failures to keep contracts, and so forth. These norms are what they are, and not some other set of norms, because they have proven that they successfully achieve the objectives of morality. This success in the service of human flourishing accounts for their moral authority, and there is no more basic explanation of or justification for their moral authority. Thus, there is no *philosophical* ethical theory that takes priority over the common morality; indeed, all philosophical theories find their grounding in the common morality.

These theories do not assume that every person accepts the norms in the common morality. It would be implausible to maintain that all persons in all societies do in fact accept moral norms. Unanimity is not the issue. Many amoral, immoral, or selectively moral persons do not care about or identify with various demands of the common morality. Some persons are morally weak; others are morally depraved. It would also be implausible to hold that a *customary* set of norms or a *consensus* set of norms in a society qualifies, as such, for inclusion in the *common* morality. The notion that moral justification is ultimately grounded in the customs and consensus agreements of particular groups is a moral travesty. Any given society's customary or consensus position may be a distorted outlook that functions to block awareness of common-morality requirements. Some societies are in the influential grip of leaders who promote religious zealotries or political ideologies that depart profoundly from the common morality.

From the perspective of those who emphasize the common morality, only universally valid norms warrant us in making intercultural and cross-cultural judgments about moral depravity, morally misguided beliefs, savage cruelty, and other moral failures. If we did not have recourse to universal norms, we could not make basic distinctions between moral and immoral behavior and therefore could not be positioned to criticize even outrageous human actions, some of which are themselves proclaimed in the name of morality. This takes us to the subject of particular moralities.

Many justifiable moral norms are particular to cultures, groups, and even individuals. The common morality contains only general moral standards. Its norms are abstract, universal, and content thin. Particular moralities tend to be the reverse: concrete, nonuniversal, and content rich. These moralities may contain norms that are often comprehensive and detailed. Business ethics, and indeed all professional ethics, are examples of particular moralities. Many examples are found in codes of professional practice, institutional codes of ethics, and the like. Although their rules are likely to be unique to some domain of business, they will generally require for their justification the norms in the common morality, such as rules of truthful disclosure, rules protecting persons from harm, and rules against conflict of interest.

Many rules have been fashioned to help control particular problems in particular environments. For example, some institutions now have elaborate rules and monitoring systems to control problems of sexual harassment. Their rules are typically designed for a particular set of problems in a specific location or industry. Such rules might be counterproductive, unnecessary, or even ludicrous in other locations.

Business ethics is fundamentally an attempt to make the moral life specific and practical. The reason why the norms of business ethics in particular cultures often differ from those of another culture is that the abstract starting points in the common morality can be coherently applied in a variety of ways to create norms that take the form of specific guidelines, institutional and public policies, and conflict resolutions. Universal norms are simply not appropriate instruments to determine practice or policy or to resolve conflicts unless they are made sufficiently specific to take account of financial constraints, social efficiency, cultural pluralism, political procedures, uncertainty about risk, and the like.

General moral norms must be specified to make them sufficiently concrete so that they can function as practical guidelines in particular contexts. Specification is not a process of producing general norms such as those in the common morality; it assumes that they are already available. Specification reduces the indeterminateness and abstractness of general norms to give them increased action-guiding capacity, without loss of the moral commitments in the original norm(s).[27] For example, the norm that we must "respect the autonomous judgment of competent persons" cannot, unless it is specified, handle complicated problems of whether workers have a right to know about potential dangers in a chemical plant. This will all have to be specified. The process of specification will have to become increasingly concrete as new problems emerge. That is, even already specified rules, guidelines, policies, and codes will almost always have to be specified further to handle new or unanticipated circumstances.

As defenders of the common morality position see it, this is the way business ethics actually works, and it is through this progressive specification that we retain the common morality and make moral progress. The common morality can be extended as far as we need to extend it to meet practical objectives. There is, of course, always the possibility of developing more than one line of specification when confronting practical problems and moral disagreements. It is to be expected—indeed, it is unavoidable—that different persons and groups will offer conflicting specifications to resolve conflicts or vagueness. In any given problematic or dilemmatic case, several competing specifications may be offered by reasonable and fair-minded parties, all of whom are serious about maintaining fidelity to the common morality.

For example, many international organizations and multinational corporations are currently struggling with the nature of their obligations to protect the privacy of patient, client, and customer records. A striking example is the problem of how to rewrite rules of privacy in the Swiss banking system, which is now undergoing massive changes in its understanding of obligations to supply information to third parties. It is apparent that there are many sincere attempts in Switzerland and elsewhere to address this issue and that obligations of disclosure and privacy will be expressed differently in different institutions. There is no reason to think that only one set of privacy-protection rules is justifiable.

This diversity does not distress defenders of a common-morality theory, because they believe that all that we can ask of moral agents is that they impartially and faithfully specify the norms of the common morality with an eye to overall moral coherence.

## A Prologue to Theories of Justice

Many rules and principles form the terms of cooperation in society. Society is laced with implicit and explicit arrangements and agreements under which individuals are obligated to cooperate or abstain from interfering with others. Philosophers are interested in the justice of these terms of cooperation. They pose questions such as these: What gives one person or group of people the right to expect cooperation from another person or group of people in some societal interchange (especially an economic one) if the former benefit and the latter do not? Is it just for some citizens to have more property than others? Is it fair for one person to gain an economic advantage over another, if both abide strictly by existing societal rules?

In their attempts to answer such questions, some philosophers believe that diverse human judgments and beliefs about justice can be brought into systematic unity through a general theory of justice. Justice has been analyzed differently, however, in rival and often incompatible theories. These general normative theories of justice are treated in Chapter 10. Here we need note only that a key distinction between just *procedures* and just *results* exists in the literature on justice.

Ideally, it is preferable to have both, but this is not always possible. For example, a person might achieve a just result in redistributing wealth but might use an unjust procedure to achieve that result, such as undeserved taxation of certain groups. By contrast, just procedures sometimes eventuate in unjust results, as when a fair trial finds an innocent person guilty. Some writers in business ethics are concerned with issues of procedural justice when they discuss such concerns as the use of ombudsmen, grievance procedures, peer review, and arbitration procedures.

Many problems of justice that a cooperative society must handle involve some system or set of procedures that foster, but do not ensure, just outcomes. Once there is agreement on appropriate procedures, the outcome must be accepted as just, even if it produces inequalities that seem unjust by other standards. If procedural justice is the best that can be attained—as, for example, is claimed in the criminal justice system—society should accept the results of its system with a certain amount of humility and perhaps make allowances for inevitable inequalities and even inequities and misfortunes.

## ANALYSIS OF CASES

Every subsequent chapter of this volume contains cases involving business activities as well as judicial opinions ("case law"). Though these cases do not derive from moral philosophy, they merit moral analysis. The *case method,* as it is often called, has long been used in law and business for such purposes. Recently philosophical ethics has drawn attention to the importance of case studies, but their use is still controversial and unsettled.

### The Case Method in Law

Case law establishes precedents of evidence and justification. The earliest developments in the law's use of the case method occurred around 1870, when Christopher Columbus Langdell revolutionized academic standards and teaching techniques by introducing this system at the Harvard Law School.[28] Langdell's textbooks contained cases selected and arranged to reveal the pervasive meaning of legal terms and the rules and principles of law. He envisioned a dialectical or Socratic manner of argument to show students how concepts, rules, and principles are found in the legal reasoning of the judges who wrote the opinions. A teacher or legal scholar was to extract fundamental principles, much in the way a skillful biographer might extract the principles of a person's reasoning by studying his or her considered judgments.

However, Langdell's "principles" did not prove to be as invariant or as consistently applied across courts, contexts, or times as Langdell had anticipated. It turned out that incompatible and rival theories or approaches by judges tended to control many of the precedent cases. Nevertheless, the case method ultimately prevailed in U.S. law schools, and still today the study of cases offers teachers and students a powerful tool for generalizing from cases. In the thrust-and-parry classroom setting, teacher and student alike reach conclusions about the rights and wrongs found in the cases they read.

### The Case Method in Business

When the Harvard Business School was opened in 1908, its first dean, Edwin F. Gay, adopted the Law School curriculum as a prototype for courses on commercial law and eventually as a model throughout the business school. By 1919 the method had taken hold, and eventually it came to dominate business schools that emphasize deliberation and decision making, weighing competing considerations, and reaching a decision in complex and difficult circumstances.[29] Judgment, rather than doctrine, principle, or fact, was taught. Cases that could not be resolved by reference to available principles or precedents were preferred for instructional purposes over those that could be readily resolved. Thus, cases were selected because they were "hard cases."

Cases prepared for study under this method typically recreate a managerial situation in which dilemmas are confronted. Cases are not primarily used to illustrate principles or rules, because the latter abstractions are generally inadequate for final resolutions in real-world business situations. The objective is to develop a capacity to grasp problems and to find novel solutions that work in very puzzling circumstances: *Knowing how* to think and act is more prized than *knowing that* something is the case or that a principle applies.

This use of the case method in business schools springs from an ideal of education that puts the student in the decision-making role after an initial immersion into the facts of a complex situation. Theories and generalizations are downplayed in this pedagogy, and the skills of thinking and acting in complex and uncertain environments are upgraded. The essence of the case method is to present a situation replete with the facts, opinions, and prejudices an executive might encounter (often in an actual case) and to help the student find a way to make decisions in such an environment.

This method makes no assumption that there is a *right* answer to any problem but maintains only that there are more or less successful ways of handling problems. Understanding argument and analysis (as discussed in the first section of this chapter) is more important than understanding substantive theories (as presented in the second section). These forms of understanding need not be antagonistic or competitive, but the case method in business schools has placed the premium on problem-based analysis, rather than on analysis by appeal to theory. This method also avoids the authority-based method relied on in law schools, where judges and the body of law are overriding authorities.

### The Case Method in Ethics

The term *casuistry* is now commonly used in ethics to refer to a method of using cases to analyze and propose solutions to moral problems. Casuists see ethics as based on seasoned experience in resolving hard cases.[30] The casuistical method is to start with *paradigm* cases whose conclusions on ethical matters are settled and then to compare and contrast the central features in the paradigm cases with the features of cases in need of a decision.

To illustrate this point, consider a comparison to case law and the doctrine of precedent. Judicial decisions have the potential to become authoritative for other judges when they confront similar cases in similar circumstances. Contemporary casuistry places a comparable premium on case authority, together with a strong preference for analogical reasoning over ethical theory and abstract principles. It is analogical reasoning that links one case to the next. Moral reasoning occurs by appeal to analogies, models, classification schemes, and even immediate intuition and discerning insight about particulars.

Casuists also maintain that principles and rules are typically too indeterminate to yield specific moral judgments. It is therefore impossible, casuists insist, that there be a unidirectional movement of thought from principles to cases—what has often been called the "application" of a principle to a case. Moreover, from a casuists' perspective, principles are merely summaries of peoples' experience in reflecting on cases, not independent norms.

There is much in these casuistical arguments that is revealing and worth serious consideration, but casuists sometimes write as though cases lead to moral paradigms or judgments entirely by their facts alone. This thesis seems mistaken. The properties that people observe to be of moral importance in cases are selected by the values that they have already accepted as being morally important or have come to appreciate while examining the case. No matter how many salient facts are assembled, there will still need to be some *value* premises in order to reach a moral conclusion.

Appeals to "paradigm cases" can easily conceal this fact. These "cases" might just as well be called "cases that contain a norm." Paradigm cases gain status as paradigms because of some commitment to central values that are preserved from one case to the next case. For someone to move constructively from case to case, one or more values must connect the cases. Even to recognize a case as a paradigm case is to accept whatever principles or values allow the paradigms to be extended to other cases. Whatever can be learned from a case and then exported to another case cannot be entirely specific to the first case; only some form of general norm (theory, principle, rule) can lead to the next case.

## Ethical Theory and Case Analysis

There are dangers in transferring the case methods in law and business to business ethics. Not much is drearier than a tedious and unrewarding exposure to the moral opinions of those ignorant of the kinds of material outlined in the first and second parts of this chapter. Studying cases in business ethics is facilitated by a knowledge of the history of ethics and types of ethical theory. Theory and history, however, also should not remain isolated from modification by case study. Several reasons support this judgment.

First, it seems mistaken to say that ethical theory is not extracted from the examination of cases but only applied to or specified in cases. Cases not only provide data for theory but also act as the testing ground for theories. Illuminating cases lead to modification and refinements of theoretical commitments, especially by pointing to limitations of theories. In thinking through the possible role of case analysis in ethics, it is useful to consider John Rawls's celebrated account of "reflective equilibrium." In developing an ethical theory, he argues, it is appropriate to start with the broadest possible set of considered moral judgments and to erect a provisional set of principles that reflects them. Reflective equilibrium views ethics as a way of testing moral beliefs to make them as coherent as possible. Starting with paradigms of what is morally proper or morally improper, one then searches for principles that are consistent with these paradigms. Widely accepted principles of right action and considered judgments are taken, as Rawls puts it, "provisionally as fixed points" but also as "liable to revision."

*Considered judgments* is a technical term referring to "judgments in which our moral capacities are most likely to be displayed without distortion." Examples are judgments about the wrongness of racial discrimination, religious intolerance, and political conflict of interest. By contrast, judgments in which one's confidence level is low or in which one is influenced by the possibility of personal gain are excluded. The goal is to match and prune considered judgments and principles in an attempt to make them coherent.[31]

In conclusion, we can recall the previous discussions in the first part of this chapter on relativism and moral disagreement. Often when discussing difficult cases, many points of view are bounced around the classroom, and the controversies may seem intractable and not subject to a persuasive form of analysis transcending personal opinion. Far from viewing their class as an environment of learning, students may perceive the class as a kind of bulletin board upon which scores of opinions are tacked. It would be a mistake, however, to conclude that such critical discussion eventuates only in opinion and monologue. Many apparent moral dilemmas do turn out to be partially resolvable in the context of such discussion, and often a consensus position emerges through dialogue, even if no one entirely agrees on the theoretical reasons for defending the consensus position.

Cases should always be examined in terms of alternative strategies and actions. Invariably, many alternatives will be proposed, but just as invariably they will not all be equally good. Even if intractable disagreement occurs, learning how to spot problems and help alleviate or deflect them may turn out to be as important as the substantive issues themselves.

## NOTES

1. Dana Milbank, "Hiring Welfare People, Hotel Chain Finds, Is Tough But Rewarding," *Wall Street Journal* (October 31, 1996).
2. Robert Lindsey, "Ancient Redwood Trees Fall to a Wall Street Takeover," *New York Times* (March 2, 1988), pp. A16–17.
3. Insurance Information Institute, "Asbestos Liability" (New York, Jan. 15, 2003): www.iii.org/media/hottopics/insurance/asbestos
4. Taken from Peter Huber, "The Press Gets Off Easy in Tort Law," *Wall Street Journal* (July 24, 1985), editorial page.

5. "Principle Sale," *Wall Street Journal* (May 22, 1985), p. 35.
6. "Bowing to the Inevitable," *Forbes* (August 12, 1985), p. 66.
7. Thomas Hobbes, *Leviathan*, Part I, Chap. 13, Par. 9.
8. This thesis is argued (without reference to philosophical theories of egoism) by Wolfgang Sauer, "Also a Concrete Self-Interest," *United Nations Chronicle* (Issue on "Global Sustainable Development: The Corporate Responsibility"), Online Edition (2002): www.un.org/pubs/chronicle/2002/issue3
9. For an act-utilitarian example in business ethics, see R. M. Hare, "Commentary on Beauchamp's Manipulative Advertising," *Business and Professional Ethics Journal*, 3 (1984): 23–28; for a rule-utilitarian example, see Robert Almeder, "In Defense of Sharks: Moral Issues in Hostile Liquidating Takeovers," *Journal of Business Ethics*, 10 (1991): 471–484.
10. Tom L. Beauchamp, ed., *Case Studies in Business, Society, and Ethics*, 5th ed. (Upper Saddle River, NJ: Prentice Hall, 2004), Chap. 3.
11. CNN.com (Sept. 3, 1999), "Online Shoppers Bid Millions for Human Kidney."
12. Madhav Goyal, et al., "Economic and Health Consequences of Selling a Kidney in India," *Journal of the American Medical Association*, 288 (October 2, 2002): 1589–93.
13. Mary Schlangenstein, "Workers Chip In to Help Southwest Employees Offer Free Labor," *The Seattle Times* (Sept. 26, 2001), p. E1.
14. See Jennifer Hull, "Unocal Sues Bank," *Wall Street Journal* (March 13, 1985), p. 22; and Charles McCoy, "Mesa Petroleum Alleges Unocal Coerced Banks," *Wall Street Journal* (March 22, 1985), p. 6.
15. See David S. Hilzenrath, "Taking Aim at Insider Bank Deals," *Washington Post* (September 30, 1991), Washington Business sec., p. 1.
16. Ralph King, "Insider Loans: Everyone Was Doing It," Business 2.0: www.business2.com/articles/mag (as posted January 15, 2003).
17. For a landmark agreement on the Island of Saipan (a class action settlement), see *The Legal Intelligencer*, 227, no. 64 (Sept. 30, 2002), National News Section, p. 4.
18. Ronald Dworkin argues that *political* morality is rights-based in *Taking Rights Seriously* (London: Duckworth, 1977), p. 171. John Mackie has applied this thesis to *morality generally* in "Can There Be a Right-Based Moral Theory?" *Midwest Studies in Philosophy*, 3 (1978): esp. p. 350. See further Judith Jarvis Thomson, *The Realm of Rights* (Cambridge, MA: Harvard University Press, 1990), pp. 122ff.
19. See further Alan Gewirth, "Why Rights are Indispensable," *Mind*, 95 (1986): 333; and Gewirth's later book, *The Community of Rights* (Chicago: University of Chicago Press, 1996).
20. See David Braybrooke, "The Firm but Untidy Correlativity of Rights and Obligations," *Canadian Journal of Philosophy* 1 (1972): 351–63; Carl P. Wellman, *Real Rights* (New York: Oxford University Press, 1995).
21. See the treatment of these distinctions in Eric Mack, ed., *Positive and Negative Duties* (New Orleans: Tulane University Press, 1985).
22. Carol Gilligan, *In a Different Voice* (Cambridge, MA: Harvard University Press, 1982).
23. Annette Baier, *Moral Prejudices* (Cambridge, MA: Harvard University Press, 1994), Chapter 4; and *Postures of the Mind* (Minneapolis: University of Minnesota Press, 1985), pp. 210–219.
24. Although there is only a single, universal common morality, there is more than one *theory* of the common morality. The common morality is universally shared; it is not a *theory* of what is universally shared. For examples of diverse theories of the common morality, see Alan Donagan, *The Theory of Morality* (Chicago: University of Chicago Press, 1977); Bernard Gert, Charles M. Culver, and K. Danner Clouser,

*Bioethics: A Return to Fundamentals* (New York: Oxford University Press, 1997); and W. D. Ross, *The Foundations of Ethics* (Oxford: Oxford University Press, 1939).

25. See Sissela Bok, *Common Values* (Columbia, MO: University of Missouri Press, 1995), pp. 13–23, 50–59. She cites a body of influential writers on the subject.
26. Compare the arguments in G. J. Warnock, *The Object of Morality* (London; Methuen & Co., 1971), esp. pp. 15–26; John Mackie, *Ethics: Inventing Right and Wrong* (London: Penguin, 1977), pp. 107ff.
27. See Henry Richardson, "Specifying Norms as a Way to Resolve Concrete Ethical Problems," *Philosophy and Public Affairs* 19 (1990), pp. 279–310; Richardson, "Specifying, Balancing, and Interpreting Bioethical Principles," *Journal of Medicine and Philosophy* 25 (2000), 285–307.
28. Christopher Columbus Langdell's first casebook on *Contracts* is treated in Lawrence M. Friedman, *A History of American Law* (New York: Simon and Schuster, 1973), pp. 531f. The general account of the case method in this section is indebted to this source, and also to G. Edward White, *Tort Law in America: An Intellectual History* (New York: Oxford University Press, 1980).
29. See M. P. McNair, ed., *The Case Method at the Harvard Business School* (New York: McGraw-Hill, 1954).
30. See Albert Jonsen and Stephen Toulmin, *Abuse of Casuistry* (Berkeley: University of California Press, 1988), pp. 11–19, 66–67, 251–254, 296–299; John Arras, "Principles and Particularity," *Indiana Law Journal* 69 (1994).
31. John Rawls, *A Theory of Justice* (Cambridge, MA: Harvard University Press, 1971), pp. 20ff, 46–48 (1999 edition, pp. 15–19, 40–46).

# Chapter Two

# The Purpose of the Corporation

THIS CHAPTER FOCUSES on corporate social responsibility. The socially responsible corporation is the good corporation. Over two thousand years ago the Greeks thought they could answer questions about the goodness of things by knowing about the purpose of things. These Greek philosophers provided a functional analysis of good. For example, if one determines what a good racehorse is by knowing the purpose of racehorses (to win races) and the characteristics—for instance, speed, agility, and discipline—horses must have to win races, then a good racehorse is speedy, agile, and disciplined. To adapt the Greeks' method of reasoning, one determines what a good (socially responsible) corporation is by investigating the purpose corporations should serve in society.

## STOCKHOLDER MANAGEMENT VERSUS STAKEHOLDER MANAGEMENT

For many, the view that the purpose of the corporation is to make a profit for stockholders is beyond debate and is accepted as a matter of fact. The classical U.S. view that a corporation's primary and perhaps sole purpose is to maximize profits for stockholders is most often associated with the Nobel Prize-winning economist Milton Friedman. This chapter presents arguments for and against the Friedmanite view that the purpose of a corporation is to maximize stockholder profits.

Friedman has two main arguments for his position. First, stockholders are the *owners* of the corporation, and hence corporate profits *belong* to the stockholders. Managers are agents of the stockholders and have a moral obligation to manage the firm in the interest of the stockholders, that is, to maximize shareholder wealth. If the management of a firm donates some of the firm's income to charitable organizations, it is seen as an illegitimate use of stockholders' money. If individual stockholders wish to donate their dividends to charity, they are free to do so since the money is theirs. But managers have no right to donate corporate funds to charity. If society decides that private charity is insufficient to meet the needs of the poor, to maintain art museums, and to finance research for curing diseases, it is the responsibility of government to raise the necessary money through taxation. It should not come from managers purportedly acting on behalf of the corporation.

Second, stockholders are entitled to their profits as a result of a contract among the corporate stakeholders. A product or service is the result of the productive efforts of a number of parties—employees, managers, customers, suppliers, the local community, and the stockholders. Each of these stakeholder groups has a contractual relationship with the firm. In return for their services, the managers and employees are paid in the form of wages; the local community is paid in the form of taxes; and suppliers, under the constraints of supply and demand, negotiate the return for their products directly with the firm. Funds remaining after these payments have been made represent profit, and by agreement the profit belongs to the stockholders. The stockholders bear the risk when they supply the capital, and profit is the contractual return they receive for risk taking. Thus each party in the manufacture and sale of a product receives the remuneration it has freely agreed to.

Friedman believes that these voluntary contractual arrangements maximize economic freedom and that economic freedom is a necessary condition for political freedom. Political rights gain efficacy in a capitalist system. For example, private employers are forced by competitive pressures to be concerned primarily with a prospective employee's ability to produce rather than with that person's political views. Opposing voices are heard in books, in the press, or on television so long as there is a profit to be made. Finally, the existence of capitalist markets limits the number of politically based decisions and thus increases freedom. Even democratic decisions coerce the opposing minority. Once society votes on how much to spend for defense or for city streets, the minority must go along. In the market, each consumer can decide how much of a product or service he or she is willing to purchase. Thus Friedman entitled his book defending the classical view of the purpose of the firm *Capitalism and Freedom.*

The classical view that a corporation's primary responsibility is to seek stockholder profit is embodied in the legal opinion *Dodge v. Ford Motor Company* included in this chapter. The Court ruled that the benefits of higher salaries for Ford workers and the benefits of lower auto prices to consumers must not take priority over stockholder interests. According to *Dodge,* the interests of the stockholder are supreme.

Some have criticized Friedman on the grounds that his view justifies anything that will lead to the maximization of profits including acting immorally or illegally if the manager can get away with it. We think that criticism of Friedman is unfair. In his classic article reprinted in this chapter Friedman says:

> In such a society, "there is one and only one social responsibility of business—to use its resources and engage in activities designed to increase its profit so long as it stays within the rules of the game, which is to say, engages in open and free competition without deception or fraud." (1970, p. 126)

Thus the manager may not do anything to maximize profits. Unfortunately, Friedman has never fully elaborated on what the rules of the game in a capitalist economy are. And some of his followers have argued for tactics that strike many as unethical. For example, Theodore Levitt has argued in defense of deceptive advertising[1] and in favor of strong industry lobbying to have the government pass laws that are favorable to business and to reject laws that are unfavorable.[2] And Albert Carr has argued that business is like the game of poker and thus, just as in poker, behavior that is unethical in everyday life is justified in business.[3] (Carr does admit that just as in poker there are some moral norms for business.)

Others have criticized Friedman on the grounds that the manager should use employees, customers, and suppliers if by doing so it can generate profit. Thus if wages can be cut to generate profit, they should be cut. Theoretically, that may indeed follow from Friedman's view and some managers and CEOs even behave that way. But as a practical matter, the manager usually can only generate profits if she treats employees, customers, and suppliers well—thus the expression "close to the customer" and books such as Jeffery Pfeiffer's *Competitive Advantage Through People* and Frederick F. Reichheld's book *The Loyalty Effect.* In 1953, the legal system acknowledged the connection between corporate philanthropy and goodwill. In the case of *A.P. Smith Manufacturing v. Barlow et al.* a charitable contribution to Princeton University was deemed to be a legitimate exercise of management authority. In the appeals case reprinted in this chapter, Judge Jacobs recognizes that an act that supports the public welfare can also be in the best interest of the corporation itself. The implication of this discussion is that in terms of behavior there may be no discernible difference between an "enlightened" Friedmanite and a manager who holds to the view that the purpose of the corporation involves more than the maximization of profit. The difference, to put it in a Kantian context, is in the motive. The enlightened Friedmanite treats employees well in order to generate profit. The non-Friedmanite treats employees well because that is one of the things a corporation is supposed to do.

Nearly all business ethicists concur with the general public that one of the purposes of a publicly held firm is to make a profit and thus making a profit is an obligation of the firm. Although many people also believe that the managers of publicly held corporations are legally required to maximize the profits for stockholders, this is not strictly true. Even in the most traditional interpretation managers have a fiduciary obligation to the corporation, which is then interpreted as a fiduciary obligation to stockholder interests. But during the merger and acquisition craze of the 1980s, several states passed laws permitting the managers to take into account the needs of the other stakeholders. Indiana was one of the first states to do so and many other states have followed. Other countries are even less enamored with the Friedman model. The London Stock Exchange has endorsed the Turnbull Committee report and as a result all companies listed on the London Stock Exchange will have to take into account "environment, reputation, business probity issues" when implementing internal controls.[4]

Although managers may not be obligated to maximize profits, they certainly do have an obligation to avoid conflicts of interest where it appears that they benefit at the expense of the stockholders. Many groups that defend stockholder rights are legitimately concerned with serious issues of corporate governance. Such issues as excessive executive pay, especially when it is not linked to performance, overly generous stock options, and golden parachutes in case of a hostile takeover or even friendly merger have all legitimately come under scrutiny.

Concerns about these issues reached a pinnacle in 2002 as a wave of corporate scandals including Enron, Arthur Andersen, and World Com swept across the United States. Federal legislation and revised industry standards have led to reform in the area of corporate governance. The success of these reforms remains to be determined. And some issues such as excessive executive compensation need further attention.

And stockholders need to be concerned about more than conflicts of interest. Managers like to keep information secret as well. Even if a case can be made for charitable contributions on the part of corporations, it would seem that stockholders have a right to know which charities receive corporate funds. But corporations have opposed a law that would require disclosing such information to shareholders.[5]

An alternative way to understand the purpose of the corporation is to consider those affected by business decisions, which are referred to as corporate stakeholders. From the stakeholders' perspective, the classical view is problematic in that all emphasis is placed on one stakeholder—the stockholder. The interests of the other stakeholders are unfairly subordinated to the stockholders' interests. Although any person or group affected by corporate decisions is a stakeholder, most stakeholder analysis has focused on a special group of stakeholders: namely, members of groups whose existence was necessary for the firm's survival. Traditionally, six stakeholder groups have been identified: stockholders, employees, customers, managers, suppliers, and the local community. Managers who manage from the stakeholder perspective see their task as harmonizing the legitimate interests of the primary corporate stakeholders. In describing stakeholder management, R. Edward Freeman proposes a set of principles that could make this kind of harmonizing possible.

Both in corporate and academic circles, stakeholder terminology has become very fashionable. For example, many corporate codes of conduct are organized around stakeholder principles.

However, many theoretical problems remain. Stakeholder theory is still in its early developmental stage. Much has been said of the obligations of managers to the other corporate stakeholders, but little has been said about the obligations of the other stakeholders, for instance, the community or employees, to the corporation. Do members of a community have an obligation to consider the moral reputation of a company when they make their purchasing decisions? Do employees have an obligation to stay with a company that has invested in their training even if they could get a slightly better salary by moving to another corporation?

Perhaps the most pressing problems for stakeholder theory are to specify in more detail the rights and responsibilities that each stakeholder group has and to suggest how the conflicting rights and responsibilities among the stakeholder groups can be resolved.

## WHICH VIEW IS BETTER?

Is the Friedmanite view that the purpose of the firm is to maximize profits or the stakeholder view that the firm is to be managed in the interests of the various stakeholders more adequate? In the two articles that conclude the chapter, John Hasnas points out inadequacies in stakeholder theory, while John Boatright presents additional difficulties for the Friedmanite position.

In his article, John Hasnas challenges those who hold that it is not wrong to spend other people's money without their consent. Even if you could increase total welfare by so doing, it would still be wrong from a nonconsequentialist perspective. And spending the money of stockholders on social responsibility is not like taxing people in a democracy for projects they do not endorse. Friedman makes a legitimate point when he says that contributions to social responsibility without the consent of the stockholders is to deprive them of profits without their consent.

In addition, stakeholder theorists are not entitled to draw some of the conclusions they do from their starting premises. A stockholder theorist could agree with Freeman that stakeholders be treated with respect and that they are entitled to participate in decisions that affect them. If one holds to a contractual theory of the nature of the firm, then the stakeholders have been treated with respect and have participated in the sense of negotiating the terms of their contracts. As for Freeman's particular suggestion that Rawls's device of the original position be used to determine management's obligations to stakeholders, Hasnas indicates that the stockholder position might be the one endorsed. Thus Hasnas maintains that stakeholder theory is without an adequate foundation.

On the other side, John Boatright asks provocatively "What's so special about stakeholders?" He argues that Friedman and his followers are mistaken in their view that a firm is a nexus of contracts and that managers are mere agents of the stockholders. As Boatright points out, managers are denied some of the powers of genuine agents in the legal sense. Simultaneously, the managers are not significantly under the control of the stockholders—a view that has been argued for over fifty years and is often expressed by corporate raiders who desire to take over a firm. Boatright concludes by showing that stockholders have been given special attention because public policy believed it was in the public interest to do so.

What is one to conclude with respect to this dispute? It seems that stockholders are in a special relationship with respect to profits but the relationship is not so special as has been traditionally thought. Moreover, it may not even be in the public interest to retain the traditional idea about the preeminence of the stockholder. Critics have argued that American managers are forced to manage to please Wall Street, which means they are forced to manage for the short term. And these critics have gone on to argue that the focus on the short term has led to inordinate cutbacks in employees and frayed relationships with top managers of corporations and the rank and file.

However, if a shift is made to consider long-term profitability, then there is a greater likelihood that in terms of managerial behavior, the stockholder theory and the stakeholder theory will coincide. Thus it can be argued that as a practical matter there may not be a great difference between the two perspectives. Even charitable giving and the attempt by corporations to solve social problems can be defended on Friedmanite grounds. In the twin cities of Minneapolis/St. Paul, it is believed that Target maintains a competitive advantage over Wal-Mart because of the former's reputation for charitable activities. What distinguishes a Friedmanite from a stakeholder theorist is the motivation a manager has for considering stakeholder interests. The Friedmanite treats stakeholders well in order to make a profit, while the stakeholder theorist treats stakeholders well because it is the right thing to do. Paradoxically, treating stakeholders well because it is right may end up being more profitable. In 1987 the Dayton Hudson Corporation was able to avoid a hostile takeover by the Hafts because the Minnesota legislature intervened to protect a good corporate citizen.

## NOTES

1. Theodore Levitt, "The Morality (?) of Advertising," *Harvard Business Review* (July–August, 1970), pp. 84–92.
2. Theodore Levitt, "The Dangers of Social Responsibility," *Harvard Business Review* (September–October, 1958), pp. 41–50.
3. Albert Z. Carr, "Is Business Bluffing Ethical?" *Harvard Business Review* (January–February, 1968), pp. 143–153.
4. *Ethical Performance,* 1 (1999).
5. Adam Bryant, "Companies Oppose Idea of Disclosing Charitable Giving," *New York Times* (April 3, 1998).

## STOCKHOLDER MANAGEMENT VERSUS STAKEHOLDER MANAGEMENT

# The Social Responsibility of Business Is to Increase Its Profits

*Milton Friedman*

When I hear businessmen speak eloquently about the "social responsibilities of business in a free-enterprise system," I am reminded of the wonderful line about the Frenchman who discovered at the age of 70 that he had been speaking prose all his life. The businessmen believe that they are defending free enterprise when they declaim that business is not concerned "merely" with profit but also with promoting desirable "social" ends; that business has a "social conscience" and takes seriously its responsibilities for providing employment, eliminating discrimination, avoiding pollution and whatever else may be the catchwords of the contemporary crop of reformers. In fact they are—or would be if they or anyone else took them seriously—preaching pure and unadulterated socialism.

---

Businessmen who talk this way are unwitting puppets of the intellectual forces that have been undermining the basis of a free society these past decades.

The discussions of the "social responsibilities of business" are notable for their analytical looseness and lack of rigor. What does it mean to say that "business" has responsibilities? Only people can have responsibilities. A corporation is an artificial person and in this sense may have artificial responsibilities, but "business" as a whole cannot be said to have responsibilities, even in this vague sense. The first step toward clarity in examining the doctrine of the social responsibility of business is to ask precisely what it implies for whom.

Presumably, the individuals who are to be responsible are businessmen, which means individual proprietors or corporate executives. Most of the discussion of social responsibility is directed at corporations, so in what follows I shall mostly neglect the individual proprietors and speak of corporate executives.

In a free-enterprise, private-property system, a corporate executive is an employee of the owners of the business. He has direct responsibility to his employers. That responsibility is to conduct the business in accordance with their desires, which generally will be to make as much money as possible while conforming to the basic rules of the society, both those embodied in law and those embodied in ethical custom. Of course, in some cases his employers may have a different objective. A group of persons might establish a corporation for an eleemosynary purpose—for example, a hospital or a school. The manager of such a corporation will not have money profit as his objective but the rendering of certain services.

In either case, the key point is that, in his capacity as a corporate executive, the manager is the agent of the individuals who own the corporation or establish the eleemosynary institution, and his primary responsibility is to them.

Needless to say, this does not mean that it is easy to judge how well he is performing his task. But at least the criterion of performance is straightforward, and the persons among whom a voluntary contractual arrangement exists are clearly defined.

Of course, the corporate executive is also a person in his own right. As a person, he may have many other responsibilities that he recognizes or assumes voluntarily—to his family, his conscience, his feelings of charity, his church, his clubs, his city, his country. He may feel impelled by these responsibilities to devote part of his income to causes he regards as worthy, to refuse to work for particular corporations, even to leave his job, for example, to join his country's armed forces. If we wish, we may refer to some of these responsibilities as "social responsibilities." But in these respects he is acting as a principal, not an agent; he is spending his own money or time or energy, not the money of his employers or the time or energy he has contracted to devote to their purposes. If these are "social responsibilities," they are the social responsibilities of individuals, not of business.

What does it mean to say that the corporate executive has a "social responsibility" in his capacity as businessman? If this statement is not pure rhetoric, it must mean that he is to act in some way that is not in the interest of his employers. For example, that he is to refrain from increasing the price of the product in order to contribute to the social objective of preventing inflation, even though a price increase would be in the best interests of the corporation. Or that he is to make expenditures on reducing pollution beyond the amount that is in the best interests of the corporation or that is required by law in order to contribute to the social objective of improving the environment. Or that, at the expense of corporate profits, he is to hire "hardcore" unemployed instead of better qualified available workmen to contribute to the social objective of reducing poverty.

In each of these cases, the corporate executive would be spending someone else's money for a general social interest. Insofar as his actions in accord with his "social responsibility" reduce returns to stockholders, he is spending their money. Insofar as his actions raise the price to customers, he is spending the customers' money. Insofar as his actions lower the wages of some employees, he is spending their money.

The stockholders or the customers or the employees could separately spend their own money on the particular action if they wished to do so. The executive is exercising a distinct "social responsibility," rather than serving as an agent of the stockholders or the customers or the employees, only if he spends the money in a different way than they would have spent it.

But if he does this, he is in effect imposing taxes, on the one hand, and deciding how the tax proceeds shall be spent, on the other.

This process raises political questions on two levels: principle and consequences. On the level of political principle, the imposition of taxes and the expenditure of tax proceeds are governmental functions. We have established elaborate constitutional, parliamentary, and judicial provisions to control these functions, to assure that taxes are imposed so far as possible in accordance with the preferences and desires of the public—after all, "taxation without representation" was one of the battle cries of the American Revolution. We have a system of checks and balances to separate the legislative function of imposing taxes and enacting expenditures from the executive function of collecting taxes and administering expenditure programs and from the judicial function of mediating disputes and interpreting the law.

Here the businessman—self-selected or appointed directly or indirectly by stockholders—is to be simultaneously legislator, executive, and jurist. He is to decide whom to tax by how much and for what purpose, and he is to spend the proceeds—all this guided only by general exhortations from on high to restrain inflation, improve the environment, fight poverty and so on and on.

The whole justification for permitting the corporate executive to be selected by the stockholders is that the executive is an agent serving the interests of his principal. This justification disappears when the corporate executive imposes taxes and spends the proceeds for "social" purposes. He becomes in effect a public employee, a civil servant, even though he remains in name an employee of a private enterprise. On grounds of political principle, it is intolerable that such civil servants—insofar as their actions in the name of social responsibility are real and not just window-dressing—should be selected as they are now. If they are to be civil servants, then they must be elected through a political process. If they are to impose taxes and make expenditures to foster "social" objectives, then political machinery must be set up to make the assessment of taxes and to determine through a political process the objectives to be served.

This is the basic reason why the doctrine of "social responsibility" involves the acceptance of the socialist view that political mechanisms, not market mechanisms, are the appropriate way to determine the allocation of scarce resources to alternative uses.

On the grounds of consequences, can the corporate executive in fact discharge his alleged "social responsibilities?" On the other hand, suppose he could get away with spending the stockholders' or customers' or employees' money. How is he to know how to spend it? He is told that he must contribute to fighting inflation. How is he to know what action of his will contribute to that end? He is presumably an expert in running his company—in producing a product or selling it or financing it. But nothing about his selection makes him an expert on inflation. Will his holding down the price of his product reduce inflationary pressure? Or, by leaving more spending power in the hands of his customers, simply divert it elsewhere? Or, by forcing him to produce less because of the lower price, will it simply contribute to shortages? Even if he could answer these questions, how much cost is he justified in imposing on his stockholders, customers, and employees for this social purpose? What is his appropriate share and what is the appropriate share of others?

And, whether he wants to or not, can he get away with spending his stockholders', customers' or employees' money? Will not the stockholders fire him? (Either the present ones or those who take over when his actions in the name of social responsibility have reduced the corporation's profits and the price of its stock.) His customers and his employees can desert him for other producers and employers less scrupulous in exercising their social responsibilities.

This facet of "social responsibility" doctrine is brought into sharp relief when the doctrine is used to justify wage restraint by trade unions. The conflict of interest is naked and clear when union officials are asked to subordinate the interest of their members to some more general purpose. If the union officials try to enforce wage restraint, the consequence is likely to be wildcat strikes, rank-and-file revolts, and the emergence of strong competitors for their jobs. We thus have the ironic phenomenon that union leaders—at least in the U.S.—have objected to Government interference with the market far more consistently and courageously than have business leaders.

The difficulty of exercising "social responsibility" illustrates, of course, the great virtue of private competitive enterprise—it forces people to be responsible for their own actions and makes it difficult for them to "exploit" other people for either selfish or unselfish purposes. They can do good—but only at their own expense.

Many a reader who has followed the argument this far may be tempted to remonstrate that it is all well and good to speak of Government's having the responsibility to impose taxes and determine expenditures for such "social" purposes as controlling pollution or training the hard-core unemployed, but that the problems are too urgent to wait on the slow course of political processes, that the exercise of social responsibility by businessmen is a quicker and surer way to solve pressing current problems.

Aside from the question of fact—I share Adam Smith's skepticism about the benefits that can be expected from "those who affected to trade for the public good"—this argument must be rejected on grounds of principle. What it amounts to is an assertion that those who favor the taxes and expenditures in question have failed to persuade a majority of their fellow citizens to be of like mind and that they are seeking to attain by undemocratic procedures what they cannot attain by democratic procedures. In a free society, it is hard for "evil" people to do "evil," especially since one man's good is another's evil.

I have, for simplicity, concentrated on the special case of the corporate executive, except only for the brief digression on trade unions. But precisely the same argument applies to the newer phenomenon of calling upon stockholders to require corporations to exercise social responsibility (the recent G.M. crusade for example). In most of these cases, what is in effect involved is some stockholders trying to get other stockholders (or customers or employees) to contribute against their will to "social" causes favored by the activists. Insofar as they succeed, they are again imposing taxes and spending the proceeds.

The situation of the individual proprietor is somewhat different. If he acts to reduce the returns of his enterprise in order to exercise his "social responsibility," he is spending his own money, not someone else's. If he wishes to spend his money on such purposes, that is his right, and I cannot see that there is any objection to his doing so. In the process, he, too, may impose costs on employees and customers. However, because he is far less likely than a large corporation or union to have monopolistic power, any such side effects will tend to be minor.

Of course, in practice, the doctrine of social responsibility is frequently a cloak for actions that are justified on other grounds rather than a reason for those actions.

To illustrate, it may well be in the long-run interest of a corporation that is a major employer in a small community to devote resources to providing amenities to that community or to improving its government. That may make it easier to attract desirable employees, it may reduce the wage bill or lessen losses from pilferage and sabotage or have other worthwhile effects. Or it may be that, given the laws about the deductibility of corporate charitable contributions, the stockholders can contribute more to charities they favor by having the corporation make the gift than by doing it themselves, since they can in that way contribute an amount that would otherwise have been paid as corporate taxes.

In each of these—and many similar—cases, there is a strong temptation to rationalize these actions as an exercise of "social responsibility." In the present climate of opinion, with its wide-spread aversion to "capitalism," "profits," the "soulless corporation," and so on, this is one way for a corporation to generate goodwill as a by-product of expenditures that are entirely justified in its own self-interest.

It would be inconsistent of me to call on corporate executives to refrain from this hypocritical window-dressing because it harms the foundations of a free society. That would be to call on them to exercise a "social responsibility"! If our institutions, and the attitudes of the public make it in their self-interest to cloak their actions in this way, I cannot summon much indignation to denounce them. At the same time, I can express admiration for those individual proprietors or owners of closely held corporations or stockholders of more broadly held corporations who disdain such tactics as approaching fraud.

Whether blameworthy or not, the use of the cloak of social responsibility, and the nonsense spoken in its name by influential and prestigious businessmen, does clearly harm the foundations of a free society. I have been impressed time and again by the schizophrenic character of many businessmen. They are capable of being extremely farsighted and clear-headed in matters that are internal to their businesses. They are incredibly short-sighted and muddle-headed in matters that are outside their businesses but affect the possible survival of business in general. This short-sightedness is strikingly exemplified in the calls from many businessmen for wage and price guidelines or controls or income policies. There is nothing that could do more in a brief period to destroy a market system and replace it by a centrally controlled system than effective governmental control of prices and wages.

The short-sightedness is also exemplified in speeches by businessmen on social responsibility. This may gain them kudos in the short run. But it helps to strengthen the already too prevalent view that the pursuit of profits is wicked and immoral and must be curbed and controlled by external forces. Once this view is adopted, the external forces that curb the market will not be the social consciences, however highly developed, of the pontificating executives; it will be the iron fist of Government bureaucrats. Here, as with price and wage controls, businessmen seem to me to reveal a suicidal impulse.

The political principle that underlies the market mechanism is unanimity. In an ideal free market resting on private property, no individual can coerce any other, all cooperation is voluntary, all parties to such cooperation benefit or they need not participate. There are no values, no "social" responsibilities in any sense other than the shared values and responsibilities of individuals. Society is a collection of individuals and of the various groups they voluntarily form.

The political principle that underlies the political mechanism is conformity. The individual must serve a more general social interest—whether that be determined by a church or a dictator or a majority. The individual may have a vote and say in what is to be done, but if he is overruled, he must conform. It is appropriate for some to require others to contribute to a general social purpose whether they wish to or not.

Unfortunately, unanimity is not always feasible. There are some respects in which conformity appears unavoidable, so I do not see how one can avoid the use of the political mechanism altogether.

But the doctrine of "social responsibility" taken seriously would extend the scope of the political mechanism to every human activity. It does not differ in philosophy from the most explicitly collectivist doctrine. It differs only by professing to believe that collectivist ends can be attained without collectivist means. That is why, in my book *Capitalism and Freedom*, I have called it a "fundamentally subversive doctrine" in a free society, and have said that in such a society, "there is one and only one social responsibility of business—to use its resources and engage in activities designed to increase its profits so long as it stays within the rules of the game, which is to say, engages in open and free competition without deception or fraud."

# A Stakeholder Theory of the Modern Corporation

*R. Edward Freeman*

## INTRODUCTION

> Corporations have ceased to be merely legal devices through which the private business transactions of individuals may be carried on. Though still much used for this purpose, the corporate form has acquired a larger significance. The corporation has, in fact, become both a method of property tenure and a means of organizing economic life. Grown to tremendous proportions, there may be said to have evolved a "corporate system"—which has attracted to itself a combination of attributes and powers, and has attained a degree of prominence entitling it to be dealt with as a major social institution.[1]

Despite these prophetic words of Berle and Means (1932), scholars and managers alike continue to hold sacred the view that managers

Portions of this essay are contained in William E. Evan and R. Edward Freeman, "A Stakeholder Theory of the Modern Corporation: Kantian Capitalism" published in the third (1988) and fourth (1993) edition of this anthology and in R. Edward Freeman, "The Politics of Stakeholder Theory," *Business Ethics Quarterly*, 4 (1994), pp. 409–21. I am grateful to the editors of this volume for their editing of these two works. Used by permission of the authors and *Business Ethics Quarterly*.

bear a special relationship to the stockholders in the firm. Since stockholders own shares in the firm, they have certain rights and privileges, which must be granted to them by management, as well as by others. Sanctions, in the form of "the law of corporations," and other protective mechanisms in the form of social custom, accepted management practice, myth, and ritual, are thought to reinforce the assumption of the primacy of the stockholder.

The purpose of this paper is to pose several challenges to this assumption, from within the framework of managerial capitalism, and to suggest the bare bones of an alternative theory, *a stakeholder theory of the modern corporation*. I do not seek the demise of the modern corporation, either intellectually or in fact. Rather, I seek its transformation. In the words of Neurath, we shall attempt to "rebuild the ship, plank by plank, while it remains afloat."[2]

My thesis is that I can revitalize the concept of managerial capitalism by replacing the notion that managers have a duty to stockholders with the concept that managers bear a fiduciary relationship to stakeholders. Stakeholders are those groups who have a stake in or claim on the firm. Specifically I include suppliers, customers, employees, stockholders, and the local community, as well as management in its role as agent for these groups. I argue that the legal, economic, political, and moral challenges to the currently received theory of the firm, as a nexus of contracts among the owners of the factors of production and customers, require us to revise this concept. That is, each of these stakeholder groups has a right not to be treated as a means to some end, and therefore must participate in determining the future direction of the firm in which they have a stake.

The crux of my argument is that we must reconceptualize the firm around the following question: For whose benefit and at whose expense should the firm be managed? I shall set forth such a reconceptualization in the form of a *stakeholder theory of the firm*. I shall then critically examine the stakeholder view and its implications for the future of the capitalist system.

## THE ATTACK ON MANAGERIAL CAPITALISM

### The Legal Argument

The basic idea of managerial capitalism is that in return for controlling the firm, management vigorously pursues the interests of stockholders. Central to the managerial view of the firm is the idea that management can pursue market transactions with suppliers and customers in an unconstrained manner.

The law of corporations gives a less clear-cut answer to the question: In whose interest and for whose benefit should the modern corporation be governed? While it says that the corporations should be run primarily in the interests of the stockholders in the firm, it says further that the corporation exists "in contemplation of the law" and has personality as a "legal person," limited liability for its actions, and immortality, since its existence transcends that of its members. Therefore, directors and other officers of the firm have a fiduciary obligation to stockholders in the sense that the "affairs of the corporation" must be conducted in the interest of the stockholders. And stockholders can theoretically bring suit against those directors and managers for doing otherwise. But since the corporation is a legal person, existing in contemplation of the law, managers of the corporation are constrained by law.

Until recently, this was no constraint at all. In this century, however, the law has evolved to effectively constrain the pursuit of stockholder interests at the expense of other claimants on the firm. It has, in effect, required that the claims of customers, suppliers, local communities, and employees be taken into consideration, though in general they are subordinated to the claims of stockholders.

For instance, the doctrine of "privity of contract," as articulated in *Winterbottom v. Wright* in 1842, has been eroded by recent developments in products liability law. Indeed, *Greenman v. Yuba Power* gives the manufacturer strict liability for damage caused by its products, even though the seller has exercised all possible care in the preparation and sale of the product and the consumer has not bought the product from nor entered into any contractual arrangement with the manufacturer. Caveat emptor has been replaced, in large part, with caveat venditor.[3] The Consumer Product Safety Commission has the power to enact product recalls, and in 1980 one U.S. automobile company recalled more cars than it built. Some industries are required to provide information to customers about a product's ingredients, whether or not the customers want and are willing to pay for this information.[4]

The same argument is applicable to management's dealings with employees. The National Labor Relations Act gave employees the right to unionize and to bargain in good faith. It set up the National Labor Relations Board to enforce these rights with management. The Equal Pay Act of 1963 and Title VII of the Civil Rights Act of 1964 constrain management from discrimination in hiring practices; these have been followed with the Age Discrimination in Employment Act of 1967.[5] The emergence of a body of administrative case law arising from labor-management disputes and the historic settling of discrimination claims with large employers such as AT&T have caused the emergence of a body of practice in the corporation that is consistent with the legal guarantee of the rights of the employees. The law has protected the due process rights of those employees who enter into collective bargaining agreements with management. As of the present, however, only 30 percent of the labor force are participating in such agreements; this has prompted one labor law scholar to propose a statutory law prohibiting dismissals of the 70 percent of the work force not protected.[6]

The law has also protected the interests of local communities. The Clean Air Act and Clean Water Act have constrained management from "spoiling the commons." In an historic case, *Marsh v. Alabama*, the Supreme Court ruled that a company-owned town was subject to the provisions of the U.S. Constitution, thereby guaranteeing the rights of local citizens and negating the "property rights" of the firm. Some states and municipalities have gone further and passed laws preventing firms from moving plants or limiting when and how plants can be closed. In sum, there is much current legal activity in this area to constrain management's pursuit of stockholders' interests at the expense of the local communities in which the firm operates.

I have argued that the result of such changes in the legal system can be viewed as giving some rights to those groups that have a claim on the firm, for example, customers, suppliers, employees, local communities, stockholders, and management. It raises the question, at the core of a theory of the firm: In whose interest and for whose benefit should the firm be managed? The answer proposed by managerial capitalism is clearly "the stockholders," but I have argued that the law has been progressively circumscribing this answer.

## The Economic Argument

In its pure ideological form managerial capitalism seeks to maximize the interests of stockholders. In its perennial criticism of government regulation, management espouses the "invisible hand" doctrine. It contends that it creates the greatest good for the greatest number, and therefore government need not intervene. However, we know that externalities, moral hazards, and monopoly power exist in fact, whether or not they exist in theory. Further, some of the legal apparatus mentioned above has evolved to deal with just these issues.

The problem of the "tragedy of the commons" or the free-rider problem pervades the concept of public goods such as water and air. No one has an incentive to incur the cost of clean-up or the cost of nonpollution, since the marginal gain of one firm's action is small. Every firm reasons this way, and the result is pollution of water and air. Since the industrial revolution, firms have sought to internalize the benefits and externalize the costs of their actions. The cost must be borne by all, through taxation and regulation; hence we have the emergence of the environmental regulations of the 1970s.

Similarly, moral hazards arise when the purchaser of a good or service can pass along the cost of that good. There is no incentive to economize, on the part of either the producer or the consumer, and there is excessive use of the resources involved. The institutionalized practice of third-party payment in health care is a prime example.

Finally, we see the avoidance of competitive behavior on the part of firms, each seeking to monopolize a small portion of the market and not compete with one another. In a number of industries, oligopolies have emerged, and while there is questionable evidence that oligopolies are not the most efficient corporate form in some industries, suffice it to say that the potential for abuse of market power has again led to regulation of managerial activity. In the classic case, AT&T, arguably one of the great technological and managerial achievements of the century, was broken up into eight separate companies to prevent its abuse of monopoly power.

Externalities, moral hazards, and monopoly power have led to more external control on managerial capitalism. There are de facto constraints, due to these economic facts of life, on the ability of management to act in the interests of stockholders.

## A STAKEHOLDER THEORY OF THE FIRM

### The Stakeholder Concept

Corporations have stakeholders, that is, groups and individuals who benefit from or are harmed by, and whose rights are violated or respected by, corporate actions. The concept of stakeholders is a generalization of the notion of stockholders, who themselves have some special claim on the firm. Just as stockholders have a right to demand certain actions by management, so do other stakeholders have a right to make claims. The exact nature of these claims is a difficult question that I shall address, but the logic is identical to that of the stockholder theory. Stakes require action of a certain sort, and conflicting stakes require methods of resolution.

Freeman and Reed (1983)[7] distinguish two senses of *stakeholder*. The "narrow definition" includes those groups who are vital to the survival and success of the corporation. The "wide-definition" includes any group or individual who can affect or is affected by the corporation. I shall begin with a modest aim: to articulate a stakeholder theory using the narrow definition.

### Stakeholders in the Modern Corporation

Figure 1 depicts the stakeholders in a typical large corporation. The stakes of each are reciprocal, since each can affect the other in terms of harms and benefits as well as rights and duties. The stakes of each are not univocal and would vary by particular corporation. I merely set forth some general notions that seem to be common to many large firms.

Owners have financial stake in the corporation in the form of stocks, bonds, and so on, and they expect some kind of financial return from them. Either they have given money directly to the firm, or they have some historical claim made through a series of morally justi-

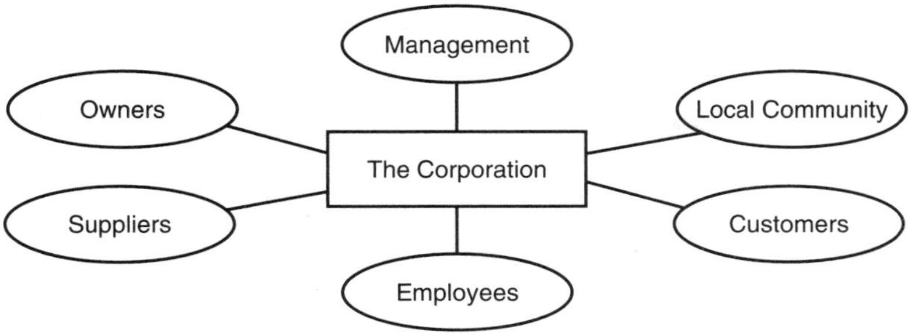


**FIGURE 1.** A Stakeholder Model of the Corporation.

fied exchanges. The firm affects their livelihood or, if a substantial portion of their retirement income is in stocks or bonds, their ability to care for themselves when they can no longer work. Of course, the stakes of owners will differ by type of owner, preferences for money, moral preferences, and so on, as well as by type of firm. The owners of AT&T are quite different from the owners of Ford Motor Company, with stock of the former company being widely dispersed among 3 million stockholders and that of the latter being held by a small family group as well as by a large group of public stockholders.

Employees have their jobs and usually their livelihood at stake; they often have specialized skills for which there is usually no perfectly elastic market. In return for their labor, they expect security, wages, benefits, and meaningful work. In return for their loyalty, the corporation is expected to provide for them and carry them through difficult times. Employees are expected to follow the instructions of management most of the time, to speak favorably about the company, and to be responsible citizens in the local communities in which the company operates. Where they are used as means to an end, they must participate in decisions affecting such use. The evidence that such policies and values as described here lead to productive company-employee relationships is compelling. It is equally compelling to realize that the opportunities for "bad faith" on the part of both management and employees are enormous. "Mock participation" in quality circles, singing the company song, and wearing the company uniform solely to please management all lead to distrust and unproductive work.

Suppliers, interpreted in a stakeholder sense, are vital to the success of the firm, for raw materials will determine the final product's quality and price. In turn the firm is a customer of the supplier and is therefore vital to the success and survival of the supplier. When the firm treats the supplier as a valued member of the stakeholder network, rather than simply as a source of materials, the supplier will respond when the firm is in need. Chrysler traditionally had very close ties to its suppliers, even to the extent that led some to suspect the transfer of illegal payments. And when Chrysler was on the brink of disaster, the suppliers responded with price cuts, accepting late payments, financing, and so on. Supplier and company can rise and fall together. Of course, again, the particular supplier relationships will depend on a number of variables such as the number of suppliers and whether the supplies are finished goods or raw materials.

Customers exchange resources for the products of the firm and in return receive the benefits of the products. Customers provide the lifeblood of the firm in the form of revenue. Given the level of reinvestment of earnings in large corporations, customers indirectly pay for the development of new products and services. Peters and Waterman (1982)[8] have argued that being close to the customer leads to success with other stakeholders and that a distinguishing characteristic of some companies that have performed well is their emphasis on the customer. By paying attention to customers' needs, management automatically addresses the needs of suppliers and owners. Moreover, it seems that the ethic of customer service carries over to the community. Almost without fail the "excellent companies" in Peters and Waterman's study have good reputations in the community. I would argue that Peters and Waterman have found multiple applications of Kant's dictum, "Treat persons as ends unto themselves," and it should come as no surprise that persons respond to such respectful treatment, be they customers, suppliers, owners, employees, or members of the local community. The real surprise is the novelty of the application of Kant's rule in a theory of good management practice.

The local community grants the firm the right to build facilities and, in turn, it benefits from the tax base and economic and social contributions of the firm. In return for the provision of local services, the firm is expected to be a good citizen, as is any person, either "natural or artificial." The firm cannot expose the community to unreasonable hazards in the form of pollution, toxic waste, and so on. If for some reason the firm must leave a community, it is expected to work with local leaders to make the transition as smoothly as possible. Of course, the firm does not have perfect knowledge, but when it discovers some danger or runs afoul of new competition, it is expected to inform the local community and to work with the community to overcome any problem. When the firm mismanages its relationship with the local community, it is in the same position as a citizen who commits a crime. It has violated the implicit social contract with the community and should expect to be distrusted and ostracized. It should not be surprised when punitive measures are invoked.

I have not included "competitors" as stakeholders in the narrow sense, since strictly speaking they are not necessary for the survival and success of the firm; the stakeholder theory works equally well in monopoly contexts. However, competitors and government would be the first to be included in an extension of this basic theory. It is simply not true that the interests of competitors in an industry are always in conflict. There is no reason why trade associations and other multi-organizational groups cannot band together to solve common problems that have little to do with how to restrain trade. Implementation of stakeholder management principles, in the long run, mitigates the need for industrial policy and an increasing role for government intervention and regulation.

## The Role of Management

Management plays a special role, for it too has a stake in the modern corporation. On the one hand, management's stake is like that of employees, with some kind of explicit or implicit employment contract. But, on the other hand, management has a duty of safeguarding the welfare of the abstract entity that is the corporation. In short, management, especially top management, must look after the health of the corporation, and this involves balancing the multiple claims of conflicting stakeholders. Owners want higher financial returns, while customers want more money spent on research and development. Employees want higher wages and better benefits, while the local community wants better parks and day-care facilities.

The task of management in today's corporation is akin to that of King Solomon. The stakeholder theory does not give primacy to one stakeholder group over another, though there will surely be times when one group will benefit at the expense of others. In general, however, management must keep the relationships among stakeholders in balance. When these relationships become imbalanced, the survival of the firm is in jeopardy.

When wages are too high and product quality is too low, customers leave, suppliers suffer, and owners sell their stocks and bonds, depressing the stock price and making it difficult to raise new capital at favorable rates. Note, however, that the reason for paying returns to owners is not that they "own" the firm, but that their support is necessary for the survival of the firm, and that they have a legitimate claim on the firm. Similar reasoning applies in turn to each stakeholder group.

A stakeholder theory of the firm must redefine the purpose of the firm. The stockholder theory claims that the purpose of the firm is to maximize the welfare of the stockholders, perhaps subject to some moral or social constraints, either because such maximization leads to the greatest good or because of property rights. The purpose of the firm is quite different in my view.

"The stakeholder theory" can be unpacked into a number of stakeholder theories, each of which has a "normative core," inextricably linked to the way that corporations should be governed and the way that managers should act. So, attempts to more fully define, or more carefully define, a stakeholder theory are misguided. Following Donaldson and Preston, I want to insist that the normative, descriptive, instrumental, and metaphorical (my addition to their framework) uses of 'stakeholder' are tied together in particular political constructions to yield a number of possible "stakeholder theories." "Stakeholder theory" is thus a genre of stories about how we could live. Let me be more specific.

A "normative core" of a theory is a set of sentences that includes among others, sentences like:

(1) Corporations ought to be governed . . .

(2) Managers ought to act to . . .

where we need arguments or further narratives which include business and moral terms to fill in the blanks. This normative core is not always reducible to a fundamental ground like the theory of property, but certain normative cores are consistent with modern understandings of property. Certain elaborations of the theory of private property plus the other institutions of political liberalism give rise to particular normative cores. But there are other institutions, other political conceptions of how society ought to be structured, so that there are different possible normative cores.

So, one normative core of a stakeholder theory might be a feminist standpoint one, rethinking how we would restructure "value-creating activity" along principles of caring and connection.[9] Another would be an ecological (or several ecological) normative cores. Mark Starik has argued that the very idea of a stakeholder theory of the *firm* ignores certain ecological necessities.[10] Exhibit 1 is suggestive of how these theories could be developed.

In the next section I shall sketch the normative core based on pragmatic liberalism. But, any normative core must address the questions in columns A or B, or explain why these questions may be irrelevant, as in the ecological view. In addition, each "theory," and I use the word hesitantly, must place the normative core within a more full-fledged account of how we could understand value-creating activity differently (column C). The only way to get on with this task is to see the stakeholder idea as a metaphor. The attempt to prescribe one and only one "normative core" and construct "a stakeholder theory" is at best a disguised attempt to smuggle a normative core past the unsophisticated noses of other unsuspecting academics who are just happy to see the end of the stockholder orthodoxy.

If we begin with the view that we can understand value-creation activity as a contractual process among those parties affected, and if

**EXHIBIT 1.** A Reasonable Pluralism

| | *A.* *Corporations ought to be governed . . .* | *B.* *Managers ought to act . . .* | *C.* *The background disciplines of "value creation" are . . .* |
|---|---|---|---|
| Doctrine of Fair Contracts | . . . in accordance with the six principles. | . . . in the interests of stakeholders. | —business theories<br>—theories that explain stakeholder behavior |
| Feminist Standpoint Theory | . . . in accordance with the principles of caring/connection and relationships. | . . . to maintain and care for relationships and networks of stakeholders. | —business theories<br>—feminist theory<br>—social science understanding of networks |
| Ecological Principles | . . . in accordance with the principle of caring for the earth. | . . . to care for the earth. | —business theories<br>—ecology<br>—other |

for simplicity's sake we initially designate those parties as financiers, customers, suppliers, employees, and communities, then we can construct a normative core that reflects the liberal notions of autonomy, solidarity, and fairness as articulated by John Rawls, Richard Rorty, and others.[11] Notice that building these moral notions into the foundations of how we understand value creation and contracting requires that we eschew separating the "business" part of the process from the "ethical" part, and that we start with the presumption of equality among the contractors, rather than the presumption in favor of financier rights.

The normative core for this redesigned contractual theory will capture the liberal idea of fairness if it ensures a basic equality among stakeholders in terms of their moral rights as these are realized in the firm, and if it recognizes that inequalities among stakeholders are justified if they raise the level of the least well-off stakeholder. The liberal ideal of autonomy is captured by the realization that each stakeholder must be free to enter agreements that create value for themselves, and solidarity is realized by the recognition of the mutuality of stakeholder interests.

One way to understand fairness in this context is to claim *a la* Rawls that a contract is fair if parties to the contract would agree to it in ignorance of their actual stakes. Thus, a contract is like a fair bet, if each party is willing to turn the tables and accept the other side. What would a fair contract among corporate stakeholders look like? If we can articulate this ideal, a sort of corporate constitution, we could then ask whether actual corporations measure up to this standard, and we also begin to design corporate structures which are consistent with this Doctrine of Fair Contracts.

Imagine if you will, representative stakeholders trying to decide on "the rules of the game." Each is rational in a straightforward sense, looking out for its own self-interest. At least *ex ante*, stakeholders are the relevant parties since they will be materially affected. Stakeholders know how economic activity is organized and could be organized. They know general facts about the way the corporate world works. They know that in the real world there are or could be transaction costs, externalities, and positive costs of contracting. Suppose they are uncertain about what other social institutions exist, but they know the range of those institutions. They do not know if government exists to pick up the tab for any externalities, or if they will exist in the nightwatchman state of libertarian theory. They know success and failure stories of businesses around the world. In short, they are behind a Rawls-like veil of ignorance, and they do not know what stake each will have when the veil is lifted. What groundrules would they choose to guide them?

The first groundrule is "The Principle of Entry and Exit." Any contract that is the corporation must have clearly defined entry, exit, and renegotiation conditions, or at least it must have methods or processes for so defining these conditions. The logic is straightforward: each stakeholder must be able to determine when an agreement exists and has a chance of fulfillment. This is not to imply that contracts cannot contain contingent claims or other methods for resolving uncertainty, but rather that it must contain methods for determining whether or not it is valid.

The second groundrule I shall call "The Principle of Governance," and it says that the procedure for changing the rules of the game must be agreed upon by unanimous consent. Think about the consequences of a majority of stakeholders systematically "selling out" a minority. Each stakeholder, in ignorance of its actual role, would seek to avoid such a situation. In reality this principle translates into each stakeholder never giving up its right to participate in the governance of the corporation, or perhaps into the existence of stakeholder governing boards.

The third groundrule I shall call "The Principle of Externalities," and it says that if a contract between A and B imposes a cost on C, then C has the option to become a party to the contract, and the terms are renegotiated. Once again the rationality of this condition is clear. Each stakeholder will want insurance that it does not become C.

The fourth groundrule is "The Principle of Contracting Costs," and it says that all parties to the contract must share in the cost of contracting. Once again the logic is straightforward. Any one stakeholder can get stuck.

A fifth groundrule is "The Agency Principle" that says that any agent must serve the interests of all stakeholders. It must adjudicate conflicts within the bounds of the other principals. Once again the logic is clear. Agents for any one group would have a privileged place.

A sixth and final groundrule we might call, "The Principle of Limited Immortality." The corporation shall be managed as if it can continue to serve the interests of stakeholders through time. Stakeholders are uncertain about the future but, subject to exit conditions, they realize that the continued existence of the corporation is in their interest. Therefore, it would be rational to hire managers who are fiduciaries to their interests and the interest of the collective. If it turns out the "collective interest" is the empty set, then this principle simply collapses into the Agency Principle.

Thus, the Doctrine of Fair Contracts consists of these six groundrules or principles:

(1) The Principle of Entry and Exit
(2) The Principle of Governance
(3) The Principle of Externalities
(4) The Principle of Contracting Costs
(5) The Agency Principle
(6) The Principle of Limited Immortality

Think of these groundrules as a doctrine which would guide actual stakeholders in devising a corporate constitution or charter. Think of management as having the duty to act in accordance with some specific constitution or charter.

Obviously, if the Doctrine of Fair Contracts and its accompanying background narratives are to effect real change, there must be requisite changes in the enabling laws of the land. I propose the following three principles to serve as constitutive elements of attempts to reform the law of corporations.

### The Stakeholder Enabling Principle

Corporations shall be managed in the interests of its stakeholders, defined as employees, financiers, customers, employees, and communities.

### The Principle of Director Responsibility

Directors of the corporation shall have a duty of care to use reasonable judgment to define and direct the affairs of the corporation in accordance with the Stakeholder Enabling Principle.

### The Principle of Stakeholder Recourse

Stakeholders may bring an action against the directors for failure to perform the required duty of care.

Obviously, there is more work to be done to spell out these principles in terms of model legislation. As they stand, they try to capture the intuitions that drive the liberal ideals. It is equally plain that corporate constitutions which meet a test like the doctrine of fair contracts are meant to enable directors and executives to manage the corporation in conjunction with these same liberal ideals.

## NOTES

1. Cf. A. Berle and G. Means, *The Modern Corporation and Private Property* (New York: Commerce Clearing House, 1932), 1. For a reassessment of Berle and Means' argument after 50 years, see *Journal of Law and Economics* 26 (June 1983), especially G. Stigler and C. Friedland, "The Literature of Economics: The Case of Berle and Means," 237–68; D. North, "Comment on Stigler and Friedland," 269–72; and G. Means, "Corporate Power in the Marketplace," 467–85.
2. The metaphor of rebuilding the ship while afloat is attributed to Neurath by W. Quine, *Word and Object* (Cambridge: Harvard University Press, 1960), and W. Quine and J. Ullian, *The Web of Belief* (New York: Random House, 1978). The point is that to keep the ship afloat during repairs we must replace a plank with one that will do a better job. Our argument is that stakeholder capitalism can so replace the current version of managerial capitalism.
3. See R. Charan and E. Freeman, "Planning for the Business Environment of the 1980s," *The Journal of Business Strategy* 1 (1980): 9–19, especially p. 15 for a brief account of the major developments in products liability law.
4. See S. Breyer, *Regulation and Its Reform* (Cambridge: Harvard University Press, 1983), 133, for an analysis of food additives.
5. See I. Millstein and S. Katsh, *The Limits of Corporate Power* (New York: Macmillan, 1981), Chapter 4.
6. Cf. C. Summers, "Protecting All Employees Against Unjust Dismissal," *Harvard Business Review* 58 (1980): 136, for a careful statement of the argument.
7. See E. Freeman and D. Reed, "Stockholders and Stakeholders: A New Perspective on Corporate Governance," in C. Huizinga, ed., *Corporate Governance: A Definitive Exploration of the Issues* (Los Angeles: UCLA Extension Press, 1983).
8. See T. Peters and R. Waterman, *In Search of Excellence* (New York: Harper and Row, 1982).
9. See, for instance, A. Wicks, D. Gilbert, and E. Freeman, "A Feminist Reinterpretation of the Stakeholder Concept," *Business Ethics Quarterly*, Vol. 4, No. 4, October 1994; and E. Freeman and J. Liedtka, "Corporate Social Responsibility: A Critical Approach," *Business Horizons*, Vol. 34, No. 4, July–August 1991, pp. 92–98.
10. At the Toronto workshop Mark Starik sketched how a theory would look if we took the environment to be a stakeholder. This fruitful line of work is one example of my main point about pluralism.
11. J. Rawls, *Political Liberalism*, New York: Columbia University Press, 1993; and R. Rorty, "The Priority of Democracy to Philosophy" in *Reading Rorty: Critical Responses to Philosophy and the Mirror of Nature (and Beyond)*, ed. Alan R. Malachowski, Cambridge, MA: Blackwell, 1990.

**WHICH VIEW IS RIGHT?**

# Two Normative Theories of Business Ethics: A Critique

*John Hasnas*

## I. INTRODUCTION

In this article I suggest that the stockholder theory is neither as outdated nor as unacceptable as it is often made to seem, and further, that there are significant problems with the stakeholder theory. To do this, I propose to summarize each theory, analyze its supporting rationale, and canvass the chief objections against it. I will then draw a tentative conclusion regarding the adequacy of each theory. Finally, on the basis of these conclusions, I suggest what must be the contours of a truly adequate normative theory of business ethics. Before turning to this, however, I feel compelled to say a word about the meaning of the phrase, 'social responsibility.'

In the business setting, 'social responsibility' is often employed as a synonym for a business's or business person's ethical obligations. This is unfortunate because this loose, generic use of the phrase can often obscure or prejudice the issue of what are a business's or business person's ethical obligations. To see why, one must appreciate that the phrase is also used to contrast a business's or business person's "social" responsibilities with its or his or her ordinary ones. A business's or business person's ordinary responsibilities are to manage the business and expend business resources so as to accomplish the specific purposes for which the business was organized. Thus, in the case of a business organized for charitable or socially beneficial purposes (e.g., nonprofit corporations such as the Red Cross or the Nature Conservancy and for-profit corporations in which the stockholders pass resolutions compelling charitable contributions), it is a manager's ordinary responsibility to attempt to accomplish these goals. Even when a business is organized strictly for profit, it may be part of a manager's ordinary responsibilities to expend business resources for socially beneficial purposes when he or she believes that such expenditures will enhance the firm's long-term profitability (e.g., through the creation of customer goodwill). When the phrase social responsibility is used in contradistinction to this, the claim that businesses or business persons have social responsibilities indicates that they are obligated to expend business resources for socially beneficial purposes even when such expenditures are not designed to help the business achieve the ends for which it was organized.

When 'social responsibility' in this narrow sense is conflated with 'social responsibility' as a synonym for a business's or business person's ethical obligations in general, it groundlessly implies that businesses or business persons do, in fact, have ethical obligations to expend business resources in ways that do not promote the business's fundamental purposes. Since not all theorists agree that this is the case, a definition that carries such an implication should be scrupulously avoided. For this reason, I intend to employ 'social responsibility'

Adapted from John Hasnas, "The Normative Theories of Business Ethics: A Guide for the Perplexed," *Business Ethics Quarterly 1998,* 8, pp. 19–42. Reprinted by permission of the author and *Business Ethics Quarterly.*

to refer exclusively to those ethical obligations, if any, that businesses or business persons have to expend business resources in ways that do not promote the specific purposes for which the business is organized. When the phrase is used in this way, it can make perfect sense to say that a business or business person has no social responsibilities. In fact, the first normative theory of business ethics that I will examine, the stockholder theory, makes precisely this claim.

## II. THE STOCKHOLDER THEORY

The first normative theory of business ethics to be examined is the stockholder theory. According to this theory, businesses are merely arrangements by which one group of people, the stockholders, advance capital to another group, the managers, to be used to realize specified ends and for which the stockholders receive an ownership interest in the venture. Under this view, managers act as agents for the stockholders. They are empowered to manage the money advanced by the stockholders, but are bound by their agency relationship to do so exclusively for the purposes delineated by their stockholder principals. The existence of this fiduciary relationship implies that managers cannot have an obligation to expend business resources in ways that have not been authorized by the stockholders regardless of any societal benefits that could be accrued by doing so. Of course, both stockholders and managers are free to spend their personal funds on any charitable or socially beneficial project they wish, but when functioning in their capacity as officers of the business, managers have a duty not to divert business resources away from the purposes expressly authorized by the stockholders. This implies that a business can have no social responsibilities.

Strictly speaking, the stockholder theory holds that managers are obligated to follow the (legal) directions of the stockholders. Thus, if the stockholders vote that the business should not close a plant without giving its employees 90-days' notice, should have no dealings with a country with a racist regime, or should endow a local public library, the management would be obligated to carry out such a directive regardless of its effect on the business's bottom line. In most cases, however, the stockholders issue no such explicit directives and purchase stock for the sole purpose of maximizing the return on their investment. When this is the purpose for which the stockholders have advanced their money, the managers' fiduciary obligation requires them to apply it to this end. For this reason, the stockholder theory is often imprecisely expressed as requiring managers to maximize the financial returns of the stockholders. The most famous statement of this shorthand description of the stockholder theory has been given by Milton Friedman who ironically refers to this as a "social responsibility." As he expresses it, "there is one and only one social responsibility of business—to use its resources and engage in activities designed to increase its profits so long as it stays within the rules of the game, which is to say, engages in open and free competition, without deception or fraud."[1]

It is important to note that even in this imprecise form, the stockholder theory does not instruct managers to do anything at all to increase the profitability of the business. It does not assert that managers have a moral blank check that allows them to ignore all ethical constraints in the pursuit of profits. Rather, it states that managers are obligated to pursue profit *by all legal, nondeceptive means.* Far from asserting that there are no ethical constraints on a manager's obligation to increase profits, the stockholder theory contends that the ethical constraints society has embodied in its laws plus the general ethical tenet in favor of honest dealing constitute the ethical boundaries within which managers must pursue increased profitability. A significant amount of the criticism that is directed against the stockholder theory results from overlooking these ethical limitations.[2]

For whatever reason, the stockholder theory has come to be associated with the type of utilitarian argument frequently advanced by free market economists.[3] Thus, supporting arguments often begin with the claim that when individual actors pursue private profit in a free market, they are led by Adam Smith's invisible hand to promote the general interest as well. It is then claimed that since, for each individual, "[b]y pursuing his own interest he frequently promotes that of the society more effectually than when he really intends to promote it,"[4] it is both unnecessary and counterproductive to exhort businesses or business persons to act directly to promote the common good. From this it is concluded that there is no justification for claiming that businesses or business persons have any social responsibilities other than to legally and honestly maximize the profits of the firm.

Although this consequentialist argument is the one most frequently cited in support of the stockholder theory, it must be noted that there is another, quite simple deontological argument for it. This argument is based on the observation that stockholders advance their money to business managers on the condition that it be used in accordance with their wishes. If the managers accepted the money on this condition and then proceed to spend it to accomplish social goals not authorized by the stockholders, they would be violating their agreement and spending other people's money without their consent, which is wrong.[5]

The stockholder theory has been subjected to some harsh criticism by several of the leading business ethicists working today. It has been described as an outmoded relic of corporate law that even the law itself has evolved beyond,[6] as containing a "myopic view of corporate responsibility" that is unfortunately held by a significant number of business practitioners, and, more pointedly, as "corporate Neanderthalism . . . with morally pernicious consequences,"[7] and as "not only foolish in theory, but cruel and dangerous in practice" and misguided "from its nonsensically one-sided assumption of responsibility to his pathetic understanding of stockholder personality as *Homo economicus*."[8] For a significant number of theorists, the stockholder theory is introduced into discussion not as a serious candidate for the proper ethical standard for the business environment, but merely as a foil for other, putatively more enlightened normative theories.

At least part of the explanation for this harsh treatment seems to be the stockholder theory's association with the utilitarian supporting argument described above. Few contemporary business ethicists have the kind of faith in the invisible hand of the market that neoclassical economists do. Most take for granted that a free market produces coercive monopolies, results in damaging externalities, and is beset by other instances of market failure such as the free rider and public goods problems, and thus cannot be relied upon to secure the common good.[9] Accordingly, to the extent that it is associated with this line of economic reasoning, the stockholder theory becomes tarred with the brush of these standard objections to laissez faire capitalism.

It should be pointed out, however, that it is not necessary to join the debate over the theoretical viability of laissez faire to demonstrate the vulnerability of the utilitarian defense of the stockholder theory. This is because contemporary economic conditions are so far removed from those of a true free market as to render the point essentially moot. Regardless of the adequacy of the stockholder theory in a world of ideal markets, the world in which we currently reside is one where businesses may gain competitive advantages by obtaining government subsidies, tax breaks, protective tariffs, and state-conferred monopoly status (e.g, utilities, the Baby Bells, cable television franchises); having health, safety, or environmental regulations written so as to burden small competitors; and otherwise purchasing governmental favor. In such a world, it is extremely unlikely that the pursuit of private profit will truly be productive of the public good. There is ample reason to be suspicious of such a claim in an environment in which 65 percent of the chief executive officers of the top 200 Fortune firms come to Washington, D.C. at least once every two weeks.[10]

It is important to note that the fact that the utilitarian argument for the stockholder theory may be seriously flawed does not mean that the theory is untenable. This is because the deontological argument for the theory, which has frequently been overlooked, is, in fact, the superior argument. To the extent that it has received serious consideration, the primary objection against it seems to consist in the contention that it is not wrong to spend other people's money without their consent *as long as it is being done to promote the public interest.* This contention is usually bolstered by the observation that this is precisely what democratic governments do all the time (at least, in theory). Since such action is presumably justified in the political realm, so the objection goes, there is no reason to think that it is not equally justified in the business realm.

There are two serious problems with this objection, however. The first is that it misses the essential point of the argument. As stated above, this argument is deontological in character. It is based on an underlying assumption that there are certain principles of conduct that must be observed regardless of the generalized benefits that must be foregone by doing so. One of the most fundamental of these principles states that individuals must honor the commitments they voluntarily and knowingly undertake. Hence, the essence of the argument is the claim that it is morally wrong to violate one's freely assumed agreement to use the stockholders' resources only in specified ways even though society could be made a somewhat better place by doing so. To assert that a manager may violate his or her agreement with the stockholders whenever this would promote the public interest is simply to deny this claim. It is to declare that one's duty to advance the common good overrides one's duty to honor one's agreements, and that the moral quality of one's actions must ultimately be judged according to a utilitarian standard. While some ethicists argue that the principle of utility is indeed the supreme ethical principle, this is far from obviously true, and any contention that merely assumes that it is cannot serve as a compelling objection to a deontological argument.

The second problem is that the objection is based on a false analogy. The assumption that democratic governments are morally justified in spending *taxpayers'* money without their consent to promote the general interest does not imply that businesses or business persons are justified in spending *stockholders'* money without their consent for the same reason. Consider that once the citizens have made their required contribution to governmental efforts to benefit society, all should be equally entitled to the control of their remaining assets. Should a citizen elect to invest them in a savings account to provide for his or her children's education or his or her old age, a banker who diverted some of these assets to other purposes, no matter how worthy, would clearly be guilty of embezzlement. For that matter, should the citizen elect to use his or her assets to purchase a new car, go on an extravagant vacation, or even take a course in business ethics, a car dealer, travel agent, or university that failed to deliver the bargained-for product in order to provide benefits to others would be equally guilty. Why should it be any different if the citizen elects to invest in a business? At least superficially, it would appear that citizens have a right to control their after-tax assets that is not abrogated merely because they elect to purchase stock and that would be violated were business managers to use these assets in unauthorized ways. If this is not the case, some showing is required to demonstrate why not.

Of course, these comments in no way establish that the stockholder theory is correct. The most that they can demonstrate is that some objections that are frequently raised against it are ill-founded. Other, more serious objections remain to be considered. However, they do suggest that the cavalier dismissal the stockholder theory sometimes receives is unjustified, and that, at least at present, it should continue to be considered a serious candidate for the proper normative theory of business ethics.

## III. THE STAKEHOLDER THEORY

The second of the leading normative theories of business ethics is the stakeholder theory. Unfortunately, 'stakeholder theory' is somewhat of a troublesome label because it is used to refer to both an empirical theory of management and a normative theory of business ethics, often without clearly distinguishing between the two. As an empirical theory of management, the stakeholder theory holds that effective management requires the balanced consideration of and attention to the legitimate interests of all stakeholders, defined as anyone who has "a stake in or claim on the firm." This has been interpreted in both a wide sense that includes "any group or individual who can affect or is affected by the corporation," and a more narrow sense that includes only "those groups who are vital to the survival and success of the corporation."[11] It is perhaps more familiar in its narrow sense in which the stakeholder groups are limited to stockholders, customers, employees, suppliers, management, and the local community. Thus, as an empirical theory, the stakeholder theory asserts that a business's financial success can best be achieved by giving the interests of the business's stockholders, customers, employees, suppliers, management, and local community proper consideration and adopting policies which produce the optimal balance among them.

When viewed as an empirical theory of management designed to prescribe a method for improving a business's performance, the stakeholder theory does not imply that businesses have any social responsibilities. In this sense, it is perfectly consistent with the normative stockholder theory since what is being asserted is the empirical claim that the best way to enhance the stockholders' return on their investment is to pay attention to the legitimate interests of all stakeholders. The essence of the stakeholder theory of *management* is that stakeholder management is required for managers to successfully meet their fiduciary obligation to the stockholders. For the purposes of this article, however, we are concerned with the stakeholder theory not as an empirical theory of management, but as a normative theory of business ethics.

When viewed as a normative theory, the stakeholder theory asserts that, regardless of whether stakeholder management leads to improved financial performance, managers *should* manage the business for the benefit of all stakeholders. It views the firm not as a mechanism for increasing the stockholders' financial returns, but as a vehicle for coordinating stakeholder interests and sees management as having a fiduciary relationship not only to the stockholders, but to all stakeholders. According to the normative stakeholder theory, management must given equal consideration to the interests of all stakeholders[12] and, when these interests conflict, manage the business so as to attain the optimal balance among them. This, of course, implies that there will be times when management is obligated to at least partially sacrifice the interests of the stockholders to those of other stakeholders. Hence, in its normative form, the stakeholder theory does imply that businesses have true social responsibilities.

The stakeholder theory holds that management's fundamental obligation is not to maximize the firm's financial success, but to ensure its survival by balancing the conflicting claims of multiple stakeholders. This obligation is to be met by acting in accordance with two principles of stakeholder management. The first, called the *principle of corporate legitimacy*, states that "the corporation should be managed for the benefit of its stakeholders: its customers, suppliers, owners, employees, and the local communities. The rights of these groups must be ensured and, further, the groups must participate, in some sense, in decisions that substantially affect their welfare."[13] The second, called the *stakeholder fiduciary principle*, states that "management bears a fiduciary relationship to stakeholders and to the corporation as an abstract entity. It must act in the interests of the stakeholders as their agent, and it must act in the interests of the corporation to ensure the survival of the firm, safeguarding the long-term stakes of each group."[14]

The stakeholder theory enjoys a considerable degree of approbation from both theorists and practitioners. In fact, it is probably fair to say that the stakeholder theory currently enjoys a breadth of acceptance equal to that the stockholder theory was said to have enjoyed in the past. To some extent, this may result from the fact that the theory seems to accord well with many people's moral intuitions, and, to some extent, it may simply be a spillover effect of the high regard in which the empirical version of the stakeholder theory is held as a theory of management. It is clear, however, that the normative theory's widespread acceptance does not derive from a careful examination of the arguments that have been offered in support of it. In fact, it is often remarked that the theory seems to lack a clear, normative foundation.

An argument that is frequently cited in support of the stakeholder theory is the one offered by Ed Freeman and William Evan in their 1988 article. That argument asserts that management's obligation to the stakeholders can be derived from Immanuel Kant's principle of respect for persons. This fundamental ethical principle holds that every human being is entitled to be treated not merely as a means to the achievement of the ends of others, but as a being valuable in his or her own right, that each person is entitled to be respected as an end in himself or herself. Since to respect someone as an end is to recognize that he or she is an autonomous moral agent, i.e., a being with desires of his or her own and the free will to act upon those desires, the principle of respect for persons requires respect for others' autonomy.

Freeman and Evan apply this principle to the world of business by claiming that businesses are bound to respect it as much as anyone else. Thus, businesses may not treat their stakeholders merely as means to the business's ends, but must recognize that as moral agents, all stakeholders are entitled "to agree to and hence participate (or choose not to participate) in the decisions to be used as such.[15] They then claim that it follows from this that all stakeholders are entitled to "participate in determining the future direction of the firm in which they have a stake.[16] However, because it is impossible to consult with all of a firm's stakeholders on every decision, this participation must be indirect. Therefore, the firm's management has an obligation to "represent" the interests of all stakeholders in the business's decision-making process. Accordingly, management is obligated to give equal consideration to the interests of all stakeholders in developing business policy and to manage the business so as to optimize the balance among these interests.

The main problem with this argument is that there is a gap in the reasoning that leads from the principle of respect for persons to the prescriptions of the stakeholder theory. It may readily be admitted that businesses are ethically bound to treat all persons, and hence all stakeholders, as entities worthy of respect as ends in themselves. It may further be admitted that this requires businesses to treat their stakeholders as autonomous moral agents, and hence, that stakeholders are indeed entitled "to agree to and hence participate (or choose not to participate) in the decisions to be used"[17] by the business. The problem is that this implies only that no stakeholder may be forced to deal with the business without his or her consent, not that all stakeholders are entitled to a say in the business's decision-making process or that the business must be managed for their benefit.

It is certainly true that respect for the autonomy of others requires that one keep one's word. To deceive someone into doing something he or she would not otherwise agree to do would be to use him or her merely as a means to one's own ends. For this reason, the principle of respect for persons requires businesses to deal honestly with all of their stakeholders. This means that businesses must honor the contracts they enter into with their customers, employees, suppliers, managers, and stockholders and live up to any representations they freely make to the local community. However, it is simply incorrect to say that respect for another's autonomy requires that the other have a say in any decision that affects his or her interests. A student's interests may be crucially affected by what grade he or she receives in a course as may a Republican's by the decision of whom the Democrats nominate for President. But the autonomy of neither the student nor the Republican is violated when he or she is denied a say in these decisions.

An adherent of the stockholder theory could point out that employees (including managers), suppliers, and customers negotiate for and autonomously accept wage and benefit packages, purchasing arrangements, and sales contracts, respectively. It does not violate their autonomy or treat them with a lack of the respect they are due as persons to fail to provide them with benefits in excess of those they freely accept. However, if managers were to break their agreement with the stockholders to use business resources only as authorized in order to provide other stakeholders with such benefits, the managers would be violating the autonomy of the stockholders. Therefore, the stockholder theorist could contend that not only is the stakeholder theory not entailed by the principle of respect for persons, but to the extent that it instructs managers to use the stockholders' money in ways they have not approved, it is, in fact, violative of it.

Perhaps because of the problems with this argument, efforts have recently been made to provide a more adequate normative justification for the stakeholder theory. Indeed, Freeman and Evan have themselves offered an alternative argument that claims that changes in corporate law imply that businesses consist in sets of multilateral contracts among stakeholders that must be administered by managers.[18] Asserting that "all parties that are affected by a contract have a right to bargain about the distribution of those effects,"[19] they then apply a Rawlsian "veil of ignorance" decision procedure to deduce that "fair contracting" requires that all stakeholders be entitled to "participate in monitoring the actual effects of the firm on them,"[20] i.e., have a say in the business's decision-making process.

Unfortunately, this argument seems to have even more problems than the one it replaces. In the first place, Rawls's decision procedure was specifically designed to guide the construction of the basic structure of society, and it is at least open to question whether it may be appropriately employed in the highly specific context of business governance issues. Further, deriving ethical conclusions from observations of the state of the law comes dangerously close to the classic fallacy of assuming that what is legally required must be ethically correct. More significantly, however, this new argument seems to suffer from the same defect as its predecessor because the assumption that all parties that are affected by a contract have a right to bargain about the distribution of those effects is virtually equivalent to the earlier argument's problematic assumption that all parties affected by a business's actions have a right to participate in the business's decision-making process. As in the earlier argument, this is the assertion that must be established, not assumed.

In sum, the lacunae in each of these supporting arguments suggest that, despite its widespread acceptance, the normative version of the stakeholder theory is simply not well grounded. At this point, its adequacy as a normative theory of business ethics must be regarded as open to serious question.

## IV. CONCLUSION

In this article, I have subjected the two leading normative theories of business ethics to critical examination. I have argued that the stockholder theory is not as obviously flawed as it is sometimes supposed to be and that several of the objections conventionally raised against it are misdirected. I have also suggested that the deontological argument in support of the stockholder theory is not obviously unsound, although I have admittedly not subjected this argument to the scrutiny that would be necessary to establish its soundness. Further, I have argued that the supporting arguments for the stakeholder theory are significantly flawed. Thus, I have suggested that the amount of confidence that is currently placed in the stakeholder theory is not well founded.

Although it may appear surprising given these conclusions, I do not view this article as a brief for the stockholder theory. Rather, I view it as a compass that can point us in the direction of a truly adequate normative theory of business ethics. I should add, however, that I also believe it points to a serious difficulty that must be overcome in order to arrive at any such theory.

To see what I mean, I would ask you to consider that both normative theories share a common feature; They both either explicitly or implicitly recognize the preeminent moral value of individual consent. The stockholder theory is explicitly based on consent. The ethical obligations it posits are claimed to derive directly from the voluntary agreement each business officer makes on accepting his or her position to use the stockholders' resources strictly in accordance with their wishes. Similarly, the stakeholder theory is at least implicitly based on consent. The ethical obligation it places on business officers to manage the firm in the interest of all stakeholders is supposed to derive from the claim that every stakeholder is entitled to a say in decisions that affect his or her interests, which itself contains the implicit recognition of each individual's right to control his or her own destiny.

The fact that both normative theories of business ethics rely on the moral force of individual consent should come as no surprise given a proper understanding of what a business is, i.e., "a voluntary association of individuals, united by a network of contracts"[21] organized to achieve a specified end. Because businesses consist in nothing more than a multitude of voluntary agreements among individuals, it is entirely natural that the ethical obligations of the parties to these agreements, including those of the managers of the business, should derive from the individual consent of each. Clearly, any attempt to provide a general account of the ethical obligations of businesses and business people must ultimately rely on the moral force of the individual's freely given consent.

Recognizing this tells us much about what an adequate normative theory of business ethics must look like. If businesses are merely voluntary associations of individuals, then the ethical obligations of business people will be the ethical obligations individuals incur by joining voluntary associations, i.e., the ordinary ethical obligations each has as a human being plus those each has voluntarily assumed by agreement. Just as individuals do not take on ethical obligations beyond those they agree to by joining a chess club, a political party, or a business school faculty, so too individuals do not become burdened with unagreed upon obligations by going into or joining a business. There is no point in time at which the collection of individuals that constitutes a business is magically transformed into a new, separate, and distinct entity that is endowed with rights or laden with obligations not possessed by the individual human beings that comprise it.

This implies that an adequate normative theory of business ethics must capture the ethical obligations generated when an individual voluntarily enters the complex web of contractual agreements that constitutes a business. Of the two theories I have examined, the stockholder theory comes closest to achieving this because it focuses on the actual agreement that exists between the stockholders and managers. It is woefully incomplete, however, because it (1) does not adequately address the limits managers' ordinary ethical obligations as human beings place on the actions they may take in the business environment, and (2) entirely fails to address the managerial obligations that arise out of the actual agreements made with the nonstockholder participants in the business enterprise. Of course, recognizing these deficiencies of the stockholder theory also highlights the essential difficulty in constructing a satisfactory normative theory of business ethics; the need to generalize across the myriad individual contractual agreements that are the constituent elements of the business.

## NOTES

1. Milton Friedman, *Capitalism and Freedom* 133 (1962). I should point out that Friedman does not always describe the constraints on the pursuit of profit this precisely. Often, he merely states that businesses should "make as much money as possible while conforming to the basic rules of society, both those embodied in law and those embodied in ethical custom." Milton Friedman, "The Social Responsibility of Business is to Increase Its Profits," *New York Times Magazine*, September 13, 1970 at 32–33. Of course, when stated this broadly, Friedman's injunction becomes a triviality asserting nothing more than that one should pursue profits ethically. Although this has been the source of much criticism of Friedman's particular expression of the stockholder theory, it need not concern us in the present context. The more specific statement given in the text does define a substantive position worthy of serious consideration, and so, that is the formulation that will be used in this article.
2. It must be kept in mind at all times that the version of the stockholder theory that asserts that the manager is ethically obliged to increase the company's profits is true only for those for-profit companies in which it is reasonable to interpret the stockholders' wishes as the maximization of profit. Whenever the stockholders have indicated that they wish their resources to be used for other purposes, the stockholder theory requires managers to attempt to fulfill those purposes, even if doing so comes at the expense of profits.
3. See, e.g., Dennis P. Quinn & Thomas M. Jones, "An Agent Morality View of Business Policy," 20 *Acad. Mgmt. Rev.* 22, 24 (1995); William M. Evan & R. Edward Freeman, "A Stakeholder Theory of the Modern

Corporation: Kantian Capitalism," *in Ethical Theory and Business* 75, 77 (Tom L. Beauchamp & Norman E. Bowie eds., 4th ed., 1993).

4. Adam Smith, *The Wealth of Nations,* bk. IV, Chap. 2, para. 9.

5. This argument can be expressed in more philosophically sophisticated language by stating that one who breaches an agreement that induced another to deal with him or her is treating the other merely as a means to his or her own ends, and is thus violating the Kantian principle of respect for persons.

   It is useful to note that Friedman himself offers this deontological argument in support of the stockholder theory, not the utilitarian argument described previously.

6. See Evan & Freeman, op. cit. Thomas Donaldson & Lee E. Preston, "The Stakeholder Theory of the Corporation: Concepts, Evidence, and Implications," 20, *Acad. Mgmt Rev.*, 65, 81–2 (1995).

7. Thomas Donaldson, *The Ethics of International Business,* 45 (1989).

8. Robert C. Solomon, *Ethics and Excellence,* 45 (1992).

9. Evan & Freeman, op. cit.

10. See James D. Gwartney and Richard E. Wagner, "Public Choice and the Conduct of Representative Government," in *Public Choice and Constitutional Economics,* 3, 23 (James D. Gwartney and Richard E. Wagner, eds., 1988).

11. Evan and Freeman, op. cit., *See also* E. Freeman & D. Reed, *Stockholders and Stakeholders: A New Perspective on Corporate Governance,* in Corporate Governance: A Definitive Exploration of the Issues (C. Huizinga ed., 1983).

12. In stating that management must give *equal* consideration to the interests of *all* stakeholders, I am not ignoring the work being done to distinguish among different classes of stakeholders. See, e.g., Max B. E. Clarkson, "A Stakeholder Framework for Analyzing and Evaluating Corporate Social Performance," 20 *Acad. Mgmt. Rev.*, 92, 105–8 (1995). On this point, it is essential to distinguish between the stakeholder theory as a normative theory of business ethics on the one hand and as either a theory of corporate social responsibility or a theory of management on the other. For purposes of either evaluating a business's responsiveness to societal demands or describing effective management techniques, it can make perfect sense to distinguish among different classes of stakeholders. However, given the arguments that have been provided in support of the stakeholder theory as a normative theory of business ethics (to be discussed below), it cannot. The logic of these arguments, whether Kantian, Rawlsian, or derived from property rights, makes no allowance for stakeholders of differing moral status. Each implies that all stakeholders are entitled to equal moral consideration. In my opinion, this represents a major difference between the normative and nonnormative versions of the stakeholder theory, and one that is likely to generate confusion if not carefully attended to.

13. Evan & Freeman, op. cit.

14. Ibid.

    This feature of the normative stakeholder theory immediately gives rise to the objection that it is based on an oxymoron. Given the meaning of the word 'fiduciary,' it is impossible to have a fiduciary relationship to several parties who, like the stakeholders of a corporation, have potentially conflicting interests. Further, even if this did make sense, placing oneself in such a position would appear to be unethical. For example, an attorney who represented two parties with conflicting interests would clearly be guilty of a violation of the canon of ethics. This objection clearly deserves a fuller treatment than it can be given in a footnote.

15. Ibid.

16. Ibid.

17. Ibid.

18. R. Edward Freeman & William Evan, "Corporate Governance: A Stakeholder Interpretation," 19 J. *Behav. Econ.*, 337 (1990).

19. *Id.* at 352.

20. *Id.* at 353.

21. Robert Hessen, "A New Concept of Corporations: A Contractual and Private Property Model," 30, *Hastings L. J.*, 1327, 1330 (1979).

# What's So Special About Shareholders?

*John R. Boatright*

## INTRODUCTION

It is well-established in law that officers and directors of corporations are fiduciaries. Much of the debate on corporate social responsibility from the 1930s to the present has focused on the questions: For whom are managers fiduciaries? And what are their specific fiduciary duties? The common-law view is that officers and directors are fiduciaries primarily for shareholders, who are legally the owners of a corporation, and their main fiduciary duty is to operate the corporation in the interests of the shareholders. As a result, the social responsibility of corporations is sharply restricted. In the words of Milton Friedman, "there is one and only one social responsibility of business," and that is to make as much money for the shareholders as possible.[1]

Those who argue for an expanded view of social responsibility offer a different answer to the question, for whom are managers fiduciaries? Merrick Dodd contended in 1932 that the powers of management are held in trust for the whole community. The modern corporation, he maintained, "has a social service as well as a profit-making function," and managers ought to take the interests of many different constituencies into account.[2] More recently, R. Edward Freeman has popularized the stakeholder approach, in which every group with a stake in a corporation has claims that rival those of stockholders.[3] Consequently, the fiduciary duties of management include serving the interests of employees, customers, suppliers, and the local community in addition to the traditional duties to shareholders. . . .

Whether the relation between managers and shareholders is "ethically different," . . . is a question that requires some understanding of the ethical basis of the duties of management to different constituencies. The stakeholder approach focuses largely on the basis of the duties of management to constituencies other than shareholders, which is to say, duties to employees, suppliers, customers, and the like. Another procedure, however, is to look more closely at the ethical basis of the fiduciary duties of officers and directors of corporations to shareholders. Since the common-law view is that shareholders are special in that managers have a fiduciary duty to run the corporation in their interests alone, we need to ask, what entitles them to this status? In short, what's so special about shareholders?

## SHAREHOLDERS AS OWNERS

There is no question but that the fiduciary duties of management have been based, historically, on the assumption that shareholders are the owners of a corporation. In *The Modern Corporation and Private Property*, Berle and Means observed that our thinking about the shareholder-management relation derives, in part, from the notion of equity in the treatment of property owners, dating from the time when business ventures were undertaken by individuals with their own assets. About the origin of the fiduciary relation they wrote:

> Taking this doctrine back into the womb of equity, whence it sprang, the foundation becomes plain. Wherever one man or a group of men

From John R. Boatright, "Fiduciary Duties and the Shareholder Management Relation: Or, What's So Special About Shareholders?," *Business Ethics Quarterly*, 4 (1994). Reprinted by permission of the author and *Business Ethics Quarterly*.

> entrusted another man or group with the management of property, the second group became fiduciaries. As such they were obliged to act conscionably, which meant in fidelity to the interests of the persons whose wealth they had undertaken to handle.[4]

Ownership of a corporation is different, of course, from the ownership of personal assets. Most notably, shareholders do not have a right to possess and use corporate assets as they would their own; instead, they create a fictitious person to conduct business, with the shareholders as the beneficiaries. To the extent that shareholders do not manage a corporation but leave control to others, there is a problem of ensuring that the hired managers run the corporation in the interests of the shareholders.

The law of corporate governance has addressed this problem by creating a set of shareholder rights along with a set of legal duties for corporate officers and directors. The most important rights of shareholders are to elect the board of directors and to receive the earnings of a corporation in the form of dividends. A main duty of officers and directors is to act as fiduciaries in the management of the corporation's assets. Since these various rights and duties are legally enforceable, they provide a relatively effective solution to the problem of accountability.

Now, even if it is granted that shareholders are the owners of a corporation in the sense of possessing these rights, it does not follow that officers and directors have a fiduciary duty to run the corporation in the interests of shareholders. It is entirely consistent to hold that shareholders are the owners of a corporation and that the managers have a fiduciary duty to run the corporation in the interests of other constituencies. There is a logical gap, in other words, between the property rights of shareholders and the fiduciary duties of management. This does not mean that ownership is irrelevant to fiduciary duties. J. A. C. Hetherington has described ownership as "the formal legal substructure on which the fiduciary duty of management rests."[5] The point is, rather, that some further premises are needed for the argument to go through.

The most common argument for the fiduciary duties of officers and directors is that the property interests which holders have in a corporation can be protected only by a stringent set of duties to act in the interests of shareholders. Shareholders, as equity suppliers, are different from bondholders and others who provide debt—and they are different, as well, from suppliers, employees, customers, and others who have dealings with a corporation. The difference, as explained by Oliver E. Williamson, is: "The whole of their investment in the firm is potentially placed at hazard."[6] Bondholders, suppliers, and so on, are protected by contracts and other safeguards, leaving shareholders, as the owners of a corporation, to bear the preponderance of risk. The various rights of shareholders are thus important means for protecting the shareholders' investment.

Williamson observes that shareholders are unique in several other respects. He writes:

> They are the only voluntary constituency whose relation with the corporation does not come up for periodic renewal. . . . Labor, suppliers . . . debt-holders, and consumers all have opportunities to renegotiate terms when contracts are renewed. Stockholders, by contrast, invest for the life of the firm. . . .[7]

Shareholders are also unique in that "their investments are not associated with particular assets." This feature makes it more difficult to devise contracts and other safeguards like those which protect other constituencies, who can generally withdraw what they have provided. A shareholder, who has only a residual claim, can be protected only by assurance that the corporation will continue to prosper.

This argument—let us call it the equity argument—is an important justification for shareholder rights. Since shareholders are different in certain respects, and since their investment ought to be protected, it is necessary to create a governance structure which assigns them a significant role. The argument does not succeed, however, in supporting the strong claim that managers have fiduciary duties to shareholders and to shareholders alone.

First, if the only justification for fiduciary duties is the need to protect the shareholders' investment, then it is unclear why this end is not achieved by existing shareholder rights and, hence, why fiduciary duties are also necessary. That is, the rights of shareholders to elect the board of directors, vote on shareholder resolutions, and so on, constitute a kind of protection which other constituencies lack and which would seem to be adequate. Some of the fiduciary duties of management, especially those which prohibit self-dealing, may also be important safeguards, but the protection of shareholders can be achieved without a strong profit-maximizing imperative which imposes a fiduciary duty to act solely in the interests of shareholders. This more stringent fiduciary duty needs some further justification.

Second, shareholders have another important source of protection that is denied to other constituencies. Through the stock market, a shareholder can, with little effort or cost, dispose of disappointing stock.[8] Banks, by contrast, are often stuck with bad loans; employees can change employers only with great difficulty; and communities must be content with the businesses located in their midst. The stock market also provides protection in the form of *ex ante* compensation, since stockholders have the opportunity to purchase stock that may increase in value. Investors are compensated for their risk by the opportunity to reap great rewards, and usually the greater the risk, the greater the potential rewards. Further, the stock market allows for diversification, so that a properly diversified investor should face little risk. Indeed, managers and employees of firms generally have far more at stake in the success of a corporation than do the shareholders.

For these reasons, then, the equity argument does not justify the view that officers and directors have a fiduciary duty to run a corporation in the interests of the shareholders. Insofar as shareholders are owners, they have property interests which ought to be protected, but doing so does fully account for the special status that common law gives to shareholders. Indeed, the argument treats shareholders as one class of investors among many, albeit an especially vulnerable class. Some observers have even suggested that shareholders are not properly the "owners" of the corporation at all. Just as bondholders own their bonds, so shareholders, they claim, are merely the owners of their stock.[9]

## CONTRACTS AND AGENCY

Another possible basis for fiduciary duties is provided by the supposition of a contract between shareholders and management and, in particular, of an agency relation whereby the managers of a corporation agree specifically to act as agents of shareholders in the latter's pursuit of wealth. This basis is logically independent of ownership, but if we ask what enables shareholders to contract with management or act as a principal, one answer is their status as owners. Thus, the logical gap between ownership and fiduciary duties might be bridged by the idea that owners hire other persons by means of a contract to become the managers of their property. . . .

In order to base the fiduciary duties of management to shareholders on a contract between management and shareholders—and, in particular, to argue that the relation is a principal-agent relationship—it is necessary, obviously, to show that some kind of contract exists.[10] There is, of course, no *express* contract between the two parties that spells out in writing the terms of the relation, but a defender of the argument might contend that there is still an *implied* contract, which is a kind recognized in law. The courts have frequently found implied contracts to exist in the relations between buyers and sellers and between employers and employees. Why not between shareholders and management?

The case for an implied contract is not very promising. In most cases, a shareholder buys shares of a corporation from previous owners, not from the corporation itself, and even in the case of original purchases of stock, there is no agreement beyond the prospectus. The available evidence suggests that shareholders buy stock with roughly the same expectations as those who make any other financial investment. The conclusion of one study is that "shareholders expect to be treated as 'investors,' much like bondholders, for example, and expect corporate managers to consider a wide constituency when making corporate decisions."[11] Moreover, the lack of any face-to-face dealings between the two parties and the lack of any specific representations by management to individual shareholders further mitigate against any presumption that an implied contract exists. In short, the standard legal conditions for an implied contract are absent in the shareholder-management relation.

Even if there is no legal contract, it is still possible to argue that the idea of a contract provides the best means for understanding the moral features of the shareholder-management relation. The classical social contract theories of Hobbes, Locke, and others provide a means for establishing political obligations, and recently some philosophers have made use of a social contract to provide a framework for the responsibility of corporations to society. Although social contract theory may be a useful normative model in some contexts, it is not easily applied to the shareholder-management relation.

First, the idea of a contract is most at home in situations in which two parties are able to negotiate a set of mutual obligations which governs specific interactions. In the case of shareholders and management, however, there is virtually no opportunity for the two parties to negotiate the terms of their relation. (As noted earlier, Williamson considers the fact that the relation never comes up for periodic renewal to be a reason for regarding shareholders as owners and not ordinary investors.) Also, the "terms" of any supposed contract are set largely by the laws of corporate governance, which have been created by legislatures and courts for reasons unrelated to any contract between shareholders and the management of a corporation. While employers and employees are free to negotiate on specific details, such as wages and working conditions, shareholders are offered shares of stock on a "take it or leave it" basis.

Second, and more important, there is relatively little interaction between shareholders and the managers with whom they are supposed to be related by means of a contract, and most of the obligations which are placed on managers are not related directly to shareholders, as the contractual model suggests. The fiduciary duties of management, for example, cover a wide variety of matters which make no reference to shareholders. . . .

## THE AGENCY RELATION

Just as the shareholder-management relation does not meet the conditions for an implied contract, so too does it not fit the conditions for agency. As a matter of law, officers are agents, but they are agents of the corporation, not the shareholders; and directors, who in a sense are the corporation, are not agents at all. Furthermore, many of the fiduciary duties of management involve activities which are, for the most part, unrelated to shareholders, . . . Thus, the claim that managers are agents for shareholders, even if true, could not account for all of the fiduciary duties of management.

That corporate managers are not agents of the shareholders follows from the standard legal definition given by the second *Restatement of Agency*, Section 1 (1), which reads: "Agency is the fiduciary relation which results from the manifestation of consent by one person to another that the other shall act on his behalf and subject to his control, and consent by the other so to act." The crucial elements in this definition are: (1) consent to the relation, (2) the power to act on another's behalf, and (3) the element of control. None of these is present in the shareholder-management relation.

First, directors and officers, upon assuming their positions, agree to abide by a set of duties, which are largely those prescribed by the laws of a state concerning corporate governance. It is unrealistic to suppose that these managers do anything that can be described as "manifesting consent" to serve the shareholders' interests. Further, none of the fine distinctions used by the courts to decide when an agency relation has been created or terminated ("actual" versus "implied" agency, for example) or to distinguish among kinds of agency (such as "special" and "universal" agency) is usefully applied to the relation between shareholders and management.

Second, officers and directors have no power to act on behalf of the shareholders insofar as this is understood in the legal sense of changing a legal relation of the principal with regard to a third party. In fact, all decisions which change the legal relation of shareholders with regard to third parties (merging with another company, for example, or changing the bylaws of the corporation) must be approved by shareholders; management is barred by law from making decisions of this kind on its own authority. If managers were agents of the shareholders, they ought to have a right to make some decisions of this kind.

Third, management is in no significant sense under the control of the shareholders. Day-to-day operations of a corporation, along with long-term strategic planning, are the province of the officers and directors. Shareholders have no right to intervene, and even shareholder suits over mistaken decisions are generally blocked by the business judgment rule. As long as their fiduciary duties are met, management can enter into new lines of business and abandon old lines, undertake rapid expansion or cut back, and, in short, make virtually all ordinary business decisions without regard for the desires of shareholders. . . .

The inescapable conclusion is that officers and directors of corporations are not, legally, in a contractual or an agency relation with shareholders and that, moreover, there are no good ethical reasons for regarding them as being in such a relation. As a result, Goodpaster's claim—that the shareholder-management relation is fiduciary in character because of a contract or agency relation—is untenable. This cannot be the basis for the fiduciary duties of management and hence for the claim that such duties are owed to shareholders alone.

## PUBLIC POLICY AS A BASIS

. . . It is necessary, however, to find some basis for fiduciary duties, if they are to exist at all. And if fiduciary duties are confined to the shareholder-management relation, then a basis must be found which singles out shareholders as a special constituency. That is, there must be something special about shareholders which makes them, and no other constituency, the object of the fiduciary duties of management. . . . [It could be argued] that the value of maintaining the private, profit-making nature of the corporation comes from considerations of public policy. Put simply, the argument is that institutions in which management is accountable primarily to shareholders provides the most socially beneficial system of economic organization.

One exponent of this view was A. A. Berle, who conducted a debate with Merrick Dodd in the 1930s over a version of the stakeholder approach. Both Dodd and Berle recognized that the assumption that shareholders are the owners of a corporation no longer serves as a basis for the fiduciary duties of management. With the separation of ownership and control, the "traditional logic of property" became outmoded, with the result that shareholders lost any special status based on property rights. According to Berle and Means:

> . . . [T]he owners of passive property, by surrendering control and responsibility over the active property, have surrendered the right that the corporation should be operated in their sole interest,—they have released the community from the obligation to protect them to the full extent implied in the doctrine of strict property rights.[12]

But by taking control away from the owners, managers have not thereby conferred upon themselves the right to run the corporation for their benefit.

> The control groups have, rather, cleared the way for the claims of a group far wider than either the owners or the control. They have placed the community in a position to demand that the modern corporation serve not alone the owners or the control but all society.[13]

Dodd's position (and Freeman's, as well) is that the fiduciary duties of management should be extended now to include all other constituencies. Berle rejected this alternative, however, because he feared that extending the range of constituencies would result, not in benefits to these constituencies but in absolute power for management. In his response to Dodd, Berle wrote, "When the fiduciary obligation of the corporate management and 'control' to stockholders is weakened or eliminated, the management and 'control' become for all practical purposes absolute."[14] Thus, it would be dangerous to the community and harmful to business to remove the strong fiduciary duties which the law imposes on managers. He wrote:

> Unchecked by present legal balances, a social-economic absolutism of corporate administrators, even if benevolent, might be unsafe; and in any case it hardly affords the soundest base on which to construct the economic commonwealth which industrialism seems to require. Meanwhile . . . we had best be protecting the interests we know, being no less swift to provide for the new interests as they successively appear.[15]

Ultimately, Berle's argument is that corporations ought to be run for the benefit of shareholders, not because they "own" the corporation, or because of some contract or agency relation, but because all other constituencies are better off as a result. The underlying assumption is that the fiduciary duties of management are and ought to be determined by considerations of public policy. The present state of corporate governance is not ideal, but it is a workable arrangement that had been fashioned by historical forces. Any reform, therefore, should be incremental, so as to avoid unwanted disruptions.

Courts and legislatures in the United States have largely followed Berle's advice and have been very reluctant to weaken the strict profit-maximizing imperative that the law of fiduciary duties imposes on management. Managers, by law, must consider primarily the interests of shareholders in certain matters, and shareholders may bring suit against officers and directors for failing to do so.

The fiduciary duties of management have been weakened to some extent by so-called "other constituency" statutes, which permit (but do not require) officers and directors to consider the impact of their decisions on constituencies besides shareholders.[16] This is an exception that proves the rule, however, since these statutes have been enacted mainly to protect management from shareholder suits in the adoption of anti-takeover measures in the belief that the interests of the public are best served by allowing a wider range of considerations in defending against hostile takeovers. . . .

These considerations tend to support the Berle view that the basis for the fiduciary duties of management is public policy. If this is so, then the shareholder-management relation is not "ethically different" for any reason that is unique to that relation. . . . Many of the fiduciary duties of officers and directors are owed not to shareholders but to the corporation as an entity with interests of its own, which can, on occasion, conflict with those of shareholders. Further, corporations have some fiduciary duties to other constituencies, such as creditors (to remain solvent so as to repay debts) and to employees (in the management of a pension fund, for example). . . .

In corporate law, a fairly sharp distinction is made between the fiduciary duties of officers and directors, for which they can be held personally liable, and their other obligations and responsibilities for which they are not personally liable. Traditionally, the fiduciary duties of management are those of obedience and diligence, which require that they act within the scope of their authority and exercise ordinary care and prudence. These duties constitute a minimal level of oversight for which managers are held to a high degree of personal accountability. As long as they fulfill these fiduciary duties and act in ways which they believe to be in the best interests of the corporation, officers and directors are shielded from personal liability for any losses that occur. Losses that occur because of honest mistakes of judgment are covered, instead, by the business judgment rule, which prevents the courts from "second-guessing" the judgment of management.

As a result of this distinction, the obligations of management to shareholders are themselves divisible into fiduciary and nonfiduciary. The shareholder-management relation is not a single relation that is fiduciary in character; rather, it is a manifold relation in which management has some obligations to shareholders which are fiduciary duties and other obligations which are nonfiduciary duties. The fiduciary duties of officers and directors in the corporation are limited, moreover, to the most general matters of organization and strategy, so that in the ordinary conduct of business, where the business judgment rule applies, the interests of other constituencies may be taken into account without the possibility of a successful shareholder suit for the breach of any fiduciary duty.

## CONCLUSION

. . . Whether shareholders should continue to occupy the status that they do is also a matter to be decided by considerations of public policy. Since the 1930s, there has been a steady erosion in shareholder power, largely as a result of the increasing separation of ownership and control and the rise of large institutional investors. This has not occasioned much concern, since market forces and government regulation, along with a limited role for shareholders, have been regarded as sufficient checks on the power of management to ensure that corporate activity is generally beneficial. In recent years, there has been a movement to increase the influence of shareholders in major corporate decisions, but the main arguments have come from economists who believe that shareholder activism would force corporations to be more efficient.

The strongest force for change at the present time comes from once passive institutional investors who, in their role as fiduciaries for their own investors, have objected to antitakeover measures, high executive compensation, and other matters that advance the interests of incumbent management over those of shareholders. Some of the largest pension funds have also taken an active role in major restructurings and the selection of CEOs. Pressure is also being placed on the SEC to change the interpretation of Rule 14a-8 to allow shareholder resolutions on a broader range of issues.

The current debate over the role of shareholders suggests that the delicate balance of shareholder power, market forces, and government regulation has not fully succeeded in achieving maximum efficiency or in preventing some management abuses. Whether the answer lies in increasing shareholder power, changing the conditions of competition, or imposing more government regulation—or in some combination of the three—remains to be decided. What is clear is that the current debate is being conducted, not on the basis of ownership or of a contract or an agency relation, but in terms of public policy. Thus, to answer the question posed in the title: except for the useful role they play in corporate governance, there is nothing special about shareholders.

## NOTES

1. Milton Friedman, *Capitalism and Freedom* (Chicago: University of Chicago Press, 1962), 133; and "The Social Responsibility of Business Is to Increase Its Profits," *The New York Times Magazine*, September 13, 1970, p. 33.
2. E. Merrick Dodd, Jr., "For Whom Are Corporate Managers Trustees?" *Harvard Law Review*, 45 (1932), 1148.
3. R. Edward Freeman, *Strategic Management: A Stakeholder Approach* (Boston: Pitman, 1984). See also, R. Edward Freeman and Daniel R. Gilbert, Jr., *Corporate Strategy and the Search for Ethics* (Englewood Cliffs, NJ: Prentice Hall, 1988), and William M. Evan and R. Edward Freeman, "A Stakeholder Theory of the Modern Corporation: Kantian Capitalism," in Tom L. Beauchamp and Norman E. Bowie, eds., *Ethical Theory and Business*, 4th ed. (Englewood Cliffs, NJ: Prentice Hall, 1993), 75–84.
4. A. A. Berle, Jr., and Gardiner C. Means, *The Modern Corporation and Private Property* (New York: Macmillan, 1932), 336.
5. J. A. C. Hetherington, "Fact and Legal Theory: Shareholders, Managers, and Corporate Social Responsibility," *Stanford Law Review*, 21 (1969), 256.
6. Oliver E. Williamson, *The Economic Institutions of Capitalism* (New York: The Free Press, 1985), 304.
7. Williamson, *The Economic Institutions of Capitalism*, 304–5.
8. Williamson replies that although individual investors can protect themselves by selling stock, shareholders as a class cannot. Williamson, *The Economic Institutions of Capitalism*, 304.
9. See Bayless Manning, review of *The American Stockholder* by J. A. Livingston, *Yale Law Journal*, 67 (1958), 1492.
10. The idea that corporations are a "nexus" of contracting relations among individuals is familiar from the work of agency theorists. See, for example, Michael C. Jensen and William H. Meckling. "Theory of the Firm: Managerial Behavior, Agency Costs and Ownership Structure," *Journal of Financial Economics*, 3 (1976), 310. Agency theory does not suppose that the relations in question are contracts that create obligations, however; it asks us, rather, to think of the relation involving shareholders, along with those of all other constituencies, *as though they were a multitude of contracts* for explanatory purposes only. On this point, see Robert C. Clark, "Agency Costs *versus* Fiduciary Duties," in John W. Pratt and Richard J. Zeckhauser, eds., *Principles and Agents: The*

*Structure of Business* (Boston: Harvard Business School Press, 1985), 59–62.

11. Larry D. Sonderquist and Robert P. Vecchio, "Reconciling Shareholders' Rights and Corporate Responsibility: New Guidelines for Management," *Duke Law Journal*, 1978, p. 840.
12. Berle and Means, *The Modern Corporation and Private Property*, 355.
13. Berle and Means, *The Modern Corporation and Private Property*, 355–56.
14. A. A. Berle, Jr., "For Whom Corporate Managers Are Trustees: A Note," *Harvard Law Review*, 45 (1932), 1367.
15. Berle, "For Whom Corporate Managers Are Trustees," 1372.
16. At least 28 states have adopted other constituency statutes. In some states this has been accomplished by legislative enactments; in others, by court decisions interpreting state law. For an overview, see Charles Hansen, "Other Constituency Statutes: A Search for Perspective," *The Business Lawyer*, 46 (1991), 1355–75. A penetrating analysis that criticizes Hansen is Eric W. Orts, "Beyond Shareholders: Interpreting Corporate Constituency Statutes," *The George Washington Law Review*, 61 (1992), 14–135.

**LEGAL PERSPECTIVES**

# *Dodge v. Ford Motor Co.*

*Michigan Supreme Court*

. . . When plaintiffs made their complaint and demand for further dividends, the Ford Motor Company had concluded its most prosperous year of business. The demand for its cars at the price of the preceding year continued. It could make and could market in the year beginning August 1, 1916, more than 500,000 cars. Sales of parts and repairs would necessarily increase. The cost of materials was likely to advance, and perhaps the price of labor; but it reasonably might have expected a profit for the year of upwards of $60,000,000. . . . Considering only these facts, a refusal to declare and pay further dividends appears to be not an exercise of discretion on the part of the directors, but an arbitrary refusal to do what the circumstances required to be done. These facts and others call upon the directors to justify their action, or failure or refusal to act. In justification, the defendants have offered testimony tending to prove and which does prove, the following facts: It had been the policy of the corporation for a considerable time to annually reduce the selling price of cars, while keeping up, or improving, their quality. As early as in June, 1915, a general plan for the expansion of the productive capacity of the concern by a practical duplication of its plant had been talked over by the executive officers and directors and agreed upon; not all of the details having been settled, and no formal action of directors having been taken. The erection of a smelter was considered, and engineering and other data in connection therewith secured. In consequence, it was determined not to reduce the selling price of cars for the year beginning August 1, 1915, but to maintain the price to accumulate a large surplus to pay for the proposed expansion of plant and equipment, and perhaps to build a plant for smelting ore. It is hoped, by Mr. Ford, that eventually

204 Mich. 459, 170 N.W. 668, 3 A.L.R. 413 (1919). Majority opinion by Justice J. Ostrander.

1,000,000 cars will be annually produced. The contemplated changes will permit the increased output.

The plan, as affecting the profits of the business for the year beginning August 1, 1916, and thereafter, calls for a reduction in the selling price of the cars. . . . In short, the plan does not call for and is not intended to produce immediately a more profitable business, but a less profitable one; not only less profitable than formerly, but less profitable than it is admitted it might be made. The apparent immediate effect will be to diminish the value of shares and the returns to shareholders.

It is the contention of plaintiffs that the apparent effect of the plan is intended to be the continued and continuing effect of it, and that it is deliberately proposed, not of record and not by official corporate declaration, but nevertheless proposed, to continue the corporation henceforth as a semieleemosynary institution and not as a business institution. In support of this contention, they point to the attitude and to the expressions of Mr. Henry Ford. . . .

> "My ambition," said Mr. Ford, "is to employ still more men, to spread the benefits of this industrial system to the greatest possible number, to help them build up their lives and their homes. To do this we are putting the greatest share of our profits back in the business."
>
> "With regard to dividends, the company paid sixty per cent, on its capitalization of two million dollars, or $1,200,000, leaving $58,000,000 to reinvest for the growth of the company. This is Mr. Ford's policy at present, and it is understood that the other stockholders cheerfully accede to this plan."

He had made up his mind in the summer of 1916 that no dividends other than the regular dividends should be paid, "for the present."

> "Q. For how long? Had you fixed in your mind any time in the future, when you were going to pay—A. No."
>
> "Q. That was indefinite in the future? A. That was indefinite; yes, sir."

The record, and especially the testimony of Mr. Ford, convinces that he has to some extent the attitude towards shareholders of one who has dispensed and distributed to them large gains and that they should be content to take what he chooses to give. His testimony creates the impression, also, that he thinks the Ford Motor Company has made too much money, has had too large profits, and that, although large profits might be still earned, a sharing of them with the public, by reducing the price of the output of the company, ought to be undertaken. We have no doubt that certain sentiments, philanthropic and altruistic, creditable to Mr. Ford, had large influence in determining the policy to be pursued by the Ford Motor Company—the policy which has been herein referred to.

It is said by his counsel that—

> "Although a manufacturing corporation cannot engage in humanitarian works as its principal business, the fact that it is organized for profit does not prevent the existence of implied powers to carry on with humanitarian motives such charitable works as are incidental to the main business of the corporation." . . .

In discussing this proposition counsel have referred to decisions [citations omitted]. These cases, after all, like all others in which the subject is treated, turn finally upon the point, the question, whether it appears that the directors were not acting for the best interests of the corporation. We do not draw in question, nor do counsel for the plaintiffs do so, the validity of the general proposition stated by counsel nor the soundness of the opinions delivered in the cases cited. The case presented here is not like any of them. The difference between an incidental humanitarian expenditure of corporate funds for the benefit of the employees, like the building of a hospital for their use and the employment of agencies for the betterment of their condition, and a general purpose and plan to benefit mankind at the expense of others, is obvious. There should be no confusion (of which there is evidence) of the duties which Mr. Ford conceives that he and the stockholders owe to the general public and the duties which in law he and his codirectors owe to protesting, minority stockholders. A business corporation is organized and carried on primarily for the profit of the stockholders. The powers of the directors are to be employed for that end. The discretion of directors is to be exercised in the choice of means to attain that end, and does not extend to a change in the end itself, to the reduction of profits, or to the nondistribution of profits among stockholders in order to devote them to other purposes. . . . As we have pointed out, and the proposition does not require argument to sustain it, it is not within the lawful powers of a board of directors to shape and conduct the affairs of a corporation for the merely incidental benefit of shareholders and for the primary purpose of benefiting others, and no one will contend that, if the avowed purpose of the defendant directors was to sacrifice the interests of shareholders, it would not be the duty of the courts to interfere. . . . It is obvious that an annual dividend of 60 per cent, upon $2,000,000, or $1,200,000, is the equivalent of a very small dividend upon $100,000,000, or more.

The decree of the court below fixing and determining the specific amount to be distributed to stockholders is affirmed. . . .

# *A. P. Smith Manufacturing Co. v. Barlow*

*Supreme Court of New Jersey*

The Chancery Division, in a well-reasoned opinion by Judge Stein, determined that a donation by the plaintiff The A.P. Smith Manufacturing Company to Princeton University was *intra vires.* Because of the public importance of the issues presented, the appeal duly taken to the Appellate Division has been certified directly to this court under Rule 1:5–1(a).

The company was incorporated in 1896 and is engaged in the manufacture and sale of valves, fire hydrants, and special equipment, mainly for water and gas industries. Its plant is located in East Orange and Bloomfield and it has approximately 300 employees. Over the years the company has contributed regularly to the local community chest and on occasions to Upsala College in east Orange and Newark University, now part of Rutgers, the State University. On July 24, 1951 the board of directors adopted a resolution which set forth that it was in the corporation's best interests to join with others in the 1951 Annual Giving to Princeton University, and appropriated the sum of $1,500 to be transferred by the corporation's treasurer to the university as a contribution towards its maintenance. When this action was questioned by stockholders the corporation instituted a declaratory judgment action in the Chancery Division and trial was had in due course.

Mr. Hubert F. O'Brien, the president of the company, testified that he considered the contribution to be a sound investment, that the

96 A 2d 581 (1953). Opinion by Judge J. Jacobs.

public expects corporations to aid philanthropic and benevolent institutions, that they obtain good will in the community by so doing, and that their charitable donations create favorable environment for their business operations. In addition, he expressed the thought that in contributing to liberal arts institutions, corporations were furthering their self-interest in assuring the free flow of properly trained personnel for administrative and other corporate employment. Mr. Frank W. Abrams, chairman of the board of the Standard Oil Company of New Jersey, testified that corporations are expected to acknowledge their public responsibilities in support of the essential elements of our free enterprise system. He indicated that it was not "good business" to disappoint "this reasonable and justified public expectation," nor was it good business for corporations "to take substantial benefits from their membership in the economic community while avoiding the normally accepted obligations of citizenship in the social community." Mr. Irving S. Olds, former chairman of the board of the United States Steel Corporation, pointed out that corporations have a self-interest in the maintenance of liberal education as the bulwark of good government. He stated that "Capitalism and free enterprise owe their survival in no small degree to the existence of our private, independent universities" and that if American business does not aid in their maintenance it is not "properly protecting the long-range interest of its stockholders, its employees, and its customers." Similarly, Dr. Harold W. Dodds, President of Princeton University, suggested that if private institutions of higher learning were replaced by governmental institutions our society would be vastly different and private enterprise in other fields would fade out rather promptly. Further on he stated that "democratic society will not long endure if it does not nourish within itself strong centers of non-governmental fountains of knowledge, opinions of all sorts not governmentally or politically originated. If the time comes when all these centers are absorbed into government, then freedom as we know it, I submit, is at an end." . . .

When the wealth of the nation was primarily in the hands of individuals they discharged their responsibilities as citizens by donating freely for charitable purposes. With the transfer of most of the wealth to corporate hands and the imposition of heavy burdens of individual taxation, they have been unable to keep pace with increased philanthropic needs. They have therefore, with justification, turned to corporations to assume the modern obligations of good citizenship in the same manner as humans do. Congress and state legislatures have enacted laws which encourage corporate contributions, and much has recently been written to indicate the crying need and adequate legal basis therefor[e]. . . .

During the first world war corporations loaned their personnel and contributed substantial corporate funds in order to insure survival; during the depression of the '30s they made contributions to alleviate the desperate hardships of the millions of unemployed; and during the second world war they again contributed to insure survival. They now recognize that we are faced with other, though nonetheless vicious, threats from abroad which must be withstood without impairing the vigor of our democratic institutions at home and that otherwise victory will be pyrrhic indeed. More and more they have come to recognize that their salvation rests upon sound economic and social environment which in turn rests in no insignificant part upon free and vigorous nongovernmental institutions of learning. It seems to us that just as the conditions prevailing when corporations were originally created required that they serve public as well as private interests, modern conditions require that corporations acknowledge and discharge social as well as private responsibilities as members of the communities within which they operate. Within this broad concept there is no difficulty in sustaining, as incidental to their proper objects and in aid of the public welfare, the power of corporations to contribute corporate funds within reasonable limits in support of academic institutions. But even if we confine ourselves to the terms of the common-law rule in its application to current conditions, such expenditures may likewise readily be justified as being for the benefit of the corporation; indeed, if need be the matter may be viewed strictly in terms of actual survival of the corporation in a free enterprise system. The genius of our common law has been its capacity for growth and its adaptability to the needs of the times. Generally courts have accomplished the desired result indirectly through the molding of old forms. Occasionally they have done it directly through frank rejection of the old and recognition of the new. But whichever path the common law has taken it has not been found wanting as the proper tool for the advancement of the general good. . . .

In the light of all of the foregoing we have no hesitancy in sustaining the validity of the donation by the plaintiff. There is no suggestion that it was made indiscriminately or to a pet charity of the corporate directors in furtherance of personal rather than corporate ends. On the contrary, it was made to a preeminent institution of higher learning, was modest in amount and well within the limitations imposed by the statutory enactments, and was voluntarily made in the reasonable belief that it would aid the public welfare and advance the interests of the plaintiff as a private corporation and as part of the community in which it operates. We find that it was a lawful exercise of the corporation's implied and incidental powers under common-law principles and that it came within the express authority of the pertinent state legislation. As has been indicated, there is now widespread belief throughout the nation that free and vigorous non-governmental institutions of learning are vital to our democracy and the system of free enterprise and that withdrawal of corporate authority to make such contributions within reasonable limits would seriously threaten their continuance. Corporations have come to recognize this and with their enlightenment have sought in varying measures, as has the plaintiff by its contribution, to insure and strengthen the society which gives them existence and the means of aiding themselves and their fellow citizens. Clearly then, the appellants, as individual stockholders whose private interests rest entirely upon the well-being of the plaintiff corporation, ought not be permitted to close their eyes to present day realities and thwart the long-visioned corporate action in recognizing and voluntarily discharging its high obligations as a constituent of our modern social structure.

The judgment entered in the Chancery Division is in all respects Affirmed.

## Johnson & Johnson: Our Credo

We believe our first responsibility is to the doctors, nurses and patients, to mothers and fathers and all others who use our products and services.
In meeting their needs everything we do must be of high quality.
We must constantly strive to reduce our costs in order to maintain reasonable prices.
Customers' orders must be serviced promptly and accurately.
Our suppliers and distributors must have an opportunity to make a fair profit.

We are responsible to our employees, the men and women who work with us throughout the world.
Everyone must be considered as an individual.
We must respect their dignity and recognize their merit.
They must have a sense of security in their jobs.
Compensation must be fair and adequate, and working conditions clean, orderly and safe.
We must be mindful of ways to help our employees fulfill their family responsibilities.
Employees must feel free to make suggestions and complaints.
There must be equal opportunity for employment, development and advancement for those qualified.
We must provide competent management, and their actions must be just and ethical.

We are responsible to the communities in which we live and work and to the world community as well.
We must be good citizens—support good works and charities and bear our fair share of taxes.
We must encourage civic improvements and better health and education.
We must maintain in good order the property we are privileged to use, protecting the environment and natural resources.

Our final responsibility is to our stockholders.
Business must make a sound profit.
We must experiment with new ideas.
Research must be carried on, innovative programs developed and mistakes paid for.
New equipment must be purchased, new facilities provided and new products launched.
Reserves must be created to provide for adverse times.
When we operate according to these principles, the stockholders should realize a fair return.

## CASES

# CASE 1. *Shutdown at Eastland*

When Speedy Motors Company closed its assembly plant in Eastland, Michigan, lobbyists for organized labor cited the case as one more reason why the Federal government should pass a law regulating plant closings. With less than a month's notice, the company laid off nearly 2,000 workers and permanently shut down the facility, which had been in operation more than 20 years. The local union president called the action "a callous and heartless treatment of the workers and of the community."

Company executives defended the decision as inevitable in view of the harsh competitive realities of the automotive industry. "Purchases of the Speedy model produced at Eastland have fallen to almost nothing and there is nothing we can do about changes in consumer preferences," a company spokesman said.

Labor lobbyists insist that instances such as this show the need for a Federal law which would require companies to give as much as two years' notice before closing a major factory, unless they can demonstrate that an emergency exists. The proposed legislation would also require the employer to provide special benefits to workers and the community affected by the shutdown.

"Closing plants needlessly and without warning is an antisocial, criminal act," a union leader said. "Giant corporations don't give a thought to the hardships they are imposing on long-time employees and communities that depend on their jobs. The only thing they consider is their profit."

Opponents of the legislation maintain that the proposed law would strike at the heart of the free enterprise system. "Companies must be free to do business wherever they choose without being penalized," a corporate spokesman argued. "Plant closing legislation would constitute unjustified interference in private decision making. Laws which restrict the ability of management to operate a business in the most efficient manner are counterproductive and in direct conflict with the theory of free enterprise."

### Questions

1. Does the closing of a plant when it ceases to be profitable violate the "moral minimum"?
2. Who are the affected stakeholders, and how should their interests be considered?
3. Who should take primary responsibility for those laid off or terminated because of a plant closing?

# CASE 2. *Merck & River Blindness*

Merck & Co., Inc. is one of the world's largest pharmaceutical products and services companies. Headquartered in Whitehouse Station, New Jersey, Merck has over 70,000 employees and sells products and services in approximately 150 countries. Merck had revenues of $47,715,700,000 in 2001, ranked 24th on the 2002 Fortune 500 list of America's largest companies, 62nd on the Global 500 list of the World's Largest Corporations, and 82nd on the Fortune 100 list of the Best Companies to Work For.

In the late 1970s Merck research scientists discovered a potential cure for a severely debilitating human disease known as river blindness (onchocerciasis). The disease is caused by a parasite that enters the body through the bite of black flies that breed on the rivers of Africa and Latin America. The parasite causes severe itching, disfiguring skin infections, and, finally, total and permanent blindness. In order to demonstrate that it was safe and effective, the drug needed to undergo expensive clinical trials. Executives were concerned because they knew that those who would benefit from using it could not afford to pay for the drug, even if it was sold at cost. However, Merck research scientists argued that the drug was far too promising from a medical standpoint to abandon. Executives relented and a seven-year clinical trial proved the drug both efficacious and safe. A single annual dose of Mectizan, the name Merck gave to the drug, kills the parasites inside the body as well as the flies that carry the parasite.

Once Mectizan was approved for human use, Merck executives explored third-party payment options with the World Health Organization, the U.S. Agency for International Development, and the U.S. Department of State without success. Four United States Senators went so far as to introduce legislation to provide U.S. funding for the worldwide distribution of Mectizan. However, their efforts were unsuccessful, no legislation was passed and, and no U.S. government funding was made available. Finally, Merck executives decided to manufacture and distribute the drug for free.

Since 1987, Merck has manufactured and distributed over 700 million tablets of Mectizan at no charge. The company's decision was grounded in its core values:

1. Our business is preserving and improving human life.
2. We are committed to the highest standards of ethics and integrity.
3. We are dedicated to the highest level of scientific excellence and commit our research to improving human and animal health and the quality of life.
4. We expect profits, but only from work that satisfies customer needs and benefits humanity.
5. We recognize that the ability to excel—to most competitively meet society's and customers' needs—depends on the integrity, knowledge, imagination, skill, diversity, and teamwork of employees, and we value these qualities most highly.

This case was prepared by Denis G. Arnold and is based on Erik Eckholm, "River Blindness: Conquering an Ancient Scourge," *The New York Times*, January 8, 1989; David Pilling, "Public Private Health Deal Aims to End Elephantiasis," *The Financial Times* (London), January 21, 2000; Karen Lowry Miller, "The Pill Machine," *Newsweek*, November 19, 2001; "The Merck Mectizan Donation Program," www.merck.com/about/cr/policies_performance/social/mectizan_donation.html (03 October 2002); "The Story of Mectizan," www.merck.com/about/cr/mectizan/ (03 October 2002); "MERCK Annual Report 2001" http://www.anrpt2001.com/index.html (03 October 2002); "About Merck: Mission Statement," www.merck.com/about/mission.html (03 October 2002); "The 2002 Fortune 500," www.fortune.com/lists/F500/index.html (03 October 2002); "The 2002 Global 500," www.fortune.com/lists/G500/index.html (03 October 2002); and "Best Companies to Work For," http://www.fortune.com/lists/bestcompanies/index.html www.fortune.com/lists/F500/index.html (03 October 2002).

George W. Merck, the company's president from 1925 to 1950, summarized these values when he wrote, "medicine is for the people. It is not for the profits. The profits follow, and if we have remembered that, they have never failed to appear. The better we have remembered that, the larger they have been."

Today, the Merck Mectizan Donation Program includes partnerships with numerous nongovernmental organizations, governmental organizations, private foundations, the World Health Organization, The World Bank, UNICEF, and the United Nations Development Program. In 1998, Merck expanded the Mectizan Donation Program to include the prevention of elephantiasis (lymphatic filariasis) in African countries where the disease coexists with river blindness. In total, approximately 30 million people in 32 countries are now treated annually with Mectizan. Merck reports that it has no idea how much the entire program has cost, but estimates that each pill is worth $1.50. The United Nations reports that river blindness may be eradicated as soon as 2007.

### Questions

1. Given the fact that Merck is spending corporate resources to manufacture and distribute Mectizan, is the Merck Mectizan Donation Program morally justifiable? Explain.
2. Would Friedman approve of the Merck Mectizan Donation Program? Explain.
3. Should the fact that Merck's values are clearly stated in corporate publications that are widely available to investors make a difference to someone who accepts Friedman's position? Explain.
4. Should the Merck Mectizan Donation Program serve as a model for other pharmaceutical companies who are in a unique position to facilitate the eradication of other diseases in the developing nations? Explain.

## CASE 3. *H. B. Fuller in Honduras: Street Children and Substance Abuse*

Kativo Chemical Industries, a wholly owned foreign subsidiary of H. B. Fuller, sells a solvent-based adhesive (glue) in several countries in Latin America. The brand name of the glue is Resistol. In 1985 it came to H. B. Fuller's attention that large numbers of street children in the Central American country of Honduras were sniffing glue and that Resistol was among the glues being abused. Indeed all these children who sniff glue are being referred to as *Resistoleros.*

Resistol has a number of industrial uses, although one of its primary uses is in small shoe repair shops. The glue has properties that are not possible to attain with a water-based formula. These properties include rapid set, strong adhesion, and water resistance. Resistol is similar to airplane glue.

Widespread inhalant abuse among street children in Honduras can be attributed to the depth of poverty there. Honduras is one of the poorest countries in Latin America. The unemployment rate is high. Infant and child mortality rates are high, life expectancy for adults is 64 years, and the adult literacy rate is estimated to be about 60 percent. Its exports,

This case is based on a much longer case with the same name authored by Norman E. Bowie and Stefanie Lenway. The full "H. B. Fuller in Honduras: Street Children and Substance Abuse" was the Case award winner in the Columbia University Graduate School of Business Ethics in Business Program.

bananas and coffee, are commodities that are subject to the vagaries of the weather and the volatility of commodity markets. Government deficits caused in part by mismanagement and corruption have prevented desirable spending on public services.

Migrants to the urban areas typically move first to cuarterias (rows) of connected rooms. The rooms are generally constructed of wood with dirt floors, and they are usually windowless. The average household contains about seven persons who live together in a single room. For those living in rooms facing an alley, the narrow way between buildings serves both as a sewage and waste disposal area and as a courtyard for as many as 150 persons.

That the name of a Fuller product should be identified with a social problem was a matter of great concern to the H. B. Fuller Company. H. B. Fuller was widely known as a socially responsible corporation. Among its achievements were an enlightened employee relations policy that included giving each employee a day off on his or her birthday and, on the 10th anniversary of employment, bonus vacation time and a substantial check so that employees could travel and see the world. H. B. Fuller contributes 5 percent of its pretax profits to charity and continually wins awards for its responsibility to the environment. A portion of its corporate mission statement reads as follows:

> H. B. Fuller Company is committed to its responsibilities, in order of priority, to its customers, employees and shareholders. H. B. Fuller will conduct business legally and ethically, support the activities of its employees in their communities, and be a responsible corporate citizen.

The issue of the abuse of glue by Honduran street children received attention in the Honduran press as early as 1983.

The man on the spot at Kativo was Vice President Humberto Larach (Beto) who headed Kativo's North Adhesives Division. Beto had proved his courage and his business creativity when he was among 105 taken hostage in the Chamber of Commerce building in downtown San Pedro Sula by Honduran guerrillas from the Communist Popular Liberation Front. Despite firefights between the guerrillas and government troops, threats of execution, and being used as a human shield, Beto had convinced two fellow hostages to buy from Kativo rather than from a competitor. Not surprisingly, Beto had a reputation for emphasizing the importance of making the bottom line that was an important part of the Kativo corporate culture.

Initial responses to the problem were handled by officials at Kativo. These responses included requests to the press not to use "Resistolero" as a synonym for a street child glue sniffer and attempts to persuade the Honduran legislature not to require the addition of oil of mustard to its glue. Beto had requested H. B. Fuller's U.S. headquarters to look into the viability of oil of mustard as an additive to the glue. H. B. Fuller's Corporate industrial hygiene staff found evidence that indicated that oil of mustard was a carcinogen and hence was potentially dangerous to employees and consumers. Kativo officials believed that glue sniffing was a social problem and that Kativo was limited in what it could do about the problem. The solution was education.

From 1985 through 1989, officials at H. B. Fuller headquarters in St. Paul, Minnesota, were only dimly aware of the problem. While some of these officials assisted their Kativo subsidiary by providing information on the dangers of oil of mustard, the traditional policy of H. B. Fuller was to give great autonomy to foreign-owned subsidiaries.

However, in late April 1986 Elmer Andersen, H. B. Fuller chairman of the board received a letter from a stockholder who pointedly asked how a company with its enlightened business philosophy could be responsible for selling a product that was causing harm to the children of Honduras. Three years later, on June 7, 1989, Vice President for Corporate Relations Dick Johnson received a call from a stockholder whose daughter was in the Peace Corps in Honduras. The stockholder's question was how can a company like H. B. Fuller claim to have a social conscience and continue to sell Resistol which is "literally burning out the brains" of children in Latin America. Johnson knew that headquarters should become actively involved in addressing the problem. But given the nature of the problem and H. B. Fuller's policy of local responsibility, what should headquarters do?

## Questions

1. To what extent can Honduran street children who obtain an H. B. Fuller product illegitimately be considered stakeholders? If they are stakeholders, how can their interests be represented?
2. What obligations does a company have to solve social problems?
3. Where does the responsibility for solving this problem rest—with the local subsidiary Kativo or with H. B. Fuller headquarters?
4. To what extent should officials at H. B. Fuller headquarters be concerned about potential criticisms that they are meddling in a problem where they don't understand the culture?

## *Suggested Supplementary Readings*


BOATRIGHT, JOHN, R. *Ethics In Finance*, Malden, MA: Blackwell Publishers, 1999.

CARSON, THOMAS. "Friedman's Theory of Corporate Social Responsibility." *Business and Professional Ethics Journal*, 12 (Spring 1993), 3–32.

CLARKSON, MAX B. E. "A Stakeholder Framework for Analyzing and Evaluating Corporate Social Performance." *The Academy of Management Review*, 20 (January 1995), 92–117.

DONALDSON, THOMAS and LEE E. PRESTON. "The Stakeholder Theory of the Corporation: Concepts, Evidence, and Implications." *Academy of Management Review*, 20 (January 1995), 65–91.

FORT, TIMOTHY L. "Business as Mediating Institution," *Business Ethics Quarterly* 6: 149–164.

FREEMAN, R. EDWARD. *Strategic Management: A Stakeholder Approach.* Boston: Pitman, 1984.

FREEMAN, R. EDWARD and DANIEL R. GILBERT, JR. *Corporate Strategy and the Search for Ethics.* Englewood Cliffs, NJ: Prentice Hall, 1998.

FRIEDMAN, MILTON. *Capitalism and Freedom.* Chicago University Press, 1962.

GOODPASTER, KENNETH E. "Business Ethics and Stakeholder Analysis." *Business Ethics Quarterly*, 1, 1991, 53–73.

JENSEN, MICHAEL C. "Value Maximization, Stakeholder Theory, and the Corporate Objective Function." *Business Ethics Quarterly*, 12 (April 2002), 235–256.

JONES, THOMAS M. "Instrumental Stakeholder Theory: A Synthesis of Ethics and Economics." *The Academy of Management Review*, 20 (April 1995), 404–37.

JONES, THOMAS M. and ANDREW C. WICKS. "Convergent Stakeholder Theory." *Academy of Management Review*, 24 (April 199), 191–221. Commentaries by Linda Klebe Trevino and Gary R. Weaver, Dennis Gioia, R. Edward Freeman, and Thomas Donaldson follow in the same volume.

JONES, THOMAS M., ANDREW C. WICKS, and R. EDWARD FREEMAN. "Stakeholder Theory: The State of the Art," in *Blackwell Guide to Business Ethics*, Norman E. Bowie, ed. (2002), pp. 19–37.

LANGTRY, BRUCE. "Stakeholders and the Moral Responsibilities of Business." *Business Ethics Quarterly*, 4 (October 1994), 431–43.

LEVITT, THEODORE. "The Dangers of Social Responsibility." *Harvard Business Review*, 36 (September–October 1958), 41–50.

MAITLAND, IAN. "The Morality of the Corporation: An Empirical or Normative Disagreement?" *Business Ethics Quarterly*, 4 (October 1994), 445–58.

MARENS, RICHARD and ANDREW WICKS. "Getting Real: Stakeholder Theory, Managerial Practice, and the General Irrelevance of Fiduciary Duties Owed to Shareholders." *Business Ethics Quarterly*, 9 (April 1999), pp. 273–292.

MINTZBERG, HENRY. "The Case for Corporate Social Responsibility." *Journal of Business Strategy* 4 (Fall 1983), 3–15.

MITCHELL, RONALD, K. BRADLEY, R. AGLE, and DONNA WOOD, "Toward A Theory of Stakeholder Identification and Salience: Defining The Principle of Who and What Really Counts," *Academy of Management Review*, 22 (1997), 853–886.

SCHLOSSBERGER, EUGENE. "A New Model of Business: Dual Investor Theory." *Business Ethics Quarterly*, 4 (October 1994), 459–74.

WICKS, ANDREW C., DANIEL R. GILBERT, JR., and R. EDWARD FREEMAN. "A Feminist Reinterpretation of the Stakeholder Concept." *Business Ethics Quarterly*, 4 (October 1994), 475–97.

# *Chapter Three*

# Corporate Character and Individual Responsibility

## INTRODUCTION

CHAPTER 2 ADDRESSED the general problem of corporate responsibility by asking what is the purpose or the function of the corporation. This chapter explores some of the issues surrounding how society can make businesses and those individuals who manage them accountable for their actions. Do we look simply to the individuals within the corporation or is there a sense in which the corporation as an entity can be held accountable? Is a corporation the kind of entity that can be responsible or is responsibility a characteristic that applies only to human beings?

The business ethics literature has many riveting cases that involve accidents and product defects. One of the earliest product defect cases was the Ford Pinto. On the positive side Johnson and Johnson has been lauded for how it handled the Tylenol crisis. These cases have been followed by the Challenger disaster, the Exxon Valdez oil spill, and most recently the Firestone/Ford defective tire issue. In addition to these high profile cases, it is estimated that there are 100,000 deaths each year in the United States from medical error. Everyone agrees that these mistakes and accidents should be minimized but how is that to be accomplished? Some would insist that we look for the responsible individuals. They argue that individuals too often hide behind the shield of a large corporation and as a result escape punishment when they have committed a misdeed. The corporation provides the cover of anonymity. Others argue that the search for individuals is often misguided and counterproductive. Many corporate misdeeds or untoward events are the result of corporate structures and incentive systems. To avoid future accidents and errors, some of which could result in catastrophes, the focus should be on the organizational structures and technological fixes rather than on the search for responsible individuals to punish. This chapter considers all these issues in depth.

## ACCOUNTABILITY: THE CORPORATION OR INDIVIDUALS WITHIN

One way to ensure good behavior is to make bad behavior punishable by law. The U.S. government used this approach when, in 1991, it passed the Federal Sentencing Guidelines (selections are reproduced in this chapter). The attempt to make business behave ethically through specific laws with appropriate penalties is called the *compliance approach to business ethics.* Under the Federal Sentencing Guidelines, should a business firm fail to have compliance systems in place and should the firm or someone acting in the name of the firm commit a federal tort, the fines that could be levied are severe enough to put the firm out of business. Even if they are not that draconian, the fines could do serious damage to the bottom line. At first many in business and academe were skeptical that the significant fines under the law would ever be imposed. All that changed in 1996 when Daiwa Bank was fined $340 million under the Guidelines. At that time that was the largest criminal fine in U.S. history. And it resulted from the actions of a Bank employee, Toshihide Iguchi, who had lost $1.1 billion in concealed securities trading. Daiwa Bank had investigated Iguchi's confession and replaced the lost pension account funds with its own money. But it did not disclose these crimes to the public or to the U.S. government until it could do so as part of its regularly scheduled reporting. That delay put Daiwa Bank in violation of a U.S. law that requires that a "Criminal Referral Form" be filed within thirty days of learning of an employee's offense. The delay also meant that Daiwa Bank needed to falsify certain records and thus compounded its offenses. Moreover, Daiwa Bank had no compliance system in place. And this omission cost Daiwa Bank. At the sentencing, Assistant U.S. Attorney Reid Figel told the court,

> It is virtually impossible for any financial institution to protect itself against every potential criminal act by its employees, particularly given the highly specialized nature and complexity of the securities now traded in the world's capital markets. It is precisely because of this complexity, however, that it is essential that corporations institute and insist upon a corporate culture of absolute compliance with the rules and regulations of the marketplace. One of the most important ways to do this is to establish and enforce a system of checks and balances that are designed to protect against the criminal acts of corporate employees.[1]

More recently, pharmaceutical giant Hoffman-LaRoche, Ltd. was fined $500 million, the largest fine ever imposed under the Federal Sentencing Guidelines, following their conviction for antitrust conspiracy in the vitamin market. The penalties could have been much worse, as the company was in fact liable for a fine of as high as $1.3 billion under the Guidelines.[2]

Of philosophical significance is the fact that the Guidelines punish and reward organizations as organizations rather than individuals within the corporation. Is this defensible? In her article that opens this chapter, Jennifer Moore provides a defense for the notion of corporate culpability upon which the Guidelines depend. In her defense she makes use of "corporate character theory" as the grounding for a theory of corporate culpability. The key to the corporate character theory is the fact that decisions in the corporation are not simply the result of a manager's giving orders. Rather devices such as standard operating procedures, decision procedures, and punitive sanctions are relevant as well. The existence of such devices gives rise to a corporate character. However, these devices can be defective as well and can rise to a corporate culture or character that is conducive to wrongdoing. It is the existence of this deviant corporate character that provides the justification for the punishment of the corporation. Moore then shows how the Guidelines are consistent with the theory of corporate character and are thus able "to pursue a wider range of sentencing aims than is traditional in the sentencing of corporations."

In his article, Manuel Velasquez criticizes the notion that a corporation can be held morally responsible separate from the moral responsibility of its agents. Velasquez points out that only intentional agents can be said to be the morally responsible cause of something. Velasquez then goes on to show that corporations are not intentional agents in the relevant sense. Many proponents of the corporate responsibility thesis try to argue that a corporation has characteristics that are truly predicated of it, but cannot be truly predicated of any corporate agents. However, Velasquez argues that having uniquely predicable characteristics does not turn the corporation into a metaphysical entity that can be held morally responsible. Another argument of the proponents of corporate moral responsibility is that if an action is not predicable of an individual, then the individual cannot be causally responsible for the action. Using a number of vivid counterexamples, Velasquez challenges this claim. We leave to the reader whether Jennifer Moore's view of corporate character can also be challenged on these grounds.

## DETERMINING RESPONSIBILITY

Many of the most dramatic cases in business ethics are cases that involve accidents or other catastrophic events. Airline crashes, the Challenger explosion, and the Chernobyl nuclear power accident are perfect examples. But some of the accidents do not make the news headlines, although they are just as tragic for the individuals involved. Medical mistakes when people are misdiagnosed, given the wrong medicine, or given the wrong amount of medicine are illustrations. When events like this occur, there is a natural tendency to want to find who was responsible and often to punish them. However, philosophers know that assigning responsibility is a difficult task—both factually and conceptually. The task can be difficult factually because the facts are hard to determine. The task can be difficult conceptually because an event can have multiple causes and it can be extremely difficult to parse out the responsibility among the multiple causes. The assignment of responsibility becomes particularly difficult when the problem results from the way an organization is structured or the way the organization has arranged the incentives that indicate success within the organization. For example, in October 1999, there was a terrible train accident outside Paddington Station in London. Many were killed. Subsequent investigation showed that one engineer ran a red light, but the investigation also showed that the red lights were often placed in positions that were obscure and hard to see. How much of the responsibility for the accident rests with the engineer who perished and how much with those who designed the placement of the lights?

Some believe that the organizational structure is so important that when an accident happens, the organization and society should often not try to find who is individually responsible and thereby put all the blame and often the punishment on them. An early example of this kind of thinking occurred with 1979 crash of Air New Zealand TE-901 into Mt. Erebus in Antarctica. The Royal Commission that investigated the crash identified the essential cause as the failure of the airline to inform Captain Collins of the change of the coordinates in the aircraft's internal computer system. Further investigation indicated that this communication failure was not simply the oversight of one individual. Rather the communications gap resulted from general flaws in management procedure. To avoid another disaster, the management needed to improve the means of communication so that pilots were given complete information concerning the coordinates placed into the aircraft's computer. In her article, "How Can We Save the Next Victim?," Lisa Belkin investigates a particularly poignant tragedy in which a young child was given ten times the dose of medication as was prescribed and died as a result. Her recommendation on the basis of this study is that often we should seek organizational or technical solutions rather than search for a person to blame.

On the other hand, some feel it is too easy for irresponsible individuals to avoid responsibility for their actions by invoking organizational structures, managerial practices and incentive systems. In the article by Russell Boisjoly et al., the authors are critical of the Rogers Commission that investigated the Challenger disaster on just such grounds. The Rogers Commission had concluded that the problem was with management systems and that decisions became collective rather than individual. However, Boisjoly et al. argue that there were individuals who could have stopped the launch and the responsibility for the accident rests on them.

Reflection indicates that we should strike a balance between these two positions. Some accidents are clearly the responsibility of an easily identified individual or set of individuals. Others result from a combination of perverse incentives, management practices and organizational structures. Some, like the train crash in London, result from both factors. The ethical corporation needs both supportive organizational structures and responsible individuals if accidents like those discussed are to be minimized.

## NOTES

1. Jeffrey M. Kaplan, "Why Daiwa Bank Will Pay $340 Million Under the Sentencing Guidelines," *Ethikos*, 9 (May/June 1996): 1–3, 11.
2. Kaplan, Jeff, "Legal Update." *EOA News* (Summer/Fall, 1999), p. 12.

**ACCOUNTABILITY AND RESPONSIBILITY**

# Corporate Culpability under the Federal Sentencing Guidelines

*Jennifer Moore*

## INTRODUCTION

In 1984, Congress created the United States Sentencing Commission to promulgate criminal sentencing guidelines for the federal courts. The first task of the Commission was the development of sentencing guidelines for individuals. When these were completed in 1987, the Commission began to formulate guidelines for organizations. The fourth and final draft of the organizational guidelines became law on November 1, 1991.

The new organizational guidelines take an explicitly "carrot and stick" approach to sentencing. Under section 8C2, calculating the appropriate fine for an organizational offender begins with the determination of a "base fine" chosen to reflect the seriousness of the offense. The base fine is then adjusted according to a series of aggravating and mitigating factors: the participation of authority personnel, the history of the organization, cooperation with law enforcement authorities, and the presence or absence of a program to prevent and detect crime. In part, these factors are intended to provide an incentive for organizations to "strengthen internal mechanisms for deterring, detecting and reporting criminal conduct by their agents and employees." But an additional result of the Guidelines is to make corporate punishment proportional to what would, in an individual, be called "culpability": the deliberateness of the offense, the extent of the offender's involvement, and the offender's "character." Indeed, the Guidelines explicitly use the term "culpability" and refer to the list of aggravating and mitigating factors as the organization's "culpability score."

Although the Guidelines are applicable to all "organizations," they were designed with corporations in mind, and it is on corporations that they are expected to have their greatest impact. Yet the Guidelines' use of organizational culpability represents a departure from the traditional principles of substantive corporate criminal law. The dominant aim of corporate criminal law has been deterrence rather than retribution, rehabilitation, or incapacitation. This has meant that culpability has played a relatively minor role. To be sure, courts have had to develop theories of corporate mens rea in order to hold corporations liable for crimes requiring intent. But these theories are the products of necessity rather than careful analysis or conceptual rigor; they stem less from a belief in the importance of corporate culpability than from the perceived need to extend criminal liability to corporations. The Guidelines, in contrast, employ a well-considered, theoretically satisfying conception of corporate culpability that is driven by the purposes of sentencing set out in 18 U.S.C. § 3553 (a) (2): just punishment, adequate deterrence, protection of the public, rehabilitation of the offender, proportionality with the seriousness of the offense, and the need to promote respect for the law.

This article examines the use of corporate culpability in the Federal Sentencing Guidelines and addresses three major questions: In light of the traditional unimportance of culpability in corporate criminal law, is corporate culpability an appropriate concern of the

From Jennifer Moore, "Corporate Culpability Under the Federal Sentencing Guidelines," *Arizona Law Review*, 34 (1992).

Guidelines? If so, how is corporate culpability best conceptualized? Finally, how do the Guidelines understand corporate culpability, and how close do they come to embodying this most satisfying theory? Part I of the Article discusses the principal reasons why culpability has been important at the trial and sentencing of individual criminals, and argues that similar reasons justify concern with culpability in the sentencing of corporate offenders. Although culpability is not the only important factor in corporate sentencing, Part I concludes, it is a legitimate concern of the Guidelines. Part II sets out three alternative conceptions of corporate culpability, those implicit in the two prevailing theories of corporate criminal liability—the doctrine of respondeat superior and the doctrine of Section 2.07 of the *Model Penal Code*—and a third conception that has received considerable support from scholars of corporate crime. Part II argues that it is this third conception, termed the "corporate character theory," that provides the most adequate understanding of corporate culpability, and that this theory is particularly well-suited for use in the sentencing of organizational criminals. Finally, Part III explores the use of culpability by the organizational guidelines themselves, and contends that they employ a conception of corporate culpability that is closely related to the corporate character theory. In addition, it attempts to show how the adoption of the corporate character theory allows the Guidelines to pursue a wider range of sentencing aims than is traditional in the sentencing of corporations. . . .

## I. CULPABILITY AND THE CRIMINAL LAW

* * *

### C. Corporate Culpability

. . . There are several reasons why one might believe that corporate culpability is not an appropriate concern. Corporations are artificial entities, not biological persons, and thus may seem unsuitable objects of moral blame and accompanying "stigma." Even if there is a sense in which corporations can be "culpable," they are likely to have weaker claims to the fair treatment, liberty, and reduction of anxiety emphasized by Hart than individuals do. Finally, the high number of strict liability offenses for which corporations can be liable suggests a lack of legislative concern with the issue of corporate culpability. These arguments are ultimately unpersuasive, however. I will argue that, although corporations cannot be blameworthy in the literal sense in which individuals can, corporations cause and direct the acts of their agents in a way that makes it natural to call them "culpable." Once this is conceded, corporate culpability merits attention in the criminal law for the same reasons that individual culpability does.

Although corporations always act through individual agents, and it is always an individual agent or group of agents who breaks the law, it is fair to say that corporations frequently *cause* their agents to violate the law. The behavior of individuals in corporations is not merely the product of individual choice; it is stimulated and shaped by goals, rules, policies, and procedures that are features of the corporation as an entity. How to design these features to ensure that agents act predictably and in the interest of the organization—that is, how to control the behavior of corporate agents—is the central question of organizational theory. Establishing a chain of command, delegating to each member a sphere of authority, setting up standard operating procedures, training members, and controlling the flow of information are all part of this task. Ultimately, organizational theorist Herbert Simon explains, the goal is for the organization to "take[] from the individual some of his decisional autonomy, and substitute[] for it an organization decision-making process."[1] Where this process is likely to result in violations on behalf of the corporation on the part of its agents, it seems natural to say that the corporation is "culpable" or "at fault."

It is important to distinguish this argument from the claim that it is sometimes difficult to locate the specific corporate agents responsible for a criminal act. Although this claim is true, it is an evidentiary point rather than a philosophical one. My argument is somewhat different: Because of the diffusion of responsibility in organizations and the ways in which individual decisions are channelled by corporate rules, policies and structures, there may in fact *be* no individual or group of individuals that is "justly to blame" for the crime. Individuals in corporations frequently operate in a kind of "twilight zone" of autonomy; they may simply exert insufficient choice or control to be suitable recipients of blame. In this situation, the "overflow" blame is properly attributed to the corporation.

Scholars of corporate crime recognize that characteristics of the corporation can cause criminal behavior on the part of its agents. Martin and Carolyn Needleman, for example, argue that "at least some criminal behavior usefully may be viewed not as personal deviance, but rather as a predictable product of the individual's membership in or contact with certain organizational systems."[2] Many theorists have identified a corporate character or "corporate culture"[3] which endures over time and transcends the character of the corporation's members. Christopher Stone has found that corporations, like political administrations, have distinct and characteristic attitudes toward the demands of law and morality.[4] "In [the corporate] setting," Stone writes, "each man's own wants, ideas—even his perceptions and emotions—are swayed and directed by an institutional structure so pervasive that it might be construed as having a set of goals and constraints (if not a mind and purpose) of *its* own."[5] . . . There appear to be "good" and "bad" corporations, law-abiding corporations and recidivists, and there is a remarkable consensus as to which corporations are which. The ability of theorists to identify corporate characters is evidence that it is not inappropriate to speak of corporate culpability.

The idea of corporate culpability is not merely a product of organizational theory and research on corporate crime; it is part of ordinary moral discourse. People behave in ways that suggest they blame corporations and feel retributive sentiments toward them. They frequently voice moral judgments about corporations, such as "Union Carbide is indifferent to safety" or "Johns-Manville took advantage of its employees." Such statements may be merely shorthand ways of blaming corporate executives whose identities are unknown to the speaker. But they can also be read as judgments passed on the character or policies of the corporation. This interpretation is strengthened when the judgments apply to the corporation over a substantial period of time, or are accompanied by acts directed at the corporation as an entity, such as picketing or boycotts. Moreover, there is evidence that the stigma of moral blameworthiness that accompanies these judgments is capable of seriously injuring not merely individuals, but the corporation as a whole. The effect of such stigma is so strong that several commentators have suggested the use of court-ordered adverse publicity as a criminal sanction against corporate offenders. . . .

## II. CONCEPTUALIZING CORPORATE CULPABILITY

* * *

### C. The Corporate Character Theory

Neither of the theories of corporate culpability currently employed at the trial stage, then, is completely satisfactory. The respondeat superior theory, [which essentially inputs any crime committed by an employee within the scope of employment,] assigns culpability to the corporation even when the agent's crime was the work of a "rogue employee," with no link to corporate character or policy. Moreover, without substantial gerrymandering, the theory is unable to find corporations culpable for acts that cannot be attributed to an identifiable agent or group of agents. These problems plague the theory of respondeat superior because it does not provide a genuine theory of corporate entity culpability, but rather works by borrowing the culpability of a corporate agent. The *Model Penal Code*, in contrast, does contain a theory of corporate entity culpability, but its conception is too narrow. . . . [It makes corporate culpability dependent on the direct participation, authorization or tolerance of high managerial officials, and fails to take account of the fact that corporations may be "justly to blame" even when such officials are not involved.] What is needed is a concept of corporate culpability capable of assigning fault not only when high managerial officials are involved, but also when corporate rules, policies, structures or procedures encourage criminal acts in less direct, more subtle, ways.

For such a concept, we must turn to a theory of corporate culpability that has received considerable attention from academics, but has not been explicitly adopted by the courts. This theory builds on the findings of organizational research by recognizing that corporations shape and control the behavior of their agents not only through direct supervision by high managerial officials, but also through the use of such devices as standard operating procedures, hierarchical structures, decision rules and disciplinary sanctions. As noted in Part I, rules, structures, policies and procedures are appropriate loci of corporate fault because they are intended to replace agents' decisional autonomy with an organizational decision-making process. Their effect is to create a corporate "culture" or "character" which endures over time and which channels behavior in ways that are in the interest of the corporation. Because this third theory of corporate culpability makes fault depend upon the character of the corporation, it will be termed the "corporate character theory." Under the corporate character theory, a corporation is culpable when its policies, structures, or procedures—features of the corporate character—cause its agents to commit illegal acts on its behalf. Generally, the corporate character theory is advanced as an alternative to the two theories of corporate criminal liability presently in use at the trial stage. However, it can also be used to assess the degree of a corporate offender's liability at sentencing. Indeed, in Part II.C.3., I will contend that the corporate character theory is *more* suitable for use at sentencing than at trial. In Part III, I will argue that a version of this theory has been adopted by the Federal Sentencing Guidelines for organizations.

***1. Contours of the Corporate Character Theory.*** There are many proponents of the corporate character theory, and each has articulated the theory in a slightly different way. Nevertheless, it is possible to discern from the literature three distinct sets of circumstances under which most corporate character theorists would find the corporation at fault. First, and most straightforwardly, a corporation is culpable under the corporate character theory if it has adopted a policy that is illegal, and an agent of the corporation carries out that policy. In such a case, it is clear that the resulting illegal act is a product of the corporate character, rather than the act of a rogue employee, and that the corporation is "justly to blame." . . .

Second, like the *Model Penal Code*, most versions of the corporate character theory find the corporation culpable when an illegal act is committed, authorized, ordered or endorsed by a high managerial official in the corporation. As the drafters of the *Model Penal Code* recognized, some corporate officials are so closely identified with the organization and have so much authority within it, that their acts per se count as "corporate policy." The participation of a high managerial official in an illegal act makes it extremely likely that the act will be carried out. It is difficult to imagine an organization with a "good" character whose officials tolerate or participate in criminal activity. Of course, the question of who counts as a high managerial official is a difficult one, heavily dependent on the circumstances in each case. Generally, the higher an official, the more likely it is that he or she does represent corporate policy; but lower officials may also represent corporate policy if they have been delegated sufficient discretion.

Third, several corporate character theorists argue that a corporation should be found culpable of an employees' illegal act if it implicitly ratifies or endorses the violation. There are at least two ways in which such ratification can take place. First, the organization may fail to correct a particular violation once it is discovered. Even if an act is initially committed by a rogue employee, failure to correct it suggests that the violation is consistent with corporate policy. Second, the organization may have a history of similar violations. Such a history suggests that the crimes are not mere anomalies, but are the result of some feature of the corporation; failure to correct the circumstances leading to the violation endorses it by implication. In both cases, there is strong evidence that the bad act is a product of the corporate character. Similar assumptions are commonly made in making judgments about the culpability of individuals. While a first offender can plausibly repudiate his crime by arguing that the crime does not genuinely reflect his character, this argument is not persuasive for a recidivist. Repetition of a crime, and failure to respond appropriately to the harms it caused, suggests that the crime was not a mistake, but a genuine outgrowth of the character of the offender. . . .

## III. THE CORPORATE CHARACTER THEORY AND THE FEDERAL SENTENCING GUIDELINES

. . . Under the corporate character theory, a corporation is culpable when a corporate policy or custom causes an agent of the corporation to violate the law on the corporation's behalf. Although use of the corporate character theory at the trial stage presents several difficulties, the theory is well-suited for use at sentencing, where judges have traditionally engaged in a broad-based assessment of the character of offenders. In this section of the paper, I explain the ways in which the Federal Sentencing Guidelines are informed by the corporate character theory.

Given the traditional unimportance of culpability in corporate criminal law, one would expect the Guidelines to ignore culpability altogether. At most, the Guidelines would be expected to employ a concept of imputed culpability, consistent with the doctrine of respondeat superior used at the trial stage in the federal courts. Instead, Part III shows, the Guidelines adopt a genuine theory of organizational entity culpability, and give it concrete content through the device of the "culpability score." The argument of Part III is threefold: Section A describes the evolution of the Guidelines and the decision of the Sentencing Commission to make culpability a significant part of the sentencing process. Section B analyzes the "culpability score" and concludes that the Guidelines require an assessment of the organization's character strikingly similar to that prescribed by the corporate character theory. Section C shows how the adoption of a version of the corporate character theory enables the Guidelines to pursue a wider range of sentencing aims than is traditional in the sentencing of organizations.

## A. The Use of Culpability in the Organizational Sentencing Guidelines

. . . The new Guidelines are complex and reflect a broad range of sentencing principles. Section 8B requires offenders to remedy any harm resulting from an offense and to compensate victims. It also provides for restitution orders, remedial orders, community service, and notice to victims. Section 8C1 subjects "criminal purpose organizations" to the organizational equivalent of the death penalty—a fine large enough to divest them of all their assets. Criminal purpose organizations are defined as organizations operating "primarily for criminal purposes or primarily for criminal means." Section 8C2.9 provides for the disgorgement of any gain from an offense that is not removed by fine or restitution order. The central portions of the Guidelines, however, are the provisions for fines for non-criminal purpose organizations and the provisions for probation. In both portions, culpability plays a substantial role.

The principle underlying section 8C2 (fines for non-criminal purpose organizations) is that "the fine range . . . should be based on the seriousness of the offense and the culpability of the organization." The seriousness of an offense is represented by its appropriate "base fine." An organization's culpability depends on its "culpability score." A sentencing judge is directed to start with the base fine, and multiply it by a set of numbers derived from its culpability score to arrive at the "guideline fine range." Adjustments within the range and, in special cases, departures from the range, determine the final fine. . . .

Once the court has determined the base fine, it calculates the organization's culpability score. Convicted organizations begin the sentencing process with a culpability score of five. The score can be raised to as high as ten or reduced to as little as zero by the presence of one or more aggravating or mitigating factors. The four aggravating factors are 1) the involvement in or tolerance of criminal activity by "high level" or "substantial authority" personnel; 2) a recent history of similar misconduct on the part of the organization; 3) violation of a judicial order or condition of probation; and 4) obstruction of justice. The two mitigating factors are 1) the presence of "an effective program to prevent and detect violations of law" on the part of corporate agents and 2) cooperation with law enforcement officials. . . .

The court is entitled to consider both offense seriousness and culpability again once the Guideline fine range is determined. The organization's role in the offense, any prior criminal or civil misconduct that was not taken into account in determining the culpability score, an unusually high or low culpability score, or the presence of any aggravating or mitigating factor may warrant adjustments within the range. . . .

Culpability also plays a major role in section 8D, on probation. The "culpability score" is not referred to explicitly in this section, but several of the aggravating and mitigating factors from the score re-appear. For organizations with over fifty employees, for example, a court is required to order a term of probation if the organization does not have an effective program to prevent and detect violations of law. Where the organization or a high-level official within the organization recently engaged in similar misconduct, probation is likewise required. . . . But the most significant feature of the probation section is its authorization of intrusion into the organizational decision-making process to change features of the organization that lead to crime. Development of a program to prevent and detect violations of the law, for example, may be made a condition of probation. This "incapacitation" and "rehabilitation" of the organization is predicated on the possibility of organizational culpability.

## B. The Organizational Guidelines and the Corporate Character Theory

The Guidelines not only make organizational culpability a central feature of their provisions on fines and probation, they give concrete content to the notion of organizational culpability through the device of the organization's "culpability score." Significantly, the aggravating and mitigating factors in the score include the same features of the organization which serve as the locus for organizational culpability under the corporate character theory: the conduct of high managerial officials, prior history, and corporate policies, customs, and procedures. The Guidelines never explicitly adopt any theory of corporate culpability, and they are not consistent with the corporate character theory in every respect. Nevertheless, the determination of an organization's culpability score under the Guidelines is best understood as an assessment of the character of the organization.

*1. Participation of High Managerial Officials.* As noted in Part II, corporate character theorists generally agree that some organizational officials are so closely identified with the organization that their acts can be said to represent corporate policy. Where such an official authorizes, participates in, or knowingly tolerates a criminal act on the part of an employee of the organization, the organization is therefore culpable. The Guidelines adopt a similar principle, stating that "an organization is more culpable when individuals who manage the organization or who have substantial discretion in acting for the organization participate in, condone, or are willfully ignorant of criminal conduct." In keeping with this principle, the Guidelines make the participation of high managerial officials an aggravating factor in an organizational offender's culpability score. Depending on the size of the organization, the Guidelines add as many as five points to the score when "an individual within high-level personnel of the organization [or the unit of the organization within which the offense was committed] participated in, condoned, or was willfully ignorant of the offense." The additional five points result in a 100–200% increase in the organization's base fine. "High-level personnel" are defined as

> individuals who have substantial control over the organization or who have a substantial role in the making of policy within the organization. The term includes: a director; an executive officer; an individual in charge of a major business or functional unit of the organization . . . an individual with substantial ownership interest.

"High level personnel" are not the only officials whose actions can result in organizational culpability, however. As noted in Part II, even the participation of agents who do not have official authority to make policy may have sufficient de facto authority to "send a message" to other members of the organization that illegal acts "will be countenanced." Whether a given individual has such de facto authority is a difficult, fact-dependent question; nevertheless, an attempt to avoid the issue by adopting a formalistic definition of persons with policy-making authority is likely to result in culpable organizations being judged not at fault. The Guidelines avoid this temptation. Instead, they add as many as five points to an organization's culpability score where "tolerance by substantial authority personnel was pervasive throughout the organization." "Substantial authority personnel" are "individuals who within the scope of their authority exercise a measure of discretion in acting on behalf of the organization. . . . Whether an individual falls within this category must be determined on a case-by-case basis." "Pervasiveness" depends upon

> the number, and degree of responsibility, of individuals within substantial authority personnel who participated in, condoned, or were willfully

> ignorant of the offense. Fewer individuals need to be involved for a finding of pervasiveness if those individuals exercised a relatively high degree of authority.

The requirement that tolerance by substantial authority personnel must be "pervasive" before points are added to the culpability score represents an oversimplification, and may result in underestimating the culpability of some organizations. Nevertheless, the Guidelines' approach is consistent with the corporate character theory. When a practice is pervasive, it becomes a way of doing business, part of the organizational decision-making process. It has an influence that it would not have if only a single employee with "substantial authority" had engaged in it. The more "pervasive" tolerance of illegal activity is, in other words, the more likely it is that the activity represents an organizational custom or policy, and the more likely it is that the organization is culpable. . . .

*2. **Prior History.*** The question of whether a defendant is a first-time or repeat offender has long been central to the sentencing of individual criminals. Before the advent of the "just deserts" school, information about an offender's prior conduct was considered essential because it enabled the court to determine the need for incapacitation and the offender's susceptibility to rehabilitation. As Andrew von Hirsch points out, however, an offender's past conduct is also relevant to his or her culpability and "desert." A first offender can plausibly argue that an offense was an anomaly, a lone departure from past standards of behavior. The act should not really be attributed to him, the offender can argue, because it was not "in character." After the first offense, however, this claim lacks credibility. Repetition has the effect of "endorsing" the earlier offense. It becomes safe to conclude that subsequent offenses are genuinely a product of the offender's character.

A similar argument can be made in the organizational context. Repeat offenses by an organization suggest that the offenses are not mere anomalies, but were caused by some feature of the organizational entity. Moreover, the fact that the organization has not changed this feature to prevent further offenses indicates that the offenses are consistent with the organization's policy or character. The corporate character theory builds on this insight by holding that repeated misconduct on the part of an organization constitutes a "ratification" or "endorsement" of its agent's criminal acts. Where the organization is a recidivist, its crimes cannot be dismissed as the acts of a "rogue employee."

Consistent with the corporate character theory, the Guidelines take account or prior history by adding one point to the culpability score of an organizational offender if it "committed any part of the instant offense" within ten years after either a "criminal adjudication based on similar misconduct" or a "civil or administrative adjudication based on two or more separate instances of similar misconduct." Two points are added if the instant offense took place within five years of the criminal or civil adjudication. "Similar misconduct" is defined as "prior conduct that is similar in nature to the instant offense, without regard to whether or not such conduct violated the same statutory provision." For example, the Guidelines explain that prior Medicare fraud would constitute misconduct similar to an offense involving another type of fraud. Additional points are added to the culpability score if the offense violated a judicial order, injunction, or condition of probation. . . .

*3. **Obstruction of Justice and Cooperation with Authorities.*** The Guidelines add three points to the organization's culpability score if the organization willfully obstructed justice, attempted to obstruct justice, or failed to prevent obstruction of justice during the investigation, prosecution or sentencing of the organization's offense. This aggravating factor is best understood in conjunction with a mitigating factor of "self-reporting, cooperation, and acceptance of responsibility." An organization that cooperates with prosecutors not only avoids the addition of three points to its culpability score; it may subtract five points from its score if "prior to an imminent threat of disclosure" and "within a reasonably prompt time after becoming aware of the offense, [it] reported the offense to appropriate governmental authorities, fully cooperated in the investigation, and clearly demonstrated recognition and affirmative acceptance of responsibility for its criminal conduct." If the organization did not report the offense, but fully cooperated and demonstrated acceptance of responsibility, it is entitled to subtract two points from its culpability score. Acceptance of responsibility alone entitles the organization to subtract one point from its score.

At first glance, ex-post obstruction of justice and cooperation with authorities seem to have little to do with culpability. The corporate character theory makes no mention of such post-offense behavior. The twin aggravating/mitigating factors seem primarily a way to lower law enforcement costs and increase the likelihood of conviction. By making entry of a guilty plea and admission of involvement in the offense "significant evidence of affirmative acceptance of responsibility," the Guidelines encourage organizations to plead guilty. In addition, self-reporting must be "thorough" in order for the organization to qualify for the mitigation credit, and the Guidelines state that "[a] prime test of whether the organization has disclosed all pertinent information is whether the information is sufficient for law enforcement personnel to identify the nature and extent of the offense and the individual(s) responsible for the criminal conduct." These provisions encourage organizations to uncover violations by their agents and to turn in the individuals responsible.

Nevertheless, cooperation with authorities and acceptance of responsibility are not irrelevant to culpability. They have long been important in the sentencing of individuals. Although cooperation and acceptance of responsibility can involve an admission of guilt, they also express remorse, contrition, and renunciation of the crime. They are thus relevant to the broad-based character assessment of the offender that has traditionally taken place at the sentencing stage. Like the first offender who plausibly argues that his crime is not "in character," the genuinely remorseful criminal distances himself from the commission of the crime and expresses an intent to reform. Obstruction of justice, in contrast, represents a continued identification with and continuation of the crime.

Obstruction of justice and cooperation with authorities are also capable of revealing organizational character. When an organization attempts to conceal a crime, it ratifies it, endorses it, and accepts it as its own. The protection of an employee who has violated the law implies that it is the corporation's policy to support such violations; an organization with a "good" character would likely have disciplined or fired the offending employee. Eliminating a criminal employee from the organizational decision-making process improves the corporate character and represents an important first step in the reform of the organization. . . .

*4. **Program to Prevent and Detect Violations of the Law.*** The corporate character theory holds that an organization is at fault, even when there is no involvement by policy-making officials, if an organizational policy or custom causes an agent of the organization to commit a violation on the organization's behalf. The policy or custom need not have been formally adopted, nor is it necessary for the policy itself to be illegal. Rather, a corporation is justly to blame for the illegal act of an agent whenever it was reasonably foreseeable that a corporate policy or practice would lead to the crime. The Guidelines provide no aggravating factor for offenses that are caused by organizational policy or custom. Instead, they appear to assume a causal link between policy and offense, and offer the organization the opportunity to rebut this assumption. To do so, the organization must show that the offense occurred, "despite an effective program to prevent and detect violations of law." If it is successful, three points are subtracted from its culpability score. . . .

## CONCLUSION

Although corporations cannot be culpable in the same way that individuals can, this Article has argued that there is a sense in which they may be "justly held to blame" for the acts of their agents. Corporate crime is not always the result of individual choice. Often, it is the product of goals, rules, policies and procedures that are features of the organization as an entity. By substituting an organizational decision-making process for its agents' individual autonomy, the corporation shapes and controls their behavior. When this process is likely to result in violations on behalf of the corporation on the part of its agents, the corporate entity may be said to be at fault.

Corporate criminal law has generally failed to take adequate account of the culpability of the corporate entity. The principal doctrine of corporate criminal liability, that of respondeat superior, works by imputing to the corporation the culpability of the agent who committed the crime. The *Model Penal Codes*'s location of corporate culpability in the participation of high managerial officials is more promising, but ultimately too narrow. The lack of a coherent theory of corporate culpability at the trial stage results in the risk that some corporations will be held liable even when they are not culpable, and, conversely, that some culpable corporations will succeed in evading liability. At the sentencing stage, failure to recognize corporate culpability has led to an impoverished vision of the range of sentencing options and of the purposes of corporate sentencing.

The Federal Sentencing Guidelines for organizations represent a significant advance over the current treatment of corporate culpability in the criminal law. In a marked departure from tradition, the Guidelines give culpability an explicit and important role in organizational sentencing. They flesh out the concept of organizational culpability concretely through the device of the culpability score. The Guidelines employ a version of the most theoretically satisfying of three competing theories of corporate culpability, the "corporate character theory." The theory builds on the insights of organizational scholars by holding that an organization is culpable when its policies, customs and procedures—features of the organizational character—cause its agents to violate the law on its behalf. Adopting the corporate character theory, I have argued, makes it possible for the Guidelines to employ innovative organizational sentencing strategies and to pursue the full range of sentencing aims. . . .

## NOTES

1. Herbert A. Simon, *Administrative Behavior* 8 (3d ed. 1976).
2. Martin Needleman & Carolyn Needleman, *Organizational Crime: Two Models of Criminogenesis,* 20 Soc. Q. 517 (1979). *See also* Marshall B. Clinard & Peter C. Yeager, Corporate Crime 58–60, 63–67 (1980) (cultural norms of the corporation can encourage criminal behavior); Laura S. Schrager & James R. Short, Jr., *Toward a Sociology of Organizational Crime,* 25 Soc. Probs. 407, 410 (1978) (criminal behavior is caused more by roles assigned to members of the corporation than by personalities of the members); Note, *Increasing Community Control over Corporate Crime—A Problem in the Law of Sanctions,* 71 Yale L.J. 280, 282 (1961) (goal of criminal acts by members of corporations is frequently enrichment of the corporation rather than of individuals).
3. *See, e.g.,* Terence E. Deal & Allen A. Kennedy, Corporate Cultures (1982); Thomas J. Peters & Robert H. Waterman, Jr., In Search of Excellence (1982); Christopher. D. Stone, Where the Law Ends, 228–48 (1975). Although the cor-

porate culture is strongly influenced by top management, it is independent of it. Clinard and Yeager argue that corporate executives "are subject . . . to the same kinds of indoctrination into the corporate mind as are employees at lower levels." Clinard & Yeager, *supra* note 58, at 66.

4. Stone, *supra* note 3, at 237. Stone discusses a study finding that coal mines owned by steel firms have significantly better worker safety records than coal mines owned by coal mining companies. One of the most commonly given explanations for the discrepancy, he reports, is simply a difference in attitude between steel companies and coal companies: "[t]he steel companies have just not evolved what was called 'a "coal mentality"' that accepts a great loss of life and limb as the price of digging coal." *Id.* at 238 (citing *Coal-Mines Study Shows Record Can Be Improved When Firms Really Try*, Wall St. J., Jan. 18, 1973, at p. 1, col. 6).
5. Stone, *supra* note 3, at 7.

# Debunking Corporate Moral Responsibility

*Manuel Velasquez*

In this essay I address three topics. First, I try to bring out by means of an example the reasons why the issue of corporate moral responsibility is important. Second, I examine the core argument underlying the claim that corporate organizations are separate moral agents and show it is based on an unnoticed but elementary mistake. Third, I examine the claim that corporate organizations themselves sometimes act intentionally and show that this claim is mistaken.

Before beginning, however, it is important to say a few words about the notions of "moral responsibility" and "corporate organization" that I discuss. The terms "responsible" and "responsibility" are sometimes used to mean "obligation" or "duty" as in "The social responsibility of business is to serve its stakeholders," or "Business is responsible for serving its stakeholders." This is not the sense of "responsibility" I discuss here. Sometimes, however, we use these terms to identify the party or parties that caused, or were to blame for, something that happened as in "The storm is responsible for the damage," or "The ultimate responsibility for World War II belongs to Hitler." This is the kind of responsibility that I discuss here. The responsible party in this sense is the party (or parties) that is identified as the (or one of the) primary, or most salient, or most significant, cause of the past act or event. But there are two kinds of causal responsibility: natural and moral. Natural causal responsibility is the kind of responsibility that we attribute to non-intentional agents such as hurricanes, avalanches, tornadoes, earthquakes, and other natural agents that often are responsible for inflicting damage on the world. Moral responsibility, on the other hand, is the kind of causal responsibility that we attribute to intentional agents—like human beings—when they caused (or helped to cause) some past event and did so intentionally. I will try to show that corporate organizations are not morally responsible in this latter sense. Moreover, by "corporate organization" I mean nothing more than an organized group of people who collectively carry on some range of business activities and which we recognize as a single body distinct from its environment. A corporate

From Manual Velasquez, "Debunking Corporate Moral Responsibility," *Business Ethics Quarterly* 13:4 (2003). Reprinted with permission of the author and publisher *Business Ethics Quarterly*.

organization, as I understand the term, need not have the legal status of a corporation. Consequently, none of what follows depends on the organization's possession of the legal status of a corporation nor on what the law says about the legal entity it calls the "corporation".[1]

## 1. THE SIGNIFICANCE OF THE ISSUE

Let me begin . . . with a concrete case that, I think, brings out much of what is at stake in the debate over whether corporate organizations are ever morally responsible for their acts in the sense I just explained. The case involves National Semiconductor, a company headquartered in Santa Clara, California, that designs and manufactures the silicon chips that form the hearts of computers and other electronic devices[2]:

> On March 6, 1984, the Department of Defense (DoD) charged that between 1978 and 1981 National Semiconductor had sold them some 26 million computer chips that had not been properly tested and then had falsified records to cover up the fraud. These potentially defective chips had been placed in airplane guidance systems, nuclear weapons systems, guided missiles, rocket launchers, and other sensitive military environments. Unfortunately, the chips were installed in scattered locations around the world and could no longer be tracked down. A government official commented that if one of these computer chips malfunctioned, "You could have a missile that would end up in Cleveland instead of the intended target."
>
> Semiconductors manufactured for such military purposes are supposed to undergo lengthy, costly, and highly rigorous tests to guarantee that each works perfectly. Officials at National Semiconductor, however, admitted the company had omitted the tests between 1978 and 1981 when it fell behind its contract deadlines because of worker strikes, technical production problems, and because intense infighting about the company's direction had led to the resignation of several key managers.
>
> To cover up the omissions, National Semiconductor managers set up teams in the company's production department to falsify the documents testifying that each chip had been tested. One employee told a reporter:
>
> I'd say that over 100 employees had to know. . . . Just about everybody in production control knew about it who had been there for six months. . . . There was a lot of documentation I personally dummied up. . . . When I realized how deeply things were being falsified, I just couldn't believe it. . . . I asked, "How did things get the way they were?" Nobody seemed to be able to give me a good answer.
>
> Not all employees went along with the large-scale deception. Workers in the company's plant in Singapore, for example, refused to falsify their records when ordered to do so.
>
> National Semiconductor agreed to pay $1.75 million in penalties for defrauding the government. However the company refused to provide the names of any of the individuals who had participated in the decision to omit the tests and falsify the documents, or any who had participated in carrying out these decisions. The Department of Defense objected. It wanted those individuals who had actually carried out the fraud to be punished and to be barred from holding the positions from which they had executed the fraud. "My concern," said the legal counsel for the Department of Defense, "is simply that a corporation acts only through its employees and officers." Moreover, the Department of Defense argued, if those individuals continued to work at the company, the government would have no assurance that the company would not engage in the fraud again.
>
> Charles Sporck, then CEO of National Semiconductor, adamantly opposed the idea. In a public statement he said: "We totally disagree with the Defense Department's proposal. We have repeatedly stated that we accept responsibility as a company and we steadfastly continue to stand by that statement." A Company spokesperson later reiterated that position. "We will see [our individual people] are not harmed. We feel it's a company responsibility, [and this is] a matter of ethics." Sporck prevailed. No individual member of National Semiconductor was ever held criminally or civilly liable for the crime. Only the company "as a company" was penalized.

I have spent considerable time developing the National Semiconductor case because it illustrates, I think, the kinds of contexts in which the issue of organizational versus individual responsibility becomes significant. The CEO of National Semiconductor was arguing that the organization as such was responsible for the fraud and had paid the penalty of $1.75 million, and that no individual member of the company should be held responsible or punished. Implicit in his position was the view that in some cases corporate organizations are responsible for their acts and should be punished and that in at least some such cases no member of the organization is responsible for what the organization has done and so no individual should be subjected to punishment. The view of the legal counsel for the DoD was exactly the opposite. While he did not contest the view that the organization as such should be fined $1.75 million, he clearly felt that this penalty upon the organization did not touch the parties who were in reality responsible for the corporate act. His statement that "a corporation acts only through its employees and officers" was intended to remind us that an organization's actions are brought about by the members of the corporate organization and so it is these members who in actuality are responsible for what the corporate organization does and so it is they who should be punished. However, because the view of the CEO of National Semiconductor prevailed, only the corporate organization was penalized and no individuals were ever directly punished for the crime.

Now there are four reasons why this decision to accept the view that the corporate organization was responsible for the crime was significant. First, and most obviously, the issue was significant because it bore directly on the question of who ended up getting punished for the company's fraud. Because the corporate organization as such was held responsible, it was penalized $1.75 million and because it was accepted that no member of the organization was responsible, none of the individuals who participated in the crime had to suffer. If the view of the DoD had prevailed, on the other hand, several individuals would likely have found themselves in jail or, at least, subjected to heavy fines and job losses. Attributions of responsibility have real consequences on who is punished when things go wrong.

The decision to accept the view that the corporate organization but no individual was responsible for the fraud was also significant for a second reason: because it bore directly on the issue of whether the punishments that were in fact imposed reasonably could be expected to deter future occurrences of fraud and thus effectively control the behavior of this company. If only the corporate organization as such was held responsible for the crime and if no individuals were directly punished and removed from their positions, then, the DoD worried, the fraud might reoccur. It might reoccur because the people who had carried out the fraud would remain in a position to carry it out again and, not having been punished, they would have no incentive to refrain from such crimes. On the contrary, since what they had done had benefited their company and so ingratiated them to their managers, and since nothing had happened to them personally as a result, one could reasonably conclude that they would be encouraged to commit fraud should similar circumstances arise again. Punishment of the corporate organization as the entity responsible for a crime can fail to touch the individuals who in reality carried out the crime and thus fail to control effectively the socially injurious behavior of the corporate organization.[3]

The decision to accept the view that the organization as such—and not any individual—was responsible for the fraud was significant for yet a third reason. It is clear that not everyone at National Semiconductor knew about the fraud, and that not all participated in the fraud. During the fraud many National Semiconductor employees and managers were working on unrelated projects and so knew nothing about it. In addition, at least one group of workers, those employed at the company's plant in Singapore, knew about the fraud but explicitly refused to participate. On the other hand, several of the workers and managers in the company's production department in California knew about the fraud. Some of them actively participated by intentionally omitting tests and intentionally falsifying documents while others passively participated by failing to do anything to stop the fraud they knew was in progress. The organization, then, was comprised of two groups: those who knowingly participated in the fraud either actively or passively, and those who were ignorant of the fraud and did nothing to advance it. When the organization as such was held responsible for the fraud, publicly chastised as an organization, and fined $1.75 million as an organization, these two very different groups were in effect treated the same. The innocent as well as the guilty suffered public embarrassment and the innocent as well as the guilty suffered equally whatever detrimental effects the corporate loss of $1.75 million had on their personal well being. In short, the decision to hold the organization as such responsible for the crime, and the related decision to punish the organization as such, resulted in the innocent being forced to suffer along with the guilty.

Finally, the decision to accept the view that the organization was responsible for the fraud was significant for a fourth reason. If we assume that a corporate organization is morally responsible for a corporate action we will naturally conclude that the corporate organization must be punished for its crimes. We may then be led to conclude that since punishment has been levied on the significant guilty party, there is no real need to inflict any additional punishments on any other parties. After all, the responsible and large party—the corporate organization—has been punished, so why pursue the minor actors? The result is exactly what happened in the National Semiconductor case: the individuals through whom the corporate organization acted—that is, the individuals who actually brought about the corporate act—are never brought to justice and never given an effective deterrent. The National Semiconductor case strongly suggests that once a company as such is held responsible for a crime, and once the decision to punish the company as such is made, then authorities can come to feel that the crime has been adequately punished and will not bother to go through the trouble of bringing other "minor" parties to justice.

The National Semiconductor case suggests, then, that accepting the view that a corporate organization as such is morally responsible for its actions is important for four reasons: (1) it has consequences on who we punish or fail to punish for those actions, (2) it has implications on how the behavior of corporate organizations is to be controlled and whether we can reasonably expect punishment to deter them from inflicting future injuries on society, (3) it can lead us to punish the innocent (who did nothing to cause the act) along with the guilty, and (4) it can lead us to be satisfied with punishing the organization without imposing effective deterrents on those individuals who brought the act about.

I want to turn now to showing that the view defended by the DoD in the National Semiconductor case is correct. Before doing so, however, it may help to note that the opposing view, the view that the corporate organization is sometimes, at least, a moral agent distinct from its members, has traditionally been referred to as the collectivist view. On the other hand, the view that the corporate organization is a number of individuals who (all or some) are themselves responsible for the organization's acts, has traditionally been characterized as the individualist view. In what follows I am going to use this traditional terminology to refer to the two main views on moral responsibility that I want to discuss, although I do not believe that the terminology is altogether satisfactory.[4] The collectivist, then, holds that both individual human beings and corporate organizations can be morally responsible agents. The individualist holds that human beings, but not corporate organizations, can be morally responsible agents.

## 2. THE COLLECTIVIST ARGUMENT FOR TAKING THE CORPORATE ORGANIZATION AS ONE

Let us again consider the National Semiconductor case. I have mentioned that Charles Sporck, the CEO of National Semiconductor, gave voice to the collectivist position when he claimed that National Semiconductor was the agent that was morally responsible for the company fraud and that none of the members of the organization were themselves morally responsible for the act. This claim, of course, makes a key assumption: it assumes that National Semiconductor is a real individual entity that acts on the world and that possesses an identity and an existence that is distinct from that of its members.[5] For if National Semiconductor were simply identical with its members, then the moral responsibility of the corporate organization would be identical with the moral responsibility of its members. In fact, the fundamental assumption underlying the collectivist view that the corporate organization is a morally responsible agent distinct from its members, is the assumption that the corporate organization is a real individual entity that acts on the world and that is distinct from its members. This key assumption, as some have remarked, is an ontological assumption. But whatever kind of assumption it is, it is an assumption that plays an essential role in our (prelegal) views on moral responsibility. For if the assumption is false, then we cannot claim coherently that corporate organizations bear a share of responsibility for their actions that is separate from the share allotted to their members.

Let us ask the question, then, why anyone would think that National Semiconductor is a real individual entity that is distinct from its members? What arguments can be given for this view? . . . There is one argument . . . that has been repeatedly advanced by collectivists in a variety of guises. I am going to call this argument "the collectivist argument." The argument is this: National Semiconductor must be a real individual entity distinct from its members because it has characteristics that cannot be reduced to those of its individual members. National Semiconductor, for example, has contracts with the government, it owns things, it has a corporate mission, it violated an agreement with the government, it defrauded the government, and it endures indefinitely. Yet no individual can be said to have those contracts with the government, or to own those things, or to have that corporate mission, or to endure indefinitely, etc. Since these characteristics cannot be said to be characteristics of the company's individual members, they must be characteristics of the corporate entity that is National Semiconductor. And since National Semiconductor has characteristics that the members do not have, it must be an individual entity that is distinct from these members. . . .

. . . What I have called the collectivist argument, then, comes down to this:

1. If X has properties that cannot be attributed to its individual members, then X is a real individual entity distinct from its members.
2. But corporate organizations have properties that cannot be attributed to their members.
3. So the corporate organization is a real individual entity distinct from its members.

What I am going to argue now is that the first premise of this argument is based on an elementary logical mistake. . . .

As any teacher of elementary logic knows, every collection of objects (no matter how unrelated the objects are) has properties that can be attributed only to the collection as a whole and not to its individual members (and vice versa). Logicians, in fact, have a special name, the "fallacy of division," for the logical fallacy of attributing the characteristics of a collection to one or more of its members. It may be true, for example, that a pile of sand is big but wrong to infer that each grain in the pile is big. The fact that groups have properties their members lack, then, is certainly not a mystery that needs to be explained by positing ghostly group entities. In fact, precisely because the group is not identical with any one of its members one expects the group to have features that the members do not share. It is not a surprising fact, therefore, that many of the properties that can be attributed to a corporate group cannot be attributed to its individual members. But this fact does not turn the corporate organization into a new real individual entity any more than any random collection of objects is constituted into a new individual entity by the fact that it has characteristics that cannot be attributed to its members.

To show that groups of people do not become individual entities when they have characteristics that their members do not have, we need only examine a counter example. Consider, then, this arbitrary set of three objects: {Monica Lewinsky, President William Clinton, a cigar}. No one, I hope, will make the mistake of thinking that the three objects I have arbitrarily collected into this new set now constitute a new individual entity. Nevertheless, this set may make you smile although it may produce puzzlement in some. I find myself forced to treat the set with a bit of respect since it is (to use the language of set theory) a well-defined set and so, as a person committed to the truth, I know I have a moral obligation to treat it as a well-defined set. I am even willing to say that the set has the right to be treated as a well-defined set. The set, then, does some things (it makes you smile); it exhibits a kind of "intentional causality"[6] (the thought of the set causes puzzlement in some of us); it is the object of at least one of my moral obligations; and it even can be considered the bearer of a right. Moreover these acts and characteristics can be attributed only to the set as a whole and not to any of its members taken individually. It is not, for example, the thought of a cigar alone that makes you smile, or that has a right to be treated as a well-defined set. It is only the abstract set itself—the arbitrary collocation of two people and a physical object—that has these characteristics. But in spite of the fact that the abstract set has characteristics that cannot be attributed to any of its members taken individually, it obviously does not follow that the set is a new individual entity. As this example shows, a group is not a real individual entity merely in virtue of the fact that what is attributed to it is an action, or (intentional) causality, or moral rights, or moral obligations.

Peter French and others[7] have made much, however, of one particular property that is attributed to the corporate organization and not to its members. This is the property of the corporate organization's continuous identity through time. The corporate organization has a continuing identity through time that is independent of the discontinuous identities of any of its members. A corporate organization, for example, may endure for decades and remain the some corporate organization even as its original members retire and are replaced. As French puts it, the corporate organization is a "conglomerate collectivity," or "an organization of individuals such that its identity is not exhausted by the conjunction of the identities of the persons in the organization. The existence of a [corporate organization] is compatible with a varying membership"[8]

But again, although it is true that the continuing identity attributed to the corporate organization cannot be attributed to any of its members, this fact does not by itself imply that the corporate organization is a real individual entity distinct from its members. We have here, again, merely a particular instance of the general logical fact that from a statement attributing a property to a group, it is fallacious to infer statements attributing the same property to its members. Take, for example, a pile of sand my young son has shaped into a replica of the Great Pyramid of Cheops. Suppose he then gently removes some of its grains and replaces them with other grains of sand, being careful not to change the shape that identifies the pile as his replica of the Pyramid of Cheops. Surely we would readily say that his replica pyramid of sand is still there even after some (perhaps even all) of its individual grains have been changed. Yet clearly the pile of sand is not an individual entity but merely an aggregate of entitles. Consequently, even when we quite willingly agree that the existence of a collective object "is compatible with a varying membership" it does not follow that the object is an individual entity.

I conclude, then, that the collectivist argument is based on a fallacy: the fallacy embodied in premise (1). The fact that a collection of entities has properties that cannot be attributed to any of its individual members, does not show that the collection is a distinct real individual entity. And if the corporate organization is not a distinct real individual entity, then it cannot be said to bear a share of responsibility for its actions that is distinct from the share we can attribute to its members.

## 3. CORPORATE ACTIONS AND INTENTIONS

I have argued that from the fact that corporate organizations have characteristics that their members do not have, it does not follow that they are distinct morally responsible agents. The confirmed collectivist will respond, however, that there is something special about corporate organizations that nevertheless makes them appropriate subjects of moral responsibility. Moral responsibility, as I noted above, is the kind of responsibility for an event that we attribute to intentional agents like human beings when they caused the event and did so intentionally.[9] On the basis of this kind of analysis of moral responsibility, the collectivist will argue as follows:

1. An agent is morally responsible for an act or event, when the agent both: (1) is causally responsible for the act or event, and (2) had the intention to so act.
2. Now sometimes corporate organizations (1) are causally responsible for acts and events, and (2) have intentions to so act.
3. Consequently, we can attribute moral responsibility to corporate organizations.

I want now to show that this argument of the collectivist is also mistaken. The mistake lies in the second premise, the claim that corporate organizations are causally responsible for some acts or events, and that they have intentions. Let me start with the first part of this claim, the claim that corporate organizations are causally responsible for some acts or events. What leads the collectivist to make this claim? Some collectivists feel that the crucial fact about corporate organizations that forces us to recognize that they are causally responsible entities is the fact that they carry out actions that are not the actions of any of their members. National Semiconductor, for example, entered a contract with the government, once merged with another organization, and defrauded the government. Yet no individual member of the company herself made such a contract, or herself merged, or herself defrauded the government. Since these acts are acts of the organization and not acts of any individual member of the organization, the collectivist argues, causal responsibility for these acts must be attributed to the corporate organization itself and not to its members: these are the acts, par excellence, for which the organization as such has to be causally responsible.

This collectivist argument, I believe, is based on two fallacies. The first is similar to the fallacy that I exposed in the last section and I will not discuss it at length. It must be granted as a fact that there are some act descriptions that, like many other characteristics, can be predicated of a collection but not of its members. But from this fact nothing follows about the collection's causal powers. As we saw repeatedly in the previous section, given any arbitrary collection of objects there will be characteristics, even actions, that we can attribute to the collection but not to its members. This is simply a logical feature of differentiating between a collection and its members: there must be differences between them or we could not differentiate them.

The collectivist claim that organizations are causally responsible for some acts and events makes a second and more insidious fallacious assumption. The claim assumes that if an action or event cannot be predicated of an individual, the individual cannot be causally responsible for the action: if an action is not an action of mine then I am not the one who causally brought the action about. This assumption is clearly wrong. Suppose I wind up a toy car, and place it on the floor where it starts moving in circles. Then the act of moving in circles is not an act of mine, but an act of the toy; that is, while it is true that the toy is moving in circles, it is false that I am moving in circles. Nevertheless, I am causally responsible for this act since I am the one that causally brought the act about by winding up the toy. Causal responsibility lies with me, although the act is predicated of the toy, and it is just a mistake to assume that the act of the toy must on this account be caused by the toy. The culprit here is the word "of." To say that an action is the action "of" an object can mean either that the action can be predicated of that object, or that the object is causally responsible for the action. The collectivist trades on this ambiguity. Seeing that some actions can be predicated only of the organization, the collectivist concludes that the organization is causally responsible for the action. But collective acts that can be predicated only of the collective itself can nevertheless be caused by, and so can be and are the causal responsibility of, the individual members of the collective.

The point I am making is simple and, I hope, obvious: the corporate organization acts only if and to the extent that, its individual members bring about those actions. If the members of the organization do nothing, then the corporate organization does nothing. Every organizational act, therefore, including those that cannot be predicated of its individual members (and so those that are not "reducible" to acts of individuals), is nevertheless causally produced by the organization's members. In order to make explicit the causal origins of organizational acts, I will lay down the following thesis:

> Thesis (1): Where A is an organizational act that can be predicated truly of an organization, but not necessarily of any individual member, there is always some individual member or members of the organization, x, y, . . . and z, such that x, y, . . . and z are causally responsible for A.[10]

Thesis (1) does not imply, of course, that the members of an organization are necessarily morally responsible for those corporate actions for which they are causally responsible. Moral responsibility requires intention, as well as causality. All that thesis (1) is meant to do is indicate where causal responsibility for corporate actions must lodge, and to separate this causal aspect of moral responsibility from its intentional aspect which I will discuss below.

Thesis (1) also does not say that organizations never exert causal influences on their members, although it does have implications for how these may be explained. Recall the words of the employee at National Semiconductor commenting on how increasing numbers of workers in the production department went along with the decision to falsify documents:

> I'd say that over 100 employees had to know. . . . Just about everybody in production control knew about it who had been there for six months. . . . When I realized how deeply things were being falsified, I just couldn't believe it. . . . I asked, "How did things get the way there were?" Nobody seemed to be able to give me a good answer.

It is a plain fact that when individuals gather together in groups they can get each other, or lead each other, to behave in ways that none would engage in if they were acting alone.[11] But this fact need not lead us to reify the group and to attribute to it causal powers it does not have. . . .

I will return to thesis (1) about the causality of organizational acts in a short while. But first I want to turn to the other part of the collectivist's claim: the claim that when corporate organizations act, they can do so intentionally or, more simply, the claim that when corporate organizations have intentions and beliefs. French and others have pointed out that we attribute intentions, purposes, and beliefs to organizations and that such intentional qualities cannot be "reduced" to the intentions, purposes and beliefs of their members. . . . It makes perfectly good sense to say, for example, that National Semiconductor intended to make millions by defrauding the government, although perhaps none of its members had that particular intention in mind. Intentional properties, such as purposes and beliefs, can be attributed to groups on the basis of a pattern which the activities of its members exhibit. . . . And because the pattern is the result of the activities of many of the group's members, the intentional property that is attributed on the basis of the pattern cannot be attributed to any single member. For example, when the activities of the members of a group exhibit a goal-directed pattern, we may say that the group is "trying" to reach that goal, that its "purpose" is to reach that goal, that it "believes" it will reach that goal, and so on. Yet it may be a fact that no individual member of the group is trying to reach that goal, nor has that purpose or belief in mind. . . .

What I now want to argue, however, is that from this fact nothing follows about whether a group is really an intentional agent. That is, just because we attribute intentional qualities to a collection of objects it does not follow that the collection has real intentions in a literal sense. An example will make the point clear. Surely no one will say that a group comprised of all those people in the United States who happen to be buying and selling the same commodity constitute a distinct intentional agent. All the people in the United States, for example, who happen to be buying and selling houses or all the people who happen to be buying and selling stocks do not constitute a distinct intentional agent. Yet their activities, as expressed in the prices they bid or take for the commodities they are buying or selling, can exhibit a goal-directed pattern. That is, housing markets and stock markets can exhibit a goal-directed pattern. Business commentators, for example, might tell us that last year the housing market was "trying" to break the $200,000 mark, that the housing market was "seeking" or "searching" for a new low, that the housing market "believed" that the cost of building materials would rise, and so on. Yet no house buyer or seller is individually trying to break the $200,000 mark, nor individually seeking a new market low, and perhaps no individual buyer or seller of a house even thought about the cost of building materials, much less thought that it would rise. So as a group (i.e., as a market) the activities of all those in and around the United States who are buying and selling houses, stocks, or anything else, can exhibit a pattern on the basis of which we attribute purposes, intentions, and beliefs to the group (i.e., to the market), which we cannot attribute to the individual members of the group. Yet such a collection of individuals is not a distinct intentional agent, and certainly not a morally responsible one. The fact that we attribute intentional qualities to groups—including corporate organizations—that are not attributable to their members, then, does not imply that those groups have real intentions. The intentions that we attribute to groups are metaphorical, based on analogies to the literal intentions we attribute to humans (I will say more on this below).

Some philosophers, notably Peter French, have repeatedly claimed that the intentions we attribute to organizations are somehow special because they can be the result of the organization's "decision structure." The decision structure of an organization consists of those procedures and policies through which the individuals of an organization reach collective decisions and engage in collective actions that are then describable as the intentional actions of the organization itself.[12] In a simple organization such as a club, for example, the decision procedure might consist solely of voting according to a simple majority rule, while more complex organizations might employ formal rules and routines that would take several volumes to transcribe. The problem with French's claim, however, is that there is nothing about procedures and policies that can enable them to transform a metaphorical intention into a real one. Procedures and policies, however simple or complex, cannot create group mental states nor group minds in any literal sense. Neither French nor any other collectivist has given us an argument that proves that by following rules and procedures a group can generate real intentionality where none was present before. . . . Absent such arguments, we have no reason to abandon the intuitive and plausible view that group intentions are metaphorical, in favor of the counterintuitive view that group intentions are literal.

To clarify what I mean when I say that intentions are attributed to groups metaphorically, let me invoke a distinction proposed by John Searle some twenty years ago.[13] Searle points out that we often use intentional language in a literal or what he calls an "intrinsic" sense. We say, for example, that humans think, feel, believe, and intend certain things, and when we say these things we mean them literally. . . . Searle points out that we sometimes also use intentional language in a non-literal or as-if sense. When I start up the car on a cold morning, for example, and the car engine turns over a few times but does not start, I may say that the car is "trying" to start, as if the car has the intention of starting but is just not succeeding in carrying out its intention. Similarly, if I have a little metal wind-up walking toy robot that has been stopped by an object in front of it, and if the toy robot continues to make walking movements into the object, I may say that it "thinks" there is nothing in front of it, as if it had beliefs and thoughts about the world around it. But in neither of these cases am I implying that these objects have some sort of mind nor that they have intentions and beliefs in any literal sense. Instead, I am in these cases simply describing their actions on analogy with the intentional behavior of people: these objects are acting as if they had intentions and beliefs.

In terms of the distinction between intrinsic and as-if intentionality, I am claiming that the intentionality we sometimes attribute to a collection of people is a form of as-if intentionality. The collection of people that constitute a market, for example, does not have a literal group mind in which conscious beliefs, intentions, and purposes inhere, and so it cannot have intrinsic intentionality. . . .

There is, however, a second group of "as-if" cases where something different is going on. I have in mind situations in which we attribute an intentional state to a group even though the intentional state can be attributed truthfully to only a few, or perhaps even none of its members, but in which we clearly are not *describing* the group. The cases I have in mind are those where the organization or its surrounding society authorizes some of the organization's members to speak or act for, or on behalf of, the organization. A duly authorized spokesperson of National Semiconductor, for example, said of the fraud that "We feel it's a company responsibility." Since she, the authorized spokesperson, said this, we are justified in attributing to the organization the belief that the fraud is a company responsibility. Yet it is entirely possible, even probable, that neither the spokesperson, nor anyone else in the company, really believed this. What is going on in such cases? . . .

To understand what is going on here, we need to distinguish two kinds of as-if intentionality. One form of as-if intentionality, the form I have been discussing thus far, is descriptive. We have already seen several instances of descriptive as-if intentionality. When I say that the toy robot thinks that there is nothing in front of it, for example, I am using as-if intentionality to describe the actions of the toy by analogy to human intentionality. The second form of as-if intentionality is prescriptive. Suppose, for example, that my six year old boy takes two toy soldiers and proposes that we play a game with them. He says: "My toy soldier thinks that he's the enemy of your toy soldier." This is clearly an attribution of as-if intentionality. But it is not descriptive. Instead, my son is prescribing: he is declaring that we are to behave toward the toy soldier as if it had these beliefs. In a prescriptive attribution of as-if intentionality, a person or group of persons asserts, declares, or authorizes that some object or group is to be dealt with as if it had a certain kind of (intrinsic) intentionality. . . .

Let me return now to the person who was authorized to be a spokesperson for National Semiconductor. When an authorized spokesperson declares that her organization has certain beliefs she might be saying that the organization is acting as if it had these beliefs. This would be a descriptive attribution of as-if intentionality. But the authorized spokesperson in the National Semiconductor case more likely was declaring that the group was to be treated as if it had those beliefs. This was a prescriptive attribution of as-if intentionality. Such prescriptive attributions are common in corporate organizations and other kinds of organized groups. For example, when the CEO of a company convenes a committee and authorizes them to write up a mission statement indicating the fundamental beliefs and vision of the organization, the resulting attribution of beliefs and vision to the organization is prescriptive. When a club or other small organization votes in favor of a certain resolution, the members authorize the attribution of that resolution to the organization and that attribution is prescriptive. And when the members of a corporate organization employ what, as I noted above, French calls the "decision structure" of the organization to carry out an act, responsibility for which is then attributed to the organization, the resulting attribution is, again, prescriptive.

Let me summarize my discussion of corporate intentionality, then, by laying out the following thesis about group intentionality:

> Thesis (2): Where X is an intentional state that is attributed to a collection of people and X cannot be attributed to any of the individual members of X, it is always the case that X is either a descriptive or a prescriptive attribution of "as if" intentionality.

. . . [T]hesis (2), makes clear a fundamental mistake that has misled all collectivists who have argued that a corporate organization can be morally responsible for its actions. All such collectivists have failed to see that attributions of intentionality can be prescriptive and instead have assumed that attributions of intentionality to corporate organizations are always descriptive. Having made this mistaken assumption, collectivists then are forced into building elaborate theories that purport to show that corporate organizations must be the kind of entities that can have intentions just like those that we attribute to human individuals. . . .

Human intentions, beliefs, and desires are mental; that is, they are essentially, by definition, the sort of things that can be present to, and in, our conscious minds: the sorts of things that we can be conscious of. This means that if an organization has such intentions, beliefs, and desires, it must have a conscious mind, a mind with a unified consciousness that encompasses within a single field of awareness all of its nonpathological intentions, plans, beliefs, and desires. All the intentions and beliefs, for example, that at this moment I own as my intentions and beliefs are intentions and beliefs that are present within my single field of awareness. The corporation as such does not have such a unified consciousness. At best the corporation consists of a multitude of disconnected consciousnesses.

But if organizations are never morally responsible for their actions, who then is morally responsible when an organization injures someone and no human individual is morally responsible for the action? In organizations, it is often the case that corporate actions are the result of the aggregated actions of many individuals, none of whom was aware of what the aggregate result would be. One individual designs the product, another individual chooses the materials, a third individual uses the design to manufacture the product from those materials, and a fourth individual markets the result. Yet none of these individuals may realize that this particular combination of design, materials, manufacturing method, and marketing will result in a product that is highly dangerous to its users. So no individual is morally responsible for the injuries that result. Who then will be held morally responsible for those injuries if the organization is not responsible? Barring negligent behavior on anyone's part, the obvious answer, I think, is: no one. Cases like these are cases where the concept of accident applies, not the concept of moral responsibility. This does not mean, of course, that there is no answer to the question, "Who should pay the costs of the injuries?" We legitimately may decide that in cases like these we should require the organization to pay these costs for a variety of reasons unrelated to moral responsibility, including: because the organization is in a better position to absorb those costs than anyone else is, because the organization has accumulated the benefits (financial and otherwise) that accrued from carrying on the activity associated with those costs and so can pay the costs from those accumulated benefits, because the organization can better ensure that these external costs are internalized so that the price of the activity that produced those external costs is properly adjusted, etc. Requiring the organization to pay such costs, of course, does not imply that the organization is *morally responsible* for the injury. It simply means that when no one is morally responsible for an injury, we have to find some fair way of distributing the costs of the injury among the various non-responsible parties and often the fairest way is by charging those costs to the organization's treasury. If by "compensatory liability" we mean merely the obligation to pay compensation for the costs of an injury, then nothing I have said here implies that organizations cannot or should not bear compensatory liability for injuries produced by their actions. Compensatory liability is not the same as moral responsibility and in many cases both ethics and practicality require that an organization should be held liable for the injuries its actions have produced.

## 4. CONCLUSION

. . . In the case before us, the Counsel for the Department of Defense was correct: National Semiconductor's corporate crime, although perhaps correctly predicated of the corporate organization as a whole, was the moral responsibility of those particular individuals who intentionally caused the organizational fraud. And it was those individuals, not merely National Semiconductor as an organization that should have been punished for the crime, because punishment of the individual wrongdoers—not the corporate organization as such—is the most effective way to control the behavior of large corporate organizations like National Semiconductor. Cases like that of National Semiconductor clearly demonstrate the importance of being clear about what corporate moral responsibility is and what it is not.

## NOTES

1. The material in brackets is the author's own compressed introduction to this essay, written especially for this textbook. Also, note that much of the text and most of the endnotes to this essay have been removed from this version of the article. The original version should be consulted for several qualifications and explanations that are omitted from this version.
2. This case is based on the following sources: David Sylvester, "The Day 2 Million Soviet Missiles 'Attacked' the U.S.," *San Jose Mercury News*, 3 June 1984, p. 13A; . . . David Willman and David Sylvester, "2 Workers Tried to Stop the Cheating," *San Jose Mercury News*, 3 June 1984, p. 12A; David Willman and David Sylvester, "How Tests Were Faked at National," *San Jose Mercury News*, 3 June 1984, p. 1. "National Semi Pleads Guilty to Scheme," *San Jose Mercury News*, 7 March 1984, p. 1. David Sylvester, "National Semi May Lose Defense Jobs," *San Jose Mercury News*, 31 May 1984, p. 1.
3. This view is, in fact, the view that has remained as a steadfast principle in state and federal courts in spite of vicarious liability. As one court put it: "The corporate form normally insulates shareholders, officers, and directors from liability for corporate obligations; but when these individuals abuse the corporate privilege, courts will disregard the corporate fiction and hold them individually liable." See the 1986 decision of the Supreme Court of Texas in *Castleberry v. Branscum* (1986) which is particularly instructive on this matter. (721 S. W. 2d 270 (Tex. 1986).
4. The individualist, for example, is usually defined as holding that while individuals are "real," groups are not. Yet the individualist can hold (as I in fact do) that both individuals and groups are real and that both really exist, but that they are nevertheless different kinds of things and so exist in different ways. Also, the individualist is sometimes defined as holding that groups are "nothing more than" their members. But the individualist can hold (as I do) that in addition to its mere members, the existence of a group requires also that there exist certain relationships and properties linking its members to each other that set these members off from their larger environment and that provides a basis for us to differentiate the group from its environment. It is thus impossible to "reduce" a group to "nothing more than" its members.
5. By "real" I simply mean actual. The more important concept is that of an "individual entity that acts on the world and that possesses an identity and an existence that is distinct from that of its members." Here and elsewhere in this paper I use the term "individual entity" to refer to the category of things we commonly recognize as ordinary *individuals*, such as people, horses, cows, frogs, trees, plants, insects, amoebas, bacteria, etc., and distinguish from the category of *groups* of individuals, when such groups are not themselves seen as constituting individuals, such as crowds, herds, flocks, groves, piles, heaps, collections, etc. While the collectivist wants to allow corporations—at least sometimes—into the first of these categories, the individualist wants to keep them firmly in the second category. . . I appeal to what Aristotle calls a "primary substance" in his *Categories*, 2a, 11, and what Thomas Aquinas calls a "substance as subject" in his *Commentary on Aristotle's Metaphysics*, Bk. VII, L. 2 as further explanations of my concept of an individual entity. . . Aristotle's primary substances (and what Aquinas calls "substances as subjects") include ordinary concrete individuals such as individual human beings, animals, birds, plants. On the other hand, it excludes the qualities possessed by concrete individuals such as colors, sizes, positions, and relationships, and excludes also abstract objects such as numbers, arbitrary sets, and concepts, as well as aggregates such as a pile of rocks or of sand. . . .
6. Intentional causality is the kind of causality that a thing exhibits when one's *thought* of that thing or *perception* of that thing (or some other intentional state of which the thing is the intensional object) causes a reaction or response in oneself. In such cases, where it is accurate to

say that it was the thought or the perception of the thing that exerted causality on oneself, the thing itself is nothing more than the intensional object of the thought or perception. I label this kind of causality "intentional" causality to distinguish it from what I call "efficient causality." By "efficient causality" I mean the kind of causality that a thing exhibits when it causes some effect but not by being the intensional object of a thought or perception that can itself be said to have caused the effect. . . . It is useful to note that an implication of the characterization I am giving of intentional causality, is that expressions of intentional causality are referentially opaque, while, by contrast, expressions of what I call "efficient causality" generally are not. . . .

7. John Ladd, "Corporate Mythology and Individual Responsibility," *International Journal of Applied Philosophy*, 2 (Spring 1984), pp. 1–21.
8. French, *Collective and Corporate Responsibility*, (New York: Columbia University Press, 1984), p. 13. French goes on to remark that it is this characteristic that makes it possible to attribute responsibility to a conglomerate as an entity distinct from its members: "What is predicable of a conglomerate is not necessarily predicable of all of those or of any of those individuals associated with it, and this is also true of predications of responsibility. . . . Statements ascribing responsibility to a conglomerate are not reducible to a conjunction of statements ascribing responsibility to the individuals associated with the conglomerate." *Ibid.*
9. We need, of course, to interpret "cause" broadly enough to include omissions. I may be morally responsible for an event if I could have acted to prevented it, but deliberately did nothing to stop it. . . .
10. The causality here is what I have labeled efficient causality in note [5] and not what I there defined as intentional causality. . . . [The distinction between intentional causality and efficient causality is important since I claim that the individual members of a corporate organization are always the efficient causes of the organization's acts, yet I also allow that a corporate organization can be the intentional object of thoughts, perceptions, or desires that cause responses or events in us and so can be the intentional causes of such responses or events.]
11. The fact that individuals in groups do things they would never do if acting alone was noticed long before sociologists attested to that fact with elaborate social experiments. The modern experiments I have in mind are, of course, the Milgram and the Zimbardo experiments. But several centuries ago, toward the end of the Roman era, St. Augustine, analyzing in his *Confessions*, Bk. 2, ch. 9, an incident in his early life when he and some friends stole some fruit from another person's orchard, noted: "By myself I would not have committed that theft in which what pleased me was not what I stole, but the fact that I stole. This would have pleased me not at all if I had done it alone, nor by myself would I have done it at all!"
12. See Peter French, *The Scope of Morality* (Minneapolis: University of Minnesota Press, 1979) where he writes (p. 27): "These decision structures accomplish a subordination and synthesis of the intentions and acts of various biological persons into a conglomerate decision. Hence, these decision structures license the descriptive transformation of events, seen under another aspect as the acts of biological persons (those who occupy various stations on the organizational chart), into conglomerate acts done for conglomerate reasons."
13. John Searle, "Intrinsic Intentionality: Reply to Criticisms of Minds, Brains, and Programs," *Behavioral and Brain Sciences*, 3:450–456; for a more recent discussions of the distinction see his *The Rediscovery of Mind* (Cambridge, MA: MIT Press, 1992), pp. 78 ff, and *Mind, Language, and Society* (New York: Oxford, 1999), pp. 93 ff. Note, also, that my discussion of prescriptive attributions of intentionality is inspired by (but is not the same as) Searle's discussion of "institutional facts" and attributions of "functions" in John Searle, *The Construction of Social Reality* (New York: The Free Press, 1995).

# Roger Boisjoly and the *Challenger* Disaster: The Ethical Dimensions

*Russell P. Boisjoly*
*Ellen Foster Curtis*
*Eugene Mellican*

## INTRODUCTION

On January 28, 1986, the space shuttle *Challenger* exploded 73 seconds into its flight, killing the seven astronauts aboard. As the nation mourned the tragic loss of the crew members, the Rogers Commission was formed to investigate the causes of the disaster. The Commission concluded that the explosion occurred due to seal failure in one of the solid rocket booster joints. Testimony given by Roger Boisjoly, Senior Scientist and acknowledged rocket seal expert, indicated that top management at NASA and Morton Thiokol had been aware of problems with the O-ring seals, but agreed to launch against the recommendation of Boisjoly and other engineers. Boisjoly had alerted management to problems with the O-ring as early as January 1985, yet several shuttle launches prior to the *Challenger* had been approved without correcting the hazards. This suggests that the management practice of NASA and Morton Thiokol had created an environment which altered the framework for decision making, leading to a breakdown in communication between technical experts and their supervisors, and top level management, and to the acceptance of risks that both organizations had historically viewed as unacceptable. With human lives and the national interest at stake, serious ethical concerns are embedded in this dramatic change in management practice.

In fact, one of the most important aspects of the *Challenger* disaster—both in terms of the causal sequence that led to it and the lessons to be learned from it—is its ethical dimension. Ethical issues are woven throughout the tangled web of decisions, events, practices, and organizational structures that resulted in the loss of the *Challenger* and its seven astronauts. Therefore, an ethical analysis of this tragedy is essential for a full understanding of the event itself and for the implications it has for any endeavor where public policy, corporate practice, and individual decisions intersect.

The significance of an ethical analysis of the *Challenger* disaster is indicated by the fact that it immediately presents one of the most urgent, but difficult, issues in the examination of corporate and individual behavior today, i.e., whether existing ethical theories adequately address the problems posed by new technologies, new forms of organization, and evolving social systems. At the heart of this issue is the concept of responsibility. No ethical concept has been more affected by the impact of these changing realities. Modern technology has so transformed the context and scale of human action that not only do the traditional parameters of responsibility seem inadequate to contain the full range of human acts and their consequences, but even more fundamentally, it is no longer the individual that is the primary locus of power and responsibility, but public and private institutions. Thus, it would seem, it is no longer the character and virtues of individuals that determine the standards of moral conduct, it is the policies and structures of the institutional settings within which they live and work.

Many moral conflicts facing individuals within institutional settings do arise from matters pertaining to organizational structures or questions of public policy. As such, they are resolvable only at a level above the responsibilities of the individual. Therefore, some writers argue that the ethical responsibilities of the engineer or manager in a large corporation have as much to do with the organization as with the individual. Instead of expecting individual engineers or managers to be moral heroes, emphasis should be on the creation of organizational structures conducive to ethical behavior among all agents under their aegis. It would be futile to attempt to establish a sense of ethical responsibility in engineers and management personnel and ignore the fact that such persons work within a sociotechnical environment which increasingly undermines the notion of individual, responsible moral agency (Boling and Dempsey, 1981; De George, 1981).

Yet, others argue that precisely because of these organizational realities individual accountability must be re-emphasized to counteract the diffusion of responsibility within large organizations and to prevent its evasion under the rubric of collective responsibility. Undoubtedly institutions do take on a kind of collective life of their own, but they do not exist, or act, independently of the individuals that constitute them, whatever the theoretical and practical complexities of delineating the precise relationships involved. Far from diminishing individuals' obligations, the reality of organizational life increases them because the consequences of decisions and acts are extended and amplified through the reach and power of that reality. Since there are pervasive and inexorable connections between ethical standards and behavior of individuals within an organization and its structure and operation, "the sensitizing of professionals to ethical considerations should be increased so that institutional structures will reflect enhanced ethical sensitivities as trained professionals move up the organizational ladder to positions of leadership" (Mankin, 1981, p. 17).

By reason of the courageous activities and testimony of individuals like Roger Boisjoly, the *Challenger* disaster provides a fascinating illustration of the dynamic tension between organizational and individual responsibility. By focusing on this central issue, this article seeks to accomplish two objectives: first, to demonstrate the extent to which the *Challenger* disaster not only gives concrete expression to the ethical ambiguity that permeates the relationship between organizational and individual responsibility, but also, in fact, is a result of it; second, to reclaim the meaning and importance of individual responsibility within the diluting context of large organizations.

In meeting these objectives, the article is divided into two parts: a case study of Roger Boisjoly's efforts to galvanize management support for effectively correcting the high risk O-ring problems, his attempt to prevent the launch, the scenario which resulted in the launch decision, and Boisjoly's quest to set the record straight despite enormous personal and professional consequences; and an ethical analysis of these events.

## PREVIEW FOR DISASTER

On January 24, 1985, Roger Boisjoly, Senior Scientist at Morton Thiokol, watched the launch of Flight 51-C of the space shuttle program. He was at Cape Canaveral to inspect the solid rocket boosters from Flight 51-C following their recovery in the Atlantic Ocean and to conduct a training session at Kennedy Space Center (KSC) on the proper methods of inspecting the booster joints. While watching the launch, he noted that the temperature that day was much cooler than recorded at other launches, but was still much warmer than the 18 degree temperature encountered three days earlier when he arrived in Orlando. The unseasonably cold weather of the past several days had produced the worst citrus crop failures in Florida history.

When he inspected the solid rocket boosters several days later, Boisjoly discovered evidence that the primary O-ring seals on two field joints had been compromised by hot combustion gases (i.e., hot gas blow-by had occurred) which had also eroded part of the primary O-ring. This was the first time that a primary seal on a field joint had been penetrated. When he discovered the large amount of blackened grease between the primary and secondary seals, his concern heightened. The blackened grease was discovered over 80 degree and 110 degree arcs, respectively, on two of the seals, with the larger arc indicating greater hot gas blow-by. Post-flight calculations indicated that the ambient temperature of the field joints at launch time was 53 degrees. This evidence, coupled with his recollection of the low temperature the day of the launch and the citrus crop damage caused by the cold spell, led to his conclusion that the severe hot gas blow-by may have been caused by, and related to, low temperature. After reporting these findings to his superiors, Boisjoly presented them to engineers and management at NASA's Marshall Space Flight Center (MSFC). As a result of his presentation at MSFC, Roger Boisjoly was asked to participate in the Flight Readiness Review (FRR) on February 12, 1985 for Flight 51-E which was scheduled for launch in April, 1985. This FRR represents the first association of low temperature with blow-by on a field joint, a condition that was considered an "acceptable risk" by Larry Mulloy, NASA's Manager for the Booster Project, and other NASA officials.

Roger Boisjoly had twenty-five years of experience as an engineer in the aerospace industry. Among his many notable assignments were the performance of stress and deflection analysis on the flight control equipment of the Advanced Minuteman Missile at Autonetics, and serving as a lead engineer on the lunar module of Apollo at Hamilton Standard. He moved to Utah in 1980 to take a position in the Applied Mechanics Department as a Staff Engineer at the Wasatch Division of Morton Thiokol. He was considered the leading expert in the United States on O-rings and rocket joint seals and received plaudits for his work on the joint seal problems from Joe C. Kilminster, Vice President of Space Booster Programs, Morton Thiokol (Kilminster, July, 1985). His commitment to the company and the community was further demonstrated by his service as Mayor of Willard, Utah from 1982 to 1983.

The tough questioning he received at the February 12th FRR convinced Boisjoly of the need for further evidence linking low temperature and hot gas blow-by. He worked closely with Arnie Thompson, Supervisor of Rocket Motor Cases, who conducted subscale laboratory tests in March, 1985, to further test the effects of temperature on O-ring resiliency. The bench tests that were performed provided powerful evidence to support Boisjoly's and Thompson's theory: Low temperatures greatly and adversely affected the ability of O-rings to create a seal on solid rocket booster joints. If the temperature was too low (and they did not know what the threshold temperature would be), it was possible that neither the primary or secondary O-rings would seal!

One month later the post-flight inspection of Flight 51-B revealed that the primary seal of a booster nozzle joint did not make contact during its two minute flight. If this damage had occurred in a field joint, the secondary O-ring may have failed to seal, causing the loss of the flight. As a result, Boisjoly and his colleagues became increasingly concerned about shuttle safety. This evidence from the inspection of Flight 51-B was presented at the FRR for Flight 51-F on July 1, 1985; the key engineers and managers at NASA and Morton Thiokol were now aware of the critical O-ring problems and the influence of low temperature on the performance of the joint seals.

During July, 1985, Boisjoly and his associates voiced their desire to devote more effort and resources to solving the problems of O-ring erosion. In his activity reports dated July 22 and 29, 1985, Boisjoly expressed considerable frustration with the lack of progress in this area, despite the fact that a Seal Erosion Task Force had been informally appointed on July 19th. Finally, Boisjoly wrote the following memo, labelled "Company Private," to R. K. (Bob) Lund, Vice President of Engineering for Morton Thiokol, to express the extreme urgency of his concerns. Here are some excerpts from that memo:

> This letter is written to insure that management is fully aware of the seriousness of the current O-ring erosion problem. . . . The mistakenly accepted position on the joint problem was to fly without fear of failure . . . is now drastically changed as a result of the SRM 16A nozzle joint erosion which eroded a secondary O-ring with the primary O-ring never sealing. If the same scenario should occur in a field joint (and it could), then it is a jump ball as to the success or failure of the joint. . . . The result would be a catastrophe of the highest order—loss of human life. . . .
>
> It is my honest and real fear that if we do not take immediate action to dedicate a team to solve the problem, with the field joint having the number one priority, then we stand in jeopardy of losing a flight along with all the launch pad facilities (Boisjoly, July, 1985a).

On August 20, 1985, R. K. Lund formally announced the formation of the Seal Erosion Task Team. The team consisted of only five full-time engineers from the 2500 employed by Morton Thiokol on the Space Shuttle Program. The events of the next five months would demonstrate that management had not provided the resources necessary to carry out the enormous task of solving the seal erosion problem.

On October 3, 1985, the Seal Erosion Task Force met with Joe Kilminster to discuss the problems they were having in gaining organizational support necessary to solve the O-ring problems. Boisjoly later stated that Kilminster summarized the meeting as a "good bullshit session." Once again frustrated by bureaucratic inertia, Boisjoly wrote in his activity report dated October 4th:

> . . . NASA is sending an engineering representative to stay with us starting Oct. 14th. We feel that this is a direct result of their feeling that we (MTI) are not responding quickly enough to the seal problem . . . upper management apparently feels that the SRM program is ours for sure and the customer be damned (Boisjoly, October, 1985b).

Boisjoly was not alone in his expression of frustration. Bob Ebeling, Department Manager, Solid Rocket Motor Igniter and Final Assembly, and a member of the Seal Erosion Task Force, wrote in a memo to Allan McDonald, Manager of the Solid Rocket Motor Project, "HELP! The seal task force is constantly being delayed by every possible means. . . . We wish we could get action by verbal request, but such is not the case. This is a red flag" (McConnell, 1987).

At the Society of Automotive Engineers (SAE) conference on October 7, 1985, Boisjoly presented a six-page overview of the joints and the seal configuration to approximately 130 technical experts in hope of soliciting suggestions for remedying the O-ring problems. Although MSFC had requested the presentation, NASA gave strict instructions not to express the critical urgency of fixing the joints, but merely to ask for suggestions for improvement. Although no help was forthcoming, the conference was a milestone in that it was the first time that NASA allowed information on the O-ring difficulties to be expressed in a public forum. That NASA also recognized that the O-ring problems were not receiving appropriate attention and manpower considerations from Morton Thiokol management is further evidenced by Boisjoly's October 24 log entry, ". . . Jerry Peoples (NASA) has informed his people that our group needs more authority and people to do the job. Jim Smith (NASA) will corner Al McDonald today to attempt to implement this direction."

The October 30 launch of Flight 61-A of the *Challenger* provided the most convincing, and yet to some the most contestable, evidence to date that low temperature was directly related to hot gas blow-by. The left booster experienced hot gas blow-by in the center and aft field joints without any seal erosion. The ambient temperature of the field joints was estimated to be 75 degrees at launch time based on post-flight calculations. Inspection of the booster joints revealed that the blow-by was less severe than that found on Flight 51-C because the seal grease was a grayish black color, rather than the jet black hue of Flight 51-C. The evidence was now consistent with the bench tests for joint resiliency conducted in March. That is, at 75 degrees the O-ring lost contact with its sealing surface for 2.4 seconds, whereas at 50 degrees the O-ring lost contact for 10 minutes. The actual flight data revealed greater hot gas blow-by for the O-rings on Flight 51-C which had an ambient temperature of 53 degrees than for Flight 61-A which had an ambient temperature of 75 degrees. Those who rejected this line of reasoning concluded that temperature must be irrelevant since hot gas blow-by had occurred even at room temperature (75 degrees). This difference in interpretation would receive further attention on January 27, 1986.

During the next two and one-half months, little progress was made in obtaining a solution to the O-ring problems. Roger Boisjoly made the following entry into his log on January 13, 1986, "O-ring resiliency tests that were requested on September 24, 1985 are now scheduled for January 15, 1986."

## THE DAY BEFORE THE DISASTER

At 10 a.m. on January 27, 1986, Arnie Thompson received a phone call from Boyd Brinton, Thiokol's Manager of Project Engineering at MSFC, relaying the concerns of NASA's Larry Wear, also at MSFC, about the 18 degree temperature forecast for the launch of flight 51-L, the *Challenger*, scheduled for the next day. This phone call precipitated a series of meetings within Morton Thiokol, at the Marshall Space Flight Center; and at the Kennedy Space Center that culminated in a three-way telecon involving three teams of engineers and managers, that began at 8:15 p.m. E.S.T.

Joe Kilminster, Vice President, Space Booster Programs, of Morton Thiokol began the telecon by turning the presentation of the engineering charts over to Roger Boisjoly and Arnie Thompson. They presented thirteen charts which resulted in a recommendation against the launch of the *Challenger*. Boisjoly demonstrated their concerns with the performance of the O-rings in the field joints during the initial phases of *Challenger's* flight with charts showing the effects of primary O-ring erosion, and its timing, on the ability to maintain a reliable secondary seal. The tremendous pressure and release of power from the rocket boosters create rotation in the joint such that the metal moves away from the O-rings so that they cannot maintain contact with the metal surfaces. If, at the same time, erosion occurs in the primary O-ring for any reason, then there is a reduced probability of maintaining a secondary seal. It is highly probable that as the ambient temperature drops, the primary O-ring will not seat, that there will be hot gas blow-by and erosion of the primary O-ring, and that a catastrophe will occur when the secondary O-ring fails to seal.

Bob Lund presented the final chart that included the Morton Thiokol recommendations that the ambient temperature including wind must be such that the seal temperature would be greater than 53 degrees to proceed with the launch. Since the overnight low was predicted to be 18 degrees, Bob Lund recommended against launch on January 28, 1986, or until the seal temperature exceeded 53 degrees.

NASA's Larry Mulloy bypassed Bob Lund and directly asked Joe Kilminster for his reaction. Kilminster stated that he supported the position of his engineers and he would not recommend launch below 53 degrees.

George Hardy, Deputy Director of Science and Engineering at MSFC, said he was "appalled at that recommendation," according to Allan McDonald's testimony before the Rogers Commission. Nevertheless, Hardy would not recommend to launch if the contractor was against it. After Hardy's reaction, Stanley Reinartz, Manager of Shuttle Project Office at MSFC, objected by pointing out that the solid rocket motors were qualified to operate between 40 and 90 degrees Fahrenheit.

Larry Mulloy, citing the data from Flight 61-A which indicated to him that temperature was not a factor, strenuously objected to Morton Thiokol's recommendation. He suggested that Thiokol was attempting to establish new Launch Commit Criteria at 53 degrees and that they couldn't do that the night before a launch. In exasperation Mulloy asked, "My God, Thiokol, when do you want me to launch? Next April?" (McConnell, 1987). Although other NASA officials also objected to the association of temperature with O-ring erosion and hot gas blow-by, Roger Boisjoly was able to hold his ground and demonstrate with the use of his charts and pictures that there was indeed a relationship: The lower the temperature the higher the probability of erosion and blow-by and the greater the likelihood of an accident. Finally, Joe Kilminster asked for a five-minute caucus off-net.

According to Boisjoly's testimony before the Rogers Commission, Jerry Mason, Senior Vice President of Wasatch Operations, began the caucus by saying that "a management decision was necessary." Sensing that an attempt would be made to overturn the no-launch decision, Boisjoly and Thompson attempted to re-review the material previously presented to NASA for the executives in the room. Thompson took a pad of paper and tried to sketch out the problem with the joint, while Boisjoly laid out the photos of the compromised joints from Flights 51-C and 61-A. When they became convinced that no one was listening, they ceased their efforts. As Boisjoly would later testify, "There was not one positive pro-launch statement ever made by anybody" (Report of the Presidential Commission, 1986, IV, p. 792, hereafter abbreviated as R.C.).

According to Boisjoly, after he and Thompson made their last attempts to stop the launch, Jerry Mason asked rhetorically, "Am I the only one who wants to fly?" Mason turned to Bob Lund and asked him to "take off his engineering hat and put on his management hat." The four managers held a brief discussion and voted unanimously to recommend *Challenger's* launch.

Exhibit 1 shows the revised recommendations that were presented that evening by Joe Kilminster after the caucus to support management's decision to launch. Only one of the rationales presented that evening supported the launch (demonstrated erosion sealing

**EXHIBIT 1** MTI Assessment of Temperature Concern on SRM-25 (51L) Launch

- CALCULATIONS SHOW THAT SRM-25 O-RINGS WILL BE 20° COLDER THAN SRM-15 O-RINGS
- TEMPERATURE DATA NOT CONCLUSIVE ON PREDICTING PRIMARY O-RING BLOW-BY
- ENGINEERING ASSESSMENT IS THAT:
  - CODER O-RINGS WILL HAVE INCREASED EFFECTIVE DUROMETER ("HARDER")
  - "HARDER" O-RINGS WILL TAKE LONGER TO "SEAT"
  - MORE GAS MAY PASS PRIMARY O-RING BEFORE THE PRIMARY SEAL SEATS (RELATIVE TO SRM-15)
  - DEMONSTRATED SEALING THRESHOLD IS 3 TIMES GREATER THAN 0.038" EROSION EXPERIENCED ON SRM-15
  - IF THE PRIMARY SEAL DOES NOT SEAT, THE SECONDARY SEAL WILL SEAT
  - PRESSURE WILL GET TO SECONDARY SEAL BEFORE THE METAL PARTS ROTATE
  - O-RING PRESSURE LEAK CHECK PLACES SECONDARY SEAL IN OUTBOARD POSITION WHICH MINIMIZES SEALING TIME
- MTI RECOMMENDS STS-51L LAUNCH PROCEED ON 28 JANUARY 1986
- SRM-25 WILL NOT BE SIGNIFICANTLY DIFFERENT FROM SRM-15

Joe C. Kilminster, Vice President Space Booster Programs.

threshold is three times greater than 0.038" erosion experienced on SRM-15). Even so, the issue at hand was sealability at low temperature, not erosion. While one other rationale could be considered a neutral statement of engineering fact (O-ring pressure leak check places secondary seal in outboard position which minimizes sealing time), the other seven rationales are negative, anti-launch, statements. After hearing Kilminster's presentation, which was accepted without a single probing question, George Hardy asked him to sign the chart and telefax it to Kennedy Space Center and Marshall Space Flight Center. At 11 p.m. E.S.T. the teleconference ended.

Aside from the four senior Morton Thiokol executives present at the teleconference, all others were excluded from the final decision. The process represented a radical shift from previous NASA policy. Until that moment, the burden of proof had always been on the engineers to prove beyond a doubt that it was safe to launch. NASA, with their objections to the original Thiokol recommendation against the launch, and Mason, with his request for a "management decision," shifted the burden of proof in the opposite direction. Morton Thiokol was expected to prove that launching *Challenger* would not be safe (R.C., IV, p. 793).

The change in the decision so deeply upset Boisjoly that he returned to his office and made the following journal entry:

> I sincerely hope this launch does not result in a catastrophe. I personally do not agree with some of the statements made by Joe Kilminster's written summary stating that SRM-25 is okay to fly (Boisjoly, 1987).

## THE DISASTER AND ITS AFTERMATH

On January 28, 1986, a reluctant Roger Boisjoly watched the launch of the *Challenger*. As the vehicle cleared the tower, Bob Ebeling whispered, "We've just dodged a bullet." (The engineers who opposed the launch assumed that O-ring failure would result in an explosion almost immediately after engine ignition.) To continue in Boisjoly's words, "At approximately T+60 seconds Bob told me he had just completed a prayer of thanks to the Lord for a successful launch. Just thirteen seconds later we both saw the horror of the destruction as the vehicle exploded" (Boisjoly, 1987).

Morton Thiokol formed a failure investigation team on January 31, 1986, to study the *Challenger* explosion. Roger Boisjoly and Arnie Thompson were part of the team that was sent to MSFC in Huntsville, Alabama. Boisjoly's first inkling of a division between himself and management came on February 13 when he was informed at the last minute that he was to testify before the Rogers Commission the next day. He had very little time to prepare for his testimony. Five days later, two Commission members held a closed session with Kilminster, Boisjoly, and Thompson. During the interview Boisjoly gave his memos and activity reports to the Commissioners. After that meeting, Kilminster chastised Thompson and Boisjoly for correcting his interpretation of the technical data. Their response was that they would continue to correct his version if it was technically incorrect.

Boisjoly's February 25th testimony before the Commission, rebutting the general manager's statement that the initial decision against the launch was not unanimous, drove a wedge further between him and Morton Thiokol management. Boisjoly was flown to MSFC before he could hear the NASA testimony about the pre-flight telecon. The next day, he was removed from the failure investigation team and returned to Utah.

Beginning in April, Boisjoly began to believe that for the previous month he had been used solely for public relations purposes. Although given the title of Seal Coordinator for the redesign effort, he was isolated from NASA and the seal redesign effort. His design information had been changed without his knowledge and presented without his feedback. On May 1, 1986, in a briefing preceding closed sessions before the Rogers Commission, Ed Garrison, President of Aerospace Operations for Morton Thiokol, chastised Boisjoly for "airing the company's dirty laundry" with the memos he had given the Commission. The next day, Boisjoly testified about the change in his job assignment. Commission Chairman Rogers criticized Thiokol management, ". . . if it appears that you're punishing the two people or at least two of the people who are right about the decision and objected to the launch which ultimately resulted in criticism of Thiokol and then they're demoted or feel that they are being retaliated against, that is a very serious matter. It would seem to me, just speaking for myself, they should be promoted, not demoted or pushed aside" (R.C., V, p. 1586).

Boisjoly now sensed a major rift developing within the corporation. Some co-workers perceived that his testimony was damaging the company image. In an effort to clear the air, he and McDonald requested a private meeting with the company's three top executives, which was held on May 16, 1986. According to Boisjoly, management was unreceptive throughout the meeting. The CEO told McDonald and Boisjoly that the company "was doing just fine until Al and I testified about our job reassignments" (Boisjoly, 1987). McDonald and Boisjoly were nominally restored to their former assignments, but Boisjoly's position became untenable as time passed. On July 21, 1986, Roger Boisjoly requested an extended sick leave from Morton Thiokol.

## ETHICAL ANALYSIS

It is clear from this case study that Roger Boisjoly's experiences before and after the *Challenger* disaster raise numerous ethical questions that are integral to any explanation of the disaster and applicable to other management situations, especially those involving highly complex technologies. The difficulties and uncertainties involved in the management of these technologies exacerbate the kind of bureaucratic syndromes that generate ethical conflicts in the first place. In fact, Boisjoly's experiences could well serve as a paradigmatic case study for such ethical problems, ranging from accountability to corporate loyalty and whistleblowing. Underlying all these issues, however, is the problematic relationship between individual and organizational responsibility. Boisjoly's experiences graphically portray the tensions inherent in this relationship in a manner that discloses its importance in the causal sequence leading to the *Challenger* disaster. The following analysis explicates this and the implications it has for other organizational settings.

By focusing on the problematic relationship between individual and organizational responsibility, this analysis reveals that the organizational structure governing the space shuttle program became the locus of responsibility in such a way that not only did it undermine the responsibilities of individual decision makers within the process, but it also became a means of avoiding real, effective responsibility throughout the entire management system. The first clue to this was clearly articulated as early as 1973 by the board of inquiry that was formed to investigate the accident which occurred during the launch of *Skylab 1*:

> The management system developed by NASA for manned space flight places large emphasis on rigor, detail, and thoroughness. In hand with this emphasis comes formalism, extensive documentation, and visibility in detail to senior management. While nearly perfect, such a system can submerge the concerned individual and depress the role of the intuitive engineer or analyst. It may not allow full play for the intuitive judgment or past experience of the individual. An emphasis on management systems can, in itself, serve to separate the people engaged in the program from the real world of hardware (Quoted in Christiansen, 1987, p. 23).

To examine this prescient statement in ethical terms is to see at another level the serious consequences inherent in the situation it describes. For example, it points to a dual meaning of responsibility. One meaning emphasizes carrying out an authoritatively prescribed review process, while the second stresses the cognitive independence and input of every individual down the entire chain of authority. The first sense of responsibility shifts the ethical center of gravity precipitously away from individual moral agency onto the review process in such a way that what was originally set up to guarantee flight readiness with the professional and personal integrity of the responsible individuals, instead becomes a means of evading personal responsibility for decisions made in the review process.

A crucial, and telling, example of this involves the important question asked by the Rogers Commission as to why the concerns raised by the Morton Thiokol engineers about the effects of cold weather on the O-rings during the teleconference the night before the launch were not passed up from Level III to Levels II or I in the preflight review process. The NASA launch procedure clearly demands that decisions and objections methodically follow a prescribed path up all levels. Yet, Lawrence Mulloy, operating at Level III as the Solid Rocket Booster Project Manager at MSFC, did not transmit the Morton Thiokol concerns upward (through his immediate superior, Stanley Reinartz) to Level II. When asked by Chairman Rogers to explain why, Mr. Mulloy testified:

> At that time, and I still consider today, that was a Level III issue, Level III being a SRB element or an external tank element or Space Shuttle main engine element or an Orbiter. There was no violation of Launch Commit Criteria. There was no waiver required in my judgment at that time and still today (R.C., I, p. 98).

In examining this response in terms of shifting responsibility onto the review process itself, there are two things that are particularly striking in Mr. Mulloy's statement. The first is his emphasis that this was a "Level III issue." In a formal sense, Mr. Mulloy is correct. However, those on Level III also had the authority—and, one would think, especially in this instance given the heated discussion on the effects of cold on the O-rings, the motivation—to pass objections and concerns on to Levels II and I. But here the second important point in Mr. Mulloy's testimony comes into play when he states, "there was no violation of Launch Commit Criteria." In other words, since there was no Launch Commit Criteria for joint temperature, concerns about joint temperature did not officially fall under the purview of the review process.

Therefore, the ultimate justification for Mr. Mulloy's position rests on the formal process itself. He was just following the rules by staying within the already established scope of the review process.

This underscores the moral imperative executives must exercise by creating and maintaining organizational systems that do not separate the authority of decision makers from the responsibility they bear for decisions, or insulate them from the consequences of their actions or omissions.

Certainly, there can be no more vivid example than the shuttle program to verify that, in fact, "an emphasis on management systems can, in itself, serve to separate the people engaged in the program from the real world of hardware." Time and time again the lack of communication that lay at the heart of the Rogers Commission finding that "there was a serious flaw in the decision making process leading up to the launch of flight 51-L" (R.C., I, p. 104) was explained by the NASA officials or managers at Morton Thiokol with such statements as, "that is not my reporting channel," or "he is not in the launch decision chain," or "I didn't meet with Mr. Boisjoly, I met with Don Ketner, who is the task team leader" (R.C., IV, p. 821, testimony of Mr. Lund). Even those managers who had direct responsibility for line engineers and workmen depended on formalized memo writing procedures for communication to the point that some "never talked to them directly" (Feynman, 1988, p. 33).

Within the atmosphere of such an ambiguity of responsibility, when a life-threatening conflict arose within the management system and individuals (such as Roger Boisjoly and his engineering associates at Morton Thiokol) tried to reassert the full weight of their individual judgments and attendant responsibilities, the very purpose of the flight readiness review process, i.e., to arrive at the "technical" truth of the situation, which includes the recognition of the uncertainties involved as much as the findings, became subverted into an adversary confrontation in which "adversary" truth, with its suppression of uncertainties, became operative (Wilmotte, 1970).

What is particularly significant in this radical transformation of the review process, in which the Morton Thiokol engineers were forced into "the position of having to prove that it was unsafe instead of the other way around" (R.C., IV, p. 822; see also p. 793), is that what made the suppression of technical uncertainties possible is precisely that mode of thinking which, in being challenged by independent professional judgments, gave rise to the adversarial setting in the first place: groupthink. No more accurate description for what transpired the night before the launch of the *Challenger* can be given than the definition of groupthink as:

> . . . a mode of thinking that people engage in when they are deeply involved in a cohesive in-group, when the members' strivings for unanimity override their motivation to realistically appraise alternative courses of action. . . . Groupthink refers to the deterioration of mental efficiency, reality testing, and moral judgment that results from in-group pressures (Janis, 1972, p. 9).

From this perspective, the full import of Mr. Mason's telling Mr. Lund to "take off his engineering hat and put on his management hat" is revealed. He did not want another technical, reality-based judgment of an independent professional engineer. As he had already implied when he opened the caucus by stating "a management decision was necessary," he wanted a group decision, specifically one that would, in the words of the Rogers Commission, "accommodate a major customer" (R.C., I, p. 104). With a group decision the objections of the engineers could be mitigated, the risks shared, fears allayed, and the attendant responsibility diffused.

This analysis is not meant to imply that groupthink was a pervasive or continuous mode of thinking at either NASA or Morton Thiokol. What is suggested is a causal relationship between this instance of groupthink and the ambiguity of responsibility found within the space shuttle program. Whenever a management system such as NASA's generates "a mindset of 'collective responsibility'" by leading "individuals to defer to the anonymity of the process and not focus closely enough on their individual responsibilities in the decision chain" (N.R.C. Report, 1988, p. 68), and there is a confluence of the kind of pressures that came to bear on the decision making process the night before the launch, the conditions are in place for groupthink to prevail.

A disturbing feature of so many of the analyses and commentaries on the *Challenger* disaster is the reinforcement, and implicit acceptance, of this shift away from individual moral agency with an almost exclusive focus on the flaws in the management system, organizational structures and/or decision making process. Beginning with the findings of the Rogers Commission investigation, one could practically conclude that no one had any responsibility whatsoever for the disaster. The Commission concluded that "there was a serious flaw in the decision making process leading up to the launch of flight 51-L. A well structured and managed system emphasizing safety would have flagged the rising doubts about the Solid Rocket Booster joint seal." Then the Commission report immediately states, "Had these matters been clearly stated and emphasized in the flight readiness process in terms reflecting the views of most of the Thiokol engineers and at least some of the Marshall engineers, it seems likely that the launch of 51-L might not have occurred when it did" (R.C., I, p. 104). But the gathering and passing on of such information was the responsibility of specifically designated individuals, known by name and position in the highly structured review process. Throughout this process there had been required "a series of formal, legally binding certifications, the equivalent of airworthiness inspections in the aviation industry. In effect the myriad contractor and NASA personnel involved were guaranteeing *Challenger's* flight readiness with their professional and personal integrity" (McConnell, 1987, p. 17).

When the Commission states in its next finding that "waiving of launch constraints appears to have been at the expense of flight safety," the immediate and obvious question would seem to be: Who approved the waivers and assumed this enormous risk? And why? This is a serious matter! A launch constraint is only issued because there is a safety problem serious enough to justify a decision not to launch. However, the Commission again deflects the problem onto the system by stating, "There was no system which made it imperative that launch constraints and waivers of launch constraints be considered by all levels of management" (R.C., 1986, I, p. 104).

There are two puzzling aspects to this Commission finding. First, the formal system already contained the requirement that project offices inform at least Level II of launch constraints. The Commission addressed the explicit violation of this requirement in the case of a July 1985 launch constraint that had been imposed on the Solid Rocket Booster because of O-ring erosion on the nozzle:

> NASA Levels I and II apparently did not realize Marshall had assigned a launch constraint within the Problem Assessment System. This communication failure was contrary to the

requirement, contained in the NASA Problem Reporting and Corrective Action Requirements System, that launch constraints were to be taken to Level II (R.C., 1986, I, pp. 138–139; see also p. 159).

Second, the Commission clearly established that the individual at Marshall who both imposed and waived the launch constraint was Lawrence Mulloy, SRB Project Manager. Then why blame the management system, especially in such a crucial area as that of launch constraints, when procedures of that system were not followed? Is that approach going to increase the accountability of individuals within the system for future flights?

Even such an independent-minded and probing Commission member as Richard Feynman, in an interview a year after the disaster, agreed with the avoidance of determining individual accountability for specific actions and decisions. He is quoted as saying, "I don't think it's correct to try to find out which particular guy happened to do what particular thing. It's the question of how the atmosphere could get to such a circumstance that such things were possible without anybody catching on." Yet, at the same time Feynman admitted that he was not confident that any restructuring of the management system will ensure that the kinds of problems that resulted in the *Challenger* disaster—"danger signs not seen and warnings not heeded"—do not recur. He said, "I'm really not sure that any kind of simple mechanism can cure stupidity and dullness. You can make up all the rules about how things should be, and they'll go wrong if the spirit is different, if the attitudes are different over time and as personnel change" (Chandler, 1987, p. 50).

The approach of the Rogers Commission and that of most of the analyses of the *Challenger* disaster is consistent with the growing tendency to deny any specific responsibility to individual persons within corporate or other institutional settings when things go wrong. Although there are obviously many social changes in modern life that justify the shift in focus from individuals to organizational structures as bearers of responsibility, this shift is reinforced and exaggerated by the way people think about and accept those changes. One of the most pernicious problems of modern times is the almost universally held belief that the individual is powerless, especially within the context of large organizations where one may perceive oneself, and be viewed, as a very small, and replaceable, cog. It is in the very nature of this situation that responsibility may seem to become so diffused that no one person IS responsible. As the National Research Council committee, in following up on the Rogers Commission, concluded about the space shuttle program:

> Given the pervasive reliance on teams and boards to consider the key questions affecting safety, 'group democracy' can easily prevail . . . in the end all decisions become collective ones . . . (N.R.C. Report, pp. 68 and 70).

The problem with this emphasis on management systems and collective responsibility is that it fosters a vicious circle that further and further erodes and obscures individual responsibility. This leads to a paradoxical—and untenable—situation (such as in the space shuttle program) in which decisions are made and actions are performed by individuals or groups of individuals but not attributed to them. It thus reinforces the tendency to avoid accountability for what anyone does by attributing the consequences to the organization or decision making process. Again, shared, rather than individual, risktaking and responsibility became operative. The end result can be a cancerous attitude that so permeates an organization or management system that it metastasizes into decisions and acts of life-threatening irresponsibility.

In sharp contrast to this prevalent emphasis on organizational structures, one of the most fascinating aspects of the extensive and exhaustive investigations into the *Challenger* disaster is that they provide a rare opportunity to re-affirm the sense and importance of individual responsibility. With the inside look into the space shuttle program these investigations detail, one can identify many instances where personal responsibility, carefully interpreted, can properly be imputed to NASA officials and to its contractors. By so doing, one can preserve, if only in a fragmentary way, the essentials of the traditional concept of individual responsibility within the diluting context of organizational life. This effort is intended to make explicit the kind of causal links that are operative between the actions of individuals and the structures of organizations.

The criteria commonly employed for holding individuals responsible for an outcome are two: (1) their acts or omissions are in some way a cause of it; and (2) these acts or omissions are not done in ignorance or under coercion (Thompson, 1987, p. 47). Although there are difficult theoretical and practical questions associated with both criteria, especially within organizational settings, nevertheless, even a general application of them to the sequence of events leading up to the *Challenger* disaster reveals those places where the principle of individual responsibility must be factored in if our understanding of it is to be complete, its lessons learned, and its repetition avoided.

The Rogers Commission has been criticized—and rightly so—for looking at the disaster "from the bottom up but not from the top down," with the result that it gives a clearer picture of what transpired at the lower levels of the *Challenger's* flight review process than at its upper levels (Cook, 1986). Nevertheless, in doing so, the Commission report provides powerful testimony that however elaborately structured and far reaching an undertaking such as the space shuttle program may be, individuals at the bottom of the organizational structure can still play a crucial, if not deciding, role in the outcome. For in the final analysis, whatever the defects in the *Challenger's* launch decision chain were that kept the upper levels from being duly informed about the objections of the engineers at Morton Thiokol, the fact remains that the strenuous objections of these engineers so forced the decision process at their level that the four middle managers at Morton Thiokol had the full responsibility for the launch in their hands. This is made clear in the startling testimony of Mr. Mason, when Chairman Rogers asked him: "Did you realize, and particularly in view of Mr. Hardy's (Deputy Director of Science and Engineering at MSFC) point that they wouldn't launch unless you agreed, did you fully realize that in effect, you were making a decision to launch, you and your colleagues?" Mr. Mason replied, "Yes, sir" (R.C., 1986, IV, p. 770).

If these four men had just said no, the launch of the *Challenger* would not have taken place the next day. . . .

Although fragmentary and tentative in its formulation, this set of considerations points toward the conclusion that however complex and sophisticated an organization may be, and no matter how large and remote the institutional network needed to manage it may be, an active and creative tension of responsibility must be maintained at every level of the operation. Given the size and complexity of such endeavors, the only way to ensure that tension of attentive and effective responsibility is to give the primacy of responsibility to that ultimate principle of all moral conduct: the human individual—even if this does necessitate, in too many instances under present circumstances, that individuals such as Roger Boisjoly, when they attempt to exercise their responsibility, must step forward as moral heroes. In so doing, these individuals do not just bear witness to the desperate need for a system of full accountability in the face of the immense power and reach of modern technology and institutions. They also give expression to the very essence of what constitutes the moral life. As Roger

Boisjoly has stated in reflecting on his own experience, "I have been asked by some if I would testify again if I knew in advance of the potential consequences to me and my career. My answer is always an immediate 'yes'. I couldn't live with any self-respect if I tailored my actions based upon the personal consequences. . ." (Boisjoly, 1987).

## REFERENCES

Boisjoly, Roger M.: 1985a, Applied Mechanics Memorandum to Robert K. Lund, Vice President, Engineering, Wasatch Division, Morton Thiokol, Inc., July 31.

Boisjoly, Roger M.: 1985b, Activity Report, SRM Seal Erosion Task Team Status, October 4.

Boisjoly, Roger M.: 1987, Ethical Decisions: Morton Thiokol and the Shuttle Disaster. Speech given at Massachusetts Institute of Technology, January 7.

Boling, T. Edwin and Dempsey, John: 1981, "Ethical dilemmas in government: Designing an organizational response," *Public Personnel Management Journal* 10, 11–18.

Chandler, David: 1987. "Astronauts gain clout in 'revitalized' NASA," *Boston Globe* 1 (January 26):50.

Christiansen, Donald: 1987, "A system gone awry," *IEEE Spectrum* 24(3):23.

Cook, Richard C.: 1986, "The Rogers commission failed," *The Washington Monthly* 18 (9), 13–21.

De George, Richard T.: 1981, "Ethical responsibilities of engineers in large organizations: The Pinto Case," *Business and Professional Ethics Journal* 1, 1–14.

Feynman, Richard P.: 1988, "An outsider's view of the Challenger inquiry," *Physics Today* 41 (2): 26–37.

Janis, Irving L.: 1972, *Victims of Groupthink*, Boston, MA: Houghton Mifflin Company.

Kilminster, J. C.: 1985, Memorandum (E000-FY86-003) to Robert Lund, Vice President, Engineering, Wasatch Division, Morton Thiokol, Inc., July 5.

Mankin, Hart T.: 1981, "Commentary on 'Ethical responsibilities of engineers in large organizations: The Pinto Case,'" *Business and Professional Ethics Journal* 1, 15–17.

McConnell, Malcolm: 1987, *Challenger, A Major Malfunction: A True Story of Politics, Greed, and the Wrong Stuff*, Garden City, N.J.: Doubleday and Company, Inc.

National Research Council: 1988, *Post-Challenger Evaluation of Space Shuttle Risk Assessment and Management*, Washington, D.C.: National Academy Press.

*Report of the Presidential Commission on the Space Shuttle Challenger Accident*: 1986, Washington, D.C.: U.S. Government Printing Office.

Thompson, Dennis F.: 1987, *Political Ethics and Public Office*, Cambridge, MA: Harvard University Press.

Wilmotte, Raymond M.: 1970, "Engineering truth in competitive environments," *IEEE Spectrum* 7 (5): 45–49.

# How Can We Save the Next Victim?

*Lisa Belkin*

On a Friday afternoon last summer, tiny Jose Eric Martinez was brought to the outpatient clinic of Hermann Hospital in Houston for a checkup. The 2-month-old looked healthy to his parents, and he was growing well, so they were rattled by the news that the infant had a ventricular septal defect, best described as a hole between the pumping chambers of his heart.

He was showing the early signs of congestive heart failure, the doctors said, and those symptoms would need to be brought under control by a drug, Digoxin, which would be given intravenously during a several-day stay.

From Lisa Belkin, "How Can We Save the Next Victim?" *The New York Times Magazine*, June 15, 1997. Reprinted with permission.

The child's long-term prognosis was good, the doctors explained. Time would most likely close the hole, and if it did not, routine surgery in a year or so would fix things. The Digoxin was a bridge between here and there. There was nothing to worry about.

The lesson of what happened next is not one of finger-pointing or blame. In fact, the message of this story is quite the opposite: that finger-pointing does not provide answers, and that often no one—no *one*—is to blame.

No single person caused the death of that child in the pediatric special care unit of Hermann Hospital on Aug. 2, 1996. No isolated error led his heart to slow and then stop, suddenly and irreversibly, while his mother, Maria, was cuddling him and coaxing him to suck on a bottle. No one person was responsible, because it is virtually impossible for one mistake to kill a patient in the highly mechanized and backstopped world of a modern hospital. A cascade of unthinkable things must happen, meaning catastrophic errors are rarely a failure of a single person, and almost always a failure of a system. It seems an obvious point, one long understood in other potentially deadly industries like aviation, aerospace, nuclear power. In those realms, a finding of human error is likely to be the *start* of an investigation, not its conclusion.

"If a pilot taxis out and takes off with the flaps up, yes, it's human error," says John Nance, an airline pilot and aviation analyst who has spent much of his time this past year as an adviser to the health care industry. "But the next question is, 'What caused the error?' It's not because the folks in the cockpit say, 'O.K., guys, we can go take off with the flaps up and die, or we can put them down and make it home for dinner.'

"Were they confused? Tired? Misinformed? That's still not an answer. What caused them to be confused or tired or misinformed? That's where you learn something useful." This systems approach to errors has been slow in coming to the health care industry. Perhaps it is because operating room slips are far less obvious and dramatic than plane crashes, and to discuss error as an integral part of medicine is to shine a light on how many errors there actually are. Or maybe it is because we accept that machines are in charge of the space shuttle, but still want to believe that human beings are in charge of our health. Possibly it is because doctors have long been trained to think that they can be—must be—perfect, and patients have been conditioned to accept no less.

Whatever the reason, medicine continues to focus on *who* while other fields try to focus on *why*.

"The mentality has always been: 'Who's the person? Who do I blame? Give me a name,'" says James Conway, who became chief operating officer of the Dana-Farber Cancer Institute in Boston in 1995 during the restructuring after the death of a patient and the injury of another from a medication error. "But that 'going for the jugular' approach hides problems in the system, problems you don't see if you don't look at it as a system error.

"People don't make errors because they want to, or because they're bad people. Everybody makes errors. Every human being. What we need to focus on is how to best design our systems so that those efforts are caught before they reach the patient."

Slowly, tentatively and very recently, health care started to shift that focus. Patient safety is coming to be recognized as a systems problem, for a chain of reasons—the death at Dana-Farber, the tort reform movement in Congress, fears that quality is suffering under managed care.

That awareness is growing throughout medicine—at the American Medical Association, at several major malpractice insurers, in the offices of academic researchers and at dozens of medical centers nationwide. Soon it will be everywhere, because the organization that accredits hospitals has announced that systemic evaluation of errors will be required at all hospitals that report a serious mistake.

One of the newly converted is Hermann Hospital, which stumbled into this burgeoning revolution by accident and as a result of an accident. The significance of the death of one baby, therefore, lies not only in how he died, but also in what happened at the hospital after he died.

"The entire organization was mobilized to go back and look at this from a systemic point of view," says Lynn Walts, Hermann's chief operating officer. The internal investigation found that six separate people had noticed, or had a chance to notice, that the infant was being given 10 times the appropriate dose of Digoxin. As a result, nearly every procedure at Hermann is now being looked at anew.

These changes in philosophy and procedure, Walts knows, will not undo the damage already done. They will not ease the anguish of the Martinez family nor soothe the psyches of their baby's doctors and nurses. Nor will the new approach absolve the hospital of liability for its mistake. But what it can do—indeed, is already doing—is to keep mistakes like that from happening again. And it can replace a paralyzing atmosphere of blame with the healing sense of moving forward, toward a goal.

"If we had looked at things differently five years ago," Walts says, "maybe this mistake wouldn't have happened. We can't change it, but we can make sure we don't look back with the same regret five years from now."

The night Jose Martinez died, Hermann Hospital was two weeks away from a visit from the Joint Commission on the Accreditation of Healthcare Organizations, a body with the power to take away a hospital's economic lifeblood by making it ineligible for payments from H.M.O.'s and other health care organizations.

The commission, sanctioned by organizations like the A.M.A. and the American Hospital Association, is an example of an industry's governing itself. It has its share of critics, who call it a watchdog with no teeth; in fact, the joint commission rarely removes hospital accreditations. But whatever teeth it has, they are sharp enough to cause great stress at hospitals preparing for a joint commission inspection. At Hermann, those preparations had been under way for a year, and in the final weeks employees were given lists of possible questions, with the proper answers. Administrators walked around conducting mock reviews: What do you do in case of a fire? What is your job? How does it fit into the hospital system?

When word spread about the overdose given to Jose Martinez, therefore, the first question asked on the executive floors at Hermann was, "How did this happen?" The question asked immediately after that was, "Should we tell the joint commission?"

"They don't directly ask you, 'Did you have a sentinel event?'" Walts says, using the commission's term for a major mishap. "And it was so recent that they probably wouldn't have discovered it in our paper trail."

It was soon decided, she says, that full confession would serve the hospital best. Joanne Turnbull, chief quality and utilization officer, was assigned the task of figuring out what happened and explaining it to the visitors.

Turnbull, a take-charge woman who is a social worker and psychologist by training, spoke with each of the central figures in the case, and each interview seemed to widen the circle. Within a few days, in time for the all-important meeting, she had a sense of the scenario that had caused Jose Martinez to die.

On the Friday afternoon that the boy was admitted, she says, the attending doctor discussed the Digoxin order in detail with the resident. First, the appropriate dose was determined in micrograms, based on the baby's weight, then the micrograms were converted to milligrams. They did those calculations together, double-checked them and determined that the correct dose was .09 milligrams, to be injected into an intravenous line.

They went on to discuss a number of tests that also needed to be done, and the resident left to write the resulting list of orders on the baby's chart. With a slip of the pen that would prove fatal, the resident ordered 0.9 milligrams of Digoxin rather than .09.

The list complete, the resident went back to the attending doctor and asked, "Is there anything else I need to add on here?" The attending scanned the list, and said no, there was nothing to add. The error went unnoticed.

A copy of the order was faxed to the pharmacy, and a follow-up original copy was sent by messenger. The pharmacist on duty read the fax and thought that the amount of Digoxin was too high. The pharmacist paged the resident, and then put the order on top of the pharmacy's coffeepot, site of the unofficial "important" pile. What the pharmacist did not know was that the resident had left for the day and did not receive the page.

Sometime later, the backup copy of the as-yet-unfilled order arrived at the pharmacy. This time a technician looked at it and filled a vial with 0.9 milligrams of Digoxin. The technician then set the order and the vial together on the counter so that the pharmacist could double-check the work.

The pharmacist verified that the dosage on the prescription matched the dosage in the vial, and did not remember questioning the dosage in the first place. The order of the Digoxin was sent up to the pediatric floor.

A nurse there took the vial, read its dosage and worried that it was wrong. She approached a resident who was on call but had not personally gone over the drug calculation with the attending.

"Would you check this order," she asked. Or maybe she said, "Is this what you want me to give?"

The resident took out a calculator, redid the math and came up with .09, the correct dose. Looking from the calculator to the vial, the resident saw a "0" and a "9" on both and did not notice the difference in the decimal point.

There was one remaining step. Following procedure, the first nurse asked a second nurse to verify that the order in the chart was the same as the label on the vial. She did, and it was.

At 9:35 P.M., a troubled nurse gave Jose Martinez a dose of Digoxin that was 10 times what was intended. It took 20 minutes for the entire dose to drip through his IV tube. At 10 P.M., the baby began to vomit while drinking a bottle, the first sign of a drug overdose.

Digoxin works by changing the flux of ions in the heart, altering the cell membranes. Too much allows the heart to flood with calcium, so it cannot contract. There is an antidote, called Digibind, and the nurse, her fears confirmed, called for it immediately. But even immediately was too late.

"They killed my son," the boy's father, Jose Leonel Martinez, sobbed on the local TV news. "Those people who work there are not professional and they shouldn't be there." A restaurant worker who had moved his family from Mexico a few years earlier, Martinez was shocked that the world's best health care system could make such a mistake.

"When I asked the doctor if the medicine they were going to put in him was strong, the doctor said no, that it was normal," he said through an interpreter. "That it was just so the child would function better."

The residents and the nurse were "given some time off" during the investigation, Walts says; no one was fired. "It sobered us to realize that we've always dealt with errors as a discipline problem, yet we're not eliminating errors by firing people," she adds.

All those in the chain of error are back at work, and all are still haunted by the death of Jose Martinez. When the system fails, the patient is not the only victim. "It was an absolutely devastating thing," the attending doctor says. "The loss to the parents was indescribable. There are no words. . . . The only thing that made it possible for me to struggle through was my concern for these young people"—meaning the two residents. "I had to make them understand that this did not mean they were bad doctors."

After hearing Turnbull's account, the joint commission placed Hermann on "accreditation watch," a category so new that the hospital was in the first group to receive the designation. It required that Hermann analyze the root cause of the error—not only what went wrong, but also why it went wrong—and develop a plan to fix it.

The change of approach at Hermann, the change of approach throughout medicine, all of it had its start those frightening, disorienting, reorienting months in 1995. That was the year, says Dr. Dennis S. O'Leary, the joint commission's president, that "medicine went to hell in a handbasket."

It is impossible to tell whether errors increased significantly in 1995 and, if so, whether the increasing complexity of medicine and the concomitant cost-cutting of managed care were to blame. What is clear is that it seemed as if error was everywhere, as if the system was out of control.

The year began with the news that Betsy Lehman, 39, a health columnist for The Boston Globe, had died not of breast cancer but of a fourfold miscalculation in the amount of Cytoxan she was being given at Dana-Farber to battle her breast cancer. It happened because the total dose to be given over four days was instead given on *each* of the four days, an error that was not corrected by doctors, nurses or pharmacists.

At about the same time, a vascular surgeon at University Community Hospital, in Tampa, Fla., was accused of amputating the wrong leg. Then came reports that the wrong side of a brain had been operated on at Memorial Sloan-Kettering Cancer Center in New York. In an echo of the Dana-Farber error, a patient at the University of Chicago Hospitals died of a huge overdose of chemotherapy medication, also because the wrong dose was written down and the error wasn't noticed until the drug was administered.

The joint commission had recently visited and accredited all those hospitals. That fact alone was reason for concern at the commission's headquarters in Oakbrook Terrace, Illinois, and the immediate response was to conduct some surprise reinspections. The accreditation of the Tampa hospital was temporarily lifted, and Dana-Farber was placed on probation.

The longer-term response was to create the category of "accreditation watch." It was intended to replace the punishment of probation with a more collaborative, problem-solving approach. "The policy should not focus on what happened from an action standpoint, because you can't undo what's been done," O'Leary says. "What can be done is to reduce the likelihood of this happening in the future."

While the public feared more mistakes, and the joint commission feared overlooking mistakes, doctors began to fear something else entirely. What sobered and stunned organized medicine was not only the enormity of these errors, but also how quickly they became infamous single-sentence sound bites. The stories took on lives of their own, told and retold with no room for nuance, no blame for anyone but the bungling idiot of a doctor.

The wrong side of the brain incident at Sloan-Kettering, for instance, was quickly abbreviated into a description of a doctor who could not tell his left from right. In reality, the case was never that simple. When the surgeon stood at the operating table and cut into the wrong side of a patient's brain, it was because he was being guided by a CAT scan and an M.R.I. showing a large tumor on the same side of the brain as he cut into. The wrong set of films, those belonging to another patient, was brought into the operating room. The surgeon was fired. Now the policy at Sloan-Kettering requires a more comprehensive preoperation check, including matching X-rays with the patient's ID bracelet.

The case of the wrong leg, in Tampa, was similarly simplified into a story of a doctor who could not tell the difference between a diseased leg and a healthy one. To the contrary, the patient had two seriously diseased legs, a result of diabetes. The circulation in both was so poor that there was no pulse present in either leg and both feet were cold to the touch. A mistake on the surgical schedule said that the left leg was to be amputated. The error was noticed, but only one copy of the schedule was corrected.

When the surgeon scrubbed for the actual operation, therefore, he did so staring at an O.R. schedule saying that the left leg should be amputated. He then walked into the operating room, past a blackboard at the control desk, when also indicated that the left leg was to be amputated. The schedule inside the O.R. said the same thing. When the surgeon approached the operating table, he found his patient already completely draped, save for his ulcerated and swollen left leg, which had been prepped by the nurse for amputation. The surgeon was placed on probation for two years (but his license was reinstated after six months), and he was fined $10,000. The hospital has changed its policy so that corrections on one copy of the schedule must appear on all copies of the schedule.

For decades, the American Medical Association's approach to error has been to describe it as an aberration in a system that is basically safe. For instance, when researchers at Harvard University released a 1993 study estimating that one million preventable injuries and 120,000 preventable deaths occurred in American hospitals in a single year, the A.M.A. dismissed the study's methods as unsound and its conclusions as alarmist.

"We were very defensive on the Harvard study," says Martin J. Hatlie, executive director of the National Patient Safety Foundation at the A.M.A. "We found ourselves in a position of denying it had any validity at all," a position that sounded hollow and disingenuous, even to those within the A.M.A.

But in 1995, when everything seemed to go wrong, the denials stopped. Not directly because of the errors, but because of the fallout from the errors. Things were bad enough for medicine when doctors were seen merely as arrogant and insensitive. Now a new popular caricature was taking shape, portraying doctors as inept, if not downright murderous.

Hatlie marks the moment of change as an afternoon when the new, 104th Congress began a debate long at the center of the A.M.A.'s agenda—limits on the amount patients can be awarded in malpractice suits. Hatlie remembers losing all hope for that provision when Representative Greg Ganske, a Republican from Iowa who is also a doctor, tried to speak in favor of the bill and was interrupted by a fellow Republican, Ed Bryant of California.

"Last week a member of the gentleman's profession did some surgery down in Florida," Bryant drawled. "I heard on the radio, he was supposed to cut off a person's foot. He amputated it, and when the person woke up, they had cut off the wrong foot."

Ganske, flustered, did not respond eloquently: "It is inevitable that mistakes are going to be made."

That was when insiders at the A.M.A. stopped quibbling over how many mistakes doctors make and decided to be seen as trying to do something about those mistakes. It is when they stopped arguing about the methodology of the Harvard study and instead turned for help to Dr. Lucien Leape, the report's primary author, who was a surgeon for 20 years and now studies medical errors. That two-year-old partnership has become the basis of some tangible, structured efforts. The National Patient Safety Foundation, for instance, was designed to root out and reduce error in the way that a similar organization, the Anesthesia Patient Safety Foundation, revolutionized that segment of the industry in the 1980's. Similarly, the U.S. Pharmacopeia Convention established the National Coordinating Council for Medication Reporting and Prevention to track medication errors. And the Institute for Healthcare Improvement began a project to reduce adverse drug events.

There are also less tangible but equally important results. Specifically, all these separate efforts add up to a growing recognition that the health of health care may lie in its ability to admit and to prevent its mistakes.

"In hockey," says Nancy W. Dickey, a Texas family practitioner and chairman of the A.M.A. board of trustees, "you don't go where the puck is. You go where the puck is going to be. We're trying to go where the puck is going to be."

Human factors experts are a patient group. They sit in their laboratories and huddle over their research papers, waiting until whole industries are ready—really ready—to hear what they have to say. Skeptics turn into believers, they know, during times of confusion and remorse.

The human factors field first began in the 1940s, when psychologists and engineers came together to prevent assembly-line errors that were threatening the war effort. The 1970s brought another burst of interest, with the Three Mile Island nuclear accident and a series of plane crashes. In 1986 came the Challenger explosion.

Now it seems to be medicine's turn, and human factors researchers have been expecting the call. Even before anyone asked for their help, they had spent a lot of time analyzing that industry. From where they sat, health care was the pinnacle of challenges, the most complex of industries, the ultimate test of systems theory.

"Health care is really interesting from our point of view because it straddles the entire span, the spectrum of accidents," says James Reason, a psychology professor at the University of Manchester and one of the first human factors researchers.

In other industries, the relationships are between operators and equipment—pilots and their airplanes, nuclear plant personnel and their walls of confusing displays and dials. In medicine, the relationships involve operators, equipment and patients—patients who, by definition, are not in perfect working order, creating infinitely more ways for things to go wrong.

It was inevitable, human factors experts agree, that medicine would eventually shed its resistance to being seen as a system in which human beings were but one fallible component. That it took a string of tragedies to spur that realization is probably also inevitable. The first step, researchers are telling clinicians, is to accept that perfect human performance is not an attainable goal. People are not perfect outside a hospital. Half asleep, they spray deodorant on their heads and hair spray under their arms. Distracted, they write the wrong dates on checks. On autopilot, they leave their phone numbers when they mean to leave their fax numbers.

They are equally imperfect inside a hospital. They write the cumulative chemotherapy dose instead of the daily dose. They write "left leg" when they mean "right leg."

Admitting to imperfection is a first step for medicine, because many in the profession seem to believe that they can be perfect, says Robert L. Helmreich, a human factors expert at the University of Texas at Austin who spent years helping airlines teach pilots that they were fallible. "They think they're bullet-proof," Helmreich says.

He cites a 1988 survey of pilots in which 42 percent agreed with the statement, "Even when I am fatigued, I perform effectively." He was amazed by that until 1996, when he gave the same survey to surgeons, anesthesiologists and nurses and found that 60 percent agreed with the statement.

The central problem with the belief in perfection is that hospital systems are designed around it. They rely on concentration—that the nurse, for instance, will connect the nutrition bag to the nutrition line and not to the dialysis line. But things should be designed, human factors experts would argue, so that the connective port on the nutrition bag fits only into the connective port on the nutrition line.

Systems based on perfection also deny the possibility of confusion—trusting that a nurse will always double-check whether she is dispensing the right drug and not a similarly packaged or a similarly named one. And they depend on memory—on a resident remembering to write down the correct dose of Digoxin, rather than on a computer system devised so that it won't accept a prescription with an erroneous dose of Digoxin.

The possible remedies for this dependence are many, and they vary with the problems of each hospital, which leads to perhaps the most important message of human factors research. "You cannot solve your problems," says David Woods, a professor of cognitive systems engineering at Ohio State University, "until you know what they are. And you will not know what they are unless you create an environment where people feel free to tell you."

Every industry that has substantially reduced error, experts say, has created a blame-free environment for reporting errors. And that includes not only actual errors, but also near misses, which have traditionally been seen as evidence of the strength of the system, but are more likely examples of errors waiting to happen.

For instance, an airline pilot must carry a form as part of the Aviation Safety Reporting System. When he makes or sees a major foulup, Helmreich says, he fills out that form—including his name—and sends it to NASA. The agency has a week to contact the pilot for amplification or clarification. Then the information is put in a computer, but without the pilot's name.

While the thorough and honest reporting of error is a central message of the experts, it is the trickiest for medicine to hear. Some hospitals are trying: James Conway at Dana-Farber, for one, has sent thank-you notes to staff members who report errors. But this zealous honesty does not come easily to a profession trained to understand that anything written down is discoverable evidence in a malpractice suit; it doesn't help that many states have chosen to confront error by publishing lists of doctors who have been disciplined or sued. In fact, no one is more interested in these latest changes by doctors than malpractice lawyers.

"On the surface, it does sound intriguing," says Judith A. Livingston, a personal injury lawyer at Kramer, Dillof, Tessel, Duffy & Moore in Manhattan. "But of course I'm skeptical." She does not see health care workers the same way human factors researchers do, and worries that this is merely a way for doctors to avoid blame. Yes, she says, the system often fails, but that does not mean that the individuals in that system are not responsible for their contributory actions.

"You can't just say, 'Everyone makes mistakes,'" she says. "If a reporter makes a mistake in a magazine article, you can run a correction," but when health care workers make a mistake, "someone dies. The gravity is so much greater. The responsibility should be greater, too."

It is too early to tell, malpractice lawyers say, what the effects of this systems approach will be on medical malpractice suits. If the new thinking does in fact reduce errors, it follows that it will reduce lawsuits. But the very methods used to root out error—admitting it, measuring it, discussing it—have the side effect of providing evidence of error, evidence that plaintiffs' lawyers are eager to see.

In most states the results of internal surveys would be protected by laws of privilege. But

Thomas Demetrio of the Chicago personal injury firm Corboy & Demetrio believes public pressure might cause that to change. If hospitals begin legitimate investigations of their error rate, "the consumer is entitled to know the findings," he says. "If the numbers are there, and they are solid, they'll come out."

To hospitals, anything that intrigues malpractice lawyers is unsettling, which is the major stumbling block for those who would like to see a human factors takeover of health care. When the joint commission created the category of accreditation watch, for instance, the agency saw it as a nonpunitive way to monitor hospital error. The hospitals saw it as something else entirely.

"It was supposed to be a neutral, nonjudgmental designation," says O'Leary, of the joint commission. "We thought we were saying, 'You tell us about your sentinel events, and we'll work together on the solutions.'"

Turnbull, of Hermann Hospital, responds: "They say, 'Report, report, report,' and then when you report, they punish you. They give the information to the newspapers."

O'Leary admits that "the policy is a work in progress—I would not be surprised to see us come back with a further iteration this fall."

Ben Kolb was scared when he arrived at Martin Memorial Hospital, in Stuart, Fla., in December 1995. This was to be the third ear operation on the 7-year-old Ben. His doctor wanted to remove scar tissue that was left from the prior surgeries, at ages 2 and 5.

So his mother, Tammy, spent the time before surgery joking with her son, talking about soccer (he was the captain of his team) and Christmas (when he would be singing in the yearly pageant at school). By the time an orderly came to take the boy into surgery, he was calm.

"Give your mom a kiss," the nurse said, and he did. "Have fun," his mother said, waving as he left.

Ben was given general anesthesia, and about 20 minutes later it took full effect. His surgeon was handed what everyone thought was a syringe of lidocaine, a local anesthetic, which reduces bleeding. He injected it inside and behind Ben's ear. Moments later, for no apparent reason, Ben's heart rate and blood pressure increased alarmingly. Dr. George McLain, an anesthesiologist on standby for emergencies, was summoned. McLain helped to stabilize the child, but a short time later Ben's heart rate and blood pressure dropped precipitously. For an hour and 40 minutes, frantic doctors performed CPR on the boy, knowing it was futile.

More than a year later, the memories are fresh, and McLain sits at lunch, crying as he speaks. The other diners stare, but he makes no attempt to hide the tears.

How long would he have kept up the CPR?

"If it was my kid, I would want them to keep trying," he says. "I think we were never going to stop."

Ben's heart did begin to beat again, and he was transferred to Martin Memorial's intensive-care unit. The surgeon, who had known Ben since he was a baby, went with McLain to talk to Tammy Kolb. "There has been a serious problem with your son," McLain remembers telling the woman. "His heart stopped. We had to restart his heart. He is extremely critical, in a comalike state."

He winces at the memory: "You don't know how strong to be to get your point across. You want her to understand, but you can't stick a knife in her."

At first, Tammy Kolb did not seem to understand. "I know he's going to wake up just fine," she said.

"I don't—," McLain said.

"I've seen this on TV. As soon as he wakes up I have a Christmas present for him. I brought it for him early."

Ben remained in a coma for nearly 24 hours. His parents and older sister remained at his bedside as their fog of denial slowly lifted. The next day they agreed that his ventilator should be removed, and he was declared brain dead. As with the death of Jose Martinez, a lot can be learned by what happened after Ben Kolb died.

First, the hospital's risk manager, Doni Haas, had all the syringes and vials used on Ben locked away, then sent to an independent laboratory for analysis. Second, Haas promised Ben's parents that she "was going to find them an answer, if there was one."

There was. Tests showed that there had been a mixup, a mistake, a human error in a system that made that error more likely. Ben Kolb, lab reports showed, was never injected with lidocaine at all. The syringe that was supposed to contain lidocaine actually contained adrenaline, a highly concentrated strength that was intended only for external use.

Procedure in the Martin Memorial operating room at the time was for topical adrenaline to be poured into one cup, made of plastic, and lidocaine to be poured into a cup nearby, made of metal. The lidocaine syringe was then filled by placing it in the metal cup. It is a procedure used all over the country, a way of getting a drug from container to operating table. According to Richmond Harman, the hospital's C.E.O., "It has probably been done 100,000 times in our facility without error."

But it is a flawed procedure, the hospital learned. It allows for the possibility that the solution can be poured into or drawn out of the wrong cup. Instead, a cap, called a spike, could be put on the vial of lidocaine, allowing the drug to be drawn directly out of the labeled bottle and into a labeled syringe. The elimination of one step eliminates one opportunity for the human factor to get in the way.

Haas received the lab results three weeks after Ben died. The family had hired an attorney by then, and Haas and McLain drove two hours and met with the Kolbs at Krupnick, Campbell, Malone, Roselli, Buser, Slama & Hancock.

"It was very unusual," says Richard J. Roselli, one of Florida's most successful malpractice lawyers and the president of the Academy of Florida Trial Lawyers. "This is the first occasion where I ever had a hospital step forward, admitting their responsibility and seeking to do everything they can to help the family."

A financial settlement was reached by nightfall, but neither side will confirm the amount paid to the Kolbs.

After the papers were signed, the family asked for a chance to talk with the doctors at the hospital. The first thing Ben's father, Tim, did when he entered the emotion-filled room was to hug his son's surgeon. Then came the torrent of questions, questions that had kept the Kolbs awake at night, questions they might never have been able to ask had the case spent years in court.

Was Ben scared when his heart rate started dropping? Was he in pain? How much did he suffer?

The doctors explained what the Kolbs did not know, that Ben had been put under general anesthesia long before anything went wrong.

"The decisions I made for him were the same I would have made if it were my child," McLain said.

Just before the family left, they asked if it would be O.K. for them to continue to use Martin Memorial for their medical care.

"Of course," Haas said, grateful and amazed.

Would the hospital promise to spread the word about how Ben died, so that the procedure in question could be changed in other places?

Haas promised.

With that, the Kolb case was closed, but it wasn't over. Tom Kolb still coaches his son's soccer team. The family still grieves.

The doctors in the operating room that day still have nightmares of their own. "I let that child's life slip through my fingers," McLain says. "They tell me there was nothing I could do. I know there was nothing I could do. But it's like I was a lifeguard and he died on my watch. There must have been something."

And the lawyers at Krupnick, Campbell are still searching, too.

"We're not done with this yet," Roselli says. Why, he asks, was it possible to mix up the lidocaine and the adrenaline? Did the two bottles look alike? "We're still investigating the product liability aspect of it," he says. "The questions of packaging and labeling."

Joanne Turnbull did not fully realize she was part of a sea change until she was in a Palm Springs auditorium last October—two months after the death of Jose Martinez, nearly two years after the death of Betsy Lehman, one day after what would have been Ben Kolb's eighth birthday—and marveled at what was going on around her.

At the front of the room were representatives from Martin Memorial Hospital. Keeping their promise to the Kolb family, the group spent nearly two hours retelling the story of how and why the boy died. In the audience, fighting tears as they took notes, were more than 300 doctors, nurses, pharmacists and administrators, each of whom had been given a smiling photograph of the child at the three-day conference on "Examining Errors in Health Care."

"Five years ago if we'd held this conference, very few people would have come," Leape, of Harvard, said at the operating session. But the list of sponsors included not only the A.M.A. and the joint commission, but also four medical insurance organizations, three pharmaceutical groups and the American Hospital Association.

"This is a miracle that this is happening," Turnbull remembers thinking as the session concluded. "Everyone's telling the truth."

In the months since Jose Martinez died, Turnbull has become an expert herself on the world of human factors research. She has done her root-cause analysis for the joint commission and learned a lot more about what went wrong that night: that the hospital's pharmacy was short one technician because someone called in sick and that policies there require that the phone be answered in four rings and visitors greeted within five seconds of their arrival; that the nurse who questioned the order was trained in a country where women rarely confront men and nurses rarely confront doctors; that the first resident was distracted by personal problems. Turnbull has made changes, too, ones she hopes will be strong enough to make such human imperfections matter less. Hermann Hospital's computer now flags questionable orders for the most dangerous drugs, including Digoxin. The hospital is looking into a paging system that alerts a caller when the person being paged has his beeper turned off. Double copies of a prescription are no longer sent to the pharmacy unless it is a prescription that must be filled within 15 minutes.

Administrators even asked the joint commission to schedule its accreditation review for April, not August, to ease the stress during the hospital's busiest month. Two research experiments are being planned to increase error reporting.

As a result of Turnbull's analysis, and the accompanying changes, Hermann Hospital is no longer under "accreditation watch." On Dec. 27, 1996, it was given full accreditation, with commendation, the highest designation given by the joint commission.

That brings satisfaction, she says, but mostly she feels sadness for the little boy and his family and concern for the staff members who are also still burdened by the event. She is wary, too, because everything she has learned tells her that no institution can ever be certain that something like this will not happen again. And she feels a sense of responsibility, an understanding that this moment and movement might well be seen as a crossroads for medicine. "We've become part of something," she says. "We want to make sure it is something that's done right."

**LEGAL PERSPECTIVES**

# Federal Sentencing Guidelines—Sentencing of Organizations

## INTRODUCTORY COMMENTARY

*The guidelines and policy statements in this chapter apply when the convicted defendant is an organization. Organizations can act only through agents and, under federal criminal law, generally are vicariously liable for offenses committed by their agents. At the same time, individual agents are responsible for their own criminal conduct. Federal prosecutions of organizations therefore frequently involve individual and organizational co-defendants. Convicted individual agents of organizations are sentenced in accordance with the guidelines and policy statements in the preceding chapters. This chapter is designed so that the sanctions imposed upon organizations and their agents, taken together, will provide just punishment, adequate deterrence, and incentives for organizations to maintain internal mechanisms for preventing, detecting, and reporting criminal conduct.*

*This chapter reflects the following general principles: First, the court must, whenever practicable, order the organization to remedy any harm caused by the offense. The resources expended to remedy the harm should not be viewed as punishment, but rather as a means of making victims whole for the harm caused. Second, if the organization operated primarily for a criminal purpose or primarily by criminal means, the fine should be set sufficiently high to divest the organization of all its assets. Third, the fine range for any other organization should be based on the seriousness of the offense and the culpability of the organization. The seriousness of the offense generally will be reflected by the highest of the pecuniary gain, the pecuniary loss, or the amount in a guideline offense level fine table. Culpability generally will be determined by the steps taken by the organization prior to the offense to prevent and detect criminal conduct, the level and extent of involvement in or tolerance of the offense by certain personnel, and the organization's actions after an offense has been committed. Fourth, probation is an appropriate sentence for an organizational defendant when needed to ensure that another sanction will be fully implemented, or to ensure that steps will be taken within the organization to reduce the likelihood of future criminal conduct.*

## PART A—GENERAL APPLICATION PRINCIPLES

### §8A1.1. Applicability of Chapter Eight

This chapter applies to the sentencing of all organizations for felony and Class A misdemeanor offenses.

### Commentary

Application Notes:

1. "Organization" means "a person other than an individual." 18 U.S.C. § 18. The term includes corporations, partnerships, associations, joint-stock companies, unions, trusts, pension funds, unincorporated organizations, governments and political subdivisions thereof, and non-profit organizations. . . .
3. The following are definitions of terms used frequently in this chapter:

* * *

Reprinted with permission from *The United States Law Week*, Vol. 50 pp. 4226–29 (March 26, 1991). Published by The Bureau of National Affairs, Inc. (800–372–1033)

(k) An "effective program to prevent and detect violations of law" means a program that has been reasonably designed, implemented, and enforced so that it generally will be effective in preventing and detecting criminal conduct. Failure to prevent or detect the instant offense, by itself, does not mean that the program was not effective. The hallmark of an effective program to prevent and detect violations of law is that the organization exercised due diligence in seeking to prevent and detect criminal conduct by its employees and other agents. Due diligence requires at a minimum that the organization must have taken the following types of steps:

(1) The organization must have established compliance standards and procedures to be followed by its employees and other agents that are reasonably capable of reducing the prospect of criminal conduct.

(2) Specific individual(s) within high-level personnel of the organization must have been assigned overall responsibility to oversee compliance with such standards and procedures.

(3) The organization must have used due care not to delegate substantial discretionary authority to individuals whom the organization knew, or should have known through the exercise of due diligence, had a propensity to engage in illegal activities.

(4) The organization must have taken steps to communicate effectively its standards and procedures to all employees and other agents, e.g., by requiring participation in training programs or by disseminating publications that explain in a practical manner what is required.

(5) The organization must have taken reasonable steps to achieve compliance with its standards, e.g., by utilizing monitoring and auditing systems reasonably designed to detect criminal conduct by its employees and other agents and by having in place and publicizing a reporting system whereby employees and other agents could report criminal conduct by others within the organization without fear of retribution.

(6) The standards must have been consistently enforced through appropriate disciplinary mechanisms, including, as appropriate, discipline of individuals responsible for the failure to detect an offense. Adequate discipline of individuals responsible for an offense is a necessary component of enforcement; however, the form of discipline that will be appropriate will be case specific.

(7) After an offense has been detected, the organization must have taken all reasonable steps to respond appropriately to the offense and to prevent further similar offenses—including any necessary modifications to its program to prevent and detect violations of law.

The precise actions necessary for an effective program to prevent and detect violations of law will depend upon a number of factors. Among the relevant factors are:

(i) Size of the organization—The requisite degree of formality of a program to prevent and detect violations of law will vary with the size of the organization: the larger the organization, the more formal the program typically should be. A larger organization generally should have established written policies defining the standards and procedures to be followed by its employees and other agents.

(ii) Likelihood that certain offenses may occur because of the nature of its business—If because of the nature of an organization's business there is a substantial risk that certain types of offenses may occur, management must have taken steps to prevent and detect those types of offenses. For example, if an organization handles toxic substances, it must have established standards and procedures designed to ensure that those substances are properly handled at all times. If an organization employs sales personnel who have flexibility in setting prices, it must have established standards and procedures designed to prevent and detect price-fixing. If an organization employs sales personnel who have flexibility to represent the material characteristics of a product, it must have established standards and procedures designed to prevent fraud.

(iii) Prior history of the organization—An organization's prior history may indicate types of offenses that it should have taken actions to prevent. Recurrence of misconduct similar to that which an organization has previously committed casts doubt on whether it took all reasonable steps to prevent such misconduct.

An organization's failure to incorporate and follow applicable industry practice or the standards called for by any applicable governmental regulation weighs against a finding of an effective program to prevent and detect violations of law.

## PART B—REMEDYING HARM FROM CRIMINAL CONDUCT

### Introductory Commentary

*As a general principle, the court should require that the organization take all appropriate steps to provide compensation to victims and otherwise remedy the harm caused or threatened by the offense. A restitution order or an order of probation requiring restitution can be used to compensate identifiable victims of the offense. A remedial order or an order of probation requiring community service can be used to reduce or eliminate the harm threatened, or to repair the harm caused by the offense, when that harm or threatened harm would otherwise not be remedied. An order of notice to victims can be used to notify unidentified victims of the offense. . . .*

* * *

### 2. Determining the Fine—Other Organizations

* * *

### §8C2.4. Base Fine

(a) The Base Fine is the greatest of:
  (1) the amount from the table in subsection (d) below corresponding to the offense level determined under §8C2.3 (Offense Level); or
  (2) the pecuniary gain to the organization from the offense; or
  (3) the pecuniary loss from the offense caused by the organization, to the extent the loss was caused intentionally, knowingly, or recklessly.

(b) *Provided*, that if the applicable offense guideline in Chapter Two includes a special instruction for organizational fines, that special instruction shall be applied, as appropriate.

(c) *Provided, further*, that to the extent the calculation of either pecuniary gain or pecuniary loss would unduly complicate or prolong the sentencing process, that amount, *i.e.*, gain or loss as appropriate, shall not be used for the determination of the bass fine.

(d) Offence Level Fine Table

| *Offense Level* | *Amount* |
|---|---|
| 6 or less | $5,000 |
| 7 | $7,500 |
| 8 | $10,000 |
| 9 | $15,000 |
| 10 | $20,000 |
| 11 | $30,000 |
| 12 | $40,000 |
| 13 | $60,000 |
| 14 | $85,000 |
| 15 | $125,000 |
| 16 | $175,000 |
| 17 | $250,000 |
| 18 | $350,000 |
| 19 | $500,000 |
| 20 | $650,000 |
| 21 | $910,000 |
| 22 | $1,200,000 |
| 23 | $1,600,000 |
| 24 | $2,100,000 |
| 25 | $2,800,000 |
| 26 | $3,700,000 |
| 27 | $4,800,000 |
| 28 | $6,300,000 |
| 29 | $8,100,000 |
| 30 | $10,500,000 |
| 31 | $13,500,000 |
| 32 | $17,500,000 |
| 33 | $22,000,000 |
| 34 | $28,500,000 |
| 35 | $36,000,000 |
| 36 | $45,500,000 |
| 37 | $57,500,000 |
| 38 or more | $72,500,000 |

* * *

## §8C2.5. Culpability Score

(a) Start with 5 points and apply subsetions (b) through (g) below.

(b) Involvement in or Tolerance of Criminal Activity

If more than one applies, use the greatest:

(1) If—

(A) the organization had 5,000 or more employees and

(i) an individual within high-level personal of the organization participated in, condoned, or was willfully ignorant of the offense; or

(ii) tolerance of the offense by substantial authority personnel was pervasive throughout the organization; or

(B) the unit of the organization within which the offense was committed had 5,000 or more employees and

(i) an individual within high-level personnel of the unit participated in, condoned, or was willfully ignorant of the offense; or

(ii) tolerance of the offense by substantial authority personnel was pervasive throughout such unit, add 5 points; or

(2) If—

(A) the organization had 1,000 or more employees and

(i) an individual within high-level personnel of the organization participated in, condoned, or was willfully ignorant of the offense; or

(ii) tolerance of the offense by substantial authority personnel was pervasive throughout the organization; or

(B) the unit of the organization within which the offense was committed had 1,000 or more employees and

(i) an individual within high-level personnel of the unit participated in, condoned, or was willfully ignorant of the offense; or

(ii) tolerance of the offense by substantial authority personnel was pervasive throughout such unit, add 4 points; or

(3) If—

(A) the organization had 200 or more employees and

(i) an individual within high-level personnel of the organization participated in, condoned, or was willfully ignorant of the offense; or

(ii) tolerance of the offense by substantial authority personnel was pervasive throughout the organization; or

(B) the unit of the organization within which the offense was committed had 200 or more employees and

(i) an individual within high-level personnel of the unit participated in, condoned, or was willfully ignorant of the offense; or

(ii) tolerance of the offense by substantial authority personnel was pervasive throughout such unit, add 3 points; or

(4) If the organization had 50 or more employees and an individual within substantial authority personnel participated in, condoned, or was willfully ignorant of the offense, add 2 points; or

(5) If the organization had 10 or more employees and an individual within substantial authority personnel participated in, condoned, or was willfully ignorant of the offense, add 1 point.

(c) Prior History

If more than one applies, use the greater:

(1) If the organization (or separately managed line of business) committed any part of the instant offense less than 10 years after (A) a criminal adjudication based on similar misconduct; or (B) civil or administrative adjudication(s) based on two or more separate instances of similar misconduct, add 1 point; or

(2) If the organization (or separately managed line of business) committed any part of the instant offense less than 5 years after (A) a criminal adjudication based on similar misconduct; or (B) civil or administrative adjudication(s) based on two or more separate instances of similar misconduct, add 2 points.

(d) Violation of an Order

If more than one applies, use the greater:

(1) (A) If the commission of the instant offense violated a judicial order or injunction, other than a violation of a condition of probation; or (B) if the organization (or separately managed line of business) violated a condition of probation by engaging in similar misconduct, *i.e.*, misconduct similar to that for which it was placed on probation, add 2 points; or

(2) If the commission of the instant offense violated a condition of probation, add 1 point.

(e) Obstruction of Justice

If the organization willfully obstructed or impeded, attempted to obstruct or impede, or aided, abetted, or encouraged obstruction of justice during the investigation, prosecution, or sentencing of the instant offense, or, with knowledge thereof, failed to take reasonable steps to prevent such obstruction or impedance or attempted obstruction or impedance, add 3 points.

(f) Effective Program to Prevent and Detect Violations of Law

If the offense occurred despite an effective program to prevent and detect violations of law, subtract 3 points.

*Provided*, that this subsection does not apply if an individual within high-level personnel of the organization, a person within high-level personnel of the unit of the organization within which the offense was committed where the unit had 200 or more employees, or an individual responsible for the administration or enforcement of a program to prevent and detect violations of law participated in, condoned, or was willfully ignorant of the offense. Participation of an individual within substantial authority personnel in an offense results in a rebuttable presumption that the organization did not have an effective program to prevent and detect violations of law.

*Provided, further*, that this subsection does not apply if, after becoming aware of an offense, the organization unreasonably delayed reporting the offense to appropriate governmental authorities.

(g) Self-Reporting, Cooperation, and Acceptance of Responsibility

If more than one applies, use the greatest:

(1) If the organization (A) prior to an imminent threat of disclosure or government investigation; and (B) within a reasonably prompt time after becoming aware of the offense, reported the offense to appropriate governmental authorities, fully cooperated in the investigation, and clearly demonstrated recognition and affirmative acceptance of responsibility for its criminal conduct, subtract 5 points; or

(2) If the organization fully cooperated in the investigation and clearly demonstrated recognition and affirmative acceptance of responsibility for its criminal conduct, subtract 2 points; or

(3) If the organization clearly demonstrated recognition and affirmative acceptance of responsibility for its criminal conduct, subtract 1 point. . . .

## §8C.2.6. Minimum and Maximum Multipliers

Using the culpability score from §8C2.5 (Culpability Score) and applying any applicable special instruction for fines in Chapter Two, determine the applicable minimum and maximum fine multipliers from the table below.

| *Culpability Score* | *Minimum Multiplier* | *Maximum Multiplier* |
|---|---|---|
| 10 or more | 2.00 | 4.00 |
| 9 | 1.80 | 3.60 |
| 8 | 1.60 | 3.20 |
| 7 | 1.40 | 2.80 |
| 6 | 1.20 | 2.40 |
| 5 | 1.00 | 2.00 |
| 4 | 0.80 | 1.60 |
| 3 | 0.60 | 1.20 |
| 2 | 0.40 | 0.80 |
| 1 | 0.20 | 0.40 |
| 0 or less | 0.05 | 0.20 |

* * *

## §8C2.8. Determining the Fine Within the Range (Policy Statement)

(a) In determining the amount of the fine within the applicable guideline range, the court should consider:

(1) the need for the sentence to reflect the seriousness of the offense, promote respect for the law, provide just punishment, afford adequate deterrence, and protect the public from further crimes of the organization;
(2) the organization's role in the offense;
(3) any collateral consequences of conviction, including civil obligations arising from the organization's conduct;
(4) any nonpecuniary loss caused or threatened by the offense;
(5) whether the offense involved a vulnerable victim;
(6) any prior criminal record of an individual within high-level personnel of the organization or high-level personnel of a unit of the organization who participated in, condoned, or was willfully ignorant of the criminal conduct;
(7) any prior civil or criminal misconduct by the organization other than that counted under §8C2.5(c);
(8) any culpability score under §8C2.5 (Culpability Score) higher than 10 or lower than 0;
(9) partial but incomplete satisfaction of the conditions for one or more of the mitigating or aggravating factors set forth in §8C2.5 (Culpability Score); and
(10) any factor listed in 18 U.S.C. § 3572(a).

(b) In addition, the court may consider the relative importance of any factor used to determine the range, including the pecuniary loss caused by the offense, the pecuniary gain from the offense, any specific offense characteristic used to determine the offense level, and any aggravating or mitigating factor used to determine the culpability score.

# *United States v. Bank of New England*

*United States Court of Appeals for the First Circuit*

## THE ISSUES

The Bank was found guilty of having failed to file CTRs* on cash withdrawals made by James McDonough. It is undisputed that on thirty-one separate occasions between May 1983 and July 1984, McDonough withdrew from the Prudential Branch of the Bank more than $10,000 in cash by using multiple checks—each one individually under $10,000—presented simultaneously to a single bank teller. The Bank contends that such conduct did not trigger the Act's reporting requirements. It also urges that felony liability should not have been imposed because it did not engage in a pattern of illegal activity. In addition, the Bank avers that, if it did commit a felony violation, it did not commit thirty-one of them. The Bank also argues that the trial judge's instructions on willfulness were fatally flawed, and that, in any event, the evidence did not suffice to show that it willfully failed to file CTRs on McDonough's transactions. Finally, the Bank submits that during her charge to the jury, the trial judge erroneously alluded to evidence of the Bank's conduct after the dates specified in the indictment.

The Bank had been named in a federal grand jury indictment which was returned on October 15, 1985. Count One of the indictment alleged that between May 1983 and May 1985, James McDonough, the Bank, and Carol Orlandella and Patricia Murphy—both of whom were former head tellers with the Bank's Prudential Branch—unlawfully conspired to conceal from the IRS thirty-six of McDonough's currency transactions. The trial court directed a verdict of acquittal on this count. Defendants

*Currency Transaction Reports (ed.)

821 F. 2nd 844 (1987). Opinion by Judge Bownes.

Murphy and Orlandella were found not guilty of charges that they individually aided and abetted the failure to file CTRs on McDonough's transactions.

The bulk of the indictment alleged that the Bank, as principal, and McDonough, as an aider and abettor, willfully failed to file CTRs on thirty-six occasions between May 1983 and July 1984. Five counts were dismissed because, on those occasions, McDonough received cashier's checks from the Bank, rather than currency. McDonough was acquitted of all charges against him. The Bank was found guilty on the thirty-one remaining counts. We affirm. . . .[†]

## IV. WILLFULNESS OF THE BANK'S CONDUCT

### A. The Trial Court's Instruction on Willfulness

Criminal liability under 31 U.S.C. § 5322 only attaches when a financial institution "willfully" violates the CTR filing requirement. A finding of willfulness under the Reporting Act must be supported by "proof of the defendant's knowledge of the reporting requirements and his specific intent to commit the crime." Willfulness can rarely be proven by direct evidence, since it is a state of mind; it is usually established by drawing reasonable inferences from the available facts.

The Bank contends that the trial court's instructions on knowledge and specific intent effectively relieved the government of its responsibility to prove that the Bank acted willfully. The trial judge began her instructions on this element by outlining generally the concepts of knowledge and willfulness:

> Knowingly simply means voluntarily and intentionally. It's designed to exclude a failure that is done by mistake or accident, or for some other innocent reason. Willfully means voluntarily, intentionally, and with a specific intent to disregard, to disobey the law, with a bad purpose to violate the law.

The trial judge properly instructed the jury that it could infer knowledge if a defendant consciously avoided learning about the reporting requirements. The court then focused on the kind of proof that would establish the Bank's knowledge of its filing obligations. The judge instructed that the knowledge of individual employees acting within the scope of their employment is imputed to the Bank. She told the jury that "if any employee knew that multiple checks would require the filing of reports, the bank knew it, provided the employee knew it within the scope of his employment, . . ."

The trial judge then focused on the issue of "collective knowledge":

> In addition, however, you have to look at the bank as an institution. As such, its knowledge is the sum of the knowledge of all of the employees. That is, the bank's knowledge is the totality of what all of the employees know within the scope of their employment. So, if Employee A knows one facet of the currency reporting requirement, B knows another facet of it, and C a third facet of it, the bank knows them all. So if you find that an employee within the scope of his employment knew that CTRs had to be filed, even if multiple checks are used, the bank is deemed to know it. The bank is also deemed to know it if each of several employees knew a part of that requirement and the sum of what the separate employees knew amounted to knowledge that such a requirement existed.

After discussing the two modes of establishing knowledge—via either knowledge of one of its individual employees or the aggregate knowledge of all its employees—the trial judge turned to the issue of specific intent:

> There is a similar double business with respect to the concept of willfulness with respect to the bank. In deciding whether the bank acted willfully, again you have to look first at the conduct of all employees and officers, and, second, at what the bank did or did not do as an institution. The

[†]Sections II and III are omitted.

> bank is deemed to have acted willfully if one of its employees in the scope of his employment acted willfully. So, if you find that an employee willfully failed to do what was necessary to file these reports, then that is deemed to be the act of the bank, and the bank is deemed to have willfully failed to file.
>
> . . . .
>
> Alternatively, the bank as an institution has certain responsibilities; as an organization, it has certain responsibilities. And you will have to determine whether the bank as an organization consciously avoided learning about and observing CTR requirements. The Government to prove the bank guilty on this theory, has to show that its failure to file was the result of some flagrant organizational indifference. In this connection, you should look at the evidence as to the bank's effort, if any, to inform its employees of the law; its effort to check on their compliance; its response to various bits of information that it got in August and September of '84 and February of '85; its policies, and how it carried out its stated policies.
>
> . . . .
>
> If you find that the Government has proven with respect to any transaction either that an employee within the scope of his employment willfully failed to file a required report or that the bank was flagrantly indifferent to its obligations, then you may find that the bank has willfully failed to file the required reports.

The Bank contends that the trial court's instructions regarding knowledge were defective because they eliminated the requirement that it be proven that the Bank violated a known legal duty. It avers that the knowledge instruction invited the jury to convict the Bank for negligently maintaining a poor communications network that prevented the consolidation of the information held by its various employees. The Bank argues that it is error to find that a corporation possesses a particular item of knowledge if one part of the corporation has half the information making up the item, and another part of the entity has the other half.

A collective knowledge instruction is entirely appropriate in the context of corporate criminal liability. The acts of a corporation are, after all, simply the acts of all of its employees operating within the scope of their employment. The law on corporate criminal liability reflects this. Similarly, the knowledge obtained by corporate employees acting within the scope of their employment is imputed to the corporation. Corporations compartmentalize knowledge, subdividing the elements of specific duties and operations into smaller components. The aggregate of those components constitutes the corporation's knowledge of a particular operation. It is irrelevant whether employees administering one component of an operation know the specific activities of employees administering another aspect of the operation:

> [A] corporation cannot plead innocence by asserting that the information obtained by several employees was not acquired by any one individual who then would have comprehended its full import. Rather the corporation is considered to have acquired the collective knowledge of its employees and is held responsible for their failure to act accordingly.

Since the Bank had the compartmentalized structure common to all large corporations, the court's collective knowledge instruction was not only proper but necessary.

Nor do we find any defects in the trial court's instructions on specific intent. The court told the jury that the concept of willfulness entails a voluntary, intentional, and bad purpose to disobey the law. Her instructions on this element, when viewed as a whole, directed the jury not to convict for accidental, mistaken or inadvertent acts or omissions. It is urged that the court erroneously charged that willfulness could be found via flagrant indifference by the Bank toward its reporting obligations. With respect to federal regulatory statutes, the Supreme Court has endorsed defining willfulness, in both civil and criminal contexts, as "a disregard for the governing statute and an indifference to its requirements." Accordingly, we find no error in the court's instruction on willfulness.

### B. Evidence of Willfulness

The Bank asserts that the evidence did not suffice to show that it had willfully failed to comply with the Act's reporting requirements. We review the evidence in the light most favorable to the government.

As already discussed, the language of the Treasury regulations itself gave notice that cash withdrawals over $10,000 were reportable, regardless of the number of checks used. Primary responsibility for CTR compliance in the Bank's branch offices was assigned to head tellers and branch managers. Head tellers Orlandella and Murphy, who knew of the nature of McDonough's transactions, also knew of the CTR filing obligations imposed by the Bank. The jury heard testimony from former bank teller Simona Wong, who stated that she knew McDonough's transactions were reportable, and that the source of her knowledge was head teller Murphy.

Even if some Bank personnel mistakenly regarded McDonough as engaging in multiple transactions, there was convincing evidence that the Bank knew that his withdrawals were reportable. An internal memo sent in May 1983 by project coordinator Jayne Brady to all branch managers and head tellers stated that "'reportable transactions are expanded to include multiple transactions which aggregate more than $10,000 in any *one day*.' This includes deposits or withdrawals by a customer to or from more than one account." The Prudential Branch Manual instructed that if Bank personnel know that a customer has engaged in multiple transactions totalling $10,000 or more, then such transactions should be regarded as a single transaction. In addition, since 1980, the instructions on the back of CTR forms have directed that reports be filed on multiple transactions which aggregate to over $10,000. Finally, a Bank auditor discussed with Orlandella and Murphy, the Bank's obligation to report a customer's multiple transactions in a single day which amount to more than $10,000. We do not suggest that these evidentiary items in themselves legally bound the Bank to report McDonough's transactions; it is the language of the regulations that impose such a duty. This evidence, however, proved that the Bank had ample knowledge that transactions like McDonough's came within the purview of the Act.

Regarding the Bank's specific intent to violate the reporting obligation, Simona Wong testified that head teller Patricia Murphy knew that McDonough's transactions were reportable but, on one occasion, deliberately chose not to file a CTR on him because he was "a good customer." In addition, the jury heard testimony that bank employees regarded McDonough's transactions as unusual, speculated that he was a bookie, and suspected that he was structuring his transactions to avoid the Act's reporting requirements. An internal Bank memo, written after an investigation of the McDonough transactions, concluded that a "person managing the branch would have to have known that something strange was going on." Given the suspicions aroused by McDonough's banking practices and the abundance of information indicating that his transactions were reportable, the jury could have concluded that the failure by Bank personnel to, at least, inquire about the reportability of McDonough's transactions constituted flagrant indifference to the obligations imposed by the Act.

We hold that the evidence was sufficient for a finding of willfulness. . . .

# *State of South Dakota v. Hy Vee Food Stores, Inc.*

*Supreme Court of South Dakota*

## OPINION

A corporation appeals its misdemeanor conviction for selling an alcoholic beverage to a person under age, twenty-one. We affirm.

As part of an undercover sting operation Sioux Falls police sent a nineteen-year-old college student into a Hy Vee grocery store on March 19, 1993 to attempt to purchase liquor. Wearing a college sweatshirt and football jacket, the police infiltrator carried a bottle of whiskey to the checkout counter. Too young to sell liquor herself the cashier asked an older employee to scan the item. The cashier then took the purchase money and rang up the sale. Neither employee asked for identification to verify the purchaser's age.

Based upon the actions of these two employees, Hy Vee Food Stores, Inc. was charged with and found guilty in magistrate court of violating SDCL 35-4-78(1) by selling an alcoholic beverage to a person under twenty-one. The magistrate imposed a $200 fine. Neither employee was charged with committing a crime. Hy Vee appealed to circuit court seeking to have the statute declared unconstitutional. The circuit court upheld the conviction. Hy Vee asserts that the individual employees committed the wrongful acts, not the corporation, and appeals on the following issue:

> Did Hy Vee's conviction under SDCL 35-4-78 violate its substantive due process rights by imposing vicarious criminal liability on the company for the illegal acts of its employees?

## DECISION

Hy Vee concedes its employees sold alcohol to an underage person in violation of SDCL 35-4-78(1): "No licensee may sell any alcoholic beverage: (1) To any person under the age of twenty-one years. . . ." A violation of this section is a Class 1 misdemeanor punishable by one year in jail or a one thousand dollar fine, or both. . . . Hy Vee avers that the imposition of criminal penalties on it under SDCL 35-4-78 for acts of its employees constitutes an impermissible infringement upon Hy Vee's substantive due process rights in violation of both Article VI of the South Dakota Constitution and the 14th Amendment of the United States Constitution. The question is whether criminal liability can be imposed against an alcoholic beverage corporate licensee for the unlawful acts of its employees?

All legislative enactments arrive before us with a presumption in favor of their constitutionality; Hy Vee bears the burden of proving beyond a reasonable doubt that the law is unconstitutional. . . . "The constitution is not a grant but a limitation upon the lawmaking power of the state legislature and it may enact any law not expressly or inferentially prohibited by state and federal constitutions." . . .

> "Due process of law," when applied to substantive rights, means that the government is without the right to deprive a person of life, liberty or property by an act that has no reasonable relation to any proper governmental purpose by which it is so far beyond the necessity of the case

533 N.W.2d 147; 1995. Opinion by Justice Konenkamp.

as to be an arbitrary exercise of governmental power.

. . . Under this criterion we determine if the statute as applied to Hy Vee has "a real and substantial relation to the objects sought to be attained." . . .

The law disfavors statutes which impose criminal liability without fault, much less those enactments which impose such liability vicariously. . . . Yet states "have power to legislate against what are found to be injurious practices in their internal commercial and business affairs so long as their laws do not run afoul of some specific federal constitutional prohibition." . . .

We begin our analysis with the rather mundane observation that a corporation cannot act but through its agents. Well settled is the basic principle that criminal liability for certain offenses may be imputed to corporate defendants for the unlawful acts of its employees, provided that the conduct is within the scope of the employee's authority whether actual or apparent. . . .

Hy Vee urges us to avert constitutional entanglement by reading into the statute a knowledge or scienter requirement and hold that a corporate superior must know that an employee is selling liquor to an underage person and either consent to or ratify the act. . . . We decline to do so in this instance because "legislative acts which are essentially public welfare regulatory measures may omit the knowledge element without violating substantive due process guarantees." . . . Where "penalties commonly are relatively small, and conviction does no grave damage to an offender's reputation" under such circumstances statutes dispensing with a mens rea component have been upheld. . . .

Hy Vee asserts that criminal liability should not be imputed here because it adopted a firm, oft-reiterated policy that its employees, new and old, must not sell liquor to underage persons. Its employee manual states:

> **Beer and alcohol sales-21 years old. I.D. check required.** Cigarette/tobacco sales-Must be 18 years of age. If in doubt-check their I.D. If you are charged with selling to a minor you could be subject to a fine and possible jail time. Hy Vee does not pay employees fines. This is your responsibility. (Original emphasis.)

Constitutional questions aside for the moment, the general rule is that merely stating or promulgating policies will not insulate a corporation from liability. . . . Moreover, corporations may be held responsible for violations "even though its employees or agents acted contrary to express instructions when they violated the law, so long as they were acting for the benefit of the corporation and within the scope of their actual or apparent authority." . . .

As the statute provides for a potential one year jail sentence, Hy Vee argues that the enactment goes beyond being a mere regulatory measure with minor consequences for its violation. If the defendant was not a corporation, this argument might carry serious merit. In this case, however, a fine was all that could have been imposed; corporations cannot be imprisoned. . . . We will not speculate over the law's applicability to persons not before us or assume that some future court will impose a jail sentence upon such persons. Hy Vee's maximum criminal exposure was a $1,000 fine. "A defendant cannot claim that a statute is unconstitutional in some of its reaches if it is constitutional as applied to him." . . . As Justice Holmes wrote, "If we free our minds from the notion that criminal statutes must be construed by some artificial and conventional rule, the natural inference, when a statute prescribes two independent penalties, is that it means to inflict them so far as it can, and that, if one of them is impossible, it does not mean, on that account, to let the defendant escape." . . .

South Dakota's alcoholic beverage laws manifest an unwavering public interest in prohibiting liquor sales to persons under twenty-one. The serious problems associated with youth who abuse alcohol justify stringent enforcement against those who dispense it. By establishing vicarious liability against a corporate alcoholic beverage licensee, our laws hold accountable the true beneficiary of illegal sales and encourage such licensees to exercise intensified supervision over employees delegated with liquor sale responsibilities. Thus, the challenged statute has a real and substantial relation to the objects sought to be attained.

Was Hy Vee's $200 fine a constitutionally permissible sanction under the circumstances? Wayne R. LaFave & Austin W. Scott, Jr., supports the view that:

> Imposition of a fine is consistent with the rationale behind vicarious criminal liability. Vicarious liability is imposed because of the nature and inherent danger of certain business activities and the difficulties of establishing actual fault in the operation of such businesses. A fine, unlike imprisonment, is less personal and is more properly viewed as a penalty on the business enterprise.

As noted in *Koczwara*, public welfare demands certain regulatory control:

> Many states have enacted detailed regulatory provisions in fields which are essentially noncriminal, e.g., pure food and drug acts, speeding ordinances, building regulations, and child labor, minimum wage and maximum hour legislation. Such statutes are generally enforceable by light penalties, and although violations are labelled crimes, the considerations applicable to them are totally different from those applicable to true crimes, which involve moral delinquency and which are punishable by imprisonment or another serious penalty. Such so-called statutory crimes are in reality an attempt to utilize the machinery of criminal administration as an enforcing arm for social regulations of a purely civil nature, with the punishment totally unrelated to questions of moral wrongdoing or guilt. It is here that the social interest in the general well-being and security of the populace has been held to outweigh the individual interest of the particular defendant. The penalty is imposed despite the defendant's lack of a criminal intent or mens rea.

The magistrate's imposition of a $200 fine was consistent with the nature of regulatory offenses and did not offend Hy Vee's state and federal constitutional due process rights.

## CASES

# CASE 1. *An Auditor's Dilemma*

Sorting through a stack of invoices, Alison Lloyd's attention was drawn to one from Ace Glass Company. Her responsibility as the new internal auditor for Gem Packing is to verify all expenditures, and she knew that Ace had already been paid for the June delivery of the jars that are used for Gem's jams and jellies. On closer inspection, she noticed that the invoice was for deliveries in July and August that had not yet been made. Today was only June 10. Alison recalled approving several other invoices lately that seemed to be misdated, but the amounts were small compared with the $130,000 that Gem spends each month for glass jars. I had better check this out with purchasing, she thought.

Over lunch, Greg Berg, the head of purchasing, explains the system to her. The jam and jelly division operates under an incentive plan whereby the division manager and the heads of the four main units—sales, production, distribution, and purchasing—receive substantial bonuses for meeting their quota in pre-tax profits for the fiscal year, which ends on June 30. The bonuses are about one-half of annual salary and constitute one-third of the managers' total compensation. In addition, meeting quota is weighted heavily in evaluations, and missing even once is considered to be a death blow to the career of an aspiring executive at Gem. So the pressure on these managers is intense. On the other hand, there is nothing to be gained from exceeding a quota. An exceptionally good year is likely to be rewarded with an even higher quota the next year, since quotas are generally set at corporate headquarters by adding 5 percent to the previous year's results.

Greg continues to explain that several years ago, after the quota had been safely met, the jam and jelly division began prepaying as many expenses as possible—not only for glass jars but for advertising costs, trucking charges, and some commodities, such as sugar. The practice has continued to grow, and sales also helps out by delaying orders until the next fiscal year or by falsifying delivery dates when a shipment has already gone out. "Regular suppliers like Ace Glass know how we work," Greg says, "and they sent the invoices for July and August at my request." He predicts that Alison will begin seeing more irregular invoices as the fiscal year winds down. "Making quota gets easier each year," Greg observes, "because the division gets an ever increasing head start, but the problem of finding ways to avoid going too far over quota has become a real nightmare." Greg is not sure, but he thinks that other divisions are doing the same thing. "I don't think corporate has caught on yet," he says. "But they created the system, and they've been happy with the results so far. If they're too dumb to figure out how we're achieving them, that's their problem."

Alison recalls that upon becoming a member of the Institute of Internal Auditors, she agreed to abide by the IIA code of ethics. This code requires members to exercise "honesty, objectivity, and diligence" in the performance of their duties, but also to be loyal to the employer. However, loyalty does not include being a party to any "illegal or improper activity." As an internal auditor, she is also responsible for evaluating the adequacy and effectiveness of the company's system of financial control. But what is the harm of shuffling a little paper around? she thinks. Nobody is getting hurt, and it all works out in the end.

### Questions

1. Is the IAA code of ethics really helpful in resolving Alison's dilemma? Why or why not?
2. Greg blames the incentive system for the dilemma. Is he right?
3. Could Gem Packing be subject to prosecution under the Federal Sentencing Guidelines, and if so would Gem Packing be subject to increased fines?
4. What should Alison do?

## CASE 2. *Sears Auto Centers*

On June 11, 1992, the CEO of Sears, Roebuck and Company, Edward A. Brennan, learned that the California Department of Consumer Affairs (DCA) was seeking to shut down the 72 Sears Auto Centers in that state. A year-long undercover investigation by the DCA had found numerous instances in which Sears employees had performed unnecessary repairs and services. Officials in New Jersey quickly announced similar charges against six local Sears Auto Centers, and several other states, including Florida, Illinois, and New York, opened their own probes into possible consumer fraud. In the wake of this adverse publicity, revenues from the auto centers fell 15 percent, and the public's trust in Sears was badly shaken.

Sears Auto Centers, which were generally connected with a Sears department store, concentrated on basic "undercar" services involving tires, brakes, mufflers, shock absorbers, and steering mechanisms. Investigators from the DCA's Bureau of Automotive Repair purchased old vehicles in need of minor repairs and disassembled the brakes and suspension systems. After examining and photographing each part, the investigators towed the automobiles to a shop where they requested a brake inspection. In 34 of 38 instances, Sears employees recommended unnecessary repairs and services, and some auto centers charged for parts that were not installed or work that was not performed. The average overcharge was $235, but in two cases the amount overcharged exceeded $500.

Brennan had been notified in December 1991 of early results from the investigation, and Sears executives negotiated for six months with California officials. The company objected to the state's position that no part should be replaced unless it had failed and claimed that many repairs were legitimate preventive maintenance. For example, there is disagreement in the industry on whether brake calipers should be reconditioned whenever the pads are replaced. In addition, some of the automobiles used in the investigation showed sign of damage from worn parts that had already been replaced, thus leading mechanics to believe that repairs were needed. The DCA moved to revoke the licenses of all Sears Auto Centers in the state after the negotiations broke down over details of the financial settlement.

California officials charged that the problems at the Sears Auto Centers were not confined to a few isolated events but constituted systemic consumer fraud. According to a deputy attorney general, "There was a deliberate decision by Sears management to set up a structure that made it totally inevitable that the consumer would be oversold." Until 1991, service advisers, who make recommendations to customers, were paid a flat salary, but subsequently their compensation included a commission incentive. The service advisers were also required to meet quotas for a certain number of parts and services in a fixed period of time. The new incentive system also affected the mechanics, who perform the work on the customers' automobiles. Instead of an hourly wage, they were now compensated by a lower base hourly figure plus a fixed dollar amount based on the time required to install a part or perform a service. Under this system, a mechanic would receive the former hourly wage only by doing an hour's worth of work, but a mechanic could also earn more by working faster.

Commissions and quotas are commonly used in competitive sales environments to motivate and monitor employees. However, critics of Sears charge that there were not enough safeguards to protect the public. One former auto center manager in Sacramento complained that quotas were not based on realistic activity and were constantly escalating. He said that "sales goals had turned into conditions of employment" and that managers were "so busy with charts and graphs" that they could not properly supervise employees. A mechanic in San Bruno, California, alleged that he was fired for not doing 16 oil changes a day and that his manager urged him to save his job by filling the oil in each car only halfway. This illustrated, he said, the "pressure, pressure, pressure to get the dollar."

The changes in the compensation system at Sears Auto Centers were part of a company wide effort to boost lagging performance. In 1990, net income for all divisions, including Allstate (insurance), Coldwell Banker (real estate), and Dean Witter (brokerage), dropped 40 percent. Net income for the merchandising group, which included the department stores and the auto centers, fell 60 percent. Brennan, CEO since 1985, was under strong pressure to cuts costs and increase revenues. Some dissident shareholders were urging the board of directors to spin off the more profitable insurance, real estate, and brokerage divisions and focus on the ailing merchandising group. Brennan's response was to cut jobs, renovate stores, and motivate people. The overall thrust, according to a story in *Business Week*, was to "make every employee, from the sales floor to the chairman's suite focus on profits." Some critics of Sears attribute the problems at the auto centers to an unrealistic strategic plan that sought to wring more revenue out of the auto repair business than was possible. Robert Monk, who unsuccessfully sought a seat on the company's board, said, "Absent a coherent growth strategy, these sorts of things can happen."

At a press conference on June 22, 1992, Edward Brennan announced that, effective immediately, Sears would eliminate its incentive compensation system for automotive service advisers and all product-specific sales goals. Although he admitted that the company's compensation program "created an environment where mistakes did occur," Brennan continued: "We deny allegations of fraud and systemic problems in our auto centers. Isolated errors? Yes. But a pattern of misconduct? Absolutely not." He reaffirmed his belief that the California investigation was flawed and that Sears was practicing responsible preventive maintenance. He further announced that the company would retain an independent organization to conduct random "shopping audits" to ensure that no overcharging would occur. Sears also paid $8 million to settle claims in California and gave auto center customers $50 coupons that were expected to cost the company another $3 million. The total cost, including legal bills and lost sales, is estimated to be $60 million.

On September 30, 1992, Sears revealed plans to spin off its three nonretail divisions, Allstate, Coldwell Banker, and Dean Witter, and to reorganize the merchandising group. A new CEO, Arthur C. Martinez, succeeded Brennan and began a turnaround of the company. In describing his vision, Martinez said, "I want to revisit and intensify the theme of our customer being the center of our universe." A cornerstone of Martinez's strategy, according to the *New York Times*, was "clean business ethics."

### Questions*

1. Is Sears as a corporation guilty of wrongdoing in this case or is the wrong doing limited to the repair people?
2. Should we be looking for individuals to hold responsible in the Sears case or is the problem one of incentives and organizational structure?
3. Should Sears be found culpable under the Federal Sentencing Guidelines?

* Questions supplied by editor.

## CASE 3. *H. J. Heinz Company: The Administration of Policy*

In April 1979 James Cunningham, H.J. Heinz Company's president and chief operating officer, learned that since 1972 certain Heinz divisions had allegedly engaged in improper income transferal practices. Payments had been made to certain vendors in a particular fiscal year, then repaid or exchanged for services in the succeeding fiscal year.[1]

These allegations came out during the investigation of an unrelated antitrust matter. Apparent improprieties were discovered in the records of the Heinz USA division's relationship with one of its advertising agencies. Joseph Stangerson—senior vice president, secretary, and general counsel for Heinz—asked the advertising agency about the alleged practices. Not only had the agency personnel confirmed the allegation about Heinz USA, it indicated that similar practices had been used by Star-Kist Foods, another Heinz division. The divisions allegedly solicited improper invoices from the advertising agency in fiscal year (FY) 1974 so that they could transfer income to FY 1975. While the invoices were paid in FY 1974, the services described on the invoices were not rendered until sometime during FY 1975. Rather than capitalizing the amount as a prepaid expense, the amount was charged as an expense in FY 1974. The result was an understatement of FY 1974 income and an equivalent overstatement of FY 1975 income.

Stangerson reported the problem to John Bailey, vice chairman and chief executive officer; to Robert Kelly, senior vice president—finance and treasurer; and to Cunningham. Bailey, CEO since 1966, had presided over 13 uninterrupted years of earnings growth. He was scheduled to retire as vice chairman and CEO on July 1 and would remain as a member of the board of directors. James Cunningham, who had been president and chief operating officer since 1972, was to become chief executive officer on July 1, 1979.

Subsequent reports indicate that neither the scope of the practice nor the amounts involved were known. There was no apparent reason to believe that the amounts involved would have had a material effect on Heinz's reported earnings during the time period, including earnings for FY 1979 ending May 2. (Heinz reported financial results on the basis of a 52–53 week fiscal year ending on the Wednesday closest to April 30.) Stangerson was not prepared to say whether the alleged practices were legal or illegal. "This thing could be something terrible or it could be merely a department head using conservative accounting practices; we don't know,"[2] one Heinz senior official stated to the press.

## BACKGROUND

Henry J. Heinz, on founding the company in 1869 in Pittsburgh, Pennsylvania, said: "This is my goal—to bring home-cooking standards into canned foods, making them so altogether wholesome and delicious and at the same time so reasonable that people everywhere will enjoy them in abundance."[3] The company's involvement in food products never changed, and in 1979 Heinz operated some 30 companies with products reaching 150 countries. Heinz reported sales of over $2.2 billion and net income of $99.1 million in FY 1978.

After a sluggish period in the early 1960s, a reorganization was undertaken to position Heinz for growth. Under the guidance of John Bailey and James Cunningham, Heinz prospered through a major recession, government price controls, and major currency fluctuations. The 1978 annual report reflected management's pride in Heinz's remarkably consistent growth:

> Fiscal 1978 went into the books as the fifteenth consecutive year of record results for Heinz. Earnings rose to another new high. Sales reached more than $2 billion only six years after we had passed the $1 billion mark for the first time in our century-long history. We are determined to maintain the financial integrity of our enterprise and support its future growth toward ever-higher levels.

Although Heinz was a multinational firm, domestic operations accounted for 62% of sales and 67% of earnings in FY 1978. Five major divisions operated in the United States in 1979.

Throughout the 1970s Heinz's major objective was consistent growth in earnings. While Heinz management did not consider acquisitions to be crucial to continuing growth, it looked favorably on purchase opportunities in areas where Heinz had demonstrated capabilities. Bailey and Cunningham stressed profit increases through the elimination of marginally profitable products. Increased advertising of successful traditional products and new product development efforts also contributed to Heinz's growth. Heinz's commitment to decentralized authority as an organizational principle aided the management of internal growth as well as acquisitions.

## ORGANIZATION

In 1979 Heinz was organized on two primary levels. The corporate world headquarters, located in Pittsburgh, consisted of the principal corporate officers and historically small staffs (management described the world headquarters as lean). World headquarters had the responsibility for "the decentralized coordination and control needed to set overall standards and ensure performance in accordance with them."[4] Some Heinz operating divisions reported directly to the president; others reported through senior vice presidents who were designated area directors. World headquarters officers worked with division senior managers in areas such as planning, product and market development, and capital programs.

Heinz's divisions were largely autonomous operating companies. Division managers were directly responsible for the division's products and services, and they operated their own research and development, manufacturing, and marketing facilities. Division staff reported directly to division managers and had neither formal reporting nor dotted-line relationships with corporate staff.

World headquarters officers monitored division performance through conventional business budgets and financial reports. If reported performance was in line with corporate financial goals, little inquiry into the details of division operation was made. On the other hand, variations from planned performance drew a great deal of attention from world headquarters; then, divisions were pressured to improve results. A review was held near the end of the third fiscal quarter to discuss expected year-end results. If shortfalls were apparent, other divisions were often encouraged to improve their performance. The aim was to meet projected consolidated earnings and goals. Predictability was a watchword and surprises were to be avoided.[5] A consistent growth in earnings attended this management philosophy.

## MANAGEMENT INCENTIVE PLAN

Designed by a prominent management consulting firm, the management incentive plan (MIP) was regarded as a prime management tool used to achieve corporate goals.[6] MIP comprised roughly 225 employees, including corporate officers, senior world headquarters personnel, and senior personnel of most divisions. Incentive compensation was awarded on the basis of an earned number of MIP points and in some cases reached 40% of total compensation.

MIP points could be earned through the achievement of personal goals. These goals were established at the beginning of each fiscal year in consultation with the participant's immediate supervisor. Points were awarded by the supervisor at the end of the year, based on goal achievement. In practice, personal goal point awards fell out on a curve, with few individuals receiving very high or very low awards.

MIP points were also awarded based on net profit after tax (NPAT) goals. (On occasion, other goals such as increased inventory turnover or improved cash flow were included in MIP goals.) Corporate NPAT goals were set at the beginning of the fiscal year by the management development and compensation committee (MDC) of the board of directors. The chief executive officer, the chief operating officer, the senior vice president-finance, and the senior vice president-corporate development then set MIP goals for each division, with the aggregate of division goals usually exceeding the corporate goal. Two goals were set—a fair goal, which was consistently higher than the preceding year's NPAT, and a higher outstanding goal. The full number of MIP points was earned by achieving the outstanding goal.

Senior corporate managers were responsible for executing the system. While divisional input was not uncommon, division NPAT goals were set unilaterally and did not necessarily reflect a division's budgeted profits. Once set, goals were seldom changed during the year. The officers who set the goals awarded MIP points at the end of the fiscal year. No points were awarded to personnel in a division that failed to achieve its fair goal, and points were weighted to favor results at or near the outstanding goal. One or more bonus points might be awarded if the outstanding goal was exceeded. Corporate officers also had the authority to make adjustments or award arbitrary points in special circumstances. The basis for these adjustments was not discussed with division personnel.

MIP points for consolidated corporate performance were awarded by the MDC committee of the board. Corporate points were credited by all MIP participants except those in a division that did not achieve its fair goal. The MDC committee could also award company bonus points.

Heinz also had a long-term incentive plan based on a revolving three-year cycle. Participation was limited to senior corporate management and division presidents or managing directors for a total of 19 persons.

## CORPORATE ETHICAL POLICY

Heinz had an explicit corporate ethical policy that was adopted in May 1976.[7] Among other things, it stated that no division should:

1. Have any form of unrecorded assets or false entries on its books or records
2. Make or approve any payment with the intention or understanding that any part of such payment was to be used for any purpose other than that described by the documents supporting the payment
3. Make political contributions
4. Make payments or gifts to public officials or customers
5. Accept gifts or payments of more than a nominal amount

Each year the president or managing director and the chief financial officer of each division were required to sign a representation letter which, among other things, confirmed compliance with the corporate Code of Ethics.

## APRIL 1979

Heinz itself had originated the antitrust proceedings that led to the discovery of the alleged practices. In 1976 Heinz filed a private antitrust suit against the Campbell Soup Company, accusing Campbell of monopolistic practices in the canned soup market. Campbell promptly countersued, charging that Heinz monopolized the ketchup market.[8] Campbell attorneys, preparing for court action, subpoenaed Heinz documents reflecting its financial relationships with one of its advertising agencies. In April 1979, while taking a deposition from Arthur West, president of the Heinz USA division, Campbell attorneys asked about flows of funds, "certain items which can be called off-book accounts." West refused to answer, claiming Fifth Amendment protection from self-incrimination.[9] Stangerson then spoke with the advertising agency and received confirmation of the invoicing practices.

## Questions*

1. To what extent are individuals to blame for the manipulation of the financial data?
2. Since Heinz has a specific corporate ethics policy and since they themselves discovered the financial manipulation, should that reduce any penalty if Heinz had been subject to the Federal Sentencing Guidelines?
3. Should we hold some person or persons morally or legally responsible for the incentive system that led to the financial manipulation?

* Questions supplied by editor.

## NOTES

1. H. J. Heinz Company, form 8-K, April 27, 1979, p. 2.
2. "Heinz to Probe Prepayments to Suppliers by Using Outside Lawyers, Accountants," *Wall Street Journal*, April 30, 1979, p. 5.
3. H. J. Heinz Company, annual report, 1976.
4. H. J. Heinz Company, form 8-K, May 7, 1980, p. 7.
5. Ibid. p. 8.
6. Ibid. pp. 10–12.
7. Ibid. p. 12.
8. "Heinz Slow Growth behind Juggling Tactic?" *Advertising Age*, March 24, 1980, p. 88.
9. "Results in Probe of Heinz Income Juggling Expected to Be Announced by Early April," *Wall Street Journal*, March 18, 1980, p. 7.

## *Suggested Supplementary Readings*


CORLETT, J. ANGELO. "Corporate Responsibility and Punishment." *Public Affairs Quarterly* 2 (January, 1988): 1–16.

DAVIS, MICHAEL. "Technical Decisions: Time to Rethink the Engineer's Responsibilities?" 11 (Fall-Winter, 1992): 41–55.

DE GEORGE, RICHARD T. "GM and Corporate Responsibility." *Journal of Business Ethics* 5 (June, 1986): 177–79.

FRENCH, PETER. *Corporate Ethics.* Fort Worth: Harcourt Brace College Publishers, 1995.

FRENCH, PETER. *Collective and Corporate Responsibility.* New York: Columbia University Press, 1984.

GAWANDE, ATUL. "When Doctors Make Mistakes." *The New Yorker* (February 1, 1999), p. 40–55.

GRUNDER, RICHARD S. "Just Punishment and Adequate Deterrence for Organizational Misconduct: Scaling Economic Penalties Under the New Corporate Sentencing Guidelines." *Southern California Law Review* 66 (1993): 225–88.

HOFFMAN, W. MICHAEL, JENNIFER MILLS MOORE, and DAVID FEDO, eds. *Corporate Governance and Institutionalizing Ethics.* Lexington, MA: Lexington Books, 1984.

HUMMELS, HARRY. "Safety and Aircraft Maintenance: A Moral Evaluation." *International Journal of Value-Based Management* 10 (2) (1997).

LADD, JOHN. "Corporate Mythology and Individual Responsibility," *International Journal of Applied Philosophy* (Spring, 1984) 1–21.

MARTIN, MIKE W. "Whistleblowing: Professionalism, Personal Life and Shared Responsibility for Safety in Engineering." *Business and Professional Ethics Journal* 12 (1992) 21–40.

NAGEL, ILENE H., and WINTHROP W. SWENSON. "The Federal Sentencing Guidelines For Corporations: Their Development, Theoretical Underpinnings, and Some Thoughts About Their Future." *Washington University Law Quarterly* 71 (1993): 205–59.

NIELSEN, RICHARD P. "What Can Managers Do About Unethical Management?" *Journal of Business Ethics* 6 (May, 1987): 309–20.

PHILLIPS, MICHAEL J. "Corporate Moral Responsibility." *Business Ethics Quarterly* 5 (July, 1995): 555–76.

SANDERS, JOHN T. "Assessing Responsibility: Fixing Blame versus Fixing Problems." *Business and Professional Ethics Journal* 12 (1993) 73–86.

STONE, CHRISTOPHER D. *Where the Law Ends: The Social Control of Corporate Behavior.* New York: Harper and Row, 1975.

WERHANE, PATRICIA H. "Engineers and Management: The Challenge of the *Challenger* Incident." *Journal of Business Ethics* 10 (August, 1991): 605–16.

# *Chapter Four*

# Acceptable Risk

## INTRODUCTION

GOVERNMENT IS CONSTITUTED to protect citizens from risk to the environment, risk from external invasion, risk to health, risk from crime, risk from fire, risk of highway accidents, and similar risks. A natural extension of this idea is that the social contract obligates government to protect citizens against risks to health, bodily safety, financial security, and the environment. However, society has not yet decided on the extent to which government should restrain business activities in order to protect persons against risks of harm to health, financial security, and environmental degradation.

Corporate activities present several types of risk of harm. This chapter concentrates on judgments of acceptable risk for consumers, investors, workers, and the environment. The focus is more on the responsibilities of business and methods for reducing risk and less on the nature and types of harm caused. These risk-reduction methods include disclosure of information about risks as well as risk-reduction techniques.

### Nature and Types of Risk

***The Nature of Harm.*** Competing conceptions of "harm" exist, but Joel Feinberg has supplied a particularly helpful definition:

> [Interests] can be blocked or defeated by events in impersonal nature or by plain bad luck. But they can only be "invaded" by human beings, . . . singly, or in groups and organizations . . . one person harms another in the present sense, then, by invading, and thereby thwarting or setting back, his interest. The test . . . of whether such an invasion has in fact set back an interest is whether that interest is in a worse condition than it would otherwise have been in had the invasion not occurred at all. . . . Not all invasions of interest are wrongs, since some actions invade another's interests excusably or justifiably, or invade interests that the other has no right to have respected.[1]

Causing a setback to interests in health, financial goals, or the environment can constitute a harm without necessarily being an unjustifiable harm. Almost everyone would agree that harming another person's interests is blameworthy if the harm results in little compensating benefit and if the damage could easily be avoided. But people rarely, if ever, experience such a clear and uncomplicated scenario. Benefits that offset risk usually exist, and the risk of harm is often expensive to eliminate or control. Some heated debates over products that appeared to be harmful—for example, presweetened children's cereals—have shown that they also create benefits. In the workplace it has become increasingly difficult simply to banish dangerous chemicals that provide major social benefits. In each case their risks must be weighed against their benefits.

***Kinds of Risk.*** Different kinds of risk raise distinct issues. For example, risks of psychological harm, physical harm, legal harm, and economic harm require different analyses and different remedies. Some representative risks pertinent to the material in this chapter are the following:

***Risks to Consumers (and their Families)***
Prepared foods (increased fat and sugar)
Drugs (side effects such as gastrointestinal bleeding)
Cigarettes (lung cancer)

***Risks to Workers (and their Families)***
Benzene (leukemia)
Asbestos (asbestosis)
Lead (impairment of reproductive capacities)

***Risks to the Public and the Environment***
Coal-dust emissions (respiratory complications)
Carbon and other fuel emissions (respiratory complications)
Toxic chemicals (genetic defects)

***Risks to Investors***
Savings accounts (decline in the rate of return)
Stocks (decline of principal)
Real estate (loss of liquidity)

***Problems of Risk Assessment.*** It is difficult for society to adequately grasp the extent of the risks inherent in thousands of toxic chemicals, foods, drugs, energy sources, machines, and environmental emissions. Some conditions have serious, irreversible consequences; others do not. Moreover, the *probability* of exposure to a risk may be known with some precision, whereas virtually nothing may be known about the harm's *magnitude*; or the magnitude may be precisely expressible, whereas the probability remains too indefinite to be calculated accurately. "Wild guess" sometimes best describes the accuracy with which physical and chemical risks may be determined, for example, for a worker who constantly changes locations, who works with multiple toxic substances, and whose physical problems can be attributed in part to factors independent of the workplace, such as smoking.

## Product Safety and Risk to Consumers

We all consume products that carry minor, significant, or unknown risks. No household is complete without several dozen potentially hazardous products, including ovens, electrical lines, furniture cleaners, spray paints, insecticides, medicines, and video display terminals. Millions of people in North America are the victims of household and office accidents involving these products every year, and more of our young people die from failures and accidents involving products than from disease. Thousands of lawsuits are filed by businesses against other businesses each year because of product failure, hazard, and harm, and there are related problems about deceptive marketing practices and inadequate warranties.

Some responsibility for the occurrence of these harms rests primarily on the consumer, who may carelessly use products or fail to read clearly written instructions. However, some risks can be described as inherent in the product: A cautious and reasonable judgment of acceptable risk has been made that the product cannot be made less risky without unduly increasing cost or limiting use. Still other problems of risk derive from use of cheap materials, careless design, poor construction, or new discovery about risk in an already marketed product.

***Disclosure of Risk Information.*** A consumer presumably controls what to purchase, because the seller must satisfy consumers or fail to sell the product and be driven from the market; yet serious questions exist about whether the information supplied to the consumer is adequate for making an informed and free choice. For example, is a customer to be told how a kerosene heater should be cleaned and stored and how often new filters should be installed? Are the side effects of a drug to be disclosed when a prescription is filled? Sellers may list only a minimal set of facts about known hazards, especially regarding technologically advanced products, because a seller attempts to sell in the most cost-effective manner. Disclosure of risk information costs money and adversely affects sales. Thus, the seller has an economic incentive to keep disclosure to a selective minimum.

These topics of disclosure and understanding have been under intense discussion in recent years. By the late 1970s a major right-to-know movement had taken hold in consumer affairs and in the U.S. workplace. Numerous laws were passed, notably the Consumer Product Safety Act of 1972, to protect consumers by setting safety standards, examining consumer product marketing, providing more adequate risk information, and upgrading the quality of warranty statements.

***Product Safety and Quality Control.*** Quality control supplements disclosure of risk information as a strategy to protect consumers. Corporations such as Johns Manville (asbestos), A.H. Robins (the Dalkon Shield), and Dow-Corning (silicone breast implants) have faced massive product liability judgments. Although higher standards of quality control would presumably protect manufacturers as well as customers, both theoretical and practical problems exist in establishing and enforcing such standards. Consumer protection methods incur significant costs that increase product price and frequently force companies to abandon the market. For example, some lawn-mower prices almost doubled after the introduction of new safety requirements, with the result that several companies floundered. Liberty issues are also at stake. For instance, the freedom to put a new "junk food" on the market might be jeopardized (in theory, the freedom to produce junk foods would be eliminated), and the freedom to buy cheap, substandard products would be lost (because they could not be marketed).

These quality-control controversies raise questions about liability and manufacturer warranties, discussed in this chapter in *Henningsen v. Bloomfield Motors and Chrysler Corporation.* In this case, the court held both Chrysler and the car dealer liable for an injury caused by a defective steering gear, without finding any evidence of negligence. The court argued that an implied warranty of suitability for use is owed the purchaser and contended that a major assumption behind free-market "contracting" or bargaining among equals can be questioned when products prove to be defective. Because the *Henningsen* case cast doubt on the efficacy of disclaimers by manufacturers, it quickly came to be applied to many products, including glass doors, guns, and stoves.

Manuel G. Velasquez considers in his essay how to differentiate between the obligations of consumers to themselves and the obligations of manufacturers to consumers. He distinguishes three theories of business obligations, showing that each strikes a different balance between consumer and manufacturer obligations. The first theory rests on an account of the social contract between consumers and business (under which Velasquez cites *Henningsen* as a classic example), and the second provides a theory of due care. The third theory presents an account of strict liability, a discussion of which follows.

***Liability for Harm.*** Two tests affecting liability are that professionals should conform to the minimally acceptable professional standards and that they should perform any actions that a reasonably prudent person would perform in the circumstances. Sometimes, even when the utmost care has been exercised, an accident, lack of information, or lack of documents might cause harm. However, if due care has been exercised to make a product safe (and affected parties have been apprised of known risks), a business is far less likely to be at fault for any harm caused, even if the business helped bring about the harm.

This rule suggests that a manufacturer can be held liable for unsafe or inefficacious products or unsafe workplaces only if the manufacturer knew or *should have known* about the risks involved. However, difficulties arise regarding what an employer or manufacturer "should have known." A product or technique may be so thoroughly researched and thus delayed that the time involved will ensure a manufacturer's loss rather than profit. Should businesses be held to this kind of economic risk? If so, how can it be determined that enough research and development had been carried out? Can the problem be handled through adequate insurance? Or is a modified conception of liability needed?

Some argue that manufacturers should be held liable not only to a standard of prudent behavior but also to a stronger standard: liability for injuries caused to parties by defects in the manufacturing process, even if the manufacturer exercised due diligence and still could not have reasonably foreseen the problem. This principle is referred to as *strict product liability,* that is, liability without fault. Here questions of good faith, negligence, and absence of knowledge are not pertinent to a determination of liability. The advocates of this no-fault principle use primarily utilitarian arguments. They maintain that manufacturers are in the best position to pay and recover the costs of injury because they can pass the costs on through the product's price and, moreover, will have the added benefit of increasing manufacturers' objectivity, diligence, and prudence before marketing a product. This argument constitutes a shift from the traditional doctrine of "let the buyer beware" (*caveat emptor*) to "let the seller beware."

This utilitarian justification is controversial and is assessed in this chapter by George G. Brenkert, who thinks it more important to ask whether strict liability conforms to principles of justice, and in particular, whether it is just to ask manufacturers to bear the cost of injury merely because they are in the best position to do so. Brenkert maintains that in a free market society it is just to use strict liability because it is essential to maintain a consumer's equal opportunity to function.

## Protecting Investors Against Risk

Many of the problems regarding risk of economic harm to consumers apply equally well to investors. At issue is a complex set of relationships encompassing problems of conflict of interest as well as problems of deception and manipulation through improper disclosures. Brokerage houses, money managers, and investment counselors demand as much freedom as possible to deal with their clients. The time spent making disclosures to customers is uncompensated and restricted by business requirements. Brokers with a large client base often do not adequately grasp the risk attached to the financial instruments they sell. Monitoring systems are usually loose, and direct supervisors do not closely track how investments are sold or which, if any, disclosures are made to clients.

Small investors who use brokerage houses and banks usually do not have the same access to relevant information that is available to professional investors. Amateur investors, not having such information, can only hope that their brokers are well informed or that the market price already reflects the relevant information. Even if brokers are sufficiently informed, the house policy may be more aggressive and thus may introduce more risk than the average customer wishes. For example, the firm may be primarily interested in limited partnerships in real estate, fully margined common stock, futures and commodities, and oil and gas drilling partnerships, rather than the more mundane unit investment trusts, certificates of deposit, and municipal bonds that a particular customer needs.

A broker has little incentive to match client needs with investments aside from the desire to maintain a business relationship. Although brokerage firms often advertise a full range of products and free financial planning by experts, brokers dislike financial planning per se, because it requires a heavy investment of time and carries no commission. They also dislike pedestrian forms of investing such as certificates of deposit and no-load mutual funds. Riskier investments generally carry higher commissions, and brokerage houses typically give brokers complete discretion to recommend a range of investments to their clients. At the same time, brokers are skillfully taught to be salespersons, to avoid lengthy phone calls, and to flatter clients who pride themselves on making their own decisions. In some firms brokers are taught to make recommendations to clients based primarily on the commission. Consequently, these brokers are motivated to sell risky and complicated forms of investment to unsuspecting clients.

An inherent conflict of interest troubles many industry critics. The broker has a fiduciary responsibility to make recommendations based on the client's financial best interest, but the broker is also a salesperson who makes a living by selling securities and who is obligated to maximize profits for the brokerage house. The more trades that are made, the better it is for the broker, but this rule seldom works to the client's advantage. Commissions are an ever-present temptation influencing a recommendation, and the structure of incentives drives up the risk for the client.

The law requires securities firms to disclose commissions to clients. However, statistics on the full range of fees involved in many instruments are rarely mentioned to clients. When available, the figures are often buried beneath a pile of information in a thick prospectus that clients do not read prior to a purchase. Most clients do not obtain the prospectus until after the purchase, which often places no dollar figure on the commission. Brokers are not legally required to disclose commissions in advance of a sale to clients, nor are they required to disclose that they are given additional, free vacations for selling a large number of shares in certain mutual funds. Moreover, clients rarely ask about the commission amount or the range of fees, not because of lack of interest, but because they fear that the inquiry might harm their relationship with the broker.

The U.S. Securities and Exchange Commission (SEC) was created by the Securities Exchange Act of 1933 to regulate manipulative stock practices. Although sensitive to issues such as insider trading, the SEC does not set ceilings on commissions and does not require brokers to receive written consent from clients prior to purchase. The SEC occasionally determines that a brokerage house's markup is so high that the commission amounts to fraud, but these cases are rare.

In recent years ethical brokerage houses have increasingly realized that tighter SEC control and a more developed sense of moral responsibility may serve their best interest. Ethical lapses are so common to the financial markets that the whole industry has been tarred with the brush of greed. Although significant reforms are beginning to emerge, their outline is not yet clear.

One proposal for protecting investors, considered in this chapter's essay by Robert E. Frederick and W. Michael Hoffman, is that the at-risk investor be denied access to securities markets to safeguard the investor from financial harm. They point out that even an investor with accurate information about stocks and bonds may not understand how to make a wise investment decision. They suggest that the at-risk investor should be required by law "to engage the services of an expert"—though they would allow some exceptions to this rule. In a second article on the ethics of investment, John R. Boatright examines several issues facing the financial services industry in its attempts to gain customer confidence and maintain its moral integrity.

He looks at issues of unethical sales practices involving deception, manipulation, and concealment, and he too considers issues of (1) the responsibility of brokers to protect the interests of those who buy financial products and (2) whether some forms of risky personal trading should be banned. He points to the complexities involved in reaching general positions in this area and attempts to achieve balanced or centrist answers to the major questions.

## Worker Safety, Occupational Risk, and the Right to Know

Critics of business and government have long contended that uninformed workers are routinely, and often knowingly, exposed to dangerous conditions. For example, employers did not tell asbestos workers for many years of the known dangers of contracting asbestosis. Although little is currently understood about the knowledge and comprehension of workers, evidence from at least some industries indicates that ignorance is a causal factor in occupational illness or injury. The simplest solution is to ban hazardous products from use, but to do so would involve shutting down a large segment of industrial manufacturing. Hundreds of products still contain asbestos either because no functional substitute is available or replacement is not cost efficient.

The implications of worker ignorance are chillingly present in the following worker's testimony before an Occupational Safety and Health Administration (OSHA) hearing on the toxic agent DBCP:

> We had no warning that DBCP exposure might cause sterility, testicular atrophy, and perhaps cancer. If we had known that these fumes could possibly cause the damage that we have found out it probably does cause, we would have worn equipment to protect ourselves. As it was, we didn't have enough knowledge to give us the proper respect for DBCP.[2]

The regulation of workplace risks has consistently sought to determine an objective level of acceptable risk and then to ban or limit exposure above that level. However, the goal of safety is not the primary justification for disclosures of risk. Individuals need the information upon which the objective standard is based to determine whether the risk it declares acceptable is *acceptable to them.* Here a subjective standard of acceptable risk seems more appropriate than an objective standard established by "experts." Choosing to risk testicular atrophy seems rightly a worker's personal choice, one not fully decidable by health and safety standards established for groups of workers. Even given objective standards, substantial ambiguity prevails when the experts are uncertain about the risks and dangerous dose levels cannot be established.

Problems also surface about the strategy of information disclosure and the strategy of protective schemes—especially if one or the other is used in isolation. Often there are no meaningful figures to define the relationship between acceptable risk and the ease with which the risk can be eliminated or controlled. There also may be no consensus about which levels of probability of serious harm, such as death, constitute risks sufficiently high to require that steps be taken to reduce or eliminate the risk or to provide information to those affected.

Both the employer's responsibility to inform employees and the employee's right to refuse hazardous job assignments are the concerns of the essay by Ruth Faden and Tom L. Beauchamp. They support a standard of information disclosure and consider three possible standards for determining the justifiability of a refusal to work or of a safety walkout. In a second essay in this section, John R. Boatright focuses on the worker's right to receive information from employers and the effectiveness of the current system. He also looks at the worker's right to refuse to work and the government's obligation to regulate the workplace. He concentrates on particularly controversial regulatory programs and policies and how they impact on the rights to know and refuse. Also included in the legal perspectives section of this chapter is the case of *Automobile Workers v. Johnson Controls, Inc.*, which determined that employers cannot legally adopt "fetal protection policies" that exclude women of childbearing age from a hazardous workplace, because such policies involve illegal sex discrimination. However, the Supreme Court decision was, in some respects, narrow; it left U.S. corporations in a state of uncertainty over an acceptable policy for protecting fetuses from reproductive hazards.

## Risk to the Environment and Health

Controversy over protecting the environment and preventing the depletion of natural resources has mushroomed in the last four decades, a period that has caught business, government, and the general public unprepared to handle environmental problems. In the 1960s and 1970s, the government first instituted regulatory programs, and ever since the public has become increasingly concerned about the environmental impact of chemical dumping, supersonic transport, burning coal, nuclear power, oil spills, and the like. In this debate, environmental deterioration is often linked to corporate actions, and thus corporate responsibility has become a major issue.

Environmental issues have traditionally been conceived in free-market terms: Natural resources are available to entrepreneurs who are free to purchase and use them. Markets transfer resources, and conflicts are handled by relatively simple procedures that balance conflicting interests. Those who pollute, for example, can be prosecuted and fined. People assume that the environment, once properly tended to, is sufficiently resilient to return to its former state.

Recently, this optimistic outlook has been vigorously challenged. First, it became apparent that a market conception of resource-use did not fit the environment, because air, water, and much of the land environments are owned in common, and their value is not determined by prices in the market. Also, new technology and increased production have damaged the environment to a point at which unrectifiable and uncontrollable global imbalances may emerge. Yet, corporations still "externalize" rather than internalize costs by passing on the costs of pollution to the public. Attempts to bring market "externalities" such as pollution into standard pricing mechanisms—by, for instance, taxing effluents—have generally proved to be inadequate in handling environmental problems.

Some writers depict the environment as analogous to a common rangeland where competing cattle ranchers graze so many cattle in search of profits (as it is economically rational for each cattle rancher to do) that eventually the common land is overgrazed and can no longer support animal life. As businesspersons pursue their economic interests, collectively they work toward the ruin of all humanity. This analysis has been disputed by those who see environmental problems as involving tradeoffs that need not do irreversible damage to "the commons." However, society acknowledges that some tradeoffs will require additional tradeoffs that may only mortgage the future. For example, air-pollution scrubbers used in industry to remove sulfur dioxide from flue gas produce three to six tons of sludge for every ton of sulfur dioxide they remove. The sludge is then buried in landfills, creating a risk of water pollution. Efforts to clean the air thereby risk polluting the water.

Classic conflicts between public and private interests have emerged in these environmental debates. For example, there have been attempts to show that fluorocarbons in aerosol spray cans so badly damage the earth's ozone shield that serious repercussions may occur from continued use; possible consequences include melting the polar ice caps, flooding the cities along the world's coasts, and producing radioactive contamination. Critics have charged that the food industry rapes the land by its failure to balance high-level methods of food production with the land's lower-level production capacity. Environmentalists have accused the timber industry of deforestation without replenishment. Responsibility for various forms of pollution has been attributed to bottle and can industries, plastics industries, smelters, chemical industries, and the oil industry. In recent years industrial disposal of hazardous wastes, including mercury, benzene, and dioxin, has been condemned because of the contamination of groundwater, landfills, and even waste recovery plants.

Those who promote a new environmental ethic argue that western culture has a special problem because of entrenched attitudes about the use of nature for human enjoyment and betterment. In this conception, humans live not as part of the ecosystem, but as external dwellers. Others argue, however, that people should view the environment in a different way only to the extent that doing so would improve their quality of life and continued existence. They maintain that environmental concerns are valid only if they improve the human situation and not because animals, plants, or ecosystems have rights. This approach emphasizes the freedom of businesses to use the environment unless their activities harm other individuals in society.

Many now believe that only severe curbs on industry and severe judicial penalties will protect the environment, whereas others believe that environmental impact statements and various now-standard practices are sufficient. The core of the environmental problem is how to balance the liberty rights of those who want to use the environment in typical free-market style with the rights of those who want safe workplaces, safe products, and the right to a contamination-free environment.

Three readings in this chapter examine these problems of environmental risk and protection. The article by Richard T. De George deals with the complexities present in cases of corporate pollution. He explores a range of issues about environmental responsibility and the conflicting principles at work. In the end, he offers three practical and "justified" approaches to "ethically handling" corporate pollution. In the ensuing article, Manuel Velasquez is concerned with moral problems centering on the finite limits of our natural resources, which he insists cannot be indefinitely exploited. He argues that substitutes will have to be developed, and that the longer the delay the greater the costs and the environmental losses. Velasquez gives an explanation of the nature of an "ecological ethics" and relates it to a number of alleged environmental rights and needed cost-benefit controls. Along the way, he considers several different theories and remedies—that is, alternative moral frameworks that can be used to address current environmental problems.

Finally, the Supreme Court of the United States, in the 1998 case of *U.S. v. Bestfoods et al.*, deals with the issue of whether a parent corporation may be held liable for the polluting activities of one of its subsidiaries. The court maintains that liability depends on the level of active participation and control by the corporation, especially where wrongful purposes are involved (most notably fraud). This opinion explores several levels of corporate responsibility to avoid disposal of hazardous materials.

## NOTES

1. Joel Feinberg, *Harm to Others* (New York: Oxford University Press, 1984), pp. 34–35.
2. Occupational Safety and Health Administration, "Access to Employee Exposure and Medical Records—Final Rules," *Federal Register* (May 23, 1980), p. 35222.

## CONSUMER RISK

# The Ethics of Consumer Production

*Manuel G. Velasquez*

Where . . . does the consumer's duty to protect his or her own interests end, and where does the manufacturer's duty to protect consumers' interests begin? Three different theories on the ethical duties of manufacturers have been developed, each one of which strikes a different balance between the consumer's duty to himself or herself and the manufacturer's duty to the consumer: the contract view, the "due care" view, and the social costs view. The contract view would place the greater responsibility on the consumer, while the "due care" and social costs views place the larger measure of responsibility on the manufacturer. We will examine each of these views.

## THE CONTRACT VIEW OF BUSINESS'S DUTIES TO CONSUMERS

According to the contract view of the business firm's duties to its customers, the relationship between a business firm and its customers is essentially a contractual relationship, and the firm's moral duties to the customer are those created by this contractual relationship.[1] When a consumer buys a product, this view holds, the consumer voluntarily enters into a "sales contract" with the business firm. The firm freely and knowingly agrees to give the consumer a product with certain characteristics and the consumer in turn freely and knowingly agrees to pay a certain sum of money to the firm for the product. In virtue of having voluntarily entered this agreement, the firm then has a duty to provide a product with those characteristics, and the consumer has a correlative right to get a product with those characteristics. . . .

Traditional moralists have argued that the act of entering into a contract is subject to several secondary moral constraints:

1. Both of the parties to the contract must have full knowledge of the nature of the agreement they are entering.
2. Neither party to a contract must intentionally misrepresent the facts of the contractual situation to the other party.
3. Neither party to a contract must be forced to enter the contract under duress or undue influence.

These secondary constraints can be justified by the same sorts of arguments that Kant and Rawls use to justify the basic duty to perform one's contracts. Kant, for example, easily shows that misrepresentation in the making of a contract cannot be universalized, and Rawls argues that if misrepresentation were not prohibited, fear of deception would make members of a society feel less free to enter contracts. However, these secondary constraints can also be justified on the grounds that a contract cannot exist unless these constraints are fulfilled. For a contract is essentially a *free agreement* struck between two parties. Since an agreement cannot exist unless both parties know what they are agreeing to, contracts require full knowledge and the absence of misrepresentation. Since freedom implies the absence of coercion, contracts must be made without duress or undue influence.

The contractual theory of business's duties to consumers, then, claims that a business has four main moral duties: The basic duty of (1) complying with the terms of the sales contract, and the secondary duties of (2) disclosing the nature of the product, (3) avoiding misrepresentation, and (4) avoiding the use of duress and undue influence. By acting in accordance with these duties, a business respects the right of consumers to be treated as free and equal persons, that is, in accordance with their right to be treated only as they have freely consented to be treated.

## The Duty to Comply

The most basic moral duty that a business firm owes its customers, according to the contract view, is the duty to provide consumers with a product that lives up to those claims that the firm expressly made about the product, which led the customer to enter the contract freely, and which formed the customer's understanding concerning what he or she was agreeing to buy. In the early 1970s, for example, Winthrop Laboratories marketed a painkiller that the firm advertised as "nonaddictive." Subsequently, a patient using the painkiller became addicted to it and shortly died from an overdose. A court found Winthrop Laboratories liable for the patient's death because, although it had expressly stated that the drug was nonaddictive, Winthrop Laboratories had failed to live up to its duty to comply with this express contractual claim.[2]

As this example suggests, our legal system has incorporated the moral view that firms have a duty to live up to the express claims they make about their products. The Uniform Commercial Code, for example, states in Section 2-314:

> Any affirmation of fact or promise made by the seller to the buyer that related to the goods and becomes part of the basis of the bargain creates an express warranty that the goods shall conform to the affirmation or promise.

In addition to the duties that result from the *express* claim a seller makes about the product, the contract view also holds that the seller has a duty to carry through on any *implied* claims he or she knowingly makes about the product. The seller, for example, has the moral duty to provide a product that can be used safely for the ordinary and special purposes for which the customer, relying on the seller's judgment, has been led to believe it can be used. . . .

The express or implied claims that a seller might make about the qualities possessed by the product range over a variety of areas and are affected by a number of factors. Frederick Sturdivant classifies these areas in terms of four variables: "The definition of product quality used here is: the degree to which product performance meets predetermined expectation with respect to (1) reliability, (2) service life, (3) maintainability, and (4) safety."[3]

***Reliability*** Claims of reliability refer to the probability that a product will function as the consumer is led to expect that it will function. If a product incorporates a number of interdependent components, then the probability that it will function properly is equal to the result of multiplying together each component's probability of proper functioning.[4] As the number of components in a product multiplies, therefore, the manufacturer has a corresponding duty to ensure that each component functions in such a manner that the total product is as reliable as he or she implicitly or expressly claims it will be. This is especially the case when malfunction poses health or safety hazards. The U.S. Consumer Product Safety Commission lists hundreds of examples of hazards from product malfunctions in its periodic announcements.[5]

***Service Life*** Claims concerning the life of a product refer to the period of time during which the product will function as effectively as the consumer is led to expect it to function. Generally, the consumer implicitly understands that service life will depend on the amount of wear and tear to which one subjects the product. In addition, consumers also base some of their expectations of service life on the explicit guarantees the manufacturer attaches to the product.

A more subtle factor that influences service life is the factor of obsolescence.[6] Technological advances may render some products obsolete when a new product appears that carries out the same functions more efficiently. Or purely stylistic changes may make last year's product appear dated and less desirable. The contract view implies that a seller who knows that a certain product will become obsolete has a duty to correct any mistaken beliefs he or she knows buyers will form concerning the service life they may expect from the product.

***Maintainability*** Claims of maintainability are claims concerning the ease with which the product can be repaired and kept in operating condition. Claims of maintainability are often made in the form of an express warranty. Whirlpool Corporation, for example, appended this express warranty on one of its products:

> During your first year of ownership, all parts of the appliance (except the light bulbs) that we find are defective in materials or workmanship will be repaired or replaced by Whirlpool free of charge, and we will pay all labor charges. During the second year, we will continue to assume the

> same responsibility as stated above except you pay any labor charges.[7]

But sellers often also imply that a product may be easily repaired even after the expiration date of an express warranty. In fact, however, product repairs may be costly, or even impossible, because of the unavailability of parts.

***Product Safety*** Implied and express claims of product safety refer to the degree of risk associated with using a product. Since the use of virtually any product involves some degree of risk, questions of safety are essentially questions of *acceptable known levels* of risk. That is, a product is safe if its attendant risks are known and judged to be "acceptable" or "reasonable" by the *buyer* in view of the benefits the buyer expects to derive from using the product. This implies that the seller complies with his or her part of a free agreement if the seller provides a product that involves only those risks he or she says it involves, and the buyer purchases it with that understanding. The National Commission on Product Safety, for example, characterized "reasonable risk" in these terms:

> Risk of bodily harm to users are not unreasonable when consumers understand that risks exist, can appraise their probability and severity, know how to cope with them, and voluntarily accept them to get benefits they could not obtain in less risky ways. When there is a risk of this character, consumers have reasonable opportunity to protect themselves; and public authorities should hesitate to substitute their value judgments about the desirability of the risk for those of the consumers who choose to incur it. But preventable risk is not reasonable (a) when consumers do not know that it exists; or (b) when, though aware of it, consumers are unable to estimate its frequency and severity; or (c) when consumers do not know how to cope with it, and hence are likely to incur harm unnecessarily; or (d) when risk is unnecessary in that it could be reduced or eliminated at a cost in money or in the performance of the product that consumers would willingly incur if they knew the facts and were given the choice.[8]

Thus, the seller of a product (according to the contractual theory) has a moral duty to provide a product whose use involves *no greater risks* than those the seller *expressly* communicates to the buyer or those the seller *implicitly* communicates by the implicit claims made when marketing the product for a use whose normal risk level is well known. . . .

### The Duty of Disclosure

An agreement cannot bind unless both parties to the agreement know what they are doing and freely choose to do it. This implies that the seller who intends to enter a contract with a customer has a duty to disclose exactly what the customer is buying and what the terms of the sale are. At a minimum, this means the seller has a duty to inform the buyer of any facts about the product that would affect the customer's decision to purchase the product. For example, if the product the consumer is buying possesses a defect that poses a risk to the user's health or safety, the consumer should be so informed. Some have argued that sellers should also disclose a product's components or ingredients, its performance characteristics, costs of operation, product ratings, and any other applicable standards.[9]

Behind the claim that entry into a sales contract requires full disclosure is the idea that an agreement is free only to the extent that one knows what alternatives are available: Freedom depends on knowledge. The more the buyer knows about the various products available on the market and the more comparisons the buyer is able to make among them, the more one can say that the buyer's agreement is voluntary. . . .[10]

Since entry into a contract requires *freely* given consent, the seller has a duty to refrain from exploiting emotional states that may induce the buyer to act irrationally against his or her own best interests. For similar reasons, the seller also has the duty not to take advantage of gullibility, immaturity, ignorance, or any other factors that reduce or eliminate the buyer's ability to make free rational choices.

### Problems with the Contractual Theory

The main objections to the contract theory focus on the unreality of the assumptions on which the theory is based. First, critics argue, the theory unrealistically assumes that manufacturers make direct agreements with consumers. Nothing could be farther from the truth. Normally, a series of wholesalers and retailers stand between the manufacturer and the ultimate consumer. The manufacturer sells the product to the wholesaler, who sells it to the retailer, who finally sells it to the consumer. The manufacturer never enters into any direct contract with the consumer. How then can one say that manufacturers have contractual duties to the consumer?

Advocates of the contract view of manufacturers' duties have tried to respond to this criticism by arguing that manufacturers enter into "indirect" agreements with consumers. Manufacturers promote their products through their own advertising campaigns. These advertisements supply the promises that lead people to purchase products from retailers who merely function as "conduits" for the manufacturer's product. Consequently, through these advertisements, the manufacturer forges an indirect contractual relationship not only with the immediate retailers who purchase the manufacturer's product but also with the ultimate consumers of the product. The most famous application of this doctrine of broadened indirect contractual relationships is to be found in a 1960 court opinion, *Henningsen v. Bloomfield Motors*. . . .[11]

A second objection to the contract theory focuses on the fact that a contract is a two-edged sword. If a consumer can freely agree to buy a product *with* certain qualities, the consumer can also freely agree to buy a product *without* those qualities. That is, freedom of contract allows a manufacturer to be released from his or her contractual obligations by explicitly *disclaiming* that the product is reliable, serviceable, safe, and so on. Many manufacturers fix such disclaimers on their products. . . .

The contract view, then, implies that if the consumer has ample opportunity to examine the product and the disclaimers and voluntarily consents to buy it anyway, he or she assumes the responsibility for the defects disclaimed by the manufacturer, as well as for any defects the customer may carelessly have overlooked. Disclaimers can effectively nullify all contractual duties of the manufacturer.

A third objection to the contract theory criticizes the assumption that buyer and seller meet each other as equals in the sales agreement. The contractual theory assumes that buyers and sellers are equally skilled at evaluating the quality of a product and that buyers are able to adequately protect their interests against the seller. . . .

In fact, sellers and buyers do not exhibit the equality these doctrines assume. A consumer who must purchase hundreds of different kinds of commodities cannot hope to be as knowledgeable as a manufacturer who specializes in producing a single product. Consumers have neither the expertise nor the time to acquire and process the information on which they must base their purchase decisions. Consumers, as a consequence, must usually rely on the judgment of the seller in making their purchase decisions, and are particularly vulnerable to being harmed by the seller. Equality, far from being the rule, as the contract theory assumes, is usually the exception.

## THE DUE CARE THEORY

The "due care" theory of the manufacturer's duties to consumers is based on the idea that consumers and sellers do not meet as equals and that the consumer's interests are particularly vulnerable to being harmed by the manufacturer who has a knowledge and an expertise that the consumer does not have. Because manufacturers are in a more advantaged position, they have a duty to take special "care" to ensure that consumers' interests are not harmed by the products that they offer them. The doctrine of "caveat emptor" is here replaced with a weak version of the doctrine of "caveat vendor": let the seller take care. . . .

The "due care" view holds, then, that because consumers must depend on the greater expertise of the manufacturer, the manufacturer not only has a duty to deliver a product that lives up to the express and implied claims about it, but in addition the manufacturer has a duty to exercise due care to prevent others from being injured by the product, *even if the manufacturer explicitly disclaims such responsibility and the buyer agrees to the disclaimer.* The manufacturer violates this duty and is "negligent" when there is a failure to exercise the care that a reasonable person could have foreseen would be necessary to prevent others from being harmed by use of the product. Due care must enter into the design of the product, into the choice of reliable materials for constructing the product, into the manufacturing processes involved in putting the product together, into the quality control used to test and monitor production, and into the warnings, labels, and instructions attached to the product. In each of these areas, according to the due care view, the manufacturer, in virtue of a greater expertise and knowledge, has a positive duty to take whatever steps are necessary to ensure that when the product leaves the plant it is as safe as possible, and the customer has a right to such assurance. Failure to take such steps is a breach of the moral duty to exercise due care and a violation of the injured person's right to expect such care, a right that rests on the consumer's need to rely on the manufacturer's expertise. . . .

### The Duty to Exercise Due Care

According to the due care theory, manufacturers exercise sufficient care only when they take adequate steps to prevent whatever injurious effects they can foresee that the use of their product may have on consumers after having conducted inquiries into the way the product will be used and after having attempted to anticipate any possible misuses of the product. A manufacturer, then, is *not* morally negligent when others are harmed by a product and the harm was not one that the manufacturer could possibly have foreseen or prevented. Nor is a manufacturer morally negligent after having taken all reasonable steps to protect the consumer and to ensure that the consumer is informed of any irremovable risks that might still attend the use of the product. A car manufacturer, for example, cannot be said to be negligent from a moral point of view when people carelessly misuse the cars the manufacturer produces. A car manufacturer would be morally negligent only if the manufacturer had allowed unreasonable dangers to remain in the design of the car that consumers cannot be expected to know about or that they cannot guard against by taking their own precautionary measures.

What specific responsibilities does the duty to exercise due care impose on the producer? In general, the producer's responsibilities would extend to three areas:

***Design*** The manufacturer should ascertain whether the design of an article conceals any dangers, whether it incorporates all feasible safety devices, and whether it uses materials that are adequate for the purposes the product is intended to serve. The manufacturer is responsible for being thoroughly acquainted with the design of the item, and to conduct research and tests extensive enough to uncover any risks that may be involved in employing the article under various conditions of use. . . .

***Production*** The production manager should control the manufacturing processes to eliminate any defective items, to identify any weaknesses that become apparent during production, and to ensure that short-cuts, substitution of weaker materials, or other economizing measures are not taken during manufacture that would compromise the safety of the final product. To ensure this, there should be adequate quality controls over materials that are to be used in the manufacture of the product and over the various stages of manufacture.

***Information*** The manufacturer should fix labels, notices, or instructions on the product that will warn the user of all dangers involved in using or misusing the item and that will enable the user to adequately guard himself or herself against harm or injury. These instructions should be clear and simple, and warnings of any hazards involved in using or misusing the product should also be clear, simple, and prominent. . . .

### Problems with "Due Care"

The basic difficulty raised by the "due care" theory is that there is no clear method for determining when one has exercised enough "due care." That is, there is no hard and fast rule for determining how far a firm must go to ensure the safety of its product. Some authors have proposed the general utilitarian rule that the greater the probability of harm and the larger the population that might be harmed, the more the firm is obligated to do. But this fails to resolve some important issues. Every product involves at least some small risk of injury. If the manufacturer should try to eliminate even low-level risks, this would require that the manufacturer invest so much in each product that the product would be priced out of the reach of most consumers. Moreover, even *attempting* to balance higher risks against added costs involves measurement problems: How does one quantify risks to health and life?

A second difficulty raised by the "due care" theory is that it assumes that the manufacturer can discover the risks that attend the use of a product before the consumer buys and uses it. In fact, in a technologically innovative society new products whose defects cannot emerge until years or decades have passed will continually be introduced into the market. Only years after thousands of people were using and being exposed to asbestos, for example, did a correlation emerge between the incidence of cancer and exposure to asbestos. Although manufacturers may have greater expertise than consumers, their expertise does not make them omniscient. Who, then, is to bear the costs of injuries sustained from products whose defects neither the manufacturer nor the consumer could have uncovered beforehand?

Third, the due care view appears to some to be paternalistic. For it assumes that the *manufacturer* should be the one who makes the important decisions for the consumer, at least with respect to the levels of risks that are proper for consumers to bear. One may wonder whether such decisions should not be left up to the free choice of consumers who can decide for themselves whether or not they want to pay for additional risk reduction.

## THE SOCIAL COSTS VIEW OF THE MANUFACTURER'S DUTIES

A third theory on the duties of the manufacturer would extend the manufacturer's duties beyond those imposed by contractual relationships and beyond those imposed by the duty to exercise due care in preventing injury or harm. This third theory holds that a manufacturer should pay the costs of *any* injuries sustained through any defects in the product, *even when the manufacturer exercised all due care in the design and manufacture of the product and has taken all reasonable precautions to warn users of every foreseen danger.* According to this third theory, a manufacturer has a duty to assume the risks of even those injuries that arise out of defects in the product that no one could reasonably have foreseen or eliminated. The theory is a very strong version of the doctrine of "caveat vendor": let the seller take care.

This third theory, which has formed the basis of the legal doctrine of "strict liability," is founded on utilitarian arguments. The utilitarian arguments for this third theory hold that the "external" costs of injuries resulting from unavoidable defects in the design of an artifact constitute part of the costs society must pay for producing and using an artifact. By having the manufacturer bear the external costs that result from these injuries as well as the ordinary internal costs of design and manufacture, all costs will be internalized and added on as part of the price of the product. Internalizing all costs in this way, according to proponents of this theory, will lead to a more efficient use of society's resources. First, since the price will reflect *all* the costs of producing and using the artifact, market forces will ensure that the product is not overproduced, and that resources are not wasted on it. (Whereas if some costs were not included in the price, then manufacturers would tend to produce more than is needed.) Second, since manufacturers have to pay the costs of injuries, they will be motivated to exercise greater care and to thereby reduce the number of accidents. Manufacturers will, therefore, strive to cut down the social costs of injuries, and this means a more efficient care for our human resources. In order to produce the maximum benefits possible from our limited resources, therefore, the social costs of injuries from defective products should be internalized by passing them on to the manufacturer, even when the manufacturer has done all that could be done to eliminate such defects. Third, internalizing the costs of injury in this way enables the manufacturer to distribute losses among all the users of a product instead of allowing losses to fall on individuals who may not be able to sustain the loss by themselves.

Underlying this third theory on the duties of the manufacturer are the standard utilitarian assumptions about the values of efficiency. The theory assumes that an efficient use of resources is so important for society that social costs should be allocated in whatever way will lead to a more efficient use and care of our resources. On this basis, the theory argues that a manufacturer should bear the social costs for injuries caused by defects in a product, even when no negligence was involved and no contractual relationship existed between the manufacturer and the user.

## Problems with the Social Costs View

The major criticism of the social costs view of the manufacturer's duties is that it is unfair.[12] It is unfair, the critics charge, because it violates the basic canons of compensatory justice. Compensatory justice implies that a person should be forced to compensate an injured party only if the person could foresee and could have prevented the injury. By forcing manufacturers to pay for injuries that they could neither foresee nor prevent, the social costs theory (and the legal theory of "strict liability" that flows from it) treats manufacturers unfairly. Moreover, insofar as the social costs theory encourages passing the costs of injuries on to all consumers (in the form of higher prices), consumers are also being treated unfairly.

A second criticism of the social costs theory attacks the assumption that passing the costs of all injuries on to manufacturers will reduce the number of accidents.[13] On the contrary, critics claim, by relieving consumers of the responsibility of paying for their own injuries, the social costs theory will encourage carelessness in consumers. An increase in consumer carelessness will lead to an increase in consumer injuries.

A third argument against the social costs theory focuses on the financial burdens the theory imposes on manufacturers and insurance carriers. Critics claim that a growing number of consumers successfully sue manufacturers for compensation for any injuries sustained while using a product, even when the manufacturer took all due care to ensure that the product was safe.[14] Not only have the number of "strict liability" suits increased, critics claim, but the amounts awarded to injured consumers have also escalated. Moreover, they continue, the rising costs of the many liability suits that the theory of "strict liability" has created have precipitated a crisis in the insurance industry because insurance companies end up paying the liability suits brought against manufacturers. . . .

The arguments for and against the social costs theory deserve much more discussion than we can give them here. The theory is essentially an attempt to come to grips with the problem of allocating the costs of injuries between two morally innocent parties: The manufacturer who could not foresee or prevent a product-related injury, and the consumer who could not guard himself or herself against the injury because the hazard was unknown. This allocation problem will arise in any society that, like ours, has come to rely on technology whose effects do not become evident until years after the technology is introduced. Unfortunately, it is also a problem that may have no "fair" solution.

## NOTES

1. See Thomas Garrett and Richard J. Klonoski, *Business Ethics*, 2nd ed. (Englewood Cliffs, New Jersey: Prentice Hall, 1986), p. 88.
2. *Crocker v. Winthrop Laboratories, Division of Sterling Drug, Inc.*, 514 Southwestern 2d 429 (1974).
3. Frederick D. Sturdivant, *Business and Society*, 3rd. ed. (Homewood, IL: Richard D. Irwin, Inc., 1985), p. 392.
4. *Ibid.*, p. 393.
5. The U.S. Consumer Products Safety Commission's notices of dangerous consumer products are accessible on the Commission's Web page at gopher://cpsc.gov.
6. A somewhat dated but still incisive discussion of this issue is found in Vance Packard, *The Wastemakers* (New York: David McKay Co., Inc., 1960).
7. Quoted in address by S. E. Upton (vice-president of Whirlpool Corporation) to the American Marketing Association in Cleveland, OH: 11 December 1969.
8. National Commission on Product Safety, *Final Report*, quoted in William W. Lowrance, *Of Acceptable Risk* (Los Altos, CA: William Kaufmann, Inc., 1976), p. 80.
9. See Louis Stern, "Consumer Protection via Increased Information," *Journal of Marketing*, 31, no. 2 (April 1967).
10. Lawrence E. Hicks, *Coping with Packaging Laws* (New York: AMACOM, 1972). p. 17.
11. *Henningsen v. Bloomfield Motors, Inc.*, 32 New Jersey 358, 161 Atlantic 2d 69 (1960).
12. George P. Fletcher, "Fairness and Utility in Tort Theory," *Harvard Law Review*, 85, no. 3 (January 1972): 537–73.
13. Posner, *Economic Analysis of Law*, pp. 139–42.
14. See "Unsafe Products: The Great Debate Over Blame and Punishment," *Business Week*, 30 April 1984; Stuart Taylor, "Product Liability: the New Morass," *New York Times*, 10 March 1985; "The Product Liability Debate," *Newsweek*, 10 September 1984.

# Strict Products Liability and Compensatory Justice

*George G. Brenkert*

## I

Strict products liability is the doctrine that the seller of a product has legal responsibilities to compensate the user of that product for injuries suffered because of a defective aspect of the product, even when the seller has not been negligent in permitting that defect to occur.[1] Thus, even though a manufacturer, for example, has reasonably applied the existing techniques of manufacture and has anticipated and cared for nonintended uses of the product, he may still be held liable for injuries a product user suffers if it can be shown that the product was defective when it left the manufacturer's hands.

To say that there is a crisis today concerning this doctrine would be to utter a commonplace which few in the business community would deny. The development of the doctrine of strict products liability, according to most business people, threatens many businesses financially. Furthermore, strict products liability is said to be a morally questionable doctrine, since the manufacturer or seller has not been negligent in permitting the injury-causing defect to occur. On the other hand, victims of defective products complain that they deserve full compensation for injuries sustained in using a defective product whether or not the seller is at fault. Medical expenses and time lost from one's job are costs no individual should have to bear by himself. It is only fair that the seller share such burdens.

In general, discussions of this crisis focus on the limits to which a business ought to be held responsible. Much less frequently, discussions of strict products liability consider the underlying question of whether the doctrine of strict products liability is rationally justifiable. But unless this question is answered it would seem premature to seek to determine the limits to which businesses ought to be held liable in such cases. In the following paper I discuss this underlying philosophical question and argue that there is a rational justification for strict products liability which links it to the very nature of the free enterprise system.

## II

. . . To begin with, it is crucial to remember that what we have to consider is the relationship between an entity doing business and an individual. The strict liability attributed to business would not be attributed to an individual who happened to sell some product he had made to his neighbor or a stranger. If Peter sold an article he had made to Paul and Paul hurt himself because the article had a defect which occurred through no negligence of Peter's, we would not normally hold Peter morally responsible to pay for Paul's injuries. . . .

It is different for businesses. They have been held to be legally and morally obliged to pay the victim for his injuries. Why? What is the difference? The difference is that when Paul is hurt by a defective product from corporation X, he is hurt by something produced in a socioeconomic system purportedly embodying free enterprise. In other words, among other things:

Used by permission of the author.

1. Each business and/or corporation produces articles or services it sells for profit.
2. Each member of this system competes with other members of the system in trying to do as well as it can for itself not simply in each exchange, but through each exchange for its other values and desires.
3. Competition is to be "open and free, without deception of fraud."
4. Exchanges are voluntary and undertaken when each party believes it can benefit thereby. One party provides the means for another party's ends if the other party will provide the first party the means to its ends.
5. The acquisition and disposition of ownership rights—that is, of private property—is permitted in such exchanges.
6. No market or series of markets constitutes the whole of a society.
7. Law, morality, and government play a role in setting acceptable limits to the nature and kinds of exchange in which people may engage.

What is it about such a system which would justify claims of strict products liability against businesses? . . . In the free enterprise system, each person and/or business is obligated to follow the rules and understandings which define this socioeconomic system. Following the rules is expected to channel competition among individuals and businesses to socially positive results. In providing the means to fulfill the ends of others, one's own ends also get fulfilled.

Though this does not happen in every case, it is supposed to happen most of the time. Those who fail in their competition with others may be the object of charity, but not of other duties. Those who succeed, qua members of this socioeconomic system, do not have moral duties to aid those who fail. Analogously, the team which loses the game may receive our sympathy but the winning team is not obligated to help it to win the next game or even to play it better. Those who violate the rules, however, may be punished or penalized, whether or not the violation was intentional and whether or not it redounded to the benefit of the violator. Thus, a team may be assessed a penalty for something that a team member did unintentionally to a member of the other team but which injured the other team's chances of competition in the game by violating the rules.

This point may be emphasized by another instance involving a game that brings us close to strict products liability. Imagine that you are playing table tennis with another person in his newly constructed table tennis room. You are both avid table tennis players and the game means a lot to both of you. Suppose that after play has begun, you are suddenly and quite obviously blinded by the light over the table—the light shade has a hole in it which, when it turned in your direction, sent a shaft of light unexpectedly into your eyes. You lose a crucial point as a result. Surely it would be unfair of your opponent to seek to maintain his point because he was faultless—after all, he had not intended to blind you when he installed that light shade. You would correctly object that he had gained the point unfairly, that you should not have to give up the point lost, and that the light shade should be modified so that the game can continue on a fair basis. It is only fair that the point be played over.

Businesses and their customers in a free enterprise system are also engaged in competition with each other. The competition here, however, is multifaceted as each tries to gain the best agreement he can from the other with regard to the buying and selling of raw materials, products, services, and labor. Such agreements must be voluntary. The competition which leads to them cannot involve coercion. In addition, such competition must be fair and ultimately result in the benefit of the entire society through the operation of the proverbial invisible hand.

Crucial to the notion of fairness of competition are not simply the demands that the competition be open, free, and honest, but also that each person in a society be given an equal opportunity to participate in the system in order to fulfill his or her own particular ends. . . .

Equality of opportunity requires that one not be prevented by arbitrary obstacles from participating (by engaging in a productive role of some kind or other) in the system of free enterprise, competition, and so on in order to fulfill one's own ends ("reap the benefits"). Accordingly, monopolies are restricted, discriminatory hiring policies have been condemned, and price collusion is forbidden.

However, each person participates in the system of free enterprise *both* as a worker/producer *and* as a consumer. The two roles interact; if the person could not consume he would not be able to work, and if there were no consumers there would be no work to be done. Even if a particular individual is only (what is ordinarily considered) a consumer, he or she plays a theoretically significant role in the competitive free enterprise system. The fairness of the system depends upon what access he or she has to information about goods and services on the market, the lack of coercion imposed on that person to buy goods, and the lack of arbitrary restrictions imposed by the market and/or government on his or her behavior.

In short, equality of opportunity is a doctrine with two sides which applies both to producers and to consumers. If, then, a person as a consumer or a producer is injured by a defective product—which is one way his activities might arbitrarily be restricted by the action of (one of the members of) the market system—surely his free and voluntary participation in the system of free enterprise will be seriously affected. Specifically, his equal opportunity to participate in the system in order to fulfill his own ends will be diminished.

Here is where strict products liability enters the picture. In cases of strict liability the manufacturer does not intend for a certain aspect of his product to injure someone. Nevertheless, the person is injured. As a result, he is at a disadvantage both as a consumer and as a producer. He cannot continue to play either role as he might wish. Therefore, he is denied that equality of opportunity which is basic to the economic system in question just as surely as he would be if he were excluded from employment by various unintended consequences of the economic system which nevertheless had racially or sexually prejudicial implications. Accordingly, it is fair for the manufacturer to compensate the person for his losses before proceeding with business as usual. That is, the user of a manufacturer's product may justifiably demand compensation from the manufacturer when its product can be shown to be defective and has injured him and harmed his chances of participation in the system of free enterprise.

Hence, strict liability finds a basis in the notion of equality of opportunity which plays a central role in the notion of a free enterprise system. That is why a business which does *not* have to pay for the injuries an individual suffers in the use of a defective article made by that business is felt to be unfair to its customers. Its situation is analogous to that of a player's unintentional violation of a game rule which is intended to foster equality of competitive opportunity.

A soccer player, for example, may unintentionally trip an opposing player. He did not mean to do it; perhaps he himself had stumbled. Still, he has to be penalized. If the referee looked the other way, the tripped player would rightfully object that he had been treated unfairly. Similarly, the manufacturer of a product may be held strictly liable for a product of his which injures a person who uses that product. Even if he is faultless, a consequence of his activities is to render the user of his product less capable of equal participation in the socioeconomic system. The manufacturer should be penalized by way of compensating the victim. Thus, the basis upon which manufacturers are held strictly liable is compensatory justice.

In a society which refuses to resort to paternalism or to central direction of the economy and which turns, instead, to competition in order to allocate scarce positions and resources, compensatory justice requires that the competition be fair and losers be protected.[2] Specifically, no one who loses should be left so destitute that he cannot reenter the competition. Furthermore, those who suffer injuries traceable to defective merchandise or services which restrict their participation in the competitive system should also be compensated.

Compensatory justice does not presuppose negligence or evil intentions on the part of those to whom the injuries might ultimately be traced. It is not perplexed or incapacitated by the relative innocence of all parties involved. Rather, it is concerned with correcting the disadvantaged situation an individual experiences due to accidents or failures which occur in the normal working of that competitive system. It is on this basis that other compensatory programs which alleviate the disabilities of various minority groups are founded. Strict products liability is also founded on compensatory justice.

An implication of the preceding argument is that business is not morally obliged to pay, as such, for the physical injury a person suffers. Rather, it must pay for the loss of equal competitive opportunity—even though it usually is the case that it is because of a (physical) injury that there is a loss of equal opportunity. Actual legal cases in which the injury which prevents a person from going about his or her daily activities is emotional or mental, as well as physical, support this thesis. If a person were neither mentally nor physically harmed, but still rendered less capable of participating competitively because of a defective aspect of a product, there would still be grounds for holding the company liable.

For example, suppose I purchased and used a cosmetic product guaranteed to last a month. When used by most people it is odorless. On me, however, it has a terrible smell. I can stand the smell, but my co-workers and most other people find it intolerable. My employer sends me home from work until it wears off. The product has not harmed me physically or mentally. Still, on the above argument, I would have reason to hold the manufacturer liable. Any cosmetic product with this result is defective. As a consequence my opportunity to participate in the socioeconomic system is curbed. I should be compensated.

## III

There is another way of arriving at the same conclusion about the basis of strict products liability. To speak of business or the free enterprise system, it was noted above, is to speak of the voluntary exchanges between producer and customer which take place when each party believes he has an opportunity to benefit. Surely customers and producers may miscalculate their benefits; something they voluntarily agreed to buy or sell may turn out not to be to their benefit. The successful person does not have any moral responsibilities to the unsuccessful person—at least as a member of this economic system. If, however, fraud is the reason one person does not benefit, the system is, in principle, undermined. If such fraud were universalized, the system would collapse. Accordingly, the person committing the fraud does have a responsibility to make reparations to the one mistreated.

Consider once again the instance of a person who is harmed by a product he bought or used, a product that can reasonably be said to be defective. Has the nature of the free enterprise system also been undermined or corrupted in this instance? Producer and consumer have exchanged the product but it has not been to their mutual benefit; the manufacturer may have benefited, but the customer has suffered because of the defect. Furthermore, if such exchanges were universalized, the system would also be undone.

Suppose that whenever people bought products from manufacturers the products turned out to be defective and the customers were always injured, even though the manufacturers could not be held negligent. Though one party to such exchanges might benefit, the other party always suffered. If the rationale for this economic system—the reason it was adopted and is defended—were that in the end both parties share the equal opportunity to gain, surely it would collapse with the above consequences. Consequently, as with fraud, an economic system of free enterprise requires that injuries which result from defective products be compensated. The question is: Who is to pay for the compensation?

There are three possibilities. The injured party could pay for his own injuries. However, this is implausible since what is called for is compensation and not merely payment for injuries. If the injured party had simply injured himself, if he had been negligent or careless, then it is plausible that he should pay for his own injuries. No compensation is at stake here. But in the present case the injury stems from the actions of a particular manufacturer who, albeit unwittingly, placed the defective product on the market and stands to gain through its sale.

The rationale of the free enterprise system would be undermined, we have seen, if such actions were universalized, for then the product user's equal opportunity to benefit from the system would be denied. Accordingly, since the rationale and motivation for an individual to be part of this socioeconomic system is his opportunity to gain from participation in it, justice requires that the injured product user receive compensation for his injuries. Since the individual can hardly compensate himself, he must receive compensation from some other source.

Second, some third party—such as government—could compensate the injured person. This is not wholly implausible if one is prepared to modify the structure of the free enterprise system. And, indeed, in the long run this may be the most plausible course of action. However, if one accepts the structure of the free enterprise system, this alternative must be rejected because it permits the interference of government into individual affairs.

Third, we are left with the manufacturer. Suppose a manufacturer's product, even though the manufacturer wasn't negligent, always turned out to be defective and injured those using his products. We might sympathize with his plight, but he would either have to stop manufacturing altogether (no one would buy such products) or else compensate the victims for their losses. (Some people might buy and use his products under these conditions.) If he forced people to buy and use his products he would corrupt the free enterprise system. If he did not compensate the injured users, they would not buy and he would not be able to sell his products. Hence, he could partake of the free enterprise system—that is, sell his products—only if he compensated his user/victims. Accordingly, the sale of this hypothetical line of defective products would be voluntarily accepted as just or fair only if compensation were paid the user/victims of such products by the manufacturer.

The same conclusion follows even if we consider a single defective product. The manufacturer put the defective product on the market. Because of his actions others who seek the opportunity to participate on an equal basis in this system in order to benefit therefrom are unable to do so. Thus, a result of his actions, even though unintended, is to undermine the system's character and integrity. Accordingly, when a person is injured in his attempt to participate in this system, he is owed compensation by the manufacturer. The seller of the defective article must not jeopardize the equal opportunity of the product user to benefit from the system. The seller need not guarantee that the buyer/user will benefit from the purchase of the product; after all, the buyer may miscalculate or be careless in the use of a nondefective product. But if he is not careless or has not miscalculated, his opportunity to benefit from the system is illegitimately harmed if he is injured in its use because of the product's defectiveness. He deserves compensation.

It follows from the arguments in this and the preceding section that strict products liability is not only compatible with the system of free enterprise but that if it were not attributed to the manufacturer the system itself would be morally defective. And the justification for requiring manufacturers to pay compensation when people are injured by defective products is that the demands of compensatory justice are met.[3]

## NOTES

1. This characterization of strict products liability is adapted from Alvin S. Weinstein et al., *Products Liability and the Reasonably Safe Product* (New York: John Wiley & Sons, 1978), ch. 1. I understand the seller to include the manufacturer, the retailer, distributors, and wholesalers. For the sake of convenience, I will generally refer simply to the manufacturer.
2. I have drawn heavily, in this paragraph, on the fine article by Bernard Boxhill, "The Morality of Reparation," reprinted in *Reverse Discrimination*, ed. Barry R. Gross (Buffalo, New York: Prometheus Books, 1977), pp. 270–278.
3. I would like to thank the following for providing helpful comments on earlier versions of this paper: Betsy Postow, Jerry Phillips, Bruce Fisher, John Hardwig, and Sheldon Cohen.

## INVESTMENT RISK

# The Individual Investor in Securities Markets: An Ethical Analysis

*Robert E. Frederick*
*and W. Michael Hoffman*

Securities markets are full of pitfalls for individual investors. Examples of fraud and regulatory violations in the markets are common. For instance, a recent *Business Week* cover story reports that investors are being duped out of hundreds of millions a year in penny stock scams in spite of SEC regulations.[1] A report in the *Wall Street Journal* on the Chicago futures trading fraud highlights the "danger of being ripped off in futures markets" by unscrupulous floor brokers filling customers' "market orders"—a type of order that "individual investors should avoid using."[2]

But securities markets present risks to individual investors that go beyond clear violations of regulations and fraud. The above *Wall Street Journal* story, for example, also issued a more general warning to investors:

> Futures are fast moving, risky investment vehicles that are unsuitable for anyone who can't afford to lose and who doesn't have time to pay close attention to trading positions.[3]

*Journal of Business Ethics* 9 (1990): 579–89. 

Furthermore, it is not only the high risk futures and commodities markets that are perilous for investors. For example, the North American Securities Administration reports that "the securities industry isn't responding well to the problems of small investors in the wake of the stock market crash," problems such as poor execution of trades and being misled by brokers.[4] Even the bond markets, which in the past at least gave the outside appearance of stability, are in increasing turmoil. For instance, the SEC is now investigating the possibility that securities firms dumped billions of dollars of risky municipal bonds on individual investors because they were unable to sell them to institutions.[5] And MetLife is suing RJR-Nabisco on the grounds that individual investors were unjustifiably harmed when the A rated corporate bonds they purchased lost millions in value due to the junk bond financing of the RJR-Nabisco leveraged buyout.[6]

In light of these and many other examples that could be given, suppose the SEC announced that individual investors, for their own protection, no longer have access to securities markets. They are no longer permitted to buy stocks, bonds, or commodities or futures options. If this were to happen there surely would be a public outcry of protest, even moral outrage. The reasons for such outrage probably would revolve around the belief that some fundamental right had been violated, perhaps the presumed right that markets should be free and open so that everyone has an opportunity to better his or her position and enjoy the goods and services of society.

A quick look, however, reveals that not all markets have unrestricted access. Nor is there a generally accepted belief that any rights are being unjustifiably violated in such cases. In consumer markets, for example, individuals under a certain age are prohibited from voting, buying alcoholic beverages, and seeing certain movies. Regardless of age, not just anyone can buy a fully automatic rifle or order a few dozen hand grenades. In fact, not just anyone can drive a car; one must pass a test and be licensed to do that. Furthermore, even after being allowed to drive, this privilege can be revoked if it is abused. And, of course, none of our citizens is legally permitted to participate in certain drug markets, such as cocaine.

But it will be argued that there is good reason for these and other such restrictions. We are attempting to prevent people, the argument goes, from harming themselves or causing harm to others. This is what makes it morally permissible, or even obligatory, to restrict access to certain kinds of consumer products. The ethical principle here is that, when possible, persons ought to be protected from undue harm. Hence, the restrictions in question are justified.

Yet might not this be exactly the rationale behind a possible SEC ban against individual investors entering securities markets? Just as unrestricted access to some drugs is thought to present unacceptable risks to consumers, trading in today's securities markets may present unacceptable risks to many investors, resulting in great financial rather than physical harm. And since we feel justified in prohibiting consumers from buying what we take to be highly dangerous drugs or other consumer products, shouldn't we, by analogy, be justified in prohibiting certain investors from buying highly risky financial instruments? . . .

## EXACTLY WHAT KIND OF INVESTOR ARE WE TALKING ABOUT?

The type of investor we will be concerned with, and the type we take to be the most likely candidate for the SEC prohibition mentioned earlier, is one that (a) is at relatively *high risk*, where risk is a function of the probability of a certain market event occurring and the degree of harm the investor would suffer were the event to occur, and (b) an investor who is relatively *unsophisticated* about the functioning of the market and hence unappreciative of the degree of risk he or she faces. For example, suppose Jones invests his life savings in high yield bonds issued to finance an LBO, and suppose a few months later the company that issued the bonds suddenly announces that it is going into Chapter 11 bankruptcy. The value of the bonds drops precipitously and, for all practical purposes, in a matter of hours Jones' savings are wiped out. If Jones did not realize that the high return he was initially receiving was a reflection of the risky nature of the bonds, then he would fall within the category of investors with which we are concerned even assuming he had several million dollars invested. . . .

## DO AT-RISK INVESTORS HAVE A RIGHT TO PARTICIPATE IN SECURITIES MARKETS?

Obviously at-risk investors are legally permitted to invest in securities markets, but do they have a right to do so? And if they do, what kind of right is it? These questions are important since how they are answered will determine in large part what kind of justification will be required to restrict or suspend investments by at-risk investors, or whether a justification is possible at all.

Since the word "right" is used in many different senses, we will give rough definitions of the sense in which we will use "right" and associated terms. A "claim right," as we will understand it, is a right established within a systems of rules. To have such a right is to have a valid or justified claim for action or forbearance against some person or institution. The notion of a "liberty" is weaker than that of a right. To have a liberty is not to have a duty or obligation to act toward a person or institution in a certain way. Rights imply liberties, but one may have a liberty without an associated right. A still weaker notion is that of a "privilege." To have a privilege is to have revocable permission to act in a certain way.[7]

Claim rights, liberties, and privileges can be either legal or moral depending on whether the rules in question are established by legislative action or follow from a system of morality. It is important to see that legal rights and moral rights need not be the same. A moral right may not be recognized by law, and one may have a legal right to engage in an immoral action.

If at-risk investors have claim rights to invest in the market, then the government has a corresponding duty not to interfere with their activity. On the other hand, if they have a liberty to invest, they have no duty not to invest. If they have a privilege, then they are permitted to invest but such permission can be withdrawn. Now, if at-risk investors have a claim right to invest, as opposed to a weaker liberty or an even weaker privilege to invest, then the justification required for infringing on that right will be very different from that required if they have a liberty or privilege. Hence, it is important to decide, as best we can, exactly which they have.

We believe a strong case can be made that at-risk investors have a moral claim right to invest in the market, and that this right follows from the classic "right to freedom" that is so much a part of the American tradition. . . .

It follows from the right to freedom that it is morally permissible for persons to choose to invest in any way they deem appropriate within the bounds of law and a proper regard for the wrongful effects their actions may have on the lives of others.

If this is correct, then any interference with this right, whether by some individual or government agency, is prima facie unjustified. There are, however, several objections that could be raised. One of them is that persons simply have no such moral right because they have no rights at all other than those granted by law. Thus, no moral right is violated if the legal right to invest is altered or eliminated. Another is that although persons have moral rights, they do not have the right to freedom that we have attributed to them. . . .

There is one other objection to the right of freedom that we proposed. It is that even if all competent persons have an equal right to freedom, it still does not follow that they have the right to make any choice within the sphere of choices that do not wrongfully harm others. It does not follow, for example, that they have the right to make choices that seriously harm themselves. Intervention in such cases may be justified to prevent harm.

But is it? In order to decide, we must consider the possible justifications for interfering with the choices of others.

## WHAT SORT OF JUSTIFICATION MIGHT BE OFFERED FOR RESTRICTING THE INVESTMENTS OF AT-RISK INVESTORS?

One kind of justification that might be proposed is paternalistic. By paternalism we roughly mean interfering with a person's actions or preferences by restricting their freedom of action or the range of choices normally available to them for the reason that such a restriction promotes or preserves their good, welfare, happiness, or interests. A paternalistic justification for restricting at risk investors would be that exposure to risk for many investors is too great to permit them to continue without some sort of protection that reduces the risk to an acceptable degree. For certain investors an acceptable degree may be no risk at all. For others some risk may be permissible.

In either case, the argument goes, as long as the intent of intervention is to protect or promote the good of at risk investors, and as long as it does not wrong other persons, then intervention is at least permissible and may be obligatory. It is only in this way that harm to many investors can be prevented.

The standard objection to paternalistic justifications is something like this: If people choose to run the risk to gain what they believe will be the rewards, who are we to interfere? From where do we derive a special dispensation to overrule their choices and interfere with their lives?

Although there is a kernel of truth in this objection, it is much too facile. Some paternalistic acts are clearly justified. Paternalistic reasoning is commonly used to justify restricting the choices of children and people judged incompetent or otherwise unable rationally to consider the consequences of their acts. Moreover, paternalistic justifications are not obviously unreasonable even in cases where the competence of the person is not in question. It is at least initially credible that some consumer products, such as prescription drugs, are not in unrestricted circulation precisely because of paternalistic reasons.

Let us confine our discussion to those persons ordinarily taken to be competent and rational. We still do not believe that paternalism *per se* justifies restricting at-risk investors that fall within this category. One reason is that it may be impossible to find out just what the good or welfare of an individual investor is. Not only is there the thorny problem of trying to reach a common and precise understanding of the vague idea of the "good" of a person, there are immense practical difficulties in discovering whether a certain individual's good is served by restricting his or her access to the market. There may be situations where an individual's good is not served, and intervention in those cases would be a wrongful violation of his or her rights.

But suppose regulators do know the good of some individuals. Would paternalism then justify intervening to preserve or promote their good? We believe not in cases where regulators and the person in question have differing conceptions of that person's good. Even if regulators happen to know a person's "true" good better than he or she does themselves, imposing on that person a conception of his or her good they do not accept is not justified. Regulators may attempt to persuade at-risk investors to take a different course or provide them with information that they need to make an informed decision, but it is not permissible to deny them the right to direct their lives. . . .

Although paternalism as characterized thus far does not justify interference with the choices of at-risk investors, there are circumstances in which intervention is justified. This can best be explained by using an example not related to investing. Suppose Jones mistakenly believes the food he is about to eat is wholesome but we have good reason to think it is contaminated with botulism. As he raises the fork to his mouth, we only have time to strike it away. At first he is angry, but after we explain the reason for our action he is grateful. The act of striking the fork away is an example of paternalistic intervention since it is done for Jones' good but against his wishes. It seems obvious, however, that we acted properly. Intervention in this case is justified since if Jones were fully aware of the circumstances he would act differently or would agree to have us intervene on his behalf. He would consent to our action. Hence, intervention here respects his right to freedom since it is compatible with his goals and does not force upon him some version of his good he would not accept.

Note that it is not merely our superior knowledge of the situation that justifies interference, but also our judgment that Jones would agree that our actions preserve or promote his good. The case would be different were Jones attempting suicide instead of trying to have a decent meal. Paternalistic intervention may not be justified when a person voluntarily undertakes an action harmful to him- or herself, provided that person has a reasonably complete understanding of his or her circumstances and the consequences of the action. But it is at least prima facie justified, we suggest, when an action is based on incomplete information and thus is, in one sense, less than fully voluntary.

Now suppose there are compelling grounds to believe that some otherwise competent investors are unappreciative of the high degree of risk they face, and that if they were presented with information about those risks they would act either to reduce or eliminate them, or would consent to having restrictions placed on the kinds of investments they could make. Since they would consent to intervention or act differently were they fully aware of the circumstances, intervention on their behalf is justified just as it was justified for Jones. Their rights are not violated since nothing is imposed on them that they would not consent to were they fully aware of the dangers they faced.

A major difference between the Jones case and at-risk investors is that we dealt with Jones as an individual, but a regulatory or legislative body would have to deal with at-risk investors as a group. There simply is no way to reach them all individually. Furthermore, although such bodies may be able to make reasonable assumptions about the kinds of risks acceptable to most at-risk investors, and about the kinds of restrictions to which most of them would agree, it seems inevitable that there will be some investors who would not consent to restrictions because, for example, they have an unusual conception of their good or welfare, or because they find the restrictions highly offensive. For these people restrictions on investing will impose a foreign conception of their good on them and thus is not compatible with their right to direct their lives. . . .

If the *reason* given for intervening is promoting the good of at-risk investors as a group, then, as we have tried to argue, it is not justified. Suppose, however, the reason is not only that the good of some investors is promoted, but that there is a duty to intervene to protect certain *rights*, in particular, the right of investors not to be harmed. The argument would go something like this: There is good reason to believe that some at-risk investors would consent to having restrictions placed on them to protect their financial position and prevent them from suffering financial harm. Since it is a basic function of government to protect its citizens from harm, there is a duty to protect these investors. Hence, placing restrictions on their investment activities is justified even though such restrictions may violate the right of other investors to direct their lives as they see fit.

If this argument is plausible, then there is a conflict of rights between two groups of at-risk investors. This is a genuine moral dilemma that can only be resolved by deciding whose rights are to prevail. We believe it should be the right not to be harmed. An analogy with prescription drugs may be helpful here. One reason there are restrictions on access to drugs is to prevent harm to persons who do not know how to use them correctly. These restrictions are justified, in our view, even supposing there are some individuals willing to take the risk. The right to freedom of this latter group should be and should remain a serious consideration in devising restrictions on drugs, but it does not override the right of others not to be exposed to excessive risk and possible serious harm.

The same holds true of at-risk investors. The right of some of them not to be exposed to excessive risk and possible serious financial harm overrides the right of others to invest without restrictions. We emphasize, however, that the right to freedom cannot be lightly dismissed, and must be given due consideration when formulating policies and regulations governing the markets. . . .

## IF SOME INVESTORS ARE RESTRICTED, HOW SHOULD IT BE DONE?

Since we are not experts in the regulation of securities markets, the best we can do here is make a few suggestions that seem to us worthy of additional investigation. It is a basic premise, essential for any just system of regulation and law, that relevantly different classes of persons be treated in relevantly different ways. Hence, it clearly would be unjust to restrict the activities of all investors to protect some of them. It also follows from this basic premise that distinctions must be drawn within the class of at-risk investors. It may turn out in the end that there is no workable method of protecting some at-risk investors while preserving the rights of all of them, but it would be a mistake to begin with this assumption.

In light of this it might be suggested that the only plausible course of action is to make sure that at-risk investors have all the information they need to make investment decisions. This has at least three advantages. The first is that providing information does not seriously infringe any rights. And establishing stringent policies to ensure that the information is received also may be reasonable. For example, suppose that to demonstrate a minimum level of competence persons must pass an examination before investing, just as they have to pass a driving exam before driving. Different kinds of exams could be given for different kinds of investments. Would such a procedure violate any rights? It certainly would be costly and inconvenient, but we doubt that it is an inordinate restriction on the right to freedom.

A second advantage is that providing information is already one function of the Securities and Exchange Commission. According to the Commission's pamphlet "Consumers' Financial Guide" the three main responsibilities of the Commission are:

1. To require that companies that offer their securities for sale in "interstate commerce" register with the Commission and make available to investors complete and accurate information.
2. To protect investors against misrepresentation and fraud in the issuance and sale of securities.
3. To oversee the securities markets to ensure they operate in a fair and orderly manner.

Although the pamphlet goes on to advise investors that "whatever the choice of investment, make sure that you have complete and accurate information before investing to ensure that you use your funds wisely," it also emphasizes that the SEC does not see itself as the guarantor of investments:

> Registration . . . does not insure investors against loss of their investments, but serves rather to provide information upon which investors may base an informed and realistic evaluation of the worth of a security.

Thus, providing information to at-risk investors is consistent with the mission of the SEC and would not require massive restructuring of the Commission.

The third advantage is that providing information would be the most direct way to discover whether investors would consent to restrictions. Earlier we argued that restrictions on some at-risk investors are justified because they would consent to intervention if they were fully aware of the risk they faced. But instead of imposing regulations based on what investors *would* do were they to have all the relevant information, it is preferable to give them the information whenever possible and see what they *actually* do. This would avoid the danger of imposing on them a conception of their good that they do not accept.

We agree that providing information to at-risk investors is a good idea, and propose that methods be initiated that ensure that investors receive the information, rather than just having it available for those that seek it out. However, this may not be enough to eliminate unacceptable risks for at-risk investors. Consider the prescription drug market again, and assume that the FDA made strenuous efforts to provide consumers with complete information about drugs. Supposing for a moment that it is legally permissible for consumers to buy drugs, as it is in some countries, this might be enough to eliminate unacceptable risk of harm from drugs for the few that had the time, energy, and expertise to use the information. But for most people it would be an overwhelming blizzard of paper that would be of no real use. As Steven Kelman has argued, the cost of organizing and understanding the information may be so high that the most sensible course of action for most people would be to assign their right to select drugs to some individual or institution with special expertise, provided the choice was made with their best interests in mind.[8] Merely providing information about drugs does not protect persons from harm unless the information is understood. When it appears unlikely that a large class of people will devote the time needed to understand it, then it is appropriate, we believe, to place legal restrictions on their choices. This protects them from harm, but is not an intolerable limitation of freedom.

The same reasoning applies in the securities markets. So much information is available and it is so complex that for many investors beyond a certain point it would be too costly to make the investment in time required to assimilate it all. Having "complete and accurate information," as the SEC suggests, is not enough. Leaving aside the issue of how one determines whether it is complete and accurate (note that not even the SEC does that), there remains the problem of understanding it well enough to make a wise investment decision. Perhaps it could be done, but would it be done by most at-risk investors? We are inclined to think not. So we suggest that, just as with prescription drugs, at-risk investors be required by law to engage the services of an expert. This would go a long way toward eliminating unacceptable risks for them, and given the significant possibility of harm many investors face, we do not feel it would be an excessive restriction on their freedom. Exceptions would have to be made for those investors willing to become expert in the markets (since they would no longer meet the definition of an at-risk investor), and some system of qualifications would need to be established to identify investment counselors capable of advising the other investors. . . .

## NOTES

1. "The Penny Stock Scandal," *Business Week*, 23 (Jan. 1989), pp. 74–82.
2. "Investors Can Take a Bite Out of Fraud," *Wall Street Journal*, (Jan. 24, 1989), p. C1.
3. *Wall Street Journal*, (Jan. 24, 1989), p. C1.
4. "Many Crash Complaints Unresolved," *Wall Street Journal*, (Oct. 10, 1988), p. C1. For additional information on problems faced by individual investors, see John L. Casey, *Ethics in the Financial Marketplace* (Scudder, Stevens & Clark, New York, 1988).
5. "SEC Studies Municipals in Trusts," *Wall Street Journal*, (Oct. 11, 1988), p. C1.
6. "Bondholders Are Mad as Hell—And No Wonder," *Business Week*, (Dec. 5, 1988), p. 28.
7. Joel Feinberg, *Social Philosophy* (Prentice Hall, Englewood Cliffs, NJ, 1973), pp. 55–56. These definitions are based on the ones given by Feinberg.
8. Steven Kelman, "Regulation and Paternalism," in *Ethical Theory and Business*, eds. T. L. Beauchamp and N. E. Bowie (Prentice Hall, Englewood Cliffs, NJ, 1988), p. 153.

# Ethical Issues in Financial Services

*John R. Boatright*

The financial services industry still operates largely through *personal selling*. Although more and more investors are sending their money in envelopes to faceless mutual funds and dealing with banks via cash machines and 800 numbers, many people still buy and sell securities through a broker whom they know personally. Most people know their insurance agents personally and deal with financial planners, tax advisers, and other finance professionals face-to-face. Personal selling creates innumerable opportunities for abuse, and although finance professionals take pride in the level of integrity in the industry, misconduct still occurs. However, customers who are unhappy over failed investments or rejected insurance claims, for example, are quick to blame the seller of the product, sometimes unfairly.

There are "bad apples" in every business, of course, but many critics fault the industry itself. Critics cite the need for better training of sales personnel, more stringent rules and procedures, more aggressive oversight, more disclosure to investors, and changes in the compensation system. The full-service brokerage business is facing a crisis as wary customers, who have felt vulnerable relying on individual brokers, now have many options for their investment dollars. Mutual funds and even banks now offer investors the opportunity to invest without the fear of being "ripped off" by a broker. . . .

## SALES PRACTICES

Two real estate limited partnerships launched by Merrill Lynch & Co. in 1987 and 1989 lost close to $440 million for 42,000 investor-clients.[1] Known as Arvida I and Arvida II, these highly speculative investment vehicles projected double-digit returns on residential developments in Florida and California, but both stopped payments to investors in 1990. At the end of 1993, each $1,000 unit of Arvida I was worth $125, and each $1,000 unit of Arvida II, a mere $6.

Not every investment is a success, of course, and aggressive investors reap higher rewards for assuming greater risk. However, the Arvida partnerships were offered by the Merrill Lynch sales force to many retirees of modest means as safe investments with good income potential. The brokers themselves were told by the firm that Arvida I entailed only "moderate risk," and company-produced sales material said little about risk, while emphasizing the projected performance. Merrill Lynch advised its own brokers that the Arvida funds were appropriate for investors with $30,000 in income and a $30,000 net worth, or with a $75,000 net worth—which is to say, most of the brokers' clients. Left out of the material was the fact that the projections included a return of some of the investors' own capital, that the track record of the real estate company was based on commercial, not residential projects, and that eight of the top nine managers of the company had left just before Arvida I was offered to the public.

Merrill Lynch insists that the brokers acted properly in selling the Arvida limited partnerships to clients, but several questions can be raised about the firm's sales practices. First, were some investors *deceived* by the brokers' sales pitches? The prospectus for an offering is typically scrutinized by the SEC and the issuing firm's legal staff in order to ensure full disclosure of all legally required information. However, investors seldom read all of the fine print and do not always understand what they do read. Much of their understanding of an investment comes from conversations with brokers, and here there is ample opportunity for deception. Second, did the Merrill Lynch brokers have a responsibility to protect the interests of their clients? At one extreme, brokers can be viewed as sellers of a product whose obligations do not extend beyond those of any seller, which include, of course, a prohibition on deception. The other extreme is to view brokers as agents who are pledged to advance the interests of clients to the best of their abilities. However, the responsibilities of brokers lie at neither extreme and vary with the client and circumstances. . . .

### Deception and Concealment

Deception is a broad term without clear boundaries. The Federal Trade Commission (FTC) was charged by Congress in 1914 with the task of protecting consumers from deceptive advertising, and the Commission struggles to this day to develop an adequate definition. Federal securities law prohibits practices that would "operate as a fraud or deceit" on a person; the Investment Company Act, which regulates mutual funds, contains similar language; and state insurance laws also prohibit fraud and deception in the sale of insurance. Most legal action has focused on fraud, with the result that the concept of deception in finance lacks a clear legal definition.

Despite the vagueness of the term, some guidelines have been developed for identifying deception. In general, a person is deceived when that person holds a false belief as a result of some claim made by another. That claim may be either a false or misleading statement or a statement that is incomplete in some crucial way. Even if every claim made by Merrill Lynch brokers is literally true, deception is still possible if the clients formed mistaken beliefs because of statements made or not made. Indeed, some investors in the Arvida limited partnerships claimed that the distinction between return *on* capital and a return *of* capital was not clearly explained to them and that, as a result, they misunderstood the cash-flow projections. In short, the investors complained that the brokers' sales pitches were deceptive.

The FTC, the SEC, and other regulators employ a three-factor test: (1) How reasonable is the person who is deceived? (2) How easily could a person avoid being deceived? And (3) how significantly is the person harmed by the deception?

First, some people are more easily deceived than others, and some claims could mislead only a few, rather gullible individuals. Regulations that seek to protect even the most ignorant consumer would prohibit all but the most straightforward of claims and would severely hamper advertising and promotion. Regulators have generally employed a *reasonable person* standard that asks whether a customer or client of ordinary intelligence and knowledge would draw a mistaken conclusion from a claim. For example, advertising for credit cards and bank loans often features a low "teaser" rate that applies for an initial period. Even though the attractive rate is featured prominently in advertisements, a reasonable person, it is assumed, can read the fine print and compare the various offers. On the other hand, a misleading comparison of mutual fund performance that would lead even careful readers to conclude that a poorly performing fund is superior to the competition is arguably deceptive.

Second, potentially deceptive claims that can be easily countered by readily accessible information are less objectionable than claims that most people can accept only at face value. Information on mutual fund performance is so widely available—albeit in confusing abundance—that a single misleading comparison is not as serious as a misstatement of the fees for a particular fund, since this is information that an investor can obtain only from a company's own material. Third, deception that would lead a person to suffer a significant financial loss or some other grave harm is of greater concern to regulators. For this reason, claims about finance and health care receive more scrutiny than claims about, say, clothing or perfumes, and misleading claims for home-equity loans, where a person's home is at risk, are more likely to be considered deceptive than equally misleading claims for credit cards or installment loans.

False and misleading claims, which are generally easy to identify, are morally objectionable because they are forms of dishonesty. More problematical is the concealment of information, because whether a claim is false or misleading is a matter of fact, whereas what information *ought* to be revealed involves a value judgment. Furthermore, the moral objection to concealment is not that concealing certain information is dishonest but that it is *unfair.* Whether a sales practice is deceptive cannot be determined, therefore, without considering the conditions for fair market transactions. . . .

Market theory generally considers economic exchanges to be fair if each party makes a *rational choice*—or at least has the opportunity to make a rational choice. Consequently, sales practices in finance are unfair, and hence deceptive, when they substantially interfere with the ability of people to make rational choices about financial matters. The concept of rational choice in economics is complicated, but the details need not concern us here. It is sufficient to note that economic theory assumes that in any economic transaction, each party gives up something (a cost) and receives something in return (a benefit). In addition, economic actors make choices that produce (or are expected to produce) the greatest net return for themselves. In short, economic actors are assumed to be egoistic utility maximizers.

This concept of economic rationality further presupposes that:

1. Both the buyer and the seller are capable of making a rational choice.
2. Both the buyer and the seller have sufficient information to make a rational choice.
3. Neither the buyer nor the seller is denied the opportunity to make a rational choice. (This condition excludes coercion, for example.)

All three of these conditions are fraught with difficulties. A misleading claim may constitute manipulation, and thus cross a line between legitimate persuasion and illegitimate coercion. But where should that line be drawn? The capacity for rational choice is an uncertain standard, not only because many people are unsophisticated about financial matters but because even experienced investors may not understand complex transactions. This condition does not specify how people who are unable to make a rational choice should be treated. . . .

## The Responsibility to Protect

The responsibility of any salesperson can range from *caveat emptor* to paternalism. However, *caveat emptor* ("let the buyer beware") is not the rule of the modern marketplace because every seller is bound by a substantial body of law, including the Uniform Commercial Code, which requires "honesty in fact and the observance of reasonable commercial standards of fair dealing in trade." According to the Uniform Commercial Code, sellers also warrant that their products are of an acceptable level of quality and fit for the purpose for which they are ordinarily used. The underlying assumption is that a seller generally has superior knowledge, so that it is more cost effective to place the burden of consumer protection on sellers rather than buyers of products. If a sales clerk at a hardware store has a legal obligation to protect consumers in the sale of a wrench, then it is not unreasonable to expect at least as high a level of conduct from a broker selling limited partnerships.

However, the focus of a seller's obligations is on the product itself and on the way in which it is represented. The decision to buy is left to the buyer, and the typical seller has no obligation to ensure that the buyer makes a wise choice. An underlying assumption of the market system is that buyers are the best judge of their own interests and should be free to make their own decisions once they are fully informed. The alternative is *paternalism*, which is generally deplored as an unjustified limitation on people's freedom. However, a responsibility to protect clients—and hence some paternalism—is supported by two considerations. One is that the broker is more than a seller when he or she is serving as an adviser because an agency relation is thereby created by a kind of contract. The other consideration is that people are generally more vulnerable in making investment decisions than in making typical consumer purchases, so that a failure to protect their interests may be regarded as abuse or unfair advantage-taking. These two considerations raise the questions: What is the nature of the relation between a salesperson and a client or customer? And what constitutes abuse?

Unfortunately, these questions are difficult to answer without examining specific cases because each one is different. Aside from the responsibility of all sellers in a buyer-seller relation, some responsibilities are imposed as a matter of market efficiency or public policy. Thus, there is concern that pushing unprepared investors into stock mutual funds endangers the market if they are not prepared to withstand a long downturn. Perhaps the main basis of the responsibility of any seller of financial products and services is the "shingle theory." Under this theory, many different relations are possible, but any seller should be held to whatever level of responsibility he or she offers in "hanging our a shingle" and thereby opening up a business. Thus, to call oneself a broker is to create a certain expectation of competent and fair treatment.

For example, investment advisers represent themselves to clients as objective, independent consultants who will offer, for a fee, sound investment advice. Some advisers are "fee-only," which is to say that they seek to gain further client confidence by advertising that they do not accept commission or other compensation for investments made on behalf of clients. Whether investment advisers who are not "fee-only" have an obligation to reveal commissions and other compensation is more problematical. For example, investment advisers and brokerage firms set up "soft-dollar" deals in which the adviser pays a higher-than-normal fee for trades in clients' accounts in return for investment research and other goods and services. Such arrangements are legal as long as they are disclosed to clients. However, some "soft-dollar" deals include office expenses and other resources that do not directly benefit clients. . . . The SEC is holding investment advisers to a high level of client responsibility while permitting brokerage firms to tempt these same clients with lucrative, potentially illegal arrangements, on the grounds that the brokerage firms have no responsibility to an adviser's clients. . . .

## PERSONAL TRADING

The explosive growth in mutual funds has brought Wall Street to Main Street. The stock market, which was once the province of the very rich, is now easily accessible to millions of ordinary investors. This revolutionary development has drawn attention to the men and women who manage billion-dollar portfolios and has even made celebrities of a few. When Jeffrey Vinik, the idolized manager of Fidelity's $54-billion Magellan Fund, touted Silicon Graphics in 1995, people took note and the share price rose—before it collapsed. The financial writer Michael Lewis, who bought 500 shares of Silicon Graphics on the way up, recalled, "As my money disappeared, my warm feelings toward Jeff Vinik went with it."[2] This fund manager's stock picks turned into an ethics case when, as Lewis reports, "Vinik was quoted by journalists singing the praises of two companies—Micron Technologies and Goodyear Tire and Rubber—at virtually the same time that he was selling his own stake in these companies."[3]

Cases like this remind us that mutual fund managers wear two hats: They manage money for others, but they often trade for their own account. Even though most fund managers toil in obscurity and refrain from giving stock tips, they still have immense opportunities to benefit personally from their privileged position. The potential for abuse was recognized in 1940 by the drafters of the Investment Company Act (ICA), which governs mutual funds. In 1970, Congress added section 17(j) to the original legislation, which gave the SEC the power to set rules that require each investment company to adopt a code of ethics and develop procedures for detecting and preventing abuse, including the collection of information on employees' personal trading activities. Because of this long-standing regulation, personal trading in the mutual fund industry has led to very little abuse, and the occasional instances have drawn a vigorous response. . . .

### The Scope of the Problem

Investment companies, of which mutual funds are the best-known type, invest their capital in other companies, usually by purchasing stock or other securities. Closed-end mutual funds have a fixed number of shares which are commonly traded on a market, while open-ended mutual funds sell new shares to the public and stand ready to redeem them at any time. Among the benefits of mutual funds over direct investments in securities are diversification, lower transaction costs, liquidity, and professional management. Like the managers of a corporation, mutual fund managers have a fiduciary duty to act in all matters solely in the interests of the shareholder-investors. Specifically, the managers of mutual funds have an obligation to avoid conflicts of interest that would lead them to put their own interests ahead of those they are duty bound to serve. In addition, mutual funds serve the role of an investment adviser, which also carries with it a fiduciary duty. . . .

Conflicts of interest from personal trading are possible for so-called "access people," that is, investment company personnel such as portfolio managers, analysts, and traders who have access to proprietary research and information about pending transactions. Access people are in a position to use this information to trade ahead of a fund's purchase (called *frontrunning*) and benefit from any upward price movement. If frontrunning raises the price of a stock, then the fund pays more for a security than it would otherwise. Similarly, an access person with advance knowledge of a fund's sale of a stock could capitalise on the information by selling short. An access person might be in a position to influence transactions that serve primarily to protect or promote that person's investment in a security. Conflicts of interest also arise when a fund manager allocates a security that is in short supply, such as shares in a "hot" initial public offering, or distributes gains and losses between different funds in ways that benefit the manager at the expense of some investors. . . .

Several studies in the 1960s revealed substantial personal trading that posed conflicts of interest, and so in 1970 Congress added section 17(j) to the 1940 ICA. This addition granted rule-making power to the SEC in order to prohibit any fraudulent, deceptive, or manipulative act by an access person in the purchase or sale of any security. Using its power, the SEC promulgated rule 17j–1 in 1980. In brief, the rule:

1. prohibits directors, officers, and employees of investment companies (and the investment advisers and principal underwriters) from engaging in fraudulent, manipulative or deceptive conduct in connection with their personal trading of securities held or to be acquired by the investment company;
2. requires investment companies (and their investment advisers and principal underwriters) to adopt codes of ethics and procedures reasonably designed to prevent trading prohibited by the rule;
3. requires every "access person" to file reports with the firm concerning his or her personal securities transactions, within ten days of the end of the quarter in which the transaction was effected; and
4. requires investment companies (and their investment advisers and principal underwriters) to maintain records related to the implementation of their procedures.[4]

Section 17(j) and rule 17j–1 reflect three important points in the approach of Congress and the SEC toward personal trading. First, the regulation of personal trading by investment company personnel is best done by the companies themselves. That is, an employee's own firm provides a strong first line of oversight. Second, every mutual fund is different, and they can provide better oversight if they are given flexibility to develop a code of ethics and specific procedures that fit their individual circumstances. Third, there is a recognition that not all personal trading poses a conflict of interest and that judgment is required for carefully evaluating each case. Thus, both a complete ban on personal trading and rigid rules are inappropriate forms of regulation.

## Should Personal Trading Be Banned?

Both the SEC and ICI reports contain lengthy sections on the question of a complete ban on personal trading. This attention suggests that the issue is not closed, despite the firm rejection of a ban in each report.

Two points should be noted at the outset. First, the question addressed in both reports is whether personal trading by access people in mutual fund companies ought to be banned industrywide, not whether any given company should impose such a ban on its own employees. The reports reject a *mandatory* ban for the industry but leave the door open to a *voluntary* ban by individual mutual fund companies. Second, personal trading by access people is already subject to considerable restrictions, and a complete ban is merely one end of a long continuum. . . .

The arguments for a complete ban can be summarized as follows:

***1. The image of the industry.*** Regardless of the seriousness of the actual problem (which may be slight), the success of the mutual fund industry depends on a "squeaky-clean" image that reassures investors, especially those new to the market. Personal trading creates a perception of conflict of interest that may be worse than the reality, and a unequivocal policy is the only effective means for countering this perception.

*2. The heavy responsibility of managing funds.* The sheer volume of assets currently under management by mutual funds and the importance of mutual funds to the savings plans of Americans create a responsibility to adhere to the highest level of ethics, and to avoid even the remote possibility of harm to investors from mismanagement. Aside from any direct loss to investors due to personal trading, there is a possible indirect loss if fund managers devote their time and energies to their own portfolios rather than attending to the work at hand.

*3. The (in)effectiveness of regulation.* Any regulation short of a complete ban creates too many opportunities to take advantage of loopholes and fuzzy lines. Fund managers, analysts, and other access people who are intent on benefiting from their positions may be tempted to skirt the edge of ethical and legal trading without overstepping the line. A simple complete ban can be better understood and more easily enforced than complicated rules and regulations.

*4. Fairness to other investors.* Access people are insiders who are privy to information that other investors lack, so that personal trading may constitute insider trading and be objectionable for the same reasons. Like proprietary corporate information, information about pending transactions is provided to access people in order for them to perform a job. Trading on the basis of this information is thus a misappropriation of company property for personal use. . . .

The arguments against a complete ban include the following:

*1. The lack of need.* A complete ban is unnecessary for several reasons. First, a multitude of funds compete fiercely with each other on the basis of performance, and in this environment, no company can succeed if it does not put the interests of the customer first. In short, the market is a powerful force for motivating companies to protect investors against abuses from personal trading. Second, fund managers compete against each other and are judged by the returns that they achieve. . . .

Third, personal trading is already stringently regulated, and the lack of apparent abuse indicates that the current regulatory system works well.

*2. No benefit to investors.* A ban on personal trading would make it difficult for mutual fund companies to attract and retain the best analysts, traders, and fund managers. Competition for the most talented people is already stiff, and a complete ban would put investment companies at a disadvantage with pension plans, insurance companies, investment banking firms, commercial bank trust departments, and other financial institutions which permit personal trading. Mutual fund customers would lose the benefit that they now derive from the skills of top-performing professionals if a complete ban were imposed.

*3. Unfairness to fund personnel.* The opportunity to invest is vital to people's economic well-being, and so a ban on personal trading that would limit people's freedom on such an important matter requires weighty justification. In general, people's freedom should not be restricted any more than is necessary to achieve the desired ends. . . .

In evaluating these arguments, the SEC considers three factors: "the prevalence of abusive securities transactions by access persons; the potential harm to fund shareholders caused by access persons' personal investment activities; and the likelihood that a ban would curb abusive trading by access persons."[5] The available data suggest that abusive personal trading is not prevalent, that it is not harmful to investors, and that any gains to investors from a complete ban would be slight. The SEC also questions whether a complete ban would deter more determined wrongdoers, some of whom are not deterred by current regulation. Banning all personal trading in an attempt to prevent the last vestiges of abuse is a misguided enterprise. The SEC report concludes that even though an industrywide ban on personal trading is not warranted at this time, the directors of mutual funds have a responsibility to assess the benefits of personal trading for shareholders and adopt more restrictive rules and procedures, or even a complete ban, if such a step is in the shareholders' interests.

## Remaining Questions . . .

### *Codes of Ethics*

Although rule 17j–1 requires investment companies to adopt a code of ethics, the content of these codes is not legally mandated. The ICI Advisory Group on Personal Investing recommends that every code of ethics incorporate certain general principles:

> These principles should, at a minimum, reflect the following: (1) the duty at all times to place the interests of shareholders first; (2) the requirement that all personal securities transactions be conducted consistent with the code of ethics and in such a manner as to avoid any actual or potential conflict of interest or any abuse of an individual's position of trust and responsibility; and (3) the fundamental standard that investment company personnel should not take inappropriate advantage of their positions.[6]

The implementation of these general principles in specific rules and procedures raises many questions, including who is covered, what transactions are prohibited, and what transactions must be reported. The term *access people* covers a range of personnel who may not be easily identified, and some distinctions among them may be appropriate. . . . Although mutual fund companies are legally required to adopt a code of ethics, there is no legal obligation to disclose it to the public. The SEC and ICI reports each recommend that mutual fund companies disclose their policy on personal trading and provide an overview of their rules and procedures in the prospectus for each fund. . . .[7]

### *Trading Practices*

Other remaining questions about trading practices are (1) the personal purchase of initial public offerings (IPOs) and private placements (2) short-term trading and (3) short-selling stocks that are held by a company's funds.

IPOs raise the possibility of a conflict of interest because the intense interest in certain "hot" new issues limits the number of investors who can participate. Fund shareholders may rightly ask why a fund manager who had the opportunity to purchase shares did so for his or her personal account and not for the fund. Private placements do not raise this concern because they generally do not involve securities that could be purchased by a fund. Still, the opportunity to participate in a private placement may be regarded by fund shareholders as a conflict of interest if, for example, it was offered by a start-up firm as an incentive for the manager to invest for the fund should the venture go public in an IPO. . . .

Short-term trading—which is generally interpreted as holding securities for less than 90 days—is prohibited by some mutual fund companies for the reason that quick profit-taking is more likely to utilize information about fund transactions. A rule against short-term trading is an especially effective precaution against frontrunning that, at the same time, does not prevent employees from realizing long-term gain in the stock market. Thus, the benefits to the company and its shareholders are likely to outweigh any small losses to fund managers and other access people.

Neither the SEC nor the ICI report addresses short-selling—which is the practice of borrowing a stock and selling it in the hopes of replacing it later at a lower price—although shorting might fall under the category of short-term trading. Short-selling is practiced by investors who believe that the price of a stock will decline, which raises the question of why a prudent fund manager does not reduce the fund's holdings. Shorting evades restrictions on matching transactions because there is no sale by the fund, and the conflict of interest arises when a fund manager makes a biased decision *not* to sell in order to short the stock for personal gain. Few companies have addressed the issue of short-selling.

## NOTES

1. "Burned by Merrill," *Business Week*, April 25, 1994, 122–5.
2. Michael Lewis, "Fidelities Revisited," *New York Times Magazine*, January 21, 1996, 18.
3. See also Robert McGough and Jeffrey Taylor, "SEC Boosts Its Scrutiny of Magellan Fund," *Wall Street Journal*, December 11, 1995, C1; Jeffrey Taylor, "SEC Has Array of Tools in Magellan Probe," *Wall Street Journal*, December 26, 1995, C19; and Jeffrey Taylor, "SEC Action Is Unlikely on Vinik," *Wall Street Journal*, May 9, 1996, C1.
4. This summary is taken from *Report of the Advisory Group on Personal Investing*, Investment Company Institute, May 9, 1994, 10.
5. *Personal Investment Activities of Investment Company Personnel*, Report of the Division of Investment Management, United States Securities and Exchange Commissions, September 1994, 28.
6. *Report of the Advisory Group on Personal Investing*, 27.
7. *Personal Investment Activities of Investment Company Personnel, 33; Report of the Advisory Group on Personal Investing*, 50.

## OCCUPATIONAL RISK

# The Right to Risk Information and the Right to Refuse Workplace Hazards

*Ruth R. Faden*
*and Tom L. Beauchamp*

Chemicals pose numerous hazards in the American workplace, ranging from health conditions of cancer, lung damage, and irritation to physical hazards such as flammable liquids and corrosive materials. It is widely agreed that workers have a moral and legal right to know about the risks involved in exposure to these chemicals. However, the nature and scope of the right of employees to be informed about health hazards remains indeterminate. It is unclear who must discover and communicate the information, under which conditions it must be communicated, and how to determine that a successful communication has occurred. We focus on several philosophical and policy-oriented problems concerning the right to

 This article derives from revisions in 1987, 1992, 1996, and 1999 of an article that appeared in the *Canadian Journal of Philosophy*, Supplementary Volume, 1982. We are indebted to John Cuddihy and Ilise Feitshans for helpful comments and criticisms.

know and correlative obligations to communicate relevant information. Related rights are also addressed, notably the right to refuse hazardous work.

## I

A government and industry consensus has gradually evolved that workers have a right to know about occupational risks, and correlatively that there is a moral and a legal obligation to communicate relevant information to workers. The National Institute for Occupational Safety and Health (NIOSH) and other U.S. federal agencies informed the U.S. Senate as early as July, 1977 that "workers have the right to know whether or not they are exposed to hazardous chemical and physical agents regulated by the Federal Government."[1] The Occupational Safety and Health Administration (OSHA) implemented regulations in 1980 guaranteeing workers access to medical and exposure records,[2] and then developed regulations from 1983 through the early years of the twenty-first century regarding the right to know about hazardous chemicals and requiring right-to-know training programs in many industries. These issues are now widely discussed using the language of OSHA's "Hazard Communication Standard" (HCS) because OSHA's standards of information dissemination have de facto become the standard of practice.[3] States and municipalities have passed additional legislation, and OSHA requires conformity to many of these local rules.[4]

Although some form of right to risk information—that is, the right to know about exposure to workplace hazards—is now well established in law and ethics, no consensus exists about the nature and extent of a producer's, importer's, distributor's, or employer's obligation to communicate such information—or about how employers must implement the standards in their facilities. Considerable ambiguity attends the nature and scope of the right—that is, which protections and actions the right entails, to whom these rights apply, when notification should occur, and under which conditions. OSHA requires that chemical producers, importers, and distributors "evaluate" the hazards of their chemicals, place labels on containers, and provide training programs for exposed employees. However, government agencies, corporations, and workers often do not distinguish between the obligation to communicate currently available information, the obligation to seek new information through searches of the scientific literature, the obligation to generate information through new research, and the like. The "right to know" can be understood as correlative to only one of these obligations—or to all of them. This is a critical ambiguity at the heart of "the right to know."

Further, those who purchase and distribute hazardous products currently meet their legal obligations by passing on risk information about a product; they are not obligated to evaluate the adequacy of the information provided by manufacturers or suppliers. As OSHA states, "the HCS is designed so that employers who simply use chemicals . . . are not required to evaluate the hazards of those chemicals. Hazard determination is the responsibility of the producers and importers."[5] The relevant literature also does not adequately discuss the central question in business ethics: Do corporations owe workers information that exceeds federal and state requirements?

## II

A diverse set of U.S. laws and federal regulations reflects the belief that citizens in general, and workers in particular, have a right to learn about significant risks. These include The Freedom of Information Act, The Federal Insecticide, Fungicide, and Rodenticide Amendments and Regulations, The Federal Food, Drug, and Cosmetic Act, The Consumer Product Safety Act, The Worker Retraining Notification Act, and The Toxic Substances Control Act. Taken together, this body of legislation communicates the message that manufacturers and other businesses have a moral and legal obligation to communicate information needed by individuals to decide about their participation, employment, or enrollment.

Developments in the right to know in the workplace have consistently held to this general trend toward disclosure and have included an expanded notion of corporate responsibility to provide adequate information to workers. These developments could revolutionize corporate workplace practices. Until the 1983 OSHA HCS went into effect in 1986 for the manufacturing sector and in 1988 for the nonmanufacturing sector, workers did not receive extensive information (if any) from a great many employers. Not until October 2001 was there a "HazCom" rule governing chemical hazards in the vast territory of sand, gravel, and crushed stone operations; this rule was passed in November 2000 by the Mine Safety and Health Administration (MSHA).[6]

Subsequent to some of these developments, various corporations quickly established model programs. For example, in the early years of this legislation the Monsanto Company created a right-to-know program in which it distributes information on hazardous chemicals to its employees, and both notifies and monitors past and current employees exposed to carcinogenic and toxic chemicals. Hercules Inc. developed videotape training sessions that incorporate frank discussions of workers' anxieties. The tapes depict workplace dangers and on-the-job accidents. Those employees who view the Hercules film are then taught how to read safety data and how to protect themselves.[7]

Job-training programs, safety data sheets, proper labels, and a written program are all HCS-mandated. Employers must establish hazard-communication programs that transmit information to their employees. Updated information may be provided to employees through computers, microfiche, the Internet, CD-ROM, and the like. The training of new employees must occur before they are exposed to hazardous substances, and each time a new hazard is introduced. Each employee must sign a written acknowledgment of training, and OSHA inspectors may interview employers and employees to check on the effectiveness of the training sessions.

The sobering statistics on worker exposure and injury and on dangerous chemicals in the workplace make such corporate programs essential. OSHA has estimated that 3 million work sites in the United States expose 32 million workers to approximately 650,000 hazardous chemicals.[8] Six thousand U.S. workers die from workplace injuries each year, and perhaps as many as 100,000 deaths annually are caused to some degree by workplace exposure and consequent disease. Roughly 1 percent of the labor force is exposed to known carcinogens.[9]

Despite OSHA's HCS regulations and use of inspections by compliance officers, compliance problems persist. OSHA has recorded thousands of HCS violations in the workplace. The agency once described the noncompliance rate as "incredible."[10]

## III

The most developed models of general disclosure obligations and the right to know have long been found in the literature on informed consent, which also treats the topic of informed refusal. Medical professionals have broadly recognized moral and legal obligations to communicate known risks (and benefits) that are associated with a proposed treatment or form of research. No parallel fiduciary obligation has traditionally been recognized in relationships between management and workers. Workmen's compensation laws have governed risks in this environment, but these laws were originally designed for problems of accident in instances of immediately assessable damage. Obligations to warn or to communicate were irrelevant under the "no-fault" conception in workmen's compensation.

However, the importance of information that will decrease occupational risk has been increasingly appreciated in recent years. In particular, knowledge is needed about the serious long-term risks of injury, disease, and death presented by exposure to toxic substances and forms of physical injury. These risks to health carry increased need for information on the basis of which a person may wish to take various actions, including choosing to forego employment completely, to refuse certain work environments within a place of employment, to request improved protective devices, and to request lowered levels of exposure.[11]

Employee–employer relationships, unlike physician-patient relationships, are often confrontational and present to workers a constant danger of undisclosed or underdisclosed risk. This danger and the relative powerlessness of employees justify employer disclosure obligations in all hazardous conditions. By what criteria, then, shall such disclosure obligations be determined?

One plausible argument is the following: Because large employers, unions, and government agencies must deal with multiple employees and complicated causal conditions, no standard should be more demanding than the so-called reasonable-person standard, which remains today the standard in Department of Labor literature. This standard is what a fair and informed member of the relevant community believes is needed. Under this standard, no employer, union, or other party should be held responsible for disclosing information beyond that needed to make an informed choice about the adequacy of safety precautions, industrial hygiene, long-term hazards, and the like, as determined by what the reasonable person in the community would judge to be the worker's need for information.

However, this reasonable-person standard of disclosure is not adequate for all disclosures. In the case of serious hazards, such as those involved in short-term, concentrated doses of radiation, a standard tied to individual persons is more appropriate. When disclosures to individual workers may be expected to have a subjective impact that varies with each individual, the reasonable-person standard should be supplemented by a standard that addresses each worker's personal informational needs.

The best solution to the problem of a general standard is a compromise between a reasonable-person standard and a subjective standard: Whatever a reasonable person would judge material to the decision-making process should be communicated, and in addition any remaining information that is material to an individual worker should be provided through a process of asking whether he or she has any additional or special concerns. This standard avoids a narrow focus on the employer's obligation to communicate information and promotes a worker's understanding and consent. These problems center on the importance of communication, rather than on legal standards of disclosure. The key to effective communication is to invite participation by workers in a dialogue. Asking questions, eliciting concerns, and establishing a climate that encourages questions may be more meaningful than the full corpus of communicated information. Different levels of education, linguistic ability, and sophistication about the issues need to be accommodated.

The majority of the nation's workplaces are presently exempted from OSHA regulations, leaving these workers largely uninformed. Even in workplaces that are covered, former workers often have as much of a need for the information as do presently employed workers. The federal government has the names of hundreds of thousands of former workers whose risk of cancer, heart disease, and lung disease has been increased by exposure to asbestos, polyvinyl chloride, benzene, arsenic, betanaphthalamine, and dozens of other chemicals. Employers have the names of several million such workers.

The U.S. Congress once passed a bill to notify workers at greatest risk,[12] so that checkups and diagnosis of disease can be made before a disease's advanced stage. However, neither industry nor the government has developed a systematic program with teeth. It has often been stated that the expense of notification would be prohibitive, that many workers would be unduly alarmed, and that existing screening and surveillance programs should prove adequate in monitoring and treating disease. Critics rightly charge, however, that existing programs are inadequate and that workers have a right to know strong enough to enable them to investigate potential problems at their initiative.

## IV

Despite the apparent consensus on the desirability of having some form of right to know in the workplace, it has proven difficult to implement this right. Complicated questions arise about the kinds of information to be communicated, by whom, to whom, under what conditions, and with what warrant. Trade secrets have also been a thorn in the side of progress, because companies resist disclosing information about an ingredient or process claimed as a trade secret.[13] They insist that they should not be required to reveal their substances or processes if their competitors might then obtain the information. OSHA therefore regards itself as duty-bound to balance the protection of workers through disclosure against the protection of corporate interests in nondisclosure.[14] In addition, economic and social constraints sometimes inhibit workers from exercising their full range of workplace options. For example, in industries in which ten—or even a hundred—people apply for every available position, bargaining for increased protection is an unlikely event.

We here set aside this sort of problem in order to consider perhaps the most perplexing difficulty about the right to know in the workplace: the right to refuse hazardous work assignments and to have effective mechanisms for workers to reduce the risks they face. Shortly after the HCS went into effect, labor saw that the right to know was often of little practical use unless it was accompanied by a meaningful right to escape and modify hazardous working conditions. Although U.S. law generally makes unsafe working conditions a punishable offense, the United States Occupational Safety and Health Act (OSH Act of 1970[15]) limited rights of refusal to work that presented life-threatening conditions and risks of serious bodily injury. Specifically, the OSH Act grants workers the right to request an OSHA inspection if they believe an OSHA standard has been violated or an imminent danger exists. Under the Act, employees also have the right to participate in OSHA inspection tours of the worksite and to consult freely with the compliance officer. Most importantly, the OSH Act protects employees who request an inspection or otherwise exercise their rights under the OSH Act from discharge or any discriminatory treatment in retaliation for *legitimate* safety and health complaints.[16]

These worker rights under the OSH Act are essential, but they do not assure that all workers have effective mechanisms for initiating inspections of suspected health hazards. The OSH Act does not cover small businesses (those employing fewer than ten workers) or federal, state, and municipal employees.[17] Questions also remain about OSHA's ability to enforce these provisions of the OSH Act. The agency tends to develop policy on the basis of cost-benefit principles, rather than strict enforcement of the right to know. If workers are to use disclosed information on health hazards effectively, they must have access to an inclusive, workable, and efficient regulatory system. The OSH Act is also written to protect the rights of individuals, not groups (although there are provisions for "authorized employee representatives" such as a union representative chosen by the employee). It has no provisions for collective action by workers and does not mandate workplace health and safety committees, as does legislation in some countries. Workers therefore still need an adequately protected right to refuse unsafe work and a meaningful right to refuse an employer's request that they sign OSHA-mandated forms acknowledging that they have been trained about hazardous chemicals. One cannot easily determine the current extent to which these rights are protected.[18]

OSHA regulations allow workers to walk off the job if there is a genuine danger of death or serious injury, while the LMRA permits refusals only under "abnormally dangerous conditions."[19] Under the LMRA, the nature of the occupation determines the extent of danger justifying refusal, while under OSHA the character of the threat, or so-called "imminent danger," determines worker action. Here "imminent danger" is defined in terms of a reasonable expectation of "death or possible serious physical harm" that might occur before normal enforcement procedures could be acted upon.[20]

By contrast, under the NLRA a walk-out by two or more workers may be justified for even minimal safety problems, so long as the action can be construed as a "concerted activity" for mutual aid and protection and a no-strike clause does not exist in any collective bargaining agreements. While the NLRA appears to provide the broadest protection to workers, employees refusing to work under the NLRA can lose the right to be reinstated in their positions if permanent replacements can be hired.

The current legal situation concerning the right to refuse hazardous work also fails to resolve other questions, such as whether the right to refuse hazardous work entails an obligation to continue to pay nonworking employees or to award the employees back-pay if the issue is resolved in their favor. On the one hand, workers without union strike benefits or other income protections would be unable to exercise their right to refuse unsafe work due to economic pressures. On the other hand, to permit such workers to draw a paycheck is to legitimize strike with pay, a practice traditionally considered unacceptable by management and by Congress.

The situation does not resolve whether the right to refuse unsafe work should be restricted to cases of obvious, imminent, and serious risks to health or life (the current OSHA and LMRA position) or should be expanded to include lesser risks and uncertain risks—for example, exposure to suspected toxic or carcinogenic substances that, although not immediate threats, may prove more dangerous over time. In order for "the right to know" to allow for meaningful worker action, workers would have to be able to remove themselves from exposure to suspected hazards, as well as obvious or known hazards.

The question of the proper standard for determining whether a safety walkout is justified is connected to this issue. At least three different standards have been applied in the past: (1) a good-faith subjective standard, which requires only that the worker honestly believe that a health hazard exists; (2) a reasonable-person standard, which requires that the belief be reasonable under the circumstances, as well as sincerely held; and (3) an objective standard, which requires evidence—commonly established by expert witnesses—that the threat in fact exists.[21]

No less important is whether the right to refuse hazardous work should be protected only until a formal review of the situation is initiated (at which time the worker must return to the job) or whether the walk-out should be permitted until the alleged hazard is at least temporarily removed. Requirements that workers continue to be exposed while OSHA or the NLRB conduct investigations is unacceptable if the magnitude of potential harm is significant. However, compelling employers to remove suspected hazards during the evaluation period may also result in unacceptable economic burdens. This situation is worsened by the fact that workers are often not in a position to act on information about health hazards by seeking alternative employment elsewhere.

We need, then, to delineate the conditions under which workers may be compelled to return to work during an alleged hazard investigation and the conditions that can compel employers to remove alleged hazards.

## V

Legal rights are useless if workers remain ignorant of their options or cannot exercise their rights. Despite recent requirements that employers initiate training programs, it remains doubtful that many workers, particularly nonunion workers, are aware that they have a legally protected right to refuse hazardous work. Even if workers were to learn of such a right, they could probably not weave their way through the maze of legal options unaided.

Programs of information and training in hazards are as important for employers and managers as for workers. Workplace disease and injury are expensive, and they profoundly affect morale. Occupational deaths can be investigated as homicides. Corporate executives have been tried, and in some cases convicted, for murder and manslaughter, on grounds that they negligently caused worker deaths by failing to notify of hazards. An improved system of corporate disclosures of risk and the rights of workers therefore stands to benefit everyone.

## NOTES

1. NIOSH, et al., "The Right to Know: Practical Problems and Policy Issues Arising from Exposures to Hazardous Chemical and Physical Agents in the Workplace" (Washington, D.C.: July 1977), pp. 1 and 5; see also Ilise L. Feitshans, "Hazardous Substances in the Workplace: How Much Does the Employee have the Right to Know?" *Detroit Law Review* 3 (1985).
2. Occupational Safety and Health Administration, "Access to Employee Exposure and Medical Records—Final Rules," *Federal Register*, May 23, 1980, pp. 35212–77.
3. Dept. of Labor, OSHA, www.osha.gov (2003); see, in particular, "Laws and Regulations," "OSHA Regulations," 29 CFR 1910.1200.
4. Dept. of Labor, OSHA, www.osha.gov, 29 CFR 1910.1200 App E, sec. 1.
5. Dept. of Labor, OSHA, www.osha.gov, 29 CFR 1910.1200 App E.
6. U.S. Dept. of Labor, Mine Safety and Health Administration, 30 CFR, Part 47—Hazard Communication. See also Charlotte S. Garvey, "Mine Operators Face New Hazard Communication Rule," *Primedia Business Magazines and Media*, Washington Letter Section (Nov. 2000), as posted, with copyright, by Lexis-Nexis.
7. Laurie Hays, "New Rules on Workplace Hazards Prompt Intensified On the Job Training Programs" *The Wall Street Journal*, July 8, 1986, p. 31; Cathy Trost, "Plans to Alert Workers," *The Wall Street Journal*, March 28, 1986, p. 15.
8. U. S. Dept. of Labor, OSHA, www.osha.gov, "Safety/Health Topics," "Hazard Communication" (as posted January 2003).
9. Department of Labor, Bureau of Labor and Statistics: www.bls.gov/iif/oshwc/cfoi/cftb0155.pdf. The 6000 figure remained remarkably stable from 1996–2001, varying only from 5900 to 6202 in these years. See earlier 48 CFR 53, 282 (1983); Office of Technology Assessment, *Preventing Illness and Injury in the Workplace* (Washington: U.S. Government Printing Office, 1985); Sheldon W. Samuels, "The Ethics of Choice in the Struggle against Industrial Dis-

ease." *American Journal of Industrial Medicine* 23 (1993): 43–52, and David Rosner and Gerald E. Markowitz, eds. *Dying for Work: Workers' Safety and Health in Twentieth-Century America* (Bloomington: University of Indiana Press, 1987).

10. Current Reports, *O.S.H. Reporter* (March 15, 1989), p. 1747.
11. See the articles by Gregory Bond, Leon Gordis, John Higgenson and Flora Chu, Albert Jonsen, and Paul A. Schulte in *Industrial Epidemiology Forum's Conference on Ethics in Epidemiology*, ed. William E. Fayerweather, John Higgenson, and Tom L. Beauchamp. New York: Pergamon Press, 1991.
12. High Risk Occupational Disease Notification and Prevention Act, HR 1309.
13. An employer is not required to disclose the name or any information about a hazardous chemical that would require disclosure of a bona fide trade secret; but in a medical emergency the company must disclose this information to physicians or nurses as long as confidentiality is assured. Under the HCS, even nonemergency disclosure is required under specified conditions of occupational health necessity.
14. For the current language, which is often vague, see 29 CFR 1910.1200(i) and 1910.1200 App D (Definition of "Trade Secret") (as posted on January 22, 2003).
15. OSHA was first authorized by the OSH Act of 1970 (29 USC §651 *et seq.*).
16. OSH Act, Section 8. If the health or safety complaint (filed by the employee) is not determined to be legitimate, there are no worker protections.
17. OSHA regulations govern only business with 11 or more employees. They also do not apply to government agencies, self-employed individuals, and family farms.
18. The right to refuse an employer's request to sign a training acknowledgment form is upheld in *Beam Distilling Co. v. Distillery and Allied Workers' International,* 90 Lab. Arb. 740 (1988). See also Ronald Bayer, ed. *The Health and Safety of Workers.* New York: Oxford University Press, 1988; James C. Robinson, *Toil and Toxics: Workplace Struggles and Political Strategies for Occupational Health.* Berkeley: University of California Press, 1991.
19. 29 USC §143 (1976), and 29 CFR §1977.12 (1979).
20. Dept. of Labor, OSHA, www.osha.gov (2003), "Worker's Page," "Imminent Danger."
21. OSHA's current general standard is that "employees do have the right to refuse to do a job if they believe in good faith that they are exposed to an *imminent danger.* 'Good faith' means that even if an imminent danger is not found to exist, the worker had reasonable grounds to believe that it did exist." Dept. of Labor, OSHA, www.osha.gov (2003), "Worker's Page," "Refusing to Work Because Conditions are Dangerous."

# Occupational Health and Safety

*John R. Boatright*

## THE SCOPE OF THE PROBLEM

Many Americans live with the possibility of serious injury and death every working day. For some workers, the threat comes from a major industrial accident, such as the collapse of a mine or a refinery explosion, or from widespread exposure to a hazardous substance, such as asbestos, which is estimated to have caused more than 350,000 cancer deaths since 1940.[1] The greatest toll on the workforce is exacted, however, by little-publicized injuries to individual workers, some of which are gradual, such as hearing loss from constant noise or nerve damage from repetitive motions. Some of the leading causes of death, such as heart disease,

Ethics and the Conduct of Business by John R. Boatright. Adapted by permission of Pearson Education Inc., Upper Saddle River, NJ.

cancer, and respiratory conditions, are thought to be job-related, although causal connections are often difficult to make. Even stress on the job is now being recognized as a workplace hazard that is responsible for headaches, back and chest pains, stomach ailments, and a variety of emotional disorders.

## The Distinction between Safety and Health

Although the term *safety* is often used to encompass all workplace hazards, it is useful to make a distinction between *safety* and *health.* Safety hazards generally involve loss of limbs, burns, broken bones, electrical shocks, cuts, sprains, bruises, and impairment of sight or hearing. These injuries are usually the result of sudden and often violent events involving industrial equipment or the physical environment of the workplace. . . .

Health hazards are factors in the workplace that cause illnesses and other conditions that develop over a lifetime of exposure. Many diseases associated with specific occupations have long been known. In 1567, Paracelsus identified pneumoconiosis, or black lung disease, in a book entitled *Miners' Sickness and Other Miners' Diseases.* . . . Mercury poisoning, once common among felt workers, produces tremors, known as "the hatters' shakes," and delusions and hallucinations, which gave rise to the phrase "mad as a hatter."

In the modern workplace, most occupational health problems result from routine exposure to hazardous substances. Among these substances are fine particles, such as asbestos, . . . heavy metals, gases, . . . solvents, . . . and certain classes of chemicals. Pesticides pose a serious threat to agricultural workers, and radiation is an occupational hazard to X-ray technicians and workers in the nuclear industry.

Because occupationally related diseases result from long-term exposure and not from identifiable events on the job, employers have generally not been held liable for them, and they have not, until recently, been recognized in workers' compensation programs. The fact that the onset of many diseases occurs years after the initial exposure—thirty or forty years in the case of asbestos—hides the causal connection. The links are further obscured by a multiplicity of causes. The textile industry, for example, claims that byssinosis among its workers results from their own decision to smoke and not from inhaling cotton dust on the job. Lack of knowledge, especially about cancer, adds to the difficulty of establishing causal connections.

## Regulation of Occupational Health and Safety

Prior to the passage of the Occupational Safety and Health Act (OSH Act) in 1970, government regulation of occupational health and safety was almost entirely the province of the states. Understaffed and underfunded, the agencies charged with protecting workers in most states were not very effective. Only a small percentage of workers in many states were even under the jurisdiction of regulatory agencies; often, powerful economic interests were able to influence their activities. Because the agencies lacked the resources to set standards for exposure to hazardous substances, they relied heavily on private standard-setting organizations and the industries themselves. The emphasis in most states was on education and training, and prosecutions for violations were rare. State regulatory agencies were also concerned almost exclusively with safety rather than with health.

States still play a major role in occupational health and safety through workers' compensation systems, but in 1970, primary responsibility for the regulation of working conditions passed to the federal government. The "general duty clause" of the OSH Act requires employers "to furnish to each of his employees employment and a place of employment which are free from recognized hazards that are causing or are likely to cause death or serious injury."[2] In addition, employers have a specific duty to comply with all the occupational safety and health standards that OSHA is empowered to make. Employees also have a duty, under Section 5(b), to "comply with occupational safety and health standards and all rules, regulations, and orders issued pursuant to this Act which are applicable to his own actions and conduct." OSHA regulates occupational health and safety primarily by issuing standards, which are commonly enforced by workplace inspections. Examples of standards are permissible exposure limits (PELs) for toxic substances and specifications for equipment and facilities, such as guards on saws and the height and strength of railings.

### The Right To a Safe and Healthy Workplace

At first glance, the right of employees to a safe and healthy workplace might seem to be too obvious to need any justification. This right—and the corresponding obligation of employers to provide working conditions free of recognized hazards—appears to follow from a more fundamental right—namely, the right of survival. Patricia H. Werhane writes, for example, "Dangerous working conditions threaten the very existence of employees and cannot be countenanced when they are avoidable." Without this right, she argues, all other rights lose their significance.[3] Some other writers base a right to a safe and healthy workplace on the Kantian ground that persons ought to be treated as ends rather than as means. Mark MacCarthy has described this view as follows:

> People have rights that protect them from others who would enslave them or otherwise use them for their own purposes. In bringing this idea to bear on the problem of occupational safety, many people have thought that workers have an inalienable right to earn their living free from the ravages of job-caused death, disease, and injury.[4]

Congress, in passing the OSH Act granting the right to all employees of a safe and healthy workplace, was apparently relying on a cost-benefit analysis, balancing the cost to industry with the savings to the economy as a whole. Congress, in other words, appears to have been employing essentially utilitarian reasoning. Regardless of the ethical reasoning used, though, workers have an undeniable right not to be injured or killed on the job.

It is not clear, though, what specific protection workers are entitled to or what specific obligations employers have with respect to occupational health and safety. One position, recognized in common law, is that workers have a right to be protected against harm resulting directly from the actions of employers where the employer is at fault in some way. Consider the case of the owner of a drilling company in Los Angeles who had a twenty-three-year-old worker lowered into a thirty-three-foot-deep, eighteen-inch-wide hole that was being dug for an elevator shaft. No test was made of the air at the bottom of the hole, and while he was being lowered, the worker began to have difficulty breathing. Rescue workers were hampered by the lack of shoring, and the worker died before he could be pulled to the surface. The owner of the drilling company was convicted of manslaughter, sentenced to forty-five days in jail, and ordered to pay $12,000 in compensation to the family of the victim. A prosecutor in the Los Angeles County district attorney's office explained the decision to bring criminal charges with the words, "Our opinion is you can't risk somebody's life to save a few bucks. That's the bottom line."

Few people would hesitate to say that the owner of the company in this case violated an employee's rights by recklessly endangering his life. In most workplace accidents, however, employers can defend themselves against the charge of violating the rights of workers with two arguments. One is that their actions were not the *direct cause* of the death or injury, and the other is that the worker *voluntarily assumed the risk.* These defenses are considered in turn.

### The Concept of a Direct Cause

Two factors enable employers to deny that their actions are a direct cause of an accident in the workplace. One factor is that industrial accidents are typically caused by a combination of factors, frequently including the actions of workers themselves. When there is such a multiplicity of causes, it is difficult to assign responsibility to any one person. The legal treatment of industrial accidents in the United States incorporates this factor by recognizing two common-law defenses for employers: that a workplace accident was caused in part by (1) lack of care on the part of the employee (the doctrine of "contributory negligence") or by (2) the negligence of co-workers (the "fellow-servant rule"). As long as employers are not negligent in meeting minimal obligations, they are not generally held liable for deaths or injuries resulting from industrial accidents.

The second factor is that it is often not practical to reduce the probability of harm any further. It is reasonable to hold an employer responsible for the incidence of cancer in workers who are exposed to high levels of a known carcinogen, especially when the exposure is avoidable. But a small number of cancer deaths can be statistically predicted to result from very low exposure levels to some widely used chemicals. Is it reasonable to hold employers responsible when workers contract cancer from exposure to carcinogens at levels that are considered to pose only a slight risk? The so-called Delaney amendment, for example, forbids the use of any food additive found to cause cancer. Such an absolute prohibition is practicable for food additives, because substitutes are usually readily available. But when union and public-interest groups petitioned OSHA in 1972 to set zero tolerance levels for ten powerful carcinogens, the agency refused on the ground that workers should be protected from carcinogens "to the maximum extent practicable *consistent with continued use.*"[5] The position of OSHA, apparently, was that it is unreasonable to forgo the benefit of useful chemicals when there are no ready substitutes and the probability of cancer can be kept low by strict controls. This is also the position of philosopher Alan Gewirth, who argues that the right of persons not to have cancer inflicted on them is not absolute. He concluded, "Whether the use of or exposure to some substance should be prohibited should depend on the degree to which it poses the risk of cancer. . . . If the risks are very slight . . . and if no substitutes are available, then use of it may be permitted, subject to stringent safeguards."[6] . . .

### The Voluntary Assumption of Risk

A further common-law defense is that employees voluntarily assume the risk inherent in work. Some jobs, such as coal mining, construction, longshoring, and meat-packing, are well-known for their high accident rates, and yet some individuals freely choose these lines of work, even when safer employment is available. The risk itself is sometimes part of the allure, but more often the fact that hazardous jobs offer a wage premium in order to compensate for the greater risk leads workers to prefer them to less hazardous, less well-paying jobs. Like people who choose to engage in risky recreational activities, such as mountain climbing, workers in hazardous occupations, according to the argument, knowingly accept the risk in return for benefits that cannot be obtained without it. Injury and even death are part of the price they may have to pay. And except when an employer or a fellow employee is negligent in some way, workers who have chosen to work under dangerous conditions have no one to blame but themselves.

A related argument is that occupational health and safety ought not to be regulated because it interferes with the freedom of individuals to choose the kind of work that they want to perform. Workers who prefer the higher wages of hazardous work ought to be free to accept such employment, and those with a greater aversion to risk ought to be free to choose other kinds of employment or to bargain for more safety, presumably with lower pay. To deny workers this freedom of choice is to treat them as persons incapable of looking after their own welfare. . . .

The argument that employees assume the risk of work can be challenged on several grounds. First, workers need to possess a sufficient amount of information about the hazards involved. They cannot be said to assume the risk of performing dangerous work when they do not know what the risks are. Also, they cannot exercise the right to bargain for safer working conditions without access to the relevant information. Yet, employers have generally been reluctant to notify workers or their bargaining agents of dangerous conditions or to release documents in their possession. Oftentimes, hazards in the workplace are not known by the employer or the employee until after the harm has been done. In order for employers to be relieved of responsibility for injury or death in the workplace, though, it is necessary that employees have adequate information *at the time they make a choice.*

Second, the choice of employees must be truly free. When workers are forced to perform dangerous work for lack of acceptable alternatives, they cannot be said to assume the risk. For many people with few skills and limited mobility in economically depressed areas, the only work available is often in a local slaughterhouse or textile mill, where they run great risks. Whether they are coerced into accepting work of this kind is a controversial question. Individuals are free in one sense to accept or decline whatever employment is available, but the alternatives of unemployment or work at poverty-level wages may be so unacceptable that people lack freedom of choice in any significant sense.

## Risk and Coercion

In order to determine whether workers assume the risk of employment by their free choice, we need some account of the concept of coercion. A paradigm example is the mugger who says with a gun in hand, "Your money or your life." The "choice" offered by the mugger contains an undesirable set of alternatives that are imposed on the victim by a threat of dire consequences. A standard analysis of coercion that is suggested by this example involves two elements: (1) getting a person to choose an alternative that he or she does not want, and (2) issuing a threat to make the person worse off if he or she does not choose that alternative.

Consider the case of an employer who offers a worker who already holds a satisfactory job higher wages in return for taking on new duties involving a greater amount of risk. The employer's offer is not coercive because there is no threat involved. The worker may welcome the offer, but declining it leaves the worker still in possession of an acceptable position. Is an employer acting like a mugger, however, when the offer of higher pay for more dangerous work is accompanied by the threat of dismissal? Is "Do this hazardous work or be fired!" like or unlike the "choice" offered by the mugger? The question is even more difficult when the only "threat" is not to hire a person. Is it coercive to say, "Accept this dangerous job or stay unemployed!" because the alternative of remaining out of work leaves the person in exactly the same position as before? Remaining unemployed, moreover, is unlike getting fired, in that it is not something that an employer inflicts on a person.

In order to answer these questions, the standard analysis of coercion needs to be supplemented by an account of what it means to issue a threat. A threat involves a stated intention of making a person worse off in some way. To fire a person from a job is usually to make that person worse off, but we would not say that an employer is coercing a worker by threatening dismissal for failure to perform the normal duties of a job. Similarly, we would not say that an employer is making a threat in not hiring a person who refuses to carry out the same normal duties. A person who turns down a job because the office is not provided with air conditioning, for example, is not being made worse off by the employer. So why would we say that a person who chooses to remain unemployed rather than work in a coal mine that lacks adequate ventilation is being coerced?

The answer of some philosophers is that providing employees with air conditioning is not morally required; however, maintaining a safe mine is. Whether a threat is coercive because it would make a person worse off can be determined only if there is some baseline that answers the question, worse off compared with what? Robert Nozick gives an example of an abusive slave owner who offers not to give a slave his daily beating if the slave will perform some disagreeable task the slave owner wants done.[7] Even though the slave might welcome the offer, it is still coercive, because the daily beating involves treating the slave in an immoral manner. For Nozick and others, what is *morally required* is the relevant baseline for determining whether a person would be made worse off by a threatened course of action.

It follows from this analysis that coercion is an inherently ethical concept that can be applied only after determining what is morally required in a given situation. As a result, the argument that the assumption of risk by employees relieves employers of responsibility involves circular reasoning. Employers are freed from responsibility for workplace injuries on the ground that workers assume the risk of employment only if they are not coerced into accepting hazardous work. But whether workers are coerced depends on the right of employees to a safe and healthy workplace—and the obligation of employers to provide it. . . .

## Whirlpool Corporation

The Whirlpool Corporation operates a plant in Marion, Ohio, for the assembly of household appliances.[8] Components for the appliances are carried throughout the plant by an elaborate system of overhead conveyors. To protect workers from the objects that occasionally fall from the conveyors, a huge wire mesh screen was installed approximately twenty feet above the floor. The screen is attached to an angle-iron frame suspended from the ceiling of the building. Maintenance employees at the plant spend several hours every week retrieving fallen objects from the screen. Their job also includes replacing paper that is spread on the screen to catch dripping grease from the conveyors, and occasionally they do maintenance work on the conveyors themselves. Workers are usually able to stand on the frame to perform these tasks, but occasionally it is necessary to step on to the screen.

In 1973, several workers fell partway through the screen, and one worker fell completely through to the floor of the plant below but survived. Afterward, Whirlpool began replacing the screen with heavier wire mesh, but on June 28, 1974, a maintenance employee fell to his death through a portion of the screen that had not been replaced. The company responded by making additional repairs and forbidding employees to stand on the angle-iron frame or step on to the screen. An alternative method for retrieving objects was devised using hooks.

Two maintenance employees at the Marion plant, Virgil Deemer and Thomas Cornwell, were still not satisfied. On July 7, 1974, they met with the maintenance supervisor at the plant to express their concern about the safety of the screen. At a meeting two days later with the plant safety director, they requested the name, address, and telephone number of a representative in the local office of the Occupational Safety and Health Administration. The safety director warned the men that they "had better stop and think about what they were doing," but he gave them the requested information. Deemer called the OSHA representative later that day to discuss the problem.

When Deemer and Cornwell reported for the night shift at 10:45 P.M. the next day, July 10, they were ordered by the foreman to perform routine maintenance duties above an old section of the screen. They refused, claiming that the work was unsafe whereupon the foreman ordered the two employees to punch out. In addition to losing wages for the six hours they did not work that night, Deemer and Cornwell received written reprimands, which were placed in their personnel files.

## THE RIGHT TO KNOW ABOUT AND REFUSE HAZARDOUS WORK

The Whirlpool case illustrates a cruel dilemma faced by many American workers. If they stay on the job and perform hazardous work, then they risk serious injury and even death. On the other hand, if they refuse to work as directed, then they risk disciplinary action, which can include loss of wages, unfavorable evaluation, demotion, and dismissal. Many people believe that it is unjust for workers to be put into the position of having to choose between safety and their job. Rather, employees ought to be able to refuse orders to perform hazardous work without fear of suffering adverse consequences. Even worse are situations in which workers face hazards of which they are unaware. Kept in the dark about dangers lurking in the workplace, employees have no reason to refuse hazardous work and are unable to take other steps to protect themselves.

### Features of the Right to Know and Refuse

The right to refuse hazardous work is different from a right to a safe and healthy workplace. If it is unsafe to work above the old screen, as Deemer and Cornwell contended, then their right to a safe and healthy workplace was violated. A right to refuse hazardous work, however, is only one of several alternatives that workers have for securing the right to a safe and healthy workplace. Victims of racial or sexual discrimination, for example, also suffer a violation of their rights, but it does not follow that they have a right to disobey orders or to walk off the job in an effort to avoid discrimination. Other means are available for ending discrimination and for receiving compensation for the harm done. The same is true for the right to a safe and healthy workplace.

The right to know is actually an aggregation of several rights. Thomas O. McGarity classifies these rights by the correlative duties that they impose on employers. These are (1) the duty to *reveal* information already possessed; (2) the duty to *communicate* information about hazards through labeling, written communications, and training programs; (3) the duty to *seek out* existing information from the scientific literature and other sources; and (4) the duty to *produce* new information (for example, through animal testing) relevant to employee health.[9] Advocates of the right of workers to know need to specify which of these particular rights are included in their claim.

Disagreement also arises over questions about what information workers have a right to know and which workers have a right to know it. In particular, does the information that employers have a duty to reveal include information about the past exposure of workers to hazardous substances? Do employers have a duty to notify past as well as present employees? The issue at stake in these questions is a part of the "right to know" controversy commonly called *worker notification.*

The main argument for denying workers a right to refuse hazardous work is that such a right conflicts with the obligation of employees to obey all reasonable directives from an employer. An order for a worker to perform some especially dangerous task may not be reasonable, however. The foreman in the Whirlpool case, for example, was acting contrary to a company rule forbidding workers to step on the screen. Still, a common-law principle is that employees should obey even an improper order and file a grievance afterward, if a grievance procedure is in place, or seek whatever other recourse is available. The rationale for this principle is that employees may be mistaken about whether an order is proper, and chaos would result if employees could stop work until the question is decided. It is better for workers to obey now and correct any violation of their rights later.

The fatal flaw in this argument is that later may be too late. The right to a safe and healthy workplace, unlike the right not to be discriminated against, can effectively provide protection for workers only if violations of the right are prevented in the first place. Debilitating injury and death cannot be corrected later; neither can workers and their families ever be adequately compensated for a loss of this kind. The right to refuse hazardous work, therefore, is necessary for the existence of the right to a safe and healthy workplace.

## The Justification for Refusing Hazardous Work

A right to a safe and healthy workplace is empty unless workers have a right in some circumstances to refuse hazardous work, but there is a tremendous amount of controversy over what these circumstances are. In the *Whirlpool* case, the Supreme Court cited two factors as relevant for justifying a refusal to work. These are (1) that the employee reasonably believes that the working conditions pose an imminent risk of death or serious injury, and (2) that the employee has reason to believe that the risk cannot be avoided by any less disruptive course of action. Employees have a right to refuse hazardous work, in other words, only as a last resort—when it is not possible to bring unsafe working conditions to the attention of the employer or to request an OSHA inspection. Also, the hazards that employees believe to exist must involve a high degree of risk of serious harm. Refusing to work because of a slight chance of minor injury is less likely to be justified. The fact that a number of workers had already fallen through the screen at the Whirlpool plant, for example, and that one had been killed strengthens the claim that the two employees had a right to refuse their foreman's order to step on to it.

The pivotal question, of course, is the proper standard for a reasonable belief. How much evidence should employees be required to have in order to be justified in refusing to work? Or should the relevant standard be the actual existence of a workplace hazard rather than the belief of employees, no matter how reasonable? A minimal requirement, which has been insisted on by the courts, is that employees act in *good faith.* Generally, acting in good faith means that employees have an honest belief that a hazard exists and that their only intention is to protect themselves from the hazard. The "good faith" requirement serves primarily to exclude refusals based on deliberately false charges of unsafe working conditions or on sabotage by employees. Whether a refusal is in good faith does not depend on the reasonableness or correctness of the employees' beliefs about the hazards in the workplace. Thus, employees who refuse an order to fill a tank with a dangerous chemical in the mistaken but sincere belief that a valve is faulty are acting in good faith, but employees who use the same excuse to conduct a work stoppage for other reasons are not acting in good faith, even if it should turn out that the valve is faulty. . . .

## The Justification of a Right to Know

Unlike the right to refuse hazardous work, the right to know about workplace hazards is not necessary for the right to a safe and healthy workplace. This latter right is fully protected as long as employers succeed in ridding the workplace of significant hazards. Some argue that the right to know is still an effective, if not an absolutely essential, means for securing the right to a safe and healthy workplace. Others maintain, however, that the right to know is not dependent for its justification on the right to a safe and healthy workplace; that is, even employees who are adequately protected by their employers against occupational injury and disease still have a right to be told what substances they are handling, what dangers they pose, what precautions to take, and so on.

***The Argument from Autonomy.*** The most common argument for the right to know is one based on autonomy. This argument begins with the premise that autonomous individuals are those who are able to exercise free choice in matters that affect their welfare most deeply. Sometimes this premise is expressed by saying that autonomous individuals are those who are able to *participate* in decision making about these matters. One matter that profoundly affects the welfare of workers is the amount of risk that they assume in the course of earning a living. Autonomy requires, therefore, that workers be free to avoid hazardous work, if they so choose, or have the opportunity to accept greater risks in return for higher pay, if that is their choice. In order to choose freely, however, or to participate in decision making, it is necessary to possess relevant information. In the matter of risk assumption, the relevant information includes knowledge of the hazards present in the workplace. Workers can be autonomous, therefore, only if they have a right to know.

In response, employers maintain that they can protect workers from hazards more effectively than workers can themselves without informing workers of the nature of those hazards. Such a paternalistic concern, even when it is sincere and well-founded, is incompatible, however, with a respect for the autonomy of workers. A similar argument is sometimes used to justify paternalism in the doctor–patient relation. For a doctor to conceal information from a patient even in cases where exclusive reliance on the doctor's greater training and experience would result in better medical care is now generally regarded as unjustified. If paternalism is morally unacceptable in the doctor–patient relation, where doctors have an obligation to act in the patient's interest, then it is all the more suspect in the employer–employee relation, where employers have no such obligation.[10]

Although autonomy is a value, it does not follow that employers have an obligation to further it in their dealings with employees. The autonomy of buyers in market transactions is also increased by having more information, but the sellers of a product are not generally required to provide this information except when concealment constitutes fraud. The gain of autonomy for employees must be balanced, moreover, against the not inconsiderable cost to employers of implementing a "right to know" policy in the workplace. In addition to the direct cost of assembling information, attaching warning labels, training workers, and so on, there are also indirect costs. Employees who are aware of the risk they are taking are more likely to demand higher wages or else safer working conditions. They are more likely to avail themselves of workers' compensation benefits and to sue employers over occupational injury and disease. Finally, companies are concerned about the loss of valuable trade secrets that could occur from informing workers about the hazards of certain substances.

***Bargaining Over Information.*** An alternative to a right to know policy that respects the autonomy of both parties is to allow bargaining over information. Thomas O. McGarity has described this alternative in the following way:

> Because acquiring information costs money, employees desiring information about workplace risks should be willing to pay the employer (in reduced wages) or someone else to produce or gather the relevant information. A straightforward economic analysis would suggest that employees would be willing to pay for health and safety information up to the point at which the value in wage negotiations of the last piece of information purchased equaled the cost of that additional information.[11]

Although promising in theory, this alternative is not practical. It creates a disincentive for employers, who possess most of the information, to yield any of it without some concession by employees, even when it could be provided at little or no cost. Bargaining is feasible for large unions with expertise in safety matters, but reliance on it would leave members of other unions and nonunionized workers without adequate means of protection. In the absence of a market for information, neither employers nor employees would have a basis for determining the value of information in advance of negotiations. Finally, there are costs associated with using the bargaining process to decide any matter—what economists call "transaction costs"—and these are apt to be quite high in negotiations over safety issues. It is unlikely, therefore, that either autonomy or worker health and safety would be well served by the alternative of bargaining over matters of occupational health and safety.

## Utilitarian Arguments for a Right to Know

There are two arguments for the right to know as a means to greater worker health and safety. Both are broadly utilitarian in character. One argument is based on the plausible assumption that workers who are aware of hazards in the workplace will be better equipped to protect themselves. Warning labels or rules requiring protective clothing and respirators are more likely to be effective when workers fully appreciate the nature and extent of the risks they are taking. Also, merely revealing information about hazardous substances in the workplace is not apt to be effective without extensive training in the procedures for handling them safely and responding to accidents. Finally, workers who are aware of the consequences of exposure to hazardous substances will also be more likely to spot symptoms of occupational diseases and seek early treatment.

The second utilitarian argument is offered by economists who hold that overall welfare is best achieved by allowing market forces to determine the level of acceptable risk. In a free market, wages are determined in part by the willingness of workers to accept risks in return for wages. Employers can attract a sufficient supply of workers to perform hazardous work either by spending money to make the workplace safer, thereby reducing the risks, or by increasing wages to compensate workers for the greater risks. The choice is determined by the marginal utility of each kind of investment. Thus, an employer will make the workplace safer up to the point that the last dollar spent equals the increase in wages that would otherwise be required to induce workers to accept the risks. At that point, workers indicate their preference for accepting the remaining risks rather than forgoing a loss of wages in return for a safer workplace.

Unlike the autonomy argument, in which workers bargain over risk information, this argument proposes that workers bargain over the trade-off between risks and wages. In order for a free market to determine this trade-off in a way that achieves overall welfare, it is necessary for workers to have a sufficient amount of information about the hazards in the workplace. Thomas O. McGarity has expressed this point as follows:

> A crucial component of the free market model of wage and risk determination is its assumption that workers are fully informed about the risks that they face as they bargain over wages. To the extent that risks are unknown to employees, they will undervalue overall workplace risks in wage negotiations. The result will be lower wages and an inadequate incentive to employers to install health and safety devices. In addition, to the extent that employees can avoid risks by taking action, uninformed employees will fail to do so. Society will then under invest in wages and risk prevention, and overall societal wealth will decline. Moreover, a humane society is not likely to require diseased or injured workers to suffer without proper medical attention. In many cases, society will pick up the tab. . . .[12]

Although these two utilitarian arguments provide strong support for the right to know, they are both open to the objection that there might be more efficient means, such as more extensive OSHA regulation, for securing the goal of worker health and safety. Could the resources devoted to complying with a right-to-know law, for example, be better spent on formulating and enforcing more stringent standards on permissible exposure limits and on developing technologies to achieve these standards? Could the cost of producing, gathering, and disseminating information be better borne by a government agency than by individual employers? These are difficult empirical questions for which conclusive evidence is largely lacking.

## NOTES

1. The estimate is made in W. J. Nicholson, "Failure to Regulate—Asbestos: A Lethal Legacy," U.S. Congress, Committee of Government Operations, 1980.
2. Sec. 5(a) (1).
3. Patricia H. Werhane, *Persons, Rights, and Corporations* (Upper Saddle River, NJ: Prentice Hall, 1985), 132.
4. Mark MacCarthy, "A Review of Some Normative and Conceptual Issues in Occupational Safety and Health," *Environmental Affairs*, 9 (1981), 782–83.
5. *Federal Register*, 39, no. 20 (29 January 1974), 3758. Emphasis added.
6. Gewirth, "Human Rights and the Prevention of Cancer," in *Human Rights: Essays on Justification and Applications* (Chicago: University of Chicago Press, 1982), 189.
7. Robert Nozick, "Coercion," in *Philosophy, Science and Method*, Sidney Morgenbesser, Patrick Suppes, and Morton White, eds. (New York: St. Martin's Press, 1969). 440–72.
8. *Whirlpool Corporation v. Marshall*, 445 U.S. 1 (1980).
9. Thomas O. McGarity, "The New OSHA Rules and the Worker's Right to Know," *The Hastings Center Report*, 14 (August 1984), 38–39.
10. This point is made in Ruth R. Faden and Tom L. Beauchamp, "The Right to Risk Information and the Right to Refuse Health Hazards in the Workplace," in *Ethical Theory and Business*, 4th ed., Tom L. Beauchamp and Norman E. Bowie, eds. (Upper Saddle River, NJ: Prentice Hall, 1993), 205.
11. McGarity, 40.
12. McGarity, 41.

ENVIRONMENTAL RISK

# Safety, Risk, and Environmental Protection

*Richard T. De George*

## ENVIRONMENTAL HARM

Who should decide how clean our air and water should be? Since these are common goods, the decisions should be made by all those affected. Since it is a public policy question, the population in general should make it through the political process. Yet voters are often given little information about the tradeoffs they as a society are actually making. Americans have typically left it up to government to determine what degree of pollution is dangerous, to decide what degree is acceptable, and to come up with regulations that will punish violations beyond that level. The public has rarely voted on alternatives or been told just what the alternatives are or what it is trading off against what. In some states voters have been asked to vote on specific issues—for instance, whether they want to construct nuclear power plants or establish toxic waste centers. Generally speaking, the public has voted on no comprehensive environmental package. Guidelines determined by various parts of government have been prescribed piecemeal. The claim might be made that the subject is technical and best left to the technicians, but we have seen that any choice of levels involves value judgments and there is little reason to assume that technicians represent or hold the same values as even the majority of the society. Many plausibly claim that, as rational agents, people have a right to decide issues that directly concern and affect them.

The blame for the deterioration of the environment frequently falls squarely on business. Factories pollute; manufacturers pour toxic substances into rivers and streams and bury noxious substances, often without regard to public safety; greedy entrepreneurs denude forests, strip-mine the land, and heedlessly eliminate increasing numbers of species. Business has had a serious and often deleterious effect on the environment. Yet the fact that, with respect to the degradation of their environment, socialist countries have fared no better, and often worse, than free-enterprise countries indicates that the harm may be due more to modern technology and its abuse than to business greed alone.

With the development of modern chemistry and increasing industrialization, a great many possibilities have been created and realized without adequate concern for their side effects and for the sometimes hidden costs of their production. For instance, pesticides and herbicides have been a boon for farmers, increasing crop yield and ridding food products of the pests that have plagued farmers for centuries. But pesticides and herbicides can also have deleterious effects. They can seep into the ground and eventually pollute ground water and wells. They can wend their way into streams and rivers, killing fish, or contaminating them. Eventually, they find their way through the food chain to humans, causing cancer, birth deformities, and other ills. The price of introducing new products often involves a certain amount of risk. In many instances the harm done was, at least at first, not intentional and was unknown. It was only after the incidence of disease and birth defects increased that scientists sought the causes and identified the chemical culprits. Can pesticides and herbicides be developed that do not eventually and indirectly harm people? The answer seems to be yes; and promoting their development is one purpose of governmental controls. Knowing there are safer and equally effective alternatives makes it unreasonable to accept the greater risks and actual harm produced by the outlawed products.

A similar analysis can be given of other activities. Strip-mining and denuding the land of forests are both short-sighted activities. We know that cutting down forests without replanting the trees leads to loss of topsoil and to flooding, both of which cause harm, and both of which can be prevented. Yet in underdeveloped countries the local timber often provides the only source of fuel and of housing material for the local people. They have no resources for reforestation and are concerned with present survival rather than with the long-term impact of their deeds. Large paper mills have less excuse for deforestation, but even they provide some good by their activities—namely, the goods they produce and are able to provide for less cost than they could otherwise.

The issues of pollution raise serious concerns about harm. Other environmental issues are less clear. Treatment of animals is of very great concern to some people and of considerably less to others, and what is proper treatment is debated. Questions such as whether the redwood forests of the U.S. West coast should be opened to lumber companies, and whether and how much land should be preserved as wilderness and kept from commercial development are issues on which there is no consensus. Similarly, how much harm is done by industrial processes and development that lead in one way or another to the elimination of animal species is a debated issue. While some argue in terms of the rights of those species, others claim that only human beings properly speaking have rights. The ground then often switches to whether harm can be demonstrated to human beings by felling the redwoods; or acting so as to endanger different animal, insect, or plant species; or treating animals with hormones and other drugs, and keeping them in crowded pens in which they can barely move.

In many instances of environmental harm, the harm done is not wanton and produces some good. From a utilitarian point of view we must ask whether more good is done than harm, looking at all those affected, not only immediately but in the long run as well. From a deontological perspective we need to ask whether the activities violate people's rights. From either perspective we must remember that though harming the environment is bad, at least to the extent that it directly or indirectly harms people, the actions that cause the harm frequently have positive effects as well, as in the case of pesticides, which can be of great help in keeping people alive because of higher crop yields than would otherwise be possible.

In dealing with environmental harm, therefore, the task is to minimize the harm done while maximizing the benefits made available by increased scientific knowledge and technological advances, and while respecting the rights of all those affected.

There is no need to belabor the point that direct, intentional, preventable harm is morally wrong. Manufacturers who knowingly dump harmful by-products and chemicals into streams or onto the ground are guilty of willfully harming others. Those involved in the production of radioactive waste know full well the damage such products can cause and the care they must take in disposing of these products. If they fail to take the appropriate measures, they are knowingly causing harm to others. The same is true with respect to farmers who knowingly misuse pesticides and herbicides, to foresters who do not plant trees to replace those they cut, and to strip-miners who do not heal the land they scar.

The problem of environmental harm and pollution is much more complex than this, however. Although the problems of pollution are only one aspect of the ethical problems involved with the environment, pollution raises a number of issues that illustrate an approach to dealing with environmental problems.

## POLLUTION AND ITS CONTROL

We can distinguish intentional from unintentional pollution, and major from minor polluters. In all cases, what we mean by *pollution* is crucial, and defining it is no easy task. As far as nature is concerned, there is no strict sense of pollution. When the volcano Mount St. Helens, in the State of Washington, erupted in May 1980, it damaged 220,000 acres of timberland; befouled the Touttle, Cowlitz, and Columbia rivers; emitted enormous amounts of sulfur; and spread its emissions in measurable amounts across the United States. In one sense the eruption polluted the air. But the eruption was natural, and the larger amount of sulfur in the air was no more unnatural than the smaller amount in the air prior to the eruption. In a literal sense, nature did not care about the amount of sulfur in the air. Human beings did, because they were adversely affected. What we often mean by *pollution* is the contamination of air, water, and land with substances that harm us or our interests, and in pollution control we are primarily concerned with preventing harm that can be avoided and that results from human activity. That is the only kind of activity that we can classify as moral or immoral.

*Pollution,* moreover, is sometimes a relative term. Certain gases and chemicals are not dangerous in very small amounts but are dangerous in large amounts. When present in small amounts, they are not usually considered pollutants; they become pollutants only when they reach a certain, dangerous level. Other substances are noxious in even minute amounts and are considered pollutants in whatever amounts they are present. What is considered to be a pollutant in drinking water may not be considered a pollutant in river water.

Since pollution is linked with harm, we wish to prevent the type of pollution that causes harm. For many years people used a variety of materials that either because of their small use did not in fact cause harm or because of ignorance were not known to cause harm. Thus, asbestos for a long while was used both as a fire retardant and as an insulator, with no knowledge that asbestos could cause cancer. When it was determined that asbestos could cause cancer, it became a pollutant to be withdrawn from the human living environment to the extent possible. Those who built with asbestos materials and had no knowledge of its harmful effects had no intention of harming others. (At what point they began to have suspicions, and then knowledge, and what they did thereafter, are questions with moral import.) Similarly, many manufacturers used rivers as dumps for their wastes, and in many instances the ratio of waste to the water into which it was dumped was sufficiently low that no harm was done. The ecosystem was able to dispose of the waste through natural means. In like manner, early motorists were few enough in number that the exhausts that their cars emitted were not dangerous and were carried away by the wind.

Pollution became a major issue when the free use of land, water, and air as means of waste disposal started to cause known harmful effects on others. This happened because of the increasing toxicity of the wastes, the better knowledge of the links between waste and human disease, and the growing number of sources of contamination. The sulfur emitted by one car might be harmless; but the sulfur emitted by millions of cars in a large city can produce harm. There is a threshold above which certain substances become harmful. Determining that level is the job of scientists. The aim of society is to keep such substances below their harmful level. And those who willfully produce those substances in such a way as to create harm are morally guilty of harming others.

One question is how much of given substances is necessary to cause harm. This level is sometimes disputed, and scientists as well as nations may vary in what they consider safe. Once a level is determined, the next step is to try to prevent crossing the harm threshold. The problem here is that very often there is no one person or firm that produces the harmful level. If the harm is caused by the wastes of a single firm, then the solution is relatively simple—namely, to preclude that firm from polluting. Determining how to do that may be a difficult problem both technically and politically, but the situation is exacerbated when multiple sources produce the harmful pollution.

Because pollution can involve harm to others, it has a moral dimension, but because it can be controlled or handled in a number of ways, it has a social dimension that may vary from city to city, state to state, and nation to nation.

Consider the following case. Jason City, a community of 150,000 people, has five factories in an industrially zoned section on the east side of the city. One of the factories is much older than the others and emits three times more sulfur into the atmosphere than the newer plants, each of which emits about the same amount of sulfur as the others. The atmosphere can absorb a certain amount of pollution and carry it away without ill effects to either people or property. Therefore, the city has had no need to do anything about the emissions from the factories, and the factories have not invested in any pollution control equipment. A sixth factory is built. It emits the same amount of sulfur as the other four new factories, but it adds just enough so that now a possibly dangerous level of sulfur is discharged into the air. The pollution may now cause harm. We have said that corporations have a moral obligation not to cause harm to people or property. Who is morally responsible to do what? The oldest factory claims that it was in the town first, and although it produces the most pollution, it caused no harm until the sixth factory arrived. The other four claim that they are minor polluters and would cause no harm if either the sixth factory had not opened or if the first factory lowered its sulfur emissions to the same level as the other factories. The sixth plant claims that it has as much right to emit sulfur into the atmosphere as the other plants, and therefore should not bear any special burden. By itself, it claims, it does no harm.

Clearly, the six plants together cause the harm, even though each one by itself would not cause harm. The moral obligation not to cause harm implies that collectively the plants must reduce and limit the total sulfur they emit. But this does not tell us what each plant should do. Ethics alone will not tell us that, because there are many ethical ways of reducing the pollution to an acceptable level. Let us consider a few.

Jason City might decide that the pollution is small enough, the harm done to residents and property slight, and the benefits to the city from having six plants great enough that nothing need be done about it. The city might decide that if anyone claims damage from the pollution, that individual should sue one or all the plants for compensation. The city could impose a limit on the amount of sulfur any plant can emit. It could prevent the construction of any more plants. It could allow future plants to be built only if they emit no sulfur whatsoever, keeping the emission level at its present rate. The city might even take it upon itself to supply emission control devices to the plants, thereby controlling pollution at the source, at city expense. It might also tell the six companies that they are causing the pollution, and that they must lower the level or face a series of fines, thus leaving it up to the plants to arrange among themselves how to lower the sulfur to an acceptable level.

There is no one right and best way for Jason City to solve the problem of sulfur pollution, but there are many ways of approaching the problem. It is appropriate, however, that the plants emitting the sulfur control their emissions because the sulfur belongs to them. They have been allowed to use the air to get rid of their wastes when doing so injured no one, but when such a procedure threatens to harm others, then the action can be rightfully curtailed. The claim that because the air belongs to all of us, any of us can discharge what we want into it cannot be successfully defended.

Wastes belong to those who produce them. Just because people do not want their wastes does not release them (or firms) of the responsibility of disposing of their wastes in a way that does not harm others. The principle is recognized with respect to garbage. Individual households in some cities pay to have their garbage disposed of; in other cities this is a service provided through tax funds; and in rural communities people are sometimes allowed to dispose of it by burning it or carrying it themselves to the town dump. Air and water pollutants are industrial wastes, which belong to the plants that produce them as truly as a household's garbage belongs to the household. The method of disposal of such wastes varies with communities. But the principle that the wastes belong to the producer and that producers have no right to harm others by their wastes is a sound moral basis for imposing limits on what pollutants are admissible, in what amounts, and how the rest are to be controlled or disposed of.

Jason City exemplifies some dimensions of the problem of pollution. But the problem has many other facets and dimensions; it is often extremely complicated, and it involves conflicting principles. There is also much uncertainty about facts, the dangers posed, and the probable effects of proposed solutions.

Pollutants produced by many chemical and manufacturing processes are highly noxious. Such chemical byproducts can clearly cause harm. Those who produce these substances have the moral obligation to dispose of them in safe ways; otherwise, they are morally guilty of the harm they produce. Their obligation to dispose of them properly and safely was a moral obligation even prior to government regulation of such waste disposal. After a number of widely publicized reports about improper disposal and the sad effects thereof, the federal government passed a law requiring a "paper trace" that covered the handling of such wastes from the producing plant through the final disposition in a proper facility. Just before the law went into effect, a number of companies—both originators of the waste and haulers—dumped toxic wastes along open roads, to save the cost of hauling the waste to the proper disposal locations. Clearly, such acts threatened the health and safety of people who would be affected by the runoff and seepage into their drinking water supplies. The action was immoral—a blot on the record of the firms involved.

Pollution, we noted, can be ethically handled in many ways. One way is for those who produce harm to reimburse those harmed for the harm done. In this way compensatory justice is brought into play after the fact. When the harm done is both serious and preventable, such pollution is not usually ethically justifiable, even though reimbursing those harmed is preferable to not reimbursing them. In some cases, however, the harm done is not serious and recompense is a satisfactory remedy. The involved parties may even agree, prior to the harm, to a fee that is to be paid those who will be damaged. This is a form of licensing the harm done by compensating those harmed. This might be the procedure, for instance, in dealing with noise pollution produced by airport traffic as it affects those living near the field. The owners of the airport might buy from the neighbors affected the right to produce the noise. (Property values decrease, and the residents suffer from the disturbance of noisy airplanes flying overhead.) One approach to pollution, as these examples show, is to allow it, but to compensate, either before or after the fact, those who are adversely affected.

A second approach allows a firm to pollute but attempts to eliminate the pollution or clean it up before it damages anyone. The cleaning up might be done by the firm that produces it, the firm might hire someone else to handle the cleanup process, or the cleanup might be carried out by some governmental agency or body. In the last-named case, the cleanup might be done at public expense (in which case the taxpayers subsidize the polluting industry) or at the expense of the polluting firms.

A third approach to pollution is to prevent it at the source. This means that the pollution will not be allowed to develop. Government might mandate this, or firms might decide on their own that preventing the damage is preferable to paying for it afterward. If government mandates the prevention of pollution, it may either specify the means to be taken to prevent the pollution or simply require that there be no effluents of a certain type produced and allow the firms involved to take whatever measures they wish to achieve the mandated end. Many firms prefer the latter approach, claiming it offers them greater incentives to find cost-effective means of preventing pollution. Government-mandated procedures are usually not individually tailored to particular needs and so are not cost effective. A variant of this approach is to set certain limits on the pollution to be tolerated, requiring that it be kept at or below a certain threshold level. . . .

The problem of pollution is complex and open to a variety of solutions. There is controversy about acceptable levels of pollution, the necessity for producing certain kinds of wastes, the relative benefits involved with producing nuclear wastes for which there are no agreed-upon disposal procedures, and so on. These issues involve corporate, social, and ethical responsibility. But the issues are not always as easy to solve as some who attack corporate policy claim. In dealing with pollution, as in dealing with other issues of social responsibility, it would be helpful to distinguish what is ethically mandatory, what is desirable but not mandatory, what is to be decided by the political process, and how goals are to be achieved. A moral audit—or a social audit, of which a moral audit is a clear part—can be constructed to include an evaluation of corporate actions with respect to pollution. We would all benefit if such instruments helped make clear what the problem is, what the variety of solutions are, and which companies are fulfilling their ethical, legal, and social responsibilities in this area.

# Ethics and the Environment

*Manuel G. Velasquez*

## THE ETHICS OF POLLUTION CONTROL

For centuries business institutions were able to ignore their impact on the natural environment, an indulgence created by a number of causes. First, business was able to treat things such as air and water as free goods—that is, as goods that no one owns and that each firm can therefore use without reimbursing anyone for their use. For several years, for example, a DuPont plant in West Virginia had been dumping 10,000 tons of chemical wastes each month into the Gulf of Mexico, until it was forced to stop. The waters of the Gulf provided a free dumping site for whose damages DuPont did not have to pay. Because such resources are not privately owned, they lack the protection that a private owner would normally provide, and businesses were able to ignore the damages they inflicted on them. Second, businesses have seen the environment as an *unlimited* good. That is, the "carrying capacity" of air and water is relatively large, and each firm's contribution of pollution to these resources is relatively small and insignificant. The amount of chemicals DuPont was dumping into the Gulf, for example, might be relatively small compared to the size of the Gulf and the effects viewed as being negligible. When the effects of its activities are seen as so slight, a firm will tend to ignore these effects. However, when *every* firm reasons in this way, the combined "negligible" effects of each firm's activities may become enormous, and potentially disastrous. The carrying capacity of the air and water is soon exceeded and these "free" and "unlimited" goods rapidly deteriorate.

Of course, pollution problems are not rooted only in business activities. Pollution also results from the use that consumers make of products and from human waste products. A primary source of air pollution, for example, is automobile use, and a primary source of water pollution is sewage. We are truly *all* polluters. Since every human being pollutes, pollution problems have increased as our population has multiplied. The world's population grew from 1 billion in 1850 to 2 billion in 1930 to 5.7 billion in 1995, and is projected to grow to between 10 and 12 billion by 2040. This population explosion has put severe strains on the air and water resources into which we dump our share of pollutants. These strains, moreover, have been aggravated by our tendency to concentrate our populations in urban centers. All over the world, urban areas are growing rapidly, and the high population densities urbanization has created multiplies the pollution burdens placed on air and water resources.

The problems of pollution, then, have a variety of origins and their treatment requires a similarly variegated set of solutions. Our focus in what follows, however, will concentrate on a single range of problems: the ethical issues raised by pollution from commercial and industrial enterprises.

## Ecological Ethics

The problem of pollution (and of environmental issues in general) is seen by some researchers as a problem that can best be framed in terms of our duty to recognize and preserve the "ecological systems" within which we live. An ecological system is an interrelated and interdependent set of organisms and environments, such as a lake—in which the fish depend on small aquatic organisms, which in turn live off of decaying plant and fish waste products. Because the various parts of an ecological system are interrelated, the activities of one of its parts will affect all the other parts. Because the various parts are interdependent, the survival of each part depends on the survival of the other parts. Now business firms (and all other social institutions) are parts of a larger ecological system, "spaceship earth."[1] Business firms depend upon the natural environment for their energy, material resources, and waste disposal and that environment in turn is affected by the commercial activities of business firms. The activities of eighteenth-century European manufacturers of beaver hats, for example, led to the wholesale destruction of beavers in the United States, which in turn led to the drying up of the innumerable swamp lands that had been created by beaver dams. Unless businesses recognize the interrelationships and interdependencies of the ecological systems within which they operate, and unless they ensure that their activities will not seriously injure these systems, we cannot hope to deal with the problem of pollution.

The fact that we are only a part of a larger ecological system has led many writers to insist that we should recognize our moral duty to protect the welfare not only of human beings, but also of other *nonhuman parts* of this system. This insistence on what is sometimes called *ecological ethics* or "deep ecology" is not based on the idea that the environment should be protected for the sake of human beings. Instead, ecological ethics are based on the idea that nonhuman parts of the environment deserve to be preserved *for their own sake*, regardless of whether this benefits human beings. Several supporters of this approach have formulated their views in a "platform" consisting of the following statements:

1. The well-being and flourishing of human and nonhuman life on Earth have value in themselves . . . These values are independent of the usefulness of the nonhuman world for human purposes.
2. Richness and diversity of life forms contribute to the realization of these values and are also values in themselves.
3. Humans have no right to reduce this richness and diversity except to satisfy vital needs.
4. The flourishing of human life and cultures is compatible with a substantial decrease of the human population. The flourishing of nonhuman life requires such a decrease.
5. Present human interference with the nonhuman world is excessive and the situation is rapidly worsening.
6. Policies must therefore be changed. The changes in policies affect basic economic, technological, and ideological structures. The resulting state of affairs will be deeply different from the present.
7. The ideological change is mainly that of appreciating life quality . . . rather than adhering to an increasingly higher standard of living.
8. Those who subscribe to the foregoing points have an obligation directly or indirectly to participate in the attempt to implement the necessary changes.[2]

An "ecological ethic" is thus an ethic that claims that the welfare of at least some nonhumans is intrinsically valuable and that because of this intrinsic value, we humans have a duty to respect and preserve them. These ethical claims have significant implications for those business activities that affect the environment. In June 1990, for example, environmentalists successfully petitioned the U.S. Fish and Wildlife Service to bar the timber industry from logging potentially lucrative old-growth forests of northern California in order to save the habitat of the spotted owl, an endangered species. The move was estimated to have cost the timber industry millions of dollars, to have lost workers as many as 36,000 lumber jobs, and to have raised the costs of consumer prices for fine wood products such as furniture and musical instruments. . . .

Attempts to extend moral rights to nonhumans or to claim that an attitude of respect for all nature is morally demanded, are highly controversial, and some authors have labeled them "incredible."[3] It is difficult, for example, to see why the *fact* that something *is* alive implies that it *should* be alive and that we therefore have a *duty* to keep it alive or to express respect or even reverence for it; and it is difficult to see why the *fact* that a river or a mountain *exists*, implies that it *should* exist and that we have a *duty* to keep it in existence or revere it. Facts do not imply values in this easy way. It is also controversial whether we can claim that animals have rights or intrinsic value. But we do not have to rely on these unusual views to develop an environmental ethic. For our purposes, we need only examine more traditional approaches to environmental issues. One is based on a theory of human rights, and the other is based on utilitarian considerations.

### Environmental Rights and Absolute Bans

In an influential article, William T. Blackstone argued that the possession of a livable environment is not merely a *desirable* state of affairs, but something to which each human being has a *right.*[4] That is, a livable environment is not merely something that we would all like to have: It is something that others have a duty to allow us to have. They have this duty, Blackstone argues, because we each have a right to a livable environment, and our right imposes on others the correlative duty of not interfering in our exercise of that right. This is a right, moreover, which should be incorporated into our legal system. . . .

To a large extent, something like Blackstone's concept of "environmental rights" is recognized in federal law. Section 101(b) of the National Environmental Policy Act of 1969, for example, states that one of its purposes is to "assure for all Americans safe, healthful, productive, and aesthetically and culturally pleasing surroundings." Subsequent acts tried to achieve this purpose. The Water Pollution Control Act of 1972 required firms, by 1977, to use the "best practicable technology" to get rid of pollution (that is, technology used by several of the least polluting plants in an industry); the Clean Water Act of 1977 required that by 1984 firms must eliminate all toxic and nonconventional wastes with the use of the "best available technology" (that is, technology used by the one least polluting plant). The Air Quality Act of 1967 and the Clean Air Amendments of 1970 and 1990 established similar limits to air pollution from stationary sources and automobiles, and provided the machinery for enforcing these limits. These federal laws did *not* rest on a utilitarian cost-benefit analysis. That is, they did not say that firms should reduce pollution so long as the benefits outweigh the costs; instead they simply imposed absolute bans on pollution regardless of the costs involved. Such absolute restrictions can best be justified by an appeal to people's rights. . . .

The main difficulty with Blackstone's view, however, is that it fails to provide any nuanced guidance on several pressing environmental choices. How much pollution control is really needed? Should we have an *absolute* ban on pollution? How far should we go in limiting property rights for the sake of the environment? What goods, if any, should we cease manufacturing in order to halt or slow environmental damage? Who should pay for the costs of preserving the environment? Blackstone's theory gives us no way of handling these questions because it imposes a simple and absolute ban on pollution. . . .

Because of the difficulties raised by absolute bans, the federal government in the early 1980s began to turn to methods of pollution control that tried to balance the costs and benefits of controlling pollution and that did not impose absolute bans. Deadlines for compliance with the standards of the Clean Air Act were extended so that the costs of compliance could be more adequately dealt with. Companies were allowed to increase discharges of pollutants that are costly to control when they agreed to make equivalent reductions of pollutants that are cheaper to control. Executive Order No. 12291, signed into law by President Reagan on February 17, 1981, required all new environmental regulations to be subjected to cost-benefit analysis before they were implemented. These new regulations are not based on the notion that people have absolute environmental rights, but on a utilitarian approach to the environment.

### Utilitarianism and Partial Controls

Utilitarianism provides a way of answering the questions that Blackstone's theory of environmental rights leaves unanswered. A fundamentally utilitarian approach to environmental problems is to see them as market defects. If an industry pollutes the environment, the market prices of its commodities will no longer reflect the true cost of producing the commodities; the result is a misallocation of resources, a rise in waste, and an inefficient distribution of commodities. Consequently, society as a whole is harmed as its overall economic welfare declines. Utilitarians, therefore, argue that individuals should avoid pollution because they should avoid harming society's welfare. . . .

### Private Costs and Social Costs

Economists often distinguish between what it cost a private manufacturer to make a product and what the manufacture of that product cost society as a whole. Suppose, for example, that an electric firm consumes a certain amount of fuel, labor, and equipment to produce one kilowatt of electricity. The cost of these resources is its *private* cost: The price it must pay out of its own pocket to manufacture one kilowatt of electricity. However, producing the kilowatt of electricity may also involve other "external" costs for which the firm does not pay. When the firm burns fuel, for example, it may generate smoke and soot that settles on surrounding neighbors, who have to bear the costs of cleaning up the grime and of paying for any medical problems the smoke creates. From the viewpoint of society as a whole, then, the costs of producing the kilowatt of electricity include not only the "internal" costs of fuel, labor, and equipment for which the manufacturer pays, but also the "external" costs of clean-up and medical care that the neighbors pay. This *sum total* of costs (the private internal costs plus the neighbors' external costs) are the social costs of producing the kilowatt of electricity: the total price society must pay to manufacture one kilowatt of electricity. Of course, private costs and *social* costs do not always diverge as in this example: Sometimes the two coincide. If a producer pays for *all* the costs involved in manufacturing a product, for example, or if manufacturing a product imposes no external costs, then the producer's costs and the total social costs will be the same.

Thus, when a firm pollutes its environment in any way, the firm's private costs are always *less* than the total social costs involved. Whether the pollution is localized and immediate, as in the neighborhood effects described in this example, or whether the pollution is global and long-range as in the "hot-house" effects predicted to follow from introducing too much carbon dioxide into the atmosphere, pollution always imposes "external" costs—that is, costs for which the person who produces the pollution does not have to pay. Pollution is fundamentally a problem of this divergence between private and social costs. . . .

### Remedies: The Duties of the Firm

There are various ways of internalizing the external costs of pollution. One way is for the polluting agent to pay to all of those being harmed, voluntarily or by law, an amount equal to the costs the pollution imposes on them. . . .

Market mechanisms then lead it to come up with ways of cutting down pollution in order to cut down its costs. . . .

A second remedy is for the polluter to stop pollution at its source by installing pollution-control devices. In this way, the external costs of polluting the environment are translated into the internal costs the firm itself pays to install pollution controls. Once costs are internalized in this way, market mechanisms again provide cost-cutting incentives and ensure that prices reflect the true costs of producing the commodity. In addition, the installation of pollution-control devices serves to eliminate the long-range and potentially disastrous worldwide effects of pollution.

### Justice

This utilitarian way of dealing with pollution (that is, by internalizing costs) seems to be consistent with the requirements of distributive justice insofar as distributive justice favors equality. Observers have noted that pollution often has the effect of increasing inequality. If a firm pollutes, its stockholders benefit because their firm does not have to absorb the external costs of pollution and this leaves them with greater profits, and those customers who purchase the firm's products also benefit because the firm does not charge them for all the costs involved in making the product. The *beneficiaries* of pollution, therefore, tend to be those who can afford to buy a firm's stock and its products. On the other hand, the external *costs* of pollution are borne largely by the poor. Property values in polluted neighborhoods are generally lower, and consequently they are inhabited by the poor and abandoned by the wealthy. Pollution, therefore, may produce a net flow of benefits away from the poor and toward the well-off, thereby increasing inequality. To the extent that this occurs, pollution violates distributive justice. Internalizing the costs of pollution, as utilitarianism requires, would rectify matters by removing the burdens of external costs from the backs of the poor and placing them in the hands of the wealthy: the firm's stockholders and its customers. . . .

Internalizing external costs also seems to be consistent with the requirements of retributive and compensatory justice. Retributive justice requires that those who are responsible for and who benefit from an injury should bear the burdens of rectifying the injury, while compensatory justice requires that those who have been injured should be compensated by those who injure them. Taken together, these requirements imply that (1) the costs of pollution control should be borne by those who cause pollution and who have benefited from pollution activities, while (2) the benefits of pollution control should flow to those who have had to bear the external costs of pollution. Internalizing external costs seems to meet these two requirements: (1) The costs of pollution control are borne by stockholders and by customers, both of whom benefit from the polluting activities of the firm, and (2) the benefits of pollution control flow to those neighbors who once had to put up with the firm's pollution.

**Costs and Benefits**

The technology for pollution control has developed effective but costly methods for abating pollution. Up to 60 percent of water pollutants can be removed through "primary" screening and sedimentation processes; up to 90 percent can be removed through more expensive "secondary" biological and chemical processes; and amounts over 95 percent can be removed through even more expensive "tertiary" chemical treatment. . . .[5]

Consider that the costs of controlling pollution and the benefits derived from pollution control are inversely related. . . . If a body of water is highly polluted, it will probably be quite easy and consequently quite cheap to filter out a certain limited amount of pollutants. To filter out a few more pollutants, however, will require finer and, therefore, additional and more expensive filters. Costs will keep climbing for each additional level of purity desired, and getting out the last few molecules of impurities would require astronomically expensive additional equipment. However, getting out those last traces of impurities will probably not matter much to people and will therefore be unnecessary. At the other end of the scale, however, getting rid of the first gross amounts of pollutants will be highly beneficial to people: The costs of damages from these pollutants are substantial. . . .

It is at this point, however, that a fundamental difficulty in the utilitarian approach to pollution emerges. The cost-benefit analyses just described assume that the costs and benefits of reducing pollution can be accurately measured. In some cases (limited and local in character) cost-benefit measurements are available. . . .

Measurement is . . . difficult when the effects of pollution are uncertain and, consequently, difficult to predict: What will be the effects of increasing the carbon dioxide content of our atmosphere by burning more coal, as the United States is now starting to do? In fact, perhaps the major problem involved in obtaining the measurements needed to apply cost-benefit analysis to pollution problems is the problem of estimating and evaluating *risk* (that is, the probability of future costly consequences). . . .

These failures of measurement pose significant technical problems for utilitarian approaches to pollution. In addition, the use of utilitarian cost-benefit analysis is sometimes based on assumptions that are inconsistent with people's moral rights. Advocates of utilitarian cost-benefit analysis sometimes assume that if the benefits of a certain technology or manufacturing process "clearly" outweigh its costs, then it is morally permissible to impose the process on unwilling citizens. . . .

But these assumptions seem to violate the basic moral right that underlies democratic societies: Persons have a moral right to be treated only as they have consented to be treated beforehand. If people have not consented to take on the costs of a technology (and indicate this unwillingness, for example, through local legislation, hearings, or opinion surveys), then their moral right of consent is violated when these costs are imposed on them anyway. Using only cost-benefit analysis to determine whether a new technology or manufacturing process should be used, then, ignores the question of whether the costs involved are *voluntarily* accepted by those who must bear them, or whether they are unilaterally *imposed* on them by others. . . .

In view of all the problems raised by utilitarian approaches to pollution, it may be that alternative approaches are more adequate. In particular, it may be that the absolute bans on pollution which are still incorporated in many federal laws, and the rights theory on which these absolute bans rest, are, for the present at least, a more adequate approach to pollution issues than utilitarianism. Alternatively, some writers have suggested that when risks cannot be reliably estimated it is best to choose only those projects that carry no risk of irreversible damages. . . . Others suggest that when risks cannot be assessed, we should, in justice, identify those who are most vulnerable and who would have to bear the heaviest costs if things should go wrong, and then take steps to ensure that they are protected. Future generations and children, for example, should be protected against our polluting choices. Finally, others suggest that when risks cannot be measured, the only rational procedure is to first assume that the worst will happen and then choose the option that will leave us best off when the worst happens (this is the so-called "maximin rule" of probability theory). It is unclear which, if any, of these alternative approaches should be adopted when utilitarian cost-benefit analysis fails.

## Social Ecology, Ecofeminism, and the Demands of Caring

The difficulties inherent in utilitarian and rights-based approaches to the ethical issues raised by environmental degradation have led many to look for alternative approaches. Some have argued, in fact, that utilitarian and rights-based theories embody a kind of calculative and rationalistic way of thinking that is itself responsible for environmental crises. Utilitarian thinking assumes that nature is to be measured and used "efficiently," while rights-based theories see humans and other entities in individualistic terms and ignore their relationships with the rest of nature. These ways of thinking, it has been argued, are tightly linked to the kind of society in which we live.

Many thinkers have argued that the environmental crises we face are rooted in the social systems of hierarchy and domination that characterize our society. This view, now referred to as "social ecology," holds that until those patterns of hierarchy and domination are changed, we will be unable to deal with environmental crises. In a system of hierarchy one group holds power over another and members of the superior group are able to dominate those of the inferior group and get them to serve their ends. Examples of such systems of hierarchy include social practices such as racism, sexism, and social classes, as well as social institutions such as property rights, capitalism, bureaucracies, and the mechanisms of government. Such systems of hierarchy and domination go hand in hand with the widespread environmental destruction taking place all around us and with economic ways of "managing" the environment. . . .

Success becomes identified with dominance and control: the greater the number of people who work for a person, the greater that person's wealth, power, and status, and the more successful the person is deemed to be. Success also becomes identified with the domination of nature as society comes to identify "progress" with the increasing ability to control and dominate nature and its processes. Science, technology, and agriculture, all join hands in this attempt to dominate and control nature. Utilitarian weighing of the costs and benefits of destroying nature are inevitable in this perspective. The widespread destruction of nature that results, then, cannot be halted until our societies become less hierarchical, less dominating, and less oppressive. . . .

Several feminist thinkers have argued that the key form of hierarchy connected to destruction of the environment is the domination of women by men. Ecofeminism has been described as "the position that there are important connections—historical, experiential, symbolic, theoretical—between the domination of women and the domination of nature, an understanding of which is crucial to both feminism and environmental ethics."[6] Ecofeminists have argued that the root of our ecological crisis lies in a pattern of domination of nature that is tightly linked to the social practices and institutions through which women have been subordinated to men. . . .

Many Ecofeminists have argued that instead one should try "to remedy ecological and other problems through the creation of an alternative 'women's culture' . . . based on revaluing, celebrating and defending what patriarchy has devalued, including the feminine, nonhuman nature, the body and the emotions."[7] In particular, some have argued, the destructive "masculine" perspective of domination and hierarchy must be replaced with the "feminine" perspective of caring.

From the perspective of an ethic of caring, the destruction of nature that has accompanied male hierarchies of domination must be replaced with caring for and nurturing our relationships to nature and living things. . . .

[Some] ecofeminists would hold that while the concepts of utilitarianism, rights, and justice have a limited role to play in environmental ethics, an adequate environmental ethic must also take into account in a central manner the perspectives of an ethic of care. Nature must be seen as an "other" that can be cared for, and with which one has a relationship that must be nurtured and attended to. Nature must not be seen as an object to be dominated, controlled, and manipulated.

While ecofeminist approaches to the environment are thought provoking, it is unclear yet what their specific implications may turn out to be. These approaches are too recent to have been fully articulated. The shortcomings of utilitarian and rights-based approaches to the environment, however, may prompt a much fuller development of these approaches in the near future.

## THE ETHICS OF CONSERVING DEPLETABLE RESOURCES

"Conservation" refers to the saving or rationing of natural resources for later uses. Conservation, therefore, looks primarily to the future: to the need to limit consumption now in order to have resources available for tomorrow.

In a sense, pollution control is a form of conservation. Pollution "consumes" pure air and water, and pollution control "conserves" them for the future. But there are basic differences between the problems of pollution and the problems of *resource depletion* that makes the term *conservation* more applicable to the latter problems than to the former. With some notable exceptions (such as nuclear wastes), most forms of pollution affect present generations and their control will benefit present generations. The depletion of most scarce resources, however, lies far in the future, and the effects of their depletion will be felt primarily by posterity, and not by present generations. Consequently, our concern over the depletion of resources is primarily a concern for *future* generations and for the benefits that will be available to them. . . .

## Rights of Future Generations

It might appear that we have an obligation to conserve resources for future generations because they have an equal right to the limited resources of this planet. If future generations have an equal right to the world's resources, then by depleting these resources, we are taking what is actually theirs and violating their equal right to these resources.

A number of writers, however, have claimed that it is a mistake to think that future generations have rights. It is a mistake, consequently, to think that we should refrain from consuming natural resources because we are taking what future generations have a right to. Three main reasons have been advanced to show that future generations cannot have rights.

First, future generations cannot intelligently be said to have rights because they do not now exist and may never exist. I may be able to *think* about future people, but I cannot hit them, punish them, injure them, or treat them wrongly. . . . Since there is a possibility that future generations may never exist, they cannot "possess" rights.

Second, if future generations did have rights, then we might be led to the absurd conclusion that we must sacrifice our entire civilization for their sake. . . .

Third, we can say that someone has a certain right only if we know that he or she has a certain interest which that right protects. The purpose of a right, after all, is to protect the interests of the right-holder, but we are virtually ignorant of what interests future generations will have. . . . Science might come up with technologies for creating products from raw materials that we have in abundance—minerals in sea water, for example—and might find potentially unlimited energy sources such as nuclear fusion. Moreover, future generations might develop cheap and plentiful substitutes for the scarce resources that we now need. Since we are uncertain about these matters, we must remain ignorant about the interests future generations will want to protect (who could have guessed eighty years ago that uranium rocks would one day be considered a "resource" in which people would have an interest?). Consequently, we are unable to say what rights future people might have.

If these arguments are correct, then to the extent that we are uncertain what future generations will exist or what they will be like, they do not have any rights. It does not follow, however, that we have no obligations to any future generations since our obligations may be based on other grounds.

## Justice to Future Generations

John Rawls argues that while it is unjust to impose disproportionately heavy burdens on present generations for the sake of future generations, it is also unjust for present generations to leave nothing for future generations.[8]

. . . In general, Rawls claims, this method of ascertaining what earlier generations in justice owe to later generations will lead to the conclusion that what justice demands of us is merely that we hand to the next generation a situation no worse than we received from the generation before us. . . .[9]

Justice, then, requires that we hand over to our immediate successors a world that is not in worse condition than the one we received from our ancestors.

The demands of caring that arise from an ethic of care would also suggest conservation policies that are similar to those advocated by Rawls' views on justice. While most people would agree that they have a fairly direct relationship of care and concern with the generation that immediately succeeds their own, such a direct relationship does not exist with more distant and so more abstract generations. The generation that immediately succeeds our own, for example, consists of our own children. The demands of caring, we have seen, imply that one ought to attempt to see matters from the perspective of those with whom we are thus directly related, and that we attempt to care for their specific needs. Such caring would imply that we should at least leave the immediately succeeding generation a world that is not worse than the one we received. . . .

Unfortunately, we cannot rely on market mechanisms (that is, price rises) to ensure that scarce resources are conserved for future generations. The market registers only the effective demands of present participants and the actual supplies presently being made available. The needs and demands of future generations, as well as the potential scarcities that lie far in the future, are so heavily "discounted" by markets that they hardly affect prices at all.[10] . . .

The only means of conserving for the future, then, appear to be voluntary (or politically enforced) policies of conservation.

In practical terms, Rawls's view implies that while we should not sacrifice the cultural advances we have made, we should adopt voluntary or legal measures to conserve those resources and environmental benefits that we can reasonably assume our immediate posterity will need if they are to live lives with a variety of available choices comparable, at least, to ours. . . .

## Economic Growth?

However, to many observers conservation measures fall far short of what is needed. Several writers have argued that if we are to preserve enough scarce resources so that future generations can maintain their quality of life at a satisfactory level, we shall have to change our economies substantially, particularly by scaling down our pursuit of economic growth. . . .

The conclusion that economic growth must be abandoned if society is to be able to deal with the problems of diminishing resources has been challenged. It is at least arguable that adherence to continual economic growth promises to degrade the quality of life of future generations.

The arguments for this claim are simple, stark, and highly controversial. If the world's economies continue to pursue the goal of economic growth, the demand for depletable resources will continue to rise. But since world resources are finite, at some point supplies will simply run out. At this point, if the world's nations are still based on growth economies, we can expect a collapse of their major economic institutions (that is, of manufacturing and financial institutions, communication networks, the service industries) which in turn will bring down their political and social institutions (that is, centralized governments, education and cultural programs, scientific and technological development, health care). . . .

The assumptions on which these doomsday scenarios were based have been repeatedly criticized and "debunked." The computer programs and underlying equations on which the predictions are based make controversial and highly uncertain assumptions about future population growth rates, the absence of future increases in output per unit of input, our inability to find substitutes for depleted resources, and the ineffectiveness of recycling. These assumptions can all be challenged. Although future generations will certainly have fewer of the natural resources on which we depend, we cannot be sure exactly what impact this will have on them. . . . But we also cannot assume that the impact will be entirely benign. Given the extreme uncertainties in this situation, at the very least a commitment to conservation seems to be in order. Whether a wholesale transformation of our economy is also necessary if civilization is to survive is a difficult and disturbing question that we may soon have to face. . . .

## NOTES

1. For the term "spaceship earth," see Kenneth Boulding, "The Economics of the Coming Spaceship Earth," in Henry Jarret ed., *Environmental Quality in a Growing Economy*, (Baltimore: Johns Hopkins Press for Resources for the Future, 1966).
2. Quoted in Bill Devall, *Simple in Means, Rich in Ends, Practicing Deep Ecology*, (Salt Lake City, UT: Peregrine Smith Books, 1988), pp. 14–15.
3. W. K. Frankena, "Ethics and the Environment," in K. E. Goodpaster and K. M. Sayre, eds., *Ethics and Problems of the 21st Century*, (Notre Dame, IN: University of Notre Dame Press, 1979), pp. 3–20.
4. William T. Blackstone, "Ethics and Ecology," in William T. Blackstone, ed., *Philosophy and Environmental Crisis*, (Athens, GA: University of Georgia Press, 1974).
5. Mills, *Economics of Environmental Quality*, pp. 111–12.
6. Karen J. Warren, "The Power and Promise of Ecological Feminism," *Environmental Ethics* 12 (Summer 1990), p. 126.
7. Val Plumwood, "Current Trends in Ecofeminism," *The Ecologist*, vol. 22, no. 1 (January/February 1992), p. 10.
8. John Rawls, *A Theory of Justice* (Cambridge: Harvard University Press, 1971), p. 289.
9. *Ibid.*, pp. 285 and 288.
10. Joan Robinson, *Economic Philosophy* (London: Penguin Books, 1966), p. 115.

## LEGAL PERSPECTIVES

# *Henningsen v. Bloomfield Motors, Inc. and Chrysler Corporation*

*Supreme Court of New Jersey*

Claus H. Henningsen purchased a Plymouth automobile, manufactured by defendant Chrysler Corporation, from defendant Bloomfield Motors, Inc. His wife, plaintiff Helen Henningsen, was injured while driving it and instituted suit against both defendants to recover damages on account of her injuries. Her husband joined in the action seeking compensation for his consequential losses. The complaint was predicated upon breach of express and implied warranties and upon negligence. At the trial the negligence counts were

*Atlantic Reporter* 161 A2d 69, pp. 73–75, 78–81, 83–87, 93–96, 102. This opinion was written by Justice John J. Francis.

dismissed by the court and the case was submitted to the jury for determination solely on the issues of implied warranty of merchantability.* Verdicts were returned against both defendants and in favor of the plaintiffs. Defendants appealed and plaintiffs cross-appealed from the dismissal of their negligence claim. . . .

. . . The particular car selected was described as a 1955 Plymouth, Plaza "6," Club Sedan. The type used in the printed parts of the [purchase order] form became smaller in size, different in style, and less readable toward the bottom where the line for the purchaser's signature was placed. The smallest type on the page appears in the two paragraphs, one of two and one-quarter lines and the second of one and one-half lines, on which great stress is laid by the defense in the case. These two paragraphs are the least legible and the most difficult to read in the instrument, but they are most important in the evaluation of the rights of the contesting parties. They do not attract attention and there is nothing about the format which would draw the reader's eye to them. In fact, a studied and concentrated effort would have to be made to read them. Deemphasis seems the motive rather than emphasis. . . . The two paragraphs are:

"The front and back of this Order comprise the entire agreement affecting this purchase and no other agreement or understanding of any nature concerning same has been made or entered into, or will be recognized. I hereby certify that no credit has been extended to me for the purchase of this motor vehicle except as appears in writing on the face of this agreement.

"I have read the matter printed on the back hereof and agree to it as a part of this order the same as if it were printed above my signature. . . ."

*["Merchantability": The articles shall be of the kind described and be fit for the purpose for which they were sold. Fitness is impliedly warranted if an item is merchantable. Ed.]

The testimony of Claus Henningsen justifies the conclusion that he did not read the two fine print paragraphs referring to the back of the purchase contract. And it is uncontradicted that no one made any reference to them, or called them to his attention. With respect to the matter appearing on the back, it is likewise uncontradicted that he did not read it and that no one called it to his attention.

. . . The warranty, which is the focal point of the case, is set forth [on the reverse side of the page]. It is as follows:

"7. It is expressly agreed that there are no warranties, express or implied, *made* by either the dealer or the manufacturer on the motor vehicle, chassis, or parts furnished hereunder except as follows.

"The manufacturer warrants each new motor vehicle (including original equipment placed thereon by the manufacturer except tires), chassis or parts manufactured by it to be free from defects in material or workmanship under normal use and service. Its obligation under this warranty being limited to making good at its factory any part or parts thereof which shall, within ninety (90) days after delivery of such vehicle *to the original purchaser* or before such vehicle has been driven 4,000 miles, whichever event shall first occur, be returned to it with transportation charges prepaid and which its examination shall disclose to its satisfaction to have been thus defective: *This warranty being expressly in lieu of all other warranties expressed or implied, and all other obligations or liabilities on its part,* and it neither assumes nor authorizes any other person to assume for it any other liability in connection with the sale of its vehicles. . . ." [Emphasis added] . . .

The new Plymouth was turned over to the Henningsens on May 9, 1955. No proof was adduced by the dealer to show precisely what was done in the way of mechanical or road testing beyond testimony that the manufacturer's instructions were probably followed. Mr. Henningsen drove it from the dealer's place of business in Bloomfield to their home in Keansburg. On the trip nothing unusual appeared in the way in which it operated. Thereafter, it was used for short trips on paved streets about the town. It had no servicing and no mishaps of any kind before the event of May 19. That day, Mrs. Henningsen drove to Asbury Park [New Jersey]. On the way down and in returning the car performed in normal fashion until the accident occurred. She was proceeding north on Route 36 in Highlands, New Jersey, at 20–22 miles per hour. The highway was paved and smooth, and contained two lanes for northbound travel. She was riding in the right-hand lane. Suddenly she heard a loud noise "from the bottom, by the hood." It "felt as if something cracked." The steering wheel spun in her hands; the car veered sharply to the right and crashed into a highway sign and a brick wall. No other vehicle was in any way involved. A bus operator driving in the left-hand lane testified that he observed plaintiff's car approaching in normal fashion in the opposite direction; "all of a sudden [it] veered at 90 degrees . . . and right into this wall." As a result of the impact, the front of the car was so badly damaged that it was impossible to determine if any of the parts of the steering wheel mechanism or workmanship or assembly were defective or improper prior to the accident. The condition was such that the collision insurance carrier, after inspection, declared the vehicle a total loss. It had 468 miles on the speedometer at the time. . . .

The terms of the warranty are a sad commentary upon the automobile manufacturers' marketing practices. Warranties developed in the law in the interest of and to protect the ordinary consumer who cannot be expected to have the knowledge or capacity or even the opportunity to make adequate inspection of mechanical instrumentalities, like automobiles, and to decide for himself whether they are reasonably fit for the designed purpose. . . . But the ingenuity of the Automobile Manufacturers Association, by means of its standardized form, has metamorphosed the warranty into a device to limit the maker's liability. To call it an "equivocal" agreement, as the Minnesota Supreme Court did, is the least that can be said in criticism of it.

The manufacturer agrees to replace defective parts for 90 days after the sale or until the car has been driven 4,000 miles, whichever is first to occur, *if the part is sent to the factory, transportation charges prepaid, and if examination discloses to its satisfaction that the part is defective.* . . .

Chrysler points out that an implied warranty of merchantability is an incident of a contract of sale. It concedes, of course, the making of the original sale to Bloomfield Motors, Inc., but maintains that this transaction marked the terminal point of its contractual connection with the car. Then Chrysler urges that since it was not a party to the sale by the dealer to Henningsen, there is no privity of contract* between it and the plaintiffs, and the absence of this privity eliminates any such implied warranty.

There is no doubt that under early common-law concepts of contractual liability only those persons who were parties to the bargain could sue for a breach of it. In more recent times a noticeable disposition has appeared in a number of jurisdictions to break through the narrow barrier of privity when dealing with sales of goods in order to give realistic recognition to a universally accepted fact. The fact is that the dealer and the ordinary buyer do not, and are not expected to, buy goods, whether they be foodstuffs or automobiles, exclusively for their own consumption or use. Makers and manufacturers know this and advertise and market their products on that assumption; witness the "family" car, the baby foods, etc. The limitations of privity in contracts for the sale of goods developed their place in the law when marketing conditions were simple, when maker and buyer frequently met face to face on an

*["Privity of contract": A contractual relation existing between parties that is sufficiently close to confer a legal claim or right. Ed.]

equal bargaining plane and when many of the products were relatively uncomplicated and conducive to inspection by a buyer competent to evaluate their quality. With the advent of mass marketing, the manufacturer became remote from the purchaser, sales were accomplished through intermediaries, and the demand for the product was created by advertising media. In such an economy it became obvious that the consumer was the person being cultivated. Manifestly, the connotation of "consumer" was broader than that of "buyer." He signified such a person who, in the reasonable contemplation of the parties to the sale, might be expected to use the product. Thus, where the commodities sold are such that if defectively manufactured they will be dangerous to life or limb, then society's interests can only be protected by eliminating the requirement of privity between the maker and his dealers and the reasonably expected ultimate consumer. In that way the burden of losses consequent upon use of defective articles is borne by those who are in a position to either control the danger or make an equitable distribution of the losses when they do occur. . . .

Under modern conditions the ordinary layman, on responding to the importuning of colorful advertising, has neither the opportunity nor the capacity to inspect or to determine the fitness of an automobile for use; he must rely on the manufacturer who has control of its construction, and to some degree on the dealer who, to the limited extent called for by the manufacturer's instructions, inspects and services it before delivery. In such a marketing milieu his remedies and those of persons who properly claim through him should not depend "upon the intricacies of the law of sales. The obligation of the manufacturer should not be based alone on privity of contract. It should rest, as was once said, upon 'the demands of social justice.'" . . .

In a society such as ours, where the automobile is a common and necessary adjunct of daily life, and where its use is so fraught with danger to the driver, passengers, and the public, the manufacturer is under a special obligation in connection with the construction, promotion, and sale of his cars. Consequently, the courts must examine purchase agreements closely to see if consumer and public interests are treated fairly. . . .

What influence should these circumstances have on the restrictive effect of Chrysler's express warranty in the framework of the purchase contract? As we have said, warranties originated in the law to safeguard the buyer and not to limit the liability of the seller or manufacturer. It seems obvious in this instance that the motive was to avoid the warranty obligations which are normally incidental to such sales. The language gave little and withdrew much. In return for the delusive remedy of replacement of defective parts at the factory, the buyer is said to have accepted the exclusion of the maker's liability for personal injuries arising from the breach of the warranty, and to have agreed to the elimination of any other express or implied warranty. An instinctively felt sense of justice cries out against such a sharp bargain. But does the doctrine that a person is bound by his signed agreement, in the absence of fraud, stand in the way of any relief? . . .

The warranty before us is a standardized form designed for mass use. It is imposed upon the automobile consumer. He takes it or leaves it, and he must take it to buy an automobile. No bargaining is engaged in with respect to it. In fact, the dealer through whom it comes to the buyer is without authority to alter it; his function is ministerial—simply to deliver it. The form warranty is not only standard with Chrysler but, as mentioned above, it is the uniform warranty of the Automobile Manufacturers Association. . . . Of these companies, the "Big Three" (General Motors, Ford, and Chrysler) represented 93.5% of the passenger-car production for 1958 and the independents 6.5%.[1] And for the same year the "Big Three" had 86.72% of the total passenger vehicle registrations. . . .

*In the context* of this warranty, only the abandonment of all sense of justice would permit us to hold that, as a matter of law, the phrase "its obligation under this warranty being limited to making good at its factory any part or parts thereof" signifies to an ordinary reasonable person that he is relinquishing any personal injury claim that might flow from the use of a defective automobile. Such claims are nowhere mentioned. . . .

In the matter of warranties on the sale of their products, the Automobile Manufacturers Association has enabled them to present a united front. From the standpoint of the purchaser, there can be no arm's-length negotiating on the subject. Because his capacity for bargaining is so grossly unequal, the inexorable conclusion which follows is that he is not permitted to bargain at all. He must take or leave the automobile on the warranty terms dictated by the maker. He cannot turn to a competitor for better security.

Public policy is a term not easily defined. Its significance varies as the habits and needs of a people may vary. It is not static and the field of application is an ever increasing one. A contract, or a particular provision therein, valid in one era may be wholly opposed to the public policy of another. Courts keep in mind the principle that the best interests of society demand that persons should not be unnecessarily restricted in their freedom to contract. But they do not hesitate to declare void as against public policy contractual provisions which clearly tend to the injury of the public in some way. . . .

In the framework of this case, illuminated as it is by the facts and the many decisions noted, we are of the opinion that Chrysler's attempted disclaimer of an implied warranty of the merchantability and of the obligations arising therefrom is so inimical to the public good as to compel an adjudication of its invalidity. . . .

The principles that have been expounded as to the obligation of the manufacturer apply with equal force to the separate express warranty of the dealer. This is so, irrespective of the absence of the relationship of principle and agent between these defendants, because the manufacturer and the Association establish the warranty policy for the industry. The bargaining position of the dealer is inextricably bound by practice to that of the maker and the purchaser must take or leave the automobile, accompanied and encumbered as it is by the uniform warranty. . . .

Under all of the circumstances outlined above, the judgments in favor of the plaintiffs and against the defendants are affirmed.

## NOTES

1. Standard and Poor (Industrial Surveys, Autos, Basic Analysis, June 25, 1959), p. 4109.

# *Automobile Workers v. Johnson Controls, Inc.*

*Supreme Court of the United States*

In this case we are concerned with an employer's gender-based fetal-protection policy. May an employer exclude a fertile female employee from certain jobs because of its concern for the health of the fetus the woman might conceive?

89 U.S. 1215 (1991). Opinion delivered by Justice Blackmun.

## I

Respondent Johnson Controls, Inc., manufactures batteries. In the manufacturing process, the element lead is a primary ingredient. Occupational exposure to lead entails health risks, including the risk of harm to any fetus carried by a female employee.

Before the Civil Rights Act of 1964, 78 Stat. 241, became law, Johnson Controls did not employ any woman in a battery-manufacturing job. In June 1977, however, it announced its first official policy concerning its employment of women in lead-exposure work. . . .

Johnson Controls "stopped short of excluding women capable of bearing children from lead exposure," *id.*, at 138, but emphasized that a woman who expected to have a child should not choose a job in which she would have such exposure. The company also required a woman who wished to be considered for employment to sign a statement that she had been advised of the risk of having a child while she was exposed to lead. . . .

Five years later, in 1982, Johnson Controls shifted from a policy of warning to a policy of exclusion. Between 1979 and 1983, eight employees became pregnant while maintaining blood lead levels in excess of 30 micrograms per deciliter. Tr. of Oral Arg. 25, 34. This appeared to be the critical level noted by the Occupational Health and Safety Administration (OSHA) for a worker who was planning to have a family. See 29 CFR §1910.1025 (1989). The company responded by announcing a broad exclusion of women from jobs that exposed them to lead:

> . . . [I]t is [Johnson Controls'] policy that women who are pregnant or who are capable of bearing children will not be placed into jobs involving lead exposure or which could expose them to lead through the exercise of job bidding, bumping, transfer or promotion rights." App. 85-86.

The policy defined "women . . . capable of bearing children" as "[a]ll women except those whose inability to bear children is medically documented." *Id.*, at 81. It further stated that an unacceptable work station was one where, "over the past year," an employee had recorded a blood lead level of more than 30 micrograms per deciliter or the work site had yielded an air sample containing a lead level in excess of 30 micrograms per cubic meter. *Ibid.*

## II

In April 1984, petitioners filed in the United States District Court for the Eastern District of Wisconsin a class action challenging Johnson Controls' fetal-protection policy as sex discrimination that violated Title VII of the Civil Rights Act of 1964, as amended, 42 U.S. C. §2000e *et seq.* Among the individual plaintiffs were petitioners [such as] Mary Craig, who had chosen to be sterilized in order to avoid losing her job. . . .

## III

The bias in Johnson Controls' policy is obvious. Fertile men, but not fertile women, are given a choice as to whether they wish to risk their reproductive health for a particular job. Section 703(a) of the Civil Rights Act of 1964, 78 Stat. 255, as amended, 42 U.S.C. §2000e-2(a), prohibits sex-based classifications in terms and conditions of employment, in hiring and discharging decisions, and in other employment decisions that adversely affect an employee's status. Respondent's fetal-protection policy explicitly discriminates against women on the basis of their sex. The policy excludes women with childbearing capacity from lead-exposed jobs and so creates a facial classification based on gender. Respondent assumes as much in its brief before this Court. Brief for Respondent 17, n. 24.

Nevertheless, the Court of Appeals assumed, as did the two appellate courts who already had confronted the issue, that sex-specific fetal-protection policies do not involve facial discrimination. . . . The court assumed that because the asserted reason for the sex-based exclusion (protecting women's unconceived offspring) was ostensibly benign, the policy was not sex-based discrimination. That assumption, however, was incorrect.

First, Johnson Controls' policy classifies on the basis of gender and childbearing capacity, rather than fertility alone. Respondent does not seek to protect the unconceived children of all its employees. Despite evidence in the record about the debilitating effect of lead exposure on the male reproductive system, Johnson Controls is concerned only with the harms that may befall the unborn offspring of its female employees. . . . Johnson Controls' policy is facially discriminatory because it requires only a female employee to produce proof that she is not capable of reproducing.

Our conclusion is bolstered by the Pregnancy Discrimination Act of 1978 (PDA), 92 Stat. 2076, 42 U.S. C. §2000e(k), in which Congress explicitly provided that, for purposes of Title VII, discrimination "on the basis of sex" includes discrimination "because of or on the basis of pregnancy, childbirth, or related medical conditions." "The Pregnancy Discrimination Act has now made clear that, for all Title VII purposes, discrimination based on a woman's pregnancy is, on its face, discrimination because of her sex." *Newport News Shipbuilding & Dry Dock Co. v. EEOC*, 462 U.S. 669, 684 (1983). In its use of the words "capable of bearing children" in the 1982 policy statement as the criterion for exclusion, Johnson Controls explicitly classifies on the basis of potential for pregnancy. Under the PDA, such a classification must be regarded, for Title VII purposes, in the same light as explicit sex discrimination. Respondent has chosen to treat all its female employees as potentially pregnant; that choice evinces discrimination on the basis of sex. . . .

The beneficence of an employer's purpose does not undermine the conclusion that an explicit gender-based policy is sex discrimination under §703(a) and thus may be defended only as a BFOQ [bona fide occupational qualification].

The enforcement policy of the Equal Employment Opportunity Commission accords with this conclusion. On January 24, 1990, the EEOC issued a Policy Guidance in the light of the Seventh Circuit's decision in the present case. . . .

In sum, Johnson Controls' policy "does not pass the simple test of whether the evidence shows 'treatment of a person in a manner which but for that person's sex would be different.'" . . .

## IV

Under §703(e)(1) of Title VII, an employer may discriminate on the basis of "religion, sex, or national origin in those certain instances where religion, sex, or national origin is a bona fide occupational qualification reasonably necessary to the normal operation of that particular business or enterprise." 42 U.S. C. §2000e-2(e)(1). We therefore turn to the question whether Johnson Controls' fetal-protection policy is one of those "certain instances" that come within the BFOQ exception. . . .

The PDA's amendment to Title VII contains a BFOQ standard of its own: Unless pregnancy employees differ from others "in their ability or inability to work," they must be "treated the same" as other employees "for all employment-related purposes." 42 U.S. C. §2000e(k). This language clearly sets forth Congress' remedy for discrimination on the basis of pregnancy and potential pregnancy. Women who are either pregnant or potentially pregnant must be treated like others "similar in their ability . . . to work." *Ibid.* In other words, women as capable of doing their jobs as their male counterparts may not be forced to choose between having a child and having a job. . . .

## V

We have no difficulty concluding that Johnson Controls cannot establish a BFOQ. Fertile women, as far as appears in the record, participate in the manufacture of batteries as efficiently as anyone else. Johnson Controls' professed moral and ethical concerns about the welfare of the next generation do not suffice to establish a BFOQ of female sterility. Decisions about the welfare of future children must be left to the parents who conceive, bear, support, and raise them rather than to the employers who hire those parents. Congress has mandated this choice through Title VII, as amended by the Pregnancy Discrimination Act. Johnson Controls has attempted to exclude women because of their reproductive capacity. Title VII and the PDA simply do not allow a woman's dismissal because of her failure to submit to sterilization.

Nor can concerns about the welfare of the next generation be considered a part of the "essence" of Johnson Controls' business. . . .

Johnson Controls argues that it must exclude all fertile women because it is impossible to tell which women will become pregnant while working with lead. This argument is somewhat academic in light of our conclusion that the company may not exclude fertile women at all; it perhaps is worth noting, however, that Johnson Controls has shown no "factual basis for believing that all or substantially all women would be unable to perform safely and efficiently the duties of the job involved." *Weeks v. Southern Bell Tel. & Tel. Co.*, 408 F. 2d 228, 235 (CA5 1969), quoted with approval in *Dothard*, 433 U.S., at 333. Even on this sparse record, it is apparent that Johnson Controls is concerned about only a small minority of women. Of the eight pregnancies reported among the female employees, it has not been shown that any of the babies have birth defects or other abnormalities. The record does not reveal the birth rate for Johnson Controls' female workers but national statistics show that approximately nine percent of all fertile women become pregnant each year. The birthrate drops to two percent for blue collar workers over age 30. See Becker, 53 U. Chi. L. Rev., at 1233. Johnson Controls' fear of prenatal injury, no matter how sincere, does not begin to show that substantially all of its fertile women employees are incapable of doing their jobs. . . .

It is no more appropriate for the courts than it is for individual employers to decide whether a woman's reproductive role is more important to herself and her family than her economic role. Congress has left this choice to the woman as hers to make.

The judgment of the Court of Appeals is reversed and the case is remanded for further proceedings consistent with this opinion.

## *United States, Petitioner v. Bestfoods et al.*

*Supreme Court of the United States*

JUSTICE SOUTER delivered the opinion of the Court.

The United States brought this action for the costs of cleaning up industrial waste generated by a chemical plant. The issue before us, under the Comprehensive Environmental Response, Compensation, and Liability Act of 1980 (CERCLA), 94 Stat. 2767, as amended, 42 U.S. C. §9601 *et seq.*, is whether a parent corporation that actively participated in, and exercised control over, the operations of a subsidiary may, without more, be held liable as an operator of a polluting facility owned or operated by the subsidiary. We answer no, unless the corporate veil may be pierced. But a corporate parent that actively participated in, and exercised control over, the operations of the facility itself may be held directly liable in its own right as an operator of the facility.

## I

In 1980, CERCLA was enacted in response to the serious environmental and health risks posed by industrial pollution. See *Exxon Corp. v. Hunt*, 475 U.S. 355, 358–359 (1986). "As its name implies, CERCLA is a comprehensive statute that grants the President broad power to command government agencies and private parties to clean up hazardous waste sites" *Key Tronic Corp. v. United States*, 511 U.S. 809, 814 (1994). If it satisfies certain statutory conditions, the United States may, for instance, use the "Hazardous Substance Superfund" to finance cleanup efforts, see 42 U.S. C. §§9601 (11), 9604; 26 U.S. C. §9507, which it may then replenish by suits brought under §107 of the Act against, among others, "any person who at the time of disposal of any hazardous substance owned or operated any facility." 42 U.S. C. §9607(a) (2). So, those actually "responsible for any damage, environmental harm, or injury from chemical poisons [may be tagged with] the cost of their actions," S. Rep. No. 96–848, p. 13 (1980). The term "person" is defined in CERCLA to include corporations and other business organizations, see 42 U.S. C. §9601 (21), and the term "facility" enjoys a broad and detailed definition as well, see §9601 (9). The phrase "owner or operator" is defined only by tautology, however, as "any person owning or operating" a facility, §9601 (20) (A) (ii), and it is this bit of circularity that prompts our review. *Cf. Exxon Corp. v. Hunt, supra*, at 363 (CERCLA, "unfortunately, is not a model of legislative draftsmanship").

* * *

## II

It is a general principle of corporate law deeply "ingrained in our economic and legal systems" that a parent corporation (so-called because of control through ownership of another corporation's stock) is not liable for the acts of its subsidiaries. Douglas & Shanks, Insulation from Liability Through Subsidiary Corporations, 39 Yale L. J. 193 (1929) (hereinafter Douglas) . . . Thus it is hornbook law that "the exercise of the 'control' which stock ownership gives to the stockholders . . . will not create liability beyond the assets of the subsidiary. That 'control' includes the election of directors, the making of by-laws . . . and the doing of all other acts incident to the legal status of stockholders. Nor will a duplication of some or all of the directors or executive officers be fatal." Douglas 196 (footnotes omitted). Although this respect for corporate distinctions when the subsidiary is a polluter has been severely criticized in the literature, see, *e.g.*, Note, Liability of Parent Corporations for Hazardous Waste Cleanup and Damages, 99 Harv. L. Rev. 986 (1986), nothing in CERCLA purports to reject this bedrock principle, and against this venerable common-law backdrop, the congressional silence is audible. Cf. *Edmonds v. Compagnie Generale Transatlantique*, 443 U.S. 256, 266–267 (1979) ("silence is most eloquent, for such reticence while contemplating an important and controversial change in existing law is unlikely"). The Government has indeed made no claim that a corporate parent is liable as an owner or an operator under §107 simply because its subsidiary is subject to liability for owning or operating a polluting facility.

But there is an equally fundamental principle of corporate law, applicable to the parent-subsidiary relationship as well as generally, that the corporate veil may be pierced and the shareholder held liable for the corporation's conduct when, *inter alia*, the corporate form would otherwise be misused to accomplish certain wrongful purposes, most notably fraud, on the shareholder's behalf. . . . Nothing in CERCLA purports to rewrite this well-settled rule, either. CERCLA is thus like many another congressional enactment in giving no indication "that the entire corpus of state corporation law is to be replaced simply because a plaintiff's cause of action is based upon a federal statute," *Burks v. Lasker*, 441 U.S. 471, 478 (1979), and the failure of the statute to speak to a matter as fundamental as the liability implications of corporate ownership demands application of the rule that "[i]n order to abrogate a common-law principle, the statute must speak directly to the question addressed by the common law," *United States v. Texas*, 507 U.S. 529, 534 (1993) (internal quotation marks omitted). The Court of Appeals [for the Sixth Circuit] was accordingly correct in holding that when (but only when) the corporate veil may be pierced, may a parent corporation be charged with derivative CERCLA liability for its subsidiary's actions.

## III

### A

If the act rested liability entirely on ownership of a polluting facility, this opinion might end here; but CERCLA liability may turn on operation as well as ownership, and nothing in the statute's terms bars a parent corporation from direct liability for its own actions in operating a facility owned by its subsidiary. As Justice (then-Professor) Douglas noted almost 70 years ago, derivative liability cases are to be distinguished from those in which "the alleged wrong can seemingly be traced to the parent through the conduit of its own personnel and management" and "the parent is directly a participant in the wrong complained of." Douglas 207, 208. In such instances, the parent is directly liable for its own actions. . . . The fact that a corporate subsidiary happens to own a polluting facility operated by its parent does nothing, then, to displace the rule that the parent "corporation is [itself] responsible for the wrongs committed by its agents in the course of its business," *Mine Workers v. Coronado Coal Co.*, 259 U.S. 344, 395 (1922), and whereas the rules of veil-piercing limit derivative liability for the actions of another corporation, CERCLA's "operator" provision is concerned primarily with direct liability for one's own actions. See, e.g., *Sidney S. Arst Co. v. Pipefitters Welfare Ed. Fund*, 25 F. 3d 417, 420 (CA7 1994) ("the direct, personal liability provided by CERCLA is distinct from the derivative liability that results from piercing the corporate veil") (internal quotation marks omitted). It is this direct liability that is properly seen as being at issue here.

Under the plain language of the statute, any person who operates a polluting facility is directly liable for the costs of cleaning up the pollution. See 42 U.S. C. §9607 (a) (2). This is so regardless of whether that person is the facility's owner, the owner's parent corporation or business partner, or even a saboteur who sneaks into the facility at night to discharge its poisons out of malice. If any such act of operating a corporate subsidiary's facility is done on behalf of a parent corporation, the existence of the parent-subsidiary relationship under state corporate law is simply irrelevant to the issue of direct liability. See *Riverside Market Dev. Corp. v. International Bldg. Prods., Inc.*, 931 F. 2d 327, 330 (CA5) ("CERCLA prevents individuals from hiding behind the corporate shield when, as 'operators,' they themselves actually participate in the wrongful conduct prohibited by the Act"), cert. denied, 502 U.S. 1004 (1991); *United States v. Kayser-Roth Corp.*, 910 F.2d 24, 26 (CA1 1990) ("a person who is an operator of a facility is not protected from liability by the legal structure of ownership").

This much is easy to say; the difficulty comes in defining actions sufficient to constitute direct parental "operation." Here of course we may again rue the uselessness of CERCLA's definition of a facility's "operator" as "any person . . . operating" the facility, 42 U.S. C. §9601(20)(A)(ii), which leaves us to do the best we can to give the term its "ordinary or natural meaning." *Bailey v. United States*, 516 U.S. 137, 145 (1995) (internal quotation marks omitted). In a mechanical sense, to "operate" ordinarily means "[t]o control the functioning of; run: *operate a sewing machine.*" American Heritage Dictionary 1268 (3d ed. 1992); see also

Webster's New International Dictionary 1707 (2d ed. 1958) ("to work; as, to *operate* a machine"). And in the organizational sense more obviously intended by CERCLA, the word ordinarily means "[t]o conduct the affairs of; manage: *operate a business.*" *American Heritage Dictionary,* supra, at 1268; see also Webster's New International Dictionary, supra, at 1707 ("to manage"). So, under CERCLA, an operator is simply someone who directs the workings of, manages, or conducts the affairs of a facility. To sharpen the definition for purposes of CERCLA's concern with environmental contamination, an operator must manage, direct, or conduct operations specifically related to pollution, that is, operations having to do with the leakage or disposal of hazardous waste, or decisions about compliance with environmental regulations.

**B**

* * *

In our enquiry into the meaning Congress presumably had in mind when it used the verb "to operate," we recognized that the statute obviously meant something more than mere mechanical activation of pumps and valves, and must be read to contemplate "operation" as including the exercise of direction over the facility's activities. . . . The Court of Appeals recognized this by indicating that a parent can be held directly liable when the parent operates the facility in the stead of its subsidiary or alongside the subsidiary in some sort of a joint venture. See 113 F. 3d, at 579. We anticipated a further possibility . . . that a dual officer or director might depart so far from the norms of parental influence exercised through dual officeholding as to serve the parent, even when ostensibly acting on behalf of the subsidiary in operating the facility. . . . Yet another possibility, suggested by the facts of this case, is that an agent of the parent with no hat to wear but the parent's hat might manage or direct activities at the facility.

Identifying such an occurrence calls for line drawing yet again, since the acts of direct operation that give rise to parental liability must necessarily be distinguished from the interference that stems from a normal relationship between parent and subsidiary. Again norms of corporate behavior (undisturbed by any CERCLA provision) are crucial reference points. Just as we may look to such norms in identifying the limits of the presumption that a dual officeholder acts in his ostensible capacity, so here we may refer to them in distinguishing a parental officer's oversight of a subsidiary from such an officer's control over the operation of the subsidiary's facility. . . . The critical question is whether, in degree and detail, actions directed to the facility by an agent of the parent alone are eccentric under accepted norms of parental oversight of a subsidiary's facility.

## CASES

# CASE 1. *Protecting Consumers Against Tobacco*

The dangers of smoking cigarettes are now almost universally recognized, and consequently, efforts to regulate their use and advertisement have become increasingly pronounced. The figures cited often tell of the thousands of people who die every year due to smoking related illnesses. Despite this knowledge, the major tobacco companies (Philip Morris, R.J. Reynolds, Brown & Williamson, and Lorillard) have consistently opposed most attempts to regulate their

This case was written by Tom Beauchamp and Joe Folio.

products. Over time their position has shifted from a denial of the harms of tobacco to a protection of an individual's right to choose. While the industry's position on a whole has remained fairly consistent, the U.S. government has expressed a growing interest in the regulation of tobacco.

The federal government has both supported and attempted to regulate the tobacco industry. For more than 30 years, the government subsidized tobacco farmers, and until the 1970s, cigarettes were standard issue to soldiers in the military. Additionally, the government currently imposes a 34 cent tax on every pack of cigarettes, which nets the government several billion dollars annually. In 2001 a presidential commission reported that the federal tax on cigarettes should be increased by 17 cents so as to further fund subsidies.[1] On the other side, various government agencies have felt political pressures to regulate tobacco consumption. In 1996, the FDA declared nicotine to be an addictive drug, thereby placing it under its own jurisdiction. Though this maneuver was eventually reversed by the Supreme Court, which stated that the job of regulation remained a job for Congress, the 2001 presidential commission again recommended increased power to regulate tobacco.

George Will, the syndicated columnist, was puzzled by these events. Writing in the *Washington Post* in 1999, Will said:

> The government, which now blames tobacco companies' duplicities for some substantial health costs, has, since the 1964 surgeon general's report, officially certified cigarettes as dangerous. For more than three decades, the government has required increasingly stern health warnings to be printed on cigarette packs and advertising. Of course, this government still subsidizes the growing of tobacco and writes budgets of tobacco tax revenues assumed.[2]

## Questions

1. Are the actions of the federal government a legitimate attempt to protect the consumer from a risky product? If not, then who should be responsible for such protection?
2. Does the federal government's regulation of tobacco and its simultaneous support and financial benefit from the industry represent a conflict of interest?
3. If tobacco is a legitimate product that consumers must be protected from, then do other products, such as fast-food and alcohol, warrant increased regulation?

## NOTES

1. "Panel Seeks New Cigarette Tax and Limits on Tobacco Industry," *The New York Times*, May 13, 2001, p. 24.
2. George Will, "Victims of 'Coffin Nails'?" *The Washington Post*, October 3, 1999, p. B7.

# CASE 2. *Exposing Workers to Plutonium*

In August 1999 it was learned that several thousand uranium workers in a 750-acre plant in Paducah, Kentucky had been exposed to plutonium and other radioactive materials. The exposures occurred at the Paducah Gaseous Diffusion Plant, which is owned by the Department of Energy of the U.S. government and is still in operation today. The 1800 workers in the plant once labored to produce material for bombs from uranium dust. The radioactive contaminants that caused the exposure also spilled into ditches and eventually were carried into wildlife areas and private water wells. Some of the material had been deliberately dumped into land-

This case was prepared by Tom Beauchamp, based in part on reports by J. Warrick in *The Washington Post*, August 8, 1999 (p. A1); August 29, 1999 (p. A1); September 16, 1999 (p. A1); January 29, 2000 (p. A8); April 12, 2000 (p. A1); and October 5, 2000 (p. A3).

fills and nearby fields. In the last few years the enriched uranium produced at the plant has been sold to commercial nuclear power plants.

Many records on plutonium contamination were kept in archives, but workers were never told of potential risks to health. Recent studies indicate that the workers have experienced higher rates of cancers from the ionizing radiation. Because they were never alerted to the risks, workers did not wear sufficient protection while working with the harmful products. Workers were told that there were insignificant amounts of plutonium and were not monitored to determine the actual levels of exposure. High levels of radiation have been discovered in the plant and, more recently, reports indicate that plutonium has been found up to one mile from the plant. In several locations half a mile from the plant, tests in year 2000 revealed that plutonium levels were above 20 times the maximally acceptable limit. Groundwater cleanups have been underway since 1988, when the serious levels of pollution in wells was discovered. Individuals continue not to draw water from personal wells that may be contaminated.

Union Carbide managed the plant for a 32-year period, when most of the pollution occurred. Lockheed Martin and Martin Marietta managed the plant during the 1980s and 1990s. The federal government for decades took the position that the amounts of exposure were too small to amount to a threat to health. However, internal documents show that Martin Marietta was very concerned during this same period about significant environmental damage that had occurred. Workers now maintain that even if their health was not jeopardized, not disclosing levels of pollution and failing to monitor for health problems were serious moral failures.

In September 1999 the Clinton administration announced that it would spend several million dollars to compensate workers harmed by the exposures at the Paducah Gaseous Diffusion Plant. According to the plan, workers may receive a lump sum of $100,000 or may negotiate another compensation package that covers medical costs, lost wages, and job retraining. The Department of Energy announced that it would allot $21.8 million in new spending for environmental cleanup in the region.

### Questions

1. Should management in the plant make a full disclosure of known risks, even when the risks are believed to be insignificant?
2. Did the government have the responsibility to pay the workers for the risks that they were asked to undertake as well as the health effects that resulted?
3. In failing to make a full disclosure, are the plant owner and managers guilty of a moral violation? What is the moral violation, and is some form of punishment in order?

## CASE 3. *The McDonald's Polystyrene Case*

Environmental consciousness has increased dramatically in the United States in the past fifteen years. More and more people are conscious of toxic wastes, of pollution, of the mountains of garbage that pour into landfills, of the depletion of forests. McDonald's, the largest restaurant chain in the world, presents a notable environmental case study.

For years McDonald's, like most other quick-food chains, used polystyrene containers—the famous Big Mac clamshell—for its hamburgers. This container was lightweight, did not absorb grease, and kept the hamburgers warm. McDonald's had chosen polystyrene over paperboard for these projects and had joined with others in a $16 million project to build seven

This case was written by Richard T. De George, *Business Ethics* (Prentice-Hall, 5th ed., 1999).

polystyrene-recycling plants around the country. But by the end of 1990 it was to change its mind.[1] Because of its size and dominant position, McDonald's became the target of the Environmental Defense Fund, which claimed that making polystyrene packaging created toxic fumes, that it took up too much landfill, and that it took too long to biodegrade. In addition, a lobby called the Pro-Environment Packaging Council, funded by paper companies, started targeting schools with a campaign about the adverse impact of polystyrene products. McDonald's was soon faced with what *Forbes Magazine* called a "children's crusade," which involved a Send-It-Back campaign, letters written by classes of children, and a threatened boycott.[2] On November 2, 1990, McDonald's announced that within sixty days it would phase out its polystyrene clams and replace them with coated paperboard.

The announcement was hailed as a victory for environmentalists and as a demonstration of the power of public opinion. Newspaper editorials across the country congratulated McDonald's for taking the leadership in environmental issues and put pressure on other chains to follow McDonald's lead.

Although no one spoke against the importance of environmental concern, several voices were raised, but scarcely heard, that questioned the soundness of McDonald's decision. Edward H. Rensi, head of McDonald's U.S. operations, who had long defended the clamshell boxes, said, "Although some scientific studies indicate that foam packaging is environmentally sound, our customers just don't feel good about it."[3] Jay Beyea, a scientist at the National Audubon Society, noted that the change would result in using a lot more paper and that "using a lot more paper means a lot more pollution."[4] It also means cutting a lot more trees. A study by the Stanford Research Institute concluded that there was no sound basis for claiming that using paper products was environmentally superior to using polystyrene or other such plastic-based materials.[5] Nor would the change affect the landfill problems, since such material accounts for only one-third of 1 percent of landfill waste by volume. Lynn Scarlett, vice-president of research at Reason Foundation, pointed out that manufacturing polystyrene clamshells used 30 percent less energy than paperboard and produced 40 percent less air pollution and 42 percent less water pollution.[6]

## Questions

1. In the end, environmentalists had won—or had a certain wing, together with large paper interests, won? Public opinion had had its way. But who informed grade school children of the facts that led to their uncharacteristic assertiveness on this issue, and did they get the whole story?
2. McDonald's move to paper products was probably a good business decision, given the circumstances and the pressure it was under. Was it the best environmental decision? Was it morally obliged to take the action it did?

## NOTES

1. Details of the case come from the sources noted below, as well as from *New York Times,* November 1, 1990, p. A1; November 2, 1990, p. A1; December 31, 1990, p. A3; and April 17, 1991, p. A14.
2. "McDonald's Caves In," *Forbes,* (February 4, 1991): 73–74.
3. *Fortune* (June 3, 1991), p. 92.
4. John Holusha, "Packaging and Public Image: McDonald's Fills a Big Order," *New York Times,* (November 2, 1990), p. A1.
5. Benjamin Zycher, "Self-Flagellation Among the Capitalists," *Regulation* 14 (Winter 1991): 25–26.
6. Lynn Scarlett, "Make Your Environment Dirtier—Recycle," *Wall Street Journal* (January 14, 1991), p. A12.

# CASE 4. *Enron and Employee Investment Risk*

In order to determine appropriate and acceptable levels of risk in their retirement funds, employee-investors must be knowledgeable about how those funds are invested. Often employees are unaware of the level of risk taken by their employers in maintaining a fund. A famous recent case of the problem emerged from the ashes of the collapse of Enron.

After greatly expanding its operations during the 1990s, Enron, an energy broker, experienced unprecedented financial growth and soaring stock prices. Much of this growth, however, was not legitimate, and the details, as a result, were not disclosed to investors or to employees.

Using the lawful practice of "mark-to-market" accounting, Enron's financial analysts and advisors were able to record potential, future profits as immediate gains. To boost these apparent profits even more, Enron also created businesses and partnerships to hide its debt. These practices inflated stock prices while falsely establishing the company's financial position and stability. The success and prominence of the company seemed to minimize concerns about investment risk in Enron stock. Seeing immediate and extensive gains, however, such employee-investors saw little incentive in questioning the risk of their investments. They were not concerned when Enron used company stock as the sole unit of deposit in employee 401(k) earnings. While this involved tremendous risk, given Enron's true instability, the details of the company's financial state remained undisclosed. Only after uncovering the fraudulent accounting practices was the true level of the risk assessed. By this time, however, employee-investors and employees with retirement savings invested in stock had lost all of their investments and all of their retirement funds.

Enron-style investing is commonplace in employee retirement accounts, where diversification in types of investment is not generally recognized as a legal or a moral requirement. While the collapse of Enron is everywhere recognized to be a scandal, the underlying questions of investor risk in company retirement plans is one feature of this scandal that remains largely unaddressed.

## Questions

1. Should businesses, like Enron, encourage employees to buy stock in their own companies? Why or why not? What are some of the risks involved in permitting such practices?
2. While, legally, not all information must be disclosed, should companies be obligated to reveal the true nature of investor risk? Or, are investors individually responsible for determining such risk?
3. Does Enron's overstating of profit amount to a manipulation of investors? Was the manipulation intentional? Should investors assume a high level of risk unless expressly told otherwise?

This case was prepared by David Lawrence and Tom L. Beauchamp.

# CASE 5. *OSHA Noncompliance and Security*

TMW Corporation produces three-quarters of the world's microsynchronizers, an integral part of apartment vacuum systems. This corporation has plants mostly in the Midwest, although a few are scattered on both the east and west coasts. The plants in the Midwest employ Electronic Worker's Union members under a contract that became effective last August and is in force for three years. This union is strong, and the employees will do anything to preserve and maintain the strong union benefits that have been won.

Last year an OSHA official visited the St. Louis plant and discovered several discrepancies with the standards established by the OSH Act, including the absence of safety goggles on employees who weld tiny wires together and also an automatic shutoff switch on the wire-splicing machine. OSHA issued warnings to TMW for the noncompliance and informed company officials that it would impose drastic fines if they did not correct them.

The company immediately proceeded to correct the problems. They had to shut down parts of the Midwest plants on a rotating basis to alter the wire-splicing.

This case was prepared by Professor Kenneth A. Kovach. Printed with permission.

# CASE 6. *Texaco in the Ecuadorean Amazon*

Ecuador is a small nation on the northwest coast of South America. During its 173-year history, Ecuador has been one of the least politically stable South American nations. In 1830 Ecuador achieved its independence from Spain. Ecuadorean history since that time has been characterized by cycles of republican government and military intervention and rule. The period from 1960 to 1972 was marked by instability and military dominance of political institutions. From 1972 to 1979 Ecuador was governed by military regimes. In 1979 a popularly elected president took office, but the military demanded and was granted important governing powers. The democratic institutional framework of Ecuador remains weak. Decreases in public sector spending, increasing unemployment, and rising inflation have hit the Ecuadorean poor especially hard. World Bank estimates indicate that in 1994 35 percent of the Ecuadorean population lived in poverty, and an additional 17 percent were vulnerable to poverty.

The Ecuadorean Amazon is one of the most biologically diverse forests in the world and is home to an estimated 5 percent of Earth's species. It is home to cicadas, scarlet macaws, squirrel monkeys, freshwater pink dolphins, and thousands of other species. Many of these species have small populations, making them extremely sensitive to disturbance. Indigenous Indian populations have lived in harmony with these species for centuries. They have fished

This case was prepared by Denis G. Arnold and is based on James Brooke, "New Effort Would Test Possible Coexistence of Oil and Rain Forest," *The New York Times*, February 26, 1991; Dennis M. Hanratty, Ed., *Ecuador: A Country Study*, 3rd ed. (Washington D.C.: Library of Congress, 1991); Anita Isaacs, *Military Rule and Transition in Ecuador*, 1972-92 (Pittsburgh: University of Pittsburgh Press, 1993); *Ecuador Poverty Report* (Washington D.C.: The World Bank, 1996); Joe Kane, *Savages* (New York: Vintage Books, 1996); Eyal Press, "Texaco on Trial," *The Nation*, May 31, 1999; and "Texaco and Ecuador," *Texaco: Health, Safety & the Environment*, 27 September 1999, www.texaco.com/she/index.html (16 December, 1999); and *Aguinda v. Texaco, Inc.*, 142 F. Supp. 2d 534 (S.D.N.Y. 2001).

and hunted in and around the rivers and lakes; and they have raised crops of cacao, coffee, fruits, nuts, and tropical woods in *chakras*, models of sustainable agroforestry.

Ten thousand feet beneath the Amazon floor lays one of Ecuador's most important resources: rich deposits of crude oil. Historically, the Ecuadorean government regarded the oil as the best way to keep up with the country's payments on its $12 billion foreign debt obligations. For 20 years American oil companies, lead by Texaco, extracted oil from beneath the Ecuadorean Amazon in partnership with the government of Ecuador. (The United States is the primary importer of Ecuadorean oil.) They constructed 400 drill sites and hundreds of miles of roads and pipelines, including a primary pipeline that extends for 280 miles across the Andes. Large tracts of forest were clear-cut to make way for these facilities. Indian lands, including *chakras*, were taken and bulldozed, often without compensation. In the village of Pacayacu the central square is occupied by a drilling platform.

Officials estimate that the primary pipeline alone has spilled more than 16.8 million gallons of oil into the Amazon over an 18-year period. Spills from secondary pipelines have never been estimated or recorded; however, smaller tertiary pipelines dump 10,000 gallons of petroleum per week into the Amazon, and production pits dump approximately 4.3 million gallons of toxic production wastes and treatment chemicals into the forest's rivers, streams, and groundwater each day. (By comparison, the Exxon Valdez spilled 10.8 million gallons of oil into Alaska's Prince William Sound.) Significant portions of these spills have been carried downriver into neighboring Peru.

Critics charge that Texaco ignored prevailing oil industry standards that call for the reinjection of waste deep into the ground. Rivers and lakes were contaminated by oil and petroleum; heavy metals such as arsenic, cadmium, cyanide, lead, and mercury; poisonous industrial solvents; and lethal concentrations of chloride salt, and other highly toxic chemicals. The only treatment these chemicals received occurred when the oil company burned waste pits to reduce petroleum content. Villagers report that the chemicals return as black rain, polluting what little fresh water remains. What is not burned off seeps through the unlined walls of the pits into the groundwater. Cattle are found with their stomachs rotted out, crops are destroyed, animals are gone from the forest, and fish disappear from the lakes and rivers. Health officials and community leaders report adults and children with deformities, skin rashes, abscesses, headaches, dysentery, infections, respiratory ailments, and disproportionately high rates of cancer. In 1972 Texaco signed a contract requiring it to turn over all of its operations to Ecuador's national oil company, Petroecuador, by 1992. Petroecuador inherited antiquated equipment, rusting pipelines, and uncounted toxic waste sites. Independent estimates place the cost of cleaning up the production pits alone at 600 million dollars. From 1995 to 1998 Texaco spent 40 million dollars on cleanup operations in Ecuador. In exchange for these efforts the government of Ecuador relinquished future claims against the company.

Numerous international accords—including the 1972 Stockholm Declaration on the Human Environment signed by over 100 countries, including the United States and Ecuador—identify the right to a clean and healthy environment as a fundamental human right and prohibit both state and private actors from endangering the needs of present and future generations. Ecuadorean and Peruvian plaintiffs, including several indigenous tribes, have filed billion-dollar class-action lawsuits against Texaco in U.S. courts under the Alien Tort Claims Act (ACTA). Enacted in 1789, the law was designed to provide noncitizens access to U.S. courts in cases involving a breach of international law, including accords. Texaco maintains that the case should be tried in Ecuador. However, Ecuador's judicial system does not recognize the concept of a class-action suit and has no history of environmental litigation. Furthermore, Ecuador's judicial system is notoriously corrupt (a poll by George Washington University found that only 16 percent of Ecuadoreans have confidence in their judicial system) and lacks the infrastructure necessary to handle the case (e.g., the city in which the case would be tried lacks a courthouse). Texaco defended its actions by arguing that it is in full compliance with Ecuadorean law and that it had full approval of the Ecuadorean government.

In May 2001 U.S. District Judge Jed Rakoff rejected the applicability of the ACTA and dismissed the case on grounds of forum non conveniens. Judge Rakoff argued that since "no act taken by Texaco in the United States bore materially on the pollution-creating activities," the case should be tried in Ecuador and Peru. In October 2001 Texaco completed a merger with Chevron Corporation. Chevron and Texaco are now known as ChevronTexaco Corporation. In August 2002 the U.S. Court of Appeals for the Second Circuit upheld Judge Rakoff's decision.

## Questions

1. Given the fact that Texaco operated in partnership with the Ecuadorean government, is Texaco's activity in the Amazon morally justifiable? Explain.
2. Does Texaco (now ChevronTexaco) have a moral obligation to provide additional funds and technical expertise to clean up areas of the Amazon it is responsible for polluting? Does it have a moral obligation to provide medical care for the residents of the Amazon region who are suffering from the effects of the pollution? Explain.
3. Does the fact that the military plays a dominant role in Ecuadorean political life undermine Texaco's claim that its environmental practices are justified because the government of Ecuador permitted them? Explain.
4. Does the example of Texaco's conduct in Ecuador indicate a need for enforceable regulations governing transnational corporate activity? Explain.

## *Suggested Supplementary Readings*

*Consumer Protection*

BOYLAN, MICHAEL. *Ethical Issues in Business.* New York: Harcourt Brace, 1995.

BROBECK, STEPHEN. *The Modern Consumer Movement.* Boston: G.K. Hall & Co., 1990.

CAVANILLAS MUGICA, SANTIAGO. "Protection of the Weak Consumer Under Product Liability Rules." *Journal of Consumer Policy*, 13 (1990).

DIENHART, JOHN W., and JORDAN CURNUTT. "Product Safety and Liability." In their *Business Ethics: A Reference Handbook.* California: ABC-CLIO, Inc., 1998, pp. 52–96.

SORELL, TOM. "The Customer Is Not Always Right." *Journal of Business Ethics*, 13 (November 1994): 913–18.

VISCUSI, W. KIP. "Toward a Proper Role for Hazard Warnings in Products Liability Cases." *Journal of Products Liability*, 13 (1991).

*Investor Protection*

ALMEDER, ROBERT F., and MILTON SNOEYENBOS. "Churning: Ethical and Legal Issues." *Business and Professional Ethics Journal*, 6 (Spring 1987).

ALMEDER, ROBERT F., and DAVID CAREY. "In Defense of Sharks: Moral Issues in Hostile Liquidating Takeovers." *Journal of Business Ethics*, 10 (1991): 471–84.

BOATRIGHT, JOHN. "Trade Secrets and Conflict of Interest." In his *Ethics and the Conduct of Business.* Upper Saddle River, NJ: Prentice Hall, 2000, pp. 128–58.

BROWN, DONNA. "Environmental Investing: Let the Buyer Beware." *Management Review*, 79 (June 1990).

BRUNER, ROBERT F., and LYNN SHARP PAINE. "Management Buyouts and Managerial Ethics." *California Management Review*, 30 (Winter 1988): 89–106.

FRANKS, JULIAN, and COLIN MAYER. *Risk, Regulation, and Investor Protection: The Case of Investment Management.* Oxford: Clarendon Press, 1989.

HEACOCK, MARIAN, and others. "Churning: An Ethical Issue in Finance." *Business and Professional Ethics Journal,* 6 (Spring 1987).

HOFFMAN, W. MICHAEL, and RALPH J., MCQUADE. "A Matter of Ethics." *Financial Strategies and Concepts,* 4 (1986).

KESTER, W. C., and T. A. LUEHRMAN. "Rehabilitating the Leveraged Buyout." *Harvard Business Review,* 73 (May–June 1995): 119–30.

MACKENZIE, CRAIG, and ALAN LEWIS. "Morals and Markets: The Case of Ethical Investing." *Business Ethics Quarterly,* 9 (July 1999): 439–52.

SCHADLER, F. P., and J. E. KARNS. "The Unethical Exploitation of Shareholders in Management Buyout Transactions." *Journal of Business Ethics,* 9 (July 1990): 595–602.

WILLIAMS, OLIVER, and others. *Ethics and the Investment Industry.* Savage, MD: Rowman and Littlefield, 1989.

*Worker Protection*

ANDERSON, ELIZABETH. "Values, Risks and Market Norms." *Philosophy and Public Affairs,* 17 (1988): 54–65.

BEAUCHAMP, TOM L. *Case Studies in Business, Society, and Ethics.* 5th ed. Upper Saddle River, NJ: Prentice Hall, 2004.

BERITIC, T. "Workers at High Risk: The Right to Know." *Lancet,* 341 (April 10, 1993): 933–34.

BOATRIGHT, JOHN. "Occupational Health and Safety." In his *Ethics and the Conduct of Business.* Upper Saddle River, NJ: Prentice Hall, 2000, pp. 307–35.

EZORSKY, GERTRUDE, Ed. *Moral Rights in the Workplace.* Albany: State University of New York Press, 1987.

GIBSON, MARY. *Workers' Rights.* Totowa, NJ: Rowman and Littlefield, 1983.

LURIE, SUE GENA. "Ethical Dilemmas and Professional Roles in Occupational Medicine." *Social Science and Medicine,* 38 (May 1994): 1367–74.

MCGARITY, THOMAS O. "The Nature of the Worker's Right to Know." *The Hastings Center Report,* 14 (August 1984): 38–42.

ROSNER, DAVID, and GERALD MARKOWITZ. "Workers, Industry, and the Control of Information: Silicosis and the Industrial Hygiene Foundation." *Journal of Public Health Policy,* 16 (1995): 29–58.

SASS, ROBERT. "The Worker's Right to Know, Participate, and Refuse Hazardous Work: A Manifesto Right." *Journal of Business Ethics,* 5 (April 1986).

WALTERS, VIVIENNE, and MARGARET DENTON. "Workers' Knowledge of Their Legal Rights and Resistance to Hazardous Work." *Industrial Relations,* 45 (Summer 1990).

*Environmental Protection*

DALLMEYER, DORINDA, and ALBERT F. IKE, Eds. *Environmental Ethics and the Global Marketplace.* Athens: University of Georgia Press, 1998.

DES JARDINS, JOSEPH R. *Environmental Ethics: An Introduction to Environmental Philosophy.* Belmont, CA: Wadsworth, 1993.

ENGEL, J. RONALD, and JOAN GIBB ENGEL, Eds. *Ethics of Environment and Development.* Tucson: University of Arizona Press, 1991.

*Environmental Ethics.* "An Interdisciplinary Journal Dedicated to the Philosophical Aspects of Environmental Problems."

FREEMAN, R. EDWARD, JESSICA PIERCE, and RICHARD DODD, "Shades of Green: Business, Ethics, and the Environment." *The Business of Consumption: Environmental Ethics and the Global Economy.* Eds. Laura Westra and Patricia H. Werhane. Lanham, Maryland: Rowman and Littlefield Publishers, 1998.

GIBSON, MARY. *To Breathe Freely: Risk, Consent, and Air.* Totowa, NJ: Rowman and Littlefield, 1985.

HOFFMAN, W. MICHAEL, and others, Eds. *Business, Ethics, and the Environment: The Public Policy Debate.* New York: Quorum Books, 1990.

———, Eds. *The Corporation, Ethics, and the Environment.* New York: Quorum Books, 1990.

LEDGERWOOD, GRANT. *Environmental Ethics and the Corporation.* Basingstoke: Macmillan, 1999.

LUDWIG, DEAN C., and JUDITH A. LUDWIG. "The Regulation of Green Marketing: Learning Lessons from the Regulation of Health and Nutrition Claims." *Business and Professional Ethics Journal,* 11 (Fall–Winter 1992): 73–91.

MCEWAN, TOM. "Environmental Protection." In his *Managing Values and Beliefs in Organizations.* New York: Prentice Hall, 2001. 247–68.

MILLER, ALAN S. *Gaia Connections: An Introduction to Ecology, Ecoethics, and Economics.* Totowa, NJ: Rowman and Littlefield, 1991.

NAESS, ARNE. *Ecology, Community, and Lifestyle*, trans. by D. Rothenberg. New York: Cambridge University Press, 1990.

NEWTON, LISA H. "The Chainsaws of Greed: The Case of Pacific Lumber." *Business and Professional Ethics Journal*, 8 (Fall 1989): 29–61.

REGAN, TOM, Ed. *Earthbound: New Introductory Essays in Environmental Ethics.* New York: Random House, 1984.

ROLSTON, HOLMES, III. *Philosophy Gone Wild: Environmental Ethics.* Buffalo: Prometheus Books, 1991.

ROSENTHAL, SANDRA B., and R. A. BUCHHOLZ. "Bridging Environmental and Business Ethics: A Pragmatic Framework." *Environmental Ethics*, 20 (1998): 393–408.

SAGOFF, MARK. *The Economy of the Earth.* New York: Cambridge University Press, 1990.

SINGH, JANG B., and EMILY F. CARASCO. "Business Ethics, Economic Development and Protection of the Environment in the New World Order." *Journal of Business Ethics*, 15 (1996): 297–307.

SINGH, JANG B., and V. C. LAKHAN. "Business Ethics and the International Trade in Hazardous Wastes." *Journal of Business Ethics*, 8 (1989): 889–99.

SKORPEN, ERLING. "Images of the Environment in Corporate America." *Journal of Business Ethics*, 10 (1991).

SMITH, DENIS, Ed. *Business and the Environment: Implications of the New Environmentalism.* New York: St. Martin's Press, 1993.

STARIK, MARK. "Should Trees Have Managerial Standing? Toward Stakeholder Status for Non-Human Nature." *Journal of Business Ethics*, 14 (March 1995): 207–17.

VANDEVEER, DONALD, and CHRISTINE PIERCE. *Environmental Ethics and Policy Book: Philosophy, Ecology and Economics.* Belmont, CA: Wadsworth Publishing Co., 1994.

# CHAPTER FIVE

# ETHICAL TREATMENT OF EMPLOYEES

## INTRODUCTION

TRADITIONALLY, BUSINESS FIRMS are organized hierarchically, with production line employees at the bottom and the CEO at the top. Also the interests of the stockholders are given priority over the interests of the other stakeholders. However, much recent literature presents a challenge to these arrangements, especially to underlying classical economic assumptions whereby labor is treated as analogous to land, capital, and machinery, that is, as replaceable and as a means to profit. Employees primarily want to be treated as persons who are genuine partners in the business enterprise. They want decent salaries and job security, as well as appreciation from supervisors, a sense of accomplishment, and fair opportunities to display their talents. Many employees are also interested in participating in planning the future directions of the company, defining the public responsibilities of the corporation, evaluating the role and quality of management, and—most especially—helping to set the tasks assigned to their jobs. These new developments in labor relations are all to the good, but they must be understood in light of a very different tradition whereby an employee is clearly subordinate to the employer, is legally obligated to obey the employer's orders, and has few rights except the right to quit.

### Status and Scope of Employee Rights

In the traditional view, the freedom of the employee to quit, the freedom of the employer to fire, and the right of the employer to order the employee to do his or her bidding define the essence of the employment contract. The legal principle behind the traditional view is called the *employment-at-will principle.* This principle says that in the absence of a specific contract or law, an employer may hire, fire, demote, or promote an employee whenever the employer wishes. Moreover, the employer may act with justification, with inadequate justification, or with no justification at all. In the selection that opens this chapter, Patricia Werhane and Tara Radin consider several arguments for the employment-at-will doctrine and find them wanting.

Over the years this master-servant relationship, which is at the core of the employment-at-will doctrine, has been legally constrained. Once unions were given legal protection, collective bargaining produced contracts that constrained the right of employers to fire at will. Employees who were protected by union contracts usually could be fired only for cause and then only after a lengthy grievance process. During the height of the union movement, the chief protection against an unjust firing was the union-negotiated contract. However, during the 1980s and early 1990s the percentage of the U.S. workforce belonging to unions fell into the teens, and as a result the protection offered by the union-negotiated contract covers millions fewer workers.

Some might argue that the decline in the number of U.S. workers who belong to unions has not significantly increased the number of employees who are at risk of an unjust dismissal. These people argue that a large number of enlightened companies have adopted policies that provide the same type of protection against unjust dismissal as was previously found in union-negotiated contracts. Moreover, where such policies exist they have the force of law. For example, on May 9, 1985, the New Jersey Supreme Court held that Hoffman-LaRoche Inc. was bound by job security assurances that were implied in an employee manual. The manual seemed to pledge that employees could be fired only for just cause and then only if certain procedures were followed. Hoffman-LaRoche argued that although the company manual gave company policy, adherence to it was voluntary and not legally enforceable. The court, however, said employers cannot have it both ways without acting unfairly and so illegally. Hoffman-LaRoche had to reinstate an employee who had been fired on grounds that his supervisor had lost confidence in his work.

In response to this and similar rulings, a number of corporations have taken steps to make it more difficult for employees to use company manuals and policy statements to protect their jobs. Some are simply eliminating the manuals and dismantling their grievance procedure apparatus. Sears Roebuck and other employers have their employees sign a form declaring that they can be fired "with or without just cause."

Others point out that during the 1980s and early 1990s, certain grounds for firing employees have been made illegal by federal or state law. Antidiscrimination statutes protect workers from being fired because of their race or sex, because they are handicapped, or because of age. Federal law also protects workers from being fired because they resist sexual advances from their bosses or refuse to date them. The protection given employees from this and other forms of sexual harassment is discussed in Chapter Six.

Yet another important development is the evolution of a common law protection to one's job if an employee disobeys an employer on the grounds that the employer ordered him or her to do something illegal or immoral. The notion that employees should not lose their jobs because they refuse to behave illegally or immorally might seem obvious, but as the two recent New Jersey cases included in this chapter show, the situation is more complex than it might appear. On some issues there is near unanimity that a course of action is right or wrong. But on other matters there is considerable difference of opinion. As we saw in the discussions of the *Challenger* in Chapter Three, conflicts concerning what is morally appropriate often occur between managers and engineers. As a practical matter, a large corporation cannot allow employees to refuse to abide by a corporate decision whenever it conflicts with a personal moral position. On the other hand, the public must support employees who refuse to obey an order or accept a decision that threatens the public with serious harm. *Potter v. Village Bank of New Jersey and Warthen v. Toms River Community Memorial Hospital* illustrate how the courts try to balance the public interest and legitimate business concerns on this issue.

Even more important, these laws do not provide sufficient protection for what many employees consider their most important workplace right—the right to a job. From the perspective of most employees, the most important contribution of capitalism is providing work. Job security is often ranked higher than increased pay in terms of what employees most want from employers. The desire for job security is captured in employee demands that workers have a right to a job and that this right deserves protection. The claim that a person has a right to a job has two components. First, workers believe they have a right to a job in the first place. Second, as employees continue to work at a job, they believe they have a right to retain that job. Provision of the right to a job in the first place is usually considered to be the responsibility of government and is not discussed here. However, the notion that employees gain rights to a job that they have been holding is a new idea. In an era in which downsizing has destroyed even the traditional social contract, the idea that a person can come to hold a right to one's job is not widely held.

Indeed, some scholars, especially from the law and economics school, have continued to support the traditional employment-at-will doctrine. For example, Richard A. Epstein has argued, in the article reprinted in this chapter, that employment-at-will is both fair and efficient. Spokespersons from the law and economics school take efficiency concerns very seriously, and Epstein spends considerable time developing some of these concerns.

## The Right to Privacy

Although a right to one's job may be the workplace right that employees most value and want honored, they believe they have other rights that should be honored as well. Many people believe that the rights guaranteed by the Bill of Rights in the Constitution are rights that each U.S. citizen has in all aspects of his or her life. But this is not the case. Americans are protected against government infringements of the Bill of Rights, but they are not protected against corporate infringement of these rights. The Bill of Rights does not apply within the corporation. Thus there is no right to free speech within the corporation. Many believe that such a gap in the protection of the Constitution for individual citizens seems unjustified. They argue that since business activity takes place within U.S. society, business activity should be conducted consistent with the Bill of Rights. Others argue, however, that applying the Bill of Rights in the corporate setting would create great inefficiencies because discipline would break down. Besides, there are many companies in the United States for which a person can work, but there is only one U.S. government. Therefore, it is more important to have a Bill of Rights to protect individuals from government than to have a Bill of Rights to protect individuals from their boss.

The right to privacy is not explicitly listed as a right protected by the Constitution. Supreme Court Justice Louis Brandeis argued that right to privacy can be inferred from a number of other rights that are protected by the Constitution. He and Samuel Warren in a famous article defined privacy as "the right to be left alone." Philosophers have criticized this definition and few today find it satisfactory. Most philosophers argue that the right to privacy should be understood as a right that one must have to exercise personal autonomy. Without zones of privacy, we could not be fully autonomous persons.

Debates regarding the extent and scope of privacy rights are commonplace in U.S. business. Theft by employees and customers is a huge problem, accounting for billions of dollars in losses every year. At one time a common technique for deterring theft was to subject employees to Polygraph (lie detector) tests. However, doubts about their accuracy and arguments that the tests invaded the privacy of employees led to a legal prohibition of their use, enacted initially by some states and then by the federal government. In 1988 Congress passed the Employee Polygraph Protection Act (EPPA) that banned polygraphs, voice-stress analyzers, and other physiological tests. Exceptions are made for pharmaceutical firms, security guards, and the government. Now employers are turning to honesty tests that are based on statistical correlations between the answers to certain questions on the honesty test and the likelihood that an employee will commit theft.[1] The same issues of accuracy and invasion of privacy that confronted the use of polygraphs confront the use of honesty tests. However, the American Psychological Association has certified the validity of some tests, and the tests have escaped serious legal challenge up to the present time.[2]

Not all invasions of privacy can be justified as a means for protecting a company from the wrongful acts of others. Sometimes a business tries to justify an intrusion of privacy by the fact that profits are greatly increased as a result.

As computer technology matures, the number of concerns about privacy issues grows. Computer technology makes the invasion of privacy easier. Companies can build databases on individuals by monitoring purchases offline and databases online. They can then target ads to individuals. This practice is called *profiling*. In 1999, the online music distributor RealNetworks Inc., was roundly criticized for its surreptitious collection of the listening habits of those who visited its site. The information included the format a person stores his or her music in, the number of songs on a person's hard disk and the person's favorite type of music, among other things. RealNetworks has 13.5 million registered users. When the invasion of privacy was discovered, the information was put on the internet. Twenty-four hours later RealNetworks halted the practice and admitted that it had made a mistake.[3]

Another serious problem facing corporate America is the rising cost of health insurance. In order to reduce their insurance premiums, many corporations are taking a great interest in the personal habits of their employees. Some will not hire people who smoke.[4] Ford Meter Box of Wabash, Indiana is one of those companies who will not hire smokers and who will fire those who do smoke. Indiana has now passed a law that forbids companies from firing employees who smoke. However, companies are still permitted to charge higher health insurance premiums to persons who smoke.[5] Other companies will insist that employees lose weight, exercise, and abstain from risky activities off the job.[6] Rules that prohibit an employee from smoking tobacco violate both an employee's right to liberty and an employee's right to privacy. Employers argue that such violations are necessary with respect to tobacco in order to keep the cost of health insurance under control.

A concern with health insurance has also sparked an interest in genetic testing. In a 1996 University of Illinois study, more than one-third of Fortune 500 firms that responded admitted to using the medical records of employees in making job-related decisions.[7] Pre-hiring medical screening has already begun and has already generated legal disputes. Rockwell International Corporation screens potential hires to make sure they can perform certain jobs. In 1993 William Cowie was subjected to a test where electrodes were attached to his fingers, hands, and wrists, and he was given painful electric shocks. The purpose of the test was to measure nerve-ending conduction. Cowie was not hired on the basis of that test, which showed that he had a potential to develop carpal tunnel syndrome. In 1998 Cowie was one of 80 workers represented by the EEOC, which is charging Rockwell International with violating antidiscrimination laws. The alleged discrimination would be behavior in violation of The Americans With Disabilities Act.

Given the potential of genetic testing for identifying the propensity for a certain illness, genetic testing only increases the temptation for business firms to sacrifice privacy. Some employees already report that companies are testing for genetic markers that indicate a potential to develop breast cancer, colon cancer, and Huntington's disease.[8] In a series called 21 Ideas for the 21st Century, *Business Week* referred to genetic testing as the idea that the risk of disease will be treated as a disease. The moral implications of this "idea" are huge. None other than Nobel Prize Laureate in Economics Kenneth Arrow has addressed the epistemological and ethical issues. The dilemma occurs because a person with a genetic predisposition to a disease may not be hired because the employer would not want his of her health care premiums to go up. In theory, there is an economic solution to this dilemma. Assuming the person could afford it, he or she could purchase insurance to protect him or her from an unfavorable diagnosis. However, Arrow goes on to argue that such insurance does not make economic sense, and as a result, the proper ethical stance is that information obtained in prognostic tests should be disregarded in the setting of insurance premiums.[9]

These issues are discussed in two articles, one by Andrew C. Wicks et. al. focuses on five broad issues concerning genetic testing and the other by Joseph Kupfer that points out some of the epistemological and ethical issues surrounding genetic testing. For example, Kupfer shows that even though a genetic marker may show a disposition for a disease, nonetheless relatively few people who have the marker contract the disease—even though a greater percentage may contract the disease than in the population at large. Wicks et. al. are cognizant of these issues and thus attempt to formulate guidelines with respect to genetic testing.

Yet another privacy issue involves the electronic monitoring of employees. New technology makes it easier to monitor employee behavior. Surely everyone has received the message "this call may be monitored for quality performance" when calling a company or civil agency. The number of keystrokes per minute is easily monitored when a person is working on a computer. The United Parcel Service has developed monitoring into a fine art. Each day the UPS worker picks up a personal box at the depot that contains the day's itinerary timed to the minute. As tasks are completed, that information is entered. Supervisors can, at any point, tell if the driver is on schedule. Each night all the day's information is entered into a computer that can be checked by a supervisor. Overnight the next day's itinerary is programmed into the box. And the UPS delivery person's freedom to make decisions on his or her own is seriously curtailed. The black box contains management's view of what is to be done and how it is to be done, right down to the precise routes the delivery person should follow, the number of pickups and deliveries, and the exact amount of time to be spent on each.[10]

And professionals are not immune from this kind of monitoring. Accountants, bank officers, insurance underwriters, personnel managers, and health maintenance organization (HMO) employees are subject to similar monitoring. HMOs tend to limit doctor-to-doctor conversations because they tend to talk too long. Rather, doctors are to consult the HMO database. HMO executives claim that such databases are superior to conversations with other doctors because the system has an extensive memory and huge calculating power that, the executives say, provides rules for dealing with practically every conceivable situation. The doctors are supposed to follow the system's recommendations. If a doctor deviates from the proscribed rule, he or she has some serious explaining to do.[11] In cases such as these, privacy issues interact with issues of employee freedom and empowerment. As management increases its ability to monitor, it also increases its power to limit employee discretion as well.

Despite the concerns about loss of privacy, there are those who say that we have too much privacy and that the right to privacy must be balanced against other rights and social goals. Let us return to expert systems in medicine. At LDS hospital in Salt Lake City, Utah, 5,000 interlinked microcomputers instantaneously transmit medical data from 25 different clinical areas and feed it into electronic patient charts. An artificial intelligence system then scans this "real-time" data for potential medical missteps. The computers can override incorrect prescriptions and change intravenous drip rates. Recall the terrible accident discussed in Chapter Three. This system would have prevented that accident. In addition, the system automatically pages nurses if it encounters anomalous lab results. Physicians can log on at every bedside and order tests or view x-rays. Who could oppose such a system? Privacy advocates. The Department of Health and Human Services is thinking of taking the LDS Hospital idea national. It is considering a medical identifier for every citizen, much like a social security number, that would enable health professionals to obtain data from a variety of databases. As Dr. David Bates has said, "Confidentiality and safety are competing interests."[12] The idea of a national identifier is still very much alive as this book goes to press.

We also readily surrender privacy in more mundane cases. Many of us have received a call from our credit card companies asking us to verify certain purchases. The credit card companies have people monitoring our purchases to see if there are deviations from the pattern that might indicate fraudulent behavior. Most of us feel relief rather than indignation at this "invasion" of privacy. We also accept screening at airports and cameras on subway platforms and in public parking garages. In Europe the police photograph every car that passes a certain spot to see if there has been a violation such as running a red light. As Jonathan Franzen has said:

> When Americans do genuinely sacrifice privacy, moreover, they do so for tangible gains in health or safety or efficiency. Most legalized infringements—H.I.V. notification, airport X-rays, Megan's Law, Breathalyzer roadblocks, the drug testing of student athletes, . . . remote monitoring of automobile emissions, county-jail strip searches, . . . —are essentially public health measures.[13]

## WHISTLEBLOWING AND THE DUTY OF LOYALTY

To suggest that the moral problems in employee-employer relationships are all about employee rights would, of course, be one-sided. No less important are employee obligations. Employees have moral obligations to respect the property of the corporation, to abide by employment contracts, and to operate within the bounds of the company's procedural rules. Indeed, it is legally established that an employer has a right to loyalty. This right is captured in the so-called law of agency. For example, Section 387 of the Restatement of Agency (1958) expresses the general principle that "an agent is subject to his principal to act solely for the benefit of the principal in all matters connected with his agency."[14] Specifically, the "agent is also under a duty not to act or speak disloyally," and the agent is to keep confidential any information acquired by him as an employee that might damage the agent or his business.[15]

Early scholarship by philosophers on whistleblowing focused on the conditions that constitute justified whistleblowing. That focus was caused in large part by the belief that whistleblowing breached a duty of loyalty of the employee to the employer. As a result of that analysis, a fairly standard list of conditions was drawn up that needed to be met if whistleblowing was morally justifiable. In the final articles in this chapter, two authors challenge the standard view in two very different ways. Michael Davis argues that the standard list is incorrect because it does not adequately deal with paradigm cases of justified whistleblowing. To remedy this situation, he proposes an alternative theory that he calls the *complicity* theory.

Ronald Duska's critique is even more radical. He challenges the assumption that the employee has a duty of loyalty to the employer. He has argued that loyalty can apply only in a relationship that transcends self-interest and must be based on a stable relationship of trust and confidence. The relationship of an employee to the corporation is not that kind of relationship, in his view, because it is a relationship of mutual self-interest. In this form of relationship, the employee does not have an obligation of loyalty to the employer.

If a corporation takes the position advocated by Milton Friedman in Chapter Two, then Duska's argument seems persuasive and indeed Friedman himself would probably accept it. In Friedman's view the only concern of the firm is to manage its assets in order to obtain profits for the stockholders, and the only concern of the workers is to get the best working conditions they can. Loyalty simply isn't in the picture. But if a broader stakeholder theory like R. Edward Freeman's is adopted, the corporation does have genuine obligations to employees. In a stakeholder-managed firm, the relationship between the employer and the employee is more likely to be characterized as a relationship of trust and confidence that transcends self-interest. If Duska accepted this characterization of the stake-holder account, these firms would be morally entitled to loyalty.

However, the duty of loyalty is not absolute. That an employee should be loyal is a *prima facie* duty. The object of the employee's duty must be deserving if the duty is genuine and overriding rather than *prima facie*. The virtue of loyalty does not require that the employee accept blindly the boss or corporate cause to which he or she is loyal. Nor does it require that when loyalty to the employer conflicts with other duties—such as protecting the public from harm—the duty to the employer is always overriding. Indeed, when a corporation is engaged in activity that is seriously wrong, employees may have a higher obligation to be disloyal to their employer and blow the whistle.

Well-publicized cases of whistleblowing bring public acclaim to the whistleblower but little else. The whistleblower finds it nearly impossible to get an equivalent job in the same industry and difficult enough to get another job at all. Many corporate executives share the sentiments of the former president of General Motors James M. Roche:

> Some of the enemies of business now encourage an employee to be disloyal to the enterprise. They want to create suspicion and disharmony, and pry into the proprietary interests of the business. However this is labelled—industrial espionage, whistleblowing, or professional responsibility—it is another tactic for spreading disunity and creating conflict.[16]

Although Roche illegitimately confuses industrial espionage and whistleblowing, the attitude expressed by his remarks explains why it is so difficult for the whistleblower to find another job. Roche's point may seem extreme but whistleblowing does undermine trust and it should not be undertaken lightly. Both the whistleblower and the corporation have responsibilities toward a wide range of stakeholders. In 2002 *Time* named three whistleblowers as persons of the year and whistleblowers received some protection under the Sarbanes-Oxley Act passed by Congress in the Summer of 2002. In 1999 the United Kingdom adopted the Public Interest Disclosure Act that provides financial compensation for whistleblowers who act in the public interest.

In conclusion, many of the moral grounds for employee loyalty have been destroyed. Commentators refer to the collapse of the social contract between a company and its employees. Each day seems to bring another announcement of a corporate downsizing. Yet there are some minimum requirements of loyalty based in law. Even today the most disgruntled employees usually treat others who whistleblow negatively; for them whistleblowing seems to violate a moral obligation to loyalty. Thus it is important pragmatically as well as ethically that whistleblowing be justifiable.

## NOTES


1. Peggy Schmidt, "Lie-Detector Tests in a New Guise," *New York Times* (October 1, 1989), pp. 29, 31.
2. Gilbert Fuchsberg, "Prominent Psychologists Group Gives Qualified Support to Integrity Tests," *Wall Street Journal* (March 2, 1991).
3. The information on this incident was taken from "The Privacy Lobby Is Starting to Sting," *Business Week* (November 15, 1999), p. 57 and "A Few RealProblems for RealNetworks," *Newsweek* (November 15, 1999), p. 71.
4. "If You Light Up on Sunday, Don't Come in on Monday," *Business Week* (August 26, 1991), pp. 68–72.
5. Ellen Alderman and Caroline Kennedy, "Privacy," *Across the Board* (March 1996), pp. 43–45.
6. "Privacy," *Business Week* (March 28, 1988), pp. 61–68.
7. Cited in Maggie Scarf, "Brave New World," *The New Republic* (July 1999): p. 17.
8. Kirsten Downey Grimsley, "Pre-Hiring Medical Screening Put to Test," *The Washington Post* (October 27, 1998), C 1–2.
9. Kenneth J. Arrow, "The Use of Genetic and Other Medical Information: Ethical and Market Dilemmas," delivered as The George Seltzer Distinguished Lecture, The University of Minnesota, 1995.
10. Simon Head, "Big Brother in a Black Box," *Civilization* (August/September 1999): pp. 53–55.
11. Ibid.
12. Katherine Eban Finkelstein, "The Computer Cure," in *The New Republic* (September 14 & 21, 1998), p. 30. All the facts regarding this case are taken from this article.
13. Jonathan Frazen, "Imperial Bedoom," *The New Yorker* (October 12, 1998).
14. Quoted from Phillip I. Blumberg, "Corporate Responsibility and the Employee's Duty of Loyalty and Obedience," in *Ethical Theory and Business,* edited by Thomas Beauchamp and Norman E. Bowie (Englewood Cliffs, NJ: Prentice Hall, 1979), 307.
15. Ibid., pp. 308, 307.
16. James M. Roche, "The Competitive System, to Work, to Preserve, and to Protect," *Vital Speeches of the Day* (May 1971), p. 445.

**THE HIRING AND FIRING OF EMPLOYEES**

# Employment at Will and Due Process

*Patricia H. Werhane*
*and Tara J. Radin*

In 1980, Howard Smith III was hired by the American Greetings Corporation as a materials handler at the plant in Osceola, Arkansas. He was promoted to forklift driver and held that job until 1989, when he became involved in a dispute with his shift leader. According to Smith, he had a dispute with his shift leader at work. After work he tried to discuss the matter, but according to Smith, the shift leader hit him. The next day Smith was fired.

Smith was an "at-will" employee. He did not belong to, nor was he protected by, any union or union agreement. He did not have any special legal protection, for there was no apparent question of age, gender, race, or handicap discrimination. And he was not alleging any type of problem with worker safety on the job. The American Greetings Employee Handbook stated that "We believe in working and thinking and planning to provide a stable and growing business, to give such service to our customers that we may provide maximum job security for our employees." It did not state that employees could not be fired without due process or reasonable cause. According to the common law principle of Employment at Will (EAW), Smith's job at American Greetings could, therefore, legitimately be terminated at any time without cause, by either Smith or his employer, as long as that termination did not violate any law, agreement, or public policy.

Smith challenged his firing in the Arkansas court system as a "tort of outrage." A "tort of outrage" occurs when employer engages in "extreme or outrageous conduct" or intentionally inflicts terrible emotional stress. If such a tort is found to have occurred, the action, in this case, the dismissal, can be overturned.

Smith's case went to the Supreme Court of Arkansas in 1991. In court the management of American Greetings argued that Smith was fired for provoking management into a fight. The Court held that the firing was not in violation of law or a public policy, that the employee handbook did not specify restrictions on at-will terminations, and that the alleged altercation between Smith and his shift leader "did not come close to meeting" criteria for a tort of outrage. Howard Smith lost his case and his job.[1]

The principle of EAW is a common-law doctrine that states that, in the absence of law or contract, employers have the right to hire, promote, demote, and fire whomever and whenever they please. In 1887, the principle was stated explicitly in a document by H. G. Wood entitled *Master and Servant.* According to Wood, "A general or indefinite hiring is prima facie a hiring at will."[2] Although the term "master-servant," a medieval expression, was once used to characterize employment relationships, it has been dropped from most of the recent literature on employment.[3]

In the United States, EAW has been interpreted as the rule that, when employees are not specifically covered by union agreement, legal statute, public policy, or contract, employers "may dismiss their employees at will . . . for good cause, for no cause, *or even for causes morally wrong,* without being thereby guilty of legal wrong."[4] At the same time, "at will" employees enjoy rights parallel to employer prerogatives, because employees may quit their jobs for any reason whatsoever (or no reason) without having to give any notice to their employers. "At will" employees range from part-time contract workers to CEOs, including all those workers and managers in the private sector of the economy not covered by agreements, statutes, or contracts. Today at least 60 percent of all employees in the private sector in the United States are "at-will" employees. These employees have no rights to due process or to appeal employment decisions, and the employer does not have any obligation to give reasons for demotions, transfers, or dismissals. Interestingly, while employees in the *private* sector of the economy tend to be regarded as "at-will" employees, *public*-sector employees have guaranteed rights, including due process, and are protected from demotion, transfer, or firing without cause.

Due process is a means by which a person can appeal a decision in order to get an explanation of that action and an opportunity to argue against it. Procedural due process is the right to a hearing, trial, grievance procedure, or appeal when a decision is made concerning oneself. Due process is also substantive. It is the demand for rationality and fairness: for good reasons for decisions. EAW has been widely interpreted as allowing employees to be demoted, transferred or dismissed without due process, that is, without having a hearing and without requirement of good reasons or "cause" for the employment decision. This is not to say that employers do not have reasons, usually good reasons, for their decisions. But there is no moral or legal obligation to state or defend them. EAW thus sidesteps the requirement of procedural and substantive due process in the workplace, but it does not preclude the institution of such procedures or the existence of good reasons for employment decisions.

EAW is still upheld in the state and federal courts of this country, as the Howard Smith case illustrates, although exceptions are made when violations of public policy and law are at issue. According to the *Wall Street Journal*, the court has decided in favor of the employees in 67 percent of the wrongful discharge suits that have taken place during the past three years. These suits were won not on the basis of a rejection of the principle of EAW but, rather, on the basis of breach of contract, lack of just cause for dismissal when a company policy was in place, or violations of public policy. The court has carved out the "public policy" exception so as not to encourage fraudulent or wrongful behavior on the part of employers, such as in cases where employees are asked to break a law or to violate state public policies, and in cases where employees are not allowed to exercise fundamental rights, such as the rights to vote, to serve on a jury, and to collect worker compensation. For example, in one case, the court reinstated an employee who was fired for reporting theft at his plant on the grounds that criminal conduct requires such reporting.[5] In another case, the court reinstated a physician who was fired from the Ortho Pharmaceutical Corporation for refusing to seek approval to test a certain drug on human subjects. The court held that safety clearly lies in the interest of public welfare, and employees are not to be fired for refusing to jeopardize public safety.[6]

During the last ten years, a number of positive trends have become apparent in employment practices and in state and federal court adjudications of employment disputes. Shortages of skilled managers, fear of legal repercussions, and a more genuine interest in employee rights claims and reciprocal obligations have resulted in a more careful spelling out of employment contracts, the development of elaborate grievance procedures, and in general less arbitrariness in employee treatment.[7] While there has not been a universal revolution in thinking about employee rights, an increasing number of companies have qualified their EAW prerogatives with restrictions in firing without cause. Many companies have developed grievance procedures and other means for employee complaint and redress.

Interestingly, substantive due process, the notion that employers should give good reasons for their employment actions, previously dismissed as legal and philosophical nonsense, has also recently developed positive advocates. Some courts have found that it is a breach of contract to fire a long-term employee when there is not sufficient cause—under normal economic conditions even when the implied contract is only a verbal one. In California, for example, 50 percent of the implied contract cases (and there have been over 200) during the last five years have been decided in favor of the employee, again, without challenging EAW.[8] In light of this recognition of implicit contractual obligations between employees and employers, in some unprecedented court cases *employees* have been held liable for good faith breaches of contract, particularly in cases of quitting without notice in the middle of a project and/or taking technology or other ideas to another job.[9]

These are all positive developments. At the same time, there has been neither an across-the-board institution of due process procedures in all corporations nor any direct challenges to the *principle* (although there have been challenges to the practice) of EAW as a justifiable and legitimate approach to employment practices. Moreover, as a result of mergers, downsizing, and restructuring, hundreds of thousands of employees have been laid off summarily without being able to appeal those decisions.

"At-will" employees, then, have no rights to demand an appeal to such employment decisions except through the court system. In addition, no form of due process is a requirement preceding any of these actions. Moreover, unless public policy is violated, the law has traditionally protected employers from employee retaliation in such actions. It is true that the scope of what is defined as "public policy" has been enlarged so that "at-will" dismissals without good reason are greatly reduced. It is also true that many companies have grievance procedures in place for "at will" employees. But such procedures are voluntary, procedural due process is not *required*, and companies need not give any reasons for their employment decisions.

In what follows we shall present a series of arguments defending the claim that the right to procedural and substantive due process should be extended to all employees in the private sector of the economy. We will defend the claim partly on the basis of human rights. We shall also argue that the public/private distinction that precludes the application of constitutional guarantees in the private sector has sufficiently broken down so that the absence of a due process requirement in the workplace is an anomaly.

## EMPLOYMENT AT WILL

EAW is often justified for one or more of the following reasons:

1. The proprietary rights of employers guarantee that they may employ or dismiss whomever and whenever they wish.
2. EAW defends employee and employer rights equally, in particular the right to freedom of contract, because an employee voluntarily contracts to be hired and can quit at any time.
3. In choosing to take a job, an employee voluntarily commits herself to certain responsibilities and company loyalty, including the knowledge that she is an "at-will" employee.
4. Extending due process rights in the workplace often interferes with the efficiency and productivity of the business organization.
5. Legislation and/or regulation of employment relationships further undermine an already overregulated economy.

Let us examine each of these arguments in more detail. The principle of EAW is sometimes maintained purely on the basis of proprietary rights of employers and corporations.

In dismissing or demoting employees, the employer is not denying rights to *persons*. Rather, the employer is simply excluding that person's *labor* from the organization.

This is not a bad argument. Nevertheless, accepting it necessitates consideration of the proprietary rights of employees as well. To understand what is meant by "proprietary rights of employees" it is useful to consider first what is meant by the term "labor." "Labor" is sometimes used collectively to refer to the workforce as a whole. It also refers to the activity of working. Other times it refers to the productivity or "fruits" of that activity. Productivity, labor in the third sense, might be thought of as a form of property or at least as something convertible into property, because the productivity of working is what is traded for remuneration in employee-employer work agreements. For example, suppose an advertising agency hires an expert known for her creativity in developing new commercials. This person trades her ideas, the product of her work (thinking), for pay. The ideas are not literally property, but they are tradable items because, when presented on paper or on television, they are sellable by their creator and generate income. But the activity of working (thinking in this case) cannot be sold or transferred.

Caution is necessary, though, in relating productivity to tangible property, because there is an obvious difference between productivity and material property. Productivity requires the past or present activity of working, and thus the presence of the person performing this activity. Person, property, labor, and productivity are all different in this important sense. A person can be distinguished from his possessions, a distinction that allows for the creation of legally fictional persons such as corporations or trusts that can "own" property. Persons cannot, however, be distinguished from their working, and this activity is necessary for creating productivity, a tradable product of one's working.

In dismissing an employee, a well-intentioned employer aims to rid the corporation of the costs of generating that employee's work products. In ordinary employment situations, however, terminating that cost entails terminating that employee. In those cases the justification for the "at-well" firing is presumably proprietary. But treating an employee "at will" is analogous to considering her a piece of property at the disposal of the employer or corporation. Arbitrary firings treat people as things. When I "fire" a robot, I do not have to give reasons, because a robot is not a rational being. It has no use for reasons. On the other hand, if I fire a person arbitrarily, I am making the assumption that she does not need reasons either. If I have hired people, then, in firing them, I should treat them as such, with respect, throughout the termination process. This does not preclude firing. It merely asks employers to give reasons for their actions, because reasons are appropriate when people are dealing with other people.

This reasoning leads to a second defense and critique of EAW. It is contended that EAW defends employee and employer rights equally. An employer's right to hire and fire "at will" is balanced by a worker's right to accept or reject employment. The institution of any employee right that restricts "at-will" hiring and firing would be unfair unless this restriction were balanced by a similar restriction controlling employee job choice in the workplace. Either program would do irreparable damage by preventing both employees and employers from continuing in voluntary employment arrangements. These arrangements are guaranteed by "freedom of contract," the right of persons or organizations to enter into any voluntary agreement with which all parties of the agreement are in accord.[10] Limiting EAW practices or requiring due process would negatively affect freedom of contract. Both are thus clearly coercive, because in either case persons and organizations are forced to accept behavioral restraints that place unnecessary constraints on voluntary employment agreements.[11]

This second line of reasoning defending EAW, like the first, presents some solid arguments. A basic presupposition upon which EAW is grounded is that of protecting equal freedoms of both employees and employers. The purpose of EAW is to provide a guaranteed balance of these freedoms. But arbitrary treatment of employees extends prerogatives to managers that are not equally available to employees, and such treatment may unduly interfere with a fired employee's prospects for future employment if that employee has no avenue for defense or appeal. This is also sometimes true when an employee quits without notice or good reason. Arbitrary treatment of employees *or* employers therefore violates the spirit of EAW—that of protecting the freedoms of both the employees and employers.

The third justification of EAW defends the voluntariness of employment contracts. If these are agreements between moral agents, however, such agreements imply reciprocal obligations between the parties in question for which both are accountable. It is obvious that, in an employment contract, people are rewarded for their performance. What is seldom noticed is that, if part of the employment contract is an expectation of loyalty, trust, and respect on the part of an employee, the employer must, in return, treat the employee with respect as well. The obligations required by employment agreements, if these are free and noncoercive agreements, must be equally obligatory and mutually restrictive on both parties. Otherwise one party cannot expect—morally expect—loyalty, trust, or respect from the other.

EAW is most often defended on practical grounds. From a utilitarian perspective, hiring and firing "at will" is deemed necessary in productive organizations to ensure maximum efficiency and productivity, the goals of such organizations. In the absence of EAW unproductive employees, workers who are no longer needed, and even troublemakers, would be able to keep their jobs. Even if a business *could* rid itself of undesirable employees, the lengthy procedure of due process required by an extension of employee rights would be costly and time-consuming, and would likely prove distracting to other employees. This would likely slow production and, more likely than not, prove harmful to the morale of other employees.

This argument is defended by Ian Maitland, who contends

> [I]f employers were generally to heed business ethicists and institute workplace due process in cases of dismissals and take the increased costs or reduced efficiency out of workers' paychecks—then they would expose themselves to the pirating of their workers by other employers who would give workers what they wanted instead of respecting their rights in the workplace. . . . In short, there is good reason for concluding that the prevalence of EAW does accurately reflect workers' preferences for wages over contractually guaranteed protections against unfair dismissal.[12]

Such an argument assumes (a) that due process increases costs and reduces efficiency, a contention that is not documented by the many corporations that have grievance procedures, and (b) that workers will generally give up some basic rights for other benefits, such as money. The latter is certainly sometimes true, but not always so, particularly when there are questions of unfair dismissals or job security. Maitland also assumes that an employee is on the same level and possesses the same power as her manager, so that an employee can choose her benefit package in which grievance procedures, whistleblowing protections, or other rights are included. Maitland implies that employers might include in that package of benefits their rights to practice the policy of unfair dismissals in return for increased pay. He also at least implicitly suggests that due process precludes dismissals and layoffs. But this is not true. Procedural due process demands a means of appeal, and substantive due process demands good reasons, both of which are requirements for other managerial decisions and judgments. Neither demands benevolence, lifetime employment, or prevents dismissals. In fact, having good reasons gives an employer a justification for getting rid of poor employees.

In summary, arbitrariness, although not prohibited by EAW, violates the managerial ideal of rationality and consistency. These are independent grounds for not abusing EAW. Even if EAW itself is justifiable, the practice of EAW, when interpreted as condoning arbitrary employment decisions, is not justifiable. Both procedural and substantive due process are consistent with, and a moral requirement of, EAW. The former is part of recognizing obligations implied by freedom of contract, and the latter, substantive due process, conforms with the ideal of managerial rationality that is implied by a consistent application of this common law principle.

## EMPLOYMENT AT WILL, DUE PROCESS, AND THE PUBLIC/PRIVATE DISTINCTION

The strongest reasons for allowing abuses of EAW and for not instituting a full set of employee rights in the workplace, at least in the private sector of the economy, have to do with the nature of business in a free society. Businesses are privately owned voluntary organizations of all sizes from small entrepreneurships to large corporations. As such, they are not subject to the restrictions governing public and political institutions. Political procedures such as due process, needed to safeguard the public against the arbitrary exercise of power by the state, do not apply to private organizations. Guaranteeing such rights in the workplace would require restrictive legislation and regulation. Voluntary market arrangements, so vital to free enterprise and guaranteed by freedom of contract, would be sacrificed for the alleged public interest of employee claims.

In the law, courts traditionally have recognized the right of corporations to due process, although they have not required due process for employees in the private sector of the economy. The justification put forward for this is that since corporations are public entities acting in the public interest, they, like people, should be afforded the right to due process.

Due process is also guaranteed for permanent full-time workers in the public sector of the economy, that is, for workers in local, state and national government positions. The Fifth and Fourteenth Amendments protect liberty and property rights such that any alleged violations or deprivation of those rights may be challenged by some form of due process. According to recent Supreme Court decisions, when a state worker is a permanent employee, he has a property interest in his employment. Because a person's productivity contributes to the place of employment, a public worker is entitled to his job unless there is good reason to question it, such as poor work habits, habitual absences, and the like. Moreover, if a discharge would prevent him from obtaining other employment, which often is the case with state employees who, if fired, cannot find further government employment, that employee has a right to due process before being terminated.[13]

This justification for extending due process protections to public employees is grounded in the public employee's proprietary interest in his job. If that argument makes sense, it is curious that private employees do not have similar rights. The basis for this distinction stems from a tradition in Western thinking that distinguishes between the public and private spheres of life. The public sphere contains that part of a person's life that lies within the bounds of government regulation, whereas the private spheres contains that part of a person's life that lies outside those bounds. The argument is that the portion of a person's life that influences only that person should remain private and outside the purview of law and regulation, while the portion that influences the public welfare should be subject to the authority of the law.

Although interpersonal relationships on any level—personal, family, social, or employee-employer—are protected by statutes and common law, they are not constitutionally protected unless there is a violation of some citizen claim against the state. Because entrepreneurships and corporations are privately owned, and since employees are free to make or break employment contracts of their choice, employee-employer relationships, like family relationships, are treated as "private." In a family, even if there are no due process procedures, the state does not interfere, except when there is obvious harm or abuse. Similarly, employment relationships are considered private relationships contracted between free adults, and so long as no gross violations occur, positive constitutional guarantees such as due process are not enforceable.

The public/private distinction was originally developed to distinguish individuals from the state and to protect individuals and private property from public—i.e., governmental—intrusion. The distinction, however, has been extended to distinguish not merely between the individual or the family and the state, but also between universal rights claims and national sovereignty, public and private ownership, free enterprise and public policy, publicly and privately held corporations, and even between public and private employees. Indeed, this distinction plays a role in national and international affairs. Boutros Boutros-Ghali, the head of the United Nations, recently confronted a dilemma in deciding whether to go into Somalia without an invitation. His initial reaction was to stay out and to respect Somalia's right to "private" national sovereignty. It was only when he decided that Somalia had fallen apart as an independent state that he approved U.N. intervention. His dilemma parallels that of a state, which must decide whether to intervene in a family quarrel, the alleged abuse of a spouse or child, the inoculation of a Christian Scientist, or the blood transfusion for a Seventh-Day Adventist.

There are some questions, however, with the justification of the absence of due process with regard to the public/private distinction. Our economic system is allegedly based on private property, but it is unclear where "private" property and ownership end and "public" property and ownership begin. In the workplace, ownership and control is often divided. Corporate assets are held by an everchanging group of individual and institutional shareholders. It is no longer true that owners exercise any real sense of control over their property and its management. Some do, but many do not. Moreover, such complex property relationships are spelled out and guaranteed by the state. This has prompted at least one thinker to argue that "private property" should be defined as "certain patterns of human interaction underwritten by public power."[14]

This fuzziness about the "privacy" of property becomes exacerbated by the way we use the term "public" in analyzing the status of businesses and in particular corporations. For example, we distinguish between privately owned business corporations and government-owned or -controlled public institutions. Among those companies that are not government owned, we distinguish between regulated "public" utilities whose stock is owned by private individuals and institutions; "publicly held" corporations whose stock is traded publicly, who are governed by special SEC regulations, and whose financial statements are public knowledge; and privately held corporations and entrepreneurships, companies and smaller businesses that are owned by an individual or group of individuals and not available for public stock purchase.

There are similarities between government-owned, public institutions and privately owned organizations. When the air controllers went on strike in the 1980s, Ronald Reagan fired them, and declared that, as public employees, they could not strike because it jeopardized the public safety. Nevertheless, both private and public institutions run transportation, control banks, and own property. While the goals of private and public institutions differ in that public institutions are allegedly supposed to place the public good ahead of profitability, the simultaneous call for businesses to become socially responsible and the demand for governmental organizations to become efficient and accountable further question the dichotomy between "public" and "private."

Many business situations reinforce the view that the traditional public/private dichotomy has been eroded, if not entirely, at least in large part. For example, in 1981, General Motors (GM) wanted to expand by building a plant in what is called the "Poletown" area of Detroit. Poletown is an old Detroit Polish neighborhood. The site was favorable because it was near transportation facilities and there was a good supply of labor. To build the plant, however, GM had to displace residents in a nine-block area. The Poletown Neighborhood Council objected, but the Supreme Court of Michigan decided in favor of GM and held that the state could condemn property for private use, with proper compensation to owners, when it was in the public good. What is particularly interesting about this case is that GM is not a government-owned corporation; its primary goal is *profitability*, not the common good. The Supreme Court nevertheless decided that it was in the *public* interest for Detroit to use its authority to allow a company to take over property despite the protesting of the property owners. In this case the public/private distinction was thoroughly scrambled.

The overlap between private enterprise and public interests is such that at least one legal scholar argues that "developments in the twentieth century have significantly undermined the 'privateness' of the modern business corporations, with the result that the traditional bases for distinguishing them from public corporations have largely disappeared."[15] Nevertheless, despite the blurring of the public and private in terms of property rights and the status and functions of corporations, the subject of employee rights appears to remain immune from conflation.

The expansion of employee protections to what we would consider just claims to due process gives to the state and the courts more opportunity to interfere with the private economy and might thus further skew what is seen by some as a precarious but delicate balance between the private economic sector and public policy. We agree. But if the distinction between public and private institutions is no longer clear-cut, and the traditional separation of the public and private spheres is no longer in place, might it not then be better to recognize and extend constitutional guarantees so as to protect all citizens equally? If due process is crucial to political relationships between the individual and the state, why is it not central in relationships between employees and corporations since at least some of the companies in question are as large and powerful as small nations? Is it not in fact inconsistent with our democratic tradition *not* to mandate such rights?

The philosopher T.M. Scanlon summarizes our institutions about due process. Scanlon says,

> The requirement of due process is one of the conditions of the moral acceptability of those institutions that give some people power to control or intervene in the lives of others.[16]

The institution of due process in the workplace is a moral requirement consistent with rationality and consistency expected in management decision-making. It is not precluded by EAW, and it is compatible with the overlap between the public and private sectors of the economy. Convincing business of the moral necessity of due process, however, is a task yet to be completed.

## NOTES

1. *Howard Smith III* v. *American Greetings Corporation*, 304 Ark. 596; 804 S.W. 2d 683.
2. H. G. Wood, *A Treatise on the Law of Master and Servant* (Albany, NY: John D. Parsons, Jr., 1877), p. 134.
3. Until the end of 1980 the *Index of Legal Periodicals* indexed employee-employer relationships under this rubric.
4. Lawrence E. Blades, "Employment at Will versus Individual Freedom: On Limiting the Abusive Exercise of Employer Power," *Columbia Law Review*, 67 (1967), p. 1405, quoted from *Payne* v. *Western*, 81 Tenn. 507 (1884), and *Hutton* v. *Watters*, 132 Tenn. 527, S.W. 134 (1915).
5. *Palmateer* v. *International Harvester Corporation*, 85 III. App. 2d 124 (1981).
6. *Pierce* v. *Ortho Pharmaceutical Corporation* 845 NJ 58 (NJ 1980), 417 A. 2d 505. See also Brian Heshizer, "The New Common Law of Employment: Changes in the Concept of Employment at Will," *Labor Law Journal*, 36 (1985), pp. 95–107.
7. See David Ewing, *Justice on the Job: Resolving Grievances in the Nonunion Workplace* (Boston: Harvard Business School Press, 1989).
8. See R. M. Bastress, "A Synthesis and a Proposal for Reform of the Employment at Will Doctrine," *West Virginia Law Review*, 90 (1988), pp. 319–51.
9. See "Employees' Good Faith Duties," *Hastings Law Journal*, 39 (198). See also *Hudson v. Moore Business Forms*, 609 Supp. 467 (N.D. Cal. 1985).
10. See *Lockner* v. *New York*, 198 U.S. (1905), and Adina Schwartz, "Autonomy in the Workplace," in Tom Regan, ed., *Just Business* (New York: Random House, 1984), pp. 129–40.
11. Eric Mack, "Natural and Contractual Rights," *Ethics*, 87 (1977), pp. 153–59.
12. Ian Maitland, "Rights in the Workplace: A Nozickian Argument," in Lisa Newton and Maureen Ford, eds., *Taking Sides* (Guilford, CT: Dushkin Publishing Group), 1990, pp. 34–35.
13. Richard Wallace, "Union Waiver of Public Employees' Due Process Rights," *Industrial Relations Law Journal*, 8 (1986), pp. 583–87.
14. Morris Cohen, "Dialogue on Private Property," *Rutgers Law Review* 9 (1954), pp. 357. See also *Law and the Social Order* (1933) and Robert Hale, "Coercion and Distribution in a Supposedly Non-Coercive State," *Political Science Quarterly*, 38 (1923), pp. 470; John Brest, "State Action and Liberal Theory," *University of Pennsylvania Law Review* (1982), 1296–1329.
15. Gerald Frug, "The City As a Legal Concept," *Harvard Law Review*, 93 (1980), p. 1129.
16. T. M. Scanlon, "Due Process," in J. Roland Pennock and John W. Chapman, eds., *Nomos XVIII: Due Process* (New York: New York University Press, 1977), p. 94.

# In Defense of the Contract at Will

*Richard A. Epstein*

The persistent tension between private ordering and government regulation exists in virtually every area known to the law, and in none has that tension been more pronounced than in the law of employer and employee relations. During the last fifty years, the balance of power has shifted heavily in favor of direct public regulation, which has been thought strictly necessary to redress the perceived imbalance between the individual and the firm. In particular the employment relationship has been the subject of at least two major statutory revolutions.

From: Richard A. Epstein, "In Defense of the Contract at Will," *University of Chicago Law Review* 34 (1984). Reprinted by permission of the University of Chicago Law Review.

The first, which culminated in the passage of the National Labor Relations Act in 1935, set the basic structure for collective bargaining that persists to the current time. The second, which is embodied in Title VII of the Civil Rights Act of 1964, offers extensive protection to all individuals against discrimination on the basis of race, sex, religion, or national origin. The effect of these two statutes is so pervasive that it is easy to forget that, even after their passage, large portions of the employment relation remain subject to the traditional common law rules, which when all was said and done set their face in support of freedom of contract and the system of voluntary exchange. One manifestation of that position was the prominent place that the common law, especially as it developed in the nineteenth century, gave to the contract at will. The basic position was set out in an oft-quoted passage from *Payne v. Western & Atlantic Railroad:*

> [M]en must be left, without interference to buy and sell where they please, and to discharge or retain employees at will for good cause or for no cause, or even for bad cause without thereby being guilty of an unlawful act *per se.* It is a right which an employee may exercise in the same way, to the same extent, for the same cause or want of cause as the employer.[1]

* * *

In the remainder of this paper, I examine the arguments that can be made for and against the contract at will. I hope to show that it is adopted not because it allows the employer to exploit the employee, but rather because over a very broad range of circumstances it works to the mutual benefit of both parties, where the benefits are measured, as ever, at the time of the contract's formation and not at the time of dispute. To justify this result, I examine the contract in light of the three dominant standards that have emerged as the test of the soundness of any legal doctrine: intrinsic fairness, effects upon utility or wealth, and distributional consequences. I conclude that the first two tests point strongly to the maintenance of the at-will rule, while the third, if it offers any guidance at all, points in the same direction.

## I. THE FAIRNESS OF THE CONTRACT AT WILL

The first way to argue for the contract at will is to insist upon the importance of freedom of contract as an end in itself. Freedom of contract is an aspect of individual liberty, every bit as much as freedom of speech, or freedom in the selection of marriage partners or in the adoption of religious beliefs or affiliations. Just as it is regarded as prima facie unjust to abridge these liberties, so too is it presumptively unjust to abridge the economic liberties of individuals. The desire to make one's own choices about employment may be as strong as it is with respect to marriage or participation in religious activities, and it is doubtless more pervasive than the desire to participate in political activity. Indeed for most people, their own health and comfort, and that of their families, depend critically upon their ability to earn a living by entering the employment market. If government regulation is inappropriate for personal, religious, or political activities, then what makes it intrinsically desirable for employment relations?

It is one thing to set aside the occasional transaction that reflects only the momentary aberrations of particular parties who are overwhelmed by major personal and social dislocations. It is quite another to announce that a rule to which vast numbers of individuals adhere is so fundamentally corrupt that it does not deserve the minimum respect of the law. With employment contracts we are not dealing with the widow who has sold her inheritance for a song to a man with a thin mustache. Instead we are dealing with the routine stuff of ordinary life; people who are competent enough to marry, vote, and pray are not unable to protect themselves in their day-to-day business transactions.

Courts and legislatures have intervened so often in private contractual relations that it may seem almost quixotic to insist that they bear a heavy burden of justification every time they wish to substitute their own judgment for that of the immediate parties to the transactions. Yet it is hardly likely that remote public bodies have better information about individual preferences than the parties who hold them. This basic principle of autonomy, moreover, is not limited to some areas of individual conduct and wholly inapplicable to others. It covers all these activities as a piece and admits no ad hoc exceptions, but only principled limitations.

This general proposition applies to the particular contract term in question. Any attack on the contract at will in the name of individual freedom is fundamentally misguided. As the Tennessee Supreme Court rightly stressed in *Payne*, the contract at will is sought by both persons.[2] Any limitation upon the freedom to enter into such contracts limits the power of workers as well as employers and must therefore be justified before it can be accepted. In this context the appeal is often to an image of employer coercion. To be sure, freedom of contract is not an absolute in the employment context, any more than it is elsewhere. Thus the principle must be understood against a backdrop that prohibits the use of private contracts to trench upon third-party rights, including uses that interfere with some clear mandate of public policy, as in cases of contracts to commit murder or perjury.

In addition, the principle of freedom of contract also rules out the use of force or fraud in obtaining advantages during contractual negotiations; and it limits taking advantage of the young, the feeble-minded, and the insane. But the recent wrongful discharge cases do not purport to deal with the delicate situations where contracts have been formed by improper means or where individual defects of capacity or will are involved. Fraud is not a frequent occurrence in employment contracts, especially where workers and employers engage in repeat transactions. Nor is there any reason to believe that such contracts are marred by misapprehensions, since employers and employees know the footing on which they have contracted: the phrase "at will" is two words long and has the convenient virtue of meaning just what it says, no more and no less.

An employee who knows that he can quit at will understands what it means to be fired at will, even though he may not like it after the fact. So long as it is accepted that the employer is the full owner of his capital and the employee is the full owner of his labor, the two are free to exchange on whatever terms and conditions they see fit, within the limited constraints just noted. If the arrangement turns out to be disastrous to one side, that is his problem; and once cautioned, he probably will not make the same mistake a second time. More to the point, employers and employees are unlikely to make the same mistake once. It is hardly plausible that contracts at will could be so pervasive in all businesses and at all levels if they did not serve the interests of employees as well as employers. The argument from fairness then is very simple, but not for that reason unpersuasive.

## II. THE UTILITY OF THE CONTRACT AT WILL

The strong fairness argument in favor of freedom of contract makes short work of the various for-cause and good-faith restrictions upon private contracts. Yet the argument is incomplete in several respects. In particular, it does not explain why the presumption in the case of silence should be in favor of the contract at will. Nor does it give a descriptive account of *why* the contract at will is so commonly found in all trades and professions. Nor does the argument meet on their own terms the concerns voiced most frequently by the critics of the contract at will. Thus, the commonplace belief today (at least outside the actual world of business) is that the contract at will is so unfair and one-sided that it cannot be the outcome of a rational set of bargaining processes any more than, to take the extreme case, a contract for total slavery. While we may not, the criticism continues, be able to observe them, defects in capacity at contract formation nonetheless must be present: the ban upon the contract at will is an effective way to reach abuses that are pervasive but difficult to detect, so that modest government interference only strengthens the operation of market forces.

In order to rebut this charge, it is necessary to do more than insist that individuals as a general matter know how to govern their own lives. It is also necessary to display the structural strengths of the contract at will that explain why rational people would enter into such a contract, if not all the time, then at least most of it. The implicit assumption in this argument is that contracts are typically for the mutual benefit of both parties. Yet it is hard to see what other assumption makes any sense in analyzing institutional arrangements (arguably in contradistinction to idiosyncratic, nonrepetitive transactions). To be sure, there are occasional cases of regret after the fact, especially after an infrequent, but costly, contingency comes to pass. There will be cases in which parties are naive, befuddled, or worse. Yet in framing either a rule of policy or a rule of construction, the focus cannot be on that biased set of cases in which the contract aborts and litigation ensues. Instead, attention must be directed to standard repetitive transactions, where the centralizing tendency powerfully promotes expected mutual gain. It is simply incredible to postulate that either employers or employees, motivated as they are by self-interest, would enter routinely into a transaction that leaves them worse off than they were before, or even worse off than their next best alternative.

From this perspective, then, the task is to explain how and why the at-will contracting arrangement (in sharp contrast to slavery) typically works to the mutual advantage of the parties. Here, as is common in economic matters, it does not matter that the parties themselves often cannot articulate the reasons that render their judgment sound and breathe life into legal arrangements that are fragile in form but durable in practice. The inquiry into mutual benefit in turn requires an examination of the full range of costs and benefits that arise from collaborative ventures. It is just at this point that the nineteenth-century view is superior to the emerging modern conception. The modern view tends to lay heavy emphasis on the need to control employer abuse. Yet, as the passage from *Payne* indicates, the rights under the contract at will are fully bilateral, so that the employee can use the contract as a means to control the firm, just as the firm uses it to control the worker.

The issue for the parties, properly framed, is not how to minimize employer abuse, but rather how to maximize the gain from the relationship, which in part depends upon minimizing the sum of employer and employee abuse. Viewed in this way the private contracting problem is far more complex. How does each party create incentives for the proper behavior of the other? How does each side insure against certain risks? How do both sides minimize the administrative costs of their contracting practices? . . .

***1. Monitoring Behavior.*** The shift in the internal structure of the firm from a partnership to an employment relation eliminates neither bilateral opportunism nor the conflicts of interest between employer and employee. Begin for the moment with the fears of the firm, for it is the firm's right to maintain at-will power that is now being called into question. In all too many cases, the firm must contend with the recurrent problem of employee theft and with the related problems of unauthorized use of firm equipment and employee kickback arrangements. . . .

[The] proper concerns of the firm are not limited to obvious forms of criminal misconduct. The employee on a fixed wage can, at the margin, capture only a portion of the gain from his labor, and therefore has a tendency to reduce output. The employee who receives a commission equal to half the firm's profit attributable to his labor may work hard, but probably not quite as hard as he would if he received the entire profit from the completed sale, an arrangement that would solve the agency-cost problem only-by undoing the firm. . . .

The problem of management then is to identify the forms of social control that are best able to minimize these agency costs. . . . One obvious form of control is the force of law. The state can be brought in to punish cases of embezzlement or fraud. But this mode of control requires extensive cooperation with public officials and may well be frustrated by the need to prove the criminal offense (including mens rea) beyond a reasonable doubt, so that vast amounts of abuse will go unchecked. Private litigation instituted by the firm may well be used in cases of major grievances, either to recover the property that has been misappropriated or to prevent the individual employee from further diverting firm business to his own account. But private litigation, like public prosecution, is too blunt an instrument to counter employee shirking or the minor but persistent use of firm assets for private business. . . .

Internal auditors may help control some forms of abuse, and simple observation by coworkers may well monitor employee activities. (There are some very subtle tradeoffs to be considered when the firm decides whether to use partitions or separate offices for its employees.) Promotions, bonuses, and wages are also critical in shaping the level of employee performance. But the carrot cannot be used to the exclusion of the stick. In order to maintain internal discipline, the firm may have to resort to sanctions against individual employees. It is far easier to use those powers that can be unilaterally exercised: to fire, to demote, to withhold wages, or to reprimand. These devices can visit very powerful losses upon individual employees without the need to resort to legal action, and they permit the firm to monitor employee performance continually in order to identify both strong and weak workers and to compensate them accordingly. The principles here are constant, whether we speak of senior officials or lowly subordinates, and it is for just this reason that the contract at will is found at all levels in private markets. . . .

In addition, within the employment context firing does not require a disruption of firm operations, much less an expensive division of its assets. It is instead a clean break with consequences that are immediately clear to both sides. The lower cost of both firing and quitting, therefore, helps account for the very widespread popularity of employment-at-will contracts. There is no need to resort to any theory of economic domination or inequality of bargaining power to explain at-will contracting, which appears with the same tenacity in relations between economic equals and subordinates and is found in many complex commercial arrangements, including franchise agreements, except where limited by statutes.

Thus far, the analysis generally has focused on the position of the employer. Yet for the contract at will to be adopted ex ante, it must work for the benefit of workers as well. And indeed it does, for the contract at will also contains powerful limitations on employers' abuses of power. To see the importance of the contract at will to the employee, it is useful to distinguish between two cases. In the first, the employer pays a fixed sum of money to the worker and is then free to demand of the employee whatever services he wants for some fixed period of time. In the second case, there is no fixed period of employment. The employer is free to demand whatever he wants of the employee, who in turn is free to withdraw for good reason, bad reason, or no reason at all.

The first arrangement invites abuse by the employer, who can now make enormous demands upon the worker without having to take into account either the worker's disutility during the period of service or the value of the worker's labor at contract termination. A fixed-period contract that leaves the worker's obligations unspecified thereby creates a sharp tension between the parties, since the employer receives all the marginal benefits and the employee bears all the marginal costs.

Matters are very different where the employer makes increased demands under a contract at will. Now the worker can quit whenever the net value of the employment contract turns negative. As with the employer's power to fire or demote, the threat to quit (or at a lower level to come late or leave early) is one that can be exercised without resort to litigation. Furthermore, that threat turns out to be most effective when the employer's opportunistic behavior is the greatest because the situation is one in which the worker has least to lose. To be sure, the worker will not necessarily make a threat whenever the employer insists that the worker accept a less favorable set of contractual terms, for sometimes the changes may be accepted as an uneventful adjustment in the total compensation level attributable to a change in the market price of labor. This point counts, however, only as an additional strength of the contract at will, which allows for small adjustments *in both directions* in ongoing contractual arrangements with a minimum of bother and confusion. . . .

***2. Reputational Losses.*** Another reason why employees are often willing to enter into at-will employment contracts stems from the asymmetry of reputational losses. Any party who cheats may well obtain a bad reputation that will induce others to avoid dealing with him. The size of these losses tends to differ systematically between employers and employees—to the advantage of the employee. Thus in the usual situation there are many workers and a single employer. The disparity in number is apt to be greatest in large industrial concerns, where the at-will contract is commonly, if mistakenly, thought to be most unsatisfactory because of the supposed inequality of bargaining power. The employer who decides to act for bad reason or no reason at all may not face any legal liability under the classical common law rule. But he faces very powerful adverse economic consequences. If coworkers perceive the dismissal as arbitrary, they will take fresh stock of their own prospects, for they can no longer be certain that their faithful performance will ensure their security and advancement. The uncertain prospects created by arbitrary employer behavior is functionally indistinguishable from a reduction in wages unilaterally imposed by the employer. At the margin some workers will look elsewhere, and typically the best workers will have the greatest opportunities. By the same token the large employer has more to gain if he dismisses undesirable employees, for this ordinarily acts as an implicit increase in wages to the other employees, who are no longer burdened with uncooperative or obtuse coworkers.

The existence of both positive and negative reputational effects is thus brought back to bear on the employer. The law may tolerate arbitrary behavior, but private pressures effectively limit its scope. Inferior employers will be at a perpetual competitive disadvantage with enlightened ones and will continue to lose in market share and hence in relative social importance. The lack of legal protection to the employees is therefore in part explained by the increased informal protections that they obtain by working in large concerns.

***3. Risk diversification and Imperfect Information.*** The contract at will also helps workers deal with the problem of risk diversification. . . . Ordinarily, employees cannot work more than one, or perhaps two, jobs at the same time. Thereafter the level of performance falls dramatically, so that diversification brings in its wake a low return on labor. The contract at will is designed in part to offset the concentration of individual investment in a single job by allowing diversification among employers *over time.* The employee is not locked into an unfortunate contract if he finds better opportunities elsewhere or if he detects some weakness in the internal structure of the firm. A similar analysis applies on the employer's side where he is a sole proprietor, though ordinary diversification is possible when ownership of the firm is widely held in publicly traded shares.

The contract at will is also a sensible private adaptation to the problem of imperfect information over time. In sharp contrast to the purchase of standard goods, an inspection of the job before acceptance is far less likely to guarantee its quality thereafter. The future is not clearly known. More important, employees, like employers, *know what they do not know.* They are not faced with a bolt from the blue, with an "unknown unknown." Rather they face a known unknown for which they can plan. The at-will contract is an essential part of that planning because it allows both sides to take a wait-and-see attitude to their relationship so their new and more accurate choices can be made on the strength of improved information. ("You can start Tuesday and we'll see how the job works out" is a highly intelligent response to uncertainty.) To be sure, employment relationships are more personal and hence often stormier than those that exist in financial markets, but that is no warrant for replacing the contract at will with a for-cause contract provision. The proper question is: will the shift in methods of control work a change for the benefit of both parties, or will it only make a difficult situation worse?

***4. Administrative Costs.*** There is one last way in which the contract at will has an enormous advantage over its rivals. It is very cheap to administer. Any effort to use a for-cause rule will in principle allow all, or at least a substantial fraction of, dismissals to generate litigation. Because motive will be a critical element in these cases, the chances of either side obtaining summary judgment will be negligible. Similarly, the broad modern rules of discovery will allow exploration into every aspect of the employment relation. Indeed, a little imagination will allow the plaintiff's lawyer to delve into the general employment policies of the firm, the treatment of similar cases, and a review of the individual file. The employer for his part will be able to examine every aspect of the employee's performance and personal life in order to bolster the case for dismissal. . . .

## III. DISTRIBUTIONAL CONCERNS

Enough has been said to show that there is no principled reason of fairness or utility to disturb the common law's longstanding presumption in favor of the contract at will. It remains to be asked whether there are some hitherto unmentioned distributional consequences sufficient to throw that conclusion into doubt. . . .

The proposed reforms in the at-will doctrine cannot hope to transfer wealth systematically from rich to poor on the model of comprehensive systems of taxation or welfare benefits. Indeed it is very difficult to identify in advance any deserving group of recipients that stands to gain unambiguously from the universal abrogation of the at-will contract. The proposed rules cover the whole range from senior executives to manual labor. At every wage level, there is presumably some differential in worker's output. Those who tend to slack off seem on balance to be most vulnerable to dismissal under the at-will rule; yet it is very hard to imagine why some special concession should be made in their favor at the expense of their more diligent fellow workers.

The distributional issues, moreover, become further clouded once it is recognized that any individual employee will have interests on both sides of the employment relation. Individual workers participate heavily in pension plans, where the value of the holdings depends in part upon the efficiency of the legal rules that govern the companies in which they own shares. If the regulation of the contract at will diminishes the overall level of wealth, the losses are apt to be spread far and wide, which makes it doubtful that there are any gains to the worst off in society that justify somewhat greater losses to those who are better off. The usual concern with maldistribution gives us situations in which one person has one hundred while each of one hundred has one and asks us to compare that distribution with an even distribution of, say, two per person. But the stark form of the numerical example does not explain how the skewed distribution is tied to the concrete choice between different rules governing employment relations. Set in this concrete context, the choices about the proposed new regulation of the employment contract do not set the one against the many but set the many against each other, all in the context of a shrinking overall pie. The possible gains from redistribution, even on the most favorable of assumptions about the diminishing marginal utility of money, are simply not present.

If this is the case, one puzzle still remains: who should be in favor of the proposed legislation? One possibility is that support for the change in common law rules rests largely on ideological and political grounds, so that the legislation has the public support of persons who may well be hurt by it in their private capacities. Another possible explanation could identify the hand of interest-group politics in some subtle form. For example, the lawyers and government officials called upon to administer the new legislation may expect to obtain increased income and power, although this explanation seems insufficient to account for the current pressure. A more uncertain line of inquiry could ask whether labor unions stand to benefit from the creation of a cause of action for wrongful discharge. Unions, after all, have some skill in working with for-cause contracts under the labor statutes that prohibit firing for union activities, and they might be able to promote their own growth by selling their services to the presently nonunionized sector. In addition, the for-cause rule might give employers one less reason to resist unionization, since they would be unable to retain the absolute power to hire and fire in any event. Yet, by the same token, it is possible that workers would be less inclined to pay the costs of union membership if they received some purported benefit by the force of law without unionization. The ultimate weight of these considerations is an empirical question to which no easy answers appear. What is clear, however, is that even if one could show that the shift in the rule either benefits or hurts unions and their members, the answer would not justify the rule, for it would not explain why the legal system should try to skew the balance one way or the other. The bottom line therefore remains unchanged. The case for a legal requirement that renders employment contracts terminable only for cause is as weak after distributional considerations are taken into account as before. . . .

## CONCLUSION

The recent trend toward expanding the legal remedies for wrongful discharge has been greeted with wide approval in judicial, academic, and popular circles. In this paper, I have argued that the modern trend rests in large measure upon a misunderstanding of the contractual processes and the ends served by the contract at will. No system of regulation can hope to match the benefits that the contract at will affords in employment relations. The flexibility afforded by the contract at will permits the ceaseless marginal adjustments that are necessary in any ongoing productive activity conducted, as all activities are, in conditions of technological and business change. The strength of the contract at will should not be judged by the occasional cases in which it is said to produce unfortunate results, but rather by the vast run of cases where it provides a sensible private response to the many and varied problems in labor contracting. All too often the case for a wrongful discharge doctrine rests upon the identification of possible employer abuses, as if they were all that mattered. But the proper goal is to find the set of comprehensive arrangements that will minimize the frequency and severity of abuses by employers and employees alike. Any effort to drive employer abuses to zero can only increase the difficulties inherent in the employment relation. Here, a full analysis of the relevant costs and benefits shows why the constant minor imperfections of the market, far from being a reason to oust private agreements, offer the most powerful reason for respecting them. The doctrine of wrongful discharge is the problem and not the solution. This is one of the many situations in which courts and legislatures should leave well enough alone.

## NOTES

1. *Payne v. Western & Atl. R.R.*, 81 Tenn. 507, 518–19 (1884), overruled on other grounds, *Hutton v. Watters*, 132 Tenn. 527, 544, 179 S.W. 134, 138 (1915). . . .
2. Ibid.

## PRIVACY

# The Ethics of Genetic Screening in the Workplace

*Joseph Kupfer*

Today we are witnessing the onslaught of "testing" in the workplace. We test for personality, aptitude, competence, "truthfulness," drugs, and now genetic make-up. Clearly, some of this testing may well be warranted, but genetic "screening" as it's called raises some peculiar questions of its own—questions of meaning and questions of morality. In what follows, I shall spell out the nature of genetic screening, its possible purposes or values, and then raise some moral questions about it.

## THE ISSUE AND ITS BACKGROUND

Genetic research is one of those areas of science which has clear practical benefits. If we know that we are carrying a gene for an inheritable illness, such as Huntington's disease, we can make a more informed choice about procreation. Knowledge of our genetic disposition toward heart disease or high blood pressure can prompt us to change our patterns of eating and exercise. And once informed of our genetically based vulnerability to lung disease, we are able to avoid threatening work conditions. Indeed, this was the first goal of genetic screening in the workplace: to enable the employee to steer clear of work situations which were liable to call forth a disabling condition or disease (henceforth, simply "disorder").

Obviously, businesses also had an interest in this goal. Fewer disabled workers means reduction in costs caused by illness, absenteeism, health insurance, workers' compensation, and

From Joseph Kupfer, "The Ethics of Genetic Screening in the Workplace," *Business Ethics Quarterly* 3:1 (1993). Reprinted with permission, of the author and *Business Ethics Quarterly*.

turnover. In addition, the first workplace screening was a response by business to 1970s legislation making business responsible for health in the workplace. DuPont, Dow Chemical, and Johnson and Johnson were among the first companies to implement genetic screening.[1] The tests were voluntary and there was no threat of job loss, rather, "warning" and "relocating" to less hazardous conditions or functions were the procedure. Indeed, DuPont's testing for sickle cell trait was requested by its own black workers! So, at its inception, genetic screening of workers seemed to be a mutually agreed upon practice aimed at mutual benefits— workers and owners cooperating for the good of all.

If this were all there was to genetic screening in the workplace, obviously, there would be little need for moral discussion. But, corporations have an interest in extending the purpose of screening beyond its original scope—to deny people work. What began as a benign program can be modified to serve only the interests of business. After all, relocating workers or modifying existing conditions so that they will be less hazardous takes time, effort, and money. It's just plain cheaper to fire or not hire a worker who is at "genetic risk." The facts of the matter, however, make the whole issue more complicated. They also point to moral difficulties with the use of genetic screening to exclude workers from jobs, what we shall consider "discriminatory genetic screening."

Before investigating the moral issues involved, we must get clear on the scientific ones concerning *how* genetic screening, in fact, works. There are serious limitations to what we can learn from genetic screening and they have moral implications. The limitations on the knowledge afforded by genetic screening are of two sorts—technical and causal. Technical limitations are determined by the level of sophistication of our techno-scientific understanding. Causal constraints depend upon how genes actually bring about disorders.

Each kind of limitation itself involves two sets of variables. Technical restrictions on genetic knowledge turn on (1) whether the gene itself has been located or simply correlated with other DNA material, and (2) whether knowledge of other family members is necessary to determine the presence of the affecting gene. Causal restrictions on genetic knowledge involve (1) whether the affecting gene requires other genes to produce the disorder, and (2) whether the gene causes the disorder with inevitability or just creates a vulnerability to it. We shall consider the two sorts of limitations on genetic knowledge by examining in order these sets of variables for their significance for the practice of genetic screening.

## TECHNICAL LIMITATIONS

First is the question of whether the gene itself has been located. Hemophilia, Duchenne muscular dystrophy, and cystic fibrosis are among the few exceptions where the genetic test actually identifies the gene in question. What is more typical are DNA "probes" or "markers" which indicate the likelihood of the gene's presence. "Most of today's probes aren't capable of pinpointing a bad gene. They can only detect sequences of healthy genes called markers, that are usually found near a bad one."[2] When "restriction" enzymes are introduced into the chromosome material, DNA fragments are generated: specifically, strips of genetic material called restriction fragment length polymorphisms (RFLPs), whose patterns can be statistically associated with the occurrence of a particular disorder.[3] In the case of Huntington's disease, for example, the probe detects "a piece of DNA that is so close to the as yet unidentified Huntington's gene that it is inherited along with the gene."[4]

This technical limitation—inability to locate the particular gene in question—means that we are usually dealing with statistical correlations. The marker can be inherited without the defective gene; therefore, uncovering the marker must be treated with caution. Conversely, as Marc Lappe warns,[5] failure to turn up the marker does not guarantee the gene's absence!

In order to establish the correlation between the marker and the disorder, collateral data may be needed. One kind, "linkage analysis," points to our second set of variables—whether or not reference to family members is needed. Linkage analysis is comparing a given individual's DNA pattern with both affected and unaffected family members. The marker for Huntington's disease, for example, is useless if there are no living family members *with* the disease. This is because what is needed is to identify the piece of DNA material *as* a marker for Huntington's disease. Its association with the disease must be ascertained by comparison with DNA fragments of surviving relatives.

This is obviously very time consuming and expensive, prohibitively so for workplace application. It also requires the consent of family members who may not be employed by the company (over whom the company can exert little leverage). In contrast, "direct markers" indicate a genetic connection with a disorder without linkage analysis. The marking of the genes for hemophilia, cystic fibrosis, and adult polycystic kidney disease can be ascertained directly. These are more feasible for workplace screening.

Another sort of collateral data that is frequently needed involves the use of "flanking probes" in order to ascertain the presence of "modifier" genes. This leads us to consideration of the causal limitations of the knowledge gleaned from genetic screening.

## CAUSAL LIMITATIONS

Our third set of variables concerns how the genetic material generates the disorder: whether the disorder is caused by one or several genes. When a disorder is coded for by more than a single gene, the gene in question must interact with these other genes in order to be expressed (as a disorder). For screening to have predictive value it must indicate the presence (or absence) of these auxiliary, "modifier" genes. For instance, in the case of Gaucher's disease, the gene marked by the DNA probe is associated with three forms of the disease. While one of the varieties of this neurological disorder is severe, the other two are fairly mild.[6] Without corroboration from modifier genes, which form of Gaucher's disease the individual will develop can't be determined.

One interesting combination of variables occurs in Huntington's disease. It is caused by a single gene; however, that gene has not yet been located. Therefore, it is identified by means of other DNA material, *and* correlation of the material with the disease requires linkage analysis. Because it is caused by a single gene, if that gene can be identified, then linkage analysis won't be needed. In addition, it will be known with virtual certainty that the individual will be afflicted. As with adult polycystic kidney disease, all carriers of the gene for Huntington's disease develop the disorder. The causal tie between the gene and the disorder is virtually absolute.

But this is the rare exception. The great majority of genes do not lead inevitably to the disorder. They create a susceptibility or vulnerability, not a certainty of expression. Our last set of variables concerns this—the nature of the gene's causal efficacy. Conditions such as high cholesterol levels and high blood pressure, and diseases such as Alzheimer's disease and diabetes, are determined by "contingency" genes. Certain contingencies must be met before these genes bring about their respective disorders.

One of these contingencies is the presence of other genes, as we have just noted. In addition, the expression of most genetically based disorders requires the influence of biological, social, or psychological factors. It is already common knowledge that diet and exercise (biological and social influences) can affect the onset of coronary artery disease and high blood pressure. The same also holds for diabetes and back arthritis.

What does it *mean* to say that the gene produces a disposition or susceptibility to a disorder? One fourth of the people with the genetic marker for "ankylosing spondylitis" develop this debilitating back arthritis. Put another way, someone with the marker is between forty and one hundred times more likely to develop ankylosing spondylitis than is someone without this genetic material.[7] Even in such "high odds" cases like this one, however, 75 percent of the people with the genetic marker do *not* develop the arthritis. Work and work conditions, for instance, contribute greatly to its onset. For many genetically determined disorders, the individual may have considerable control over whether and how severely the disorder occurs. Knowledge of our genetic constitution can be helpful in making practical decisions rather than simply forecasting our fate.

## CONSIDERATIONS OF PRIVACY

We come now to the moral questions of whether and to what extent genetic screening in the workplace is justified. Recall that we are talking about discriminatory screening which is designed to exclude workers from jobs, rather than to "warn and relocate." I shall argue that considerations of privacy and justice mitigate against screening or at least its untrammeled deployment.

Let's begin with considerations of privacy. When information is gathered about us our privacy may be infringed upon in varying degrees. Whether our privacy is violated depends on such things as whether we consent to the gathering of the information, the nature of the information, and what happens as a result of its gathering. What I would like to focus on here is the issue of control and autonomy. Many different sorts of information can be obtained, most of it valuable to the company. Some information concerns such things as credit ratings or religious affiliations, other involves ascertaining physical facts by monitoring drug use. Is genetic screening any different in principle from drug screening, polygraph tests, or surveillance? In at least one regard it seems to be. Although in most cases, we have some control over whether a gene is expressed as a disorder, we cannot control whether we *have* the gene in the first place. Whether we have the disposition, the vulnerability to the disorder, is out of our hands.

We have some say over our work, religion, credit rating, and most of us can choose to use drugs or not. But not so with genes. They are in and of us, forever. This lack of control is especially compounded in the workplace because of related lack of power in this context. First, most workers are not in a position to refuse to cooperate with demands for screening. When this is the case, they have no control over the gathering of information about which they also lack control. This lack of power is magnified by workers' overall status in the workplace. In spite of unionization, most workers have little say over working conditions, product manufacture, wages, promotions, and firing.

We need to see testing in general, and genetic screening in particular, within the context of the employer-employee relationship. Testing workers gives employers and managers still greater control over workers' lives. Screening of all sorts would be different, and experienced differently, in a context in which power were more equitably distributed in the workplace. This seems especially important in the area of testing for genetically based disorders, precisely because we have no control over our genetic makeup.

This sense of powerlessness is critical to the special type of stigmatization associated with genetic defects. When screening uncovers a genetic abnormality, the individual can feel morally defective—cursed or damned. This could and has happened simply from acquiring genetic information under the most benign circumstances. Thus, Madeleine and Lenn Goodman found considerable stigmatization among Jewish people identified as carriers of Tay-Sachs disease even though no obvious disadvantages followed from such identification.[8] But when the information is used prejudicially, as in the workplace discrimination we are here considering, the likelihood and intensity of stigmatization increases. As Thomas Murray notes, diagnosing an illness as genetically caused may *label* the person as *constitutionally* weak, making finding another job difficult.[9]

All of these aspects of the situation help explain why the loss of privacy suffered in genetic screening in the workplace is serious. The screening is for properties over which the worker has no control and is not responsible; it occurs in a context of relative powerlessness; and it is likely to result in stigmatization with profound costs to his or her life-chances. The genetic screening as described here involves loss of privacy, but the stigmatization and its repercussions, as we shall see, are a matter of *injustice.* Loss or forfeiture of privacy is less defendable the less just the situation under which it occurs and the less just the purposes for which it is used.

The invasion of privacy is greater when the genetic screening is "across the board" rather than selective. When businesses screen for *any* potential disease or debilitating condition, it is like having the police come and search your house just to see what they'll turn up. In both cases, there is clearly an "interest" in uncovering the relevant danger. The state and employer reduce their respective risks. But such interests are not overriding, not in a society which claims to value the individual's autonomy and privacy. The employer has no more right to a total genetic profile than he has to information about one's sexual habits, recreational activities, or religious and political beliefs—even though knowledge of these and other details of our lives might well be of use to him.

Testing for job-specific susceptibilities is more warranted since directly connected to the work context and the employer's role in bringing about the disorder. It is more like searching someone's home for specific items, such as guns or counterfeit money. Presumably, there is a good reason for looking in both sorts of case. Since screening for just a *few,* job-related genetic dispositions, less of the self is being "searched." Therefore, there is probably less sense of being violated or stigmatized. The individual is told that she is unfit to do this particular job, for example, heavy lifting because of the disposition to back arthritis. She is not labelled as constitutionally weak due to some general condition, such as vulnerability to heart disease.

Even here, however, another threat looms. It is all too likely that employers will tend to use such information to fire employees rather than improve workplace conditions. It's cheaper. But perhaps it's the employer's responsibility to make the workplace safe, even for those with susceptibilities to environmentally-triggered disorders. People who have a disposition to lung disease, for example, might be able to work in this particular factory at no increased risk *if* the employer provided better air ventilation and circulation. This issue seems to be a matter of justice: who should bear the burden of workplace danger.

## CONSIDERATIONS OF JUSTICE

We turn now directly to considerations of justice. The first sort of consideration focuses on the individual and the nature of genetic causation. The second concerns these individuals as members of a paying public.

In the great majority of cases, genetic markers indicate merely a predisposition for a disorder, not the inevitability of its onset. (Even when inevitable, in many cases the degree of severity remains unpredictable.) It seems unjust to penalize an individual for something that has not yet come to pass and which may well be prevented by him. It is unjust to act as if the individual is already diseased or disabled, especially when he may run a *lower* risk than others without the marker because of healthful life-choices made on the basis of this information.

It is like treating someone as though guilty until proven innocent. In the case of genetically caused susceptibility to a disorder, it is worse because carrying the gene is beyond the person's control. Considerations of justice suggest that there is something wrong in penalizing people for conditions which are beyond their control. Of course, sometimes people are justly denied benefits or privileges on account of uncontrollable conditions. Thus, we don't allow blind people to drive or people who have slow reaction times to be air-traffic controllers. But this is not penalizing someone so much as finding them unqualified for performance of a task. Public safety certainly does and should operate as a constraint on opportunity. However, this kind of consideration is rare in the case of genetically based disorders; moreover, it should come into play only with the onset of the disabling conditions, not with the mere discovery of a genetic propensity toward it. In a society proclaiming commitment to egalitarian principles, we shouldn't further handicap people who may become disabled by depriving them of work while they are still able to do the job.

The question of the justness of discriminatory genetic screening can also be posed from the larger, social perspective. It arises from the social nature and purpose of genetic research. Genetic research, including testing individuals and groups, was developed to help people. By diagnosing genetic predispositions, testing could enable people to make beneficial decisions concerning themselves, family members, and potential offspring. When individuals already manifested certain disorders, voluntary genetic counselling was designed to help provide diagnosis, prognosis, and information for vital decisions.

This is analogous to diagnostic reading tests conducted in the public schools. These are designed to help students get remedial help when needed. Instead, imagine a situation where such tests were used to "weed out" the weakest students so that they didn't clutter up the classroom and drain teaching resources. Surely we would find such a policy unjust, if not outrageous! This would be similar to the discriminatory use of genetic screening. Like individuals with contingency markers, slow readers often can *alter* their futures. In both cases, the diagnostic tests can be used to assist the individual to deal with his problem and make life-enhancing choices. On the other hand, the tests can be used to exclude the individual from certain beneficial opportunities: jobs in the case of genetic screening, and instruction to improve reading skills in the case of the reading tests.

Each use of the diagnostic test can be viewed as part of a larger model. The "diagnostic-therapeutic" model takes as primary the interests of the individuals being tested. The "competition" model, however, takes as primary the interests of some other group or institution: the business in the case of genetic testing, the school or superior students in the case of reading diagnosis. On the competition model, the "defective" worker or student is displaced in favor of the competing interests.

My analogy between the school reading test and genetic screening being used against the diagnosed individuals faces the following objection. In the case of the reading test, public education is paid for by public monies; therefore, everybody has an equal right to instruction, including those with reading disabilities. But in the case of genetic screening, the employer is operating privately. She is under no obligation to serve the interests of the employee (or prospective employee). The parallel between people with reading disabilities and those genetically marked for disorders would then break down on the basis of the public/private distinction.

My reply is that genetic research and the procedures employed in genetic screening were developed with public monies. They were carried out by means of government grants and publicly financed facilities such as state universities. Even private universities and research institutes rely greatly on government monies for equipment and salaries, as well as the findings generated by the public institutions. Moreover, these public funds were allocated for the expressed purposes of increasing scientific knowledge and helping society's members. Promotion of these social goods was used to legitimate if not justify investing society's taxes in genetic research. For private businesses to use the knowledge and technology developed through this research in order to deny some of its members employment seems unjust. This is so even if private companies market instruments and procedures for the genetic screening; the technologies *these* private companies are selling could only have been developed on the shoulders of publicly financed (and publicly available) research.

This brings us to the importance of health. Health is unlike most other goods because it is a prerequisite for so many things we value. Without it, we are cut off from the joys of recreation, travel, the arts, work, socializing, sometimes even life itself. Depending on the degree of infirmity, even such simple, apparently available delights as reading, talking, or walking may be denied the individual. The economic benefits of work are usually needed for people to receive adequate long term health care, so that depriving them of work is likely to be condemning people to lack of health.

Denying a person work on the basis of the *disposition* to develop a disorder may, ironically, increase its likelihood of occurrence. Prevention of its occurrence might require repeated diagnostic tests, treatment, or therapy; it might require the economic wherewithal for a particular health regimen, such as exercise. Even if the lack of work doesn't contribute to the onset of the genetically marked disorder through economic deprivation, it compounds the individual's plight. He not only suffers from the potential to develop this particular disorder, but is now unemployed (and probably uninsured) to boot. He is now economically unprotected against *other* misfortunes and subjected to the psychological stress which could foster other disorders.

What should we conclude from all this? It seems to me that these considerations of privacy and justice argue strongly against general, discriminatory genetic screening in the workplace. Thomas Murray has a list of requirements that a morally defensible exclusion policy must meet. Among them are two that especially turn on considerations of justice.[10] The policy must exclude workers from but a few jobs so that those affected stand a good chance of finding other employment. Otherwise, we'd be treating them unjustly by virtually denying them the opportunity to work at all. In addition, the exclusion shouldn't single out groups that have already been unjustly treated. This is important since genetic dispositions are often inherited along racial and ethnic lines such as the high black incidence of sickle cell anemia and the high Jewish incidence of Tay-Sachs. This, too, is a matter of justice. We shouldn't compound prior injustices with present ones.

I would qualify Murray's conditions with the following restrictions. Corporate screening should be confined to work-specific disorders, rather than probe for a general genetic profile. Moreover, the company should make it a policy to try to relocate the employee to a less hazardous work site or activity, just as the first companies engaged in screening did. This degree of constraint seems minimal in light of the importance of privacy and justice.

## NOTES

1. William Pat Patterson, "Genetic Screening: How Much Should We Test Employees?," *Industry Week* (June 1, 1987), pp. 47–48.
2. Kathleen McAuliffe, "Predicting Diseases," *U.S. News and World Report* (May 25, 1987), p. 65.
3. Kathleen Nolan and Sara Swenson, "New Tools, New Dilemmas: Genetic Frontiers," *The Hastings Center Report* (October/November, 1988), p. 65.
4. Gina Kolati, "Genetic Screening Raises Questions For Employers and Insurers," *Research News* (April 18, 1986), p. 317.
5. Marc Lappe, "The Limits of Genetic Inquiry," *The Hastings Center Report* (August, 1987), p. 7.
6. Ibid., p. 8.
7. Marc Lappe, *Genetic Politics* (New York: Simon and Schuster, 1979), p. 61.
8. Madeleine and Lenn Goodman, "The Overselling of Genetic Anxiety," *The Hastings Center Report* (October, 1982), p. 249. There was, however, fear of loss of marriage eligibility among many of the people tested. The Goodmans also cite a study of sickle cell trait in Greece, where "possession of sickle cell trait had become a socially stigmatized status; introducing new anxieties into this rural community," p. 26.
9. Thomas Murray, "Warning: Screening Workers for Genetic Risk," *The Hastings Center Report* (February, 1983).
10. Ibid., p. 8. Murray also includes the following: sound scientific basis linking anomaly to exposure to disease; risk should be very large and the disease should be severe and irreversible; and that the number of people excluded should be very small. This last stricture doesn't strike me as all that convincing. It isn't the number of people affected that *makes* a policy unjust. Although many suffering an injustice is worse than few suffering it, injustice done even to few is still injustice and weighs against the policy.

# Screening Workers for Genetic Hypersusceptibility: Potential Ethical, Legal, and Social Implications from the Human Genome Project

*Andrew C. Wicks, Lowell E. Sever, Rebekah Harty, Steven W. Gajewski, Miriam Marcus-Smith*

## INTRODUCTION

The protection of workers' health has been of increasing concern throughout recent history. We are now on the verge of developing new methods for risk reduction as the Human Genome Project increases our understanding of genetic factors as they relate to disease risk, including potential methods of identifying susceptibilities to environmental and workplace toxicants. (In the context the authors are considering, hypersusceptibility is a statistical statement regarding increased risk and is not a prediction that a particular individual will develop a disease.) The focus of this discussion is on genetic screening programs that can identify or classify people based on their likelihood or probability of developing a particular disease following exposure to a hazardous agent.

Reprinted with the permission of *Journal of Health and Human Services Administration.* Vol. 21 (1) (1999): 116–32.

According to Hennekens and Buring (1987:184), "Screening refers to the application of a test to people who are as yet asymptomatic for the purpose of classifying them with respect to their likelihood of having a particular disease." Screening is contrasted with monitoring and surveillance which "involve the repeated performance of an observation or measurement used to detect an unfavorable trend that may be altered by appropriate intervention" (Ashford et al., 1990:321).

Caporaso and Goldstein (1995) claim that the genetic screening for insurance or occupation is an "ethically repugnant" application of genetic screening. In contrast, these authors concur with Vineis and Schulte (1995) that genetic screening in the workplace may offer promising new possibilities to improve worker health protection. They will analyze relevant ethical, legal, and social issues to support this position and offer parameters for policy formulation. Although the discussion is meant to be broad and applicable to a wide range of workplace settings, they will contextualize the discussion within the health care setting.

In this article, the authors explore a wide range of issues surrounding the use of genetic screening in the workplace: issues of risk, the rationale and legal basis for screening, the privacy concerns of workers, the confidentiality of test results, and potential discrimination. In the final segment, they will draw together the various strands of the discussion and suggest some guidelines for developing screening policies.

Although the authors consider a variety of moral concepts and arguments, they use a set of five ethical principles as a framework. . . . These principles, which can be used to express a range of ethical concerns, are: 1) respect for autonomy (protection of person's ability to act as an autonomous agent); 2) nonmaleficence (protecting persons from harm); 3) beneficence (providing benefit or assistance to others); 4) justice (giving each person his or her due); and 5) self-interest (the legitimate interest of individuals in pursuing their own projects and protecting their interests). . . .

These moral principles are *prima facie* binding; they have a presumptive moral weight but conflict within and among principles occur; critical analysis or balancing must be done to determine what is morally right or best. . . .

## Criteria of an Effective and Acceptable Screening Program

For screening programs to be considered acceptable, certain minimum criteria need to be fulfilled. For example, Annas (1990) has suggested a group of factors should be used to evaluate screening programs prior to implementation: (1) the frequency and severity of the condition screened for; (2) the availability of treatment of documented efficacy; (3) the extent to which detection by screening improves outcomes; (4) the validity and safety of screening tests; (5) the adequacy of resources to assure effective screening and counseling follow-up; (6) the costs of the program; and (7) the acceptance of the program by the community (including physicians and the public). Particular importance is placed on the accuracy and reliability of the tests including specificity and sensitivity. These criteria reflect the belief that, in order to be appropriate and justifiable, genetic screening must be far more than technically feasible.

## Reasons to Test

A variety of reasons to perform screening have been identified. The authors will indicate the range of these motivations and clarify some of the moral principles embedded in them.

There are several reasons why employers might want to institute genetic screening programs. The first reason to test, and the motivation that has been described as most powerful, is to cut costs and increase productivity (self-interest). Testing might be able to identify individuals who are at greater risk for disease and illness and remove them from the workplace, thereby saving on insurance costs. For example, if such genetic tests were available, identified hypersusceptible clinicians at higher risk of contracting hepatitis, tuberculosis or HIV could be assigned to work with patient populations where their risk of contact with such patients is substantially reduced. Indeed, in the current health care environment, insurance companies could apply significant pressure to perform testing as a way to save on insurance costs.

Second, some have projected that screening might be a valuable tool in decreasing the frequency and costs of workers compensation claims. Here again, self-interest of the employer in a desire for increased profits is the motivation. Genetic tests might be effective in showing that some claimants had genetic predisposition to illness or that workplace exposure played only a small role in the onset of the illness, thereby reducing employer liability.

Third, there is concern for public safety (beneficence and nonmaleficence), arising from a concern that workers who become ill on the job may pose a threat to public safety (e.g., a pilot who becomes suddenly ill while in flight). If genetic screening can help predict the presence or likelihood of the onset of illness before disease state is detectable, then it may play an important role in protecting public safety.

Fourth, employers have also expressed concern for the health and wellbeing of workers (beneficence and nonmaleficence). Particularly in high-risk environments, some workers may be at greater risk for adverse health effects from various chemicals or toxicants. If generic screening can help determine which individuals are at (higher) risk for ill-effects from exposure, it could enable employers to prevent harm to their workers.

However, employers also face certain disincentives to introduce genetic screening. As the OTA's 1990 report makes clear, employers are in a "double bind"—there is a variety of constraints existing on how they can use testing (and others that may be developed) and there may be penalties for not using testing results, particularly when risks to particular individuals are found. There are also concerns that, if screening programs are unpopular with workers, there may be a variety of negative effects from testing programs ranging from the tangible (strikes, protests, sabotage, etc.) to the less tangible (lower morale, increased mistrust between workers and managers, etc.), both of which can affect the overall "cost" of testing.

Workers have two main interests in testing. One motivation is to increase their knowledge base and ability to make informed choices about their lives, particularly regarding something as serious as the risk of major illness (autonomy). Other related interests include a desire to help prevent harm to themselves and facilitate prompt and effective medical treatment for any illness (non maleficence and beneficence). Particularly when screening is highly accurate and capable of providing clear evidence that certain activities will substantially increase the risk of serious illness, testing may prove very helpful on the ability of workers to avoid harm.

The public, through the government, also has an interest in testing for reasons of health and wellbeing of its citizens as well as in reducing or avoiding medical costs whenever possible (justice and maleficence). It is also interested in helping business to flourish and remain competitive nationally and internationally, to reduce costs, and to provide jobs, services, and products that are necessary for a vibrant community. Part of this interest is in making sure that business does not bear undue burdens in protecting the health of workers, Thus, society may have an interest in testing if it can help businesses from paying excessive or unfair costs (justice).

### Legal Basis for Testing

The legal framework regarding testing can be found in several sources. Of particular importance is the obligation of employers to provide a safe environment. The standard set by the Occupational Safety and Health Act under the General Duty Clause (5(a)(1)OSH Act) that employers provide a workplace "free from recognized hazards" leaves open the possibility that genetic screening may be included as a technique to help fulfill this obligation.

## PRIVACY

Considerations regarding privacy are frequently raised in connection with genetic screening in the workplace. Significant potential exists for genetic screening to reveal sensitive information about health implications beyond the susceptibility issue which could cause concern about other family members and future offspring. Occupational genetic screening, unlike drug screening, may raise privacy issues affecting an "extended familial class." (Such collateral results may give rise to additional duties on the part of the physician and employer).

The Supreme Court has recognized a fundamental right to privacy as implicit in several of the amendments to the Bill of Rights. In the realm of medicine, the moral right of persons to be free of tests, procedures, and even unwanted touching are all well recognized and protected in law. Patients, or surrogates acting on their behalf, must provide informed consent before any testing or treatment is performed unless it is an emergency and health care workers are unable to obtain consent.

Motives for emphasizing the privacy rights of workers are related to the potential for misuse of information and the tendency to undermine the voluntariness of consent. In the case of making screening a condition of employment, the issue of economic coercion arises particularly for applicants who may have few job opportunities. The lure of a job may lead applicants to give consent that is not sufficiently voluntary and, therefore, may violate the moral rights of workers.

The primary "misuses" of information are discussed in greater detail in the confidentiality and discrimination sections but the authors suggest that they also shape the question of privacy rights. Workers see the risks of misuse (even if there are stringent confidentiality protections) and the consequences of misuse as combining to provide grounds for more extensive privacy rights than might otherwise be extended. If these claims are found to be persuasive, one might well conclude that their rights outweigh the interests of employers and that it is morally impermissible to conduct genetic screening without the voluntary and informed consent of workers.

## CONFIDENTIALITY

Among the most pressing concerns of workers is protecting information about themselves that they consider confidential, including the results. Of particular importance is the issue of who should have access to medical records and what specific information may be disclosed. One of the reasons that confidentiality issues have taken on such significance in discussions about screening is the nature of the information in question. Many have suggested that generic information is "special"—somehow more private, personal, and threatening to persons than most other information. Unlike drug testing or a polygraph where one can learn about past deeds, genetic information gets at things about us that are unchangeable and inextricable part of who we are. Thus, although a polygraph might reveal that a person is an alcoholic, a genetic screening test might show that a person has "bad genes." While a person probably has some responsibility for and to do something about the former, genetic characteristics are beyond a person's control and cannot be changed. . . .

Some have argued that, because of how insurance works, if one is turned down for insurance because of health problems (such as genetic defects or predispositions), it becomes that much more difficult to obtain insurance from other sources. Similar problems exist regarding employment and these effects, combined with larger social attitudes about genetics, could lead to wholesale discrimination that drastically inhibits one's opportunities in virtually every sphere of activity. The history of eugenic practices in the United States, the problems faced by persons with sickle cell trait, and the experience of people who are HIV-positive provide further evidence that such concerns are not extreme but may be all too realistic if there are no adequate safeguards in place to protect individuals from genetic-based discrimination. . . .

## DISCRIMINATION

Gostin (1991:110) offers a useful operating definition of general discrimination as "the denial of rights, privileges or opportunities on the basis of information obtained from genetically diagnostic and prognostic tests." Discrimination questions potentially revolve around two major issues: the use of genetic information to deny individuals what are rightfully theirs and the use of genetic information as a mechanism to further discriminate against minorities. Discrimination issues are especially important in our society given that fairness, respect for the individual, and equality of opportunity are values that our society treats as fundamental.

The potential use of genetic screening raises concerns about discrimination for a variety of reasons. The history of eugenics in the United States (including forced sterilization) during the early parts of the twentieth century provides a sober reminder that genetic information can be a powerful tool to generate comprehensive patterns of discrimination (see, for example, Justice Holmes' opinion in the Supreme Court case of *Buck v. Bell*). While we have gained more knowledge about genetics, there are other procedures that make the concern salient, particularly the myriad ways in which people with HIV have been discriminated against. As discussed in the section on confidentiality, if genetic information is used to deny people jobs or insurance opportunities—even without malevolent intent—it is a form of stigmatization.

Indeed, there is evidence that genetic testing has been used to discriminate against African Americans (screening for sickle cell trait), males (screening for glucose-6-phosphate dehydrogenase deficiency), and workers with alphal-antitrypsin deficiency (Council of Ethical and Judicial Affairs, 1991; Gostin, 1991). Thus, we need to be extremely careful that genetic screening is not used in ways that revisit these tragic episodes.

The law provides several forms of protection from genetic discrimination. The two primary federal statues are Title VII of the Civil Rights Act and the Americans with Disabilities Act (ADA). Individuals with genetic disease would be considered to have a disability, therefore covered under federal and state disability discrimination laws, but it is less clear whether an individual with a sensitive genotype or genetic predispositions to disease would be so considered.

Title VII, which bars discrimination based on race, color, religion, sex or national origin, becomes important because of the link between many forms of particular minority groups and genetic disease (e.g., African Americans and sickle cell disease; Ashkenazi Jews and Bloom's syndrome and Tay-Sachs disease; Armenians and familial mediterranean fever). Title VII offers two possible defenses that minorities may have against such practice: that a given activity is a pretext for discrimination or that it has disproportionate impact on minority groups even though the policy itself is neutral.

The ADA outlaws discrimination against individuals based on a basis on which to establish screening programs. While it is legitimate and morally justifiable that firms pursue their economic wellbeing, there are some basic limits on this imperative, including the moral and legal implications against discrimination and violation of equal opportunity. Any form of testing must show an ability to avoid both a discrimination intent as well as differential effects in its impact. The first two rationales for testing clearly fail this test. Even though employers are rightly concerned about their economic wellbeing, such concerns should not be allowed to infringe on the legitimate rights of workers. Unless there can be a direct link between testing and some valid purpose that would not entail discrimination, such as current ability to perform one's work task, then testing appears to be illegitimate.

The appeal of public safety seems to be a much more compelling and defensible rationale for testing. If there are instances where genetic screening can prove effective in preventing specific and significant harm to the public without violating the prohibitions against discrimination, screening may well be justified. However, as the AMA's Council on Ethics and Judicial Affairs (1991) has noted, genetic screening is currently not even an effective means of determining high risks of harm to the public, let alone providing a unique or especially valuable means of determining risk, It suggests that "genetic tests will have a poor predictive value when used to identify workers who might pose risks to public safety. Incomplete penetrance, variable expression, and delayed manifestation are problems." It also maintains that direct testing by more routine methods to determine workers' ability to perform their tasks is a far more effective and less costly method of protecting public safety.

These arguments do not rule out the possibility that future developments in technology would allow genetic screening to play a significant, and perhaps even an indispensable, role in averting harm to the public. As the technology becomes more sophisticated and capable of detecting harm, complex questions are likely to arise as to whether screening is appropriate if it is only slightly more effective than more routine direct testing for functional abilities, particularly if there are significant concerns about discrimination, privacy violation, and other issues not associated with nongenetic evaluation methods.

The protection of workers' health and safety also appears to have considerable merit as a rationale for testing. This may serve as a compelling justification to test, particularly where strong and direct disability. In March of 1995, the Equal Employment Opportunity Commission (EEOC) defined disability, under the ADA, to include persons who were presymptomatic for or predisposed to a disabling disease. It is not clear that this interpretation will be sustained by the courts (Mehlman et al., 1996). Gostin (1991) makes a compelling case that future disability should be covered by the ADA and that there should be legislative action to specify this condition.

## CONCLUSION

. . . Having highlighted some of the key issues surrounding genetic screening, the authors suggest legitimate grounds for testing and broad constraints that should structure a screening policy. While this discussion has been tailored to the social context of the U.S., many of the issues are translatable to the international debates about genetic screening. Indeed, it may be vital that policy discussions take place at this level, particularly as economies are being more interconnected, to ensure that adequate protections and enforcement mechanisms are in place.

The authors began by highlighting four potential rationales for employers to carry out genetic screening: cost savings and increased productivity, decreases in the frequency and cost of workers compensation claims, public safety, and the health and well-being of workers.

The authors suggest that the first two reasons are illegitimate. Links can be made between workplace exposures and susceptibility to serious illness. Given the broader responsibilities placed on corporations to look out for the welfare of their workers and past precedents for testing and removal of employees on the basis of likelihood of occupational injury, employers can make a strong case for genetic screening.

Tenuous connections between test results and harm from workplace exposure (risks), however, will weaken the grounds for testing. General criteria regarding screening must be considered in evaluating the merits of genetic screening as a whole, as well as genetic tests for specific illnesses or disease risks. As technology advances based on new insights arising from the Human Genome Project, the authors believe there will be instances where genetic screening may meet the criteria for screening programs, potentially providing unique and justifiable means for reducing the risk of harm to workers from workplace exposure.

The discussion of privacy issues suggests that employers strive as far as possible to make informed consent a part of any testing protocol. In addition, to alleviate concerns about abuse and involuntariness, some have argued that it would be appropriate for employers to encourage employees to seek testing through their own physician rather than through an occupational physician (CEJA, 1991). Such an approach could also help mitigate concerns about employer liability. However, if testing is to be done on a voluntary basis or performed by an employee's physician, it will be necessary to adjust OSHA and workers compensation to reflect this arrangement so that employers will not be penalized for collecting and acting on this information. Also, any screening protocol should address the possibility of discovering collateral health or health risk information that goes beyond the specific occupational exposure concern and/or that has implications for the tested individual's family or future offspring.

Finally, there should be extensive and rigorous mechanisms for protecting the confidentiality of information about employees. This applies to medical records in general but especially with respect to genetic information. Policies should ensure that employers will not be given information to which they are not entitled and that workers can be confident that their interests are being looked after. Such an arrangement ensures the interests of both parties, seeing testing as a benevolent initiative that will help workers and boost morale rather then another method of corporate control and intimidation.

The possible incentives that corporations have for misuse of the information make it especially important to provide strong protections and safeguards that testing that appears warranted does not allow for such misuse. One of the stronger incentives for misuse may come from insurance companies in an effort to reduce health care costs. The current state of flux in the health care industry and the pressure for more inclusive coverage may lead to a system in which these incentives will be significantly reduced. It is far less likely, however, that such incentives will be removed entirely. Such developments could play an important role in evaluating the justifiability of programs of genetic screening and the various moral considerations of any screening program.

Questions about the degree of risk and the use of screening techniques must also be carefully examined. Given the backdrop of power inequalities between workers and management and the devastating impact that misuse of genetic information could have on individuals and their ability to pursue their life plans, there should be a strong presumption for monitoring, surveillance, and other modes of evaluation that are not as potentially morally problematic or controversial as genetic screening. However, it should also be noted that screening, when it meets the parameters outlined in this section, has clear potential advantages that merit its consideration. Particularly as compared to monitoring and surveillance, in which one waits for evidence of potential harm and then reacts, screening is proactive and seeks to avoid potential damage before it occurs.

In this context, it is instructive to look at other related models for testing and exclusion. Of particular importance is the *UAW vs. Johnson Controls, Inc.* (59 U.S.L.W. 4209, 1993) case and the development of fetal protection policies (and, by implication, female exclusion policies.) Such policies are relevant not only because gender is a genetically based factor but it also deals with the same issues of screening and health risks. The company in question, Johnson Controls, sought to protect fertile women from perceived high risk teratogenic exposures (lead) in some jobs out of concern that this would substantially increase the likelihood of birth defects.

The policy was challenged and ruled unlawful discrimination against women. The case highlights that worker autonomy is an important social value that has substantial legal protection and that any proposed policies need to avoid "paternalistic" rationales and seek to respect worker autonomy, particularly the ability of workers to make decisions about risk. Such protections are not universal as there are valid instances where pregnancy can be used as a basis for removal of workers (e.g., when this status affects the "essence" or "the central mission of the employer's business" according to Supreme Court decisions) but they provide a strong presumption for individual autonomy in making such decisions.

In addition, viewing screening as a panacea, as our society has done with other technologies, poses the disturbing possibility that the emphasis will be shifted from what the law mandates (creating a safe workplace) to what is convenient and cost-effective for corporations (removing workers from the workplace). Such a shift not only violates the sense of fairness embodied in current regulations, it risks creating a false sense of safety among workers who are not found to be hypersusceptible and places substantial burdens onto workers and away from corporations.

Not only would such arrangements violate fundamental individual rights and (ironically) increase the background risks for workers from occupational exposures, they would enable corporations to pass on extensive costs to society in the form of a large group of potentially unemployable and/or uninsurable individuals. There is no question that employers should not be forced to incur any and every cost of making the workplace safer. Reasonable limits must be established to ensure that their burdens are not excessive but it appears that the more likely risk comes from excesses in the other direction if employers are too quick to rely on testing and to see removal as the first and best option rather than making improvements in the workplace.

In conclusion, genetic screening capabilities raise important policy issues at the intersection of technology, ethics, law, and socioeconomic concerns. It is important to develop policies and protocols for the management of these issues as the Human Genome Project unfolds so that the ability of genetic screening to serve proper ends is not eclipsed by the potential misuse of genetic information in the workplace.

## REFERENCES

Annas, G.J. (1990). "Mapping the Human Genome and the Meaning of Monster Mythology." *Emory Law Journal* 39(3):629–664.

Caporaso, N., and A. Goldstein (1995). "Cancer Genes: Single and Susceptibility: Exposing the Differences." *Pharmacogenetics*, 5(5):59–63.

Council on Ethics and Judicial Affairs (AMA) (1991). "Use of Genetic Testing by Employers." *Journal of the American Medical Association*, 266(13): 1827–1830.

Gostin. L. (1991). "Genetic Discrimination: The Use of Genetically Based Diagnostic and Prognostic Tests by Employers and Insurers." *American Journal of Law and Medicine*, 17(1–2):109–144.

Hennekens, C.H., and J.E. Buring (1987). *Epidemiology in Medicine.* Boston: Little, Brown.

Mehlman, M.S., and Colleagues (1996). "The Need for Anonymous Genetic Counseling and Testing." *American Journal of Human Genetics*, 58(2):393–397.

Vineis, P., and P.A. Schulte (1995). "Scientific and Ethical Aspects of Genetic Screening of Workers for Cancer Risk: The Case of the N-Acetyltransferase Phenotype." *Journal of Clinical Epidemiology*, 48(2):189–97.

## WHISTLEBLOWING

# Some Paradoxes of Whistleblowing

*Michael Davis*

## INTRODUCTION

By "paradox" I mean an apparent—and, in this case, real—inconsistency between theory (our systematic understanding of whistleblowing) and the facts (what we actually know, or think we know, about whistleblowing). What concerns me is not a few anomalies, the exceptions that test a rule, but a flood of exceptions that seems to swamp the rule.

This paper has four parts. The first states the standard theory of whistleblowing. The second argues that the standard theory is paradoxical, that it is inconsistent with what we know about whistleblowers. The third part sketches what seems to me a less paradoxical theory of whistleblowing. The fourth tests the new theory against one classic case of whistleblowing, Roger Boisjoly's testimony before the presidential commission investigating the *Challenger* disaster ("the Rogers Commission"). I use that case because the chief facts are both uncontroversial enough and well-known enough to make detailed exposition unnecessary. For the same reason, I also use that case to illustrate various claims about whistleblowing throughout the paper.

## JUSTIFICATION AND WHISTLEBLOWING

The standard theory is not about whistleblowing, as such, but about justified whistleblowing—and rightly so. Whether this or that is, or is not, whistleblowing is a question for lexicographers. For the rest of us, mere moral agents, the question is—when, if ever, is whistleblowing justified?

We may distinguish three (related) senses in which an act may be "justified." First, an act may be something morality permits. Many acts, for example, eating fruit at lunch, are morally

Michael Davis, "Some Paradoxes of Whistleblowing." *Business & Professional Ethics Journal*, Vol. 15 (1) (1996). Reprinted by permission.

justified in this weak sense. They are (all things considered) morally all right, though some of the alternatives are morally all right too. Second, acts may be morally justified in a stronger sense. Not only is doing them morally all right, but doing anything else instead is morally wrong. These acts are *morally* required. Third, some acts, though only morally justified in the weaker sense, are still required all things considered. That is, they are mandatory because of some non-moral consideration. They are *rationally* (but not morally) required.

I shall be concerned here only with *moral* justification, that is, with what morality permits or requires. I shall have nothing to say about when other considerations, for example, individual prudence or social policy, make (morally permissible) whistleblowing something reason requires. . . .

Most acts, though permitted or required by morality, need no justification. There is no reason to think them wrong. Their justification is too plain for words. Why then is whistleblowing so problematic that we need *theories* of its justification? What reason do we have to think whistleblowing might be morally wrong?

Whistleblowing always involves revealing information that would not ordinarily be revealed. But there is nothing morally problematic about that; after all, revealing information not ordinarily revealed is one function of science. Whistleblowing always involves, in addition, an actual (or at least declared) intention to prevent something bad that would otherwise occur. There is nothing morally problematic in that either. That may well be the chief use of information.

What seems to make whistleblowing morally problematic is its organizational context. A mere individual cannot blow the whistle (in any interesting sense); only a member of an organization, whether a current or a former member can do so. Indeed, he can only blow the whistle on his own organization (or some part of it). So, for example, a police officer who makes public information about a burglary ring, though a member of an organization, does not blow the whistle on the burglary ring (in any interesting sense). He simply alerts the public. Even if he came by the information working undercover in the ring, his revelation could not be whistleblowing. While secret agents, spies, and other infiltrators need a moral justification for what they do, the justification they need differs from that which whistleblowers need. Infiltrators gain their information under false pretenses. They need a justification for that deception. Whistleblowers generally do not gain their information under false pretenses. . . .

What then is morally problematic about the whistleblower's organizational context? The whistleblower cannot blow the whistle using just any information obtained in virtue of membership in the organization. A clerk in Accounts who, happening upon evidence of serious wrong-doing while visiting a friend in Quality Control, is not a whistleblower just because she passes the information to a friend at the *Tribune.* She is more like a self-appointed spy. She seems to differ from the whistleblower, or at least from clear cases of the whistleblower, precisely in her relation to the information in question. To be a whistleblower is to reveal information with which one is *entrusted.*

But it is more than that. The whistleblower does not reveal the information to save his own skin (for example, to avoid perjury under oath). He has no excuse for revealing what his organization does not want revealed. Instead, he claims to be doing what he should be doing. If he cannot honestly make that claim—if, that is, he does not have that intention—his revelation is not whistleblowing (and so, not justified as whistleblowing), but something analogous, much as pulling a child from the water is not a rescue, even if it saves the child's life, when the "rescuer" merely believes herself to be salvaging old clothes. What makes whistleblowing morally problematic, if anything does, is this high-minded but unexcused misuse of one's position in a generally lawabiding, morally decent organization, an organization that *prima facie* deserves the whistleblower's loyalty (as a burglary ring does not).

The whistleblower must reveal information the organization does not want revealed. But, in any actual organization, "what the organization wants" will be contested, with various individuals or groups asking to be taken as speaking for the organization. Who, for example, did what Thiokol wanted the night before the *Challenger* exploded? In retrospect, it is obvious that the three vice presidents, Lund, Kilminster, and Mason, did not do what Thiokol wanted—or, at least, what it would have wanted. At the time, however, they had authority to speak for the company—the conglomerate Morton-Thiokol headquartered in Chicago—while the protesting engineers, including Boisjoly, did not. Yet, even before the explosion, was it obvious that the three were doing what the company wanted? To be a whistleblower, one must, I think, at least temporarily lose an argument about what the organization wants. The whistleblower is disloyal only in a sense—the sense the winners of the internal argument get to dictate. What can justify such disloyalty?

## The Standard Theory

According to the theory now more or less standard[1], such disloyalty is morally permissible when:

(S1) The organization to which the would-be whistleblower belongs will, through its product or policy, do serious and considerable harm to the public (whether to users of its product, to innocent bystanders, or to the public at large);
(S2) The would-be whistleblower has identified that threat of harm, reported it to her immediate superior, making clear both the threat itself and the objection to it, and concluded that the superior will do nothing effective; and
(S3) The would-be whistleblower has exhausted other internal procedures within the organization (for example, by going up the organizational ladder as far as allowed)—or at least made use of as many internal procedures as the danger to others and her own safety make reasonable.

Whistleblowing is morally required (according to the standard theory) when, in addition:

(S4) The would-be whistleblower has (or has accessible) evidence that would convince a reasonable, impartial observer that her view of the threat is correct; and
(S5) The would-be whistleblower has good reason to believe that revealing the threat will (probably) prevent the harm at reasonable cost (all things considered).

Why is whistleblowing morally required when these five conditions are met? According to the standard theory, whistleblowing is morally required, when it is required at all, because "people have a moral obligation to prevent serious harm to others if they can do so with little cost to themselves." In other words, whistleblowing meeting all five conditions is a form of "minimally decent Samaritanism" (a doing of what morality requires) rather than "good Samaritanism" (going well beyond the moral minimum).[2]

A number of writers have pointed out that the relation between the first three conditions and the full five does not seem to be that between the morally permissible and the morally required.[3] If, for example, the whistleblower lacks evidence that would convince a reasonable, impartial observer of the threat in question (S4), her whistleblowing could not prevent harm. Since it could not prevent harm, her whistleblowing would not be even morally permissible: what could make morally permissible an attempt to help a stranger when the attempt will probably fail and the cost be high both to the would-be Samaritan and to those to whom she owes a competing obligation? The most that can be said for blowing the whistle where only conditions S1–S3 are met seems to be that the whistleblower has an excuse when (without negligence) she acts on inadequate evidence. So, for many writers, the standard view is that S1–S5 state sufficient conditions for morally *required* whistleblowing even though S1–S3 do not state sufficient conditions for morally permissible whistleblowing but (at best) for morally *excusable* whistleblowing.

The standard theory is not a definition of whistleblowing or even of justified whistleblowing. The theory purports to state sufficient conditions, not necessary conditions (a "when" but *not* an "only when"). But these sufficient conditions are supposed to identify the central cases of morally justified whistleblowing. Since a theory that did only that would be quite useful, we cannot object to the theory merely because it is incomplete in this way. Incomplete only in this way, the theory would be about as useful as theories of practical ethics ever are.

### Three Paradoxes

That's the standard theory—where are the paradoxes? The first paradox I want to call attention to concerns a commonplace of the whistleblowing literature. Whistleblowers are not minimally decent Samaritans. If they are Samaritans at all, they are good Samaritans. They always act at considerable risk to career, and generally, at considerable risk to their financial security and personal relations.[4]

In this respect, as in many others, Roger Boisjoly is typical. Boisjoly blew the whistle on his employer, Thiokol; he volunteered information, in public testimony before the Rogers Commission, that Thiokol did not want him to volunteer. As often happens, both his employer and many who relied on it for employment reacted hostilely. Boisjoly had to say goodbye to the company town, to old friends and neighbors, and to building rockets; he had to start a new career at an age when most people are preparing for retirement.

Since whistleblowing is generally costly to the whistleblower in some large way as this, the standard theory's minimally decent Samaritanism provides *no* justification for the central cases of whistleblowing. That is the first paradox, what we might call "the paradox of burden."

The second paradox concerns the prevention of "harm." On the standard theory, the would-be whistleblower must seek to prevent "serious and considerable harm" in order for the whistleblowing to be even morally permissible. There seems to be a good deal of play in the term "harm." The harm in question can be physical (such as death or disease), financial (such as loss of or damage to property), and perhaps even psychological (such as fear or mental illness). But there is a limit to how much the standard theory can stretch "harm." Beyond that limit are "harms" like injustice, deception, and waste. As morally important as injustice, deception, and waste can be, they do not seem to constitute the "serious and considerable harm" that can require someone to become even a minimally decent Samaritan.

Yet, many cases of whistleblowing, perhaps most, are not about preventing serious and considerable physical, financial, or psychological harm. For example, when Boisjoly spoke up the evening before the *Challenger* exploded, the lives of seven astronauts sat in the balance. Speaking up then was about preventing serious and considerable physical, financial, and psychological harm—but it was not whistleblowing. Boisjoly was then serving his employer, not betraying a trust (even on the employer's understanding of that trust); he was calling his superiors' attention to what he thought they should take into account in their decision and not publicly revealing confidential information. The whistleblowing came after the explosion, in testimony before the Rogers Commission. By then, the seven astronauts were beyond help, the shuttle program was suspended, and any further threat of physical, financial, or psychological harm to the "public" was—after discounting for time—negligible. Boisjoly had little reason to believe his testimony would make a significant difference in the booster's redesign, in safety procedures in the shuttle program, or even in reawakening concern for safety among NASA employees and contractors. The *Challenger's* explosion was much more likely to do that than anything Boisjoly could do. What Boisjoly could do in his testimony, what I think he tried to do, was prevent falsification of the record.[5]

Falsification of the record is, of course, harm in a sense, especially a record as historically important as that which the Rogers Commission was to produce. But falsification is harm only in a sense that almost empties "harm" of its distinctive meaning, leaving it more or less equivalent to "moral wrong." The proponents of the standard theory mean more by "harm" than that. De George, for example, explicitly says that a threat justifying whistleblowing must be to "life or health."[6] The standard theory is strikingly more narrow in its grounds of justification than many examples of justified whistleblowing suggest it should be. That is the second paradox, the "paradox of missing harm."

The third paradox is related to the second. Insofar as whistleblowers are understood as people out to prevent harm, not just to prevent moral wrong, their chances of success are not good. Whistleblowers generally do not prevent much harm. In this too, Boisjoly is typical. As he has said many times, the situation at Thiokol is now much as it was before the disaster. Insofar as we can identify cause and effect, even now we have little reason to believe that—whatever his actual intention—Boisjoly's testimony actually prevented any harm (beyond the moral harm of falsification). So, if whistleblowers must have, as the standard theory says (S5), (beyond the moral wrong of falsification) "good reason to believe that revealing the threat will (probably) prevent the harm," then the history of whistleblowing virtually rules out the moral justification of whistleblowing. That is certainly paradoxical in a theory purporting to state sufficient conditions for the central cases of justified whistleblowing. Let us call this "the paradox of failure."

## A Complicity Theory

As I look down the roll of whistleblowers, I do not see anyone who, like the clerk from Accounts, just happened upon key documents in a cover-up.[7] Few, if any, whistleblowers are mere third-parties like the good Samaritan. They are generally deeply involved in the activity they reveal. This involvement suggests that we might better understand what justifies (most) whistleblowing if we understand the whistleblower's obligation to derive from *complicity* in wrongdoing rather than from the ability to prevent harm.

Any complicity theory of justified whistleblowing has two obvious advantages over the standard theory. One is that (moral) complicity itself presupposes (moral) wrongdoing, not harm. So, a complicity justification automatically avoids the paradox of missing harm, fitting the facts of whistleblowing better than a theory which, like the standard one, emphasizes prevention of harm.

That is one obvious advantage of a complicity theory. The second advantage is that complicity invokes a more demanding obligation than the ability to prevent harm does. We are morally obliged to avoid doing moral wrongs. When, despite our best efforts, we nonetheless find ourselves engaged in some wrong, we have an obligation to do what we reasonably can to set things right. If, for example, I cause a traffic accident, I have a moral (and legal) obligation to call help, stay at the scene until help arrives, and render first aid (if I know how), even at substantial cost to myself and those to whom I owe my time, and even with little likelihood that anything I do will help much. Just as a complicity theory avoids the paradox of missing harm, it also avoids the paradox of burden.

What about the third paradox, the paradox of failure? I shall come to that, but only after remedying one disadvantage of the complicity theory. That disadvantage is obvious-we do not yet have such a theory, not even a sketch. Here, then, is the place to offer a sketch of such a theory.

*Complicity Theory.* You are morally required to reveal what you know to the public (or to a suitable agent or representative of it) when:

(C1) what you will reveal derives from your work for an organization;
(C2) you are a voluntary member of that organization;
(C3) you believe that the organization, though legitimate, is engaged in serious moral wrongdoing;
(C4) you believe that your work for that organization will contribute (more or less directly) to the wrong if (but *not* only if) you do not publicly reveal what you know;
(C5) you are justified in beliefs C3 and C4; and
(C6) beliefs C3 and C4 are true.

The complicity theory differs from the standard theory in several ways worth pointing out here. The first is that, according to C1, what the whistleblower reveals must derive from his work for the organization. This condition distinguishes the whistleblower from the spy (and the clerk in Accounts). The spy seeks out information in order to reveal it; the whistleblower learns it as a proper part of doing the job the organization has assigned him. The standard theory, in contrast, has nothing to say about how the whistleblower comes to know of the threat she reveals (S2). For the standard theory, spies are just another kind of whistleblower.

A second way in which the complicity theory differs from the standard theory is that the complicity theory (C2) explicitly requires the whistleblower to be a *voluntary* participant in the organization in question. Whistleblowing is not—according to the complicity theory—an activity in which slaves, prisoners, or other involuntary participants in an organization engage. In this way, the complicity theory makes explicit something implicit in the standard theory. The whistleblowers of the standard theory are generally "employees." Employees are voluntary participants in the organization employing them.

What explains this difference in explicitness? For the Samaritanism of the standard theory, the voluntariness of employment is extrinsic. What is crucial is the ability to prevent harm. For the complicity theory, however, the voluntariness is crucial. The obligations deriving from complicity seem to vary with the voluntariness of our participation in the wrongdoing. Consider, for example, a teller who helps a gang rob her bank because they have threatened to kill her if she does not; she does not have the same obligation to break off her association with the gang as someone who has freely joined it. The voluntariness of employment means that the would-be whistleblower's complicity will be more like that of one of the gang than like that of the conscripted teller.

A third way in which the complicity theory differs from the standard theory is that the complicity theory (C3) requires moral wrong, not harm, for justification. The wrong need not be a new event (as a harm must be if it is to be *prevented*). It might, for example, consist in no more than silence about facts necessary to correct a serious injustice.

The complicity theory (C3) does, however, follow the standard theory in requiring that the predicate of whistleblowing be "serious." Under the complicity theory, minor wrongdoing can no more justify whistleblowing than can minor harm under the standard theory. While organizational loyalty cannot forbid whistleblowing, it does forbid "tattling," that is, revealing minor wrongdoing.

A fourth way in which the complicity theory differs from the standard theory, the most important, is that the complicity theory (C4) requires that the whistleblower believe that her work will have contributed to the wrong in question if she does nothing, but it does *not* require that she believe that her revelation will prevent (or undo) the wrong. The complicity theory does not require any belief about what the whistleblowing can accomplish (beyond ending complicity in the wrong in question). The whistleblower reveals what she knows in order to prevent complicity in the wrong, not to prevent the wrong as such. She can prevent complicity (if there is any to prevent) simply by publicly revealing what she knows. The revelation itself breaks the bond of complicity, the secret partnership in wrongdoing, that makes her an accomplice in her organization's wrongdoing. The complicity theory thus avoids the third paradox, the paradox of failure, just as it avoided the other two.

The fifth difference between the complicity theory and the standard theory is closely related to the fourth. Because publicly revealing what one knows breaks the bond of complicity, the complicity theory does not require the whistleblower to have enough evidence to convince others of the wrong in question. Convincing others, or just being able to convince them, is not, as such, an element in the justification of whistleblowing.

The complicity theory does, however, require (C5) that the whistleblower be (epistemically) justified in believing both that his organization is engaged in wrongdoing and that he will contribute to that wrong unless he blows the whistle. Such (epistemic) justification may require substantial physical evidence (as the standard theory says) or just a good sense of how things work. The complicity theory does not share the standard theory's substantial evidential demand (S4).

In one respect, however, the complicity theory clearly requires more of the whistleblower than the standard theory does. The complicity theory's C6-combined with C5-requires not only that the whistleblower be *justified* in her beliefs about the organization's wrongdoing and her part in it, but also that she be *right* about them. If she is wrong about either the wrongdoing or her complicity, her revelation will not be justified whistleblowing. This consequence of C6 is, I think, not as surprising as it may seem. If the would-be whistleblower is wrong only about her own complicity, her revelation of actual wrongdoing will, being otherwise justified, merely fail to be justified *as whistleblowing* (much as a failed resuce, though justified as an attempt, cannot be justified as a rescue). If, however, she is wrong about the wrongdoing itself, her situation is more serious. Her belief that wrong is being done, though fully justified on the evidence available to her, cannot justify her disloyalty. All her justified belief can do is *excuse* her disloyalty. Insofar as she acted with good intentions and while exercising reasonable care, she is a victim of bad luck. Such bad luck will leave her with an obligation to apologize, to correct the record (for example, by publicly recanting the charges she publicly made), and otherwise to set things right.

The complicity theory says nothing on at least one matter about which the standard theory says much-going through channels before publicly revealing what one knows. But the two theories do not differ as much as this difference in emphasis suggests. If going through channels would suffice to prevent (or undo) the wrong, then it cannot be true (as C4 and C6 together require) that the would-be whistleblower's work will contribute to the wrong if she does not publicly reveal what she knows. Where, however, going through channels would *not* prevent (or undo) the wrong, there is no need to go through channels. Condition C4's if-clause will be satisfied. For the complicity theory, going through channels is a way of finding out what the organization will do, not an independent requirement of justification. That, I think, is also how the standard theory understands it.[8]

A last difference between the two theories worth mention here is that the complicity theory is only a theory of morally required whistleblowing while the standard theory claims as well to define circumstances when whistleblowing is morally permissible but not morally required. This difference is another advantage that the complicity theory has over the standard theory. The standard theory, as we saw, has trouble making good on its claim to explain how whistleblowing can be morally permissible without being morally required.

### Testing the Theory

Let us now test the theory against Boisjoly's testimony before the Rogers Commission. Recall that under the standard theory any justification of that testimony seemed to fail for at least three reasons: First, Boisjoly could not testify without substantial cost to himself and Thiokol (to whom he owed loyalty). Second, there was no serious and substantial harm his testimony could prevent. And, third, he had little reason to believe that, even if he could identify a serious and considerable harm to prevent, his testimony had a significant chance of preventing it.

Since few doubt that Boisjoly's testimony before the Rogers Commission constitutes justified whistleblowing, if anything does, we should welcome a theory that—unlike the standard one—justifies that testimony as whistleblowing. The complicity theory sketched above does that:

(C1) Boisjoly's testimony consisted almost entirely of information derived from his work on Booster rockets at Thiokol.

(C2) Boisjoly was a voluntary member of Thiokol.

(C3) Boisjoly believed Thiokol, a legitimate organization, was attempting to mislead its client, the government, about the causes of a deadly accident. Attempting to do that certainly seems a serious moral wrong.

(C4) On the evening before the *Challenger* exploded, Boisjoly gave up objecting to the launch once his superiors, including the three Thiokol vice presidents, had made it clear that they were no longer willing to listen to him. He also had a part in preparing those superiors to testify intelligently before the Rogers Commission concerning the booster's fatal field joint. Boisjoly believed that Thiokol would use his failure to offer his own interpretation of his retreat into silence the night before the launch, and the knowledge that he had imparted to his superiors, to contribute to the attempt to mislead Thiokol's client.

(C5) The evidence justifying beliefs C3 and C4 consisted of comments of various officers of Thiokol, what Boisjoly had seen at Thiokol over the years, and what he learned about the rocket business over a long career. I find this evidence sufficient to justify his belief both that his organization was engaged in wrongdoing and that his work was implicated.

(C6) Here we reach a paradox of *knowledge*. Since belief is knowledge if, but only if, it is *both* justified *and* true, we cannot *show* that we know anything. All we can show is that a belief is now justified and that we have no reason to expect anything to turn up later to prove it false. The evidence now available still justifies Boisjoly's belief both about what Thiokol was attempting and about what would have been his part in the attempt. Since new evidence is unlikely, his testimony seems to satisfy C6 just as it satisfied the complicity theory's other five conditions.

Since the complicity theory explains why Boisjoly's testimony before the Rogers Commission was morally required whistleblowing, it has passed its first test, a test the standard theory failed.

## NOTES

I should thank Vivian Weil for several discussions provoking this paper, as well as for commenting on several drafts; members of the Program in Ethics, Science, and Environment, Oregon State University, for raising several hard questions after I read an early version of this paper to them, April 24, 1996; those who asked questions (including my copanelist, Roger Boisjoly) at a session of the annual meeting of the Northwest Section of the American Society of Engineering Educators, Oregon Institute of Technology, Klamath Falls, Oregon, April 26, 1996;

attendees at a symposium sponsored by the Centre for Professional Ethics, University of Central Lancashire, Preston, England, November 12, 1996; and the editors of *Business and Professional Ethics Journal.*

1. Throughout this paper, I take the standard theory to be Richard T. De George's version in *Business Ethics*, 3rd. Edition (New York: Macmillan, 1990), pp. 200–214 (amended only insofar as necessary to include non-businesses as well as businesses). Why treat De George's theory as standard? There are two reasons: first, it seems the most commonly cited; and second, people offering alternatives generally treat it as the one to be replaced. The only obvious competitor, Norman Bowie's account, is distinguishable from De George's on no point relevant here. See Bowie's *Business Ethics* (Englewood Cliffs, NJ: Prentice-Hall, 1982), p. 143.
2. There is now a significant literature on the responsibilities of the minimally decent Samaritan. See, for example: Peter Singer, "Famine, Affluence, and Morality," *Philosophy and Public Affairs*, Vol. 7, No. 2 (1972): 229–243; Alan Gewirth, *Reason and Morality* (Chicago: University of Chicago Press, 1978), pp. 217–230; Patricia Smith, "The Duty to Rescue and the Slippery Slope Problem," *Social Theory and Practice*, Vol. 16, No. 1 (1990): 19–41; John M. Whelan, "Charity and the Duty to Rescue," *Social Theory and Practice*, Vol. 17, No. 3 (1991): 441–456; and David Copp, "Responsibility for Collective Inaction," *Journal of Social Philosophy*, Vol. 22, No. 2 (1991): 71–80.
3. See, for example, David Theo Goldberg. "Tuning In to Whistle Blowing," *Business and Professional Ethics Journal*, Vol. 7, No. 2 (1988): 85–94.
4. For an explanation of why whistleblowing is inevitably a high risk undertaking, see my "Avoiding the Tragedy of Whistleblowing," *Business and Professional Ethics Journal*, Vol. 8, No. 4 (1989): 3–19.
5. After I presented this paper in Klamath Falls, Boisjoly told me that, though his motive for testifying as he did was (as I surmised) to prevent falsification of the record, part of his reason for wanting to prevent that was that he wanted to do what he could to prevent the managers responsible for the disaster from having any part in redesigning the boosters. This *secondary* motive is, of course, consistent with the complicity theory.
6. De George, p. 210: "The notion of *serious* harm might be expanded to include serious financial harm, and kinds of harm other than death and serious threats to health and body. But as we noted earlier, we shall restrict ourselves here to products and practices that produce or threaten serious harm or danger to life and health."
7. See Myron Peretz Glazer and Penina Migdal Glazer, *The Whistleblowers: Exposing Corruption in Government and Industry* (New York: Basic Books, 1989) for a good list of whistleblowers (with detailed description of each); for an older list (with descriptions), see Alan F. Westin, *Whistleblowing! Loyalty and Dissent in the Corporation* (New York: McGraw-Hill, 1981).
8. Compare De George, p. 211: "By reporting one's concern to one's immediate superior or other appropriate person, one preserves and observes the regular practices of firms, which on the whole promote their order and efficiency; this fulfills one's obligation of minimizing harm, and *it precludes precipitous whistle blowing.*" (Italics mine.)

# Whistleblowing and Employee Loyalty

*Ronald Duska*

There are proponents on both sides of the issue—those who praise whistleblowers as civic heroes and those who condemn them as "finks." Maxwell Glen and Cody Shearer, who wrote about the whistleblowers at Three Mile Island say, "Without the *courageous* breed of assorted company insiders known as whistleblowers—workers who often risk their

Reprinted by permission of the author.

livelihoods to disclose information about construction and design flaws—the Nuclear Regulatory Commission itself would be nearly as idle as Three Mile Island. . . . That whistleblowers deserve both gratitude and protection is beyond disagreement."[1]

Still, while Glen and Shearer praise whistleblowers, others vociferously condemn them. For example, in a now infamous quote, James Roche, the former president of General Motors said:

> Some critics are now busy eroding another support of free enterprise—the loyalty of a management team, with its unifying values and cooperative work. Some of the enemies of business now encourage an employee to be *disloyal* to the enterprise. They want to create suspicion and disharmony, and pry into the proprietary interests of the business. However this is labeled—industrial espionage, whistle blowing, or professional responsibility—it is another tactic for spreading disunity and creating conflict.[2]

From Roche's point of view, not only is whistleblowing not "courageous" and not deserving of "gratitude and protection" as Glen and Shearer would have it, it is corrosive and impermissible.

Discussions of whistleblowing generally revolve around three topics: (1) attempts to define whistleblowing more precisely, (2) debates about whether and when whistleblowing is permissible, and (3) debates about whether and when one has an obligation to blow the whistle.

In this paper I want to focus on the second problem, because I find it somewhat disconcerting that there is a problem at all. When I first looked into the ethics of whistleblowing it seemed to me that whistleblowing was a good thing, and yet I found in the literature claim after claim that it was in need of defense, that there was something wrong with it, namely that it was an act of disloyalty.

If whistleblowing is a disloyal act, it deserves disapproval, and ultimately any action of whistleblowing needs justification. This disturbs me. It is as if the act of a good Samaritan is being condemned as an act of interference, as if the prevention of a suicide needs to be justified.

In his book *Business Ethics,* Norman Bowie claims that "whistleblowing . . . violate(s) a *prima facie* duty of loyalty to one's employer." According to Bowie, there is a duty of loyalty that prohibits one from reporting his employer or company. Bowie, of course, recognizes that this is only a *prima facie* duty, that is, one that can be overridden by a higher duty to the public good. Nevertheless, the axiom that whistleblowing is disloyal is Bowie's starting point.[3]

Bowie is not alone. Sissela Bok sees "whistleblowing" as an instance of disloyalty:

> The whistleblower hopes to stop the game; but since he is neither referee nor coach, and since he blows the whistle on his own team, his act is seen as a *violation of loyalty.* In holding his position, he has assumed certain obligations to his colleagues and clients. He may even have subscribed to a loyalty oath or a promise of confidentiality. . . . Loyalty to colleagues and to clients comes to be pitted against loyalty to the public interest, to those who may be injured unless the revelation is made.[4]

Bowie and Bok end up defending whistleblowing in certain contexts, so I don't necessarily disagree with their conclusions. However, I fail to see how one has an obligation of loyalty to one's company, so I disagree with their perception of the problem and their starting point. I want to argue that one does not have an obligation of loyalty to a company, even a *prima facie* one, because companies are not the kind of things that are properly objects of loyalty. To make them objects of loyalty gives them a moral status they do not deserve and in raising their status, one lowers the status of the individuals who work for the companies. Thus, the difference in perception is important because those who think employees have an obligation of loyalty to a company fail to take into account a relevant moral difference between persons and corporations.

But why aren't companies the kind of things that can be objects of loyalty? To answer that we have to ask what are proper objects of loyalty. John Ladd states the problem this way, "Granted that loyalty is the wholehearted devotion to an object of some kind, what kind of thing is the object? Is it an abstract entity, such as an idea or a collective being? Or is it a person or group of persons?" [5] Philosophers fall into three camps on the question. On one side are the idealists who hold that loyalty is devotion to something more than persons, to some cause or abstract entity. On the other side are what Ladd calls "social atomists," and these include empiricists and utilitarians, who think that at most one can only be loyal to individuals and that loyalty can ultimately be explained away as some other obligation that holds between two people. Finally, there is a moderate position that holds that although idealists go too far in postulating some super-personal entity as an object of loyalty, loyalty is still an important and real relation that holds between people, one that cannot be dismissed by reducing it to some other relation.

There does seem to be a view of loyalty that is not extreme. According to Ladd, "'loyalty' is taken to refer to a relationship between persons—for instance, between a lord and his vassal, between a parent and his children, or between friends. Thus the object of loyalty is ordinarily taken to be a person or a group of persons."[6]

But this raises a problem that Ladd glosses over. There is a difference between a person or a group of persons, and aside from instances of loyalty that relate two people such as lord/vassal, parent/child, or friend/friend, there are instances of loyalty relating a person to a group, such as a person to his family, a person to this team, and a person to his country. Families, countries, and teams are presumably groups of persons. They are certainly ordinarily construed as objects of loyalty.

But to what am I loyal in such a group? In being loyal to the group am I being loyal to the whole group or to its members? It is easy to see the object of loyalty in the case of an individual person. It is simply the individual. But to whom am I loyal in a group? To whom am I loyal in a family? Am I loyal to each and every individual or to something larger, and if to something larger, what is it? We are tempted to think of a group as an entity of its own, an individual in its own right, having an identity of its own.

To avoid the problem of individuals existing for the sake of the group, the atomists insist that a group is nothing more than the individuals who comprise it, nothing other than a mental fiction by which we refer to a group of individuals. It is certainly not a reality or entity over and above the sum of its parts, and consequently is not a proper object of loyalty. Under such a position, of course, no loyalty would be owed to a company because a company is a mere mental fiction, since it is a group. One would have obligations to the individual members of the company, but one could never be justified in overriding those obligations for the sake of the "group" taken collectively. A company has no moral status except in terms of the individual members who comprise it. It is not a proper object of loyalty. But the atomists go too far. Some groups, such as a family, do have a reality of their own, whereas groups of people walking down the street do not. From Ladd's point of view the social atomist is wrong because he fails to recognize the kinds of groups that are held together by "the ties that bind." The atomist tries to reduce these groups to simple sets of individuals bound together by some externally imposed criteria. This seems wrong.

There do seem to be groups in which the relationships and interactions create a new force or entity. A group takes on an identity and a reality of its own that is determined by its purpose, and this purpose defines the various relationships and roles set up within the group. There is a division of labor into roles necessary for the fulfillment of the purposes of the group. The membership, then, is not of individuals who are the same but of individuals who have specific relationships to one another determined by the aim of the group. Thus we get specific relationships like parent/child, coach/player, and so on, that don't occur in other groups. It seems then that an atomist account of loyalty that restricts loyalty merely to individuals and does not include loyalty to groups might be inadequate.

But once I have admitted that we can have loyalty to a group, do I not open myself up to criticism from the proponent of loyalty to the company? Might not the proponent of loyalty to business say: "Very well. I agree with you. The atomists are short-sighted. Groups have some sort of reality and they can be proper objects of loyalty. But companies are groups. Therefore companies are proper objects of loyalty."

The point seems well taken, except for the fact that the kinds of relationships that loyalty requires are just the kind that one does not find in business. As Ladd says, "The ties that bind the persons together provide the basis of loyalty." But all sorts of ties bind people together. I am a member of a group of fans if I go to a ball game. I am a member of a group if I merely walk down the street. What binds people together in a business is not sufficient to require loyalty.

A business or corporation does two things in the free enterprise system: It produces a good or service and it makes a profit. The making of a profit, however, is the primary function of a business as a business, for if the production of the good or service is not profitable, the business would be out of business. Thus nonprofitable goods or services are a means to an end. People bound together in a business are bound together not for mutual fulfillment and support, but to divide labor or make a profit. Thus, while we can jokingly refer to a family as a place where "they have to take you in no matter what," we cannot refer to a company in that way. If a worker does not produce in a company or if cheaper laborers are available, the company—in order to fulfill its purpose—should get rid of the worker. A company feels no obligation of loyalty. The saying "You can't buy loyalty" is true. Loyalty depends on ties that demand self-sacrifice with no expectation of reward. Business functions on the basis of enlightened self-interest. I am devoted to a company not because it is like a parent to me; it is not. Attempts of some companies to create "one big happy family" ought to be looked on with suspicion. I am not devoted to it at all, nor should I be. I work for it because it pays me. I am not in a family to get paid, I am in a company to get paid.

The cold hard truth is that the goal of profit is what gives birth to a company and forms that particular group. Money is what ties the group together. But in such a commercialized venture, with such a goal, there is no loyalty, or at least none need be expected. An employer will release an employee and an employee will walk away from an employer when it is profitable for either one to do so.

Not only is loyalty to a corporation not required, it more than likely is misguided. There is nothing as pathetic as the story of the loyal employee who, having given above and beyond the call of duty, is let go in the restructuring of the company. He feels betrayed because he mistakenly viewed the company as an object of his loyalty. Getting rid of such foolish romanticism and coming to grips with this hard but accurate assessment should ultimately benefit everyone.

To think we owe a company or corporation loyalty requires us to think of that company as a person or as a group with a goal of human fulfillment. If we think of it in this way we can be loyal. But this is the wrong way to think. A company is not a person. A company is an instrument, and an instrument with a specific purpose, the making of profit. To treat an instrument as an end in itself, like a person, may not be as bad as treating an end as an instrument, but it does give the instrument a moral status it does not deserve; and by elevating the instrument we lower the end. All things, instruments and ends, become alike.

Remember that Roche refers to the "management team" and Bok sees the name "whistleblowing" coming from the instance of a referee blowing a whistle in the presence of a foul. What is perceived as bad about whistleblowing in business from this perspective is that one blows the whistle on one's own team, thereby violating team loyalty. If the company can get its employees to view it as a team they belong to, it is easier to demand loyalty. Then the rules governing teamwork and team loyalty will apply. One reason the appeal to a team and team loyalty works so well in business is that businesses are in competition with one another. Effective motivation turns business practices into a game and instills teamwork.

But businesses differ from teams in very important respects, which makes the analogy between business and a team dangerous. Loyalty to a team is loyalty within the context of sport or a competition. Teamwork and team loyalty require that in the circumscribed activity of the game I cooperate with my fellow players, so that pulling all together, we may win. The object of (most) sports is victory. But winning in sports is a social convention, divorced from the usual goings on of society. Such a winning is most times a harmless, morally neutral diversion.

But the fact that this victory in sports, within the rules enforced by a referee (whistleblower), is a socially developed convention taking place within a larger social context makes it quite different from competition in business, which, rather than being defined by a context, permeates the whole of society in its influence. Competition leads not only to victory but to losers. One can lose at sport with precious few consequences. The consequences of losing at business are much larger. Further, the losers in business can be those who are not in the game voluntarily (we are all forced to participate) but who are still affected by business decisions. People cannot choose to participate in business. It permeates everyone's lives.

The team model, then, fits very well with the model of the free market system, because there competition is said to be the name of the game. Rival companies compete and their object is to win. To call a foul on one's own teammate is to jeopardize one's chances of winning and is viewed as disloyalty.

But isn't it time to stop viewing corporate machinations as games? These games are not controlled and are not ended after a specific time. The activities of business affect the lives of everyone, not just the game players. The analogy of the corporation to a team and the consequent appeal to team loyalty, although understandable, is seriously misleading, at least in the moral sphere where competition is not the prevailing virtue.

If my analysis is correct, the issue of the permissibility of whistleblowing is not a real issue since there is no obligation of loyalty to a company. Whistleblowing is not only permissible but expected when a company is harming society. The issue is not one of disloyalty to the company, but of whether the whistleblower has an obligation to society if blowing the whistle will bring him retaliation.

## NOTES


1. Maxwell Glen and Cody Shearer, "Going After the Whistle-blowers," *Philadelphia Inquirer*, Tuesday, August 2, 1983, Op-ed page, p. 11A.
2. James M. Roche, "The Competitive System, to Work, to Preserve, and to Protect," *Vital Speeches of the Day* (May 1971): 445.
3. Norman Bowie, *Business Ethics* (Englewood Cliffs, N.J.: Prentice Hall, 1982), pp. 140–143.
4. Sissela Bok, "Whistleblowing and Professional Responsibilities," *New York University Education Quarterly* 2 (1980): 3.
5. John Ladd, "Loyalty," *The Encyclopedia of Philosophy* 5: 97.
6. Ibid.


### LEGAL PERSPECTIVES

# *Warthen v. Toms River Community Memorial Hospital*

*Superior Court of New Jersey*

Plaintiff Corrine Warthen appeals from a summary judgment of the Law Division dismissing her action against defendant Toms River Community Memorial Hospital (Hospital). Plaintiff sought to recover damages for her allegedly wrongful discharge in violation of public policy following her refusal to dialyze a terminally ill double amputee patient because of her "moral, medical and philosophical objections" to performing the procedure.

The facts giving rise to this appeal are not in dispute and may be summarized as follows. The Hospital, where plaintiff had been employed for eleven years as a registered nurse, terminated plaintiff from its employment on August 6, 1982. For the three years just prior to her discharge, plaintiff had worked in the Hospital's kidney dialysis unit. It is undisputed that plaintiff was an at-will employee.

Plaintiff alleges that during the summer of 1982 her supervisor periodically assigned her to dialyze a double amputee patient who suffered from a number of maladies. On two occasions plaintiff claims that she had to cease treatment because the patient suffered cardiac arrest and severe internal hemorrhaging during the dialysis procedure. During the first week of 1982 plaintiff again was scheduled to dialyze this patient. She approached her head nurse and informed her that "she had moral, medical, and philosophical objections" to performing this procedure on the patient because the patient was terminally ill and, she contended, the procedure was causing the patient additional complications. At that time the head nurse granted plaintiff's request for reassignment.

On August 6, 1982, the head nurse again assigned plaintiff to dialyze the same patient. Plaintiff once again objected, apparently stating that she thought she had reached agreement with the head nurse not to be assigned to this particular patient. She also requested the opportunity to meet with the treating physician, Dr. DiBello. Dr. DiBello informed plaintiff that the patient's family wished him kept alive through dialysis and that he would not survive without it. However, plaintiff continued to refuse to dialyze the patient, and the head nurse informed her that if she did not agree to perform the treatment, the Hospital would dismiss her. Plaintiff refused to change her mind, and the Hospital terminated her.

488 A.2d 299 (1985). Opinion by Judge Michels.

Plaintiff subsequently instituted this action alleging that she was wrongfully discharged by the Hospital without justification and in violation of public policy. The Hospital denied liability to plaintiff and alleged, by way of a separate defense, that plaintiff's termination was appropriate because she had the status of an at-will employee. Following completion of pretrial discovery, the Hospital moved for summary judgement; which the trial court denied because it perceived "that there [was] . . . a question of fact as to whether or not there is a public policy as articulated in the nurses' code of ethics that would permit somebody in the nursing profession to refuse to participate in a course of treatment which is against her principles in good faith." However, upon reconsideration, the trial court granted the motion, concluding that "the nurses' code of ethics is a personal moral judgment and permits the nurse to have a personal moral judgement, but it does not rise to a public policy in the face of the general public policies that patients must be cared for in hospitals and patients must be treated basically by doctors and doctors' orders must be carried out." This appeal followed.

Plaintiff contends that the trial court erred in granting summary judgment because her refusal to dialyze the terminally ill patient was justified as a matter of law by her adherence to the *Code for Nurses*, a code of ethics promulgated by the American Nurses Association, and that determining whether adherence to the *Code* "constitutes a public policy question" is a question of fact which should be resolved by a jury, not by the trial court. We disagree. . . .

Plaintiff relies on the "public policy" exception to the "at-will employment" doctrine to justify her claim that defendant wrongfully discharged her. As has often been stated at common law, "in the absence of an employment contract, employers or employees have been free to terminate the employment relationship with or without cause." . . . Recently, in *Pierce v. Ortho Pharmaceutical Corp., supra*, the Supreme Court recognized a developing exception to the traditional "at-will employment" doctrine, holding that "an employee has a cause of action for wrongful discharge when the discharge is contrary to a clear mandate of public policy." . . .

As a preliminary matter plaintiff contends that identifying the "clear mandate of public policy" constitutes a genuine issue of material fact for the jury rather than, as occurred in the instant case, a threshold question for the trial judge. To support her contention plaintiff cites *Kalman v. Grand Union Co.*, . . . in which we said:

> It is the employee's burden to identify "a specific expression" or "a clear mandate" of public policy which might bar his discharge. [Citation omitted]. What constitutes a qualifying mandate is a fact question. . . .

However, quoting the following explanatory language from *Ortho Pharmaceutical*, we went on to emphasize that " the judiciary must define the cause of action in case-by-case determinations." . . .

In *Ortho Pharmaceutical* plaintiff, a physician and research scientist, was dismissed because of her opposition to continued laboratory research, development and testing of the drug loperamide, which Ortho intended to market for the treatment of diarrhea. The plaintiff was opposed to the drug because it contained saccharin and because she believed that by continuing work on loperamide she would violate her interpretation of the Hippocratic oath. The Court held, *as a matter of law*, that where plaintiff merely contended saccharin was controversial, not dangerous, and the FDA had not yet approved human testing of loperamide, the Hippocratic oath did not contain a clear mandate of public policy preventing the physician from continuing research. Then, not finding any issue of material fact, the Supreme Court remanded the case to the trial court for the entry of summary judgment.

Thus, identifying the mandate of public policy is a question of law, analogous to interpreting a statute or defining a duty in a negligence case. . . . As the Chancery Court said in *Schaffer v. Federal Trust Co.*, . . .

> "Public policy has been defined as that principle of law which holds that no person can lawfully do that which has a tendency to be injurious to the public, or against the public good." . . . The term admits of no exact definition. . . . The source of public policy is the statutes enacted by the legislature and in the decisions of the courts; there we find what acts are considered harmful to the public and therefore unlawful.
>
> Public policy is not concerned with minutiae, but with principles. Seldom does a single clause of a statute establish public policy; policy is discovered from study of the whole statute, or even a group of statutes *in pari materia*. . . .

Based on the foregoing, we hold that where a discharged at-will employee asserts wrongful discharge on public policy grounds, the trial court must, as a matter of law, determine whether public policy justified the alleged conduct. Then, assuming the pleadings raise a genuine issue of material fact, it is for the jury to determine the truth of the employee's allegations. Here, therefore, the issue of whether the *Code for Nurses* represented a clear expression of public policy did not present a genuine issue of material fact precluding the entry of summary judgment.

Plaintiff next contends that, as a matter of law, the *Code for Nurses* constitutes an authoritative statement of public policy which justified her conduct and that the trial court therefore improperly granted defendant's motion for summary judgment. In *Ortho Pharmaceutical* the Supreme Court discussed the role of professional codes of ethics as sources of public policy in "at-will employment" cases:

> In certain instances, a professional code of ethics may contain an expression of public policy. However, not all such sources express a clear mandate of public policy. For example, a code of ethics designed to serve only the interests of a profession or an administrative regulation concerned with technical matters probably would not be sufficient. Absent legislation, the judiciary must define the cause of action in case-by-case determinations. An employer's right to discharge an employee at will carries a correlative duty not to discharge an employee who declines to perform an act that would require a violation of a clear mandate of public policy. However, unless an employee at will identifies a specific expression of public policy, he may be discharged with or without cause. . . .

The Court carefully warned against confusing reliance on professional ethics with reliance on personal morals:

> Employees who are professionals owe a special duty to abide not only by federal and state law, but also by the recognized codes of ethics of their professions. That duty may oblige them to decline to perform acts required by their employers. However, an employee should not have the right to prevent his or her employer from pursuing its business because the employee perceives that a particular business decision violates the employee's personal morals, as distinguished from the recognized code of ethics of the employee's profession. . . .

The burden is on the professional to identify "a specific expression" or "a clear mandate" of public policy which might bar his or her dismissal. . . .

Here, plaintiff cites the *Code for Nurses* to justify her refusal to dialyze the terminally ill patient. She refers specifically to the following provisions and interpretive statement:

> THE NURSE PROVIDES SERVICES WITH RESPECT FOR HUMAN DIGNITY AND THE UNIQUENESS OF THE CLIENT UNRESTRICTED BY CONSIDERATIONS OF SOCIAL OR ECONOMIC STATUS, PERSONAL ATTRIBUTES, OR THE NATURE OF HEALTH PROBLEMS.
>
> 1.4 THE NATURE OF HEALTH PROBLEMS
>
> The nurse's concern for human dignity and the provision of quality nursing care is not limited by personal attitudes or beliefs. If personally opposed to the delivery of care in a particular case because of the nature of the health problem or the procedures to be used, the nurse is justified in refusing to participate. Such refusal should be made known in advance and in time for other appropriate arrangements to be made for the client's nursing care. If the nurse must knowingly enter such a case under emergency circumstances or enters unknowingly, the obligation to provide the best possible care is observed. The nurse withdraws from this type of

> situation only when assured that alternative sources of nursing care are available to the client. If a client requests information or counsel in an area that is legally sanctioned but contrary to the nurse's personal beliefs, the nurse may refuse to provide these services but must advise the client of sources where such service is available. [American Nurses Association, *Code for Nurses with Interpretive Statements*. . . .

Plaintiff contends that these provisions constitute a clear mandate of public policy justifying her conduct. . . .

It is our view that as applied to the circumstances of this case the passage cited by plaintiff defines a standard of conduct beneficial only to the individual nurse and not to the public at large. The overall purpose of the language cited by plaintiff is to preserve human dignity; however, it should not be at the expense of the patient's life or contrary to the family's wishes. The record before us shows that the family had requested that dialysis be continued on the patient, and there is nothing to suggest that the patient had, or would have, indicated otherwise. . . .

Recently, in *In re Conroy, supra*, our Supreme Court confirmed this State's basic interest in the preservation of life, . . . and our recognition, embraced in the right to self-determination, that all patients have a fundamental right to expect that medical treatment will not be terminated against their will. . . . This basic policy mandate clearly outweighs any policy favoring the right of a nurse to refuse to participate in treatments which he or she personally believes threatens human dignity. Indeed, the following passage from the *Code for Nurses* echoes the policy cited by *Conroy* and severely constrains the ethical right of nurses to refuse participation in medical procedures:

> 1.4 THE NATURE OF HEALTH PROBLEMS
>
> The nurse's respect for the worth and dignity of the individual human being applies irrespective of the nature of the health problem. It is reflected in the care given the person who is disabled as well as the normal; the patient with the long-term illness as well as the one with the acute illness, or the recovering patient as well as the one who is terminally ill or dying. It extends to all who require the services of the nurse for the promotion of health, the prevention of illness, the restoration of health, and the alleviation of suffering. [American Nurses Association, *Code for Nurses with Interpretive Statements*. . . .

The position asserted by plaintiff serves only the individual and the nurses' profession while leaving the public to wonder when and whether they will receive nursing care. . . . Moreover, as the Hospital argues, "[i]t would be a virtual impossibility to administer a hospital if each nurse or member of the administration staff refused to carry out his or her duties based upon a personal private belief concerning the right to live. . . ."

Concededly, plaintiff had to make a difficult decision. Viewing the facts in a light most beneficial to plaintiff, she had dialyzed the particular patient on several occasions in the past, and on two of those occasions plaintiff says the patient had suffered cardiac arrest and severe internal hemorrhaging during the dialysis procedure. The first time plaintiff objected to performing the procedure her head nurse agreed to reassign her, and at that time plaintiff apparently believed she had an agreement with the head nurse not to be assigned to this particular patient. She also believed she had fulfilled her ethical obligation by making her refusal to participate in the procedure "known in advance and in time for other appropriate arrangements to be made for the client's nursing care."

Nonetheless, we conclude as a matter of law that even under the circumstances of this case the ethical considerations cited by plaintiff do not rise to the level of a public policy mandate permitting a registered nursing professional to refuse to provide medical treatment to a terminally ill patient, even where that nursing professional gives his or her superiors advance warning. Beyond this, even if we were to make the dubious assumption that the *Code for Nurses* represents a clear expression of public policy, we have no hesitancy in concluding on this record that plaintiff was motivated by her own personal morals, precluding application of the "public policy" exception to the "at-will employment" doctrine. Plaintiff alleged that each time she refused to dialyze the patient she told the head nurse that she had "moral, medical and philosophical objections" to performing the procedure. She makes no assertion that she ever referred to her obligations and entitlements pursuant to her code of ethics. In addition, the very basis for plaintiffs reliance on the *Code for Nurses* is that she was personally opposed to the dialysis procedure. By refusing to perform the procedure she may have eased her own conscience, but she neither benefited the society-at-large, the patient, nor the patient's family.

Accordingly, the judgment under review is affirmed.

# *Potter v. Village Bank of New Jersey*

*Superior Court of New Jersey*

The crucial question raised in this appeal is whether a bank president and chief executive officer who blows the whistle on suspected laundering of Panamanian drug money is protected from retaliatory discharge by the public policy of this State. We answer in the affirmative. We also hold that the retaliatory discharge in this case constituted an intentional tort which exposed defendants to compensatory and punitive damages. We affirm the judgment.

## A

Plaintiff Dale G. Potter became the president and chief executive officer of the Village Bank of New Jersey (Village Bank) on November 15, 1982. His employment was terminated in May or June 1984. On June 13, 1984 plaintiff filed a complaint in the Chancery Division against Village Bank alleging that his job had been wrongfully terminated. Plaintiff sought reinstatement to his position as chief executive officer and president of the bank. . . .

After the matter was transferred to the Law Division, plaintiff filed an amended complaint. . . . In the four-count amended complaint plaintiff sought compensatory and punitive damages based on (1) fraudulent inducement, (2) breach of contract, (3) tortious interference with the employment relationship and (4) wrongful termination.

The case was tried to a jury over a four-day period. . . . At the end of plaintiff's case, the trial judge granted defendants' motion for involuntary dismissal of plaintiff's claims of fraudulent inducement, breach of contract and wrongful interference with the employment relationship. The only remaining claim was for wrongful discharge. . . .

The claim of wrongful discharge was submitted to the jury as to the remaining defendants, Village Bank and Em Kay. The jury answered the following special interrogatories:

> Q1. Did the Defendants wrongfully discharge the plaintiff?
> A. Yes.
> Q2. Was the plaintiff damaged by such wrongful discharge?
> A. Yes.
> Q3. What amount of compensatory damages, if any, should the plaintiff be awarded for such wrongful discharge?
> A. $50,000.
> Q4. What amount of punitive damages, if any, should the plaintiff be awarded for such wrongful discharge?
> A. $100,000.

543 A.2d 80 (1985). Opinion by Judge J.H. Coleman.

After the trial judge denied defendants' motion for judgment notwithstanding the verdict, final judgment was entered in the sum of $162,575.40, which consisted of $100,000 in punitive damages, $50,000 in compensatory damages plus $12,575.40 in prejudgment interest on the compensatory damages.

Village Bank and Em Kay Holding Corporation have appealed from the entire judgment. Plaintiff has cross-appealed from the involuntary dismissals at the end of plaintiff's evidence.

The pivotal issue presented to the jury was whether plaintiff resigned or was discharged in violation of a clear mandate of public policy. Based on the evidence presented, the jury concluded he was fired contrary to a clear mandate of public policy. The following evidence supports that finding. Em Kay Holding Corporation (Em Kay) owns 93% of the stock of Village Bank. The remaining 7% is distributed among other shareholders. Em Kay is owned by the Em Kay Group which has its headquarters in Panama City, Panama. Em Kay Group is owned by Mory Kraselnick and Moises Kroitoro.

Bart and Kraselnick negotiated with plaintiff for employment at Village Bank. In September 1982 when the president of Village Bank suffered a heart attack, plaintiff was offered and accepted a position with the bank as a "holding company consultant." Plaintiff became president and chief executive officer of Village Bank two months later. Between then and January 1983, Kraselnick frequently telephoned plaintiff to request that Village Bank make large loans to companies that did business with Kraselnick and companies owned by Kraselnick. With few exceptions, plaintiff refused these requests.

After a January 21, 1983 meeting Kraselnick told plaintiff: "[I]f I ever ask you to do anything wrong, I'll stand up in front of you." At the time, plaintiff did not understand the meaning of the statement. Over the next couple of months, however, many cash deposits of between $8,000 and $9,300 were made into the accounts of Kraselnick, Bart, Noel Kinkella (office manager of Em Kay Equities whose president was Bart) and several of the companies in the Em Kay Group.

On March 24, 1983 plaintiff learned that Village Bank was advertising his job in the *Wall Street Journal*. When plaintiff confronted Kraselnick about this, he was told "You're not as outspoken and enthusiastic as I want you to be when you meet me." After plaintiff defended his position, the two temporarily reconciled.

On March 31, 1983 Kinkella went to Village Bank with a shopping bag filled with money. She made seven $9,000 deposits to accounts held by Kraselnick, Bart, Kinkella and four Em Kay related companies. Plaintiff became suspicious that drug money was being laundered so he called the New Jersey Commissioner of Banking and reported the transactions and requested advice. Before plaintiff could meet with the Commissioner, Kinkella deposited another package of about $50,000 in cash. When plaintiff asked Bart about the money, Bart told him that it was for lease payments between two related aeronautical companies in the Em Kay Group. Plaintiff became more suspicious that the large cash deposits were related to laundering of Panamanian drug money. When the Commissioner eventually met with plaintiff, he told plaintiff to maintain anonymity and that a full investigation would be undertaken. The jury was not informed about the details of plaintiff's suspicions.

Audits of the bank were conducted starting around the end of April or the beginning of May 1983. On June 28, 1983 plaintiff advised Village Bank's board of directors of the examination, but not of his meeting with the Commissioner. In July 1983 plaintiff filed currency transaction reports with the Department of the Treasury reporting the cash deposits.

In September 1983 Village Bank's board of directors raised plaintiff's salary from $65,000 to $75,000. Kraselnick also offered plaintiff a $10,000 bonus in cash so he "wouldn't pay income taxes" on it. When plaintiff refused to accept the bonus in cash, the bonus was not paid. In December 1983 the United States Attorney's Office for

New Jersey issued subpoenas to the bank for the production of documents "on a list of accounts" related to the Em Kay Group. Plaintiff was also interviewed by representatives from that office.

On January 6, 1984 plaintiff executed his first written employment contract with Village Bank. The term was for one year beginning November 15, 1983. The contract provided for a base salary of $75,000, with a bonus at the discretion of the board of directors.

At some time between July and December 1983, plaintiff told Steven S. Radin, secretary to the Village Bank board of directors, that he "had gone to the Commissioner and reported the [cash] transactions." In January 1984 Radin informed Bart and Kraselnick of what plaintiff had told him. This angered Kraselnick. At the next scheduled board meeting, the directors were informed.

Immediately after the board meeting, Kraselnick asked plaintiff why he went to the Commissioner of Banking. When plaintiff responded "I thought that it was drug money," Kraselnick stated "you're probably right." From that point on, plaintiff contended that he was isolated from running the bank effectively since his subordinates in the bank were ordered not to talk to him. Further, there were several instances where Kraselnick questioned plaintiff's judgment and accused him of doing things incorrectly.

Plaintiff testified that Radin and at least two of Village Bank's directors advised him that he was about to be fired before plaintiff wrote a letter on May 22, 1984. The letter was written to Kraselnick which stated in pertinent part:

> I wanted to be able to communicate directly with you and since my requests for a face to face meeting with you have been rejected, I am using this as my only recourse. At this point in time, I am considering myself "de facto" fired since Allan Bart has told several directors and John Bjerke, among others, that "Potter's gone" and in turn at least one director has communicated the same to several customers who have even discussed it with people in the Bank including myself. Needless to say, the lack of discretion in discussing this situation in this way can only serve to hurt the Bank and the people in it. However, it has been done and the effect of it, in my opinion, has been that I consider myself at this point in time essentially to be terminated only without the prerequisite action of the Board of Directors.

Shortly after the letter was written, plaintiff told members attending a board meeting that the letter was not intended as a letter of resignation. He reiterated this point in a May 31, 1984 letter to Radin.

By letter dated June 1, 1984, Radin notified plaintiff that

> . . . it was the consensus of the Board that the Bank pay you full salary until the termination (November 15, 1984) of your present contract. During that period of time you would have the use of a car, office and secretarial assistance. Also you would receive all ordinary employee benefits. In consideration of these severance terms the Board requested a general release from you for the Bank, its directors and officers. The Board gave you until June 1, 1984 to accept or reject this offer. From May 24, 1984 until June 1, 1984 you were placed on leave of absence with pay.

Plaintiff rejected the proposal made by the board. When plaintiff attempted to attend a June 11 board meeting with his attorney, the board asked him to leave the bank. . . .

## B

Subsequent to the trial in this matter Kraselnick, Bart, Bjerke and Village Bank were indicted by a federal grand jury for the District of New Jersey for allegedly conspiring to defraud the United States and making fraudulent statements in violation of 31 *U.S.C.* § 5311 *et seq.*, 31 *C.F.R.* § 103.22 *et seq.*, and 18 *U.S.C.* §§ 371, 1001 and 1002. The alleged criminal violations are based on their failure to report large cash transactions at Village Bank during the time Potter was president and chief executive officer.

31 *U.S.C.* § 5313(a) provides, in pertinent part:

> (a) When a domestic financial institution is involved in a transaction for the . . . receipt . . . of United States coins or currency (or other mon-

> etary instruments the Secretary of the Treasury prescribes), in an amount, denomination, or amount and denomination, or under circumstances the Secretary prescribes by regulation, the institution and any other participant in the transaction the Secretary may prescribes shall file a report on the transaction at the time and in the way the Secretary prescribes. A participant acting for another person shall make the report as the agent or bailee of the person and identify the person for whom the transaction is being made.

Pursuant to this authority, the Secretary of the Treasury promulgated regulations which mandate the reporting of transactions in currency of more than $10,000.

Because the deposits in this case were slightly less than $10,000, plaintiff was not required by the strict wording of the statute and regulations to report the cash transactions. However, there is existing authority holding that a bank officer may not structure a single transaction in currency as multiple transactions to avoid the reporting requirements. A financial institution must aggregate all transactions by one customer in one day.

. . . Potter did much more than "protest [] [the] directors' improprieties" relating to a regulatory scheme. He blew the whistle on suspected criminal conduct involving one or more directors. Hence, Potter's termination relates to the public policy designed to encourage citizens to report suspected criminal violations to the proper authorities in order to ensure proper enforcement of both state and federal penal laws. . . . Nowhere in our society is the need for protection greater than in protecting well motivated citizens who blow the whistle on suspected white collar and street level criminal activities. If "no person can lawfully do that which has a tendency to be injurious to the public or against the public good" because of public policy, *Allen v. Commercial Casualty Insurance Co.*, . . . surely whistle blowers of suspected criminal violations must be protected from retaliatory discharge. It stands to reason that few people would cooperate with law enforcement officials if the price they must pay is retaliatory discharge from employment. Clearly, that would have a chilling effect on criminal investigations and law enforcement in general.

Additionally, after the plaintiff's employment was terminated, the Legislature enacted the Conscientious Employee Protection Act, . . . effective September 5, 1986. Under the act, an employee who has been terminated because of reporting suspected criminal violations, has the right to file a retaliatory tort claim in addition to other remedies. We read this legislative enactment as a codification of public policy established through judicial decisions. . . .

We hold that the public policy of the State of New Jersey should protect at will employees—including bank presidents—who in good faith blow the whistle on one or more bank directors suspected of laundering money from illegal activities. . . .

## C

We hold that an at will employee who has sustained a retaliatory discharge in violation of a clear mandate of public policy is entitled to recover economic and noneconomic losses. Such an employee may recover (1) the amount he or she would have earned from the time of wrongful discharge for a reasonable time until he or she finds new employment, including bonuses and vacation pay, less any unemployment compensation received in the interim, . . . (2) expenses associated with finding new employment and mental anguish or emotional distress damages proximately related to the retaliatory discharge, . . . and (3) the replacement value of fringe benefits such as an automobile and insurance for a reasonable time until new employment is obtained. . . .

The jury awarded $50,000 in compensatory damages. In addition, the jury awarded $100,000 in punitive damages. We are completely satisfied that both the compensatory and punitive damages awarded are supported by sufficient credible evidence and were consonant with the law. . . .

## CASES

# CASE 1. *The Reluctant Security Guard*

David Tuff, 24, is a security guard who has been working for the past 17 months for the Blue Mountain Company in Minneapolis, Minnesota. Blue Mountain manages and operates retail shopping malls in several midwestern states. The company has a security services division that trains and supplies mall security guards, including those for the Village Square Mall where Tuff has been employed.

Minnesota state and local laws require that security officers be licensed and approved by the county police department. Security officers are required to obey the police unit's rules. Tuff completed the required training, passed the security guard compulsory examination, and was issued a license. Tuff has consistently carried out his guard duties conscientiously. Previously a four-year military policeman in the U.S. Marine Corps. his commanding officer had praised both his service and his integrity.

Part of his job training at Blue Mountain required that Tuff learn the procedures found in the *Security Officer's Manual*, which uses military regulations as a model. Two sections of this manual are worded as follows:

> **Section V, subsection D.**
> Should a serious accident or crime, including all felonies, occur on the premises of the licensee, it shall be the responsibility of the licensee to notify the appropriate police department immediately. Failure to do so is a violation of the provisions of this manual.

Furthermore, the manual permits the following action if the provisions are violated:

> **Section XI—disciplinary and deportment**
> **A. General**
> 1. The Private Security Coordinator may reprimand a licensee as hereinafter provided. In cases of suspension or revocation, the licensee shall immediately surrender his identification card and badge to the County Police Department. . . .
> **B. Cause for Disciplinary Action**
> 13. Any violation of any regulation or rule found in this manual is cause for disciplinary action.

The reverse side of a security officer's license bears these statements:

> Obey The Rules and Regulations Promulgated By The Superintendent Of Police.
> We will obey all lawful orders and rules and regulations pertaining to security officers promulgated by the superintendent of police of the country or any officer placed by him over me.

Given this language, Tuff believed that his license could be revoked or suspended for *any* failure to report illegal behavior such as drunk driving and selling narcotics. He had sworn to uphold these regulations at the end of his training and had later signed a statement acknowledging that he knew a police officer could ask for his badge if a conflict should arise.

Fourteen months after Tuff joined the company, Blue Mountain issued new rules of procedure outlining certain assigned duties of its security guards. These rules required security officers "to order and escort intoxicated persons, including persons driving under the influence of alcohol, off its parking lots and onto the public roads." The rules did not instruct

From Anna Pinedo and Tom L. Beauchamp, "The Reluctant Security Guard." *Case Studies in Business, Society and Ethics*, edited by Tom L. Beauchamp, Prentice Hall, Upper Saddle River, NJ. 1998. Reprinted with permission.

security officers to either arrest the drivers or to contact or alert the police.

Tuff immediately, and publicly, opposed the company's new policy. Over the ensuing months, he expressed his dissatisfaction to every company officer he could locate. He complained to his immediate superiors, sometimes several times a day, that he was being asked to set a drunk out on the road who might later kill an innocent person. Tuff described to these supervisors imagined scenarios in which a drunk clearly violated the law, and he then asked them what he would be expected to do in these circumstances under the new rules.

His immediate supervisor, Director of Security Manuel Hernandez, told him that if any such situation arose he should contact the supervisor in charge, who would make the decision. Hernandez noted that most drunks do not weave down the road and hit someone. Tuff was not satisfied and used abusive language in denouncing the rules. Hernandez became angry and told Tuff that his complaints irritated his supervisors and that they could tolerate only so much of his behavior. Hernandez also cautioned him that he should worry less about his license and more about his paycheck. Neither man put any complaint in writing. Tuff never received a written warning or reprimand from any company official. Tuff maintained that he considered the policy to be illegal, violative of the rules he had sworn to uphold, and dangerous to the maintenance of his license. Neither his supervisor nor the company manager agreed with his interpretation. They encouraged him to continue his job as usual, but under the new rules.

Tuff then contacted a volunteer organization working to prevent drunk driving. At first he simply sought the organization's interpretation of the law, but later, he voiced a specific complaint about the Blue Mountain policy. His supervisors were approached by some representatives of the volunteer organization, who expressed strong opposition to Blue Mountain's policy for security guards and treatment of drunk drivers.

In the following weeks, Tuff discussed the company policy with several other concerned security guards. He met with security officers Fred Grant and Robert Ladd at a restaurant after work. They discussed the company procedure and its conflict with their licensing requirements and sworn commitments. They considered going to the local newspaper with their grievances against the company policy.

Tuff then contacted a local television news station and a local newspaper. He talked to four reporters about several drunk driving incidents at Blue Mountain parking lots. The reporters pursued Tuff's complaint by talking to company officials about the policy. The reporters proved to their editors' satisfaction that Tuff's complaints to the media were not given in reckless disregard of the truth and were, in fact, entirely truthful.

Hernandez called Tuff into his office to discuss these disclosures to the newspaper. Hernandez asked Tuff to sign a document acknowledging that he had spoken with news reporters concerning Blue Mountain company policies, but he refused to sign. Hernandez reminded him of a company policy prohibiting an employee from talking to the media about company policies. This policy is mentioned on a list of company rules distributed to all employees that states that violation of the rules could result in dismissal or in disciplinary procedures. Tuff knew the company rule but did not consider his revelations a violation, because he had not spoken with the press *on company time.*

Hernandez considered Tuff's interpretation of the rule's scope ridiculous. He consulted with the company's Council of Managers that afternoon. Every manager agreed that Tuff's interpretation of the rule showed a blatant disregard for company policy and that Tuff's excuse was an ad hoc rationalization. They also agreed that Tuff had shown himself to be a complainer and a man of poor judgment, qualities that rendered him unsuitable to be a Blue Mountain security guard. The discussion of this problem at the meeting took little more than five minutes. Council members instructed Hernandez to give Tuff a few days' leave to reflect on the situation. Hernandez duly reported this conclusion to Tuff, who then departed for his home. The number of days of leave he should take was not specified, but both men agreed in an amicable though tense setting that they would be in touch.

Three days later an article about the company's policies appeared in the local newspaper, along with a picture of Tuff in the mall, about to report for work. This story prompted an editorial that was critical of the company on a local television station. The story relied entirely on data provided by Tuff, some of which had been copied from his nightly shift reports.

The newspaper had also interviewed Sergeant Shriver of the county police department. He corraborated Tuff's interpretation that any failure by a security guard to report those driving while intoxicated or those under the influence of drugs constituted a violation of the security manual and the specific terms of the officer's license. He also confirmed Tuff's statement that police officers routinely inspect security officers' activities and that the police have instructions to look for failures to comply with license requirements.

After the television editorial, Blue Mountain began to receive phone calls at a rate of approximately 15 per hour, with over 90 percent of the callers expressing opposition to the company's policies. Several callers indicated that they would no longer patronize the malls mentioned in the newspaper story.

The Council of Managers immediately reconvened to consider this escalation of the problem. Its members agreed that Tuff had to be fired for his violation of the company rule against disclosures to the news media. The managers considered Tuff's revelations an unforgivable act of disloyalty. They discussed whether the proper and precise reason for Tuff's dismissal was his disclosure of confidential information or his approaching the media. Their decision on this point required a sharpening of a vaguely worded corporate rule; a careful process of interpretation revealed that approaching the media is grounds for dismissal even if no disclosure of confidential information is made.

Five working days later, Tuff was called into the company manager's office and dismissed. The manager informed him that the reason for this dismissal was his discussions with the press, a violation of company policy.

Tuff then issued a public statement. He explained that his complaints against Blue Mountain Company's procedures had stemmed from his concern to protect the public and other security officers. Tuff had discussed the policy with the company's other security guards, who had all expressed some degree of concern over the policy because it forced them to violate their licensing requirements and subjected them to possible license suspension or revocation. Based on these encounters, Tuff believed that he was acting on their behalf as well as on his own.

Tuff also disclosed a legal argument he wanted to pursue: He contended that his admissions to the media and his complaints about company policy were protected activities. The company interfered with, restrained, and coerced its employees in the exercise of their rights, as protected by the National Labor Relations Act of 1935, by suspending and eventually dismissing Tuff for his disclosures to the press, which violated company policy.

Tuff brought his case to the National Labor Relations Board (NLRB), whose members determined that Blue Mountain was within its legal rights to fire him. The board found that whistleblowers are legally protected only if they engage in "concerted activity" together with their fellow workers, Because Tuff had acted alone for the most part, he was not protected. However, a NLRB spokesperson said the board made no moral judgment on either the employer's or the employee's conduct. The parties' moral behavior, he said, was not at stake in the NLRB decision.

### Questions

1. Was the security guard right to take the action he did? Would you have taken the same action? Why or why not?
2. Is this a case of an unjust dismissal?
3. Should there be a law to protect employees from losing their jobs for this kind of activity?
4. Think of some creative ways other than dismissal to handle this situation.

## CASE 2. *A Matter of Principle*

Nancy Smith was hired May 1, 1988, as the associate director of Medical Research at a major pharmaceutical company. The terms of Ms. Smith's employment were not fixed by contract, and as a result she is considered to be an "at-will" employee. Two years later Ms. Smith was promoted to Director of Medical Research Therapeutics, a section that studied nonreproductive drugs.

One of the company's research projects involved the development of loperamide—a liquid treatment for acute and chronic diarrhea to be used by infants, children, and older persons who were unable to take solid medication. The formula contained saccharin in an amount that was 44 times higher than that the Food and Drug Administration permitted in 12 ounces of an artificially sweetened soft drink. There are, however, no promulgated standards for the use of saccharin in drugs.

The research project team responsible for the development of loperamide unanimously agreed that because of the high saccharin content, the existing formula loperamide was unsuitable for distribution in the United States (apparently the formula was already being distributed in Europe). The team estimated that the development of an alternative formula would take at least three months.

The pharmaceutical's management pressured the team to proceed with the existing formula, and the research project team finally agreed. Nancy Smith maintained her opposition to the high saccharin formula and indicated that the Hippocratic Oath prevented her from giving the formula to old people and children. Nancy Smith was the only medical person on the team, and the grounds for her decision was that saccharin was a possible carcinogen. Therefore Nancy Smith was unable to participate in the clinical testing.

Upon learning that she was unwilling to participate in the clinical testing, the management removed her from the project and gave her a demotion. Her demotion was posted, and she was told that management considered her unpromotable. She was charged specifically with being irresponsible, lacking in good judgment, unproductive, and uncooperative with marketing. Nancy Smith had never been criticized by supervisors before. Nancy Smith resigned because she believed she was being punished for refusing to pursue a task she thought unethical.

This case was prepared by Norman E. Bowie on the basis of the appeal decision in *Pierce v. Ortho Pharmaceutical Corporation*, Superior Court of New Jersey, 1979.

### Questions

1. Was Nancy Smith terminated, or did she resign voluntarily?
2. Should the pharmaceutical's management have the right to terminate Nancy Smith if she refused to participate in the clinical testing?
3. Under the circumstances of her "resignation," should she have the right to sue for reinstatement to her position as Director of Medical Research Therapeutics?
4. If you were the judge in such a court case, how would you rule and on what grounds?

## CASE 3. *Health and Genetic Screening*

During the past decade, biologists have made significant strides in the field of genetics. Media attention has focused on gene splicing, the creation of new forms of life, and the increase in the quality, size, and disease resistance of agricultural products.

However, this new technology is also enabling biologists to delve into complex genetic information. Soon DNA tests will be able to provide full physical and mental profiles of human beings. Apart from the issues that such testing will present for parents-to-be, complexities could develop in the workplace as well.

The Office of Technology Assessment of the House Committee on Science and Technology surveyed the five hundred largest U.S. industrial companies, fifty private utilities, and eleven unions and found that seventeen had used genetic testing to screen employees for the sickle-cell trait or enzyme deficiencies.

Genetic screening also could reveal an individual's tolerance for or susceptibility to chemicals used in the workplace. With health insurance costs increasing exponentially, employers are trying to improve employee health with routine medical screening, creation of smoke-free environments, and drug testing. Genetic profile tests could be used to hire only those individuals who meet certain minimum health requirements and are thus likely to keep health insurance costs down.

Insurers have used AIDS screening as a prerequisite for medical insurance coverage; similarly, genetic tests could predict susceptibility to heart disease and cancer. Genetic tests allow insurers to screen applicants and either deny coverage or create high-risk pools for those in high risk groups.

Scientist Robert Weinberg has stated:

> A belief that each of us is ultimately responsible for our own behavior has woven our social fabric. Yet in the coming years, we will hear more and more from those who write off bad behavior to the inexorable forces of biology and who embrace a new astrology in which alleles rather than stars determine individuals' lives. It is hard to imagine how far this growing abdication of responsibility will carry us.
>
> As a biologist, I find this prospect a bitter pill. The biological revolution of the past decades has proven extraordinarily exciting and endlessly fascinating, and it will, without doubt, spawn enormous benefit. But as with most new technologies, we will pay a price unless we anticipate the human genome project's dark side. We need to craft an ethic that cherishes our human ability to transcend biology, that enshrines our spontaneity, unpredictability, and individual uniqueness. At the moment, I find myself and those around me ill equipped to respond to the challenge.[1]

Starting in 1972, DuPont screened its black employees for sickle-cell anemia, which affects one in every four to six hundred black Americans. Requested by the Black DuPont Employees

Association to perform the genetic screening. DuPont administered the voluntary test not to deny jobs, but to offer employees relocation to chemical-free areas where the disease would not be triggered.

Critics of DuPont said the testing allowed the company to transfer workers rather than clean up its work environment. DuPont's medical director responded,

> This is a very naive view. No one can operate at zero emissions, exposures—zero anything. There has to be an agreed-upon practical, safe limit. But there are some employees who are more susceptible to certain diseases than others. It's only common sense to offer them the opportunity to relocate.[2]

In the 1960s, certain workers at an Israeli dynamite factory became ill with acute hemolytic anemia, which causes the walls of the red blood cells to dissolve, thus decreasing the cells' ability to circulate oxygen throughout the body. The workers were transferred to other parts of the plant, but genetic screening revealed that all of them had a G-6-PD deficiency, which causes hemolytic anemia upon exposure to chemicals. The information allowed the factory to place workers properly and led it to reduce chemical levels in the plant.[3]

## Questions

1. What impact does genetic screening have on an employee's privacy?
2. In what ways should employers regard genetic screening as necessary?
3. Discuss how genetic screening might lead to discrimination.
4. Will genetic screening help employers increase safety in the workplace?

## NOTES

1. Robert Weinberg, "Genetic Screening," *Technology Review* (April 1991): 51.
2. William P. Patterson, "Genetic Screening," *Industry Week* (1 June, 1987): 48.
3. Thomas H. Murray, "Genetic Testing at Work: How Should It Be Used?" *Personnel Administrator* (September 1985): 90–92.

## *Suggested Supplementary Readings*

ADLER G. STONEY, "Ethical Issues in Electronic Performance Monitoring" *Journal of Business Ethics* (1998) 17, 729–43.

ALDERMAN, ELLEN, and CAROLINE KENNEDY. *The Right to Privacy.* New York: Alfred A. Knopf, 1995.

ARVEY, RICHARD D., and GARY L. RENZ. "Fairness in the Selection of Employees." *Journal of Business Ethics* (May 1992): 331–40.

BRENKERT, GEORGE. "Freedom, Participation and Corporations: The Issue of Corporate (Economic) Democracy." *Business Ethics Quarterly,* 2 (July 1992): 251–69.

BRENKERT, GEORGE. "Privacy, Polygraphs, and Work." *Business Professional Ethics Journal,* 1 (Fall 1981): 19–34.

BROCKETT, PATRICK L., and SUSANE E. TANKERSLEY, "The Genetics Revolution, Economics, Ethics, and Insurance." *Journal of Business Ethics,* 16 (1997), 1661–76.

DALTON, DAN R., and MICHAEL B. METZGER. "Integrity Testing' for Personnel Selection: An Unsparing Perspective." *Journal of Business Ethics,* 12 (February 1993): 147–56

DANDEKAR, NATALIE. "Can Whistleblowing Be FULLY Legitimated?" *Business and Professional Ethics Journal,* 10 (Spring 1991): 89–108.

DECEW, JUDITH WAGNER. In Pursuit of Privacy. Ithaca: Cornell University Press, 1997.

DE GEORGE, RICHARD. "The Right to Work: Law and Ideology." *Valparaiso University Law Review,* 19 (Fall 1984): 15–35.

DESJARDINS, JOSEPH R., and JOHN J. MCCALL. "A Defense of Employee Rights." *Journal of Business Ethics* 4 (October 1985): 367–76.

ETZIONI, AMITAI. *The Limits of Privacy.* New York: Basic Books, 1999.

EWIN, R. E. "Corporate Loyalty: Its Objects and Its Grounds." *Journal of Business Ethics* 12 (May 1993): 387–96.

EWING, DAVID W. *Freedom Inside the Organization: Bringing Civil Liberties to the Workplace.* New York: E. P. Dutton, 1977.

EZORSKY, GERTRUDE, ed. *Moral Rights in the Workplace.* Albany, N.Y.: State University of New York Press, 1987.

FIELDER, JOHN H. "Organizational Loyalty." *Business and Professional Ethics Journal* 11 (Spring 1992): 71–90.

GLAZER, M. P., and P. M. GLAZER. *The Whistle Blowers: Exposing Corruption in Government and Industry.* New York: Basic Books, 1989.

HANSON, KAREN. "The Demands of Loyalty." *Idealistic Studies* 16 (April 1986): 195–204.

HAUGHEY, JOHN C. "Does Loyalty In the Workplace Have a Future?" *Journal of Business Ethics* 3 (January 1993): 1–16.

HIRSCHMAN, ALBERT. *Exit, Voice and Loyalty.* Cambridge, MA: Harvard University Press, 1970.

HUBBARD, RUTH, and ELIJAH WALD. *Exploding the Gene Myth.* Boston: Beacon Press, 1993.

KEELEY, MICHAEL, and JILL W. GRAHAM. "Exit, Voice and Ethics." *Journal of Business Ethics* 10 (May 1991): 349–55.

KOEHN, DARYL. "Whistleblowing and Trust: Some Lessons from ADM Scandal." *The Online Journal of Ethics,* http: //www.sthom.edu/cbes.

KUPFER, JOSEPH. "Privacy, Autonomy, and Self-Concept." *American Philosophical Quarterly* 24 (January 1987): 81–89.

LEE, BARBARA A. "Something Akin to a Property Right: Protections for Job Security." *Business and Professional Ethics Journal* 8 (Fall 1989): 63– 81.

LIPPKE, RICHARD L. "Work, Privacy, and Autonomy." *Public Affairs Quarterly* 3 (April 1989): 41–53.

MAITLAND, IAN. "Rights in the Workplace: A Nozickian Argument." *Journal of Business Ethics* 8 (December 1989): 951–54.

NEAR, JANEY P., and Marcia P. Miceli. "WhistleBlowers in Organizations: Dissidents or Reformers?" *Research in Organizational Behavior* 9 (1987): 321–68.

NIXON, JUDY L., and Judy F. West. "The Ethics of Smoking Policies." *Journal of Business Ethics* 8 (December 1989): 409–14.

PETTIT, PHILIP. "The Paradox of Loyalty." *American Philosophical Quarterly* 25 (April 1988): 163–71.

PFEIFFER, RAYMOND S. "Owing Loyalty to One's Employer." *Journal of Business Ethics* 11 (July 1992): 535–43.

PHILLIPS, MICHAEL J. "Should We Let Employees Contract Away. Their Rights Against Arbitrary Discharge?" *Journal of Business Ethics* 13 (April 1994): 233–42.

WESTIN, ALAN F., and STEVEN SALISBURY. *Individual Rights in the Corporation: A Reader on Employee Rights.* New York: Pantheon, 1980.

# Chapter Six

# Diversity and Discrimination in the Workplace

## INTRODUCTION

For decades women and various minorities were barred from some of the most desirable institutions and positions in North America. Even when declared unconstitutional, discrimination persisted in many quarters. This discrimination has led to a widespread demand for effective policies that will provide justice for those previously and presently discriminated against. However, policies that establish goals, timetables, target numbers, and quotas intended to ensure more equitable opportunities continue to provoke controversy. Recent controversy has centered on whether programs designed to increase diversity and other strategies to offset gender-based and race-based discrimination are appropriate forms of remedy.

The term "affirmative action" refers to positive steps taken to hire persons from groups previously and presently discriminated against. This term has been used to refer to everything from open advertisement of positions to employment and admission quotas.

For over two decades U.S. federal laws have encouraged or required corporations to advertise jobs fairly and to promote the hiring of members of formerly abused groups. As a result, corporate planning has often used employment goals or targeted employment outcomes to eliminate the vestiges of discrimination.

The term "preferential hiring" refers to hiring that gives preference in recruitment and ranking to groups previously and presently affected by discrimination. This preference can be in the form of goals or quotas or in the act of choosing minorities over other candidates with equal credentials; or it can come in more camouflaged forms, such as the policy of a state university to accept every student in the top 10 percent of her or his graduating class (irrespective of school district).

### The Moral Basis of Preferential Policies

Affirmative action programs and various attempts to achieve diversity in the workplace have had a profound impact on U.S. businesses. Consider, for example, the impact of these policies on the Monsanto Chemical Company. In 1971 Monsanto found itself with few black and few female employees. In that same year the Department of Labor announced that diversity was noticeably lacking in the company and that affirmative action must be enforced. In complying, Monsanto tripled the number of minority employees in the next 14 years, aggressively promoted women and African American into middle management positions, and eliminated racial hiring patterns in technical and craft positions. Monsanto reported that it achieved these goals without diluting the quality of its employees. The firm has also said that it has no intention of abandoning its affirmative action programs.

Such preferential policies are often said to have their foundations in the principle of compensatory justice, which requires that if an injustice has been committed, just compensation or reparation is owed to the injured person(s). Everyone agrees that if an individual has been injured by past discrimination, he or she should be compensated for the past injustice. However, controversy has arisen over whether past discrimination against *groups* such as women and minorities justifies compensation for current group members. Critics of group preferential policies hold that only identifiable discrimination against individuals requires compensation.

Ronald Reagan was the first U.S. president to oppose preferential hiring. He and his successor, George Bush, campaigned against quotas and then sought to roll them back. The Department of Justice was the administration's vanguard, but other government agencies were intimately involved. In 1985, Chairman of the U.S. Civil Rights Commission, Clarence Pendleton, reported to then President Bush his conviction that the Commission had succeeded in making racial and group quotas a "dead issue." He maintained that public controversy over preferential treatment had been replaced with a vision of a color-blind society that is an "opportunity society" rather than a "preference society."[1] President George W. Bush later pursued the same policy when his term of office began at the start of the twenty-first century.

Although it is doubtful that quotas are a dead issue, given current civil rights law and business practice, Pendleton's comment illustrates the split that existed then, and still today, between two primary, competing positions in U.S. society: (1) that the only means to the end of a color-blind, sex-blind society is preferential treatment of women and/or minorities and (2) that a color-blind, sex-blind society can be achieved by guaranteeing equal opportunities to all citizens, irrespective of race or sex. According to the second position, employers must never use criteria favoring color, sex, or any such irrelevant consideration when hiring or promoting personnel. The goal is to eradicate discrimination, not to perpetuate it through reverse discrimination. These two competing positions agree that compensation is justified if particular victims of discrimination have been harmed, but they disagree about whether compensation is owed to individuals as members of groups.

Many disputes in the literature on the subject center on whether policies or practices of preferential treatment are (1) just, (2) unjust, or (3) not just, but still permissible.

1. Those who claim that such compensatory measures are just, or are required by justice, generally argue that past discrimination warrants present remedies for those discriminated against in the past. Proponents note, for example, that African Americans who were victims of past discrimination are still handicapped or discriminated against, whereas the families of past slave owners are still being unduly

enriched by inheritance laws. Those who have inherited wealth accumulated by iniquitous practices have no more right to their wealth than the sons of slaves, who have some claim to it as a matter of compensation. In the case of women, the argument is that our culture is structured to foster in women a lack of self-confidence, that it still prejudicially excludes them from much of the domestic and international work forces, and that it treats them as a low-paid auxiliary labor unit. Consequently, only highly independent women can be expected to compete with males on initially fair terms; and even these women may not be able to compete equally in the setting of multinational corporations with operations in many countries.

2. Those who claim that group compensatory measures are unjust argue that no criteria exist for measuring just compensation, that employment discrimination in society is presently minor and controllable, and that those harmed by past discrimination are no longer alive to be compensated. Instead of providing compensation, they argue, strict equality as well as merit hiring and promotion should be enforced, while attacking the roots of discrimination. Also, some now successful but once underprivileged minority groups argue that their long struggle for equality is being jeopardized by programs of "favoritism" to African Americans and women.

In the opening article, George Sher considers whether preferential treatment is needed in order to increase diversity in the workplace. He maintains that diversity arguments take multiple forms, but that every version involves some appeal to past wrongdoing. Sher finds it difficult to pin down what sort of past wrongness justifies present preferences. He finds that many half-truths and half-arguments have been involved in attempts to justify the use of preferential treatment. On the whole, he finds arguments from compensatory justice and preferential treatment to be "immensely problematic."

In his contribution, Scott Arnold argues that most of the controversial affirmative action programs are unjustified. He tries to cut across competing ideologies by using arguments based on management's fiduciary responsibility to its shareholders to act in the firm's best financial interest and the state's responsibilities to its citizens. Arnold presents the striking thesis that "even if the demands of justice require preferential treatment programs, the government is not justified in requiring or encouraging them."

3. The third view is that some compensatory measures are not just because they violate principles of justice, but are still justifiable by moral arguments. Thomas Nagel, a proponent of this view, argues that "there is an element of individual unfairness" in strong affirmative action plans, but these plans are justified as a means to the end of eradicating an intolerable social situation. Tom L. Beauchamp argues that even some forms of *reverse* discrimination can be justified as a means to the end of a nondiscriminatory society. Beauchamp discusses both the voluntary preferential treatment programs that have been of special interest to senior management and state-mandated programs. He concludes that both can be justified under certain circumstances.

Among writers who support affirmative action policies, a mainline approach has been to argue that under certain conditions compensation owed for past wrongs justifies present preferential policies. Sher primarily attacks arguments that are, in this way, backward-looking. However, Beauchamp does not employ arguments that compensation is owed to classes for *past* wrongs; he maintains that reverse discrimination is permissible to eliminate or alleviate *present* discriminatory practices that affect whole classes of persons (especially practices of minority exclusion). He mentions factual evidence for his claim that invidious discrimination is pervasive in society. Because discrimination now prevails, Beauchamp contends that policies that may eventuate in reverse discrimination are unavoidable in reaching the end of eliminating ongoing discrimination.

Opponents of this position argue that reverse discrimination violates fundamental, overriding principles of justice and cannot be justified. As Arnold points out, there exist quite a variety of arguments in opposition to affirmative action. Arguments that have received widespread attention include the following: (1) Some persons who are not responsible for the past discrimination (for example, qualified young white males) pay the price; preferential treatment is invidiously discriminatory because innocent persons are penalized solely on the basis of their race or sex. (2) Male members of minority groups such as Polish, Irish, Arabic, Chinese, and Italian members of society—who were previously discriminated against—inevitably will bear a heavy and unfair burden of compensating women and other minority groups. (3) Many members of any class selected for preferential treatment have never been unjustly treated and therefore do not deserve preferential policies. (4) Compensation can be provided to individuals who were previously treated unfairly without resorting to reverse discrimination.

## Decisions in the Courts

The U.S. Supreme Court has held that federal law permits private employers to create plans that favor groups traditionally discriminated against. However, the moral and legal justifications, if any, for such plans and the acceptability of any particular plan remain controversial. As the court cases in this chapter indicate, the problems associated with preferential and discriminatory hiring are surprisingly complicated. In two cases decided in the late 1980s, the Supreme Court supported the permissibility of specific numerical goals in affirmative action plans that are intended to combat a manifest imbalance in traditionally segregated job categories (even if the particular workers drawn from minorities were not victims of past discrimination). In *Local 28 v. Equal Employment Opportunity Commission*, otherwise known as *Sheet Metal Workers*, a specific minority hiring goal of 29.23 percent had been established. The Court held that quotas involved in the 29 percent goal are justified when dealing with persistent or egregious discrimination. The Supreme Court held that the history of Local 28 was one of complete "foot-dragging resistance" to the idea of hiring without discrimination in their apprenticeship training programs from minority groups. The Court argued that

> even where the employer or union formally ceases to engage in discrimination, informal mechanisms may obstruct equal employment opportunities. An employer's reputation for discrimination may discourage minorities from seeking available employment. In these circumstances, affirmative race-conscious relief may be the only means available to assure equality of employment opportunities and to eliminate those discriminatory practice and devices which have fostered racially stratified job environments to the disadvantage of minority citizens.

However, in a 1989 opinion included in this chapter, the Supreme Court held in *City of Richmond v. J. A. Croson* that Richmond, Virginia, officials could not require contractors to set aside 30 percent of their budget for subcontractors who owned "minority business enterprises." The Court held that this plan did not exhibit sufficient government interest to justify the plan and that the plan was not written to remedy the effects of prior discrimination. The Court found that this way of fixing a percentage based on race, in the absence of evidence of identified past discrimination, denied citizens an equal opportunity to compete for the subcontracts. (Parts of the reasoning in *Croson* were affirmed in the 1995 case of *Adarand Constructors Inc. v. Pena.)*

Some writers have interpreted *Croson* and other recent cases as the dismantling of affirmative action, specifically all affirmative action plans that contain specific numerical goals. Other readers of these cases, however, find a continuation of the Supreme Court's long line of vigorous defenses of minority rights and the protection of those rights, including the implementation of the rights in corporate policies. As important as these cases are, no comprehensive criteria have yet been established for legally valid affirmative action plans.

### Problems of Sexual Harassment

Sexual discrimination in the workplace has long been a major issue in business ethics, but sexual harassment is a relatively new topic in the literature of this field. Statistics on the prevalence of sexual harassment are somewhat unreliable, but various studies and surveys suggest that between 15 percent and 65 percent of working women encounter some form of sexual harassment, depending on type of job, work force, location, and the like—and also depending on one's definition of "sexual harassment." Studies also reveal an increase of sexual harassment complaints during the past decade or two. The landmark U.S. Supreme Court case of *Meritor Savings Bank v. Vinson* (reprinted in this chapter) was decided in 1986. This case established that a hostile or abusive work environment can result from many activities in the workplace that constitute sexual harassment. This case, which was brought under Title VII of the Civil Rights Act of 1964, has significantly impacted discussions and policies of workplace discrimination—especially as it relates to first amendment issues of free speech.

The most widespread form of sexual harassment now seems to be offensive sexual innuendos that generate embarrassment and anger, rather than coercive threats demanding sexual favors or physical abuse. Some studies suggest that sexual harassment has recently become less overt, but not less commonplace. Forms of sexual harassment that condition a job or promotion on sexual favors have declined, but an increase has occurred in unwanted sexual advances such as propositions, offensive posters, degrading comments, kisses and caresses, and improper joking and teasing. Weighing an individual's right to "free speech" against an employee's right to a "nonhostile workplace" is the focus of much of the contemporary debate.

Men and women often have different views of what constitutes an unwelcome sexual advance, comment, or environment. However, in *Meritor*, the Supreme Court extended protections against sexual harassment beyond circumstances of asking for sexual favors to any form of offensive remark or sexual conduct that creates a hostile working environment. Before *Meritor*, sexual harassment had often been thought to involve attempted coercion—that is, an attempt to present a threat the person approached could not reasonably resist. In the typical case, a person's job, promotion, or company benefit was conditioned on performing a sexual favor. However, after

*Meritor*, it has been widely agreed that many forms of true sexual harassment do not involve an irresistible threat and are not coercive.

In the case in this chapter of *Teresa Harris v. Forklift Systems*, a central issue is whether *noncoercive* comments based on employee gender cause an abusive work environment. In this case it is found that gender insults, gender ridicule, and sexual innuendo can constitute sexual harassment when they negatively alter the conditions of a victim's employment and constitute an abusive environment. The court finds that conduct may constitute sexual harassment even if that conduct does not involve a serious disturbance of psychological well-being or an injury. This case reaffirms the finding in *Meritor* that "an objectively hostile or abusive environment" is enough for sexual harassment.

Establishing a precise definition of *sexual harassment* has proved difficult. The centerpiece of many definitions has been how to take account of persistent behavior involving unwelcome sexual remarks, advances, or requests that negatively affect working conditions and put these behaviors in the form of a definition. The conduct need not involve making a sexual favor a condition of employment or promotion, and it need not be imposed on persons who are in no position to resist the conduct. Even someone who is in a strong position to resist the approach can be sexually harassed. Derogatory gestures, offensive touching, and leering can affect a worker's performance and create a sense that the workplace is inhospitable, irrepective of a worker's ability to resist. The conduct need not be "sexual" in a narrow sense or even sexually motivated. For example, the conduct can be gender specific, involving demeaning remarks about how women underperform in their job assignments.

The notion of causing or allowing a "hostile working environment" has been at the forefront of recent attempts in government, law, and philosophy to define "sexual harassment," but it has proved difficult to define both terms so that they are not overly broad. What makes for a hostile or intimidating workplace? Do teasing and denigrating remarks count? What is it to denigrate? Which forms of conduct overstep the bounds of being friendly and humorous? Employees in some corporations have complained that corporate policies are written so that asking someone out for a drink after work or expressing sexual humor can be construed as unwelcome conduct that creates a hostile working environment.

Standards of offensive or unwelcome sexual behavior have also been difficult to formulate. The "reasonable person" standard of what counts as offensive or unwelcome has been replaced in some courts with a "reasonable woman" standard that tries to determine whether a male's comments or advances directed toward a woman would be considered offensive by taking the reasonable woman's point of view rather than the reasonable person's point of view. This shift from a gender-neutral standard should make it easier for women to file lawsuits successfully, because men might not find offensive what a woman would. However, if one takes the view, as many now do, that harassment is largely a matter of how the individual feels when approached by another person, then the standard of the reasonable woman will be too weak. The standard would have to be whether *this person* finds conduct offensive, not whether *the reasonable woman* so finds it. Although the law is not likely to move in the direction of a subjective standard, the ethics literature is increasingly moving in that direction.

Efforts to remove sexual harassment from the corporate workplace appear to have increased since the 1986 *Meritor* decision, although there is controversy about how seriously to take the increased interest. Many major corporations now have some form of training and grievance policies. Corporations with sexual harassment policies for all management levels report that unwelcome comments and touching have declined significantly after initiating the policies. One reason for increased corporate interest is that corporations have been held legally liable for the behavior of their supervisors, even when corporate officials above the supervisors were unaware of the behavior. Although these lawsuits and corporate policies have made corporations more sensitive to the issues, little evidence exists that top executives have given urgent priority to the improvement and enforcement of sexual harassment policies.

Various current legal issues centered on the problem of a conflict between the right to "free speech" and the right to a nonhostile environment are taken up in two articles in this chapter by Deborah Epstein and Eugene Volokh. Epstein maintains (in part against Volokh's publications) that legal restrictions on harassing workplaces do not seriously conflict with legal protections of free speech. She thinks it would be a mistake to narrow the laws that protect rights against harassment in order to protect rights of speech. Epstein believes that harassment law generates a fundamental conflict between equal employment opportunity (in particular, a woman's right to be on an equal level with men) and freedom of expression. She attempts to strike a balance between the two—that is, a balance between the captivity that women can feel in the workplace and the free speech rights of all workers.

In response, Volokh argues that there is a constant danger, given the loose terms at work in harassment law, that the law will function to suppress core areas of protected speech. He maintains that the policy Epstein proposes would end up barring all gender-specific or sexual speech so long as anyone finds it objectionable, because employers will need to restrict any statement that might be construed as contributing to a hostile environment. A cautious employer, then, will find it necessary to ban all forms of political speech as long as one person in the workplace finds it offensive. Volokh concludes that harassment law, as it stands, seriously endangers rights of free speech.

## NOTES

1. Juan Williams, "Quotas Are a 'Dead Issue,' Rights Panel Chairman Says," *Washington Post*, January 30, 1985, p. A2.

## DIVERSITY AND AFFIRMATIVE ACTION

# Diversity

*George Sher*

My topic in this article is the argument that preferential treatment is needed to increase diversity in educational institutions and the workplace. Although this argument has achieved considerable currency, and although it is often thought to sidestep the complications that arise when preferential treatment is viewed as a form of compensation, its normative basis has rarely

 *Philosophy & Public Affairs 28*, no. 2.

been made explicit. Thus, one aim of my discussion is simply to explore the different forms that the diversity argument can take. However, a further and more substantive aim is to show that its alleged advantages are illusory—that in every version, the appeal to diversity raises difficult questions whose most plausible answers turn on tacit appeals to past wrongdoing.

## I

Justifications of preferential treatment come in two main types. Arguments of one type—often called backward-looking—make essential reference to the discrimination and injustice that blacks, women, and members of certain other groups have suffered in the past. These arguments urge that current group members be given preference in employment or admission to educational institutions to make amends for or rectify the effects of such wrongdoing—to put things right or, as far as possible, "make the victims whole." By contrast, the other type of justification—often called forward-looking—makes *no* essential reference to past wrongdoing, but instead defends preferential treatment entirely as a means to some desirable future goal. Even when the goal is to eliminate inequalities or disadvantages that *were in fact* caused by past wrongdoing, the reason for eliminating them is not *that* they were caused by past wrongdoing. Rather, their continued existence is said to violate some purely *non*-historical principle or ideal—for example, the principle of utility or some ideal of equality.

Of the two types of argument, the forward-looking type is often viewed as more straightforward. Those who look exclusively to the future are spared both the daunting task of documenting the effects of past injustice on specific individuals and the even more difficult task of specifying *how much* better off any given individual would now be in its absence. In a more theoretical vein, they need not answer the troublesome question of whether (and if so why) we must compensate persons who would not even have existed, and so *a fortiori* would not be better off, if historical wrongs such as slavery had not taken place; and neither need they specify how many generations must elapse before claims to compensation lose their force. Perhaps for these reasons, defenders of preferential treatment seem increasingly inclined to eschew the backward-looking approach and to cast their lot with forward-looking arguments.

It seems to me, however, that this strategy is badly misguided for two distinct but related reasons: first, because the forward-looking defenses of preferential treatment are only superficially less problematic than their backward-looking counterparts, and, second, because the most promising way of rectifying their inadequacies is to reintroduce precisely the sorts of reference to the past that their proponents have sought to avoid. . . .

If selecting a less-than-best-qualified applicant is to be an acceptable way of promoting utility when the chosen applicant is black or female but not when that applicant is white male, the reason is very likely to be that blacks and women, but not white males, were often treated unjustly in the past. . . .

My topic here, however, is neither the general contrast between the forward- and backward-looking defenses of preferential treatment nor the prospects for mounting a successful utilitarian or egalitarian defense. Instead, I mention these matters only to frame what I want to say about a different forward-looking defense that has recently come to the fore. This new defense is, of course, the one I mentioned at the outset—the argument that preferential treatment is justified by the need to promote racial, sexual, and ethnic diversity in such crucial sectors of our society as the academy and the workplace. A bit more precisely, it is the argument that preferential treatment is justified when, and because, it moves us closer to a situation in which the holders of every (desirable) type of job and position include representatives of all racial, sexual, and ethnic groups in rough proportion to their overall numbers.

The rhetoric of this new argument is all around us. . . .

## II

I can envision four possible ways of arguing that racial, sexual, and ethnic diversity is morally important. To show this, someone might argue that such diversity is either (1) a requirement of justice or (2) intrinsically valuable or (3) conducive to the general welfare or (4) conducive to some value *other* than well-being. However, as we will see, each version of the diversity argument remains vulnerable to essentially the same objection that I advanced against the other forward-looking defenses of preferential treatment—namely, that when we ask why the argument focuses only on certain groups, we are invariably thrown back on the injustice or discrimination that their past members have suffered.

Consider first the claim that diversity is a requirement of justice. To defend this claim, one must first specify the relevant conception of justice and then show why it requires that every desirable job and position be distributed among all racial, sexual and ethnic groups in rough proportion to their numbers. Although there are obviously many ways of filling in the blanks, I shall consider only two that I think may actually exert some influence. Of these two proposals, one construes racial, sexual, and ethnic groups as morally fundamental entities with claims of justice of their own, while the other takes these groups to be only derivatively relevant.

Suppose, first, that racial, sexual, and ethnic groups do themselves have claims of justice; and suppose, further, that the best theory of justice is egalitarian. In that case, the best theory of justice will require that all racial, sexual, and ethnic groups be made roughly equally well off. Because such groups are not organized entities, and so are incapable either of having experiences or of pursuing goals, their well-being cannot reside either in the quality of their subjective states or in their success in achieving their goals. Instead, each group's well-being must be a function of the well-being of its individual members, which in turn can be expected to vary with the members' income and social standing. Because these connections hold, any society that wishes to implement a conception of justice that requires that all racial, sexual, and ethnic groups be made equally well off may indeed have to distribute all desirable jobs and positions among all relevant groups in rough proportion to their numbers.

Here, then, is one way of grounding the case for racial, sexual, and ethnic diversity in a broader conception of justice. But should we accept this argument? Elsewhere, I have contended that racial, sexual, and ethnic groups are in fact *un*likely to have independent claims of justice;[1] I also doubt that the best theory of justice is straightforwardly egalitarian. However, in the current discussion, I shall simply grant both premises and focus only on the argument's further assumption that not all groups, but only some subset that includes racial, sexual, and ethnic groups, have independent claims of justice.

Why exactly, must the argument make this further assumption? One answer is simply that if enough other groups *did* have independent claims of justice, then even distributing every desirable position among all racial, sexual, and ethnic groups in exact proportion to their numbers would at best eliminate only a small fraction of a society's unjust inequalities. However, while this answer is not wrong, it does not go far enough. The more decisive answer is that if enough other groups also had independent claims of justice, then no increase in a society's diversity could bring *any* increase in its overall justice. . . .

There are, of course, many other possible ways of arguing that mixed groups lack the moral status of racial, sexual, and ethnic groups. Thus, the mere fact that the cited arguments fail is hardly decisive. Still, in the absence of any better argument, the best explanation of the impulse to single out certain racial, sexual, and ethnic groups is again that it reflects a desire to make amends for (or rectify the lingering effects of) the discrimination that their past members have suffered. As Paul Taylor has put it, the guiding thought appears to be that the relevant groups were "as it were, *created* by the original unjust practice[s]."[2] I think, in fact, that this way of formulating the moral importance of past injustice is highly misleading, but I shall not argue that point here. Instead, in keeping with my broader theme, I shall simply observe that if anyone *were* to elaborate the diversity argument in these terms, he would be abandoning all pretense that his argument is purely forward-looking.

## III

What, next, of the suggestion that racial, sexual, and ethnic diversity is a requirement of justice for individuals? Unlike its predecessor, this suggestion does not presuppose a problematic moral ontology. Yet just because the suggestion does not construe groups as morally fundamental, it raises a difficult new question—namely, why should justice for individuals call for *any* special distribution of positions among groups?

Although this question, too, can be answered in various ways, I shall consider only the single answer that I think proponents of diversity would be most likely to give. Put most briefly, that answer is, first, that the operative principle of justice is one of equality of opportunity, and, second, that a lack of racial, sexual, and ethnic diversity is significant precisely because it shows that opportunities remain *un*equal. Even though legal barriers are a thing of a past, the fact that relatively few blacks, women, and members of other minorities hold well-paying, authoritative positions is often viewed as compelling evidence that the members of these groups have lacked, and continue to lack, equal opportunity. That in turn may be thought to show that using preferential treatment to bring about their representation within desirable professions in proportion to their numbers is justified by the fact that it will make opportunities *more* equal. . . .

This observation does not show that such uses of preferential treatment cannot make opportunities more equal; but it does show that any relevant gains must be long-term rather than immediate. The point must be not that opportunities will be more equal *when* the preferential treatment is used, but rather that they will be more equal *afterwards*. This will be true (the argument must run) because the proportional distribution of desirable positions among all racial, sexual, and ethnic groups will convey to the members of previously excluded groups the message that people like them can successfully acquire and hold such positions, and that in turn will raise the aspirations of many. Because this reasoning appeals to the effects of diversity upon the motivation of future group members, it is, in essence, a variant of the familiar "role model" argument. . . .

If all preferences and attitudes were either innate or else the results of past wrongdoing, we could end this part of our discussion here. However, in fact, these alternatives are not exhaustive. Many people have acquired their current attitudes from cultures that did *not* evolve in response to wrongdoing or oppression; and such attitudes, too, can lead the relevant groups to be underrepresented within professions. It may be, for example, that the reason relatively few members of a given group have pursued careers that require academic success or extended training is simply that the group's culture, which was shaped by its earlier agrarian lifestyle, does not attach much value to education. If internalizing this attitude also counts as being denied equal opportunity, and if increasing the group's presence within various professions would help eventually to dispel the attitude, then using preferential treatment to promote such diversity may indeed be justified on purely forward-looking grounds.

How significant is the challenge to my thesis that every ostensibly forward-looking defense of diversity has a backward-looking core? That depends I think, on the answers to several further questions. It depends, most obviously, on whether equal opportunity *does* require that no one be brought up in a culture that instills attitudes unconducive to success in the modern world; but it depends, as well, on whether equal opportunity trumps respect for ancestral cultures; whether increasing diversity would effectively diminish the transmission of counterproductive attitudes; and whether, even if it would, we can more effectively alter these attitudes in some other way. . . . Thus, pending further discussion, this issue must simply remain unresolved.

## IV

So far, I have discussed only the first of the four possible arguments for racial, sexual, and ethnic diversity. That argument, which construes such diversity as a requirement of justice, predictably raised a variety of complications. By contrast, the second and third arguments—that diversity is intrinsically valuable and that it is conducive to the general welfare—raise fewer new issues and so can be dealt with much more quickly.

The challenge to someone who holds that racial, sexual, and ethnic diversity is *intrinsically* valuable is to provide some justification of this claim that goes beyond the bare fact that he believes it. He cannot simply assert that the claim is self-evident because such assertions are equally available to his opponents; yet once we ask what else can be said, we almost immediately run out of argument. I say "almost immediately" because many of the metaphors that are commonly used in this connection—for example, descriptions of a diverse society as a tapestry or a "gorgeous mosaic"—can themselves be viewed as arguments that the relevant intrinsic values are familiar aesthetic ones. However, I hope it goes without saying that the aesthetic appeal of a given pattern of distribution is not a proper basis for any decision about social policy.

Because the appeal to intrinsic value is essentially a nonargument, I cannot pinpoint the exact place at which it goes historical. Yet just because that appeal has so little to recommend it, the best explanation of whatever influence it has—and, though I cannot prove it, I think it does have some influence—is again that it provides cover for a policy whose real aim is to benefit members of unjustly disadvantaged groups.

The third possible argument for diversity—that it is conducive to the general welfare—is very different; for unlike the appeal to intrinsic value, this argument can be developed in various ways. One obvious possibility is to exploit our earlier observation that the members of many racial, sexual, and ethnic groups identify strongly with the fortunes and accomplishments of other group members; for given this mutual identification, increasing diversity will benefit not only those group members who actually gain prestigious, well-paying positions, but also the many others who take pride and pleasure in their success. Alternatively or in addition, it can be argued that working closely with members of unfamiliar groups breaks down barriers and disrupts stereotypes, and that increasing racial, sexual, and ethnic diversity will therefore increase overall well-being by fostering understanding and harmony.

Because diversity yields these and other benefits, there is an obvious case for the use of preferential treatment to promote it. However, when the issue is framed in these terms, the diversity argument is no longer an alternative to a utilitarian defense of preferential treatment, but rather is itself such a defense. Despite its interposition of diversity, its essential message is precisely that preferential treatment is justified by its beneficial consequences. Thus, if my conjecture about the other utilitiarian defenses was correct—if the disparity between the difficulties they confront and the confidence with which they are advanced suggests that their proponents' real impulse is compensatory—then that conjecture must apply here too.

## V

That leaves only the fourth argument for diversity's importance—the argument that it promotes some value *other* than well-being. Although there are many nonwelfarist values to which appeal might theoretically be made, the only live version of this argument is one that appeals to the intellectual values of the academy.

That increasing racial, sexual, and ethnic diversity will advance the academic enterprise is an article of faith among many academics. Neil Rudenstine, the president of Harvard, expressed the conventional wisdom this way: "A diverse educational environment challenges [students] to explore ideas and arguments at a deeper level—to see issues from various sides, to rethink their own premises, to achieve the kind of understanding that comes only from testing their own hypotheses against those of people with other views."[3] Although these claims obviously do not support all forms of preferential treatment—they are, for example, irrelevant both to nonacademic hiring and to contractual "set-asides"—they do purport to justify, through an appeal to values internal to the academy's own mission, both preferential admission to many educational institutions and preferential hiring across the curricular spectrum.

Like many of the other arguments we have considered, this one can itself be fleshed out in various ways. Some of its proponents, including Rudenstine himself, stress the value *to students* of exposure to different perspectives, while others stress the value of diversity in research. Of those who focus on research, some argue that including hitherto excluded groups will open up new areas of investigation, while others emphasize the value of diverse challenges to all hypotheses, including, or especially, hypotheses in traditional, well-worked areas. Of those who emphasize challenges to hypotheses, some stress the importance of confronting all hypotheses with the broadest possible range of potentially falsifying tests, while others focus on exposing the hidden biases of investigators. Because the appeal to diversity's contribution to intellectual inquiry is so protean, I cannot work systematically through its variants, but will pose only a single question that applies to each. That question, predictably enough, is why we should single out the contributions of any small set of groups such as those on the official Affirmative Action list.

For even if diversity yields every one of the intellectual benefits that are claimed for it, why should we benefit most when the scholarly community contains substantial numbers of blacks, women, Hispanics, (American) Indians, Aleuts, and Chinese-Americans? Why not focus instead, or in addition, on Americans of Eastern European, Arabic, or (Asian) Indian extraction? For that matter, can't we achieve even greater benefit by extending preference to *native* Africans, Asians, Arabs, and Europeans? And why understand diversity only in terms of gender, ethnicity, and national origin? Why should a population that is diverse in this dimension provide any more educational or scholarly benefit than one that is ethnically homogeneous but includes suitable number of gays, religious fundamentalists, the young, the old, the handicapped, ex-military officers, conservatives, Marxists, Mormons, and blue-collar workers? These groups, too, have characteristic concerns, types of experience, and outlooks on the world. . . .

The most salient feature of the groups on the official list is of course the discrimination they have suffered. This may not entirely explain why just these groups are included—that may in part be traceable to the play of political forces—but it does explain the prominence of such core groups as blacks and women. This strongly suggests that the current argument is also covertly backward-looking. However, before we can draw this conclusion, we must consider an important alternative—namely, that the real reason for concentrating on previously oppressed groups is not that their members alone are owed compensation, but rather that beliefs and attitudes shaped by oppression are better suited than others to advance educational or scholarly aims.

For although we obviously cannot assume that all the members of any group think alike, a history of discrimination may indeed affect the way many of a group's members tend to view the world. In addition to the already-noted high degree of collective identification, the perspective of the oppressed is often said to include a keen awareness of the motives, prejudices, and hidden agendas of others, a heightened sense of the oppressive effects of even seemingly benign social structures, and a strong commitment to social change. As a corollary, that perspective may include a degree of antagonism toward received opinion and a certain impatience with abstraction. Thus, the question that remains to be addressed is whether, and if so how, any of these beliefs, attitudes, or traits might make a special contribution to education or research. . . .

Yet while such knowledge may contribute significantly to mutual understanding and social harmony, the beliefs, attitudes, traits, and experiences that are characteristic of oppressed groups are in the end only one class of facts among innumerable others. Considered simply as objects of study—and that is how we must consider them if the current argument is not to be yet another tributary of the great utilitarian river—the beliefs, attitudes, traits, and experiences of the oppressed are no more important than those of the nonoppressed, which in turn are no more important than indefinitely many other possible objects of inquiry.

Thus, to give their variant of the argument a fighting chance, those who attach special educational and scholarly value to the perspective of the oppressed must take the other path. They must locate its special educational or scholarly value not in anyone's *coming to know* that oppressed groups hold certain beliefs, attitudes, etc., but rather in the contribution of those beliefs and attitudes to the acquisition of *other* knowledge. Their argument must be that this perspective uniquely enhances our collective ability to pose or resolve questions across much of the intellectual spectrum. To show that the perspective of the oppressed generates new lines of inquiry, friends of diversity often cite the tendency of women to pursue scientific research with humanitarian rather than militaristic applications and the contributions that various minorities have made to history and other fields by studying their own past and present. To show that this perspective contributes to the investigation of established topics, they point out that black and female investigators tend to be specially attuned to the inclusion of blacks and women in experimental control groups, that black students bring to the study of law a well-founded mistrust of the police, and that enhanced sensitivity to power relations has opened up fruitful new ways of interpreting literary texts.

We certainly must agree that the beliefs, attitudes, and traits of oppressed groups have made important contributions to the way academic questions are now formulated and addressed. However, what friends of diversity must show is not merely that these beliefs, attitudes, and traits make *some* significant contribution to effective inquiry, but that they are *more* conducive to it, all things considered, than any of the alternative mixtures that would emerge if there were no Affirmative Action or if preference were given to other sorts of groups. . . .

My own view is that we will make the most progress if we simply stock the academy with persons who display the traditional academic excellences to the highest degree. The students and faculty members who are most likely to help us progress toward true beliefs, powerful explanations, deep understanding, and a synoptic world-view are just the ones with the greatest analytical ability, the most imagination, the best memory, and the strongest desire to pursue the truth wherever it leads. However, while these are things that I deeply believe, my argument does not require any premise this strong. Instead, it requires only the much weaker premise that indefinitely many traits of intellect or character are sometimes useful in advancing cognitive or pedagogical aims, and that we have no reason to expect the beliefs and attitudes of the oppressed to be preeminent among these.

This reasoning of course presupposes that the aims of the academy *are* to be understood in terms of truth, understanding, explanation, and the rest. If they are not—if, for example, the basic aim is instead to promote social change—then the case for favoring the beliefs and attitudes of the oppressed may well be stronger. However, if someone does take the basic aim to be social change, and if he urges the hiring and admission of more members of oppressed groups to expedite the desired changes, then he will no longer be appealing to the very academic values that even his opponents share. He will, instead, be mounting an appeal to some further conception of social justice—one whose evaluation must await its more precise articulation. Thus, pending further discussion, my main thesis—that every major defense of diversity is either incomplete or backward-looking—remains intact. . . .

## VI

The motivation I have stressed—a desire to rationalize the use of preferential treatment to benefit members of previously wronged groups—is a complex mixture of the admirable and the base. It is admirable because it reflects a high-minded conception of what justice requires, base because it substitutes the use of half-truths, half-arguments, and persuasive slogans for a frank willingness to acknowledge what is really at stake. In fact, compensatory justice *is* immensely problematic, and the moral status of preferential treatment is immensely problematic too. We do not advance the cause of justice, but only degrade public discourse, if we blur these difficulties instead of seeking to overcome them.

## NOTES

1. The argument appears in "Groups and Justice," *Ethics* 87. no. 1 (October 1977): 81–87; reprinted in *Approximate Justice*, pp. 55–64.
2. Paul W. Taylor, "Reverse Discrimination and Compensatory Justice," in Steven M. Cahn, editor, *The Affirmative Action Debate* (New York: Routledge, 1995), p. 14.
3. Neil L. Rudenstine. "Why a Diverse Student Body Is So Important." *The Chronicle of Higher Education*, April 19, 1996 p. B1.

## AFFIRMATIVE ACTION AND REVERSE DISCRIMINATION

# A Defense of Affirmative Action

*Thomas Nagel*

The term "affirmative action" has changed in meaning since it was first introduced. Originally it referred only to special efforts to ensure equal opportunity for members of groups that had been subject to discrimination. These efforts included public advertisement of positions to be filled, active recruitment of qualified applicants from the formerly excluded groups, and special training programs to help them meet the standards for admission or appointment. There was also close attention to procedures of appointment, and sometimes to the results, with a view to detecting continued discrimination, conscious or unconscious.

More recently the term has come to refer also to some degree of definite preference for members of these groups in determining access to positions from which they were formerly excluded. Such preference might be allowed to influence decisions only between candidates who are otherwise equally qualified, but usually it involves the selection of women or minority members over other candidates who are better qualified for the position.

Let me call the first sort of policy "weak affirmative action" and the second "strong affirmative action." It is important to distinguish them, because the distinction is sometimes blurred in practice. It is strong affirmative action—the policy of preference—that arouses controversy. Most people would agree that weak or precautionary affirmative action is a good thing, and worth its cost in time and energy. But this does not imply that strong affirmative action is also justified.

I shall claim that in the present state of things it is justified, most clearly with respect to blacks. But I also believe that a defender of the practice must acknowledge that there are serious arguments against it, and that it is defensible only because the arguments for it have great weight. Moral opinion in this country is sharply divided over the issue because significant values are involved on both sides. My own view is that while strong affirmative action is intrinsically undesirable, it is a legitimate and perhaps indispensable method of pursuing a goal so important to the national welfare that it can be justified as a temporary, though not short-term, policy for both public and private institutions. In this respect it is like other policies that impose burdens on some for the public good.

## THREE OBJECTIONS

I shall begin with the argument against. There are three objection to strong affirmative action: that it is inefficient; that it is unfair; and that it damages self-esteem.

The degree of inefficiency depends on how strong a role racial or sexual preference plays in the process of selection. Among candidates meeting the basic qualifications for a position, those better qualified will on the average

Testimony before the Subcommittee on the Constitution of the Senate Judiciary Committee, June 18, 1981. Reprinted by permission of Professor Nagel.

perform better, whether they are doctors, policemen, teachers, or electricians. There may be some cases, as in preferential college admissions, where the immediate usefulness of making educational resources available to an individual is thought to be greater because of the use to which the education will be put or because of the internal effects on the institution itself. But by and large, policies of strong affirmative action must reckon with the costs of some lowering in performance level: the stronger the preference, the larger the cost to be justified. Since both the costs and the value of the results will vary from case to case, this suggests that no one policy of affirmative action is likely to be correct in all cases, and that the cost in performance level should be taken into account in the design of a legitimate policy.

The charge of unfairness arouses the deepest disagreements. To be passed over because of membership in a group one was born into, where this has nothing to do with one's individual qualifications for a position, can arouse strong feelings of resentment. It is a departure from the ideal—one of the values finally recognized in our society—that people should be judged so far as possible on the basis of individual characteristics rather than involuntary group membership.

This does not mean that strong affirmative action is morally repugnant in the manner of racial or sexual discrimination. It is nothing like those practices, for though like them it employs race and sex as criteria of selection, it does so for entirely different reasons. Racial and sexual discrimination are based on contempt or even loathing for the excluded group, a feeling that certain contacts with them are degrading to members of the dominant group, that they are fit only for subordinate positions or menial work. Strong affirmative action involves none of this: it is simply a means of increasing the social and economic strength of formerly victimized groups, and does not stigmatize others.

There is an element of individual unfairness here, but it is more like the unfairness of conscription in wartime, or of property condemnation under the right of eminent domain. Those who benefit or lose out because of their race or sex cannot be said to deserve their good or bad fortune.

It might be said on the other side that the beneficiaries of affirmative action deserve it as compensation for past discrimination, and that compensation is rightly exacted from the group that has benefited from discrimination in the past. But this is a bad argument, because as the practice usually works, no effort is made to give preference to those who have suffered most from discrimination, or to prefer them especially to those who have benefited most from it, or been guilty of it. Only candidates who in other qualifications fall on one or other side of the margin of decision will directly benefit or lose from the policy, and these are not necessarily, or even probably, the ones who especially deserve it. Women or blacks who don't have the qualifications even to be considered are likely to have been handicapped more by the effects of discrimination than those who receive preference. And the marginal white male candidate who is turned down can evoke our sympathy if he asks, "Why me?" (A policy of explicitly *compensatory* preference, which took into account each individual's background of poverty and discrimination, would escape some of these objections, and it has its defenders, but it is not the policy I want to defend. Whatever its merits, it will not serve the same purpose as direct affirmative action.)

The third objection concerns self-esteem, and is particularly serious. While strong affirmative action is in effect, and generally known to be so, no one in an affirmative action category who gets a desirable job or is admitted to a selective university can be sure that he or she has not benefited from the policy. Even those who would have made it anyway fall under suspicion, from themselves and from others: it comes to be widely felt that success does not mean the same thing for women and minorities. This painful damage to esteem cannot be avoided. It should make any defender of strong affirmative action want the practice to end as soon as it has achieved its basic purpose.

## JUSTIFYING AFFIRMATIVE ACTION

I have examined these three objections and tried to assess their weight, in order to decide how strong a countervailing reason is needed to justify such a policy. In my view, taken together they imply that strong affirmative action involving significant preference should be undertaken only if it will substantially further a social goal of the first importance. While this condition is not met by all programs of affirmative action now in effect, it is met by those which address the most deep-seated, stubborn, and radically unhealthy divisions in the society, divisions whose removal is a condition of basic justice and social cohesion.

The situation of black people in our country is unique in this respect. For almost a century after the abolition of slavery we had a rigid racial caste system of the ugliest kind, and it only began to break up twenty-five years ago. In the South it was enforced by law, and in the North, in a somewhat less severe form, by social convention. Whites were thought to be defiled by social or residential proximity to blacks, intermarriage was taboo, blacks were denied the same level of public goods—education and legal protection—as whites, were restricted to the most menial occupations, and were barred from any positions of authority over whites. The visceral feeling of black inferiority and untouchability that this system expressed were deeply ingrained in the members of both races, and they continue, not surprisingly, to have their effect. Blacks still form, to a considerable extent, a hereditary social and economic community characterized by widespread poverty, unemployment, and social alienation.

When this society finally got around to moving against the caste system, it might have done no more than to enforce straight equality of opportunity, perhaps with the help of weak affirmative action, and then wait a few hundred years while things gradually got better. Fortunately it decided instead to accelerate the process by both public and private institutional action, because there was wide recognition of the intractable character of the problem posed by this insular minority and its place in the nation's history and collective consciousness. This has not been going on very long, but the results are already impressive, especially in speeding the advancement of blacks into the middle class. Affirmative action has not done much to improve the position of poor and unskilled blacks. That is the most serious part of the problem, and it requires a more direct economic attack. But increased access to higher education and upper-level jobs is an essential part of what must be achieved to break the structure of drastic separation that was left largely undisturbed by the legal abolition of the caste system.

Changes of this kind require a generation or two. My guess is that strong affirmative action for blacks will continue to be justified into the early decades of the next century, but that by then it will have accomplished what it can and will no longer be worth the costs. One point deserves special emphasis. The goal to be pursued is the reduction of a great social injustice, not proportional representation of the races in all institutions and professions. Proportional racial representation is of no value in itself.

It is not a legitimate social goal, and it should certainly not be the aim of strong affirmative action, whose drawbacks make it worth adopting only against a serious and intractable social evil.

This implies that the justification for strong affirmative action is much weaker in the case of other racial and ethnic groups, and in the case of women. At least, the practice will be justified in a narrower range of circumstances and for a shorter span of time than it is for blacks. No other group has been treated quite like this and no other group is in a comparable status. Hispanic-Americans occupy an intermediate position, but it seems to me frankly absurd to include persons of oriental descent as beneficiaries of affirmative action, strong or weak. They are not a severely deprived and excluded minority, and their eligibility serves only to swell the numbers that can be included on affirmative action reports. It also suggests that there is a drift in the policy toward adopting the goal of racial proportional representation for its own sake. This is a foolish mistake, and should be resisted. The only legitimate goal of the policy is to reduce egregious racial stratification.

With respect to women, I believe that except over the short term, and in professions or institutions from which their absence is particularly marked, strong affirmative action is not warranted and weak affirmative action is enough. This is based simply on the expectation that the social and economic situation of women will improve quite rapidly under conditions of full equality of opportunity. Recent progress provides some evidence for this. Women do not form a separate hereditary community, characteristically poor and uneducated, and their position is not likely to be self-perpetuating in the same way as that of an outcast race. The process requires less artificial acceleration, and any need for strong affirmative action for women can be expected to end sooner than it ends for blacks.

I said at the outset that there was a tendency to blur the distinction between weak and strong affirmative action. This occurs especially in the use of numerical quotas, a topic on which I want to comment briefly.

A quota may be a method of either weak or strong affirmative action, depending on the circumstances. It amounts to weak affirmative action—a safeguard against discrimination—if, and only if, there is independent evidence that average qualifications for the positions being filled are no lower in the group to which a minimum quota is being assigned than in the applicant group as a whole. This can be presumed true of unskilled jobs that most people can do, but it becomes less likely, and harder to establish, the greater the skill and education required for the position. At these levels, a quota proportional to population, or even to representation of the group in the applicant pool, is almost certain to amount to strong affirmative action. Moreover it is strong affirmative action of a particularly crude and indiscriminate kind, because it permits no variation in the degree of preference on the basis of costs in efficiency, depending on the qualification gap. For this reason I should defend quotas only where they serve the purpose of weak affirmative action. On the whole, strong affirmative action is better implemented by including group preference as one factor in appointment or admission decisions, and letting the results depend on its interaction with other factors.

I have tried to show that the arguments against strong affirmative action are clearly outweighed at present by the need for exceptional measures to remove the stubborn residues of racial caste. But advocates of the policy should acknowledge the reasons against it, which will ensure its termination when it is no longer necessary. Affirmative action is not an end in itself, but a means of dealing with a social situation that should be intolerable to us all.

# Affirmative Action and the Demands of Justice

*N. Scott Arnold*

This essay is about the moral and political justification of affirmative action programs in the United States. Both legally and politically, many of these programs are under attack, though they remain ubiquitous. The concern of this essay, however, is not with what the law says but with what it should say. The main argument advanced in this essay concludes that most of the controversial affirmative action programs are unjustified. . . .

## I. AFFIRMATIVE ACTION PROGRAMS

Affirmative action programs exist in a variety of institutional settings. They can be found as a part of the policies that govern hiring, promotion, and retention (in both the public and private sectors); the awarding of contracts; and admissions to training programs, universities, and professional schools. All such programs can be classified in two broad categories, what can be called "outreach efforts" and "preferential treatment programs." Outreach efforts are intended to broaden the search for the best talent, where "best" is defined by reference to the institution's goals and objectives. One purpose of such programs is to seek to reassure women and minorities that the institution in question does not discriminate on the basis of race, gender, or ethnicity, and that the institution is genuinely concerned to recruit the best talent or award the contract to the most deserving firm. Such programs include advertising in minority-targeted media (e.g., black-owned newspapers), taking extra time and effort to examine the credentials of minority applicants (time and effort that would not be extended to majority applicants with identical records), and setting up or attending special job-fairs or minority-owned business exhibitions to get acquainted with talent that firms and organizations would otherwise not be aware of. Some may complain about these programs on the grounds of unfairness to those not targeted, but such complaints are not widely voiced and are not the subject of the main controversy over affirmative action.

Preferential treatment programs are another matter. These involve taking race, gender, or ethnicity into account as a positive factor in the awarding of contracts, in hiring, or in admissions. It may be a small factor, breaking ties between otherwise equally qualified applicants or contractors, or it may be a rather more important factor, which operates to give preference to the minimally qualified or the less qualified over the more qualified applicants or contractors. Let us consider the various categories of preferential treatment programs in a bit more detail:

***1. Minority set-asides.*** Minority set-aside programs require or encourage government agencies or general contractors who do business with the government to set aside a certain percentage of the total dollar value of a contract for minority-owned (or women-owned) businesses. This may involve an inflexible requirement, or there may be financial incentives for general contractors to do this, or there may even be a form of "bid-rigging" by government agencies to ensure that minority firms are awarded the contract.

*2. **Preferential hiring.*** Hiring policies in the public sector or in the private sector sometimes take race into account as a positive factor in hiring decisions. The operation of preferential hiring programs results in the hiring of members of minorities who would not be hired if race were not a non-negligible factor in the decision. Those doing the hiring may have in mind target percentages that they would like to meet for minority hires ("goals," as they are sometimes called), or they may be operating with relatively hard quotas. The line between goals and quotas is never a clear one, however; few quotas are insensitive to (other) qualifications, and few goals are mere aspirations. What makes something a quota is that those doing the hiring will not seriously consider nonminority candidates for a position or a range of positions for an extended period of time while they search for suitable minority candidates. The mind-set is to find the best qualified minority person for the job. A nonminority candidate would be considered only if no minimally qualified minority candidate could be found at a reasonable search cost.

Quotas are of dubious legality in most settings, since Section 703(j) of Title VII of the 1964 Civil Rights Act states:

> [N]othing contained in this subchapter shall be interpreted to require any employer . . . to grant preferential treatment to any individual or to any group because of the race, color, religion, sex, or national origin of such individual or group on account of an imbalance which may exist with respect to the total number or percentage of persons of any race, color, religion, sex, or national origin employed by any employer . . . in comparison with the total number of percentage of persons of such race, color, religion, sex, or national origin in any community. . . .[1]

However, in some settings quotas have been upheld.[2] Indeed, the courts have sometimes ordered hiring by the numbers as a remedy in discrimination suits.[3] In any event, the dubious legality of quotas does not prevent them from being used. If a manager is in part evaluated and rewarded on the basis of his contribution to his organization's affirmative action goals, minority status will be an important factor in his hiring decisions. As historian Herman Belz has written, describing preferential treatment programs developed in the private sector:

> Many corporations used an equal employment opportunity measurement system that offered rewards and penalties intended to change the behavior of managers, showing them how to arrive at an "ideal" number of minorities in the work force. . . . [C]ompany executives increasingly included equal employment opportunity performance along with traditional business indicators as a standard in overall evaluation.[4]

An important subcategory of preferential treatment programs in the private sector are what might be called *defensive preferential hiring programs.* Firms that do business with the U.S. government and have more than fifty employees, or contracts with the government worth more than $50,000, are required to submit elaborate affirmative action plans, complete with minority hiring goals and timetables within which those goals are to be achieved. Failure to meet these goals according to the timetables can result in an investigation by the Office of Federal Contract Compliance Programs (OFCCP). This is turn can mean enormous administrative burdens for the firm, law-suits, and/or the loss of the contract. To avoid these burdens, risks, and the sheer intrusiveness of the bureaucracy, very often the rational thing for firms to do is to hire by the numbers. This is certainly more efficient than designing and implementing ever more elaborate outreach programs whose prospects for success are uncertain.

Another situation in which defensive preferential hiring programs are used is to avoid what are called "disparate impact lawsuits." Anytime a company with fifteen or more employees (whether or not it is a government contractor) has job requirements, uses tests, or has hiring practices that have a negative "disparate impact" on minorities, it is risking a discrimination lawsuit from disappointed job applicants or from public-spirited lawyers who recruit clients to bring these suits. For example, suppose that 12 percent of the relevant population is African American and the use of a test or job-qualification results in hiring only 6 percent African Americans. This test or job qualification is said to have a (negative) disparate impact on African Americans and can serve as a basis for a lawsuit. The company can still use the test or qualification, but it faces certain hurdles. It can argue that the definition of the reference population that serves to define the disparate impact should be restricted to those with certain job-related qualifications or to those who actually applied for the position, or it can contest the definition of the firm's workforce (e.g., does the workforce include other divisions of the firm located elsewhere?). Perhaps most importantly, the company can argue that the test or qualification that produced the disparate impact is job-related and consistent with business necessity. This can defeat a claim of discrimination based on disparate impact. For example, if one is hiring physicians, applicants must be licensed to practice medicine, and if this requirement has a disparate impact on a protected minority population, that would be legally acceptable. Once the business necessity of the challenged practice has been established, it is then open to the plaintiff to argue that there are other selection criteria that would have a less disparate impact which the employer could have used in place of the challenged practice.

The way the law is currently interpreted has had some perverse effects. It is often very difficult or expensive to establish that a test or requirement is in fact a business necessity, at least given the stringent way the courts have interpreted this.[5] Consequently, it is often rational for companies to drop the requirement or practice before it is challenged and hire by the numbers as best they can, so as to ward off a disparate-impact lawsuit. Or they can continue to use the practice that has a disparate impact and bundle it with a more subjective screening device (e.g., an interview) and use the latter to get the numbers to "come out right." Although the government does not mandate these strategies—and indeed specifically prohibits them in Section 703(j), as quoted above—these strategies are clearly encouraged by the way Title VII of the Civil Rights Act has been interpreted to allow hiring practices with disparate impact to serve to get a lawsuit started. . . .

This essay offers a rather different argument against preferential treatment programs. I want to begin by discussing a relatively rare variant of these programs—purely voluntary preferential treatment programs in publicly traded corporations in the private sector. These programs are *not* defensive in nature but are voluntarily instigated by senior management. For example, the Disney Corporation instituted a set-aside program for minority contractors in the planned expansion of its California facilities. There seems to have been no pressure on the firm to do this from any layer of government, but they decided to set aside $450 million for minority contractors out of a total budget of $3 billion.[6] Similarly, a corporation might have a preferential hiring program that is voluntary in the sense that it would remain in place even if the law were changed so that firms did not need to maintain such programs in order to receive government contracts or to avoid lawsuits. Although there may be few such programs in either hiring or contracting, a discussion of them will prove a useful preliminary to a discussion of the much more common mandated set-asides and defensive preferential hiring programs. More specifically, the next section argues that, subject to some qualifications and exceptions, these voluntary set-asides and hiring programs are wrong; subsequent sections apply the same reasoning to more common types of preferential treatment programs that are mandated or encouraged by the government.

## II. THE PROBLEM WITH PURELY VOLUNTARY PREFERENTIAL TREATMENT PROGRAMS

The argument to be advanced in this section is a moral one, not a legal one. The law introduces complications that will he addressed shortly, but the main argument of this section concerns the morality of purely voluntary preferential treatment programs in contracting and hiring. The first premise is that management has a fiduciary responsibility to its shareholders to act in the firm's best financial interests, subject to the constraints imposed by the law. There may be exceptions to this general principle, and thus it is a rebutable presumption, but typically when a board of directors hires a chief executive officer (CEO) or a management team, there is a shared understanding that management will act in the firm's best financial interests. This shared understanding is the basis of the fiduciary responsibility (and thus the moral obligation) of the CEO or management team. Possible exceptions to one side, there is an ambiguity in the concept of what constitutes the firm's best financial interests. Is it maximizing profits in the near term? Increasing market share? Maximizing shareholoder value? Or some combination of these? Answers to these questions can be variable and indeterminate, though they may be addressed at the time the board hires the CEO or management team. Nevertheless, as agents for the firm's principals(i.e., the stockholders), management's primary goal and responsibility is to advance the financial interests of the firm. However the ambiguity about the firm's best financial interests is resolved, there is the further difficulty of identifying which policies will actually further that goal. Management's moral responsibility to the shareholders does not require perfection in the choice of policies, but it does require that managers act according to their best judgment about what will advance the financial interests of the firm. One thing this implies is that managers are not permitted to further their own conception of justice by instituting programs such as Disney's, at least when they foresee that this is not financially advantageous to the firm. . . .

Now for the exceptions and complications. Note that this argument does not apply to privately held firms owned and managed by one individual. An owner of such a firm might decide on his own to implement a preferential treatment program; if there is any thing morally objectionable about this, it is not because the managers have violated a fiduciary obligation to the owners. Similarly, the owners of a closely held corporation might jointly agree to order management (which might consist of one or more of their number) to institute a preferential treatment program not required or encouraged by law. Finally, there could be cases in which the owners of a privately held company announce, upon making an initial public offering of stock, that the company will pursue such programs as a matter of company policy, even if it is detrimental to the firm's financial interests. Or they could go before the shareholders at the annual shareholders' meeting and announce their intention to pursue preferential policies that are not in the firm's financial interests, detailing their best estimates of the costs and benefits (both financial and otherwise) of these policies. Under the circumstances, shareholders would have no grounds for complaint. Let us suppose, however, that a firm's management does not do either of these things. Suppose instead that they simply decide, perhaps with the acquiescence of the board of directors, to pursue a social-justice agenda (or an environmental agenda, or a charitable-giving agenda) that foreseeably harms the firm's financial interests. They do not tell the shareholders about it, or if they do, they do so after the fact and mislead them about its costs and benefits. Under such circumstances, they have violated their fiduciary obligations to the shareholders and thus have acted wrongly.

One objection to this argument would be to charge that purely voluntary preferential treatment programs in contracting and hiring really are in a firm's best financial interests. Proponents of affirmative action often claim that a diverse workforce is in the company's best financial interests, and indeed can point to an array of diversity programs that large corporations have instituted and an army of diversity consultants whom companies have hired to run them.

It is difficult to evaluate this objection for the simple reason that it is difficult to determine how many preferential treatment programs in contracting or hiring are truly voluntary in the sense that they would persist in the absence of any legal pressure to maintain them. The proliferation of diversity programs does not prove very much in this context for at least two reasons. First, and most obviously, antidiscrimination law is extremely far-reaching in its coverage. As I noted above, disparate-impact lawsuits can be brought against any firm with more than fifteen employees. As for set-asides, an estimated 27 million people work for firms that do business with the federal government. . . . An expensive and elaborate diversity program is part of a well-conceived defensive preferential treatment program for large companies.

Second, diversity programs include much more than preferential programs in hiring and contracting. They often include attempts to achieve a more harmonious and effective workforce by sensitizing workers to cultural and gender differences. They also try to prevent, or at least insulate the company from, other types of lawsuits (e.g., those arising from the Americans with Disabilities Act, sexual harassment lawsuits). For these reasons, the percentage of preferential hiring and contracting programs that would continue to exist in the absence of threats of Title VII litigation or the loss of government contracts is impossible to determine. For the sake of argument, however, let us grant that there could be purely voluntary preferential treatment programs which management reasonably believes are in a firm's best financial interests; the above argument would not apply to such programs, if in fact they do exist. . . .

## III. NONVOLUNTARY PREFERENTIAL TREATMENT PROGRAMS: THE PEROTIAN ARGUMENT AND THE DEMANDS OF JUSTICE

The argument of Section II does not address the most common types of preferential treatment programs that are currently in force—those which the state mandates or encourages. These include minority set-asides and preferential hiring programs involving government contractors, as well as defensive programs in the private sector that are instituted to avoid disparate-impact lawsuits. When people talk about the affirmative action controversy, these are the programs (along with similar programs in higher education) that they are taking about.

It seems that an argument parallel to the one set out above could be mounted against these programs as well. Government bureaus are analogous to firms, with citizens occupying a role analogous to that of shareholders. Because former presidential candidate Ross Perot reminds us that in a democracy the citizens own their government, let us call this "the Perotian Argument."[7] Whether or not citizens literally own their government as Perot maintains, it is clear that they have a legitimate expectation that the government will try to get the best mix of quality and price in the goods and services that it buys from the private sector. They also have a legitimate expectation that the government will not gratuitously impose added costs or reduced quality on goods and services exchanged in purely private business dealings. Of course, the legitimacy of these expectations is purely moral, not epistemic. Only the very naive believe that governments generally meet these expectations. Most citizens are well aware that governments very often do not. But they should. By mandating and encouraging preferential treatment programs, however, the government violates citizen's legitimate expectations about how their government will behave.

There are two premises in this argument: that the citizens of a democracy have a legitimate expectation that the government will not act in such a way as to raise the price and/or reduce the quality of goods and services in both the public and private sectors; and that nonvoluntary preferential treatment programs violate this expectation. The first is hard to argue with, at least as a general proposition. It is simply a demand that government act efficiently in procuring goods and services and in affecting the private sector. There are undoubtedly exceptions to this general proposition, and thus it is a rebuttable presumption; indeed, proponents of preferential treatment programs may insist that in this area an exception should be made because of the demands of justice. This claim will be taken up in due course, but for now it is sufficient to note that those who control the government in a democracy do not own the resources they control. They have a fiduciary relationship with the citizenry that closely parallels the relationship between corporate officers and shareholders; this serves as the basis for the legitimate expectations just mentioned. . . .

Proponents of these programs might agree with all this and yet insist that even though these programs do impose real costs, that is simply the price of justice. Justice, John Rawls asserts, is the first virtue of social institutions.[8] If justice requires preferential treatment programs, so be it. This is essentially the same objection raised against the purely voluntary programs considered in the last section. It is now time to give it full consideration. I shall argue that even if the demands of justice require preferential treatment programs, the government is not justified in requiring or encouraging them. In other words, the argument that follows grants, for the sake of discussion, that justice requires preferential treatment programs, and yet concludes that these programs are, all things considered, unjustified.

This argument starts with some suggestive parallels with Locke's observations about the problems of a state of nature. Recall that a state of nature is a pre-political society in which people have various natural rights, including the rights to life, liberty, and property. In addition, they have the right to punish those who violate their other rights. All this gives rise to what Locke calls the "inconveniences of a state of nature." These include the following: Some people cannot enforce their rights. Some people do not correctly apply the natural law, or they tend to be biased when judging in their own cases, or they tend to mispunish, overpunish, etc. They use the demands of justice as a cloak to further their own interests and/or the interests of their friends at the expense of others and at the expense of justice. This worry is a special case of the central worry of Western political philosophy, at least in the liberal tradition: How is government to be limited? Whether or not one believes in Lockean rights, there is no doubt that the state faces a permanent threat—very often realized—of being hijacked to serve private interests. Historically, state power has been used to advance private interests at the expense of the public interest, including the demands of justice, however one understands these concepts. . . .

Two plausible requirements . . . must be met if the power of the state is to be used to further some conception of the demands of (distributive or compensatory) justice:

(i) Proponents of state action must get a political consensus for doing what justice requires. A political consensus does not require unanimity among the people or their elected representatives, but it does require that supporters of government intervention make their case publicly and get an on-the-record vote from the legislature or from the electorate through a referendum. Let us call this the *Public Justification requirement*. . . .

(ii) Proponents of state action must explain how and why their proposal will not permit state power to be systematically abused to further private interests at the expense of those disadvantaged by the policies in question. Very often, proposed legislation will foreseeably but unavoidably help groups and individuals it is not intended to help at the expense of groups and individuals it is not intended to harm; if this is so, that fact has to be made public and a case has to be made that this is a cost worth paying. . . .

## IV. MINORITY SET-ASIDE PROGRAMS

The main question this section and the next will address is whether minority set-aside programs and nonvoluntary preferential hiring programs satisfy the two requirements. Let us begin with the former. Minority set asides began in 1968 with the Small Business Administration. The SBA served as prime contractor for other governmental agencies, awarding procurement contracts to small businesses. It interpreted its statutory authority to allow it to set aside a certain percentage of its contracts to businesses owned by "socially and economically disadvantaged" individuals, which was further interpreted to apply primarily to "minority business enterprises" (MBEs). The first set-aside program legislated by Congress was included in the 1977 Public Works Employment Act (PWEA).[9] It required each prime contractor to set aside 10 percent of the dollar value of the contract for MBEs, which were explicitly defined as businesses at least 50 percent owned by members of minority groups; or, if the business was a joint stock company, at least 51 percent of the stock had to be owned by minorities. Targeted minorities included African Americans, Hispanics, Asians, Native Americans, Eskimos, and Aleuts. The PWEA contained a provision to suspend the requirement if there were no available minority firms. In subsequent years, state and local governments instituted their own minority set-aside programs modeled on federal programs. Other set-aside programs at the federal level were introduced piecemeal, either by executive order or as part of other legislation.

Do minority set-aside programs meet the Public Justification requirement? Set-aside programs instituted by the executive branch (such as the SBA's program) were not subject to any public debate and discussion in Congress; they were simply imposed by the executive branch, so they clearly do not meet the requirement. The case of set-asides mandated by Congress is not as simple, since set-aside provisions can be found in many pieces of legislation that Congress passed and that the president signed into law. The crucial issue is the legislative history of a given set-aside provision.

The first of these provisions—the one included in the PWEA—is especially important, since it set the precedent; proponents of subsequent programs appealed to it as conferring presumptive validity on their proposals. One would expect that the first modern attempt to introduce race-conscious programs by legislation would occasion considerable congressional debate and discussion, but in fact that did not happen. There were no committee hearings or reports relating to the minority set-aside provision in the PWEA, probably because the provision was offered as a floor amendment in the House of Representatives. It passed on a voice vote and was accorded similar treatment in the Senate. . . .

## V. PREFERENTIAL TREATMENT IN HIRING

Though minority set-asides are an important form of preferential treatment, preferential hiring programs are more significant. They impact many more people and seem to have provoked more passionate debate. The vast majority of preferential hiring programs are mandated or encouraged by the government and would likely not exist but for that pressure. They fall into three categories: (1) those mandated by the courts in response to successful discrimination suits; (2) defensive preferential hiring programs encouraged by the executive branch for contractors doing business with the federal government; and (3) defensive preferential hiring programs undertaken to ward off disparate-impact lawsuits. Let us consider each of these in turn to see if the Public Justification and Anti-Hijacking requirements were satisfied when these programs were instituted.

*1. Court-ordered preferential hiring programs.* Courts occasionally order hiring (or promotions) by the numbers in response to successful lawsuits brought under Title VII of the 1964 Civil Rights Act. Section 706 of Title VII of the 1964 Civil Rights Act. Section 706 of Title VII gives a court considerable discretion in ordering remedies for discriminatory practices. In response to a finding of discrimination, Section 706(g) (1) says,

> the court may enjoin the respondent from engaging in such unlawful employment practice and may order such affirmative action as may be appropriate which may include but is not limited to reinstatement or hiring of employees, with or without back pay . . . or any other equitable relief that the court deems appropriate.[10]

Though it is doubtful whether "quota relief" is consistent with Section 703(j) of Title VII, the courts have assumed that it is and have on occasion ordered hiring or promotion by the numbers. They have forced employers to hire a certain percentage of minorities against whom no discrimination has been proven or even alleged. Typically, these remedies are imposed on employers who seem particularly racist or sexist in their policies and practices. This remedy fails to satisfy the Public Justification requirement, even if it is legally permissible, since nowhere in the Civil Rights Act is this remedy explicitly mentioned. Congress never debated and sanctioned hiring or promotion by the numbers as a remedy for discrimination, no matter how egregious. The fact, if indeed it is a fact, that Congress somehow left the door open for quota remedies is irrelevant for the purposes of the Public Justification requirement, since this requirement imposes burdens on the legislature. This form of affirmative action is relatively rare, however, in comparison to the next two types to be considered, so perhaps we should not make too much of this failure.

*2. Preferential hiring under various executive orders.* In 1965, President Lyndon Johnson issued Executive Order 11246, which created the Office of Federal Contract Compliance (later renamed the Office of Federal Contract Compliance Programs) and led to the establishment of defensive preferential hiring programs by government contractors. Later, President Richard Nixon extended preferential hiring requirements to cover the civil service in Executive Order 11478. The story of the development of this policy has been told elsewhere. The "goals and timetables" approach to hiring was inaugurated under these executive orders, which remain in effect to this day. The OFCCP has considerable power over firms doing business with the government. Many such firms do business exclusively (or nearly exclusively) with the government and can ill-afford to walk away from government contracts. Though firms are nominally prohibited from hiring by the numbers, they must submit an affirmative action plan, complete with goals and timetables. The failure of so-called "good faith efforts" to yield the right hiring numbers can bring the OFCCP down on a contractor with a vengeance. This office has much more power than the EEOC, since it can deny contracts without a court finding that a company has been guilty of discrimination. OFCCP officials can simply refuse to certify a company as able to bid on contracts. Although this sanction has seldom been applied, the threat of it is usually sufficient to get compliance. . . .

*3. **Other defensive preferential hiring programs.*** Defensive preferential hiring programs among firms not doing business with the federal government came into existence in response to judicial interpretation of Title VII of the 1964 Civil Rights Act. In *Griggs v. Duke Power* (1971)[11] and subsequent cases, the Supreme Court ruled that hiring practices and policies having a disparate impact on minorities were prima facie suspect and could be grounds for a Title VII lawsuit. Moreover, the EEOC has made it clear that it will not bring disparate-impact lawsuits against employers who abide by what is called "the 80 percent rule."[12] This rule states that if the percentage of women or minorities a firm hires is at least 80 percent of their percentage in the relevant populations, the firm will not ordinarily be subject to an investigation and a disparate-impact lawsuit. Rational firms have responded to these pressures by instituting preferential hiring programs to reach safe harbor from such lawsuits. In 1989, the Supreme Court pulled back from the standards imposed by *Griggs* and its progeny in *Ward's Cove Packing Co. v. Antonio.*[13] It lessened the pressure on businesses to engage in preferential hiring by redistributing the burden of proof in disparate-impact cases. In response to the Court's ruling in *Ward's Cove*, Congress reimposed the *Griggs* standards in the Civil Rights Act of 1991. Were the Public Justification and Anti-Hijacking requirements satisfied for preferential hiring programs anywhere in this series of events? Let us begin with the original legislation: Title VII of the 1964 Civil Rights Act.

If one purpose of Title VII was to foster preferential hiring programs, proponents of the law would have had to make clear that employment practices that have a disparate impact on minorities create a rebuttable presumption of discrimination. Under this construal of Title VII, the intended beneficiaries would be the women and minorities who successfully sued, as well as those who would be hired to avoid such suits, and presumably other women and minorities who might indirectly benefit from preferential hirings and promotions. The intended victims would be the owners of the businesses who, for whatever reason, used employment practices (or hired managers who used such practices) that created a disparate impact. Others in the firm, such as other managers who would have to struggle with affirmative action regulations and other employees who would be negatively affected in a variety of ways, might also count as intended victims of the policy, though that depends on how the argument is framed. The argument would have to be made that the benefits of the law, as so interpreted, outweigh the costs.

What about the unintended beneficiaries and victims? The Anti-Hijacking requirement stipulates that they have to be identified as well. The main unintended victims are, of course, the nonminority candidates who otherwise would have gotten the jobs. Academic defenders of preferential hiring are quick to point out that their being excluded is not a result of stereotyping and does not stigmatize them in the way ordinary racial discrimination would. Moreover, if there were ways to solve the underlying social problems without hurting these people, defenders of preferential hiring programs would probably embrace them. All this makes the victim status of disappointed majority job candidates unintended, however foreseeable their plight is. However, they are still adversely affected, and whatever the demands of justice, the lack of stigmatization is cold comfort to someone who did not get a job or promotion because of his or her race or gender. The unintended beneficiaries of preferential hiring programs are a little harder to identify. Clearly, government bureaucrats and lawyers in the equal employment opportunity/affirmative action industry count as foreseen though unintended beneficiaries. In addition, the private sector has its affirmative action officers, "diversity consultants," and others who profit from attempts to eliminate (perceived) social injustice.

The above identifies the intended and unintended beneficiaries and victims of preferential hiring programs, an identification essential to satisfying the Public Justification and Anti-Hijacking requirements. The main problem for defenders of preferential hiring programs is that legislators supporting Title VII never made this case. . . .

## NOTES

1. 42 U.S.C. 2000e-2(j).
2. Kaiser Aluminum had a training program that used racial preferences for blacks over whites, which was upheld by the Supreme Court in *United Steelworkers of America v. Weber*, 443 U.S. 193 (1979).
3. See, e.g., *Morrow v. Crisler*, 491 F.2d 1053 (1974), and *NAACP v. Allen*, 493 F.2d 614 (1974).
4. Herman Belz, *Equality Transformed* (New Brunswick, NJ: Transaction Publishers, 1991), p. 105. See also Theodore V. Purcell, S.j., et al., "What Are the Social Responsibilities of Psychologists in Industry? A Symposium." *Personnel Psychology*, 27 (Autumn 1974): 436.
5. See Richard Epstein, *Forbidden Grounds: The Case against Employment Discrimination Laws* (Cambridge, MA: Harvard University Press, 1992), pp. 212–22.
6. Chris Woodyard,"Disney to Boost Minority Builders," *Los Angels Times* (June 16, 1992), p. D2. Subsequently, the planned expansion was significantly scaled back.
7. Or is it the taxpayers who own the government? Not all citizens are taxpayers and not all taxpayers are citizens, though the two groups substantially overlap. Since I do not wish to claim that anyone literally owns the government, this complication need not be pursued. All that is claimed in what follows is that citizens or taxpayers have a principal-agent relationship with their government analogous to shareholders' relationship to management, at least when it comes to the government's dealings in the economy.
8. John Rawls, *A Theory of Justice* (Cambridge, MA: The Belknap Press of Harvard University Press, 1971), p. 3.
9. Information in this and subsequent paragraphs on the set-aside provision in the PWEA comes from the *Congressional Record*, 95th Congress, 1st session (1977), pp. 5327–30.
10. 42 U.S.C. 2000e-(g) (1).
11. 401 U.S. 424 (1971).
12. Uniform Guidelines on Employee Selection Procedures (1978), 29 C.F.R. Section 1607.4D (1989).
13. 490 U.S. 642 (1989). [See the case presentation below in this volume. Ed.]

# Goals and Quotas in Hiring and Promotion

*Tom L. Beauchamp*

Since the 1960s, government and corporate policies that set goals for hiring women and minorities have been sharply criticized. Their opponents maintain that many policies establish indefensible quotas and discriminate in reverse against sometimes more qualified white males. In 1991 President George Bush referred to the word "quota" as the "dreaded q-word." Quotas, he said, had "finally" been eliminated from government policies.

Although it must be acknowledged that some policies with target goals or quotas do violate rules of fair and equal treatment, I believe that such policies can be justified. My objective is to defend corporate policies that set goals of representing groups in the pools from which corporations draw their employees. I argue that goals and quotas, rightly conceived, are congenial to management—not hostile as they are often depicted. Both the long-range interest of corporations and the public interest are served by carefully selected preferential policies.

## I. TWO POLAR POSITIONS

In 1965 President Lyndon Johnson issued an executive order that announced a toughened federal initiative requiring goals and timetables for equal employment opportunity.[1] This initiative was the prevailing regulatory approach for many years. But eventually two competing schools of thought on the justifiability of preferential programs have come into sharp conflict. The first stands in opposition to quotas, accepting the view that all persons are entitled to an equal opportunity and to constitutional guarantees of equal protection in a color-blind, nonsexist society. Civil rights laws, in this approach, should offer protection only to *individuals* who have been victimized by forms of discrimination, not to *groups* (though it is controversial whether individuals can be harmed merely by virtue of a group membership[2]). Hiring goals, timetables, and quotas only work to create new victims of discrimination.

The second school supports strong affirmative action policies. The justification of affirmative action programs is viewed as the correction of discriminatory employment practices, not group compensation for prior injustice. The terms "affirmative action" and "quotas" have proved troublesome, because they have been defined in both minimal and maximal ways. The original meaning of "affirmative action" was minimalist. It referred to plans to safeguard equal opportunity, to protect against discrimination, to advertise positions openly, and to create scholarship programs to ensure recruitment from specific groups.[3] Few now oppose open advertisement and the like, and if this were all that were meant by "affirmative action," few would oppose it. However, "affirmative action" has assumed new and expanded meanings. Today it is typically associated with quotas and preferential policies that target specific groups, especially women or minority members.

Although the meaning of "affirmative action" is inherently contestable, I will here stipulate the meaning as functionally equivalent to the following statement (in 2002) of the Hewlett-Packard Company:

> *Affirmative action* at HP means that the company extends its commitment beyond equal opportunity to proactively recruit, hire, develop and promote qualified women, minorities, people with disabilities, and Vietnam-era veterans. In addition, HP has a commitment to supporting external educational and community organizations that support these objectives.[4]

Thus, I will use "affirmative action" to refer to positive steps taken to hire persons from groups previously and presently discriminated against, leaving open what will count as a "positive step" to remove discrimination.

The supporters of affirmative action—the second school, to which I belong—view the first school as construing "equal opportunity" and "civil rights" so narrowly that persons affected by discrimination do not receive adequate aid in overcoming the effects of prejudice. This second school believes that mandated hiring protects minorities and erodes discrimination, whereas the identification of individual victims of discrimination would be, as the editors of *The New York Times* once put it, the "project of a century and [would] leave most victims of discrimination with only empty legal rights."[5]

These two schools may not be as far apart morally as they first appear. If legal enforcement of civil rights law could efficiently and comprehensively identify discriminatory treatment and could protect its victims, both schools would agree that the legal-enforcement strategy is preferable. But there are at least two reasons why this solution will not be accepted by the second school. First, there is the unresolved issue of whether those in contemporary society who have been advantaged by *past* discrimination (for example, wealthy owners of family businesses) deserve their advantages. Second, there is the issue of whether *present*, ongoing discrimination can be successfully, comprehensively, and fairly combatted by identifying and prosecuting violators without resorting to quotas. This second issue is the more pivotal one and is closely related to the justification of specific targets.

A "quota," as used here, does not mean that fixed numbers of employees should be hired regardless of an individual's qualification for a position. Quotas are simply target employment percentages. In some cases a less-qualified person may be hired or promoted; but it has never been a part of affirmative action to hire below the threshold of "basically qualified,"[6] and often significant questions exist in the employment situation about the exact qualifications needed for positions.[7] Quotas, then, are numerically expressible goals that one is obligated to pursue with good faith and due diligence. If it is impossible to hire the basically qualified persons called for by the goals in a given time frame, the schedule can be relaxed, as long as the target goals, the due diligence, and the good faith continue. The word *quota* does not mean "fixed number" in any stronger sense.

Today the language of "quotas" is almost nonexistent in corporate policy statements, but this fact should not be taken to indicate that corporations now deviate from the principles that originally gave rise to the language and use of quotas. For example, in December 2002, General Motors stated its policy on "Workplace Diversity" as follows:

> GM recognizes that it is essential for [its] work force to reflect both the marketplace and customers. . . . General Motors remains committed to affirmative action. . . . GM monitors its programs to determine whether recruitment, hiring, and other personnel practices are operating in a nondiscriminatory manner. It also includes outreach programs designed to identify and reach qualified individuals of any race or gender that have not been fully represented in the talent pools from which GM selects and promotes employees.[8]

Similarly, ExxonMobil announced in 2002 that although its "total employment has declined in recent years, the percentage representation of women and minorities in our workforce has steadily increased." ExxonMobil announced that, by program design, among its "officials and managers," women increased 34 percent and minorities 55 percent over the previous decade; among its "professionals," women increased 9 percent and minorities 25 percent over the same period.[9]

## II. DATA ON DISCRIMINATION

Discrimination in hiring and promotion is, of course, not present throughout American society, but it is pervasive. An impressive body of statistics constituting (prima facie) evidence of discrimination has been assembled in recent years. These data indicate that in sizable parts of American society white males continue to receive the highest entry-level salaries when compared to all other social groups; that women with similar credentials and experience to those of men are commonly hired at lower positions or earn lower starting salaries than men and are promoted at one-half the rate of their male counterparts, with the consequence that the gap between salaries and promotion rates is still growing at an increasing rate; that 70 percent or more of white-collar positions are held by women, although they hold only about 10 percent of management positions; that three out of seven U.S. employees occupy white-collar positions, whereas the ratio is but one of seven for African Americans; and, finally, that a significant racial gap in unemployment statistics is a consistent pattern in the United States, with the gap now greatest for college-educated, African-American males.[10]

Such statistics are not decisive indicators of discrimination, but additional facts also support the conclusion that racist and sexist biases powerfully influence the marketplace.

***Housing.*** For example, studies of real estate rentals, housing sales, and home mortgage lending show a disparity in loan rejection rates between white applicants and minority applicants with comparable bank and credit histories. Wide disparities exist even after statistics are adjusted for economic differences; minority applicants are over 50 percent more likely to be denied a loan than white applicants of equivalent economic status. Other studies indicate that discrimination in sales of houses is prevalent in the United States. Race appears to be as important as socioeconomic status in failing to secure both houses and loans, and studies also show that the approval rate for African Americans increases in lending institutions with an increase in the proportion of minority employees in that institution.[11]

***Jobs.*** A similar pattern is found in employment. In 1985 the Grier Partnership and the Urban League produced independent studies that reveal striking disparities in the employment levels of college-trained African Americans and whites in Washington, D.C., one of the best markets for African Americans. Both studies found that college-trained African Americans have much more difficulty than their white counterparts in securing employment. Both cite discrimination as the major underlying factors.[12] In a 1991 study by the Urban Institute, employment practices in Washington, D.C. and Chicago were examined. Equally qualified, identically dressed white and African American applicants for jobs were used to test for bias in the job market, as presented by newspaper-advertized positions. Whites and African Americans were matched identically for speech patterns, age, work experience, personal characteristics, and physical build. Investigators found repeated discrimination against African-American male applicants. The higher the position, the higher the level of discrimination. The white men received job offers three times more often than the equally qualified African Americans who interviewed for the same position. The authors of the study concluded that discrimination against African-American men is "widespread and entrenched."[13] Very similar results were found in other studies in the 1990s.[14]

These statistics and empirical studies help frame racial discrimination in the United States. Anyone who believes that only a narrow slice of surface discrimination exists will be unlikely to agree with what I have been and will be arguing, at least if my proposals entail strong affirmative action measures. By constrast, one who believes that discrimination is securely and almost invisibly entrenched in many sectors of society will be more likely to endorse or at least tolerate resolute affirmative action policies.

These statistics help frame the significance of racial discrimination in the United States. Although much is now known about patterns of discrimination, much remains to be discovered, in part because it is hidden and subtle.

## III. PROBLEMS OF PROOF AND INTENTION

Although racism and sexism are commonly envisioned as intentional forms of favoritism and exclusion, intent to discriminate is not a necessary condition of discrimination. Institutional networks can unintentionally hold back or exclude persons. Hiring by personal friendships and word of mouth are common instances, as are seniority systems. Numerical targets are important remedies for these camouflaged areas, where it is particularly difficult to shatter patterns of discrimination and reconfigure the environment.[15]

The U.S. Supreme Court once held unanimously that persons may be guilty of discriminating against the handicapped when there is no "invidious animus, but rather [a discriminatory effect] of thoughtlessness and indifference— of benign neglect." The Court held that discrimination would be difficult and perhaps impossible to prove or to prevent if *intentional* discrimination alone qualified as discrimination.[16] The Court acknowledged that discrimination is often invisible to those who discriminate. This, in my judgment, is the main reason goals and quotas are an indispensable government and management tool: They may be the only way to break down patterns of discrimination and bring meaningful diversity to the workplace.

Courts in the United States have on a few occasions resorted to quotas because an employer had an intractable history and a bullheaded resistance to change that necessitated strong measures. The Supreme Court has never directly supported quotas using the term "quota,"[17] but it has upheld affirmative action programs that contain numerically expressed hiring formulas that are intended to reverse the patterns of both intentional and unintentional discrimination.[18] At the same time, the Supreme Court has suggested that some affirmative action programs using numerical formulas have gone too far.[19] Whether the formulas are excessive depends on the facts in the individual case. The case of *Adarand Constructors Inc. v. Pena* (1995) defended a standard requiring that there be a compelling governmental interest for race-based preferences in construction contracts for minority-owned companies; it continued the long line of cases that weigh and balance different interests.

I believe the Supreme Court has consistently adhered to this balancing strategy and that it is the right moral perspective as well as the proper framework for American law.[20] It allows use of race and sex as relevant bases of policies if and only if it is essential to do so in order to achieve a larger and justified social purpose.

These reasons for using race and sex in setting employment goals are far distant from the role of these properties in invidious discrimination. Racial discrimination and sexual discrimination typically spring from feelings of superiority and a sense that other groups deserve lower social status. Affirmative action entails no such attitude or intent. Its purpose is to restore to persons a status they have been unjustifiably denied, to help them escape stigmatization, and to foster relationships of interconnectedness in society.[21]

Affirmative action in pockets of vicious and visceral racism will likely be needed for another generation, after which we should have reached our goals of fair opportunity and equal consideration. Once these goals are achieved, affirmative action will no longer be justified and should be abandoned. The goal to be reached at that point is not proportional representation, which has occasionally been used as a basis for fixing target numbers in affirmative action policies, but as such is merely a means to the end of discrimination, not an end to be pursued for its own sake. The goal is simply fair opportunity and equal consideration.

Issues about the breadth and depth of discrimination may divide us as a society more than any other issue about affirmative action. Discriminatory attitudes and practices are likely to be deep-seated in some institutions, while shallow or absent in others. Society is not monolithic in the depth and breadth of discrimination. In some cases affirmative action programs are not needed; in other cases only modest good faith programs are in order; and in still others enforced quotas are necessary to break down discriminatory patterns.

Because we deeply disagree about the depth, breadth, and embeddedness of discrimination, we disagree further over the social policies that will rid us of the problem. Those who believe discrimination is relatively shallow and detectable look for formulas and remedies that center on *equal opportunity*. Those who believe discrimination is deep, camouflaged, and embedded in society look for formulas that center on *measurable outcomes*.[22]

## IV. WHY CORPORATIONS SHOULD WELCOME GOALS AND QUOTAS

Little has been said to this point about corporate policy. I shall discuss only *voluntary* programs that use target goals and quotas. They stand in sharp contrast to *legally enforced* goals and quotas. There are at least three reasons why it is in the interest of responsible businesses to use aggressive plans that incorporate goals and quotas: (1) an improved work force, (2) maintenance of a bias-free corporate environment, and (3) congeniality to managerial planning.

(1) First, corporations that discriminate will fail to look at the full range of qualified persons in the market and, as a result, will employ a higher percentage of second-best employees. Numerous American institutions have learned that discrimination causes the institution to lose opportunities to make contact with the full range of qualified persons who might be contacted. Their competitive position is thereby weakened, just as a state university would be weakened if it hired faculty entirely from its own state. These institutions have found that promoting diversity in the workforce is correlated with high quality employees, reductions in the costs of discrimination claims, a lowering of absenteeism, less turnover, and increased customer satisfaction.[23]

In fiscal year 2003 the Dell Computer Corporation announced that, by design, it had substantially increased its diversity recruiting and global diversity. Dell noted that "companies that diversify work force and supply bases are more successful in gaining access to multicultural markets. Mutually beneficial relationships with minority suppliers open doors for Dell to market its products and services to women and minority customers, provide growth opportunities for our suppliers, and benefit our communities."[24]

Maintaining a high-quality work force is consistent with the management style already implemented in many companies. For example, James R. Houghton, chairman of Corning Glass, established voluntary quotas to increase the quality of employees, not merely the number of women and black employees. Corning began by establishing the following increased-percentage targets for the total employment population to be met between 1988 and 1991: women professionals to increase from 17.4 percent to 23.2 percent, black professionals to increase from 5.1 percent to 7.4 percent, the number of black senior managers to increase from 1 to 5, and the number of women senior managers to increase from 4 to 10. Corning management interpreted the targets as follows: "Those numbers were not commandments set in stone. We won't hire people just to meet a number. It will be tough to meet some of [our targets]." Corning found that it could successfully recruit in accordance with these targets, but also found severe difficulty in maintaining the desired target numbers in the work force because of an attrition problem. The company continued thereafter to take the view that in an age in which the percentage of white males in the employment pool is constantly declining, a "total quality company" must vigorously recruit women and minorities using target goals.[25]

(2) Second, pulling the foundations from beneath affirmative action hiring would open old wounds in many institutions that have been

developing plans through consent-decree processes with courts as well as direct negotiations with minority groups and unions. Many corporations report that they have invested heavily in eliminating managerial biases and stereotypes while training managers to hire appropriately. They are concerned that without the pressure of an affirmative action plan, which they draft internally, managers will fail to recognize their own biases and stereotypes. Removal of voluntary programs might additionally stigmatize a business by signalling to minorities that a return to older patterns of discrimination is permissible. Such stigmatization is a serious blow in today's competitive market.

(3) Third, affirmative action programs involving quotas have been successful for the corporations that have adopted them, and there is no need to try to fix what is not broken. As the editors of *Business Week* once maintained, "Over the years business and regulators have worked out rules and procedures for affirmative action, including numerical yardsticks for sizing up progress, that both sides understand. It has worked and should be left alone."[26] It has worked because of the above-mentioned improved work force and because of a businesslike approach typical of managerial planning: Managers set goals and timetables for almost everything—from profits to salary bonuses. From a manager's point of view, setting goals and timetables is simply a way of measuring progress.

One survey of 200 major American corporations found that the same approach has often been taken to the management of affirmative action: Over 75 percent of these corporations already use "voluntary internal numerical objectives to assess [equal employment opportunity] performance." Another survey of 300 top corporate executives reported that 72 percent believe that minority hiring improves rather than hampers productivity, while 64 percent said there is a need for the government to help bring women and minorities into the mainstream of the work force. Many corporations have used their records in promotion and recruitment to present a positive image of corporate life in public reports and recruiting brochures.[27]

Affirmative action has also worked to increase productivity and improve consumer relationships. Corporations in consumer goods and services industries report increased respect and increased sales after achieving affirmative action results. They report that they are able to target some customers they otherwise could not reach, enjoy increased competitiveness, and better understand consumer complaints as a result of a more diverse work force. Corporations with aggressive affirmative action programs have also been shown to outperform their competitors.[28]

## V. CONCLUSION

If the social circumstances of discrimination were to be substantially altered, my conclusions in this paper would be modified. The introduction of preferential treatment on a large scale undoubtedly runs the risk of producing economic advantages to individuals who do not deserve them, protracted court battles, congressional lobbying by power groups, a lowering of admission and work standards, reduced social and economic efficiency, increased racial and minority hostility, and the continued suspicion that well-placed minorities received their positions purely on the basis of quotas. These reasons constitute a strong case against affirmative action policies that use numerical goals and quotas. However, this powerful case is not sufficient to overcome the still stronger counterarguments.

## NOTES


1. Executive Order 11246. C.F.R. 339 (1964–65). This order required all federal contractors to develop affirmative action policies. For subsequent developments, see Bernard E. Anderson, "The Ebb and Flow of Enforcing Executive Order 11246," *American Economic Review Papers and Proceedings*, 86 (1996): 298–301.
2. See J. Angelo Corlett, "Racism and Affirmative Action," *Journal of Social Philosophy* 24 (1993): 163–75; and Cass R. Sunstein, "The Limits of Compensatory Justice," *Nomos XXXIII: Compensatory Justice*, Ed. John Chapman (New York: New York University Press, 1991): 281-310.
3. See Thomas Nagel, "A Defense of Affirmative Action," Testimony before the Subcommittee on the Constitution of the Senate Judiciary Committee, June 18, 1981; and Louis Pojman, "The Moral Status of Affirmative Action," *Public Affairs Quarterly*, 6 (1992): 181–206.
4. http://www.hp.com/hpinfo/abouthp/diversity/nondisc.htm
5. "Their Right to Remedy, Affirmed," *The New York Times*, July 3, 1986, p. A30.
6. This standard has been recognized at least since *EEOC v. AT&T*, No. 73–149 (E.D. Pa. 1973). See also U.S. Department of Labor, Employment Standards Administration, Office of Federal Contract Compliance Programs, "OFCCP: Making EEO and Affirmative Action Work," January 1987 OFCCP-28.
7. See Harry Holzer and David Neumark, "Are Affirmative Action Hires Less Qualified? Evidence from Employer-Employee Data on New Hires," *Journal of Labor Economics*, 17 (1999): 534–69; Laura Purdy, "Why Do We Need Affirmative Action?" *Journal of Social Philosophy*, 25 (1994): 133–43. Holzer and Neumark make a basic distinction between educational qualifications and job performance.
8. http://www.gm.com/company/gmability/diversity/ people/workforce.html
9. http://www.exxonmobil.com/news/publications/diversity/c_whyfocus.html
10. Bron Taylor, *Affirmative Action at Work: Law, Politics, and Ethics* (Pittsburgh: University of Pittsburgh Press, 1991); Morley Gunderson, "Pay and Employment Equity in the United States and Canada," *International Journal of Manpower*, 15 (1994): 26–43; Patricia Gaynor and Garey Durden, "Measuring the Extent of Earnings Discrimination: An Update," *Applied Economics*, 27 August (1995): 669–76; Marjorie L. Baldwin and William G. Johnson, "The Employment Effects of Wage Discrimination Against Black Men," *Industrial & Labor Relations Review*, 49 (1996): 302–16; Franklin D. Wilson, Marta Tienda, and Lawrence Wu, "Race and Unemployment: Labor Market Experiences of Black and White Men, 1968–1988," *Women & Occupations*, 22 (1995): 245-270; Betty M. Vetter, Ed., *Professional Women and Minorities: A Manpower Data Resource Service*, 8th ed. (Washington: Commission on Science and Technology, 1989); (anonymous) "Less Discrimination for Women but Poorer Prospects at Work than Men," *Management Services*, 40 (1996): 6; Cynthia D. Anderson and Donald Tomaskovic-Devey, "Patriarchal Pressures: An Exploration of Organizational Processes that Exacerbate and Erode Gender Earnings Inequality," *Work & Occupations*, 22 (1995): 328–56; Thomas J. Bergman and G. E. Martin, "Tests for Compliance with Phased Plans to Equalize Discriminate Wages," *Journal of Applied Business Research*, 11 (1994/1995): 136–43.
11. Helen F. Ladd, "Evidence on Discrimination in Mortgage Lending," *Journal of Economic Perspectives*, 12 (1998), 41–62; Brent W. Ambrose, William T. Hughes, Jr., and Patrick Simmons, "Policy Issues concerning Racial and Ethnic Differences in Home Loan Rejection Rates," *Journal of Housing Research*, 6 (1995): 115–35; *A Common Destiny: Blacks and American Society*, Ed. Gerald D. Jaynes and Robin M. Williams, Jr., Committee on the Status of Black Americans, Commission on Behavioral and Social Sciences and Education, National Research Council (Washington: NAS Press, 1989), pp. 12–13, 138–48; Sunwoong Kim, Gregory D. Squires, "Lender Characteristics and Racial Disparities in Mortgage Lending," *Journal of Housing Research*, 6 (1995): 99–133; Glenn B. Canner and Wayne Passmore, "Home Purchase Lending in Low-Income Neighborhoods and to Low-Income Borrowers," *Federal Reserve Bulletin*, 81 February 1995): 71–103; John R. Walter, "The Fair Lending Laws and their Enforcement,"

*Economic Quarterly*, 81 (Fall 1995): 61–77; Stanley D. Longhofer, "Discrimination in Mortgage Lending: What Have We Learned?" *Economic Commentary* [Federal Reserve Bank of Cleveland], August 15, 1996: 1–4.

12. As reported by Rudolf A. Pyatt, Jr., "Significant Job Studies," *The Washington Post*, April 30, 1985, pp. D1–D2. See also Paul Burstein, *Discrimination, Jobs, and Politics* (Chicago: University of Chicago Press, 1985). Bureau of Labor Statistics, *Employment and Earnings* (Washington: U.S. Dept. of labor, January 1989). *A Common Destiny*, op. cit., pp. 16–18, 84–88.
13. See Margery Austin Turner, Michael Fix, and Raymond Struyk, *Opportunities Denied, Opportunities Diminished: Discrimination in Hiring* (Washington, D.C.: The Urban Institute, 1991).
14. William A. Darity and Patrick L. Mason, "Evidence on Discrimination in Employment: Codes of Color, Codes of Gender," *Journal of Economic Perspectives*, 12 (1998), 63–90; Francine Blau, et al., *The Economics of Women, Men, and Work*, 3rd ed. Upper Saddle River, NJ: Prentice-Hall, 1998.
15. See Laura Purdy, "Why Do We Need Affirmative Action?" *Journal of Social Philosophy* 25 (1994): 133–43; Farrell Bloch, *Antidiscrimination Law and Minority Employment: Recruitment Practices and Regulatory Constraints* (Chicago: University of Chicago Press, 1994); Joseph Sartorelli, "Gay Rights and Affirmative Action." In *Gay Ethics*, ed. Timothy F. Murphy (New York: Haworth Press, 1994); Taylor, *Affirmative Action at Work.*
16. *Alexander v. Choate*, 469 U.S. 287, at 295.
17. But the Court comes very close in *Local 28 of the Sheet Metal Workers' International Association v. Equal Employment Opportunity Commission*, 106 S.Ct. 3019—commonly known as *Sheet Metal Workers.*
18. *Fullilove v. Klutznick*, 448 U.S. 448 (1980); *United Steelworkers v. Weber*, 443 U.S. 193 (1979); *United States v. Paradise*, 480 U.S. 149 (1987); *Johnson v. Transportation Agency*, 480 U.S. 616 (1987).
19. *Firefighters v. Stotts*, 467 U.S. 561 (1984); *City of Richmond v. J. A. Croson Co.*, 109 S.Ct. 706 (1989); *Adarand Constructors Inc. v. Federico Pena*, 63 LW 4523 (1995); *Wygant v. Jackson Bd. of Education*, 476 U.S. 267 (1986); *Wards Cove Packing v. Atonio*, 490 U.S. 642.
20. For a very different view, stressing inconsistency, see Yong S. Lee, "Affirmative Action and Judicial Standards of Review: A Search for the Elusive Consensus." *Review of Public Personnel Administration*, 12 September–December 1991): 47–69.
21. See Robert Ladenson, "Ethics in the American Workplace, "*Business and Professional Ethics Journal*, 14 (1995): 17–31; Gertrude Ezorsky, *Racism and Justice: The Case for Affirmative Action*, op. cit.; Thomas E. Hill, Jr., "The Message of Affirmative Action," *Social Philosophy and Policy*, 8 (1991): 108–29; Jorge L. Garcia, "The Heart of Racism," *Journal of Social Philosophy*, 27 (1996): 5–46.
22. For a balanced article on this topic, see Robert K. Fullinwider, "Affirmative Action and Fairness," *Report from the Institute for Philosophy & Public Policy* 11 (University of Maryland, Winter 1991), pp. 10–13.
23. John Yinger, *Closed Doors, Opportunities Lost* (New York: Russell Sage Foundation, 1995); Jerry T. Ferguson and Wallace R, Johnston. "Managing Diversity," *Mortgage Banking*, 55 (1995); 32–36L; Joseph Semien, "Opening the Utility Door for Women and Minorities," *Public Utilities Fortnightly*, July 5, 1990, pp. 29–31.
24. http://www.dell.com/us/en/gen/corporate/vision_diversity.htm
25. Tim Loughran, "Corning Tries to Break the Glass Ceiling," *Business & Society Review* 76 (Winter 1991), pp. 52–55.
26. Editorial, "Don't Scuttle Affirmative Action," *Business Week*, April 5, 1985, p. 174.
27. "Rethinking *Weber*: The Business Response to Affirmative Action," *Harvard Law Review*, 102 January 1989), p. 661, note 18.
28. See "Rethinking *Weber*, "esp. pp. 668–70; Joseph Michael Pace and Zachary Smith, "Understanding Affirmative Action: From the Practitioner's Perspective," *Public Personnel Management*, 24 (Summer 1995): 139–147.

## ARTICLES

# Can a "Dumb Ass Woman" Achieve Equality in the Workplace? Running the Gauntlet of Hostile Environment Harassing Speech

*Deborah Epstein*

## INTRODUCTION

Sandra Bundy may have guessed that her new job with the District of Columbia Department of Corrections would be a challenge. What she may not have expected was that she would have to meet the challenge under very different conditions than those faced by her male coworkers. Ms. Bundy's work was continually interrupted by one of her supervisors, who kept calling her into his office and forcing her to listen to his theories about how women ride horses to obtain sexual gratification.[1] He repeatedly asked Ms. Bundy to come home with him in order to view his collection of pictures and books on this topic. Another supervisor repeatedly propositioned her, asking her to come with him to a motel or on a trip to the Bahamas.

None of Ms. Bundy's male counterparts, in contrast, had to listen to their boss's sexual fantasies and proposals. When Ms. Bundy tried to remove this gender-based obstacle to her job performance by reporting it to a third supervisor and pleading for help, he only exacerbated the problem, telling her that "any man in his right mind would want to rape you," and asking her to have sex with him.

Ms. Bundy successfully sued the Department of Corrections for sexual harassment in violation of Title VII, the federal statute outlawing workplace discrimination. Title VII forbids sexual harassment when it creates a discriminatory hostile work environment, that is, when the harassment is sufficiently severe or pervasive that it adversely affects the terms or conditions of employment for workers of a single gender.[2] In Ms. Bundy's case, the court held that her supervisors' repeated sexual comments and propositions met this standard, even though their harassment was entirely verbal. . . .

Several scholars take the opposite position and argue that most or all of Title VII's restrictions on harassing workplace speech run afoul of the First Amendment. The two proponents of this view who have engaged in the most extensive analysis are Professors Kingsley Browne and Eugene Volokh. Professor Browne argues that free speech interests require a drastic reduction in the scope of hostile environment harassment law, limiting its reach to cases involving unwanted physical contact. Professor Volokh also recommends narrowing the law to cover verbal harassment only when it is intentionally directed at a particular individual; undirected expressions of gender-based intolerance, he believes, should go unregulated.

This article stakes out a middle ground between Sangree on the one hand and Browne and Volokh on the other, and it responds to the principal arguments they have marshaled. Unlike Professor Sangree, I believe that hostile environment harassment law generates a fundamental conflict between equality of opportunity and freedom of expression. But a thorough examination of the nature and weight of each of these fundamental interests, in the distinct context of the workplace, demonstrates that a balance can be struck. . . .

## I. THE HARM INFLICTED BY HOSTILE ENVIRONMENT HARASSING SPEECH

A full understanding of the harm inflicted by harassing workplace speech is a necessary prerequisite to any attempt to determine the appropriate balance between the government's interest in protecting citizens from such speech and the First Amendment's guarantee of free expression. As Professor Charles Lawrence has noted, "To engage in a debate about the first amendment and [discriminatory] speech without a full understanding of the nature and extent of the harm of [such] speech risks making the first amendment an instrument of domination rather than a vehicle of liberation."[3]

Sexual harassment has been called the most widespread problem faced by women on the job. A 1981 United States Merit Systems Protection Board ("MSPB") survey of approximately 23,000 federal employees found that 42% of all women and 15% of all men had experienced some form of sexual harassment at work.[4] When the MSPB conducted a follow-up study in 1988, these numbers remained virtually identical. Recent surveys conducted in the private sector demonstrate that about 59% of women executives are harassed at some point in their careers. Other surveys have shown that women experience sexual harassment in the workplace at even higher rates, ranging from 42% to 88%. Approximately 15% of women working for Fortune 500 companies experience sexual harassment on an annual basis.

Harassing speech accounts for a substantial portion of the problem. The majority of sexual harassment complaints involve allegations of verbal harassment. One survey shows that two-thirds of working women have been subjected to verbal harassment on the job. In 1994, a survey of 2000 lawyers at twelve large law firms across the nation showed that 91% of the women and 13% of the men had been subjected to unwelcome verbal harassment within the past year. A recent survey of 182 women who work in traditionally male industries (including plumbers, electricians, carpenters, fire fighters, and police officers) revealed that 83% received unwelcome sexual remarks, and 88% were forced to view pictures of naked or partially dressed women in the workplace.

Professors Browne and Volokh acknowledge that gender-based verbal harassment can result in employment discrimination, but neither recognizes the seriousness of the problem. This is particularly true of Professor Browne, who fails to engage in any substantial discussion of the harm that discriminatory harassing speech can inflict on a female worker and how that harm can create substantial obstacles to her success on the job. . . .

Gender-based harassment of female employees subjects them to an extensive range of harms not experienced by their male colleagues. These harms often include an adverse effect on a woman's job performance. The 1981 MSPB Survey showed that harassment victims suffered in terms of the quantity and quality of their work, their ability to work with others, and their attendance record.[5] Other studies have found that between 45% and 75% of sexual harassment victims experience some adverse effect on their work performance. . . .

The cases challenging gender-specific abuse and gender-based sexually harassing speech provide compelling examples of the harms identified above. In *Robinson v. Jacksonville Shipyards, Inc.*,[6] for example, Lois Robinson worked as a welder and as one of a few female skilled craftworkers employed by a shipyard. At work,

Ms. Robinson was repeatedly subjected to sexual and gender-specific harassing comments: a male welder told her that he wished her shirt would blow over her head so he could look at her breasts; a shipfitter told her that he wished her shirt was tighter; another told her that "women are only fit company for something that howls," and that "there's nothing worse than having to work around women"; and a foreman asked her to sit on his lap. Coworkers further harassed Ms. Robinson by placing gender-specific abusive and sexual graffiti on the workplace walls. For example, a coworker wrote over the place where Ms. Robinson hung her jacket, "lick me you whore dog bitch"; and another wrote "pussy" on a wall of her work area when she left to get a drink of water.

Ms. Robinson also was surrounded by prominently displayed pictures that depicted women in various stages of undress and in sexually suggestive or submissive poses, including: a dart board made out of a drawing of a woman's breast, with her nipple as the bull's eye; a picture of a naked woman with long blond hair, wearing high heels and holding a whip (Ms. Robinson found this picture particularly troubling because she has long blond hair and works with a welding tool known as a "whip"); a picture of a nude woman, with legs spread and breasts and genitals exposed; a drawing of a naked woman with fluid flowing from her genital area; a picture of a woman's pubic area with a spatula pressed on it; a drawing of a naked woman with the caption "USDA Choice"; a picture of a naked woman playing with a piece of cloth between her legs; and calendar photos depicting nude and partially nude women. Ms. Robinson's male coworkers made frequent sexual comments about these pictures in her presence, such as "I'd like to have some of that" and "I'd like to get into bed with that." No similar pictures of men were displayed.

After Ms. Robinson complained to shipyard management, the number of displayed pornographic pictures actually increased. Ms. Robinson testified that this constant barrage of sexual and gender-based hostile comments and pictures made her feel extremely anxious, caused her to have difficulty sleeping, and resulted in her having to miss several days of work each year.

In *Harris v. Forklift Systems, Inc.*,[7] Terasa Harris spent more than three years working as a manager for an equipment rental company. During that time, she was frequently subjected to gender-specific abusive speech. The company's president, Charles Hardy, repeatedly stated to Ms. Harris, in the presence of her fellow employees, "You're a woman, what do you know?," called her a "dumb ass woman," and told her that the company needed a man to do her job. Hardy also made numerous sexually suggestive requests, asking Ms. Harris to retrieve coins from his front pants pocket by saying, "Teresa, I have a quarter way down there. Would you get that out of my pocket?" He threw objects on the ground in front of Ms. Harris, asking her to bend over and pick them up, and suggested that female Forklift Systems employees should dress in a way that would expose their breasts. He also told women workers that he had heard that eating corn would make their breasts grow. In the presence of other employees, Hardy proposed that he and Ms. Harris "go to the Holiday Inn to negotiate [her] raise." Hardy also suggested to Ms. Harris that they should start "screwing around." There was no evidence that similar gender-specific abuse or sexually suggestive remarks were made to male employees.

Ms. Harris asked her boss to stop making these comments, and he promised to do so. But soon afterwards, when Ms. Harris was negotiating a deal with a customer, Hardy asked her, in front of her fellow employees, "What did you do promise the guy . . . some bugger Saturday night?"

In *Rabidue v. Osceola Refining Co.*,[8] Vivienne Rabidue, an administrative assistant, was forced to work with a supervisor who routinely referred to women as "whore," "cunt," "pussy," and "tits," all gender-specific derogatory terms focused on female sexuality or sexual body parts. With respect to Ms. Rabidue, the supervisor stated, "All that bitch needs is a good lay." Ms. Rabidue was exposed on a daily basis to posters and pinups of naked and partially naked women, including one poster, which remained on the wall for eight years, depicting a prone woman with a golf ball on her breasts with a man standing over her, golf club in hand, shouting "Fore." No evidence was submitted suggesting similar treatment of Ms. Rabidue's male counterparts.

As these examples demonstrate, Professor Browne is wrong when he claims that expression of racist and sexist sentiments are no longer socially acceptable and, accordingly, there is no longer a need for the "protectionist doctrine" of workplace harassment laws. In fact, gender-based harassing speech continues to force women to perform their jobs under adverse conditions not imposed on men. This discrimination perpetuates the historic inequality between men and women in the workplace that Title VII was designed to remedy, "operat[ing] as overt exclusion once did to erect a significant barrier to equality in the work-place."[9]

## II. POORLY DEFINED LAW OR POORLY INFORMED CRITICS? HOSTILE ENVIRONMENT HARASSMENT AND THE DOCTRINES OF VAGUENESS, OVERBREADTH, AND CHILLING EFFECT

. . . The First Amendment requires specificity in any restriction on expression. Although a law need not be defined with "mathematical certainty," it must provide potential violators with adequate notice of what is prohibited. Although some limited elaboration of what constitutes actionable harassing speech would be useful, examination of the legal definition of harassing speech and its stringent proof requirements makes clear that, contrary to the claims of Professors Browne and Volokh, the law is far from vague.

### A. Forms of Prohibited Workplace Harassment

Congress enacted Title VII as part of the Civil Rights Act of 1964 to eliminate certain forms of workplace discrimination. Specifically, Title VII makes it "an unlawful employment practice for an employer . . . to discriminate against any individual with respect to his compensation, terms, conditions, or privileges of employment, because of such individual's race, color, religion, sex, or national origin."

Although Title VII clearly prohibits gender-based workplace discrimination, it does not expressly set forth a cause of action for harassment. Approximately ten years after the statute's enactment, however, the courts began to recognize that certain forms of harassment, when inflicted on workers of only one gender, constitute prohibited discrimination. This concept was later adopted by the Equal Employment Opportunity Commission ("EEOC") in its *Guidelines on Discrimination Because of Sex*,[10] and in 1986 it was unanimously embraced by the Supreme Court in *Meritor Savings Bank v. Vinson*.[11] Seven years later, in its most recent pronouncement on harassment law, the Court unanimously reaffirmed that Title VII's prohibition on gender discrimination incorporates a ban on gender-based harassment.[12]

Perhaps the most widely discussed form of gender-based harassment is *sexual* harassment, defined by the EEOC as "[u]nwelcome sexual advances, requests for sexual favors, and other verbal or physical conduct of a sexual nature," directed at members of one gender and not the other. Illegal sexual harassment exists in two distinct forms. In a "quid pro quo" case, the target of the harassment, because of her gender, is coerced into performing an unwelcome sexual act as part of a bargain to obtain an employment benefit or avoid an employment disadvantage. Quid pro quo harassment is essentially the equivalent of extortion or blackmail, and, accordingly, it is not subject to First Amendment protection.

The second form of sexual harassment prohibited under the *Guidelines*, "hostile environment" harassment, exists when an employee, in contrast to similarly situated workers of another gender, is subjected to a workplace so "permeated with discriminatory intimidation, ridicule, and insult that [it] is sufficiently severe or pervasive to alter the conditions of [her] employment and create an abusive working environment."

Other forms of gender-based workplace harassment that are not sexual in nature also may constitute illegal discrimination. The EEOC has recognized that gender-specific abuse is actionable if it is sufficiently severe or pervasive to create a hostile work environment. Recently, in *Harris v. Forklift Systems, Inc.*, the Court upheld the imposition of Title VII liability based in part on a supervisor's abusive but nonsexual comments to a woman subordinate that were based specifically on her gender, such as "You're a woman, what do you know"; "We need a man [to do your job]"; and "[You're] a dumb ass woman."

Although gender-specific harassment and gender-based sexual harassment are conceptually different, most courts and numerous commentators have failed to distinguish between the two, referring to both as "sexual." This confusion may stem in part from the frequency with which both forms of harassment arise in a single case, and from the identical standard of proof, the creation of a hostile environment, which applies to both.

## B. The Elements of a Hostile Environment Harassment Claim

Professors Browne and Volokh perpetuate the widespread misunderstanding of hostile environment harassment law by consistently referring to it as a prohibition on all speech that subjectively "offends" the listener, and by inventing a misleading parade of horribles designed to create the impression that harassment law censors all speech that fails a politically correct litmus test. But in fact, as an examination of the requisite elements of a hostile evironment harassment claim demonstrates, the "mere utterance of an . . . epithet which engenders offensive feelings in an employee . . . does not sufficiently affect the conditions of employment to implicate Title VII."[13]

1. Harassment Must Be Gender-Based.
   A victim of workplace harassment must show that, but for her gender, she would not have been the object of harassment. . . .

2. The Employer or Its Agent Must Perpetrate or Condone the Harassment.
   Title VII applies to employers, not to the individual personnel who engage in harassing or otherwise discriminatory behavior. As a result, hostile environment liability may be imposed on an employer only if it had sufficient notice of its occurrence and, despite this fact, failed to take prompt and effective remedial action. . . .

3. Harassment Must Be Severe or Pervasive.
   Harassment will trigger Title VII liability only if it is "sufficiently sever or pervasive to alter the [terms, privileges, or] conditions of the [the target's] employment and creates an abusive working environment."[14] . . .

4. Harassment Must Be Unwelcome to Its Target.
   Another prerequisite for imposition of Title VII hostile environment liability is that the harassment must be "unwelcome." Harassment is unwelcome if the victim did not invite it and regards it as offensive or undesirable. This requirement evolved out of a recognition that consensual sexual relationships can occur in the workplace; even conduct or speech that discriminates, by creating a different environment for members of one gender and not the other, is not illegal if the target appreciates it and does not view it as harmful. . . .

5. Harassment Must Create a Subjectively and Objectively Hostile Work Environment.

   Finally, hostile environment harassment law requires the victim to prove not only that she personally found that the harassment created a hostile or abusive work environment, but also that a "reasonable person" would agree with her. The reasonableness requirement ensures that gender-based abusive or sexual acts are not restricted whenever they offend the fragile sensibilities of a hypersensitive listener, but only when they rise to an objectively abusive level.

Taken together, these five proof requirements create a concrete definition of illegal gender-specific abuse and gender-based sexual harassment, and they focus the law's regulatory reach on its most objectively extreme, persistent, and unwelcome forms. . . .

## III. THE IMPORTANCE OF CONTEXT

### A. The Physical Context of the Workplace

Whether the workplace is a factory, office, or construction site, it is a setting in which employees are typically unable to avoid gender-based harassing speech. Outside of the workplace, an individual has a far greater degree of choice, and in most instances can avoid erotic, pornographic, or gender-specific abusive expression. "Girlie" magazines typically are not openly displayed on newsstands; radios and television sets have power switches and channel changers; and movies are rated for sex, violence, and profanity. A pedestrian on the street is free to walk away and avoid all but the initial impact of unwanted, gender-based abusive or sexually harassing expression; this may constitute a painful blow, but at least additional rounds may be avoided.

The workplace is different. If pornography or gender-specific abusive slogans are openly displayed in areas that a female worker must frequent to perform her job, she loses the power to avoid such speech. When a woman must choose between routinely viewing gender-based demeaning or abusive expression and quitting her job, her choice can hardly be labelled a "free" one.

The Court has long recognized that physical context places limits on a person's ability to avoid unwanted speech. The "captive audience" doctrine evolved out of this recognition, and it creates a context-based balance between the listener's right to personal privacy and the speaker's right to express himself freely. As a general rule, the doctrine gives priority to the speaker's rights over the listener's and dictates that if a listener is offended or otherwise harmed by speech, First Amendment principles require her to avoid it. Whenever possible, a person must walk away from speech that she does not wish to hear. Any other rule would cede too much censorship power to the government and enable it to restrict otherwise protected speech solely on the basis of speculation that the targeted audience may be offended or unwilling to listen. . . .

Because women are less captive outside of the workplace, hostile environment harassment law has only a limited application there. Once a potential harasser leaves work, he is free to express any view he wishes without interference, regardless of the extent to which it could harm members of one gender and not the other. Consider the example of a man who bumps into a female colleague in a bar across the street from the office. If he makes comments about her physical appearance, asks her to go out on a date, or asks her to have sex with him, she is likely to feel more free to choose whether to listen to him, engage in a conversion, or leave without risking her job. If she is indeed not captive, she may be required to bear the burden of avoiding speech when it is unwelcome. Hostile environment harassment law, as interpreted by the courts and the *EEOC Guidelines*, appropriately distinguishes between these two different contexts in regulating expression. . . .

Of course, the "workplace" is not a single, uniform physical setting. Professor Sangree errs by analyzing the physical location of the job site as a monolithic entity. Many work sites contain areas that are relatively avoidable, such as personal lockers or work stations. In these enclaves, the captivity argument diminishes in strength. If a woman worker has no work-related need to enter an area and can readily avoid it, then she cannot be deemed "captive" to expression that is verbalized or posted there.

The difficulty lies in defining what part of the workplace is avoidable. Consider the example of an individual's personal office. If the office belongs to a supervisor, it may be critically important for other workers to have access to it, either to accomplish their jobs effectively or to make personal connections that could result in a raise, promotion, or other job-related benefit. A rule of law that allows a supervisor to plaster the walls of his office with nude photographs of people of one gender, or gender-specific abusive slogans, presents workers of the targeted gender with an unacceptable choice: face abuse on the basis of your gender or avoid contact with management and weaken your position on the job. . . .

### B. The Interpersonal Context of the Workplace

Another factor that influences the First Amendment analysis of hostile environment harassing speech is the interpersonal context, or power hierarchy, of the workplace. The power disparity between harasser and targeted worker contributes to the worker's captivity and restricts her freedom to respond. In many situations, the woman worker knows that she must choose between listening in silence or responding and risking some adverse action by her employer. "Women and minorities often use the same word to describe individuals who confront . . . their bosses [about discrimination]—unemployed."[15]

This problem is exacerbated by the power structure of most workplaces, which continues to be largely sex-segregated. Although women now constitute nearly half of the U.S. workforce, their relatively recent entry into many fields means that most of them hold jobs that fall in the low range of the professional hierarchy, with men occupying the vast majority of supervisory and managerial positions. For example, in March 1995, the Federal Glass Ceiling Commission reported that although women make up 45.7% of the U.S. workforce, 97% of senior managers at the Fortune 1000 industrial corporations are white men, and only 5% of the top managers at Fortune 2000 industrial and service companies are women. The picture is similar outside of the business community. A 1991 *National Law Journal* survey showed that women constituted 37% of the associates at the 250 largest U.S. law firms but only 11% of the partners. The lower status of most women workers leads them to perceive their own position in the workplace as marginal or precarious, making them especially reluctant to take employment-related risks.

Modern First Amendment jurisprudence has recognized that the power hierarchy present in the workplace justifies some regulation of management speech to ensure the adequate protection of workers' rights. Professor Browne admits that the Court "has endorsed a higher degree of regulation of speech in the workplace in limited situations," but he does not explore whether the special characteristics of the workplace justify restrictions on hostile environment harassing speech. Instead, he summarily concludes that there is no "general governmental right to regulate speech in the workplace"; the government may limit certain forms of coercive speech to protect its interest in economic regulation, but harassing speech is not one of them. Professor Volokh conducts an even more limited analysis, concluding that the Court treats workplace speech differently only if it falls within what he dubs the "threat-or-promise" exception: "both employees and employers have [full] First Amendment rights in the workplace, as long as the communications do not contain a threat of reprisal or force or promise of benefit."[16] . . .

In sum, both the physical and the interpersonal contexts of the workplace create special pressures on women workers, making them captive to harassers' hostile and abusive speech. Here, as in other situations recognized by the courts, the context in which the speech occurs reduces the strength of First Amendment protections.

### C. Viewpoint Neutrality and Harassing Speech

One could argue, as do Professors Browne and Volokh, that the deference given to context in First Amendment jurisprudence is never sufficient to overcome the requirement that restrictions on expression be viewpoint neutral. The argument against viewpoint-based regulation of speech is that it invites abusive enforcement by allowing officials to censor only expression critical of the state and thus distort the marketplace of ideas. Courts and commentators frequently articulate the principle that viewpoint-discriminatory regulations of expression are more constitutionally suspect than those that are viewpoint neutral.

I agree with Professors Browne and Volokh that Title VII's restrictions on hostile environment harassment are viewpoint discriminatory. The law prohibits expression only if it voices the view that women and men should be treated differently. . . .

By restricting expression of only one point of view, the law does exactly what the viewpoint-neutrality requirement was designed to prevent: it distorts the underlying debate on the issue of gender equality. . . .

There are powerful reasons to demand viewpoint neutrality in the regulation of expression. But as with any doctrine, situations exist in which those reasons diminish. Workplace harassment law is one of them, in part because the captive nature of the victim and the coercive power of the harasser contribute to the strength of the government's interest in preventing workplace harassment. As demonstrated in Part IV of this article, the compelling nature of this interest and the narrow tailoring of existing restrictions on harassing speech combine to demonstrate that the law survives First Amendment strict scrutiny analysis. . . .

## CONCLUSION

To determine the constitutionality of the law's restrictions on hostile environment harassing speech, one must weigh the obstacles it creates to equal employment opportunity against harassers' rights of free expression on the job. Professors Browne and Volokh have given inadequate weight to the equal opportunity side of the scale by seriously underestimating the harm that verbal harassment inflicts on women workers. Harassing speech subjects women to severe or pervasive abuse while their male counterparts are free to perform their jobs without facing such obstacles. It causes many women to suffer physically and psychologically, and often has an adverse effect on their job performance. The government's interest in eradicating discriminatory harassing speech from the workplace could hardly be more compelling. . . .

Workers, like any other group of citizens, have a vital need to express themselves freely, and the First Amendment forcefully protects their right to do so before or after work, on the streets, and in their homes. But what Professors Browne and Volokh fail to recognize is that the workplace is different. Both commentators focus on the content of workplace harassing speech . . . and ignore the context in which it occurs. The physical context of the job site effectively traps the victims of harassing and abusive speech so that they cannot avoid it. And because harassing speech is prohibited only when it is explicitly or implicitly condoned by the target's employer, the power hierarchy that operates in the workplace makes "more speech" an unrealistic option. These factors reduce the strength of First Amendment interests in the workplace; what may be said with impunity outside of the workplace may be regulated within it.

Professor Sangree, in contrast, places so much emphasis on the importance of the workplace context that she abdicates any real concern about workers' free speech rights. Her focus on the captivity of female employees blinds her to the reality that most worksites have within them relatively private settings, in which women are not captive and can avoid gender-specific abusive or harassing speech. She fails to recognize that in these portions of the workplace, such as a personal locker or a protected corner of a private office, pornography or other gender-based material will not create a differential, adverse environment for women workers. In these avoidable areas, an employee should be free to post or engage in whatever speech he desires.

**NOTES**

1. Bundy v. Jackson, 641 F.2d 934, 939, 940 n. 2 (D.C. Cir. 1981).
2. *See, e.g.*, Harris v. Forklift Sys., Inc., 114 S.Ct. 367, 370 (1993); Meritor Sav. Bank v. Vinson, 477 U.S. 57, 66 (1986).
3. Charles R. Lawrence III, *If He Hollers Let Him Go: Regulating Racist Speech on Campus*, 1990 Duke L. J. 431, 459; *see also* Mari J. Matsuda, *Public Response to Racist Speech: Considering the Victim's Story*, 87 Mich. L. Rev. 2320 (1989).
4. U.S. Merit Sys. Protection Bd., Sexual Harassment in the Federal Workplace—Is It a Problem? 81 (1981) [hereinafter 1981 MSPB Survey].
5. 1981 MSPB Survey, at 81.
6. 760 F. Supp. 1486 (M.D. Fla. 1991).
7. 47. 114 S.Ct. 367 (1993).
8. 805 F.2d 611 (6th Cir. 1986).
9. Strauss, at 5.
10. EEOC Guidelines on Discrimination Because of Sex, 29 C.F.R. § 1604 (1995).
11. 477 U.S. 57 (1986).
12. Harris v. Forklift Sys., Inc., 114 S.Ct. 367 (1993).
13. *Harris*, 114 S.Ct. at 370.
14. Meritor Sav. Bank v. Vinson, 477 U.S. 57, 67 (1986).
15. Brief Amici Curiae of the NAACP Legal Defense and Education Fund, Inc. and the National Council of Jewish Women at 24, 114 S.Ct. 367 (1993) (No. 92–1168).
16. Volokh, at 1821.

# What Speech Does "Hostile Work Environment" Harassment Law Restrict?

*Eugene Volokh*

The first step in evaluating a speech restriction is figuring out exactly what it restricts. The debate about the constitutionality of "hostile work environment" harassment law is in large part a debate about this.

If harassment law bans only hard-core pornography, personal slurs, and repeated indecent propositions, people might have one view about it. If, on the other hand, it restricts political and religious statements, prints of

Francisco de Goya paintings, sexually themed (perhaps not even misogynistic) jokes, and the like, people's views might be quite different. Some might condemn the law in either event, and some might approve of it in either event, but for quite a few people the decision may be influenced by the law's scope.

I'm deeply flattered that Professor Epstein chose to respond to my article on freedom of speech and workplace harassment.[1] We disagree on many points, but I very much respect her contribution to the literature. . . .

I want to focus briefly on the one area to which (perhaps surprisingly) a little less attention has been paid: Exactly what speech does "hostile work environment" harassment law restrict?

## I. POLITICAL, ARTISTIC, RELIGIOUS, AND SOCIALLY THEMED SPEECH QUALIFIES

The first place to look for an answer, of course, is the definition of harassment. Speech can be punished as workplace harassment if it's

- "severe or pervasive" enough to
- create a "hostile or abusive work environment"
- based on race, religion, sex, national origin, age, disability, veteran status, or, in some jurisdictions, sexual orientation, political affiliation, citizenship status, marital status, or personal appearance,
- for the plaintiff and for a reasonable person.[2]

Note what the definition does *not* require. It does not require that the speech consist of obscenity or fighting words or threats or other constitutionally unprotected statements. It does not require that the speech be profanity or pornography, which some have considered "low value." Under the definition, it is eminently possible for political, religious, or social commentary, or "legitimate" art, to be punished.

"David Duke for President" posters, after all, might well be quite offensive to many reasonable people based on their race, religion, or national origin, and may create a hostile environment. This would be even more true of bigoted or insensitive remarks about minority or female political candidates. Many reasonable people might view strident denunciations of Catholicism, whether political or religious, as creating a hostile environment for devout Catholics. . . .

One court has said that coworkers' use of job titles such as "foreman" and "draftsman" may constitute sexual harassment,[3] and a Kentucky human rights agency has gotten a company to change its "Men Working" signs (at a cost of over $35,000) on the theory that the signs "perpetuat[e] a discriminatory work environment and could be deemed unlawful under the Kentucky Civil Rights Act."[4] . . .

Another court has found a hostile environment based largely (though not entirely) on "caricatures of naked men and women, animals with human genitalia, . . . a cartoon entitled 'Highway Signs You Should Know' [that showed] twelve drawings of sexually graphic 'road signs' (entitled, for example, 'merge,' 'road open,' etc.)," and so on.[5] Though "[m]any of the sexual cartoons and jokes . . . depicted both men and women," the court concluded that "widespread verbal and visual sexual humor—particularly vulgar and degrading jokes and cartoons . . . may tend to demean women."[6] The court ultimately held that "every incident reported by [plaintiff]"—the jokes as well as the other conduct—"involves sexual harassment."[7] An official U.S. Department of Labor pamphlet likewise defines harassment as including cases where "[s]omeone made sexual jokes or said sexual things that you didn't like," with no requirement that the jokes be insulting or even misogynistic.[8]

If there is anything about harassment law that prevents liability based on this sort of speech, it has to be the severity/pervasiveness component: The fact-finder—judge or jury—must conclude not only that the speech was offensive, based on race, religion, sex, or some other attribute, but also that it was either "severe" or "pervasive" enough to create a hostile or abusive environment for the plaintiff and for a reasonable person. And if the outcomes in the above cases were, as Professor Epstein suggests, "bizarre judicial misapplications," "exception[s] to the rule" that should be ignored in determining the rule's true scope, it could only be because the speech in those cases didn't meet the severity or pervasiveness thresholds.[9]

But how exactly can we condemn the fact-finders here of being guilty of "bizarre judicial misapplications"? After all, nothing in the rule they were told to apply says that religious proselytizing, political commentary, or off-color jokes are insulated from liability. Perhaps you or I can say that a reasonable person ought not find Bible verses or the phrase "Men Working" or jokes about sexually graphic road signs to be "severe" or "pervasive" enough to create a hostile environment; but obviously other people, who probably thought themselves to be quite reasonable, have disagreed.

"Severe," "pervasive," "hostile," and "abusive" are mushy terms. I'm not completely sure what it means to say that people have "bizarre[ly] misappli[ed]" such terms. They might just have had a different notion of how offensive something must be to be "severe," or how frequent it most be to be "pervasive." . . .

## II. STEERING WIDE OF THE UNLAWFUL ZONE

So we see that, on its face, harassment law can suppress core protected speech. Whatever shelter there is for such speech must come from the "severe or pervasive" requirement. The heart of a defense of harassment law, I take it, would be an assertion that this requirement—despite the examples I gave above—will shield all protected speech except the most obnoxious.

Let's consider, though, how this would work out in practice. Imagine you're an employment lawyer, and an employer comes to you and says: "Help me out. One of my employees is complaining that her coworkers' political posters and lunchroom conversations have created a hostile environment based on her [race/religion/sex/national origin/age/disability/veteran status/sexual orientation/marital status]. The speech sounds to me like normal political argument, and I don't want to suppress it. But I also don't want to be stuck with a big lawsuit."

What can you say in response? Saying "Well, you're OK if the speech isn't severe or pervasive enough to create a hostile or abusive environment" obviously gets you nowhere: The employer will just ask you "Well, is it severe or pervasive enough or isn't it?"

Your answer would probably have to be "We won't know until it gets to court." With vague words like "severe," "pervasive," "hostile," and "abusive," that's generally all you can say. And because of this, the safe advice would be: "Shut the employees up." After all, the typical employer doesn't profit from its employees' political discussions; it can only lose because of them. The rational response is suppression, even if the lawyer personally believes that the speech probably doesn't reach the severe-or-pervasive threshold. . . .

Employees can thus only say "gender-specific or sexual" things—and I assume this includes supposedly sexist political or social statements, sexually themed jokes, and so on—*until one listener objects.* At that point, they must either shut up or schedule a meeting with a "designated EEO officer" before speaking further.

Gone is any requirement that the speech be "severe or pervasive," or that it create a hostile or abusive environment, or that it even be offensive to a reasonable person. The policy Professor Epstein suggests would bar *any* "gender-specific or sexual" speech so long as there's any objection, at least until one gets clearance from above. This is "a narrow, speech-protective antiharassment policy that minimizes any chilling effect"? . . .

Of course, harassment law, like many other laws, is underenforced as well as overenforced. Many employers, because of ignorance or bigotry or whatever else, ignore the risk of liability and don't suppress speech or conduct that should be restricted. And though I have no idea whether "in the vast majority of cases, the judiciary is not engaging in overbroad enforcement, but instead is failing to impose liability," I'm sure this underenforcement happens in some cases, perhaps many cases.

But other employers pay attention to the risk and consequently suppress any speech that might possibly be seen as harassment, even if you and I would agree that it's not severe or pervasive enough that a reasonable person would conclude that it creates a hostile environment. Likewise, some fact-finders are imposing fairly low thresholds of severity or pervasiveness, even as other fact-finders are imposing higher ones. In those cases, the law may pose First Amendment problems regardless of whether it's underenforced in other situations.

## III. THE LAW'S EFFECT ON INDIVIDUAL STATEMENTS

We see, then, that the "severe or pervasive" requirement is too vague to provide much protection for speech, and even Professor Epstein's own proposed policy essentially eliminates this requirement. This, though, isn't some slight drafting flaw that can be corrected with a bit of tinkering: harassment law by its nature restricts individual statements, even when they're clearly not severe or pervasive enough to generate a hostile environment.

Recall that a hostile environment can be created by many different employees, each making only one or a few offensive statements. Individually, the statements might not be "severe or pervasive" enough to create liability, but in the aggregate they may be actionable.

An employer can't just announce to its employees: "Say whatever you like, so long as the aggregate of all your statements and all the other employees' statements isn't so severe or pervasive that it creates a hostile environment." Most employees have no idea what their coworkers may have said days, weeks, or months ago. If the employer wants to protect itself, it must tell each employee what speech that employee must avoid.

The employer's only reliable protection is a zero-tolerance policy, one which prohibits any statement that, when aggregated with other statements, may lead to a hostile environment. This is what many employment experts in fact advise. . . .

There's no proviso that an occasional sexually themed joke or "sexually oriented picture" is permissible, so long as it's neither severe nor pervasive. The policies—just like Professor Epstein's proposed policy—on their face condemn every such incident; and, of course, what else could they do? These are not hysterical overreactions of the misinformed. They are exactly what one should expect from reasonable, prudent lawyers giving advice on how to avoid liability in the real world. . . .

The employers' need to restrict any statement that might contribute to a hostile environment—even when the statement doesn't create the environment by itself—also illustrates another important point: Court decisions that even partly rely on certain statements tend to suppress that sort of statement more generally. Consider, for instance, *Makhayesh v. Great Lakes Steel*,[10] in which a Muslim employee of

Syrian descent sued for national origin and religious harassment. Part of the alleged harassment was direct, personal insults, but part was coworkers generally referring to Muslim religious leaders as "toilet seat[s]" and suggesting, in the context of the Gulf War, that the United States "nuke Iraq and Syria" and "go back [to Libya] and wipe them off the face of the earth."[11] The Michigan Court of Appeals reversed a grant of summary judgment for the employer, and held that the evidence was sufficient to let the harassment claims to go to trial.[12]

How should a cautious employer respond to a holding such as this? It can't just say to its employees "It's fine for you to make offensive political statements about Iraq, Syria, Libya, and Muslim religious leaders, *unless* some other people are also mistreating the offended worker in other ways (about which you, the employee, might not even know)." So long as courts say that certain speech can contribute to a hostile environment, the cautious employer would be wise to restrict it. . . .

## IV. THE SPEECH THAT HARASSMENT LAW RESTRICTS

The scope of harassment law is thus molded by three facts:

1. On its face, harassment draws no distinction among slurs, pornography, political, religious, or social commentary, jokes, art, and other forms of speech. All can be punished, so long as they are "severe or pervasive" enough to create a "hostile environment."
2. The vagueness of the terms "severe" and "pervasive"—and the fact that the law is implemented by employers, who have an incentive to oversuppress—means that the law may practically restrict any speech that an employer concludes *might* be found by a fact-finder to be "severe or pervasive" enough.
3. Finally, because an employer is liable for the aggregate of all its employees' speech, wise employers will bar any sort of statement that might, if repeated by enough people, be "severe or pervasive" enough to create a hostile environment.

Putting all this together, harassment law potentially burdens any workplace speech that's offensive to at least one person in the workplace based on that person's race, religion, sex, national origin, age, disability, veteran status or, in some jurisdictions, sexual orientation, marital status, political affiliation, citizenship status, or personal appearance, even when the speech is political and even when it's not severe or pervasive enough to itself be actionable. . . .

Of course, the speech-restrictive potential of harassment law won't be realized in every situation. Many employers will live dangerously—from prejudice, ignorance, or even a commitment to free expression. Many offended employees won't complain. Many fact-finders will apply high thresholds of "severity" and "pervasiveness" rather than low ones.

But this is true of all speech restrictions. Sexually themed literature wasn't completely suppressed by pre-1960s restrictive obscenity laws. Sedition laws are notoriously ineffective at suppressing sedition. Even the broadest libel laws would be vastly underenforced, and juries can exhibit unjustified hostility towards libel plaintiffs as well as unjustified sympathy.

To properly measure harassment law's impact on speech, we should ask: What restrictions would prudent, law-abiding employers—employers who heed the EEOC's statement that "Prevention is the best tool for the elimination of sexual harassment"[13]—impose in trying to avoid liability? The answer appears to be what I outline above: a broad prohibition on a wide range of isolated statements.

It's a mistake to hide behind the supposed shield of the severity and pervasiveness requirements. Harassment law puts at risk speech—including religious proselytizing, bigoted political statements, sexually themed humor, and sexually suggestive art—whether or not it's severe or pervasive. Whether this burden is justified is a matter that's been extensively debated elsewhere; but there should be no denying that the burden exists.

## NOTES

1. Deborah Epstein, *Can a "Dumb Ass Woman" Achieve Equality in the Workplace? Running the Gauntlet of Hostile Environment Harassing Speech,* 84 GEO. L. J. 399 (1996).
2. *See, e.g.*, Harris v. Forklift Sys. Inc., 510 U.S. 17, 21–22 (1993) (barring harassment based on race, religion, sex, or national origin).
3. Tunis v. Corning Glass Works, 747 F. Supp. 951, 959 (S.D.N.Y. 1990), *aff'd without opinion*, 930 F.2d 910 (2d Cir. 1991).
4. Kentucky Comm'n on Human Rights, Human Rights Report, Spring 1994, at 2.
5. Cardin v. Via Tropical Fruits, Inc., No. 88–14201, 1993 U.S. Dist. LEXIS 16302, at *24–25 & n. 4 (S.D. Fla. July 9, 1993).
6. *Id.* at *45.
7. *Id.* at *61.
8. U. S. Dep't of Labor, Sexual Harassment: Know Your Rights (1994).
9. Epstein, at 417–18.
10. No. 91-108394-CZ (Mich. Ct. App. Apr. 10, 1995) (per curiam) (unpublished opinion).
11. *Id.* at 1; *id.* at 3 (Taylor, J., concurring in part and dissenting in part).
12. *Id.* at 2.
13. 29 C.F.R. § 1604.11(f) (1996) (the regulation covering sexual harassment).

## LEGAL PERSPECTIVES

# *Local 28 of the Sheet Metal Worker's International Association v. Equal Employment Opportunity Commission*

*Supreme Court of the United States*

In 1975, petitioners were found guilty of engaging in a pattern and practice of discrimination against black and Hispanic individuals (nonwhites) in violation of Title VII of the Civil Rights Act of 1964, 42 U.S.C. § 2000e *et seq.*, and ordered to end their discriminatory practices, and to admit a certain percentage of nonwhites to union membership by July 1981. In 1982 and again in 1983, petitioners were found guilty of civil contempt for disobeying the District Court's earlier orders. They now challenge the District Court's contempt finding, and also the remedies the court ordered both for the Title VII violation and for contempt. Principally, the issue presented is whether the remedial provision of Title VII, see 42 U.S.C. § 2000e-5(g), empowers a district court to order race-conscious relief that may benefit individuals who are not identified victims of unlawful discrimination.

Petitioner Local 28 of the Sheet Metal Workers' International Association (Local 28) represents sheet metal workers employed by contractors in the New York City metropolitan area. Petitioner Local 28 Joint Apprenticeship Committee (JAC) is a management-labor com-

106 S.Ct. 3109 (1986).

mittee which operates a 4-year apprenticeship training program designed to teach sheet metal skills. . . .

Petitioners joined by the EEOC, argue that the membership goal, the [Employment, Training, Education and Recruitment Fund ("the Fund")] order, and other orders which require petitioners to grant membership preferences to nonwhites are expressly prohibited by § 706(g), 42 U.S.C. § 2000e-5(g), which defines the remedies available under Title VII. Petitioners and the EEOC maintain that § 706(g) authorizes a district court to award preferential relief only to the actual victims of unlawful discrimination. They maintain that the membership goal and the Fund violate this provision, since they require petitioners to admit to membership, and otherwise to extend benefits to, black and Hispanic individuals who are not the identified victims of unlawful discrimination. We reject this argument, and hold that § 706(g), does not prohibit a court from ordering, in appropriate circumstances, affirmative race-conscious relief as a remedy for past discrimination. Specifically, we hold that such relief may be appropriate where an employer or a labor union has engaged in persistent or egregious discrimination, or where necessary to dissipate the lingering effects of pervasive discrimination.

Section 706(g) states: "If the court finds that the respondent has intentionally engaged in or is intentionally engaging in an unlawful employment practice . . . , the court may enjoin the respondent from engaging in such unlawful employment practice, and order such affirmative action as may be appropriate, which may include, but is not limited to, reinstatement or hiring of employees, with or without back pay . . . , or any other equitable relief as the court deems appropriate. . . . No order of the court shall require the admission or reinstatement of an individual as a member of a union, or the hiring, reinstatement, or promotion of an individual as an employee, or the payment to him of any back pay, if such individual was refused admission, suspended, or expelled, or was suspended or discharged for any reason other than discrimination on account of race, color, religion, sex, or national origin in violation of . . . this title." 78 Stat. 261, as amended and as set forth in 42 U.S.C. § 2000e-5(g).

The language of § 706(g) plainly expresses Congress' intent to vest district courts with broad discretion to award "appropriate" equitable relief to remedy unlawful discrimination. . . . Nevertheless, petitioners and the EEOC argue that the last sentence of § 706(g) prohibits a court from ordering an employer or labor union to take affirmative steps to eliminate discrimination which might incidentally benefit individuals who are not the actual victims of discrimination. This reading twists the plain language of the statute.

The last sentence of § 706(g) prohibits a court from ordering a union to admit an individual who was "refused admission . . . for any reason other than discrimination." It does not, as petitioners and the EEOC suggest, say that a court may order relief only for the actual victims of past discrimination. The sentence on its face addresses only the situation where a plaintiff demonstrates that a union (or an employer) has engaged in unlawful discrimination, but the union can show that a particular individual would have been refused admission even in the absence of discrimination, for example, because that individual was unqualified. In these circumstances, § 706(g) confirms that a court could not order the union to admit the unqualified individual. . . . In this case, neither the membership goal nor the Fund order required petitioners to admit to membership individuals who had been refused admission for reasons unrelated to discrimination. Thus, we do not read § 706(g) to prohibit a court from ordering the kind of affirmative relief the District Court awarded in this case.

The availability of race-conscious affirmative relief under § 706(g) as a remedy for a violation of Title VII also furthers the broad purposes underlying the statute. Congress enacted Title VII based on its determination that racial minorities were subject to pervasive and systematic discrimination in employment. . . . Title VII was designed "to achieve equality of employment opportunities and remove barriers that have operated in the past to favor an identifiable group of white employees over other employees. . . . In order to foster equal employment opportunities, Congress gave the lower courts broad power under § 706(g) to fashion "the most complete relief possible" to remedy past discrimination. . . .

In most cases, the court need only order the employer or union to cease engaging in discriminatory practices, and award make-whole relief to the individuals victimized by those practices. In some instances, however, it may be necessary to require the employer or union to take affirmative steps to end discrimination effectively to enforce Title VII. Where an employer or union has engaged in particularly longstanding or egregious discrimination, an injunction simply reiterating Title VII's prohibition against discrimination will often prove useless and will only result in endless enforcement litigation. In such cases, requiring recalcitrant employers or unions to hire and to admit qualified minorities roughly in proportion to the number of qualified minorities in the work force may be the only effective way to ensure the full enjoyment of the rights protected by Title VII. . . .

Affirmative race-conscious relief may be the only means available "to assure equality of employment opportunities and to eliminate those discriminatory practices and devices which have fostered racially stratified job environments to the disadvantage of minority citizens." . . .

Finally, a district court may find it necessary to order interim hiring or promotional goals pending the development of nondiscriminatory hiring or promotion procedures. In these cases, the use of numerical goals provides a compromise between two unacceptable alternatives: an outright ban on hiring or promotions, or continued use of a discriminatory selection procedure. . . .

Many opponents of Title VII argued that an employer could be found guilty of discrimination under the statute simply because of a racial imbalance in his work force, and would be compelled to implement racial "quotas" to avoid being charged with liability. *Weber,* 443 U.S., at 205. 99 S.Ct., at 2728. At the same time, supporters of the bill insisted that employers would not violate Title VII simply because of racial imbalance, and emphasized that neither the Commission nor the courts could compel employers to adopt quotas solely to facilitate racial balancing, *Id.*, at 207, n 7, 99 S.Ct, at 2729, n. 7. The debate concerning what Title VII did and did not require culminated in the adoption of 703(j), which stated expressly that the statute did not require an employer of labor union to adopt quotas or preferences simply because of a racial imbalance. However, while Congress strongly opposed the use of quotas or preferences merely to maintain racial balance, it gave no intimation as to whether such measures should be acceptable as *remedies* for Title VII violations. . . .

The purpose of affirmative action is not to make identified victims whole, but rather to dismantle prior patterns of employment discrimination and to prevent discrimination in the future. Such relief is provided to the class as a whole rather than to individual members; no individual is entitled to relief, and beneficiaries need not show that they were themselves victims of discrimination. In this case, neither the membership goal nor the Fund order required petitioners to indenture or train particular individuals, and neither required them to admit to membership individuals who were refused admission for reasons unrelated to discrimination. . . .

The court should exercise its discretion with an eye toward Congress' concern that race-conscious affirmative measures not be invoked simply to create a racially balanced work force. In the majority of Title VII cases, the court will not have to impose affirmative action as a remedy for past discrimination, but need only order the employer or union to cease engaging in discriminatory practices and award make-whole relief to the individuals victimized by those practices. However, in some cases, affirmative action may be necessary in order effectively to enforce Title VII. As we noted before, a court may have to resort to race-conscious affirmative action when confronted with an employer or labor union that has engaged in persistent or egregious discrimination. Or such relief may be necessary to dissipate the lingering effects of pervasive discrimination. Whether there might be other circumstances that justify the use of court-ordered affirmative action is a matter that we need not decide here. We note only that a court should consider whether affirmative action is necessary to remedy past discrimination in a particular case before imposing such measures, and that the court should also take care to tailor to fit the nature of the violation it seeks to correct. In this case, several factors lead us to conclude that the relief ordered by the District Court was proper.

First, both the District Court and the Court of Appeals agreed that the membership goal and Fund order were necessary to remedy petitioners' pervasive and egregious discrimination. The District Court set the original 29 percent membership goal upon observing that "[t]he record in both state and federal courts against [petitioners] is replete with instances of their bad faith attempts to prevent or delay affirmative action." 401 F.Supp., at 488. The court extended the goal after finding petitioners in contempt for refusing to end their discriminatory practices and failing to comply with various provisions of RAAPO. In affirming the revised membership goal, the Court of Appeals observed that "[t]his court has twice recognized Local 28's long continued and egregious racial discrimination . . . and Local 28 has presented no facts to indicate that our earlier observations are no longer apposite." 753 F.2d, at 1186. In light of petitioners' long history of "foot-dragging resistance" to court orders, simply enjoining them from once again engaging in discriminatory practices would clearly have been futile. Rather, the District Court properly determined that affirmative race-conscious measures were necessary to put an end to petitioners' discriminatory ways.

Both the membership goal and Fund order were similarly necessary to combat the lingering effects of past discrimination. In light of the District Court's determination that the union's reputation for discrimination operated to discourage nonwhites from even applying for membership, it is unlikely that an injunction would have been sufficient to extend to nonwhites equal opportunities for employment. Rather, because access to admission, membership, training, and employment in the industry had traditionally been obtained through informal contacts with union members, it was necessary for a substantial number of nonwhite workers to become members of the union in order for the effects of discrimination to cease. The Fund, in particular, was designed to insure that non-whites would receive the kind of assistance that white apprentices and applicants had traditionally received through informal sources. On the facts of this case, the District Court properly determined that affirmative, race-conscious measures were necessary to assure the equal employment opportunities guaranteed by Title VII.

Second, the District Court's flexible application of the membership goal gives strong indication that it is not being used simply to achieve and maintain racial balance, but rather as a benchmark against which the court could gauge petitioners' efforts to remedy past discrimination. The court has twice adjusted the deadline for achieving the goal, and has continually approved of changes in the size of the apprenticeship classes to account for the fact that economic conditions prevented petitioners from meeting their membership targets; there is every reason to believe that both the court and the administrator will continue to accommodate *legitimate* explanations for petitioners' failure to comply with the court's orders. Moreover, the District Court expressly disavowed any reliance on petitioners' failure to meet the goal as a basis for the contempt finding, but instead viewed this failure as symptomatic of petitioners' refusal to comply with various subsidiary provisions of RAAPO. In sum, the District Court has implemented the membership goal as a means by which it can measure petitioners' compliance with its orders, rather than as a strict racial quota.

Third, both the membership goal and the Fund order are temporary measures. Under AAAPO "[p]referential selection of [union members] will end as soon as the percentage of [minority union members] approximates the percentage of [minorities] in the local labor force." *Weber*, 443 U.S., at 208–209, 99 S.Ct., at 2730; see *United States v. City of Alexandria*, 614 F.2d, at 1366. Similarly, the Fund is scheduled to terminate when petitioners achieve the membership goal, and the court determines that it is no longer needed to remedy past discrimination. The District Court's orders thus operate "as a temporary tool for remedying past discrimination without attempting to 'maintain' a previously achieved balance." *Weber*, 443 U.S., at 216, 99 S.Ct., at 2734 (Blackmun, J., concurring).

Finally, we think it significant that neither the membership goal nor the Fund order "unnecessarily trammel[s] the interests of white employees." *Id.* 443 U.S., at 208, 99 S.Ct., at 2730; *Teamsters*, 431 U.S., at 352–353, 97 S.Ct., at 1863–1864. Petitioners concede that the District Court's orders did not require any member of the union to be laid off, and did not discriminate against existing union members. See *Weber, supra*, 443 U.S., at 208, 99 S.Ct., at 2729–2730; see also 30 St. Louis U.L.J., at 264. While whites seeking admission into the union may be denied benefits extended to their nonwhite counterparts, the court's orders do not stand as an absolute bar to such individuals; indeed, a majority of new union members have been white. See *City of Alexandria, supra*, at 1366. Many provisions of the court's orders are race-neutral (for example, the requirement that the [Joint Apprenticeship Committee (JAC)] assign one apprentice for every four journeyman workers), and petitioners remain free to adopt the provisions of AAAPO and the Fund order for the benefit of white members and applicants.

Petitioners also allege that the membership goal and Fund order contravene the equal protection component of the Due Process Clause of the Fifth Amendment because they deny benefits to white individuals based on race. We have consistently recognised that government bodies constitutionally may adopt racial classifications as a remedy for past discrimination. . . . We conclude that the relief ordered in this case passes even the most rigorous test—it is narrowly tailored to further the Government's compelling interest in remedying past discrimination.

In this case, there is no problem . . . with a proper showing of prior discrimination that would justify the use of remedial racial classifications. Both the District Court and Court of Appeals have repeatedly found petitioners guilty of egregious violations of Title VII, and have determined that affirmative measures were necessary to remedy their racially discriminatory practices. More importantly, the District Court's orders were properly tailored to accomplish this objective. First, the District Court considered the efficacy of alternative remedies, and concluded that, in light of petitioners' long record of resistance to official efforts to end their discriminatory practices, stronger measures were necessary. . . . Again, petitioners concede that the District Court's orders did not disadvantage *existing* union members. While white applications for union membership may be denied certain benefits available to their nonwhite counterparts, the court's orders do not stand as an absolute bar to the admission of such individuals; again, a majority of those entering the union after entry of the court's orders have been white. We therefore conclude that the District Court's orders do not violate the equal protection safeguards of the Constitution.

Finally, Local 28 challenges the District Court's appointment of an administrator with broad powers to supervise its compliance with the court's orders as an unjustifiable interference with its statutory right to self-governance. See 29 USC § 401(a). Preliminarily, we note that while AAAPO gives the administrator broad powers to oversee petitioners' membership practices, Local 28 retains complete control over its other affairs. Even with respect to membership, the administrator's job is to insure that petitioners comply with the court's orders and admit sufficient numbers of non-whites; the administrator does not select the particular individuals that will be admitted, that task is left to union officials. In any event, in light of the difficulties inherent in monitoring compliance with the court's orders, and especially petitioners' established record of resistance to prior state and federal court orders designed to end their discriminatory membership practices, appointment of an administrator was well within the District Court's discretion. . . .

To summarize our holding today, six members of the Court agree that a district court may, in appropriate circumstances, order preferential relief benefiting individuals who are not the actual victims of discrimination as a remedy for violations of Title VII, . . . that the District Court did not use incorrect statistical evidence in establishing petitioners' nonwhite membership goal, that the contempt fines and Fund order were proper remedies for civil contempt, and that the District Court properly appointed an administrator to supervise petitioners' compliance with the court's orders. Five members of the Court agree that in this case, the District Court did not err in evaluating petitioners' utilization of the apprenticeship program, and that the membership goal and the Fund order are not violative of either Title VII or the Constitution. The judgment of the Court of Appeals is hereby *Affirmed.* . . .

# *City of Richmond v. J. A. Croson Company*

*Supreme Court of the United States*

In this case, we confront once again the tension between the Fourteenth Amendment's guarantee of equal treatment to all citizens, and the use of race-based measures to ameliorate the effects of past discrimination on the opportunities enjoyed by members of minority groups in our society. . . .

## I

On April 11, 1983, the Richmond City Council adopted the Minority Business Utilization Plan (the Plan). The Plan required prime contractors to whom the city awarded construction contracts to subcontract at least 30 percent of the dollar amount of the contract to one or more Minority Business Enterprises (MBEs). Ordinance No. 83-69-59, codified in Richmond, Va., City Code, § 12-156(a) (1985). The 30 percent set-aside did not apply to city contracts awarded to minority-owned prime contractors. *Ibid.*

The Plan defined an MBE as "[a] business at least fifty-one (51) percent of which is owned and controlled . . . by minority group members." § 12-23, p. 941. "Minority group members" were defined as "[c]itizens of the United

109 S.Ct.706 (1989).

States who are Blacks, Spanish-speaking, Orientals, Indians, Eskimos, or Aleuts." *Ibid.* There was no geographic limit to the Plan; an otherwise qualified MBE from anywhere in the United States could avail itself of the 30 percent set-aside. The Plan declared that it was "remedial" in nature, and enacted "for the purpose of promoting wider participation by minority business enterprises in the construction of public projects." § 12-158(a). The Plan expired on June 30, 1988, and was in effect for approximately five years. *Ibid.*

The Plan authorized the Director of the Department of General Services to promulgate rules which "shall allow waivers in those individual situations where a contractor can prove to the satisfaction of the director that the requirements herein cannot be achieved." § 12-157. To this end, the Director promulgated Contract Clauses, Minority Business Utilization Plan (Contract Clauses). Section D of these rules provided: "No partial or complete waiver of the foregoing [30 percent set-aside] requirement shall be granted by the city other than in exceptional circumstances. To justify a waiver, it must be shown that every feasible attempt has been made to comply, and it must be demonstrated that sufficient, relevant, qualified Minority Business Enterprises . . . are unavailable or unwilling to participate in the contract to enable meeting the 30 percent MBE goal." . . .

The Plan was adopted by the Richmond City Council after a public hearing. App. 9-50. Seven members of the public spoke to the merits of the ordinance: five were in opposition, two in favor. Proponents of the set-aside provision relied on a study which indicated that, while the general population of Richmond was 50 percent black, only .67 percent of the city's prime construction contracts had been awarded to minority businesses in the 5-year period from 1978 to 1983. . . .

There was no direct evidence of race discrimination on the part of the city in letting contracts or any evidence that the city's prime contractors had discriminated against minority-owned subcontractors. . . .

. . . On September 6, 1983, the city of Richmond issued an invitation to bid on a project for the provision and installation of certain plumbing fixtures at the city jail. On September 30, 1983, Eugene Bonn, the regional manager of J. A. Croson Company (Croson), a mechanical plumbing and heating contractor, received the bid forms. The project involved the installations of stainless steel urinals and water closets in the city jail. Products of either of two manufacturers were specified, Acorn Engineering Company (Acorn) or Bradley Manufacturing Company (Bradley). Bonn determined that to meet the 30 percent set-aside requirement, a minority contractor would have to supply the fixtures. The provision of the fixtures amounted to 75 percent of the total contract price. . . .

Bonn subsequently began a search for potential MBE suppliers. The only potential MBE fixture supplier was Melvin Brown, president of Continental Metal Hose, hereafter referred to as "Continental." However, because of Continental's inability to obtain credit approval, Continental was unable to submit a bid by the due date of October 13, 1983. Shortly thereafter and as a direct result, Croson submitted a request for a waiver of the 30 percent set-aside. Croson's waiver request indicated that Continental was "unqualified" and that the other MBEs contacted had been unresponsive or unable to quote. Upon learning of Croson's waiver request, Brown contacted an agent of Acorn, the other fixture manufacturer specified by the city. Based upon his discussions with Acorn, Brown subsequently submitted a bid on the fixtures to Croson. Continental's bid was $6,183.29 higher than the price Croson had included for the fixtures in its bid to the city. This constituted a 7 percent increase over the market price for the fixtures. With added bonding and insurance, using Continental would have raised the cost of the project by $7,663.16. On the same day that Brown contacted Acorn, he also called city procurement officials and told them that Continental, an MBE, could supply the fixtures specified in the city jail contract. On November 2, 1983, the city denied Croson's waiver request, indicating that Croson had 10 days to submit an MBE Utilization Commitment Form, and warned that failure to do so could result in its bid being considered unresponsive.

Croson wrote the city on November 8, 1983. In the letter, Bonn indicated that Continental was not an authorized supplier for either Acorn or Bradley fixtures. He also noted that Acorn's quotation to Brown was subject to credit approval and in any case was substantially higher than any other quotation Croson had received. Finally, Bonn noted that Continental's bid had been submitted some 21 days after the prime bids were due. In a second letter, Croson laid out the additional costs that using Continental to supply the fixtures would entail, and asked that it be allowed to raise the overall contract price accordingly. The city denied both Croson's request for a waiver and its suggestion that the contract price be raised. The city informed Croson that it had decided to rebid the project. On December 9, 1983, counsel for Croson wrote the city asking for a review of the waiver denial. The city's attorney responded that the city had elected to rebid the project, and that there is no appeal of such a decision. Shortly thereafter Croson brought this action under 42 U.S.C. § 1983 in the Federal District Court for the Eastern District of Virginia, arguing that the Richmond ordinance was unconstitutional on its face and as applied in this case.

The District Court upheld the Plan in all respects . . . [and held that] the 30 percent figure was "reasonable in light of the undisputed fact that minorities constitute 50 percent of the population of Richmond." *Ibid.*

Croson sought certiorari from this Court. We granted the writ, vacated the opinion of the Court of Appeals, and remanded the case for further consideration in light of our intervening decision in *Wygant v. Jackson Board of Education*, 476 U.S. 267, 106 S.Ct. 1842, 90 L.Ed.2d 260 (1986). . . .

On remand, a divided panel of the Court of Appeals struck down the Richmond set-aside program as violating both prongs of strict scrutiny under the Equal Protection Clause of the Fourteenth Amendment. *J.A. Croson Co. v. Richmond*, 822 F.2d 1355 (CA4 1987) *(Croson II)*. . . .

In this case, the debate at the city council meeting "revealed no record of prior discrimination by the city in awarding public contracts. . . ." *Croson II, supra*, at 1358. Moreover, the statistics comparing the minority population of Richmond to the percentage of *prime* contracts awarded to minority firms had little or no probative value in establishing prior discrimination in the relevant market, and actually suggested "more of a political than a remedial basis for the racial preference." 822 F.2d, at 1359. The court concluded that, "[i]f this plan is supported by a compelling governmental interest, so is every other plan that has been enacted in the past or that will be enacted in the future." *Id.*, at 1360.

The Court of Appeals went on to hold that even if the city had demonstrated a compelling interest in the use of a race-based quota, the 30 percent set-aside was not narrowly tailored to accomplish a remedial purpose. The court found that the 30 percent figure was "chosen arbitrarily" and was not tied to the number of minority subcontractors in Richmond or to any other relevant number. *Ibid.* The dissenting judge argued that the majority had "misconstrue[d] and misapplie[d]" our decision in Wygant. 822 F.2d, at 1362. We noted probable jurisdiction of the city's appeal, . . . and we now affirm the judgment.

## II

. . . Congress, unlike any State or political subdivision, has a specific constitutional mandate to enforce the dictates of the Fourteenth

Amendment. The power to "enforce" may at times also include the power to define situations which *Congress* determines threaten principles of equality and to adopt prophylactic rules to deal with those situations. . . .

That Congress may identify and redress the effects of society-wide discrimination does not mean that, *a fortiori*, the States and their political subdivisions are free to decide that such remedies are appropriate. Section 1 of the Fourteenth Amendment is an explicit *constraint* on state power, and the States must undertake any remedial efforts in accordance with that provision. To hold otherwise would be to cede control over the content of the Equal Protection Clause to the 50 state legislatures and their myriad political subdivisions. The mere recitation of a benign or compensatory purpose for the use of a racial classification would essentially entitle the States to exercise the full power of Congress under § 5 of the Fourteenth Amendment and insulate any racial classification from judicial scrutiny under § 1. We believe that such a result would be contrary to the intentions of the Framers of the Fourteenth Amendment, who desired to place clear limits on the States' use of race as a criterion for legislative action, and to have the federal courts enforce those limitations. . . .

It would seem equally clear, however, that a state or local subdivision (if delegated the authority from the State) has the authority to eradicate the effects of private discrimination within its own legislative jurisdiction. This authority must, of course, be exercised within the constraints of § 1 of the Fourteenth Amendment. . . . As a matter of state law, the city of Richmond has legislative authority over its procurement policies, and can use its spending powers to remedy private discrimination, if it identifies that discrimination with the particularity required by the Fourteenth Amendment. . . .

Thus, if the city could show that it had essentially become a "passive participant" in a system of racial exclusion practiced by elements of the local construction industry, we think it clear that the city could take affirmative steps to dismantle such a system. It is beyond dispute that any public entity, state or federal, has a compelling interest in assuring that public dollars, drawn from the tax contributions of all citizens, do not serve to finance the evil of private prejudice. . . .

## III.A

The Equal Protection Clause of the Fourteenth Amendment provides that "[N]o State shall . . . deny to *any person* within its jurisdiction the equal protection of the laws" (emphasis added). As this Court has noted in the past, the "rights created by the first section of the Fourteenth Amendment are, by its terms, guaranteed to the individual. The rights established are personal rights." *Shelley v. Kraemer*, 334 U.S. 1, 22, 68 S.Ct. 836, 846, 92 L.Ed. 1161 (1948). The Richmond Plan denies certain citizens the opportunity to compete for a fixed percentage of public contracts based solely upon their race. To whatever racial group these citizens belong, their "personal rights" to be treated with equal dignity and respect are implicated by a rigid rule erecting race as the sole criterion in an aspect of public decision making. . . .

Classifications based on race carry a danger of stigmatic harm. Unless they are strictly reserved for remedial settings, they may in fact promote notions of racial inferiority and lead to a politics of racial hostility. . . .

## III.B

The District Court found the city council's "findings sufficient to ensure that, in adopting the Plan, it was remedying the present effects of past discrimination in the *construction industry.*" Supp. App. 163 (emphasis added). Like the "role model" theory employed in *Wygant*, a generalized assertion that there has been past discrimination in an entire industry provides no guidance for a legislative body to determine the precise scope of the injury it seeks to remedy. It "has no logical stopping point." *Wygant, supra,* at 275, 106 S.Ct., at 1847 (plurality opinion). "Relief" for such an ill-defined wrong could extend until the percentage of public contracts awarded to MBEs in Richmond mirrored the percentage of minorities in the population as a whole.

Appellant argues that it is attempting to remedy various forms of past discrimination that are alleged to be responsible for the small number of minority businesses in the local contracting industry. Among these the city cites the exclusion of blacks from skilled construction trade unions and training programs. This past discrimination has prevented them "from following the traditional path from laborer to entrepreneur." Brief for Appellant 23–24. The city also lists a host of nonracial factors which would seem to face a member of any racial group attempting to establish a new business enterprise, such as deficiencies in working capital, inability to meet bonding requirements, unfamiliarity with bidding procedures, and disability caused by an inadequate track record. *Id.,* at 25–26, and n. 41.

While there is no doubt that the sorry history of both private and public discrimination in this country has contributed to a lack of opportunities for black entrepreneurs, this observation, standing alone, cannot justify a rigid racial quota in the awarding of public contracts in Richmond, Virginia. Like the claim that discrimination in primary and secondary schooling justifies a rigid racial preference in medical school admissions, an amorphous claim that there has been past discrimination in a particular industry cannot justify the use of an unyielding racial quota.

It is sheer speculation how many minority firms there would be in Richmond absent past societal discrimination, just as it was sheer speculation how many minority medical students would have been admitted to the medical school at Davis absent past discrimination in educational opportunities. Defining these sorts of injuries as "identified discrimination" would give local governments license to create a patchwork of racial preferences based on statistical generalizations about any particular field of endeavor.

These defects are readily apparent in this case. The 30 percent quota cannot in any realistic sense be tied to any injury suffered by anyone. . . .

There is nothing approaching a prima facie case of a constitutional or statutory violation by *anyone* in the Richmond construction industry. . . .

The District Court accorded great weight to the fact that the city council designated the Plan as "remedial." But the mere recitation of a "benign" or legitimate purpose for a racial classification, is entitled to little or no weight. . . . Racial classifications are suspect, and that means that simple legislative assurances of good intention cannot suffice. . . .

In this case, the city does not even know how many MBEs in the relevant market are qualified to undertake prime or subcontracting work in public construction projects. . . . Nor does the city know what percentage of total city construction dollars minority firms now receive as subcontractors on prime contracts let by the city.

To a large extent, the set-aside of subcontracting dollars seems to rest on the unsupported assumption that white prime contractors simply will not hire minority firms. . . . Without any information on minority participation in subcontracting, it is quite simply impossible to evaluate overall minority representation in the city's construction expenditures.

The city and the District Court also relied on evidence that MBE membership in local contractors' associations was extremely low. Again, standing alone this evidence is not probative of any discrimination in the local construction industry. There are numerous explanations for this dearth of minority participation, including past societal discrimination in education and economic opportunities as well as both black and white career and entrepreneurial choices. Blacks may be disproportionately attracted to industries other than construction. . . . The mere fact that black membership in these trade organizations is low, standing alone, cannot establish a prima facie case of discrimination. . . .

While the States and their subdivisions may take remedial action when they possess evidence that their own spending practices are exacerbating a pattern of prior discrimination, they must identify that discrimination, public or private, with some specificity before they may use race-conscious relief. . . .

In sum, none of the evidence presented by the city points to any identified discrimination in the Richmond construction industry. We, therefore, hold that the city has failed to demonstrate a compelling interest in apportioning public contracting opportunities on the basis of race. To accept Richmond's claim that past societal discrimination alone can serve as the basis for rigid racial preferences would be to open the door to competing claims for "remedial relief" for every disadvantaged group. The dream of a Nation of equal citizens in a society where race is irrelevant to personal opportunity and achievement would be lost in a mosaic of shifting preferences based on inherently unmeasurable claims of past wrongs. . . .

### IV

Since the city must already consider bids and waivers on a case-by-case basis, it is difficult to see the need for a rigid numerical quota. . . .

Given the existence of an individualized procedure, the city's only interest in maintaining a quota system rather than investigating the need for remedial action in particular cases would seem to be simple administrative convenience. But the interest in avoiding the bureaucratic effort necessary to tailor remedial relief to those who truly have suffered the effects of prior discrimination cannot justify a rigid line drawn on the basis of a suspect classification. . . . Under Richmond's scheme, a successful black, Hispanic, or Oriental entrepreneur from anywhere in the country enjoys an absolute preference over other citizens based solely on their race. We think it obvious that such a program is not narrowly tailored to remedy the effects of prior discrimination.

### V

. . . Because the city of Richmond has failed to identify the need for remedial action in the awarding of its public construction contracts, its treatment of its citizens on a racial basis violates the dictates of the Equal Protection Clause. Accordingly, the judgment of the Court of Appeals for the Fourth Circuit is Affirmed.

## *Meritor Savings Bank, FSB v. Vinson, et al.*

*Supreme Court of the United States*

This case presents important questions concerning claims of workplace "sexual harassment" brought under Title VII of the Civil Rights Act of 1964, 78 Stat. 253, as amended, 42 U.S.C. § 2000e *et seq.*

477 U.S. 84 (1986).

## I

In 1974, respondent Mechelle Vinson . . . started as a teller-trainee, and thereafter was promoted to teller, head teller, and assistant branch manager. She worked at the same branch for four years, and it is undisputed that her advancement there was based on merit alone. In September 1978, respondent notified her supervisor, Sidney Taylor, that she was taking sick leave for an indefinite period. On November 1, 1978, the bank discharged her for excessive use of that leave.

Respondent brought this action against Taylor and the bank, claiming that during her four years at the bank she had "constantly been subjected to sexual harassment" by Taylor in violation of Title VII. She sought injunctive relief, compensatory and punitive damages against Taylor and the bank, and attorney's fees.

At the 11-day bench trial, the parties presented conflicting testimony about Taylor's behavior during respondent's employment.* Respondent testified that during her probationary period as a teller-trainee, Taylor treated her in a fatherly way and made no sexual advances. Shortly thereafter, however, he invited her out to dinner and, during the course of the meal, suggested that they go to a motel to have sexual relations. At first she refused, but out of what she described as fear of losing her job she eventually agreed. According to respondent, Taylor thereafter made repeated demands upon her for sexual favors, usually at the branch, both during and after business hours; she estimated that over the next several years she had intercourse with him some 40 or 50 times. In addition, respondent testified that Taylor fondled her in front of other employees, followed her into the women's restroom when she went there alone, exposed himself to her, and even forcibly raped her on several occasions. These activities ceased after 1977, respondent stated, when she started going with a steady boyfriend.

Respondent also testified that Taylor touched and fondled other women employees of the bank, and she attempted to call witnesses to support this charge. But while some supporting testimony apparently was admitted without objection, the District Court did not allow her "to present wholesale evidence of a pattern and practice relating to sexual advances to other female employees in her case in chief, but advised her that she might well be able to present such evidence in rebuttal to the defendants' cases." *Vinson v. Taylor*, 22 EPD §30, 708, p. 14,693, n. 1, 23 FEP Cases 37, 38–39, n. 1 (DC 1980). Respondent did not offer such evidence in rebuttal. Finally, respondent testified that because she was afraid of Taylor she never reported his harassment to any of his supervisors and never attempted to use the bank's complaint procedure.

Taylor denied respondent's allegations of sexual activity, testifying that he never fondled her, never made suggestive remarks to her, never engaged in sexual intercourse with her, and never asked her to do so. He contended instead that respondent made her accusations in response to a business-related dispute. The bank also denied respondent's allegations and asserted that any sexual harassment by Taylor was unknown to the bank and engaged in without its consent or approval.

The District Court denied relief and . . . ultimately found that respondent "was not the victim of sexual harassment and was not the victim of sexual discrimination" while employed at the bank.

Although it concluded that respondent had not proved a violation of Title VII, the District Court nevertheless went on to address the bank's liability. After noting the bank's express

---

*Like the Court of Appeals, this Court was not provided a complete transcript of the trial. We therefore rely largely on the District Court's opinion for the summary of the relevant testimony.

policy against discrimination, and finding that neither respondent nor any other employee had ever lodged a complaint about sexual harassment by Taylor, the court ultimately concluded that "the bank was without notice and cannot be held liable for the alleged actions of Taylor."

The Court of Appeals for the District of Columbia Circuit reversed.... The court stated that a violation of Title VII may be predicated on either of two types of sexual harassment: harassment that involves the conditioning of concrete employment benefits on sexual favors, and harassment that, while not affecting economic benefits, creates a hostile or offensive working environment.... Believing that "Vinson's grievance was clearly of the [hostile environment] type," and that the District Court had not considered whether a violation of this type had occurred, the court concluded that a remand was necessary.

The court further concluded that the District Court's findings that any sexual relationship between respondent and Taylor "was a voluntary one" did not obviate the need for a remand....

As to the bank's liability, the Court of Appeals held that an employer is absolutely liable for sexual harassment practiced by supervisory personnel, whether or not the employer knew or should have known about the misconduct. The court relied chiefly on Title VII's definition of "employer" to include "any agent of such a person," 42 U.S.C. §2000e(b), as well as on the EEOC Guidelines. The court held that a supervisor is an "agent" of his employer for Title VII purposes, even if he lacks authority to hire, fire, or promote, since "the mere existence—or even the appearance—of a significant degree of influence in vital job decisions gives any supervisor the opportunity to impose on employees."...

In accordance with the foregoing, the Court of Appeals reversed the judgment of the District Court and remanded the case for further proceedings....

## II

Title VII of the Civil Rights Act of 1964 makes it "an unlawful employment practice for an employer ... to discriminate against any individual with respect to his compensation, terms, conditions, or privileges for employment, because of such individual's race, color, religion, sex, or national origin."...

Respondent argues, and the Court of Appeals held, that unwelcome sexual advances that create an offensive or hostile working environment violate Title VII. Without question, when a supervisor sexually harasses a subordinate because of the subordinate's sex, that supervisor "discriminate[s]" on the basis of sex....

First, the language of Title VII is not limited to "economic" or "tangible" discrimination. The phrase "terms, conditions, or privileges of employment" evinces a congressional intent "'to strike at the entire spectrum of disparate treatment of men and women'" in employment....

Second, in 1980 the EEOC issued Guidelines specifying that "sexual harassment," as there defined, is a form of sex discrimination prohibited by Title VII....

In defining "sexual harassment," the Guidelines first describe the kinds of workplace conduct that may be actionable under Title VII. These include "[u]nwelcome sexual advances, requests for sexual favors, and other verbal or physical conduct of a sexual nature." 29 CFR § 1604.11(a) (1985). Relevant to the charges at issue in this case, the Guidelines provide that such sexual misconduct constitutes prohibited "sexual harassment," whether or not it is directly linked to the grant or denial of an economic *quid pro quo,* where "such conduct has the purpose or effect of unreasonably interfering with an individual's work performance or creating an intimidating, hostile, or offensive working environment." . . .

In concluding that so-called "hostile environment" (*i.e.*, non *quid pro quo*) harassment violates Title VII, the EEOC drew upon a substantial body of judicial decisions and EEOC precedent holding that Title VII affords employees the right to work in an environment free from discriminatory intimidation, ridicule, and insult. . . .

Since the Guidelines were issued, courts have uniformly held, and we agree, that a plaintiff may establish a violation of Title VII by proving that discrimination based on sex has created a hostile or abusive work environment. . . .

For sexual harassment to be actionable, it must be sufficiently severe or pervasive "to alter the conditions of [the victim's] employment and create an abusive working environment." *Ibid.* Respondent's allegations in this case—which include not only pervasive harassment but also criminal conduct of the most serious nature—are plainly sufficient to state a claim for "hostile environment" sexual harassment. . . .

The fact that sex-related conduct was "voluntary," in the sense that the complainant was not forced to participate against her will, is not a defense to a sexual harassment suit brought under Title VII. The gravamen of any sexual harassment claim is that the alleged sexual advances were "unwelcome." 29 CFR § 1604.11(a) (1985). While the question whether particular conduct was indeed unwelcome presents difficult problems of proof and turns largely on credibility determinations committed to the trier of fact, the District Court in this case erroneously focused on the "voluntariness" of respondent's participation in the claimed sexual episodes. The correct inquiry is whether respondent by her conduct indicated that the alleged sexual advances were unwelcome, not whether her actual participation in sexual intercourse was voluntary. . . .

## III

Although the District Court concluded that respondent had not proved a violation of Title VII, it nevertheless went on to consider the question of the bank's liability. Finding that "the bank was without notice" of Taylor's alleged conduct, and that notice to Taylor was not the equivalent of notice to the bank, the court concluded that the bank therefore could not be held liable for Taylor's alleged actions. The Court of Appeals took the opposite view, holding that an employer is strictly liable for a hostile environment created by a supervisor's sexual advances, even though the employer neither knew nor reasonably could have known of the alleged misconduct. The court held that a supervisor, whether or not he possesses the authority to hire, fire, or promote, is necessarily an "agent" of his employer for all Title VII purposes, since "even the appearance" of such authority may enable him to impose himself on his subordinates. . . .

The EEOC, in its brief as *amicus curiae*, contends that courts formulating employer liability rules should draw from traditional agency principles. Examination of those principles has led the EEOC to the view that where a supervisor exercises the authority actually delegated to him by his employer, by making or threatening to make decisions affecting the employment status of his subordinates, such actions are properly imputed to the employer whose delegation of authority empowered the supervisor to undertake them. . . . Thus, the courts have consistently held employers liable for the discriminatory discharges of employees by supervisory personnel, whether or not the employer knew, should have known, or approved of the supervisor's actions. . . .

The EEOC suggests that when a sexual harassment claim rests exclusively on a "hostile environment" theory, however, the usual basis for a finding of agency will often disappear.

In that case, the EEOC believes, agency principles lead to

> a rule that asks whether a victim of sexual harassment had reasonably available an avenue of complaint regarding such harassment, and, if available and utilized, whether that procedure was reasonably responsive to the employee's complaint. If the employer has an expressed policy against sexual harassment and has implemented a procedure specifically designed to resolve sexual harassment claims, and if the victim does not take advantage of that procedure, the employer should be shielded from liability absent actual knowledge of the sexually hostile environment (obtained, *e.g.*, by the filing of a charge with the EEOC or a comparable state agency). In all other cases, the employer will be liable if it has actual knowledge of the harassment or if, considering all the facts of the case, the victim in question had no reasonably available avenue for making his or her complaint known to appropriate management officials." Brief for United States and EEOC as *Amici Curiae* 26.

As respondent points out, this suggested rule is in some tension with the EEOC Guidelines, which hold an employer liable for the acts of its agents without regard to notice. 29 CFR § 1604.11(c) (1985). The Guidelines do require, however, an "examin[ation of] the circumstances of the particular employment relationship and the job [f]unctions performed by the individual in determining whether an individual acts in either as supervisory or agency capacity."

We hold that the Court of Appeals erred in concluding that employers are always automatically liable for sexual harassment by their supervisors. For the same reason, absence of notice to an employer does not necessarily insulate that employer form liability. *Ibid.*

Finally, we reject petitioner's view that the mere existence of a grievance procedure and a policy against discrimination, coupled with respondent's failure to invoke that procedure, must insulate petitioner from liability. While those facts are plainly relevant, the situation before us demonstrates why they are not necessarily dispositive. Petitioner's general nondiscrimination policy did not address sexual harassment in particular, and thus did not alert employees to their employer's interest in correcting that form of discrimination. App. 25. Moreover, the bank's grievance procedure apparently required an employee to complain first to her supervisor, in this case Taylor. Since Taylor was the alleged perpetrator, it is not altogether surprising that respondent failed to invoke the procedure and report her grievance to him. Petitioner's contention that respondent's failure should insulate it from liability might be substantially stronger if its procedures were better calculated to encourage victims of harassment to come forward.

## IV

In sum, we hold that a claim of "hostile environment" sex discrimination is actionable under Title VII, that the District Court's findings were insufficient to dispose of respondent's hostile environment claim, and that the District Court did not err in admitting testimony about respondent's sexually provocative speech and dress. As to employer liability, we conclude that the Court of Appeals was wrong to entirely disregard agency principles and impose absolute liability on employers for the acts of their supervisors, regardless of the circumstances of a particular case.

Accordingly, the judgment of the Court of Appeals reversing the judgment of the District Court is affirmed, and the case is remanded for further proceedings consistent with this opinion.

# *Teresa Harris, Petitioner v. Forklift Systems, Inc.*

OCTOBER 13, 1993, ARGUED

NOVEMBER 9, 1993, DECIDED

*Supreme Court of the United States*

In this case we consider the definition of a discriminatorily "abusive work environment" (also known as a "hostile work environment") under Title VII of the Civil Rights Act of 1964, 78 Stat. 253, as amended, 42 U.S.C. § 2000e *et seq.* (1988 ed., Supp. III).

Teresa Harris worked as a manager at Forklift Systems, Inc., an equipment rental company, from April 1985 until October 1987. Charles Hardy was Forklift's president.

The Magistrate found that, throughout Harris' time at Forklift, Hardy often insulted her because of her gender and often made her the target of unwanted sexual innuendos. Hardy told Harris on several occasions, in the presence of other employees, "You're a woman, what do you know" and "We need a man as the rental manager"; at least once, he told her she was "a dumb ass woman." App. to Pet. for Cert. A-13. Again in front of others, he suggested that the two of them "go to the Holiday Inn to negotiate [Harris'] raise." *Id.*, at A-14. Hardy occasionally asked Harris and other female employees to get coins from his front pants pocket. *Ibid.* He threw objects on the ground in front of Harris and other women, and asked them to pick the objects up. *Id.*, at A-14 to A-15. He made sexual innuendos about Harris' and other women's clothing. *Id.*, at A-15.

In mid-August 1987, Harris complained to Hardy about his conduct. Hardy said he was surprised that Harris was offended, claimed he was only joking, and apologized. *Id.*, at A-16. He also promised he would stop, and based on this assurance Harris stayed on the job. *Ibid.* But in early September, Hardy began anew: While Harris was arranging a deal with one of Forklift's customers, he asked her, again in front of other employees, "What did you do, promise the guy . . . some [sex] Saturday night?" *Id.*, at A-17. On October 1, Harris collected her paycheck and quit.

Harris then sued Forklift, claiming that Hardy's conduct had created an abusive work environment for her because of her gender. The United States District Court for the Middle District of Tennessee, adopting the report and recommendation of the Magistrate, found this to be "a close case," *id.*, at A-31, but held that Hardy's conduct did not create an abusive environment. The court found that some of Hardy's comments "offended [Harris], and would offend the reasonable woman," *id.*, at A-33, but that they were not

> so severe as to be expected to seriously affect [Harris'] psychological well-being. A reasonable woman manager under like circumstances would have been offended by Hardy, but his conduct would not have risen to the level of interfering with that person's work performance.
>
> Neither do I believe that [Harris] was subjectively so offended that she suffered injury. . . . Although Hardy may at times have genuinely offended [Harris], I do not believe that he created a working environment so poisoned as to be intimidating or abusive to [Harris]." *Id.*, at A-34 to A-35. . . .

510 U.S 17; 114 S.Ct. 367; 126 L.Ed.2d 295; 1993 U.S. LEXIS 7155; 62 U.S.L.W. 4004; 63 Fair Empl. Prac. Cas. (BNA) 225; 62 Empl. Prac. Dec. (CCH) P42,623; 93 Cal. Daily Op. Service 8330; 93 Daily Journal DAR 14212; 7 Fla. L. Weekly Fed. S 655.

. . . Title VII of the Civil Rights Act of 1964 makes it "an unlawful employment practice for an employer . . . to discriminate against any individual with respect to his compensation, terms, conditions, or privileges of employment, because of such individual's race, color, religion, sex, or national origin." 42 U.S.C. § 2000e-2(a)(1). As we made clear in *Meritor Savings Bank, FSB v. Vinson,* 477 U.S. 57, 91 L.Ed. 2d 49, 106 S.Ct. 2399 (1986), this language "is not limited to 'economic' or 'tangible' discrimination. The phrase 'terms, conditions, or privileges of employment' evinces a congressional intent 'to strike at the entire spectrum of disparate treatment of men and women' in employment, "which includes requiring people to work in a discriminatorily hostile or abusive environment. *Id.*, at 64, quoting *Los Angeles Dept. of Water and Power v. Manhart,* 435 U.S. 702, 707, n.13, 55 L.Ed.2d 657, 98 S.Ct. 1370 (1978) (some internal quotation marks omitted). When the workplace is permeated with "discriminatory intimidation, ridicule, and insult," 477 U.S. at 65, that is "sufficiently severe or pervasive to alter the conditions of the victim's employment and create an abusive working environment," *id.*, 67 (internal brackets and quotation marks omitted), Title VII is violated.

This standard, which we reaffirm today, takes a middle path between making actionable any conduct that is merely offensive and requiring the conduct to cause a tangible psychological injury. As we pointed out in *Meritor,* "mere utterance of an. . . . epithet which engenders offensive feelings in a employee," *ibid.* (internal quotation marks omitted) does not sufficiently affect the conditions of employment to implicate Title VII. Conduct that is not severe or pervasive enough to create an objectively hostile or abusive work environment—an environment that a reasonable person would find hostile or abusive—is beyond Title VII's purview. Likewise, if the victim does not subjectively perceive the environment to be abusive, the conduct has not actually altered the conditions of the victim's employment, and there is no Title VII violation.

But Title VII comes into play before the harassing conduct leads to a nervous breakdown. A discriminatorily abusive work environment, even one that does not seriously affect employees' psychological well-being, can and often will detract from employees' job performance, discourage employees from remaining on the job, or keep them from advancing in their careers. Moreover, even without regard to these tangible effects, the very fact that the discriminatory conduct was so severe or pervasive that it created a work environment abusive to employees because of their race, gender, religion, or national origin offends Title VII's broad rule of workplace equality. The appalling conduct alleged in *Meritor,* and the reference in that case to environments "'so heavily polluted with discrimination as to destroy completely the emotional and psychological stability of minority group workers,'" *id.*, at 66, quoting *Rogers v. EEOC,* 454 F.2d 234, 238 (CA5 1971), cert. denied, 406 U.S. 957, 32 L. Ed. 2d 343, 92 S.Ct. 2058 (1972), merely present some especially egregious examples of harassment. They do not mark the boundary of what is actionable.

We therefore believe the District Court erred in relying on whether the conduct "seriously affected plaintiff's psychological well-being" or led her to "suffer injury." Such an inquiry may needlessly focus the factfinder's attention on concrete psychological harm, an element Title VII does not require. Certainly Title VII bars conduct that would seriously affect a reasonable person's psychological well-being, but the statute is not limited to such conduct. So long as the environment would reasonably be perceived, and is perceived, as hostile or abusive, *Meritor, supra,* at 67, there is no need for it also to be psychologically injurious.

This is not, and by its nature cannot be, a mathematically precise test. We need not answer today all the potential questions it raises, nor specifically address the Equal Employment Opportunity Commission's new regulations on this subject, see 58 Fed. Reg. 51266 (1993) (proposed 29 CFR § 1609.1, 1609.2); see also 29 CFR § 1604.11 (1993). But we can say that whether an environment is "hostile" or "abusive" can be determined only by looking at all the circumstances. These may include the frequency of the discriminatory conduct; its severity; whether it is physically threatening or humiliating, or a mere offensive utterance; and whether it unreasonably interferes with an employee's work performance. The effect on the employee's psychological well-being is, of course, relevant to determining whether the plaintiff actually found the environment abusive. But while psychological harm, like any other relevant factor, may be taken into account, no single factor is required.

Forklift, while conceding that a requirement that the conduct seriously affect psychological well-being is unfounded, argues that the District Court nonetheless correctly applied the *Meritor* standard. We disagree. Though the District Court did conclude that the work environment was not "intimidating or abusive to [Harris],"App. to Pet. for Cert. A-35, it did so only after finding that the conduct was not "so severe as to be expected to seriously affect plaintiff's psychological well-being," *id.*, at A-34, and that Harris was not "subjectively so offended that she suffered injury," *ibid.* The District Court's application of these incorrect standards may well have influenced its ultimate conclusion, especially given that the court found this to be a "close case," *id.*, at A-31.

We therefore reverse the judgment of the Court of Appeals, and remand the case for further proceedings consistent with this opinion.

So ordered.

## CASES

## CASE 1. *Increasing Minority Coaches in the NFL*

The National Football League, founded in 1920, currently has 32 franchises located in major cities around the United States. While some people consider the league merely a sports league, it is fundamentally a business enterprise—and a massive financial success for owners, league management, players, and coaches. However, NFL owners have frequently been accused of racial prejudice as a result of their failure to hire an adequate percentage of minority coaches and administrators. While minorities represent the bulk of the players in the league, there is a far lower percentage of minority head coaches (and assistant coaches). On this fact virtually everyone agrees; but there is disagreement regarding what, if anything, should be done about it.

From 1986 to 2002 a total of five black head coaches were hired by teams in the NFL. At the start of the 2002 season, only two of the five remained. Critics argue that minority groups are routinely overlooked and judged according to

This case was prepared by David Lawrence, based on the Cochran-Mehri report entitled "Black Coaches in the National Football League: Superior Performance, Inferior Opportunities," and also based on various articles in the *Washington Post* and *Sports Illustrated.*

a different standard. One economist reports that black coaches average at least one more win per season than white coaches and earn playoff berths 67 percent of the time, compared to 39 percent of the time for white coaches. Despite these favorable statistics, black coaches are not routinely given opportunities and are fired at higher rates.

Because so few head coaches are from minority groups, lawyers Johnnie Cochran and Cyrus Mehri have proposed a plan to increase this number to an acceptable level. The basics of their plan are as follows: Because draft choices represent the NFL's essential currency, those teams that hire minority head coaches will receive extra draft picks as incentives and rewards for their responsible management. However, those teams that decide to refrain from hiring minority coaches and managers will lose some of their current draft picks.

Gene Upshaw, the players Association executive director (and himself African American), argues that the current hiring practices ensure that the most competent and experienced individuals are offered positions. He believes that sufficient progress is indicated by the fact that minorities are being given increasing consideration within franchises (even if not an increasing number of jobs). Mehri and Cochran maintain that unless their plan is enacted, minorities will continue to be overlooked and therefore will not be given the opportunities that they deserve to coach in the NFL.

### Questions

1. Do you believe that Mehri and Cochran's proposal is a viable plan for increasing the number of minority head coaches? If not, why?
2. Given the opportunity, would you adopt their plan, devise a new plan, or maintain current policy? If you were to propose a new plan, what would it be? Or should there be no plan at all?

## CASE 2. *Sing's Chinese Restaurant*

The Bali Hai Corporation started as a small Chinese restaurant in Boston, Massachusetts, in 1959. The restaurant was an exact replica of a Chinese pagoda. Over the years, the restaurant, owned and managed by Arnold Sing, became known for its food and atmosphere. Customers were made to feel as if they were actually in China. In the last few years, Sing decided to incorporate and open other similar restaurants throughout the country. Sing, who had come to the United States from China in the early 1940s, was very strict in keeping up his reputation for good food and atmosphere. He had a policy of hiring only waiters of Asian descent. He felt this added to his customers' dining pleasure and made for a more authentic environment. For kitchen positions, though, Sing hired any qualified applicants.

About a year ago at Sing's Bali Hai in Washington, DC, there was a shortage of waiters. An advertisement was placed in the newspaper for waiters, and the manager of the store was instructed by Sing to hire only Asians. The manager was also reminded of Bali Hai's commitment to a reputation for good food and atmosphere. Two young men, one black and one white, both with considerable restaurant experience, applied for the waiter's jobs. The manager explained the policy of hiring only Asians to the young men, and he also told them he could get them work in his kitchen. The two men declined the positions and instead went directly to the area Equal Employment Office and filed a complaint. Sing's defense was that the policy was only to preserve the atmosphere of the restaurant. He said the Asian waiters were needed to make it more authentic. Sing also added that he hired blacks, whites, and persons of other races for his kitchen help.

**Questions**

1. Is Sing's defense a good one under the law? Why or why not?
2. Is Sing's defense a good one under the standards of morality? Why or why not?
3. Is this a case of "preferential hiring"? Of "reverse discrimination"?

## CASE 3. *Wards Cove Packing Co. v. Atonio*

Two companies operated salmon canneries in remote areas of Alaska, which canneries functioned only during the summer salmon runs. There were two general types of jobs at the canneries: cannery line jobs, which were unskilled positions, and "noncannery" jobs, which were predominantly skilled positions but varied from engineers and bookkeepers to cooks and boat crew members. The cannery workers were predominantly nonwhite, mainly Filipinos, whom the companies hired through a hiring hall agreement with a predominantly Filipino union local in Seattle, and Alaska Natives, hired from villages near the canneries. The noncannery workers were predominantly white and were hired during the winter through the companies' offices in Washington and Oregon. Virtually all of the noncannery jobs paid more than the cannery jobs, and noncannery workers used dormitory and mess hall facilities that were separate from and allegedly superior to those of the cannery workers. A class of nonwhite cannery workers who were or had been employed at the canneries in question brought an action against the companies in the United States District Court for the Western District of Washington, which action charged the companies with employment discrimination on the basis of race in violation of a provision of Title VII of the Civil Rights Act of 1964 (42 USCS 2000e-2(a)). Specifically, it was alleged that the racial stratification of the work force was caused by several of the companies' hiring and promotion practices, including a rehire preference, a lack of objective hiring criteria, the separate hiring channels, and a practice of not promoting from within. . . .

On certiorari, the United States Supreme Court . . . held that (1) racial imbalance in one segment of an employer's work force is not sufficient to establish a prima facie case of disparate impact with respect to the selection of workers for the employer's other positions; (2) in this case, the comparison between the percentage of cannery workers who are nonwhite and the percentage of noncannery workers who are nonwhite did not make out a prima facie disparate-impact case; (3) the plaintiff in such a case bears the burden of isolating and identifying the specific employment practices that are allegedly responsible for any observed statistical disparities; and (4) if the plaintiff establishes a prima facie disparate-impact case, the employer bears the burden of producing evidence of a business justification for its employment practice, but the burden of persuasion on this issue remains with the plaintiff.

Supreme Court of the United States. 490 U.S. 642; 109 S.Ct. 2115; 1989 U.S. Lexis 2794; 104 L.Ed.2d 733; 57 U.S.L.W. 4583; 49 Fair Empl. Prac. Cas. (BNA) 1519; 50 Empl. Prac. Dec. (CCH) P39,021.

Blackmun, J., joined by Brennan and Marshall, JJ., dissented, expressing the view that the opinion of the court took three major strides backwards in the battle against racial discrimination by (1) upsetting the long-standing distribution of burdens of proof in Title VII disparate-impact cases; (2) barring the use of internal work force comparisons in the making of a prima facie case of discrimination, even where the structure of the industry in question rendered any other statistical comparison meaningless; and (3) requiring practice-by-practice statistical proof of causation, even where such proof would be impossible.

### Questions

1. Are the canneries' hiring practices discriminatory? If so, what company policies should be adopted?
2. Is there a correlation between the hiring practices for cannery workers and noncannery workers? Should the practices be the same or separate, even though the positions are different?
3. Is it an acceptable practice for the cannery to rehire skilled noncannery workers it has worked with previously? Is it acceptable even if the noncannery workers are predominantly white?

## CASE 4. *Weber and the Kaiser Aluminum Steelworkers Plan*

In 1974 the United Steelworkers of America and Kaiser Aluminum & Chemical Corp. established an employment agreement that addressed an overwhelming racial imbalance in employment in Kaiser plants. Of primary concern was the lack of skilled black crafts workers. This concern arose because of an ongoing exclusion of black crafts workers. In an attempt to remove the disparity and create a fair employment policy, an affirmative action plan ("the plan") was agreed to,

> whereby black craft-hiring goals were set for each Kaiser plant equal to the percentage of blacks in the respective local labor forces . . . [and] to enable plants to meet these goals, on-the-job training programs were established to teach unskilled workers—black and white—the skills necessary to become craftsworkers (443 U.S. 198 [1979]).

Under the guidelines of the plan, 50 percent of those selected for the newly instituted training program were to be black employees *until* the goals of the plan were accomplished, after which the 50 percent provision would be discontinued.

Such a plan was instituted at the Gramercy, Louisiana, plant from which the major problems had arisen and where blacks constituted less than 2 percent of the skilled craftsworkers, although they were approximately 39 percent of the Gramercy labor force. Subsequently, thirteen trainees, of which seven were black, were selected in accordance with the guidelines of the plan. The black trainees had less seniority than many white production workers who were denied training status. Brian Weber, one such production worker, argued that he and others had been unduly discriminated against. He thought the plan was a violation of Title VII of the Civil Rights Act of 1964. A District Court and a Court of Appeals held that Title VII had been violated. The U.S. Supreme Court then addressed the issue of whether employers were forbidden from enacting such affirmative action plans to alleviate racial imbalances.

The Supreme Court held that forbidding such affirmative action plans under Title VII would be in direct contradiction to its purpose, because the statutory words call upon "employers and unions to self-examine and to self-

This case was abstracted from Supreme Court materials by Katie Marshall and Tom L. Beauchamp.

evaluate their employment practices and to endeavor to eliminate, so far as possible, the vast vestiges of an unfortunate and ignominious page in this country's history" (433 U.S. 204 [1978]). The Supreme Court concluded that the Kaiser plan purposes "mirror[ed] those of the statute," because both the plan and the statute "were designed to break down old patterns of racial segregation [and] both were structured to open employment opportunities for Negroes in occupations which have been traditionally closed to them." The Supreme Court reversed the opinions of the lower courts (433 U.S. 208 [1978]).

## Questions

1. Are the percentage figures in this case "quotas"? Are they justified under the circumstances?
2. Does Kaiser have a fair employment policy? If not, how should it be revised?
3. Is there reverse discrimination against Weber? If so, is it justified?

# CASE 5. *Firefighters Local Union No. 1784 v. Stotts*

Respondent Carl Stotts, a black member of petitioner Memphis, Tennessee, Fire Department, filed a class action in Federal District Court charging that the Department and certain city officials were engaged in a pattern or practice of making hiring and promotion decisions on the basis of race in violation of, *inter alia*, Title VII of the Civil Rights Act of 1964.

This action was consolidated with an action filed by respondent Fred Jones, also a black member of the Department, who claimed that he had been denied a promotion because of his race. Thereafter, a consent decree was entered with the stated purpose of remedying the Department's hiring and promotion practices with respect to blacks. Subsequently, when the city announced that projected budget deficits required a reduction of city employees, the District Court entered an order preliminarily enjoining the Department from following its seniority system in determining who would be laid off as a result of the budgetary shortfall, since the proposed layoffs would have a racially discriminatory effect and the seniority system was not a bona fide one. A modified layoff plan, aimed at protecting black employees so as to comply with the court's order, was then presented and approved, and layoffs pursuant to this plan were carried out. This resulted in white employees with more seniority than black employees being laid off when the otherwise applicable seniority system would have called for the layoff of black employees with less seniority. The Court of Appeals affirmed, holding that although the District Court was wrong in holding that the seniority system was not bona fide, it had acted properly in modifying the consent decree. . . .

JUSTICE WHITE delivered the opinion of the Court. Petitioners challenge the Court of Appeals' approval of an order enjoining the City of Memphis from following its seniority system in determining who must be laid off as a result of a budgetary shortfall. Respondents contend that the injunction was necessary to effectuate the terms of a Title VII consent decree in which the City agreed to undertake certain obligations in order to remedy past hiring and promotional practices. Because we conclude that the order cannot be justified, either as an effort to enforce the consent decree or as a valid modification, we reverse.

Supreme Court of the United States: 467 U.S. 561; 104 S.Ct. 2576; 1984 U.S. Lexis 108; 81 L.Ed.2d 483; 52 U.S.L.W. 4767; 34 Fair Empl. Prac. Cas. (BNA) 1702; 34 Empl. Prac. Dec. (CCH) P34, 415.

## Questions

1. Is seniority or diversity upheld in this instance? What do each of the courts argue?
2. Is it justifiable for the Department to lay off new minority workers and maintain seniority even if it has a discriminatory effect?
3. Is the Supreme Court decision concerning the Memphis Fire Department applicable to business or is it only relevant to emergency services?

# CASE 6. *Promotions at Uptown Bottling and Canning Company*

Lincoln Grant, a 31-year-old African-American employee, has been working for six years, as a technician at Uptown Bottling and Canning Co. in Baltimore, MD. On four separate occasions, he has unsuccessfully sought a promotion to a managerial position. As the only member in his department who has completed graduate study, Grant questions how the company has treated him. He also knows that only four African-American employees have been promoted during the previous nine years, compared to 41 white employees who have been offered promotions over the same period of time. Baltimore city is more than 50 percent African American, and the surrounding metropolitan region is about 25 percent African American.

On one occasion, the company posted a listing for a managerial position and encouraged current employees to apply. According to the job description, eligible applicants should have at least five years of prior experience with the company and should hold a graduate degree in either business or engineering. Furthermore, each applicant would be required to take a written exam. Although Grant applied, the company awarded the position to Henry Thompson, a white male with only two years of experience and no graduate degree. Grant, as it turned out, was the only applicant with five years of prior experience and a graduate degree.

In making its final selections for jobs, Uptown Bottling and Canning considers test scores and leadership potential. Grant's test scores were significantly above average, but his supervisors told him that he lacked the leadership skills required of managers. Based on observed performance, they pointed out, Grant has never demonstrated leadership skills while working at Uptown. At the same time, Grant has also never been given any form of leadership training. Most of the 41 white employees who were promoted had been given leadership training within the first five years of their employment with the company.

## Questions

1. Are the facts in this case sufficient to indicate that the Uptown Bottling and Canning Co. discriminated against Lincoln Grant on the basis of race?
2. Given the promotion statistics, should the company do more to see that African-American employees are considered for both leadership training and promotions? Are statistics irrelevant, or do they point to underlying failures of fair employment?

---

This case was prepared by David Lawrence.

## CASE 7. *Freedom of Expression in the Workplace*

Barbara Hill was employed at American Plastic Products Co. beginning in June 1999. As a member of the engineering department, part of her job description included identifying defects in the equipment that formed the plastic products. She was expected to report on these defects at production meetings, which were held every morning.

In order to enter the engineering laboratory to perform this research, Barbara had to walk down a long corridor that was the only entrance to the room in which production meetings were held. As she walked down this hall every morning, she could not escape noticing pin-up photographs and provocative calendars on the walls that had been placed there by male employees. Barbara complained to her supervisor, who proceeded to remove all of the offending materials, including even a postcard located on a desk in an office with glass doors opening into the corridor.

The following day, as she was walking down the corridor to the laboratory, Barbara overheard a conversation between two male employees. Though not directed at her, she could not help but overhear that they were agreeing, with intensely expressed conviction, that women should not be given detail-oriented jobs, such as hers, because men are better able to focus in the workplace. Their conversation was punctuated with the language of "chicks," "bitches," and the like.

Barbara complained to her supervisor again, this time claiming that such behavior created a hostile work environment. When approached by the supervisor, the two male employees contended that they were simply expressing their political and business opinions—nothing more. The supervisor considered whether he should place the two men on probation and warn them to refrain from such conversations in the future. However, the supervisor decided to sit on this idea for a few days.

### Questions

1. Should the pin-up photographs and calendars have been taken down? Why or why not? Why might a supervisor deem it necessary to do so?
2. Should employees be permitted to voice their opinions at work even if other employees find them misguided or offensive? Does the right to free expression outweigh the right to a nonhostile working environment?

This case was prepared by David Lawrence.

## CASE 8. *"Harassment" at Brademore Electric*

Maura Donovan is a recent graduate of UCLA who now works as a low-level administrative assistant for Keith Sturdivant at the Brademore Electric Corporation, a large Los Angeles electrical contractor. Keith interviewed and hired Maura to work directly under him.

Maura had been employed at Brademore only three weeks when Keith approached her

This case was prepared by Tom L. Beauchamp.

to go out on the weekend. Maura was taken somewhat by surprise and declined, thinking it best not to mix business and pleasure. But two days later Keith persisted, saying that Maura owed him something in return for his "getting" her the job. Maura was offended by this comment, knowing that she was well qualified for the position, but Keith seemed lonely, almost desperate, and she agreed to go with him to the Annual Renaissance Fair on Saturday afternoon. As it turned out, she did not have an enjoyable time. She liked the fair, but found Keith a bit crude and at times almost uncivil in the way he treated employees at the Fair. She hoped he would not ask her out again.

But Monday morning he came back with the idea that they go on an overnight sailboat trip with some of his friends the next weekend. Maura politely declined. But Keith persisted, insisting that she owed her job to him. Maura found herself dreading the times she saw Keith coming down the corridor. What had been a very nice work environment for her had turned into a place of frequent dread. She spent a lot of time working to avoid Keith.

For four straight weeks, Keith came up with a different idea for how they might spend the weekend—always involving an overnight trip. Maura always declined. After the second week, she lied and told him that she was dating a number of other men. She said she was quite interested in two of these men and that she did not see any future with Keith. Keith's reaction was to become even more insistent that they had a future together and to continue to ask her out.

Keith had become quite infatuated with Maura. He watched her every movement, whenever he had the opportunity. Sometimes he openly stared at her as she walked from one office to another. He began to have sexual fantasies about her, which he disclosed to two male supervisors. However, he never mentioned to Maura that he had in mind any form of sexual relationship.

Keith's direct supervisor, Vice President B. K. Singh, became aware of Keith's interest in Maura from two sources. First, he was told about the sexual fantasies by one of Keith's two male friends to whom Keith made the disclosures. Second, Maura had that same day come to his office to complain about what she considered sexual harassment. Mr. Singh became concerned about a possible contaminated work environment, but he did not think that he or Maura could make any form of harassment charge stick. The company had no corporate policy on harassment. Mr. Singh considered the situation to be just another case of one employee asking another out and being overly persistent. Mr. Singh decided not to do anything right away, not even to discuss the problem with Keith. He was worried that if he did take up the matter with Keith at such an early stage, he would himself be creating a hostile work environment. He believed Keith's advances would have to worsen before he should intervene or take the problem to the President.

## Questions

1. Is Keith's conduct a case of sexual harassment? Is it a clear case, a borderline case, or no case at all?
2. Is it justifiable for Mr. Singh to adopt a position of nonintervention? Should he speak with Keith? What would you do if you were in his position?
3. Does the fact that Maura agreed once to go out with Keith mean that she has encouraged him to make further requests? If so, was she sufficiently discouraging at a later point?

## *Suggested Supplementary Readings*


ALBERTS, ROBERT J., and LORNE H. SEIDMAN. "Sexual Harassment by Clients, Customers, and Suppliers: How Employers Should Handle an Emerging Legal Problem." *Employee Relations Law Journal*, 20 (Summer 1994): 85–100.

BAUGH, S. GAYLE. "On the Persistence of Sexual Harassment in the Workplace," *Journal of Business Ethics*, 16 (1997): 899–908.

BEAUCHAMP, TOM L. "In Defense of Affirmative Action." *Journal of Ethics*, 2 (1998): 143–158.

BLOCH, FARRELL. *Antidiscrimination Law and Minority Employment: Recruitment Practices and Regulatory Constraints*. Chicago, IL: The University of Chicago Press, 1994.

BOOKER, M. J. "Can Sexual Harassment Be Salvaged?" *Journal of Business Ethics*, 17 (August 1998): 1171–1177.

BOXILL, BERNARD. *Blacks and Social Justice*. Totowa, NJ: Rowman and Littlefield, 1992.

BROWNE, KINGSLEY R. "Title VII as Censorship: Hostile-Environment Harassment and the First Amendment." *Ohio State Law Journal*, 52 (1991).

CAVA, ANITA. "Sexual Harassment Claims: New Framework for Employers." *Business and Economic Review*, 47 (2001): 13–16.

COHEN, MARSHALL, THOMAS NAGEL, and THOMAS SCANLON, Eds. *Equality and Preferential Treatment*. Princeton, NJ: Princeton University Press, 1977.

CRAIN, KAREN A., and KENNETH A. HEISCHMIDT. "Implementing Business Ethics: Sexual Harassment." *Journal of Business Ethics*, 14 (April 1995): 299–308.

CROUCH, MARGARET A. "The 'Social Etymology' of 'Sexual Harassment'." *Journal of Social Philosophy*, 29 (1998): 19–40.

DANDEKER, NATALIE. "Contrasting Consequences: Bringing Charges of Sexual Harassment Compared with Other Cases of Whistleblowing." *Journal of Business Ethics*, 9 (1990).

DODDS, SUSAN M., LUCY FROST, ROBERT PARGETTER, and ELIZABETH W. PRIOR. "Sexual Harassment." *Social Theory and Practice*, 14 (Summer 1988): 111–30.

EGLER, THERESA DONAHUE. "Five Myths About Sexual Harassment." *HR Magazine*, 40 (January 1995): 27–30.

EPSTEIN, DEBORAH. "Freedom of Speech vs. Workplace Harassment." *Slate*: Http://Slate.msn.com. September 17, 1997.

EPSTEIN, DEBORAH. "Freedom of Speech vs. Workplace Harassment." *Slate*: Http://Slate.msn.com. October 17, 1997.

ERLER, EDWARD J. "The Future of Civil Rights: Affirmative Action Redivivus." *Notre Dame Journal of Law and Ethics*, 11 (1997): 15–65.

EYRING, ALISON, and BETTE ANN STEAD. "Shattering the Glass Ceiling: Some Successful Corporate Practices." *Journal of Business Ethics*, 17 (February 1998): 245–251.

EZORSKY, GERTRUDE. *Racism and Justice*. Ithaca, NY: Cornell University Press, 1991.

FICK, BARBARA J. "The Case for Maintaining and Encouraging the Use of Voluntary Affirmative Action in Private Sector Employment." *Notre Dame Journal of Law and Ethics*, 11 (1997): 159–70.

FINE, LESLIE M., C. DAVID SHEPHERD, and SUSAN L. JOSEPHS. "Sexual Harassment in the Sales Force: The Customer Is NOT Always Right." *Journal of Personal Selling & Sales Management*, 14 (Fall 1994): 15–30.

FULLINWIDER, ROBERT K. "The Life and Death of Racial Preferences." *Philosophical Studies*, 85 (1997): 163–180.

FULLINWIDER, ROBERT K. *The Reverse Discrimination Controversy*. Totowa. NJ: Rowman and Allanheld, 1980.

GRIFFITH, STEPHEN. "Sexual Harassment and the Rights of the Accused." *Public Affairs Quarterly*, 13 (1999): 43–71.

HOLMES, ROBERT L. "Sexual Harassment and the University." *Monist*, 79 (1996): 499–518.

HORNE, GERALD. *Reversing Discrimination: The Case for Affirmative Action*. New York: International Publishers, 1992.

IRVINE, WILLIAM B. "Beyond Sexual Harassment." *Journal of Business Ethics*, 28 (December 2000): 353–60.

KALANTARI, BEHROOZ. "Dynamics of Job Evaluation and the Dilemma of Wage Disparity in the United States." *Journal of Business Ethics*, 14 (1995): 397–403.

KERSHNAR, STEPHEN. "Uncertain Damages to Racial Minorities and Strong Affirmative Action." *Public Affairs Quarterly*, 13 (1999): 83–98.

KEYTON, JOANN, and RHODES, STEVEN C. "Sexual Harassment: A Matter of Individual Ethics, Legal Definitions, or Organizational Policy?" *Journal of Business Ethics*, 16 (1997): 129–46.

LADENSON, ROBERT. "Ethics in the American Workplace." *Business and Professional Ethics Journal*, 14 (1995): 17–31.

LEAP, TERRY L., and LARRY R. SMELTZER. "Racial Remarks in the Workplace: Humor or Harassment?" *Harvard Business Review* , 62 (1984).

LEMONCHECK, LINDA, and HAJDIN, MANE. *Sexual Harassment: A Debate.* Lanham, MD: Rowman & Littlefield, 1997.

MOSLEY, ALBERT G., and CAPALDI, NICHOLAS. *Affirmative Action: Social Justice or Unfair Preference?* Lanham, MD: Rowman & Littlefield, 1996.

MORRIS, CELIA. *Bearing Witness: Sexual Harassment and Beyond—Everywoman's Story.* Boston: Little, Brown, & Company, 1994.

MOY, PATRICIA, DAVID DOMKE, and KEITH STAMM. "The Spiral of Silence and Public Opinion on Affirmative Action." *Journalism and Mass Communication Quarterly*, 78 (Spring 2001): 7–25.

PACE, JOSEPH MICHAEL, and ZACHARY SMITH. "Understanding Affirmative Action: From the Practitioner's Perspective." *Public Personnel Management*, 24 (1995): 139–47.

PETERSEN, DONALD J., and DOUGLAS P. MASSENGILL. "Sexual Harassment Cases Five Years After Meritor Savings Bank v. Vinson." *Employee Relations Law Journal*, 18 (1992–93): 489–515.

PHILIPS, MICHAEL. "Preferential Hiring and the Question of Competence." *Journal of Business Ethics*, 10 (1991).

PLATT, ANTHONY M. "The Rise and Fall of Affirmative Action." *Notre Dame Journal of Law and Ethics*, 11 (1997): 67–78.

POJMAN, LOUIS P. "The Case against Affirmative Actions." *International Journal of Applied Philosophy*, 12 (1998): 97–115.

PURDY, LAURA. "Why Do We Need Affirmative Action?" *Journal of Social Philosophy*, 25 (1994): 133–43.

ROSENFELD, MICHEL. *Affirmative Action and Justice: A Philosophical and Constitutional Inquiry.* New Haven: Yale University Press, 1991.

SEGRAVE, KERRY. *The Sexual Harassment of Women in the Workplace, 1600 to 1993.* Jefferson, NC: McFarland & Company, Inc., Publisher, 1994.

SHANEY, MARY JO. "Perceptions of Harm: The Consent Defense in Sexual Harassment Cases." *Iowa Law Review*, 71 (1986).

SINGER, M. S., and A. E. SINGER. "Justice in Preferential Hiring." *Journal of Business Ethics*, 10 (1991).

SUNSTEIN, CASS R. "The Limits of Compensatory Justice." *Nomos*, 33 (1991): 281–310.

THOMAS, LAURENCE. "On Sexual Offers and Threats." In *Moral Rights in the Workplace*, edited by Gertrude Ezorsky. Albany, NY: State University of New York Press, 1987.

VOLOKH, EUGENE. "Freedom of Speech and Workplace Harassment." *UCLA Law Review*, 39 (1992).

VOLOKH, EUGENE. "Freedom of Speech vs. Workplace Harassment." *Slate*: Http://Slate.msn.com. September 23, 1997.

WAGNER, ELLEN J. *Sexual Harassment in the Workplace: How to Prevent, Investigate, and Resolve Problems in Your Organization.* New York: Amacom [American Management Association], 1992.

WALL, EDMUND, Ed. *Sexual Harassment: Confrontations and Decisions.* Buffalo, NY: Prometheus Books, 1992.

WARNKE, GEORGIA. "Affirmative Action, Neutrality, and Integration." *Journal of Social Philosophy*, 29 (1998): 87–103.

WELLS, DEBORAH L., and BEVERLY J. KRACHER. "Justice, Sexual Harassment, and the Reasonable Victim Standard." *Journal of Business Ethics*, 12 (1993): 423–31.

YORK, KENNETH M. "Defining Sexual Harassment in Workplaces: A Policy-Capturing Approach." *Academy of Management Journal*, 32 (1989).

# *Chapter Seven*

# Marketing and the Disclosure of Information

## INTRODUCTION

Marketing ethics explores decision making that emerges at several different levels in corporate life, such as whether to place a new product on the market, how to price a product, how to advertise, and how to conduct sales. Marketing research, pricing, advertising, selling, and international marketing have all come under close ethical scrutiny in recent years. Ethical issues about marketing are often centered on obligations to disclose information. Advertising is the most visible way businesses present information to the public, but not the only way, or even the most important. Sales information, annual reports containing financial audits, public relations presentations, warranties, trade secrets, and public education and public health campaigns are other vital means by which corporations manage, communicate, and limit information.

A classic defense of American business practice is that business provides the public with products that the public wants; the consumer is king in the free enterprise system, and the market responds to consumer demands. This response is often said to represent the chief strength of a market economy over a collectivist system. Freedom of consumer choice is unaffected by government and corporate controls. But consider the following controversy about freedom of choice. In the mid-1980s the Federal Trade Commission (FTC) "reconsidered" its rule prohibiting supermarket advertising of items when those items are not in stock. The rule had been enacted in 1971 to combat frustration among shoppers who found empty shelves in place of advertised goods and often wound up substituting more expensive items. FTC officials suggested that the rule may have been unduly burdensome for the supermarket industry and that "market forces" would eliminate or curtail those who dishonestly advertise. Consumer groups argued that relaxing the rule would permit more expensive stores to lure shoppers by advertising low prices leading many shoppers to spend more overall than they would have spent in a low-budget store. Mark Silbergeld of the Consumers Union argued that the Commission was acting in ignorance of the *real purpose* of supermarket advertising, which is to present a "come-on to get people into their stores."[1]

In the last 30 years or so it has been widely appreciated that this problem is only one among many that confronts marketers of goods and services. Some problems are commonplace—for example, withholding vital information, distortion of data, and bluffing. Other problems of information control are more subtle; these include the use of flashy information to entice customers, the use of annual reports as public relations devices, and the use of calculated "news releases" to promote products. Rights of autonomy and free choice are at the center of these discussions. In some forms, withholding information and manipulating advertising messages threaten to undermine the free choice of consumers, clients, stockholders, and even colleagues. Deceptive and misleading statements can limit freedom by restricting the range of choice and can cause a person to do what he or she otherwise would not do.

Aside from these *autonomy*-based problems, there are *harm*-based problems that may have little to do with making a choice. For example, in a now classic case, the Nestlé corporation was pressured to suspend infant formula advertising and aggressive marketing tactics in developing countries. This controversy focused less on the freedom-based issue of the right to the dissemination of information than on preventing a population from harming itself through inadequate breastfeeding and inadequate appreciation of the risks of the use of infant formula. Such harm–based issues are mentioned in this chapter, but the restriction of free choice by manipulative influence is the central issue.

The inception of the problem is that consumers are frequently unable to evaluate information about the variety of goods and services available to them without assistance. There is a large "knowledge gap," as it is commonly called, between consumer and marketer. The consumer either lacks vital information or lacks the skills to evaluate the good or service. This circumstance leads to a situation in which the consumer must place trust in a service agency, producer, or retailer. Many marketers are well aware of this situation and feel acutely that they must not abuse their position of superior information. Many also engage in marketing their own trustworthiness while simultaneously marketing a product or service. When the felt or proclaimed trust is breached (whether intentionally or by accident), the marketer-consumer relationship is endangered.

## Advertising

Many critics deplore the values presented in advertising as well as the effects advertising has on consumers. Other critics are more concerned about specific practices of advertising directed at vulnerable groups such as children, the poor, and the elderly; advertising that exploits women or uses fear appeals; advertising that uses subliminal messages; and the advertising of liquor and tobacco products. Although critics have long denounced misleading or information-deficient advertising, the moral concerns and concepts underlying these denunciations have seldom been carefully examined. What is a deceptive or misleading advertisement? Is it, for example, deceptive or misleading to advertise a heavily sweetened cereal as "nutritious" or as "building strong bodies"? Are such advertisements forms of lying? Are they manipulative, especially when children are the primary targets or people are led to make purchases they do not need and would not have made had they not seen the advertising? If so, does the manipulation derive from some form of deception? For example, if an advertisement that touts a particular mouthwash as germ-killing manipulates listeners into purchasing the mouthwash, does it follow that these consumers have been deceived?

Does such advertising represent a deprivation of free choice, or is it rather an example of how free choice determines market forces? Control over a person is exerted through various kinds of influences, but not all *influences* actually *control* behavior. Some forms of influence are desired and accepted by those who are influenced, whereas others are unwelcome. Many influences can easily be resisted by most persons; others are irresistible. Human reactions to influences such as corporate-sponsored information and advertising presentations cannot in many cases be determined or easily studied. Frank Dandrea, vice president of marketing for Schiefflin & Co., the importer of Hennessy's Cognac, once said that in their advertisements "The idea is to show a little skin, a little sex appeal, a little tension."[2] This effect is accomplished by showing a scantily clad woman holding a brandy snifter and staring provocatively in response to a man's interested glance. Hennessy tries in a subtle manner to use a mixture of sex and humor, just as Coors Beer uses the technique in less than subtle ways. Other companies use rebates and coupons. All these methods are attempts to influence, and it is well known that they are at least partially successful. However, the degree of influence of these strategies and the moral acceptability of these influences have been less carefully examined.

There is a continuum of controlling influence in our daily lives, running from coercion, at the most controlling end of the continuum, to persuasion and education, both of which are noncontrolling influences. Other points on the continuum include indoctrination, seduction, and the like. Coercion requires an intentional and successful influence through an irresistible threat of harm. A coercively induced action deprives a person of freedom because it entirely controls the person's action. Persuasion, by contrast, involves a successful appeal to reason in order to convince a person to accept freely what is advocated by the persuader. Like informing, persuading is entirely compatible with free choice.

Many choices are not substantially free, although we commonly think of them as free. These include actions under powerful family and religious influences, purchases made under partial ignorance of the quality of the merchandise, and deference to an authoritative physician's judgment. Many actions fall short of ideal free action either because the agent lacks critical information or because the agent is under the control of another person. The central question is whether actions are sufficiently or adequately free, not whether they are ideally or wholly free.

*Manipulation* is a general term that refers to the great gray area of influence. It is a catchall category that suggests the act of getting people to do what is advocated without resorting to coercion but also without appealing to reasoned argument. In the case of *informational* manipulation, on which several selections in this chapter concentrate, information is managed so that the manipulated person will do what the manipulator intends. Whether such uses of information necessarily compromise or restrict free choice is an unresolved issue. One plausible thesis is that some manipulations—for instance, the use of rewards such as free trips or lottery coupons in direct mail advertising—are compatible with free choice, whereas others—such as deceptive offers or tantalizing ads aimed at young children—are not compatible with free choice. Beer, wine, and tobacco advertising aimed at teenagers and young adults has been under particularly harsh criticism in recent years, on grounds that sex, youth, fun, and beauty are directly linked in the advertising to dangerous products, with noticeable marketing success.

As Robert L. Arrington and John Douglas Bishop point out in their essays, these issues raise complex questions of moral responsibility in the advertising of products. Arrington notes that puffery, subliminal advertising, and indirect information-transfer are typical examples of the problem. After he examines criticisms and defenses of such practices, he analyzes four of the central concepts at work in the debate: (1) autonomous desire, (2) rational desire, (3) free choice, and (4) control. He tries to show that, despite certain dangers, advertising should not be judged guilty of frequent violations of the consumer's autonomy in any relevant sense of this notion.

Bishop concentrates on a specific form of advertising labelled "self-identity image advertising." It "persuades" by presenting an idealized type of person, such as a beautiful woman or a sexy teenager. The product is presented as the symbol of the ideal, and consumers are targeted to use the product to project a self-image to themselves and others. Bishop argues that such ads need not be false or misleading, but also that the ads can undermine a consumer's self-esteem by omitting images that are authentic for that person. While he thinks that the ads need not undermine autonomous choice, he does acknowledge that they can result in specific harms if not used properly.

Many problems with advertising fall somewhere between acceptable and unacceptable manipulation. Consider these two examples: Anheuser-Busch ran a television commercial for its Budweiser Beer showing some working men heading for a brew at day's end. The commercial began with a shot of the Statue of Liberty in the background, included close-up shots of a construction crew working to restore the Statue, and ended with the words, "This Bud's for you, you know America takes pride in what you do." This statement may seem innocent, but the Liberty-Ellis Island Foundation accused Anheuser-Busch of a "blatant attempt to dupe [i.e., manipulate] consumers" by implying that Budweiser was among the sponsors helping to repair the Statue. The Foundation was particularly annoyed because Anheuser-Busch had refused such a sponsorship when invited by the Foundation, whereas its rival, Stroh Brewing Company, had subsequently accepted an exclusive brewery sponsorship.[3]

A second case comes from Kellogg's advertising for its All-Bran product. The company ran a campaign linking its product to the prevention of cancer, apparently causing an immediate increase in sales of 41 percent for All-Bran. Although many food manufacturers advertise the low-salt, low-fat, low-calorie, or high-fiber content of their products, Kellogg went further, citing a specific product as a way to combat a specific disease. It is illegal to make claims about the health benefits of a specific food product without Food and Drug Administration (FDA) approval, and Kellogg did not have this approval. Even so, officials at both the National Cancer Institute and the FDA were not altogether critical of the ads. On the one hand, officials at these agencies agree that a high-fiber, low-fat diet containing some of the ingredients in All-Bran does help prevent cancer. On the other hand, no direct association exists between eating a given product and preventing cancer, and certainly no single food product can function like a drug as a preventative or remedy for such a disease.

The Kellogg ad strongly suggested that eating All-Bran is what one needs to do to prevent cancer. Such a claim is potentially misleading in several respects. The ad did not suggest how much fibre people should eat, nor did it note that people can consume too much fiber while neglecting other essential minerals. Further, no direct scientific evidence linked the consumption of this product with the prevention of cancer, and this product could not be expected to affect all types of cancer. Is the Kellogg promise manipulative, or is the ad, as Kellogg claims, basically a truthful, health-promotion campaign? Does it contain elements of both?

One of the court cases in this chapter—*Coca-Cola Co. v. Tropicana Products, Inc.*—focuses on a central question of the ethics of advertising. In this case, the two main competitors in the United States for the chilled orange juice market came into a direct conflict. The Coca-Cola Co., maker of Minute Maid orange juice sued Tropicana Products on grounds of false advertising. Tropicana had claimed in its advertisements that its brand of orange juice is "as it comes from the orange" and the only "brand not made with concentrate and water." Coke asserted that this claim is false and that Tropicana is pasteurized and sometimes frozen prior to packaging. Coke also claimed that it had lost sales of its product as a result of this misrepresentation. The court agrees with Coke both that the company has lost sales and that consumers have been misled by Tropicana's advertising campaign.

In a second case in the legal section, the United States Court of Appeals, Seventh Circuit, takes up a set of issues presented in the case of *B.Sanfield, Inc. v. Finlay Fine Jewelry Corp.* The issues concern one of the most commonly used forms of bargain advertising, which is to offer a percentage reduction from the advertiser's own former price for an article. Had the original price been a bona fide price at which the article was being offered to the public, over the course of a substantial period of time, the price comparison would be a legitimate basis for an advertisement. But if the alleged "former price" was not bona fide, but rather fictitious—for example, an inflated price that makes the subsequent offer appear to be a large reduction—then the "bargain" being advertised is itself fictitious. In this case, Sanfield (a locally owned retailer) contends that when Finlay (a nationwide retailer) advertises its jewelry at around 50 percent off the "regular" price, the ad is nothing more than a way of deceiving consumers; the "bargain" that Finlay advertises is no bargain at all, as Sanfield sees it. Sanfield believes that its business is suffering by its competitors' misleading advertisements with phony discounting and fake percentage markdowns. Nonetheless, the court finds in this case that "deception, like beauty, is in the eye of the beholder." Whether the ad is deceptive therefore turns entirely on the perception of the consumer, not the ad itself.

These examples illustrate the broad categories on the continuum of controlling influences that are under examination in this chapter. They indicate that the difference between *manipulation* and *persuasion* is the key matter. Of course, the question must be addressed whether *unjustifiably* manipulative advertising occurs frequently, or even at all.

## Sales

Some of these issues about disclosure, deception, and manipulation are as prominent in sales as in advertising. The attractive pricing of products is a first step in sales, and questions have been raised about pricing itself. For example, there have been accusations of price gouging of specific populations, such as those in poor neighborhoods and the elderly. The more common problems, however, concern failures (intentional or not) to disclose pertinent information about a product's function, quality, or price. A simple example is the common practice of selling a product at a low price because it is the previous year's model, although it is not disclosed that the latest models are already out and in stock.

As the marketplace for products has grown more complex and the products themselves more sophisticated, buyers have become more dependent upon salespersons to know their products and to tell the truth about them. The implicit assumption in some sales contexts is that bargaining and deception about a selling price are parts of the game, just as they are in real estate and labor negotiations. Nevertheless, this "flea-market" and "horse-trader" model of sales is unsuited to other contemporary markets. The salesperson is expected to have superior knowledge and is treated as an expert on the product, or at least as one who obtains needed information about a product. In this climate, it seems unethical for salespersons to take advantage of a buyer's implicit trust by using deceptive or manipulative techniques. But even if it is unethical to disclose too little, does it follow that the ethical salesperson has an obligation to disclose everything that might be of interest to the customer? For example, must the salesperson disclose that his or her company charges more than a competitor? What principles rightly govern the transfer of information during sales?

In an article on sales practices in this chapter, David M. Holley probes the social role of the salesperson. He concludes that there is a general obligation to disclose all information that a consumer would need to make a reasonable judgment about whether to purchase a product or service. Holley argues that this rule is superior to several alternatives that have been proposed in the literature. Partially in response to Holley, Thomas Carson argues in "Deception and Withholding Information in Sales" that salespeople have (prima facie) duties to do each of the following: (1) warn customers of dangers or hazards; (2) refrain from all acts of lying and deception; (3) honestly respond to all questions about items being sold; and (4) refrain from steering customers toward purchases that they believe may harm customers. Carson thus does not accept the view that salespersons are free to sell products under the model of *caveat emptor* (let the buyer beware); nor does he quite accept the other extreme, namely that salespersons should see their role as fundamentally that of paternalistic protector of the customer's interests.

Changes in the climate of sales of the sort proposed in the articles in this chapter could potentially have a massive impact in business. More persons are employed in sales than any other area of marketing, and sales has commonly been criticized as a poorly monitored area of business activity. Salespersons appear to be more prone to unethical conduct if substantial portions of their income are dependent on commissions, competition is fierce and unregulated, dubious practices of disclosure have become common, sales managers are removed from actual selling practices, and codes of ethics are widely disregarded in the industry.

## Bluffing and Strategic Disclosure

Whether marketing practices can be justified by the "rules of the game" in business is another major question. Some have argued that marketing strategies should be understood as by their nature attempts to influence us, but against which we should also be expected to protect ourselves—as in the proverbial case of purchasing a used automobile. By the very rules of the game, bluffing, bidding, and rhetorical overstatement invite similar countermoves. Although abuse and contempt are not tolerated, deception is tolerated and even encouraged as long as all players know the rules of the game and occupy roughly equal bargaining positions. This model suggests, on the one hand, that some deceptive practices and sharp practices can be justifiable. On the other hand, limits must be set to restrict deception, manipulation, and cunning maneuvers that take advantage of a competitor's misfortune.

Manipulation can take many forms: offering rewards, threatening punishments, instilling fear, and so forth. The principal form discussed in this chapter is the manipulation of information. Here the manipulator modifies a person's sense of options by affecting the person's understanding of the situation. Deception, bluffing, and the like are used by the manipulator to change not the person's *actual* options but only the person's *perception* of the options. The more a person is deprived of a relevant understanding in the circumstances, the greater the effect on the person's free choice.

One does not need extensive experience in business to know that many deceptive practices, like bluffing and slick sales techniques, are widely practiced and widely accepted. It is common knowledge that automobile dealers do not expect people to pay the sticker price for automobiles; but it is a closely guarded secret as to how much can be knocked off that price. A certain amount of quoting of competitors, bargaining, moving "extras" under the basic price, and going to managers for approval is part of the game. A similar situation prevails in real estate transactions, in which the asking price for a house is seldom the anticipated selling price, as well as at bargaining sessions, in which labor leaders overstate wage demands and management understates the wage increases it is willing to grant. The intent is to manipulate, however gently.

In his article "Is Business Bluffing Ethical?" Albert Z. Carr recognizes that such practices are characteristic of many business contexts and maintains that they are analogous to the game of poker. According to Carr, just as conscious misstatement, concealment of pertinent facts, exaggeration, and bluffing are morally acceptable in poker, they are acceptable in business. What makes such practices acceptable, Carr says, is that all parties understand the rules of the game. In advertising, for example, exaggeration and bluffing are understood to be part of the selling game. Only an extraordinarily naive person would believe advertisements without casting a skeptical eye on the images and words issuing from a television set.

Yet there are moral limits to the game, even if the rules of the game are grasped by all. Suppose that Pamela is willing to sell her home for $160,000, if that is the best price she can get. She puts the home on the market at $170,000. A potential buyer's initial offer is $160,000. Pamela turns the offer down, telling him that $165,000 is her rock-bottom price. He then purchases the home for $165,000. Many people would characterize her behavior as shrewd bluffing and certainly not an immoral lie. Many people would think more of her, rather than less. However, suppose she manufactured the claim that another party was writing up a contract to buy the house for $165,000 and that she would sell it to him for the same $165,000 price because both she and he are Baptists. In this case, many people would maintain that she had told at least one lie, probably two, but are the lies unjustified or merely part of the game? Would it make any moral difference if she were to have her brother pretend to make her an offer and draw up a fake contract so that the prospective buyer would be pressured to buy?

The sophistication of the audience, standard practice in the business, and intention of the informer all need to be considered to decide whether gilded information is unacceptable. Manipulation and deception can result as much from what is not said as from what is said. For example, true information can be presented out of context and thereby be misleading.

A classic problem about disclosure of information appears in *Backman v. Polaroid Corporation.* In this case, investors alleged that Polaroid had obtained negative information about its product Polavision but had failed to disclose to investors unfavorable facts that were known about the product. In effect, the claim is that Polaroid manipulated investors into purchasing its stock at a higher value than its actual worth. A similar charge led to accusations against Salomon, Inc., in late 1991 for both moral and legal failures to disclose properly to shareholders a stock option plan and cash bonus plan that benefited top corporate executives. Investors charged that the level of compensation diluted the value of the stock. Salomon responded that it had "followed the rules" of disclosure in its mailings to stockholders.[4]

Despite such examples, Carr maintains that it is morally permissible to deceive others in these ways as long as everyone knows that such actions are accepted in the business world as standard practice. Carr would presumably say that neither Polaroid nor Salomon did anything wrong so long as it is accepted that the unfavorable facts about a product or compensation scheme do not have to be disclosed. However, this perception raises many problems. For example, bluffing, active deception, and lack of disclosure interfere with the way markets work when good information is available and may also create instability in markets and hurt productivity and stifle competition.

Carr's criteria are either rejected or restated in a more guarded form in the next article by Thomas Carson. Carson argues that people commonly misstate their bargaining positions in the course of business negotiations, but that these misstatements often do not involve lying. He maintains that bluffing and other forms of negotiation are legitimate when one has good reason to believe that the other party understands the rules and is engaging in the same form of activity. However, it is impermissible to misstate one's negotiating or bargaining position whenever one does not have good reason to believe that the other party is engaging in a similar form of misstatement. Thus, by contrast to Carr, Carson argues that bluffing is often immoral when the attempt to lie or bluff is unilateral. To follow out the game metaphor, Carson is insisting not only that the rules of the game be understood but that the game be on a level playing surface for all players.

## NOTES

1. Sari Horwitz, "FTC Considers Letting Food Stores Advertise Out-of-Stock Items," *Washington Post* (December 27, 1984), p. E1.
2. As quoted in Amy Dunkin and others, "Liquor Makers Try the Hard Sell in a Softening Market," *Business Week* (May 13, 1985), p. 56.
3. "Anheuser-Busch Sued on Ad Showing Statue of Liberty," *Wall Street Journal* (November 28, 1984), p. 43.
4. Robert J. McCartney, "Investors Hit Salomon on Bonuses," *Washington Post* (October 23, 1991), pp. C1, C5.

## ADVERTISING

# Advertising and Behavior Control

*Robert L. Arrington*

Consider the following advertisements:

1. "A woman in *Distinction Foundation* is so beautiful that all other women want to kill her."
2. Pongo Peach color from Revlon comes "from east of the sun . . . west of the moon where each tomorrow dawns". It is "succulent on your lips" and "sizzling on your finger tips (And on your toes, goodness knows)". Let it be your "adventure in paradise".
3. "Musk by English Leather—The Civilized Way to Roar."
4. "Increase the value of your holdings. Old Charter Bourbon Whiskey—The Final Step Up."
5. Last Call Smirnoff Style: "They'd never really miss us, and it's kind of late already, and its quite a long way, and I could build a fire, and you're looking very beautiful, and we could have another martini, and its awfully nice just being home . . . you think?"
6. A Christmas Prayer. "Let us pray that the blessings of peace be ours—the peace to build and grow, to live in harmony and sympathy with others, and to plan for the future with confidence." New York Life Insurance Company.

These are instances of what is called puffery—the practice by a seller of making exaggerated, highly fanciful or suggestive claims about a product or service. Puffery, within ill-defined limits, is legal. It is considered a legitimate, necessary, and very successful tool of the advertising industry. Puffery is not just bragging; it is bragging carefully designed to achieve a very definite effect. Using the techniques of so-called motivational research, advertising firms first identify our often hidden needs (for security, conformity, oral stimulation) and our desires (for power, sexual dominance and dalliance, adventure) and then they design ads which respond to these needs and desires. By

*Journal of Business Ethics* 1 (1982) 3–12. 

associating a product, for which we may have little or no direct need or desire, with symbols reflecting the fulfillment of these other, often subterranean interests, the advertisement can quickly generate large numbers of consumers eager to purchase the product advertised. What woman in the sexual race of life could resist a foundation which would turn other women envious to the point of homicide? Who can turn down an adventure in paradise, east of the sun where tomorrow dawns? Who doesn't want to be civilized and thoroughly libidinous at the same time? Be at the pinnacle of success—drink Old Charter. Or stay at home and dally a bit—with Smirnoff. And let us pray for a secure and predictable future, provided for by New York Life, God willing. It doesn't take very much motivational research to see the point of these sales pitches. Others are perhaps a little less obvious. The need to feel secure in one's home at night can be used to sell window air conditioners, which drown out small noises and provide a friendly, dependable companion. The fact that baking a cake is symbolic of giving birth to a baby used to prompt advertisements for cake mixes which glamorized the 'creative' housewife. And other strategies, for example involving cigar symbolism, are a bit too crude to mention, but are nevertheless very effective.

Don't such uses of puffery amount to manipulation, exploitation, or downright control? In his very popular book *The Hidden Persuaders*, Vance Packard points out that number of people in the advertising world have frankly admitted as much:

> As early as 1941 Dr. Dichter (an influential advertising consultant) was exhorting ad agencies to recognize themselves for what they actually were—"one of the most advanced laboratories in psychology". He said the successful ad agency "manipulates human motivations and desires and develops a need for goods with which the public has at one time been unfamiliar—perhaps even undesirous of purchasing". The following year *Advertising Agency* carried an ad man's statement that psychology not only holds promise for understanding people but "ultimately for controlling their behavior"[1].

Such statements lead Packard to remark: "With all this interest in manipulating the customer's subconscious, the old slogan 'let the buyer beware' began taking on a new and more profound meaning".

B. F. Skinner, the high priest of behaviorism, has expressed a similar assessment of advertising and related marketing techniques. Why, he asks, do we buy a certain kind of car?

> Perhaps our favorite TV program is sponsored by the manufacturer of that car. Perhaps we have seen pictures of many beautiful or prestigeful persons driving it—in pleasant or glamorous places. Perhaps the car has been designed with respect to our motivational patterns: the device on the hood is a phallic symbol; or the horsepower has been stepped up to please our competitive spirit in enabling us to pass other cars swiftly (or, as the advertisements say, 'safely'). The concept of freedom that has emerged as part of the cultural practice of our group makes little or no provision for recognizing or dealing with these kinds of control.[2]

In purchasing a car we may think we are free, Skinner is claiming, when in fact our act is completely controlled by factors in our environment and in our history of reinforcement. Advertising is one such factor. . . .

Puffery, indirect information transfer, subliminal advertising—are these techniques of manipulation and control whose success shows that many of us have forfeited our autonomy and become a community, or herd, of packaged souls? The business world and the advertising industry certainly reject this interpretation of their efforts. *Business Week*, for example, dismissed the charge that the science of behavior, as utilized by advertising, is engaged in human engineering and manipulation. It editorialized to the effect that "it is hard to find anything very sinister about a science whose principle conclusion is that you get along with people by giving them what they want"[3]. The theme is familiar: businesses just give the consumer what he/she wants; if they didn't they wouldn't stay in business very long. Proof that the consumer wants the products advertised is given by the fact that he buys them, and indeed often returns to buy them again and again.

The techniques of advertising we are discussing have had their more intellectual defenders as well. For example, Theodore Levitt, Professor of Business Administration at the Harvard Business School, has defended the practice of puffery and the use of techniques depending on motivational research.[4] What would be the consequences, he asks us, of deleting all exaggerated claims and fanciful associations from advertisements? We would be left literal descriptions of the empirical characteristics of products and their functions. Cosmetics would be presented as facial and bodily lotions and powders which produce certain odor and color changes; they would no longer offer hope or adventure. In addition to the fact that these products would not then sell as well, they would not, according to Levitt, please us as much either. For it is hope and adventure we want when we buy them. We want automobiles not just for transportation, but for the feelings of power and status they give us. Quoting T. S. Eliot to the effect that "Human kind cannot bear very much reality", Levitt argues that advertising is an effort to "transcend nature in the raw", to "augment what nature has so crudely fashioned". He maintains that "everybody everywhere wants to modify, transform, embellish, enrich and reconstruct the world around him". Commerce takes the same liberty with reality as the artist and the priest—in all three instances the purpose is "to influence the audience by creating illusions, symbols, and implications that promise more than pure functionality". For example, "to amplify the temple in men's eyes, (men of cloth) have, very realistically, systematically sanctioned the embellishment of the houses of the gods with the same kind of luxurious design and expensive decoration that Detroit puts into a Cadillac". A poem, a temple, a Cadillac—they all elevate our spirits, offering imaginative promises and symbolic interpretations of our mundane activities. Seen in this light, Levitt claims, "Embellishment and distortion are among advertising's legitimate and socially desirable purposes". To reject these techniques of advertising would be "to deny man's honest needs and value".

Philip Nelson, a Professor of Economics at SUNY-Binghamton, has developed an interesting defense of indirect information advertising.[5] He argues that even when the message (the direct information) is not credible, the fact that the brand is advertised, and advertised frequently, is valuable indirect information for the consumer. The reason for this is that the brands advertised most are more likely to be better buys—losers won't be advertised a lot, for it simply wouldn't pay to do so. Thus even if the advertising claims made for a widely advertised product are empty, the consumer reaps the benefit of the indirect information which shows the product to be a good buy. Nelson goes so far as to say that advertising, seen as information and especially as indirect information, does not require an intelligent human response. If the indirect information has been received and has had its impact, the consumer will purchase the better buy even if his explicit reason for doing so is silly, e.g., he naively believes an endorsement of the product by a celebrity. Even though his behavior is overtly irrational, by acting on the indirect information he is nevertheless doing what he ought to do, i.e., getting his money's worth. "'Irrationality' is rational", Nelson writes, "if it is cost-free". . . .

The defense of advertising which suggests that advertising simply is information which allows us to purchase what we want, has in turn been challenged. Does business, largely through its advertising efforts, really make available to the consumer what he/she desires and demands? John Kenneth Galbraith has denied that the matter is as straightforward as this.[6] In his opinion the desires to which business is supposed to respond, far from being original to the consumer, are often themselves created by business. The producers make both the product and the desire for it, and the "central function" of advertising is "to create desires". Galbraith coins the term 'The Dependence Effort' to designate the way wants depend on the same process by which they are satisfied.

David Braybrooke has argued in similar and related ways.[7] Even though the consumer is, in a sense, the final authority concerning what he wants, he may come to see, according to Braybrooke, that he was mistaken in wanting what he did. The statement 'I want *x*', he tells us, is not incorrigible but is "ripe for revision". If the consumer had more objective information than he is provided by product puffing, if his values had not been mixed up by motivational research strategies (e.g., the confusion of sexual and automotive values), and if he had an expanded set of choices instead of the limited set offered by profit-hungry corporations, then he might want something quite different from what he presently wants. This shows, Braybrooke thinks, the extent to which the consumer's wants are a function of advertising and not necessarily representative of his real or true wants.

The central issue which emerges between the above critics and defenders of advertising is this: do the advertising techniques we have discussed involve a violation of human autonomy and a manipulation and control of consumer behavior, *or* do they simply provide an efficient and cost effective means of giving the consumer information on the basis of which he or she makes a free choice. Is advertising information, or creation of desire?

To answer this question we need a better conceptual grasp of what is involved in the notion of autonomy. This is a complex, multifaceted concept, and we need to approach it through the more determinate notions of (a) autonomous desire, (b) rational desire and choice, (c) free choice, and (d) control or manipulation. In what follows I shall offer some tentative and very incomplete analyses of these concepts and apply the results to the case of advertising.

(a) *Autonomous Desire.* Imagine that I am watching T.V. and see an ad for Grecian Formula 16. The thought occurs to me that if I purchase some and apply it to my beard, I will soon look younger—in fact I might even be myself again. Suddenly I want to be myself! I want to be young again! So I rush out and buy a bottle. This is our question: was the desire to be younger manufactured by the commercial, or was it 'original to me' and truly mine? Was it autonomous or not?

F. A. von Hayek has argued plausibly that we should not equate nonautonomous desires, desires which are not original to me truly mine, with those which are culturally induced.[8] If we did equate the two, he points out, then the desires for music, art, and knowledge could not properly be attributed to a person as original to him, for these are surely induced culturally. The only desires a person would really have as his own in this case would be the purely physical ones for food, shelter, sex, etc. But if we reject the equation of the nonautonomous and the culturally induced, as von Hayek would have us do, then the mere fact that my desire to be young again is caused by the T.V. commercial—surely an instrument of popular culture transmission—does not in and of itself show that this is not my own, autonomous desire. Moreover, even if I never before felt the need to look young, it doesn't follow that this new desire is any less mine. I haven't always liked 1969 Aloxe Corton Burgundy or the music of Satie, but when the desires for these things first hit me, they were truly mine.

This shows that there is something wrong in setting up the issue over advertising and behavior control as a question whether our desires are truly ours *or* are created in us by advertisements. Induced and autonomous desires do not separate into two mutually exclusive classes. To obtain a better understanding of autonomous and non-autonomous desires, let us consider some cases of a desire which a person does not *acknowledge* to be his own even though he *feels* it. The kleptomaniac has a desire to steal which in many instances he repudiates, seeking by treatment to rid himself of it. And if I were suddenly overtaken by a desire to attend an REO concert, I would immediately disown this desire, claiming possession or momentary madness. These are examples of desires which one might have but with which one would not identify. They are experienced as foreign to one's character or personality. Often a person will have what Harry Frankfurt calls a second-order desire, that is to say, a desire *not* to have another desire.[9] In such cases, the first-order desire is thought of as being nonautonomous, imposed on one. When on the contrary a person has a second-order desire to maintain and fulfill a first-order desire, then the first-order desire is truly his own, autonomous, original to him. So there is in fact a distinction between desires which are the agent's own and those which are not, but this is not the same as the distinction between desires which are innate to the agent and those which are externally induced. . . .

What are we to say in response to Braybrooke's argument that insofar as we might choose differently if advertisers gave us better information and more options, it follows that the desires we have are to be attributed more to advertising than to our own real inclinations? This claim seems empty. It amounts to saying that if the world we lived in, and we ourselves, were different, then we would want different things. This is surely true, but it is equally true of our desire for shelter as of our desire for Grecian Formula 16. If we lived in a tropical paradise we would not need or desire shelter. If we were immortal, we would not desire youth. What is true of all desires can hardly be used as a basis for criticizing some desires by claiming that they are nonautonomous.

(b) *Rational Desire and Choice.* Braybrooke might be interpreted as claiming that the desires induced by advertising are often irrational ones in the sense that they are not expressed by an agent who is in full possession of the facts about the products advertised or about the alternative products which might be offered him. Following this line of thought, a possible criticism of advertising is that it leads us to act on irrational desires or to make irrational choices. It might be said that our autonomy has been violated by the fact that we are prevented from following our rational wills or that we have been denied the 'positive freedom' to develop our true, rational selves. It might be claimed that the desires induced in us by advertising are false desires in that they do not reflect our essential, i.e., rational, essence.

The problem faced by this line of criticism is that of determining what is to count as rational desire or rational choice. If we require that the desire or choice be the product of an awareness of *all* the facts about the product, then surely every one of us is always moved by irrational desires and makes nothing but irrational choices. How could we know all the facts about a product? If it be required only that we possess all of the *available* knowledge about the product advertised, then we still have to face the problem that not all available knowledge is *relevant* to a rational choice. If I am purchasing a car, certain engineering features will be, and others won't be, relevant, *given what I want in a car.* My prior desires determine the relevance of information. Normally a rational desire or choice is thought to be one based upon relevant information, and information is relevant if it shows how other, prior desires may be satisfied. It can plausibly be claimed that it is such prior desires that advertising agencies acknowledge, and that the agencies often provide the type of information that is relevant in light of these desires. To the extent that this is true, advertising does not inhibit our rational wills or our autonomy as rational creatures.

It may be urged that much of the puffery engaged in by advertising does not provide relevant information at all but rather makes claims which are not factually true. If someone buys Pongo Peach in anticipation of an adventure in paradise, or Old Charter in expectation of increasing the value of his holdings, then he/she is expecting purely imaginary benefits. In no literal sense will the one product provide adventure and the other increased capital. A purchasing decision based on anticipation of imaginary benefits is not, it might said, a rational decision, and a desire for imaginary benefits is not a rational desire. . . .

Some philosophers will be unhappy with the conclusion of this section, largely because they have a concept of true, rational, or ideal desire which is not the same as the one used here. A Marxist, for instance, may urge that any desire felt by alienated man in a capitalistic society is foreign to his true nature. Or an existentialist may claim that the desires of inauthentic men are themselves inauthentic. Such concepts are based upon general theories of human nature which are unsubstantiated and perhaps incapable of substantiation. Moreover, each of these theories is committed to a concept of an ideal desire which is normatively debatable and which is distinct from the ordinary concept of a rational desire as one based upon relevant information. But it is in the terms of the ordinary concept that we express our concern that advertising may limit our autonomy in the sense of leading us to act on irrational desires, and if we operate with this concept we are driven again to the conclusion that advertising may lead, but probably most often does not lead, to an infringement of autonomy.

(c) *Free Choice.* It might be said that some desires are so strong or so covert that a person cannot resist them, and that when he acts on such desires he is not acting freely or voluntarily but is rather the victim of irresistible impulse or an unconscious drive. Perhaps those who condemn advertising feel that it produces this kind of desire in us and consequently reduces our autonomy.

This raises a very difficult issue. How do we distinguish between an impulse we do not resist and one we *could* not resist, between freely giving in to a desire and succumbing to one? I have argued elsewhere that the way to get at this issue is in terms of the notion of acting for a reason.[10] A person acts or chooses freely if he does so for a reason, that is, if he can adduce considerations which justify in his mind the act in question. Many of our actions are in fact free because this condition frequently holds. Often, however, a person will act from habit, or whim, or impulse, and on these occasions he does not have a reason in mind. Nevertheless he often acts voluntarily in these instances, i.e., he could have acted otherwise. And this is because if there *had been* a reason for acting otherwise of which he was aware, he would in fact have done so. Thus acting from habit or impulse is not necessarily to act in an involuntary manner. If, however, a person is aware of a good reason to do *x* and still follows his impulse to do *y*, then he can be said to be impelled by irresistible impulse and hence to act involuntarily. Many kleptomaniacs can be said to act involuntarily, for in spite of their knowledge that they likely will be caught and their awareness that the goods they steal have little utilitarian value to them, they nevertheless steal. Here their 'out of character' desires have the upper hand, and we have a case of compulsive behavior.

Applying these notions of voluntary and compulsive behavior to the case of behavior prompted by advertising, can we say that consumers influenced by advertising, act compulsively? The unexciting answer is: sometimes they do, sometimes not. I may have an overwhelming, T.V. induced urge to own a Mazda Rx-7 and all the while realize that I can't afford one without severely reducing my family's caloric intake to a dangerous level. If, aware of this good reason not to purchase the car, I nevertheless do so, this shows that I have been the victim of T.V. compulsion. But if I have the urge, as I assure you I do, and don't act on it, or if in some other possible world I could afford an Rx-7, then I have not been the subject of undue influence by Mazda advertising. Some Mazda Rx-7 purchasers act compulsively; others do not. The Mazda advertising effort *in general* cannot be condemned, then, for impairing its customers' autonomy in the sense of limiting free or voluntary choice. Of course the question remains what should be done about the fact that advertising may and does *occasionally* limit free choice. We shall return to this question later.

In the case of subliminal advertising we may find an individual whose subconscious desires are activated by advertising into doing something his calculating, reasoning ego does not approve. This would be a case of compulstion. But most of us have a benevolent subconsciousness which does not overwhelm our ego and its reasons for action. And therefore most of us can respond to subliminal advertising without thereby risking our autonomy. To be sure, if some advertising firm developed a subliminal technique which drove all of us to purchase Lear jets, thereby reducing our caloric intake to the zero point, then we would have a case of advertising which could properly be censured for infringing our right to autonomy. We should acknowledge that this is possible, but at the same time we should recognize that it is not an inherent result of subliminal advertising.

(d) *Control or Manipulation.* Briefly let us consider the matter of control and manipulation. Under what conditions do these activities occur? In a recent paper on 'Forms and Limits of Control' I suggested the following criteria:[11]

A person *C* controls the behavior of another person *P iff*

(1) *C* intends *P* to act in a certain way *A*;
(2) *C*'s intention is causally effective in bringing about *A*; and
(3) *C* intends to ensure that all of the necessary conditions of *A* are satisfied.

These criteria may be elaborated as follows. To control another person it is not enough that one's actions produce certain behavior on the part of that person; additionally one must intend that this happen. Hence control is the intentional production of behavior. Moreover, it is not enough just to have the intention; the intention must give rise to the conditions which bring about the intended effect. Finally, the controller must intend to establish by his actions any otherwise unsatisfied necessary conditions for the production of the intended effect. The controller is not just influencing the outcome, not just having input; he is as it were guaranteeing that the sufficient conditions for the intended effect are satisfied.

Let us apply these criteria of control to the case of advertising and see what happens. Conditions (1) and (3) are crucial. Does the Mazda manufacturing company or its advertising agengy intend that I buy an Rx-7? Do they intend that a certain number of people buy the car? *Prima facie* it seems more appropriate to say that they *hope* a certain number of people will buy it, and hoping and intending are not the same. But the difficult term here is 'intend'. Some philosophers have argued that to intend *A* it is necessary only to desire that *A* happen and to believe that it will. If this is correct, and if marketing analysis gives the Mazda agency a reasonable belief that a certain segment of the population will buy its product, then, assuming on its part the desire that this happen, we have the conditions necessary for saying that the agency intends that a certain segment purchase the car. If I am a member of this segment of the population, would it then follow that the agency intends that I purchase an Rx-7? Or is control referentially opaque? Obviously we have some questions here which need further exploration.

Let us turn to the third condition of control, the requirement that the controller intend to activate or bring about any otherwise unsatisfied necessary conditions for the production of the intended effect. It is in terms of this condition that we are able to distinguish brainwashing from liberal education. The brainwasher arranges all of the necessary conditions for belief. On the other hand, teachers (at least those of liberal persuasion) seek only to influence their students–to provide them with information and enlightenment which they may absorb *if they wish.* We do not normally think of teachers as controlling their students, for the students' performances depend as well on their own interests and inclinations. . . .

Let me summarize my argument. The critics of advertising see it as having a pernicious effect on the autonomy of consumers, as controlling their lives and manufacturing their very souls. The defense claims that advertising only offers information and in effect allows industry to provide consumers with what they want. After developing some of the philosophical dimensions of this dispute, I have come down tentatively in favor of the advertisers. Advertising may, but certainly does not always or even frequently, control behavior, produce compulsive behavior, or create wants which are not rational or are not truly those of the consumer. Admittedly it may in individual cases do all of these things, but it is innocent of the charge of intrinsically or necessarily doing them or even, I think, of often doing so. This limited potentiality, to be sure, leads to the question whether advertising should be abolished or severely curtailed or regulated because of its potential to harm a few poor souls in the above ways. This is a very difficult question, and I do not pretend to have the answer. I only hope that the above discussion, in showing some of the kinds of harm that can be done by advertising and by indicating the likely limits of this harm, will put us in a better position to grapple with the question.

## NOTES

1. Vance Packard, *The Hidden Persuaders* (Pocket Books, New York 1958), pp. 20–21.
2. B. F. Skinner, "Some Issues Concerning the Control of Human Behavior: A Symposium", in Karlins and Andrews (eds.), *Man Controlled* (The Free Press, New York, 1972).
3. Quoted by Packard, *op. cit.*, p. 220.
4. Theodore Levitt, "The Morality (?) of Advertising", *Harvard Business Review* 48 (1970), 84–92.
5. Phillip Nelson, "Advertising and Ethics", in Richard T. De George and Joseph A. Pichler (eds.), *Ethics, Free Enterprise and Public Policy* (Oxford University Press, New York, 1978) pp. 187–98.
6. John Kenneth Galbraith, *The Affluent Society*; reprinted in Tom L. Beauchamp and Norman E. Bowie (eds.) *Ethical Theory and Business* (Prentice-Hall Englewood Cliffs, 1979), pp. 496–501.
7. David Braybrooke, "Skepticism of Wants, and Certain Subversive Effects of Corporation on American Values", in Sidney Hook (ed.), *Human Values and Economic Policy* (New York University Press, New York, 1967); reprinted in Beauchamp and Bowie (eds.) *op. cit.*, pp. 502–508.

8. F. A. von Hayek, 'The Non Sequitur of the "Dependence Effect"', *Southern Economic Journal* (1961); reprinted in Beauchamp and Bowie (eds.) op. cit., pp. 508–512.
9. Harry Frankfurt, "Freedom of the Will and the Concept of Person", *Journal of Philosophy* LXVIII (1971), 5–20.
10. Robert L. Arrington, "Practical Reason, Responsibility and the Psychopath", *Journal for the Theory of Social Behavior* 9 (1979), 71–89.
11. Robert L. Arrington, "Forms and Limits of Control", delivered at the annual meeting of the Southern Society for Philosophy and Psychology, Birmingham, Alabama, 1980.

# Is Self-Identity Image Advertising Ethical?

*John Douglas Bishop*

For decades, criticisms of advertising have been legion. Advertising has been criticized both for its impact on society and for its impact on individuals. Criticisms have variously centred on aesthetic, economic, cultural, and other issues, but some have raised serious moral concerns. Sometimes critics have complained about specific ads or types of ads, sometimes about advertising in general. This paper confines its attention to one specific type of advertising (self-identity image ads), and to the moral issues arising out of the impact of image ads on individuals. The central moral issues raised by image ads are these: (a) whether they make false or misleading promises; (b) whether they promote false values; (c) whether they cause harm; and (d) whether they threaten the autonomy of the individual. . . .

Self-identity image ads (hereafter: image ads) create a symbolic image of an idealized person-type and invite the potential consumers of the product to identify themselves in some way with that image. The Marlboro Man is a good example is such an idealized image. Note that these ads do not try to create an image of the product; in fact, such ads often do not mention product features, price, or availability. They create an image of an idealized person-type who is usually portrayed as a user of the product, though in some cases the connection between the ideal person and the product is vague. Images can be constructed and connected or transferred to the product in various ways. To see how these ads work, we need a basic way of analyzing this construction and transference. Versions of the techniques of analysis used by Williamson (1978) and Wernick (1991) will be sufficient for our purposes. The language of these techniques is best explained by examples. Two ads are described here; the following sections of this paper analyze these ads in terms of their direct effect on the viewer's beliefs, the presuppositions that underlie their explicit content, and their use of symbols. The ads were chosen because they are typical representatives of self-identity image ads.

## EXAMPLE AD 1: THE "BEAUTIFUL" WOMAN[1]

The top 80 percent of this ad is a photo of a woman; her face, head, left shoulder, arms, and hands are shown. She is wearing glittering glass jewelry on her neck and left forearm, and no clothes are shown. Her face is turned toward the camera, and she is looking directly at the viewer of the ad. Her hair is combed back away from her face with not a single hair out of place. The edge of the bright red paint on her lips is similarly precise and neat. There is nothing pictured in the background, which is pure white. Most of the picture is her skin (face, shoulder, arms, and hands), which has absolutely no wrinkles, lines, freckles, scars, dents, dimples, or even pores; it is perfectly smooth and monotone except for some slight shading. Her face has no expression; it is relaxed and blank. In the lower right corner of the photo, superimposed on her upper arm, is a black and white jar, with black printing: "Teint Lumiere Creme Perfecting creme makeup SPF 8 CHANEL Paris New York." The bottom 20 percent of the ad is outside the photo; clear, large letters say "CHANEL." In smaller print it says; "Introducing new perfecting creme makeup. Lightweight, light-reflective formula minimizes imperfections for a flawless matte finish."

At a basic level, the interpretation of this ad is straightforward. We are meant to view this as a "beautiful" women with "flawless" skin. Various techniques connect in the viewer's mind the "flawless" skin with the product. The product and the name CHANEL are superimposed on a large expanse of bare skin; the lines of the arms, cheeks, and jewelry all point to the Chanel jar; and the position of her head and arms makes it look as though she is leaning on the word "CHANEL." We are meant to associate the beauty and flawless skin with Chanel; whether the product causes the beauty, or is a symbol of it, or is associated with it in some other way, we will examine throughout the rest of this paper.

## EXAMPLE AD 2: THE SEXY TEENAGERS[2]

This ad is a glossy heavy bond insert that opens to a 50 by 58 cm poster. Four young people (two male, two female), all white, healthy, and good looking, are shown separately on a purple carpet with 1960s-style cheap wooden basement paneling in the background. The models are scantily clad in denim—one male has only underwear and an open vest on. One male and one female model have their legs spread open exposing genital bulging underwear. All four are in seductive poses, and look coyly directly at the viewer. The models appear to be between 14 and 18 years of age. Three of the four pictures have the CK logo and words "Calvin Klein Jeans" superimposed prominently. There is no other text.

Again at a basic level, this is easy to interpret. Calvin Klein wants to associate his logo, name, and product with healthy, good looking, white (?), sexy teenagers; he is creating an image that reeks of youthful sex and trying to connect this image with Calvin Klein in the target audience's mind.

Are these two ads ethical? Are they false or misleading? Do they manipulate people by creating desires for products people would otherwise not want? Do they threaten autonomy? To address these ethical issues, we need to look carefully at how these ads are intended to work and the impact they have on viewers. The following sections will consider whether image ads are false or misleading, have unethical presuppositions, or threaten autonomy.

## FALSE PROMISES

One interpretation of the Chanel ad is that it promises to make the user as "beautiful" (or at least her skin as "flawless") as the woman in the ad. On this interpretation, the ad works by making the viewer believe that use of the product will make the user just like the model in some relevant aspect. Since all people have lines, wrinkles, and/or pores on their faces, this promise is obviously false. However, it is generally accepted that this is neither the intent nor the usual consumer interpretation of image ads (Arrington 1982, Waide 1987, Lippke 1988). Further, the fact that a product like Chanel skin cream needs repeat buyers means that the ad-induced belief would have to continue after the product has been used. This view of consumer reactions posits a consumer with beliefs so resistant to evidence that there would be little or no possibility of consumer autonomy. The fact that some consumers such as small children (cf. Paine 1983) or people not used to modern advertising (as in the marketing of infant formula in Africa; cf. Post 1986) might be prone to this interpretation suggests moral restrictions on the target or placement of image ads, but does not affect the ethics of the image ad as a type. And the empirical possibility that some purchasers are in fact duped into false beliefs by image ads does not answer the ethical question of who is responsible for the duping; consumers may choose to participate actively in the image game, even if it involves self-deception. . . .

In general, image ads are not unethical because they are false or misleading. They do not make explicit product promises, and implied product promises are discounted by consumers, and are meant to be discounted. If the ads succeed in making the product a symbol of a particular image, then the image promises may be true or be self-fulfilling. It is an empirical question whether consumers discount the ads enough, but since most of the products that use image ads are low in price and depend on repeat purchases, this does not seem an important ethical issue.

## PRESUPPOSITIONS

Ads are often criticized not for their stated or implied claims, but for the presuppositions that lie behind the explicit message of the ad. The Chanel ad, for example, presupposes that lines and wrinkles on a woman's face are "flaws" that destroy beauty. The ad assumes that such wrinkles are not to be seen as interesting and beautiful signs of maturity, experience, and lively features, which they might in a culture that respected aged women more.

The presuppositions of image ads can raise ethical concerns in several ways. First, since presuppositions are unstated, there may be concern that the viewer of image ads is receiving messages they are not aware of, and that therefore threaten their autonomy. Second, specific presuppositions of specific ads may be morally objectionable because they recommend false values. Third, there is concern about the cumulative effect of certain presuppositions common to many image ads. And finally, there are problems relating specifically to the gaze that is presupposed by many image ads. Since presuppositions in general may threaten autonomy, discussion of that issue will be postponed to section 3. We will here consider in turn: (1) the issue of specific presuppositions that may be unethical, (2) the cumulative effect of certain presuppositions, and (3) the issue of presupposed gaze.

### Specific Presuppositions

Many ethical criticisms of the presuppositions of image ads object to specific presuppositions of certain ads or types of ads, but do not necessarily see a problem with other ads. Consider the following presuppositions assumed by the Chanel ad;

(a) Beautiful women have wrinkle-free skin.
(b) This is the kind of woman you should see as beautiful.
(c) Women ought to pursue personal beauty with time and money.
(d) Women will be and should be valued for their beauty.

Once spelled out like this, these assumptions are obviously suspect, and it is precisely specific presuppositions of this sort that feminist critics of advertising and others have analyzed so clearly (Wolf 1990).

Similarly, it is the specific presuppositions of the Calvin Klein ad that have provoked criticism (Brady 1995, Crain 1995, Garfield 1995,

Lippe 1995). The ad seems to assume that teenagers are sexy, ought to be seen as sexy, and ought to have sexiness as a significant part of their personal identity. Even people who see no ethical objections to teen sexual activity *per se* may feel that such ads lead teens to put too much emphasis on sex. . . .

By their very nature, image ads recommend for adoption as a self-image a particular person-type; inherent in this is the presupposition that a person should be valued for the characteristics of that person-type. The Chanel ad, for instance, suggests that women should be valued for their complexion; the Calvin Klein ad that teenagers should be valued for their sexiness. These value judgments are inevitable in image ads precisely because these ads are proposing the adoption of a particular self-image. And these value judgements apply both to how one should judge oneself, and to how people should judge others. Is it unethical to encourage valuing people based on their youth, thinness, complexion, beauty, sexiness, or hair—to list only some of the particular values that image ads are wont to advocate—or are these "false" values? . . .

## THE CUMULATIVE EFFECT OF PRESUPPOSITIONS

Some of the objections to the presuppositions of image ads are not concerned with the presuppositions of specific ads, but rather complain about the proportion of certain kinds of presuppositions in image advertising in general. It is suggested that imbalance in advertising overall causes harm in ways that a single ad cannot. This harm may be the aggravation of false values already considered. For example, perhaps there is nothing morally wrong with the Chanel ad suggesting women should spend time and money to approximate the young, smooth-skinned beauty ideal; the problem is that too many cosmetic and fashion ads assume this, and too few assume women should spend their time and money studying, developing talents, or growing old with dignity. All fashion and cosmetic ads show the kind of "beauty" that drives sales; none show the beauty that drives sales; none show the beauty that comes from smiles, openness, cheerfulness, and liveliness. We have suggested there is nothing immoral with the presuppositions of the Tommy Hilfiger ad that young people should wear a certain style of casual clothes when having healthy outdoor fun with friends, but what is the cumulative effect of seeing thousands of ads that presuppose that having friends requires fashion, cosmetics, and special soaps, and never having it suggested that friendship depends on honesty, openness, or generosity? Is the imbalance in ads unethical? As these examples show, the cumulative effect of ads may place a "false" emphasis on values that are not inherently false. Claims of "false" emphasis are subjective in the same way that false values are, but a decent avoidance by one advertiser will not fix the cumulative problem of advertising in general. . . .

What should be done about the threat of image advertising to self-esteem? Collectively or separately image advertisers could establish and support women's magazines that publish more realistic body images. Separately, companies like Chanel could create and advertise products using models with other body types, much as cosmetics companies now have products for various racial types. They would not have to use their own name or discontinue current ads since the issue is balancing images. Thirdly, companies should avoid using camera, photographic, and other techniques to create impossible body types as ideals. Given the severity of the harm of lost self-esteem, I conclude cosmetics companies have a moral responsibility to minimize the harm done to people's self-esteem.

## Gaze

Ads are carefully constructed so that the ways they are viewed by different sorts of people create particular impacts. The Chanel ad, for example, intends a certain impact on women—it presupposes a female viewer gaze. The Calvin Klein jeans ad, on the other hand, is intended to have an impact with either a male or female viewer gaze; it presupposes a young person, or a young person wannabe, gaze.

The viewer gaze determines the impact of an ad because it determines the reading of the ad. The Chanel ad entices the female gaze to a narcissistic reading; that is, it invites the female viewer to imagine herself as being the model, to read herself into the ad by identifying with the "beautiful" woman. This creates a second type of gaze. The ad is constructed to imply that the "beautiful" woman is looking at someone, and that that someone is looking at her. If the female viewer of the ad imaginatively becomes the woman in the ad, who is it that is now receiving her gaze and doing the viewing? This is the implied gaze (as opposed to the viewer gaze). Generally, women are assumed to want to be beautiful as a means of attracting the attention of men; therefore, the usual implied gaze of the Chanel ad is male. That is, the ad presupposes that it is a man who is looking at and sharing the gaze of the woman in the ad, even though it is assumed that the viewer of the ad is a woman. It can be asked whether the implied male gaze of ads of this sort is ethically objectionable. . . .

Self-identity image ads work only if the viewer identifies themselves with the image presented—the viewer has to read themselves into the ad as being, if only in fantasy, the person-type the model portrays; they have to imaginatively consider the image as potentially forming part of their self-identity. The ubiquity of image ads means that this process can be indulged in repeatedly. This constant reexamination of one's own self-identity is a form of narcissism; it was not common in most societies prior to the onset of modern advertising, but now forms part of the "culture of narcissism" (Lasch 1979). Whether this form of narcissism is unethical is hard to say. Its impact on human welfare cannot be guessed without making uncertain comparisons with alternative ways of spending one's time. It may be entirely consistent with the cultivation of a virtuous character, though the concentration of advertising on the physical body and the portrayal of only limited roles probably does not encourage reflections on one's own character. The self-identities offered by image ads are most often of isolated individuals (Dyer 1982, p. 110), but this is compatible with liberal notions of society, justice, and human rights. Narcissism and a narcissistic culture may be distasteful, but to view their encouragement as unethical would require precise arguments.

Implied gaze is more serious because it can contribute substantially to the undermining of self-esteem. The problem here is not the content of the implied gaze because in fact that is usually undetermined. Consider the Chanel ad; many viewers would assume that the implied gaze (which in this case is also shared gaze) is male and based on desire. But there is nothing in the ad to determine this; a viewer could assume an implied gaze that is female and based on envy, or (if the viewer gaze is lesbian) an implied gaze that is female and based on desire. Queer readings of fashion ads make clear that implied gaze (or, in this case, implied gays) is usually but not always undetermined (Woods 1995, Bishop 1997).

What can affect self-esteem is not the content but the very implication of implied gaze. Most image ads imply that we are being watched and judged by an Other at all times. This is not problematic because false; what is problematic is that image ads usually present impossible identity ideals, and therefore imply that we are constantly being judged by impossible standards. This tends to undermine self-esteem. . . .

The ethical problems of undermining self-esteem are increased by the fact that this technique works best on people who belong to marginalized groups, especially women, adolescents, and minorities.

This undermining of self-esteem is further complicated by the fact that the impossible ideals presented in image ads are almost always based on the physical body, or in a few cases, particular social roles. This dramatically and unfairly undermines the self-esteem of anyone who fares poorly by those standards. In many cases this undermining is permanent, since there is often little one can do about one's body type (although, of course, one can make some effort to "stay in shape"). The implications that standards are physical also undermines the fact that it is morally more important to esteem people for their abilities, accomplishments, character, and virtues. This intentional undermining of self-esteem is the most serious ethical problem with image ads. Although this problem is greatly aggravated by the cumulative effect of many advertisers using impossible images and implied gaze, there would seem to be more than a collective responsibility in Brenkert's sense for avoiding this harm; each advertiser could individually avoid this technique and still market their products to the same target consumers. The problem is with a specific advertising technique, not with the product or consumer usage of it (as in Brenkert's example of malt liquors). Since the combination of implied gaze and impossible identity images causes harm, I conclude advertisers have an ethical responsibility for avoiding this technique. . . .

## IMAGE ADS, ETHICS, AND AUTONOMY

If it is true that image ads tend to restrict human autonomy, there are grounds for concern about the ethics of this form of advertising. Autonomy is a complex concept; three aspects of human autonomy are particularly relevant to discussion of image ads. (1) Autonomy of choice (sometimes referred to as external autonomy): can a person in fact act on a desire that they have? (2) Autonomy of desire (or internal autonomy): is a person's having a desire, or their decision to act on it, autonomous? (3) Social autonomy: how does social context enhance or restrict either choice (external autonomy) or decisions about desires or actions (internal autonomy). We will consider these in turn.

### Autonomy of Choice

In order or discuss whether a person's choice can be acted on autonomously, let us identify what choices people make with respect to image ads. . . .

***Choice Regarding Exposure to Ads.*** Do people have any (apparently free) choice about whether to look at image ads? On the one hand, people leading ordinary lives cannot help seeing bill boards and transit ads; on the other hand, people can choose not to read fashion or other ad-dominated magazines, not to watch television or listen to commercial radio, not to open junk mail, and not to shop at fashion stores. Since outdoor advertising is only 6–7 percent of advertising budgets,[3] most but not all image advertising can be avoided if a person wishes. But most people do not try to avoid image ads; they go out of their way to be exposed to them, they even pay money to buy fashion magazines that are densely packed with little else. People choose to be viewers of image ads. Most image ads are concentrated in fashion and special interest magazines that consumers pay money to look at. This willingness of consumers to actively seek and pay for image ads reduces the problem of passive exposure to the level of billboard bylaws; it is not relevant to assessing the ethics of the technique itself. I do not know of any arguments against the autonomy of choosing to buy magazines or watch television in which it is image ads themselves that restrict autonomous choice. Since the choice to be exposed to the ad must be prior to any effect of the ad, arguments purporting to show that persuasive techniques in advertising undermine autonomy do not apply to choosing to be exposed to the ad. Let us conclude that the choice of seeing or avoiding most image ads is externally autonomous.

***Choice Regarding the Creation of Symbols.*** The intention of image ads is to have the product and its logo become a symbol of a particular ideal person-type; can the viewer choose to accept or reject this symbolism? To answer this question, we need to consider how image ads create symbols. A sign is composed of a signifier (the physical object, sound, picture, etc.) and something signified (the meaning a person attaches to the signifier). If the connection between the signifier and the signified is an arbitrary cultural construction available only to people within a culture (or subculture), then we will say the sign is a symbol. For example, two small pieces of wood fixed across each other may be a signifier to a person familiar with Christianity; the signified is the large and elaborate meaning Christians attach to the crucifix. To a person unfamiliar with Christianity, the crossed pieces of wood may not be a signifier because no meaning is suggested. The crucifix is a sign for Christians, and a symbol since the connection between signified and signifier is culturally dependent. . . .

In the Chanel ad, the photo of the woman, her jewelry, lipstick, coiffure, arm position, head attitude, etc. are signifiers; the signified is an image of "elegant and beautiful" woman. This image is then transferred to the Chanel logo and the particular face cream product so that the logo and product come to be a symbol for elegant and beautiful woman. However, the ad is more complicated than that because in our culture (or at least in the subculture that reads *Vogue* regularly) viewers come to the ad with the Chanel logo already functioning as a symbol of French elegance, sophistication, and creative Parisian fashion. This ad adds to the creation of a symbol that been created and refined in many ads, displays, and feature articles on Chanel and her fashions. . . .

***Choice Regarding Accepting or Rejecting Self-images.*** If we choose to look at image ads and we do not actively resist symbol creation, the product logo will come to symbolize the image of an ideal person-type; can we choose to accept or reject this image as a role model for our self image? I want to argue that the very variety of possible self-images in image advertising gives people a choice as to which image to accept, and tends to make people more aware of this choice in selecting a personal image. Young people today are especially conscious that they can be whatever kind of person they want to be. If this is a kind of autonomy, that is morally valuable, then image advertising has great moral worth because it tends to make people aware of their autonomy, presents them with clearly defined options, and creates the symbolic language that allows them to express their choice. Indeed, Calvin Klein "Be" ads explicitly preach that the viewer can be what and whom they want to be—they preach free choice and hence one kind of autonomy in personal images. . . .

***Choice Regarding Buying the Product.*** No one makes us buy image products, we are free to do so or not—we are autonomous in the political sense of that word. And most of us have economic autonomy in that we can afford many image products, and they are certainly readily available. Granted, as a professor I cannot afford to project the image that owning an S-class Mercedes would give, but since desiring such an image is based on the desire to have a higher social status than other people, this is not morally relevant. The destitute in our society cannot afford image products at all, but destitution is not caused by image advertising, and what is morally wrong with destitution would not be fixed if there were no image ads. In fact, it is noticeable that the kinds of products sold through image ads are not the kinds that we need in any morally relevant sense of the word "need." Image ads sell beer, liquor, cigarettes, cosmetics, fashions, cars, vacations—these are sold by image advertising precisely because we have no real need for them. A person could easily choose a lifestyle that excludes all of these. . . .

## Autonomy of Desire

Many of the issues surrounding internal autonomy have been discussed in the literature on persuasive advertising (Arrington 1982, Crisp 1987, Waide 1987, Lippke 1988), and that discussion need not be revisited in the context of image ads (which, of course, are a form of persuasive advertising). In particular, we can accept Arrington's arguments that persuasive ads do not "control behaviour, [or] produce compulsive behaviour" (p. 582). There is no empirical evidence to show that the purchasing of image products is compulsive in the way that kleptomania, alcoholism, drug addiction, or gambling can be compulsive. Only in a figurative sense can a person be a "slave to fashion." "Compulsive" shopping seems to be nothing more than weakness of the will, or, if it is more serious, there is nothing to show that it is caused by advertising. Two other issues in this debate are worth commenting on; what are people's second-order desires with respect to the images of image advertising? And do image ads have an impact on the viewer by appealing to unconscious desires?

***Second-order Desires.*** Second-order desires are a way of approaching the question of whether persuasive advertising can "create wants which are not rational or truly those of the consumer" (Arrington 1982, p. 582). It is assumed that irrational and unwanted desires threaten a person's autonomy unless the person can control them. It is argued that the origins of a desire are not relevant to a person's autonomy if they can reflectively assess that desire relative to their interests, aims, and life plans, and if such reflection can create second-order desires that control the motivational force of the original desire. This concept of autonomy as based on higher-order desires has been criticized (e.g., Lehrer 1977, pp. 94–103) first because it seems to lead to an infinite regress of desires, and second because it is a poor basis for autonomy unless it can be shown that the higher-order desires themselves are autonomous. Image advertising needs to be considered in the terms set by this debate.

An image ad creates an image of an ideal person-type and attaches the product as a symbol to the image. If the viewer desires to posses the product as a result of the ad, presumably they have a desire to own a symbol of that image; if they do not intend to use the symbol ironically, then they probably have a first-order desire to use the symbol to express the self-image to themselves or to others. The ordered-desires theory of autonomy claims that the viewer is autonomous in possessing a desire if they do not have a second-order desire not to have the first-order desire; in our case, if they do not desire not to desire the expression of that self-image. The question is not whether the viewer can reject the image—if they do, there are many other images to choose from—rather, the question is, do people desire the image, and at the same time desire not to desire the image? This situation may be the simple, though not always easy, task of having to resist temptation. It would threaten a person's autonomy if an image ad created an unwanted desire that could not be resisted and if the second-order desire was rationally grounded. Whether significant numbers of people tend to be put in this situation by image ads is an empirical question; I know of no evidence that they are. Furthermore, if a person repeatedly loses their autonomy in this way, the rational thing to do is to avoid image ads, and we have already established that people have a large amount of choice in this, and that many people do the opposite—they actively seek image ads. This seems to imply a second-order desire to have the first-order desire. . . .

***Unconscious Desires.*** It is frequently argued that if advertising can create unconscious desires then it threatens our internal autonomy. This leads us to ask to what extent image ads work in a way that is unconscious to the viewer. Consider the Calvin Klein ad. "Motivational research" would say that this ad tries to persuade by using the viewer's unconscious desire of sex to control the specifics of their conscious desire for clothes (cf. Arrington, pp. 574–575). First, I am completely puzzled by any suggestion that sexual desire is unconscious, especially among the teenage target audience of this ad. The sexual content of the Calvin Klein ad is explicit—very explicit—not subliminal. Furthermore, the Calvin Klein ad is not selling sex, nor promising to satisfy sexual desires; it is selling an image and promising (truthfully) to help satisfy the desire to project a sexy personal image to oneself and others. This desire is not unconscious, nor is the appeal to the desire unconscious. People play the fashion image game quite consciously; they are well aware of the possibility of choice in fashion selection, and aware of choice in using fashion to create and project a self-image. They are also aware of looking at fashion ads for precisely this purpose. As Levitt (1970) says, "everybody everywhere wants to modify, transform, embellish, enrich and reconstruct the world around him" (p. 336). Image ads assume that people also want to reconstruct themselves and their image; this is not an unconscious desire. . . .

## Social Autonomy

The two concepts of autonomy discussed so far have been powerfully criticized for assuming that autonomy is a characteristic of isolated, independent individuals. Several philosophers, including Morwenna Griffiths whom we will rely on, have proposed an alternative concept of autonomy that recognizes that all people are embedded in social networks and dependent on other people; we will refer to this as "social autonomy."[4]

For Griffiths, the self is fragmented, always developing, and communally constructed because it is embedded in social relations with other people. The autonomous self, therefore, is not unified, static, or isolated; autonomy must be sought through an authentic "patchwork" (p. 191) of changing selves that participate in a web of fluid relationships with other people. Such relationships must avoid the traditional "master-slave" paradigm of controller and controlled; autonomy is not achieved through control or independence, but through mutual participation in creating the relationship with others. The self should not act on others, but interact with them. Autonomy is consistent with dependency. The web of the self's identity results from four attitudes toward others; wanting a relationship (love); not wanting one (resistance); being wanted (acceptance); and not being wanted (rejection). These apply to specific relations with identifiable others; they also apply to our relations with "invisible colleges"—that is, our identifying as a member of a large group, such as being a woman, being a writer, etc. (Griffiths 1995, pp. 86, 88, 90). Self-image is crucial to this continuous process of negotiating ever-changing relationships; the web of identity and the web of belonging are intertwined. . . .

## Conclusions Regarding Autonomy

Image advertising does not generally restrict autonomy of choice, autonomy of desire, nor social autonomy. One exception is that image ads can restrict autonomy of desire if they undermine self-esteem so severely that a person cannot undertake higher-order reflection on their own self-image and life plans. A second exception is the threat to social autonomy that results if image ads idealize domination and submission in personal relationships, or if they use exclusionary stereotypes of marginalized groups.

## CONCLUSIONS AND RECOMMENDATIONS

People are not passively manipulated by image ads. They actively participate when viewing image advertising, and actively participate in the image game. They seek out image ads, choose to and even pay to look at them, choose to accept the symbols they create, and choose to project self-identities through those symbols. They willingly pay large premiums to buy products they do not in any real sense need. Image ads would not work if targeted viewers were not proactive; the viewer has to read themselves into the ad or it will have no effect. . . .

Finally, we should remember that image ads create symbols that people are willing to buy; therefore, they contribute to the economy by creating something of value. Some writers have argued that persuasive advertising must be a threat to rational autonomy because in a world of purely rational logicians the persuasion would not work.[5] This is not true of image ads; even the most rational logicians could choose to buy a symbol to project an image.

And we should not forget that the image game is fun.

## NOTES

1. The ad appears in *Vogue* magazine, 1993, November issue, p. 247.
2. The ad was widely distributed as an insert in newspapers in early 1995.
3. Furthermore, ad budgets are only about 25 percent of promotion budgets; so outdoor ads are about 1.5 percent of promotion budgets. Figures are for Canada, c. 1990, from Darmon and LaRoche.
4. Griffiths's theory of autonomy is presented in her book *Feminisms and the Self: The Web of Identity*. A critique of her theory is beyond the scope of this paper; we will simply use it to assess the ethics of image ads.
5. Arrington quotes Jules Henry on this, p. 592.

## BIBLIOGRAPHY

Arrington, R. L. 1982. Advertising and Behavior Control. *Journal of Business Ethics* 1 (1982): 3–12. Republished in White 1993.

Bishop, J. D. 1997. How Gay Ads Corrupt Straight Men. Trail College Lecture presented at Trent University, March 1997.

Brady, J. 1995. Fueling, feeling the heat: Calvin Klein pushes into "different edge" with controversial jean ads. *Advertising Age* 66, no. 35, Sept. 4, 1995, p. 1.

Brenkert, G. G. 1998. Marketing to Inner-city Blacks: PowerMaster and Moral Responsibility. *Business Ethics Quarterly* 8 (1998): 1–18.

Crain, R. 1995. Rationale for CK ads feeble and hypocritical. *Advertising Age* 66, no. 35, Sept. 4, 1995, p. 16.

Crisp, R. 1897. Persuasive Advertising, Autonomy, and the Creation of Desire. *Journal of Business Ethics* 6 (1987): 413–418. Republished in Newton and Ford 1994.

Dyer, G. 1982. *Advertising as Communication.* London: Methuen.

Garfield, B. 1995. Publicity monster turns on Klein. *Advertising Age* 66, no. 35, Sept. 4, 1995, p. 17.

Griffiths, M. 1995. *Feminisms and the Self: the Web of Identity.* London: Routledge.

Lash, C. 1979. *The Culture of Narcissism.* New York: Warner.

Lehrer, K. 1997. *Self-Trust: A Study of Reason, Knowledge and Autonomy.* Oxford: Clarendon.

Levitt, T. 1970. The Morality (?) of Advertising. *Harvard Business Review* 48 (1970): 84–92. Republished in Boylan 1995.

Lippe, D. 1995. Readers rate Klein "porn" campaign. *Advertising Age* 66, no. 35, Sept. 4, 1995, p. 34.

Lippke, R. L. 1998. Advertising and the Social Conditions of Autonomy. *Business and Professional Ethics Journal* 8 (1998): 35–58. Republished in White 1993.

Paine, L. S. 1983. Children as Consumers: An Ethical Evaluation of Children's Television Advertising. *Business and Professional Ethics Journal* 3 (1983): 119–146. Republished in White 1993.

Post, J. E. 1986. The Ethics of Marketing: Nestle's Infant Formula. Published in Hoffman and Frederick.

Waide, J. 1987. The Making of Self and World in Advertising. *Journal of Business Ethics* 6 (1987): 73–79. Republished in White 1993.

Wernick, A. 1991. *Promotional Culture: Advertising, Ideology and Symbolic Expression.* London: Sage.

Williamson, J. 1978. *Decoding Advertisements: Ideology and Meaning in Advertising.* London: Marion Books.

Wolf, N. 1990. *The Beauty Myth.* Toronto: Random House.

Woods, G. 1995. We're Here, We're Queer and We're Not Going Catalogue Shopping. Published in Burston and Richardson.

# Information Disclosure in Sales

*David M. Holley*

The issue of information disclosure is an important topic for a number of areas of applied ethics. Discussions in medical ethics often deal with the question of how much information should be given to a patient by health care professionals. A central topic of journalistic ethics is what kind of information the public has a right to know. In business ethics, discussions of information disclosure have dealt with areas such as disclosure of health and safety risks to employees, financial information to stockholders, and product safety information to consumers.[1]

One area of business ethics which seems inadequately explored, but holds both theoretical and practical interest, is the question of exactly how much information a salesperson is obligated to give to a potential customer in selling a product. Unlike the field of health care in which roles such as physician or nurse are paradigms of professions which carry with them clearly recognized responsibilities to serve the best interest of the patient, a salesperson is not generally thought to have such a professional responsibility to customers. In fact it is usually expected that the activity of sales will involve a primary pursuit of the interests of the seller. While there are legal obligations to disclose certain types of information, the question of what moral responsibilities a salesperson has is open to dispute.

An attempt to resolve the matter and specify a salesperson's moral responsibilities to disclose information raises two important theoretical questions: (1) To what extent can ethical argument help to define the moral responsibilities of a social role when these are only vaguely defined in a culture? and (2) How is empirical information about common practice relevant to making normative judgments?

*Journal of Business Ethics* **17**:631–641, 1998. 

This paper considers these issues in the context of an examination of ethical responsibilities for information disclosure in sales. . . .

## MORAL GUIDELINES AND SOCIAL ROLES

Suppose we imagine the various options with regard to a salesperson's duty to disclose specific information in some situation to lie along a continuum with one end of the continuum representing a requirement for a high level of information disclosure and the other a requirement for a minimal level of information disclosure:

| Low level | | | | High level |
|---|---|---|---|---|
| 1 | 2 | 3 | 4 | 5 |

If we assume that a salesperson has a responsibility to answer a customer's questions nondeceptively, we could represent various points on the continuum as rules requiring particular levels of additional disclosure such as the following:

1. *Minimal Information Rule:* The buyer is responsible for acquiring information about the product. There is no obligation to give any information the buyer does not specifically ask about.
2. *Modified Minimal Information Rule:* The only additional information the seller is obligated to give is information a buyer might need to avoid risk of injury (safety information).
3. *Fairness Rule:* In addition to safety information, a seller is responsible for giving the buyer any information needed to make a reasonable judgment about whether to purchase the product which the buyer could not reasonably be expected to know about unless informed by the seller.
4. *Mutual Benefit Rule:* In addition to safety information, the seller is responsible for giving the buyer any information needed to make a reasonable judgment about whether to purchase the product which the buyer does not posses.
5. *Maximal Information Rule:* A seller is responsible for giving the buyer any information relevant to deciding whether to purchase the product.

What considerations might move us toward one end of the continuum or the other? One approach is to take the perspective of the buyer. A person attracted by the ideal of the golden rule might ask, "What would I want the salesperson to tell me if I were purchasing the product?" . . .

Trying to get a determinate answer from a moral ideal such as the golden rule also leads to some implausible conclusions. Suppose, for example, that what I would want as a buyer in some situation is an objective analysis of the merits and disadvantages of this product in relation to competing products. Does this automatically imply that the information should be supplied in the desired form by the salesperson? To think so is to disregard the salesperson's role as an advocate of the product. A jury member may need enough information to formulate a reasonable judgment of guilt or innocence, but it would be far-fetched to conclude that this gives the defense attorney a responsibility to provide all the necessary information. To think so overlooks the attorney's role as an advocate (as well as the responsibilities of others in the legal system).

These considerations suggest that deciding how much information a salesperson should provide depends upon an understanding of the nature of the salesperson's role. While there are various types of sales, we can say in general that a salesperson is supposed to act toward achieving a particular goal: getting people to purchase a product. Describing the activity as sales probably also implies that the method of achieving this goal is some type of persuasion rather than coercion. But determining the proper limits of this persuasion calls for some conception of the context of sales activities. If, for example, we viewed selling a product as a kind of game (a metaphor which has been applied to many business activities), then supplying or withholding information might plausibly be viewed as strategies employed to win (make the sale). If the game is like poker, we could even imagine that essentially deceptive strategies (bluffing) could be an accepted part of the game.[2] Someone adopting this picture might argue that a salesperson should disclose information only when it is strategically advantageous to do so.

However, this picture of sales activities is clearly deficient. Part of the problem is that it presupposes relatively equal parties who know that they are involved in a game and what the nature and goals of this game are. Even if this is adequate as an account of some business situations, it hardly seems to apply as a general picture of the buyer–seller relationship. Furthermore, efficient functioning of the buyer–seller relationship presupposes a higher degree of trust than game metaphors would suggest to be appropriate. Buyers must depend to some extent on information they receive from sellers, and if we imagine that the information is not reliable, we are imagining a situation which, if widespread enough, undermines the ends for which the marketplace exists.

On the other hand, the need of the buyer to depend on the seller is not as great as the need of a patient to rely on the objectivity and good judgment of a physician. In that case it seems necessary to build into the professional role a duty to seek the patient's wellbeing which limits and overrides the physician's activities as a profitseeker. The professional requirement is connected with the extreme vulnerability of patients to the pure pursuit of economic self-interest by physicians.

While buyers are generally less vulnerable than patients, there are cases where the interest involved is significant enough to call for certain limits on self-interest in the pursuit of a sale. For example, suppose that use of a product involves some danger of physical injury which the buyer is unlikely to know about. Withholding the information is in effect subjecting the buyer to a risk of physical injury which she/he does not voluntarily agree to accept. Given the importance of avoiding physical injury and the vulnerability of virtually everyone to hidden dangers, there would be a strong moral reason for modifying the minimal information rule to require that such risks be revealed. The limit here could be stated in terms of applying a general principle of non-injury to sales situations, perhaps something like "Do not act in ways which are likely to result in injury to another person without the informed and reasonable consent (explicit or implicit) of that person." . . .

## REASONABLE EXPECTATIONS AND BUYER KNOWLEDGE

The moral credentials of what I have called the fairness rule rest upon the claim that this rule assures fair treatment of all parties. I shall interpret this to mean that a system utilizing this rule gives all parties to a transaction an adequate opportunity to protect their individual interests. If information is needed but unavailable, it should be revealed; if it is needed and available the party who needs it can seek it out.

We should notice, however that applying this rule depends upon assessing what the buyer can reasonably be expected to know. How is this assessment to be made? Is the seller to think about what buyers in general can reasonably be expected to know, or about what some subgroup of buyers of which this buyer is a member can reasonably be expected to know, or perhaps about what this individual buyer can be expected to know? Different answers to this question yield different requirements about what information needs to be disclosed.

Suppose I am selling antiques, and I am dealing with a person I know to be a collector and retailer of antiques. It seems plausible to suggest that I would be justified in assuming this person to have a certain level of knowledge about the value of antiques. Suppose it becomes evident to me that this dealer is not aware of a distinction between the item I am selling and a more valuable item with which it might be confused. Do I have an obligation to enlighten him?

According to the mutual benefit rule, the answer would be yes. If we interpret the fairness rule to be relative to the individual person, we would have to determine whether this individual buyer could be expected to know this distinction, and it is unclear how such a determination is to be made. So perhaps the most promising way of applying the fairness rule is to regard "what a person can reasonably be expected to know" as applying relative to some relevant class membership. In this case I might have obligations to reveal to someone acting as an expert only what that person could not be expected to know, even with expertise in the field. Of course, in a particular case I might have good reason for revealing more: say, for example that I have a long-term relationship with this individual which has been mutually beneficial and that she would regard my withholding information I know she does not have negatively, possibly resulting in the disruption of the relationship, but this need not imply that there is a moral obligation to reveal the information.

If we interpret the fairness rule to apply relative to group membership and if we distinguish at least between cases in which the buyer is reasonably regarded as an expert in knowledge of some area from cases in which the buyer should not be regarded as an expert, the rule provides different guidance about what should be revealed to experts as opposed to what should be revealed to nonexperts. Should the class of nonexperts be subject to further division? Perhaps the general public could be divided into sophisticated consumers and unsophisticated or naive consumers. Given this distinction, the fairness rule would imply that a salesperson is obligated to reveal more when dealing with an unsophisticated consumer. The main problem with making this distinction is that it would be difficult in practice to determine the type of consumer being dealt with in a particular transaction. I might become aware that I am dealing with a particularly naive consumer, but how much effort must I expend in making such a determination?

From a practical point of view it would probably be more realistic to have some expectations of a level of information to be revealed to the general public which would result in informed and reasonable judgment in the vast majority of cases. Exactly how much information this is would depend on what level of informed judgment is high enough and what percentage of customers making such a judgment is good enough. Assuming that such a determination could be made, the fairness rule on this interpretation would require disclosure of information sufficient for a reasonable judgment by a high percentage of customers falling in the relevant class.

But what if in the course of a sales transaction it becomes evident that a particular buyer has not been given enough information to judge reasonably (e.g., because this buyer is more uninformed or naive than might be expected of the average buyer)? Or what if the buyer is using misinformation which the seller did not cause but could correct? If the fairness rule is to be interpreted to require that information be supplied in such cases, then it is functionally equivalent to the mutual benefit rule in these cases. This would probably be distasteful to most advocates of the fairness rule, since the whole point of a rule less stringent than the mutual benefit rule is to place some responsibility for acquiring information on the buyer rather than the seller. To build in a requirement that misinformation or ignorance must be corrected seems to defeat much of the purpose of the rule.

If the seller could distinguish between those buyers who could have acquired the relevant information with an appropriate level of effort and those who could not because of unavoidable deficiencies or circumstantial difficulties, it would be possible to make allowances for the latter class, but not the former. But except in obvious cases, such a distinction would often be difficult to make. So a decision to act in accordance with the fairness rule probably means deciding to withhold information both from the culpably irresponsible as well as many of the unavoidably ignorant.

## VULNERABILITY AND DEPENDENCE

It is relatively easy to think of some cases in which withholding information seems unconscionable. The financial advisor who sells to an elderly widow with very limited resources a risky investment without making the risk clear surely exemplifies substandard ethics. The failure to disclose in such a case takes advantage of one who is in a vulnerable position. Whatever we might say about exchanges in which both parties have adequate opportunity to protect their interests, we must still take into account that some individuals may be relatively defenseless, either permanently or temporarily. A disclosure rule which allows such people to be exploited when their vulnerability is apparent would fail one of the most basic of ethical tests. So if the fairness rule is to be ethically defensible, some restrictions must be built in to limit the pursuit of self-interest at the expense of those who might be persuaded to act in ways which are clearly contrary to their interests.

Some writers have raised the general question of whether a salesperson needs to behave paternalistically.[3] This way of putting the question can be misleading, since paternalistic action involves overriding or limiting another's choice or ability to choose. While a salesperson may occasionally have such a responsibility when dealing with individuals who are incompetent or behaving in clearly irrational ways, there is ordinarily no obligation to refuse to sell a legitimate product because the purchase is judged not to be in the buyer's interest. However, the question of how hard to push a sale when it appears to diverge from a customer's interest can arise fairly often. It is all very well to say that the customer is the one who should decide what is in his/her interest, but if the salesperson is strategically withholding information crucial to making such a judgment, this defense seems hollow.

Consider the case of a person of very limited education, intelligence, and sophistication who lives on a small social security income and needs roof repairs. A salesperson recommends and makes the case for a total reroofing with the finest materials available, a choice which will mean using up a small savings account and acquiring a significant debt. The salesperson makes no attempt to explore cheaper alternatives, and the customer is not sufficiently astute to inquire about them. What seems to make nondisclosure objectionable in this case is the customer's limited capacity to protect his own interests. He relies on the salesperson to provide not only information but a kind of guidance. To follow a policy or revealing only as much as an average customer would need in effect deprives this very vulnerable customer of what he needs to know, but is unable to learn without help.

Examples involving extremely vulnerable consumers suggest that even if the fairness rule were a sufficient guide to disclosure in some cases, there are situations in which the relationship between salesperson and customer involves such an imbalance of power that the customer is not adequately protected. In such cases the buyer is dependent on the seller for information, and failure to provide crucial information becomes more like a betrayal of trust than an admirable competitive move.

While cases involving extremely vulnerable individuals furnish the clearest illustrations of the limits of the fairness rule, we can see problems with this rule even in transactions involving more skillful buyers. Suppose Simon wants to buy a rocker-recliner. Because he has children who have been rough on furniture, Simon tells a salesperson that he is especially concerned about finding a piece that can endure their abuse. Simon notices that a particular manufacturer has advertised a "lifetime warranty" on its chairs. He assumes that this means that anything which goes wrong with the chair is covered. The salesperson knows that the lifetime warranty does not include the kind of damage children are likely to inflict on the chair, but does not mention this, nor does she mention that a cheaper chair of a lesser-known manufacturer with a more limited warranty is actually more likely to provide the kind of durability this customer seeks.

What is apparent from this kind of example is that ordinary customers often interpret the salesperson's role to be not merely an advocate for a particular product, but a kind of consultant who can be relied upon to help the customer satisfy particular needs. Withholding information of relevance to attaining such satisfaction would often be a refusal to accept a role the customer is expecting to be performed.

While we can imagine the marketplace working without salespeople functioning as consultants, the complexity of the modern marketplace often makes it practically necessary, even if not absolutely necessary, to rely on sellers to provide information which could have been attained with enough effort, but is not likely to be possessed by the average consumer because of a variety of limitations, including limitations of time. As a result the salesperson comes to be relied upon to provide the customer with enough information to enable him or her to satisfy particular needs.

This kind of dependence of customer on salesperson is avoidable only with great difficulty. It is a dependence brought about by complexities involved in navigating the marketplace under social conditions such as ours. The vulnerabilities brought about by such practical necessities create a need for building into the salesperson's role some degree of responsibility for providing information needed by the customer to judge how to satisfy his or her needs and desires.

Hence, the fairness rule is inadequate as a general account of what a salesperson is obligated to disclose. While there may be certain limited contexts in which such a rule can function, they would primarily involve individuals with significant expertise in a particular area and an implicit willingness to protect their own interests. Under such conditions it might be permissible to disregard the interests of the buyer, but we should not be misled into thinking of these as paradigmatic of the buyer-seller relationship generally.

## THE MUTUAL BENEFIT RULE

How far is a salesperson obligated to go in serving the customer's interests through information disclosure? The strongest kind of obligation which could be advocated would claim that a salesperson must seek to produce optimal benefit for the customer. Such a requirement would mean that a salesperson might often have to direct a customer to buy merchandise from a competitor offering superior or equal quality for a lower price. In effect it could virtually deny the salesperson's role as an advocate for her own company's products.

The maximal information rule calls upon the salesperson to provide any information relevant to deciding whether to purchase a product. Presumably this would include objective comparisons of the strengths and weaknesses of various alternatives. It would place on the salesperson the responsibility for supplying customers with the sort of analysis we expect from a *Consumer Reports* product test. While we can imagine such a requirement, it is difficult to see how it could work without undermining the competitive structure of the market.

What seems to be needed is a rule which could still allow the salesperson to function as a product advocate but limit that advocacy in ways conducive to fulfillment of the customer's needs. The mutual benefit rule requires the salesperson to disclose enough information to allow the customer to make a reasonable judgment about whether to purchase the product. How strict a requirement this is depends on how we interpret "reasonable." We need not interpret this term to designate an optimal choice. In most cases there are a range of products and purchases that could satisfy a particular customer's needs. Given varieties of product features, some may be better in some respects and worse in others, but equally satisfactory. Furthermore, there are many equally reasonable ways of evaluating how much money a particular product feature is worth or how much time and effort should be expended in shopping. It can be entirely reasonable to patronize a store with knowledgeable and reliable salespeople even if that occasionally means paying a higher price for comparable merchandise.

Thus, we could loosely interpret the mutual benefit rule to require that the salesperson provide enough information for a customer to make a judgment which is satisfactory, given his or her particular needs, desires, and budget. This need not imply a requirement to make extensive inquiries about the particular customer's situation (though some products such as life insurance or financial investments or home purchases might make such knowledge necessary). In most cases a salesperson could make general assumptions based on what most customers in the market for this kind of product are concerned about. As distinctive concerns or needs become apparent, however, this standard would require them to be taken into account. Hence, for example, in the rocker-recliner case described earlier, the customer's concern about damage children might cause is relevant to what information this customer needs.

The distinction between the mutual benefit rule and the maximal information rule is that the latter requires disclosure of all information relevant to a purchase decision while the former requires disclosure only of enough information for a reasonable judgment. Suppose we compare the two with regard to disclosure of price information. All relevant information would probably include clear cost comparisons to products with similar features sold by competitors. But given the above interpretation of "reasonable," the mutual benefit rule would allow disclosure of the price of a product without comparative information as long as the price is not so much out of line that the purchase could not be judged competitive. Requiring that comparative information about price be furnished only when the price is clearly uncompetitive is probably equivalent to a requirement to price one's products competitively, something most merchants would say the market generally requires them to do anyway.

The mutual benefit rule, even with the permissive interpretation I have given it, builds in some protection of customer vulnerabilities. The spirit of this rule of information disclosure would mean a salesperson should not knowingly encourage choices which would be against the interests of someone in the customer's position. Notice that is not the same as saying that the salesperson should always promote the choice he or she would have made in the customer's position. The salesperson is free under this rule, as I have interpreted it, to advocate a range of reasonable choices.

Such a rule would require the disclosure of defects which might significantly diminish the value of the product. Unlike the fairness rule, this requirement would apply regardless of whether the defects could be discovered with a reasonable amount of effort. It would not, however, require disclosure of all details which might be regarded as negative unless they clearly bear on a purchaser's central concerns.

Hence, one selling a house ordinarily need not disclose that the next-door neighbors are obnoxious, but would be required to disclose that the city planned to construct a major freeway a hundred yards away or that the foundation has a crack which will soon need repair.

With a relatively loose interpretation of what counts as a reasonable judgment, the mutual benefit rule comes closest to satisfying the important ethical and practical concerns. Hence, there is good reason to regard this rule as our primary norm for information disclosure in sales This conclusion is consistent with the possibility of recognizing specialized contexts in which buyers need fewer protections. So, for example, we might regard the fairness rule as adequate for situations in which buyers are representing themselves as professionals in the relevant field.

## CONCLUSION

I have attempted to use ethical argument to render more precise the extent of a salesperson's obligation to disclose information to a customer. The argument takes into account features of the contemporary marketplace which call for locating the disclosure requirement somewhere in the neighborhood of a permissively interpreted mutual benefit rule. Even if my argument is correct, it does not establish precisely what information needs to be revealed in every case since the concept of "reasonableness" used in interpreting the mutual benefit rule can be highly elastic. Nevertheless, it does furnish a guideline for ruling out some clearly unethical conduct as well as some conduct which some people's moral intuitions would allow.

## NOTES

1. E.g., Faden, R. and Tom Beauchamp: 1992, "The Right to Risk Information and the Right to Refuse Workplace Hazards," in Tom Beauchamp and Norman Bowie (eds.), *Ethical Theory and Business*, 6th ed. (Prentice-Hall, Englewood Cliffs, NJ). Frederick, Robert and Michael Hoffman: 1990, "The Individual Investor in Securities Markets: An Ethical Analysis," *Journal of Business Ethics* **9**, 579–589. Stern, Louis: 1967, "Consumer Protection via Increased Information," *Journal of Marketing* **31**, 48–52. DeGeorge, Richard: 1995: *Business Ethics*, 4th ed. "Corporate Disclosure" (Prentice-Hall, Englewood Cliffs, NJ), pp. 284–293.
2. Carr, Albert: 1968, "Is Business Bluffing Ethical?", *Harvard Business Review* **46**, 143–153.
3. Ebejer, James and Michael Morden: 1988, "Paternalism in the Marketplace: Should a Salesman Be His Buyer's Keeper?", *Journal of Business Ethics* **7**, 337–339. Walters, Kerry: 1989, "Limited Paternalism and the Pontius Pilate Plight," *Journal of Business Ethics* **8**, 955–962. Brockway, George: 1993, "Limited Paternalism and the Salesperson: A Reconsideration," *Journal of Business Ethics* **12**, 275–279.

# Deception and Withholding Information in Sales

*Thomas Carson*

## INTRODUCTION

Approximately 10 percent of the U.S. work force is involved in sales. In addition, most members of our society occasionally sell major holdings such as used cars and real estate. The ethics of sales is an important, but neglected, topic in business ethics. Only a handful of pa-

©2001. *Business Ethics Quarterly*, Volume 11, Issue 2, pp. 275–306.

pers, most of them quite short, have ever been written on this topic (no books have ever been written on the ethics of sales). David Holley's papers "A Moral Evaluation of Sales Practices" and "Information Disclosure in Sales" are the only full-length papers ever written on this topic (they are the only full-length papers that state and defend a theory about the moral duties of salespeople).[1]

Salespeople are often in a position to mislead customers and deceptive practices are common in many areas of sales. I argue that the likely harm to the buyer creates a strong presumption for thinking that deception in sales is morally wrong. Except in very unusual cases, deception in sales cannot be justified. I also argue that deception in sales is wrong because it violates the golden rule. . . .

## PRELIMINARIES

### A Conceptual Roadmap

We need to distinguish between deception, lying, withholding information, and concealing information. Roughly, to deceive someone is to cause her to have false beliefs (or intentionally cause her to have false beliefs). Standard dictionary definitions of lying say that a lie is a false statement made with the intent to deceive others. The *Oxford English Dictionary* defines a lie as: "a false statement made with the intent to deceive."[2] *Webster's International Dictionary of the English Language* (1929) gives the following definition of the verb "lie": "to utter a falsehood with the intent to deceive."[3] Lying arguably requires the intent to deceive others, but lies that don't succeed in causing others to have false beliefs are not instances of deception. A further difference between lying and deception is that, while a lie must be a false statement, deception needn't involve false statements; true statements can be deceptive and some forms of deception don't involve making statements of any sort. Thus, many instances of deception do not constitute lying. Withholding information does not constitute deception. It is not case of *causing* someone to have false beliefs; it is merely a case of failing to correct false beliefs or incomplete information. On the other hand, actively concealing information often constitutes deception. For example, if painting over the rust on a used car caused a potential buyer to believe falsely that the body of the car was in good condition, doing so would constitute deception.

### The Common-Law Principle of *Caveat Emptor*

Traditionally, many salespeople have followed the principle of *caveat emptor* ("buyer beware"). According to the common-law principle of *caveat emptor*, sellers are not legally obligated to inform prospective buyers about the properties of the goods they sell. Under *caveat emptor*, sales and contracts to sell are legally enforceable even if the seller fails to inform the buyer of serious defects in the goods that are sold. English common law sometimes called for the enforcement of sales in cases in which sellers made false or misleading statements about the goods they sold. Under *caveat emptor*, buyers themselves are responsible for determining the quality of the goods they purchase. . . .

Many salespeople take the law to be an acceptable moral standard for their conduct and claim that they have no moral duty to provide buyers with information about the goods they sell, except for information that the law requires for an enforceable sale.

### Who Is a Salesperson?

Car salespeople, realtors, sales representatives who sell supplies or equipment to businesses, and private individuals who sell their own cars or homes are paradigm cases of salespeople. A cashier in a store who rings up the bill and is not expected to advise customers in any way is not a salesperson. I will use the term "salesperson" fairly broadly to include people who "wait on customers" in stores, e.g., clothing, hardware, and shoe stores. Roughly, a salesperson is anyone who sells things and whose position requires him to advise buyers on their purchases or supply them with information about what they are purchasing. People who assist customers on the floors of large warehouse stores are borderline cases for the concept of a salesperson. . . .

## HOLLEY ON WITHHOLDING INFORMATION

Holley's theory is based on his concept of a "voluntary" or "mutually beneficial" market exchange. Holley says that a voluntary exchange occurs "only if" the following conditions are met:

1. Both buyer and seller understand what they are giving up and what they are receiving in return.
2. Neither buyer nor seller is compelled to enter into the exchange as a result of coercion, severely restricted alternatives, or other constrains on the ability to choose.
3. Both buyer and seller are able at the time of the exchange to make rational judgments about its costs and benefits.[4]

These three criteria admit of degrees of satisfaction. An ideal exchange is an exchange involving people who are fully informed, fully rational, and "enter into the exchange entirely of their own volition." The conditions for an ideal exchange are seldom, if ever, met in practice. However, Holley claims that it is still possible to have an "acceptable exchange" if the parties are "adequately informed, rational and free from compulsion."

According to Holley, "the primary duty of salespeople to customers is to avoid undermining the conditions of an acceptable exchange." He makes it clear that, on his view, acts of omission (as well as acts of commission) can undermine the conditions of an acceptable exchange. This means that a salesperson can't be morally justified in doing any of the following:

1. Coercing customers.
2. Deceiving customers.
3. Lying to customers.
4. Withholding information necessary for an acceptable exchange (which the customer lacks). [*Comment:* often, it is difficult for a salesperson to know whether or not she is doing this, because she doesn't know what sort of information customers posses. A salesperson might know that a certain piece of information is necessary for an acceptable exchange, but not know whether or not the customer possesses that information.]
5. Doing things that undermine the rationality of the other party.
6. Taking advantage of the irrationality of the other party.
7. Taking advantage of the other person's lack of options.

Because of the complexity of many goods and services, customers often lack information necessary for an acceptable exchange. Careful examination of products will not necessarily reveal problems or defects. According to Holley, *caveat emptor* is not acceptable as a moral principle, because customers often lack information necessary for an acceptable exchange. In such cases, it is not permissible for salespeople to withhold that information. In order to ensure that the conditions for an acceptable exchange are met, salespeople often need to give information to the buyer. The question then is: *what* information do salespeople need to offer buyers in order to ensure that the buyer is adequately informed? Holley attempts to answer this question in the following passage in which he appeals to the golden rule:

> Determining exactly how much information needs to be provided is not always clear-cut. We must in general rely on our assessments of what a reasonable person would want to know. As a practical guide, a salesperson might consider, "What would I want to know, if I were considering buying this product"?

This principle is very demanding, perhaps more demanding than Holley realizes. Presumably, most reasonable people would *want* to know a *great deal* about the things they are thinking of buying. They might want to know *everything* that is relevant to the decision whether or not to buy something. (This is not to say that they would always be willing to take a great deal of time, trouble, or expense to obtain that information, but just that they would *want* that information, other things being equal.)

## CRITICISMS OF HOLLEY

This section offers numerous criticisms of Holley, far more than are necessary for the purposes of refuting his theory. These criticisms, however, are not superfluous. A crucial part of the justification for my own theory is that it avoids *all* of these criticisms. My criticisms of Holley point to problems that any adequate theory about the duties of salespeople must be able to resolve. . . .

1. Often salespeople can devote only a very limited amount of time to any given customer. When time does not permit it, a salesperson cannot be morally obligated to provide all information necessary to ensure that the customer is "adequately informed" (all the information that a reasonable consumer would *want* to know were she in the buyer's position). In many cases, reasonable consumers would *want* to know a great deal of information. Often salespeople simply don't have the time to give all customers all the information that Holley deems necessary for an acceptable exchange. It cannot be a person's duty to do what is impossible—the statement that someone *ought* to do a certain act implies that she *can* do that act. I have three closely related criticisms of Holley. A. Often, salespeople don't know all of the information necessary for an acceptable exchange. In such cases, it cannot be their moral duty to provide such information. B. Even if it's *possible* for a salesperson to provide all customers with all the information that Holley requires her to give, doing so might be so time-consuming that she couldn't deal with enough customers to earn a decent income. Salespeople working on commission cannot be expected to work at a pace that makes it impossible for them to earn a decent living. C. Often salespeople simply don't know enough about the buyer's level of knowledge or ignorance to know what information they need to give the buyer in order to ensure that she is adequately informed. Usually the best clues as to the buyer's state of knowledge are the buyer's own questions. Discussions of the ethics of sales are much too focused on determining, in the abstract, what information salespeople do or do not need to give customers. They need to pay more attention to the question of how salespeople should answer questions that prospective buyers actually ask of them. . . .
2. Holley's theory implies that a salesperson in a store would be obligated to inform customers that a particular piece of merchandise in her store sells for less at a competing store if she knows this to be the case. (Presumably, she would *want* to know where she can get it for the lowest price, were she herself considering buying the product.) Not only do salespeople have no duty to provide this kind of information, (ordinarily) it would be *wrong* for them to do so.
3. (This point is related to #2.) Most salespeople work for employers, e.g., stores, auto dealers, and insurance companies. Salespeople not only have moral duties to customers, they also have duties to employers. Their duties to customers can conflict with their duties to their employers. Any adequate account of the duties of salespeople must balance the claims of customers and employers. This is part of what is wrong with Holley's use of the golden rule. It's not enough for the salesperson to ask what she would want to know were she in the position of the customer—this fails to do justice to the claims of her employer. This is not an objection to the golden rule *per se*. In cases in which an action affects more than one person, the golden rule does *not* tell us to pick *one* of those individuals and ask what we would want to be done were we in *that person's position*. The golden rule (or at least those versions of it that are *plausible*) requires that we consider the desires and interest of *all* the affected parties (see sections IX and XI).
4. Holley's theory seems to yield unacceptable consequences in cases in which the buyer's alternatives are severely constrained. Suppose that

someone who has a very modest income is attempting to buy a house in a small town. The buyer's options are severely constrained, since there is only one house for sale in her price range and very few houses or apartments for rent. According to Holley, there can't be an acceptable exchange in such cases because condition #2 is not satisfied. However, it's not clear what he thinks sellers ought to do in such cases. The seller can't be expected to remove these constraints by giving the buyer money or building more houses in the town. Holley's view seems to imply that it would be wrong for anyone to sell a house to such a person. This result is unacceptable. . . .

## TOWARD A MORE PLAUSIBLE THEORY ABOUT DECEPTION AND WITHHOLDING INFORMATION IN SALES

Salespeople have certain moral duties regarding the disclosure of information when dealing with *rational adult consumers.* I formulate and defend a provisional list of these duties below. These are *prima facie* duties that can conflict with other duties and are sometimes overridden by other duties. (A *prima facie* duty is one's actual duty, other things being equal. Alternatively, a *prima facie* duty is an actual duty in the absence of conflicting duties of greater or equal importance.) Salespeople have other duties to customers that don't concern the disclosure of information; my list does not purport to be a complete list of the moral duties of salespeople. The following are (*prima facie*) duties of salespeople concerning the disclosure of information:

1. Salespeople should provide buyers with safety warnings and precautions about the goods and services they sell. Sometimes it is enough for salespeople to call attention to written warnings and precautions that come with the goods and services in question. These warnings are unnecessary if the buyers already understand the dangers or precautions in question.
2. Sales people should refrain from lying and deception in their dealings with customers.
3. As much as their knowledge and time constraints permit, salespeople should fully answer customers' questions about the products or services they are selling. They should answer questions forthrightly and not evade questions or withhold information that has been asked for (even if this makes it less likely that they will make a successful sale). Salespeople are obligated to answer questions about the goods and services they, themselves, sell. However, they are not obligated to answer questions about competing goods and services or give information about other sellers. In such cases, the salesperson should refuse to answer the question, not evade it or pretend to answer it.
4. Salespeople should not try to "steer" customers toward purchases that they have reason to think will cause significant harm to customers (financial harm counts) or that customers will come to deeply regret. [Any means by which one tries to cause another to purchase a particular good or service counts as "steering" him toward purchasing it.]

1–4 is a minimal list of the duties of salespeople concerning the disclosure of information. I am inclined to think that the following are also *prima facie* duties of salespeople concerning the disclosure of information, but I am much less confident that these principles can be justified:

5. Salespeople should not sell customers goods or services that they have reason to think will prove to be harmful to customers (financial harm counts) or that the customers will come to regret later, without giving the customers their reasons for thinking that this is the case. [This duty does not hold if the seller has good reasons to think that the customer already possesses the information in question. Ordinarily, salespeople are not obligated to warn customers about the dangers of such things as tobacco, alcohol, and fast cars.]
6. Salespeople should not sell items they know to be defective or of poor quality without alerting customers to this. [This duty does not hold if the buyer knows or can be reasonably expected to know about the poor quality of what he is buying.]

### Connections Between 2, 4, and 6

Lying and deception in sales are not confined to lying to or deceiving customers about the goods one sells. Many salespeople misrepresent their own motives to customers/clients (case 2 from section III is a good example of this.) Almost all salespeople invite the trust of customers/clients and claim, implicitly or explicitly, to be acting in their interests. Salespeople often ask customers to defer to their judgment about what is best for them. For most salespeople, gaining the trust of customers/clients is essential for success in sales. Many salespeople are *not* interested in helping customers in the way they represent themselves as being. A salesperson who misrepresents motives and intentions to customers is guilty of violating 2 (or a least guilty of *attempting* to deceive customers/clients). This kind of simultaneous inviting and betrayal of trust is a kind of treachery. In ordinary cases, rules against lying and deception alone prohibit salespeople from steering customers toward goods or services they have reason to think will be bad for them. It is difficult to steer someone in this way without lying or deception. In order to do this, salespeople may need to deceive customers about the features of the items they sell or about the quality and availability of alternative goods and services. Salespeople are often asked to recommend what they think is best for the customer. To recommend something one knows to be unsuitable for the customer in response to such a request would be deceptive. In such a case, it would be a lie to assert that the item in question is, in one's opinion, the one that is best for they buyer. Similar remarks apply to selling defective goods. Often it is impossible to do this without lying to or deceiving customers. In practice, most violations of rules 4 and 6 are also violations of rule 2.

## A JUSTIFICATION FOR MY THEORY

I have two different lines of argument for my theory. First, 1–4 yield intuitively plausible results in concrete cases and avoid *all* of the objections I raised against Holley and Ebejer and Morden. Second, I justify 1–4 by appeal to the golden rule and consistency requirement for moral judgments. Some readers may regard this second line of argument as redundant. However, I disagree. People don't always agree in their moral intuitions about moral issues in sales. Mere appeal to intuitions cannot settle these or any other controversial moral questions. The appeal to "our" moral intuitions doesn't give us any answer to skeptical challenges to morality or any answer to those who attempt to justify or rationalize ostensibly wrong acts that serve their own self-interests. These individuals—I'm thinking of people like Albert Carr—will simply report conflicting moral intuitions. Answering such individuals (and attempting to show *why* they are mistaken) is part of the task of business ethics. Work in business ethics cannot simply appeal to the moral intuitions or shared beliefs of the converted.

Taken together, 1–4 give us an intuitively plausible theory about the duties of salespeople regarding the disclosure of information; they give more acceptable results in actual cases than the theories of Holley and Ebejer and Morden. 1–4 don't permit salespeople to lie to or deceive customers, fail to warn them of hazards, or fail to answer their questions about the things they are selling (except in unusual cases—see below). But, unlike Holley's theory and Ebejer and Morden's theory, 1–4 do not make unreasonable demands on salespeople. They don't require that salespeople provide information that they don't have or spend more time with customers than they can spend. Nor do they require salespeople to divulge information about the virtues of what competitors are selling things to people who have limited options, nor do they employ ambiguous concepts such as the concept of "expert knowledge." My theory avoids all of the objections I raised against Holley and Ebejer and Morden.

In addition, my theory explains why different types of salespeople have different sorts of duties of their customers. For example, ordinarily, realtors have a duty to provide much more information to customers than sales clerks who sell inexpensive items in gift stores. My theory explains this difference in terms of the following: 1. the realtor's greater knowledge and expertise (the realtor is able to provide far more information than the sales clerk), 2. the much greater amount of time the realtor can devote to the customer, 3. the greater importance of the purchase of a home than the purchase of small gift and the greater potential for harm or benefit to the buyer (this means that violations of moral obligations are a much more serious matter in the case of realtors), 4. the fact that home buyers generally *ask* realtors for a great deal more information than customers ask of sales clerks in gift stores, and (in some cases) 5. implicit or explicit claims by the relator to be acting on behalf of prospective home buyers (clerks in stores rarely make such claims).

### An Objection Considered

On my view, salespeople are required to give safety warnings and answer customers' questions, but they are not obligated to ensure that customers are adequately informed. Some customers aren't sufficiently well informed to know what questions they need to ask of salespeople. It might be objected that when dealing with such individuals salespeople are obligated to do more than follow 1–4. 1–4 imply that it is *prima facie* wrong to take advantage of customers' ignorance by deceiving them or steering them toward purchases that are likely to cause them significant harm. Suppose, however, that without being steered or deceived, an ill-informed customer who doesn't know what questions to ask is about to make a purchase that will harm him. What are the seller's obligations in such a case? Often salespeople don't know enough about the customer's state of knowledge or ignorance to know whether or not the customer is asking the right questions. (A customer who doesn't ask questions, might know so much that he doesn't need any further information, or he might be so ignorant that he doesn't know what questions to ask.) Suppose that the salesperson *knows* that the buyer is ignorant and unable to ask appropriate questions. (Such cases are, I think, unusual.) What are the seller's duties in such a case? My intuitions tell me that a salesperson has a *prima facie* duty to warn the customer about the harm he is likely to suffer. However, since others report very different moral intuitions about such cases, and because there is no reason to think that my moral intuitions are more reliable than theirs, the appeal to moral intuitions alone cannot settle this matter. The ultimate answer to the question about what sellers ought to do in cases of the sort at issue depends on the success or failure of other sorts of arguments for principle 5 or principles similar to 5. (5 implies that the seller is obligated to caution the buyer in this kind of case.) For my own part, I think that it is unclear whether or not 5 can be justified (see section IX below), so I take it to be an open question whether 5 is one of the *prima facie* duties of salespeople.

The view that 1–4, and 1–4 alone, are *prima facie* duties of salespeople conflicts with some peoples' moral intuitions in cases of the sort in question. But, *by itself*, this is not a decisive objection to the view in question. Salespeople typically work for themselves or their employers. Buyers understand this. In the case of major purchases such as automobiles and houses, buyers understand the importance of the purchase and the importance of making a rational informed decision. In cases in which buyers don't know enough to ask the right questions, it is common for them to seek help from friends or family members (or even bring them along when they talk to salespeople). It is reasonable for sellers to assume that uninformed customers have sought help or advice before making major purchases. Uninformed consumers do not fare as well in the market as informed consumers. Sellers are not obligated to act as agents for customers or to compensate for their ignorance.

## The Golden Rule

The best-known version of the golden rule (at least in the West) is found in the New Testament. Jesus' version of the golden rule commands us to act toward others as we would be willing to have them act toward us. Jesus gives two statements of the golden rule in the New Testament (New Revised Standard Version): "Do to others as you would have them do to you" (Luke 6:31); "In everything do to others as you would have them do to you; for this is the law and the prophets" (Matthew 7:12). Jesus' version of the golden rule can be construed as a test of the moral rightness of actions that states a *necessary* condition for a right action. On this reading, the golden rule implies that an act is morally permissible only if the agent is willing to have others do the same act to him in similar circumstances (an act is morally wrong if the agent is unwilling to have others do the same act to him in similar circumstances). The golden rule can also be construed as a consistency principle (according to which those who violate the golden rule are guilty of inconsistency). I believe that the following version of the golden rule can be justified:

> GR. Consistency requires that if you think that it would be morally permissible for someone to do a certain act to another person, then you must consent to the idea of someone else doing the same act to you in relevantly similar circumstances.

This is consistent with, but not equivalent to, the version of the golden rule stated by Jesus. . . . I don't offer this as an interpretation of what Jesus and other religious teachers meant by the golden rule, nor I do I claim that this is the only version of the golden rule that can be justified. I claim only that this particular version of the golden rule *can* be justified and that it can be used to show that those who reject 1–4 as *prima facie* duties for salespeople are inconsistent.

### How the golden rule supports 1–4

Given this version of the golden rule, any rational and consistent moral judge who makes judgments about the moral obligations of salespeople must accept 1–4 as at least *prima facie* duties. Consider duty 1. All of us have reason to fear the hazards about us in the world and all of us depend on others to warn us of hazards. Few people would survive to adulthood were it not for the warnings of others about such things as oncoming cars, live electric wires, and approaching tornadoes. No one who values her own life can honestly say that she is willing to have others fail to warn her of dangers. 2. Like everyone else, a salesperson needs correct information in order to act effectively to achieve her goals and advance her interest. She is not willing to act on the basis of false beliefs. Consequently, she is not willing to have others deceive her or lie to her about matters relevant to her decisions in the marketplace. She is not willing to have members of other professions (such as law and medicine) make it a policy to deceive her or lie to her whenever they can gain financially from doing so. 3. Salespeople have questions about the goods and services they themselves buy. They can't say that they are willing to have others evade or refuse to answer those questions. We want our questions to be answered by salespeople or else we wouldn't ask them. We are not willing to have salespeople evade or refrain from answering our questions. [*Digression:* Principle 3 permits salespeople to refuse to answer questions that would force them to provide information about their competitors. Why should we say *this*? Why not say instead that salespeople are obligated to answer *all questions* that customers ask? The answer is that we are not willing to do this if we imagine ourselves in the position of the salesperson's employer. A salesperson's actions affect *both* her customers and her employer. In applying the golden rule to this issue she can't simply ask what kind of information she would want were she in the customer's position. (Holly poses the question in this way; see V.3.) 3 is a reasonable principle that takes into account the interests of customers, the salesperson, and her employer. 3 can probably be improved upon, but it is a decent first approximation. A reasonable person could endorse something like 3 as a policy for salespeople to follow. A disinterested person who was not trying to give preference to the interests of salespeople, employers, or customers could endorse 3. We can and must recognize the legitimacy of employers' demands for loyalty. The role of being an advocate or agent for someone who is selling things is legitimate within certain bounds—almost all of us are willing to have real estate agents work for us. A rational person could consent to the idea that everyone follow principles such as 3. *End of Digression.*] 4. All of us are capable of being manipulated by others into doing things that will harm us, especially in cases in which others are more knowledgeable than we are. No one can consent to the idea that other people (or salespeople) should manipulate us into doing things that significantly harm us whenever doing so is to their own advantage. Salespeople who claim that it would be permissible for them to make it a policy to deceive customers, fail to warn them about dangers, evade their questions, or manipulate them into doing things that are harmful to them whenever doing so is advantageous to them are inconsistent because they are not willing to have others do the same to them. They must allow that 1–4 are *prima facie* moral duties. . . .

## NOTES

1. David Holley, "A Moral Evaluation of Sales Practices." *Business and Professional Ethics Journal* 5 (1986): 3–21; "Information Disclosure in Sales," *Journal of Business Ethics* 17 (1998): 631–641. (My references to "A Moral Evaluation of Sales Practices" are to the version reprinted in *Ethical Theory and Business,* fourth edition, ed. Tom Beauchamp and Norman Bowie (Englewood Cliffs, N.J: Prentice Hall, 1993), pp. 462–472.
2. *Oxford English Dictionary,* second edition (Oxford: The Clarendon Press, 1989).
3. I think we need to add another condition to this definition of lying: in order for a false statement to be a lie the person who makes it must know or believe that it is false. (See my papers, "On the Definition of Lying: A Reply to Jones and Revisions," *Journal of Business Ethics* **7** (1988): 509–514 and "Second Thoughts on Bluffing," *Business Ethics Quarterly* 3 (1993): 317–341.)
4. Holley, "A Moral Evaluation of Sales Practices," p. 463.

## BLUFFING

# Is Business Bluffing Ethical?

*Albert Z. Carr*

A respected businessman with whom I discussed the theme of this article remarked with some heat, "You mean to say you're going to encourage men to bluff? Why, bluffing is nothing more than a form of lying! You're advising them to lie!"

I agreed that the basis of private morality is a respect for truth and that the closer a businessman comes to the truth, the more he deserves respect. At the same time, I suggested that most bluffing in business might be regarded simply as game strategy—much like bluffing in poker, which does not reflect on the morality of the bluffer.

I quoted Henry Taylor, the British statesman who pointed out that "falsehood ceases to be falsehood when it is understood on all sides that the truth is not expected to be spoken"—an exact description of bluffing in poker, diplomacy and business. I cited the analogy of the criminal court, where the criminal is not expected to tell the truth when he pleads "not guilty." Everyone from the judge down takes it for granted that the job the of the defendant's attorney is to get his client off, not to reveal the truth; and this is considered ethical practice. I mentioned Representative Omar Burleson, the Democrat from Texas, who was quoted as saying, in regard to the ethics of Congress, "Ethics is a barrel of worms"[1]—a pungent summing up of the problem of deciding who is ethical in politics.

I reminded my friend that millions of businessmen feel constrained every day to say *yes* to their bosses when they secretly believe *no* and that this is generally accepted as permissible strategy when the alternative might be the loss of a job. The essential point, I said, is that the ethics of business are game ethics, different from the ethics of religion.

He remained unconvinced. Referring to the company of which he is president, he declared: "Maybe that's good enough for some businessmen, but I can tell you that we pride ourselves on our ethics. In 30 years not one customer has ever questioned my word or asked to check our figures. We're loyal to our customers and fair to our suppliers. I regard my handshake on a deal as a contract. I've never entered into price-fixing schemes with my competitors. I've never allowed my salesmen to spread injurious rumors about other companies. Our union contract is the best in our industry. And, if I do say so myself, our ethical standards are of the highest!"

He really was saying, without realizing it, that he was living up to the ethical standards of the business game—which are a far cry from those of private life. Like a gentlemanly poker player, he did not play in cahoots with others at the table, try to smear their reputations, or hold back chips he owed them.

But this same fine man, at that very time, was allowing one of his products to be advertised in a way that made it sound a great deal better than it actually was. Another item in his product line was notorious among dealers for its "built-in obsolescence." He was holding back from the market a much-improved product because he did not want to interfere with sales of the inferior item it would have replaced. He had joined with certain of his competitors in hiring a lobbyist to push a state legislature, by methods that he preferred not to know too much about, into amending a bill then being enacted.

From Albert Z. Carr, "Is Business Bluffing Ethical?" *Harvard Business Review* (January/February 1968). Reprinted by permission of the *Harvard Business Review.* 

In his view these things had nothing to do with ethics; they were merely normal business practice. He himself undoubtedly avoided outright falsehoods—never lied in so many words. But the entire organization that he ruled was deeply involved in numerous strategies of deception.

## PRESSURE TO DECEIVE

Most executives from time to time are almost compelled, in the interests of their companies or themselves, to practice some form of deception when negotiating with customers, dealers, labor unions, government officials, or even other departments of their companies. By conscious misstatements, concealment of pertinent facts, or exaggeration—in short, by bluffing—they seek to persuade others to agree with them. I think it is fair to say that if the individual executive refuses to bluff from time to time—if he feels obligated to tell the truth, the whole truth, and nothing but the truth—he is ignoring opportunities permitted under the rules and is at a heavy disadvantage in his business dealings.

But here and there a businessman is unable to reconcile himself to the bluff in which he plays a part. His conscience, perhaps spurred by religious idealism, troubles him. He feels guilty; he may develop an ulcer or a nervous tic. Before any executive can make profitable use of the strategy of the bluff, he needs to make sure that in bluffing he will not lose self-respect or become emotionally disturbed. If he is to reconcile personal integrity and high standards of honesty with the practical requirements of business, he must feel that his bluffs are ethically justified. The justification rests on the fact that business, as practiced by individuals as well as by corporations, has the impersonal character of a game—a game that demands both special strategy and an understanding of its special ethics.

The game is played at all levels of corporate life, from the highest to the lowest. At the very instant that a man decides to enter business, he may be forced into a game situation, as is shown by the recent experience of a Cornell honor graduate who applied for a job with a large company. This applicant was given a psychological test which included the statement, "Of the following magazines, check any that you have read either regularly or from time to time, and double-check those which interest you most. *Reader's Digest, Time, Fortune, Saturday Evening Post, The New Republic, Life, Look, Ramparts, Newsweek, Business Week, U.S. News & World Report, The Nation, Playboy, Esquire, Harper's, Sports Illustrated.*"

His tastes in reading were broad, and at one time or another he had read almost all of these magazines. He was a subscriber to *The New Republic,* an enthusiast for *Ramparts,* and an avid student of the pictures in *Playboy.* He was not sure whether his interest in *Playboy* would be held against him, but he had a shrewd suspicion that if he confessed to an interest in *Ramparts* and *The New Republic,* he would be thought a liberal, a radical, or at least an intellectual, and his chances of getting the job, which he needed, would greatly diminish. He therefore checked five of the more conservative magazines. Apparently it was a sound decision, for he got the job.

He had made a game player's decision, consistent with business ethics.

A similar case is that of a magazine space salesman who, owing to a merger, suddenly found himself out of a job:

> This man was 58, and, in spite of a good record, his chance of getting a job elsewhere in a business where youth is favored in hiring practice was not good. He was a vigorous, healthy man, and only a considerable amount of gray in his hair suggested his age. Before beginning his job search he touched up his hair with a black dye to confine the gray to his temples. He knew that the truth about his age might well come out in time, but he calculated that he could deal with that situation

> when it arose. He and his wife decided that he could easily pass for 45, and he so stated his age on his résumé.

This was a lie: yet within the accepted rules of the business game, no moral culpability attaches to it.

## THE POKER ANALOGY

We can learn a good deal about the nature of business by comparing it with poker. While both have a large element of chance, in the long run the winner is the man who plays with steady skill. In both games ultimate victory requires intimate knowledge of the rules, insight into the psychology of the other players, a bold front, a considerable amount of self-discipline, and the ability to respond swiftly and effectively to opportunities provided by chance.

No one expects poker to be played on the ethical principles preached in churches. In poker it is right and proper to bluff a friend out of the rewards of being dealt a good hand. A player feels no more than a slight twinge of sympathy, if that, when—with nothing better than a single ace in his hand—he strips a heavy loser, who holds a pair, of the rest of his chips. It was up to the other fellow to protect himself. In the words of an excellent poker player, former President Harry Truman, "If you can't stand the heat, stay out of the kitchen." If one shows mercy to a loser in poker, it is a personal gesture, divorced from the rules of the game.

Poker has its special ethics, and here I am not referring to rules against cheating. The man who keeps an ace up his sleeve or who marks the cards is more than unethical; he is a crook, and can be punished as such—kicked out of the game or, in the Old West, shot.

In contrast to the cheat, the unethical poker player is one who, while abiding by the letter of the rules, finds ways to put the other players at an unfair disadvantage. Perhaps he unnerves them with loud talk. Or he tries to get them drunk. Or he plays in cahoots with someone else at the table. Ethical poker players frown on such tactics.

Poker's own brand of ethics is different from the ethical ideals of civilized human relationships. The game calls for distrust of the other fellow. It ignores the claim of friendship. Cunning deception and concealment of one's strength and intentions, not kindness and openheartedness, are vital in poker. No one thinks any the worse of poker on that account. And no one should think any the worse of the game of business because its standards of right and wrong differ from the prevailing traditions of morality in our society. . . .

## "WE DON'T MAKE THE LAWS"

Wherever we turn in business, we can perceive the sharp distinction between its ethical standards and those of the churches. Newspapers abound with sensational stories growing out of this distinction:

> We read one day that Senator Philip A. Hart of Michigan has attacked food processors for deceptive packaging of numerous products.[2]
>
> The next day there is a Congressional to-do over Ralph Nader's book, *Unsafe At Any Speed*, which demonstrates that automobile companies for years have neglected the safety of car-owning families.[3]
>
> Then another Senator, Lee Metcalf of Montana, and journalist Vic Reinemer show in their book, *Overcharge*, the methods by which utility companies elude regulating government bodies to extract unduly large payments from users of electricity.[4]

These are merely dramatic instances of a prevailing condition; there is hardly a major industry at which a similar attack could not be aimed. Critics of business regard such behavior as unethical, but the companies concerned know that they are merely playing the business game.

Among the most respected of our business institutions are the insurance companies. A group of insurance executives meeting recently in New England was startled when their guest speaker, social critic Daniel Patrick Moynihan, roundly berated them for "unethical" practices. They had been guilty, Moynihan alleged, of using outdated actuarial tables to obtain unfairly high premiums. They habitually delayed the hearings of lawsuits against them in order to tire out the plaintiffs and win cheap settlements. In their employment policies they use ingenious devices to discriminate against certain minority groups.[5]

It was difficult for the audience to deny the validity of these charges. But these men were business game players. Their reaction to Moynihan's attack was much the same as that of the automobile manufacturers to Nader, of the utilities to Senator Metcalf, and of the food processors to Senator Hart. If the laws governing their businesses change, or if public opinion becomes clamorous, they will make the necessary adjustments. But morally they have in their view done nothing wrong. As long as they comply with the letter of the law, they are within their rights to operate their businesses as they see fit.

The small business is in the same position as the great corporation in this respect. For example:

> In 1967 a key manufacturer was accused of providing master keys for automobiles to mail-order customers, although it was obvious that some of the purchasers might be automobile thieves. His defense was plain and straightforward. If there was nothing in the law to prevent him from selling his keys to anyone who ordered them, it was not up to him to inquire as to his customers' motives. Why was it any worse, he insisted, for him to sell car keys by mail, than for mail-order houses to sell guns that might be used for murder? Until the law was changed, the key manufacturer could regard himself as being just as ethical as any other businessman by the rules of the business game.[6]

Violations of the ethical ideals of society are common in business, but they are not necessarily violations of business principles. Each year the Federal Trade Commission orders hundreds of companies, many of them of the first magnitude, to "cease and desist" from practices which, judged by ordinary standards, are of questionable morality but which are stoutly defended by the companies concerned.

In one case, a firm manufacturing a well-known mouthwash was accused of using a cheap form of alcohol possibly deleterious to health. The company's chief executive, after testifying in Washington, made this comment privately:

> "We broke no law. We're in a highly competitive industry. If we're going to stay in business, we have to look for profit wherever the law permits. We don't make the laws. We obey them. Then why do we have to put up with this 'holier than thou' talk about ethics? It's sheer hypocrisy. We're not in business to promote ethics. Look at the cigarette companies, for God's sake! If the ethics aren't embodied in the laws by the men who made them, you can't expect businessmen to fill the lack. Why, a sudden submission to Christian ethics by businessmen would bring about the greatest economic upheaval in history!" It may be noted that the government failed to prove its case against him.

## CAST ILLUSIONS ASIDE

Talk about ethics by businessmen is often a thin decorative coating over the hard realities of the game. . . .

The illusion that business can afford to be guided by ethics as conceived in private life is often fostered by speeches and articles containing such phrases as, "It pays to be ethical," or, "Sound ethics is good business." Actually, this is not an ethical position at all; it is a self-serving calculation in disguise. The speaker is really saying that in the long run a company can make more money if it does not antagonize competitors, suppliers, employees, and customers by squeezing them too hard. He is saying that oversharp policies reduce ultimate gains. That is true, but it has nothing to do with ethics. The underlying attitude is much like that in the familiar story of the shopkeeper who finds an extra $20 bill in the cash register, debates with himself the ethical problem—should he tell his partner?—and finally decides to share the money because the gesture will give him an edge over the s.o.b. the next time they quarrel.

I think it is fair to sum up the prevailing attitude of businessmen on ethics as follows:

We live in what is probably the most competitive of the world's civilized societies. Our customs encourage a high degree of aggression in the individual's striving for success. Business is our main area of competition, and it has been ritualized into a game of strategy. The basic rules of the game have been set by the government, which attempts to detect and punish business frauds. But as long as a company does not transgress the rules of the game set by law, it has the legal right to shape its strategy without reference to anything but its profits. If it takes a long-term view of its profits, it will preserve amicable relations, so far as possible, with those with whom it deals. A wise businessman will not seek advantage to the point where he generates dangerous hostility among employees, competitors, customers, government, or the public at large. But decisions in this area are, in the final test, decisions of strategy, not of ethics.

... If a man plans to make a seat in the business game, he owes it to himself to master the principles by which the game is played, including its special ethical outlook. He can then hardly fail to recognize that an occasional bluff may well be justified in terms of the game's ethics and warranted in terms of economic necessity. Once he clears his mind on this point, he is in a good position to match his strategy against that of the other players. He can then determine objectively whether a bluff in a given situation has a good chance of succeeding and can decide when and how to bluff, without a feeling of ethical transgression.

To be a winner, a man must play to win. This does not mean that he must be ruthless, cruel, harsh, or treacherous. On the contrary, the better his reputation for integrity, honesty, and decency, the better his chances of victory will be in the long run. But from time to time every businessman, like every poker player, is offered a choice between certain loss or bluffing within the legal rules of the game. If he is not resigned to losing, if he wants to rise in his company and industry, then in such a crisis he will bluff—and bluff hard. . . .

In the last third of the twentieth century even children are aware that if a man has become prosperous in business, he has sometimes departed from the strict truth in order to overcome obstacles or has practiced the more subtle deceptions of the half-truth or the misleading omission. Whatever the form of the bluff, it is an integral part of the game, and the executive who does not master its techniques is not likely to accumulate much money or power.

## NOTES

1. *The New York Times*, March 9, 1967.
2. *The New York Times*, November 21, 1966.
3. New York, Grossman Publishers, Inc., 1965.
4. New York, David McKay Company, Inc., 1967.
5. *The New York Times*, January 17, 1967.
6. Cited by Ralph Nader in "Business Crime," *The New Republic*, July 1, 1967, p. 7.

# Second Thoughts About Bluffing

*Thomas Carson*

## INTRODUCTION

In the United States it is common, perhaps even a matter of course, for people to misstate their bargaining positions during business negotiations. I have in mind the following kinds of cases, all of which involve deliberate false statements about one's bargaining position, intentions, or preferences in a negotiation: 1) I am selling a house and tell a prospective buyer that $90,000 is absolutely the lowest price that I will accept, when I know that I would be willing to accept as little as $80,000 for the house. 2) A union negotiator says that $13.00 an hour is the very lowest wage that his union is willing to consider when, in fact, he has been authorized by the union to accept a wage as low as $12.00 an hour. 3) I tell a prospective buyer that I am in no hurry to sell my house when, in fact, I am desperate to sell it within a few days.[1] Such statements would seem to constitute lies—they are deliberate false statements made with the intent to deceive others about the nature of one's own bargaining position. 1) and 2) clearly constitute lies according to standard dictionary definitions of lying. The *Oxford English Dictionary* defines the word "lie" as follows: "a false statement made with the intent to deceive." Also see *Webster's International Dictionary of the English Language* (1929), "to utter a falsehood with the intent to deceive."

The cases described above should be contrasted with instances of bluffing which do not involve making false statements. An example of the latter case would be saying "I want more" in response to an offer which I am willing to accept rather than not reach an agreement at all. This paper will focus on cases of bluffing which involve deliberate false statements about one's bargaining position or one's "settlement preferences."

I will defend the following two theses:

(a) Appearances to the contrary, this kind of bluffing typically does not constitute lying. (I will argue that standard dictionary definitions of lying are untenable and defend an alternative definition hinted at, but never clearly formulated, by W. D. Ross. On my definition, deliberate false statements about one's negotiating position usually do not constitute lies *in this society*.)

(b) It is usually permissible to misstate one's bargaining position or settlement preferences when one has good reason to think that one's negotiating partner is doing the same and it is usually impermissible to misstate one's negotiating position if one does not have good reason to think that the other party is misstating her position (preferences).

There are significant puzzles and uncertainties involved in applying my definition of lying to cases of misstating one's bargaining position. Because of this, I intend to make my argument for (b) independent of my argument for (a). My arguments for (b) are compatible with (but do not presuppose) the view that misstating one's position is lying and that lying is *prima facie* wrong. I will conclude the paper with a brief examination of other related deceptive stratagems in negotiations.

## THE ECONOMIC SIGNIFICANCE OF BLUFFING

In a business negotiation there is typically a range of possible agreements that each party would be willing to accept rather than reach no agreement at all. For instance, I might be willing to sell my home for as little as $80,000. (I would prefer to sell the house for $80,000 *today*, rather than continue to try to sell the house.) My range of acceptable agreements extends upward without limit—I would be willing to accept any price in excess of $80,000 rather than fail to make the sale today. Suppose that a prospective buyer is willing to spend as much as $85,000 for the house. (She prefers to buy the house for $85,000 today rather than not buy it at all today.) The buyer's range of acceptable agreements presumably extends downward without limit—she would be willing to purchase the house for any price below $85,000. In this case the two bargaining positions overlap and an agreement is possible (today). Unless there is some overlap between the minimum bargaining positions of the two parties, no agreement is possible. For example, if the seller's lowest acceptable price is $80,000 and the buyer's highest acceptable price is $70,000 no sale will be possible unless at least one of the parties alters her position.

If there is an overlap between the bargaining positions of the negotiators, then the actual outcome will depend on the negotiations. Consider again our example of the negotiation over the sale of the house. The owner is willing to sell the house for as little as $80,000 and the prospective buyer is willing to pay as much as $85,000. Whether the house sells for $80,000, $85,000, somewhere between $80,000 and $85,000, or even whether it sells at all will be determined by the negotiations. In this case, it would be very advantageous for either party to know the other person's minimum acceptable position and disadvantageous for either to reveal her position to the other. For example, if the buyer knows that the lowest price that the seller is willing to accept is $80,000, she can drive him towards the limit of his range of acceptable offers. She knows that he will accept an offer of $80,000 rather than have her break off the negotiations. In negotiations both buyer and seller will ordinarily have reason to keep their own bargaining positions and intentions secret.

It can sometimes be to one's advantage to mislead others about one's own minimum bargaining position. In the present case, it would be to the seller's advantage to cause the buyer to think that $85,000 is the lowest price that he (the seller) will accept. For in this case the buyer would offer $85,000 for the house—the best possible agreement from the seller's point of view. (It would also be easy to imagine cases in which it would be to the buyer's advantage to mislead the seller about her bargaining position.) There are various ways in which the seller might attempt to bluff the buyer in order to mislead her about his position. (1) He might set a very high "asking price," for example, $100,000. (2) He might initially refuse an offer and threaten to cut off the negotiations unless a higher offer is made while at the same time being prepared to accept the offer before the other person breaks off the negotiations. (I have in mind something like the following. The prospective buyer offers $80,000 and the seller replies: "I want more than that. I'm not happy with $80,000. Why don't you think about it and give me a call tomorrow.") (3) He might misrepresent his own bargaining position.

The kind of deception involved in (1) and (2) does not (or need not) involve lying or making false statements. (3) involves a deliberate false statement intended to deceive the other party and thus constitutes lying according to the standard definition of lying.

Attempting to mislead the other person about one's bargaining position can backfire and prevent a negotiation from reaching a mutually acceptable settlement which both parties would have preferred to no agreement at all. For example, suppose that the seller tells the buyer that he won't accept anything less than $95,000 for the house. If the buyer believes him she will break off the negotiations, since, by hypothesis, she is not willing to pay $95,000 for the house. Unless he knows the other person's bargaining position, a person who misrepresents his own position risks losing the opportunity to reach an acceptable agreement. By misstating one's position one also risks angering the other party and thereby causing him to modify his position or even break off the negotiations. (Truthful statements about one's own position might be perceived as lies and thus also risk alienating one's counterpart.)

## THE CONCEPT OF LYING

### A New Definition of Lying

. . . My definition of lying is inspired by Ross's claim that the duty not to lie is a special case of the duty to keep promises. Ross holds that (at least in ordinary contexts) we make an implicit promise to be truthful when we use language to communicate with others. To lie is to break an implicit promise to be truthful.[2]

Ross's view that making a statement (ordinarily) involves making an implicit promise that what one says is true suggests the following provisional definition of "lying" (Ross himself never attempts to define "lying"):

> A lie is a false statement which the "speaker" does not believe to be true made in a context in which the speaker warrants the truth of what he says.

This definition handles the earlier counter-example. Not only is the implicit warranty of truthfulness in force in the case of the witness's testimony in court, the witness explicitly warrants the truth of what he says by swearing an oath. Another virtue of the present analysis is that it makes sense of the common view that lying involves a violation of trust. To lie, on my view, is to invite trust and encourage others to believe what one says by warranting the truth of what one says and at the same time to betray that trust by making false statements which one does not believe to be true. . . .

### Lying and Bluffing

What are the implications of my analysis of lying for the issue of bluffing? Negotiations between experienced and "hardened" negotiators in our society (e.g., horse traders and realtors) are akin to a game of "Risk." It is understood that any statements one makes about one's role or intentions as a player during a game of "Risk" are not warranted to be true. In negotiations between hardened and cynical negotiators statements about one's intentions or settlement preferences are not warranted to be true. But it would be too strong to hold that nothing that one says in negotiations is warranted to be true. Convention dictates that other kinds of statements concerning the transaction being contemplated, e.g., statements to the effect that one has another offer, are warranted as true. So, for example, on my view, it would be a lie if I (the seller) were to falsely claim that someone else has offered me $85,000 for my house.

I am strongly inclined to believe that statements about one's minimum negotiating position are not warranted to be true in negotiations between "hardened negotiators" who recognize each other as such. I cannot here propose general criteria for determining when one may be said to warrant the truth of what one says. Therefore, what follows is somewhat conjectural. A cynical negotiator typically does not expect (predict) that her counterpart will speak truthfully about his minimum negotiating position. This alone is not enough to remove the implicit warranty of truth. A pathological liar who denies his every misdeed warrants the truth of what he says, even if those he addresses do not *expect* (predict) that what he says is true. The crucial feature of a negotiation which distinguishes it from the foregoing case is that in ordinary negotiations each party *consents* to renouncing the ordinary warranty of truth. There are various ways in which people consent to removing the default warranty of truth. Business negotiations are ritualized activities to which certain unstated rules and expectations (both in the sense of predictions and demands) apply. It is not expected that one will speak truthfully about one's negotiating position. Those who understand this and who enter into negotiations with other parties who are known to share this understanding implicitly consent to the rules and expectations of the negotiating ritual. In so doing, they consent to remove the warranty of truth for statements about one's minimum negotiating position. . . .

Before moving on to other issues, I would again like to stress the following two points: (1) my application of my definition of lying to this case is tentative and conjectural, and (2) my arguments concerning the moral status of bluffing do not depend on the assumption that misstating one's bargaining position or intentions is (typically) not a case of lying (my arguments are compatible with the view that misstating one's position or intentions is lying).

## THE MORAL STATUS OF BLUFFING (PRELIMINARY CONSIDERATIONS)

### Carr's Defense of Bluffing

In a well-known paper Albert Carr argues that misstating one's negotiating position is morally permissible.[3] Business, he argues, is a game like poker—a game in which special norms apply. The moral norms appropriate to the game of business or a game of poker are different from those appropriate to ordinary contexts.

> No one expects poker to be played on the ethical principles preached in churches. In poker it is right and proper to bluff a friend out of the rewards of being dealt a good hand. . . . Poker's own brand of ethics is different from the ethical ideals of civilized human relationships. The game calls for distrust of the other fellow. It ignores the claim of friendship. Cunning, deception, and concealment of one's strength and intentions, not kindness and openheartedness, are vital in poker. No one thinks any the worse of poker on that account. And no one should think any the worse of business because its standards of right and wrong differ from the prevailing traditions of morality in our society. . . .[4]

Carr claims that just as bluffing is permissible according to the special rules of poker, so it is permissible according to the rules of business.

What are the rules of the business game? How can we determine whether or not a particular rule or practice is part of the business game? Carr's position is confused on this point. At a number of points he suggests that the "rules of the business game" are simply our society's conventional moral standards for business, i.e., those standards which are thought by most people to govern the conduct of businesspeople. Carr defends a number of questionable business practices and argues that they are all morally justifiable, *because* they are standard practice and are regarded as permissible by conventional morality.

> In his view these things had nothing to do with ethics; they were merely normal business practice.[5]
>
> This was a lie; yet within the accepted rules of the business game, no moral culpability attaches to it.[6]

In other passages Carr seems to assume that the appropriate rules for business are those set by the law.

> If the laws governing their business change, or if public opinion becomes clamorous, they will make the necessary adjustments. But morally they have in their view done nothing wrong. As long as they comply with the letter of the law, they are within their rights to operate their businesses as they see fit.[7]

There are three possible ways to interpret the principle to which Carr appeals in trying to justify bluffing and other questionable business practices.

(a) Any action or practice engaged in by businesspeople in a given society is morally permissible provided that it is consistent with the ethical rules or principles which are generally accepted in that society.

(b) Any action or practice engaged in by businesspeople in a given society is morally permissible provided that it is consistent with the laws of that society.

(c) Any action or practice engaged in by businesspeople in a given society is morally permissible provided that it is consistent with *both* i) the society's conventional ethical rules or principles governing those actions and practices, *and* ii) the laws of that society.

On any of these readings, Carr's argument is most implausible. One can't justify an act or practice *simply because* it is consistent with conventional morality. Similarly, the fact that an action or practice is permitted by the law does not suffice to establish its moral permissibility. Conventional morality and the law are not infallible moral guidelines. In the past, many immoral practices, most notably slavery, were condoned by the conventional morality and legal codes of our own and many other societies. . . .

## VARIATIONS ON THE EXAMPLE

1. *Is lying worse than mere deception?* Consider the following case. Suppose that I want the other party to hold false beliefs about my minimum bargaining position. I want him to think that $90,000 is the lowest price that I'm willing to accept for my house when, in fact, I'm willing to sell it for a little as $80,000. However, I am very much averse to lying about this and I believe that misstating my own position would be a lie. I am willing to try to deceive or mislead him about my intentions, but I am not willing to lie about them. Here, as in many cases, it is possible to think of true but equally misleading things to say so as to avoid lying. Suppose that our lowest acceptable selling price is $80,000, but I want you to think that it is actually around $85,000. Instead of lying, I could say "my wife told me to tell you that $85,000 is absolutely the lowest price that we will accept." The trick here would be to have my wife utter the words "tell the buyer that $85,000 is absolutely the lowest price that we are willing to accept." In saying this she would not be stating our minimum position, but rather helping to create the ruse to fool the buyer. It is very doubtful that this is morally preferable to lying. Intuitively, it strikes me as worse. Many people (perhaps most) seem to believe that making true but deceptive statements is preferable to lying. This is demonstrated by the fact that many (most?) of us will, on occasion, go through verbal contortions or give very careful thought to exactly what we say in order to mislead others without lying. In this kind of case lying does not seem to be morally preferable to "mere deception."

Consider another example in which the difference between lying and mere deception does not seem to be morally significant. Suppose that two parents go out of town for the weekend leaving their two adolescent children home alone. The parents give their son strict orders that under no circumstances is he permitted to entertain his girlfriend in the house while they are away. The parents call during the weekend to "check up" on the children. They speak with their daughter. "What's going on there? What is your brother up to? He doesn't have Nora [his girlfriend] there does he?" The son is entertaining Nora in the house at the time that they call. The daughter does not want to get her brother in trouble, but, on the other hand, she doesn't want to lie. She does not answer the last question directly, but replies with the following true, but misleading, statement. "He's fine; he's watching the ball game with Bob." (Bob is a male friend who *is* there but is about to leave.)

2. *Claiming to have another offer.* On my view, the fact that misstating one's position is a very common practice can often help justify misstating one's own position. Because misstating one's bargaining position is such a widespread practice in our society, one is often justified in assuming that one's negotiating partner is misrepresenting her position. If the other person states a minimum bargaining position, then one is justified in thinking that she is misrepresenting that position, in the absence of reasons for thinking that she is not.

There are other ways of deceiving others about one's bargaining position which are not common practice. The following two cases are among the kinds that I have in mind here:

> Case #1. I (the seller) say to a prospective buyer "I have another offer for $80,000, but I'll let you have it if you can beat the offer" when, in fact, I don't have another offer.

Case #2. I (the seller) want you to think that I have another offer. I have my brother come over and in your presence pretend to offer me $80,000 for the condo. (You don't know that he is my brother.) I say to my brother "the other person was here first. I'll have to let him/her see if he/she wants to meet the offer." I turn to the seller and say "It's yours for $80,000."

What I say in the first case is clearly a lie. It is a deliberate false statement which is warranted to be true and is intended to deceive others. My action in this case is *prima facie* very wrong. I am putting extreme pressure on the other person and may panic her into a rash decision. Falsely claiming to have another offer could, in principle, be justified by appeal to SD [the principle of self-defense]. If the buyer was falsely representing the possibility of another comparable deal, then a Rossian theory might conceivably justify me in doing the same. This is very unlikely in the ordinary course of things. This means that it is unlikely that one could defend lying in such a case by appeal to the need to defend one's own interests. My actions in case #2 seem intuitively even worse than those in #1. Case #2 does not involve lying but it does involve an elaborate scheme of deception and is potentially very harmful to the buyer. The same general things that I said about case #1 apply here. My actions in this case are *prima facie* very wrong. In principle, a Rossian theory could justify those actions, but that is very unlikely.

## NOTES

1. This example is taken from "Shrewd Bargaining on the Moral Frontier: Towards a Theory of Morality in Practice," J. Gregory Dees and Peter C. Crampton, *Business Ethics Quarterly*, 1 (2) (April 1991): 143.
2. W. D. Ross, *The Right and the Good* (Oxford, 1930), p. 21.
3. Albert Carr, "Is Business Bluffing Ethical?" in *Ethical Issues in Business*, third edition, Thomas Donaldson and Patricia Werhane, eds. (Englewood Cliffs, NJ: Prentice Hall, 1988).
4. Carr, pp. 72–73; see also pp. 69 and 70.
5. Carr, p. 70.
6. Carr, p. 72.
7. Carr, p. 73; also see p. 75.

## LEGAL PERSPECTIVES

# *Irving A. Backman v. Polaroid Corporation*

*United States Court of Appeals (First Circuit)*

This is a class action brought by Irving A. Backman on behalf of himself and all other persons who purchased shares of stock of defendant Polaroid Corporation on the open market between January 11 and February 22, 1979, allegedly misled by defendant's conduct that violated Section 10 (b) of the Securities Exchange Act of 1934 and Rule 10b-5 of the regulations promulgated thereunder. Suit was filed in June 1979. . . . The improprieties asserted, both in the complaint and in plaintiffs' opening to the jury, as responsible for plaintiffs'

910 F. 2d 10 (1st Cir. 1990).

purchasing shares before a substantial drop in the market, were defendant's failure to disclose unfavorable facts about its new product, Polavision, an instant movie camera. Following trial on liability, the jury found for plaintiffs. . . . On appeal, a divided panel . . . granted a new trial. On this rehearing en banc we reverse and order judgment for defendant. . . .

In their amended complaint plaintiffs alleged that defendant failed to disclose that Polavision, introduced in the spring, had been unprofitable throughout 1978, and would continue so, significantly, at least through 1979; that it had been excessively inventoried and had suffered lagging sales; that little, if any, information had been made public; that defendant knew that this undisclosed information was material to investors, and that major investment research firms had publicly projected defendant's earnings based on assumptions defendant knew were contrary to the true facts, all of which nondisclosure was in violation of the securities laws.

Secondly, plaintiffs re-alleged the above, and added that over the years defendant had advertised that it was a growth company, and that, through its successes, the investment community had come to consider it the best of the growth companies, and that its failing to make the above disclosures operated as a fraud and deceit on the investing public, was a "fraud on the market," and constituted an unlawful manipulation thereof. . . .

However, mere market interest is no basis for imposing liability. We said [in a former case] the materiality of the information claimed not to have been disclosed . . . is not enough to make out a sustainable claim of securities fraud. Even if information is material, there is no liability under Rule 10b-5 unless there is a duty to disclose it.

A duty to disclose "does not arise from the mere possession of non-public information." . . .

In a twelve day trial [the plaintiffs] precisely followed their opening, alleging, simply, nondisclosure of material information. As summarized in their final argument,

> Polaroid . . . violated the federal securities laws which require full disclosure so that people who purchase and sell securities do so on a fair playing field; that people have the same information and people can make their investment decisions based on having all of the information and having truthful information. . . . [Y]ou have to find that Polaroid had adverse information, that information was material—i.e., that it was important—and that Polaroid knowingly and deliberately withheld it. *And that's all we're asking you to do here.* (Emphasis supplied.)

The summation was not an inadvertence, but was in accord with plaintiffs's own testimony.

**Q.** Now, Mr. Backman, in this action you are not claiming, are you, that the financial information put out by Polaroid was in any way false and misleading, are you?
**A.** I think you'll have to refer to the complaint. I believe the failure to disclose is just as improper as providing false information. And I believe the essence of my suit deals with the failure to disclose. . . . I do claim it was false and misleading because the failure to disclose is just as misleading a (sic) improper disclosure.

This, of course, is not so, "Silence, absent a duty to disclose, is not misleading under Rule 10b-5." . . .

We have gone into this at length, not so much to show the emptiness of plaintiff's first claim—agreed to by the full panel—but to accent our finding that there had been no falsity or misleading by defendant in any respect. In eight years of preparation and twelve days of trial, the words misrepresentation and misleading never crossed plaintiffs' lips. . . .

It appeared that Dr. Edwin H. Land, the founder and at all times president or C.E.O. of Polaroid, had added to his invention of the world-famous instant still camera another exceptional invention—an instant movie camera,

Polavision. It appeared throughout the case, however, that Polavision's sales appeal did not correspond with the quality of the invention. Launched in early 1978 with great fanfare, the estimates for fall, to which production had been geared, proved to be substantially excessive. As a result, in late October, Eumig, the Austrian manufacturer, having earlier been told to increase production, was instructed to reduce by 20,000. In mid-November Eumig was told to take out another 90,000 sets, and to halt production. Plaintiffs' panel brief, quoting the fortuitous language of Eumig's cable acknowledgement, "to now finally stop production entirely," gives the impression that the halt was intended to be permanent. Conveniently, from plaintiffs' standpoint, dots in the quotation replace the subsequent sentence, "Steps have been taken to ensure a quick new start-up of production on a reduced scale." This omission aids plaintiffs in their recitation, the regrettable incorrectness of which we will come to, that "management knew that Polavision was a commercial failure." Thereafter, fourth quarter internal figures, not publicly released, confirmed that the original Polavision estimates (also not released) had been substantially excessive.

The next event was a newspaper release published on January 9, 1979, that Rowland Foundation, a charitable trust established by Dr. and Mrs. Land, was to sell 300,000 shares of Polaroid, in part for funds for a new project, and in part to diversify its portfolio. Defendant participated in the preparation of the release, but not in the action itself. It is not claimed that the release was in any way untrue. Plaintiff's claim is misleading because additional information should then have been given the public. The sale was consummated on January 11. . . .

On February 22, 1979, immediately following the annual meeting, defendant announced further facts about Polavision's lack of success, and the market fell, shortly, by some 20%. . . .

Plaintiffs' brief now finds assisted misrepresentation because "Polaroid featured Polavision on the cover," plaintiffs point out that after President McCune "announced record worldwide sales and earnings for both the third quarter and the first nine months of 1978, . . . Mr. McCune noted that the Company's worldwide manufacturing facilities continue to operate at close to maximum capacity," whereas, in fact, Polavision's contract supplier, Eumig, was told, shortly before the report, to hold up on 20,000 units. We note, first, that the statement, taken as a whole, was true; it expressly recognized an absence of totality. Of more specific importance, it flagged, on three of its three and half pages of text, that Polavision's effect on earnings was negative. . . . With this emphasized three times, we ask did this report mislead investors to buy stock because Polavision was doing so well?

Plaintiffs quote *Roeder*, 814 F.2d at 26, that even a voluntary disclosure of information that a reasonable investor would consider material must be "complete and accurate." This, however, does not mean that by revealing one fact about a product, one must reveal all others, that, too, would be interesting, market-wise, but means only such others, if any, that are needed so that what was revealed would not be "so incomplete as to mislead." . . . Disclosing that Polavision was being sold below cost was not misleading by reason of not saying how much below. Nor was it misleading not to report the number of sales, or that they were below expectations. . . .

We come, next, to the January 9 Rowland Foundation sale release. There was nothing untrue or misleading in the release itself, but plaintiffs say, with support from the panel opinion, that it should have contained additional information in order to keep the November report from being misleading. . . .

Obviously, if a disclosure is in fact misleading when made, and the speaker thereafter learns of this, there is a duty to correct it. . . . In special circumstances, a statement, correct at the time, may have a forward intent and connotation upon which parties may be expected to rely. If this is a clear meaning, and there is a change, correction, more exactly, further disclosure, may be called for. . . . Fear that statements of historical fact might be claimed to fall within it, could inhibit disclosures altogether. And what is the limit? In the present case if the shoe were on the other foot, and defendant could have, and had, announced continued Polavision profits, for how long would it have been under a duty of disclosure if the tide turned? Plaintiffs' contention that it would be a jury question is scarcely reassuring. . . .

After indicating reluctance to accept plaintiffs' contention that the Third Quarter Report was misleading when made, the panel opinion, in holding that it could be found misleading in light of later developments, said as follows.

> [E]ven if the optimistic Third Quarter Report was not misleading at the time of its issuance, there is sufficient evidence to support a jury's determination that the report's relatively brief mention of Polavision difficulties *became* misleading in light of the subsequent information acquired by Polaroid indicating the seriousness of Polavision's problems. This subsequent information included . . . Polaroid's decision to . . . stop Polavision production by its Austrian manufacturer, Eumig, *and its instruction to its Austrian supplier to keep this production cutback secret.* We feel that a reasonable jury could conclude that this subsequent information rendered the Third Quarter Report's brief mention of Polavision expenses misleading, triggering a duty to disclose on the part of Polaroid. (Emphasis in orig.)

At the time of the Rowland sale, while selling the stock had absolutely nothing to do with Polaroid's financial health . . . some might find it less than forthcoming for the press release not to have at least mentioned Polavision's difficulties so that the investing public could assess for themselves the reasons behind the sale.

That this was an improper mix was made conspicuous by plaintiffs' oral argument.

> [W]e've cited the specific passages of Mr. McCune's testimony in our brief, where Mr. McCune testified that the expression, "continued to reflect substantial expenses" was intended to convey that that condition would continue in the future. . . . What we're saying is that a jury could find that this statement, even if it wasn't misleading when issued, became misleading because of the forward-looking nature.

This is a failure to recognize that what Mr. McCune said was a single, simple, statement, that substantial expenses had made Polavision's earnings negative. Though the panel opinion characterized it as "relatively brief," it was precisely correct, initially. Even if forward-looking, it remained precisely correct thereafter. . . . In arguing that the statement did not "remain true," plaintiffs' brief, unabashedly, points solely to matters outside the scope of the initial disclosure, in no way making it incorrect or misleading, originally, or later.

The shell in plaintiffs' gun at trial . . . are all percussion cap and no powder. . . . Plaintiffs have no case.

# *B. Sanfield, Inc. v. Finlay Fine Jewelry Corp.*

*United States Court of Appeals for the Seventh Circuit*

## I.

Sanfield is a locally owned retailer. At its one and only store in Rockford, it offers jewelry, floral arrangements, plants, and other gifts for sale to the public. Finlay is a nationwide retailer that also sells jewelry to the public. It does so through fine jewelry departments that it leases

No. 98–1873, 168 F.3d 967 (1999). September 16, 1998, Argued. February 17, 1999, Decided.

from host department stores such as Bergner's, which has thirteen stores in Illinois, including two in Rockford.

Among other items, Sanfield and Finlay each sell gold earrings, gold chains, gold bangles, and gold charms; and this suit centers upon Finlay's efforts to advertise and promote the sale of those four categories of jewelry. Although Finlay prices these items in the first instance at about 5.5 times their cost, it frequently offers them for sale at 40 to 60 percent off the original price, with 50 percent being the most common discount. In fact, Finlay sells the vast majority of these types of jewelry in Rockford at the discounted, rather than the original price. See R. 183 Ex. 77 PP 9, 10.

The premise of Sanfield's suit is that the "regular" price that Finlay sets for its gold earrings, chains, bangles, and charms is a sham. Finlay sets the original price high, Sanfield alleges, with no expectation that it will make substantial sales at that price. The truly regular price is, in practice, the discounted price. Yet, Sanfield emphasizes, although reduced, even the discounted price of a given piece of Finlay jewelry may in fact be substantially higher than the regular, nondiscounted price at which other retailers, including Sanfield, customarily offer that same item. Rational consumers who take the time to price shop would, of course, opt to buy the jewelry at the regular prices offered by the other retailers. Sanfield believes, however, that "50 percent off" has such an alluring ring that many consumers are misled into thinking that Finlay's sale prices are really better than the nondiscounted prices at which Sanfield offers its own jewelry. As a result, customers are enticed away from Sanfield.

Consistent with Sanfield's theory, state and federal regulations (which we will set out in full below) both recognize the possibility that the advertising and promotion of discount prices can be deceptive. Like a number of other states, Illinois has adopted a regulation which provides that it is deceptive for a seller to compare the discounted price of an item with the regular price, unless the seller has either (1) sold a substantial number of that item at a price equal to or greater than the regular price or (2) has offered the item openly and actively at the regular price for a reasonably substantial time in good faith with the genuine intent of selling the item at that price. 14 Ill. Admin. Code § 470.220; see generally Alan M. Komensky & Mark D. Wegener, When is a Sale Not a Sale? State Regulation of Price Comparison Advertising, 5 Antitrust 28 (Summer 1991). The federal counterpart likewise recognizes the deceptive potential of advertising a reduction in a product's former price when the former price is fictitious; and it poses a similar question for the purpose of assessing whether the regular price is bona fide—has the seller in good faith offered the item at the regular price openly and actively for a reasonably substantial period of time in the regular, recent course of its business? . . .

Only if there were proof that consumers actually believe that Finlay regularly and in good faith offered its jewelry for sale at the regular price could one conclude that Finlay's advertising and promotional practices are deceptive, the court reasoned. Sanfield offered some evidence on that score (as did Finlay), but the court found it insufficient to show that consumers were actually misled. Consequently, the court found that Sanfield had not carried its burden in establishing the first element of its claim under the Illinois consumer fraud statute—that Finlay had engaged in a deceptive act or practice and the first and second elements of its Lanham Act claim—that Finlay had issued false or misleading advertisements which are actually deceiving or likely to deceive. Having so concluded, the court believed it unnecessary to consider whether Finlay's ads comported with the state and federal regulations. . . .

## II.

### A.

Exercising the regulatory authority granted him by the consumer fraud act, 815 ILCS 505/4, the Illinois Attorney General has determined that "the use of misleading price comparisons is injurious to both the consuming public and competitors and is an unfair or deceptive act and an unfair method of competition under Section 2 of the Consumer Fraud and Deceptive Practices Act. . . ." 14 Ill. Admin. Code—470.110. The following regulation identifies the circumstances under which a seller's comparison of a discounted price to its own regular price amounts to a deceptive act for purposes of the statute: It is unfair or deceptive for a seller to compare current price with its former (regular) price for any product or service (for example: "$ 99, now $ 69 Save $ 30"; "regularly $ 99, Now $ 69"; "Originally $ 99, Now $ 69"; "Save $ 30, Now $ 69") unless one of the following criteria are [sic] met:

(a) the former (regular) price is equal to or below the price(s) at which the seller made a substantial number of sales of such products in the recent regular course of its business; or
(b) the former (regular) price is equal to or below the price(s) at which the seller offered the product for a reasonably substantial period of time in the recent regular course of its business, openly and actively and in good faith, with an intent to sell the product at that price(s). . . .

One of the most commonly used forms of bargain advertising is to offer a reduction from the advertiser's own former price for an article. If the former price is the actual, bona fide price at which the article was offered to the public on a regular basis for a reasonably substantial period of time, it provides a legitimate basis for the advertising of a price comparison. Where the former price is genuine, the bargain being advertised is a true one. If, on the other hand, the former price being advertised is not bona fide but fictitious—for example, where an artificial, inflated price was established for the purpose of enabling the subsequent offer of a large reduction—the "bargain" being advertised is a false one; the purchaser is not receiving the unusual value he expects. In such a case, the reduced price is, in reality, probably just the seller's regular price.

Taking its cue from these regulatory provisions, Sanfield contends that when Finlay advertises its jewelry at 50 percent (or some other percentage) off the "regular" price, it is deceiving consumers, because in fact Finlay rarely if ever sells the jewelry at that price and (as Sanfield sees it) makes no good faith effort to do so. The "bargain" that Finlay purports to offer prospective customers is therefore no bargain at all, as Sanfield sees it, because the ostensibly discounted price is the price at which Finlay makes (and expects to make) the vast majority of its sales. . . .

Deception, like beauty, is in the eye of the beholder. If consumers generally understand that a retailer makes little or no concerted effort to sell at a stated regular price, then stating the price as regular would be neither deceptive nor misleading. It might impact the efficacy of the promoted sale, but it would not deceive. If the consuming public held the opposite belief, that is, that [the] regular price is the price that defendant regularly and genuinely offers the advertised items for sale at, then that would evidence deception. Absent consumer perceptions, however, whether defendant actually offers or sells the items at [the] regular price proves little, if anything, in this context.

# *Coca-Cola Company v. Tropicana Products, Inc.*

*United States Court of Appeals for the Second Circuit*

A proverb current even in the days of ancient Rome was "seeing is believing." Today, a great deal of what people see flashes before them on their TV sets. This case involves a 30-second television commercial with simultaneous audio and video components. We have no doubt that the byword of Rome is as valid now as it was then. And, if seeing something on TV has a tendency to persuade a viewer to believe, how much greater is the impact on a viewer's credulity when he both sees and hears a message at the same time?

In mid-February of 1982 defendant Tropicana products, Inc. (Tropicana) began airing a new television commercial for its Premium Pack orange juice. The commercial shows the renowned American Olympic athlete Bruce Jenner squeezing an orange while saying "It's pure, pasteurized juice as it comes from the orange," and then shows Jenner pouring the fresh-squeezed juice into a Tropicana carton while the audio states "It's the only leading brand not made with concentrate and water."

Soon after the advertisement began running, plaintiff Coca-Cola Company (Coke, Coca-Cola), maker of Minute Maid orange juice, brought suit in the United States District Court for the Southern District of New York, 538 F. Supp. 1091, against Tropicana for false advertising in violation of section 43(a) of the Lanham Act. The statute provides that anyone who uses a false description or representation in connection with goods placed in commerce "shall be liable to a civil action by [anyone]. . . . Who believes that he is or is likely to be damaged by the use of. . . such false description or representation." 15 U.S.C. § 1125(a) (1976). Coke claimed the commercial is false because it incorrectly represents that Premium Pack contains unprocessed, fresh-squeezed juice when in fact the juice is pasteurized (heated to about 200 degrees Fahrenheit) and sometimes frozen prior to packaging. The court below denied plaintiff's motion for a preliminary injunction to enjoin further broadcast of the advertisement pending the outcome of this litigation. In our view preliminary injunctive relief is appropriate.

Perhaps the most difficult element to demonstrate when seeking an injunction against false advertising is the likelihood that one will suffer irreparable harm if the injunction does not issue. It is virtually impossible to prove that so much of one's sales will be lost or that one's goodwill will be damaged as a direct result of a competitor's advertisement. Too many market variables enter into the advertising-sales equation. Because of these impediments, a Lanham Act plaintiff who can prove actual lost sales may obtain an injunction even if most of his sales decline is attributable of factors other than a competitor's false advertising. In fact, he need not even point to an actual loss or diversion of sales.

The Lanham Act plaintiff must, however, offer something more than a mere subjective belief that he is likely to be injured as a result of the false advertising, Id. at 189; he must submit proof which provides a reasonable basis for that belief. The likelihood of injury and causation will not be presumed, but must be demonstrated in some manner.

Two recent decisions of this Court have examined the type of proof necessary to satisfy this requirement Relying on the fact that the products involved were in head-to-head competition, the Court in both cases directed the issuance of a preliminary injunction under the Lanham Act. Vidal Sassoon, 661 F.2d at 227; Johnson & Johnson, 631 F.2d at 189–91. In both decisions the Court reasoned that sales of the plaintiffs' products would probably be harmed if the competing products' advertising tended to mislead consumers in the manner alleged. Market studies were used as evidence that some consumers were in fact misled by the advertising in issue. Thus, the market studies supplied the causative link between the advertising and the plaintiffs' potential lost sales, and thereby indicated a likelihood of injury.

Applying the same reasoning to the instant case, if consumers are misled by Tropicana's commercial, Coca-Cola probably would suffer irreparable injury. Tropicana and Coca-Cola are the leading national competitors for the chilled (ready-to-serve) orange juice market. If Tropicana's advertisement misleads consumers into believing that Premium Pack is a more desirable product because it contains only fresh-squeezed, unprocessed juice, then it is likely that Coke will lose a portion of the chilled juice market and thus suffer irreparable injury.

Evidence in the record supports the conclusion that consumers are likely to be misled in this manner. A consumer reaction survey conducted by ASI Market Research, Inc. and a Burke test, measuring recall of the commercial after it was aired on television, were admitted into evidence, though neither one was considered by the district court in reference to irreparable injury. The trial court examined the ASI survey regarding the issue of likelihood of success on the merits, and found that it contained various flaws which made it difficult to determine for certain whether a large number of consumers were misled. We do not disagree with those findings. We note, moreover, that despite these flaws the district court ruled that there were at least a small number of clearly deceived ASI interviewees. Our examination of the Burke test results leads to the same conclusion, i.e., that a not insubstantial number of consumers were clearly misled by the defendant's ad. Together these tests provide sufficient evidence of a risk of irreparable harm because they demonstrate that a significant number of consumers would be likely to be misled. The trial court should have considered these studies on the issue of irreparable injury. . . .

Once the initial requisite showing of irreparable harm has been made, the party seeking a preliminary injunction must satisfy either of the two alternatives regarding the merits of his case. We find that Coca-Cola satisfies the more stringent first alternative because it is likely to succeed on the merits of its false advertising action.

Coke is entitled to relief under the Lanham Act if Tropicana has used a false description or representation in its Jenner commercial. When a merchandising statement or representation is literally or explicitly false, the court may grant relief without reference to the advertisement's impact on the buying public. When the challenged advertisement is implicitly rather than explicitly false, its tendency to violate the Lanham Act by misleading, confusing or deceiving should be tested by public reaction.

In viewing defendant's 30-second commercial at oral argument, we concluded that the trail court's finding that this ad was not facially false is an error of fact. Since the trial judge's finding on this issue was based solely on the inference it drew from reviewing documentary evidence, consisting of commercial, we are in as good a position as it was to draw an appropriate inference. We find, therefore, that the squeezing-pouring sequence in the Jenner commercial is false on its face. The visual component of the ad makes an explicit representation that Premium Pack is produced by squeezing oranges and pouring the freshly squeezed juice directly into the carton. This is not a true representation of how the product is prepared. Premium Pack juice is heated and sometimes frozen prior to packaging. Additionally, the simultaneous audio component of the ad states that Premium Pack is "pasteurized juice as it comes from the oranges." This statement is blatantly false—pasteurized juice does not come from oranges. Pasteurization entails heating the juice to approximately 200 degrees Fahrenheit to kill certain natural enzymes and microorganisms which cause spoilage. Moreover, even if the addition of the word "pasteurized" somehow made sense and effectively qualified the visual image, Tropicana's commercial nevertheless represented that the juice is only squeezed, heated and packaged when in fact it may actually also be frozen.

Hence, Coke is likely to succeed in arguing that Tropicana's ad is false and that it is entitled to relief under the Lanham Act. The purpose of the Act is to insure truthfulness in advertising and to eliminate misrepresentations with reference to the inherent quality or characteristic of another's product. The claim that Tropicana's Premium Pack contains only fresh-squeezed, unprocessed juice is clearly a misrepresentation as to that product's inherent quality or characteristic. Since the plaintiff has satisfied the first preliminary injunction alternative, we need not decide whether the balance or hardships tips in its favor.

Because Tropicana has made a false representation in its advertising and Coke is likely to suffer irreparable harm as a result, we reverse the district court's denial of plaintiff's application and remand this case for issuance of a preliminary injunction preventing broadcast of the squeezing-pouring sequence in the Jenner commercial.

**CASES**

# CASE 1. *More HorsePOWER?*

A television advertisement praises next year's model of the popular pickup truck, the Mammoth, claiming that "This sleek and stylish truck is the most powerful in its class." The company that produces the truck traditionally sells luxury sedans and sports cars, which are among the best rated and the safest in the industry. While trucks like the Mammoth are often used for hauling heavy equipment, this model has a smaller capacity and is not well suited for hauling, though it does have a powerful engine. Critics have pointed out, probably correctly, that if the Mammoth were produced by any other company, few consumers would have interest in it because of its limited capacity and decidedly awkward design.

The ad begins with a young man preparing himself for a night at the opera. Dressed in a tuxedo, he looks in the mirror and appears uncomfortable and without confidence. He then gets behind the wheel of the Mammoth, which is beautifully styled on the inside with wood interior and leather seats. The next scene presents the same man as he arrives at the opera house. Reporters and photographers, interviewing the music director, suddenly flock toward the Mammoth and surround it. As the man exits the truck, five well-known models flock to his side and escort him inside the theater. The once unconfident man is now the guest of honor, and appears suave and collected. As the commercial ends, a narrator comments, "The Mammoth. Power, Beauty, Style."

## Questions

1. Is this a case of puffery in advertising? Does the advertisement unduly focus on qualities not necessarily connected with the product?
2. Is it permissible for advertisements to use "hidden human needs" in order to sell products? Should they simply state the facts?

This case was prepared by David Lawrence and Dianna Spring.

## CASE 2. *Self-Identity Advertising*

A fitness company has done research and has concluded that after people eat in fast-food restaurants, they are more likely to buy products associated with glamour, exercise, and health. So, this company has concentrated ads for its newest gym outside of numerous fast-food franchises so that individuals will see the ads as they leave.

Each ad is split down the middle into two parts. On the left is a man on a treadmill at the gym. He is wearing a tight shirt with the gym's name on it; the shirt reveals large muscles, and the man appears to be in incredible shape. On the right, the same man is entering an office building at work. He appears to be walking down a corridor, and everyone is turning to look at him as he passes.

### Questions

1. Does this ad purposefully challenge the consumer's self-identity in order to sell the company's product? Is there anything wrong with such advertising?
2. If persons leaving a fast-food restaurant are more vulnerable to irrational persuasion or manipulation by advertisements, should such advertising be banned? Is there any basis for objecting to such advertisements?

This case was prepared by David Lawrence.

## CASE 3. *Advertising Joe Camel*

According to the Centers for Disease Control and Prevention in Atlanta, the cigarette industry is currently losing a half million customers a year in the United States to lung cancer and smoking-related deaths. The percentage of adults who smoke has also dropped dramatically. As a result of this declining market, cigarette manufacturers need customers in alternative population segments. They favor advertisements that depict an optimum lifestyle, suggesting one could enjoy that lifestyle when smoking certain cigarettes.

Statistics show that almost 50 percent of smokers begin by age 15. A few tobacco companies have been criticized for crossing the fine line between general advertising and advertising directed at children. Although companies insist that advertising themes such as the animated "Joe Camel" and his female counterpart "Josephine Camel," introduced in 1994, do nothing more than promote the product to users, these advertisements have been severely criticized. The California Supreme Court in San Francisco decided in 1994 to hear the case brought by a California woman against RJR's "Joe Camel" campaign. The court upheld the lawsuit because "the allegations against R.J. Reynolds were based not on smoking and health, but on a 'more general' duty imposed under state law 'not to engage in unfair competition by advertising illegal conduct,' namely, smoking by minors." (Paul Barrett, "Supreme Court Gives Green Light to Suit Against Tobacco Concern's Cartoon Ads," *The Wall Street Journal*, November 29, 1994, p. A24.)

Opposition to cigarette advertising is not confined to the American market. As of October 1, 1991, all cigarette advertising on television was banned throughout Europe. In addition, each European country began some form of prohibition. For example, the United Kingdom began to require tobacco advertisers to place one of six warning labels on cigarette packages including one that reads "smoking kills." In France, tobacco ads must devote 20 percent of the space to warning labels.

## Questions

1. Is there an ethical issue about advertising in this case, or is the only real objection that smoking cigarettes is harmful to health?
2. Should cigarette advertising using the media be banned altogether?
3. Does it make any moral difference whether the advertising a U.S. company does is at home or abroad?

# CASE 4. *Green Advertising*

In an environmental study, 83 percent of respondents said they prefer buying environmentally safe products, and 37 percent claimed they would pay up to 15 percent more for environmentally safe packaging. These findings present the marketer with a tangible incentive. The practice of so-called green promotion and advertising is an attempt to use corporate publicity to create a message of corporate initiative in creating a healthier, improved natural environment. In a typical example, Japan's Kirin Beer launched its "Earth Beer" to be marketed worldwide with a picture of the earth on a green label. Promotionally, Kirin claimed that the product was "earth friendly." However, this beer was not produced or packaged differently from Kirin's original products or the products of other beer manufacturers. Kirin has not been the only company to try to fill the consumer's desire for environmental friendly products. In 1988 only 2.8 percent of all new products touted an environmental advantage, but this number jumped to 13.0 percent in 1993 and 10.5 percent in 1994.

The rise of green promotion poses this question: Are companies taking action to improve the environment, or is it purely publicity? Friends of the Earth President Brent Blackwelder claims that, in many cases, green advertising is not warranted by the conduct of the corporation. For example, he claims that DuPont is not a conscientious protector of the environment, although it uses green advertising. Blackwelder contends that "it's morally reprehensible to portray this type of image [in advertising] when they have this type of track record."

The background of his position on DuPont is as follows. In September 1991, DuPont launched a television ad campaign featuring barking sea lions, jumping dolphins, and other animals enjoying fresh, unpolluted seas. The ad strongly implied that Dupont was making major changes to protect the environment. A Friends of the Earth report, by contrast, claimed that DuPont had the highest ratio of pollution to profit (14 percent) and that the company paid nearly $1 million monthly from 1989 to June 1991 in fines for environmental infractions. The report also noted that after the devastating 1990 Exxon tanker accident, DuPont's oil-marketing subsidiary promoted its plans to build two new double-hulled tankers to prevent oil spills as a unique environmental strategy. However, since one out of every six crude oil tankers was already double hulled, DuPont's "change" was not a new initiative.

In response to these claims, DuPont issued a public statement that said, "It seems to be a rehash of several of DuPont's most serious environmental challenges—all of which we are working diligently to resolve." DuPont also noted that it had begun working on several new projects to benefit the environment. For example, DuPont had begun developing a chemical to reduce ozone-depleting fluorocarbons

This case was prepared by Katy Cancro and revised by Jeff Greene, using articles in *Advertising Age* in May, June and September 1991, a Reuters report in *The Washington Post,* August 28, 1991, and *The Journal of Advertising,* Summer 1995, special issue.

and had initiated a buyback of fluorocarbon-producing products in an effort to preserve the ozone layer.

The Federal Trade Commission held public hearings in the summer of 1991 to investigate claims of deceptive green advertising. The following year, in July 1992, the commission issued *Guides for the Use of Environmental Marketing Claims.* The publication attempted to prevent some of the bogus claims that companies were making about their products and to assist the consumer in identifying products that really are making a difference in improving the environment.

### Questions

1. Is environmental advertising sometimes no more than a new form of *deceptive* advertising? What makes it deceptive, if it is?
2. Does green advertising damage the consumer, or is it a harmless method of developing the reputation of the corporation?
3. To what extent should companies be held responsible for demonstrating a track record of environmental preservation that corresponds to its green advertising?
4. Should green advertising be federally regulated?

## CASE 5. *Sales at World Camera and Electronics*

Sales personnel at World Camera and Electronics are given a financial incentive to sell overstocked cameras; each week, the management identifies a particular camera that salespeople should try to sell over other brands. When such cameras are sold, the salesperson receives a 20 percent commission instead of the usual 10 percent.

Matthew Anderson, a college student, wishes to purchase a camera. After carefully researching different styles, he decides to buy a manual 35 mm camera that he believes is ideal for student photographers. He finds the exact model that he desires at World Camera. The salesperson agrees that this model would be a fine purchase.

However, rather than simply sell this camera, the salesperson shows Matthew another camera. This one is far more expensive and a bit less practical for his needs. The salesperson has a financial incentive to sell this camera and convinces Matthew that it is indeed a better buy. While this model is widely recognized as having numerous advanced features, Matthew does not require these additions—and is not likely in the future to need such sophisticated options. In the end, Matthew buys the more expensive camera believing that the salesperson's expertise is valuable in finding the "perfect fit" for his future needs.

### Questions

1. Is this a case of deceptive sales? Does the fact that the salesperson sold a "better" camera with sophisticated features justify the sale? Is the fact that she will receive a financial bonus relevant to a moral assessment of her actions?
2. Does the salesperson's "steering" toward a particular product, in this case a more expensive camera, represent a "significant harm" to the customer? Should customers expect that salespeople be objective, with the customer's best interest in mind, or should they accept the principle of "Buyer beware"?

This case was prepared by David Lawrence.

## CASE 6. *Marketing Malt Liquor*

During the summer of 1991, the surgeon general of the United States and advocacy groups led by the Center for Science in the Public Interest (CSPI) launched a campaign to remove G. Heileman Brewing Company's malt liquor PowerMaster from store shelves. The LaCrosse, Wisconsin-based brewer had experienced a series of financial setbacks. In January 1991 the company filed for protection from creditors in a New York bankruptcy court, claiming to be "struggling under a huge debt load." (Alix Freedman, "Heileman Will Be Asked to Change Potent Brew's Name," *The Wall Street Journal*, June 20, 1991, p. B1.) In an attempt to reverse its financial decline, Heileman introduced PowerMaster with a 5.9 percent alcohol content. Most malt liquors (defined by law as beers with alcohol levels above 4 percent) have a 5.5 percent average content, as compared with the typical 3.5 percent alcohol level of standard beers.

PowerMaster came under fire from both anti-alcohol and African-American activists. These groups charged that Heileman had created the name and the accompanying advertising campaign, which featured a black male model, with the intent of targeting young black men, who consume roughly one-third of all malt liquors. U.S. Surgeon General Antonia Novello joined the Heileman critics, calling the PowerMaster marketing campaign insensitive. Citing the economic burden that a legal contest to retain the brand name would entail, the company discontinued the product. However, beer industry executives and members criticized the government's role in the controversy. One newspaper columnist cited race as the critical factor in the campaign to remove PowerMaster, noting that the "It's the power" advertising slogan used in the marketing of Pabst Brewing Co.'s Olde English 800 malt liquor had gone unchallenged. James Sanders, president of the Washington, DC-based Beer Institute, contended that the government focused on the PowerMaster label to avoid having to focus on other factors such as unemployment and poverty, the real problems that the black community confronts.

### Questions

1. Would it be deceptive or manipulative advertising to call your beer "PowerMaster" and to use black male models?
2. Is it ethically insensitive for a company to target a specific market identified by race and gender?

## CASE 7. *The Conventions of Lying on Wall Street*

Salomon Brothers is among an elite group authorized to purchase U.S. Treasury notes from the U.S. government for resale to private investors. These notes are sold periodically at Treasury auctions. Before each auction, a firm receives "buy" orders from customers. The firm then tries to buy securities at the lowest possible price. The government places some restrictions on the bidding. First, a firm may purchase no more than 35 percent of the notes offered at a given auction for its portfolio. Second, if a firm holds large orders from an investor, it can buy bonds directly for that customer, and these bonds are *not* included in

This case was prepared by Tom L. Beauchamp and revised by Jeff Greene.

the 35 percent limit. If a firm is unable to purchase enough securities to fill the orders from its customers, the firm must then buy from competing firms at a higher rate than the auction rate.

In July 1991 Salomon Brothers, Inc., confessed to illegally purchasing U.S. Treasury notes on three separate occasions. They exploited the system in two ways. First, at the December, February, and May auctions, Salomon used customers' names to submit false bids. That is, they ordered bonds for customers who had *not* placed orders and did not know their names were being used. After the auction, Salomon added these bonds to its own portfolio. On second occasion, Salomon worked with a customer to purchase a large quantity of bonds in the customer's name. Salomon then bought back a portion of the bonds, effectively making a net purchase from the auction greater than 35 percent. Using this strategy, Salomon purchased 46 percent of Treasury notes sold on one occasion and 57 percent of the securities sold on another occasion.

Treasury auctions are also affected by the prevalent practice of sharing information. Current and former traders at several prominent Wall Street investment banks admit they regularly have shared "secrets" about the size and price of their bids at government auctions. This collusion to create a low bidding strategy results in firms paying less to the federal government. Consequently, the government makes less money to finance debt, causing an increase in taxes and interest rates.

This collusion is further complicated by strategies of deception. Lying has been tolerated and indeed has been expected for many years as part of the competition for trading. "It is part of the playing field. It's ingrained in the way the Street operates," one industry executive says, "I've stood out there on that trading floor and they lie to each other (before the auctions). That's part of the game. It was an exception when traders actually told the truth to each other about their bidding strategy." He adds, "They lie through their teeth to each other. You want to catch the [other] guy in an awkward position and pick him off."

In a report to the U.S. Congress, the Federal Home Mortgage Company claimed that two-thirds of Wall Street firms that it regularly deals with have lied to the agency to increase the chances of buying as many of the agency's securities as possible. Such deceit is so pervasive and routine on Wall Street that it has come to be regarded as the preferred and accepted way of doing business—the "standard of practice," as some put it. The common practice of submitting inflated orders has come under scrutiny from securities firms and the Federal Trade Commission, but the practice is so pervasive that it cannot be easily remedied. A small group of dealers holds purchasing power on the market and has long operated with financial success and with no serious challenges to its mode of operation.

One bond market specialist says, "I'm not condoning it or excusing it or saying it didn't go to an extreme . . . but people forget that the markets which are under the spotlight are part of that kind of distribution activity which for centuries has [been] associated with a fair amount of caveat emptor and puffery." The traditions of bluffing, deception, and puffery have created an environment in which every player in the "game" expects deception as the condition for playing.

## Questions

1. Is Wall Street actually a "game," and can these allegations and expectations be applied equally to every participant?
2. Should the FTC ignore deceit and collusion on Wall Street since it is ingrained in the system? Why or why not?
3. Does Wall Street have a valid standard of practice for disclosing information?

## *Suggested Supplementary Readings*


ALLMON, DEAN E., and JAMES GRANT. "Real Estate Sales Agents and the Code of Ethics." *Journal of Business Ethics*, 9 (October 1990).

ATTAS, DANIEL. "What's Wrong with 'Deceptive' Advertising?" *Journal of Business Ethics* 21 (1999): 49–59.

BEAUCHAMP, TOM L. "Manipulative Advertising." *Business and Professional Ethics Journal*, 3 (Spring–Summer 1984): 1–22.

BEAUCHAMP, TOM L. *Case Studies in Business, Society, and Ethics*. 5th ed. Upper Saddle River, NJ: Prentice-Hall, 2004, Chaps. 2, 4.

BOWIE, NORMAN, and RONALD F. DUSKA. "Applying the Moral Presuppositions of Business to Advertising and Hiring." In *Business Ethics*, 2nd ed., Norman E. Bowie and Ronald F. Duska. Englewood Cliffs, NJ: Prentice-Hall, 1990.

BRENKERT, G. G. "Marketing to Inner-City Blacks: PowerMaster and Moral Responsibility." *Business Ethics Quarterly*, 8 (1998): 1–18.

BROCKWAY, GEORGE. "Limited Paternalism and the Salesperson: A Reconsideration." *Journal of Business Ethics*, 12 (April 1993): 275–80.

*Business and Professional Ethics Journal*, 3 (Spring–Summer 1984). The entire issue is devoted to ethical issues in advertising.

CAMENISCH, PAUL. "Marketing Ethics." *Journal of Business Ethics*, 10 (April 1991).

CARSON, THOMAS L. "Ethical Issues in Sales: Two Case Studies." *Journal of Business Ethics*, 17 (May 1998): 725–28.

COHAN, JOHN ALAN. "Towards a New Paradigm in the Ethics of Women's Advertising." *Journal of Business Ethics*, 33 (October 2001): 323–37.

CRISP, ROGER. "Persuasive Advertising, Autonomy, and the Creation of Desire." *Journal of Business Ethics*, 6 (1987): 413–18.

DABHOLKAR, PRATIBHA A., and JAMES J. KELLARIS. "Toward Understanding Marketing Students' Ethical Judgement of Controversial Personal Selling Practices." *Journal of Business Research*, 24 (June 1992): 313–29.

DE CONINCK, J. B., and D. J. GOOD. "Perceptual Differences of Sales Practitioners and Students Concerning Ethical Behavior." *Journal of Business Ethics*, 8 (September 1989): 667–76.

EBEJER, JAMES M., and MICHAEL J. MORDEN. "Paternalism in the Marketplace: Should a Salesman Be His Buyer's Keeper?" *Journal of Business Ethics*, 7 (1998): 337–39.

GREENLAND, LEO. "Advertisers Must Stop Conning Consumers." *Harvard Business Review* (July/Aug. 1974): 18–28, 156.

HAMILTON III, J.B., JAMES R. LUMPKIN, and DAVID STRUTTON. "An Essay on When to Fully Disclose in Sales Relationships: Applying Two Practical Guidelines for Addressing Truth-Telling Problems." *Journal of Business Ethics*, 16 (April 1997): 545–60.

HARE, R. M. "Commentary on Beauchamp's 'Manipulative Advertising'." *Business Professional Ethics Journal*, 3 (Spring–Summer 1984): 23–28.

HITE, ROBERT E., and others. "A Content Analysis of Ethical Policy Statements Regarding Marketing Activities." *Journal of Business Ethics*, 7 (October 1988).

HOLLEY, DAVID M. "A Moral Evaluation of Sales Practices." *Business and Professional Ethics Journal*, 5 (1986–87): 3–21.

KAUFMANN, PATRICK J., N. CRAIG SMITH, and GWENDOLYN K. ORTMEYER. "Deception in Retailer High-Low Pricing: A 'Rule of Reason' Approach." *Journal of Retailing*, 70 (Summer 1994): 115–38.

KOEHN, DARYL. "Business and Game-Playing: The False Analogy." *Journal of Business Ethics*, 16 (1997): 1447–52.

KING, CAROLE. "It's Time to Disclose Commissions." *National Underwriter*, 94 (November 19, 1990).

LACZNICK, GENE R. "Marketing Ethics: Onward Toward Greater Expectations." *Journal of Public Policy and Marketing*, 12 (1993): 91–96.

LACZNICK, GENE R., and PATRICK E. MURPHY. *Ethical Marketing Decisions: The Higher Road*. Boston: Allyn and Bacon, 1993.

LEVITT, THEODORE. "The Morality (?) of Advertising." In *Ethical Issues in Business*, ed. Michael Boylan. Fort Worth, TX: Harcourt Brace and Company, 1995.

LIPPKE, RICHARD L. "Advertising and the Social Conditions of Autonomy." *Business and Professional Ethics Journal*, 8 (1989): 35–58.

———. "The 'Necessary Evil' Defense of Manipulative Advertising." *Business and Professional Ethics Journal*, 18 (1999): 3–21.

MAES, JEANNE D, and others. "The American Association of Advertising Agencies (4As) Standards of Practice: How Far Does this Professional Association's Code of Ethics Influence Reach?" *Journal of Business Ethics*, 17 (1998): 1155–61.

MCCLAREN, NCHOLAS. "Ethics in Personal Selling and Sales Management: A Review of the Literature Focusing on Empirical Findings and Conceptual Foundations." *Journal of Business Ethics*, 27 (October 2000): 285–303.

MICHALOS, ALEX C. "Advertising: Its: Logic, Ethics, and Economics." *A Pragmatic Approach to Business Ethics*. Thousand Oaks, CA: Sage Publications, 1995.

MURPHY, PATRICK E., and PRIDGEN, M. D. "Ethical and Legal Issues in Marketing," *Advances in Marketing and Public Policy*, 2 (1991): 185–244.

OAKES, G. "The Sales Process and the Paradoxes of Trust." *Journal of Business Ethics*, 9 (August 1990): 67–79.

PERKINS, ANNE G. "Advertising: The Costs of Deception." *Harvard Business Review*, 72 (May–June 1994): 10–11.

PETERSON, ROBIN T. "Physical Environment Television Advertisement Themes." *Journal of Business Ethics*, 10 (March 1991).

POLONSKY, MICHAEL JAY, and others. "Communicating Environmental Information: Are Marketing Claims on Packaging Misleading?" *Journal of Business Ethics*, 17 (1998): 281–94.

PHILLIPS, BARBARA J. "In Defense of Advertising: A Social Perspective." *Journal of Business Ethics*, 16 (1997): 109–18.

PHILLIPS, MICHAEL J. "The Inconclusive Case Against Manipulative Advertising." *Business and Professional Ethics Journal*, 13 (1994).

PREDMORE, CAROLYN E., and TARA J. RADIN. "The Myth of the Salesperson: Intended and Unintended Consequences of Product-Specific Sales Incentives." *Journal of Business Ethics*, 36 (March 2002); 79–92.

QUINN, JOHN F. "Moral Theory and Defective Tobacco Advertising and Warnings." *Journal of Business Ethics*, 8 (November 1989).

SMITH, N. CRAIG, and JOHN A. QUELCH. *Ethics in Marketing Management*. Homewood, IL: Irwin, 1992.

SNEDDON, ANDREW. "Advertising and Deep Autonomy." *Journal of Business Ethics*, 33 (September 2001): 15–28.

SULLIVAN, ROGER J. "A Response to 'Is Business Bluffing Ethical?'" *Business and Professional Ethics Journal*, 3 (Winter 1984).

VALLANCE, ELIZABETH. *Business Ethics at Work*. New York: Cambridge University Press, 1995.

WONG, KENMAN L. "Tobacco Advertising and Children: The Limits of First Amendment Protection." *Journal of Business Ethics*, 15 (1996): 1051–64.

# Chapter Eight

# Ethical Issues in Information Technology

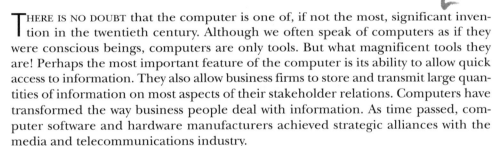

## INTRODUCTION

There is no doubt that the computer is one of, if not the most, significant invention in the twentieth century. Although we often speak of computers as if they were conscious beings, computers are only tools. But what magnificent tools they are! Perhaps the most important feature of the computer is its ability to allow quick access to information. They also allow business firms to store and transmit large quantities of information on most aspects of their stakeholder relations. Computers have transformed the way business people deal with information. As time passed, computer software and hardware manufacturers achieved strategic alliances with the media and telecommunications industry.

With this transformation in information gathering, storage, retrieval, and transmittal, a number of ethical issues have surfaced. In almost every case, the ethical issue is not new. However, the computer and surrounding information technology have added layers of complexity to the issue. Consider the issue of pornography. Before the computer, it was fairly easy to keep pornography out of the hands of children. Adult bookstores were off limits to children. There were relatively few movie theaters that showed x-rated films, and these tended to be away from schools and middle class residential areas. Should a child get Playboy into the house, parents had an uncanny ability to discover it. The computer provided easy access to a wide range of pornography. The pornographic images could be viewed in the privacy of a child's room and once the child signed out of the site, it was not obvious that anything was amiss. Chat rooms provided an additional opportunity for young people to be taken advantage of by sexual predators. Keeping children safe from sexual predators and away from pornography has always been an issue; however, the computer has greatly complicated that task.

The computer has had an impact on most of the issues that one would find in a text on contemporary moral problems. Whole texts are now devoted to ethical issues in information technology. In this business ethics text, we limit our discussion to two-privacy and intellectual property rights. Protecting one's privacy and protecting one's intellectual property have been a challenge before the computer came into widespread use. However, the computer has vastly complicated the when and how privacy and intellectual property should be protected. For example in her article, Deborah Johnson points out that computer technology has changed the scale of information gathering, the kind of information that can be gathered, and the scale of information exchange.

## COMPUTERS AND PRIVACY

Deborah Johnson provides an overview of the many privacy issues that face computer users. She begins with a series of scenarios that presents specific issues that require theoretical ethical resolution. Johnson points out that the normal way of addressing these issues is to speak of tradeoffs between the right to privacy of those individuals whom the information is about and the needs of those who use the information. Those who want the information argue that it makes for better decision making. Imagine how putting medical records on computer would help avoid some of the medical errors discussed in the Lisa Belkin article in Chapter 3. What is needed, Johnson believes, are arguments on behalf of privacy that counterbalance the benefits of information gathering. Since improved decision making is a social good, Johnson is attracted to arguments that make privacy a social good as well. The exercise of autonomy is a social good and since privacy is necessary for one to exercise his or her autonomy, Johnson believes that she has the argument that will best counterbalance the improved decision-making argument.

Daren Charters provides a specific instance of this issue in his article on DoubleClick reprinted in this chapter. DoubleClick has always used cookies. A cookie works as follows: A user clicks on a site and asks for information. A small computer file (cookie) that identifies a computer with a unique tracking number is installed on the user's computer. The firm that places the cookie there can now track the users of this computer on Web sites in its network. The firm then stores that information and can send ads to that computer and/or sell information to a third party that allows that third party to send information to a computer. Suppose you email a ski shop because you are interested in a new pair of skis. If the right cookie is attached to your computer, you may start receiving ads to motels and condos from ski areas all over the country and beyond. The use of cookies creates obvious privacy concerns. But DoubleClick had proposed going further. It had proposed buying Abacus, which was a source of personally identifiable information (PPI) on 88 million American households. That would give DoubleClick the ability to track the user of a computer on the network and know who the user is. That information could be sold to third parties. When the impending merger became public, people were sufficiently outraged to convince DoubleClick not to proceed with the merger. However, other companies have quietly completed mergers that would give them the ability to secure the kind of PPI that DoubleClick had wanted to secure.

Basically your privacy is not protected on the Internet. Many Web sites have privacy policies and it is possible to get privacy seals. Many Web sites that have privacy policies enable you to indicate that you do not want to receive ads from the site or have information the site has on you sold to third parties. This is called opting out. Privacy advocates would require a strategy called opting in. Only if you opt in could you receive ads and you would have to explicitly agree to have the site sell the information it has about you to third parties. Some privacy advocates argue that the United States should adopt strict privacy laws similar to those adopted by the European Union. Others argue that self-regulation through the use of privacy seals or technical fixes are sufficient to protect a person's right to privacy on the Internet.

Microsoft is developing a new operating system called Palladium. This system, still in development, would revolutionize how individuals and institutions use and make secure the information they receive and send out on the Internet. According to press reports, Palladium will tell you whom you are dealing with and what they are doing, it will protect information, stop viruses and worms, eliminate spam, safeguard privacy, and control the information you send. It would also enable companies to protect their intellectual property.[1]

Supporters of stronger laws point out that corporations cannot be trusted to regulate themselves. Even as Microsoft develops Palladium to protect user privacy and intellectual property, it has been accused of creating products now on the market that hinder individual privacy. For example, Passport is a digital wallet that includes people's addresses and credit card information. Its purpose is to make shopping online easier. However, it also provides the company with a detailed profile of a person's buying habits.[2]

## INTELLECTUAL PROPERTY

Intellectual property appears at a number of points in the new information technology. There are the computer software programs that enable users to accomplish their goals. One thinks of Word, Excel, and other programs that are needed to accomplish word processing and data analysis. Then there are items like computer games that are designed for use on computers. Finally, there are intellectual property issues when a computer operator accesses an item that is under copyright protection but which can be transmitted to anyone who wants to have it without collecting any copyright fee.

The issue of intellectual property rights most familiar to readers of this text is the dowloading of music. The courts declared that Napster infringed on copyrights and was ordered to change its way of doing business. Its new business model failed and Naptster is now in bankruptcy court. It is interesting to note that it is legal to tape a program on your VCR, but it is illegal to download a song under copyright protection. Selections from the two court cases, *Sony Corp v. Universal City Studios Inc.*, and *A&M Records v. Napster* are included in this chapter. The concern of Universal City Studios was unauthorized copying. Suppose you recorded a program and then gave your tape to others to copy. The court found that the impact on individual viewers would be too great to justify forbidding the copying. However, the sharing of music would have a great impact on those who held copyright. Presumably the sales of CD's would plunge if one could download a song and then share it with anyone else on the Internet.

However, Napster like companies that allow the downloading of music for free and arguably illegally are still in existence. Even *The Wall Street Journal* published an article that provides a five-step process for downloading music, and with just a bit of reading both explicitly and between the lines you can tell how to download the music for free.[3]

The music industry itself has stepped into the fray. MusicNet was the cooperative result of AOL Time Warner Inc., EMI Group PLC, Bertelsmann AG and the Seattle software company RealNetworks.[4] MusicNet is not a success. Critics point out that it does not allow consumers to keep the songs permanently, the songs cannot be transferred to portable devices and they cannot be exchanged with friends who have not signed up for the service. As of mid-2002, there were only 40,000 subscribers while millions download music from free sites.

Issues such as these are the concern of Richard De George in his article "Intellectual Property and the Information Age." De George notes three characteristics of intellectual property: (1) It is infinitely sharable and one person's having the property is compatible with many other persons having it as well; (2) any expression of an idea builds on prior knowledge that is not one's own creation; and (3) it is fundamentally social in the sense that it can be further developed when shared. There are good reasons not to have a property right in such knowledge. Indeed that idea was behind the Linux operating system and Shareware. De George then examines the ethical justification for copyright. There is a utilitarian argument that copyright protection is necessary to encourage the production of these works. There is also a fairness argument that says that those who take the time, energy, and money to develop the ideas should be compensated. De George then looks at the issue of whether or not intellectual property deserves copyright protection from four different perspectives: (1) the view of scholars and authors who are concerned about honesty and proper attribution; (2) the view of the entrepreneur who views copying as taking one's property and in so doing increasing the risk that the entrepreneur would be driven out of business; (3) the view of the buyers; and (4) view of society as a whole. De George then considers what would be right with respect to copying programs for personal use and the peer-to-peer exchange of copyrighted material. Although protection may be more justified for the latter, De George points out how difficult it is and would be to enforce this copyright protection.

Exactly, Lawrence Lessig would argue. He thinks that the issue of intellectual property cannot be settled by extending copyright law. Rather we need to look to the technology itself—to computer code as he refers to it. Lessig puts it this way: "In cyberspace we must understand how code regulates—how the software and hardware that make cyberspace what it is *regulate* cyberspace as it is. . . . *Code is law.*"[5] Moreover, we should use code to provide copyright protection rather than law, because the law will overreact and go beyond the rationale for copyright protection in the first place. Indeed that is already happening. Lessig analyzes the Sony and Napster cases and admits that the likelihood of unauthorized copying is much greater with Napster. However, Lessig thinks we should look for less draconian solutions. One suggestion is compulsory license. Lessig refers to this as compensation without control. He uses cable television as an example. Cable television is not permitted to take content from the networks—reruns of old shows for example—and broadcast them without paying a fee. On the other hand, the networks cannot prevent the cable companies from showing the reruns so long as they pay a fee. This is a perfect example of compensation without control. Lessig concludes by urging Congress to adopt something analogous to the solution found with cable television rather than "handing over the keys to Hollywood."

## NOTES

1. Palladium is described by Steven Levy, "The BIG Secret," *Newsweek*, July 1, 2002, pp. 42–44.
2. See "A Window Into Your Personal Life" *Business Week* July 2, 2001, pp. 63–64.
3. Nick Wingfield, "Even You Can Download Music," *The Wall Street Journal*, May 15, 2002, D1, D3.
4. Anna Wilde Matthews, Martin Peers, and Nick Wingfield, "The Music Industry is Finally Online, But Few Listen," *The Wall Street Journal* May 7, 2002, A1, A20.
5. Lawrence Lessig, *Code and Other Laws of Cyberspace*, New York: Basic Books, 1999.

## COMPUTERS AND PRIVACY

# Privacy

*Deborah Johnson*

### SCENARIO 5.1 Fund-Raising and Potential Donors

Jan Perez began college as a computer science major. She loves computers and has always been very good at figuring out how to do things on the Internet and the Web. However, after a year and a half of college, Jan decides that as much as she likes computing, she doesn't want to major in it; she chooses, instead, a major that is more likely to lead to a career involving contact and interaction with people. She also wants something that involves public service or promoting good causes.

After college, Jan is delighted to find that the development office of a large, private university wants to hire her. She accepts the job enthusiastically, thinking she will do some good by raising money for a great university.

Jan's supervisor is extremely pleased to find out how much Jan knows about computers and the Internet. Within a few months of starting the job, Jan is asked to find out all she can about a Frank Doe. Mr. Doe has never been approached by the university; Jan's supervisor only recently heard from another donor that Mr. Doe has a very positive impression of the university and has the capacity to make a major contribution.

The fund-raising unit needs to know how wealthy Mr. Doe is to determine what kind of contribution to ask for. They need to know about his life and interests to know which of their projects he might want to support. And, they need to know about him personally so they can approach him, put him at ease, and not offend him in any way. Jan is given some suggestions about where to look, but she is also told to find out whatever she can.

Using the Internet, Jan does the following:

1. She searches a variety of public databases which give her information about his real estate holdings, his memberships on the boards of public corporations, a list of corporations for which he is a major stockholder.
2. She searches other databases to find out if he has made contributions to political parties or campaigns.
3. She searches archives of newspapers to see if Mr. Doe has ever been written about in the news.
4. She searches other databases to see if he has had any encounters with law enforcement agencies.
5. She searches other databases to find out what religious organizations he supports.
6. She contacts credit agencies and requests his credit history.
7. Jan wonders if Amazon.com would tell her what types of books, if any, Mr. Doe purchases.
8. Jan wonders which Internet service provider Mr. Doe uses; she contemplates what she could learn about Mr. Doe if his service provider would tell her about his online activities. For example, he may keep a portfolio of stock holdings in his account.
9. Mr. Doe is a local resident. Jan's supervisor mentions in passing that Mr. Doe, she has been told, uses the university's medical complex for all his medical treatment. Jan decides to see whether she can access patient files at the university medical complex. Much to her surprise, she is able to access Mr. Doe's insurance records and this tells her that in the last several years, he has been receiving frequent treatment for a kidney ailment. She wonders if this will make him interested in contributing to the hospital or for kidney research.

At the end of several weeks of research, Jan has an enormous amount of information about Mr. Doe. As she acquired each bit of information from a separate database, there didn't seem anything wrong with doing that; now, however, the cumulative effect of putting all of this information together makes Jan feel uncomfortable. She wonders if this is right. She feels a bit like a voyeur or stalker.

Has Jan done anything wrong?

### SCENARIO 5.2 Taking data home.

Max Brown works in the Department of Alcoholism and Drug Abuse of a northeastern state. The agency administers programs for individuals with alcohol and drug problems and maintains huge databases of information on the clients who use their services. Max has been asked to take a look at the track records of the treatment programs. He is to put together a report that contains information about such factors as number of clients seen in each program each month for the past five years, length of each client's treatment, number of clients who return after completion of a program, criminal histories of clients, and so on.

To put together this report, Max has been given access to all files in the agency's mainframe computer. It takes Max several weeks to find the information he needs because it is located in a variety of places in the system. As he finds information, he downloads it to the computer in his office; that is, he copies the information from the mainframe onto the hard disk of his office microcomputer.

Under pressure to get the report finished by the deadline, Max finds that he is continuously distracted at work. He decides that he will have to work at home over the weekend to finish on time. This will not be a problem. He copies the information (containing, among other things, personal information on clients) onto several disks and takes them home. He finishes the report over the weekend. To be safe, he leaves a copy of the report on his home computer as well as copying it onto a disk which he takes up to work.

Was Max wrong in moving personal information from the mainframe to his office computer? In moving the information from his office computer to a disk? To his home computer? In leaving the information on his computer at home? What could happen as a result of Max's treatment of the data? Should the agency for which Max works have a policy on use of personal information stored in its system? What might such a policy specify?

## Scenario 5.3 Workplace Monitoring

Estelle Cavello was recently hired to supervise a large unit of a medical insurance company. Estelle will be in charge of a unit responsible for processing insurance claims. When she was hired, the vice president made it clear to Estelle that he expects her to significantly increase the efficiency of the unit. The company has targets for the number of claims that should be processed by each unit and Estelle's unit has never been able to meet its target.

One of the first things Estelle does when she starts this job is to install a software system that will allow her to monitor the work of each and every claims processor. The software allows Estelle to record the number of keystrokes made per minute on any terminal in the unit. It also allows her to bring the work of others up on her computer screen so that she can watch individual work as it is being done. As well, Estelle can access copies of each employee's work at the end of each day. She can find out how much time each worker spent with the terminal off; she can see what correspondence the person prepared; she can review e-mail that the worker sent or received; and so on.

Should Estelle use this software to monitor her employees?

## Scenario 5.4 Data Mining

Ravi Singh works for one of the major credit card companies in their data-processing center. The company is continuously developing new products to offer to customers and add revenue to the corporation. He is an avid reader of computer magazines and recently has been reading about data-mining tools that are now available for a reasonable cost. Ravi goes to his supervisor with the suggestion that their unit purchase one of these tools and use it to find out more about their customers. The information may be telling in terms of customer interest and capability.

The supervisor likes the idea. After exploring the systems that are available, the unit purchases one and Ravi is assigned to explore patterns in the database of information on the company's customers and their purchasing habits.

Ravi discovers that certain zip codes are highly correlated with loan defaults. These zip codes must be in low-income areas for the mined and analysed data indicate that the company could reduce its losses significantly by refusing to extend credit to anyone living in twenty-five zip codes, while at the same time not significantly reducing their revenues. In other words, on average losses due to default generated by individuals in those zip codes were greater than revenue generated.

Ravi continues with his data mining. Next he discoverers a correlation between those who use their credit cards to make contributions to Hindu charitable organizations and those who charge over $40,000 a year on their credit cards.

This information seems important. If the company made a special effort to solicit Hindus as customers, it might be able to increase its revenues significantly.

Ravi goes to his supervisor with the suggestion that they adopt these strategies. Has Ravi done anything wrong? If his company adopts these strategies, have they done anything wrong?

These scenarios depict just a few of the ways that information can be created, gathered, moved, and used with computer technology. Of all the social and ethical concerns surrounding computer technology, the threat to personal privacy was probably the first to capture public attention. And this issue persists in drawing public concern and leading to action by policy makers. One hears about it frequently in the popular media; major studies continue to be undertaken; new books continue to be written; and new legislation continues to be passed to regulate electronic information. It will be helpful to begin by laying out just why and how computer technology facilitates information gathering and seems to threaten personal privacy.

## IS THERE ANYTHING NEW HERE?

I suggest that computer and information technology, like other new technologies, creates new possibilities; it creates possibilities for behavior and activities that were not possible before the technology. Public concern about computers and privacy arises for precisely this reason. Computers make it possible (and in many cases, cheap and easy) to gather detailed information about individuals to an extent never possible before. Federal, state, and local government agencies now maintain extensive records of individual behavior including such things as any interactions with criminal justice agencies, income taxes, employment history for social security, use of human services agencies, motor vehicle registration, and so on. As well, private organizations maintain extensive databases of information on individual purchases, airline travel, credit worthiness, health records, telephone or cellular phone usage, employment, and so on.

We have the technological capacity for the kind of massive, continuous surveillance of individuals that was envisioned in such frightening early twentieth-century science fiction works as George Orwell's *1984* (1949) and Zamyatin's *We* (1920). The only differences between what is now possible and what was envisioned then is that much of the surveillance of individuals that takes place now is done by private institutions (marketing firms, insurance companies, credit agencies), *and* much of the surveillance now is via electronic records instead of by direct human observation or through cameras. . . .

We can ask whether there is anything fundamentally different about today as compared to fifty years ago or a century ago. Record-keeping is far from a new phenomenon. Government agencies and private corporations have been keeping records for thousands of years and using this information in variety of ways. So, is there anything different about the kind or degree of privacy that we have today as compared to fifty or a hundred years ago?

Computer technology has changed record-keeping activities in a number of undeniable and powerful ways. First, the *scale of information gathering* has changed. Second, the *kind of information* that can be gathered has changed. And, third, the *scale of exchange* of information has changed enormously.

In the precomputer, "paper-and-ink" world, the mere fact that records were paper and stored in file cabinets, imposed some limitations on the amount of data gathered, who had access, how long records were retained, and so on. Electronic records do not have these limitations. We can collect, store, manipulate, exchange, and retain practically infinite quantities of data. The point is that technology no longer limits what can be done; now only time and money and, perhaps, human capabilities impose limits on the quantity of information that can be gathered and processed.

The kind of information that it is now possible to collect and use is also new. Think about the workplace monitoring scenario at the beginning of this chapter. Employers can keep records of every keystroke an employee makes. Before computers, finger movements of this kind would not have been thought to be important, let alone the kind of thing that could be recorded. Employers can monitor their employees' uses of the Web, their participation in chat rooms, not to mention their e-mail.

One particularly important new form of information is referred to as transaction generated information (TGI). TGI includes purchases made with a credit card, telephone calls, entry and exit from intelligent highways, and so on. As you move about in the world, your activities (transactions) are automatically recorded. . . .

There is no single government or private organization accumulating all of the information. TGI gathering seems to be fragmented and, therefore, seems not to pose the threat of Big Brother.

Indeed, in the very early days of computing, especially in the 1960s and 1970s, many social commentators expressed concern about the information gathering potential of computer technology and these fears were articulated as fears of Big Brother—fears that all the information would be funneled to a highly centralized U.S. government. The fear was that electronic information gathering practices would give too much power to government. It would create a potentially totalitarian government, a surveillance society. Those fears wained in part because legislation was passed that restricted government information gathering.

Fear also weakened because computer technology changed. It became smaller and cheaper, and, consequently, became available much more widely. On the one hand, this diffused fear of Big Brother because it promised computer power in the hands of "many" rather than just big government. At the same time, however, smaller computers in the hands of many companies and individuals facilitated the exchange of information to an extent previously unimaginable. Typically information of one kind will be gathered and stored separately from information of another kind; for example, marketing firms will gather and store information on buying habits, one government agency will record income tax information, another government agency will record criminal justice activities, and so on.

With computer technology, however, it is technically possible to combine all this information. In the private sector this is done routinely. Think of the fund-raising example at the beginning of this chapter. Within government this happens less frequently because the Privacy Act of 1974 restricted data matching. . . .

The restriction on matching mentioned in the Privacy Act of 1974 did not apply to private organizations, just to the federal government. What was called "matching" in the 1970s is today called data mining and is quite common in private organizations. Indeed, you can now purchase data-mining tools, sometimes called knowledge discovery instruments (kdi) that help find patterns of behavior among groups of individuals. Their use is described in Scenario 5.4.

Add to these changes in the scale and kind of information gathered with computer technology, a further element. Because computerized information is electronic, it is easy to copy and distribute. Before computers were connected by telephone lines, information could be fairly easily copied using tapes or disks. Now that computers are connected via telecommunication lines, information can go anywhere in the world where there are telephone lines. Hence, the extent to which information can be exchanged is now practically limitless. Once information about an individual is recorded in a machine or on a disk, it can be easily transferred to another machine or disk. It can be bought and sold, given away, traded, and even stolen. The information can spread instantaneously from one company to another, from one sector to another, and from one country to another.

The Max Brown case (Scenario 5.2) is illustrative here. He takes sensitive data home on a disk. From a technical point of view, he could have simply accessed the data from home. But in either case, the data moves around. Once it moves out of its source, it is very difficult to keep track of all the places it might exist, be it on disks or hard drives.

Movement of data happens when you subscribe to a magazine and your name and address are sold to a marketing firm. The marketing firm infers from the subscription that you have certain tastes and begins sending you a variety of opportunities to buy the things you like. Forester and Morrison (1990) report the case of a women who took her landlord to court after he refused to do anything about the pest problem in her apartment. He did not show up for court but evicted her shortly after the court date. When she went looking for another apartment, she found that she was repeatedly turned down by landlords. She would look at an apartment, notify the landlord that she wanted it, and within a few days hear back that the apartment was already rented to someone else. It turned out that a database of names of individuals who take landlords to court is maintained and the information is sold to landlords. Needless to say, landlords don't want to rent to individuals who may take them to court.

As far as the technology goes, the distribution of information can take place with or without the knowledge of the person whom the information is about, and it can take place intentionally as well as unintentionally. There is an unintentional distribution when records are provided that contain more information than is requested. As well, when information is stolen, the exchange is unintentional from the point of view of the agency that gathered or maintained the records. Think again of the Max Brown scenario; Brown's wife, children, or friends might (while using his home computer) inadvertently access the data on individuals in the state's treatment programs and see the names of clients in the state programs.

If all of this were not cause enough for concern, there is more. Information stored in a computer can be erroneous, and, at the same time, can be readily distributed. The effect of a small error can be magnified enormously. Information can be erroneous due to unintentional human error or because someone has intentionally altered it to harm a competitor or enhance their own records. It is important to remember that databases of information are not always as secure as we would like them to be. When computers are connected via telecommunications lines, the possibilities of data being tampered with or stolen are increased. . . .

Suppose John A. Smith's file is inadvertently combined with John B. Smith's. John A. Smith is turned down for a loan on the basis of erroneous information since John A. has *never* failed to pay his debts, has a good job, and has a sizeable holding of stocks, but John B. has a low-paying job, declared bankruptcy three years ago, and is once again deeply in debt. John A. is wronged when he is turned down for a loan. Moreover, suppose that after a series of inquires and complaints by John A., the error is identified, and John A.'s file is corrected. (This is not always as easy as it sounds. Companies are often very slow in responding to complaints about errors in records.) John A. asks his bank to send for the updated report, and the bank changes its mind about the loan when it sees the accurate information. It would appear that the injury to John A. has been remedied. Not necessarily. The inaccurate information may have been given to other companies before it was corrected, and they, in turn, may have given it to others. As a result, it may be difficult, if not impossible, to track down all the databases in which the error is now stored. It may be impossible to completely expunge the erroneous information from John A.'s records.

When information is stored in a computer, there is little incentive to get rid of it; hence, information may stay with an individual for a long period of time. Information stored in a computer takes up very little space and is easy to maintain and transfer. Because of this, details can be carried in a record forever. Something insignificant that happened to an individual when he was 10 years old may easily follow him through life because the information has been recorded once and there is little motivation to delete it. In the past, the inconvenience of paper served to some degree as an inhibitor to keeping and exchanging apparently useless information.[1]

Because it is so easy to keep information, some fear that individuals will get categorized and stigmatized at early stages in their lives. One way to see this is to imagine what it would be like if elementary and secondary school records were put into a national database where prospective employers, government agencies, or insurance companies could get access. We might find decisions being made about us on the basis of testing done when we were in elementary school or on the basis of disciplinary incidents in our teenage years.

When decision makers are faced with making decisions about individuals, they want data. They want data both to insure a good decision and to justify their decision to others. When they must choose between making a decision on the basis of little or no data, and making it on the basis of lots of data known to be unreliable, many prefer the latter. Hence, information tends to get used if it is available even though it may not be relevant or reliable.

In summary, while record-keeping is, by no means, a new activity, it appears that computer and information technology has changed record-keeping activities in the following ways: (1) it has made a *new scale* of information gathering possible; (2) it has made *new kinds* of information possible, especially transaction generated information; (3) it has made *a new scale of* information *distribution and exchange* possible; (4) the *effect* of erroneous information can be *magnified*; and (5) information about events in one's life may *endure* much longer than ever before. These five changes make the case for the claim that the world we live in is more like a panopticon than ever before.

As an aside here, you may be tempted to say that computers are not really the problem or the cause of the problem. It is individuals and organizations that are creating, gathering, exchanging, and using information. Computers, according to this line of argument, are simply tools: If there is a problem, the problem is the people who use computers, not the computers themselves.

While there is some truth to this, it is important to remember that computer technology facilitates certain kinds of activities. Computer technology makes it possible for individuals to do things they could not do before. Individuals and organizations are more likely to engage in activities when they are possible (not to speak of easy and inexpensive). For example, in Scenario 5.4, Estelle would not have monitored employees to the extent she did or in quite the way that she did if computers and the monitoring software were not available. Individuals choose actions because they find themselves in a world which has certain possibilities; in a world with different possibilities, they would behave differently. Insofar as computer technology changes what it is possible for human beings to do, it can be a major factor in determining what people do and the kind of society in which we live.

## UNDERSTANDING THE "COMPUTERS AND PRIVACY" ISSUE

### Uses of Information

Information about individuals would not exist if organizations did not have an interest in using it. Information is created, collected, and exchanged because organizations can use it to further their interests and activities. Information about individuals is used to make decisions about those individuals, and often the decisions profoundly affect the lives of those individuals whom the information is about. Information about you, stored in a database, may be used to decide whether or not you will be hired by a company; whether or not you will be given a loan; whether or not you will be called to the police station for interrogation, arrest, or prosecution; whether or not you will receive education, housing, social security, unemployment compensation, and so on.

The computers and privacy issue is often framed as an issue that calls for a balancing of the needs of those who use information about individuals (typically government agencies and private institutions) *against* the needs or rights of those individuals whom the information is about. Later in this chapter, I will argue against this framing of the issue on grounds that it is biased in favor of information gathering, but for the moment it is important to understand why organizations want information.

In general, those who want information about individuals want it because they believe that it will help them to make better decisions. Several examples quickly illustrate this point. Banks believe that the more information they have about an individual, the better they will be able to make judgments about that individual's ability to pay back a loan or about the size of the credit line the individual can handle. The FBI's National Crime Information Center (NCIC) provides criminal histories of individuals to all the states. Law enforcement agencies justify the existence of this database on grounds that the more information they have about individuals, the better they will be able to identify and capture criminals. We might also bring in examples from the insurance industry where decisions are made about which individuals to insure at what rate, or from the Department of Health and Human Services where decisions are made about who qualifies for various welfare and medical benefits. And, of course, don't forget the fund-raising organization, data-mining and workplace monitoring scenarios at the beginning of this chapter. In theory, the more and better the information these organizations have, the better their decision making will be.

Companies also claim that they need information about their customers to serve them better. If a company like Amazon.com keeps track of the books that you buy, it can infer from this information what new books you are likely to be interested in. When they send you information on these new books, they claim they are providing a service to you (even if it is one that you didn't ask for and one that happens also to serve their interest in selling more books). If an advertising firm knows what I buy at the grocery store, it can use that information to send me coupons for items I am likely to buy. If television stations know what I watch on television and when I change the channel, they can use that information to develop programming more suited to my tastes. If marketing companies know about my income level and my tastes in clothes, food, sports, and music, they can send me catalogues or special offers for products and services that fit my precise tastes.

In the standard understanding of the computers and privacy issue we have public and private institutions that want information about individuals. They make a powerful case for how this information improves their decision making and helps them to do their job better and more efficiently. In theory, all of that means better serving us, as consumers and citizens. It means, for example, better law enforcement; more efficient government; better, more customized services; and so on.

Personal privacy is generally put on the other side of the balancing scales. The issue is framed so that we have to balance all the good things that are achieved through information gathering and exchange *against* the desire or need for personal privacy. Some even claim that we have a right to personal privacy for if that were true, the scales would weigh heavily on the side of personal privacy. From a legal and constitutional point of view, however, we have, at most, a limited and complex right to privacy.

This framing of the issue seems to be skewed heavily in favor of information gathering and exchange. The only way to counter the powerful case made on behalf of information gathering and exchange is, it would seem, to make a more powerful case for protecting and ensuring privacy in the lives of individuals. Either we must show that there is a grave risk or danger to these information-gathering activities—a danger so great that it counterbalances the benefits of the activity. Or we must show that there is a greater benefit to be gained from constraining these activities. To put this another way, once the benefits of information gathering and exchange are on the table, the burden of proof is on privacy advocates to show either that there is something harmful about information gathering and exchange or that there is some benefit to be gained from constraining information gathering. Either way, there is a daunting hurdle to overcome.

Many of us feel uncomfortable with the amount of information that is gathered about us. We do not like not knowing who has what information about us and how it is being used. Why are we so uncomfortable? What do we fear? Part of the fear is, no doubt, related to our mistrust of large, faceless organizations, and part of it is related to mistrust of government. The challenge is to translate this discomfort and fear into an argument that counterbalances the benefits of information gathering.

Odd as it may seem, the case for protecting personal privacy has not been easy to make. From the point of view of public policy, arguments on behalf of personal privacy have not "won the day." I am going to discuss a number of ways that the case for individual privacy can be and has been made, but I am also going to argue for a somewhat different framing of the issue. At least part of the problem, I believe, lies in framing the issue as a matter of balancing the interests of private and public institutions against the interests of individuals. We ought, instead, to recognize that privacy is both an individual and a social good, one that goes to the heart of the kind of beings we are and important to the realization of a democratic society.

### Personal Privacy

Two big questions have dominated the philosophical literature on privacy: What is it and why is it valuable? Needless to say, the two questions are intertwined. Neither has been easy to answer. The term *privacy* seems to be used to refer to a wide range of social practices and domains, for example, what we do in the privacy of our own homes, domains of life in which the government should not interfere, things about ourselves that we tell only our closest friends. Privacy seems, also, to overlap other concepts such as freedom or liberty, seclusion, autonomy, secrecy, controlling information about ourselves. So, privacy is a complex and, in many respects, elusive concept. A variety of arguments have been put forward to explain the value of personal privacy.

As we review several of these, it will be helpful to keep in mind a distinction between privacy as an instrumental good and privacy as an intrinsic good. When privacy is presented as being valuable because it leads to something else, then it is cast as an instrumental good. In such arguments, privacy is presented as a means to an end. Its value lies in its connection to something else. On the other hand, when privacy is presented as good in itself, it is presented as a value in and of itself. As you might predict, the latter argument is harder to make for it requires showing that privacy has value even when it leads to nothing else or even when it may lead to negative consequences.

The most important arguments on behalf of privacy as an instrumental good have focused either on its being necessary for special relationships or on its being necessary for democracy. Charles Fried (1968), for example, argued that we have to have privacy to have relationships of intimacy and trust. In a society in which individuals were always being observed (as in the panopticon), he argued, friendship, intimacy, and trust could not develop. If we want such relationships, we must create domains of privacy. Others argue that privacy is necessary for democracy. Here the important idea is that if individuals are constantly being observed, they will not be able to exercise the kind of independent thinking that is essential for democracy to work.

The arguments on behalf of privacy as an instrumental good begin to cross over into privacy as an intrinsic good when they suggest a connection between privacy and autonomy. You'll remember from the discussion of Kantian theory that autonomy is not just one among many values; autonomy is fundamental to what it means to be human, to our value as human beings. If privacy is essential to autonomy, then the loss of privacy would be a threat to our most fundamental values. But the connection between privacy and autonomy is often presented not exactly as a means-ends relationship. Rather the suggestion is that autonomy is inconceivable without privacy.

It will take us too far afield to explore all of these arguments. In what follows, I am going to explore several of the most salient arguments on behalf of privacy, and I will move from a focus on privacy as an individual good to privacy as a *social good.*

### Information Mediates Relationships

To begin with what seems most clear, information about an individual seems to be a fundamental precondition for establishing a relationship with that individual. Moreover, the information determines the character of the relationship. James Rachels (1975) has argued that people need to control information about themselves in order to maintain a diversity of relationships. His insight is that individuals maintain a variety of relationships (e.g., with parents, spouses, employers, friends, casual acquaintances, and so on), and each of these relationships is different because of the different information that each party has. Think, for example, about what your best friend knows about you as compared with what your teacher, your employer, or your dentist knows about you. These diverse relationships are a function of differing information.

Take your relationship with your dentist. Suppose she has been your dentist for five years but she knows relatively little about you, except, of course, for what she knows about your teeth. Now suppose you need extensive work done on your teeth, and you begin to go to her office regularly at a time of the day when she is not rushed. You strike up conversations about your various interests. Each time you talk to her, she learns more about you and you learn more about her. Suppose you discover you have several hobbies and sports interests in common. She suggests that if you schedule your appointment next week so you are her last appointment, you could go out and play tennis afterward. The story can go on about how this relationship might develop from one of patient-professional, to good friends, perhaps to one of intimate friends. The changes in the relationship will in large measure be a function of the amount and kind of information you acquire about one another.

Rachels uses this insight to argue that privacy is important because it allows us to maintain a diversity of relationships. If everything were open to all (that is, if everyone knew the same things about you), then diversity would not be possible. You would have similar relationships with everyone.

Rachels seems right about the way information affects relationships. We control relationships by controlling the information that others have about us. When we lose control over information, we lose significant control over how others perceive and treat us. However, while Rachels seems right about this, his analysis does not quite get at what is worrisome about all the information gathering that is facilitated by computer technology. That is, the information gathering and exchange that goes on via computer technology does not seem, on the face of it, to threaten the diversity of personal relationships each of us has. For example, despite the fact that huge quantities of data now exist about my purchases, phone calls, medical condition, work history, and so on, I am able to maintain a diversity of personal relationships. Rachels seems slightly off target in putting the emphasis on the diversity of relationships, rather than simply on the loss of control of relationships that comes with loss of control of information. Perhaps, this is not surprising given that Rachels focused on personal relationships rather than relationships between individuals and organizations.

What happens when you lose control of information is better thought of on the model of an everyday case in which gossip generates some (false) information about you and the information is spread from one person to another. You are interested in being viewed and treated in a certain way and you know the information (true or false) will affect the way people see you and treat you. Once the information begins to move from person to person, you have no way of knowing who has heard it. If it is false information, you have no way contacting everyone and correcting their repository of information about you. Even if the information is true, there may be individuals that will treat you unfairly on the basis of this information and yet since you don't know who has it, you can't protect yourself. So, loss of control of information reduces your ability to establish and influence the relationships you have and the character of those relationships.

### Individual-Organization Relationships

In trying to understand the threat to privacy posed by the new type and scale of personal information gathering made possible by computer technology, the relationships most at issue are those between *individuals and formal organizations.*[2] In these relationships what is important to the individual is that the individual have some power or control in establishing or shaping the relationship (not that he or she has diversity of such relationships). Information about us is what allows an organization such as a marketing firm, a credit card company, or a law enforcement agency to establish a relationship with us. And, information determines how we are treated in that relationship. One is sent an offer to sign up for a credit card when the credit card company gets your name and address and finds out how much you earn and/or own. How much credit is extended depends on the information. Similarly, a relationship between you and your local police force is created when the police force receives information about you; the nature of the relationship depends on the information received.

Currently, organizations may establish (or try to establish) a relationship with you without any action on your part. That is, you may subscribe to a magazine or open a bank account and establish a relationship with one organization, but when that organization sells information about you, another organization creates a file on you and begins to evaluate you for their purposes.

As an aside, let me point out that the twentieth century was a period of enormous growth in the size of public and private organizations (facilitated in part by the development of computer and information technology). This growth is likely to continue in the twenty-first century on a global scale. What this trend means is that instead of interacting with small, local, family-owned businesses wherein one might know or come to know the decision makers personally, most of us now (and in the future will) interact mostly with large national or international organizations operating with complex rules and regulations. Indeed, it is often a computer that makes the decision about our credit line or loan application. We may shop at grocery stores, department stores, or franchises that are local units of national companies. We may purchase items from catalogues or on the Internet and have no idea where the offices of the company are located. We may deal with banks that are national or international, go to large impersonal agencies for government services such as driver's licenses or building permits, attend colleges of 2,000 to 40,000 students, and so on. While our dealings with these organizations may have the most powerful effects on our lives, we may know little about these organizations and the people who own or manage them. Yet they will have (or have access to) an enormous amount of information about us—be it accurate or relevant. And unless we make an exerted effort, we are not likely to know what information they have about us to use when making decisions.

Everything that I have said here was recognized in the 1977 report of the Privacy Protection Study Commission when computer technology was in its early stages of development (i.e., when record-keeping practices were relatively primitive as compared with today's practices). Contrasting face-to-face relationships with relationships to record-keeping organizations, the report explains:

> What two people divulge about themselves when they meet for the first time depends on how much personal revelation they believe the situation warrants and how much confidence each has that the other will not misinterpret or misuse what is said. If they meet again, and particularly if they develop a relationship, their self-revelation may expand both in scope and detail. All the while, however, each is in a position to correct any misrepresentation that may develop and to judge whether the other is likely to misuse the personal revelations or pass them on to others without asking permission. Should either suspect that the other has violated the trust on which the candor of their communication depends, he can sever the relationship altogether, or alter its terms, perhaps by refusing thereafter to discuss certain topics or to reveal certain details about himself. Face-to-face encounters of this type, and the human relationships that result from them, are the threads from which the fabric of society is woven. The situations in which they arise are inherently social, not private, in that the disclosure of information about oneself is expected.
>
> An individual's relationship with a record-keeping organization has some of the features of his face-to-face relationships with other individuals. It, too, arises in an inherently social context, depends on the individual's willingness to divulge information about himself or to allow others to do so, and often carries some expectation as to its practical consequences. Beyond that, however, the resemblance quickly fades.
>
> By and large it is the organization's sole prerogative to decide what information the individual shall divulge for its records or allow others to divulge about him and the pace at which he must divulge it. If the record-keeping organization is a private-sector one, the individual theoretically can take his business elsewhere if he objects to the divulgences required of him. Yet in a society in which time is often at a premium, in which organizations performing similar functions tend to ask similar questions, and in which organizational record-keeping practices and the differences among them are poorly perceived or understood, the individual often has little real opportunity to pick and choose. Moreover, if the record-keeping organization is a public-sector one, the individual may have no alternative but to yield whatever information is demanded of him.

So, private and public organizations are powerful actors in the everyday lives of most individuals in our society, and yet it would seem that individuals have very little power in those relationships. One major factor making this possible is that these organizations can acquire, use, and exchange information about us, without our knowledge or consent. . . .

## REFRAMING THE COMPUTERS AND PRIVACY ISSUE—PRIVACY AS A SOCIAL GOOD

A major part of the problem seems to come from the combination of taking a piecemeal approach and then framing the computers and privacy issue as one involving a trade-off between social goods, such as law enforcement and government efficiency, and the interests of individuals in controlling information about themselves. Instead of thinking comprehensively about what record-keeping and exchanging practices would be best for our society, the problem has been framed as one in which interests are pitted against one another and business and government seem to be pitted against individuals. This is odd when one remembers that ultimately business and government are justified in terms of their service to individuals as consumers and citizens.

In her 1995 book, *Legislating Privacy*, Priscilla M. Regan examined three privacy policy debates that took place in the United States in recent years—information privacy, communications privacy, and psychological privacy. She concludes that when individual privacy is pitted against social goods such as law enforcement or government efficiency, personal privacy loses. Regan suggests that privacy should be seen not as an individual good but rather as a social good. As an important social good, privacy would be on par with other social goods such as law enforcement or government efficiency. Instead of a social good outweighing an individual good, it would be clear that we have two social goods at stake. In reframing the issue in this way, privacy would be more likely to be treated as equally important, if not more important, than other social goods.

How, then, can the case be made for privacy as a social good? Earlier I argued that loss of control of information about us significantly reduces our autonomy—our power in relationships with formal organizations. Now I want to push this line of thinking even further. Instead of emphasizing loss of control, however, I want to return to the idea of the panopticon. If most everything that we do is recorded, then it would seem that the world that we live in is fundamentally changed from the world that existed in the past. And with this change comes an extremely important loss of freedom. We are unable to go places or do things without a record being created. The act of making a phone call is now the act of making a phone call *and* creating a record. We no longer have the option of making a phone call and not creating a record. Therefore, we have lost a degree of freedom. The loss of this freedom might be justified if you are in prison after having been fairly prosecuted and found guilty. But it hardly seems justified if you have done nothing wrong.

Even more important are the changes that take place in individuals as a result of constant surveillance. When a person is being watched, they tend to take on the perspective of the observer. When you know that decisions will be made about you on the basis of your activities (e.g., your educational records, work records, political activities, criminal activities), you think about that fact before you act. You take on the view of the private and public institutions that will make decisions about you. This can have a powerful effect both on how individuals behave and on how they see themselves. Individuals may come more and more to view themselves as they are viewed by those who watch them.

You may think of this as a good thing insofar as it means more social control and perhaps fewer crimes, fewer loan defaults, people working harder, and so on. The consequences of this kind of social control are, however, insidious.

For one thing, it means that formal organizations exert an enormous amount of social control that may or may not be justified. Individuals may be inhibited about what they buy at the grocery store when they learn that their purchases are being recorded and analyzed. Remember that freedom is one of the most fundamental aspects of democracy. Yet freedom is eroded (or at least threatened) when every move is recorded. The result may be individuals who are ill-equipped to live in a democracy.

Consider how Jeffrey Reiman (1995), drawing on other authors, describes the situation:

> To the extent that a person experiences himself as subject to public observation, he naturally experiences himself as subject to public review. As a consequence, he will tend to act in ways that are publicly acceptable. People who are shaped to act in ways that are publicly acceptable will tend to act in safe ways, to hold and express and manifest the most widely-accepted views, indeed, the lowest-common denominator of conventionality. . . . Trained by society to act conventionally at all times, people will come so to think and so to feel. . . . As the inner life that is subject to social convention grows, the still deeper inner life that is separate from social convention contracts and, given little opportunity to develop, remains primitive. . . . You lose both the practice of making your own sense out of your deepest and most puzzling longings, and the potential for self-discovery and creativity that lurk within a rich inner life. . . . To say that people who suffer this loss will be easy to oppress doesn't say enough. They won't have to be oppressed, since there won't be anything in them that is tempted to drift from the beaten path.

The idea of democracy is the idea of citizens having the freedom to exercise their autonomy and in so doing to develop their capacities to do things that have not been thought of and to be critical. All of this makes for a citizenship that is active and pushing the world forward progressively. But if the consequences of trying something new, expressing a new idea, acting unconventionally are too negative, then there is no doubt that few citizens will take the risks. Democracy will diminish.

When the argument for privacy is framed in this way, privacy is shown to be something which is not just an individual good that can be diminished for the sake of a social good; rather, it is shown to be a social good in its own right and more important than other social goods such as efficiency and better consumer services. . . .

## CONCLUSION

Privacy is, perhaps, the most important of the ethical issues surrounding computer and information technology. I have tried to show this by making clear the importance of privacy to democratic society and the subtle ways in which our lives are changed when we are being watched. Individuals who walk through life knowing that each step creates a record that may or may not end up in a database somewhere are very different from individuals who walk through life feeling free and confident that they live in a open society in which the rules are known and fair.

Protecting personal privacy is not easy and is not likely to get easier. The most effective approach to privacy protection is a many-pronged approach. One thing is for sure, the use of personal information is not going to diminish of its own accord. Information about individuals is extremely valuable both in the private and in the public sector. This issue is not going to go away until we do something about it.

## REFERENCES

Fried, Charles. "Privacy," *Yale Law Journal*, 77 (1968), p. 477.

Orwell, George. *1984* (New York: Harcourt, Brace & World, 1949).

Rachels, James. "Why Privacy Is Important," *Philosophy and Public Affairs*, 4 (Summer 1975), pp. 323–33.

Regan, Pricilla M. *Legislating Privacy, Technology, Social Values, and Public Policy* (Chapel Hill, NC: University of North Carolina Press, 1995).

Reiman, Jeffrey "Hl. Driving to the Panopticon: A Philosophical Exportation of the Risks to Privacy Posed by the Highway Technology of the Future," *Computer and High Technology Law Journal*, 11 (1995) pp. 27–44.

Zamyatin, Yl. *We* (Harmonsworth, England: Penguin Books, 1972). Originally published in Russia, 1920).

## NOTES

1. Ironically, it can work the other way as well. Sometimes, that is, changes in technology may result in data being forgotten. In other words, where paper records stored in boxes in an archive may be obtained (even with difficulty), data stored on an old computer may be much more difficult to access because the technology is obsolete.
2. Of course, information stored in databases could affect personal relationships and gossip can spread on the Internet, but most large-scale, massive databases are maintained by formal organizations who make powerful decisions about individuals.

# Electronic Monitoring and Privacy Issues in Business-Marketing: The Ethics of the DoubleClick Experience

*Darren Charters*

> If we would've known we wouldn't have done it. We moved into a grey area where there's a tremendous amount of confusion and that's not good. We're a very innovative company and sometimes you get ahead. We made a mistake.
>
> Mr. Kevin O'Connor CEO DoubleClick Inc.

## INTRODUCTION

Businesses have long been aware of the value of targeted advertising. DoubleClick Inc. (DoubleClick) is an advertising company that operates in the Internet banner and pop-up advertising business space. The ability to continually tailor Internet advertising to the interests of a user is an advance on previous advertising mediums and represents an opportunity to develop a competitive advantage in the industry. Once trends are detected in a user's Internet activity advertising can be customized to the user's revealed interests.

A company such as DoubleClick sits between the advertiser and the end user and acts as a facilitator between companies who want to advertise to specific types of users and users who may be interested in receiving such advertising. End-users arguably benefit as they obtain the advantages of customized advertising content while the receipt of unwanted advertising is minimized. Until November 1999, DoubleClick had always tracked user activity by attaching user histories to anonymous user identifications. Accordingly, while user activity could be tracked the actual identity of the user was unknown. However, the ability to further refine data profiles was made possible through a series of acquisitions of other companies and their proprietary databases.

Daren Charters, "Electronic Monitoring and Privacy Issues in Business-Marketing: The Ethics of the DoubleClick Experience" *Journal of Business Ethics* (2002) V. 35 pp. 243–254. With kind permission of Kluwer Academic Publishers.

In November 1999 DoubleClick announced an amendment to its existing practice. DoubleClick intended to match anonymous existing data with specific user names, personal information, and e-mail addresses. There was no initial public response to the proposed activity. However, in February 2000 the Electronic Privacy Information Center, a privacy advocate, publicly stated that the linkage of such information might have negative implications for users. The negative public response after the statement was immediate and forceful. DoubleClick was forced to back away from the proposed activity. DoubleClick's CEO offered the comment preceding the introduction in response to DoubleClick's failed proposal.

Mr. O'Connor's statement suggests that DoubleClick did nothing wrong from an ethical perspective. Rather, if DoubleClick was guilty of anything, it was just of being too far ahead in anticipating customer tolerance for such activity. Reflecting on the aborted initiative, Mr. O'Connor indicated that DoubleClick would not combine personally identifiable information with anonymous user activity profiles until such time as industry-wide privacy standards exist. Once again, however, there was no suggestion that DoubleClick will not engage in such activity, only that it would wait until some standards are developed before doing so. . . .

The following discussion will focus solely on electronic monitoring in the business-marketing context. Electronic monitoring is also a relevant issue in the business employment context. However, the nature of the employer-employee relationship creates different issues in workplace electronic monitoring including the harm potentially caused to individual and organizational morale, and the impact that the express contractual right to conduct such activity may or may not have on the ethics of the issue. Accordingly this paper will not attempt to discuss the ethical issues surrounding workplace electronic monitoring. When the term electronic monitoring is used throughout the remainder of the paper it will refer only to electronic monitoring primarily for business-marketing purposes. To understand how electronic monitoring is made possible on the Internet one needs to understand "cookies", which are the basic enabling technology.

## COOKIES AND ELECTRONIC MONITORING

### i. Cookie Technology

Cookies are small data structures used by websites or servers to store and retrieve information on the user's side of the Internet connection. They are sent by a host website or server and reside in the user's computer. A cookie allows websites and servers to "remember" information about specific users. Cookies are a relatively recent phenomenon and were created with very early editions of Internet browsers. In the brief period following the introduction of cookies but prior to the development of the Internet as a medium for commerce the primary use for cookies was as a tool of convenience. For example, cookies could be used to store password codes so that a user would not have to re-type a password when re-entering a site. The intent behind cookies was not to create a tool for gathering knowledge about users but to benefit users through increased convenience. More recently this user convenience has also manifested itself in ability to create customized content through personalized news service subscriptions and other services.

As business has developed on the Internet cookies have been adapted for business purposes including "shopping carts" for carrying electronic purchases and tracking website activity. By downloading a cookie, servers hosting a website have the power to track and record information such as the previous website from which the user arrived, all web pages the user visits while on the given site, and finally the website address to which the user departs. This information is multiplied in power if the user can be successfully prompted to provide personal information and data while at the site. The knowledge can then be tied to a specific individual. This power has been taken one step further by Internet marketers, who developed the ability to monitor and profile user activity across thousands of sites. In addition the ability to tie such history to a specific individual has been achieved, not just through the voluntary action of users, but also through industry wide database consolidation.

### ii. Browser Capabilities

Practically speaking, most Internet users would have no knowledge as to when their Internet activity is being electronically monitored. The normal practice is to download cookies onto a user's hard drive without notice to the user. In this respect there is no choice given to the user, and the downloading and subsequent monitoring is involuntary from the user's perspective. However, it must be acknowledged that software already exists that can give users complete power with respect to what cookies, if any, are allowed to be stored on a computer. More recent Internet browser versions have given users the ability to control cookies. Users can elect to prohibit all cookie downloads or, alternatively, be notified of, and have the right to accept or reject, any attempted cookie downloads by a server. Based on this it might be asserted that user's cannot take the position that there is an ethical issue created by, or an invasion of privacy resulting from, electronic monitoring when it is within their power to completely prohibit or selectively control the activity.

On a theoretical level this argument may have some merit, but it fails for three practical reasons. First, Internet users may still be utilizing browser software that does not contain such cookie control options. Second, even if all users had such browser software, it is a distinct possibility that many users would still be unaware of the capability such software contained. Many computer and Internet users regularly utilize, and only have limited knowledge of, a minimal amount of a software program's capabilities. Third, and most important, the technology that enables electronic monitoring is constantly evolving.

Soon after technology was developed that gave control of cookies to users, marketers seized on new technologies, such as web "bugs", that can evade user detection thus allowing continued surveillance. The ongoing tension between user and marketer control in the development of surveillance technology ensures that the ethics of electronic monitoring will be a relevant issue for the foreseeable future. Further, while the technological means to monitor electronically may differ the same ethical issues are poised to play themselves out, or are already emerging in other spheres of business activity. For example the same issues are already developing in the field of telecommunications. In addition, the same issues will likely surface in the context of location based wireless Internet advertising, thus providing additional incentive to develop a greater understanding of the ethical principles involved in the current Internet advertising debate. . . .

## ETHICAL PRINCIPLES UNDERLYING THE RIGHT TO PRIVACY

As with most, if not all, moral and legal rights there is an ethical basis underpinning the right. The right to privacy is no exception. It is built on both Utilitarian and Kantian foundations:

### i. Utilitarian Foundation

The Utilitarian basis for acknowledging a right to privacy is two-fold (Boatright, 2000). First, there is the concern that the invasion of privacy can result in significant actual harm to individuals. To evaluate whether a practice is ethical in Utilitarian terms, the harm realized is measured against the benefit flowing from the activity. The ethical evaluation is based on the collective benefits and collective harm resulting to society, although each is experienced at the individual level. If the overall harm exceeds the overall benefit then the practice is deemed to be unethical.

In the context of electronic marketing the potential harm results from the fact that the organization developing user profiles can accumulate potentially sensitive information about a user, based on his or her Internet activities. For example, a gay individual may have elected not to publicly disclose his or her sexual orientation. However, the same individual may, with presumed anonymity, visit websites with gay content or participate as part of a gay Internet community. A company that is able to electronically monitor the individual's computer use could potentially gain intimate knowledge of the individual's situation as a result of the Internet sites the individual visited. The organization developing the profile may intend to use such information solely for the purpose of advertising, however it is not difficult to see the potential harm to the individual's practical interests if such information came into the hands of another party. Another example is potentially sensitive medical condition that might be accessed by employers doing pre-hiring checks or insurers contemplating the issuance of a policy. Profile information generated by electronic monitoring has the potential to be used against the individuals in a manner that harms their personal practical interests.

Opponents of electronic marketing frequently dwell on potential harm but little mention is made of an actual weighing of harms against benefits. The balancing in the electronic monitoring context involves weighing potential serious harm to a limited number of people against the marginal benefit, such as increased convenience and knowledge of consumer products, which might flow to many people from such activity. If the total harm exceeds the total benefit the invasion of privacy through electronic monitoring cannot be considered ethical. However, if it can be claimed that benefits exceed harm the foundation exists for an ethical invasion of privacy.

The second utilitarian basis for acknowledging a right to privacy is based on a wider concept of harm. As stated succinctly by Boatright, "a certain amount of privacy is necessary for the enjoyment of some activities, so that invasions of privacy change the character of our experiences and deprive us of the opportunity for gaining pleasure from them" (Boatright, 2000, p. 169). The "harm" resulting from the loss of the ability to gain maximum pleasure is presumed to exceed any benefit, such as increased convenience in the electronic monitoring context, such activity might have. A similar argument is that invasions of privacy harm the development and maintenance of personal identity, and that such harm exceeds all benefits (Boatright, 2000). There has been little reference to either of the above arguments made by privacy advocates in the electronic monitoring debate.

### ii. Kantian Foundation

The right to privacy can also be supported on the basis of Kant's second categorical imperative. It provides that individuals should act in a manner that treats other individuals as an end and never as a means only (Boatright, 2000). This imperative captures the themes that people should be respected and treated as autonomous individuals capable of rational choice. To quote Stanley Benn:

> Covert observation—spying—is objectionable because it deliberately deceives a person about his world, thwarting . . . his attempts to make a rational choice. One cannot be said to respect a man . . . if one knowingly and deliberately alters his conditions of action, concealing the fact from him (Boatright, 2000, p. 170).

Arguments against electronic monitoring that are premised on Kantianism base their position on the argument that electronic monitoring violates the principle of respect for individuals and prohibits them from acting as autonomous beings capable of rational choice.

To date, there has been little public opposition expressed against electronic monitoring on the foregoing basis. However, this is not surprising. In terms of generating public support against electronic monitoring, concerns over potential harm will have a greater mobilizing influence than a more esoteric, albeit relevant, ethical theory such as Kantianism. The fact that Kantian theories supporting a right to privacy have not been part of popular debate makes them no less a valid basis on which to base an objection to, or alternatively support for, electronic monitoring.

## PRIVACY AND ETHICAL THEORIES APPLIED

### i. Electronic Monitoring and Privacy

Reduced to its simplest form, electronic monitoring as it is currently practiced amounts to unauthorized observance. Many individuals using the Internet have no knowledge of when their online activity is being monitored for the purpose of developing an advertising profile. When discussing concepts of privacy theorists have sometimes resorted to the analogy of one individual watching another individual in a shower without the showering individual's knowledge or consent (McCloskey, 1980). Such action is almost always considered an unethical invasion of privacy. The foregoing analogy generally applies to the context of electronic monitoring. The fundamental similarity is that Internet users can be observed without knowledge or express consent. That said, personal reaction to such observance by users has ranged from significant concern to complete disinterest. Although many people consider their bodies to be a very private aspect of themselves, they may feel less so about Internet activities that are capable of being observed electronically. Accordingly, this may account for the relative indifference of some users.

When the previously discussed concepts of privacy are considered, one would conclude that electronic monitoring without consent constitutes an invasion of privacy. Electronic monitoring violates the right to privacy if it is conceived of as the right to be left alone, or the right to control access to one's personal information. There is a possible argument that there is no violation of the right to withhold certain facts from public knowledge. It might be argued that if current user apathy about electronic monitoring is substantial, most users have little concern over whether their activity is widely known. As such, electronic monitoring does not meet the threshold test that most members of society consider it to be information that should not be widely known. However this argument can just as easily be made the opposite way. As such, even considering the various understandings attached to the concept of privacy it is difficult to argue that electronic monitoring does not violate the privacy right.

### ii. Electronic Monitoring and Ethical Foundations

The interesting fact is that electronic monitoring still occurs notwithstanding that it amounts to an invasion of privacy. The justification for, and tolerance of, electronic monitoring rests in the minor differences that exist with the shower analogy. With electronic monitoring the observed information may be electronically collected, organized, and distilled before another individual views it. It is even possible that another individual will never view such information and that any advertising that is tailored to an Internet user will be done completely by electronic intelligent agents. The possibility of harm is minimized still further once Internet advertising companies such as DoubleClick make additional efforts to ensure user profiles remain anonymous.

From a Kantian perspective the minimization of harm is relatively meaningless in terms of ethically justifying the activity. If electronic monitoring is carried out in such a way that it fundamentally respected the autonomy of individuals then it is ethically permissible on a Kantian basis even with isolated incidents of harm. It is still ethically permissible in instances of significant harm provided the principle of individual autonomy is respected. Using Benn's quote above as the analytical tool, it is evident that the guarantee that profiles will not be matched against other identifying information is meaningless in terms of making the practice of electronic monitoring ethical from a Kantian perspective. Most users still had no knowledge of the situation and DoubleClick and other companies could not, from an ethical perspective, be judged to be treating users as individuals capable of rational choice.

However, the minimization of harm is fundamental to justifying electronic monitoring on a Utilitarian basis. As noted above the right to privacy is a relatively weak right. Accordingly, it is open to being subverted based on an appeal to Utilitarianism. Utilitarian based arguments would allow electronic monitoring regardless of its design provided the harms do not exceed its benefits to society as a whole. On this basis, the argument is that any serious albeit intermittent harm that comes to individuals (i.e., the example of the user and the medical condition) is more than offset by the benefits that accrue to the public. Advertising promotes economic efficiency, and advertising that can be tailored directly to individuals, only serves to further promote economic efficiency and thus, generally benefits the public. Further, by initiating the blind profile Internet advertisers could claim that the potential for harm was significantly minimized. Proponents of electronic monitoring could then claim the invasion of privacy was ethically justified. In reality, it was only justifiable based on one ethical perspective, Utilitarianism. Further, in DoubleClick's situation, had it proceeded with its intention to link user profiles with identified individuals it would have undermined the very ethical foundation that justified its electronic monitoring practice.

## DOUBLECLICK'S RESPONSE TO OPPOSITION

It is apparent from the foregoing discussion that linking user data to personally identifiable information could result in a formerly ethical invasion of privacy becoming unethical. DoubleClick responded to the privacy concerns in a variety of ways after aborting its plan. DoubleClick also initiated a significant media campaign to explain how users could opt-out of DoubleClick's service. DoubleClick had an operable opt-out service for over three years preceding the most recent controversy but had not promoted it extensively. The opt-out mechanism requires a user to visit a site and download a cookie. This cookie serves as notice to DoubleClick that they are not to download any cookies on the user's computer. DoubleClick would be free to download a cookie onto a hardrive as long as the "opt-out cookie" is not present.

In theory, it could be argued that this gives autonomous individuals a choice with respect to electronic monitoring and thus provides a Kantian justification for the activity. However, this option is little known and is likely to remain so notwithstanding advertising efforts. Accordingly it is difficult to claim that this truly gives control to users and respects their individual autonomy.

A Chief Privacy Officer (CPO) was also hired along a Privacy Advisory Board Chair to act as a consumer ombudsman. Overall the response was indicative of a company that developed a greater sensitivity to privacy issues (perhaps for commercial reasons) but that had not developed a deeper understanding of the ethical issues at stake. That is, the actions do not suggest that they have analyzed and understood the ethical issues and tried to develop a principled response. To give DoubleClick some benefit of the doubt, it may be that the new CPO and privacy advisory board chair will infuse the organization with a deeper understanding of the ethical issues at stake and develop ethically based approaches to dealing with such issues. DoubleClick's share price largely recovered after the implementation of the foregoing measures suggesting that even if the response was ethically unsatisfactory in the short-term, at least the market was satisfied with DoubleClick's immediate response.

As noted above DoubleClick indicated it would not engage in such activity until such time as industry wide privacy standards were developed. This was relevant in that DoubleClick could still justify its electronic monitoring on a Utilitarian basis. That said, they probably lost some degree of public trust on the issue. DoubleClick has been directly involved in the development of the Interactive Advertising Bureau's (IAB) recently developed Privacy Guidelines. The Privacy Guidelines are intended to form the foundation of a self-regulatory regime with respect to personally identifiable information gathered by electronic means on the Internet. Unfortunately, regarding the use of cookies in electronic monitoring, the guidelines state only that IAB member organizations should notify users, through privacy policies, of such technologies in use and provide users the ability to disable such cookies or other information gathering system. This represents no change from the current situation and for the reasons outlined above, does not provide a proper foundation for the ethical use of cookies in electronic monitoring.

The Privacy Guidelines have also proposed measures that allow individuals to place limits on the use of personally identifiable information that an organization may possess. Once again, it is premised on an opt-out format. That is, organizations are generally free to collect and use personally identifiable information in the first instance subject to an individual informing an organization of limits to be placed on use of such information. It is an ingenious approach that appears to place control of personally identifiable information in the hands of individuals that, realistically, requires minimal change in the current practices of organizations that use electronic monitoring to gather such information.

Further, the Privacy Guidelines have a fundamental problem in that their only real value is as a tool of moral suasion. Although the Privacy Guidelines encourage Internet businesses to adopt the practices established therein, there is no mechanism whatsoever for disciplining businesses who elect to ignore them. For all the effort put into the exercise, the Privacy Guidelines amount to nothing more than best practice suggestions for Internet marketers with respect to privacy issues.

If DoubleClick respects the initial basis on which it proceeded with electronic monitoring, it can claim to have an ethical basis for such conduct. However, considering DoubleClick's willingness to discontinue the previously protective practice one has to wonder how vigilant DoubleClick, or other companies, will be about supporting the privacy of Internet users in a highly competitively market. Since DoubleClick maintains profiles for their own business benefit, it is not possible to claim that they stand in a position of trust with respect to managing such information. However, their position is ethically more sensitive than they appeared to originally comprehend. Based on this, there is cause to argue that it is no longer sufficient to continue to permit electronic monitoring in its current state. This is buttressed by the inherent weakness of relying on a self-regulatory regime that effectively has no sanctioning authority or disciplinary power.

The alternative, and it is not a mutually exclusive option, would be move to a permission-based form of electronic monitoring. This option will be discussed below. The practice of electronic monitoring would still be ethically justifiable in such circumstance. However, it is apparent that DoubleClick's current opt-out practice is not the platform on which such permission based electronic marketing should be premised. This is due to the fact that users have extremely limited knowledge of it and, more fundamentally, it places the onus on the user to take active steps to prevent electronic monitoring. The same argument applies with respect to the ethical suitability of building such capabilities into Internet browser software.

## AN ALTERNATIVE ETHICAL JUSTIFICATION

If one accepts that privacy is the right to control access to information about one's self then the solution to electronic monitoring is apparent. The choice about whether or not to be monitored in the first instance should be made by the individual user. In fact, in the wake of the DoubleClick experience many commentators and privacy advocates have taken the position that express consent by a user should be a regulatory precondition to downloading cookies that enable electronic monitoring. Placing the power to control electronic monitoring with users is ethically justifiable on a Kantian basis.

First, giving users a choice to be monitored gives individuals autonomy and appears to respect their capabilities of rational choice. However, it could be argued in a wider sense that Internet advertisers are still utilizing individuals as a means to profit and that this violates Kant's second categorical imperative. However, if an individual knowingly and rationally elects to permit such monitoring this must undermine, at least to a minimum degree, such an argument. Accordingly, any electronic monitoring that occurs with express rational permission can be claimed to be ethical on a Kantian basis. This is a significant step, because it provides an alternative basis for ethically justifying electronic monitoring.

A corollary to the foregoing discussion is that while electronic monitoring is most frequently opposed on the basis of potential harm, which is a Utilitarian concern, the permission-based approach in no way guarantees an outcome that will make the practice ethically justifiable on a Utilitarian basis. In other words, the solution being proposed by many commentators is at ethical odds to the frequently stated concern of potential significant harm. If everyone freely elects to permit electronic monitoring the potential for harm is no different than it was prior to such a practice. For example, it is not difficult to imagine that information based on website usage, if in the hands of certain groups, could be used to make decisions about individuals that cause harm. The only difference is that now users have voluntarily accepted the risk. It should also be recognized however, that providing choice to users necessarily undermines the concept that there is a private sphere that should generally be respected irrespective of individual opinion. As such, it is a fundamental rejection of one concept of the right to privacy.

Even if the foregoing is accepted it has little application to the profiles that have been generated to date. In fact there will likely be continual pressure to exploit the marketing advantages that such databases provide. Further, there appears to be limited willingness for companies to zealously regulate themselves at an individual or even an industry-wide level. In this respect there is a regulatory role for governments to play. There is a possibility that individual harm will result from such database consolidation. In addition, regulations should be developed which aim to provide at least minimal individual privacy protection with respect to such database management and/or consolidation. It is apparent that this represents as much a threat to individual privacy as electronic monitoring in the first instance. . . .

## REFERENCES

Boatright, M.: 2000, 'Privacy', *Ethics and the Conduct of Business*, 3rd ed. (Prentice-Hall, Saddle River New Jersey), pp. 159–183.

McCloskey, H.: 1980, 'Privacy and the Right to Privacy', *Philosophy* 55(211), 17–38.

'IAB Privacy Guidelines.' *Internet Advertising Bureau.* 2000. <http//www.ia.net/priracy guidelines/htm> (August 7, 2000).

## TECHNOLOGICAL CHALLENGES TO INTELLECTUAL PROPERTY

# Intellectual Property and the Information Age

*Richard T. De George*

When VCRs first became available in the United States, both the movie and the TV industries felt them as a threat to their commercial interests. They sued to block the use of VCRs, arguing they were a tool devised to violate copyright laws. The courts ruled otherwise, finding that VCRs had many legitimate uses, even though they might be used to violate copyright laws, and holding that users could legally make copies of material presented on TV for personal viewing and use at a later time. They justified this under the "fair use" clause of the copyright law, which allows individuals to make certain reasonable use of copyrighted material for personal use. The commercial use of such copies is illegal, as is the copying of rented movies and other copyrighted material available in tape format. The movie and TV industries responded creatively by turning the presence of home VCRs into an additional profit stream through the sale and rental of movies and TV programs.

Last evening Joe taped the popular movie *Sound of Music*, which was playing on one of the TV channels. He was away for the evening and intended to look at the movie when it better fit his schedule. This is both common and legal. He may tape as many programs and movies as he wishes for later viewing. His taped version is his to use, even though the same movie is also available for rent or sale at his local video rental store. His friend, Richard, intended to tape the movie, but by mistake set his VCR to the wrong channel, and hence taped some other program instead. When he learned this, he asked Joe if he could copy Joe's tape. He reasoned that since it was legal for him to copy the movie directly from the TV, and he would have if he had not made a mistake, there seems to be no difference in principle for him to copy Joe's tape. Another friend, Tom, also meant to tape the movie, but forgot to set his machine. Rather than phone friends to see if any of them had taped it, he simply went to the Internet and asked if anyone had made a copy from the TV broadcast that they would let him copy. His reasoning was similar to Richard's. It was legal for him to make a copy from the TV—there is no difference in principle between his recording it directly or his getting it from someone else who recorded it directly, and it does not make any difference whether or not the person he copies it from is a friend, as long as he or she copied it legally. Now whether this reasoning is correct from a legal point of view is questionable, since lending a copy of one's tape for someone else to copy does not seem to be "personal use." Yet the reasoning of Richard and Tom does seem to have some plausibility. For if they could have made legal copies directly themselves, then there is nothing wrong in their having the copy from that source, and getting it second hand rather than first hand does not seem pertinent from an ethical point of view. No harm is done to the commercial interests of any of the parties.

From *The Ethics of Information Technology and Business* by Richard T. De George, Blackwell Publishers 2003 © by Richard T. De George. Reprinted by permission of Blackwell Publishers.

The small number of viewers who did not tape directly and got their copy second hand would not likely change the station's Nielsen ratings, and neither Richard nor Tom would buy or rent the film, nor would Joe. They simply wanted a copy of that and other films to look at when the TV offerings on a given evening were not to their liking.

In addition to taping the *Sound of Music*, Joe also taped some songs that were being played on MTV. He not only videotaped them, but he also taped just the audio part on his tape recorder. Since he could tape the whole video, it seems he is also allowed to tape only a portion of it. Richard and Tom, having the same tastes as Tom and being in the same situations as they were with the movie, copy from Joe or from whomever has a copy and is willing to share the videos and the songs.

Since he may make copies for his personal use, Joe reasons that he may also make copies of music played by DJs on the radio or that he gets via the Internet. The principle of fair use seems to be the same, whether one uses a VCR or a CD writer on one's computer.

Napster is a firm that carried this scenario one step further. It developed technology that would allow anyone using the Internet to request a certain song, and Napster would serve as an intermediary between the requester and someone willing to supply the song. There were two important differences, however, from the cases of Joe, Richard, and Tom. First, although some of the songs that were supplied and copied were not covered by copyright, others were so covered. They were copies on CDs that the owner had purchased. And purchasing the CD gives one a right to listen to the songs on it, but it does not give one the right to copy the songs or to allow others to copy them. The same is true of rented or purchased tapes of movies. They may not legally be copied and such copying does not come under the doctrine of fair use. The second important difference is that the service provided by Napster proved to be so attractive that it was used by millions of people to download music free that they would otherwise have paid for. Why buy a CD when one can get the same songs free? Why buy all the songs on a CD when one is only interested in one song and one can download it free?

The rock band Mettalica sued Napster for copyright infringement. A U.S. District Court ordered Napster to shut down its services. In October 2000, a U.S. Appellate Court affirmed the lower court's action and ruled that Napster could only provide access to those songs that were not protected by copyright, and that it had a way to do this before it could continue its operation. Some music companies then sought to enter into various agreements with Napster whereby they would get a fee for each of their songs downloaded. On July 1, 2001, Napster shut down to integrate the technology the courts mandated it have installed to block the trading of copyrighted material.

In the meantime, however, other programmers devised programs that did not require an intermediary such as Napster, and that allowed individuals to contact each other and trade or download music on a peer-to-peer basis. Gnutella was one of these programs, which users could download for free and then use to contact and trade music with others who used the program. Gnutella, like Napster, can be used to download the newest amateur band that wants to get an audience by giving its music away, as well as copyrighted music. By mid-July 2001, six alternative services had sprung up and were providing peer-to-peer copying capabilities involving no intermediary. Over 1 million users downloaded Music City's program Morpheus, and over 900,000 downloaded Audiogalaxy' Satellite program. The companies, which hope to make money by running banner ads, claim that they are not responsible for what users do with the programs they provide.

* * *

Two questions arise. First, is the development of such technology itself ethically defensible, and does the same kind of argument that justifies the use of VCRs justify their use as well? Second, is the copying of material, such as music, from someone else's hard drive using this technology ethically defensible if the material, for instance, is played over steaming audio sites on the Internet?

Central to answering these questions is the notion of intellectual property and its ethical and legal status.

Intellectual property refers to certain products of the mind or intellect that a society decides can be owned in some sense. One trait that distinguishes intellectual property from other types of property is that intellectual property is infinitely shareable. If I have an idea I can give it away and still have it. Unlike other kinds of property, someone can borrow or take or steal my idea and I still have it. I no longer have exclusive use of it if others have it as well; but their having it does not preclude my also having it. It is this key feature of products of the mind that makes discussions of intellectual property significantly different from discussions about other kinds of property. One may have the right to exclusive use, but not the right to destroy it (which would make no sense), and one's possession of the intellectual property is compatible with others having the same property. Because I can have an idea and you may independently come to have a similar idea, ideas in general are not considered the type of thing that can be owned. There would be no way of knowing if someone else had an idea first and if so, whether the idea belonged to that person. There would be no social utility in trying to have ownership of ideas. Nor would there be any social utility in trying to assign ownership rights to mathematics or to facts or to scientific discoveries and theories. But 'idea' is a very broad term and covers some things to which some societies give property rights. What is usually proprietary is the expression of an idea in some tangible form, such as a book or an invention, although this is a rough characterization, since it is debatable whether one can have an idea that one does not express in some sense.

A second feature that influences the bundle of rights that constitutes intellectual property is the fact that any expression of an idea builds on prior knowledge that is not of one's creation. Newton and Leibniz hit upon the calculus independently, and there was a dispute about who had the idea first. But it makes no difference to others who had the idea first since both shared their insight and made their mathematical discoveries available to all. The more or less simultaneous development of the calculus demonstrates the notion that ideas are built on other ideas. By the time of Newton and Leibniz mathematical knowledge had developed to the level where the next step was the calculus. Had Leibniz and Newton not developed it, someone else within a reasonable amount of time would undoubtedly have done so. We each stand on the shoulders of others who have gone before us and who have passed on their ideas. We absorb them and in turn build on them before passing them on. So we cannot make complete claim to them, the way we might with physical objects we build or make or own.

The third aspect of intellectual property that makes it distinctive is that such property is fundamentally social. It is not only socially developed but information and knowledge are most useful when shared, because sharing allows others to develop them further. For this reason some societies do not and have not recognized any property right to the products of the mind or to any claimed sort of intellectual property. Those that do recognize intellectual property must balance the social nature against individual claims to certain rights with respect to it, and this directly influences the bundle of rights any society assigns to intellectual property.

These three characteristics form the foundation for the widely held belief that each generation has the responsibility to pass on to the next generation the knowledge that has been socially acquired and developed. It is this aspect of human beings—the ability to develop and pass on knowledge—that clearly separates them from other species. Colleges and universities in turn are established in order to preserve, transmit, and develop the social knowledge base, and they have the responsibility to do so.

This social view of knowledge informed the early development of the computer and the mind set of the early programmers, who freely shared their work. It similarly was an important aspect in the early development of the Internet, which was seen as free and open to all. . . .

## PROTECTION OF INTELLECTUAL PROPERTY

In the United States, the legal basis for the protection of intellectual property comes from the U. S. Constitution, Article 1, Section 8, which includes under the Powers of Congress the power "To promote the Progress of Science and useful Arts, by securing for limited Times to Authors and Inventors the exclusive Right to their respective Writings and Discoveries." Two aspects of this basis for the protection of intellectual property are noteworthy. The first is that the main purpose of the protection of intellectual property is not the right of the author or inventor but the progress of science and the useful arts. The purpose of the protection is the benefit of the common good. The second is that unlike other property rights which exist indefinitely, the rights granted for intellectual property are limited in time. . . .

### Copyright

**Copyright**, as the name implies, governs the exclusive right of the author to reproduce or copy the work, distribute it, display or perform it publicly, prepare derivative works based upon it, and authorize others to do these things. We have seen that ideas cannot be owned. What one can have a legal right to is the protection of the expression of one's ideas, and it is this that copyright grants. We can express our ideas in a variety of ways. Language is the most obvious, and copyright covers verbal expressions in books, articles, plays, poetry, and other written media. Copyright includes also the expression of ideas in other forms—music, film, video, painting, and recordings. It protects authorship in that it makes it illegal for anyone but the author to claim authorship. It also gives the author the exclusive right to sell the expression of his idea or to otherwise profit from it. This in turn prohibits others from copying it or from selling or profiting from it without the author's permission. The exception is fair use which allows certain uses, such as quoting a portion of a work in a review or in a scholarly publication (giving appropriate attribution), or making a partial copy for legitimate personal use. . . .

The ethical justification for copyright is twofold. The first is a basically utilitarian justification. This says that since society wishes to encourage the production of such works, the best way to promote such production is by making it possible for those who produce them to benefit financially therefrom. We have the history of the development of works that are covered by copyright that tends to show the result has been to society's benefit. Of course, we do not know what would have been produced without the financial incentives copyright provides, and we do know that people continue to have ideas, to develop mathematics, to develop scientific formulas, and to produce knowledge that cannot be protected by copyright. There are some societies that deny any protection for ideas in any form and hence do not recognize the validity of claims of intellectual property rights. For centuries there was no copyright protection, yet works of art, literature, music, and so on were produced. Shakespeare borrowed many of his plots from others and had no copyright protection for what he produced.

Nonetheless, in modern societies the financial inducement is certainly at least one motivating force encouraging the production of literary, artistic and other works.

The second justification for copyright is one of fairness. It says that those who expend time, energy, and money on developing the expression of their ideas, deserve recompense for that time, energy, and money. Moreover, if such protection did not exist, and the item were sold commercially, then those who did not expend the time, energy and money would reap the rewards instead of the originator of the work. The one who did profit without the prior effort and expense would be a free rider, and since the free rider had no prior expenses to be recouped, could undersell the legitimate producer. This would be clearly unfair.

This argument is challenged by some who contend that the claim of authorship is legitimate, but that there is no inherent right to any reward from the production of any such work. Despite the possible and actual objections by some, the justifications are widely accepted and ground the legitimacy of copyright worldwide. . . .

If one asks about the relation of intellectual property, ethics, and copyright protection, four different moral intuitions are applicable and represent four different perspectives. The perspectives represent the four major parties involved in copyright issues.

The first intuition is that from an ethical point of view what is appropriate in this domain is not property rights but honesty of attribution. This is the view of scholars and of some authors. One should not claim that an idea is one's own when it comes from another. But ideas are not the sort of thing that we can or should in general restrict. They can be shared and if useful can be built upon and developed. Since ideas and knowledge are infinitely shareable, the general rule is that we all benefit from correct ideas and knowledge, and the way to make sure the ideas and knowledge are correct is to test them against other ideas and knowledge claims that are contrary to them. This is the view of ideas prevalent in most areas of a university, where ideas are usually shared rather than sold or traded. To take one area, in a university teachers of philosophy share their philosophical ideas with their colleagues, in their classes, at meetings and conventions, in articles, and in books. They do not steal each others ideas by using, criticizing, or developing them. But they cannot ethically claim them as their own when they are not. Most philosophy journals do not pay for the articles they publish, and most books in philosophy are not written with the intent of making a great deal of money. If that is the goal, it is rarely achieved. That does not prevent articles and books from being written and published. This is the point of view adopted by many of the writers of programs, who argue that software should be treated the same as many other products of intellectual activity and that this is the best way to guarantee their development.

A second widely shared ethical intuition is that of the entrepreneur. Just as someone should not copy another's work and claim it is one's own, if a product is sold it is prima facie wrong simply to copy that product and sell it as if it were one's own. Selling it while acknowledging that it is not one's own satisfies the criterion of honesty of attribution. It violates property rights if these have been developed in a legal system of property, such as the one we have. Vendors of software want people to buy their products, and are not interested in simply having others acknowledge the source. They spend money to develop and market the product, and they want a return on that investment. It is blatantly unfair for some other company simply to copy and market the product, under the same or a different name, and get the profit without having invested in the development. Even worse is undercutting the original producer and driving it out of business. Hence if a society wants commercial products, they should be protected at least until the original producers can recoup their expenses. This intuition is part of the basis for the claim of legal protection by the commercial vendors of software. They argue in addition for continuous protection for as long as possible for them to reap profits—a claim that goes beyond the moral intuition.

The third intuition is that of the buyers of software that what they buy is their own to use in any way they like comparable to their use of other products they buy. Thus if I have three computers in my home and I buy a word processing program, I tend to feel I have the right to use it on all three machines rather than buying three copies, or physically carrying the program from machine to machine and loading it each time, as some software vendors claim I should. The rights I have with respect to most of the other items I buy are not restricted, except insofar as they violate the second intuition. But if I do not engage in selling the product or copying it for sale, it is mine to do with as I like.

The fourth group is society as a whole. And the appropriate intuition is that intellectual knowledge and intellectual products are essentially social for the reasons we have already seen. They should be used for the common good. And if there is a conflict between the common good and individual claims to property rights in intellectual property, the former may well take precedence over the latter.

Although the interests of the four groups overlap to some extent, in many ways they are importantly different. To argue either in ethics or law from only one of these perspectives is not to do justice to the others. The law has tended to favor the interests of the marketers of software, since the law has been formed in part by the claims of the marketers and the cases have involved primarily suits brought by them.

## UNAUTHORIZED COPYING OF SOFTWARE

The four intuitions are applicable in considering the unauthorized copying of software. . . .

### 1. Copying Programs for Personal Use

Some of the writers of programs have opted for free exchange of software or for shareware. This is perfectly appropriate. It is interesting to note that authors of books have not objected to copyright laws, while programmers have. The reasons for the difference in attitude are significant and should be taken more seriously than they have by the courts and legislatures. Although the co-existence of shareware and commercial programs is not obviously unfair or counterproductive to the needs of society, the protection given commercial programs must not be such as to stifle or preclude the development of shareware or of software. Claims that they do stifle or preclude the development of some software have so far fallen on deaf legislative and judicial ears.

The views of marketers rather than the views of many writers of software who did not market their products but shared them became the accepted legal norm in areas where those two intuitions conflict.

The views of marketers have also trumped the views of the users of software marketed on a large scale or of the recipients of custom-designed software, and the marketers' views have been written into law. The views of the marketers of software concerning their legal claims were also put forth as morally binding. Those views almost uncritically have become the conventional ethical norm that is preached, even though widely flouted. Users of programs such as WordPerfect and Lotus 1-2-3 are told that it is unethical to share such programs with others, and there is even an attempt to make users feel guilty if they use a program they buy on more than one machine within their own homes.

Lending a book to a friend is not unethical. Lending a program is said to be. Why? The usual answer is that lending a program to a friend is not considered comparable to lending a book to a friend, since typically one retains the use of one's copy of the program. Hence lending a program is compared to photocopying a book. The argument against lending software is based on an analogy with books, copyrights of written material, and fair use doctrines established to protect written material. Although the items lent (books and programs) are very different, the analogy of copying rather than of lending or sharing has come to dominate ethical discussions. Yet the analogy between books and software breaks down at various points, and only some of these are considered, despite the arguable importance of some of the other differences. The ease of copying software is a technological boon to users and to society that one could argue should be capitalized on as a means of transferring knowledge and technology broadly. Yet that aspect of technology is precisely what mass producers of software with the help of copyright wish to stem. Insufficient thought has been given to the results.

Focusing on the preceding third intuition, the users of programs would like the right to use what they buy. By analogy with many other products, how one uses the product after one buys it is up to the owners. They may sell it, change it, and so on. What is precluded is copying it and selling it in competition with the original seller. What copyright grants in most cases is the right of initial sale. Thus if a student buys a textbook for a class, for instance, he or she may sell it after the course is over, and it is then resold to another student. Neither the publisher nor the author receives any compensation beyond the initial sale. Soon publishers find that the market becomes saturated with second-hand copies of the book, and sales fall dramatically. To protect their interests many textbook publishers and authors come out with a new edition of the book after three or so years, forcing the sale of the new edition and rendering the old edition obsolete and unsaleable. But the sellers of software make more radical claims for ownership and wish to prevent resale on the basis of the claim that they did not sell the product but only licensed it on certain conditions which they specify.

From a legal point of view they place a great deal of emphasis on the fact that one signs an agreement that comes with purchased software—which one does not do when one buys a book. However, the agreement is one that is forced by the seller on the buyer after having paid one's $400 or $500 if one wants to get technical support and the options to upgrade when new versions of the program come out. The borrower of a program gets neither the documentation nor the servicing—items that do not come with books, and that help justify the higher prices of programs. One typically buys a program to use it, not to read it. The extension of copyright laws to programs ignores these and other very important differences.

Since the marketers of software cannot effectively police or enforce the agreements or prevent such violations of copyright, they attempt to protect their products through moral claims. Indirectly through the agreements that are included with software there has been an attempt to inculcate a view on the morality of copying software. The moral claims do not automatically follow from the developments in the legal realm. It is not necessarily the case that everything that is illegal is immoral. Copying or lending software is not in itself immoral. It is claimed to be immoral primarily because it is illegal. But whether a law that is neither enforced nor enforceable has the force of law, and hence whether one is ethically bound by such a legal statute in this case is at least open to question. The argument from analogy with other items one buys provides grounds for arguing the moral justifiability of lending and copying software for personal use. . . .

The legal property rights one has in software are a function of the system of property and law in which the software develops and becomes embedded. It is the commercial possibilities that drive the analogies and definitions. For this reason the proper question is not some abstract notion of rights or of intellectual property. The right questions are whether the present state of affairs is satisfactory to all concerned and to society's best interests, and if not how it can be improved. . . .

## PEER TO PEER EXCHANGE OF COPYRIGHTED MATERIAL

This brings us to the kind of case with which we started and exemplified by the legal charges brought against Napster.

When it comes to downloading MP3 music files (or eventually other copyrighted material such as movies in digital format), most people do not consider it the same as placing commercial programs on the Web for the taking. Two of their intuitions, they feel, conflict. The one is that making a copyrighted item freely available for downloading by anyone is unethical as well as illegal; the other is that one has a moral if not a legal right to share whatever one buys with a friend if one so chooses.

The courts found Napster guilty of abetting the violation of copyright law by serving as an intermediary between those wishing to swap or share copyrighted as well as non-copyrighted music. It was not seen as comparable to a VCR, which might be used for copyright violation but also had legitimate uses. It was Napster, not its 80 million individual users, that was targeted for legal action. But shutting Napster down even temporarily did not solve the problem because users quickly developed and shared peer-to-peer programs that eliminated the need for a middle man who could be identified, sued and shut down.

Moral suasion and possible legal action has not stopped the downloading by millions of copyrighted music. While lending a copy of a song to a friend might plausibly be claimed to be covered by fair use, and while the 1992 Audio Home Recording Act allows the taping of a CD on a tape for personal use, e.g., in a car, the indiscriminate copying of copyrighted material from unknown peers on the Internet is arguably hardly comparable.

The defense of the practice that is often given is not that those who produce the music and who market it do not deserve any return for their effort. Many who engage in the practice claim that they would be willing to pay what they consider a reasonable amount for the music they wish. But the music distributors had not made available the music they want for purchase on-line, and the marketing strategy of many music companies has been to mix on a single CD a popular song with many that the customer does not want. The customer must buy the whole CD to get the item he or she wants, and to the customer the cost of the CD is greater than the perceived value of the one song. In addition, those who defend the practice argue, the music industry itself gives its music away on MTV, for instance, or by providing it on the radio or other formats available over the Internet. Vendors of computer programs do not do this. If music is provided free to the listener in these ways, and if taping videos is legally fair use, by analogy taping or downloading music should be fair use.

These arguments do not, of course, show that downloading the music one wants freely is justifiable either legally or ethically. But they do indicate that the music industry and its marketing techniques have not kept pace with technology and that there are anomalies in the way music is distributed. With the advent of VCRs, movie makers found they had to adopt a different marketing strategy from the one on which they previously relied and found that they could use the prevalence of VCRs to their commercial interests by renting movies at a very reasonable rate.

The extent to which music companies and artists are harmed is a matter of controversy. One side argues that obviously those who download won't buy the music; this deprives the companies and artists of legitimate income. They will be adversely affected. Furthermore the incentive for other companies and artists to produce more music is diminished, since the rewards are less. This in turn means less music available for society and for music lovers themselves who do the downloading. The other side argues that in many cases those who download would not buy the disk anyway, so there is no lost revenue in those cases. Others download to listen. If they like what they hear, then they buy that artist's CDs, which increases rather than decreases sales. Forrester Research claimed that Napster increased sales. CD sales jumped 8 percent in the first quarter of 2000 over 1999. Both sides can point to some statistics. Similarly, the results on society are speculative. One side argues the demise of the music industry, the other the freeing up of creativity from the straight jacket of the big five record companies. Hence the utilitarian arguments are not decisive. But neither is the argument based on property rights, except insofar as they are presently reflected in copyright law and judicial decisions based thereon.

The problem facing the music industry and legislators in the face of the rising peer-to-peer technology that is replacing Napster is that the law is all but unenforceable. Prosecuting even a small fraction of those who download copyrighted music using the new technology from the Internet is unfeasible. Even if the worse perpetrators were caught and fined, the chance of any individual being caught would be slight, unless more resources were put into policing and prosecuting such action than it seems socially responsible to do. The alternative seems to find some solution that does justice to both intuitions, that protects the legitimate commercial interests of those in the music industry, and that makes available at a reasonable price—determined as in most cases by the market—the music that consumers wish to download. While some question whether anyone will pay even a nominal price to download music when they can download the same music free, there are built-in incentives for users to do so. Peer-to-peer technology opens one's computer to access by anyone on the Internet, and those who download music from unknown sources take the risk of downloading viruses or other dangers. Students who download music using the fast Internet access provided by their colleges and universities open up their institutions to possible lawsuit, as well as opening themselves up to various penalties if the institution prohibits such downloading, as the institutions might do both to avoid possible suit and to avoid the need of expanding its bandwidth to accommodate the traffic and difficulties that massive downloading of music by students can create. Burning one's own CDs, moreover, requires that one buy a CD-write drive, which might more than offset what one saves from free downloads. Those who download to their hard drives do not have the portability that makes music CDs so popular.

Only so much can be legislated. It would be a great cost to society to try to outlaw any technology, such as peer-to-peer, which holds great promise as a means of easy, inexpensive exchange of all things digital.

At this stage it seems likely that accommodation will be made, that present copyright laws with reference to music and other products on the Internet is inadequate, and that changes are both necessary and will be forthcoming. The important thing is to make sure that all affected parties and their claims and arguments are adequately heard and taken into account, and that no one of the intuitions or groups is given special privilege, consideration, or legislative preference.

The great advantage of information is that it is infinitely shareable with others while it is retained by oneself. Everyone in the world is thus a potential recipient of information and all can share in these benefits without depriving others of them. The information age thus provides an opportunity to move from individuality to community, away from private ownership rights and toward concern for sharing for the common good. Yet, paradoxically, the information age, by focusing on the importance of information, has highlighted its commercial value. A result has been an attempt not to share freely but to control information for commercial purposes. Technology and ownership rules are at odds in the case of the copying of software and anything else in digitalized form, in the development of peer-to-peer exchanges, in the open source code movement, and in the trend toward licensing rather than the ownership acquired in purchasing.

The problem then becomes twofold. The first issue is whether the present law can be enforced if millions of users are trading copyrighted material, even if it is illegal. Is an unenforceable law a law? There is a long tradition that claims it is not. The problem is exacerbated by the fact that downloading material easily crosses borders. If something comparable to Napster is located in a country that does not prohibit its activities, the server outlawed in the United States can perform its function from a different jurisdiction. . . .

# Controlling the Wired

*Lawrence Lessig*

When the Net emerged into the popular press, there was an anxiety among many about what the Net would make possible. People could do things *there* that we had discouraged or made illegal *here.*

Pornography was the most dramatic example of this anxiety. The freedom of the Net meant, the world quickly learned, the freedom of anyone—regardless of age—to read the obscene. The news was filled with instances of kids getting access to material deemed "harmful to minors." The demand of many was that Congress do something to respond.

In 1996, Congress did respond, by passing the Communications Decency Act (CDA). Its aim was to protect children from "indecent content" in cyberspace. The act was stupidly drafted, practically impaling itself upon the First Amendment, but its aim was nothing new. Laws have long been used to protect children from material deemed "harmful to minors." Congress was attempting to extend that protection here.

Congress failed. It failed because the CDA was overbroad, regulating speech that could not be regulated constitutionally. And it failed because it had not properly considered the burden this regulation would impose upon activity in cyberspace. The statute required adult IDs before adult content could be made available. But to require sites to keep and run ID machines was to burden Internet speech too severely. Congress would have to guarantee that the burden it was imposing on the Internet generally was no greater than necessary to advance its legitimate state interest—protecting children.

In 1998, Congress tried again. This time it focused on clearly regulable speech—speech that was "harmful to minors." And it was much more forgiving about the technology that would permissibly block kids from "harmful to minors" speech. Still, federal courts struck down the law on the ground that the burden it would impose on the Internet generally was just too great

These cases evince a distinctive attitude. Though the state's interest in protecting children is compelling, courts have insisted that this compelling state interest be pursued with care. In effect, a demonstration that the regulation won't harm the Net too broadly is required before this state interest can be promoted. Facts, and patient review, are the rule in this area of the law of cyberspace.

Keep this picture in mind. . . . For the meaning of *Reno v. ACLU* is not that porn is okay for kids or that the state's interest in enabling parents to protect their kids from porn is outdated. The Court in *Reno* was quite explicit: Protecting children from speech harmful to minors is a "compelling" state interest. But this compelling interest must be advanced in ways that are consistent with the other free speech values. The state was free to advance its compelling state interest; but it was required, in so doing, not to kill the rest of the Net.

About the same time that parents were panicking about porn on the Net, copyright holders were panicking about copyright on the Net. Just as parents worried that there was no way to keep control over their kids, copyright holders worried that there was no way to keep control over copyrighted content. The same features of the Internet that made it hard to keep kids from porn also made it hard to keep copyrights under control.

Both forms of panicking were premature. While it is true that the Net as it was originally built made it hard to control content (by either keeping it from kids or keeping it from being copied by kids), the Net as it was originally built is not the Net as it must be. Code made the Net as it was; that code could change. And the real issue for policy makers should be whether we can expect code to be developed that would solve this problem of control.

In *Code* I argued that in the context of copyright, we should certainly expect such code to be developed.[1] And if it were developed as its architects described, then the real danger, I argued, is not that copyrighted material would be uncontrolled: the real danger is that copyrighted material would be *too perfectly* controlled. That the technologies that were possible and that were being deployed would give content owners more control over copyrighted material than the law of copyright ever intended.

This is precisely what we have seen in the past two years, but with a twist that I never expected. Content providers have been eager to deploy code to protect content; that much I and others expected. But now, not only Congress but also the courts have been doubly eager to back up their protections with law.

This part I didn't predict. And indeed, in light of *Reno v. ACLU*, one would be justified in not predicting it. If parents must go slowly before demanding that the law protect their kids, why would we expect Hollywood to get expedited service?

The answer to that question is best left until after we have surveyed the field. So consider the work of the courts, legislatures, and code writers in their crusade to expand the protections for a kind of "property" called IP.

## INCREASING CONTROL

### Copyright Bots

In dorm rooms around the country, there are taped copies of old LPs. Taped to the windows, there are posters of rock stars. Books borrowed from friends are on the shelves in some of these rooms. Photocopies of class material, or chapters from assigned texts, are strewn across the floor. In some of these rooms, *fans* live; they have lyrics to favorite songs scribbled on notepads; they may have pictures of favorite cartoon characters pinned to the wall. Their computer may have icons based on characters from *The Simpsons.*

The content in these dorm rooms is being used without direct compensation to the original creator. No doubt, no permission was granted for the taping of the LPs. Posters displayed to the public are not displayed with the permission of the poster producers. Books may have been purchased, but there was no contract forbidding passing them to other friends. Photocopying goes on without anyone knowing what gets copied. The lyrics from songs copied down from a recording are not copied with the permission of the original author. Cartoon characters, the exclusive right of their authors, are not copied and posted, on walls or on computer desktops, with the permission of anyone.

All these *uses* occur without the express permission of the copyright holder. They are unlicensed and uncompensated ways in which copyrighted works get used.

Not all of these uses are impermissible uses. Many are protected by exceptions built into the Copyright Act. When you buy a book, you are free to loan it to someone else. You are free to copy a small section of the book and give it to a friend. Under the Audio Home Recording Act, you are free to copy music from one medium to another. Taped recordings of records are therefore quite legal.

But some of these uses of copyrighted works may well be illegal. To post the poster may be a public display of the poster not authorized by the purchase. To use icons on your computer of *Simpsons* cartoons is said by Fox to violate its rights. And if too much of an assigned text has simply been copied by the student, then that copying may well exceed the scope of "fair use."

The reality of dorm rooms, however—and, for that matter, most private space in real space—is that these violations, if they are violations, don't matter much. Whether or not the law technically gives a student the right to have a *Simpsons* cartoon on his desktop, there is no practical way for Fox Broadcasting Company to enforce its rights against overeager fans. The friction of real space sets the law of real space. And that friction means that for most of these "violations," there is no meaningful violation at all.

Now imagine all this activity moved to cyberspace. Rather than a dorm room, imagine that a student builds a home page. Rather than taped LPs, imagine he produces MP3 translations of the original records. *The Simpsons* cartoon is no longer just on his desktop; imagine it is also on his Web server. And likewise with the poster: the rock star, we can imagine, is now scanned into an image file and introduces this student's Web page.

How have things changed?

Well, in one sense, one might say the change is quite dramatic. Now, rather than simply posting this content to a few friends who might pass through the dorm room, this student is making this content available to millions around the world. After all, pages on the World Wide Web are available anywhere in the world. Millions use the World Wide Web. Millions can now, for free, download the content that this student posted.

But there's a gap in this logic. There are millions who use the World Wide Web. But there are billions of Web pages. The chances that anyone will stumble across this student's page are quite slight. Search engines balance this point, though that depends upon what's on a particular page. Most Web pages are not even seen by the author's mother. The World Wide Web has amazing potential for publishing; but a potential is not a million-hit site.

Thus, in reality, this page is effectively the same as the student's dorm room. Probably more people view the poster on the dorm room window than will wade through the student's Web page. In terms of exposure, then, moving to cyberspace doesn't change much.

But in terms of the capacity for monitoring the use of this copyrighted material, the change in the move from real space to cyberspace is quite significant. The dorm room in cyberspace is subject to a kind of monitoring that the dorm room in real space is not. Bots, or computer programs, can scan the Web and find content that the bot author wants to flag. The bot author can then collect links to that content and follow through however it seems most sensible.

Consider the story of fans of *The Simpsons* who find themselves summoned to court when their *Simpsons* fan pages are discovered by a bot hired by the television network Fox. The fans are not allowed, Fox said, to collect friends and strangers around these images of Bart Simpson and his dad. These images are "owned" by Fox, and Fox has the right to exercise perfect control. Though "[t]he sites are the Internet equivalent of taping posters of favorite actors to a bedroom wall," they are not permitted by copyright law.

Fan sites are not the only examples here. Dunkin' Donuts used the threat of a copyright lawsuit to force a site devoted to criticism of the nationwide chain to sell the site to the company. The company claimed it could "more effectively capture the comments and inquiries" if it owned the site. Maybe, but it is also certainly true that it could more effectively edit the content the site made public.

A more telling example is the history of OLGA—an on-line guitar archive started by James Bender at the University of Nevada, Las Vegas. As the Web site describes it:

> OLGA is a library of files that show you how to play songs on guitar. The files come from other Internet guitar enthusiasts like yourself, who took the time to write down chords or tablature and send them to the archive or to the newsgroups rec.music.makers.guitar.tablature and alt.guitar.tab. Since they come from amateur contributors, the files vary greatly in quality, but they should all give you somewhere to start in trying to play your favorite tunes.

In 1996, the University of Nevada, Las Vegas, was contacted by EMI Publishing, which alleged that the site violated EMI's copyright. The university shut the site down. The then-current archivist, cathal woods, moved the archive to another host. Then in 1998, OLGA was contacted again, this time by the Harry Fox Agency, which, like EMI, complained of copyright violations without specifying precisely what was being infringed. OLGA closed the archive in that year and then began a long (and as yet unresolved) campaign to establish the right of hobbyists to exchange chord sequences.

The pattern here is extremely common. Copyright holders vaguely allege copyright violations; a hosting site, fearing liability and seeking safe harbor, immediately shuts down the site. The examples could be multiplied thousands of times over, and only then would you begin to have a sense of the regime of control that is slowly emerging over content posted by ordinary individuals in cyberspace. Yahoo!, MSN, and AOL have whole departments devoted to the task of taking down "copyrighted" content from any Web site, however popular, simply because the copyright holder demands it. Machines find this content; ISPs are ordered to remove it; fearing liability, and encouraged by a federal law that gives them immunity if they remove the content quickly,[2] they move quickly to take down the content.

This is the second side of the effect that cyberspace will have on copyright. Copyright interests obsess about the ability for content to be "stolen"; but we must also keep in view the potential for use to be more perfectly controlled. And the pattern so far has tracked that potential. Increasingly, as activity that would be permitted in real space (either because the law protects it or because the costs of tracking it are too high) moves to cyberspace, control over that activity has increased.

This is not a picture of copyrights imperfectly protected; this is a picture of copyright control out of control. As millions move their life to cyberspace, the power of copyright owners to monitor and police the use of "their" content only increases. This increase, in turn, benefits the copyright holders, but with what benefit to society and with what cost to ordinary users? Is it progress if every use must be licensed? If control is maximized? . . .

## MP3

My.MP3 [is] an innovative new service whose users could "beam" the content of their CD collection to a Web site and then get access to their music at that Web site. This service was provided by the company MP3.com. To provide access to this music, MP3.com had to purchase a very large collection of CDs. It then copied those CDs into its computer database. When a user of My.MP3 placed a CD into the Beam-it program, the system identified whether that CD was in MP3.com's library. If it was, then that user account got access to the content of that CD whenever he or she accessed the account.

Ten days after launching the service, MP3.com received a letter from RIAA attorneys. Its service was a "blatant" violation of copyright laws, said the letter, and MP3.com should take the service down immediately. MP3.com refused, and the lawyers did what lawyers do when someone refuses: they filed suit in U.S. district court, asking for over $100 million in damages.

The RIAA lawyers had a point, if you looked at the statute quite literally. MP3.com may have purchased a bunch of CDs, but it had clearly "copied" these CDs when it created its single, massive database. There was, on its face, then, an unauthorized copy of each of these CDs, and the question became whether or not this copy was nonetheless fair use.

Applying the ordinary standard for fair use, the RIAA argued that it was clearly not. This was for a commercial purpose. Thus, fair use was not a defense, and the blatant and willful copying was then a prosecutable offense.

When lawyers have such a clean, slam-dunk case, they get very, very sure of themselves. And the papers in the My.MP3 case are filled with outrage and certainty.

But when you stand back from the outrage and ask, "What's really going on here?," this case looks a lot different. First, as should be clear, My.MP3 was not facilitating the theft of any music. You had to insert a real CD into your computer before you could get access to the copy on MP3.com's server. Of course, you could borrow someone else's CD and hence trick the system into thinking you were the rightful owner of the CD. But you could borrow someone else's CD and copy it anyway. The existing system permits theft; My.MP3 didn't add to that.

Second, it should be fairly clear that this service would increase the value of any given CD. Using this technology, a consumer could listen to his or her CD in many different places. Once the system recognized your rights to the music on the CD, the system gave you those rights whenever you were at a browser. That means that the same piece of plastic is now more valuable. That increase in value should only increase the number of CDs that are purchased. And that increase would benefit the sellers of CDs.

Third, it is also fairly clear that exactly the sort of thing that MP3.com was doing could easily have been done by the consumers themselves. Any number of companies have created free disk space on the Internet. Anyone could "rip" his or her CDs and then post them to this site. This ripped content could then be downloaded from any computer. And this download could be "streamed" to be just like the service MP3.com was providing.

The difference is simply that users don't have to upload their CDs. On a slow connection, that could take hours; on a fast connection, it still can be quite tedious. And a second difference is that the duplication that would be necessary for everyone to have his or her CDs on-line would be much less. Ironically, by shutting down MP3.com, the RIAA was inducing the production of many more copies of the very same music.

Thus the battle here was between two ways of viewing the law—one very strict and formal and the other much more sensitive to the consequences of one outcome over the other. And the claim of MP3.com was simply that the court should consider the facts in the case before it shut down this innovative structure for distributing content. MP3.com was arguing for a right to "space-shift" content, so that a user's content could be accessible anywhere.

But the court had no patience for MP3.com's innovation. In a stunning decision, the court not only found MP3.com guilty of copyright violation, it also found the violation "willful." And rather than giving nominal or minimal damages for this violation, the court imposed $110 million in damages. For experimenting with a different way to give consumers access to their data, MP3.com was severely punished. . . .

**Napster**

Napster enables individuals to identify and transfer music from other individuals. It enables *peers*, that is, to get music from *peers*. It does this not through a completely peer-to-peer architecture—there is a centralized database of who has what, and who, at any particular moment, is on-line. But the effect is peer-to-peer. Once the service identifies that X has the song that Y wants, it transfers control to the clients of X and Y, and these clients oversee the transfer. The Napster server has just made the link.

But that was enough in the eyes of the recording industry. And with predictably lightning speed, it filed suit here as well. Napster was just a system for stealing copyrighted material. It should, the RIAA demanded, be shut down.

Against the background of MP3.com, Napster does look a bit dicey. After all, the service at issue in MP3.com was a service to give individuals access to content that they presumptively had purchased. On Napster, the presumption is the opposite. There seems little reason for me to download music I already own.

But even that is not quite correct. I've been a Napster user, though I am not an imaginative user, and I am generally quite lazy. I know exactly what I want to hear, and I know that because I own the music already. But it is easier simply to download and play the music I own on Napster than it is for me to go through the CDs I own (most of which are at home, anyway) and insert the one I want in a player. Thus, while I won't say that none of the music I have listened to on Napster is music I don't own, probably only 5 percent is.

That the user owned the music, however, didn't stop the court in the MP3.com case. And the assurance that users were only downloading music they already owned was not likely to satisfy the RIAA. Most people, the RIAA argued, used Napster's technology to "steal" copyrighted work. It was a technology designed to enable stealing; it should be banned like burglar's tools.

Copyright law is not new to a technology said to be designed solely to facilitate theft. Think of the VCR. The VCR records content from television sets. It is designed to record content from television sets. The designers could well have chosen to disable the record button when the input was from a TV. They could, that is, have permitted recording when the input was from a camera and not a TV. But instead, they designed it so that television content could be copied for free.

No one in the television industry gave individuals the right to copy television content. The television industry instead insisted that copying television content was a crime. The industry launched a massive legal action against producers of VCRs, claiming that it was a technology designed to enable stealing and that it should be banned like burglar's tools. As Motion Picture Association of America president Jack Valenti testified, the VCR was the "Boston Strangler" of the American film industry.

This legal campaign ended up in the courtroom of Judge Warren Ferguson. After "three years of litigation, five weeks of trial and careful consideration of extensive briefing by both sides," the trial court judge found that the use of VCRs should be considered "fair use" under the copyright act. The court of appeals quickly reversed, but the important work had been done in the trial court. The judge had listened to the facts. Sony was permitted weeks of testimony to demonstrate that, in fact, the VCR would not harm the industry. Sony was permitted, in other words, to show how this technology should be influenced by the law.

These findings were critical in the appellate review of the case. And when the case finally reached the Supreme Court, it gave the Supreme Court sufficient ground to understand matters in a balanced and reasonable way. Though the VCR was designed to steal, the Court concluded that it could not be banned as an infringing technology unless there was no "potential" for a "substantial noninfringing use."

*Potential.* For a *substantial* noninfringing use. Notice what this standard does not say. It does not require that a majority of the uses of the technology be noninfringing. It requires only that a "substantial" portion be noninfringing. And it does not require that this noninfringement be proven today. It requires only that there be a potential for this noninfringing use. As long as one can demonstrate how the technology could be used in a way that was legitimate, the technology would not be banned by a court.

The Supreme Court's test is rightly permissive. The tradition of American law is not to ban technologies, but to punish infringing use. And that test should have had an obvious answer in the context of the Napster case. Here there are no doubt lots of infringing uses. But there are also lots that under any fair estimation constitute fair or noninfringing use. Music that has been released to the Net to be freely distributed is freely distributed through Napster. That use is clearly noninfringing and is substantial. Music that has fallen into the public domain is available on Napster. That use is clearly noninfringing, and is substantial. And lots of recordings that are not music—lectures, for example—can be made available on Napster. The Electronic Frontier Foundation has a series of lectures that are traded on Napster; they are offered as content that is free.

But when this claim was made to Judge Marilyn Hall Patel in California, she, unlike Judge Ferguson in the Sony case, had no patience for the argument. Without a trial, and with barely contained contempt, she ordered the site shut down.

Within thirty-six hours, Napster attorney David Boies had received a stay of that order from the Ninth Circuit Court of Appeals. And after hearing arguments in the case, that court affirmed much in the injunction of Judge Patel. The court did, however, make one important modification: Napster was not responsible for contributory infringement unless the copyright holder made Napster aware of the violation. Napster therefore wasn't closed down by the court; it wasn't required to become the copyright police. But it was required to remove music posted contrary to the copyright holder's wish. So, like the circuits of the computer Hal in the movie *2001*, the music in the memory of the Napster system will be slowly turned off, as copyright holders will demand the right to control the sharing of their content. . . .

## CONSEQUENCES OF CONTROL

The Internet in its nature shocks real-space law. That's often great; it is sometimes awful. The question policy makers must face is how to respond to this shock.

Courts are policy makers, and they too must ask how best to respond. Should they respond by intervening immediately to remedy the "wrong" said to exist? Or should they wait to allow the system to mature and to see just what harm there is?

In the context of porn, the courts' response is to wait and see. And indeed, this is the response of the government in many different contexts. Porn, privacy, taxation: in each case, courts and the government have insisted we should wait to see how the network develops.

In the context of copyright, the response has been different. Pushed by an army of high-powered lawyers, greased with piles of money from PACs, Congress and the courts have jumped into action to defend the old against the new. They have legislated, and litigated, quickly to assure that control of the old is not completely undermined by the new.

Ordinary people might find these priorities a bit odd. After all, the recording industry continues to grow at an astounding rate. Annual CD sales have tripled in the past ten years.[3] Yet the law races to support the recording industry, without any showing of harm. (Indeed, possibly the opposite: when Napster usage fell after the court restricted access, album sales fell as well. Napster may indeed have helped sales rather than hurt them.)[4]

At the same time, it can't be denied that the Net has reduced the ability that parents have to protect their children. Yet the law says, "Wait and see, let's make sure we don't harm the growth of the Net." In one case—where the harm is the least—the law is most active; and in the other—where the harm is most pronounced—the law stands back.

Indeed, the contrast is even stronger than this, and it is this that gets to the heart of the matter.

The Internet exposes much more copyrighted content to theft than in the world that existed before the Internet. This much of the content holders' claim is plainly true.

But as I've argued, the Internet does two other things as well. First, the Internet makes it possible (if the proper code is deployed) to control the use of copyrighted material much more fully than in the world before the Internet. And second, the Internet opens up a range of technologies for production and distribution that threaten the existing concentrations of media power.

In responding to the shock that the Internet presents to copyright law, it is of course important to account for the increased exposure to theft. But the law must also draw a balance to assure that this proper response to an increased risk of theft does not simultaneously erase the important range of access and use rights traditionally protected under copyright law. If the Net creates an initial imbalance, the response by Congress should not create an equal and opposite imbalance, where traditional rights are lost in the name of perfect control by content holders . . .

But now we should add a second concern to that same story: The response by Congress should also not be such as to permit this concentrated industry of today to leverage its control from the old world into the new. Artists deserve compensation. But their right to compensation should not translate into the industry's right to control how innovation in a new industry should develop.

*Control*, however, is precisely Hollywood's and the recording labels' objective. In the context of copyright law, the industry has been very clear: Its aim, as RIAA president Hilary Rosen has described it, is to assure that no venture capitalist invests in a start-up that aims to distribute content unless that start-up has the approval of the recording industry. This industry thus demands the right to veto new innovation, and it invokes the law to support its veto right.

Michael Robertson of MP3.com agrees that this is the aim and effect. "[T]his litigation," Robertson told me, "is as much about straddling the competition as anything else."[5] And it has had its effect.

> [W]hat they've done very successfully is dried up the capital markets for any digital music company. [W]e went public a little over a year ago [and] raise[d] $400 million from going public. Today, if you took a digital music company business plan, you couldn't get a buck and a half from a venture capital company.[6]

This is the reality that the current law has produced. In the name of protecting original copyright holders against the loss of income they never expected, we have established a regime where the future will be as the copyright industry permits. This puny part of the American economy has grabbed a veto on how creative distribution will occur.

One could quibble about whether current law is properly interpreted to give existing interests this control. Some see these cases (in particular the MP3.com and Napster cases) as simple; I find them very hard. But whether they are simple or hard, the underlying law is not unchangeable. Congress could play a role in making sure that the power of the old does not trump innovation in the new. It could, that is, intervene to strike a balance between the right of copyright holders to be compensated and the right of innovators to innovate.

The model for this intervention is something we've already seen: the compulsory license. For recall, the first real Napster-type case: cable television. It, like Napster, made its money by "stealing" the content of others. Congress in remedying this theft required that the cable companies pay content holders compensation. But at the same time, Congress gave cable television companies the right to license broadcasting content, whether or not the copyright holder wanted to.

Congress's aim in part was to assure that the cable industry could develop free of the influence of the broadcasters. The broadcasters were a powerful industry; Congress felt (rightly) that cable would grow more quickly and innovate more broadly if it was not beholden to the power of broadcasters. So Congress cut any dependency that the cable industry might have, by assuring it could get access to content without yielding control.

Compensation without control.

The same solution is available today. But the recording industry is doing everything it can to keep Congress far from this solution. For it knows that if it has the absolute right to veto distribution that it can't control, then it can strike deals with companies offering distribution that won't threaten the labels' power. The courts, whether rightly or not, have handed the labels this veto power; Congress, if it weren't flustered by the emotion of the recording industry, could well intervene to strike a very different balance.

We find that balance by looking for a balance—not by giving copyright interests a veto over how new technologies will develop. We discover what best serves both interests by allowing experimentation and alternatives.

But this is not how the law is treating copyright interests just now. Instead, they are in effect getting more control over copyright in cyberspace than they had in real space, even thought the need for more control is less clear. We are locking down the content layer and handing over the keys to Hollywood. . . .

If the extremes of these constraints are not necessary, if there is no good showing that they do any good, if they limit the range of creativity by virtue of the system of control they erect, why do we have them?

For this is a change. The content layer—the ability to use content and ideas—is closing. It is closing without a clear showing of the benefit this closing will provide and with a fairly clear showing of the harms it will impose. . . . This closing of the content layer is control without any showing of a return. Mindless locking up of resources that spur innovation. Control without reason.

This closing will not be without cost. Making it harder for innovations to enter, making resources more universally controlled—this will drive new competitors off the field, leaving the field once again safe for the old.

## NOTES


1. Lawrence Lessig, *Code and Other Laws of Cyberspace* (New York: Basic Books, 1999), 225.
2. See Digital Millennium Copyright Act, 105 P. L. 304, Sec. 202(c)(1)(iii) (1998).
3. Recording Industry Association of America, 2000 Year-end Statistics (2001), at http://www.riaa.com/pdf/Year_End_2000.pdf.
4. Jeff Leeds, "Album Sales Test the Napster Effect," *Los Angeles Times*, June 20, 2001, C1.
5. Telephone interview with Michael Robertson, November 16, 2000.
6. Ibid.


## LEGAL PERSPECTIVES

# *Sony Corp. v. Universal City Studios Inc.*

*U.S. Supreme Court*

Petitioners manufacture and sell home video tape recorders. Respondents own the copyrights on some of the television programs that are broadcast on the public airwaves. Some members of the general public use video tape recorders sold by petitioners to record some of these broadcasts, as well as a large number of other broadcasts. The question presented is whether the sale of petitioners' copying equipment to the general public violates any of the rights conferred upon respondents by the Copyright Act.

Respondents commenced this copyright infringement action against petitioners in the United States District Court for the Central District of California in 1976. Respondents alleged that some individuals had used Betamax video tape recorders (VTRs) to record some of respondents' copyrighted works which had been exhibited on commercially sponsored television and contended that these individuals had thereby infringed respondents' copyrights. Respondents further maintained that petitioners were liable for the copyright infringement allegedly committed by Betamax consumers because of petitioners' marketing of the Betamax VTRs. Respondents sought no relief against any Betamax consumer. Instead, they sought money damages and an equitable accounting of profits from petitioners, as well as an injunction against the manufacture and marketing of Betamax VTRs.

After a lengthy trial, the District Court denied respondents all the relief they sought and entered judgment for petitioners. The United States Court of Appeals for the Ninth Circuit reversed the District Court's judgment on respondents' copyright claim, holding petitioners liable for contributory infringement and ordering the District Court to fashion appropriate relief. We granted certiorari, since we had not completed our study of the case last Term, we ordered reargument. We now reverse.

An explanation of our rejection of respondents' unprecedented attempt to impose copyright liability upon the distributors of copying equipment requires a quite detailed recitation of the findings of the District Court. In summary, those findings reveal that the average member of the public uses a VTR principally to record a program he cannot view as it is being televised and then to watch it once at a later

---

464 U.S. 417 (1984) majority opinion by Justice Stevens.

time. This practice, known as "time-shifting," enlarges the television viewing audience. For that reason, a significant amount of television programming may be used in this manner without objection from the owners of the copyrights on the programs. For the same reason, even the two respondents in this case, who do assert objections to time-shifting in this litigation, were unable to prove that the practice has impaired the commercial value of their copyrights or has created any likelihood of future harm. Given these findings, there is no basis in the Copyright Act upon which respondents can hold petitioners liable for distributing VTR's to the general public. The Court of Appeals' holding that respondents are entitled to enjoin the distribution of VTR's, to collect royalties on the sale of such equipment, or to obtain other relief, if affirmed, would enlarge the scope of respondents' statutory monopolies to encompass control over an article of commerce that is not the subject of copyright protection. Such an expansion of the copyright privilege is beyond the limits of the grants authorized by Congress.

## I

The two respondents in this action, Universal City Studios, Inc., and Walt Disney Productions, produce and hold the copyrights on a substantial number of motion pictures and other audiovisual works. In the current marketplace, they can exploit their rights in these works in a number of ways: by authorizing theatrical exhibitions, by licensing limited showings on cable and network television, by selling syndication rights for repeated airings on local television stations, and by marketing programs on prerecorded videotapes or videodiscs. Some works are suitable for exploitation through all of these avenues, while the market for other works is more limited.

Petitioner Sony manufactures millions of Betamax video tape recorders and markets these devices through numerous retail establishments, some of which are also petitioners in this action. Sony's Betamax VTR is a mechanism consisting of three basic components: (1) a tuner, which receives electromagnetic signals transmitted over the television band of the public airwaves and separates them into audio and visual signals; (2) a recorder, which records such signals on a magnetic tape; and (3) an adapter, which converts the audio and visual signals on the tape into a composite signal that can be received by a television set.

Several capabilities of the machine are noteworthy. The separate tuner in the Betamax enables it to record a broadcast off one station while the television set is tuned to another channel, permitting the viewer, for example, to watch two simultaneous news broadcasts by watching one "live" and recording the other for later viewing. Tapes may be reused, and programs that have been recorded may be erased either before or after viewing. A timer in the Betamax can be used to activate and deactivate the equipment at predetermined times, enabling an intended viewer to record programs that are transmitted when he or she is not at home. Thus a person may watch a program at home in the evening even though it was broadcast while the viewer was at work during the afternoon. The Betamax is also equipped with a pause button and a fast-forward control. The pause button, when depressed, deactivates the recorder until it is released, thus enabling a viewer to omit a commercial advertisement from the recording, provided, of course, that the viewer is present when the program is recorded. The fast-forward control enables the viewer of a previously recorded program to run the tape rapidly when a segment he or she does not desire to see is being played back on the television screen.

The respondents and Sony both conducted surveys of the way the Betamax machine was used by several hundred owners during a sample period in 1978. Although there were some differences in the surveys, they both showed that the primary use of the machine for most owners was "time-shifting"—the practice of recording a program to view it once at a later time, and thereafter erasing it. Time-shifting enables viewers to see programs they otherwise would miss because they are not at home, are occupied with other tasks, or are viewing a program on another station at the time of a broadcast that they desire to watch. Both surveys also showed, however, that a substantial number of interviewees had accumulated libraries of tapes. Sony's survey indicated that over 80% of the interviewees watched at least as much regular television as they had before owning a Betamax. Respondents offered no evidence of decreased television viewing by Betamax owners.

Sony introduced considerable evidence describing television programs that could be copied without objection from any copyright holder, with special emphasis on sports, religious, and educational programming. For example, their survey indicated that 7.3% of all Betamax use is to record sports events, and representatives of professional baseball, football, basketball, and hockey testified that they had no objection to the recording of their televised events for home use.

Respondents offered opinion evidence concerning the future impact of the unrestricted sale of VTR's on the commercial value of their copyrights. The District Court found, however, that they had failed to prove any likelihood of future harm from the use of VTR's for time-shifting. . . .

## II

Article I, 8, of the Constitution provides:

> The Congress shall have Power . . . To Promote the Progress of Science and useful Arts, by securing for limited Times to Authors and Inventors the exclusive Right to their respective Writings and Discoveries.

The monopoly privileges that Congress may authorize are neither unlimited nor primarily designed to provide a special private benefit. Rather, the limited grant is a means by which an important public purpose may be achieved. It is intended to motivate the creative activity of authors and inventors by the provision of a special reward, and to allow the public access to the products of their genius after the limited period of exclusive control has expired. . . .

As the text of the Constitution makes plain, it is Congress that has been assigned the task of defining the scope of the limited monopoly that should be granted to authors or to inventors in order to give the public appropriate access to their work product. Because this task involves a difficult balance between the interests of authors and inventors in the control and exploitation of their writings and discoveries on the one hand, and society's competing interest in the free flow of ideas, information, and commerce on the other hand, our patent and copyright statutes have been amended repeatedly.

From its beginning, the law of copyright has developed in response to significant changes in technology. Indeed, it was the invention of a new form of copying equipment—the printing press—that gave rise to the original need for copyright protection. Repeatedly, as new developments have occurred in this country, it has been the Congress that has fashioned the new rules that new technology made necessary. . . .

The judiciary's reluctance to expand the protections afforded by the copyright without explicit legislative guidance is a recurring theme. Sound policy, as well as history, supports our consistent deference to Congress when major technological innovations alter the market for copyrighted materials. Congress has the constitutional authority and the institutional ability to accommodate fully the varied permutations of competing interests that are inevitably implicated by such new technology.

In a case like this, in which Congress has not plainly marked our course, we must be circumspect in construing the scope of rights created by a legislative enactment which never contemplated such a calculus of interests. . . .

## III

If vicarious liability is to be imposed on Sony in this case, it must rest on the fact that it has sold equipment with constructive knowledge of the fact that its customers may use that equipment to make unauthorized copies of copyrighted material. There is no precedent in the law of copyright for the imposition of vicarious liability on such a theory. . . .

## IV

The question is . . . whether the Betamax is capable of commercially significant noninfringing uses. . . .

### A. Authorized Time-Shifting

Each of the respondents owns a large inventory of valuable copyrights, but in the total spectrum of television programming their combined market share is small. The exact percentage is not specified, but it is well below 10%. If they were to prevail, the outcome of this litigation would have a significant impact on both the producers and the viewers of the remaining 90% of the programming in the Nation. . . .

### B. Unauthorized Time-Shifting

Even unauthorized uses of a copyrighted work are not necessarily infringing. An unlicensed use of the copyright is not an infringement unless it conflicts with one of the specific exclusive rights conferred by the copyright statute. Moreover, the definition of exclusive rights in 106 of the present Act is prefaced by the words "subject to sections 107 through 118." Those sections describe a variety of uses of copyrighted material that "are not infringements of copyright" "notwithstanding the provisions of section 106." The most pertinent in this case is 107, the legislative endorsement of the doctrine of "fair use."

That section identifies various factors that enable a court to apply an "equitable rule of reason" analysis to particular claims of infringement. Although not conclusive, the first factor requires that "the commercial or nonprofit character of an activity" be weighed in any fair use decision. If the Betamax were used to make copies for a commercial or profit-making purpose, such use would presumptively be unfair. The contrary presumption is appropriate here, however, because the District Court's findings plainly establish that time-shifting for private home use must be characterized as a noncommercial, nonprofit activity. Moreover, when one considers the nature of a televised copyrighted audiovisual work, and that time-shifting merely enables a viewer to see such a work which he had been invited to witness in its entirety free of charge, the fact that the entire work is reproduced, see 107(3), does not have its ordinary effect of militating against a finding of fair use.

This is not, however, the end of the inquiry because Congress has also directed us to consider "the effect of the use upon the potential market for or value of the copyrighted work." The purpose of copyright is to create incentives for creative effort. Even copying for noncommercial purposes may impair the copyright holder's ability to obtain the rewards that Congress intended him to have. But a use that has no demonstrable effect upon the potential market for, or the value of, the copyrighted work need not be prohibited in order to protect the author's incentive to create. The prohibition of such noncommercial uses would merely inhibit access to ideas without any countervailing benefit.

Thus, although every commercial use of copyrighted material is presumptively an unfair exploitation of the monopoly privilege that belongs to the owner of the copyright, noncommercial uses are a different matter. A challenge to a noncommercial use of a copyrighted work requires proof either that the particular use is harmful, or that if it should become widespread, it would adversely affect the potential market for the copyrighted work. Actual present harm need not be shown; such a requirement would leave the copyright holder with no defense against predictable damage. Nor is it necessary to show with certainty that future harm will result. What is necessary is a showing by a preponderance of the evidence that some meaningful likelihood of future harm exists. If the intended use is for commercial gain, that likelihood may be presumed. But if it is for a noncommercial purpose, the likelihood must be demonstrated. . . .

There was no need for the District Court to say much about past harm. "Plaintiffs have admitted that no actual harm to their copyrights has occurred to date."

On the question of potential future harm from time-shifting, the District Court offered a more detailed analysis of the evidence. It rejected respondents' "fear that persons 'watching' the original telecast of a program will not be measured in the live audience and the ratings and revenues will decrease," by observing that current measurement technology allows the Betamax audience to be reflected. It rejected respondents' prediction "that live television or movie audiences will decrease as more people watch Betamax tapes as an alternative," with the observation that "[t]here is no factual basis for [the underlying] assumption." It rejected respondents' "fear that time-shifting will reduce audiences for telecast reruns," and concluded instead that "given current market practices, this should aid plaintiffs rather than harm them." And it declared that respondents' suggestion that "theater or film rental exhibition of a program will suffer because of time-shift recording of that program" "lacks merit."

After completing that review, the District Court restated its overall conclusion several times, in several different ways. "Harm from time-shifting is speculative and, at best, minimal." "The audience benefits from the time-shifting capability have already been discussed. It is not implausible that benefits could also accrue to plaintiffs, broadcasters, and advertisers, as the Betamax makes it possible for more persons to view their broadcasts." "No likelihood of harm was shown at trial, and plaintiffs admitted that there had been no actual harm to date." "Testimony at trial suggested that Betamax may require adjustments in marketing strategy, but it did not establish even a likelihood of harm." "Television production by plaintiffs today is more profitable than it has ever been, and, in five weeks of trial, there was no concrete evidence to suggest that the Betamax will change the studios' financial picture."

The District Court's conclusions are buttressed by the fact that to the extent time-shifting expands public access to freely broadcast television programs, it yields societal benefits. In Community Television of Southern California v. Gottfried, we acknowledged the public interest in making television broadcasting more available. Concededly, that interest is not unlimited. But it supports an interpretation of the concept of "fair use" that requires the copyright holder to demonstrate some likelihood of harm before he may condemn a private act of time-shifting as a violation of federal law.

When these factors are all weighed in the "equitable rule of reason" balance, we must conclude that this record amply supports the District Court's conclusion that home time-shifting is fair use. In light of the findings of the District Court regarding the state of the empirical data, it is clear that the Court of Appeals erred in holding that the statute as presently written bars such conduct.

In summary, the record and findings of the District Court lead us to two conclusions. First, Sony demonstrated a significant likelihood that substantial numbers of copyright holders who license their works for broadcast on free television would not object to having their broadcasts time-shifted by private viewers. And second, respondents failed to demonstrate that time-shifting would cause any likelihood of nonminimal harm to the potential market for, or the value of, their copyrighted works. The Betamax is, therefore, capable of substantial noninfringing uses. Sony's sale of such equipment to the general public does not constitute contributory infringement of respondents' copyrights.

## V

> The direction of Art. I is that Congress shall have the power to promote the progress of science and the useful arts. When, as here, the Constitution is permissive, the sign of how far Congress has chosen to go can come only from Congress. [Deepsouth Packing Co. v. Laitram Corp.]

One may search the Copyright Act in vain for any sign that the elected representatives of the millions of people who watch television every day have made it unlawful to copy a program for later viewing at home, or have enacted a flat prohibition against the sale of machines that make such copying possible.

It may well be that Congress will take a fresh look at this new technology, just as it so often has examined other innovations in the past. But it is not our job to apply laws that have not yet been written. Applying the copyright statute, as it now reads, to the facts as they have been developed in this case, the judgment of the Court of Appeals must be reversed.

It is so ordered.

# *A & M Records v. Napster*

*United States District Court for the Northern District of California*

## OPINION

The matter before the court concerns the boundary between sharing and theft, personal use and the unauthorized worldwide distribution of copyrighted music and sound recordings. On December 6, 1999, A&M Records and seventeen other record companies ("record company plaintiffs") filed a complaint for contributory and vicarious copyright infringement, violations of the California Civil Code section 980(a)[2], and unfair competition against Napster, Inc., an Internet start-up that enables users to download MP3 music files without payment. On January 7, 2000, plaintiffs Jerry Leiber, Mike Stoller, and Frank Music Corporation filed a complaint for vicarious and contributory copyright infringement on behalf of a putative class of similarly-situated music publishers ("music publisher plaintiffs") against Napster, Inc. and former CEO Eileen Richardson. . . . Now before this court is the record company and music publisher plaintiffs' joint motion

114 F. Supp 2d 896 (2001) Opinion by Chief Judge Marilyn Hall Patel.

to preliminarily enjoin Napster, Inc. from engaging in or assisting others in copying, downloading, uploading, transmitting, or distributing copyrighted music without the express permission of the rights owner.

In opposition to this motion, defendant seeks to expand the "fair use" doctrine articulated in Sony Corp. of America v. Universal City Studios, Inc., 464 U.S. 417 (1984), to encompass the massive downloading of MP3 files by Napster users. Alternatively, defendant contends that, even if this third-party activity constitutes direct copyright infringement, plaintiffs have not shown probable success on the merits of their contributory and vicarious infringement claims. Defendant also asks the court to find that copyright holders are not injured by a service created and promoted to facilitate the free downloading of music files, the vast majority of which are copyrighted.

Having considered the parties' arguments, the court grants plaintiffs' motion for a preliminary injunction against Napster, Inc. The court makes the following Findings of Fact and Conclusions of Law to support the preliminary injunction under Federal Rules of Civil Procedure 65(d).

## I. FINDINGS OF FACT

### A. MP3 Technology

1. Digital compression technology makes it possible to store audio recordings in a digital format that uses less memory and may be uploaded and downloaded over the Internet. MP3 is a popular, standard format used to store such compressed audio files. Compressing data into MP3 format results in some loss of sound quality. However, because MP3 files are smaller, they require less time to transfer and are therefore better suited to transmission over the Internet.
2. Consumers typically acquire MP3 files in two ways. First, users may download audio recordings that have already been converted into MP3 format by using an Internet service such as Napster. Second, "ripping" software makes it possible to copy an audio compact disc ("CD") directly onto a computer hard-drive; ripping software compresses the millions of bytes of information on a typical CD into a smaller MP3 file that requires a fraction of the storage space.

### B. Defendant's Business

1. Napster, Inc. is a start-up company based in San Mateo, California. It distributes its proprietary file-sharing software free of charge via its Internet website. People who have downloaded this software can log-on to the Napster system and share MP3 music files with other users who are also logged-on to the system. It is uncontradicted that Napster users currently upload or download MP3 files without payment to each other, defendant, or copyright owners. According to a Napster, Inc. executive summary, the Napster service gives its users the unprecedented ability to "locate music by their favorite artists in MP3 format." Defendant boasts that it "takes the frustration out of locating servers with MP3 files" by providing a peer-to-peer file-sharing system that allows Napster account holders to conduct relatively sophisticated searches for music files on the hard drives of millions of other anonymous users.
2. Although Napster was the brainchild of a college student who wanted to facilitate music-swapping by his roommate, it is far from a simple tool of distribution among friends and family. According to defendant's internal documents, there will be 75 million Napster users by the end of 2000. At one point, defendant estimated that even without marketing, its "viral service" was growing by more than 200 percent per month. Approximately 10,000 music files are shared per second using Napster, and every second more than 100 users attempt to connect to the system.
3. Napster, Inc. currently collects no revenues and charges its clientele no fees; it is a free service. However, it has never been a nonprofit organization. It plans to delay the maximization of revenues while it attracts a large user base. The value of the system grows as the quantity and quality of available music increases. Defendant's internal documents reveal a strategy of attaining a "critical mass" of music in an "ever-expanding library" as new members bring their MP3 collections online.

   Defendant eventually plans to "monetize" its user base. Potential revenue sources include targeted email; advertising; commissions from links to commercial websites; and direct marketing of CDs, Napster products, and CD burners and rippers. Defendant also may begin to charge fees for a premium or commercial version of its software. The existence of a large user base that increases daily and can be "monetized" makes Napster, Inc. a potentially attractive acquisition for larger, more established firms. . . .

4. The evidence shows that virtually all Napster users download or upload copyrighted files and that the vast majority of the music available on Napster is copyrighted. Eighty-seven percent of the files sampled by plaintiffs' expert, Dr. Ingram Olkin, "belong to or are administered by plaintiffs or other copyright holders." After analyzing Olkin's data, Charles J. Hausman, anti-piracy counsel for the RIAA, determined that 834 out of 1,150 files in Olkin's download database belong to or are administered by plaintiffs; plaintiffs alone own the copyrights to more than seventy percent of the 1,150 files. Napster users shared these files without authorization.
5. Napster, Inc. has never obtained licenses to distribute or download, or to facilitate others in distributing or downloading, the music that plaintiffs own. . . .

## D. Plaintiffs' Business

1. The music publisher plaintiffs compose music and write songs. They depend financially upon the sale of sound recordings because they earn royalties from such sales.

   However, they do not get a royalty when a Napster user uploads or downloads an MP3 file of their compositions without payment or authorization. The record company plaintiffs' sound recordings also result from a substantial investment of money, time, manpower, and creativity.

   In contrast, defendant invests nothing in the content of the music which means that, compared with plaintiffs, it incurs virtually no costs in providing a wide array of music to satisfy consumer demand.
2. To make a profit, the record company plaintiffs largely rely on the success of "hit" or popular recordings, which may constitute as little as ten or fifteen percent of albums released. Many, or all, of their top recordings have been available for free on Napster.
3. The record company plaintiffs have invested substantial time, effort, and funds in actual or planned entry into the digital downloading market. . . .

## E. Effect of Napster on the Market for Plaintiffs' Copyrighted Works

1. The court finds that Napster use is likely to reduce CD purchases by college students, whom defendant admits constitute a key demographic. Plaintiffs' expert, Dr. E. Deborah Jay, opined that forty-one percent of her college-student survey respondents "gave a reason for using Napster or described the nature of its impact on their music purchases in a way which either explicitly indicated or suggested that Napster displaces CD sales." She also found that twenty-one percent of the college students surveyed revealed that Napster helped them make a better selection or decide what to buy. However, Jay's overall conclusion was that "[t]he more songs Napster users have downloaded," the more likely they are to admit or imply that such use has reduced their music purchases. The report of Soundscan CEO Michael Fine lends support to Jay's findings. After examining data culled from three types of retail stores near college or university campuses,[1] Fine concluded that "on-line file sharing has resulted in a loss of album sales within college markets."

   For the reasons discussed in the court's separate order, the report by defendant's expert, Dr. Peter S. Fader, does not provide credible evidence that music file-sharing on Napster stimulates more CD sales than it displaces.[2] Nor do the recording industry documents that defendant cites reliably show increased music sales due to Napster use. . . .
2. Because plaintiffs entered the digital download market very recently, or plan to enter it in the next few months, they are especially vulnerable to direct competition from Napster, Inc. The court finds that, in choosing between the free Napster service and pay-per-download sites, consumers are likely to choose Napster. . . .
3. Downloading on Napster also has the potential to disrupt plaintiffs' promotional efforts because it does not involve any of the restrictions on timing, amount; or selection that plaintiffs

impose when they offer free music files. Even if Napster users sometimes download files to determine whether they want to purchase a CD, sampling on Napster is vastly different than that offered by plaintiffs. On Napster, the user—not the copyright owner—determines how much music to sample and how long to keep it.

## II. CONCLUSIONS OF LAW

### A. Legal Standard

1. The Ninth Circuit authorizes preliminary injunctive relief for "a party who demonstrates either (1) a combination of probable success on the merits and the possibility of irreparable harm, or (2) that serious questions are raised and the balance of hardships tips in its favor."
2. The standard is a sliding scale which requires a greater degree of harm the lesser the probability of success. In a copyright infringement case, demonstration of a reasonable likelihood of success on the merits creates a presumption of irreparable harm.

### B. Proof of Direct Infringement

1. To prevail on a contributory or vicarious copyright infringement claim, a plaintiff must show direct infringement by a third party. As a threshold matter, plaintiffs in this action must demonstrate that Napster users are engaged in direct infringement.
2. Plaintiffs have established a prima facie case of direct copyright infringement. As discussed above, virtually all Napster users engage in the unauthorized downloading or uploading of copyrighted music; as much as eighty-seven percent of the files available on Napster may be copyrighted, and more than seventy percent may be owned or administered by plaintiffs.

### C. Affirmative Defense of Fair Use and Substantial Non-Infringing Use

1. Defendant asserts the affirmative defenses of fair use and substantial non-infringing use. The latter defense is also known as the staple article of commerce doctrine. . . .
2. For the reasons set forth below, the court finds that any potential non-infringing use of the Napster service is minimal or connected to the infringing activity, or both. The substantial or commercially significant use of the service was, and continues to be, the unauthorized downloading and uploading of popular music, most of which is copyrighted.
3. Section 107 of the Copyright Act provides a non-exhaustive list of fair use factors. These factors include:

    (1) the purpose and character of the use, including whether such use is of a commercial nature or is for nonprofit educational purposes;

    (2) the nature of the copyrighted work;

    (3) the amount and substantiality of the portion used in relation to the copyrighted work as a whole; and

    (4) the effect of the use upon the potential market for or value of the copyrighted work.

4. In the instant action, the purpose and character of the use militates against a finding of fair use. . . .
5. Under the first factor, the court must also determine whether the use is commercial. In Acuff-Rose, the Supreme Court clarified that a finding of commercial use weighs against, but does not preclude, a determination of fairness.
6. If a use is non-commercial, the plaintiff bears the burden of showing a meaningful likelihood that it would adversely affect the potential market for the copyrighted work if it became widespread.
7. Although downloading and uploading MP3 music files is not paradigmatic commercial activity, it is also not personal use in the traditional sense. Plaintiffs have not shown that the majority of Napster users download music to sell—that is, for profit. However, given the vast scale of Napster use among anonymous individuals, the court finds that downloading and uploading MP3 music files with the assistance of Napster are not private uses. At the very least, a host user sending a file cannot be said to engage in a personal use when distributing that file to an anonymous requester. Moreover, the fact that Napster users get for free something they would ordinarily have to buy suggests that they reap economic advantages from Napster use.

8. The court finds that the copyrighted musical compositions and sound recordings are creative in nature; they constitute entertainment, which cuts against a finding of fair use under the second factor.
9. With regard to the third factor, it is undisputed that downloading or uploading MP3 music files involves copying the entirety of the copyrighted work. The Ninth Circuit held prior to Sony that "wholesale copying of copyrighted material precludes application of the fair use doctrine." Even after Sony, wholesale copying for private home use tips the fair use analysis in plaintiffs' favor if such copying is likely to adversely affect the market for the copyrighted material.
10. The fourth factor, the effect on the potential market for the copyrighted work, also weighs against a finding of fair use. Plaintiffs have produced evidence that Napster use harms the market for their copyrighted musical compositions and sound recordings in at least two ways. First, it reduces CD sales among college students. Second, it raises barriers to plaintiffs' entry into the market for the digital downloading of music. . . .

## D. Contributory Copyright Infringement

1. Once they have shown direct infringement by Napster users, plaintiffs must demonstrate a likelihood of success on their contributory infringement claim. A contributory infringer is "one who, with knowledge of the infringing activity, induces, causes or materially contributes to the infringing conduct of another." Courts do not require actual knowledge; rather, a defendant incurs contributory copyright liability if he has reason to know of the third party's direct infringement.
2. Plaintiffs present convincing evidence that Napster executives actually knew about and sought to protect use of the service to transfer illegal MP3 files. For example, a document authored by co-founder Sean Parker mentions the need to remain ignorant of users' real names and IP addresses "since they are exchanging *pirated* music." The same document states that, in bargaining with the RIAA, defendant will benefit from the fact that "we are not just making *pirated* music available but also pushing demand." These admissions suggest that facilitating the unauthorized exchange of copyrighted music was a central part of Napster, Inc.'s business strategy from the inception.

   Plaintiff also demonstrate that defendant had actual notice of direct infringement because the RIAA informed it of more than 12,000 infringing files. Although Napster, Inc. purportedly terminated the users offering these files, the songs are still available using the Napster service, as are the copyrighted works which the record company plaintiffs identified in Schedules A and B of their complaint. . . .

## E. Vicarious Copyright Infringement

1. Even in the absence of an employment relationship, a defendant incurs liability for vicarious copyright infringement if he "has the right and ability to supervise the infringing activity and also has a direct financial interest in such activities."
2. In Fonovisa, the swap meet operator satisfied the first element of vicarious liability because it had the right to terminate vendors at will; it also controlled customers' access and promoted its services. Although Napster, Inc. argues that it is technologically difficult, and perhaps infeasible, to distinguish legal and illegal conduct, plaintiffs have shown that defendant supervises Napster use. Indeed, Napster, Inc. itself takes pains to inform the court of its improved methods of blocking users about whom rights holders complain. This is tantamount to an admission that defendant can, and sometimes does, police its service. . . .

   Moreover, a defendant need not exercise its supervisory powers to be deemed capable of doing so. The court therefore finds that Napster, Inc. has the right and ability to supervise its users' infringing conduct.
3. Plaintiffs have shown a reasonable likelihood that Napster, Inc. has a direct financial interest in the infringing activity. Citing several non-governing cases from other districts, they contend that direct financial benefit does not require earned revenue, so long as the defendant has economic incentives for tolerating unlawful behavior.

   Although Napster, Inc. currently generates no revenue, its internal documents state that it "will drive [sic] revenues directly from increases in userbase." The Napster service attracts more and more users by offering an increasing amount of quality music for free. It hopes to "monetize" its user base through one of several generation revenue models noted in the factual findings. . . .

4. Plaintiffs has shown a reasonable likelihood of success on their vicarious infringement claims. . . .

## J. Irreparable Harm

1. Because plaintiffs have shown a reasonable likelihood of success on the merits of their contributory and vicarious copyright infringement claims, they are entitled to a presumption of irreparable harm.
2. The court rejects defendant's contention that it has rebutted this presumption by demonstrating that any harm is *de minimis.* The declarations of record company executives, combined with the Teece Report, establish that plaintiffs have invested in the digital downloading market and that their business plans are threatened by a service that offers the same product for free. Moreover, while the court recognizes the limitations of a survey that only targets college students, the Jay Report suggests the tendency of Napster use to suppress CD purchases, especially among heavy users.

## K. Balance of the Hardships

1. The court cannot give much weight to defendant's lament that the requested relief will put it out of business. Although even a narrow injunction may so fully eviscerate Napster, Inc. as to destroy its user base or make its service technologically infeasible, the business interests of an infringer do not trump a rights holder's entitlement to copyright protection. Nor does defendant's supposed inability to separate infringing and non-infringing elements of its service constitute a valid reason for denying plaintiffs relief or for issuing a stay.

   Any destruction of Napster, Inc. by a preliminary injunction is speculative compared to the statistical evidence of massive, unauthorized downloading and uploading of plaintiffs' copyrighted works—as many as 10,000 files per second, by defendant's own admission. The court has every reason to believe that, without a preliminary injunction, these numbers will mushroom as Napster users, and newcomers attracted by the publicity, scramble to obtain as much free music as possible before trial. . . .

## III. CONCLUSION

For the foregoing reasons, the court GRANTS plaintiffs' motion for a preliminary injunction against Napster, Inc. Defendant is hereby preliminarily ENJOINED from engaging in, or facilitating others in copying, downloading, uploading, transmitting, or distributing plaintiffs' copyrighted musical compositions and sound recordings, protected by either federal or state law, without express permission of the rights owner. This injunction applies to all such works that plaintiffs own; it is not limited to those listed in Schedules A and B of the complaint.

Plaintiffs have shown persuasively that they own the copyrights to more than seventy percent of the music available on the Napster system. Because defendant has contributed to illegal copying on a scale that is without precedent, it bears the burden of developing a means to comply with the injunction. Defendant must insure that no work owned by plaintiffs which neither defendant nor Napster users have permission to use or distribute is uploaded or downloaded on Napster. The court ORDERS plaintiffs to cooperate with defendant in identifying the works to which they own copyrights. To this end, plaintiffs must file a written plan no later than September 5, 2000, describing the most expedient method by which their rights can be ascertained. The court also ORDERS plaintiffs to post a bond for the sum of $5,000,000.00 to compensate defendant for its losses in the event that this injunction is reversed or vacated.

IT IS SO ORDERED.

## NOTES

1. Fine's study tracked retail music sales trends in three types of stores in the United States: (1) all stores located within one mile of any college or university on a list acquired from Quality Education Data; (2) all stores located within one mile of any college or university on a list of colleges and universities that have banned Napster use; (3) all stores within one mile of any college or university listed among the "Top 40 Most Wired Colleges in 1999," according to Yahoo Internet Life. Researchers working on the Fine Report used Soundscan Point of Sale data to compare music sales totals from the latter two categories with (1) national totals and (2) sales from the first category, "All College Stores." The report tracked retail sales in the first quarter ("Q1") of 1997, 1998, 1999, and 2000.
2. The court's memorandum and order regarding the admissibility of expert reports includes a detailed discussion of flaws in the Fader Report. Among the shortcomings the court noted are Fader's heavy reliance on journalistic articles and studies that he did not conduct, the fact the centerpiece of his repor is a survey that he only distantly supervised, and the lack of tables offering statistical breakdowns of survey respondents and their answers.

## CASES

# CASE 1. *Privacy, Legality, and Information Technology*

As Chief Information Officer at the Bank of Commerce, Steve Pulley oversees all of the bank's electronic transmission and reporting, and manages the software needs of the bank's twelve branches. On this particular day, Pulley is worried about some of the fine print he is reading associated with the latest Microsoft Windows update.

Pulley is concerned that if the bank agrees to the terms of the end user license agreement (EULA) for Microsoft's Windows 2000 Service Pack 3 and XP Service Pack 1, it might be in violation of new federal privacy laws that govern financial institutions. The "automatic update" feature of the EULA allows users to obtain automatic upgrades and patches to their operating systems. But in order to get the updates, end users must agree to give Microsoft access to information on their systems.

Although many home or small office users may be willing to consent to the arrangement in order to receive the convenient automatic downloads, the arrangement raises legitimate questions regarding the protection of individual consumer identity. And while such an arrangement might concern any individual consumer on grounds of protecting privacy, it is of special concern to the Bank of Commerce because of the Gramm-Leach-Bliley Act of 1999. The regulation specifically forbids financial institutions from transferring any personal customer data to any third party without the consent of the customer. This type of legislation is not uncommon; European countries typically have even more stringent consumer data privacy regulations.

If Bank of Commerce were to comply with the Service Pack EULA, Pulley concludes, they would be in direct violation of the Gramm-Leach-Bliley Act, which would subject the institution to fines and criminal penalties. This is clearly out of the question. An immediate and

This case was prepared by Jared D. Harris. Source material for the case came from an article on the CIO Information Network website, http://cin.earthweb.com, "Is Microsoft Licensing Forcing Banks to Break the Law?" October 22, 2002, by Dan Orzech.

short term solution is for Pulley to decline the Service Pack EULA, but he worries about the bigger picture: Microsoft reportedly plans to modify future versions of the software, eliminating users' ability to "opt out" of the automatic update feature.

In reading the precise language of the EULA, it appears that Microsoft's underlying motivation behind automatic update may be to minimize the distribution of pirated copies of the Windows software. The EULA for Windows XP Service Pack 1 states that it may use the automatic update technology "to confirm that you have a licensed copy of the OS Software." This is accomplished by the use of an electronic key that is transmitted to Microsoft over the Internet. In order for the exchange of information to take place, Microsoft is in turn required to have access to the licensee's system.

Any security concerns are further complicated by the fact that users agreeing to the EULA grant system access not only to Microsoft, but also to its "designated agents." Whereas Microsoft itself isn't renown for its exceptional security, Pulley frets even more about an "agent" company that, for example, might be a small overseas firm governed by a less developed legal system.

Pulley is worried that a change in operating systems at the Bank of Commerce would be disruptive and costly. What's more, he may very well be faced with the same dilemma under a Microsoft competitor's EULA. Microsoft is not the only company that offers an automatic update service; for example, the latest Apple Computer operating system OS X has similar functionality, called "software update."

### Questions

1. What options are available to Pulley in resolving this issue?
2. Is Microsoft's use of automatic update technology justified in terms of preventing piracy? What are the legal implications?
3. What should the government's role be in attending to (or regulating) these types of issues?
4. Ignore the existence of the Gramm-Leach-Bliley Act. At what point do the consumer policies of a company overstep their moral "bounds"? To what extent should moral bounds govern individual company policies?
5. Microsoft isn't renown for exceptional security. To what extent should Microsoft be accountable for improper use of consumer information by one of its designated agents? To what extent should Microsoft be accountable for the theft of consumer information by unrelated parties who exploit the automatic update technology through "hacking"?

## CASE 2. *Privacy Pressures: The Use of Web Bugs at HomeConnection*

As Matthew Scott, president of HomeConnection, sat in his office waiting for several members of his executive team to arrive, he grew more worrisome about a story featuring his company in the morning paper. His impulse was to fight back and go on the defensive, but

Scott knew that he had to be careful. However, he did not accept the article's implicit conclusion that HomeConnection had no regard for the privacy rights of its customers, and he was anxious to hear what his colleagues had to say about the matter.

HomeConnection was an Internet Service Provider (ISP) with several million customers, primarily clustered in the mid-West. An ISP links people and businesses to the Internet, usually for a monthly fee. HomeConnection was much smaller than the industry leader, America OnLine (AOL), but it was still seen as a formidable player in this industry. Thanks to Scott's management, the company had recorded increasing profits for the past three years, 1999 through 2002. One feature that attracted customers was the opportunity to create their own personal Web page. HomeConnection made this process easy and convenient.

In the past year HomeConnection had devised an innovative promotion to help increase its subscriber base. The company encouraged its users with their own personal Web pages to carry an ad for HomeConnection. The ad would offer new subscribers a heavily discounted rate for the first year of membership. In addition, as an incentive to display the ad on their personal Web pages, the company agreed to pay its users $25 for any new members who signed up for a subscription by clicking on the ad. The response to the promotion was stronger than expected, and HomeConnection's membership had risen by over 6.5 percent since the program's inception eight months ago. Scott was quite enthused about the results, and he did not anticipate that one aspect of the program would attract some negative attention.

In consultation with his marketing manager, Scott had authorized the use of Web bugs so that when users placed the ad on their Web pages they would also get a Web bug. A Web bug is embedded as a miniscule and invisible picture on the screen and it can track everything one does on a particular Web site. Web bugs, also called "Web beacons," are usually deployed to count visitors to a Web site or to gather cumulative data about visitors to those sites without tracking any personal details. In this case the Web bug transmitted information to a major on-line ad agency, DoubleDealer. DoubleDealer would collect data about those who visited these Web pages, which ads they clicked on, and so forth.

The newspaper report cited HomeConnection as well as other ISPs and e-commerce sites for using this protocol without the permission of their customers. They quoted a well-known privacy expert: "It's extremely disturbing that these companies are using technology to gather information in such a clandestine manner; I don't see how it can be morally justified." The article had clearly resonated with some of HomeConnecton's users, and the switchboard had been busy most of the afternoon with calls from irate customers. Some wanted to cancel their subscription.

Scott felt that the company had done nothing wrong but was a victim of a pervasive paranoia about privacy. HomeConnection was not using these bugs for any untoward purposes—its purpose was to track the results of the advertising promotion, that is, how many people were clicking on these ads. Also, Scott himself had modified the company's privacy policy to indicate that Web bugs might be used sometimes. (However, there was no indication that Web bugs would be placed on the personal Web pages of its user base.)

As several of his managers made their way into the conference room adjoining his office, Scott made one last check with customer service. By now it was late in the day and the volume of calls and e-mails was dying down. It was now up to Scott to determine a response—did the company face a serious problem or was this just a tempest in a teapot?

**Questions***

1. Has HomeConnection's use of the Web bug violated the privacy of those who agreed to display the ad on their personal computers? Has the privacy of those who visit the site and click on the ad been violated?
2. Should those who display the ad on their personal computers have the right to refuse to have the Web bugs attached? In other words should they be allowed to have the right to opt-out of this arrangement?
3. Suppose a person who displays the ad agrees to the Web bug. Should that person be required to place a statement on his or her personal Web site indicating that persons clicking on the ad may receive further advertisements from a number of sources?

* Questions added by the editor.

## CASE 3. *Spiders at the Auction*

eBay, Inc. is one of the largest and most successful commercial sites on the entire World Wide Web. Founded in 1995, eBay introduced consumers to a consumer business model that brings buyers and sellers together in an engaging auction format in order to buy and sell many different items such as coins, consumer electronics, antiques, appliances, and so forth. Products sold on the Web site can range from a $1 baseball card to a $578,000 Shoeless Joe Jackson's baseball bat. With 38 million customers, sales for 2002 were projected to be $1 billion returning a net income of $150 million. eBay carries no inventory so it can keep costs low. But the biggest reason for success derives from the fact that eBay is "a master at harnessing the awesome power of the Net—not just to let customers sound off directly in the ears of the big brass, but to track their every movement so new products and services are tailored to just what customers want."[1]

eBay has had several disputes with auction aggregator services which accumulate data from different auction sites so that a consumer can see what is available at all these different sites. The advantage for the buyer is the ability to see if a product available on eBay might be available at a lower asking price on a different site. One such dispute occurred in 1999 with an aggregator service known as AuctionWatch. The AuctionWatch site offers a "Universal Search Function" which allows users to access the price, product, description, and bidding history from popular auction sites such as eBay, Yahoo, and amazon.com. For example, if a user were interested in Boston Red Sox baseball memorabilia, that individual could check the AuctionWatch site to ascertain all of the Red Sox memorabilia available for auction across multiple sites.

AuctionWatch relied on spider technology to locate this data at these different auction sites. A spider is a robotic search engine that can crawl through sites many times a day to extract shopping data. According to Karen Solomon, "The benefits of bots for consumers are indisputable, but some merchants are less than thrilled about the technology's parasitic presence."[2]

eBay officials were certainly "less than thrilled" with AuctionWatch's constant forays into its computer system. They asked the company to stop, but it refused to contain its auction bot activities. eBay claimed that its auction data was proprietary, though that data was not eligible for any copyright protection. eBay also argued that the auction bots burdened its servers and perhaps impeded performance for its regular customers.

Given AuctionWatch's categorical refusal to curtail its intrusive activities, eBay executives met with their lawyers to discuss the next step. Should they simply allow the auction bot to continue? Should they pursue legal action? One possible legal angle to deter AuctionWatch was to accuse it of "trespass to chattels." Trespass to chattels represents a tort action for the unauthorized theft, use, or interference with another's tangible property.[3] But was this bot really "trespassing" on eBay's property, including its servers? Hasn't eBay made its Web site available to the public on this public network?

## NOTES

1. R. Hof, "The People's Company," *Business Weeke.biz* (December 3, 2001), p. 15.
2. K. Solomon, "Revenge of the Bots," *Industry Standard* (November 29, 1999), p. 263.
3. Restatement (Second) of Torts, Sections 217–18 (1965).

## Questions*

1. Does the fact that eBay can track the movements of those who visit their site violate the visitor's right to privacy?
2. Should eBay's auction data be considered proprietary and thus be protected as intellectual property? Or should that data be considered public property since eBay's data are available to eBay's customers?
3. Would you agree with eBay that these "spiders" are thieves?

* Questions supplied by the editor.

# CASE 4. *Ditto.Com*

Ditto.com, a small company formerly known as Arriba Software, operates a popular visual search engine at the Web site www.ditto.com. In response to queries from users, Ditto.com will retrieve images instead of text. It produces a list of "thumbnail" pictures that are relevant to the user's query. While this functionality provides a valuable service to consumers, it has generated considerable controversy about the scope of intellectual property protection for on-line photographs and images.

Ditto.com's Web site includes a massive search index with over six million entries. Each entry is a thumbnail image that has been acquired through the use of Ditto's spider[1] which crawls its way through media Web sites that collect and store photographs or other images. According to the company's Web site, once the crawler does its work, "we then select, rank, weight, filter, and rate pictures, illustrations, clipart, photographs, drawings and other image-related material; next we index the images from the Web site."[2] All of this is done without the permission of the artist or photographer who created the image. When a user initiates a query, he or she receives the list of reduced thumbnail pictures ranked and in order of relevance. When the user clicks on one of these retrieved thumbnail images, two windows appear on the user's screen: The first is a stand-alone copy of a full-size image and the second contains the complete originating Web page where that image appeared.

The Ditto.com program presents two sets of problems for some artists and photographers. Some object to the fact that their works were indexed by Ditto.com without their knowledge or permission. They argue that when search engines like Ditto.com display images without their permission and out of context, there is copyright infringement. There are also objections to Ditto's "deep linking" to the originating Web page for the image; this deep linking bypasses the home page which often includes advertisements and other promotional messages.

And there has been at least one lawsuit filed against Ditto.com. Leslie Kelly is a photographer from Huntington California who operates a Web site called www.goldrush1849.com. This site provides users with a virtual photographic tour of Sacramento and the California gold rush country. According to court documents, 35 of Kelly's photographs have been indexed in the Ditto.com image database with thumbnail versions made available to Ditto's users. Kelly filed suit for copyright infringement, arguing that Ditto.com had no right to copy and distribute his copyrighted photos without his explicit permission. In late 1999 a federal judge ruled in Ditto.com's favor, but the case has been appealed to the United States Court of Appeals for the Ninth Circuit.

At issue is whether the reduced size of the images (i.e., thumbnail versions) exempts them from copyright infringement. Specifically, is Ditto.com's use of these images tantamount to "fair use"? In copyright law fair use is a limitation on the copyright owner's exclusive right "to reproduce the copyrighted work in copies."[3] There are four factors to be considered in a fair use decision:

1. Purpose and character of the use. (Is the use commercial or for nonprofit or educational purposes?; in general, there is a bias against commercial use)
2. Nature of the copyrighted work. (Creative works tend to receive more protection than factual ones.)
3. Amount and "substantiality of the portion used in relation to the copyrighted work as a whole."
4. Effects on the potential market for the copyrighted work.[4]

In this controversial case, the judge concluded that search engine's activities amounted to "fair use" of the copyrighted images for several reasons. Judge Taylor concluded that while the use was commercial, "it was also of a somewhat more incidental and less exploitative nature than more traditional types of commercial use."[5] The judge also found that Ditto.com's use was significantly transformative, that is, it adds something new or alters the original with a new expression. This is a highly significant factor given the Supreme Court's ruling in *Campbell v. Acuff-Rose*: "The more transformative the new work, the less will be the significance of other factors, like commercialism, that may weigh against a finding of fair use."[6] According to Judge Taylor, Ditto.com's use is notably different from the use for which the images were created: "Plaintiff's photographs are artistic works used for illustrative purposes. Defendant's visual search engine is designed to catalog and improve access to images on the Internet."[7] Judge Taylor also found that there would most likely not be a negative commercial impact since Ditto.com's activities would actually bring more users to the Web sites where the images are located. While factors (2) and (3) did weigh against the fair use defense, Judge Taylor felt that on the whole this case passed the fair use test especially because the "defendant's purposes were and are inherently transformative."[8]

Despite Judge Taylor's ruling, this case raises some nagging moral and legal questions. Is Ditto.com's functionality similar to Napster's as some have alleged? Does it allow users to steal on-line art since they can view and download images without even visiting the originating Web site? Does it support wholesale visual plagiarism? Does the reduced size of the image represent a real transformation of the original as Judge Taylor has maintained? If not, is the fair use defense really tenable here? Is the deep linking to the originating Web site morally acceptable in this case?

## NOTES

1. A spider is an automated program that "crawls" through Web sites looking for certain information.
2. Available: www.ditto.com/about_us.asp.
3. 17 U.S.C. §106 (1).
4. 17 U.S.C. §107.
5. *Leslie A. Kelly et al. v. Arriba Soft Corp.*, 77 F. Supp. 2d 1116; U.S. Dist. (1999).
6. *Campbell v. Acuff-Rose,* 510 U.S. 569 (1994).
7. *Kelly v. Arriba.*
8. Ibid.

## Questions*

1. Should the photographs that are "found" on the Internet and reduced in size by Ditto.com be considered the intellectual property of the photographer and thus subject to copyright protection?
2. Do you agree with the cited court opinions that reducing the image is sufficient for a transformation such that the photographs do not deserve copyright protection?
3. Is Ditto.com's indexing of the photographs without the permission of the artists who made them a violation of the artist's property rights in the photographs he or she takes?

* Questions supplied by editor.

# *Suggested Supplementary Readings*

AGRE, PHILIP, and MARC ROTENBERG, Eds. *Technology and Privacy: The New Landscape.* Cambridge, MA: MIT Press, 1997.

ALDERMAN, JOHN. *Sonic Boom: Napster, MP3 and the New Pioneers of Music.* Cambridge, MA: Perseus Publishing, 2001.

BENNETT, CALON J., and REBECCA GRANT. *Visions of Privacy: Policy Choices for the Digital Age.* Toronto: University of Toronto Press, 1999.

BRANDEIS, LOUIS, and SAMUEL WARREN. "The Right to Privacy." *4, 193 Harvard Law Review,* 193 (1890).

BRIN, DAVID. *The Transparent Society.* Reading, MA: Addison-Wesley, 1998.

BURK, DAN L. "Transborder Intellectual Property Issues on the Electronic Frontier." *Stanford Law & Policy Review,* 6 (1) (1994), pp. 9–16.

CHALYKOFF, JOHN, and NITIN NOHIRA. "Note on Electronic Monitoring." Boston, MA: *Harvard Business School Publications* (1990).

DAVIS, RANDALL, PAMELA SAMUELSON, MITCHELL KAPOR, and JEROME REICHMAN, "A New View of Intellectual Property and Software." *Communications of the ACM,* 39 (3) (March 1996), pp. 21–30.

DECEW, JUDITH WAGNER. *In Pursuit of Privacy, Law, Ethics and the Rise of Technology.* Ithaca: Cornell University Press, 1997.

DE GEORGE, RICHARD "*The Ethics of Information Technology and Business.*" Oxford: Blackwell Publishing Company, 2003.

ETZIONI, AMITAI. *The Limits of Privacy.* New York: Basic Books, 1999.

LYON, DAVID, and ELIA ZUREIK, Eds. *Computers, Surveillance, and Privacy.* Minneapolis: University of Minnesota Press, 1996.

MASON, RICHARD, and MARY CULNAN. *Information and Responsibility: The Ethical Challenge.* Thousand Oaks, CA: Sage Publications, 1995.

MOOR, JAMES "The Ethics of Privacy Protection." *Library Trends,* 39 (1–2) (1990), pp. 69–82.

ROSEN, JONATHAN. *The Unwanted Gaze.* New York: Random House, 2000.

SPINELLO, RICHARD. "E-Mail and Panoptic Power in the Workplace." In L. Hartman, Ed. *Perspectives on Business Ethics.* New York: McGraw-Hill, 2002.

U.S. Congress, Office of Technology Assessment, "Finding a Balance: Computer Software, Intellectual Property, and the Challenge of Technological Change," OTA-TCT-527 (Washington, DC: U.S. Government Printing Office, May 1992).

WESTIN, ALAN. *Privacy and Freedom.* New York: Atheneum, 1967.

WRIGHT, MARIE, and JOHN KAHALIK. "The Erosion of Privacy." *Computers and Society,* 27 (4) (December 1997), pp. 22–26.

## *Chapter Nine*

# Ethical Issues in International Business

## INTRODUCTION

THERE IS NO QUESTION that markets are international and that failure to recognize this fact could be fatal. Most firms realize that competitors for their market share could come from any corner of the globe. Even fairly small regional firms often attempt to market their products internationally. Of course, there is much more to the awareness of international issues than the development of international markets. As people in all parts of the world travel outside their own countries, they discover that countries differ on many matters of right and wrong. In some instances what is considered right or acceptable in one country is considered wrong or unacceptable in another. In addition, many of the problems that affect one country have an impact on other nations. Two excellent examples come to us from two very different problems—maintaining the integrity of financial markets and protecting the world environment. Radioactive material from damaged nuclear power plants has spread well beyond national borders, as witnessed by the disaster at the Russian nuclear power plant at Chernobyl. Ailing nuclear power plants in Russia and elsewhere remain an international threat. Moreover, the phenomenon of global warming is no respecter of national borders. Thus, we are all forced to think internationally whether we want to or not.

And there is plenty to think about. Bribery, extortion, and the issue of facilitating payments remain common problems. When firms try to take advantage of a lower cost structure, whether it be lower wages or lower taxes, they are often accused of exploitation. Consumers in developed countries have become increasingly aware of the alleged sweatshop conditions under which the goods they purchase are manufactured and assembled. And many would argue that the more developed countries and the companies that do business there have an obligation to help resolve the social problems, especially the problem of poverty that affects other parts of the world. However, before we can address these specific issues with much authority, an overarching problem needs to be addressed.

## Are Any Universal Moral Norms Applicable to International Business?

There is a wide variety of opinion on what is acceptable conduct in international business, and a general skepticism prevails that questions whether there are any universal norms for ethical business practice. An international company involved in business abroad must face the question, "When in Rome, should it behave as the Romans do?" For purpose of this discussion, the home country of a business firm is where it has its headquarters or where it has its charter of incorporation. A host country is any other country where that firm does business.

When the norms of the home country and the norms of the host country are in conflict, a multinational corporation has four options: (1) Follow the norms of the home country because that is the patriotic thing to do; (2) follow the norms of the host country to show proper respect for the host country's culture; (3) follow whichever norm is most profitable; (4) follow whichever norm is morally best. (The four alternatives are not mutually exclusive.)

To choose option (4) requires an appeal to international moral norms for business practice. In his article Norman Bowie shows the importance of establishing the existence and content of these international norms. Bowie bases his argument for international norms on three considerations. First, widespread agreement already exists among nations, as illustrated by the large number of signatories to the United Nations Declaration of Human Rights and by the existence of a number of international treaties establishing norms of business practice. Two excellent examples of the latter are the "Guidelines for Multinational Enterprises," adopted by the Organization of Economic Cooperation and Development, and the Caux Roundtable Principles of Business. The United Nations itself is engaged in a voluntary cooperative project to improve the social responsibility of corporations. Corporations first participate by endorsing the nine general principles of the U.N. Social Compact (reprinted in this chapter). Additionally corporations may participate in the Global Reporting Initiative whereby corporations report on their progress in adopting and implementing the nine principles. It should also be added that there are a number of industry-wide codes or agreements on the proper conduct of business matters. Industry-wide codes cover a number of important areas. A survey by the Organization for Economic Cooperation and Development has found that there are more than 240 codes of conduct and that roughly half cover the environment and that roughly half cover labor rights. Many are individual company codes, but 26 codes from associations of companies and nonprofit groups require independent inspections. For example, the U.S.-based Chocolate Manufacturers Association and British chocolate makers have signed an agreement with anti-slavery groups and the International Labor Organization to monitor cocoa farms after allegations of child slavery in West Africa.[1] In the human rights area a group of energy companies and human rights organizations have adopted a set of voluntary guidelines for respecting human rights while protecting overseas operations.[2] In some parts of the world, corporations need security forces to protect their employees and property. However, these security forces have often been accused of human rights abuses as they carry out their tasks. Sometimes corporations are seen as wittingly or unwittingly supporting governments in human rights abuses. These guidelines have been criticized on the grounds that they are voluntary and will not be monitored for compliance.[3]

Second, Bowie argues that certain moral norms must be endorsed if society is to exist at all. Corporations ought to accept the moral norms that make society and hence business itself possible. This argument is a powerful argument against the view known as ethical relativism. *Ethical relativism* asserts that whatever a country says is right or wrong for a country, *really* is right or wrong for that country. But if there are ethical norms that must be adopted if a country is to exist at all, then obviously the rightness of these norms is not justified by being endorsed in any particular country.

Third, Bowie uses certain Kantian arguments to show that business practice presupposes certain moral norms if it is to exist at all. Bowie refers to these norms as the *morality of the marketplace.* For example, there must be a moral obligation for business to keep its contracts if business is to exist at all. Bowie's argument is not merely theoretical. Russia had great difficulty in adopting a capitalist economy because businesspersons and business firms have either been unwilling or unable to pay their bills. Without institutions to enforce contracts, business practice is fragile at best. It should also be pointed out that similar arguments could be used by utilitarians. If certain moral rules or traits such as truth telling or honesty give a multinational corporation a competitive advantage, then eventually these moral norms or traits will be adopted by all multinationals because those that do not will not survive.

The claim that there are universal values or moral norms that should be followed by all multinationals whether in Rome or not is not inconsistent with the idea that there is a wide range of situations where variations in conduct are permissible. To use Donaldson and Dunfee's term, there is considerable *moral free space* even in a world where there are universal moral norms. In her article, Patricia Werhane provides a theoretical framework for moral free space. She points out that to some extent our view of the world is constructed from the society in which we live. Werhane refers to these images as mental models and she conclusively shows that we should not impose our mental models about capitalism and business practice on other cultures. Thus the task of the manager of an international firm is to avoid a rigid imposition of his or her views on foreign subsidiaries while at the same time avoiding a relativism that would ensnare the firm in violations of legitimate universal norms.

Finally, this discussion of "When in Rome Should We Do as the Romans Do?" has legal ramifications as well. What about the rights of foreigners who are injured abroad by U.S. corporations? Do they have any rights to relief in American courts? Normally, they do not under the doctrine of *forum non conveniens* (it is not the convenient forum). It makes more practical sense for foreigners to seek relief in the country where the injury took place. But, in *Dow Chemical Company and Shell Oil Company v. Domingo Castro Alfaro et al.*, the Supreme Court of Texas disagrees. The Texas Supreme Court in a majority opinion pointed out that the chief effect of the doctrine of *forum non conveniens* was to give an unjust advantage to multinationals. However, *forum non conveniens* is still the prevailing law in most states.

Recently, foreign nationals have sued American companies alleging human rights abuses. One landmark case, *John Doe I et. al., vs. Unocal,* granted summary judgment on behalf of Unocal in a case involving alleged human rights violations in Myanmar (formerly Burma.) The government of Myanmar supplied labor to Unocal that the plaintiffs claimed was forced labor or slavery. The court found that Unocal knew about and benefitted from forced labor in Myanmar. But Unocal was not a willing partner since it could not control the Myanmar military and thus was not liable under federal law. However, the U.S. Court of Appeals disagreed in part and argued that trial against Unocal could go ahead on the issues of whether Unocal aided and abetted the Myanmar military in subjecting workers to forced labor. Selections from the Appeals Court decision are included in this Chapter.

Most recently the Bush administration has attempted to create new hurdles for those who seek to sue American firms for human rights abuses. A U.S. State Department representative urged a federal judge to dismiss a case against the Exxon Mobil Corp that was accused of complicity in the murder, rape, and torture of villagers living near its natural gas operations in Indonesia. Allowing the case to go forward would compromise U.S. diplomatic efforts including efforts to fight the war on terrorism.[4] Nonetheless claims continue to be filed under an ancient law—the 1789 Alien Tort Claims Act and early court victories have gone to the plaintiffs.[5]

## Bribery

One of the norms that Bowie believes is being adopted internationally is a norm that condemns bribery. Such a norm received legal recognition in the United States with the passage of the Foreign Corrupt Practices Act in 1977. That act, which was amended in 1988, makes it illegal for U.S. companies to pay bribes in order to do business abroad. Spokespersons for American business have long criticized the law on the grounds that it puts American firms at a competitive disadvantage. Other countries operate under no such restrictions. Although the United States did take the lead in this respect, more and more organizations are passing rules outlawing bribery. For example, the European Community has done so.

Another criticism of the Foreign Corrupt Practices Act was that it was an example of American moral imperialism—a charge that is often levelled against American regulations. However, in this case, the charge of moral imperialism is false since the FCPA does not force other countries or the multinationals of other countries to follow America's lead. It simply required U.S. companies to follow American moral norms with respect to bribery when doing business abroad.

A third criticism of the FCPA is more telling, however. That criticism is that the Act does not adequately distinguish among gift giving, facilitating payments, bribery, and extortion. The FCPA does allow for facilitating payments and that allowance was expanded when the law was amended in 1988. However, the law does not sufficiently distinguish between bribery and extortion. The chief difference between bribery and extortion is who does the initiating of the act. A corporation pays a bribe when it offers to pay or provide favors to a person or persons of trust to influence the latter's conduct or judgment. A corporation pays extortion money when it yields to a demand for money in order to have accomplished what it has a legal right to have accomplished without the payment. The difference between extortion and a facilitating payment is one of degree. It is also often difficult to distinguish a gift from a bribe.

Donaldson and Dunfee argue that in many situations an international corporation should respect the moral norms of the country in which it operates, but they also show that the norm against bribery is a universal norm and thus a business is morally obligated not to bribe.

## HUMAN RIGHTS AND THE MULTINATIONAL CORPORATION

Many argue that the notion of human rights provides a set of universal standards that both individuals and organizations, including business organizations, should respect. After all nearly all countries in the world belong to the United Nations and thus have in principle endorsed the U.N. Declaration on Human Rights. (We acknowledge that countries differ on the interpretation and implementation of these rights.) However, as Thomas Donaldson has pointed out, there are three distinct ways to honor human rights: (1) To avoid depriving. (2) To help protect from deprivation. (3) To aid the deprived.[6] Donaldson maintains that while human rights should be honored in all three senses, it is not clear that it is the obligation of business to honor all human rights in all three ways. For example, if a right to an education is a human right, that does not mean that it is the obligation of a corporation to provide it.

Working out what is morally required for firms engaged in international business is a complex activity that would require a full book. However, in addition to the U.N. Declaration on Human Rights, we also endorse the nine principles of the U.N. Social Compact, reprinted in this chapter, as a starting point for determining what we can be morally expected of corporations. In addition, philosophers can provide a normative ground for human rights that can serve as a justification for claiming that business firms engaged in international business ought to take human rights issues into account.

In his article, Denis Arnold provides the required normative grounding. First, he adopts the position of Alan Gewirth[7] who asks, what are the necessary conditions for human purposive action? Answer: Freedom and well-being are necessary. Since I value my own purposes, I logically must value the conditions that make the achievement of my purposes possible. And I must endorse the corresponding rights claim with respect to freedom and well-being. Gewirth then uses a Kantian strategy to show that my concern for my own freedom and well-being logically commits me to be concerned with the freedom and well-being of all purposive agents. After all, what is true of my situation is true of the situation of all purposive agents. Arnold correctly notes that this justification transcends issues of culture since these rights are claims to the conditions that make *any* purposive action possible. Having provided justification for the rights to freedom and well-being, Arnold shows what the existence of these rights require of multinational enterprises with respect to labor practices.

Two topics are of particular concern: First, how should international firms behave when they do business in a country that is known to violate human rights. Indeed, should a corporation do business in such a country at all? Second, what are the responsibilities of a firm with respect to its suppliers? Of particular interest here is the issue of sweatshops in those countries that supply apparel and other goods to American firms.

As noted above, American internationals are now being sued for allegedly cooperating with governments engaged in the violation of human rights, In his article John Schermerhorn, Jr. considers the obligations of firms doing business in Burma (now officially called Myanmar.) Schermerhorn points out that Myanmar's neighbors all prefer constructive engagement rather than have various countries impose economic sanctions. Schermerhorn then distinguishes four kinds of engagement and provides possible ethical grounds for business to invest in Myanmar.

Perhaps the international business ethics issue that has received the most attention on college campuses is the issue of sweatshops. Foreign suppliers to such companies as Nike have been accused of operating sweatshops. The sweatshop issue has become the chief activist cause on college campuses, and there have been calls for universal standards and the monitoring of their implementation. Some calls have already been successful. On October 7, 1999, Nike reversed policy and released the location of forty-two of 365 factories. Then on October 18, 1999 Reebok International, Ltd. released the first independent factory audit of two Indonesian factories undertaken by a human rights group. A few days later Liz Claiborne, Inc. released a critical report of an audit of a Guatemalan factory and Mattel, Inc. will publish a comprehensive review of eight of its plants in four countries.[8]

Monitoring is not limited to individual companies. The Fair Labor Association is made up of industry and human rights representatives. This group was created by a Presidential task force and includes such companies as Adidas, Salomon, Levi Strauss and Co., Nike, Reebok, Liz Claiborne, and Phillips-Van Heusen.[9]

Not everyone is so quick to condemn the practices of multinationals in this area. Several prominent economists have spoken out claiming that the wages paid to the workers of foreign suppliers in the third world are hardly immoral "slave wages," but rather represent an increase in the standard of living. These arguments are summarized and defended in the article by Ian Maitland. Moreover, if child labor is the issue, the moral thing to do, economist Gary S. Becker argues, is to pay parents to keep children, especially daughters who are often less valued, in school. That approach is superior to laws that simply remove children from the workplace and derive families of an important source of income.[10]

On the other hand, Denis Arnold and Norman Bowie use Kantian arguments to show that multinational enterprises have a moral obligation to ensure that their suppliers follow local labor laws, refrain from coercion, meet minimum safety standards, and provide a living wage for employees. Only the fourth requirement—providing a living wage for employees—may seem to run afoul of the arguments Maitland articulates. However, Arnold and Bowie bring forth considerations that call into question the economic arguments Maitland brings forth and, if successful, they circumvent Maitland's moral arguments that depend on them.

Globalization and the increase in international business competition it brings forth continue to spark a number of debates in international business ethics. Multinationals need to find a way to harmonize the core values of the firm with universal ethical norms. At the same time, they need to respect the legitimate ethical norms and values of the countries in which they do business. The effort to be an ethical and profitable business at home becomes even more complicated when a business enters the international arena.

## NOTES


1. "Do-It-Yourself Labor Standards." *Business Week* November 19, 2001, 74, 76.
2. Yochi J. Dreazen. "Global Standards of Human Rights are Released." *The Wall Street Journal*, December 21, 2000, A6.
3. Ibid.
4. Peter Waldman and Timothy Mapes. "Administration Sets New Hurdles for Human-Rights Cases," *The Wall Street Journal*, August 7, 2002, B1, 3.
5. Paul Magnusson. "Making a Federal Case Out of Overseas Abuses." *Business Week*, November 22, 2002.
6. Thomas Donaldson. *The Ethics of International Business*. New York: Oxford University Press, 1989.
7. Alan Gewirth. *Reason and Morality*. Chicago: University of Chicago Press, 1978.
8. Aaron Bernstein, "Sweatshops: No More Excuses." *Business Week* (November 7, 1999), pp. 104–06.
9. Ibid.
10. Gary S. Becken. "'Bribe' Third World Parents to Keep Their Kids in School." *Business Week* (November 22, 1999).


## UNIVERSALS, RELATIVISM, AND THE PROBLEM OF BRIBERY

# Relativism and the Moral Obligations of Multinational Corporations

*Norman Bowie*

In this essay, I will focus on the question of whether U.S. multinationals should follow the moral rules of the United States or the moral rules of the host countries (the countries where the U.S. multinationals do business). A popular way of raising this issue is to ask whether U.S. multinationals should follow the advice "When in Rome, do as the Romans do." In discussing that issue I will argue that U.S. multinationals would be morally required to follow that advice if the theory of ethical relativism were true. On the other hand, if ethical uni-

This piece is composed of selections from Norman Bowie, "The Moral Obligations of Multinational Corporations," *Problems of International Justice* (edited by Steven Luper-Foy), 1988 and Norman Bowie "Relativism, Cultural and Moral," *The Blackwell Encyclopedic Dictionary of Business Ethics* (edited by Patricia Werhane and R. Edward Freeman) Blackwell, Cambridge, MA, 1997. Reprinted with permission of the author and Blackwell Publishers.

versalism is true, there will be times when the advice would be morally inappropriate. In a later section, I will argue that ethical relativism is morally suspect. Finally, I will argue that the ethics of the market provide some universal moral norms for the conduct of multinationals.

## RELATIVISM

*Cultural relativism* is a descriptive claim that ethical practices differ among cultures; that, as a matter of fact, what is considered right in one culture may be considered wrong in another. Thus the truth or falsity of cultural relativism can be determined by examining the world. The work of anthropologists and sociologists is most relevant in determining the truth or falsity of cultural relativism, and there is widespread consensus among social scientists that cultural relativism is true.

*Moral relativism* is the claim that what is really right or wrong is what the culture says is right or wrong. Moral relativists accept cultural relativism as true, but they claim much more. If a culture sincerely and reflectively adopts a basic moral principle, then it is morally obligatory for members of that culture to act in accordance with that principle.

The implication of moral relativism for conduct is that one ought to abide by the ethical norms of the culture where one is located. Relativists in ethics would say, "One ought to follow the moral norms of the culture." In terms of business practice, consider the question, "Is it morally right to pay a bribe to gain business?" The moral relativists would answer the question by consulting the moral norms of the country where one is doing business. If those norms permit bribery in that country, then the practice of bribery is not wrong in that country. However, if the moral norms of the country do not permit bribery, then offering a bribe to gain business in that country is morally wrong. The justification for that position is the moral relativist's contention that what is really right or wrong is determined by the culture.

Is cultural relativism true? Is moral relativism correct? As noted, many social scientists believe that cultural relativism is true as a matter of fact. But is it?

First, many philosophers claim that the "facts" aren't really what they seem. Early twentieth-century anthropologists cited the fact that in some cultures, after a certain age, parents are put to death. In most cultures such behavior would be murder. Does this difference in behavior prove that the two cultures disagree about fundamental matters of ethics? No, it does not. Suppose the other culture believes that people exist in the afterlife in the same condition that they leave their present life. It would be very cruel to have one's parents exist eternally in an unhealthy state. By killing them when they are relatively active and vigorous, you insure their happiness for all eternity. The *underlying* ethical principle of this culture is that children have duties to their parents, including the duty to be concerned with their parents' happiness as they approach old age. This ethical principle is identical with our own. What looked like a difference in ethics between our culture and another turned out, upon close examination, to be a difference based on what each culture takes to be the facts of the matter. This example does, of course, support the claim that as a matter of fact ethical principles vary according to culture. However, it does not support the stronger conclusion that *underlying* ethical principles vary according to culture.

Cultures differ in physical setting, in economic development, in the state of their science and technology, in their literacy rate, and in many other ways. Even if there were universal moral principles, they would have to be applied in these different cultural contexts. Given the different situations in which cultures exist, it would come as no surprise to find universal principles applied in different ways. Hence we expect to find surface differences in ethical behavior among cultures even though the cultures agree on fundamental universal moral principles. For example, one commonly held universal principle appeals to the public good; it says that social institutions and individual behavior should be ordered so that they lead to the greatest good for the greatest number. Many different forms of social organization and individual behavior are consistent with this principle. The point of these two arguments is to show that differences among cultures on ethical behavior may not reflect genuine disagreement about underlying principles of ethics. Thus it is not so obvious that any strong form of cultural relativism is true.

But are there universal principles that are accepted by all cultures? It seems so; there does seem to be a whole range of behavior, such as torture and murder of the innocent, that every culture agrees is wrong. A nation-state accused of torture does not respond by saying that a condemnation of torture is just a matter of cultural choice. The state's leaders do not respond by saying, "We think torture is right, but you do not." Rather, the standard response is to deny that any torture took place. If the evidence of torture is too strong, a finger will be pointed either at the victim or at the morally outraged country: "They do it too." In this case the guilt is spread to all. Even the Nazis denied that genocide took place. What is important is that *no* state replies that there is nothing wrong with genocide or torture.

In addition, there are attempts to codify some universal moral principles. The United Nations Universal Declaration of Human Rights has been endorsed by the member states of the UN, and the vast majority of countries in the world are members of the UN. Even in business, there is a growing effort to adopt universal principles of business practice. In a study of international codes of ethics, Professors Catherine Langlois and Bodo B. Schlegelmilch[1] found that although there certainly were differences among codes, there was a considerable area of agreement. William Frederick has documented the details of six international compacts on matters of international business ethics. These include the aforementioned UN Universal Declaration of Human Rights, the European Convention on Human Rights, the Helsinki Final Act, the OECD Guidelines for Multinational Enterprises and Social Policy, and the United Nations Conduct on Transnational Corporations (in progress). The Caux Roundtable, a group of corporate executives from the United States, Europe, and Japan, are seeking worldwide endorsement of a set of principles of business ethics. Thus there are a number of reasons to think that cultural relativism, at least with respect to basic moral principles, is not true, that is, that it does not accurately describe the state of moral agreement that exists. This is consistent with maintaining that cultural relativism is true in the weak form, that is, when applied only to surface ethical principles.

But what if differences in fundamental moral practices among cultures are discovered and seem unreconcilable? That would lead to a discussion about the adequacy of moral relativism. The fact that moral practices do vary widely among countries is cited as evidence for the correctness of moral relativism. Discoveries early in the century by anthropologists, sociologists, and psychologists documented the diversity of moral beliefs. Philosophers, by and large, welcomed corrections of moral imperialist thinking, but recognized that the moral relativist's appeal to the alleged truth of cultural relativism was not enough to establish moral relativism. The mere fact that a culture considers a practice moral does not mean that it is moral. Cultures have sincerely practiced slavery, discrimination, and the torture of animals. Yet each of these practices can be independently criticized on ethical grounds. Thinking something is morally permissible does not make it so.

Another common strategy for criticizing moral relativism is to show that the consequences of taking the perspective of moral relativism are inconsistent with our use of moral language. It is often contended by moral relativists that if two cultures disagree regarding universal moral principles, there is no way for that disagreement to be resolved. Since moral relativism is the view that what is right or wrong is determined by culture, there is no higher appeal beyond the fact that culture endorses the moral principle. But we certainly do not talk that way. When China and the United States argue about the moral rights of human beings, the disputants use language that seems to appeal to universal moral principles. Moreover, the atrocities of the Nazis and the slaughter in Rwanda have met with universal condemnation that seemed based on universal moral principles. So moral relativism is not consistent with our use of moral language.

Relativism is also inconsistent with how we use the term "moral reformer." Suppose, for instance, that a person from one culture moves to another and tries to persuade the other culture to change its view. Suppose someone moves from a culture where slavery is immoral to one where slavery is morally permitted. Normally, if a person were to try to convince the culture where slavery was permitted that slavery was morally wrong, we would call such a person a moral reformer. Moreover, a moral reformer would almost certainly appeal to universal moral principles to make her argument; she almost certainly would not appeal to a competing cultural standard. But if moral relativism were true, there would be no place for the concept of a moral reformer. Slavery is really right in those cultures that say it is right and really wrong in those cultures that say it is wrong. If the reformer fails to persuade a slaveholding country to change its mind, the reformer's antislavery position was never right. If the reformer is successful in persuading a country to change its mind, the reformer's antislavery views would be wrong—until the country did in fact change its view. Then the reformer's antislavery view would be right. But that is not how we talk about moral reform.

The moral relativist might argue that our language should be reformed. We should talk differently. At one time people used to talk and act as if the world were flat. Now they don't. The relativist could suggest that we can change our ethical language in the same way. But consider how radical the relativists' response is. Since most, if not all, cultures speak and act as if there were universal moral principles, the relativist can be right only if almost everyone else is wrong. How plausible is that?

Although these arguments are powerful ones, they do not deliver a knockout blow to moral relativism. If there are no universal moral principles, moral relativism could argue that moral relativists is the only theory available to help make sense of moral phenomena.

An appropriate response to this relativist argument is to present the case for a set of universal moral principles, principles that are correct for all cultures independent of what a culture thinks about them. This is what adherents of the various ethical traditions try to do. The reader will have to examine these various traditions and determine how persuasive she finds them. In addition, there are several final independent considerations against moral relativism that can be mentioned here.

First, what constitutes a culture? There is a tendency to equate cultures with national boundaries, but that is naive, especially today.

With respect to moral issues, what do US cultural norms say regarding right and wrong? That question may be impossible to answer, because in a highly pluralistic country like the United States, there are many cultures. Furthermore, even if one can identify a culture's moral norms, it will have dissidents who do not subscribe to those moral norms. How many dissidents can a culture put up with and still maintain that some basic moral principle is the cultural norm? Moral relativists have had little to say regarding criteria for constituting a culture or how to account for dissidents. Unless moral relativists offer answers to questions like these, their theory is in danger of becoming inapplicable to the real world.

Second, any form of moral relativism must admit that there are some universal moral principles. Suppose a culture does not accept moral relativism, that is, it denies that if an entire culture sincerely and reflectively adopts a basic moral principle, it is obligatory for members of that culture to act in accord with that principle. Fundamentalist Muslim countries would reject moral relativism because it would require them to accept as morally permissible blasphemy in those countries where blasphemy was permitted. If the moral relativist insists that the truth of every moral principle depends on the culture, then she must admit that the truth of moral relativism depends on the culture. Therefore the moral relativist must admit that at least the principle of moral relativism is not relative.

Third, it seems that there is a set of basic moral principles that every culture must adopt. You would not have a culture unless the members of the group adopted these moral principles. Consider an anthropologist who arrives on a populated island: How many tribes are on the island? To answer that question, the anthropologist tries to determine if some people on some parts of the island are permitted to kill, commit acts of violence against, or steal from persons on other parts of the island. If such behavior is not permitted, that counts as a reason for saying that there is only one tribe. The underlying assumption here is that there is a set of moral principles that must be followed if there is to be a culture at all. With respect to those moral principles, adhering to them determines whether there is a culture or not.

But what justifies these principles? A moral relativist would say that a culture justifies them. But you cannot have a culture unless the members of the culture follow the principles. Thus it is reasonable to think that justification lies elsewhere. Many believe that the purpose of morality is to help make social cooperation possible. Moral principles are universally necessary for that endeavor.

## THE MORALITY OF THE MARKETPLACE

Given that the norms constituting a moral minimum are likely to be few in number, it can be argued that the argument thus far has achieved something—that is, multinationals are obligated to follow the moral norms required for the existence of a society. But the argument has not achieved very much—that is, most issues surrounding multinationals do not involve alleged violations of these norms. Perhaps a stronger argument can be found by making explicit the morality of the marketplace. That there is an implicit morality of the market is a point that is often ignored by most economists and many businesspersons.

Although economists and businesspersons assume that people are basically self-interested, they must also assume that persons involved in business transactions will honor their contracts. In most economic exchanges, the transfer of product for money is not simultaneous. You deliver and I pay or vice versa. As the economist Kenneth Boulding put it: "without an integrative framework, exchange itself cannot develop, because exchange, even in its most primitive forms, involves trust and credibility."[2]

Philosophers would recognize an implicit Kantianism in Boulding's remarks. Kant tried to show that a contemplated action would be immoral if a world in which the contemplated act was universally practiced was self-defeating. For example, lying and cheating would fail Kant's tests. Kant's point is implicitly recognized by the business community when corporate officials despair of the immoral practices of corporations and denounce executives engaging in shady practices as undermining the business enterprise itself.

Consider what John Rawls says about contracts:

> Such ventures are often hard to initiate and to maintain. This is especially evident in the case of covenants, that is, in those instances where one person is to perform before the other. For this person may believe that the second party will not do his part, and therefore the scheme never gets going. . . . Now in these situations there may be no way of assuring the party who is to perform first except by giving him a promise, that is, by putting oneself under an obligation to carry through later. Only in this way can the scheme be made secure so that both can gain from the benefits of their cooperation.[3]

Rawls's remarks apply to all contracts. Hence, if the moral norms of a host country permitted practices that undermined contracts, a multinational ought not to follow them. Business practice based on such norms could not pass Kant's test.

In fact, one can push Kant's analysis and contend that business practice generally requires the adoption of a minimum standard of justice. In the United States, a person who participates in business practice and engages in the practice of giving bribes or kickbacks is behaving unjustly. Why? Because the person is receiving the benefits of the rules against such activities without supporting the rules personally. This is an example of what John Rawls calls freeloading. A freeloader is one who accepts the benefits without paying any of the costs.

> In everyday life an individual, if he is so inclined, can sometimes win even greater benefits for himself by taking advantage of the cooperative efforts of others. Sufficiently many persons may be doing their share so that when special circumstances allow him not to contribute (perhaps his omission will not be found out), he gets the best of both worlds. . . . We cannot preserve a sense of justice and all that this implies while at the same time holding ourselves ready to act unjustly should doing so promise some personal advantage.[4]

This argument does not show that if bribery really is an accepted moral practice in country X, that moral practice is wrong. What it does show is that practices in country X that permit freeloading are wrong and if bribery can be construed as freeloading, then it is wrong. In most countries I think it can be shown that bribery is freeloading, but I shall not make that argument here.

The implications of this analysis for multinationals are broad and important. If activities that are permitted in other countries violate the morality of the marketplace—for example, undermine contracts or involve freeloading on the rules of the market—they nonetheless are morally prohibited to multinationals that operate there. Such multinationals are obligated to follow the moral norms of the market. Contrary behavior is inconsistent and ultimately self-defeating.

Our analysis here has rather startling implications. If the moral norms of a host country are in violation of the moral norms of the marketplace, then the multinational is obligated to follow the norms of the marketplace. Systematic violation of marketplace norms would be self-defeating. Moreover, whenever a multinational establishes businesses in a number of different countries, the multinational provides something approaching a universal morality—the morality of the marketplace itself. If Romans are to do business with the Japanese, then whether in Rome or Tokyo, there is a morality to which members of the business community in both Rome and Tokyo must subscribe—even if the Japanese and Romans differ on other issues of morality.

## NOTES

1. C. Langlois and B.B. Schlegelmilch, "Do Corporate Codes of Ethics Reflect National Character? Evidence from Europe and the United States," *Journal of International Studies,* 21(a), pp. 519–539.
2. Kenneth E. Boulding, "The Basis of Value Judgments in Economics," in *Human Values and Economic Policy,* Sidney Hook, ed. (New York: New York University Press, 1967), p. 68.
3. John Rawls, *A Theory of Justice* (Cambridge, MA: Harvard University Press, 1971), p. 569.
4. Ibid., p. 497.

# Exporting Mental Models: Global Capitalism in the 21st Century

*Patricia H. Werhane*

When one is asked to enumerate the most challenging ethical issues business will face in the next century, the list is long. Environmental sustainability, international trade, exploitation, corruption, unemployment, poverty, technology transfer, cultural diversity (and thus relativism) are a few obvious candidates. Underlying these and other issues is a more serious global phenomenon: the exportation of Western capitalism.

There is a mental model of free enterprise, a model primarily created in the United States, that is being exported, albeit unconsciously, as industrialized nations expand commerce through the globalization of capitalism. This model is not one of greedy self-interested cowboy capitalists eagerly competing to take advantage of resources, low-priced employment, or offshore regulatory laxity. Rather I am referring to another model, one that has worked and worked well in most of North America and Western Europe for some time. This model contends that industrialized free enterprise in a free trade global economy, where businesses and entrepreneurs can pursue their interests competitively without undue regulations or labor restrictions, will produce growth and well-being, i.e., economic good, in every country or community where this phenomenon is allowed to operate. . . .

What is wrong with adapting a model for global capitalism out of the highly successful American model for free enterprise? What is wrong with economic growth and improved standards of living, particularly in developing countries? Isn't reduction of poverty a universally desirable outcome? The tempting answer is that there is nothing wrong with this model. In this paper I shall suggest that a more thoughtful reply requires some qualifications.

To begin, let me explain the notion of mental models. Although the term is not always clearly defined, "mental model" connotes the idea that human beings have mental representations, cognitive frames, or mental pictures of their experiences, representations that model the stimuli or data with which they are

From Patricia H. Werhane, "Exporting Mental Models: Global Capitalism in the 21st Century," *Business Ethics Quarterly,* 10(1) (2000), 353–62. Reprinted with permission of the author and *Business Ethics Quarterly.*

interacting, and these are frameworks that set up parameters through which experience, or a certain set of experiences, is organized or filtered (Werhane 1991, 1998, 1999).

> Mental models are the mechanisms whereby humans are able to generate descriptions of system purpose and form, explanations of system functioning and observed system states, and predictions of future system states. (Rouse and Morris 1986, p. 351)

Mental models might be hypothetical constructs of the experience in question or scientific theories; they might be schema that frame the experience, through which individuals process information, conduct experiments, and formulate theories; or mental models may simply refer to human knowledge about a particular set of events or a system. Mental models account for our ability to describe, explain, and predict, and may function as protocols to account for human expectations that are often formulated in accordance to these models.

Mental models function as selective mechanisms and filters for dealing with experience. In focusing, framing, organizing, and ordering what we experience, mental models bracket and leave out data, and emotional and motivational foci taint or color experience. Nevertheless, because schema we employ are socially learned and altered through religion, socialization, culture, educational upbringing, and other experiences, they are shared ways of perceiving, organizing, and learning.

Because of the variety and diversity of mental models, none is complete, and "there are multiple possible framings of any given situation" (Johnson 1993, p. 9). By that I mean that each of us can frame any situation, event, or phenomenon in more than one way, and that same phenomenon can also be socially constructed in a variety of ways. It will turn out that the way one frames a situation is critical to its outcome, because "[t]here are . . . different moral consequences depending on the way we frame the situation" (Johnson 1993).

Why is the notion of mental models of concern for business, and in particular, for global business? Let me explain by using some illustrations. One of the presuppositions of Western free enterprise, a supposition that fueled and made possible the industrial revolution, is that feudalism, at least as it is exhibited through most forms of serfdom, is humiliating, it demeans laborers, and worse, it does not allow serfs, in particular, to create or experience any sense of what it would mean to be free, free to live and work where one pleases (or to be lazy), to own property, and choose how one lives. Adam Smith even argued that feudalism is inefficient as well. It is commonly, although not universally, argued that individual property ownership is a social good. In agriculturally based economies, in particular, owning one's own farm land is considered a necessary step toward freedom and self-reliance. The industrial revolution, coupled with free commerce, wage labor, and property ownership, changes the feudal mental model, and, it is commonly argued, improves the lives of serfs, farm workers, and tenant farmers, in particular.

However, as Akiro Takahashi points out in a recent article in *Business Ethics Quarterly*, even 20th-century feudal arrangements are complex social institutions. One cannot simply free the serfs or sharecroppers, engage in redistributive land reform, and hope that a new economic arrangement will work out. Takahashi's example is from a 1960s rice-growing community in Luzon in the Philippines. From as long as anyone can remember until land reforms in the 1970s the village had operated as a fiefdom. There were a few landholders and the rest of the villagers were tenant farmers. In order to work the land, each year the tenant farmers paid rents equal to half the net production of their farms. But because the tenant farmers were always in debt to the landlords, they usually owed all the net production to the landlords. The tenant farmers in fact never paid their debts, but because of high interest rates, as much as 200 percent, their debt increased each year so that they really could never leave the property. Since in fact what was owed the landlord was the *net* produce, each sharecropper was allowed to hire workers to farm the land they rented. So tenant farmers hired workers from other landlords or from other communities to till and harvest. Each sharecropper, in turn, went to work for another landlord's sharecropper. In addition, it was common practice for the harvesters not to do a perfect job, leaving often as much as 20 to 25 percent of the rice unharvested. Gleaning was not allowed by tenant farmers or their families on the land they rented. But the wives of the farm workers and rest of the community "gleaned" the rest of the rice for themselves. In this way the poor were supported by the landlord and tenant farmers got some rice. The landlords pretended none of this occurred, still demanding the net product from each of its tenant farmers (Takahaski 1997, pp. 39–40).

The value of private ownership (as linked to personal freedom) is a perfectly fine idea in principle. But abstracting that idea and universalizing it as a mental model for all reform has severe negative moral consequences, as the following example illustrates.

> Seven years ago, the prayers of 39 families were answered when the government [of Mexico] gave them this 1,000-acre communal farm in southern Mexico to raise livestock. Today the exhausted pastures are a moonscape of dust and rock. Cattle here don't graze quietly; they root like pigs as they yank rare blades of grass from the parched earth. . . . All arable land has been split into five-acre patches of corn per family. To stay alive, the men earn 21 cents an hour cutting sugar cane in nearby fields.
>
> Farms like this one, known as ejidos, have helped the government win political support in the countryside by answering peasant demands for "land and liberty" that date back to the revolution of 1910. Unfortunately, this continuing land-redistribution plan has done a better job of carving farmland into small, barren plots than it has of growing food or providing a decent living for farmers.
>
> . . . Farmers tend to split their parcels among their sons, and with two-thirds of farms already smaller than 12.5 acres, there isn't any room in the countryside for the next generations. (Frazier 1984, pp. 1, 18)

Another example: the Neem tree is a wild scraggly tree that grows well throughout India. For thousands of years, in hundreds of villages throughout that country the Neem tree has had a special place in the community. The tree has special religious meaning in some Hindu sects. Its leaves are used as pesticides, spread on plants to protect them from insects. Various herbal medicines are made from Neem leaves and bark, its products are used as contraceptives and for skin ailments, and many Indians brush their teeth with small Neem branches. Because of its effectiveness as a pesticide, recently the W. R. Grace Company began studying the tree, and in 1992 they developed a pesticide, Neemix. Neemix works as effectively as Neem leaves and has a long shelf life, thus making it more desirable as a pesticide than the leaves. Following the guidelines of the Indian government regarding patenting, Grace patented Neemix, opened a plant in India, and manufactured the product.

However, there have been mass protests against this patenting, both from Indians and from the Foundation on Economic Trends, a biotechnology watchdog organization. The argument is that Grace committed "biopiracy" because the Neem tree belongs to Indians, and products from the tree cannot be patented. Moreover, such patenting and manufacture of Neemix and other products drives up prices of Neem such that the indigenous poor, to whom the tree belongs, can no longer have access to the trees (Severence et al. 1999; Vijayalakshmi, Radha, and Shiva, 1995).

A fourth illustration: SELF, the Solar Electric Light Fund, a United States-based NGO, for some time has been developing a project aimed at electrifying rural communities in China. SELF has promoted a small photovoltaic (PV) solar unit that produces about 20 to 60 watts of energy. SELF has a policy of not giving away its photovoltaic units. This is because, it argues, if people have to pay something, even a small amount, for this service, they will value it more. So SELF has set up complex long-term lending schemes so that some poor rural people in China can afford electricity and own their own units as well (Sonenshein et al. 1997a).

SELF has been highly successful in some rural communities in China, so it decided to export that project to South Africa, concentrating on small Zulu villages. Working with village leaders in one community, SELF tried a pilot project, with the aim of providing electricity for 75 homes in a small village of Maphephethe. Six units were installed and were well received, and those receiving the units were delighted to have reliable power. However, one serious problem developed. Previous to the introduction of PV technology all the villagers lived modest but similar lives in a fairly egalitarian community. Now, those who have PV units are able to improve their social and economic status by operating manual sewing machines at night. The distribution of PV technology has upset a very delicate social balance by creating social stratification within this community (Sonenshein et al., 1997b).

What do these examples tell us? They tell us something very simple, something we should have learned years ago from the Nestle infant formula cases. American (or in Nestle's case, Western European) mental models of property and free enterprise cannot be exported uniformly to every part of the world without sometimes producing untoward consequences. This is because the notion of what is good or a social good is a socially constructed idea that is contextually and culturally relative. Abstract ideas such as autonomy, equality, private property, ownership, and community create mental models that take on different meanings depending on the social and situational context. Differing notions of community, ownership, intellectual property, exchange, competition, equality, and fairness, what Walzer calls social goods, create cultural anomalies that cannot be overcome simply by globalizing private free enterprise and operating in the same way everywhere (see Walzer 1983, Chapter One).

Land reform based on the notion of private ownership will not be successful in every community without making drastic social changes that alter communal relationships, family traditions, and ancient practices. This does not mean that land reform is wrong-headed; it suggests that it must be reconceived in each situation, so that what falls under the rubric of "reform" is contextually relevant such that change does not destroy the cultural fabric underlying what is to be changed.

It is tempting to argue that what is needed in remote communities or in some developing countries is a rule of law, similar to Anglo-Saxon law, that respects rights and property ownership, enforces contracts, protects equal opportunity, etc., along with adequate mechanisms for enforcement. Indeed, it has been argued, I think with some merit, that one of the difficulties in Russia today is inadequate commercial laws or means to enforce them. But this argument, too, needs qualification. For example, intellectual property rights, already under siege with the electronic revolution, cannot merely be spelled out in every instance using a Western notion of ownership without infringing on some deeply rooted traditions and customs. An Anglo-Saxon model of patent protection, adapted in Indian law, may not be appropriate in many parts of rural India.

Do these examples, and there are thousands of others, point to the conclusion that because of the relativity of custom and culture, we should either abandon the ideal of global economic well-being, or, alternately, simply continue to convert the world into versions of Dallas? Is the aim a television in every village? Or is John Gray correct when he declares in his recent book that "the global economy system [based on Western *laissez-faire* free enterprise] is immoral, inequitable, unworkable, and unstable" (Zakaria 1999, p. 16)?

These two alternatives, as I have crudely stated them, present us with unnecessary dilemmas as if there were only two sorts of responses to problems of globalizing free enterprise. I want to suggest that there are other ways to deal with these issues.

The existence of widespread complex cultural, social, community, and even religious differences along with differing social goods does not imply that we can neither operate in those settings if they are alien to our own nor merely export Western versions of capitalism. To appeal again to Michael Walzer, despite the plurality and incommensurability of cross-cultural social goods, there is a thin thread of agreement, across cultures and religious difference, about the "bads," what cannot be tolerated or should not be permitted in any community. Walzer also calls these thin threads of agreement "moral minimums" (Walzer 1994). Human suffering, abject poverty, preventable disease, high mortality, and violence are abhorred wherever they occur. We are uncertain about the constitution of the "good life," but there is widespread agreement about deficient or despicable living conditions, indecencies, violations of human rights, mistreatment, and other harms.

Given that perspective, almost everyone will agree that poverty, however contextually defined, disease, high infant mortality, and violence are bads. Alleviating suffering of these sorts is surely a good. Improving economic conditions, in most cases, alleviates poverty and human suffering, if not violence. Then, is not economic value added in the form economic growth the proper solution to those evils?

We must cautiously reach that conclusion. Economic growth is not a "bad." Indeed, in most cultures it is considered a social good. But the notion cannot be identified without qualification with a Western idea of free enterprise. The model of economic growth in each context has to be framed in terms of each particular culture and its social goods. Free enterprise and private ownership, as practiced in most industrialized nations, can be, in many contexts, viable options, but only if they are modified so as not to destroy the fabric of a particular set of social goods, or replace that fabric with a new "good" that destroys, without replacing, all the elements of that culture. For example, land reform and the redistribution of property, apparently worthwhile projects to free tenant farmers from feudal bonds, will be successful only if the new landholders have means to function as economically viable farmers and in ways that do not threaten age-old traditions. As the Philippines example demonstrates, the fragile distributive system in the feudal community cannot be dismantled merely for the sake of independence and private ownership without harming complex communal relationships that maintained this system for centuries.

As purveyors of free enterprise, when moving into new communities and alien cultures corporate managers need to test their business mental models, *especially* if a particular system, service, or product has been successful in a number of markets. One needs to examine one's own mental models and try to fathom which models are operating in the community in which a company is planning to operate. In particular, it is important to find out what the operative social structures and community relationships are, what it is that this community values as its social goods, and try to imagine how those might be different given the introduction of a new kind of economic system. Because it is *not* just "the economy, stupid." What matters are social relationships; family, religious, and community traditions; and values—deeply held values about what is important and treasured—that is, those social goods a community cannot give up without sacrificing more than its lack of material well-being. If endemic poverty is an evil, we must create new ways to engage in free enterprise that takes into account, and even celebrates, cultural difference. . . .

In a new article in the *Harvard Business Review*, Stuart Hart and C. K. Prahalad make a different kind of argument for this same point. Hart and Prahalad contend that it happens to be in the long-term self-interest of global multinational companies to tread cautiously and with respect in alien cultural contexts. This is because, in brief, developing countries represent 80 percent of the population of the world and thus are an as yet untapped source of growth and development. If that growth is done carefully through working within indigenous constraints, the result could be the creation of exciting new products and services that enhance rather than destroy communities while at the same time benefiting the companies in question (Hart and Prahalad 1999).

The challenge is to create new mental models for global business that achieve the aims Hart and Prahalad propose. There is at least one such attempt by a large transnational corporation to do exactly this. Unilever is a multibillion-dollar global company with over 300,000 employees operating in almost 100 countries. Its main products are foods, fish, chemicals, and household products. Because it was founded in the Netherlands, a country one-third of which is reclaimed from the seas, Unilever has always been concerned with questions of environmental sustainability. In addition, the more recent expansion of its agricultural and fishing operations in remote communities has made Unilever increasingly aware of cultural difference. Beginning in 1993, Unilever began a process that resulted in a corporate-wide initiative that they call The Triple Bottom Line (Vis 1997). The rationale for this initiative is that if Unilever is going to continue to be successful in the next century, its success depends on its worldwide financial, ecological, and social assets. So Unilever changed the definition of "economic value added" to an expanded triple bottom line that measures economic, ecological, and community assests, liabilities, profits (or benefits), and losses. According to Unilever in its statement of corporate purpose and practice, each of these assets is of equal importance, and its aim is to be able to quantify the corporate contributions to each of these three areas. This may sound Pollyannaish, but Unilever's defense of this initiative could have been written by Milton Friedman.

> Each type of asset represents a source of value to the company and its shareholders. The sustained development of each of these sources of value ensures that the overall value accruing to shareholders is built up sustainably over the long term. This is in essence the significance of sustainable development to a company that aims at sustainable profit growth and long-term value creation for its shareholders, [customers], and employees. (Vis 1997, p. 3)

As part of this Triple Bottom Line initiative, Unilever is currently engaged in a series of small enterprises in a few small villages in India to develop new products aimed at the rural poor. These are microdevelopment projects, because the products they are supporting require little capital, they are locally produced, and of only indigenous interest. Unilever's goal, however, is to make those villages and their inhabitants economically viable managers, entrepreneurs, and customers as those notions are defined and make sense within a particular village culture and in ways that are not environmentally threatening. Whether this example will be a success story remains to be seen. There is to date no outcomes data, since the case events are still unfolding, and it will be some years before one can determine whether these projects are successes.

Is this stretching the limits of what we should expect from global corporations? Not according to Unilever. It argues that human flourishing in diverse settings creates needs for a diversity of products and services, products and services that Unilever will be able to provide. At the same time human well-being creates long-term economic value added, both for Unilever and for the cultures and communities in which it operates.

## BIBLIOGRAPHY


Frazier, Steve. 1984. "Peasant Politics: Mexican Farmers Get Grants of Small Plots, But Output is Meager." *Wall Street Journal*, June 4, pp. 1, 18.

Hart, Stuart and Prahalad, C. K. 1999. "Strategies for the Bottom of the Pyramid: Creating Sustainable Development." *Harvard Business Review*, November–December.

Johnson, Mark. 1993. *Moral Imagination.* Chicago: University of Chicago Press.

Rouse, William B. and Morris, Nancy M. 1986. " On Looking Into the Black Box: Prospects and Limits in the Search for Mental Models." *Psychological Bulletin* 100: 349–363.

Severence, Kristi; Spiro, Lisa; and Werhane, Patricia H. 1999. "W. R. Grace Co. and the Neemix Patent." *Darden Case Bibliography:* UVA-E-0157. Charlottesville: University of Virginia Press.

Sonenshein, Scott; Gorman, Michael E.; and Werhane, Patricia H. 1997a. "SELF." *Darden Case Bibliography:* UVA-0112. Charlottesville: University of Virginia Press.

———. 1997b. "Solar Energy in South Africa." *Darden Case Bibliography:* UVA-E-0145. Charlottesville: University of Virginia Press.

Takahashi, Akiro, "Ethics in Developing Economies of Asia." *Business Ethics Quarterly*, 7: 33–45.

Vijayalakshmi, K; Radha, K.S.; and Shiva, Vandana. 1996. *Neem: A User's Manual.* Madras: Centre for Indian Knowledge Systems.

Vis, Jan-Kees. 1997. *Unilever: Putting Corporate Purpose Into Action.* Unilever Publication.

Walzer, Michael. 1983. *Spheres of Justice.* New York: Basic Books.

———. 1994. *Thick and Thin.* Notre Dame: Notre Dame University Press.

Werhane, Patricia H. 1991. "Engineers and Management: The Challenge of the Challenger Incident." *Journal of Business Ethics*, 1: 605–616.

———. 1998. "Moral Imagination and Management Decision Making." *Business Ethics Quarterly*, Special Issue No. 1: 75–98.

———. 1999. *Moral Imagination and Management Decision Making.* New York: Oxford University Press.

Zakaria, Fareed. 1999. "Passing the Bucks [a review of Gray's *False Dawn*]." *New York Times Book Review*, April 25, pp. 16, 18.


# Untangling the Corruption Knot: Global Bribery Viewed through the Lens of Integrative Social Contract Theory

*Thomas W. Dunfee*
*and Thomas J. Donaldson*

Global managers often must navigate the perplexing gray zone that arises when two cultures—and two sets of ethics—meet. Consider these two scenarios:

- Competing for a bid in a foreign country, you are introduced to a "consultant" who offers to help you in your client contacts. A brief conversation makes it clear that this person is well connected in local government and business circles and knows your

"Untangling the Corruption Knot: Global Bribery Viewed through the Lens of Integrated Social Contract Theory", in *Guide to Business Ethics* by Norman E. Bowie, ed. 2002. Reprinted with permission of authors Thomas W. Dunfee and Thomas J. Donaldson and Blackwell Publishers.

customer extremely well. The consultant will help you to prepare and submit your bid and negotiate with the customer . . . for a substantial fee. Your peers tell you that such arrangements are normal in this country — and that a large part of the consulting fee will go directly to staff people working for your customer. Those who have rejected such help in the past have seen contracts go to their less-fussy competitors.

- A developing country in Africa solicits bids for a dam on a major river. Your firm submits a bid based on your substantial experience in building similar structures. The contract is awarded to an Indonesian firm having little experience in building the type of dam required. You suspect that a bribe has been paid to the government official in charge of awarding the contract. You later hear that the winning proposal involves substandard materials and design. You genuinely believe that the dam is likely to collapse in the future and cause great loss of life.

What should you do in such cases? "Bribery is just like tipping," some people say. "Whether you tip for service at dinner; or, bribe for the benefit of getting goods through customs—you pay for a service rendered." But while many of us balk at a conclusion that puts bribery on a par with tipping or that suggests we should violate our personal values when in another culture, we cannot say why. In the case of the African dam, one appears to confront a choice among evils. If one does nothing, the contract will go to a less qualified bidder, and even worse, the lives of people living near the dam may be endangered. But if one complains, it not only seems like sour grapes, but by exposing the corruption, one risks endangering the representatives of one's firm. Ultimately *can* there be any solution to such problems?

This chapter describes a systematic way to think through the problems of bribery and its possible responses. In order to untangle the corruption knot, we will show how to apply two key concepts from the "social contracts" approach we develop at length in our book, *Ties That Bind.* We focus on bribery as part of the international issue of corruption because of its enormous importance in today's global business environment. Further, we believe that public attitudes about bribery are changing, making matters even more challenging for beleaguered managers facing the temptation of bribery. Academics, public policy makers, officials of public international organizations, and corporate managers all must consider the full implications of widespread global bribery. . . .

## INTEGRATIVE SOCIAL CONTRACTS THEORY[1]

We wrote the book, *Ties that Bind,* out of our conviction that answering today's questions require a new approach to business ethics, one that exposes the implicit understandings or "contracts" that bind industries, companies, and economic systems into moral communities. It is in these economic communities, and in the often unspoken understandings that provide their ethical glue, that we believe many of the answers to business ethics quandaries lie. Further, we think that answering such questions requires the use of a yet deeper, and universal "contract" superseding even individual ones. The theory that combines both these deeper and thinner kinds of contracts we label "Integrative Social Contracts Theory," or "ISCT" for short.

ISCT does not overturn popular wisdom. While it asserts that the social contracts that arise from specific cultural and geographic contexts have legitimacy, it acknowledges a *limit* to that legitimacy. It recognizes the moral authority of key transcultural truths, for example, the idea that human beings everywhere are deserving of respect. The social contract approach we detail holds that any social contract terms existing outside these boundaries must be deemed illegitimate, no matter how completely subscribed to within a given economic community. In this sense, all particular or "micro" social contracts, whether they exist at the national, industry, or corporate level, must conform to a hypothetical "macro" social contract that lays down moral boundaries for any social contracting. ISCT thus lies midway on the spectrum of moral belief, separating relativism from absolutism. It allows substantial "moral free space" for nations and other economic communities to shape their distinctive concepts of economic fairness, but it draws the line at flagrant neglect of core human values.

ISCT is derived from a thought experiment in which rational contractors are assumed to rely upon a limited set of core assumptions in framing their search for a common economic ethics, where "economic ethics" refers to the principles establishing the boundaries of proper behavior in the context of the production and exchange of goods and services.

These are as follows:

- All humans are constrained by bounded moral rationality. This means that even rational persons knowledgeable about ethical theory cannot always divine good answers to moral problems without being acquainted with community-specific norms.
- The nature of ethical behavior in economic systems and communities helps determine the quality and efficiency of economic interactions. Higher quality and more efficient economic interactions are preferable to lower quality and less efficient economic interactions.
- All other things being equal, economic activity that is consistent with the cultural, philosophical, or religious attitudes of economic actors is preferable to economic activity that is not.

In virtue of these three propositions, we argue further that individual contractors would desire the option to join and to exit economic communities as a means of leveraging their ability to achieve the benefits of either greater efficiency or greater compatibility with preferred religious, philosophical, or community norms.

The hypothetical members of the global economic community would be capable of considering which norms would be best to guide all business activity in a way that achieves fairness. In this hypothetical state of nature, we argue that such rational global contractors would agree to the following *de minimis* macrosocial contract setting the terms for economic ethics:

1. Local economic communities have moral free space in which they may generate ethical norms for their members through microsocial contracts.
2. Norm-generating microsocial contracts must be grounded in consent, buttressed by the rights of individual members to voice and exit.
3. To become obligatory (legitimate), a microsocial contract norm must be compatible with hypernorms.
4. In cases of conflicts among norms satisfying macrosocial contract terms 1–3, priority principles must be established through the application of rules consistent with the spirit and letter of the macrosocial contract.

Here are the ISCT priority principles, or "rules of thumb":

1. Local community norms have priority unless adopting them harms members of another community.
2. Local community norms designed to resolve norm conflicts have priority unless adopting them harms members of another community.
3. The more global the source of the norm, the greater the norm's priority.
4. Norms essential to the maintenance of the economic environment in which the transaction occurs have priority over norms potentially damaging to that environment.
5. Patterns of consistency among alternative norms add weight for priority.
6. Priority is given to well-defined norms over less well-defined ones.

Thus, under the approach delineated in ISCT, it is important to make use of hypernorms, or, in other words, universal principles applicable to all cultures and actions. Second, many problems dissolve when existing microsocial contracts found within relevant communities are carefully identified and proper priority is established among them. . . .

## KEY INTERNATIONAL ISSUE: CORRUPTION[2]

Corruption is widely condemned, but also widely practiced (Donaldson and Dunfee, 1999, pp. 213–33). Some firms establish procedures to ensure that others do not bribe their employees, even as those same firms use bribes to obtain business. Surprisingly firms from countries where domestic corruption is minimal often play a major role as bribe-payers into corrupt environments. Many explanations arise for these seemingly inconsistent acts. Companies' participation in some forms of corruption may stem from competitive necessity and the belief that by bribing they are respecting local cultural norms. Or, they may feel that they are being extorted by locals, who are the real culprits. Finally, they may throw up their hands, proclaiming their inability to control rogue employees. Despite such excuses, consensus is growing in many professional sectors, as well as in the general public, that something must be done about bribery. Hence, a confluence of factors has produced a changing environment in which corruption is now viewed as a key global problem.

Consider three typical instances of sensitive payments. The first involves low-level bribery of public officials in some developing nations. In these nations it may be difficult for any company, foreign or national, to move goods through customs without paying low-level officials a few dollars. The payments are relatively small, uniformly assessed, and accepted as standard practice. Indeed, the salaries of such officials are sufficiently low that the officials require the additional income. One suspects the salary levels are set with the prevalence of bribery in mind.

Or consider a second kind of bribery where a company competes for a bid in a foreign country, and where, to win the competition, a payment must be made, not as it happens to a government official, but to the employee of a private company. Nonetheless, in this instance, it is clear that the employee of the private company, instead of passing on the money to the company, will pocket the money. In a modified version of this scenario, the bribe may even happen one level deeper. For example, a company competing for a bid may be introduced to a "consultant" who offers to help in client contacts (see the example that begins this chapter). There are many variations of this kind of bribery, including one where the payment is made to a senior manager for the approval of large, phantom, cost overruns incurred by the bribe-paying supplier.

Third, and most significant, is bribery involving large sums of money paid to public sector officials for the granting of public works projects, or permissions to buy land or do business within the bribe receivers' country. . . .

### Violating a Microsocial Norm

From the standpoint of the bribe recipient, the acceptance of a bribe usually violates a microsocial norm specifying the duties of the agent, i.e., the bribe recipient, to the principal, i.e., the employing body, such as the government, private company, etc.

Perhaps the most obvious problem with bribery is that it typically involves the violation of a duty by the person accepting the bribe to the principal for whom that person serves as an agent. Note that in the cases described above, the bribe recipient performs an action at odds with the policies established by his employer. The customs official accepts money for a service that he was supposed to provide anyway. In the case where a company competes for a bid or seeks approval of a cost overrun, the approving manager pockets the money in violation of company policy and the company is shortchanged. In other words, if the money belongs to anyone, it belongs to the customer's company, not to the individual employee. In the typical case of high-level public sector bribery, the public official violates the public trust and his obligation to society in virtue of his role.

Such policies may or may not be written down. Often they are explicit, but even where they are not, they usually reflect well-understood, implicit agreements binding the employee or official as agent to the interests of his employer or nation (the principal.) In short, even when not formally specified, such duties flow from well-understood micro-social contracts existing within the relevant economic community.

But while this rationale shows one ethical problem with bribery, it is inconclusive. To begin with, it shows the ethical problem with *accepting* a bribe, but says nothing about *offering* a bribe. Has the person making the payment also committed an ethical error? Second, while violating a duty to an employer is one reason for considering an act unethical, why could this reason not be overridden by other reasons? Perhaps other microsocial contracts in the culture firmly endorse the ethical correctness of bribe giving and bribe taking. Perhaps these microsocial contracts, along with an employee's legitimate interest in supporting his family, etc., override the prima facie obligation of the employee to follow the policies of his employer. . . .

### Violating an Authentic Norm

Bribery is typically not an authentic norm. The mythology is that bribery is accepted where it flourishes. This image is badly distorted. . . .

All countries have laws against the practice. This is a striking fact often overlooked by individuals that have something to gain by the practice. "There is not a country in the world," writes Fritz Heimann, "where bribery is either legally or morally acceptable." That bribes have to be paid secretly everywhere, and that officials have to resign in disgrace if the bribe is disclosed, makes it clear that bribery violates the moral standards of the South and the East, just as it does in the West" (Heimann, 1994).

Some countries, even ones where the practice has flourished, not only outlaw it, but prescribe draconian penalties. "In Malaysia, which is significantly influenced by the Moslem prescriptions against bribery, execution of executives for the offense of bribery is legal" (Carroll and Gannon, 1997). In China in 1994, the President of the Great Wall Machinery and Electronics High-Technology Industrial Group Corp., Mr. Shen Haifu, was executed by a bullet to the back of his neck for bribery and embezzlement offenses. In 2000, several prominent Chinese officials were sentenced to death for bribery including the former vice-chair of the national legislature. Chinese academics and managers often speak of the great social cost incurred due to the current level of bribery. Under ISCT, this has the implication that even among a community of bribe payers, bribery cannot necessarily be established as an authentic norm. And, even when a norm can be found to exist among a set of bribe-soliciting public officials and bribe-paying global managers, it is never sufficient to consider just those communities. Instead, the norms of all communities affected by the bribes must be considered. The citizens who get overpriced, poor quality public services as a result of the bribes can be expected to hold an anti-bribery norm. Similarly, the owners of the organization victimized by the betrayal of its managers would oppose the practice of bribery. Under the priority rules set forth in ISCT, these anti-bribery community norms would be expected to have priority and to override the norms of the pro-bribery communities.

In short, in many if not most instances, the necessary condition imposed by ISCT that the norm be authentic, i.e., that it is both acted on *and* believed to be ethically correct by a substantial majority of the members of a community, simply appears false. Further, whenever a bribery norm does satisfy the requirements for recognition as an authentic norm, it will be subject to being overridden by the anti-bribery norms of affected communities. To the extent that these expectations are true, most instances of bribery would fail the ISCT moral free space test.

## Hypernorm Violation

Even this last consideration, however, leaves a nagging doubt behind. In particular, is bribery only wrong because most people dislike it? Is there nothing more fundamentally *wrong* with bribery? Suppose, hypothetically, that the world came to change its mind over the next thirty years about bribery. Suppose that in some future state, a majority of people finds bribery to be morally acceptable? If so, would bribery be ethically correct? In such a world would reformers who spoke out against bribery be speaking illogical nonsense?

The answer to this question turns on the further question of whether a hypernorm disallowing bribery exists. For if such a hypernorm existed, then no legitimate microsocial norm could support bribery, and, in turn, it would deserve moral condemnation even in a world whose majority opinion endorsed it.

One can argue that high-level public sector bribery, in and of itself, violates a hypernorm. Philip Nichols (1997) cites specific references from each of the world's major religions condemning bribery. "Corruption is condemned and proscribed," he writes, "by each of the major religious and moral schools of thought. Buddhism, Christianity, Confucianism, Hinduism, Islam, Judaism, Sikhism, and Taoism each proscribe corruption. Adam Smith and David Ricardo condemned corruption, as did Karl Marx and Mao Tse Tung" (Nichols, 1997, pp. 321–2). Bribes have resulted in collapsing bridges and buildings, in the deaths of children from tainted drugs, and in the diversion of food intended for starving peoples. Many bribes have a direct negative effect on human well-being. In fact, a multicultural set of authors exploring the implications of ISCT explicitly identified a hypernorm condemning bribery (Fritzsche et al., 1995). However, the condemnation of coarse public sector bribery still leaves unresolved the status of many other forms of bribery, including private sector bribery and the many other permutations of public sector bribery. To deal with those, we now consider whether other hypernorms can be identified that condemn bribery.

At least two hypernorms may be invoked in seeking a more fundamental condemnation of bribery. The first is obvious. To the extent that one places a positive, transnational value, on a *right to political participation*, large bribes of publicly elected officials damage that value. For example, when Prime Minister Tanaka of Japan in the 1970s bought planes from the American aircraft manufacturer Lockheed, after accepting tens of millions of dollars in bribes, people questioned whether he was discharging his duties as a public official correctly. In addition to the fact that his actions violated the law, the Japanese citizenry was justified in wondering whether their interests, or Tanaka's personal political interest, drove the decision. Implicit in much of the political philosophy written in the Western world in the last three hundred years, in the writings of Rousseau, Mill, Locke, Jefferson, Kant, and Rawls, is the notion that some transcultural norm supports a public claim for the citizenry of a nation state to participate in some way in the direction of political affairs. Many—see, for example, Shue (1980), Donaldson (1989) and the *Universal Declaration of Human Rights*—have discussed and articulated the implications of this right in current contexts. If such a right exists, then it entails obligations on the part of politicians and prospective bribe givers to not violate it. In turn, large-scale bribery of highly elected public officials—the sort that the Lockheed Corporation engaged in the 1970s—would be enjoined through the application of a hypernorm. It would, hence, be wrong regardless of whether a majority of the members of an economic community, or even the majority of the world's citizens, endorsed it.

Notice, however, that the political participation hypernorm misses one kind of case. Suppose it is true that large-scale pay-offs to public officials in democratic or quasi-democratic countries are proscribed by considerations of people's right to political participation. In such countries, bribery may defeat meaningful political rights. But many countries in which bribery is prevalent are not democratic. Bribery in countries such as Zaire, Nigeria and China may nonetheless not have a direct effect on political participation by ordinary citizens that is directly repressed by authoritarian governments.

Other troubling questions may be raised. How about much smaller pay-offs to public officials? And how about bribes *not* to public officials, but to employees of corporations? It seems difficult to argue that small, uniformly structured bribes to customs officials, or bribes to purchasing agents of companies in host countries, seriously undermine the people's right to political participation. These questions prompt the search for yet another hypernorm relevant to the issue of bribery.

A second hypernorm does appear relevant to the present context. It is what we have called the economic hypernorm of "necessary social efficiency." That hypernorm requires that economic agents utilize resources efficiently concerning goods in which their society has a stake. The hypernorm arises because all societies have an interest in husbanding public resources, developing strategies to promote aggregate economic welfare and in turn, of developing efficiency parameters to do so. . . .

Formal and informal proscriptions on bribery may be viewed as informal efficiency parameters. Indeed, nations and NGOs who oppose bribery most commonly cast their opposition in terms of the damage that bribery does to the economic efficiency of the nation state. . . .

Corruption *is* inefficient for identifiable reasons. First, it limits the ability of governments to perform vital functions and may even threaten overall governmental effectiveness. The *Financial Times* reported that "deep corruption [in China] is corroding the exercise of state power" (Kynge, 1997). Falsified accounts to cover up corruption have had the effect of rendering China's official statistics "virtually meaningless" (ibid). In Ecuador, it is estimated the government could pay off its foreign debt in five years if corruption was brought under control. It is estimated that corruption costs the country $2 billion every year (Transparency International). And in Argentina, corruption in the customs department defrauded the government out of $3 billion in revenues: Officials estimated that 30 percent of all imports were being under-billed and approximately $2.5 billion of goods were brought into the country under the guise of being labeled "in transit" to another country, thus illegally avoiding import taxes altogether (Argentines Give Import to Fraud Crackdown, *Financial Time* London, 3 December 1997, p. 5.). Corruption also influences government spending, moving it out of vital functions such as education and public health, and into projects where public officials can more easily extract bribes (Mauro, 1998).

Corruption imposes tremendous costs on business. While American companies complain of lost contracts due to the FCPA, other countries complain of the bribes their firms must pay to obtain those contracts. For example, German companies are estimated to pay an aggregate of over $3 billion in bribes to obtain business contracts abroad (Guggenheim, 1996). In certain countries, the costs of doing business due to bribes significantly impair the ability to make a profit. In Indonesia, it is estimated that 20 percent of business costs are bribes to bureaucrats (Honest trade: 'A global war against bribery', *Economist*, 16 January 1999, p. 22.) In Albania, approximately one-third of potential profits are lost to bribe payments (ibid).

As the economist Kenneth Arrow noted years ago, "a great deal of economic life depends for its viability on a certain limited degree of ethical commitment" (Arrow, 1973, p. 313). To the extent that market participants bribe, they interfere with the market mechanism's rational allocation of resources, and their actions impose significant social costs. When people buy or sell on the basis of price and quality, with reasonable knowledge about all relevant factors, the market allocates resources efficiently. The best products relative to price, and, in turn, the best production mechanisms, are encouraged to develop. But when agents accept defective goods or pay more than they have to in order to divert money into personal pockets, the entire market mechanism is distorted. By misallocating resources, bribery damages economic efficiency (Sen, 1997). As economists Bliss and Di Tella (1997) note, "Corrupt agents exact money from firms." Corruption affects, they observe, the number of firms in a free entry equilibrium, and in turn increases costs relative to profits. In contrast, "the degree of deep competition in the economy increases with lower overhead costs relative to profits; and with a tendency toward similar cost structures." Corruption can even be shown to exact a cost on additional social efforts to improve economic welfare, including industrial policy initiatives (Ades and Di Tella, 1997), and on predictability in economic arrangements.

Bribery, then, is objectionable on both moral and economic grounds. Nonetheless, it is worth noting that practical solutions to problems of bribery are notoriously difficult to implement, and usually involve a shift of focus to deeper levels of society. At the precise level at which most managers confront bribery, bribery eludes a fully satisfactory solution. This is because from the standpoint of an individual manager working in some global regions, refusing to bribe can mean losing business. Sales and profits are typically lost to the more unscrupulous companies, and the unethical company benefits at the expense of the more ethical company. Indeed, both the ethical *company* and the ethical *individual* are victims. (Of course, companies mitigate the damage to employees caught in this bribery trap when they communicate clear policies, and when they support employees who follow those policies.) A fully satisfactory answer, hence, lies not at the level where individuals face bribery, but at deeper levels, i.e., at the level of the firm, the competitive environment, and ultimately, the host country's background institutions. Many theorists argue that such deeper, institutional reform entails a narrowing of the dramatic gap that now exists between civil servant and private sector pay, a new mindset or "social contract" among government officials and corporate managers, and a toughening of the sanctions designed to ensure legal compliance in host countries. In short, the practical solution to bribery demands changes in social and economic structures so as to facilitate a more level playing field that aligns incentives *away from* rather than *toward* longstanding practices of bribery.

## NOTES

1. Much of this section is derived from Thomas Donaldson and Thomas W. Dunfee, 2001, Précis for: Ties that bind. *Business and Society Review*, 105 (4), 436–43.
2. Much of this section is derived from David Hess and Thomas Dunfee, 2001, Fighting corruption: A principled approach: The C2 principles (combating corruption). *Cornell International Law Journal*, 33 (3), 593–626.

## REFERENCES

Ades, A. and Di Tella, R. 1997: *National champions and corruption: some unpleasant interventionist arithmetic.* Paper presented at the University of Pennsylvania, Philadelphia.

Arrow, K. J. 1973: Social responsibility and economic efficiency. *Public Policy*, 3 (21), 300–17.

Bliss, C. and Di Tella, R. 1997: *Does competition kill corruption?* Paper presented at the University of Pennsylvania, Philadelphia.

Carroll, S. J. and Gannon, M. J. 1997: *Ethical Dimensions of International Management.* Thousand Oaks, CA: Sage.

Donaldson, T. 1989: *The Ethics of International Business.* New York: Oxford University Press.

Donaldson, T. and Dunfee, T. 1999: *Ties that Bind: A Social Contract Approach to Business Ethics.* Harvard University Business School Press.

Fritzsche, D. J., Hou, P. Y., Sugai, S. and Dun-Hou, S. 1995: Exploring the ethical behavior of managers: A comparative study of four countries. *Asia Pacific Journal of Management*, 12 (2), 37–61.

Guggenheim, K. 1996: Corruption, not revolutions or coups, topples governments these days, *L.A. Times*, October 6, sec. A, p. 4.

Heimann, F. F. 1994: Should foreign bribery be a crime? *Transparency International*, 2.

Kynge, J. 1997: "China uncovers falsified accounts in state groups," *Financial Times* (London), Wednesday, December 24, p. 7.

MacDonald, G. M. 1988: Ethical perceptions of Hong Kong/Chinese Business managers. *Journal of Business Ethics*, 7, 835–45.

Mauro, P. 1998: Corruption: Causes, consequences, and agenda for further research. *Finance & Development*, 35, (1), 11–14.

Nichols, P. M. 1997: Outlawing transnational bribery through the World Trade Organization. *Law and Policy in International Business.* 28 (2), 305–86.

Sen, A. 1997: Economics, business principles, and moral sentiments. *Business Ethics Quarterly*, 7 (3), 5–15.

Shue, H. 1980: *Basic Rights: Subsistence, Affluence, and U.S. Foreign Policy.* Princeton, NJ: Princeton University Press.

Tsalikis, J. and Wachukwu, O. 1991: A comparison of Nigerian to American views of bribery and extortion in international commerce. *Journal of Business Ethics*, 10 (2), 85–98.

Universal Declaration of Human Rights 1948: Reprinted in T. Donaldson and P. Werhane (eds) (1979). *Ethical Issues in Business:* 252–5. Englewood Cliffs, NJ: Practice Hall.

## HUMAN RIGHTS AND THE MULTINATIONAL CORPORATION

# Human Rights and Global Labor Practices

*Denis G. Arnold*

Ethical concerns are at the core of the dispute concerning global labor practices. Critics charge multinational enterprises (MNEs) with the inhumane and unjust treatment of workers in developing nations. Economists retort that satisfying the demands of these critics will result in fewer jobs in developing nations, thereby reducing social welfare. In order to properly evaluate these claims, and other like them, it is first necessary to provide an analysis of the ethical obligations of MNEs regarding global labor practices.

One set of ethical norms that is a prominent feature of contemporary public discourse, especially as it pertains to international affairs, is that of human rights. The promulgation of the United Nations Universal Declaration of Human Rights, together with the advocacy of organizations such as Amnesty International and Human Rights Watch, has led to the widespread acceptance of human rights as a basic tool of moral evaluation by individuals of widely divergent political and religious beliefs. In-

From "Rising Above Sweatshops: Innovative Management Responses to Global Labor Challenges," L. Hartman, D. Arnold and R. Wokutch eds., Praeger Publishers, 2003. Reprinted with permission of Praeger Publishers.

creasingly, the language of human rights is a prominent feature of debates regarding globalization and global labor practices.

This essay explains how an understanding of basic human rights can help MNE managers produce morally innovative solutions to global labor challenges. The essay provides both a justification of the rights to freedom and well-being, as well as an application of those rights to the circumstances of MNE workers. Other important human rights issues confronting MNEs, such as the morally appropriate stance to take toward regimes that engage in systematic human rights violations, are necessarily beyond the scope of this essay.[1]. . .

## I. THE JUSTIFICATION OF HUMAN RIGHTS

In order to think about human rights in a meaningful way, it is necessary to answer certain philosophical questions about their nature. Three of the most basic questions are the following: How can human rights be justified? What specific human rights exist? And how do human rights differ from other rights, such as legal rights? Let us consider each question in turn.

Human rights are rights enjoyed by humans not because we are members of the species *Homo sapiens*, but because fully functional members of our species are persons. Personhood is a metaphysical category that may or may not be unique to *Homo sapiens*. To be a person one must be capable of reflecting on one's desires at a second-order level, and one must be capable of acting in a manner consistent with one's considered preferences.[2] First-order desires are the assortment of desires that occupy one's conscious mind and compete for one's attention. Second-order desires are desires about those first-order desires. When one embraces a particular first-order desire at a second-order level, it becomes a preference. A mundane example will help to illustrate this concept. Each of us is likely to have found ourselves staring at a bedside clock after having turned off an early morning alarm. Lying comfortably in bed, one might reflect on one's immediate desires: to get up and go for a run; to get up and prepare for an early morning meeting; or to roll over and return to sleep. The process of reflecting on these competing desires takes place at a second-order level of consciousness. It is the capacity to reflect on one's competing desires and to act in a manner consistent with our second-order preferences that distinguishes persons from mere animals. This is not to say that one cannot sometimes fail to act in a manner consistent with one's better judgment and still be regarded as a person. Indeed, most of us are intimately familiar with such weakness of the will. The point is that we enjoy this capacity, and we are capable of acting in a manner consistent with this capacity. Furthermore, if a human were constitutionally incapable of acting in a manner consistent with his or her second-order preferences, he or she would not be properly described as a person.[3] It is in this sense that the idea of personhood is properly understood as metaphysical rather than biological.[4]

The derivation of human rights from the concept of personhood is a complex endeavor, and one of the most important accomplishments of twenteenth century philosophy. Some of the most important work on this topic has been produced by the philosopher Alan Gewirth. In his influential book *Reason and Morality*, Gewirth provides a rigorous and detailed justification of human rights.[5] Since it is sometimes argued that human rights cannot be justified without appealing to specific religious or legal traditions, it is necessary to provide a summary of Gewirth's philosophical defense of human rights.

Gewirth begins with the idea that every person regards his or her purposes as good according to his or her own criteria. By rising each morning and pursuing their own individual goals, individuals demonstrate in a practical way those things that they value.[6] Such actions are possible only insofar as the necessary conditions of one's acting to achieve one's purposes are satisfied. In other words, via the act of pursuing their individual aims, individuals demonstrate that they value the necessary conditions of action. The necessary conditions of action are freedom and well-being. Without freedom and well-being, one cannot pursue those things which one values. Freedom is here understood as controlling one's behavior by one's unforced choice while having knowledge of relevant circumstances. Possessing well-being entails having the general abilities and conditions required for a person to be able to act in a manner consistent with his or her considered, or second-order, preferences. Anyone who pursues a particular good must, on pain of contradiction, claim that they have a right to freedom and well-being. As such, all persons must accept that others have rights to freedom and well-being. Gewirth puts the matter this way:

> Since the agent [or person] regards as necessary goods the freedom and well-being that constitute the generic features of his successful action, he logically must hold that he has rights to these generic features, and he implicitly makes a corresponding rights claim.[7]

Gewirth is not arguing, as some might think, that because persons require freedom and well-being in order to function, they are thereby entitled to freedom and well-being.[8] Such an argument, one grounded in *empirical necessity*, would not be convincing because it does not follow from the fact that one requires something, that one has a right to that thing. While Gewirth's argument does have an empirical component, it is properly understood as a transcendental argument in the Kantian tradition. A transcendental argument is one that establishes the truth of a proposition by appealing to necessary conditions of human experience. Gewirth's argument is that, as a matter of *rational consistency*, a person must acknowledge that she is a purposive being, and that the pursuit of her ends requires freedom and well-being. Hence she must claim a right to freedom and well-being; to do otherwise would be irrational. Because all other persons share these qualities, she must—again, as a matter of rational consistency—ascribe these rights to all other beings. To deny that persons have the right to freedom and well-being is to deny that one is a purposive being. Since the denial is a purposive act, it contradicts the proposition being asserted. In this way, Gewirth provides a deep and satisfying justification for human rights. Because the justification is grounded in rational reflection on the human condition, it can be embraced by individuals of diverse religious faiths and different cultural identities.

At this point in our discussion, it is worthwhile to consider an objection to the foregoing argument concerning human rights. This criticism stems from the observation that the idea of human rights emerged from the Western philosophical tradition, but is taken to be universal in its applicability. The claim is then made that human rights are of less importance in the value systems of other cultures. For example, it is argued that "Asian values" emphasize order, discipline, and social harmony, as opposed to individual rights. In this view, the freedom and well-being of individuals should not be allowed to interfere with the harmony of the community, as might be the case, for example, when workers engage in disruptive collective action in an effort to secure their rights. This view might also be used to defend the claim that the moral norms that govern Asian factory operations should emphasize order and discipline, not freedom and well-being.

Several points may be made in reply to this objection. First, Asia is a large region with a vast and heterogeneous population. As Amartya Sen and others have argued, to claim that all, or even most, Asians share a uniform set of values is to impose a level of uniformity that does not exist at present and has not existed in the past.[9] Second, in secular, democratic Asian societies such as India, respect for individual rights has a long tradition. Indeed, there are significant antecedents in the history of the civilizations of the Indian subcontinent that emphasize individual freedom and well-being. For example, in the third century B.C.E. the Emperor Ashoka granted his citizens the freedom to embrace whatever religious or philosophical system they might choose, while at the same time he emphasized the importance of tolerance and respect for philosophical and religious beliefs different than one's own.[10] Third, even if it was the case that Asian cultures shared a uniform set of values that de-emphasized human rights, this would not by itself provide good reasons for denying or disrespecting the rights to freedom and well-being. This is because the justification of human rights just provided is grounded in rational arguments that are valid across cultures. Jack Donnely makes a similar point in his recent defense of universal human rights.

> One of the things that makes us human is our capacity to create and change our culture. Cultural diversity has in recent years increasingly come to be valued in itself. Westerners have in recent centuries been especially insensitive in their approach to such differences. Nonetheless, the essential insight of human rights is that the worlds we make for ourselves, intentionally and unintentionally, must conform to relatively universal requirements that rest on our common humanity and seek to guarantee equal concern and respect from the state for every person.[11]

The critic is likely to retort that such a view reflects Western prejudices grounded in Enlightenment ideals. However, this response is unpersuasive. Diverse intellectual traditions have emphasized the importance of values derived from reason, rather than mythology, traditionalism, mere sentiment, or some other source. For example, in the sixteenth century the Moghul Emperor Akbar wrote:

> The pursuit of reason and rejection of traditionalism are so brilliantly patent as to be above the need for argument. If traditionalism were proper, the prophets would merely have followed their own elders (and not come with new messages).[12]

Akbar arranged to have philosophers representing diverse religious and philosophical beliefs engage in rational discussions regarding the merits of their competing views, and sought to identify the most persuasive features of each view. In doing so, Akbar was able to emphasize the power and force of rational analysis. Given that a similar emphasis on rational analysis concerning values may be found in the histories of other non-Western cultures, the claim that such analysis is uniquely Western is unpersuasive.

Human rights are moral rights that apply to all persons in all nations, regardless of whether the nation in which a person resides acknowledges and protects those rights. It is in this sense that human rights are said to be *inalienable.* Human rights differ from legal rights in that, unlike legal rights, the existence of human rights is not contingent upon any institution. Many nations grant their citizens certain constitutional or legal rights via foundational documents or legal precedent. However, the rights that are protected vary among nations. Some nations ensure that the rights of citizens are protected by effective policing and an independent judiciary. Frequently, however, poor citizens and disfavored groups are not provided with the same level of protection for their legal rights as the economic and political elite. Persons who are deprived of their rights do not thereby cease to have those rights. As A. I. Melden has argued,

> . . . the complaint that persons are deprived of their human rights when, for example, they are subjected to forced indenture by their employers, is a complaint that their rights have been violated and implies, clearly, that they have rights they are unjustly prevented from exercising. If

> one were deprived of one's rights in the sense in which one would be deprived of things in one's physical possession by having them taken away, one would no longer have the rights, and there would be no grounds for the complaint. So it is with the denial of a person's right—this does not consist in denying that he has the right but, rather, in denying him, by withholding from him, that to which he has the right or the means or opportunity for its exercise.[13]

Employers may deny employees their inalienable right to freedom and well-being, whether or not local governments are complicit, but in doing so they in no way diminish the legitimacy of the claims of their employees to those rights. However, by virtue of their failure to operate from the moral point of view, such employers succeed in diminishing their own standing in the community of rights holders.

## II. HUMAN RIGHTS AND LABOR PRACTICES

We have seen how a right to freedom and a right to well-being can be justified. If persons have a right to freedom and well-being, then at a minimum other persons have an obligation to refrain from interfering with those rights. It is in this sense that rights entail corresponding duties on the part of other persons. What are the specific obligations or duties of MNE managers with respect to the freedom and well-being of employers and how are these obligations to be balanced against the obligations of managers to their employers?

Because freedom and well-being are basic rights, the obligation to respect those rights is equally basic. As such, no labor practices may be undertaken that will violate a worker's right to freedom and well-being. MNEs are in a unique position to ensure that basic rights are respected in the workplace by virtue of their power and the vast resources under their command. In the words of the United Nations, "Society no longer accepts the view that the conduct of global corporations is bound only by the laws of the country in which they operate. By virtue of their global influence and power, they must accept responsibility and be accountable for upholding high human rights standards."[14] MNEs typically have well-defined internal decision structures that provide an internal mechanism for enforcing human rights standards. The internal decision structure of an organization is comprised of its offices and levels of responsibility, together with the rules that allow managers to differentiate between enterprise level decisions, and the decisions of individual employees.[15] For this reason, morally innovative managers are well positioned to play a constructive role in ensuring that the rights of workers in developing nations are respected.[16]

MNE managers should regard respect for their employees' rights to freedom and well-being as constraints on the activities they undertake on behalf of their employers. However, the rights to freedom and well-being are very general. Greater specificity regarding the content of these rights must be provided. Let us begin with freedom. Previously we characterized freedom as controlling one's behavior via one's unforced choice while having knowledge of relevant circumstances. Gewirth provides a helpful summary of the content of the right to freedom:

> This consists in a person's controlling his actions and his participation in transactions by his own unforced choice or consent and with knowledge of relevant circumstances, so that his behavior is neither compelled nor prevented by the actions of other persons. Hence, a person's right to freedom is violated if he is subjected to violence, coercion, deception, or any other procedures that attack or remove his informed control of his behavior by his own unforced choice. This right includes having a sphere of personal autonomy and privacy whereby one is let alone by others unless and until he unforcedly consents to undergo their action.[17]

Possessing freedom entails having the general abilities and conditions required for a person to be able to act in a manner consistent with his or her second-order preferences. A right to freedom, then, involves the right to pursue one's own goals and preferences without interference from others. Specifically, it includes control over one's own physical integrity, freedom of belief and expression, and freedom of association. Traditionally, the right to freedom is thought to be as extensive as is compatible with a like right to freedom for all. Such freedom is not, however, unlimited. It may be rightfully curtailed if a person's actions illegitimately infringe upon the freedom or well-being of others.

The rights one enjoys as a human being are not unlimited in the sense that one is free to exercise all of them under any circumstances. Legitimate restrictions may be placed on the exercise of one's rights by both the state and private enterprise. It is, for example, not an illegitimate infringement of one's right to freedom of belief and expression if an employer prohibits proselytizing on behalf of one's religious convictions while at work. Such activity is typically disruptive and as such incompatible with the purposes for which employees are hired. Furthermore, employees are free to engage in such activity when they are not working. Restricting employee activity in this manner does not infringe on an employee's dignity as a person. There are, however, certain restrictions on employee freedom that always violate human dignity because they treat the employee as a tool rather than as a person. Control over one's physical integrity is one such example. This freedom could, for example, be violated by a rule that permitted only one bathroom break each day.

Several international covenants and conventions are available to MNEs interested in specific guidance with respect to their global labor practices. For example, the Articles of the United Nations Universal Declaration of Human Rights (1948) provide specific examples of what it means to respect an employee's right to freedom at work (see Figure 1). Articles 3, 4, and 5 provide a basis for the prohibition of all forced labor, indentured servitude, corporeal punishment of employees by supervisors, and seriously unsafe working conditions. Article 23, Section 4 provides a basis for the prohibition of the

**FIGURE 1**

**UNIVERSAL DECLARATION OF HUMAN RIGHTS**
**Articles Concerning the Right to Freedom with Special Relevance to the Obligations of MNEs to Workers**

**Article 3.** Everyone has the right to life, liberty, and security of person.

**Article 4.** No one shall be held in slavery or servitude; slavery and the slave trade shall be prohibited in all their forms.

**Article 5.** No one shall be subjected to torture or to cruel, inhuman or degrading treatment or punishment.

**Article 23, Section 4.** Everyone has the right to form and to join trade unions for the protection of his interests.

*Source:* United Nations Department of Public Information, "Universal Declaration of Human Rights," http://www.unhchr.ch/udhr/lang/eng.htm (accessed July 31, 2002).

termination of employees for organizing or joining a trade union.

Now let us turn to well-being. As we have seen, well-being entails having the general abilities and conditions required for a person to be able to act autonomously. The most important component of well-being, and the one that we shall focus upon here, is basic goods. Basic goods are the general physical and psychological capabilities necessary for human functioning. In recent years, the relationship between well-being and human functioning has received a great deal of attention from economists and philosophers. Amartya Sen and Martha Nussbaum, have produced some of the most important work on this topic. Their distinctive variety of quality of life assessment, known as the *capabilities approach*, had become increasingly influential. This is partly due to the fact that it has been adapted by the United Nations Development Programme (UNDP) and has been incorporated into the UNDP Human Development Reports since 1993. The relationship between human functioning and well-being is usefully articulated by Sen:

> The primary feature of well-being can be seen in terms of how a person can "function," taking that term in a very broad sense. I shall refer to various doings and beings that come into this assessment as functionings. These could be activities (like eating or reading or seeing), or states of existence or being, e.g., being well nourished, being free from malaria, not being ashamed by the poverty of one's clothing or shoes (to go back to a question that Adam Smith discussed in his *Wealth of Nations*).[18]

It is important to note that not all persons will have the same capacity to function well with the same goods. Variations in the transformation of goods into constituent elements of well-being will vary significantly among persons.

> Take, for example, the consumption of food, on the one hand, and the functioning of being well nourished, on the other. The relationship between them varies with (1) metabolic rates, (2) body size, (3) age, (4) sex (and if a woman, whether pregnant or lactating), (5) activity levels, (6) medical services, (9) nutritional knowledge, and other influences.[19]

Access to the basic goods necessary for human functioning does not mean that a person who enjoys the basic goods necessary to function well will do so. Two individuals may have access to the same goods necessary for each of them to achieve the same level of well-being, yet fail to do so because one of them made choices that reduced his or her ability to function well. For this reason it is necessary to emphasize an individual's *capability* to function. What are these capabilities?

Nussbaum identifies ten capabilities as necessary for humans to enjoy well-being (see Figure 2).[20] The list is itself the product of years of cross-cultural study and discussion and

**FIGURE 2**

**Central Human Functional Capabilities**

1. **Life.** Being able to live to the end of a human life of normal length; not dying prematurely, or before one's life is so reduced as to not be worth living.
2. **Bodily Health.** Being able to have good health, including reproductive health; to be adequately nourished; to have adequate shelter.
3. **Body Integrity.** Being able to move freely from place to place; having one's bodily boundaries treated as sovereign, i.e. being able to be secure against assault, including sexual assault, child sexual abuse, and domestic violence; having opportunities for sexual satisfaction and for choice in matters of reproduction.

*(continues on next page)*

**FIGURE 2 (continued)**

4. **Senses, Imagination, and Thought.** Being able to use the senses, to imagine, think, and reason- and to do these things in a "truly human" way, a way informed and cultivated by an adequate education, including, but by no means limited to, literacy and basic mathematical and scientific training. Being able to use imagination and thought in connection with experiencing and producing self-expressive works and events of one's own choice, religious, literacy, musical and so forth. Being able to use one's mind in ways protected by guarantees of freedom of expression with respect to both political and artistic speech, and freedom of religious exercise. Being able to have pleasurable experiences, and to avoid non-necessary pain.

5. **Emotion.** Being able to have attachments to things and people outside of ourselves; to love those who love and care for us, to grieve at their absence; in general, to love, to grieve, to experience longing gratitude, and justified anger. Not having one's emotional development blighted by overwhelming fear and anxiety, or by traumatic events of abuse or neglect (Supporting this capability means supporting forms of human association that can be shown to be crucial in their development.)

6. **Practical Reason.** Being able to form a conception of the good and to engage in critical reflection about the planning of one's life. (This entails protection for the liberty of conscience.)

7. **Affiliation.**
   **A.** Being able to live with and towards others, to recognize and show concern for other human beings, to engage in various forms of social interaction; to be able to imagine the situation of another and have compassion for that situation; to have the capability for both justice and friendship. (Protecting this capability means protecting institutions that constitute and nourish such forms of affiliation, and also protecting the freedom of assembly and political speech.)
   **B.** Having the social bases of self-respect and non-humiliation; being able to be treated as a dignified being whose worth is; equal to that of others. This entails, at a minimum, protections against discrimination on the basis of race, sex, sexual orientation, religion, caste, ethnicity, or national origin. In work, being able to work as a human being, exercising practical reason and entering into meaningful relationships of mutual recognition with other workers.

8. **Other Species.** Being able to live with concern for and in relation to animals, plants, and the world of nature.

9. **Play.** Being able to laugh, play, to enjoy recreational activities.

10. **Control over One's Environment.**
    **A. Political.** Being able to participate effectively in political choices that govern one's life; having the right of political participation, protections of free speech and free association.
    **B. Material.** Being able to hold property (both land and movable goods), not just formally but in terms of real opportunity; and having property rights on an equal basis with others; having the right to seek employment on an equal basis with others; having the freedom from unwarranted search and seizure.

*Source:* Martha Nussbaum, *Women and Human Development* (New York, Cambridge University Press, 2001), pp. 78–80.

represents a sort of overlapping consensus on the part of individuals with widely disparate views of human life. Nussbaum is careful to point out both that the list is open-ended, and that items on the list may be interpreted somewhat differently in different societies. However, each item on the list is of central importance and as such it must be regarded as a significant loss when a person falls below any one of the central areas.

The Articles of the United Nations Universal Declaration of Human Rights provide a valuable resource for determining what it means for an employer to respect an employee's right to well-being (see Figure 3). Article 23, Section 2 provides a basis for the prohibition of discrimination based on arbitrary characteristics such as race or sex. Article 23, Section 2 and Article 25, Section 1 provide a basis for paying employees wages that are consistent with living with dignity. They also provide a basis for thinking that it is the responsibility of MNEs to ensure that social security and other taxes are paid to appropriate governmental authorities. Article 24 provides a basis for the view that employees are entitled to wages adequate for a dignified standard of living without working extensive overtime hours. . . .

## III. MORAL IMAGINATION AND INNOVATION

As we have seen, the Universal Declaration of Human Rights provides a valuable resource for moral managers who wish to respect the rights of employees. In addition, the International Labour Organization's (ILO) carefully developed Conventions and Recommendations on safety and health provide a detailed template for minimum safety standards. Both the U.N. and the ILO provide specific guidance to MNEs via the ILO's Tripartite Declaration of Principles concerning Multinational Enterprises and

**FIGURE 3**

**UNIVERSAL DECLARATION OF HUMAN RIGHTS**
**Articles Concerning the Right to Well-being with Special Relevance to the Obligations of MNEs to Workers**

**Article 23**

(2) Everyone, without any discrimination, has the right to equal pay for equal work.

(3) Everyone who works has the right to just and favorable remuneration ensuring for himself and his family an existence worthy of human dignity, and supplemented, if necessary, by other means of social protection.

**Article 24**

Everyone has the right to rest and leisure, including reasonable limitation of working hours and periodic holidays with pay.

**Article 25**

(1) Everyone has the right to a standard of living adequate for health and well-being of himself and of his family, including food, clothing, housing and medical care and necessary social services, and the right: to security in the event of unemployment, sickness, disability, widowhood, old age or other lack of livelihood in circumstances beyond his control.

*Source:* United Nations Department of Public Information, "Universal Declaration of Human Rights," http://www.unhchr.ch/udhr/lang/eng.htm (accessed July 31, 2002).

Social Policy (1977) and the United Nations Global Compact (1999). However, knowledge of specific examples of the rights to freedom and well-being is not by itself sufficient for the moral manager to ensure that employee rights are respected. Something more is needed. Managers must be capable of innovative moral decision making.

The claim that managers must be capable of innovative strategic decision making is so common as to be *passé*. However, the claim that managers *qua* managers must also be capable of innovative *moral* decision making has only recently been the subject of serious study. In an important recent book, Patricia Werhane provides a sustained defense of the thesis that moral imagination is a necessary condition of innovative managerial moral decision making.[21] Werhane defines the functioning of moral imagination in the following terms. First, managers must have an *awareness of the particular* that includes the following:

> 1. awareness of the character, context, situation, event, and dilemma at issue;
> 2. awareness of the script . . . in that context and role relationships entailed in that context, and
> 3. awareness of possible moral conflicts or dilemmas that might arise in that situation, including dilemmas created at least in part by the dominating script or the situation itself.[22]

Second, managers must have a *capacity for productive imagination.* A productive moral imagination involves an awareness of an "incomplete, perhaps even limiting or distorting script" and a willingness to challenge that script. Third, managers must have a *capacity for creativity* that will enable them to "envision and actualize novel, morally justifiable possibilities through a fresh point of view or conceptual scheme."[23] Managers must, in other words, be capable of understanding, evaluating, and rewriting the script.

That managers can assess an existing script regarding labor practices, recognize the limitations of that script, and produce a new script is well illustrated by the case of Mattel, Inc. In 1997, senior executives at Mattel, the world's largest manufacturer of toys, assessed their existing script concerning global labor practices, and determined it to be morally unsatisfactory. In that same year Mattel announced the creation of its Global Manufacturing Principles (GMP) and the establishment of an independent monitoring council to ensure compliance with the GMP at the 20+ factories that are owned or controlled by Mattel, and at the 300+ production facilities with which Mattel contracts.[24] According to S. Prakash Sethi, Chair of Mattel's Independent Monitoring Council for Global Manufacturing Principles, this was the first time that a major MNE "voluntarily committed itself to independent monitoring by outside observers with complete authority to make their findings available to the public."[25] Sethi reports Mattel's progress to date has been commendable:

> Mattel has already completed extensive in-house audits to ensure that its own plants, and those of the company's major suppliers, are in compliance with Mattel's Global Manufacturing Principles. Where necessary, it has also worked closely with the company's suppliers to help them improve their operations so as to meet Mattel's standards—frequently at Mattel's expense. And, in a number of cases, where suppliers have been unable or unwilling to make such an effort, Mattel has discontinued its business relationship with those suppliers.
>
> Mattel has been quite responsive to the needs of the communities where it has major plants and other types of operations. The company has committed itself to a program of coordinated activities that would (1) help the communities where it has operations, and (2) further strengthen and expand programs that would help workers—through education and training—develop non-job related skills that would enhance their productivity and income once they leave Mattel and pursue other employment and career options. Mattel has also committed the company to establishing higher standards of work and living environments for its workers in overseas operations, both in all new facilities that it would build in the future, and through upgrading of its current facilities.[26]

Mattel's efforts to substantially improve its global labor practices demonstrate both respect for the rights of employees, and moral imagination. Other MNEs such as Nike, adidas-Solomon, and Chiquita have, in recent years, implemented new initiatives regarding labor practices that are similarly innovative.[27] As these firms demonstrate, respecting employee rights is not incompatible with profitability.

## IV. CONCLUSION

The vast majority of workers in most developing nations operate outside or at the periphery of formal employment relations. As formal sector employment increases in these nations, MNEs that demonstrate respect for the rights of workers can be expected to have an influence on the local norms governing labor practices disproportionate to the number of workers that they actually employ. This is because they, together with morally innovative indigenous employers, will be setting the standard against which other employers must be measured. The result will be a substantially improved quality of life for the growing ranks of workers in the formal sector. Correspondingly, morally innovative MNEs and their suppliers can be expected to enjoy the most productive and loyal indigenous workers since they will be ranked among the most desirable employers. Furthermore, as increasing numbers of workers leave the informal sector in pursuit of better opportunities in the formal sector, less pressure will be exerted on the scarce productive resources of the informal sector. This should permit an enhanced standard of living for those remaining in the informal sector. Far from causing a decrease in overall social welfare by spurring unemployment, MNEs that demonstrate respect for worker rights are well positioned to enhance the welfare of citizens in developing nations.

## NOTES

1. An important set of arguments concerning the obligations of MNEs regarding human rights may be found in Thomas Donaldson, *The Ethics of International Business* (New York, Oxford University Press, 1989). For helpful discussions of the morally appropriate stances that MNEs should take toward repressive regimes, see John R. Schermerhorn, Jr., "Terms of Global Business Engagement in Ethically Challenged Environments: Applications to Burma," *Business Ethics Quarterly*, 9 (July 1999), pp. 485–505; S. Prakash Sethi and Oliver F. Williams, *Economic Imperatives and Ethical Values in Global Business: The South African Experience and International Codes Today* (Dordrecht: Kluwer Academic Publishers, 2000); and Michael A. Santoro, *Profits and Principles: Global Capitalism and Human Rights in China* (Ithaca, NY: Cornell University Press, 2000).
2. For a defense of this account of personhood, see Harry G. Frankfurt, *The Importance of What We Care About* (Cambridge, UK: Cambridge University Press, 1988); see also Gerald Dworkin, *The Theory and Practice of Autonomy* (Cambridge, UK: Cambridge University Press, 1988). For an important recent discussion of the hierarchical conception of personhood see Robert Kane, *The Significance of Free Will* (Oxford, UK: Oxford University Press, 1996).
3. Not surprisingly, the question of what rights humans with severe mental impairment may be said to have is a complex issue. Addressing this important topic is, however, beyond the scope of this essay.
4. For an important discussion of the relationship of personhood to rights, see A. I. Melden, *Rights and Persons* (Berkeley, CA: University of California Press, 1977).
5. Alan Gewirth, *Reason and Morality* (Chicago, IL: University of Chicago Press, 1978).
6. One might object to this view on the grounds that some people pursue ends that they themselves do not regard as valuable. Such an objection fails to undermine Gewirth's point since, on his account, one demonstrates that one regards some ends as valuable insofar as one pursues that end. Here Gewirth's position may be regarded as consistent with those social scientists who are interested in studying not what people say they value, but what they demonstrate they value through their actions.

7. Alan Gewirth, *Reason and Morality, infra* n. 5 at p. 63.
8. For example, Alasdair MacIntyre mistakenly interprets Gewirth in this manner. See MachIntyre, *After Virtue*, 2nd ed. (Notre Dame, IN: University of Notre Dame Press, 1984), pp. 66–67.
9. See Amartya Sen, "Human Rights and Asian Values." In *Business Ethics in the Global Marketplace*, Tibor R. Machan (ed.) (Stanford, CA: Hoover Institution Press, 1999), pp. 37–62; and "East and West: The Reach of Reason," *The New York Review of Books* (July 20, 2000), pp. 33–38. Much of my discussion of these issues follows that of Sen. See also Inoue Tatsuo, "Liberal Democracy and Asian Orientalism." in Joanne R. Bauer and Daniel A. Bell (Eds.), *The East Asian Challenge for Human Rights* (Cambridge, UK: Cambridge University Press, 1999), pp. 27–59; and Jack Donnely, "Human Rights and Asian Values: A Defense of 'Western' Universalism." in Joanne R. Bauer and Daniel A. Bell (Eds.), *The East Asian Challenge for Human Rights* (Cambridge, UK: Cambridge University Press, 1999), pp. 60–87.
10. Sen, "Human Rights and Asian Values," *infra* n. 9, pp. 48–53.
11. Donnely. "Human Rights and Asian Values: A Defense of 'Western' Universalism," *infra* n. 9, p. 87.
12. Quoted in Sen "East and West: The Reach of Reason," *infra* n. 9, p. 37.
13. A. I. Melden, *Rights and Persons, infra* n. 4 at pp. 167–68.
14. United National Development Programme, *Human Development Report 2000* (New York, Oxford University Press, 2000), p. 80.
15. The idea of an organizational internal decision structure was first articulated by Peter French nearly 25 years ago in his essay "The Corporation as a Moral Person," *American Philosophical Quarterly*, 16 (1979), pp. 207–17. For a statement of his current views on the subject, see his *Corporate Ethics* (Fort Worth, TX: Harcourt Brace, 1995).
16. Henry Shue argues that to make an exception on the part of MNEs with respect to the duty of not depriving other persons of their rights would be to effectively deny the existence of those rights. See Shue, *Basic Rights* (Princeton, NY: Princeton University Press, 1980), p. 170.
17. Alan Gewirth, *Human Rights: Essays on Justification and Applications* (Chicago, IL: University of Chicago Press, 1982), pp. 56–57.
18. Amartya Sen, "Well-being, Agency and Freedom: The Dewey Lectures 1984," *Journal of Philosophy*, 82 (April 1985), pp. 197–98.
19. Amartya Sen, "Well-being, Agency and Freedom: The Dewey Lectures 1984," *infra* n. 18 at pp. 198–99.
20. Martha Nussbaum, *Women and Human Development* (New York, NY: Cambridge University Press, 2001).
21. Patricia H. Werhane, *Moral Imagination and Management Decision Making* (New York, NY: Oxford University Press, 1999).
22. Patricia H. Werhane, *Moral Imagination and Management Decision Making, infra* n. 21, p. 103.
23. Patricia H. Werhane, *Moral Imagination and Management Decision Making, infra* n. 21, p. 104.
24. S. Prakash Sethi, "Codes of Conduct for Multinational Corporations: An Idea Whose Time Has Come," *Business and Society Review*, 104 (3) (1999), pp. 225–41.
25. S. Prakash Sethi, "Codes of Conduct for Multinational Corporations: An Idea Whose Time Has Come," *infra* n. 24, pp. 237–38.
26. S. Prakash Sethi, "Codes of Conduct for Multinational Corporations: An Idea Whose Time Has Come," *infra* n. 24, pp. 239–40.
27. For a detailed description of these programs, see Laura Hartman, Denis G. Arnold and Richard Wokutch, Eds., *Rising Above Sweatshops: Innovative Management Approaches to Global Labor Challenges* (New York, Praeger, 2003).

# Terms of Global Business Engagement in Ethically Challenging Environments: Applications to Burma

*John R. Schermerhorn, Jr.*

## SOCIAL AND POLITICAL CONTEXT

. . . Called "Myanmar" by its totalitarian rulers, Burma is beset by tragedy, turmoil, and great controversy. Although historically rich in culture, natural resources, and vast agricultural potential, it suffers badly in the community of nations. Only one in four Burmese children finishes primary school and the country's 45 million people are among the world's least educated. With a national income under $300, the country's fledgling market economy suffers from many problems that limit development prospects. Burma gets the lowest Freedom House ranking on economic, political, and civil liberties. The World Bank and International Monetary Fund have refused loans that would otherwise be available to countries facing such extreme economic hardships.

In 1988 Burma's dictator General U Ne Win stepped down after 36 years of imposing his authoritarian commitment to socialism. A military junta, the State Law and Order Restoration Council (SLORC), seized power and crushed student-led pro-democracy protests. Although national elections were held in 1990, the SLORC failed to honor results. The National League for Democracy (NLD), led by Daw Aung San Suu Kyi (daughter of U Aung San, hero of Burma's post-World War II independence struggle), won some 60 percent of the popular vote and over 80 percent of government seats. To date, this elected government has yet to assume office.

Daw Suu Kyi was placed under house arrest in July 1989, received the Nobel Peace Prize in 1991, and was held in detention until 1995. Her movements within the country have since been restricted; NLD members have been arrested and jailed on various charges; students participating in rallies or distributing leaflets have been arrested and mistreated by the police; large numbers of ethnic minorities have fled persecution and involuntary conscription into the military; citizens have risked being forced to labor in support of military initiatives against dissidents or to work on infrastructure projects related to tourism and business development.

The military regime defended these practices as necessary to the processes of national development, claiming that Daw Suu Kyi and the elected civilian government would be unable to hold the country together during difficult times. Through it all, the SLORC's harsh treatment of Daw Suu Kyi, her pro-democracy supporters, and the Burmese citizenry created diplomatic and social controversy. The SLORC drew sharp criticism from governments in North America and Europe, as well as from human rights groups worldwide. Burma's admission to the Association of Southeast Asian Nations (ASEAN), in July 1997, was controversial.

In November 1997, the SLORC was replaced by the State Peace and Development Council (SPDC). The state-run media announced: "For the emergence and practice of discipline democracy and for the emergence of a peace-

From "Terms of Global Business Engagement in Ethically Challenging Environments: Applications to the Case of Burma," John R. Schermehorn, Jr., *Business Ethics Quarterly* 9 (1999). Reprinted with permission from *Business Ethics Quarterly* and author.

ful and prosperous modern state and in the interest of the state and the people, the State Peace and Development Council was formed with immediate effect" (*The Nation* 1997). An anonymous Rangoon analyst described the SPDC, with its top leadership including former SLORC generals, as "merely old wine in a new bottle" (*The Nation* 1997).

Daw Suu Kyi actively challenged the SPDC to install the parliament that had been elected in 1990. The new government responded with more harassment. When her automobile was blocked on two occasions while traveling to visit supporters outside of Rangoon, she staged sit-in protests lasting several days. Growing concern for an escalation of tensions led the United States, Australia, and New Zealand, among other countries, to ask United Nations Secretary General Kofi Annan for "urgent" intervention to encourage the SPDC to open dialogue with Daw Suu Kyi and prevent the escalation of tensions (Reuters 1998). Daw Suu Kyi remained firm in a long-standing commitment to democratic determination of Burma's future, expressed in her essay "In Quest of Democracy" as "the unhappy legacies of authoritarianism can be removed only if the concept of absolute power as the basis of government is replaced by the concept of confidence as the mainspring of political authority" (Suu Kyi 1991b: 178). . . .

## FOREIGN INVESTMENT CONTROVERSIES

*Under current circumstances, it is not possible to do business without directly supporting the military government and its pervasive human rights violations.*

—Levi Strauss and Co.,
corporate announcement

*Today's operations are not commercially viable, but we believe this country has big potential.*

—Mike Nagai of Mitsui's Burma office

Foreign investment in Burma is controversial, with its most apparent beneficiaries being persons and firms with connections to the government and military. Substantial activist lobbies pursue MNCs that do business in the country, and Table 1 shows a sample of stay-go tendencies for various companies. Levi Strauss and Co. discontinued outsourcing contracts in 1992 due to concerns for Burma's human rights record. Liz Claiborne, J. Crew, Oshkosh B'Gosh, and Columbia Sportswear later exited, as have

**TABLE 1** Sample Disposition of Business Interests in Burma

| Maintained business interests in Burma | Discontinued business interests in Burma |
|---|---|
| ABB Asea Brown Boveri Ltd. | Amoco Corp. |
| Acer Inc. | Anheuser-Busch Companies Inc. |
| Asia Pacific Breweries Ltd. | Apple Computer Inc. |
| Atlantic Richfield | Carlsberg AS |
| British Petroleum PLC | Columbia Sportswear |
| Daewoo Corp. | J. Crew |
| Deutsche Telekom AG | Levi Strauss |
| Mitsubishi Corp. | Liz Claiborne |
| Mitsui & Co. Ltd. | Oshkosh B'Gosh Inc. |
| Shangri-La Hotels Ltd. | PepsiCo Inc. |
| Siemens AG | Seagram Company Ltd. |
| Total S.A. | Wente Vineyards |

*Source:* Information for this table reported in IRRC 1997.

Canada's Seagram and America's Wente Vineyards. Europe's Carlsberg canceled a planned joint venture to establish a brewery in the country, with its decision preceded by protests by the International Union of Food, Agricultural and Allied Workers Associations. PepsiCo disengaged after suffering from a campaign to boycott its products in the United States and from pressures by shareholder interest groups, among them the Franklin Research and Development Corporation and the Maryknoll Fathers and Brothers. Selective purchasing laws in several American cities, including Berkeley, California; Madison, Wisconsin; and Ann Arbor, Michigan, as well as in the State of Massachusetts, also plagued the company.

In the oil and gas sector, major controversy surrounds the Total/Unocal-led Yadana investment project in the strategic southern Tenasserim region. The US$1 billion-plus project involves a multinational consortium of Total of France (31+ percent share), Unocal of the United States (28+ percent share), PTTEP of Thailand (25+ percent share), and Burma Oil and Gas Enterprise (15 percent share). Once called the "only one project that really matters to the military junta," it has been criticized for both its potential to financially support the government (estimated to generate up to $400 million annual income) and the methods by which it is being constructed. A report by Earthwatch International and the Southeast Asian Information Network holds the Yadana business consortium responsible for human rights atrocities committed in the project's behalf. Charges include abuse of civilian populations by military personnel providing security, impression of civilians as forced labor to build roads and other infrastructure support, and forcible relocation of civilian populations along the pipeline route.

The Yadana consortium has so far held firm in its investment, with Total claiming that it is victimized by a disinformation campaign. The firm counts among the benefits of its presence the comparatively high wages paid to its Burmese workers, compensation provided for lands acquired, and a "socioeconomic programme" funded in support of local populations. Unocal has justified its involvement with the statement: "Unocal is a global energy company, not a political agency. Our participation in the Yadana project is based on resource potential, business economics and technical expertise" (Unocal 1996). The firm further argues that all work on its project is done by paid labor and that its local contractors must follow "fair hiring practices"

## SANCTIONS VERSUS CONSTRUCTIVE ENGAGEMENT DEBATE

*We always said—very, very clearly—Burma is not ripe for investment.*

—Daw Aung San Suu Kyi

*How can you influence Burma when you don't have a forum?*

—Malaysian Foreign Minister Abdullah Ahmad Badawi

Controversies over foreign investment in Burma have largely been framed as a debate between those who favor "sanctions" on the one hand—an absolutist position—and those seeking "constructive engagement" on the other—tending more toward a relativist position. Commenting on the situation in Burma, Archbishop Desmond Tutu of South Africa states the case for sanctions: "Tough sanctions, not constructive engagement finally brought the release of Nelson Mandela and the dawn of a new era in my country. This is the language that must be spoken with tyrants—for, sadly, it is the only language they understand" (Tutu 1993). Daw Suu Kyi agrees, as do most, if not all, of the activist lobbies rallied against the military government. They advocate investment prohibitions and trade boycotts designed to force the authoritarian government into dialogue with the NLD, and ultimately bring democratic government to Burma.

The call for sanctions has so far failed to gain multilateral backing, and is unlikely to do so. Governments inclined in this direction, namely Canada, the European Union countries, and the United States, have yet to take definitive action that prohibits their nations' firms from operating in the country. Australian Deputy Prime Minister Tim Fischer has spoken against sanctions, saying: "Sanctions will never work with regard to Burma. They are not practical with regard to the Burma situation" (Baker 1996).

Burma's Southeast Asian neighbors generally prefer a policy of constructive engagement. In contrast to confrontational and isolationist sanctions, this approach is supposed to work through private persuasion and economic involvement. Malaysian Prime Minister Mahathir Mohamad, for example, is quoted as saying: "We believe that the way to bring people around to our way of thinking is to talk to them, not to squeeze them or to twist their arms behind their backs" (Jayasankaran 1996). Although the Philippine and Thai governments have shown recent signs of impatience with constructive engagement, regional business support for the policy remains substantial. A survey of Asian executives by the *Far Eastern Economic Review* shows that 69 percent of respondents believe ASEAN membership has made Burma a more attractive location for investment.

Constructive engagement in concept seems consistent with Asian cultural preferences for public harmony, respect for authority, face and consensus building. It may also reflect regional geopolitical realities. China ranked number 3 as an export destination and number 1 as an import source in Burma's 1996 international trade statistics, and is a major arms supplier to the government. China is also involved in controversial territorial claims with several ASEAN countries regarding islands in the South China Sea. Continuing contact with Burma is one way for ASEAN to balance China's growing regional influence. By dealing with Burma in their own ways, furthermore, ASEAN governments also display independence from unwanted Western hegemony.

In practice, constructive engagement is criticized for encouraging Burma's government to believe that its policies are succeeding and to discourage efforts at reform and dialogue with the democratic opposition. Observers note that the truly "constructive" aspects of the approach are difficult to discern and require better explication.

No one seems to deny the complexity of the situation in Burma and the role of foreign investment in the country. As one ASEAN diplomat says: "We agree all is not well in Burma. The question is how do you bring about change" (Ching 1996: 36).

## ALTERNATIVE TERMS OF GLOBAL BUSINESS ENGAGEMENT: A FRAMEWORK

When businesses cross national and cultural boundaries their commercial agendas become associated with others of social consequence. Those who argue against or for foreign investment in Burma are expressing value judgments—in terms of what they believe is right for the country, and action preferences—in terms of what they believe should be done about it. Table 2 builds from the sanctions and constructive engagement debate to more broadly describe four alternative terms of global business engagement that can be identified with respect to Burma and that are likely to apply in other ethically challenging environments. The framework is designed to benefit interested researchers and policy makers alike. It recognizes two forms of "engagement"—unrestricted and constructive—and two forms of "non-engagement"—principled and sanctioned. The foundations for each action alternative are further identified with implied

**TABLE 2** Contrasting Terms of Global Business Engagement in Ethically Challenging Environments

| Terms of Engagement | Ethical Framework | Social Change Strategy | Cultural Orientation |
|---|---|---|---|
| Unrestricted engagement<br>——<br>*Business as usual* | Individualism view<br>——<br>*Follow self-interests* | Natural selection<br>——<br>*Survival of the fittest* | Cultural relativism<br>——<br>*Anything goes* |
| Constructive engagement<br>——<br>*Purpose-driven investment* | Utilitarianism view<br>——<br>*Seek broad positive impact* | Shared power<br>——<br>*Change takes time, comes from within* | Cultural tolerance<br>——<br>*With dialogue comes understanding* |
| Principled non-engagement<br>——<br>*Value-driven business disinvestment or refusal to invest* | Virtues view<br>——<br>*Act consistent with organizational values* | Rational persuasion<br>——<br>*Good reasons to change exist* | Cultural rejection<br>——<br>*New directions can be pursued* |
| Sanctioned non-engagement<br>——<br>*Business investment prohibited* | Rights view<br>——<br>*Support declared universal values* | Force-coercion<br>——<br>*Failure to change will be penalized* | Cultural absolutism<br>——<br>*What is wrong must be corrected* |

ethical positions, social change strategies, and cultural orientations. Likely outcomes of economic and/or social progress in the host country are also assessed.

## Unrestricted Engagement

Unrestricted engagement by foreign investors is described in Table 2 as business-as-usual behavior. The underlying ethical framework is individualism, with businesses doing what is best for their economic self-interests. The implied social change strategy is one of natural selection. The investor's commitment is to economic gain in the local business environment; it is not guided by corporate goals for specific economic and/or social contributions to the host country. The cultural orientation is relativism, showing a willingness to accept and abide by local practices in business conduct.

The likely outcome of unrestricted business engagement in ethically challenging environments is limited, perhaps highly segmented, economic contributions to the host country. In Burma, the government and its close associates seem to be the primary beneficiaries of economic gains from foreign investments in hotels and other tourism projects. Direct contributions to social progress, if any, probably trace more to natural "spill-over" effects than the investors' corporate intentions.

It is tempting to attribute unrestricted engagement to explicit choices made by foreign investors in the context of firm-specific values and self-interests. But in at least some and perhaps many cases, it may well emerge as a practice toward which business inevitably drifts when strong moral leadership or external regulatory guidance is otherwise lacking. Too many corporate leaders expect governments to set moral directions for them. Consider this statement by the president of Columbia Sportswear: "we rely on the U.S. government to be the moral equivalent of a watchdog" (AFL-CIO 1996: 3). The inherent risk of such reasoning is learned helplessness to make self-regulating business decisions. With learned helplessness, unrestricted engagement may become a point of natural tendency toward which foreign investors move.

### Constructive Engagement

The second form of engagement, constructive engagement, is described in Table 2 as purpose-driven behavior in which economic contributions by the foreign investor also advance social progress in the host country. The assumption is that with economic development will come desirable social development. The ethical foundations of constructive engagement are utilitarian, seeking at any given time the greatest good for the greatest number of people. The implied social change strategy is shared power, with dialogue between investors and hosts creating a basis for the latter to examine and perhaps reconstruct core values. The underlying cultural orientation shows tolerance for cultural differences.

The expected outcomes of constructive engagement are deliberate, perhaps slow, social progress along with increasingly universal economic progress. Although the concept is clear, the practice is hard to document. In Burma, Total and Unocal seem to consider and would like others to view their Yadana investment as constructive engagement. Criticisms of its local impact, however, make this distinction controversial at the very least. Any link between constructive engagement as an ASEAN policy and actual behavior by Asian investors is also hard to document. U Thein Tun, a Burmese businessman aligned with the government knows this only too well. "Pressure may work with investors from America and the EU," he says, "but I don't see this kind of problem in countries like Japan, Korea, Singapore, Hong Kong, and Thailand" (Fairclough 1996).

Businesses may operate under the self-perceived guise of constructive engagement even as they employ or drift toward the unrestricted practices described earlier. In the absence of clear elucidation of just what makes a business investment "constructive," furthermore, even firms that try to behave in this manner can be criticized by others as actually following business-as-usual practices.

### Principled Non-Engagement

The first of the non-engagement approaches to ethically challenging environments is described in Table 2 as principled non-engagement. The forces driving this alternative are internal to the firm. They originate in leadership and corporate values, and are manifested in specific decisions either to not invest or to discontinue investment. Principled non-engagement suggests a virtues approach to ethics where core values guide business behavior from one situation to the next. It involves a rational persuasion strategy of planned change, with the act of non-engagement serving notice to the potential host of both the benefits of change—gaining the investment, and the costs of not changing—continuing to lose its advantages. The underlying cultural orientation is rejection, communicating an unwillingness to work in or become involved in a country where the cultural values and standards are inconsistent with one's own.

The expected outcomes of principled non-engagement are no direct contribution to local economic progress and, at best, indirect or long-term contributions to social progress. Robert Haas's decision to discontinue Levi's activities in Burma are indicative of this approach. Specifically he said: "We will not source in countries where conditions, such as the human rights climate, would run counter to our values and have an adverse effect on our global brand image or damage our corporate reputation" (Haas 1994). As a result, Burma has been denied by Levi any economic advantages from doing business with the firm. Whether or not the country benefits socially from this decision remains an open question.

Principled non-engagement is anchored in leadership and organizational values and standards. It results from moral self-regulation that relies upon value-based decision making to deliver consistent outcomes as business investment opportunities are evaluated around the world. At Levi, foreign investment decisions are guided by the corporate "Code of Ethics" and a set of "Ethical Principles." The company has criteria for both country selection—including criteria of brand image, health and safety, human rights, legal requirements, and political or social stability, and business partner selection—including environmental requirements, ethical standards, health and safety, legal requirements, and employment standards.

### Sanctioned Non-Engagement

Table 2 describes sanctioned non-engagement as the prohibition of foreign investment in a given setting. The ethical foundations are universalist, with the sanctions standing for core values and basic human rights that are assumed to apply everywhere. The implied social change strategy is force-coercion, in which the loss of foreign investment becomes a penalty that is assessed in a direct attempt to change the target country's behavior. The underlying cultural orientation is absolutism, with the country expected to conform with outside ethical standards and expectations.

The forces driving sanctioned non-engagement originate external to the firm, with two distinct forms possible. *Sanctions by government regulation* are those that by law forbid business involvement in certain settings. For example, the United States Congress authorized the President to invoke sanctions to block new private investment by American firms in Burma. *Sanctions by market regulation* occur as pressures by activist lobbies and consumer groups threaten a firm doing business in a targeted country with loss of customers and sales. This power of the marketplace was mobilized against PepsiCo's involvements in Burma and certainly helped bring about the firm's eventual decision to withdraw.

Sanctioned non-engagement is expected to encourage social progress in the potential host country while, for the short term, denying any contribution to economic progress. Those who support sanctions by government or market regulation with Burma want to deny the SPDC government all opportunities for economic progress in the absence of social progress. But the impact of sanctions is limited when government-legislated boycotts lack universal appeal and activist and consumer pressures remain largely firm-specific. In the absence of internal forces to the contrary, furthermore, weaknesses in sanctions as an external form of business regulation encourage business-as-usual tendencies. Burma, as one case in point, continues to host and attract foreign investors.

## CONSIDERATIONS AND RESEARCH DIRECTIONS

The many ethical challenges already posed by global cultural diversity are likely to grow in number and significance with our passage into the 21st century. The alternative terms of global business engagement described in Table 2 introduce a number of questions worthy of consideration by scholars, corporate executives, and government policy makers. Although not an exhaustive listing, the following suggestions and research directions deserve attention.

### Constructive Engagement

Among the four alternatives in Table 2, constructive engagement is most difficult to pinpoint in actual practice. We need answers to the question: What exactly is *constructive* engagement? The concept needs clarification both as used diplomatically in respect to government policies, and as implemented practically in respect to business behaviors. Criteria must be developed to define when and under what conditions a business can justifiably claim that its behavior in a given setting is "constructive." Once the criteria exist, they can and should be used in social audits of global business performance. Such audits, if taken, have the potential to increase the accountability of global firms for their activities in ethically challenging settings.

The clarification of constructive engagement might be pursued through Donaldson's (1996) notion of core or threshold values, and Donaldson and Dunfee's (1994) concepts of macro-and micro-social contracts. At the level of the macro-social contract, agreement on core values or "hyper-norms" would set threshold standards on matters relating to human dignity, basic rights, and good citizenship. Within this trans-cultural umbrella, micro-social contracts could then be tailored to fit specific local and regional cultural contexts. Such coexistence of macro-social and micro-social contracts is described in Donaldson and Dunfee's (1994) use of Integrated Systems Theory. What remains to be seen is how this concept can be made operational to guide business behavior in ethically challenging settings such as Burma.

Efforts to develop transnational business guidelines by the United Nations, Caux Round Table, and other global social responsibility forums are important in the macro-social context. Further research and development on their behalf should continue, with the suggestions in Table 3 perhaps added to the mix of possibilities as applied to Burma. However, any "outside-in" or "top-down" approaches to social contracting will have the tendency to stall in exerting positive influence at the level of action. At this micro-social level, the contributions of local and regional forums are also necessary. They can bring to the contracting process the "inside-out" or "bottom-up" perspectives of the local culture, or at least the culture of a neighborhood. Questions must be asked and answered in regard to how local and regional social responsibility forums can be engaged to set local standards for constructive

**TABLE 3** Possible Common Ethical Ground for Business Investments in Burma

- Management control over all aspects of local operations, including labor practices, conditions of employment and subcontracting.
- Management commitment to inviolable respect for human dignity, basic rights, and good citizenship in all aspects of local operations.
- Management control over local use of the corporate identity and brand names, including government-sponsored public relations and advertising.
- Management commitment to make and control revenue set-asides to improve conditions of life for local employees and the broader citizenry, including housing, public services, education and health care.
- Management confidence in basic rights of local citizens to personal safety, freedom of movement, political participation and economic advancement.
- Management commitment to annual and objective external audits of all aspects of local operations, and to the public release of audit results.

engagement, serve as exemplars and models, and through peer pressure ensure that other investors live up to shared expectations.

The opportunity exists to test this notion in Burma. The country obviously needs business partners, and Asian ones in particular. It is possible for Burma's neighbors to make those partnerships hard to get and expensive—not in monetary terms, but in required contributions to demonstrable social and economic progress. Ideally, Southeast Asia's respected business leaders would take the initiative in setting standards for constructive engagement and providing a model for other investors to follow when dealing with their neighbor. The goal would be noble—to commit their names and corporate reputations to a statement of principles that would guide foreign investments in Burma toward truly constructive outcomes. Precedent for such a step is found in the Sullivan Principles, which provided business guidelines for dealing with apartheid South Africa.

### Moral Business Leadership

The forces of global capitalism place unique demands on business leadership. The intensity of economic competition today adds to the risk that the rule of relativism and the practice of unrestricted engagement will become default positions for too much international business conduct. This likelihood is accentuated when corporate executives, by intention or driven by learned helplessness, allow and expect governments or activist groups to make ethical decisions for them. The Burma case demonstrates limits to the effectuality of external business regulation through government-led sanctions and boycotts, and to the narrow influence of activist lobbies and consumer boycotts.

Rather than be the followers in ethical decision making, global business executives should be the leaders. Faced with a decision regarding Levi's involvement in Burma, Robert Haas met his leadership responsibility by declaring values and refusing to do business with a government that didn't meet standards. We need to examine how leadership roles shape the internal regulation of international business behavior. We need to identify the world's moral business leaders. And, we need to know why we don't have more of them.

It isn't only the individual leader who deserves attention. Peer leadership and peer group support in the executive community are important too. American corporate executives, for example, appear quite willing to join in efforts to lobby the U.S. government for favorable international trade practices and policies. Why aren't they more willing to lobby one another about ethical standards and actively work together to maintain these standards in international business conduct? The world would benefit greatly if global business executives would form together in vast peer networks committed to ethical practices. . . .

## CONCLUSION

The ethics of business operations cannot hide in foreign environments any more than they can hide at home. Tolerance is increasingly scarce for those who use ethical relativism to justify questionable behavior in any cultural milieu. But diversity in our global economy is also rendering the rule of absolutism simplistic and unrealistic as a guide to business behavior. Ultimate responsibility for ethical conduct in global business affairs rests with corporate leadership. The case of Burma reminds us that governments and international bodies have difficulty making rules for everyone to follow. It reminds us that the impact of activist lobbies varies from one corporation and situation to the next. Importantly, it reminds us that, in the meantime, a lot of business-as-usual is taking place.

There is much work yet to be done before acceptable terms of global business engagement in ethically challenging settings can be agreed upon. While the search progresses, executives would do well to reconsider the broad imperatives of moral business leadership. They might start from the perspective of a basic rule of public responsibility identified years ago by Peter Drucker—*Primum non nocer*, "not knowingly do harm" (1973: 369, 375). Although modest in concept, the rule offers the great opportunity of self-constraint. . . .

## BIBLIOGRAPHY

AFL-CIO. 1996. Statement of the American Federation of Labor Congress of Industrial Organizations to the Senate Committee on Banking, Housing, and Urban Affairs, May 22 1996.

Baker, Mark. 1996. "Burma Bans Unworkable, Says Fischer." Internet posting, South-East Asia Correspondent, Bangkok. November 3.

Ching, Frank. 1996. "Burma Wants to End its Isolation." *Far Eastern Economic Review.* August 15: 36.

Donaldson, Thomas. 1996. "Values in Tension: Ethics Away from Home." *Harvard Business Review*, 74 (September–October): 48–62.

Donaldson, Thomas and Dunfee, Thomas W. 1994. "Towards a Unified Conception of Business Ethics: Integrative Social Contracts Theory." *Academy of Management Review*, 19 (2), 252–285.

Drucker, P. F. 1973. *Management: Tasks, Responsibilities, Practices.* New York: Harper and Row.

Fairclough, Gordon. 1996. "Enter at Own Risk." *Far Eastern Economic Review.* August 15: 62–66.

Haas, Robert D. 1994. "Ethics—A Global Business Challenge." *Vital Speeches of the Day.* June 1: 506–509.

Jayasankaran, S. 1996. "Seeing Red: Lobby Groups Protest Over Burmese Visit." *Far Eastern Economic Review.* August 29: 18.

Reuters. 1998. "Albright: New Zealand joins U.S. in pressing Myanmar on Suu Kyi." *CNN Interactive CNN.com*, August 1.

Suu Kyi, 1991. "In quest of democracy." In *Freedom From Fear and Other Writings: Aung San Suu Kyi*, ed. M. Aris, pp. 167–79. London: Penguin Books.

*The Nation.* 1997. "SLORC Replaced with New Body." November 16.

Tutu, Desmond. 1993. "Burma as South Africa." *Far Eastern Economic Review.* September 16: 23.

# The Great Non-Debate Over International Sweatshops

*Ian Maitland*

In recent years, there has been a dramatic growth in the contracting out of production by companies in the industrialized countries to suppliers in developing countries. This globalization of production has led to an emerging international division of labor in footwear and apparel in which companies like Nike and Reebok concentrate on product design and marketing but rely on a network of contractors in Indonesia, China, Central America, etc., to build shoes or sew shirts according to exact specifications and deliver a high quality good according to precise delivery schedules. As Nike's vice president for Asia has put it, "We don't know the first thing about manufacturing. We are marketers and designers."

The contracting arrangements have drawn intense fire from critics—usually labor and human rights activists. These "critics" (as I will refer to them) have charged that the companies are (by proxy) exploiting workers in the plants (which I will call "international sweatshops") of

From Ian Maitland, "The Great Non-Debate Over International Sweatshops," *British Academy of Management Annual Conference Proceedings*, September, pp. 240–265, 1997. Reprinted with permission of the author.

their suppliers. Specifically the companies stand accused of chasing cheap labor around the globe, failing to pay their workers living wages, using child labor, turning a blind eye to abuses of human rights, being complicit with repressive regimes in denying workers the right to join unions and failing to enforce minimum labor standards in the workplace, and so on.

The campaign against international sweatshops has largely unfolded on television and, to a lesser extent, in the print media. What seems like no more than a handful of critics has mounted an aggressive, media-savvy campaign which has put the publicity-shy retail giants on the defensive. The critics have orchestrated a series of sensational "disclosures" on prime time television exposing the terrible pay and working conditions in factories making jeans for Levi's or sneakers for Nike or Pocahontas shirts for Disney. One of the principal scourges of the companies has been Charles Kernaghan who runs the National Labor Coalition (NLC), a labor human rights group involving 25 unions. It was Kernaghan who, in 1996, broke the news before a Congressional committee that Kathie Lee Gifford's clothing line was being made by 13-and 14-year-olds working 20-hour days in factories in Honduras. Kernaghan also arranged for teenage workers from sweatshops in Central America to testify before Congressional committees about abusive labor practices. At one of these hearings, one of the workers held up a Liz Claiborne cotton sweater identical to ones she had sewn since she was a 13-year-old working 12 hours days. According to a news report, "[t]his image, accusations of oppressive conditions at the factory and the Claiborne logo played well on that evening's network news." The result has been a circus-like atmosphere—as in Roman circus where Christians were thrown to lions.

Kernaghan has shrewdly targeted the companies' carefully cultivated public images. He has explained: "Their image is everything. They live and die by their image. That gives you a certain power over them." As a result, he says, "these companies are sitting ducks. They have no leg to stand on. That's why it's possible for a tiny group like us to take on a giant like Wal-Mart. You can't defend paying someone 31 cents an hour in Honduras. . . ."[1] Apparently most of the companies agree with Kernaghan. Not a single company has tried to mount a serious defense of its contracting practices. They have judged that they cannot win a war of soundbites with the critics. Instead of making a fight of it, the companies have sued for peace in order to protect their principal asset—their image.

Major U.S. retailers have responded by adopting codes of conduct on human and labor rights in their international operations. Levi-Strauss, Nike, Sears, J.C.Penney, Wal-Mart, Home Depot, and Philips Van-Heusen now have such codes. As Lance Compa notes, such codes are the result of a blend of humanitarian and pragmatic impulses: "Often the altruistic motive coincides with 'bottom line' considerations related to brand name, company image, and other intangibles that make for core value to the firm."[2] Peter Jacobi, President of Global Sourcing for Levi-Strauss has advised: "If your company owns a popular brand, protect this priceless asset at all costs. Highly visible companies have any number of reasons to conduct their business not just responsibly but also in ways that cannot be portrayed as unfair, illegal, or unethical. This sets an extremely high standard since it must be applied to both company-owned businesses and contractors. . . ."[3] And according to another Levi-Strauss spokesman, "In many respects, we're protecting our single largest asset: our brand image and corporate reputation."[4] Nike recently published the results of a generally favorable review of its international operations conducted by former American U.N. Ambassador Andrew Young.

Recently a truce of sorts between the critics and the companies was announced on the White House lawn with President Clinton and Kathie Lee Gifford in attendance. A presidential task force, including representatives of labor unions, human rights groups and apparel companies like L.L. Bean and Nike, has come up with a set of voluntary standards which, it hopes, will be embraced by the entire industry. Companies that comply with the code will be entitled to use a "No Sweat" label.

## OBJECTIVE OF THIS PAPER

In this confrontation between the companies and their critics, neither side seems to have judged it to be in its interest to seriously engage the issue at the heart of this controversy, namely: What are appropriate wages and labor standards in international sweatshops? As we have seen, the companies have treated the charges about sweatshops as a public relations problem to be managed so as to minimize harm to their public images. The critics have apparently judged that the best way to keep public indignation at boiling point is to oversimplify the issue and treat it as a morality play featuring heartless exploiters and victimized third world workers. The result has been a great non-debate over international sweatshops. Paradoxically, if peace breaks out between the two sides, the chances that the debate will be seriously joined may recede still further. Indeed, there exists a real risk (I will argue) that any such truce may be a collusive one that will come at the expense of the very third world workers it is supposed to help.

This paper takes up the issue of what are appropriate wages and labor standards in international sweatshops. Critics charge that the present arrangements are exploitative. I proceed by examining the specific charges of exploitation from the standpoints of both (a) their factual and (b) their ethical sufficiency. However, in the absence of any well-established consensus among business ethicists (or other thoughtful observers), I simultaneously use the investigation of sweatshops as a setting for trying to adjudicate between competing views about what those standards should be. My examination will pay particular attention to (but will not be limited to) labor conditions at the plants of Nike's suppliers in Indonesia. I have not personally visited any international sweatshops, and so my conclusions are based entirely on secondary analysis of the voluminous published record on the topic.

## WHAT ARE ETHICALLY APPROPRIATE LABOR STANDARDS IN INTERNATIONAL SWEATSHOPS?

What are ethically acceptable or appropriate levels of wages and labor standards in international sweatshops? The following three possibilities just about run the gamut of standards or principles that have been seriously proposed to regulate such policies.

1. *Home-country standards:* It might be argued (and in rare cases has been) that international corporations have an ethical duty to pay the same wages and provide the same labor standards regardless of where they operate. However, the view that home-country standards should apply in host-countries is rejected by most business ethicists and (officially at least) by the critics of international sweatshops. Thus Thomas Donaldson argues that "[b]y arbitrarily establishing U.S. wage levels as the benchmark for fairness one eliminates the role of the international market in establishing salary levels, and this in turn eliminates the incentive U.S. corporations have to hire foreign workers."[5] Richard DeGeorge makes much the same argument: If there were a rule that said that "that American MNCs [multinational corporations] that wish to be ethical must pay the same wages abroad as they do at home, . . . [then] MNCs would have little incentive to move their manufacturing abroad; and if they did move abroad they would disrupt the local labor market with artificially high wages that bore no relation to the local standard or cost of living."[6]
2. *"Living wage" standard:* It has been proposed that an international corporation should, at a minimum, pay a "living wage." Thus DeGeorge says that corporations should pay a living wage "even when this is not paid by local firms."[7] However, it is hard to pin down what this means operationally. According to DeGeorge, a living

wage should "allow the worker to live in dignity as a human being." In order to respect the human rights of its workers, he says, a corporation must pay "at least subsistence wages and as much above that as workers and their dependents need to live with reasonable dignity, given the general state of development of the society."[8] As we shall see, the living wage standard has become a rallying cry of the critics of international sweatshops. Apparently, DeGeorge believes that it is preferable for a corporation to provide no job at all than to offer one that pays less than a living wage. . . .

3. *Classical liberal standard:* Finally, there is what I will call the classical liberal standard. According to this standard a practice (wage or labor practice) is ethically acceptable if it is freely chosen by informed workers. For example, in a recent report the World Bank invoked this standard in connection with workplace safety. It said: "The appropriate level is therefore that at which the costs are commensurate with the value that informed workers place on improved working conditions and reduced risk."[9] Most business ethicists reject this standard on the grounds that there is some sort of market failure or the "background conditions" are lacking for markets to work effectively. Thus for Donaldson full (or near-full) employment is a prerequisite if workers are to make sound choices regarding workplace safety: "The average level of unemployment in the developing countries today exceeds 40 percent, a figure that has frustrated the application of neoclassical economic principles to the international economy on a score of issues. With full employment, and all other things being equal, market forces will encourage workers to make trade-offs between job opportunities using safety as a variable. But with massive unemployment, market forces in developing countries drive the unemployed to the jobs they are lucky enough to land, regardless of the safety."[10] Apparently there are other forces, like Islamic fundamentalism and the global debt "bomb," that rule out reliance on market solutions, but Donaldson does not explain their relevance.[11] DeGeorge, too, believes that the necessary conditions are lacking for market forces to operate benignly. Without what he calls "background institutions" to protect the workers and the resources of the developing country (e.g., enforceable minimum wages) and/or greater equality of bargaining power exploitation is the most likely result.[12] "If American MNCs pay workers very low wages . . . they clearly have the opportunity to make significant profits."[13] DeGeorge goes on to make the interesting observation that "competition has developed among multinationals themselves, so that the profit margin has been driven down" and developing countries "can play one company against another."[14] But apparently that is not enough to rehabilitate market forces in his eyes.

## THE CASE AGAINST INTERNATIONAL SWEATSHOPS

To many of their critics, international sweatshops exemplify the way in which the greater openness of the world economy is hurting workers. . . . Globalization means a transition from (more or less) regulated domestic economies to an unregulated world economy. The superior mobility of capital, and the essentially fixed, immobile nature of world labor, means a fundamental shift in bargaining power in favor of large international corporations. Their global reach permits them to shift production almost costlessly from one location to another. As a consequence, instead of being able to exercise some degree of control over companies operating within their borders, governments are now locked in a bidding war with one another to attract and retain the business of large multinational companies.

The critics allege that international companies are using the threat of withdrawal or withholding of investment to pressure governments and workers to grant concessions. "Today [multinational companies] choose between workers in developing countries that compete against each other to depress wages to attract foreign investment." The result is a race for the bottom — a "destructive down-ward bidding spiral of the labor conditions and wages of workers throughout the world. . . . "[15] . . . Thus, critics charge that in Indonesia wages are deliberately held below the poverty level or subsistence in order to make the country a desirable location. The results of this competitive dismantling of worker protections, living standards and worker rights are predictable: deteriorating work conditions, declining real incomes for workers, and a widening gap between rich and poor in developing countries. I turn next to the specific charges made by the critics of international sweatshops.

### Unconscionable Wages

Critics charge that the companies, by their proxies, are paying "starvation wages" and "slave wages." They are far from clear about what wage level they consider to be appropriate. But they generally demand that companies pay a "living wage." Kernaghan has said that workers should be paid enough to support their families and they should get a "living wage" and "be treated like human beings."[16] . . . According to Tim Smith, wage levels should be "fair, decent or a living wage for an employee and his or her family." He has said that wages in the maquiladoras of Mexico averaged $35 to $55 a week (in or near 1993) which he calls a "shockingly substandard wage," apparently on the grounds that it "clearly does not allow an employee to feed and care for a family adequately."[17] In 1992, Nike came in for harsh criticism when a magazine published the pay stub of a worker at one of its Indonesian suppliers. It showed that the worker was paid at the rate of $1.03 per day which was reportedly less than the Indonesian government's figure for "minimum physical need."[18]

### Immiserization Thesis

Former Labor Secretary Robert Reich has proposed as a test of the fairness of development policies that "Low-wage workers should become better off, not worse off, as trade and investment boost national income." He has written that "[i]f a country pursues policies that . . . limit to a narrow elite the benefits of trade, the promise of open commerce is perverted and drained of its rationale."[19] A key claim of the activists is that companies actually impoverish or immiserize developing country workers. They experience an absolute decline in living standards. This thesis follows from the claim that the bidding war among developing countries is depressing wages. . . .

### Widening Gap Between Rich and Poor

A related charge is that international sweatshops are contributing to the increasing gap between rich and poor. Not only are the poor being absolutely impoverished, but trade is generating greater inequality within developing countries. Another test that Reich has proposed to establish the fairness of international trade is that "the gap between rich and poor should tend to narrow with development, not widen."[20] Critics charge that international sweatshops flunk that test. They say that the increasing GNPs of some developing countries simply mask a widening gap between rich and poor. "Across the world, both local and foreign elites are getting richer from the exploitation of the most vulnerable."[21] And, "The major adverse consequence of quickening global economic integration has been widening income disparity within almost all nations. . . ."[22] There appears to be a tacit alliance between the elites of both first and third worlds to exploit the most vulnerable, to regiment and control and conscript them so that they can create the material conditions for the elites' extravagant lifestyles.

### Collusion with Repressive Regimes

Critics charge that, in their zeal to make their countries safe for foreign investment, Third World regimes, notably China and Indonesia, have stepped up their repression. Not only have these countries failed to enforce even the minimal labor rules on the books, but they have also used their military and police to break strikes and repress independent unions. They have stifled political dissent, both to retain their hold on political power and to avoid any instability that might scare off foreign investors. Consequently, critics charge, companies like Nike are profiting from political repression. "As unions spread in [Korea and Taiwan], Nike shifted its suppliers primarily to Indonesia, China and Thailand, where they could depend on governments to suppress independent union-organizing efforts."[23]

## EVALUATION OF THE CHARGES AGAINST INTERNATIONAL SWEATSHOPS

The critics' charges are undoubtedly accurate on a number of points: (1) There is no doubt that international companies are chasing cheap labor. (2) The wages paid by the international sweatshops are—by American standards—shockingly low. (3) Some developing country governments have tightly controlled or repressed organized labor in order to prevent it from disturbing the flow of foreign investment. Thus, in Indonesia, independent unions have been suppressed. (4) It is not unusual in developing countries for minimum wage levels to be lower than the official poverty level. (5) Developing country governments have winked at violations of minimum wage laws and labor rules. However, most jobs are in the informal sector and so largely outside the scope of government supervision. (6) Some suppliers have employed children or have subcontracted work to other producers who have done so. (7) Some developing country governments deny their people basic political rights. China is the obvious example; Indonesia's record is pretty horrible but had shown steady improvement until the last two years. But on many of the other counts, the critics' charges appear to be seriously inaccurate. And, even where the charges are accurate, it is not selfevident that the practices in question are improper or unethical, as we see next.

### Wages and Conditions

Even the critics of international sweatshops do not dispute that the wages they pay are generally higher than—or at least equal to—comparable wages in the labor markets where they operate. According to the International Labor Organization (ILO), multinational companies often apply standards relating to wages, benefits, conditions of work, and occupational safety and health, which both exceed statutory requirements and those practiced by local firms."[24] The ILO also says that wages and working conditions in so-called Export Processing Zones (EPZs) are often equal to or higher than jobs outside. The World Bank says that the poorest workers in developing countries work in the informal sector where they often earn less than half what a formal sector employee earns. Moreover, "informal and rural workers often must work under more hazardous and insecure conditions than their formal sector counterparts.[25]

The same appears to hold true for the international sweatshops. In 1996, young women working in the plant of a Nike supplier in Serang, Indonesia were earning the Indonesian legal minimum wage of 5,200 rupiahs or about $2.28 each day. As a report in the *Washington Post* pointed out, just earning the minimum wage put these workers among higher-paid Indonesians: "In Indonesia, less than half the working population earns the minimum wage, since about half of all adults here are in farming, and the typical farmer would make only about 2,000 rupiahs each day."[26] The workers in the Serang plant reported that they save about three-quarters of their pay. A 17-year-old woman said: "I came here one year ago from central Java. I'm making more money than my father makes." This woman also said that the she sent about 75 percent of her earnings back to her family on the farm.[27] Also in 1996, a Nike spokeswoman estimated that an entry-level factory workers in the plant of a Nike supplier made five times what a farmer makes.[28] Nike's chairman, Phil Knight, likes to teasingly remind critics that the average worker in one of Nike's Chinese factories is paid more than a professor at Beijing University.[29] There is also plentiful anecdotal evidence from non-Nike sources. A worker at the Taiwanese-owned King Star Garment Assembly plant in Honduras told a reporter that he was earning seven times what he earned in the countryside.[30] In Bangladesh, the country's fledgling garment industry was paying women who had never worked before between $40 and $55 a month in 1991. That compared with a national per capita income of about $200 and the approximately $1 a day earned by many of these women's husbands as day laborers or rickshaw drivers.[31]

The same news reports also shed some light on the working conditions in sweatshops. According to the *Washington Post*, in 1994 the Indonesian office of the international accounting firm Ernst & Young surveyed Nike workers concerning worker pay, safety conditions and attitudes toward the job. The auditors pulled workers off the assembly line at random and asked them questions that the workers answered anonymously. The survey of 25 workers at Nike's Serang plant found that 23 thought the hours and overtime hours too high. None of the workers reported that they had been discriminated against. Thirteen said the working environment was the key reason they worked at the Serang plant while eight cited salary and benefits.[32] The *Post* report also noted that the Serang plant closes for about ten days each year for Muslim holidays. It quoted Nike officials and the plant's Taiwanese owners as saying that 94 percent of the workers had returned to the plant following the most recent break. . . .

There is also the mute testimony of the lines of job applicants outside the sweatshops in Guatemala and Honduras. According to Lucy Martinez-Mont, in Guatemala the sweatshops are conspicuous for the long lines of young people waiting to be interviewed for a job.[33] Outside the gates of the industrial park in Honduras that Rohter visited "anxious on-lookers are always waiting, hoping for a chance at least to fill out a job application [for employment at one of the apparel plants]."[34]

The critics of sweatshops acknowledge that workers have voluntarily taken their jobs, consider themselves lucky to have them, and want to keep them. . . . But they go on to discount the workers' views as the product of confusion or ignorance, and/or they just argue that the workers' views are beside the point. Thus, while "it is undoubtedly true" that Nike has given jobs to thousands of people who wouldn't be working otherwise, they say that "neatly skirts the fundamental human-rights issue raised by these production arrangements that are now spreading all across the world."[35] Similarly the NLC's Kernaghan says that "[w]hether workers think they are better off in the assembly plants than elsewhere is not the real issue."[36] Kernaghan, and Jeff Ballinger of the AFL-CIO, concede that the workers desperately need these jobs. But "[t]hey say they're not asking that U.S. companies stop operating in these countries. They're asking that workers be paid a living wage and treated like human beings."[37] Apparently these workers are victims of what Marx called false consciousness, or else they would grasp that they are being exploited. According to Barnet and Cavanagh, "For many workers . . . exploitation is not a concept easily comprehended because the alternative prospects for earning a living are so bleak."[38]

### Immiserization and Inequality

The critics' claim that the countries that host international sweatshops are marked by growing poverty and inequality is flatly contradicted by the record. In fact, many of those countries have experienced sharp increases in living standards—for all strata of society. In trying to attract investment in simple manufacturing, Malaysia and Indonesia and, now, Vietnam and China, are retracing the industrialization path already successfully taken by East Asian countries like Taiwan, Korea, Singapore and Hong Kong. These four countries got their start by producing labor-intensive manufactured goods (often electrical and electronic components, shoes, and garments) for export markets. Over time they graduated to the export of higher value-added items that are skill-intensive and require a relatively developed industrial base.[39]

As is well known, these East Asian countries achieved growth rates exceeding eight percent for a quarter century. . . . The workers in these economies were not impoverished by growth. The benefits of growth were widely diffused: These economies achieved essentially full employment in the 1960s. Real wages rose by as much as a factor of four. Absolute poverty fell. And income inequality remained at low to moderate levels. It is true that in the initial stages the rapid growth generated only moderate increases in wages. But once essentially full employment was reached, and what economists call the Fei-Ranis turning point was reached, the increased demand for labor resulted in the bidding up of wages as firms competed for a scarce labor supply.

Interestingly, given its historic mission as a watchdog for international labor standards, the ILO has embraced this development model. It recently noted that the most successful developing economies, in terms of output and employment growth, have been "those who best exploited emerging opportunities in the global economy."[40] An "export oriented policy is vital in countries that are starting on the industrialization path and have large surpluses of cheap labour." Countries which have succeeded in attracting foreign direct investment (FDI) have experienced rapid growth in manufacturing output and exports. The successful attraction of foreign investment in plant and equipment "can be a powerful spur to rapid industrialization and employment creation." "At low levels of industrialization, FDI in garments and shoes and some types of consumer electronics can be very useful for creating employment and opening the economy to international markets; there may be some entrepreneurial skills created in simple activities like garments (as has happened in Bangladesh). Moreover, in some cases, such as Malaysia, the investors may strike deeper roots and invest in more capital-intensive technologies as wages rise."

According to the World Bank, the rapidly growing Asian economies (including Indonesia) "have also been unusually successful at sharing the fruits of their growth."[41] In fact, while inequality in the West has been growing, it has been shrinking in the Asian economies. They are the only economies in the world to have experienced high growth *and* declining inequality, and they also show shrinking gender gaps in education. . . .

### Profiting from Repression?

What about the charge that international sweatshops are profiting from repression? It is undeniable that there is repression in many of the countries where sweatshops are located. But economic development appears to be relaxing that repression rather than strengthening its grip. The companies are supposed to benefit from government policies (e.g., repression of unions) that hold down labor costs.

However, as we have seen, the wages paid by the international sweatshops already match or exceed the prevailing local wages. Not only that, but incomes in the East Asian economies, and in Indonesia, have risen rapidly. . . .

The critics, however, are right in saying that the Indonesian government has opposed independent unions in the sweatshops out of fear they would lead to higher wages and labor unrest. But the government's fear clearly is that unions might drive wages in the modern industrial sector *above* market-clearing levels— or, more exactly, further above market. It is ironic that critics like Barnet and Cavanagh would use the Marxian term "reserve army of the unemployed." According to Marx, capitalists deliberately maintain high levels of unemployment in order to control the working class. But the Indonesian government's policies (e.g., suppression of unions, resistance to a higher minimum wage and lax enforcement of labor rules) have been directed at achieving exactly the opposite result. The government appears to have calculated that high unemployment is a greater threat to its hold on power. I think we can safely take at face value its claims that its policies are genuinely intended to help the economy create jobs to absorb the massive numbers of unemployed and underemployed.[42]

## LABOR STANDARDS IN INTERNATIONAL SWEATSHOPS: PAINFUL TRADE-OFFS

Who but the grinch could grudge paying a few additional pennies to some of the world's poorest workers? There is no doubt that the rhetorical force of the critics' case against international sweatshops rests on this apparently self-evident proposition. However, higher wages and improved labor standards are not free. After all, the critics themselves attack companies for chasing cheap labor. It follows that, if labor in developing countries is made more expensive (say, as the result of pressures by the critics), then those countries will receive less foreign investment, and fewer jobs will be created there. Imposing higher wages may deprive these countries of the one comparative advantage they enjoy, namely low-cost labor.

We have seen that workers in most "international sweatshops" are already relatively well paid. Workers in the urban, formal sectors of developing countries commonly earn more than twice what informal and rural workers get. Simply earning the minimum wage put the young women making Nike shoes in Serang in the top half of the income distribution in Indonesia. Accordingly, the critics are in effect calling for a *widening* of the economic disparity that already greatly favors sweatshop workers.

By itself that may or may not be ethically objectionable. But these higher wages come at the expense of the incomes and the job opportunities of much poorer workers. As economists explain, higher wages in the formal sector reduce employment there and (by increasing the supply of labor) depress incomes in the informal sector. The case against requiring above-market wages for international sweatshop workers is essentially the same as the case against other measures that artificially raise labor costs, like the minimum wage. In Jagdish Bhagwati's words: "Requiring a minimum wage in an overpopulated, developing country, as is done in a developed country, may actually be morally wicked. A minimum wage might help the unionized, industrial proletariat, while limiting the ability to save and invest rapidly which is necessary to draw more of the unemployed and nonunionized rural poor into gainful employment and income."[43] The World Bank makes the same point: "Minimum wages may help the most poverty-stricken workers in industrial countries, but they clearly do not in developing nations. . . . The workers whom minimum wage legislation tries to protect—urban formal workers—already earn much more than the less favored majority. . . . And inasmuch as minimum wage and other regulations discourage formal employment by increasing wage and nonwage costs, they hurt the poor who aspire to formal employment."[44]

The story is no different when it comes to labor standards other than wages. If standards are set too high they will hurt investment and employment.The World Bank report points out that "[r]educing hazards in the workplace is costly, and typically the greater the reduction the more it costs. Moreover, the costs of compliance often fall largely on employees through lower wages or reduced employment. As a result, setting standards too high can actually lower workers' welfare. . . ."[45] Perversely, if the higher standards advocated by critics retard the growth of formal sector jobs, then that will trap more informal and rural workers in jobs which are far more hazardous and insecure than those of their formal sector counterparts.

The critics consistently advocate policies that will benefit better-off workers at the expense of worse-off ones. If it were within their power, it appears that they would reinvent the labor markets of much of Latin America. Alejandro Portes' description seems to be on the mark: "In Mexico, Brazil, Peru, and other Third World countries, [unlike East Asia], there are powerful independent unions representing the protected sector of the working class. Although their rhetoric is populist and even radical, the fact is that they tend to represent the better-paid and more stable fraction of the working class. Alongside, there toils a vast, unprotected proletariat, employed by informal enterprises and linked, in ways hidden from public view, with modern sector firms." . . .

Of course, it might be objected that trading off workers' rights for more jobs is unethical. But, so far as I can determine, the critics have not made this argument. Although they sometimes implicitly accept the existence of the trade-off (we saw that they attack Nike for chasing cheap labor), their public statements are silent on the lost or forgone jobs from higher wages and better labor standards. At other times, they imply or claim that improvements in workers' wages and conditions are essentially free. . . .

In summary, the result of the ostensibly humanitarian changes urged by critics are likely to be (1) reduced employment in the formal or modern sector of the economy, (2) lower incomes in the informal sector, (3) less investment and so slower economic growth, (4) reduced exports, (5) greater inequality and poverty.

## CONCLUSION: THE CASE FOR NOT EXCEEDING MARKET STANDARDS

It is part of the job description of business ethicists to exhort companies to treat their workers better (otherwise what purpose do they serve?). So it will have come as no surprise that both the business ethicists whose views I summarized at the beginning of this paper—Thomas Donaldson and Richard DeGeorge—objected to letting the market alone determine wages and labor standards in multinational companies. Both of them proposed criteria for setting wages that might occasionally "improve" on the outcomes of the market.

Their reasons for rejecting market determination of wages were similar. They both cited conditions that allegedly prevent international markets from generating ethically acceptable results. Donaldson argued that neoclassical economic principles are not applicable to international business because of high unemployment rates in developing countries. And DeGeorge argued that, in an unregulated international market, the gross inequality of bargaining power between workers and companies would lead to exploitation.

But this paper has shown that attempts to improve on market outcomes may have unforeseen tragic consequences. We saw how raising the wages of workers in international sweatshops might wind up penalizing the most vulnerable workers (those in the informal sectors of developing countries) by depressing their wages and reducing their job opportunities in the formal sector. Donaldson and DeGeorge cited high unemployment and unequal bargaining power as conditions that made it necessary to bypass or override the market determination of wages. However, in both cases, bypassing the market in order to prevent exploitation may aggravate these conditions. As we have seen, above-market wages paid to sweatshop workers may discourage further investment and so perpetuate high unemployment. In turn, the higher unemployment may weaken the bargaining power of workers vis-à-vis employers. Thus such market imperfections seem to call for more reliance on market forces rather than less. Likewise, the experience of the newly industrialized East Asian economies suggests that the best cure for the ills of sweatshops is more sweatshops. But most of the well-intentioned policies that improve on market outcomes are likely to have the opposite effect.

Where does this leave the international manager? If the preceding analysis is correct, then it follows that it is ethically acceptable to pay market wage rates in developing countries (and to provide employment conditions appropriate for the level of development). That holds true even if the wages pay less than so-called living wages or subsistence or even (conceivably) the local minimum wage. The appropriate test is not whether the wage reaches some predetermined standard but whether it is freely accepted by (reasonably) informed workers. The workers themselves are in the best position to judge whether the wages offered are superior to their next-best alternatives. (The same logic applies *mutatis mutandis* to workplace labor standards).

Indeed, not only is it ethically acceptable for a company to pay market wages, but it may be ethically unacceptable for it to pay wages that exceed market levels. That will be the case if the company's above-market wages set precedents for other international companies which raise labor costs to the point of discouraging foreign investment. Furthermore, companies may have a social responsibility to transcend their own narrow preoccupation with protecting their brand image and to publicly defend a system which has greatly improved the lot of millions of workers in developing countries.

## NOTES

1. Steven Greenhouse, "A Crusader Makes Celebrities Tremble." *New York Times* (June 18, 1996), p. B4.
2. Lance A. Compa and Tashia Hinchliffe Darricarrere, "Enforcement Through Corporate Codes of Conduct," in Compa and Stephen F. Diamond, *Human Rights, Labor Rights, and International Trade* (Philadelphia: University of Pennsylvania Press, 1996) p. 193.
3. Peter Jacobi in Martha Nichols, "Third-World Families at Work: Child Labor or Child Care." *The Harvard Business Review* January–February 1993).
4. David Sampson in Robin G. Givhan, "A Stain on Fashion; The Garment Industry Profits from Cheap Labor." *Washington Post* (September 12, 1995), p. B1.
5. Thomas Donaldson, *Ethics of International Business* (New York: Oxford University Press, 1989), p. 98.
6. Richard DeGeorge, *Competing with Integrity in International Business* (New York: Oxford University Press, 1993) p. 79.
7. *Ibid.*, pp. 356–357.
8. *Ibid.*, p. 78.
9. World Bank, *World Development Report 1995, "Workers in an Integrating World Economy"* (Oxford University Press, 1995) p. 77.
10. Donaldson, *Ethics of International Business*, p. 115.
11. *Ibid.*, p. 150.
12. DeGeorge, *Competing with Integrity*, p. 48.
13. *Ibid.*, p. 358.
14. *Ibid.*

15. Terry Collingsworth, J. William Goold, Pharis J. Harvey, "Time for a Global New Deal," *Foreign Affairs* (January–February 1994), p. 8.
16. William B. Falk, "Dirty Little Secrets," *Newsday* (June 16, 1996).
17. Tim Smith, "The Power of Business for Human Rights." *Business & Society Review* (January 1994), p. 36.
18. Jeffrey Ballinger, "The New Free Trade Heel." *Harper's Magazine* (August 1992), pp. 46–47. "As in many developing countries, Indonesia's minimum wage, . . . , is less than poverty level." Nina Baker, "The Hidden Hands of Nike," *Oregonian* (August 9, 1992).
19. Robert B. Reich, "Escape from the Global Sweatshop; Capitalism's Stake in Uniting the Workers of the World." *Washington Post* (May 22, 1994). Reich's test is intended to apply in developing countries "where democratic institutions are weak or absent."
20. *Ibid.*
21. Kenneth P. Hutchinson, "Third World Growth." *Harvard Business Review* (November–December 1994).
22. Robin Broad and John Cavanagh, "Don't Neglect the Impoverished South." *Foreign Affairs* (December 22, 1995).
23. John Cavanagh & Robin Broad, "Global Reach; Workers Fight the Multinationals." *The Nation*, (March 18, 1996), p. 21. See also Bob Herbert, "Nike's Bad Neighborhood." *New York Times* (June 14, 1996).
24. International Labor Organization, *World Employment 1995* (Geneva: ILO, 1995) p. 73.
25. World Bank, *Workers in an Integrating World Economy,*. p. 5.
26. Keith B. Richburg, Anne Swardson, "U.S. Industry Overseas: Sweatshop or Job Source?: Indonesians Praise Work at Nike Factory." *Washington Post* (July 28, 1996).
27. Richburg and Swardson, "Sweatshop or Job Source?" The 17 years old was interviewed in the presence of managers. For other reports that workers remit home large parts of their earnings see Seth Mydans, "Tangerang Journal; For Indonesian Workers at Nike Plant: Just Do It." *New York Times* (August 9, 1996), and Nina Baker, "The Hidden Hands of Nike."
28. Donna Gibbs, Nike spokeswoman on ABC's *World News Tonight*, June 6, 1996.
29. Mark Clifford, "Trading in Social Issues; Labor Policy and International Trade Regulation," *World Press Review* (June 1994), p. 36.
30. Larry Rohter, "To U.S. Critics, a Sweatshop; for Hondurans, a Better Life." *New York Times* (July 18, 1996).
31. Marcus Brauchli, "Garment Industry Booms in Bangladesh." *Wall Street Journal* (August 6, 1991).
32. Richburg and Swardson, "Sweatshop or Job Source?"
33. Lucy Martinez-Mont, "Sweatshops Are Better Than No Shops." *Wall Street Journal* (June 25, 1996).
34. Rohter, "To U.S. Critics a Sweatshop."
35. Barnet & Cavanagh, *Global Dreams*, p. 326.
36. Rohter, "To U.S. Critics a Sweatshop."
37. William B. Falk, "Dirty Little Secrets," *Newsday* (June 16, 1996).
38. Barnet and Cavanagh, "Just Undo It: Nike's Exploited Workers." *New York Times* (February 13, 1994).
39. Sarosh Kuruvilla, "Linkages Between Industrialization Strategies and Industrial Relations/Human Resources Policies: Singapore, Malaysia, The Philippines, and India." *Industrial & Labor Relations Review* (July 1996), p. 637.
40. The ILO's Constitution (of 1919) mentions that: ". . . . the failure of any nation to adopt humane conditions of labour is an obstacle in the way of other nations which desire to improve the conditions in their own countries." ILO, *World Employment 1995*, p. 74.
41. World Bank, *The East Asian Miracle* (New York: Oxford University Press, 1993) p. 2.
42. Gideon Rachman, "Wealth in Its Grasp, a Survey of Indonesia." *Economist* (April 17, 1993), pp. 14–15.
43. Jagdish Bhagwati & Robert E. Hudec, eds. *Fair Trade and Harmonization* (Cambridge: MIT Press, 1996), vol. 1, p. 2.
44. World Bank, *Workers in an Integrating World Economy*, p. 75.
45. *Ibid.*, p. 77. As I have noted, the report proposes that the "appropriate level is therefore that at which the costs are commensurate with the value that informed workers place on improved working conditions and reduced risk. . . ." (p. 77).

# Sweatshops and Respect for Persons

*Denis G. Arnold*
*and Norman E. Bowie*

In recent years labor and human rights activists have been successful at raising public awareness regarding labor practices in both American and off-shore manufacturing facilities. Organizations such as Human Rights Watch, United Students Against Sweatshops, the National Labor Coalition, Sweatshop Watch, and the Interfaith Center on Corporate Responsibility have accused multinational enterprises (MNEs), such as Nike, Wal-Mart, and Disney, of the pernicious exploitation of workers. Recent violations of American and European labor laws have received considerable attention.[1] However, it is the off-shore labor practices of North American- and European-based MNEs and their contractors that have been most controversial. This is partly due to the fact that many of the labor practices in question are legal outside North America and Europe, or are tolerated by corrupt or repressive political regimes. Unlike the recent immigrants who toil in the illegal sweatshops of North America and Europe, workers in developing nations typically have no recourse to the law or social service agencies. Activists have sought to enhance the welfare of these workers by pressuring MNEs to comply with labor laws, prohibit coercion, improve health and safety standards, and pay a living wage in their global sourcing operations. Meanwhile, prominent economists wage a campaign of their own in the opinion pages of leading newspapers, arguing that because workers for MNEs are often paid better when compared with local wages, they are fortunate to have such work. Furthermore, they argue that higher wages and improved working conditions will raise unemployment levels.

One test of a robust ethical theory is its ability to shed light on ethical problems. One of the standard criticisms of Immanuel Kant's ethical theory is that it is too abstract and formal to be of any use in practical decision making. We contend that this criticism is mistaken and that Kantian theory has much to say about the ethics of sweatshops.[2] We argue that Kant's conception of human dignity provides a clear basis for grounding the obligations of employers to employees. In particular, we argue that respecting the dignity of workers requires that MNEs and their contractors adhere to local labor laws, refrain from coercion, meet minimum safety standards, and provide a living wage for employees. We also respond to the objection that improving health and safety conditions and providing a living wage would cause greater harm than good.

## I. RESPECT FOR PERSONS

Critics of sweatshops frequently ground their protests in appeals to human dignity and human rights. Arguably, Kantian ethics provides a philosophical basis for such moral pronouncements. The key principle here is Kant's second formulation of the categorical imperative: "Act so that you treat humanity, whether in your own person or in that of another, always as an end and never as a means only."[3] The popular expression of this principle is that morality requires that we respect people. One significant feature of the idea of respect for persons is that its derivation and application

From Denis G. Arnold and Norman E. Bowie "Sweatshops and Respect for Persons," *Business Ethics Quarterly* 13 (2003). Reprinted with permission of authors and *Business Ethics Quarterly.*

can be assessed independently of other elements of Kantian moral philosophy. Sympathetic readers need not embrace all aspects of Kant's system of ethics in order to grant the merit of Kant's arguments for the second formulation of the categorical imperative. This is because Kant's defense of respect for persons is grounded in the uncontroversial claim that humans are capable of rational, self-governing activity. We believe that individuals with a wide range of theoretical commitments can and should recognize the force of Kant's arguments concerning respect for persons.

Kant did not simply assert that persons are entitled to respect; he provided an elaborate argument for that conclusion. Persons ought to be respected because persons have dignity. For Kant, an object that has dignity is beyond price. Employees have a dignity that machines and capital do not have. They have dignity because they are capable of moral activity. As free beings capable of self-governance they are responsible beings, since freedom and self-governance are the conditions for responsibility. Autonomous responsible beings are capable of making and following their own laws; they are not simply subject to the causal laws of nature. Anyone who recognizes that he or she is free should recognize that he or she is responsible (that he or she is a moral being). As Kant argues, the fact that one is a moral being entails that one possesses dignity.

> Morality is the condition under which alone a rational being can be an end in himself because only through it is it possible to be a lawgiving member in the realm of ends. Thus morality, and humanity insofar as it is capable of morality, alone have dignity.[4]

As a matter of consistency, a person who recognizes that he or she is a moral being should ascribe dignity to anyone who, like him or herself, is a moral being.

Although it is the capacity to behave morally that gives persons their dignity, freedom is required if a person is to act morally. For Kant, being free is more than freedom from causal necessity. This is negative freedom. Freedom in its fullest realization is the ability to guide one's actions from laws that are of one's own making. Freedom is not simply a spontaneous event. Free actions are caused, but they are caused by persons acting from laws they themselves have made. This is positive freedom. Onora O'Neill puts the point this way.

> Positive freedom is more than independence from alien causes. It would be absent in lawless or random changes, although these are negatively free, since they depend on no alien causes. Since will is a mode of causality it cannot, if free at all, be merely negatively free, so it must work by non-alien causality . . . it [free will] must be a capacity for self-determination or autonomy.[5]

When we act autonomously we have the capacity to act with dignity. We do so when we act on principles that are grounded in morality rather than in mere inclination. Reason requires that any moral principle that is freely derived must be rational in the sense that it is universal. To be universal in this sense means that the principle can be willed to be universally binding on all subjects in relevantly similar circumstances without contradiction. The fact that persons have this capability means that they possess dignity. And it is as a consequence of this dignity that a person "exacts respect for himself from all other rational beings in the world."[6] As such, one can and should "measure himself with every other being of this kind and value himself on a footing of equality with them."[7]

Respecting people requires honoring their humanity; which is to say it requires treating them as ends in themselves. In Kant's words,

> Humanity itself is a dignity; for a man cannot be used merely as a means by any man . . . but must always be used at the same time as an end. It is just

> in this that his dignity . . . consists, by which he raises himself above all other beings in the world that are not men and yet can be used, and so over all *things*.[8]

Thomas Hill, Jr. has discussed the implication of Kant's arguments concerning human dignity at length.[9] Hill argues that treating persons as ends in themselves requires supporting and developing certain human capacities, including the capacity to act on reason; the capacity to act on the basis of prudence or efficiency; the capacity to set goals; the capacity to accept categorical imperatives; and the capacity to understand the world and reason abstractly.[10] Based on Kant's writings in the *Metaphysics of Morals*, we would make several additions to the list. There Kant argues that respecting people means that we cannot be indifferent to them. Indifference is a denial of respect.[11] He also argues that we have an obligation to be concerned with the physical welfare of people and their moral well being. Adversity, pain, and want are temptations to vice and inhibit the ability of individuals to develop their rational and moral capacities.[12] It is these rational and moral capacities that distinguish people from mere animals. People who are not free to develop these capacities may end up leading lives that are closer to animals than to moral beings. Freedom from externally imposed adversity, pain, and want facilitate the cultivation of one's rational capacities and virtuous character. Thus, treating people as ends in themselves means ensuring their physical well being and supporting and developing their rational and moral capacities.

With respect to the task at hand, what does treating the humanity of persons as ends in themselves require in a business context—specifically in the context of global manufacturing facilities? In an earlier work Bowie has spelled out the implications of the Kantian view for businesses operating in developed countries.[13] Here we apply the same strategy in order to derive basic duties for MNEs operating in developing countries. Specifically, we derive duties that apply to MNEs that are utilizing the vast supplies of inexpensive labor currently available in developing economies. To fully respect a person one must actively treat his or her humanity as an end. This is an obligation that holds on every person *qua* person, whether in the personal realm or in the marketplace. As Kant writes, "Every man has a legitimate claim to respect from his fellow men and is *in turn* bound to respect every other." [14] There are, of course, limits to what managers of MNEs can accomplish. Nonetheless, we believe that the analysis we have provided entails that MNEs operating in developing nations have an obligation to respect the humanity of their employees. We discuss the implications of this conclusion next.

It is noteworthy that an application of the doctrine of respect for persons to the issue of the obligations of employers to employees in developing economies results in conclusions similar to the capabilities approach developed by Amartya Sen.[15] Over the last 20 years Sen has argued that development involves more than an increase in people's incomes and the GNP of the country. He argues that we should be concerned with certain basic human capabilities, the most important of which is freedom. Sen's perspective is similar in important respects to our own because both are concerned with providing work that enhances the positive freedom of the worker. The United Nations utilizes both the Kantian view and the capabilities view as a dual theoretical foundation for its defense of human rights. Among the rights identified by the U.N. are freedom from injustice and violations of the rule of law; freedom to decent work without exploitation; and the freedom to develop and realize one's human potential. It argues that all global actors, including MNEs, have a moral obligation to respect basic human rights.[16] . . .

## II. OUTSOURCING AND THE DUTIES OF MNES

One significant feature of globalization that is of particular relevance to our analysis is the increase in outsourcing by MNEs. Prior to the 1970s most foreign production by MNEs was intended for local markets. In the 1970s new financial incentives led MNEs to begin outsourcing the production of goods for North American, European, and Japanese markets to manufacturing facilities in developing countries. Encouraged by international organizations such as The World Bank and the International Monetary Fund, developing nations established "free trade zones" to encourage foreign investment via tax incentives and a minimal regulatory environment. In the 1980s the availability of international financing allowed entrepreneurs to set up production facilities in developing economies in order to meet the growing demand by MNEs for offshore production.[17] Outsourcing production has many distinct advantages from the perspective of MNEs. . . . Outsourcing has been especially popular in consumer products industries, and in particular in the apparel industry. Nike, for example, outsources all of its production.

Are MNEs responsible for the practices of their subcontractors and suppliers? We believe that they are. Michael Santoro has defended the view that MNEs have a moral duty to ensure that their business partners respect employees by ensuring that human rights are not violated in the workplace. Santoro argues as follows:

> multinational corporations are morally responsible for the way their suppliers and subcontractors treat their workers. The applicable moral standard is similar to the legal doctrine of *respondeat superior*, according to which a principal is "vicariously liable" or responsible for the acts of its agent conducted in the course of the agency relationship. The classic example of this is the responsibility of employers for the acts of employees. Moreover, ignorance is no excuse. Firms must do whatever is required to become aware of what conditions are like in the factories of their suppliers and subcontractors, and thereby be able to assure themselves and others that their business partners don't mistreat those workers to provide a cheaper source of supply.[18]

We concur with Santoro's judgment and offer the following twofold justification for the view that MNEs have a duty to ensure that the dignity of workers is respected in the factories of subcontractors. First, an MNE, like any other organization, is composed of individual persons and since persons are moral creatures, the actions of employees in an MNE are constrained by the categorical imperative. This means MNE managers have a duty to ensure that those with whom they conduct business are properly respected.[19] Second, as Kant acknowledges, individuals have unique duties as a result of their unique circumstances. One key feature in determining an individual's duties is the power they have to render assistance. For example, Kant famously argues that a wealthy person has a duty of charity that an impoverished person lacks. Corollary duties apply to organizations. Researchers have noted that the relationship of power between MNEs and their subcontractors and suppliers is significantly imbalanced in favor of MNEs:

> As more and more developing countries have sought to establish export sectors, local manufacturers are locked in fierce competitive battles with one another. The resulting oversupply of export factories allows U.S. companies to move from one supplier to another in search of the lowest prices, quickest turnaround, highest quality and best delivery terms, weighted according to the priorities of the company. In this context, large U.S. manufacturer-merchandisers and retailers wield enormous power to dictate the price at which they will purchase goods.[20]

MNEs are well positioned to help ensure that the employees of its business partners are respected because of this imbalance of power. In addition, MNEs can draw upon substantial economic resources, management expertise, and technical knowledge to assist their business partners in creating a respectful work environment.

## III. THE RULE OF LAW

Lawlessness contributes to poverty[21] and is deeply interconnected with human and labor rights violations. One important role that MNEs can play to help ensure that the dignity of workers is properly respected is encouraging respect for the rule of law. . . . It is commonplace for employers in developing nations to violate worker rights in the interest of economic efficiency and with the support of state institutions. Violations of laws relating to wages and benefits, forced overtime, health and safety, child labor, sexual harassment, discrimination, and environmental protection are legion. Examples include the following:

1. Human Rights Watch reports that in Mexican maquiladoras, or export processing zones, U.S. companies such as Johnson Controls and Carlisle Plastics require female job applicants to submit to pregnancy screening; women are refused employment if they test positive. Employment discrimination based on pregnancy is a violation of Mexican law.[22]
2. A Guatemalan Ministry of the Economy study found that less than 30 percent of maquiladora factories that supply MNEs make the legally required payments for workers into the national social security system which gives workers access to health care. The report was not made public by the Ministry of the Economy due to its "startling" nature.[23]
3. An El Salvadoran Ministry of Labor study funded by the United States Agency for International Development found widespread violation of labor laws, including flagrant violation of the freedom to organize and unionize, in maquiladora factories that supply MNEs. The report was suppressed by the Ministry of Labor after factory owners complained.[24]
4. In North and Central Mexico widespread violation of Mexican environmental laws by MNEs and their contractors has been documented by both U.S. and Mexican nongovernmental organizations, and local Mexican governmental officials.[25]
5. In Haiti, apparel manufacturers such as L.V. Myles Corporation, producing clothing under license with the Walt Disney Company in several contract factories, paid workers substantially less than the Haitian minimum wage. These clothes were sold in the United States at Wal-Mart, Sears, J.C. Penney and other retailers. This practice continued until the National Labor Committee documented and publicized this violation of Haitian law.[26]

Furthermore, in many nations in which MNEs operate those responsible for administering justice are violators of the law. Factory workers frequently have no legal recourse when their legal rights are violated.

The intentional violation of the legal rights of workers in the interest of economic efficiency is fundamentally incompatible with the duty of MNEs to respect workers. Indifference to the plight of workers whose legal rights are systematically violated is a denial of respect. At a minimum MNEs have a duty to ensure that their offshore factories, and those of their suppliers and subcontractors, are in full compliance with local laws. Failure to honor the dignity of workers by violating their legal rights—or tolerating the violation of those rights—is also hypocritical. In Kantian terms, it constitutes a pragmatic contradiction. A pragmatic contradiction occurs when one acts on a principle that promotes an action that would be inconsistent with one's purpose if everyone were to act upon that principle. In this case, the principle would be something like the following: "It is permissible to violate the legal rights of others when doing so is economically efficient." MNEs rely on the rule of law to ensure, among other things, that their contracts are fulfilled, their property is secure, and their copyrights are protected. When violations of the legal rights of MNEs take place, MNEs and business organizations protest vociferously. Thus, MNEs rely on the rule of law to ensure the protection of their own interests. Without the rule of law, MNEs would cease to exist. Therefore, it is inconsistent for an MNE to permit the violation of the legal rights of workers while at the same time it demands that its own rights be protected.

## IV. COERCION

We have shown why it is reasonable to believe that all persons possess dignity and that this dignity must be respected. The obligation that we respect others requires that we not use people as a means only, but instead that we treat other people as capable of autonomous law guided action. The requirement not to use people can be met passively, by not treating them in certain ways. However, the requirement to treat them as ends-in-themselves entails positive obligations. We will explore these positive obligations as they relate to sweatshops in Section VI. In this section and the next, we explore the requirement that we not use people as a means only. One common way of doing so recognized by Kant is coercion. Coercion violates a person's negative freedom. Coercion is *prima facie* wrong because it treats the subjects of coercion as mere tools, as objects lacking the rational capacity to choose for themselves how they shall act.

Are sweatshops in violation of the no coercion requirement? An answer to this question depends both on the definition of the concepts in question and on the facts of the particular case. Elsewhere Arnold has provided accounts of physical and psychological coercion.[27] Physical coercion occurs when one's bodily movements are physically forced. In cases where one person (P) physically coerces another person (Q), Q's body is used as an object or instrument for the purpose of fulfilling P's desires. We assume that readers of this essay will agree that using physical coercion to keep people working in sweatshops against their will is disrespectful and morally wrong. While comparatively rare, physical coercion (or the threat of physical coercion) does take place. For example, at a shoe factory in Guangdong, China, it is reported that 2700 workers were prevented from leaving the factory by 100 live-in security guards that patrolled the walled factory grounds.[28]

For psychological coercion to take place, three conditions most hold. First, the coercer must have a desire about the will of his or her victim. However, this is a desire of a particular kind because it can only be fulfilled through the will of another person. Second, the coercer must have an effective desire to compel his or her victim to act in a manner that makes efficacious the coercer's other regarding desire. The distinction between an other regarding desire and a coercive will is important because it provides a basis for delineating between cases of coercion and, for example, cases of rational persuasion. In both instances a person may have an other regarding desire, but in the case of coercion that desire will be supplemented by an effective first-order desire which seeks to enforce that desire on the person, and in cases of rational persuasion it will not. What is of most importance in such cases is that P intentionally attempts to compel Q to comply with an other regarding desire of P's own. These are necessary, but not sufficient conditions of coercion. In order for coercion to take place, the coercer must be successful in getting his or her victim to conform to his or her other regarding desire. In all cases of coercion P attempts to violate the autonomy of Q. When Q successfully resists P's attempted coercion, Q retains his or her autonomy. In such cases P retains a coercive will.

In typical cases, people work in sweatshops because they believe they can earn more money working there than they can in alternative employment, or they work in sweatshops because it is better than being unemployed. In many developing countries, people are moving to large cities from rural areas because agriculture in those areas can no longer support the population base. When people make a choice that seems highly undesirable because there are no better alternatives available, are those people coerced? On the definition of coercion employed here, having to make a choice among undesirable options is not sufficient for coercion. We therefore assume that such persons are not coerced even though they have no better alternative than working in a sweatshop.

Nonetheless, the use of psychological coercion in sweatshops appears widespread. For example, coercion is frequently used by supervisors to improve worker productivity. Workers throughout the world report that they are forced to work long overtime hours or lose their jobs. In Bangladesh, factory workers report that they are expected to work virtually every day of the year. Overtime pay, a legal requirement, is often not paid. Employees who refuse to comply are fired.[29] In El Salvador, a government study of maquiladora factories found that

> in the majority of companies, it is an obligation of the personnel to work overtime under the threat of firing or some other kind of reprisal. This situation, in addition to threatening the health of the workers, causes family problems in that [the workers] are unable to properly fulfill obligations to their immediate family.
>
> On some occasions, because the work time is extended into the late hours of the night, the workers find themselves obligated to sleep in the factory facilities, which do not have conditions necessary for lodging of personnel.[30]

Bangladesh, El Salvador, and other developing economies lack the social welfare programs that workers in North America and Europe take for granted. If workers lose their jobs, they may end up without any source of income. Thus, workers are understandably fearful of being fired for noncompliance with demands to work long overtime hours. When a worker is threatened with being fired by a supervisor unless she agrees to work overtime, and when the supervisor's intention in making the threat is to ensure compliance, then the supervisors actions are properly understood as coercive. Similar threats are used to ensure that workers meet production quotas, even in the face of personal injury. For example, a 26-year-old worker who sews steering wheel covers at a Mexican maquila owned by Autotrim reports the following:

> We have to work quickly with our hands, and I am responsible for sewing 20 steering wheel covers per shift. After having worked for nine years at the plant, I now suffer from an injury in my right hand. I start out the shift okay, but after about three hours of work, I feel a lot of sharp pains in my fingers. It gets so bad that I can't hold the steering wheel correctly. But still the supervisors keep pressuring me to reach 100 percent of my production. I can only reach about 70 percent of what they ask for. These pains began a year ago and I am not the only one who has suffered from them. There are over 200 of us who have hand injuries and some have lost movement in their hands and arms. The company has fired over 150 people in the last year for lack of production. Others have been pressured to quit. . . .[31]

We do not claim that production quotas are inherently coercive. Given a reasonable quota, employees can choose whether or not to work diligently to fill that quota. Employees who choose idleness over industriousness and are terminated as a result are not coerced. However, when a supervisor threatens workers who are ill or injured with termination unless they meet a production quota that either cannot physically be achieved by the employee, or can only be achieved at the cost of further injury to the employee, the threat is properly understood as coercive. In such cases the employee will inevitably feel compelled to meet the quota. Still other factory workers report being threatened with termination if they seek medical attention. For example, when a worker in El Salvador who was three months pregnant began hemorrhaging she was not allowed to leave the factory to receive medical attention. She subsequently miscarried while in the factory, completed her long work day, and took her fetus home for burial.[32] Other workers have died because they were not allowed to leave the factory to receive medical attention.[33] In cases where workers suffer miscarriages or death, rather than risk termination, we believe that it is reasonable to conclude that the workers are coerced into remaining at work.

According to the analysis provided here, workers choose to work in sweatshops because the alternatives available to them are worse. However, once they are employed coercion is often used to ensure that they will work long overtime hours and meet production quotas. Respecting workers requires that they be free to decline overtime work without fear of being fired. It also requires that if they are injured or ill—especially as a result of work-related activities—they should be allowed to consult health care workers and be given work that does not exacerbate their illnesses or injuries. Using coercion as a means of compelling employees to work overtime, to meet production quotas despite injury, or to remain at work while in need of medical attention, is incompatible with respect for persons because the coercers treat their victims as mere tools. It is important to note that even if the victim of coercion successfully resisted in some way, the attempted coercion would remain morally objectionable. This is because the coercer acts as if it is permissible to use the employees as mere tools.

## V. WORKING CONDITIONS

Critics of MNEs argue that many workers are vulnerable to workplace hazards such as repetitive motion injuries, exposure to toxic chemicals, exposure to airborne pollutants such as fabric particles, and malfunctioning machinery. One of the most common workplace hazards concerns fire safety. In factories throughout the world workers are locked in to keep them from leaving the factory. When fires break out workers are trapped. This is what happened in 1993 when a fire broke out at the Kader Industrial Toy Company in Thailand. Over 200 workers were killed and 469 injured. The factory had been producing toys for U.S. companies such as Hasbro, Toys "R" Us, J.C. Penney, and Fisher-Price.[34] In Bangladesh alone, there have been 17 fires that have resulted in fatalities since 1995. A recent fire at Chowdhury Knitwears claimed 52 lives.[35]

Workers are also exposed to dangerous toxic chemicals and airborne pollutants. For example, a Nike-commissioned Ernst & Young Environmental and Labor Practices Audit of the Tae Kwang Vina factory outside Ho Chi Minh City, Vietnam, was leaked to the press. Among the many unsafe conditions reported by Ernst & Young at this 10,000 person facility was exposure to toluene (a toxic chemical used as a solvent in paints, coatings, adhesives, and cleaning agents) at 6 to 177 times that allowed by Vietnamese law.[36] . . . In addition to toluene, workers at the Tae Kwang Vina factory were exposed to airborne fabric particles and chemical powders at dangerous levels. It is implausible to think that the (mainly) young women who work in the Tae Kwang Vina factory were informed about these health risks before they were hired. Ernst & Young reports that the employees received no training concerning the proper handling of chemicals after they were hired. Since that time Nike has overseen substantial health and safety improvements at the Tae Kwang Vina factory, and at the other Southeast Asian factories with which it contracts. Nonetheless, available evidence indicates that unsafe workplace conditions remain common among MNE factories.[37] Consider, for example, the report of Mexican maquila worker Omar Gil:

> Back in 1993 I got my first job in a maquiladora, at Delphi Auto Parts. They paid 360 pesos a week (about $40). There was a lot of pressure from the foreman on the assembly lines to work hard and produce, and a lot of accidents because of the bad design of the lines. The company didn't give

us adequate protective equipment to deal with the chemicals—we didn't really have any idea of the dangers, or how we should protect ourselves. The Union did nothing to protect us.

From Delphi I went to another company, National Auto parts. In that plant we made car radiators for Cadillacs and Camaros, and there was a lot of sickness and accidents there too. I worked in the area with the metal presses. There were not ventilators to take the fumes out of the plant, and they didn't give us any gloves. We had to handle the parts with our bare hands, and people got cut up a lot. I worked in an area with a lot of lead. If you worked with lead, you're supposed to have special clothing and your clothes should be washed separately. But the company didn't give us any of that. We had to work in our street clothes.

For all of that they paid 400 pesos a week (about $43). We had no union, and there was the same pressure for production from the foreman and the group leaders as I saw at Delphi.

Now I work at TRW, where I've been for about a month and a half. There's really no difference in the conditions in any of these plants—if anything, my situation now is even worse.[38]

If our analysis is correct, then those MNEs that tolerate such health and safety risks have a duty to improve those conditions. Lax health and safety standards violate the moral requirement that employers be concerned with the physical safety of their employees. A failure to implement appropriate safeguards means that employers are treating their employees as disposable tools rather than as beings with unique dignity.

We cannot provide industry specific health and safety guidelines in the space of this essay. However, we believe that the International Labour Organization's carefully worked out Conventions and Recommendations on safety and health provide an excellent template for minimum safety standards.[39] For example, the ILO provides specific recommendations regarding airborne pollutants in "Occupational Exposure to Airborne Substances Harmful to Health" (1980) and exposure to chemicals in "Safety in the Use of Chemicals at Work" (1993). Ethicists, business people, and labor leaders with widely divergent views on a number of issues can agree on a minimum set of health and safety standards that should be in place in factories in the developing world. We return to this issue in Section VII.

## VI. WAGES

One of the most controversial issues concerning sweatshops is the demand that employers raise the wages of employees in order to provide a "living wage." Workers from all over the world complain about low wages. For example,

> employees of a maquiladora in Ciudad Acuna, Mexico, owned by the Aluminum Company of America (Alcoa), calculated that to buy the most basic food items needed by a factory worker—items such as beans, tortilla, rice, potatoes, onions and cooking oil, and excluding such "luxuries" as milk, meat, vegetables and cereal—cost U.S. $26.87 per week. At the time, weekly wages at the plant ranged only from $21.44 to $24.60.[40]

While a living wage is difficult to define with precision, one useful approach is to use a method similar to that used by the U.S. government to define poverty. This method involves calculating the cost of a market basket of food needed to meet minimum dietary requirements and then adding the cost of other basic needs. The Council on Economic Priorities uses this approach to define a wage that meets basic needs in different countries. Their formula is as follows:

1. Establish the local cost of a basic food basket needed to provide 2100 calories per person.
2. Determine the share of the local household income spent on food. Divide into 1 to get total budget multiplier.
3. Multiply that by food spending to get the total per person budget for living expenses.
4. Multiply by half the average number of household members in the area. (Use a higher share if there are many single-parent households.)
5. Add at least 10 percentage for discretionary income.[41]

The United Nations Development Programme employs a similar method to distinguish between three different levels of poverty (see Table 1).[42]

It is our contention that, at a minimum, respect for employees entails that MNEs and their suppliers have a moral obligation to ensure that employees do not live under conditions of overall poverty by providing adequate wages for a 48-hour work week to satisfy both basic food needs and basic nonfood needs. Doing so helps to ensure the physical well-being and independence of employees, contributes to the development of their rational capacities, and provides them with opportunities for moral development. This in turn allows for the cultivation of self-esteem.[43] It is difficult to specify with precision the minimum number of hours per week that employees should work in order to receive a living wage. However, we believe that a 48-hour work week is a reasonable compromise that allows employees sufficient time for the cultivation of their rational capacities while providing employers with sufficient productivity. In addition, MNEs and their suppliers have an obligation to pay appropriate host nations taxes and meet appropriate codes and regulations to ensure that they contribute in appropriate ways to the creation and maintenance of the goods, services, and infrastructure necessary for the fulfillment of human capabilities. Anything less than this means that MNEs, or their suppliers, are not respecting employees as ends in themselves.

## VII. ECONOMIC CONSIDERATIONS

. . . In a recent paper, Ian Maitland criticizes both the labor and human rights activists who have accused MNEs of unjust labor practices, as well as MNEs, such as Nike, that have responded by acquiescing to some of the activists demands.[44] . . . In addition to assessing the veracity of claims regarding worker exploitation, he sets out to determine "the ethically appropriate levels of wages and labor standards in international sweatshops."[45] He argues that philosophers . . . who object to letting market determinations alone set wage standards, are misguided on the grounds that "attempts to improve on market outcomes may have unforeseen tragic consequences."[46] Maitland's arguments regarding ethically appropriate levels of wages and labor standards may be summarized as follows:

1. Workers in the urban, formal sector of developing nations earn better wages than do workers in the rural, informal sector.
2. The imposition of wages or labor standards greater than that demanded by the market increases costs.
3. Increased costs result in layoffs and slow investment in the formal sector.

**TABLE 1**

| Types of Poverty | Deficiencies | Measures |
|---|---|---|
| Extreme Poverty (also known as Absolute Poverty) | Lack of income necessary to satisfy basic food needs | Minimum caloric intake and a food basket that meets that requirement |
| Overall Poverty (also known as Relative Poverty) | Lack of income necessary to satisfy basic nonfood needs | Ability to secure shelter, energy, transportation, and basic health care |
| Human Poverty | Lack of basic human capabilities | Access to goods, services, and infrastructure |

4. Formal sector layoffs result in a surplus supply of labor in the informal sector.
5. A surplus of informal sector workers depresses income in the informal sector.

**Conclusion:** higher wages or labor standards increase poverty and limit economic growth in developing nations.

Appealing as it does to textbook economic theory, Maitland's conclusion retains an authoritative quality. Naive critics of MNEs fail to take into consideration rudimentary economic theory, and cynical corporate managers ignore these economic realities in order to preserve their brand images and corporate reputations. Maitland has done a valuable service by raising issues of central importance to the welfare of millions of powerless and impoverished people. However, is his conclusion correct? In the remaining portion of essay we argue that it is not.

First, despite his faith in the ability of international markets alone to generate ethically acceptable wage and labor standards for MNEs and their contractors. . . . Maitland does not himself defend an unrestricted market approach. It is not clear, however, that Maitland recognizes this fact. The most obvious evidence in support of this conclusion is his criticism of corporate managers who, he believes, merely seek to appease their critics. "Not a single company has tried to mount a serious defense of its contracting practices. They have judged that they cannot win a war of soundbites with the critics. Instead of making a fight of it, the companies have sued for peace in order to protect their principal asset—their image." [47] Thus, according to Maitland, corporate managers have made the strategic decision to respond to market forces—in this case consumers' preferences and other marketing considerations—in the manner they deem most consistent with profitability. Given Maitland's faith in the free market, one might expect him to criticize this strategy because it is inefficient.[48] However, Maitland does not pursue this approach. Instead, he argues that managers should not appease their critics—even if managers regard this as the strategy most consistent with profitability—because doing so will have undesirable economic and moral outcomes, namely, higher unemployment and slower economic growth. There is, then, a contradiction at the heart of Maitland's analysis. He argues in favor of improvements to current market outcomes, while at the same time he argues against attempts to improve on market outcomes on the grounds that doing so will result in undesirable moral consequences.[49]

Second, some of the most compelling evidence in support of the proposition that MNEs can improve workplace health and safety conditions while avoiding "tragic outcomes" comes from MNEs themselves. Companies such as Levis Strauss, Motorola, and Mattel have expended considerable resources to ensure that employees in their global sourcing operations work in healthy and safe environments. For example, Levis Strauss & Company stipulates that "We will only utilize business partners who provide workers with a safe and healthy environment." [50] Levis is known for acting in a manner consistent with this policy. Motorola explicitly endorses the idea of respect for persons in their Code of Business Conduct. The Code is built on two foundations:

> **Uncompromising integrity** means staying true to what we believe. We adhere to honesty, fairness and "doing the right thing" without compromise, even when circumstances make it difficult.
>
> **Constant respect for people** means we treat others with dignity, as we would like to be treated ourselves. Constant respect applies to every individual we interact with around the world.[51]

The physical instantiation of these principles can be seen at a Motorola's factory in Tianjin, China:

> In the company cafeteria, workers queue up politely for a variety of free and nutritious meals. One area is set aside for a pregnancy well-care program. A booth is open at which appointments can be made with the company medical staff. There is a bank branch dedicated to employee needs. It is a scene that one might expect in a Fortune 500 corporate campus in the United States. The overwhelming sense is of a pleasant, orderly place in which people are fulfilled in their work.[52]

Recently Mattel announced the creation of a global code of conduct for its production facilities and contract manufacturers. It has spent millions of dollars to upgrade its manufacturing facilities in order to improve worker safety and comfort. Furthermore, it has invited a team of academics lead by S. Prakash Sethi to monitor its progress in complying with its self-imposed standards and to make their findings public.[53] This is believed to be the first time that a major MNE has voluntarily submitted to external monitoring. The examples set by Levis, Motorola, and Mattel provide evidence that MNEs are capable of improving worker health and safety without causing further hardship in the communities in which they operate.

Finally, it is not clear that improving employee wages will inevitably lead to the "tragic consequences" that Maitland and others predict. The economic issues under consideration are complex and we cannot address them here in the detail they deserve. Nonetheless, several reasons may be provided for thinking that Maitland's conclusion is incorrect. With regard to the lowest paid formal sector wage earners in developing countries, the assumption that productivity is independent of wage levels is dubious.

> As exceptionally low wages are raised, there may be increases in productivity either because of induced management improvements or because of greater labour efficiency due to a decrease in wasteful labour turnover and industrial disputes and to improvements in workers morale and nutrition resulting, in turn, in an increase in the workers willingness and capacity to work and a reduction in the incidence of debilitating diseases, time off due to illness and accidents caused by fatigue. If higher wages, at least over a certain range, are accompanied by certain improvements in labour productivity, it is conceivable that labour costs could decrease rather than increase and to such an extent that employment would not fall.[54]

Put simply, workers whose minimum daily caloric intakes are met, and who have basic nonfood needs met, will have more energy and better attitudes at work; will be less likely to come to work ill; and will be absent with less frequency. Workers are thus likely to be more productive and loyal. Economists refer to a wage that if reduced would make the firm worse off because of a decrease in worker productivity as the efficiency wage. Empirical evidence supports the view that increased productivity resulting from better nutrition offsets the cost of higher wages.[55] Thus, if workers are being paid less than the efficiency wage in a particular market there are good economic reasons, in addition to moral reasons, for raising wages. Higher productivity per hour could also help alleviate the need for overtime work and facilitate a 48-hour work week.

One might object that our analysis implies that MNE managers are unaware of the correlation between wages and productivity, and that such ignorance on the part of MNE managers is implausible. Our reply is twofold. First, workers in developing nations *are* frequently paid less than the efficiency wage in those labor markets. Second, findings from an El Salvadoran Ministry of Labor study of maquiladora factories are instructive. Researchers found that "According to the production managers interviewed, some companies use North American and Asian efficiency and productivity levels as a parameter for establishing production goals, without considering the different nutritional conditions and technical capacity of our workers."[56] We believe that such erroneous assumptions have been widespread among MNE managers.

Part of Maitland's analysis rests on the assumption that increased labor costs will inevitably result in higher unemployment in competitive markets. Maitland is correct to identify this view as a common belief among many economists, especially as it relates to minimum wage legislation.[57] However, this view has been challenged in recent years. In their influential recent book length study of the impact of minimum wage increases on employment, David Card and Alan Krueger argue that their reanalysis of the evidence from the United States, Canada, the United Kingdom, and Puerto Rico indicates that the existing data does not provide compelling evidence for the textbook view.[58] In addition, Card and Krueger analyzed new data for recent increases in the minimum wage in the United States. Their analysis is complex, but the results of their analysis are straightforward. "In every case . . . the estimated effect of the minimum wage was either zero or positive."[59] Increased labor costs appear to have been passed on to consumers in the form of higher prices without increasing unemployment. Again, these data undermine the textbook view regarding the impact of increases in the minimum wage. Economist Richard Freeman summarizes the impact of Card and Krueger's work as follows:

> the Card-Krueger work is essentially correct: the minimum wage at levels observed in the United States has had little or no effect on employment. At the minimum, the book has changed the burden of proof in debates over the minimum, from those who stressed the potential distributional benefits of the minimum to those who stress the potential employment losses.[60] After evaluating recent work on the impact of minimum wages, economists William Spriggs and John Schmitt reached a more determinate conclusion: "The overwhelming weight of recent evidence supports the view that low-wage workers will benefit overwhelmingly from a higher federal minimum."[61]

Two points concerning wages should be distinguished. First, conclusions concerning the impact of U.S. minimum wage legislation on unemployment cannot automatically be assumed to apply to developing nations. Careful study of the unique conditions of those labor markets is necessary before corollary claims can be assessed. Nonetheless, the textbook view rests significantly on studies concerning the U.S. labor market. As such, we believe that the burden of proof remains with those who maintain that increased labor costs must inevitably result in higher unemployment. Second, we wish to emphasize that we are not taking a position in this essay on increasing federally mandated minimum wages in developing nations. Rather, our contention is that it is economically feasible for MNEs to voluntarily raise wages in factories in developing economies without causing increases in unemployment. MNEs may choose to raise wages while maintaining existing employment levels. Increased labor costs that are not offset by greater productivity may be passed on to consumers, or, if necessary, absorbed through internal cost cutting measures such as reductions in executive compensation.

## VIII. CONCLUSION

As Kant argues, it is by acting in a manner consistent with human dignity that persons raise themselves above all things. Insofar as we recognize the dignity of humanity, we have an obligation to respect both ourselves and others.[62] We have argued that MNE managers that encourage or tolerate violations of the rule of law; use coercion; allow unsafe working conditions; and provide below subsistence wages, disavow their own dignity and that of their workers. In so doing, they disrespect themselves and their workers. Further, we have argued that this moral analysis is not undermined by economic considerations. Significantly, MNEs are in many ways more readily able to honor the humanity of workers. This is because MNEs typically have well-defined internal decision structures that, unlike individual moral agents, are not susceptible to weakness of the will.[63] For this reason, MNE managers who recognize a duty to respect their employees, and those of their subcontractors, are well positioned to play a constructive role in ensuring that the dignity of humanity is respected.

## NOTES

1. See, for example, Susan Chandler, "Look Who's Sweating Now," *BusinessWeek*, October 16, 1995; Steven Greenhouse, "Sweatshop Raids Cast Doubt on an Effort By Garment Makers to Police the Factories," *New York Times*, July 18, 1997; and Gail Edmondson, et al., "Workers in Bondage," *BusinessWeek*, November 27, 2000.
2. For the purposes of this paper we define the term as any workplace in which workers are typically subject to two or more of the following conditions: income for a 48-hour workweek less than the overall poverty rate for that country (see Table 1); systematic forced overtime; systematic health and safety risks that stem from negligence or the willful disregard of employee welfare; coercion; systematic deception that places workers at risk; and underpayment of earnings.
3. Immanuel Kant, *Foundations of the Metaphysics of Morals*, Lewis White Beck, trans. (New York: Macmillan, 1990), p. 46.
4. Kant, *Foundations of the Metaphysics of Morals*, p. 52.
5. Onora O'Neill, *Constructions of Reason*, (Cambridge: Cambridge University Press, 1989), p. 53.
6. Immanuel Kant, *The Metaphysics of Morals*, Mary Gregor, trans., (Cambridge: Cambridge University Press, 1991), p. 230.
7. Ibid.
8. Ibid., 255.
9. Thomas Hill, Jr., *Dignity and Practical Reason in Kant's Moral Theory* (Ithaca: Cornell University Press, 1992).
10. Ibid. pp. 40–41.
11. Kant, *Metaphysics of Morals*, p. 245.
12. Ibid., pp. 192–93 and 196–97.
13. Norman E. Bowie, *Business Ethics: A Kantian Perspective* (Malden, MA: Blackwell, 1999). See pp. 41–81 for further discussion of the second categorical imperative.
14. Kant, *Metaphysics of Morals*, p. 255.
15. His latest book is *Development as Freedom* (New York: Anchor Books, 1999). Martha Nussbaum has developed her own version of the capabilities approach, one that pays particular attention to the unique circumstances of women's lives. *Women and Human Development: The Capabilities Approach* (Cambridge: Cambridge University Press, 2000).
16. United Nations Development Programme, *Human Development Report 2000* (New York: Oxford University Press, 2000).
17. Pamela Varley, Ed., *The Sweatshop Quandary: Corporate Responsibility on the Global Frontier* (Washington DC, Investor Responsibility Research Center, 1998), pp. 185–86.
18. Michael A. Santoro, *Profits and Principles: Global Capitalism and Human Rights in China* (Ithaca: Cornell University Press, 2000), p. 161.
19. For a fuller discussion of this matter, see Bowie, *Business Ethics: A Kantian Perspective*, esp. Chap. 2.
20. Varley, Ed., *The Sweatshop Quandary*, p. 95.
21. Better rule of law is associated with higher per capita income. See *World Development Report 2000/2001: Attacking Poverty* (New York: Oxford University Press, 2000), p. 103.
22. Human Rights Watch, "A Job or Your Rights: Continued Sex Discrimination in Mexico's Maquiladora Sector," 10 (1)(B) December 1998. Available at http://www.hrw.org/reports98/women2/.
23. Varley, ed., *The Sweatshop Quandary*, p. 131.
24. Republic of El Salvador, Ministry of Labor, Monitoring and Labor Relations Analysis Unit, "Monitoring Report on Maquilas and Bonded Areas" (July 2000). Available at http://www.nlcnet.org/elsalvador/0401/translation.htm.
25. Edward J. Williams, "The Maquiladora Industry and Environmental Degradation in the United States–Mexican Borderlands." Paper presented at the annual meeting of the Latin American Studies Association, Washington, DC, September 1995. Available at http://www.natlaw.com/pubs/williams.htm. See also, Joan Salvat, Stef Soetewey, and Peter Breuls, *Free Trade Slaves*, 58 min. (Princeton, NJ: Films for the Humanities and Sciences, 1999), videocassette.
26. National Labor Committee, "The U.S. in Haiti: How To Get Rich on 11 Cents an Hour" (1995).

Available at http://www.nlcnet.org/Haiti/0196/index.htm.

27. Denis G. Arnold, "Coercion and Moral Responsibility," *American Philosophical Quarterly*, 38 (2001): 53–67. The view of psychological coercion employed here is a slightly revised version of the view defended in that essay. In particular, the condition that cases of psychological coercion always involve psychological compulsion has been replaced with the condition that cases of psychological coercion always involve the victim's compliance with the threat.
28. Varley, Ed., *The Sweatshop Quandary*, p. 72.
29. Barry Bearak, "Lives Held Cheap In Bangladesh Sweatshops," *New York Times*, April 15, 2001.
30. Republic of El Salvador, Ministry of Labor, Monitoring and Labor Relations Analysis Unit, "Monitoring Report on Maquilas and Bonded Areas."
31. Varley, Ed., *The Sweatshop Quandary*, p. 68.
32. Salvat, et al., *Free Trade Slaves.*
33. Ibid.
34. Varley, Ed., *The Sweatshop Quandary*, p. 67.
35. Bearak, "Lives Held Cheap in Bangladesh Sweatshops."
36. "Ernst & Young Environmental and Labor Practice Audit of the Tae Kwang Vina Industrial Ltd. Co., Vietnam." Available at http://www.corpwatch.org/trac/nike/ernst/audit.html.
37. See, for example, Varley, Ed., *The Sweatshop Quandary*, esp. pp. 59–98.
38. Campaign for Labor Rights, "The Story of a Maquiladora Worker: Interview with Omar Gil by David Bacon," (September 6, 2000). Available at www.summersault.com/~agj/clr/alerts/thestoryofamaquiladoraeworker.html.
39. International Labour Organization, "SafeWork: ILO Standards on Safety and Health." Available at http://www.ilo.org/public/english/ protection/ safework/standard.htm.
40. After the complaint was raised in a shareholder meeting, Alcoa raised the wages of the workers by 25 percent. Pamela Varley, Ed., *The Sweatshop Quandary*, p. 63.
41. Aaron Bernstein, "Sweatshop Reform: How to Solve the Standoff," *BusinessWeek*, May 3, 1999.
42. *Poverty Report 2000: Overcoming Human Poverty* (New York: United Nations Development Programme, 2000).
43. Self-esteem is grounded in the conscious recognition of one's dignity as a rational being.
44. Ian Maitland, "The Great Non-Debate Over International Sweatshops," reprinted in Tom L. Beauchamp and Norman E. Bowie, *Ethical Theory and Business*, 6th ed. (Englewood Cliffs: Prentice Hall, 2001), p. 595. First published in *British Academy of Management Conference Proceedings* (September 1997), pp. 240–65.
45. Ibid.
46. Ibid., p. 603.
47. Ibid., p. 594.
48. Such an argument would likely maintain that corporate managers fail to recognize that a public relations strategy that includes higher wages and improved workplace standards is more costly than an alternative strategy that does not. The details of such a strategy would then need to be worked out.
49. Maitland, "The Great Non-Debate Over International Sweatshops," p. 602.
50. Ibid., p. 539.
51. Motorola, "Code of Business Conduct." Available at http://www.motorola.com/code/code.html.
52. Santoro, *Profits and Principles*, p. 6.
53. S. Prakash Sethi, "Codes of Conduct for Multinational Corporations: An Idea Whose Time Has Come," *Business and Society Review*, 104 (3)(1999). 225–41.
54. Gerald Starr, *Minimum Wage Fixing* (Geneva: International Labour Organization, 1981), p. 157.
55. C. J. Bliss and N. H. Stern, "Productivity, Wages, and Nutrition, 2: Some Observations." *Journal of Development Economics*, 5 (1978): 363–98. For theoretical discussion, see C. J. Bliss and N. H. Stern, "Productivity, Wages, and Nutrition, 1: The Theory." *Journal of Development Economics*, 5 (1978): 331–362.
56. Republic of El Salvador, Ministry of Labor, Monitoring and Labor Relations Analysis Unit, "Monitoring Report on Maquilas and Bonded Areas." Available at http://www.nlcnet.org/ elsalvador/0401/translation.htm.
57. See, for example, the essays collected in Simon Rottenberg, Ed., *The Economics of Legal Minimum Wages* (Washington DC: The American Enterprise Institute, 1981).
58. See David Card and Alan B. Krueger, *Myth and Measurement: The New Economics of the Minimum Wage* (Princeton: Princeton University Press,

1995. See also the special symposium on *Myth and Measurement in Industrial & Labor Relations Review* (July 1995) with contributions by Charles Brown, Richard Freeman, Daniel Hamermesh, Paul Osterman, and Finis Welch; David Neumark and William Wascher, "Minimum Wages and Employment: A Case Study of the Fast-Food Industry in New Jersey and Pennsylvania: Comment," *The American Economic Review* (December 2000): 1362–96; and David Card and Alan B. Krueger, "Minimum Wages and Employment: A Case Study of the Fast-Food Industry in New Jersey and Pennsylvania: Reply," *The American Economic Review* (December 2000): 1397–1420. For a discussion of the living wage issue in the context of the U.S. economy, see Robert Pollin and Stephanie Luce, *The Living Wage: Building a Fair Economy* (The New Press: New York, 1998).

59. Card and Krueger, *Myth and Measurement*, p. 389.
60. Richard B. Freeman, "In Honor of David Card: Winner of the John Bates Clark Medal," *Journal of Economic Perspectives* (Spring 1997): 173.
61. William Spriggs and John Schmitt, "The Minimum Wage: Blocking the Low-Wage Path," in Todd Schafer and Jeff Faux, *Reclaiming Prosperity: A Blueprint for Progressive Economic Reform* (ME Sharpe: Armonk, NY, 1996), p. 170.
62. Kant, *Foundations of the Metaphysics of Morals*, p. 255.
63. For a fuller defense of this position see Peter A. French, *Corporate Ethics* (Hartcourt Brace: Fort Worth, TX: 1995), pp. 79–87.

**LEGAL PERSPECTIVES**

# Universal Declaration of Human Rights

## Preamble

Whereas recognition of the inherent dignity and of the equal and inalienable rights of all members of the human family is the foundation of freedom, justice and peace in the world,

Whereas disregard and contempt for human rights have resulted in barbarous acts which have outraged the conscience of mankind, and the advent of a world in which human beings shall enjoy freedom of speech and belief and freedom from fear and want has been proclaimed as the highest aspiration of the common people,

Whereas it is essential, if man is not to be compelled to have recourse, as a last resort, to rebellion against tyranny and oppression, that human rights should be protected by the rule of law,

Whereas it is essential to promote the development of friendly relations between nations,

Whereas the peoples of the United Nations have in the Charter reaffirmed their faith in fundamental human rights, in the dignity and worth of the human person and in the equal rights of men and women and have determined to promote social progress and better standards of life in larger freedom,

Whereas Member States have pledged themselves to achieve, in co-operation with the United Nations, the promotion of universal respect for and observance of human rights and fundamental freedoms,

Whereas a common understanding of these rights and freedoms is of the greatest importance for the full realization of this pledge,

**Now, Therefore THE GENERAL ASSEMBLY proclaims THIS UNIVERSAL DECLARATION OF HUMAN RIGHTS** as a common standard of achievement for all peoples and all nations, to the end that every individual and every organ

*Source:* United Nations Department of Public Information, "Universal Declaration of Human Rights," http://www.unhchr.ch/udhr/lang/eng.htm (accessed March 19, 2003).

of society, keeping this Declaration constantly in mind, shall strive by teaching and education to promote respect for these rights and freedoms and by progressive measures, national and international, to secure their universal and effective recognition and observance, both among the peoples of Member States themselves and among the peoples of territories under their jurisdiction.

*Article 1.*

All human beings are born free and equal in dignity and rights. They are endowed with reason and conscience and should act towards one another in a spirit of brotherhood.

*Article 2.*

Everyone is entitled to all the rights and freedoms set forth in this Declaration, without distinction of any kind, such as race, colour, sex, language, religion, political or other opinion, national or social origin, property, birth or other status. Furthermore, no distinction shall be made on the basis of the political, jurisdictional or international status of the country or territory to which a person belongs, whether it be independent, trust, non-self-governing or under any other limitation of sovereignty.

*Article 3.*

Everyone has the right to life, liberty and security of person.

*Article 4.*

No one shall be held in slavery or servitude; slavery and the slave trade shall be prohibited in all their forms.

*Article 5.*

No one shall be subjected to torture or to cruel, inhuman or degrading treatment or punishment.

*Article 6.*

Everyone has the right to recognition everywhere as a person before the law.

*Article 7.*

All are equal before the law and are entitled without any discrimination to equal protection of the law. All are entitled to equal protection against any discrimination in violation of this Declaration and against any incitement to such discrimination.

*Article 8.*

Everyone has the right to an effective remedy by the competent national tribunals for acts violating the fundamental rights granted him by the constitution or by law.

*Article 9.*

No one shall be subjected to arbitrary arrest, detention or exile.

*Article 10.*

Everyone is entitled in full equality to a fair and public hearing by an independent and impartial tribunal, in the determination of his rights and obligations and of any criminal charge against him.

*Article 11.*

(1) Everyone charged with a penal offence has the right to be presumed innocent until proved guilty according to law in a public trial at which he has had all the guarantees necessary for his defence.

(2) No one shall be held guilty of any penal offence on account of any act or omission which did not constitute a penal offence, under national or international law, at the time when it was committed. Nor shall a heavier penalty be imposed than the one that was applicable at the time the penal offence was committed.

*Article 12.*

No one shall be subjected to arbitrary interference with his privacy, family, home or correspondence, nor to attacks upon his honour and reputation. Everyone has the right to the protection of the law against such interference or attacks.

*Article 13.*

(1) Everyone has the right to freedom of movement and residence within the borders of each state.

(2) Everyone has the right to leave any country, including his own, and to return to his country.

*Article 14.*

(1) Everyone has the right to seek and to enjoy in other countries asylum from persecution.

(2) This right may not be invoked in the case of prosecutions genuinely arising from non-political crimes or from acts contrary to the purposes and principles of the United Nations.

*Article 15.*

(1) Everyone has the right to a nationality.

(2) No one shall be arbitrarily deprived of his nationality nor denied the right to change his nationality.

*Article 16.*

(1) Men and women of full age, without any limitation due to race, nationality or religion, have the right to marry and to found a family. They are entitled to equal rights as to marriage, during marriage and at its dissolution.

(2) Marriage shall be entered into only with the free and full consent of the intending spouses.

(3) The family is the natural and fundamental group unit of society and is entitled to protection by society and the State.

*Article 17.*

(1) Everyone has the right to own property alone as well as in association with others.

(2) No one shall be arbitrarily deprived of his property.

*Article 18.*

Everyone has the right to freedom of thought, conscience and religion; this right includes freedom to change his religion or belief, and freedom, either alone or in community with others and in public or private, to manifest his religion or belief in teaching, practice, worship and observance.

*Article 19.*

Everyone has the right to freedom of opinion and expression; this right includes freedom to hold opinions without interference and to seek, receive and impart information and ideas through any media and regardless of frontiers.

*Article 20.*

(1) Everyone has the right to freedom of peaceful assembly and association.

(2) No one may be compelled to belong to an association.

*Article 21.*

(1) Everyone has the right to take part in the government of his country, directly or through freely chosen representatives.

(2) Everyone has the right of equal access to public service in his country.

(3) The will of the people shall be the basis of the authority of government; this will shall be expressed in periodic and genuine elections which shall be by universal and equal suffrage and shall be held by secret vote or by equivalent free voting procedures.

*Article 22.*

Everyone, as a member of society, has the right to social security and is entitled to realization, through national effort and international co-operation and in accordance with the organization and resources of each State, of the economic, social and cultural rights indispensable for his dignity and the free development of his personality.

*Article 23.*

(1) Everyone has the right to work, to free choice of employment, to just and favourable conditions of work and to protection against unemployment.

(2) Everyone, without any discrimination, has the right to equal pay for equal work.

(3) Everyone who works has the right to just and favorable remuneration ensuring for himself and his family an existence worthy of human dignity, and supplemented, if necessary, by other means of social protection.

(4) Everyone has the right to form and to join trade unions for the protection of his interests.

*Article 24.*

Everyone has the right to rest and leisure, including reasonable limitation of working hours and periodic holidays with pay.

*Article 25.*

(1) Everyone has the right to a standard of living adequate for the health and well-being of himself and of his family, including food, clothing, housing and medical care and necessary social services, and the right to security in the event of unemployment, sickness, disability, widowhood, old age or other lack of livelihood in circumstances beyond his control.

(2) Motherhood and childhood are entitled to special care and assistance. All children, whether born in or out of wedlock, shall enjoy the same social protection.

*Article 26.*

(1) Everyone has the right to education. Education shall be free, at least in the elementary and fundamental stages. Elementary education shall be compulsory. Technical and professional education shall be made generally available and higher education shall be equally accessible to all on the basis of merit.

(2) Education shall be directed to the full development of the human personality and to the strengthening of respect for human rights and fundamental freedoms. It shall promote understanding, tolerance and friendship among all nations, racial or religious groups, and shall further the activities of the United Nations for the maintenance of peace.

(3) Parents have a prior right to choose the kind of education that shall be given to their children.

*Article 27.*

(1) Everyone has the right freely to participate in the cultural life of the community, to enjoy the arts and to share in scientific advancement and its benefits.

(2) Everyone has the right to the protection of the moral and material interests resulting from any scientific, literary or artistic production of which he is the author.

*Article 28.*

Everyone is entitled to a social and international order in which the rights and freedoms set forth in this Declaration can be fully realized.

*Article 29.*

(1) Everyone has duties to the community in which alone the free and full development of his personality is possible.

(2) In the exercise of his rights and freedoms, everyone shall be subject only to such limitations as are determined by law solely for the purpose of securing due recognition and respect for the rights and freedoms of others and of meeting the just requirements of morality, public order and the general welfare in a democratic society.

(3) These rights and freedoms may in no case be exercised contrary to the purposes and principles of the United Nations.

*Article 30.*

Nothing in this Declaration may be interpreted as implying for any State, group or person any right to engage in any activity or to perform any act aimed at the destruction of any of the rights and freedoms set forth herein.

# *Dow Chemical Company and Shell Oil Company v. Domingo Castro Alfaro et al.*

*Supreme Court of Texas*

Because its analysis and reasoning are correct I join in the majority opinion without reservation. I write separately, however, to respond to the dissenters who mask their inability to agree among themselves with competing rhetoric. In their zeal to implement their own preferred social policy that Texas corporations not be held responsible at home for harm caused abroad, these dissenters refuse to be restrained by either express statutory language or the compelling precedent, previously approved by this very court, holding that forum non conveniens does not apply in Texas. To accomplish the desired social engineering, they must invoke yet another legal fiction with a fancy name to shield alleged wrongdoers, the so-called doctrine of *forum non conveniens.* The refusal of a Texas corporation to confront a Taxes judge and jury is to be labelled "inconvenient" when what is really involved is not convenience but connivance to avoid corporate accountability.

The dissenters are insistent that a jury of Texans be denied the opportunity to evaluate the conduct of a Texas corporation concerning decisions it made in Taxes because the only ones allegedly hurt are foreigners. Fortunately Texans are not so provincial and narrow-minded as these dissenters presume. Our citizenry recognizes that a wrong does not fade away because its immediate consequences are first felt far away rather than close to home. Never have we been required to forfeit our membership in the human race in order to maintain our proud heritage as citizens of Texas.

The dissenters argue that it is *inconvenient* and *unfair* for farmworkers allegedly suffering permanent physical and mental injuries, including irreversible sterility, to seek redress by suing a multinational corporation in a court three blocks away from its world headquarters and another corporation, which operates in Texas this country's largest chemical plant. Because the "doctrine" they advocate has nothing to do with fairness and convenience and everything to do with immunizing multinational corporations from accountability for their alleged torts causing injury abroad, I write separately.

## THE FACTS

Respondents claim that while working on a banana plantation in Costa Rica for Standard Fruit Company, an American subsidiary of Dole Fresh Fruit Company, headquartered in Boca Raton, Florida, they were required to handle dibromochloropropane ["DBCP"], a pesticide allegedly manufactured and furnished to Standard Fruit by Shell Oil Company ["Shell"] and Dow Chemical Company ["Dow"]. The Environmental Protection Agency issued a notice of intent to cancel all food uses of DBCP on September 22, 1977.42 Fed. Reg. 48026 (1977). It followed with an order suspending registrations of pesticides containing DBCP on November 3, 1977. 42 Fed. Reg. 57543 (1977). Before and after the E.P.A.'s ban of DBCP in the United States, Shell and Dow apparently shipped several hundred thousand gallons of the pesticide to Costa Rica for use by Standard Fruit. The Respondents, Domingo Castro Alfaro and other plantation workers, filed suit in

786 S.W. 2d 674 (Tex. 1990). Concurring opinion by Judge Doggett.

a state district court in Houston, Texas, alleging that their handling of DBCP caused them serious personal injuries for which Shell and Dow were liable under the theories of products liability, strict liability and breach of warranty.

Rejecting an initial contest to its authority by Shell and Dow, the trial court found that it had jurisdiction under Tex. Civ. Prac. & Rem. Code Ann. § 71.031 (Vernon 1986), but dismissed the cause on the grounds of forum non conveniens. The court of appeals reversed and remanded, holding that Section 71.031 provides a foreign plaintiff with an absolute right to maintain a death or personal injury cause of action in Texas without being subject to forum non conveniens dismissal. 751 S.W.2d 208. Shell and Dow have asked this court to reverse the judgment of the court of appeals and affirm the trial court's dismissal.

Shell Oil Company is a multinational corporation with its world headquarters in Houston, Texas. Dow Chemical Company, though headquartered in Midland, Michigan, conducts extensive operations from its Dow Chemical USA building located in Houston. Dow operates this country's largest chemical manufacturing plant within 60 miles of Houston in Freeport, Texas. The district court where this lawsuit was filed is three blocks away from Shell's world headquarters, One Shell Plaza in downtown Houston.

Shell has stipulated that all of its more than 100,000 documents relating to DBCP are located or will be produced in Houston. Shell's medical and scientific witnesses are in Houston. The majority of Dow's documents and witnesses are located in Michigan, which is far closer to Houston (both in terms of geography and communications linkages) than to Costa Rica. The respondents have agreed to be available in Houston for independent medical examinations, for depositions and for trial. Most of the respondents' treating doctors and coworkers have agreed to testify in Houston. Conversely, Shell and Dow have purportedly refused to make their witnesses available in Costa Rica.

The banana plantation workers allegedly injured by DBCP were employed by an American company on American-owned land and grew Dole bananas for export soley to American tables. The chemical allegedly rendering the workers sterile was researched, formulated, tested, manufactured, labeled and shipped by an American company in the United States to another American company. The decision to manufacture DBCP for distribution and use in the third world was made by these two American companies in their corporate offices in the United States. Yet now Shell and Dow argue that the one part of this equation that should not be American is the legal consequences of their actions.

## FORUM NON CONVENIENS—"A COMMON LAW DOCTRINE OUT OF CONTROL"

As a reading of Tex. Civ. Prac. & Rem. Code Ann. § 71.031 (Vernon 1986) makes clear, the doctrine of forum non conveniens has been statutorily abolished in Texas. The decision in *Allen v. Bass*, . . . approved by this court, clearly holds that, upon a showing of personal jurisdiction over a defendant, article 4678, now section 71.031 of the Texas Civil Practice & Remedies Code, "opens the courts of this state to citizens of a neighboring state and gives them an absolute right to maintain a transitory action of the present nature and to try their cases in the courts of this state."

Displeased that *Allen* stands in the way of immunizing multinational corporations from suits seeking redress for their torts causing injury abroad, the dissenters doggedly attempt to circumvent this precedent. Unsuccessful with arguments based upon Texas law, they criticize the court for not justifying its result on public policy grounds.

## Using the "Doctrine" to Kill the Litigation Altogether

Both as a matter of law and of public policy, the doctrine of forum non conveniens is without justification. The proffered foundations for it are "considerations of fundamental fairness and sensible and effective judicial administration." . . . In fact, the doctrine is favored by multinational defendants because a forum non conveniens dismissal is often outcome-determinative, effectively defeating the claim and denying the plaintiff recovery. . . .

Empirical data available demonstrate that less than four percent of cases dismissed under the doctrine of forum non conveniens ever reach trial in foreign court.[1] A forum non conveniens dismissal usually will end the litigation altogether, effectively excusing any liability of the defendant. The plaintiffs leave the courtroom without having had their case resolved on the merits.

## The *Gulf Oil* Factors—Balanced Toward the Defendant

Courts today usually apply forum non conveniens by use of the factors set forth at length in *Gulf Oil Corp. v. Gilbert*. . . . Briefly summarized, those factors are (i) the private interests of the litigants (ease and cost of access to documents and witnesses); and (ii) the public interest factors (the interest of the forum state, the burden on the courts, and notions of judicial comity). In the forty-three years in which the courts have grappled with the *Gulf Oil* factors, it has become increasingly apparent that their application fails to promote fairness and convenience. Instead, these factors have been used by defendants to achieve objectives violative of public policy. . . .

***The Public Interest Factors.*** The three public interest factors asserted by Justice Gonzalez may be summarized as (1) whether the interests of the jurisdiction are sufficient to justify entertaining the lawsuit; (2) the potential for docket backlog; and (3) judicial comity. . . .

The next justification offered by the dissenters for invoking the legal fiction of "inconvenience" is that judges will be overworked. Not only will foreigners take our jobs, as we are told in the popular press; now they will have our courts. The xenophobic suggestion that foreigners will take over our courts "forcing our residents to wait in the corridors of our courthouses while foreign causes of action are tried," Gonzalez dissent, 786 S.W.2d at 690, is both misleading and false.

It is the height of deception to suggest that docket backlogs in our state's urban centers are caused by so-called "foreign litigation." This assertion is unsubstantiated empirically both in Texas and in other jurisdictions rejecting forum non conveniens.[2] Ten states, including Texas, have not recognized the doctrine. Within these states, there is no evidence that the docket congestion predicted by the dissenters has actually occurred. The best evidence, of course, comes from Texas itself. Although foreign citizens have enjoyed the statutory right to sue defendants living or doing business here since the 1913 enactment of the predecessor to Section 71.031 of the Texas Civil Practice and Remedies Code, reaffirmed in the 1932 decision in *Allen*, Texas has not been flooded by foreign causes of action.

Moreover, the United States Supreme Court has indicated that docket congestion "is a wholly inappropriate consideration in virtually every other context." . . . If we begin to refuse to hear lawsuits properly filed in Texas because they are sure to require time, we set a precedent that can be employed to deny Texans access to these same courts.

Nor does forum non conveniens afford a panacea for eradicating congestion:

> Making the place of trial turn on a largely imponderable exercise of judicial discretion is

extremely costly. Even the strongest proponents of the most suitable forum approach concede that it is inappropriately time-consuming and wasteful for the parties to have to "litigate in order to determine where they shall litigate." If forum non conveniens outcomes are not predictable, such litigation is bound to occur. . . . In terms of delay, expense, uncertainty, and a fundamental loss of judicial accountability, the most suitable forum version of forum non conveniens clearly costs more than it is worth. Robertson, *supra*, 103 L.Q.Rev. at 414, 426.

Comity—deference shown to the interests of the foreign forum — is a consideration best achieved by rejecting forum non conveniens. Comity is not achieved when the United States allows its multinational corporations to adhere to a double standard when operating abroad and subsequently refuses to hold them accountable for those actions. As S. Jacob Scherr, Senior Project Attorney for the Natural Resources Defense Counsel, has noted

> There is a sense of outrage on the part of many poor countries where citizens are the most vulnerable to exports of hazardous drugs, pesticides and food products. At the 1977 meeting of the UNEP Governing Council, Dr. J.C. Kiano, the Kenyan minister for water development, warned that developing nations will no longer tolerate being used as dumping grounds for products that had not been adequately tested "and that their peoples should not be used as guinea pigs for determining the safety of chemicals." Comment, *U.S. Exports Banned For Domestic Use, But Exported to Third World Countries*, 6 Int'l Tr.L.J. 95, 98 (1980–81) [hereinafter *"U.S. Exports Banned"*].

Comity is best achieved by "avoiding the possibility of 'incurring the wrath and distrust of the Third World as it increasingly recognizes that it is being used as the industrial world's garbage can.'" Note, *Hazardous Exports from a Human Rights Perspective*, 14 Sw. U.L. Rev. 81, 101 (1983) [hereinafter "*Hazardous Exports*"] (quoting Hon. Michael D. Barnes (Representative in Congress representing Maryland)).[3] . . .

## PUBLIC POLICY AND THE TORT LIABILITY OF MULTINATIONAL CORPORATIONS IN UNITED STATES COURTS

The abolition of forum non conveniens will further important public policy considerations by providing a check on the conduct of multinational corporations (MNCs). *See Economic Approach*, 22 Geo. Wash.J. Int'l L. & Econ. at 241. The misconduct of even a few multinational corporations can affect untold millions around the world.[4] For example, after the United States imposed a domestic ban on the sale of cancer-producing TRIS-treated children's sleepwear, American companies exported approximately 2.4 million pieces to Africa, Asia and South America. A similar pattern occurred when a ban was proposed for baby pacifiers that had been linked to choking deaths in infants. *Hazardous Exports, supra*, 14 Sw. U.L.Rev. at 82. These examples of indifference by some corporations towards children abroad are not unusual.[5]

The allegations against Shell and Dow, if proven true, would not be unique, since production of many chemicals banned for domestic use has thereafter continued for foreign marketing.[6] Professor Thomas McGarity, a respected authority in the field of environmental law, explained:

> During the mid-1970s, the United States Environmental Protection Agency (EPA) began to restrict the use of some pesticides because of their environmental effects, and the Occupational Safety and Health Administration (OSHA) established workplace exposure standards for toxic and hazardous substances in the manufacture of pesticides. . . . [I]t is clear that many pesticides that have been severely restricted in the United States are used without restriction in many Third World countries, with resulting harm to fieldworkers and the global environment.

McGarity, *Bhopal and the Export of Hazardous Technologies*, 20 Tex.Int'l L.J. 333, 334 (1985) (citations omitted). By 1976, "29 percent, or 161 million pounds of all the pesticides exported by the United States were either unregistered or banned for domestic use." McWilliams, *Tom Sawyer's Apology: A Reevaluation of United States Pesticide Export Policy*, 8 Hastings Int'l & Comp.L.Rev. 61, 61 & n. 4 (1984). It is estimated that these pesticides poison 750,000 people in developing countries each year, of which 22,500 die. *Id.* at 62. Some estimates place the death toll from the "improper marketing of pesticides at 400,000 lives a year." *Id.* at 62 n. 7.

Some United States multinational corporations will undoubtedly continue to endanger human life and the environment with such activities until the economic consequences of these actions are such that it becomes unprofitable to operate in this manner. At present, the tort laws of many third world countries are not yet developed. *An Economic Approach, supra*, 22 Geo. Wash.J.Int'l L. & Econ. at 222–23. Industrialization "is occurring faster than the development of domestic infrastructures necessary to deal with the problems associated with industry." *Exporting Hazardous Industries, supra*, 20 Int'l L. & Pol. at 791. When a court dismisses a case against a United States multinational corporation, it often removes the most effective restraint on corporate misconduct. *See An Economic Approach, supra*, 22 Geo.Wash.J.Int'l L. & Econ. at 241.

The doctrine of forum non conveniens is obsolete in a world in which markets are global and in which ecologists have documented the delicate balance of all life on this planet. The parochial perspective embodied in the doctrine of forum non conveniens enables corporations to evade legal control merely because they are transnational. This perspective ignores the reality that actions of our corporations affecting those abroad will also affect Texans. Although DBCP is banned from use within the United States, it and other similarly banned chemicals have been consumed by Texans eating foods imported from Costa Rica and elsewhere. *See* D. Weir & M. Schapiro, *Circle of Poison* 28–30, 77, 82–83 (1981). In the absence of meaningful tort liability in the United States for their actions, some multinational corporations will continue to operate without adequate regard for the human and environmental costs of their actions. This result cannot be allowed to repeat itself for decades to come.

As a matter of law and of public policy, the doctrine of forum non conveniens should be abolished. Accordingly, I concur. . . .

## NOTES

1. Professor David Robertson of the University of Texas School of Law attempted to discover the subsequent history of each reported transnational case dismissed under forum non conveniens from *Gulf Oil v. Gilbert*, 330 U.S. 501, 67 S.Ct. 839, 91 L.Ed. 1055 (1947) to the end of 1984. Data was received on 55 personal injury cases and 30 commercial cases. Of the 55 personal injury cases, only one was actually tried in a foreign court. Only two of the 30 commercial cases reached trial. *See* Robertson, *supra*, at 419.
2. Evidence from the most recent and largest national study ever performed regarding the pace of litigation in urban trial courts suggests that there is no empirical basis for the dissenters' argument that Texas dockets will become clogged without forum non conveniens. The state of Massachusetts recognizes forum non conveniens. *See Minnis v. Peebles*, 24 Mass.App. 467, 510 N.E.2d 289 (1987). Conversely, the state of Louisiana has explicitly not recognized forum non conveniens since 1967. . . . Nevertheless, the study revealed the median filing-to-disposition time for tort cases in Boston to be 953 days; in New Orleans, with no forum non conveniens, the median time for the disposition of tort cases was only 405 days. The study revealed the median disposition time for contract cases in Boston to be 1580 days, as opposed to a mere 271 days in New Orleans where forum non conveniens is not used. J. Goerdt, C. Lomvardias, G. Gallas & B. Mahoney, Examining Court Delay—The Pace of Litigation in 26 Urban Trial Courts, 1987 20, 22 (1989).
3. A senior vice-president of a United States multinational corporation acknowledged that "[t]he realization at corporate headquarters that

liability for any [industrial] disaster would be decided in the U.S. courts, more than pressure from Third World governments, has forced companies to tighten safety procedures, upgrade plants, supervise maintenance more closely and educate workers and communities." Wall St. J., Nov. 26, 1985, at 22, col. 4 (quoting Harold Corbett, senior vice-president for environmental affairs at Monsanto Co.).

4. As one commentator observed, U.S. multinational corporations "adhere to a double standard when operating abroad. The lack of stringent environmental regulations and worker safety standards abroad and the relaxed enforcement of such laws in industries using hazardous processes provide little incentive for [multinational corporations] to protect the safety of workers, to obtain liability insurance to guard against the hazard of product defects or toxic tort exposure, or to take precautions to minimize pollution to the environment. *This double standard has caused catastrophic damages to the environment and to human lives.*"

   Note, *Exporting Hazardous Industries: Should American Standards Apply?*, 20 Int'l L. & Pol. 777, 780–81 (1988) (emphasis added) (footnotes omitted) [hereinafter *"Exporting Hazardous Industries"*]. *See also* Diamond, *The Path of Progress Racks the Third World, New York Times*, Dec. 12, 1984, at B1, col. 1.

5. A subsidiary of Sterling Drug Company advertised Winstrol, a synthetic male hormone severely restricted in the United States since it is associated with a number of side effects that the F.D.A. has called "virtually irreversible," in a Brazilian medical journal, picturing a healthy boy and recommending the drug to combat poor appetite, fatigue and weight loss. *U.S. Exports Banned, supra*, 6 Int'l Tr.L.J. at 96. The same company is said to have marketed Dipyrone, a painkiller causing a fatal blood disease and characterized by the American Medical Association as for use only as "a last resort," as "Novaldin" in the Dominican Republic. "Novaldin" was advertised in the Dominican Republic with pictures of a child smiling about its agreeable taste. *Id.* at 97. "In 1975, thirteen children in Brazil died after coming into contact with a toxic pesticide whose use had been severely restricted in this country." *Hazardous Exports, supra*, 14 Sw. U.L. Rev. at 82.

6. Regarding Leptophos, a powerful and hazardous pesticide that was domestically banned, S. Jacob Scherr stated that "In 1975 alone, Velsicol, a Texas-based corporation exported 3,092,842 pounds of Leptophos to thirty countries. Over half of that was shipped to Egypt, a country with no procedures for pesticide regulation or tolerance setting. In December 1976, the *Washington Post* reported that Laptophos use in Egypt resulted in the death of a number of farmers and illness in rural communities. . . . But despite the accumulation of data on Leptophos' severe neurotoxicity, Velsicol continued to market the product abroad for use on grain and vegetable crops while proclaiming the product's safety." *U.S. Exports Banned*, 6 Int'l Tr.L.J. at 96.

# *Doe 1 vs. Unocal*

*U.S. Court of Appeals, Ninth Circuit*

## OPINION

This case involves human rights violations that allegedly occurred in Myanmar, formerly known as Burma. Villagers from the Tenasserim region in Myanmar allege that the Defendants directly or indirectly subjected the villagers to forced labor, murder, rape, and torture when the Defendants constructed a gas pipeline through the Tenasserim region. The villagers base their claims on the Alien Tort Claims Act, 28 U.S.C. § 1350, and the Racketeer Influenced and Corrupt Organizations Act, 18 U.S.C. § 1961 *et seq.*, as well as state law.

The District Court, through dismissal and summary judgment, resolved all of Plaintiffs'

963 F Supp (2002). Opinion by Circuit Judge Pregerson.

federal claims in favor of the Defendants. For the following reasons, we reverse in part and affirm in part the District Court's rulings.

## I. FACTUAL AND PROCEDURAL BACKGROUND

### A. Unocal's Investment in a Natural Gas Project in Myanmar.

Burma has been ruled by a military government since 1958. In 1988, a new military government, Defendant-Appellee State Law and Order Restoration Council ("the Myanmar Military"), took control and renamed the country Myanmar. The Myanmar Military established a state owned company, Defendant-Appellee Myanmar Oil and Gas Enterprise ("Myanmar Oil"), to produce and sell the nation's oil and gas resources.

In 1992, Myanmar Oil licensed the French oil company Total S.A. ("Total") to produce, transport, and sell natural gas from deposits in the Yadana Field off the coast of Myanmar ("the Project"). Total set up a subsidiary, Total Myanmar Exploration and Production ("Total Myanmar"), for this purpose. The Project consisted of a Gas Production Joint Venture, which would extract the natural gas out of the Yadana Field, and a Gas Transportation Company, which would construct and operate a pipeline to transport the natural gas from the coast of Myanmar through the interior of the country to Thailand.

Also in 1992, Defendant-Appellant Unocal Corporation and its wholly owned subsidiary Defendant-Appellant Union Oil Company of California, collectively referred to below as "Unocal," acquired a 28% interest in the Project from Total. Unocal set up a wholly owned subsidiary, the Unocal Myanmar Offshore Company ("the Unocal Offshore Co."), to hold Unocal's 28% interest in the Gas Production Joint Venture half of the Project. Similarly, Unocal set up another wholly owned subsidiary, the Unocal International Pipeline Corporation ("the Unocal Pipeline Corp."), to hold Unocal's 28% interest in the Gas Transportation Company half of the Project. Myanmar Oil and a Thai government entity, the Petroleum Authority of Thailand Exploration and Production, also acquired interests in the Project. Total Myanmar was appointed Operator of the Gas Production Joint Venture and the Gas Transportation Company. As the Operator, Total Myanmar was responsible, *inter alia*, for "determin[ing] . . . the selection of . . . employees [and] the hours of work and the compensation to be paid to all . . . employees" in connection with the Project.

### B. Unocal's Knowledge that the Myanmar Military Was Providing Security and Other Services for the Project.

It is undisputed that the Myanmar Military provided security and other services for the Project, and that Unocal knew about this. The pipeline was to run through Myanmar's rural Tenasserim region. The Myanmar Military increased its presence in the pipeline region to provide security and other services for the Project. A Unocal memorandum documenting Unocal's meetings with Total on March 1 and 2, 1995 reflects Unocal's understanding that "[f]our battalions of 600 men each will protect the [pipeline] corridor" and "[f]ifty soldiers will be assigned to guard each survey team." A former soldier in one of these battalions testified at his deposition that his battalion had been formed in 1996 specifically for this purpose. In addition, the Military built helipads and cleared roads along the proposed pipeline route for the benefit of the Project.

There is also evidence sufficient to raise a genuine issue of material fact whether the Project *hired* the Myanmar Military, through Myanmar Oil, to provide these services, and whether Unocal knew about this. A Production Sharing

Contract, entered into by Total Myanmar and Myanmar Oil before Unocal acquired an interest in the Project, provided that "[Myanmar Oil] shall . . . supply[ ] or mak[e] available . . . security protection . . . as may be requested by [Total Myanmar and its assigns]," such as Unocal. Unocal was aware of this agreement. Thus, a May 10, 1995 Unocal "briefing document" states that "[a]ccording to *our contract*, the government of Myanmar is responsible for protecting the pipeline." (Emphasis added.) Similarly, in May 1995, a cable from the U.S. Embassy in Rangoon, Myanmar, reported that Unocal On-Site Representative Joel Robinson ("Unocal Representative Robinson" or "Robinson") "stated forthrightly that *the companies have hired* the Burmese military to provide security for the project." (Emphasis added.)

Unocal disputes that the Project hired the Myanmar Military or, at the least, that Unocal knew about this. For example, Unocal points out that the Production Sharing Contract quoted in the previous paragraph covered only the off-shore Gas Production Joint Venture but not the Gas Transportation Company and the construction of the pipeline which gave rise to the alleged human rights violations. Moreover, Unocal President John Imle ("Unocal President Imle" or "Imle") stated at his deposition that he knew of "no . . . contractual obligation" requiring the Myanmar Military to provide security for the pipeline construction. Likewise, Unocal CEO Roger Beach ("Unocal CEO Beach" or "Beach") stated at his deposition that he also did not know "whether or not Myanmar had a contractual obligation to provide . . . security." Beach further stated that he was not aware of "any support whatsoever of the military[,] . . . either physical or monetary." These assertions by Unocal President Imle and Unocal CEO Beach are called into question by a briefing book which Total prepared for them on the occasion of their April 1996 visit to the Project. The briefing book lists the "numbers of villagers" working as "local helpers hired by battalions," the monthly "amount paid in Kyats" (the currency of Myanmar) to "Project Helpers," and the "amount in Kyats" expended by the Project on "food rations (Army + Villages)."

Furthermore, there is evidence sufficient to raise a genuine issue of material fact whether the Project directed the Myanmar Military in these activities, at least to a degree, and whether Unocal was involved in this. In May 1995, a cable from the U.S. Embassy in Rangoon reported:

> [Unocal Representative] Robinson indicated . . . Total/Unocal uses [aerial photos, precision surveys, and topography maps] to show the [Myanmar] military where they need helipads built and facilities secured. . . . Total's security officials meet with military counterparts to inform them of the next day's activities so that soldiers can ensure the area is secure and guard the work perimeter while the survey team goes about its business.

A November 8, 1995 document apparently authored by Total Myanmar stated that "[e]ach working group has a security officer . . . to control the army positions." A January 1996 meeting document lists "daily security coordination with the army" as a "working procedure." Similarly, the briefing book that Total prepared for Unocal President Imle and Unocal CEO Beach on the occasion of their April 1996 visit to the Project mentions that "daily meeting[s]" were "held with the tactical commander" of the army. Moreover, on or about August 29, 1996, Unocal (Singapore) Director of Information Carol Scott ("Unocal Director of Information Scott" or "Scott") discussed with Unocal Media Contact and Spokesperson David Garcia ("Unocal Spokesperson Garcia" or "Garcia") via e-mail how Unocal should publicly address the issue of the alleged movement of villages by the Myanmar Military in connection with the pipeline. Scott cautioned Garcia that "[b]y saying *we* influenced the army not to move a village, you introduce the concept that they would do such a thing; whereas, by saying that no villages have been moved, you skirt the issue of whether it could happen or not." (Emphasis added.) This e-mail is some evidence that Unocal could influence the army not to commit human rights violations, that the army might otherwise commit such violations, and that Unocal knew this.

### C. Unocal's Knowledge that the Myanmar Military Was Allegedly Committing Human Rights Violations in Connection with the Project.

Plaintiffs are villagers from Myanmar's Tenasserim region, the rural area through which the Project built the pipeline. Plaintiffs allege that the Myanmar Military forced them, under threat of violence, to work on and serve as porters for the Project. For instance, John Doe IX testified that he was forced to build a helipad near the pipeline site in 1994 that was then used by Unocal and Total officials who visited the pipeline during its planning stages. John Doe VII and John Roe X, described the construction of helipads at Eindayaza and Po Pah Pta, both of which were near the pipeline site, were used to ferry Total/Unocal executives and materials to the construction site, and were constructed using the forced labor of local villagers, including Plaintiffs. John Roes VIII and IX, as well as John Does I, VIII and IX testified that they were forced to work on building roads leading to the pipeline construction area. Finally, John Does V and IX, testified that they were required to serve as "pipeline porters" — workers who performed menial tasks such as such as hauling materials and cleaning the army camps for the soldiers guarding the pipeline construction.

Plaintiffs also allege in furtherance of the forced labor program just described, the Myanmar Military subjected them to acts of murder, rape, and torture. For instance, Jane Doe I testified that after her husband, John Doe I, attempted to escape the forced labor program, he was shot at by soldiers, and in retaliation for his attempted escape, that she and her baby were thrown into a fire, resulting in injuries to her and the death of the child. Other witnesses described the summary execution of villagers who refused to participate in the forced labor program, or who grew too weak to work effectively. Several Plaintiffs testified that rapes occurred as part of the forced labor program. For instance, both Jane Does II and III testified that while conscripted to work on pipeline-related construction projects, they were raped at knifepoint by Myanmar soldiers who were members of a battalion that was supervising the work. Plaintiffs finally allege that Unocal's conduct gives rise to liability for these abuses.

The successive military governments of first Burma and now Myanmar have a long and well-known history of imposing forced labor on their citizens. . . . As detailed below, even before Unocal invested in the Project, Unocal was made aware—by its own consultants and by its partners in the Project—of this record and that the Myanmar Military might also employ forced labor and commit other human rights violations in connection with the Project. And after Unocal invested in the Project, Unocal was made aware—by its own consultants and employees, its partners in the Project, and human rights organizations—of allegations that the Myanmar Military was actually committing such violations in connection with the Project. . . .

## II. ANALYSIS

### Liability Under the Alien Tort Claims Act.

#### *1. Introduction*

*1.* The Alien Tort Claims Act confers upon the federal district courts "original jurisdiction of any civil action by an alien for a tort only, committed in violation of the law of nations." We have held that the ATCA also provides a cause of action, as long as "plaintiffs . . . allege a violation of 'specific, universal, and obligatory' international norms as part of [their] ATCA claim." . . . Plaintiffs allege that Unocal's conduct gave rise to ATCA liability for the forced labor, murder, rape, and torture inflicted on them by the Myanmar Military. . . . We must determine whether, viewing the evidence in the light most favorable to the nonmoving party, there are any genuine issues of material fact and whether the district court correctly applied the relevant substantive law.

*2.* One threshold question in *any* ATCA case is whether the alleged tort is a violation of the law of nations. We have recognized that torture, murder, and slavery are *jus cogens* violations and, thus, violations of the law of nations.[1] . . . Rape can be a form of torture. Moreover, forced labor is so widely condemned that it has achieved the status of a *jus cogens* violation. *See, e.g.*, Universal Declaration of Human Rights. . . . Accordingly, all torts alleged in the present case are *jus cogens* violations and, thereby, violations of the law of nations. . . .

*4.* In light of these authorities,[2] we conclude that forced labor is a modern variant of slavery that, like traditional variants of slave trading, does not require state action to give rise to liability under the ATCA.

b. Unocal may be liable under the ATCA for aiding and abetting the Myanmar Military in subjecting Plaintiffs to forced labor.

Plaintiffs argue that Unocal aided and abetted the Myanmar Military in subjecting them to forced labor. We hold that the standard for aiding and abetting under the ATCA is, as discussed below, knowing practical assistance or encouragement that has a substantial effect on the perpetration of the crime. We further hold that a reasonable factfinder could find that Unocal's conduct met this standard. . . .

We however agree with the District Court that in the present case, we should apply international law as developed in the decisions by international criminal tribunals such as the Nuremberg Military Tribunals for the applicable substantive law. "The law of nations 'may be ascertained by consulting the works of jurists, writing professedly on public law; or by the general usage and practice of nations; *or by judicial decisions recognizing and enforcing that law.*'" . . .

*7.* International human rights law has been developed largely in the context of criminal prosecutions rather than civil proceedings. . . .

*8.* The *Furundzija* standard for aiding and abetting liability under international criminal law can be summarized as knowing practical assistance, encouragement, or moral support which has a substantial effect on the perpetration of the crime. At least with respect to assistance and encouragement, this standard is similar to the standard for aiding and abetting under domestic tort law. Thus, the Restatement of Torts states: "For harm resulting to a third person from the tortious conduct of another, one is subject to liability if he . . . (b) knows that the other's conduct constitutes a breach of duty and gives *substantial assistance or encouragement* to the other so to conduct himself. . . ." *Restatement (Second) of Torts* § 876 (1979) (emphasis added). Especially given the similarities between the *Furundzija* international criminal standard and the Restatement domestic tort standard, we find that application of a slightly modified *Furundzija* standard is appropriate in the present case. In particular, given that there is—as discussed below—sufficient evidence in the present case that Unocal gave assistance and encouragement to the Myanmar Military, we do not need to decide whether it would have been enough if Unocal had only given moral support to the Myanmar Military. Accordingly, we may impose aiding and abetting liability for knowing practical assistance or encouragement which has a substantial effect on the perpetration of the crime, leaving the question whether such liability should also be imposed for moral support which has the required substantial effect to another day.

*9.* First, a reasonable factfinder could conclude that Unocal's alleged conduct met the *actus reus* requirement of aiding and abetting as we define it today, i.e., practical assistance or encouragement which has a substantial effect on the perpetration of the crime of, in the present case, forced labor.

*10.* Unocal's weak protestations notwithstanding, there is little doubt that the record contains substantial evidence creating a material question of fact as to whether forced labor was used in connection with the construction of the pipeline. Numerous witnesses, including a number of Plaintiffs, testified that they were forced to clear the right of way for the pipeline and to build helipads for the project before construction of the pipeline began. For instance, John Doe IX testified that he was forced to build a helipad near the pipeline site in 1994 that was then used by Unocal and Total officials who visited the pipeline during its planning stages. Other Plaintiffs and witnesses, including John Doe VII and John Roe X, described the construction of helipads at Eindayaza and Po Pah Pta, both of which were near the pipeline site, were used to ferry Total/Unocal executives and materials to the constructed site, and were constructed using the forced labor of local villagers, including Plaintiffs. Other Plaintiffs, such as John Roes VIII and IX, as well as John Does I, VIII and IX, testified that they were forced to work on building roads leading to the pipeline construction area. Finally, yet other Plaintiffs, such as John Does V and IX, testified that they were required to serve as "pipeline porters"—workers who performed menial tasks such as hauling materials and cleaning the army camps for the soldiers guarding the pipeline construction. These serious allegations create triable questions of fact as to whether the Myanmar Military implemented a policy of forced labor in connection with its work on the pipeline.

*11.* The evidence also supports the conclusion that Unocal gave practical assistance to the Myanmar Military in subjecting Plaintiffs to forced labor. The practical assistance took the form of hiring the Myanmar Military to provide security and build infrastructure along the pipeline route in exchange for money or food. The practical assistance also took the form of using photos, surveys, and maps in daily meetings to show the Myanmar Military where to provide security and build infrastructure.

*12.* This assistance, moreover, had a "substantial effect" on the perpetration of forced labor, which "most probably would not have occurred in the same way" without someone hiring the Myanmar Military to provide security, and without someone showing them where to do it. This conclusion is supported by the admission of Unocal Representative Robinson that "[o]ur assertion that [the Myanmar Military] has not *expanded and amplified its usual methods* around the pipeline *on our behalf* may not withstand much scrutiny," and by the admission of Unocal President Imle that "[i]f forced labor goes hand and glove with the military yes there will be *more forced labor.*" (Emphasis added.)

*13.* Second, a reasonable factfinder could also conclude that Unocal's conduct met the *mens rea* requirement of aiding and abetting as we define it today, namely, actual or constructive (i.e.,reasonable) knowledge that the accomplice's actions will assist the perpetrator in the commission of the crime. The District Court found that "[t]he evidence does suggest that Unocal knew that forced labor was being utilized and that the Joint Venturers benefitted from the practice." Moreover, Unocal knew or should reasonably have known that its conduct—including the payments and the instructions where to provide security and build infrastructure — would assist or encourage the Myanmar Military to subject Plaintiffs to forced labor.

*14.* Viewing the evidence in the light most favorable to Plaintiffs, we conclude that there are genuine issues of material fact whether

Unocal's conduct met the *actus reus* and *mens rea* requirements for liability under the ATCA for aiding and abetting forced labor. Accordingly, we reverse the District Court's grant of Unocal's motion for summary judgment on Plaintiffs forced labor claims under the ATCA.

## NOTES

1. *Jus cogens* norms are norms of international law that are binding on nations even if they do not agree to them.
2. From Section [3] which has been omitted.

## CASES

# CASE 1. *Foreign Assignment*

Sara Strong graduated with an MBA from UCLA four years ago. She immediately took a job in the correspondent bank section of the Security Bank of the American Continent. Sara was assigned to work on issues pertaining to relationships with correspondent banks in Latin America. She rose rapidly in the section and received three good promotions in three years. She consistently got high ratings from her superiors, and she received particularly high marks for her professional demeanor.

In her initial position with the bank, Sara was required to travel to Mexico on several occasions. She was always accompanied by a male colleague even though she generally handled similar business by herself on trips within the United States. During her trips to Mexico she observed that Mexican bankers seemed more aware of her being a woman and were personally solicitous to her, but she didn't discern any major problems. The final decisions on the work that she did were handled by male representatives of the bank stationed in Mexico.

A successful foreign assignment was an important step for those on the "fast track" at the bank. Sara applied for a position in Central or South America and was delighted when she was assigned to the bank's office in Mexico City. The office had about twenty bank employees and was headed by William Vitam. The Mexico City office was seen as a preferred assignment by young executives at the bank.

After a month, Sara began to encounter problems. She found it difficult to be effective in dealing with Mexican bankers—the clients. They appeared reluctant to accept her authority, and they would often bypass her in important matters. The problem was exacerbated by Vitam's compliance in her being bypassed. When she asked that the clients be referred back to her, Vitam replied, "Of course, that isn't really practical." Vitam made matters worse by patronizing her in front of clients and by referring to her as "my cute assistant" and "our lady banker." Vitam never did this when only Americans were present and in fact treated her professionally and with respect in internal situations.

Sara finally complained to Vitam that he was undermining her authority and effectiveness; she asked him in as positive a manner as possible to help her. Vitam listened carefully to Sara's complaints, then replied, "I'm glad that you brought this up, because I've been meaning to sit down and talk to you about my little

This case was prepared by Thomas Dunfee and Diana Robertson, The Wharton School.

game playing in front of the clients. Let me be frank with you. Our clients think you're great, but they just don't understand a woman in authority, and you and I aren't going to be able to change their attitudes overnight. As long as the clients see you as my assistant and deferring to me, they can do business with you. I'm willing to give you as much responsibility as they can handle your having. I *know* you can handle it. But we just have to tread carefully. You and I know that my remarks in front of clients don't mean anything. They're just a way of playing the game Latin style. I know it's frustrating for you, but I really need you to support me on this. It's not going to affect your promotions. You just have to act like it's my responsibility." Sara replied that she would try to cooperate, but that basically she found her role demeaning.

As time went on, Sara found that the patronizing actions in front of clients bothered her more and more. She spoke to Vitam again, but he was firm in his position and urged her to try to be a little more flexible, even a little more "feminine."

Sara also had a problem with Vitam over policy. The Mexico City office had five younger women who worked as receptionists and secretaries. They were all situated at work stations at the entrance of the office. They were required to wear standard uniforms that were colorful and slightly sexy. Sara protested the requirement that uniforms be worn because (1) they were inconsistent to the image of the banking business and (2) they were demeaning to the women who had to wear them. Vitam just curtly replied that he had received a lot of favorable comments about the uniforms from clients of the bank.

Several months later, Sara had what she thought would be a good opportunity to deal with the problem. Tom Fried, an executive vice president who had been a mentor for her since she arrived at the bank, was coming to Mexico City; she arranged a private conference with him. She described her problems and explained that she was not able to be effective in this environment and that she worried that it would have a negative effect on her chance of promotion within the bank. Fried was very careful in his response. He spoke of certain "realities" that the bank had to respect, and he urged her to "see it through" even though he could understand how she would feel that things weren't fair.

Sara found herself becoming more aggressive and defensive in her meetings with Vitam and her clients. Several clients asked that other bank personnel handle their transactions. Sara has just received an Average rating, which noted "the beginnings of a negative attitude about the bank and its policies."

## Questions

1. What obligations does an international company have to ensure that its employees are not harmed, for instance, by having their chances for advancement limited by the social customs of a host country?
2. What international moral code, if any, is being violated by Security Bank of the American Continent?
3. Has the bank made the correct decision by opting to follow the norms of the host country?
4. What steps can be taken on the part of the internationals and their employees to avoid or resolve situations in which employees are offended or harmed by host country practices?
5. In this situation does morality require respect for Mexican practices, or does it require respect for Sara Strong? Are these incompatible?

# CASE 2. *Facilitation or Bribery: Cultural and Ethical Disparities*

Geletex, Inc., is a U.S. telecommunications corporation attempting to expand its operations worldwide. As Geletex begins its operations in other countries, it has discovered cultural, governmental, and ethical standards that differ significantly from country to country and from those in the United States. Geletex has had a code of ethics for its U.S. operations since 1975. The company's director of compliance, Jed Richardson, provides ongoing training for employees, runs a hotline through which employees can report problems and is well known and respected throughout the company for his high standards and trustworthiness. As Geletex's international operations grow, Jed is becoming increasingly uncomfortable with what appear to be double standards for the company's U.S. operations and its operations in other countries. Jed, who has been traveling to each of the Geletex international offices, has found the following situations, which since have been causing him some sleepless nights:

- In the Lima, Peru, office, Jed, in reviewing financial records, discovered that the commissions expense for the branch is unusually high. Geletex pays its salespeople commissions for each commercial customer they recruit for cellular or long-distance services. Jed knows from experience that some companies pay unusually high sales commissions to disguise the fact that salespeople are paying kickbacks in exchange for contracts. In the United States, such payments would be commercial bribery and a violation of Geletex's code of ethics. When Jed confronted the Lima, Peru, district manager and questioned him about the high commissions, he responded, "Look, things are different down here. We've got a job to do. If the company wants results, we've got to get things moving any way we can."
- In the Stockholm, Sweden, office, Jed noted a number of college-age student employees who seemed to have little work to do. Again, Jed questioned the district manager, who responded, "Sure, Magnus is the son of a telecommunications regulator. Caryl is the daughter of a judge who handles regulatory appeals in utilities. Andre is a nephew of the head of the governing party. They're bright kids, and the contacts don't hurt us. In the Scandanavian culture, giving jobs to children is part of doing business."
- In the Bombay, India, office, Jed noted that many different payments had been made to both the Indian government and government officials. When Jed voiced his concern, the district manager responded, "I can explain every payment. On this one, we needed the utilities [water and electricity] for our offices turned on. We could have waited our turn and had no services for ninety days, or we could pay to get moved to the top of the list and have our utilities turned on in forty-eight hours. On the check for licensing, again, we could have waited six months to get licensed or pay to expedite it and be licensed."

Jed is an expert on the Foreign Corrupt Practices Act (FCPA). The act permits "facilitation" or "grease" payments but prohibits bribes. Facilitation opens doors or expedites processes; it does not purport to influence outcomes. Jed is unsure about Geletex's international operations and compliance with the law. He is very unsure about Geletex having an international code of ethics.

## Questions

1. Do any of the offices' actions violate the FCPA?
2. Must a business adopt the ethical standards of a host culture in order to succeed?
3. Are all of the actions in the various offices ethical?
4. If you were Jed, what ethical standards would you develop for international operations?
5. Does Jed's firm create any internal problems by allowing different conduct in different countries and cultures?
6. The American Bar Association reports that there have been only 16 bribery prosecutions under the FCPA since 1977. However, thousands of others have settled voluntarily rather than go to trial. Is the FCPA necessary for international business operations? Does it impede U.S. businesses' success in other countries?

# CASE 3. *Adidas-Salomon[1]: Application of Standards of Engagement to Child Labor Dilemma*

Adidas-Salomon, formerly called adidas, was founded in 1949 and was named after its founder Adolf (Adi for short) Dassler. Most of us know adidas for its shoe production but the firm also produces clothing and sports equipment.[2] This diversification helped adidas to earn a net income of 208 million euros (approximately $183 million) on net sales of 6.11 billion euros (approximately $5.35 billion) in 2001.[3] Shoes accounted for approximately 44 percentage of sales during that year.[4]

Adidas does not actually manufacture any of its products but instead contracts with approximately 950 suppliers worldwide.[5] Though it is not the case with its contract apparel factories, most of adidas' footwear suppliers produce almost exclusively for adidas. This allows the firm great leverage in footwear factories to demand compliance with certain standards with regard to labor practices or issues surrounding safety, health, and the environment. Given its leverage with suppliers, adidas asserts that "outsourcing supply does not mean outsourcing social responsibility."[6]

## ADIDAS-SALOMON'S STANDARDS OF ENGAGEMENT

Many firms have created and have published codes of conduct and other like statements *subsequent* to targeted attacks by activists. Adidas-Salomon had been subject to similar attacks but also had discovered through its own internal mechanisms that some of its supplier operations were not operating at standards equivalent to its own operations. In 1998, adidas-Salomon published its Standards of Engagement (SoE) with the aim of ensuring that all of its suppliers' factories are safe, fair places to work. Updated in 2001, the SoE are patterned after the ILO conventions and the model code of conduct of the World Federation of Sporting Goods Industries and reflect attention to the following labor, safety, health, and environmental issues:

- forced labor
- child labor
- discrimination
- wages and benefits

---

Reprinted with permission of the author, Laura P. Hartman. This case was developed based on research that serves as the foundation for "Rising above Sweatshops: Innovative Management Responses to Global Labor Challenges," edited by L. Hartman, D. Arnold, and R. Wokutch (Praeger Publishers, 2003).

- hours of work
- freedom of association and collective bargaining
- disciplinary practices
- health and safety
- environmental requirements
- community involvement

Since their inception, the most widely encountered problems in Asian supplier factories are the payment of recruitment fees, poor age documentation, wages lower than minimum wage, maximum working hours ignored, working rules not published, wages docked as punishment for violating working rules, confiscation of passports, abuse of migrant workers, and illegal status of unions.[7]

Once informed by its sourcing division that adidas-Salomon will be using a new supplier, adidas-Salomon's SoE division schedules a first-time audit to determine compliance with the SoE. At the conclusion of this or other annual audits, suppliers are informed about areas needing attention, are given performance ratings for (1) health, safety, and environment; and (2) labor standards, and are ranked using the adidas-Salomon 5-star approach. It was during one of these first time audits that adidas discovered a pervasive problem with child labor in one of its new Asian suppliers.

### Children Found in Supplier Factory

Adidas faced this particularly challenging dilemma when it performed a first-time audit of a footwear supplier in Vietnam. On her audit of the factory, the auditor found documents that did not seem to make sense and confirmed these inconsistencies through worker interviews. At the conclusion of her investigation, the auditor identified just under 200 of the factory's 2000 workers as underage, according to adidas's SoE.

The auditor found both child workers (under 16) as well as juveniles (16–18 years old). Both groups were subject to the same responsibilities, pay, hours, and overtime requirements as other workers, in violation of adidas's SoE. According to the SoE and its Guidelines on Employment Standards, child laborers are not permitted at all: Business partners may not employ children who are less than 15 years old, or who are younger than the age for completing compulsory education in the country of manufacture where such age is higher than 15. Adidas also requires that juvenile workers must be assigned to age-appropriate, safe duties, with a maximum of seven hours per day with no overtime.[8]

### Next Steps

After reporting this information, the adidas auditor realized that the solution was more complicated than simply letting the supplier terminate all of these youths. However, during the time the SoE division was contemplating its response, several dozen child workers were immediately terminated without the knowledge of adidas. Adidas SoE staff now knew that something had to be done—and quickly—to avoid losing contact with other youth workers, which might force these kids into alternatives far worse than the work environment they were forced to leave.

Adidas senior production staff immediately told the factory manager that no more youths could be encouraged to leave, under any circumstances. Adidas felt incredible pressure to act without delay in establishing some parameters for the situation, even though a more drawn out process might have resulted in greater buy-in and participation from the factory, and a longer consultation period with the youths. Adidas hired a Vietnamese education coordinator through an NGO called Verité. At the same time, adidas drafted some basic notices to the children, on behalf of the factory. The notices explained that the factory would offer a program of educational classes and vocational training to the workers under 18. The students had to decide whether they would commit to the program. The notice required them to discuss the issue with family members and to give their consent to enter into the program. It was clear to the adidas SoE team members that most of the student did not have a full understanding of what was going to happen and many of them were naturally suspicious.

### Possible Solutions?

Working with Verité and the education coordinator, adidas was able to develop what later became adidas global policy for managing similar situations, that is, a global vision:

> The supplier meets with the worker and tries to persuade them to go back to school. If the worker agrees to return to school, schooling fees and other costs are paid for by the factory until the worker completes compulsory education. Any continued employment is conditional on enrolling the workers in a work study program of continued education.
>
> The factory continues to pay the average monthly wage for the worker until the worker finishes school. This will make up for any lost income that the worker's family depends on in order to cover the basic needs of the family. The worker is required to provide the personnel manager proof of enrollment in school in order to continue receiving the monthly salary and school payments.
>
> Finally, the factory agrees to provide a job for the worker once the worker has completed compulsory education.[9]

For children up to 16 years of age, in cooperation with teachers from the local government schools, the factory put into place a full-day education program with coverage similar to that covered in local schools. Topics included math, literature, chemistry, physics, biology, and history. Children would arrive and depart from the factory at the same times they originally traveled, but would spend the workday in a large classroom in a space specifically designated for the program by the factory. Preprogram assessments were completed to accurately place each student in an education- appropriate program, and teachers were hired to conduct the classes from a local province.

For juveniles who are 16 and 17 years of age, adidas felt that it was important to offer them continuing education programs in "lifestyle skills" subjects such as topics including computer skills, the Vietnamese Labor Code, the environment, safety (both personal and in the workplace, with a focus on fire safety), AIDS/HIV, sexual education, and hygiene. Not only would these programs assist the juveniles in areas of personal development, but adidas felt that it was necessary to occupy the workers in the afternoons so they wouldn't seek other work in alternate factories, thus subverting the current efforts.

### Assessment

When the program began, they had 13 students enrolled in the younger program and 133 students in the juvenile program. As of June 2001, only 56 students remained involved in the program since many had already reached the age of 18. Eleven of these students are less than 16 years old (following an academic program equivalent to the 6th, 7th and 8th grade levels); 43 are juveniles participating in the lifestyle education programs and two are older workers who have chosen to participate in these latter courses.

While adidas was of tremendous assistance in the establishment of the programs, themselves, they did not contribute to the programs on a financial level. "We wanted them to know that we believed this was their responsibility and not a 'rescue'" says the adidas auditor. In order to facilitate payments, and because it was Verité's policy to enter into a contractual relationship with the multinational rather than the factory (to ensure payments and assure leverage between the MNE and the factory), adidas paid to Verité a quarterly advance for the work anticipated while the factory paid adidas retrospectively on a monthly basis for work performed. Under these arrangements, the risk was carried in full by adidas; but this arrangement also afforded adidas the leverage it needed in order to ensure compliance by the factory. In the final months of the program, an assessment by another NGO and local Vietnamese researches will be conducted. The assessment will be fully funded by adidas, but the results of, and any recommendations in, the assessment will be available to all the parties involved in the program.

### Questions

1. If a supplier is not in compliance with the SoE, what is the most effective way for adidas to respond? Under what circumstances would you suggest that adidas work to resolve the issues versus terminating the relationship with the supplier?
2. Do you believe that adidas's, response to the child labor challenge in its supplier was effective? What alternatives did it have in terms of a response?
3. If you were the auditor, in hindsight, what lessons can be learned from this experience?

## NOTES

1. Note: adidas-Salomon customarily uses a lowercase "a" to begin its name.
2. http://www.adidas-salomon.com/en/overview/.
3. adidas-Salomon, "Overview, History," *infra* n. 3.
4. adidas-Salomon, "Overview, History," *infra* n. 3.
5. adidas-Salomon, "Clearer: Social and Environmental Report 2001." Herzogenaurach, Germany: adidas-Salomon, 2000, p. 20.
6. adidas-Salomon, "Our World: Social and Environmental Report 2000," *infra* n. 5, p. 14.
7. adidas-Salomon. "Our world: Social and environmental report 2000," *infra* n. 5, pp. 26–27.
8. adidas-Salomon Guidelines on Employment Standards, (2001), part two, chapter 3, pp. 1–8.
9. adidas-Salomon Guidelines on Employment Standards *infra* at note 8, at part two, Chapter 3, p. 5.

## APPENDIX

# Adidas Standards of Engagement

### AUTHENTICITY. INSPIRATION. COMMITMENT. HONESTY.

These are some of the core values of the adidas brand. We measure ourselves by these values, and we measure our business partners in the same way.

Consistent with these brand values, we expect our partners—contractors, subcontractors, suppliers, and others—to conduct themselves with the utmost fairness, honesty, and responsibility in all aspects of their business.

These Standards of Engagement are tools that assist us in selecting and retaining business partners that follow workplace standards and business practices consistent with our policies and values. As a set of guiding principles, they also help identify potential problems so that we can work with our business partners to address issues of concern as they arise.

Specifically, we expect our business partners to operate workplaces where the following standards and practices are followed:

I. General Principle

Business partners shall comply fully with all legal requirements relevant to the conduct of their businesses.

II. Employment Standards
We will only do business with partners who treat their employees fairly and legally with regard to wages, benefits, and working conditions. In particular, the following guidelines apply:

**Forced labor:** Business partners shall not employ forced labor, whether in the form of prison labor, indentured labor, bonded labor, or otherwise.

**Child labor:** Business partners shall not employ children who are less than 15 years old (or 14 years old where the law of the country of manufacture allows), or who are younger than the age for completing compulsory education in the country of manufacture where such age is higher than 15.

**Discrimination:** While we recognize and respect cultural differences, we believe that workers should be employed on the basis of their ability to do the job, rather than on the basis of personal characteristics or beliefs. We will seek business partners that share this value, and that do not discriminate in hiring and employment practices on grounds of race, national origin, gender, religion, age, disability, sexual orientation, or political opinion.

**Wages and benefits:** Business partners shall pay their employees the minimum wage required by law or the prevailing industry wage, whichever is higher, and shall provide legally mandated benefits. Wages shall be paid directly to the employee in cash or check or the equivalent, and information relating to wages shall be provided to employees in a form they understand. Advances and deductions from wages shall be carefully monitored, and shall comply with law.

**Hours of work:** Employees shall not be required to work more than sixty hours per week, including overtime, on a regular basis and shall be compensated for overtime according to law. Employees shall be allowed at least 24 consecutive hours off per week, and should receive paid annual leave.

**Right of association:** Business partners shall recognize and respect the right of workers to join and organize associations of their own choosing.

**Disciplinary practices:** Every employee shall be treated with respect and dignity. No employee shall be subject to any physical, sexual, psychological or verbal harassment or abuse.

III. Health and Safety
Business partners shall provide a safe and healthy working environment, including protection from fire, accidents, and toxic substances. Lighting, heating and ventilation systems should be adequate. Employees should have access at all times to sanitary facilities, which should be adequate and clean. When residential facilities are provided for employees, the same standards should apply.

IV. Environmental Requirements
Business partners shall comply with all applicable environmental laws and regulations.

V. Community Involvement
We will favor business partners who make efforts to contribute to improving conditions in the countries and communities in which they operate.

## *Suggested Supplementary Readings*

ABENG, TANRI. "Business Ethics in Islamic Context: Perspectives of a Muslim Business Leader." *Business Ethics Quarterly*, 7 (1997): 47–54

AVIVA, GEVA, "Moral Problems of Employing Foreign Workers." *Business Ethics Quarterly*, 9 (1999): 381–403.

Brenkert, George C. "Can We Afford International Human Rights?" *Journal of Business Ethics,* 11 (July 1992): 515–21.

Brennan, Bartley A. "The Foreign Corrupt Practices Act Amendments of 1988: The Death of a Law." *North Carolina Journal of International Law & Commerce Regulation,* 15 (1990): 229–47.

Carson, Thomas L. "Bribery, Extortion, and 'The Foreign Corrupt Practices Act.'" *Philosophy and Public Affairs,* 14 (Winter 1985): 66–90.

DeGeorge, Richard. *Competing with Integrity in International Business.* New York: Oxford University Press, 1993.

———. "International Business Ethics: Russia and Eastern Europe." *Social Responsibility: Business, Journalism, Law and Medicine,* 19 (1993): 5–23.

Dollinger, Marc J. "Confucian Ethics and Japanese Management Practices." *Journal of Business Ethics,* 7 (August 1988): 575–83.

Donaldson, Thomas. *The Ethics of International Business,* New York: Oxford University Press, 1989.

———. "The Language of International Corporate Ethics," *Business Ethics Quarterly,* 2 (July 1992): 271–81.

———. "Values in Tension: Ethics Away from Home," *Harvard Business Review* (September/October 1996): 48–62.

Filatotchev, Igor, Ken Starkey, and Mike Wright. "The Ethical Challenge of Management Buy-outs as a form of Privatization in Central and Eastern Europe." *Journal of Business Ethics,* 13 (July 1994): 523–32.

Frederick, William C. "The Moral Authority of Transnational Corporate Codes." *Journal of Business Ethics,* 10 (1991): 165–177.

Getz, Kathleen. "International Codes of Conduct: An Analysis of Ethical Reasoning." *Journal of Business Ethics,* 9 (1990): 567–77.

Gillespie, Kate. "Middle East Response to the Foreign Corrupt Practices Act." *California Management Review,* 29 (Summer, 1987): 9–30.

Hazera, Alejandro. "A Comparison of Japanese and U.S. Corporate Financial Accountability." *Business Ethics Quarterly,* 5 (July, 1995): 479–97.

Hindman, Hugh D., and Charles G. Smith. "Cross-Cultural Ethics and the Child Labor Problem." *Journal of Business Ethics,* 19 (March, 1999): 21–33.

Hoffman W., Michael, and Others, eds. *Ethics and the Multinational Enterprise.* Washington, DC: University Press of America, 1985.

Husted, Bryan W. "Honor Among Thieves: A Transaction-Cost Interpretation of Corruption in Third World Countries." *Business Ethics Quarterly,* 4 (January 1994): 17–27.

——— "Culture and International Anti-Corruption Agreements in Latin America," *Journal of Business Ethics,* 37 (4) (June 2002) 413–422.

Ip, Po-Keung. "The Weizhi Group of Xian: A Chinese Virtuous Corporation," *Journal of Business Ethics,* 35 (1) (January 2002), pp. 15–26.

Koehn, Daryl, "What Can Eastern Philosophy Teach Us about Business Ethics?" *Journal of Business Ethics,* 19 (1999): 71–79.

Lane, Henry W., and Donald G. Simpson. "Bribery in International Business: Whose Problem Is It?" *Journal of Business Ethics,* 3 (February, 1984): 35–42.

Langlois, Catherine C., and Bodo B. Schlegelmilch. "Do Corporate Codes of Ethics Reflect National Character? Evidence from Europe and the United States." *Journal of International Business Studies,* 21 (Fall 1990): 519–39.

Noonan, John T. Jr. *Bribes.* New York: Macmillan and Co., 1984.

Pacini, Carl, Judyth A. Swingen, and Hudson Rogers. "The Role of the OECD and EU Conventions in Combating Bribery in Foreign Public Officials," *Journal of Business Ethics,* 37(4) (June 2002) 385–405.

Sen, Amrtya. "Human Rights and Asian Values." New York: Carnegie Council on Ethics and International Affairs, 1997.

Steidlmeier, Paul. "The Moral Legitimacy of Intellectual Property Claims: American Business and Developing Country Perspectives." *Journal of Business Ethics,* 12 (February 1993): 157–64.

Su, Chenting, and James E. Littlefield. "Entering Guanxi: A Business Ethical Dilemma in Mainland China?." *Journal of Business Ethics,* 33 (2001), 199–210.

Taka, Iwao. "Business Ethics: A Japanese View." *Business Ethics Quarterly,* 4 (1) (1994).

Transparency International Corruption Reports http://www.transparency.de

Tubbs, Walter. "Karoushi: Stress-death and the Meaning of Work." *Journal of Business Ethics,* 12 (November, 1993): 869–77.

Velasquez, Manuel. "International Business, Morality, and the Common Good." *Business Ethics Quarterly,* 2 (January 1992): 26–40.

Wokutch, Richard E., and Jon M. Shepard. "The Maturing of the Japanese Economy: Corporate Social Responsibility Implications." *Business Ethics Quarterly,* 9 (1999): 541–558.

# *Chapter Ten*

# Social and Economic Justice

## INTRODUCTION

Economic disparities among individuals and nations have generated heated controversy over systems for distributing and taxing income and wealth. Sustained moral and political conflicts in the United States concern the justification of structures of taxation, international debt relief, corporate profits, corporate gifts, executive salaries and bonuses, plant closings, and exploitative conditions in factories.

Several well-reasoned and systematic answers to these and related questions have been grounded in theories of justice—that is, theories of how social and economic benefits, protections, services, and burdens should be distributed. In Chapter 1 we briefly analyzed some problems of ethical theory and justice. In the present chapter, the major distinctions, principles, and methods of moral argument in theories of justice are treated. The first four articles address the question, "Which general system of social and economic organization is most just?" The later articles (and cases at the end of the chapter) address the justice of particular policies and circumstances.

### Theories of Distributive Justice

What a person deserves or is entitled to is often decided by specific rules and laws, such as those governing state lotteries, food stamp allocation, health care coverage, admission procedures for universities, and the like. These rules may be evaluated, criticized, and revised by reference to moral principles such as equality of persons, nondiscriminatory treatment, property ownership, protection from harm, compensatory justice, and retributive justice. The word *justice* is used broadly to cover both these principles and specific rules derived from the same principles, but developed for specific situations.

Economists have sometimes complained about philosophers' approaches to justice, on grounds that a "fair price" or "fair trade" is not a matter of moral fairness: Prices may be low or high, affordable or not affordable, but not fair or unfair. It is simply unfortunate, not unfair, if one cannot afford to pay for something or if another person is paid 40 times what you are paid. The basis of this exclusion of price as a consideration of justice is the market-established nature of prices and salaries. To speak of "unfair" prices, trade, or salaries is to express a negative opinion, of course; but these economists reason that from a market perspective any price is fair as long as it is determined by a fair market. Salaries must be treated in the same way.

However, the economist may be missing the philosopher's point. The philosopher is often asking whether the market itself is a fair arrangement. If so, what makes it fair? If not, what makes it unfair? If coercion is used in the market to set prices, is this maneuver unfair, or does it render the market not a free market? If health care and education are distributed nationally or internationally with vast inequality, can high prices on essential items such as health care goods and university tuition be fair? If a multinational company has a monopoly on an essential foodstuff, is there no such thing as a price that is too high? These questions of fairness fall under the topic of distributive justice.

The term *distributive justice* refers to the proper distribution of social benefits and burdens. A theory of distributive justice attempts to establish a connection between the properties or characteristics of persons and the morally correct distribution of benefits and burdens in society. *Egalitarian* theories emphasize equal access to primary goods (see John Rawls's article); *communitarian* theories emphasize group goals, collective control, and participation in communal life, by contrast to liberal political systems that emphasize individual welfare and rights (see Michael Walzer's article); *libertarian* theories emphasize rights to social and economic liberty and deemphasize collective control (see Robert Nozick's essay, as well as Milton Friedman's); and *utilitarian* theories emphasize a mixed use of such criteria resulting in the maximization of both public and individual interests (see Peter Singer's article).

Systematic theories of justice attempt to elaborate how people should be compared and what it means to give people what they are due. Philosophers attempt to achieve the needed precision by developing material principles of justice, so called because they put material content into a theory of justice. Each material principle of justice identifies a relevant property on the basis of which burdens and benefits should be distributed. The following list includes the major candidates for the position of principles of distributive justice.

1. To each person an equal share
2. To each person according to individual need
3. To each person according to that person's rights
4. To each person according to individual effort
5. To each person according to societal contribution
6. To each person according to merit

A theory of justice might accept more than one of these principles. Some theories accept all six as legitimate. Many societies use several, in the belief that different rules are appropriate to different situations.

## Utilitarian Theory

In utilitarianism (which is examined in detail in Chapter 1), problems of justice are viewed as one part of the larger problem of maximizing value, and it is easy to see how a utilitarian might use all of these material principles to this end. The ideal distribution of benefits and burdens is simply the one having this maximizing effect. According to utilitarian Peter Singer, in his essay in this chapter, a heavy element of political planning and economic redistribution is required to ensure that justice is done. Because utilitarianism was treated in Chapter 1, detailed considerations will be given in this introduction only to egalitarian, libertarian, and communitarian theories.

## Egalitarian Theory

Equality in the distribution of social benefits and burdens has a central place in several influential ethical theories. For example, in utilitarianism different people are equal in the value accorded their wants, preferences, and happiness, and in Kantian theories all persons are considered equally worthy and deserving of respect as ends in themselves. Egalitarian theory treats the question of how people should be considered equal in some respects (for example, in their basic political and moral rights and obligations), yet unequal in others (for example, in wealth and social burdens such as taxation).

***Radical and Qualified Egalitarianism.*** In its radical form, egalitarian theory proposes that individual differences are always morally insignificant. Distributions of burdens and benefits in a society are just to the extent that they are equal, and deviations from absolute equality in distribution are unjust. For example, the fact that in the United States more than 35 percent of the wealth is owned by less than one-half of one percent of the population makes U.S. society unjust, according to this theory, no matter how relatively "deserving" the people at both extremes might be.

However, most egalitarian accounts are guardedly formulated, so that persons are not entitled to equal shares of all social benefits and so that individual merit justifies some differences in distribution. Egalitarianism, so qualified, is concerned only with basic equalities among individuals. For example, egalitarians generally prefer *progressive* tax rates (higher incomes taxed more heavily than lower) rather than *proportional* rates (each unit taxed the same). This preference may seem odd since a proportional rate treats everyone equally. However, qualified egalitarians often reason that progressive rates tax the wealthy more and thereby distribute wealth more evenly.

***John Rawls's Theory.*** In recent years a qualified egalitarian theory in the Kantian tradition has enjoyed wide discussion. John Rawls's *A Theory of Justice* maintains that all economic goods and services should be distributed equally except when an unequal distribution would work to everyone's advantage (or at least to the advantage of the worst off in society). Rawls presents this egalitarian theory as a direct challenge to utilitarianism. He argues that social distributions produced by maximizing utility permit violations of basic individual liberties and rights. Being indifferent to the distribution of satisfactions among individuals, utilitarianism permits the infringement of people's rights and liberties in order to produce a proportionately greater utility for all concerned.

Rawls defends a hypothetical social contract procedure that is strongly indebted to what he calls the "Kantian conception of equality." Valid principles of justice are those to which all persons would agree if they could freely and impartially consider the social situation. Impartiality is guaranteed by a conceptual device Rawls calls the "veil of ignorance." Here each person is imagined to be ignorant of all his or her particular characteristics, for example, the person's sex, race, IQ, family background, and special talents or handicaps. Theoretically, this veil of ignorance would prevent the adoption of principles biased toward particular groups of persons.

Rawls argues that under these conditions people would unanimously agree on two fundamental principles of justice. The first requires that each person be permitted the maximum amount of basic liberty compatible with a similar liberty for others. The second stipulates that once this equal basic liberty is assured, inequalities in social primary goods (for example, income, rights, and opportunities) are to be allowed only if they benefit everyone. Rawls considers social institutions to be just if and only if they conform to these principles of the social contract. He rejects radical egalitarianism, arguing that inequalities that render everyone better off by comparison to being equal are desirable.

Rawls formulates what is called the *difference principle:* Inequalities are justifiable only if they maximally enhance the position of the "representative least advantaged" person, that is, a hypothetical individual particularly unfortunate in the distribution of fortuitous characteristics or social advantages. Rawls is unclear about who might qualify under this category, but a worker incapacitated from exposure to asbestos and living in poverty clearly would qualify. Formulated in this way, the difference principle could allow, for instance, extraordinary economic rewards to business entrepreneurs, venture capitalists, and corporate takeover artists if the resulting economic situation were to produce improved job opportunities and working conditions for the least advantaged members of society, or possibly greater benefits for pension funds holding stock for the working class.

The difference principle rests on the moral viewpoint that because inequalities of birth, historical circumstance, and natural endowment are undeserved, persons in a cooperative society should make more equal the unequal situation of its naturally disadvantaged members.

## Libertarian Theory

What makes a libertarian theory *libertarian* is the priority given to distinctive procedures or mechanisms for ensuring that liberty rights are recognized in social and economic practice, typically the rules and procedures governing economic acquisition and exchange in capitalist or free-market systems.

***The Role of Individual Freedom.*** The libertarian contends that it is a basic violation of justice to ensure equal economic returns in a society. In particular, individuals are seen as having a fundamental right to own and dispense with the products of their labor as they choose, even if the exercise of this right leads to large inequalities of wealth in society. Equality and utility principles, from this perspective, sacrifice basic liberty rights to the larger public interest by exploiting one set of individuals for the benefit of another. The most apparent example is the coercive extraction of financial resources through taxation.

***Robert Nozick's Theory.*** Libertarian theory is defended in this chapter by Robert Nozick, who refers to his view as an "entitlement theory" of justice. Nozick argues that a theory of justice should work to protect individual rights and should not propound a thesis intended to "pattern" society through arrangements such as those in socialist and (impure) capitalist countries in which governments take pronounced steps to redistribute wealth.

Nozick's libertarian position rejects all distributional patterns imposed by material principles of justice. He is thus committed to a form of *procedural* justice. That is, for Nozick there is no pattern of just distribution independent of fair procedures of acquisition, transfer, and rectification; in this view he is joined in this chapter by Friedman. Their claims have been at the center of controversy over the libertarian account, and competing theories of justice often react to their uncompromising commitment to pure procedural justice.

## Communitarian Theory

Moral and political theories that advocate individual responsibility, free-market exchanges, and limited community control are often called *liberal* theories. "Liberalism," which places the individual at the center of moral and political life, views the state as properly limited in the event of a conflict with individual rights such as freedom of association, expression, and religion. The state's proper role is to protect and enforce basic moral and political rights, often called *civil rights*. Rawls and Nozick are both adherents of liberalism in this sense.

In recent years a tide of communitarian theories has risen against liberalism. Although a diverse lot, communitarian theories share many ideas. They see typical liberal theories such as those of Rawls and Nozick (and even Mill and Singer) as subverting communal life and the obligations and commitments that grow out of that perspective on life. These theorists see persons as *constituted* by communal values and thus as best suited to achieve their good through communal life, not state protections or individual moral and political rights.

Communitarians object to the way Rawlsian liberalism has made justice the first virtue of social institutions and then has patterned those institutions to protect the individual against society. The communitarian believes that justice is a less central virtue of social life, one needed only when communal values have broken down into conflicts of the sort litigated in court. Rather than conceptualizing the state's role as that of enforcer of rights allowing individuals to pursue any course they wish, the communitarian takes the view that the community may rightly be expected to impose on individuals certain conceptions of virtue and the good life.

The sole representative of communitarian theories in this chapter is Michael Walzer, a moderate communitarian not as opposed to liberalism as hard-line communitarians. For him notions of justice are not based on some "rational" or "natural" foundation external to the society. Rather, standards of justice are developed internally as the community evolves. Something has to be "given-as-basic" in every ethical theory, and the communitarian sees everything as deriving from communal values and historical practices. Conventions, traditions, and loyalties therefore play a more prominent role in communitarian theories than in the other theories we encounter in this chapter.

Communitarians recognize that people sometimes have good reason to challenge and even reject values accepted by the community. To this end, Walzer argues that a community ethic must be particularly vigilant to avoid "oppressing" minorities. Although an individual has a right to challenge community values, a communitarian will not accept an individual's personal values as either moral or respectable when those values depart from the central, defining moral values of the community.

## Capitalism: Is There Justice beyond the Free Market?

Many philosophers argue that an adequate theory of economic justice must recognize a set of individual rights that is more inclusive than those acknowledged in theories of capitalist markets. "Capitalism" is here understood as a market-based, economic system governed by capital, that is, the wealth of an individual or an establishment accumulated by or employed in its business activities. Entrepreneurs and the institutions they create generate the capital with which businesses provide goods, services, and payments to workers. Defenders of capitalism argue that this system maximally distributes social freedoms and desirable resources, resulting in the best economic outcomes for everyone in society. All libertarians, but also many utilitarians, egalitarians, and communitarians, have defended capitalism using this general conception.

In his selection in this chapter, Milton Friedman offers a defense of capitalism based on the "liberal philosophy" of the freedom of the individual to "make the most of his capacities and opportunities" (so long as the individual does not interfere with like liberties for others in society). When freedom comes in conflict with an egalitarian conception of the distribution of social goods, Friedman maintains that we ought to choose in favor of economic freedom. He argues that "the so-called capitalist ethic" is not itself an ethical principle; rather, it is a corollary of more fundamental principles of freedom. These principles protect persons from economic controls that use coercion (usually through taxation) to redistribute resources. The central principle of a market system, then, should be co-operation through voluntary exchange.

Critics are skeptical of such claims, unless they are heavily qualified in favor of some form of economic rights, not merely liberty rights. Critics believe that owners and managers unfairly allocate high wages for themselves, while distributing only low wages to workers, who are not able to move freely from one job to another in many capitalist markets. Critics of capitalism generally acknowledge that capitalists do often take significant economic risks (a justification advanced for their higher wages); however, critics maintain that capitalists rarely have to assume the burdens of deprivation that workers do. The avoidance of deprivation is a major reason why some writers propose interventions in capitalist markets; they seek to secure stronger economic rights for workers—such as a higher minimum wage, continuous health insurance, and unemployment insurance (or protections against economic disaster in the circumstance of job layoffs).

Critics of capitalism challenge its proponents to answer the following questions: Why should we assume that people's economic rights extend only to the acquisition and dispensation of private property according to free-market rules? Is it not equally plausible to posit more substantive moral rights in the economic sphere—say, rights to health care, decent levels of education, and decent standards of living?

In his contribution to this chapter, Leo Groarke uses these and other questions to point to "the weaknesses of capitalism." He finds that capitalism can have "profoundly negative effects" on the moral character of society by promoting the individual's pursuit of a consumer lifestyle, while neglecting moral matters of fundamental importance. These consumptive patterns, as he sees it, spawn many other public policy problems, including the cleanup of environmental damage for which no one wants to pay. He also argues that real capitalist markets often fall far short of ideal markets in that they ignore the kinds of motivations and strategies that are involved in the accumulation of private property and wealth. He further finds that the information necessary for a market to function fairly is often not available to those who need it. For example, misinformation through misleading channels such as aggressive advertising tends to overwhelm objective sources of information. Finally, Groarke judges that unequal concentrations of wealth and power promote rather than reduce gaps in levels of income and themselves exert major influences on how markets operate. To reduce these problems, Groarke argues for what he calls "mitigated capitalism," in which the economic system is regulated by an independent government with substantial regulatory authority to ensure competitive, efficient, and fair markets.

The capitalist ideal is widely agreed to be plausible for free transactions among informed and consenting parties who start as equals in the bargaining process. However, this conception has come under significant criticism in circumstances in which contractual bargaining among equals is impossible or unlikely. Contracts, voting privileges, individuals investing in the stock market, and family relationships may involve bluffing, differentials of power and wealth, manipulation, and the like. These factors can and often do work systematically to disadvantage vulnerable individuals. For example, over the course of time in the working of capitalist markets, one group in society may gain considerable wealth and political influence, by comparison to other groups in society. Even if the *transactions* leading to this imbalance may have been legitimate, the *outcome* may not be acceptable. If an individual's bargaining position has been deeply eroded, does he or she have a right to protection from social inequalities that have emerged? If he or she is destined to poverty as a result of social conditions, is there a legitimate claim of justice, as several authors in this chapter propose?

If people have a right to a minimal level of material means (a right libertarians do not acknowledge), it seems to many writers that their rights are violated whenever economic distributions leave persons with less than that minimal level. A commitment to individual economic rights, then, may go hand-in-hand with a theory of justice that requires a more activist role for government. This may be true even if one starts with free-market assumptions. Many philosophers agree with libertarian premises that economic freedom is a value deserving of respect and protection, but they disagree with the claim that the principles and procedures of unmitigated capitalist markets adequately protect the basic values of individual and public welfare.

In reaction to these problems, some reject the pure procedural commitments of pure capitalist (often libertarian or utilitarian) theories and replace them with a principle specifying human need as the relevant respect in which people are to be compared for purposes of determining social and economic justice. Much turns here on how the notion of need is defined and implemented. For purposes of justice, a principle of need would be least controversial if it were restricted to fundamental needs. If malnutrition, bodily injury, and the withholding of certain information involve fundamental harms, we have a fundamental need for nutrition, health care facilities, and education. According to theories based on this material principle, justice places the satisfaction of fundamental human needs above the protection of economic freedoms or rights (or at least at the same level of importance).

This construal of the principle of need has been used to support rights that reach well beyond capitalism. Yet there may be room for reconciliation between the principle of need and the principles that underlie capitalist systems. Many advanced industrial countries have the capacity to produce more than is strictly necessary to meet their citizens' fundamental needs. One might argue that *after* everyone's fundamental needs have been satisfied, *then* justice requires no particular pattern of distribution. For example, some current discussions of the right to health care and the right to a job are rooted in the idea of meeting basic medical and economic needs—but *only basic* needs. In this way, a single unified theory of justice might require the maintenance of certain patterns in the distributions of basic goods (for example, a decent minimum level of income, education, and health care), while allowing the market to determine distributions of goods beyond those that satisfy fundamental needs.

This approach accepts a two-tiered system of access to goods and services: (1) social coverage for basic and catastrophic needs, and (2) private purchase of other goods and services. On the first tier, distribution is based on need, and everyone's basic needs are met by the government. Better services may be made available for purchase in an economic system on the second tier. This proposal seems to present an attractive point of convergence and negotiation for libertarians, communitarians, utilitarians, and egalitarians. It provides a premise of equal access to basic goods, while allowing additional rights to economic freedom. Theories such as utilitarianism and communitarianism may also find the compromise particularly attractive because it serves to minimize public dissatisfaction and to maximize community welfare. The egalitarian finds an opportunity to use an equal access principle, and the libertarian retains free-market production and distribution. However, the system would involve compromise by proponents of each of these theories of justice.

### Conclusion

Rawls, Nozick, and their utilitarian and communitarian opponents all capture some intuitive convictions about justice, and each theory exhibits strengths as a theory. Rawls's difference principle, for example, describes a widely shared belief about justified inequalities. Nozick's theory makes a strong appeal in the domains of property rights and liberties. Utilitarianism is widely used in Western nations in the development of public policy, and communitarian theories, in some form, supply the prevailing model of justice in many nations.

Perhaps, then, there are several equally valid, or at least equally defensible, theories of justice. There could be, based on this analysis, libertarian societies, egalitarian societies, utilitarian societies, and communitarian societies, as well as societies based on mixed theories or derivative theories of taxation and redistribution. However, this possibility raises other problems in ethical theory discussed in Chapter 1—in particular, relativism and moral disagreement, and before this conclusion is accepted, the details of the arguments in this chapter's selections should be carefully assessed.

**THEORIES OF SOCIAL JUSTICE**

# An Egalitarian Theory of Justice

*John Rawls*

## THE ROLE OF JUSTICE

Justice is the first virtue of social institutions, as truth is of systems of thought. A theory however elegant and economical must be rejected or revised if it is untrue; likewise laws and institutions no matter how efficient and well-arranged must be reformed or abolished if they are unjust. Each person possesses an inviolability founded on justice that even the welfare of society as a whole cannot override. For this reason justice denies that the loss of freedom for some is made right by a greater good shared by others. It does not allow that the sacrifices imposed on a few are outweighed by the larger sum of advantages enjoyed by many. Therefore in a just society the liberties of equal citizenship are taken as settled; the rights secured by justice are not subject to political bargaining or to the calculus of social interests. The only thing that permits us to acquiesce in an erroneous theory is the lack of a better one; analogously, an injustice is tolerable only when it is necessary to avoid an even greater injustice. Being first virtues of human activities, truth and justice are uncompromising.

These propositions seem to express our intuitive conviction of the primacy of justice. No doubt they are expressed too strongly. In any event I wish to inquire whether these contentions or others similar to them are sound, and if so how they can be accounted for. To this end it is necessary to work out a theory of justice in the light of which these assertions can be interpreted and assessed. I shall begin by considering the role of the principles of justice. Let us assume, to fix ideas, that a society is a more or less self-sufficient association of persons who in their relations to one another recognize certain rules of conduct as binding and who for the most part act in accordance with them. Suppose further that these rules specify a system of cooperation designed to advance the good of those taking part in it. Then, although a society is a cooperative venture for mutual advantage, it is typically marked by a conflict as well as by an identity of interests. There is an identity of interests since social cooperation makes possible a better life for all than any would have if each were to live solely by his own efforts. There is a conflict of interests since persons are not indifferent as to how the greater benefits produced by their collaboration are distributed, for in order to pursue their ends they each prefer a larger to a lesser share. A set of principles is required for choosing among the various social arrangements which determine this division of advantages and for underwriting an agreement on the proper distributive shares. These principles are the principles of social justice: they provide a way of assigning rights and duties in the basic institutions of society and they define the appropriate distribution of the benefits and burdens of social cooperation. . . .

## THE MAIN IDEA OF THE THEORY OF JUSTICE

My aim is to present a conception of justice which generalizes and carries to a higher level of abstraction the familiar theory of the social contract as found, say, in Locke, Rousseau, and Kant. In order to do this we are not to think of the original contract as one to enter a particular society or to set up a particular form of government. Rather, the guiding idea is that the principles of justice for the basic structure of society are the object of the original agreement. They are the principles that free and rational persons concerned to further their own interests would accept in an initial position of equality as defining the fundamental terms of their association. These principles are to regulate all further agreements; they specify the kinds of social cooperation that can be entered into and the forms of government that can be established. This way of regarding the principles of justice I shall call justice as fairness.

Thus we are to imagine that those who engage in social cooperation choose together, in one joint act, the principles which are to assign basic rights and duties and to determine the division of social benefits. Men are to decide in advance how they are to regulate their claims against one another and what is to be the foundation charter of their society. Just as each person must decide by rational reflection what constitutes his good, that is, the system of ends which it is rational for him to pursue, so a group of persons must decide once and for all what is to count among them as just and unjust. The choice which rational men would make in this hypothetical situation of equal liberty, assuming for the present that this choice problem has a solution, determines the principles of justice.

In justice as fairness the original position of equality corresponds to the state of nature in the traditional theory of the social contract. This original position is not, of course, thought of as an actual historical state of affairs, much less as a primitive condition of culture. It is understood as a purely hypothetical situation characterized so as to lead to a certain conception of justice. Among the essential features of this situation is that no one knows his place in society, his class position or social status, nor does any one know his fortune in the distribution of natural assets and abilities, his intelligence, strength, and the like. I shall even assume that the parties do not know their conceptions of the good or their special psychological propensities. The principles of justice are chosen behind a veil of ignorance. This ensures that no one is advantaged or disadvantaged in the choice of principles by the outcome of natural chance or the contingency of social circumstances. Since all are similarly situated and no one is able to design principles to favor his particular condition, the principles of justice are the result of a fair agreement or bargain. For given the circumstances of the original position, the symmetry of everyone's relations to each other, this initial situation is fair between individuals as moral persons, that is, as rational beings with their own ends and capable, I shall assume, of a sense of justice. The original position is, one might say, the appropriate initial status quo, and thus the fundamental agreements reached in it are fair. This explains the propriety of the name "justice as fairness": it conveys the idea that the principles of justice are agreed to in an initial situation that is fair. The name does not mean that the concepts of justice and fairness are the same, any more than the phrase "poetry as metaphor" means that the concepts of poetry and metaphor are the same.

Justice as fairness begins, as I have said, with one of the most general of all choices which persons might make together, namely, with the choice of the first principles of a conception of justice which is to regulate all subsequent criticism and reform of institutions. Then, having chosen a conception of justice, we can suppose that they are to choose a constitution and a legislature to enact laws, and so on, all in accordance with the principles of justice initially agreed upon. Our social situation is just if it is such that by this sequence of hypothetical agreements we would have contracted into the general system of rules which defines it.

. . . It may be observed, however, that once the principles of justice are thought of as arising from an original agreement in a situation of equality, it is an open question whether the principle of utility would be acknowledged. Offhand it hardly seems likely that persons who view themselves as equals, entitled to press their claims upon one another, would agree to a principle which may require lesser life prospects for some simply for the sake of a greater sum of advantages enjoyed by others. Since each desires to protect his interests, his capacity to advance his conception of the good, no one has a reason to acquiesce in an enduring loss for himself in order to bring about a greater net balance of satisfaction. In the absence of strong and lasting benevolent impulses, a rational man would not accept a basic structure merely because it maximized the algebraic sum of advantages irrespective of its permanent effects on his own basic rights and interests. Thus it seems that the principle of utility is incompatible with the conception of social cooperation among equals for mutual advantage. It appears to be inconsistent with the idea of reciprocity implicit in the notion of a well-ordered society. Or, at any rate, so I shall argue.

I shall maintain instead that the persons in the initial situation would choose two rather different principles: the first requires equality in the assignment of basic rights and duties, while the second holds that social and economic inequalities, for example inequalities of wealth and authority, are just only if they result in compensating benefits for everyone, and in particular for the least advantaged members of society. These principles rule out justifying institutions on the grounds that the hardships of some are offset by a greater good in the aggregate. It may be expedient but it is not just that some should have less in order that others may prosper. But there is no injustice in the greater benefits earned by a few provided that the situation of persons not so fortunate is thereby improved. The intuitive idea is that since everyone's well-being depends upon a scheme of cooperation without which no one could have a satisfactory life, the division of advantages should be such as to draw forth the willing cooperation of everyone taking part in it, including those less well situated. Yet this can be expected only if reasonable terms are proposed. The two principles mentioned seem to be a fair agreement on the basis of which those better endowed, or more fortunate in their social position, neither of which we can be said to deserve, could expect the willing cooperation of others when some workable scheme is a necessary condition of the welfare of all. Once we decide to look for a conception of justice that nullifies the accidents of natural endowment and the contingencies of social circumstance as counters in quest for political and economic advantage, we are led to these principles. They express the result of leaving aside those aspects of the social world that seem arbitrary from a moral point of view. . . .

## THE ORIGINAL POSITION AND JUSTIFICATION

. . . The idea here is simply to make vivid to ourselves the restrictions that it seems reasonable to impose on arguments for principles of justice, and therefore on these principles themselves. Thus it seems reasonable and generally acceptable that no one should be advantaged or disadvantaged by natural fortune or social circumstances in the choice of principles. It also seems widely agreed that it should be impossible to tailor principles to the circumstances of one's own case. We should insure further that particular inclinations and aspirations, and persons' conceptions of their good, do not affect the principles adopted. The aim is to rule out those principles that it would be rational to propose for acceptance, however little the chance of success, only if one knew certain things that are irrelevant from the standpoint of justice. For example, if a man knew that he was wealthy, he might find it rational to advance the principle that various taxes for welfare measures be counted unjust; if he knew that he was poor, he would most likely propose the contrary principle. To represent the desired restrictions one imagines a situation in which everyone is deprived of this sort of information. One excludes the knowledge of those contingencies which sets men at odds and allows them to be guided by their prejudices. In this manner the veil of ignorance is arrived at in a natural way. . . .

## TWO PRINCIPLES OF JUSTICE

I shall now state in a provisional form the two principles of justice that I believe would be chosen in the original position. . . .

The first statement of the two principles reads as follows.

> **First:** each person is to have an equal right to the most extensive basic liberty compatible with a similar liberty for others.
>
> **Second:** social and economic inequalities are to be arranged so that they are both (a) reasonably expected to be to everyone's advantage, and (b) attached to positions and offices open to all. . . . [The Difference Principle]

By way of general comment, these principles primarily apply, as I have said, to the basic structure of society. They are to govern the assignment of rights and duties and to regulate the distribution of social and economic advantages. As their formulation suggests, these principles presuppose that the social structure can be divided into two more or less distinct parts, the first principle applying to the one, the second to the other. They distinguish between those aspects of the social system that define and secure the equal liberties of citizenship and those that specify and establish social and economic inequalities. The basic liberties of citizens are, roughly speaking, political liberty (the right to vote and to be eligible for public office) together with freedom of speech and assembly; liberty of conscience and freedom of thought; freedom of the person along with the right to hold (personal) property; and freedom from arbitrary arrest and seizure as defined by the concept of the rule of law. These liberties are all required to be equal by the first principle, since citizens of a just society are to have the same basic rights.

The second principle applies, in the first approximation, to the distribution of income and wealth and to the design of organizations that make use of differences in authority and responsibility, or chains of command. While the distribution of wealth and income need not be equal, it must be to everyone's advantage, and at the same time, positions of authority and offices of command must be accessible to all. One applies the second principle by holding positions open, and then, subject to this constraint, arranges social and economic inequalities so that everyone benefits.

These principles are to be arranged in a serial order with the first principle prior to the second. This ordering means that a departure from the institutions of equal liberty required by the first principle cannot be justified, or compensated for, by greater social and economic advantages. The distribution of wealth and income, and the hierarchies of authority must be consistent with both the liberties of equal citizenship and equality of opportunity.

It is clear that these principles are rather specific in their content, and their acceptance rests on certain assumptions that I must eventually try to explain and justify. A theory of justice depends upon a theory of society in ways that will become evident as we proceed. For the present, it should be observed that the two principles (and this holds for all formulations) are a special case of a more general conception of justice that can be expressed as follows.

> All social values—liberty and opportunity, income and wealth, and the bases of self-respect—are to be distributed equally unless an unequal distribution of any, or all, of these values is to everyone's advantage.

Injustice, then, is simply inequalities that are not to the benefit of all. Of course, this conception is extremely vague and requires interpretation.

As a first step, suppose that the basic structure of society distributes certain primary goods, that is, things that every rational man is presumed to want. These goods normally have a use whatever a person's rational plan of life. For simplicity, assume that the chief primary goods at the disposition of society are rights and liberties, powers and opportunities, income and wealth. These are the social primary goods. Other primary goods such as health and vigor, intelligence and imagination, are natural goods; although their possession is influenced by the basic structure, they are not so directly under its control. Imagine, then, a hypothetical initial arrangement in which all the social primary goods are equally distributed: everyone has similar rights and duties, and income and wealth are evenly shared. This state of affairs provides a benchmark for judging improvements. If certain inequalities of wealth and organizational powers would make everyone better off than in this hypothetical starting situation, then they accord with the general conception.

Now it is possible, at least theoretically, that by giving up some of their fundamental liberties men are sufficiently compensated by the resulting social and economic gains. The general conception of justice imposes no restrictions on what sort of inequalities are permissible;

it only requires that everyone's position be improved. . . .

Now the second principle insists that each person benefit from permissible inequalities in the basic structure. This means that it must be reasonable for each relevant representative man defined by this structure, when he views it as a going concern, to prefer his prospects with the inequality to his prospects without it. One is not allowed to justify differences in income or organizational powers on the ground that the disadvantages of those in one position are outweighed by the greater advantages of those in another. Much less can infringements of liberty be counterbalanced in this way. Applied to the basic structure, the principle of utility would have us maximize the sum of expectations of representative men (weighted by the number of persons they represent, on the classical view); and this would permit us to compensate for the losses of some by the gains of others. Instead, the two principles require that everyone benefit from economic and social inequalities. . . .

## THE TENDENCY TO EQUALITY

I wish to conclude this discussion of the two principles by explaining the sense in which they express an egalitarian conception of justice. Also I should like to forestall the objection to the principle of fair opportunity that it leads to a callous meritocratic society. In order to prepare the way for doing this, I note several aspects of the conception of justice that I have set out.

First we may observe that the difference principle gives some weight to the considerations singled out by the principle of redress. This is the principle that undeserved inequalities call for redress; and since inequalities of birth and natural endowment are undeserved, these inequalities are to be somehow compensated for. Thus the principle holds that in order to treat all persons equally, to provide genuine equality of opportunity, society must give more attention to those with fewer native assets and to those born into the less favorable social positions. The idea is to redress the bias of contingencies in the direction of equality. In pursuit of this principle greater resources might be spent on the education of the less rather than the more intelligent, at least over a certain time of life, say the earlier years of school.

Now the principle of redress has not to my knowledge been proposed as the sole criterion of justice, as the single aim of the social order. It is plausible as most such principles are only as a prima facie principle, one that is to be weighed in the balance with others. For example, we are to weigh it against the principle to improve the average standard of life, or to advance the common good. But whatever other principles we hold, the claims of redress are to be taken into account. It is thought to represent one of the elements in our conception of justice. Now the difference principle is not of course the principle of redress. It does not require society to try to even out handicaps as if all were expected to compete on a fair basis in the same race. But the difference principle would allocate resources in education, say, so as to improve the long-term expectation of the least favored. If this end is attained by giving more attention to the better endowed, it is permissible; otherwise not. And in making this decision, the value of education should not be assessed only in terms of economic efficiency and social welfare. Equally if not more important is the role of education in enabling a person to enjoy the culture of his society and to take part in its affairs, and in this way to provide for each individual a secure sense of his own worth.

Thus although the difference principle is not the same as that of redress, it does achieve some of the intent of the latter principle. It transforms the aims of the basic structure so that the total scheme of institutions no longer emphasizes social efficiency and technocratic values. . . .

. . . The natural distribution is neither just nor unjust; nor is it unjust that men are born into society at some particular position. These are simply natural facts. What is just and unjust is the way that institutions deal with these facts. Aristocratic and caste societies are unjust because they make these contingencies the ascriptive basis for belonging to more or less enclosed and privileged social classes. The basic structure of these societies incorporates the arbitrariness found in nature. But there is no necessity for men to resign themselves to these contingencies. The social system is not an unchangeable order beyond human control but a pattern of human action. In justice as fairness men agree to share one another's fate. In designing institutions they undertake to avail themselves of the accidents of nature and social circumstance only when doing so is for the common benefit. The two principles are a fair way of meeting the arbitrariness of fortune; and while no doubt imperfect in other ways, the institutions which satisfy these principles are just. . . .

There is a natural inclination to object that those better situated deserve their greater advantages whether or not they are to the benefit of others. At this point it is necessary to be clear about the notion of desert. It is perfectly true that given a just system of cooperation as a scheme of public rules and the expectations set up by it, those who, with the prospect of improving their condition, have done what the system announces that it will reward are entitled to their advantages. In this sense the more fortunate have a claim to their better situation; their claims are legitimate expectations established by social institutions, and the community is obligated to meet them. But this sense of desert presupposes the existence of the cooperative scheme; it is irrelevant to the question whether in the first place the scheme is to be designed in accordance with the difference principle or some other criterion.

Perhaps some will think that the person with greater natural endowments deserves those assets and the superior character that made their development possible. Because he is more worthy in this sense, he deserves the greater advantages that he could achieve with them. This view, however, is surely incorrect. It seems to be one of the fixed points of our considered judgments that no one deserves his place in the distribution of native endowments, any more than one deserves one's initial starting place in society. The assertion that a man deserves the superior character that enables him to make the effort to cultivate his abilities is equally problematic, for his character depends in large part upon fortunate family and social circumstances for which he can claim no credit. The notion of desert seems not to apply to these cases. Thus the more advantaged representative man cannot say that he deserves and therefore has a right to a scheme of cooperation in which he is permitted to acquire benefits in ways that do not contribute to the welfare of others. There is no basis for his making this claim. From the standpoint of common sense, then, the difference principle appears to be acceptable both to the more advantaged and to the less advantaged individual. . . .

## BACKGROUND INSTITUTIONS FOR DISTRIBUTIVE JUSTICE

The main problem of distributive justice is the choice of a social system. The principles of justice apply to the basic structure and regulate how its major institutions are combined into one scheme. Now, as we have seen, the idea of justice as fairness is to use the notion of pure procedural justice to handle the contingencies of particular situations. The social system is to be designed so that the resulting distribution is just however things turn out. To achieve this end it is necessary to get the social and economic process within the surroundings of suitable political and legal institutions. Without an appropriate scheme of these background institutions the outcome of the distributive process will not be just. Background fairness is lacking. I shall give a brief description of these supporting institutions as they might exist in a properly organized democratic state that allows private ownership of capital and natural resources. . . .

In establishing these background institutions the government may be thought of as divided into four branches.[1] Each branch consists of various agencies, or activities thereof, charged with preserving certain social and economic conditions. These divisions do not overlap with the usual organization of government but are to be understood as different functions. The allocation branch, for example, is to keep the price system workably competitive and to prevent the formation of unreasonable market power. Such power does not exist as long as markets cannot be made more competitive consistent with the requirements of efficiency and the facts of geography and the preferences of households. The allocation branch is also charged with identifying and correcting, say by suitable taxes and subsidies and by changes in the definition of property rights, the more obvious departures from efficiency caused by the failure of prices to measure accurately social benefits and costs. To this end suitable taxes and subsidies may be used, or the scope and definition of property rights may be revised. The stabilization branch, on the other hand, strives to bring about reasonably full employment in the sense that those who want work can find it and the free choice of occupation and the deployment of finance are supported by strong effective demand. These two branches together are to maintain the efficiency of the market economy generally.

The social minimum is the responsibility of the transfer branch. . . . The essential idea is that the workings of this branch take needs into account and assign them an appropriate weight with respect to other claims. A competitive price system gives no consideration to needs and therefore it cannot be the sole device of distribution. There must be a division of labor between the parts of the social system in answering to the common sense precepts of justice. Different institutions meet different claims. Competitive markets properly regulated secure free choice of occupation and lead to an efficient use of resources and allocation of commodities to households. They set a weight on the conventional precepts associated with wages and earnings, whereas a transfer branch guarantees a certain level of well-being and honors the claims of need. . . .

It is clear that the justice of distributive shares depends on the background institutions and how they allocate total income, wages and other income plus transfers. There is with reason strong objection to the competitive determination of total income, since this ignores the claims of need and an appropriate standard of life. From the standpoint of the legislative stage it is rational to insure oneself and one's descendants against these contingencies of the market. Indeed, the difference principle presumably requires this. But once a suitable minimum is provided by transfers, it may be perfectly fair that the rest of total income be settled by the price system, assuming that it is moderately efficient and free from monopolistic restrictions, and unreasonable externalities have been eliminated. Moreover, this way of dealing with the claims of need would appear to be more effective than trying to regulate income by minimum wage standards, and the like. It is better to assign to each branch only such tasks as are compatible with one another. Since the market is not suited to answer the claims of need, these should be met by a separate arrangement. Whether the principles of justice are satisfied, then, turns on whether the total income of the least advantaged (wages plus transfers) is such as to maximize their long-run expectations (consistent with the constraints of equal liberty and fair equality of opportunity).

Finally, there is a distribution branch. Its task is to preserve an approximate justice in distributive shares by means of taxation and the necessary adjustments in the rights of property. Two aspects of this branch may be distinguished. First of all, it imposes a number of inheritance and gift taxes, and sets restrictions on the rights of bequest. The purpose of these levies and regulations is not to raise revenue (release resources to government) but gradually and continually to correct the distribution of wealth and to prevent concentrations of power detrimental to the fair value of political liberty and fair equality of opportunity. For example, the progressive principle might be applied at the beneficiary's end.[2] Doing this would encourage the wide dispersal of property which is a necessary condition, it seems, if the fair value of the equal liberties is to be maintained.

## NOTES

1. For the idea of branches of government, see R. A. Musgrave, *The Theory of Public Finance* (New York: McGraw-Hill, 1959), Ch. 1.
2. See Meade, *Efficiency, Equality and the Ownership of Property*, pp. 56f.

# The Entitlement Theory

*Robert Nozick*

The term "distributive justice" is not a neutral one. Hearing the term "distribution," most people presume that some thing or mechanism uses some principle or criterion to give out a supply of things. Into this process of distributing shares some error may have crept. So it is an open question, at least, whether *re*distribution should take place; whether we should do again what has already been done once, though poorly. However, we are not in the position of children who have been given portions of pie by someone who now makes last minute adjustments to rectify careless cutting. There is no *central* distribution, no person or group entitled to control all the resources, jointly deciding how they are to be doled out. What each person gets, he gets from others who give to him in exchange for something, or as a gift. In a free society, diverse persons control different resources, and new holdings arise out of the voluntary exchanges and actions of persons. . . .

The subject of justice in holdings consists of three major topics. The first is the *original acquisition of holdings*, the appropriation of unheld things. This includes the issues of how unheld things may come to be held, the process, or processes, by which unheld things may come to be held, the things that may come to be held by these processes, the extent of what comes to be held by a particular person, and so on. We shall refer to the complicated truth about this topic, which we shall not formulate here, as the principle of justice in acquisition. The second topic concerns the *transfer of holdings* from one person to another. By what processes may a person transfer holdings to another? How may a person acquire a holding from an-

From Robert Nozick, *Anarchy, State, and Utopia* (New York: Basic Books, Inc., Publishers, 1974), pp. 149–154, 156–157, 159–163, 168, 174–175, 178–179, 182. 

other who holds it? Under this topic come general descriptions of voluntary exchange, and gift and (on the other hand) fraud, as well as reference to particular conventional details fixed upon in a given society. The complicated truth about this subject (with placeholders for conventional details) we shall call the principle of justice in transfer. (And we shall suppose it also includes principles governing how a person may divest himself of a holding, passing it into an unheld state.)

If the world were wholly just, the following inductive definition would exhaustively cover the subject of justice in holdings.

1. A person who acquires a holding in accordance with the principle of justice in acquisition is entitled to that holding.
2. A person who acquires a holding in accordance with the principle of justice in transfer, from someone else entitled to the holding, is entitled to the holding.
3. No one is entitled to a holding except by (repeated) applications of 1 and 2.

The complete principle of distributive justice would say simply that a distribution is just if everyone is entitled to the holdings they possess under the distribution. . . .

Not all actual situations are generated in accordance with the two principles of justice in holdings: the principle of justice in acquisition and the principle of justice in transfer. Some people steal from others, or defraud them, or enslave them, seizing their product and preventing them from living as they choose, or forcibly exclude others from competing in exchanges. None of these are permissible modes of transition from one situation to another. And some persons acquire holdings by means not sanctioned by the principle of justice in acquisition. The existence of past injustice (previous violations of the first two principles of justice in holdings) raises the third major topic under justice in holdings: the rectification of injustice in holdings. If past injustice has shaped present holdings in various ways, some identifiable and some not, what now, if anything, ought to be done to rectify these injustices? . . .

## HISTORICAL PRINCIPLES AND END-RESULT PRINCIPLES

The general outlines of the entitlement theory illuminate the nature and defects of other conceptions of distributive justice. The entitlement theory of justice in distribution is *historical*; whether a distribution is just depends upon how it came about. In contrast, *current time-slice principles* of justice hold that the justice of a distribution is determined by how things are distributed (who has what) as judged by some *structural* principle(s) of just distribution. A utilitarian who judges between any two distributions by seeing which has the greater sum of utility and, if the sums tie, applies some fixed equality criterion to choose the more equal distribution, would hold a current time-slice principle of justice. As would someone who had a fixed schedule of trade-offs between the sum of happiness and equality. According to a current time-slice principle, all that needs to be looked at, in judging the justice of a distribution, is who ends up with what; in comparing any two distributions one need look only at the matrix presenting the distributions. No further information need be fed into a principle of justice. It is a consequence of such principles of justice that any two structurally identical distributions are equally just. . . .

Most persons do not accept current time-slice principles as constituting the whole story about distributive shares. They think it relevant in assessing the justice of a situation to consider not only the distribution it embodies, but also how that distribution came about. If some persons are in prison for murder or war crimes, we do not say that to assess the justice of the distribution in the society we must look only at what this person has, and that person has, and that person has, . . . at the current time.

We think it relevant to ask whether someone did something so that he deserved to be punished, *deserved* to have a lower share. . . .

## PATTERNING

. . . Almost every suggested principle of distributive justice is patterned: to each according to his moral merit, or needs, or marginal product, or how hard he tries, or the weighted sum of the foregoing, and so on. The principle of entitlement we have sketched is *not* patterned. There is no one natural dimension or weighted sum or combination of a small number of natural dimensions that yields the distributions generated in accordance with the principle of entitlement. The set of holdings that results when some persons receive their marginal products, others win at gambling, others receive a share of their mate's income, others receive gifts from foundations, others receive interest on loans, others receive gifts from admirers, others receive returns on investment, others make for themselves much of what they have, others find things, and so on, will not be patterned. . . .

To think that the task of a theory of distributive justice is to fill in the blank in "to each according to his __________" is to be predisposed to search for a pattern; and the separate treatment of "from each according to his __________" treats production and distribution as two separate and independent issues. On an entitlement view these are *not* two separate questions. Whoever makes something, having bought or contracted for all other held resources used in the process (transferring some of his holdings for these cooperating factors), is entitled to it. . . .

So entrenched are maxims of the usual form that perhaps we should present the entitlement conception as a competitor. Ignoring acquisition and rectification, we might say:

> From each according to what he chooses to do, to each according to what he makes for himself (perhaps with the contracted aid of others) and what others choose to do for him and choose to give him of what they've been given previously (under this maxim) and haven't yet expended or transferred.

This, the discerning reader will have noticed, has its defects as a slogan. So as a summary and great simplification (and not as a maxim with any independent meaning) we have:

> *From each as they choose, to each as they are chosen.*

## HOW LIBERTY UPSETS PATTERNS

It is not clear how those holding alternative conceptions of distributive justice can reject the entitlement conception of justice in holdings. For suppose a distribution favored by one of these non-entitlement conceptions is realized. Let us suppose it is your favorite one and let us call this distribution $D_1$; perhaps everyone has an equal share, perhaps shares vary in accordance with some dimension you treasure. Now suppose that Wilt Chamberlain is greatly in demand by basketball teams, being a great gate attraction. (Also suppose contracts run only for a year, with players being free agents). He signs the following sort of contract with a team: In each home game, twenty-five cents from the price of each ticket of admission goes to him. (We ignore the question of whether he is "gouging" the owners, letting them look out for themselves.) The season starts, and people cheerfully attend his team's games; they buy their tickets, each time dropping a separate twenty-five cents of their admission price into a special box with Chamberlain's name on it. They are excited about seeing him play; it is worth the total admission price to them. Let us suppose that in one season one million persons attend his home games, and Wilt Chamberlain winds up with $250,000, a much larger sum than the average income and larger even than anyone else has. Is he entitled to this income? Is this new distribution $D_2$, unjust? If so, why? There is *no* question about whether each of the people was entitled to the control over the resources they held in $D_1$; because that was the distribution (your favorite) that (for the purposes of argument) we assumed was acceptable. Each of these persons *chose* to give twenty-five cents of their money to Chamberlain. They could have spent it on going to the movies, or on candy bars, or on copies of *Dissent* magazine, or of *Monthly Review*. But they all, at least one million of them, converged on giving it to Wilt Chamberlain in exchange for watching him play basketball. If $D_1$ was a just distribution, and people voluntarily moved from it to $D_2$, transferring parts of their shares they were given under $D_1$ (what was it for if not to do something with?), isn't $D_2$ also just? If the people were entitled to dispose of the resources to which they were entitled (under $D_1$) didn't this include their being entitled to give it to, or exchange it with, Wilt Chamberlain? Can anyone else complain on grounds of justice? Each other person already has his legitimate share under $D_1$. Under $D_1$, there is nothing that anyone has that anyone else has a claim of justice against. After someone transfers something to Wilt Chamberlain, third parties *still* have their legitimate shares; *their* shares are not changed. By what process could such a transfer among two persons give a rise to a legitimate claim of distributive justice on a portion of what was transferred, by a third party who had no claim of justice on any holding of the others *before* the transfer? To cut off objections irrelevant here, we might imagine the exchanges occurring in a socialist society, after hours. After playing whatever basketball he does in his daily work, or doing whatever other daily work he does, Wilt Chamberlain decides to put in *overtime* to earn additional money. (First his work quota is set; he works time over that.) Or imagine it is a skilled juggler people like to see, who puts on shows after hours. . . .

The general point illustrated by the Wilt Chamberlain example is that no end-state principle or distributional patterned principle of justice can be continuously realized without continuous interference with people's lives. Any favored pattern would be transformed into one unfavored by the principle, by people choosing to act in various ways; for example, by people exchanging goods and services with other people, or giving things to other people, things the transferrers are entitled to under the favored distributional pattern. To maintain a pattern one must either continually interfere to stop people from transferring resources as they wish to, or continually (or periodically) interfere to take from some person's resources that others for some reason chose to transfer to them. . . .

Patterned principles of distributive justice necessitate *re*distributive activities. The likelihood is small that any actual freely-arrived-at set of holdings fits a given pattern; and the likelihood is nil that it will continue to fit the pattern as people exchange and give. From the point of view of an entitlement theory, redistribution is a serious matter indeed, involving, as it does, the violation of people's rights. (An exception is those takings that fall under the principle of the rectification of injustices.) . . .

## LOCKE'S THEORY OF ACQUISITION

. . . [Let us] introduce an additional bit of complexity into the structure of the entitlement theory. This is best approached by considering Locke's attempt to specify a principle of justice in acquisition. Locke views property rights in an unowned object as originating through someone's mixing his labor with it. This gives rise to many questions. What are the boundaries of what labor is mixed with? If a private astronaut clears a place on Mars, has he mixed his labor with (so that he comes to own) the whole planet, the whole uninhabited universe, or just a particular plot? Which plot does an act bring under ownership? . . .

Locke's proviso that there be "enough and as good left in common for others" is meant to ensure that the situation of others is not worsened. . . .

. . . I assume that any adequate theory of justice in acquisition will contain a proviso similar to [Locke's]. . . .

I believe that the free operation of a market system will not actually run afoul of the Lockean proviso. . . . If this is correct, the proviso will not . . . provide a significant opportunity for future state action.

# Rich and Poor

*Peter Singer*

One way of making sense of the non-consequentialist view of responsibility is by basing it on a theory of rights of the kind proposed by John Locke or, more recently, Robert Nozick. If everyone has a right to life, and this right is a right *against* others who might threaten my life, but not a right *to* assistance from others when my life is in danger, then we can understand the feeling that we are responsible for acting to kill but not for omitting to save. The former violates the rights of others, the latter does not.

Should we accept such a theory of rights? If we build up our theory of rights by imagining, as Locke and Nozick do, individuals living independently from each other in a 'state of nature', it may seem natural to adopt a conception of rights in which as long as each leaves the other alone, no rights are violated. I might, on this view, quite properly have maintained my independent existence if I had wished to do so. So if I do not make you any worse off than you would have been if I had had nothing at all to do with you, how can I have violated your rights? But why start from such an unhistorical, abstract and ultimately inexplicable idea as an independent individual? We now know that our ancestors were social beings long before they were human beings, and could not have developed the abilities and capacities of human beings if they had not been social beings first. In any case we are not, now, isolated individuals. If we consider people living together in a community, it is less easy to assume that rights must be restricted to rights against interference. We might, instead, adopt the view that taking rights to life seriously is incompatible with standing by and watching people die when one could easily save them. . . .

## THE OBLIGATION TO ASSIST

### The Argument for an Obligation to Assist

The path from the library at my university to the Humanities lecture theatre passes a shallow ornamental pond. Suppose that on my way to give a lecture I notice that a small child has fallen in and is in danger of drowning. Would anyone deny that I ought to wade in and pull

From Peter Singer, "Rich and Poor," in *Practical Ethics* (New York: Cambridge University Press, 1979), pp. 166, 168–179. Reprinted with permission of the publisher.

the child out? This will mean getting my clothes muddy, and either cancelling my lecture or delaying it until I can find something dry to change into; but compared with the avoidable death of a child this is insignificant.

A plausible principle that would support the judgment that I ought to pull the child out is this: if it is in our power to prevent something very bad happening, without thereby sacrificing anything of comparable moral significance, we ought to do it. This principle seems uncontroversial. It will obviously win the assent of consequentialists; but non-consequentialists should accept it too, because the injunction to prevent what is bad applies only when nothing comparably significant is at stake. Thus the principle cannot lead to the kinds of actions of which non-consequentialists strongly disapprove—serious violations of individual rights, injustice, broken promises, and so on. If a non-consequentialist regards any of these as comparable in moral significance to the bad thing that is to be prevented, he will automatically regard the principle as not applying in those cases in which the bad thing can only be prevented by violating rights, doing injustice, breaking promises, or whatever else is at stake. Most non-consequentialists hold that we ought to prevent what is bad and promote what is good. Their dispute with consequentialists lies in their insistence that this is not the sole ultimate ethical principle: that it is *an* ethical principle is not denied by any plausible ethical theory.

Nevertheless the uncontroversial appearance of the principle that we ought to prevent what is bad when we can do so without sacrificing anything of comparable moral significance is deceptive. If it were taken seriously and acted upon, our lives and our world would be fundamentally changed. For the principle applies, not just to rare situations in which one can save a child from a pond, but to the everyday situations in which we can assist those living in absolute poverty. In saying this I assume that absolute poverty, with its hunger and malnutrition, lack of shelter, illiteracy, disease, high infant mortality and low life expectancy, is a bad thing. And I assume that it is within the power of the affluent to reduce absolute poverty, without sacrificing anything of comparable moral significance. If these two assumptions and the principle we have been discussing are correct, we have an obligation to help those in absolute poverty which is no less strong than our obligation to rescue a drowning child from a pond. Not to help would be wrong, whether or not it is intrinsically equivalent to killing. Helping is not, as conventionally thought, a charitable act which it is praiseworthy to do, but not wrong to omit; it is something that everyone ought to do.

This is the argument for an obligation to assist. Set out more formally, it would look like this.

> **First premise:** If we can prevent something bad without sacrificing anything of comparable significance, we ought to do it.
>
> **Second premise:** Absolute poverty is bad.
>
> **Third premise:** There is some absolute poverty we can prevent without sacrificing anything of comparable moral significance.
>
> **Conclusion:** We ought to prevent some absolute poverty.

The first premise is the substantive moral premise on which the argument rests, and I have tried to show that it can be accepted by people who hold a variety of ethical positions.

The second premise is unlikely to be challenged. Absolute poverty is, as [Robert] McNamara put in, "beneath any reasonable definition of human decency" and it would be hard to find a plausible ethical view which did not regard it as a bad thing.

The third premise is more controversial, even though it is cautiously framed. It claims only that some absolute poverty can be prevented without the sacrifice of anything of comparable moral significance. It thus avoids the objection that any aid I can give is just 'drops in the ocean' for the point is not whether my personal contribution will make any noticeable impression on world poverty as a whole (of course it won't) but whether it will prevent some poverty. This is all the argument needs to sustain its conclusion, since the second premise says that any absolute poverty is bad, and not merely the total amount of absolute poverty. If without sacrificing anything of comparable moral significance we can provide just one family with the means to raise itself out of absolute poverty, the third premise is vindicated.

I have left the notion of moral significance unexamined in order to show that the argument does not depend on any specific values or ethical principles. I think the third premise is true for most people living in industrialized nations, on any defensible view of what is morally significant. Our affluence means that we have income we can dispose of without giving up the basic necessities of life, and we can use this income to reduce absolute poverty. Just how much we will think ourselves obliged to give up will depend on what we consider to be of comparable moral significance to the poverty we could prevent: colour television, stylish clothes, expensive dinners, a sophisticated stereo system, overseas holidays, a (second?) car, a larger house, private schools for our children. . . . For a utilitarian, none of these is likely to be of comparable significance to the reduction of absolute poverty; and those who are not utilitarians surely must, if they subscribe to the principle of universalizability, accept that at least *some* of these things are of far less moral significance than the absolute poverty that could be prevented by the money they cost. So the third premise seems to be true on any plausible ethical view—although the precise amount of absolute poverty that can be prevented before anything of moral significance is sacrificed will vary according to the ethical view one accepts.

## Objections to the Argument

***Taking Care of Our Own.*** Anyone who has worked to increase overseas aid will have come across the argument that we should look after those near us, our families and then the poor in our own country, before we think about poverty in distant places.

No doubt we do instinctively prefer to help those who are close to us. Few could stand by and watch a child drown; many can ignore a famine in Africa. But the question is not what we usually do, but what we ought to do, and it is difficult to see any sound moral justification for the view that distance, or community membership, makes a crucial difference to our obligations.

Consider, for instance, racial affinities. Should whites help poor whites before helping poor blacks? Most of us would reject such a suggestion out of hand, [by appeal to] the principle of equal consideration of interests: people's needs for food has nothing to do with their race, and if blacks need food more than whites, it would be a violation of the principle of equal consideration to give preference to whites.

The same point applies to citizenship or nationhood. Every affluent nation has some relatively poor citizens, but absolute poverty is limited largely to the poor nations. Those living on the streets of Calcutta, or in a drought-stricken region of the Sahel, are experiencing poverty unknown in the West. Under these circumstances it would be wrong to decide that only those fortunate enough to be citizens of our own community will share our abundance.

We feel obligations of kinship more strongly than those of citizenship. Which parents could give away their last bowl of rice if their own children were starving? To do so would seem unnatural, contrary to our nature as biologically evolved beings—although whether it would be wrong is another question altogether. In any case, we are not faced with that situation, but with one in which our own children are well-fed, well-clothed, well-educated, and would now like new bikes, a stereo set, or their own car. In these circumstances any special obligations we might have to our children have been fulfilled, and the needs of strangers make a stronger claim upon us.

The element of truth in the view that we should first take care of our own, lies in the advantage of a recognized system of responsibilities. When families and local communities look after their own poorer members, ties of affection and personal relationships achieve ends that would otherwise require a large, impersonal bureaucracy. Hence it would be absurd to propose that from now on we all regard ourselves as equally responsible for the welfare of everyone in the world; but the argument for an obligation to assist does not propose that. It applies only when some are in absolute poverty, and others can help without sacrificing anything of comparable moral significance. To allow one's own kin to sink into absolute poverty would be to sacrifice something of comparable significance; and before that point had been reached, the breakdown of the system of family and community responsibility would be a factor to weigh the balance in favour of a small degree of preference for family and community. This small degree of preference is, however, decisively outweighed by existing discrepancies in wealth and property.

***Property Rights.*** Do people have a right to private property, a right which contradicts the view that they are under an obligation to give some of their wealth away to those in absolute poverty? According to some theories of rights (for instance, Robert Nozick's) provided one has acquired one's property without the use of unjust means like force and fraud, one may be entitled to enormous wealth while others starve. This individualistic conception of rights is in contrast to other views, like the early Christian doctrine to be found in the works of Thomas Aquinas, which holds that since property exists for the satisfaction of human needs, "whatever a man has in superabundance is owed, of natural right, to the poor for their sustenance." A socialist would also, of course, see wealth as belonging to the community rather than the individual, while utilitarians, whether socialist or not, would be prepared to override property rights to prevent great evils.

Does the argument for an obligation to assist others therefore presuppose one of these other theories of property rights, and not an individualistic theory like Nozick's? Not necessarily. A theory of property rights can insist on our *right* to retain wealth without pronouncing on whether the rich *ought* to give to the poor. Nozick, for example, rejects the use of compulsory means like taxation to redistribute income, but suggests that we can achieve the ends we deem morally desirable by voluntary means. So Nozick would reject the claim that rich people have an "obligation" to give to the poor, in so far as this implies that the poor have a right to our aid, but might accept that giving is something we ought to do and failure to give, though within one's rights, is wrong—for rights is not all there is to ethics.

The argument for an obligation to assist can survive, with only minor modifications, even if we accept an individualistic theory of property rights. In any case, however, I do not think we should accept such a theory. It leaves too much to chance to be an acceptable ethical view. For instance, those whose forefathers happened to inhabit some sandy wastes around the Persian Gulf are now fabulously wealthy, because oil lay under those sands; while those whose forefathers settled on better land south of the Sahara live in absolute poverty, because of drought and bad harvests. Can this distribution be acceptable from an impartial point of view? If we imagine ourselves about to begin life as a citizen of either Kuwait or Chad—but we do not know which—would we accept the principle that citizens of Kuwait are under no obligation to assist people living in Chad?

***Population and the Ethics of Triage.*** Perhaps the most serious objection to the argument that we have an obligation to assist is that since the major cause of absolute poverty is overpopulation, helping those now in poverty will only ensure that yet more people are born to live in poverty in the future.

In its most extreme form, this objection is taken to show that we should adopt a policy of "triage." The term comes from medical policies adopted in wartime. With too few doctors to cope with all the casualties, the wounded were divided into three categories: those who would probably survive without medical assistance, those who might survive if they received assistance, but otherwise probably would not, and those who even with medical assistance probably would not survive. Only those in the middle category were given medical assistance. The idea, of course, was to use limited medical resources as effectively as possible. For those in the first category, medical treatment was not strictly necessary; for those in the third category, it was likely to be useless. It has been suggested that we should apply the same policies to countries, according to their prospects of becoming self-sustaining. We would not aid countries which even without our help will soon be able to feed their populations. We would not aid countries which, even with our help, will not be able to limit their population to a level they can feed. We would aid those countries where our help might make the difference between success and failure in bringing food and population into balance.

Advocates of this theory are understandably reluctant to give a complete list of the countries they would place into the 'hopeless' category; but Bangladesh is often cited as an example. Adopting the policy of triage would, then, mean cutting off assistance to Bangladesh and allowing famine, disease and natural disasters to reduce the population of that country (now around 80 million) to the level at which it can provide adequately for all.

In support of this view Garrett Hardin has offered a metaphor: we in the rich nations are like the occupants of a crowded lifeboat adrift in a sea full of drowning people. If we try to save the drowning by bringing them aboard our boat will be overloaded and we shall all drown. Since it is better that some survive than none, we should leave the others to drown. In the world today, according to Hardin, "lifeboat ethics" apply. The rich should leave the poor to starve, for otherwise the poor will drag the rich down with them. . . .

Anyone whose initial reaction to triage was not one of repugnance would be an unpleasant sort of person. Yet initial reactions based on strong feelings are not always reliable guides. Advocates of triage are rightly concerned with the long-term consequences of our actions. They say that helping the poor and starving now merely ensures more poor and starving in the future. When our capacity to help is finally unable to cope—as one day it must be—the suffering will be greater than it would be if we stopped helping now. If this is correct, there is nothing we can do to prevent absolute starvation and poverty, in the long run, and so we have no obligation to assist. Nor does it seem reasonable to hold that under these circumstances people have a right to our assistance. If we do accept such a right, irrespective of the consequences, we are saying that, in Hardin's metaphor, we would continue to haul the drowning into our lifeboat until the boat sank and we all drowned.

If triage is to be rejected it must be tackled on its own ground, within the framework of consequentialist ethics. Here it is vulnerable. Any consequentialist ethics must take probability of outcome into account. A course of action that will certainly produce some benefit is to be preferred to an alternative course that may lead to a slightly larger benefit, but is equally likely to result in no benefit at all. Only if the greater magnitude of the uncertain benefit outweighs its uncertainty should we choose it. Better one certain unit of benefit than a 10 percent chance of 5 units; but better a 50 percent chance of 3 units than a single certain unit. The same principle applies when are we trying to avoid evils.

The policy of triage involves a certain, very great evil: population control by famine and disease. Tens of millions would die slowly. Hundreds of millions would continue to live in absolute poverty, at the very margin of existence. Against this prospect, advocates of the policy place a possible evil which is greater still: the same process of famine and disease, taking place in, say, fifty years time, when the world's population may be three times its present level, and the number who will die from famine, or struggle on in absolute poverty, will be that much greater. The question is: how probable is this forecast that continued assistance now will lead to greater disasters in the future?

Forecasts of population growth are notoriously fallible, and theories about the factors which affect it remain speculative. One theory, at least as plausible as any other, is that countries pass through a "demographic transition" as their standard of living rises. When people are very poor and have no access to modern medicine their fertility is high, but population is kept in check by high death rates. The introduction of sanitation, modern medical techniques and other improvements reduces the death rate, but initially has little effect on the birth rate. Then population grows rapidly. Most poor countries are now in this phase. If standards of living continue to rise, however, couples begin to realize that to have the same number of children surviving to maturity as in the past, they do not need to give birth to as many children as their parents did. The need for children to provide economic support in old age diminishes. Improved education and the emancipation and employment of women also reduce the birthrate, and so population growth begins to level off. Most rich nations have reached this stage, and their populations are growing only very slowly.

If this theory is right, there is an alternative to the disasters accepted as inevitable by supporters of triage. We can assist poor countries to raise the living standards of the poorest members of their population. We can encourage the governments of these countries to enact land reform measures, improve education, and liberate women from a purely child-bearing role. We can also help other countries to make contraception and sterilization widely available. There is a fair chance that these measures will hasten the onset of the demographic transition and bring population growth down to a manageable level. Success cannot be guaranteed; but the evidence that improved economic security and education reduce population growth is strong enough to make triage ethically unacceptable. We cannot allow millions to die from starvation and disease when there is a reasonable probability that population can be brought under control without such horrors.

Population growth is therefore not a reason against giving overseas aid, although it should make us think about the kind of aid to give. Instead of food handouts, it may be better to give aid that hastens the demographic transition. This may mean agricultural assistance for the rural poor, or assistance with education, or the provision of contraceptive services. Whatever kind of aid proves most effective in specific circumstances, the obligation to assist is not reduced.

One awkward question remains. What should we do about a poor and already overpopulated country which, for religious or nationalistic reasons, restricts the use of contraceptives and refuses to slow its population growth? Should we nevertheless offer development assistance? Or should we make our offer conditional on effective steps being taken to reduce the birthrate? To the latter course, some would object that putting conditions on aid is an attempt to impose our own ideas on independent sovereign nations. So it is—but is this imposition unjustifiable? If the argument for an obligation to assist is sound, we have an obligation to reduce absolute poverty; but we have no obligation to make sacrifices that, to the best of our knowledge, have no prospect of reducing poverty in the long run. Hence we have no obligation to assist countries whose governments have policies which will make our aid ineffective. This could be very harsh on poor citizens of these countries—for they may have no say in the government's policies—but we will help more people in the long run by using our resources where they are most effective.

# Spheres of Justice

*Michael Walzer*

## COMPLEX EQUALITY AND PLURALISM

Distributive justice is a large idea. It draws the entire world of goods within the reach of philosophical reflection. Nothing can be omitted; no feature of our common life can escape scrutiny. Human society is a distributive community. That's not all it is, but it is importantly that: we come together to share, divide, and exchange. We also come together to make the things that are shared, divided, and exchanged; but that very making—work itself—is distributed among us in a division of labor. My place in the economy, my standing in the political order, my reputation among my fellows, my material holdings: all these come to me from other men and women. It can be said that I have what I have rightly or wrongly, justly or unjustly; but given the range of distributions and the number of participants, such judgments are never easy.

The idea of distributive justice has as much to do with being and doing as with having, as much to do with production as with consumption, as much to do with identity and status as with land, capital, or personal possessions. Different political arrangements enforce, and different ideologies justify, different distributions of membership, power, honor, ritual eminence, divine grace, kinship and love, knowledge, wealth, physical security, work and leisure, rewards and punishments, and a host of goods more narrowly and materially conceived—food, shelter, clothing, transportation, medical care, commodities of every sort, and all the odd things (paintings, rare books, postage stamps) that human beings collect. And this multiplicity of goods is matched by a multiplicity of distributive procedures, agents, and criteria. There are such things as simple distributive systems—slave galleys, monasteries, insane asylums, kindergartens (though each of these, looked at closely, might show unexpected complexities); but no fullfledged human society has ever avoided the multiplicity. We must study it all, the goods and the distributions, in many different times and places.

There is, however, no single point of access to this world of distributive arrangements and ideologies. There has never been a universal medium of exchange. Since the decline of the barter economy, money has been the most common medium. But the old maxim according to which there are some things that money can't buy is not only normatively but also factually true. What should and should not be up for sale is something men and women always have to decide and have decided in many different ways. Throughout history, the market has been one of the most important mechanisms for the distribution of social goods; but it has never been, it nowhere is today, a complete distributive system.

Similarly, there has never been either a single decision point from which all distributions are controlled or a single set of agents making decisions. No state power has ever been so pervasive as to regulate all the patterns of sharing, dividing, and exchanging out of which a society takes shape. Things slip away from the state's grasp; new patterns are worked out—familial networks, black markets, bureaucratic alliances, clandestine political and religious organizations. State officials can tax, conscript, allocate, regulate, appoint, reward, punish, but they cannot capture the full range of goods or substitute themselves for every other agent of distribution. Nor can anyone else do that: there are market coups and cornerings, but there has never been a fully successful distributive conspiracy.

And finally, there has never been a single criterion, or a single set of interconnected criteria, for all distributions. Desert, qualification, birth and blood, friendship, need, free exchange, political loyalty, democratic decision: each has had its place, along with many others, uneasily coexisting, invoked by competing groups, confused with one another.

In the matter of distributive justice, history displays a great variety of arrangements and ideologies. But the first impulse of the philosopher is to resist the displays of history, the world of appearances, and to search for some underlying unity: a short list of basic goods, quickly abstracted to a single good; a single distributive criterion or an interconnected set; and the philosopher himself standing, symbolically at least, at a single decision point. I shall argue that to search for unity is to misunderstand the subject matter of distributive justice. Nevertheless, in some sense the philosophical impulse is unavoidable. Even if we choose pluralism, as I shall do, that choice still requires a coherent defense. There must be principles that justify the choice and set limits to it, for pluralism does not require us to endorse every proposed distributive criterion or to accept every would-be agent. Conceivably, there is a single principle and a single legitimate kind of pluralism. But this would still be a pluralism that encompassed a wide range of distributions. By contrast, the deepest assumption of most of the philosophers who have written about justice, from Plato onward, is that there is one, and only one, distributive system that philosophy can rightly encompass.

Today this system is commonly described as the one that ideally rational men and women would choose if they were forced to choose impartially, knowing nothing of their own situation, barred from making particularist claims, confronting an abstract set of goods.[1] If these constraints on knowing and claiming are suitably shaped, and if the goods are suitably defined, it is probably true that a singular conclusion can be produced. Rational men and women, constrained this way or that, will choose one, and only one, distributive system. But the force of that singular conclusion is not easy to measure. It is surely doubtful that those same men and women, if they were transformed into ordinary people, with a firm sense of their own identity, with their own goods in their hands, caught up in everyday troubles, would reiterate their hypothetical choice or even recognize it as their own. The problem is not, most importantly, with the particularism of interest, which philosophers have always assumed they could safely—that is, uncontroversially—set aside. Ordinary people can do that too, for the sake, say, of the public interest. The greater problem is with the particularism of history, culture, and membership. Even if they are committed to impartiality, the question most likely to arise in the minds of the members of a political community is not, What would rational individuals choose under universalizing conditions of such-and-such a sort? But rather, What would individuals like us choose, who are situated as we are, who share a culture and are determined to go on sharing it? And this is a question that is readily transformed into, What choices have we already made in the course of our common life? What understandings do we (really) share?

Justice is a human construction, and it is doubtful that it can be made in only one way. At any rate, I shall begin by doubting, and more than doubting, this standard philosophical assumption. The questions posed by the theory of distributive justice admit of a range of answers, and there is room within the range for cultural diversity and political choice. It's not only a matter of implementing some singular principle or set of principles in different historical settings. No one would deny that there is a range of morally permissible implementations. I want to argue for more than this: that the principles of justice are themselves pluralistic in form; that different social goods ought to be distributed for different reasons, in accordance with different procedures, by different agents; and that all these differences derive from different understandings of the social goods themselves—the inevitable product of historical and cultural particularism. . . .

## MEMBERSHIP AND JUSTICE

The distribution of membership is not pervasively subject to the constraints of justice. Across a considerable range of the decisions that are made, states are simply free to take in strangers (or not)—much as they are free, leaving aside the claims of the needy, to share their wealth with foreign friends, to honor the achievements of foreign artists, scholars, and scientists, to choose their trading partners, and to enter into collective security arrangements with foreign states. But the right to choose an admissions policy is more basic than any of these, for it is not merely a matter of acting in the world, exercising sovereignty, and pursuing national interests. At stake here is the shape of the community that acts in the world, exercises sovereignty, and so on. Admission and exclusion are at the core of communal independence. They suggest the deepest meaning of self-determination. Without them, there could not be *communities of character*, historically stable, ongoing associations of men and women with some special commitment to one another and some special sense of their common life.[2]

But self-determination in the sphere of membership is not absolute. It is a right exercised, most often, by national clubs or families, but it is held in principle by territorial states. Hence it is subject both to internal decisions by the members themselves (*all* the members, including those who hold membership simply by right of place) and to the external principle of mutual aid. Immigration, then, is both a matter of political choice and moral constraint. Naturalization, by contrast, is entirely constrained: Every new immigrant, every refugee taken in, every resident and worker must be offered the opportunities of citizenship. If the community is so radically divided that a single citizenship is impossible, then its territory must be divided, too, before the rights of admission and exclusion can be exercised. For these rights are to be exercised only by the community as a whole (even if, in practice, some national majority dominates the decision making) and only with regard to foreigners, not by some members with regard to others. No community can be half-metic, half-citizen and claim that its admissions policies are acts of self-determination or that its politics is democratic.

The determination of aliens and guests by an exclusive band of citizens (or of slaves by masters, or women by men, or blacks by whites, or conquered peoples by their conquerors) is not communal freedom but oppression. The citizens are free, of course, to set up a club, make membership as exclusive as they like, write a constitution, and govern one another. But they can't claim territorial jurisdiction and rule over the people with whom they share the territory. To do this is to act outside their sphere, beyond their rights. It is a form of tyranny. Indeed, the rule of citizens over non-citizens, of members over strangers, is probably the most common form of tyranny in human history. . . .

## FREE EXCHANGE

Free exchange is obviously open-ended; it guarantees no particular distributive outcome. At no point in any exchange process plausibly called "free" will it be possible to predict the particular division of social goods that will obtain at some later point.[3] (It may be possible, however, to predict the general structure of the division.) In theory at least, free exchange creates a market within which all goods are convertible into all other goods through the neutral medium of money. There are no dominant goods and no monopolies. Hence the successive divisions that obtain will directly reflect the social meanings of the goods that are divided. For each bargain, trade, sale, and purchase will have been agreed to voluntarily by men and women who know what that meaning is, who are indeed its makers. Every exchange is a revelation of social meaning. By definition, then, no *x* will ever fall into the hands of someone who possesses *y*, merely because he possesses *y* and without regard to what *x* actually means to some other member of society. The market is radically pluralistic in its operations and its outcomes, infinitely sensitive to the meanings that individuals attach to goods. What possible restraints can be imposed on free exchange, then, in the name of pluralism?

But everyday life in the market, the actual experience of free exchange, is very different from what the theory suggests. Money, supposedly the neutral medium, is in practice a dominant good, and it is monopolized by people who possess a special talent for bargaining and trading—the green thumb of bourgeois society. Then other people demand a redistribution of money and the establishment of the regime of simple equality, and the search begins for some way to sustain that regime. But even if we focus on the first untroubled moment of simple equality—free exchange on the basis of equal shares—we will still need to set limits on what can be exchanged for what. For free exchange leaves distributions entirely in the hands of individuals, and social meanings are not subject, or are not always subject, to the interpretative decisions of individual men and women.

Consider an easy example, the case of political power. We can conceive of political power as a set of goods of varying value, votes, influence, offices, and so on. Any of these can be traded on the market and accumulated by individuals willing to sacrifice other goods. Even if the sacrifices are real, however, the result is a form of tyranny—petty tyranny, given the conditions of simple equality. Because I am willing to do without my hat, I shall vote twice; and you who value the vote less than you value my hat, will not vote at all. I suspect that the result is tyrannical even with regard to the two of us, who have reached a voluntary agreement. . . .

Free exchange is not a general criterion, but we will be able to specify the boundaries within which it operates only through a careful analysis of particular social goods. . . .

## THE MARKETPLACE

There is a stronger argument about the sphere of money, the common argument of the defenders of capitalism: that market outcomes matter a great deal because the market, if it is free, gives to each person exactly what he deserves. The market rewards us all in accordance with the contributions we make to one another's well-being.[4] The goods and services we provide are valued by potential consumers in such-and-such a way, and these values are aggregated by the market, which determines the price we receive. And that price is our desert, for it expresses the only worth our goods and services can have, the worth they actually have for other people. But this is to misunderstand the meaning of desert. Unless there are standards of worth independent of what people want (and are willing to buy) at this or that moment in time, there can be no deservingness at all. We would never know what a person deserved until we saw what he had gotten. And that can't be right.

Imagine a novelist who writes what he hopes will be a best seller. He studies his potential audience, designs his book to meet the current fashion. Perhaps he had to violate the canons of his art in order to do that, and perhaps he is a novelist for whom the violation was painful. He has stooped to conquer. Does he now deserve the fruits of his conquest? Does he deserve a conquest that bears fruit? His novel appears, let's say, during a depression when no one has money for books, and very few copies are sold; his reward is small. Has he gotten less than he deserves? (His fellow writers smile at his disappointment; perhaps that's what he deserves.) Years later, in better times, the book is reissued and does well. Has its author become more deserving? Surely desert can't hang on the state of the economy. There is too much luck involved here; talk of desert makes little sense. We would do better to say simply that the writer is entitled to his royalties, large or small.[5] He is like any other entrepreneur; he has bet on the market. It's a chancy business, but he knew that when he made the bet. He has a right to what he gets—after he has paid the costs of communal provision (he lives not only in the market but also in the city). But he can't claim that he has gotten less than he deserves, and it doesn't matter if the rest of us think that he has gotten more. The market doesn't recognize desert. Initiative, enterprise, innovation, hard work, ruthless dealing, reckless gambling, the prostitution of talent: All these are sometimes rewarded, sometimes not.

But the rewards that the market provides, when it provides them, are appropriate to these sorts of effort. The man or woman who builds a better mousetrap, or opens a restaurant and sells delicious blintzes, or does a little teaching on the side, is looking to earn money. And why not? No one would want to feed blintzes to strangers, day after day, merely to win their gratitude. Here in the world of the petty bourgeoisie, it seems only right that an entrepreneur, able to provide timely goods and services, should reap the rewards he had in mind when he went to work.

This is, indeed, a kind of "rightness" that the community may see fit to enclose and restrain. The morality of the bazaar belongs in the bazaar. The market is a zone of the city, not the whole of the city. But it is a great mistake, I think, when people worried about the tyranny of the market seek its entire abolition. It is one thing to clear the Temple of traders, quite another to clear the streets. The latter move would require a radical shift in our understanding of what material things are for and of how we relate to them and to other people through them. But the shift is not accomplished by the abolition; commodity exchange is merely driven underground; or it takes place in state stores, as in parts of Eastern Europe today, drearily and inefficiently.

The liveliness of the open market reflects our sense of the great variety of desirable things; and so long as that is our sense, we have no reason not to relish the liveliness. . . .

## THE RELATIVITY AND THE NON-RELATIVITY OF JUSTICE

Justice is relative to social meanings. Indeed, the relativity of justice follows from the classic non-relative definition, giving each person his due, as much as it does from my own proposal, distributing goods for "internal" reasons. These are formal definitions that require, as I have tried to show, historical completion. We cannot say what is due to this person or that one until we know how these people relate to one another through the things they make and distribute. There cannot be a just society until there is a society; and the adjective *just* doesn't determine, it only modifies, the substantive life of the societies it describes. There are an infinite number of possible lives, shaped by an infinite number of possible cultures, religions, political arrangements, geographical conditions, and so on. A given society is just if its substantive life is lived in a certain way—that is, in a way faithful to the shared understandings of the members. . . .

We are (all of us) culture-producing creatures; we make and inhabit meaningful worlds. Since there is no way to rank and order these worlds with regard to their understanding of social goods, we do justice to actual men and women by respecting their particular creations. And they claim justice, and resist tyranny, by insisting on the meaning of social goods among themselves. Justice is rooted in the distinct understandings of places, honors, jobs, things of all sorts, that constitute a shared way of life. To override those understandings is (always) to act unjustly.

Just as one can describe a caste system that meets (internal) standards of justice, so one can describe a capitalist system that does the same thing. But now the description will have to be a great deal more complex, for social meanings are no longer integrated in the same way. It may be the case, as Marx says in the first volume of *Capital*, that the creation and appropriation of surplus value "is peculiar good fortune for the buyer [of labor power], but no injustice at all to the seller."[6] But this is by no means the whole story of justice and injustice in capitalist society. It will also be crucially important whether this surplus value is convertible, whether it purchases special privileges, in the law courts, or in the educational system, or in the spheres of office and politics. Since capitalism develops along with and actually sponsors a considerable differentiation of social goods, no account of buying and selling, no description of free exchange, can possibly settle the question of justice. We will need to learn a great deal about other distributive processes and about their relative autonomy from or integration into the market. The dominance of capital outside the market makes capitalism unjust.

The theory of justice is alert to differences, sensitive to boundaries. It doesn't follow from the theory, however, that societies are more just if they are more differentiated. Justice simply has more scope in such societies, because there are more distinct goods, more distributive principles, more agents, more procedures. And the more scope justice has, the more certain it is that complex equality will be the form that justice takes. Tyranny also has more scope. Viewed from the outside, from our own perspective, the Indian Brahmins look very much like tyrants—and so they will come to be if the understandings on which their high position is based cease to be shared. From the inside, however, things come to them naturally, as it were, by virtue of their ritual purity. They don't need to turn themselves into tyrants in order to enjoy the full range of social goods. Or, when they do turn themselves into tyrants, they merely exploit the advantages they already posses. But when goods are distinct and distributive spheres autonomous, that same enjoyment requires exertion, intrigue, and violence. This is the crucial sign of tyranny: a continual grabbing of things that don't come naturally, an unrelenting struggle to rule outside one's own company. . . .

## JUSTICE IN THE TWENTIETH CENTURY

. . . Contemporary forms of egalitarian politics have their origin in the struggle against capitalism and the particular tyranny of money. And surely in the United States today it is the tyranny of money that most clearly invites resistance: property/power rather than power itself. But it is a common argument that without property/power, power itself is too dangerous. State officials will be tyrants, we are told, whenever their power is not balanced by the power of money. It follows, then, that capitalists will be tyrants whenever wealth is not balanced by a strong government. Or, in the alternative metaphor of American political science, political power and wealth must check one another: since armies of ambitious men and women push forward from one side of the boundary, what we require are similar armies pushing forward from the other side. John Kenneth Galbraith developed this metaphor into a theory of "countervailing powers."[7] There is also a competing argument according to which freedom is served only if the armies of capitalism are always and everywhere unopposed. But that argument can't be right, for it isn't only equality but freedom, too, that we defend when we block a large number of (the larger number of) possible exchanges. . . .

Money can buy power and influence, as it can buy office, education, honor, and so on, without radically coordinating the various distributive spheres and without eliminating alternative processes and agents. It corrupts distributions without transforming them; and then corrupt distributions coexist with legitimate ones, like prostitution alongside married love. But this is tyranny still, and it can make for harsh forms of domination. And if resistance is less heroic than in totalitarian states, it is hardly less important. . . .

The appropriate arrangements in our own society are those, I think, of a decentralized democratic socialism; a strong welfare state run, in part at least, by local and amateur officials; a constrained market; an open and demystified civil service; independent public schools; the sharing of hard work and free time; the protection of religious and familial life; a system of public honoring and dishonoring free from all considerations of rank or class; workers' control of companies and factories; a politics of parties, movements, meetings, and public debate. But institutions of this sort are of little use unless they are inhabited by men and women who feel at home within them and are prepared to defend them. It may be an argument against complex equality that it requires a strenuous defense—and a defense that begins while equality is still in the making. But this is also an argument against liberty. Eternal vigilance is the price of both.

## EQUALITY AND SOCIAL CHANGE

Complex equality might look more secure if we could describe it in terms of the harmony, rather than the autonomy, of spheres. But social meanings and distributions are harmonious only in this respect: that when we see why one good has a certain form and is distributed in a certain way, we also see why another must be different. Precisely because of these differences, however, boundary conflict is endemic. The principles appropriate to the different spheres are not harmonious with one another; nor are the patterns of conduct and feeling they generate. Welfare systems and markets, offices and families, schools and states are run on different principles: so they should be. The principles must somehow fit together within a single culture; they must be comprehensible across the different companies of men and women. But this doesn't rule out deep strains and odd juxtapositions. Ancient China was ruled by a hereditary divine-right emperor and a meritocratic bureaucracy. One has to tell a complex story to explain that sort of coexistence. A community's culture is the story its members tell so as to make sense of all the different pieces of their social life—and justice is the doctrine that distinguishes the pieces. In any differentiated society, justice will make for harmony only if it first makes for separation. Good fences make just societies.

We never know exactly where to put the fences; they have no natural location. The goods they distinguish are artifacts; as they were made, so they can be remade. Boundaries, then, are vulnerable to shifts in social meaning, and we have no choice but to live with the continual probes and incursions through which these shifts are worked out. Commonly, the shifts are like sea changes, very slow. . . . But the actual boundary revision, when it comes, is likely to come suddenly, as in the creation of a national health service in Britain after the Second World War: one year, doctors were professionals and entrepreneurs; and the next year, they were professionals and public servants. We can map a program of such revisions, based on our current understanding of social goods. We can set ourselves in opposition, as I have done, to the prevailing forms of dominance. But we can't anticipate the deeper changes in consciousness, not in our own community and certainly not in any other. The social world will one day look different from the way it does today, and distributive justice will take on a different character than it has for us. Eternal vigilance is no guarantee of eternity. . . .

## NOTES

1. See John Rawls, *A Theory of Justice* (Cambridge, MA: 1971): Jürgen Habermas, *Legitimation Crisis*, trans. Thomas McCarthy (Boston: 1975), esp. p. 113; Bruce Ackerman, *Social Justice in the Liberal State* (New Haven, 1980).
2. I have taken the term "communities of character" from Otto Bauer (see *Austro-Marxism* [13], p. 107).
3. Cf. Nozick on "patterning," *Anarchy, State, and Utopia*, pp. 155 ff [this text, Chap 10].
4. See Louis O. Kelso and Mortimer J. Adler, *The Capitalist Manifesto* (New York: 1958), pp. 67–77, for an argument that makes the distribution of wealth on the basis of contribution analogous to the distribution of office on the basis of merit. Economists like Milton Friedman are more cautious, but this is surely the popular ideology of capitalism: success is a deserved reward for "intelligence, resolution, hard work, and a willingness to take risks" (George Gilder, *Wealth and Poverty* [New York: 1981], p. 101).
5. See Robert Nozick's distinction between entitlement and desert, *Anarchy, State, and Utopia* (New York: 1974), pp. 155–60.
6. Karl Marx, *Capital*, ed. Frederick Engels (New York, 1967), p. 194; I have followed the translation and interpretation of Allen W. Wood, "The Marxian Critique of Justice," *Philosophy and Public Affairs* 1 (1972): 263ff.
7. John Kenneth Galbraith, *American Capitalism* (Boston: 1956), chap. 9.

## CAPITALISM AND ECONOMIC JUSTICE

# Capitalism and Freedom

*Milton Friedman*

### LIBERALISM AND EGALITARIANISM

The heart of the liberal philosophy is a belief in the dignity of the individual, in his freedom to make the most of his capacities and opportunities according to his own lights, subject only to the proviso that he not interfere with the freedom of other individuals to do the same. This implies a belief in the equality of men in one sense; in their inequality in another. Each man has an equal right to freedom. This is an important and fundamental

From Milton Friedman, *Capitalism and Freedom*, (the University of Chicago Press, 1982), pp. 195, 161–166, 133–136, right precisely because men are different, because one man will want to do different things with his freedom than another, and in the process can contribute more than another to the general culture of the society in which many men live.

The liberal will therefore distinguish sharply between equality of rights and equality of opportunity, on the one hand, and material equality or equality of outcome on the other. He may welcome the fact that a free society in fact tends toward greater material equality than any other yet tried. But he will regard this as a desirable by-product of a free society, not its major justification. He will welcome measures that promote both freedom and equality—such as measures to eliminate monopoly power and to improve the operation of the market. He will regard private charity directed at helping the less fortunate as an example of the proper use of freedom. And he may approve state action toward ameliorating poverty as a more effective way in which the great bulk of the community can achieve a common objective. He will do so with regret, however, at having to substitute compulsory for voluntary action.

The egalitarian will go this far, too. But he will want to go further. He will defend taking from some to give to others, not as a more effective means whereby the "some" can achieve an objective they want to achieve, but on grounds of "justice." At this point, equality comes sharply into conflict with freedom; one must choose. One cannot be both an egalitarian, in this sense, and a liberal. . . .

A Central Element in the development of a collectivist sentiment in this century, at least in Western countries, has been a belief in equality of income as a social goal and a willingness to use the arm of the state to promote it. Two very different questions must be asked in evaluating this egalitarian sentiment and the egalitarian measures it has produced. The first is normative and ethical: what is the justification for state intervention to promote equality? The second is positive and scientific: what has been the effect of the measures actually taken?

## THE ETHICS OF DISTRIBUTION

The ethical principle that would directly justify the distribution of income in a free market society is, "To each according to what he and the instruments he owns produces." The operation of even this principle implicitly depends on state action. Property rights are matters of law and social convention. . . . Their definition and enforcement is one of the primary functions of the state. The final distribution of income and wealth under the full operation of this principle may well depend markedly on the rules of property adopted.

What is the relation between this principle and another that seems ethically appealing, namely, equality of treatment? In part, the two principles are not contradictory. Payment in accordance with product may be necessary to achieve true equality of treatment. Given individuals whom we are prepared to regard as alike in ability and initial resources, if some have a greater taste for leisure and others for marketable goods, inequality of return through the market is necessary to achieve equality of total return or equality of treatment. One man may prefer a routine job with much time off for basking in the sun to a more exacting job paying a higher salary; another man may prefer the opposite. If both were paid equally in money, their incomes in a more fundamental sense would be unequal. Similarly, equal treatment requires that an individual be paid more for a dirty, unattractive job than for a pleasant rewarding one. Much observed inequality is of this kind. Differences of money income offset differences in other characteristics of the occupation or trade. In the jargon of economists, they are "equalizing differences" required to make the whole of the "net advantages," pecuniary and non-pecuniary, the same.

Another kind of inequality arising through the operation of the market is also required, in a somewhat more subtle sense, to produce equality of treatment, or to put it differently to satisfy men's tastes. It can be illustrated most simply by a lottery. Consider a group of individuals who initially have equal endowments and who all agree voluntarily to enter a lottery with very unequal prizes. The resultant inequality of income is surely required to permit the individuals in question to make the most of their initial equality. Redistribution of the income after the event is equivalent to denying them the opportunity to enter the lottery. This case is far more important in practice than would appear by taking the notion of a "lottery" literally. Individuals choose occupations, investments, and the like partly in accordance with their taste for uncertainty. The girl who tries to become a movie actress rather than a civil servant is deliberately choosing to enter a lottery, so is the individual who invests in penny uranium stocks rather than government bonds. Insurance is a way of expressing a taste for certainty. Even these examples do not indicate fully the extent to which actual inequality may be the result of arrangements designed to satisfy men's tastes. The very arrangements for paying and hiring people are affected by such preferences. If all potential movie actresses had a great dislike of uncertainty, there would tend to develop "cooperatives" of movie actresses, the members of which agreed in advance to share income receipts more or less evenly, thereby in effect providing themselves insurance through the pooling of risks. If such a preference were widespread, large diversified corporations combining risky and non-risky ventures would become the rule. The wild-cat oil prospector, the private proprietorship, the small partnership, would all become rare.

Indeed, this is one way to interpret governmental measures to redistribute income through progressive taxes and the like. It can be argued that for one reason or another, costs of administration perhaps, the market cannot produce the range of lotteries or the kind of lottery desired by the members of the community, and that progressive taxation is, as it were, a government enterprise to do so. I have no doubt that this view contains an element of truth. At the same time, it can hardly justify present taxation, if only because the taxes are imposed *after* it is already largely known who have drawn the prizes and who the blanks in the lottery of life, and the taxes are voted mostly by those who think they have drawn the blanks. One might, along these lines, justify one generation's voting the tax schedules to be applied to an as yet unborn generation. Any such procedure would, I conjecture, yield income tax schedules much less highly graduated than present schedules are, at least on paper.

Though much of the inequality of income produced by payment in accordance with product reflects "equalizing" differences or the satisfaction of men's tastes for uncertainty, a large part reflects initial differences in endowment, both of human capacities and of property. This is the part that raises the really difficult ethical issue.

It is widely argued that it is essential to distinguish between inequality in personal endowments and in property, and between inequalities arising from inherited wealth and from acquired wealth. Inequality resulting from differences in personal capacities, or from differences in wealth accumulated by the individual in question, are considered appropriate, or at least not so clearly inappropriate as differences resulting from inherited wealth.

This distinction is untenable. Is there any greater ethical justification for the high returns to the individual who inherits from his parents a peculiar voice for which there is a great demand than for the high returns to the individual who inherits property? The sons of Russian commissars surely have a higher expectation of income—perhaps also of liquidation—than the sons of peasants. Is this any more or less justifiable than the higher income expectation of the son of an American millionaire? We can look at this same question in another way. A parent who has wealth that he wishes to pass on to his child can do so in different ways. He can use a given sum of money to finance his child's training as, say, a certified public accountant, or to set him up in business, or to set up a trust fund yielding him a property income. In any of these cases, the child will have a higher income than he otherwise would. But in the first case, his income will be regarded as coming from human capacities; in the second, from profits; in the third, from inherited wealth. Is there any basis for distinguishing among these categories of receipts on ethical grounds? Finally, it seems illogical to say that a man is entitled to what he has produced by personal capacities or to the produce of the wealth he has accumulated, but that he is not entitled to pass any wealth on to his children; to say that a man may use his income for riotous living but may not give it to his heirs. Surely, the latter is one way to use what he has produced.

The fact that these arguments against the so-called capitalist ethic are invalid does not of course demonstrate that the capitalist ethic is an acceptable one. I find it difficult to justify either accepting or rejecting it, or to justify any alternative principle. I am led to the view that it cannot in and of itself be regarded as an ethical principle; that it must be regarded as instrumental or a corollary of some other principle such as freedom.

Some hypothetical examples may illustrate the fundamental difficulty. Suppose there are four Robinson Crusoes, independently marooned on four islands in the same neighborhood. One happened to land on a large and fruitful island which enables him to live easily and well. The others happened to land on tiny and rather barren islands from which they can barely scratch a living. One day, they discover the existence of one another. Of course, it would be generous of the Crusoe on the large island if he invited the others to join him and share its wealth. But suppose he does not. Would the other three be justified in joining forces and compelling him to share his wealth with them? Many a reader will be tempted to say yes. But before yielding to this temptation, consider precisely the same situation in different guise. Suppose you and three friends are walking along the street and you happen to spy and retrieve a $20 bill on the pavement. It would be generous of you, of course, if you were to divide it equally with them, or at least blow them to a drink. But suppose you do not. Would the other three be justified in joining forces and compelling you to share the $20 equally with them? I suspect most readers will be tempted to say no. And on further reflection, they may even conclude that the generous course of action is not itself clearly the "right" one. Are we prepared to urge on ourselves or our fellows that any person whose wealth exceeds the average of all persons in the world should immediately dispose of the excess by distributing it equally to all the rest of the world's inhabitants? We may admire and praise such action when undertaken by a few. But a universal "potlatch" would make a civilized world impossible.

In any event, two wrongs do not make a right. The unwillingness of the rich Robinson Crusoe or the lucky finder of the $20 bill to share his wealth does not justify the use of coercion by the others. Can we justify being judges in our own case, deciding on our own when we are entitled to use force to extract what we regard as our due from others? Or what we regard as not their due? Most differences of status or position or wealth can be regarded as the product of chance at a far enough remove. The man who is hard working and thrifty is to be regarded as "deserving"; yet these qualities owe much to the genes he was fortunate (or unfortunate?) enough to inherit.

Despite the lip service that we all pay to "merit" as compared to "chance," we are generally much readier to accept inequalities arising from chance than those clearly attributable to merit. The college professor whose colleague wins a sweepstake will envy him but is unlikely to bear him any malice or to feel unjustly treated. Let the colleague receive a trivial raise that makes his salary higher than the professor's own, and the professor is far more likely to feel aggrieved. After all, the goddess of chance, as of justice, is blind. The salary raise was a deliberate judgment of relative merit.

## THE INSTRUMENTAL ROLE OF DISTRIBUTION ACCORDING TO PRODUCT

The operative function of payment in accordance with product in a market society is not primarily distributive, but allocative. . . . The central principle of a market economy is co-operation through voluntary exchange. Individuals co-operate with others because they can in this way satisfy their own wants more effectively. But unless an individual receives the whole of what he adds to the product, he will enter into exchanges on the basis of what he can receive rather than what he can produce. Exchanges will not take place that would have been mutually beneficial if each party received what he contributed to the aggregate product. Payment in accordance with product is therefore necessary in order that resources be used most effectively, at least under a system depending on voluntary co-operation. Given sufficient knowledge, it might be that compulsion could be substituted for the incentive of reward, though I doubt that it could. One can shuffle inanimate objects around; one can compel individuals to be at certain places at certain times; but one can hardly compel individuals to put forward their best efforts. Put another way, the substitution of compulsion for co-operation changes the amount of resources available. . . .

## SOCIAL RESPONSIBILITY OF BUSINESS AND LABOR

The view has been gaining widespread acceptance that corporate officials and labor leaders have a "social responsibility" that goes beyond serving the interest of their stockholders or their members. This view shows a fundamental misconception of the character and nature of a free economy. In such an economy, there is one and only one social responsibility of business—to use its resources and engage in activities designed to increase its profits so long as it stays within the rules of the game, which is to say, engages in open and free competition, without deception or fraud. Similarly, the "social responsibility" of labor leaders is to serve the interests of the members of their unions. It is the responsibility of the rest of us to establish a framework of law such that an individual in pursuing his own interest is, to quote Adam Smith, "led by an invisible hand to promote an end which was no part of his intention. Nor is it always the worse for the society that it was no part of it. By pursuing his own interest, he frequently promotes that of the society more effectually than when he really intends to promote it. I have never known much good done by those who affected to trade for the public good."[1]

Few trends could so thoroughly undermine the very foundations of our free society as the acceptance by corporate officials of a social responsibility other than to make as much money for their stockholders as possible. This is a fundamentally subversive doctrine. If businessmen do have a social responsibility other than making maximum profits for stockholders, how are they to know what it is? Can self-selected private individuals decide what the social interest is? Can they decide how great a burden they are justified in placing on themselves or their stockholders to serve that social interest? Is it tolerable that these public functions of taxation, expenditure, and control be exercised by the people who happen at the moment to be in charge of particular enterprises, chosen for those posts by strictly private groups? If businessmen are civil servants rather than the employees of their stockholders then in a democracy they will, sooner or later, be chosen by the public techniques of election and appointment.

And long before this occurs, their decision-making power will have been taken away from them. A dramatic illustration was the cancellation of a steel price increase by U.S. Steel in April 1962 through the medium of a public display of anger by President Kennedy and threats of reprisals on levels ranging from anti-trust suits to examination of the tax reports of steel executives. This was a striking episode because of the public display of the vast powers concentrated in Washington. We were all made aware of how much of the power needed for a police state was already available. It illustrates the present point as well. If the price of steel is a public decision, as the doctrine of social responsibility declares, then it cannot be permitted to be made privately.

The particular aspect of the doctrine which this example illustrates, and which has been most prominent recently, is an alleged social responsibility of business and labor to keep prices and wage rates down in order to avoid price inflation. Suppose that at a time when there was upward pressure on prices—ultimately of course reflecting an increase in the stock of money—every businessman and labor leader were to accept this responsibility and suppose all could succeed in keeping any price from rising, so we had voluntary price and wage control without open inflation. What would be the result? Clearly product shortages, labor shortages, gray markets, black markets. If prices are not allowed to ration goods and workers, there must be some other means to do so. Can the alternative rationing schemes be private? Perhaps for a time in a small and unimportant area. But if the goods involved are many and important, there will necessarily be pressure, and probably irresistible pressure, for governmental rationing of goods, a governmental wage policy, and governmental measures for allocating and distributing labor.

Price controls, whether legal or voluntary, if effectively enforced would eventually lead to the destruction of the free-enterprise system and its replacement by a centrally controlled system. And it would not even be effective in preventing inflation. History offers ample evidence that what determines the average level of prices and wages is the amount of money in the economy and not the greediness of businessmen or of workers. Governments ask for the self-restraint of business and labor because of their inability to manage their own affairs—which includes the control of money—and the natural human tendency to pass the buck.

One topic in the area of social responsibility that I feel duty-bound to touch on, because it affects my own personal interests, has been the claim that business should contribute to the support of charitable activities and especially to universities. Such giving by corporations is an inappropriate use of corporate funds in a free-enterprise society.

The corporation is an instrument of the stockholders who own it. If the corporation makes a contribution, it prevents the individual stockholder from himself deciding how he should dispose of his funds. With the corporation tax and the deductibility of contributions, stockholders may of course want the corporation to make a gift on their behalf, since this would enable them to make a larger gift. The best solution would be the abolition of the corporate tax. But so long as there is a corporate tax, there is no justification for permitting deductions for contributions to charitable and educational institutions. Such contributions should be made by the individuals who are the ultimate owners of property in our society.

People who urge extension of the deductibility of this kind of corporate contribution in the name of free enterprise are fundamentally working against their own interest. A major complaint made frequently against modern business is that it involves the separation of ownership and control—that the corporation has become a social institution that is a law unto itself, with irresponsible executives who do not serve the interests of their stockholders. This charge is not true. But the direction in which policy is now moving, of permitting corporations to make contributions for charitable purposes and allowing deductions for income tax, is a step in the direction of creating a true divorce between ownership and control and of undermining the basic nature and character of our society. It is a step away from an individualistic society and toward the corporate state.

## NOTES

1. *Wealth of Nations*, Bk. IV, chapter ii.

# Can Capitalism Save Itself? Some Ruminations on the Fate of Capitalism

*Leo Groarke*

One might begin a history of our present economic era with the collapse of the Soviet Union's communist experiment. . . .

At the beginning of a new millennium, American-style capitalism has emerged the victor. Soviet communism is, in marked contrast, of interest only to historians. In the wake of its demise, the world economy is characterized by frontier capitalism in the former Soviet states; by the rise (and sometimes fall) of free market economies in East Asia and the developing world; by global markets; and by increasingly powerful multinational corporations. Capital and investment flow around the world with an ease and speed which was previously unimaginable. Globally and nationally, capitalism has become the socioeconomic order of the day.

Capitalism's proponents often treat its rise as a vindication of their own political perspective. To some extent this must be accepted—for the rise of capitalism does suggest that it can economically outperform communism. That said, history leaves no room for confidence in the permanence of the capitalist economy. Tribal societies, Greek city states, and feudalism in a multitude of forms all enjoyed their heydays. To many (perhaps most) who lived in their midst, their economic, social, and political structures seemed inevitable, permanent, and unassailable. But they all gave way to other forms of life that exposed their contradictions, their internal tensions, and their inability to accommodate new realities. It would be naive to think this is impossible in the case of capitalism.

Because capitalism has both strengths and weaknesses, its survival in the long term depends upon our ability to create a sociopolitical environment which can exploit its strengths and constrain its weaknesses. I will argue that a 'mitigated' capitalism can do both, but that the weaknesses of capitalism will bring about its demise if they are not adequately addressed. I will therefore criticize capitalism's most enthusiastic supporters, for they ignore these weaknesses and in this way fail to recognize and address legitimate concerns about capitalist economies. As ironic as it may sound, it is the most strident defenders of capitalism who are most likely to sow the seeds of its demise.

Excerpts from Leo Groarke, in *Ethics and Capitalism*, ed. John Douglas Bishop, University of Toronto Press © 2000. Used with permission.

## THE STRENGTHS OF CAPITALISM

Arguments for capitalism are sometimes founded on an inalienable right to private property. Such arguments maintain that individuals have a right to whatever private property they can accumulate (without resorting to violence, fraud, and the like) and, by implication, a right to trade such property in a free market.

Dan Usher has . . . noted that such arguments assume rather than justify the values inherent in capitalist economies. In answer to them, it can be said that a right to accumulate private property is not self-evident, but a source of constant and continuing controversy and debate. It follows that rights of this sort are an untenable basis for capitalism, especially as they are heavily biased in favour of the interests of those who own significant amounts of property (or have the opportunity to secure it). Those without such property can, in view of this, plausibly dismiss such rights as a covert attempt to rationalize a political point of view which is in reality designed to make the rich richer and the poor poorer.

It does not follow that the property rights on which capitalism depends cannot be justified, but only that they must be justified in a less contentious way. . . . This can most plausibly be accomplished by arguing that private property and the exchange of goods and services in a free market contribute to the common good. Ironically from an ethical point of view, the benefits this makes possible are the result of a frank recognition that humans are motivated by self-interest rather than altruistic convictions of the sort which tend to be enshrined in principles of ethics. The very success of capitalist economies thus shows that most humans are motivated by their own economic interests, which serve as a catalyst for the transactions which have made capitalist markets the economic engine of the world.[1]

Instead of bemoaning this aspect of human nature, capitalism harnesses it for the sake of economic prosperity and the common good. The exchange of goods in a free market is motivated by self-interest, but at the same time serves greater economic interests and benefits society at large. . . . As the experience of the world's capitalist markets demonstrates, competitive self-interest can in this way create an exceptionally efficient system of production and exchange which generates wealth on a scale which was previously unimagined.

As many of capitalism's advocates emphasize, the market transactions it makes possible eliminate the need to plan a whole economy. This is an important point because planned economies have in practice proved to be unworkable. The problems that attend them plagued the economy of the former Soviet Union, which could not match the performance of economies in the West. . . . A successful attempt to plan a whole economy would require the ability to predict human needs, preferences, and behavior to an extent that seems unattainable. In the process of eliminating planning of this sort, capitalism allows a pattern of production and distribution which is determined by the autonomous decisions of those who participate in the market and is as a result impressively sensitive to individual needs and preferences. . . .

By relying on the free market as the principle economic mechanism for determining the production and distribution of goods and services, capitalism reduces the need for administration and bureaucracy that would otherwise direct the running of the economy. . . .

According to many commentators, capitalism's rejection of regulation in the market is a manifestation of a deeper commitment to individual freedom. Liberty is, therefore, the basic value to which thinkers . . . appeal in propounding arguments for capitalism. While there is something to this, it is important not to exaggerate the freedom implied by capitalism's limits on the power of 'big government.' It would, in particular, be a mistake to equate market freedom and the political freedom we assume to be an essential feature of a just society. The existence of capitalist economies in many politically repressive states—Nazi Germany, Chile under Pinochet, Singapore, and Hong Kong—shows that capitalism does not require democratic rights and freedoms. . . .

Whatever one thinks of such issues, capitalism is an impressive economic system. As I have already noted, its strengths include its ability to exploit individual self-interest for the sake of the greater good; its willingness to recognize frankly that different individuals are not equal; its ability to generate great prosperity and wealth through competition; its ability to coordinate the supply and distribution of goods and services without large-scale planning and regulation (without attempting to plan a whole economy); its tolerance for different ways of doing things; and (more controversially) the commitment to freedom implicit in its commitment to economic freedom. It goes without saying that these strengths make capitalism an attractive economic system. Looked at from the point of view of ethics, they raise the question whether capitalism might provide a basis for a prosperous economic order which could be the cornerstone of just and laudatory social and political relations.

## THE WEAKNESSES OF CAPITALISM

As impressive as they are, the strengths of capitalism should not blind us to its weaknesses. From a moral point of view, one of its most serious failings is the profoundly negative effect it appears to have on the moral character of a society and the individuals whose lives it influences. In favour of capitalism it might be said that it leaves moral matters to the individual (and is in this sense amoral), and that it makes possible material prosperity which can be used in the pursuit of moral ends. While this is true to some extent, it must also be acknowledged that capitalist markets promote a consumer lifestyle which emphasizes the individual pursuit of wealth, to the detriment of things that matter more from a moral point of view. . . .

The consumptive lifestyles which have been fostered by capitalist economies are reflected in today's environmental problems, which threaten to drastically alter human (and non-human) life on planet earth. . . .

The environmental crisis . . . is bound to be exacerbated by the forces of globalization and development, which ensure the spread of capitalist economies and their consumer lifestyles. . . .

Other ethical issues arise when one considers the workings of real (as opposed to theoretical) capitalist markets, for they frequently fall short of the ideals which are touted in popular defences of the capitalist economy . . . the ideal model of capitalism . . . often ignores the motivations and strategies that guide the accumulation of private property in real markets. . . .

In many cases . . . markets are driven, not by efficiency and an openness to innovation, but by past prejudice and by conventional 'wisdom' which precludes new efficiencies. Markets can to some extent compensate for these obstacles by disseminating information via normal market mechanisms. . . . [This] allows buyers to distinguish between superior and inferior (and more and less cost-effective) goods and services. The problem is that such information is very frequently absent from real markets, which are not ideal and typically operate on the basis of poor, incomplete, or misleading information. Misinformation is often explicitly fostered and sustained by seductive and intentionally misleading advertising which overwhelms more objective sources of information. To some extent the problems this creates are inevitable, for there will always be some market players whose interests are best served by attempts to purposely thwart the dissemination of relevant information which would compromise their success.

If I am someone who manufactures inefficient electrical appliances I may, for example, protect my share of the appliance market, not by improving my product, but by doing my best to ensure that the public is not aware of innovative, cost-effective alternatives. . . . If I have significant economic resources I may in this way have a profound effect on the market. Considered only from the point of view of my own interests, such a strategy may be more cost effective than the attempt to reorganize and reinvent the way that I do business. This is especially true if manufacturers who produce superior appliances are not able to compete with me because they lack the resources needed to disseminate information in the market. . . .

The influences that often make markets irrational rather than efficient are exacerbated by the unequal concentrations of wealth and power that capitalist economies allow. Inequality is a necessary feature of the capitalist economy, for it provides the incentive which drives the market towards efficiency. The problem is that inequalities—and especially enormous inequalities of the sort that characterize free markets in the real world—can also have the opposite effect. This is an inevitable consequence of the fact that market players with great wealth can exert tremendous influence on the market, both through direct intervention (in the most extreme cases through monopoly and insider trading) and by (more subtly but often more significantly) influencing the legal, cultural, and political environment in which the market operates. . . .

Especially as capitalism promotes the pursuit of self-interest, one must expect those who participate in markets to do what they can to further their own economic interests. In the context of vastly different economic resources, this means that real markets are often plagued by market strategies which promote regulatory favouritism, thoughtless buying rather than reflection, ignorance rather than informed choices, and morally and even legally objectionable market moves. This is to be expected in markets designed to reward strategies that promote economic advantage rather than right or wrong or the efficient working of the market . . . such corruption is objectionable not only on moral grounds—because it violates a basic moral duty to be honest—but also because it undermines those benefits which justify capitalist markets in the first place. It thus works to replace fair competition and efficiency with decisions made on the basis of unjustified patronage and which serve to entrench a political status quo, promote great and unjustified differences in wealth, and encourage (and justify) a pervasive suspicion of markets and the workings of capitalist economies.

Considered from the point of view of the common good, the problems with unregulated markets are further exacerbated by their failure to consider the interests of those who do not directly participate in the market and do not, therefore, influence its 'invisible hand.' The longterm consequences of market transactions will, for example, probably affect the lives of children and future generations *more* than the lives of those who actually participate in these transactions, but such groups have no way to ensure that their interests . . . influence the direction of these transactions. Someone who suffers from the pollution produced by a papermill may be far removed from the market activities that guide its operation and so have little or no effect on its operations. More generally, the poor will have some influence on prices in the market, but relatively little influence in comparison with the rich, whose economic power allows them to influence the workings of the market much more significantly. As a decision-making mechanism, real markets therefore tend to favour, not the common good and those who need help most, but those who enjoy extensive private property and great economic power.

## MITIGATED CAPITALISM

One might easily elaborate the problems with unregulated capitalist markets in more detail. It is more important to consider what can be done about them. In the absence of attempts to constrain the weaknesses of capitalism,

I think it likely that capitalism will in the long run be undermined by a combination of pressures which will be exacerbated by free markets marred by corruption, the trust-agency problem, and other practical impediments; the negative environmental impacts of consumerist economies; the tremendous social pressures which are produced by great disparities in income and lifestyle; and ethnic, religious, and other tensions which attempt to fill a moral vacuum which capitalism perpetuates. If particular capitalist economies do not wholly succumb to such forces, they may instead be forced to deal with them by evolving in a way that no longer guarantees democratic values like the right to free speech and political protest.

A democratic capitalism which is to persevere will, therefore, have to be bolstered by measures or conditions which mitigate its weaknesses. This suggests that market regulation has an important role to play in creating a sustainable capitalism. To many of those enamoured of capitalism, this will seem something of an anathema . . . widespread scepticism about the effects and workability of government regulation is one of the hallmarks of capitalist politics today. . . . The problem is that such views caricature legitimate regulation, both by romanticizing the workings of unregulated markets (which are treated as a panacea for all social problems) and demonizing regulation (which is treated as always corrupt, incompetent, and ineffectual). For though it must be granted that regulation can be incompetent and corrupt the market, it must also be said that capitalism can be justified only if it is guided by regulation which ensures that efficiency, competition, and reasonable social consequences are characteristics of the market. This is possible within a capitalist framework because such regulation need not deny that private property and the market have a primary role in establishing the production and distribution of goods and services.

The extent to which a justifiable capitalism needs a regulated market can be seen in the case of international corruption. As Cragg argues, there are useful things which private corporations can do to improve markets from this point of view, but 'the business community must clearly recognize that there is a role here for governments acting nationally and internationally.'[2] Without national (and perhaps international) regulation, corporations which make efforts to avoid corruption and 'play fair' are likely to suffer competitive disadvantages because they cannot employ effective market strategies which are available to their competitors. As Bookchin remarks in the context of ecological issues:

> However ecologically concerned an entrepreneur may be, the harsh fact is that his or her survival in the marketplace precludes a meaningful ecological orientation. To engage in ecologically sound practices places a morally concerned entrepreneur at a striking, and indeed, fatal disadvantage in a competitive relationship with a rival—notably one who lacks any ecological concerns and thus produces at lower costs and reaps higher profits for further capital expansion.[3]

It does not follow that capitalist managers and owners should not attempt to play fair in the market, but it does follow that their behaviour is likely to have a limited effect on behaviour in the market if it is not backed by external constraints imposed by government. Market players concerned to mitigate the negative aspects of unregulated markets need, therefore, to assert unapologetically the importance of government regulation, all the more so given that they often operate within a business culture in which it is politically incorrect to say such things. In answer to popular prejudices against 'big government,' it must be said that government needs significant powers in order to institute measures to ensure that capitalist markets are and remain free and competitive, and in order to mitigate the negative aspects of capitalism we have already noted.

This is especially true in the case of global corporate capitalism, for it creates a world economy in which large multinational corporations enjoy a degree of economic and political power which rivals that of nation states. A government charged with the responsibility of ensuring that Microsoft respects the principles of a competitive market cannot be a shrinking violet that lacks substantive powers. The powers that it enjoys must be backed by a much broader appreciation of the extent to which market regulation is a necessary feature of a healthy capitalist economy.

Because one of the prime functions of government in a capitalist society should be the regulation of capitalist markets, it is important that it operate in ways which ensures that its actions and decisions are not compromised by undue control or influence exerted by players in the market. . . . Among many other things, this implies that proper regulation requires a vigilant attempt to separate public and private interests (one might compare an earlier need to separate the functions of the church and state). In practice, this is a constant problem which is evident in most capitalist economies, in which government and economic interests frequently collaborate in a way that compromises government's ability to act as an independent regulator of the market.

If this is correct, then the most defensible capitalism is a mitigated capitalism which is (contrary to popular prejudice) regulated by an independent government which has substantial regulatory powers. It is more difficult to say exactly what kinds of restrictions on the market are and are not defensible from this point of view. A detailed account of such regulation is beyond the scope of the present chapter, but it is important to end it with a general overview of justifiable and unjustifiable regulation. Our earlier discussion justifies (1) regulations which are designed to ensure that the market remains competitive and efficient, and (2) regulations designed to ensure that all players in the market respect the interests of those who do not have the ability to influence it significantly, even though they are significantly affected by its behaviour. . . .

Many of the regulations which can in this way be justified are (at least to some extent) a standard feature of contemporary capitalism. They include measures to prevent monopoly, corruption, fraud, false advertising, insider trading, and so on. More substantive policy initiatives . . . include measures designed to bolster the flow of relevant information in the market; environmental protection (to protect the interests of all of those effected by the negative impacts of market transactions on the environment); limits on inheritance (which increases the arbitrariness of success in the market); the redistribution of income and other mechanisms to prevent huge disparities in wealth and economic power (disparities which interfere with competitive markets and exclude the poor from the market); and public education to ensure the development of the intellectual capital needed to both establish an efficient market and guide government regulation (which in a democratic society depends on public opinion). As markets become increasingly global in their scope, such regulation needs to be globalized as well.

One might argue about the extent of such measures but it should be clear that they justify significant restrictions on the market. It follows that mitigated capitalism (i.e., justifiable capitalism) does not imply an unregulated market economy. To some extent, one might compare mitigated capitalism to capitalism as it exists in most capitalist economies today, for such economies often have many of the regulatory features I have already noted (among other things, this shows that mitigated capitalism can work in practice). That said, there are ways in which the mitigated capitalism I propose implies an economy which is more radically capitalist than the economies of contemporary capitalist states. This is because the governments in such states regularly intervene in the market, not in order to ensure that markets are efficient or that all market players respect the interests of those affected by market transactions (i.e., not for the reasons justified by mitigated capitalism), but in order to introduce subsidies, regulations, grants, and other advantages intended (explicitly or implicitly) to favour particular market players. In the process, they disrupt and displace the proper workings of the market, denying it its proper role in determining the production and distribution of goods and services in a capitalist economy. . . .

Consider the City of Detroit's expropriation of 'Poletown' in 1981—action it undertook in order to provide land for a GM cadillac assembly plant. Although this was the action of a municipal government it had tremendous implications for the neighbourhood, which contained some 1,400 homes, 16 churches, 144 local businesses, and a vigorous neighbourhood association which fought the move in a series of court challenges but lost in the Supreme Court. In making the move, the city favoured GM with regulatory action that was tantamount to an enormous economic subsidy. The extent of this favouritism can be better appreciated in the context of the fact that in the free market the acquisition of such land would have been impossible, for it is clear that no amount of compensation could convince the occupants to give up their homes and businesses and the more intangible roots, shared memories, relationships, and sense of place that accompanied them. . . .[4]

The mitigated capitalism I have proposed leaves no room for interventions of this sort. Rather, it rejects them on the grounds that they undermine competitive markets and in this way the efficiency that justifies free markets. Because such interventions are a frequent feature of economic activities in many contemporary capitalist economies, it follows that mitigated capitalism is, despite its commitment to regulation, committed to a very significant expansion of the free market's role in determining economic development. The capitalism I have proposed is in this way characterized by a profound commitment to the free market, although it is a commitment which expresses itself, not only in the rejection of many typical government interventions, but also in external constraints designed to ensure that the free market remains free and competitive for the sake of the common good.

## CONCLUSION

If the account of capitalism I have proposed is correct, then popular attitudes to capitalism are simplistic. Those who support capitalism tend to be characterized by an unrestrained commitment to the free market which ignores its weaknesses and naively treats it as a panacea for all social ills. Those who reject capitalism condemn it on moral grounds without recognizing its great strengths. I believe that mitigated capitalism can provide a 'middle' way which both recognizes the ways in which capitalism is superior to alternative economic systems but also recognizes that it has weaknesses that need to be constrained if capitalism is to sustain itself.

In the end the greatest barrier to a reasonable capitalism may be common prejudices for and against it. Intellectually, it may be that our greatest need is for new metaphors which allow us to see beyond the simplistic picture of capitalism that portrays the market as an unmitigated good *or* evil. We might do better to compare the unregulated market to a spoiled child who lacks discipline or a fruit tree which must be pruned regularly if it is to bear good fruit. Left to their own devices with no guiding hand to direct them, there is no reason to believe that such a child or tree will turn out well. Something similar holds of capitalism, which can bring about substantial good, but only if it is disciplined, directed, and not allowed its natural excesses. Properly constrained, capitalism is our best hope for the future. But an unconstrained capitalism is, in the long run, likely to be the cause of its own undoing.

## NOTES

1. In 'Famine, Affluence, and Morality,' *Philosophy and Public Affairs*, 1 (1972), 229–43, Peter Singer argues that famine in Africa obliges us to reduce our standard of living to that of famine victims.
2. Cragg, "Business, Globalization, and the Logic and Ethics of Corruption," 264.
3. Bookchin, quoted in Rubinoff, "Capitalism, Ethics, and Ecology: The Tyranny of the Corporate Agenda," 303.
4. See Mary Ann Glendon, *Rights Talk: The Impoverishment of Political Discourse* (New York: Free Press, 1991), 29–30.

## CASES

# CASE 1. *Baseball Economics*

In December 1981 the Baltimore Orioles Hall-of-Fame pitcher Jim Palmer gave a newspaper interview in Portland, Oregon. He was highly critical of the system of economic incentives operative in baseball. He argued that money controlled almost all decisions by management and players alike. Many players, he said, "make a lot more money than they should." He argued that the salaries are often determined through "panic" on the part of management, which plans at all cost against a situation in which star players leave and join other teams at increased salary levels. He noted that players make from $300,000 to $400,000 in their second year and sign multiyear contracts. This kind of security, he said, leads players to relax and to lose their concentration on skilled performance.

On the same day Palmer gave his interview in Portland, Baseball Commissioner Bowie Kuhn was testifying before a Congressional subcommittee on issues surrounding the costs of cable television. Kuhn described the possible introduction of massive cable television broadcasts of baseball as economically intolerable for the sport. Both gate receipts and network television revenues would decline, he held, and this would be a disaster for a sport already "treading on financial quicksand." Kuhn supported this judgment with figures to show that only nine of baseball's 26 teams had made a profit in the previous year. He argued that the aggregate loss was $25 million. He further contended that cable television would bring competing sporting events into a city without the consent or agreement of anyone in baseball management.

Ted Turner, who owned both Turner Broadcasting System (cable) and the Atlanta Braves baseball team, also testified at the same hearing as Kuhn. "If baseball is in trouble," he said, "it is because they are paying the [superstar] baseball players a million and half dollars a year. . . . There isn't one single example of a proven economic harm from cable television."

Salaries have continued to rise dramatically. A survey of New York Mets' baseball fans in 1992 indicated that most thought the salary figures outrageous and that the money should be more evenly spread across the players. In 2002, 21 years after Palmer's interview and Kuhn's testimony before Congress, players' salaries had escalated beyond what Palmer, Kuhn, or Turner could have then imagined. The New York

This case was prepared by Tom L. Beauchamp and Jeff Greene, using articles from numerous newspapers and journals.

Yankees led the league with a record-breaking payroll of $125.9 million. For the 2002 season, the average player's salary was over $4 million, with Derek Jeter at $14.6 million being the highest paid player on the Yankees (and the seventh-highest-paid player in baseball). The top six players in annual salary were Alex Rodriguez of the Texas Rangers ($22 million), Carlos Delgado of the Toronto Blue Jays ($19.4 million), Kevin J. Brown of the Los Angeles Dodgers ($15.7 million), Manny Ramirez of the Boston Red Sox ($15.4 million), and Barry Bonds of the San Francisco Giants and Sammy Sosa of the Chicago Cubs (tied for fifth place at $15 million).

With the explosion of salaries it has become harder and harder for the small market teams to compete, because the big players consistently go for big money. However, in 1994 the Montreal Expos proved, at least for one season, that in some cases more than just money matters. Their $18.6 million payroll was the second lowest in the league, yet when the season ended (because of a strike), they were six games ahead of everyone in the National League, including the Atlanta Braves. However, their dream season would be short-lived because they needed approximately $30 million merely to keep the team together, according to fair market value. Since the club could not even come close to the $30 million figure, it was inevitable that it would lose many of its best players; and it did. "I think that the world realizes that our market cannot support that sort of payroll," said Bill Stoneman, Expos' vice president of baseball operations at the time. "We'd like to re-sign all of our players, but we'd like to be in business a year from now."

Montreal's problem is not unique. Pittsburgh had to break up one of the National League's best teams in the 1990s, and San Diego had to dump its best talent just as the club seemed poised to become a serious contender. It now seems clear that if some sort of revenue sharing does not come into effect, the small market teams will not be able to compete on equal terms within the league.

### Questions

1. Does a team like the New York Yankees have an obligation to share some of their revenues with other teams that have a weaker economic base?
2. Do Bowie Kuhn's comments reflect a libertarian or a utilitarian theory of justice?
3. If Peter Singer's proposals (in this chapter) were followed, what would be the obligations of major league baseball players to help the poor both within and outside their own country?

## CASE 2. *Nike's Suppliers in Vietnam*

Following allegations of worker abuse, an investigation was launched in 1998 of Nike practices in subcontracted factories in Vietnam. This investigation created a public relations problem for the American manufacturer of athletic apparel. The report found that by not directly running the factories where its products were being made, Nike had little direct control over how employees were treated.

The report focused on Nike subcontracted factories in and around Ho Chi Minh City. It found local supervisors using abusive and

This case was written by Sasha Lyutse. Basic sources were: "*The Living Wage Project to Brief Members of Congress on Nike Labor Abuses,*" PR Newswire Association, Inc., Copyright 2001, April 3, 2001; "*Labor-rights Group: Nike, Knight not Living up to 1998 Promises,*" The Associated Press State & Local Wire, May 16, 2001; and "*Nike battles Labour Charges U.S. Firm makes Changes after Alleged Worker Abuses in Vietnam,*" Toronto Star Newspapers, Ltd., Copyright 1998, April 2, 1998.

humiliating practices to punish Vietnamese workers. Nike insisted that it did not tolerate abuse and required its manufacturers to take "immediate and effective measures to deal with it." A Nike training manager, the company said, works with subcontractors on sexual harassment, physical and verbal abuse, as well as on listening skills. The report found that Nike had "a fine code of conduct," but that its local contractors often violated it.

In 1998 Nike employees at the Sam Yang factory, just outside Ho Chi Minh City, were paid $1.84 a day. Their average monthly salary was $48— slightly better than Vietnam's $45 minimum wage for this region. With this salary, Nike workers could meet needs for food and shelter, but little else. In a 1998 survey, however, Nike suppliers were found to be paying competitive wages—no worse and no better than those paid by other foreign shoemakers.

Phillip Knight, founder of Nike's $9 billion sports-apparel empire, signs sports superstars to multimillion dollar contracts to advertise Nike sneakers that sometimes sell for $100 or more on the American market. A pair of Nike sneakers is unattainable for a worker at the Sam Yang factory, who works six days a week and makes roughly $600 a year, half the average income in Ho Chi Minh City, but about four times the annual earnings in more remote rural regions of Vietnam.

In 1999 Nike responded to mounting pressures by creating a labor monitoring department and translated its code of conduct into 11 languages so that more workers could read it. At the Sam Yang factory the local owners issued a 10-point "action plan" based on many of the 1998 report's recommendations. They held a union election, signed a labor contract with workers, and improved working conditions. The factory also got a new manager, increased trainees' wages and cut overtime. Most workers got a 5 percent raise, which came to about 8 cents more a day.

However, a 2001 report by the Global Alliance, an initiative sponsored by Nike in response to persistent criticism, documented proof of continued abusive labor practices in Southeast Asia, including physical, verbal and sexual abuse. According to the report, 96 percent of workers stated that they did not make enough money to meet their basic needs.

In its early days, before costs escalated and orders shifted to lowercost suppliers in Taiwan and South Korea, Nike imported all of its shoes from Japan. Soon, even Taiwan and South Korea became expensive, and suppliers moved their factories to China and Indonesia. In its global search for low-cost labor, Nike found Vietnam. By 1998, one out of every 10 pairs of Nike shoes came from subcontractors in Vietnam.

Vietnam is one of Southeast Asia's poorest countries. It has an official rural unemployment of about 27 percent in some regions. It aggressively seeks foreign investment to create jobs and bring manufacturing expertise. However, unlike those countries that turn a blind eye to worker abuses by overseas employers, Vietnam pays close attention to foreign investors' behavior and has some of the region's toughest laws aimed at protecting workers; it ensures a minimum wage, sets overtime limits, permits strikes, etc.

At the same time, Vietnamese government officials sometimes appear to have divided priorities. They feel that they are duty-bound to defend workers (which union leaders say is their primary responsibility), but they also feel that they must accommodate investment planners who want trade unions to back off and not scare away desperately needed foreign investments.

In 1998 Nike employed more workers than any other foreign business in Vietnam (through its five Nike-aligned shoe factories). At the time, shipments of Nike shoes accounted for 5 percent of Vietnam's total exports. If Nike were to pull out of Vietnam, 35,000 Vietnamese would be out of work.

## Questions

1. Is an average monthly salary of $48 morally indefensible, or is such a judgment relative to the expectations of a given society?
2. Are there issues of economic justice in this case, or are prices always fair when set in competitive markets?
3. If Nike were to close its factories and leave Vietnam for a country with a lower minimum wage, would this decision be morally indefensible?

# CASE 3. *Sapora's Patriarchical Society*

Sapora, a large Pacific Rim island, has for years been a leading industrial, commercial, and financial center with a flourishing market and growing trade. GlobeCom, an American telecommunications firm long established in Sapora, has decided to expand its Sapora branch and the volume of business it does with local Saporan companies. Ties with local businesses have flourished quickly, and an extremely profitable business relationship has developed. Sapora has rapidly become a major training ground for GlobeCom managers, and successful tenure in Sapora is viewed as a key step on the way to the top of GlobeCom.

Sapora, however, is a traditionally patriarchal society, and its businessmen at the executive level are just that: men. Female executives in the workplace are a rarity, and there is seldom, if ever, a managerial track available to women. Women are often given positions largely designed to make the office more comfortable, such as serving tea and performing basic services. Women are discouraged from aiming at executive positions and are not invited to after-work social functions that play a vital role in successful employee and corporate bonding—an entrenched aspect of Sapora's business culture. The overwhelmingly male majority of Saporan customers, suppliers, and government officials are also uncomfortable doing business with foreign women, preferring to work with men.

Although GlobeCom abides by strict U.S. gender equality laws in its American branches, its human resource managers who send executives abroad hesitate to violate the unwritten laws and cultural mores of Sapora. They have found over time that female managers working in Sapora tend to be less successful than males; they have a more difficult time dealing with local businesses and are generally offered fewer business opportunities than their male counterparts. Resource managers, who are responsible for the efficacy of the GlobeCom workforce, both domestically and abroad, are sending fewer and fewer woman to fill open posts in Sapora.

The American female's inability to obtain the necessary firsthand experience in dealing with Saporan businesses has become a career handicap. Female employees have found that while in the beginning they move up the company ranks fairly easily in GlobeCom's American branches, they eventually hit a career ceiling because they lack the formative, career-building experience their male counterparts receive in Sapora. It would be difficult, however, to persuade GlobeCom that female managers can succeed in Sapora's culture, which in many subtle and overt ways discourages gender equality.

This case was written by Sasha Lyutse. Sapora is fictional, but the case is based in an existing country that is a powerful player in international markets.

### Questions

1. Should GlobeCom do business in a country with a patriarchical society? In responding, imagine that GlobeCom could not survive if it stopped doing business in Sapora.
2. Assuming that GlobeCom's female employees are unable to obtain the necessary experience and suffer a career disadvantage because of the situation in Sapora, should the company use some form of handicap (for example, a bonus) to offset the career handicap? Would such a handicap be demeaning?
3. What should U.S. gender equality look like in light of GlobeCom's problem?

## CASE 4. *CEO Compensation at Qwest*

In April 2002, despite posting a net loss of $4 billion for the previous year and being strained by a $25 billion debt, Qwest Communications awarded its CEO, Joseph Nacchio, a yearly compensation and benefits package of $217.3 million, including pay and potential gains from stock option grants. At the time of this writing, Qwest shares were 83 percent off their 52-week high.

In 2001 Nacchio received a salary of almost $1.2 million, a 27 percent increase over 2000, but his bonus dropped 32 percent to $1.5 million. In addition, he obtained at least $74.5 million from exercising stock options and long-term incentive pay of $24.4 million. Other compensation of $229,705 included a $136,745 allocation for use of corporate aircraft. However, stock options, with a potential future value of $115.6 million, became worthless by September 2002, according to the Investor Responsibility Research Center, since Qwest's share price dropped lower that the $16.81 exercise price of the options. So, as of September 2002, the actual worth of the compensation and benefits package for the year was approximately $101.7 million.

According to the Investor Responsibility Research Center, this was one of the top pay packages for 2001, based on an analysis of CEO pay at 267 companies with revenue of $1 billion or more. A Qwest spokesperson, however, said that Nacchio's pay is on a scale with other firms trying to retain officers and that Qwest has outperformed many competitors. (See *USA TODAY*, April 10, 2002.)

In 2002, despite a 30-month-long stock market slump, there appeared to remain a wide disjuncture between CEO pay and company performance. There was at the time little evidence of substantial CEO-pay-package cuts even in companies that performed poorly. Executive salaries generally rose, despite an economic climate of low stock prices and greater scrutiny of directors and executives as a result of corporate financial and fraud scandals. While average worker salaries were rising just above 3.6 percent, many CEOs were receiving double-digit salary increases, bonuses, stock option grants potentially worth millions, and benefits such as company-owned apartments. (See *USA TODAY*, September 30, 2002.)

### Questions

1. Is Joseph Nacchio's yearly compensation and benefits package of $217.3 million fair, unfair, or neither fair nor unfair?
2. As a matter of fairness, should a CEO's pay be reduced when: (a) other employees are

This case was written by Sasha Lyutse.

forced to take a reduction or (b) when the company's profit margin is lower than anticipated under the society's economic condition?

3. As a matter of fairness, should the salaries of American CEOs be substantially reduced below their present level? If so, who should be authorized to lower the salary?

## CASE 5. *Cocaine at the Fortune-500 Level*

Roberto, a pure libertarian in moral and political philosophy, is deeply impressed by his reading of Robert Nozick's account of justice. He lives in Los Angeles and teaches philosophy at a local university. Roberto is also a frequent user of cocaine, which he enjoys immensely and provides to friends at parties. Neither he nor any of his close friends is addicted. Over the years Roberto has become tired of teaching philosophy and now has an opportunity, through old friends who live in Peru, to become a middleman in the cocaine business. Although he is disturbed about the effects cocaine has in some persons, he has never witnessed these effects firsthand. He is giving his friends' business offer serious consideration.

Roberto's research has told him the following: Selling cocaine is a $35 billion plus industry. Although he is interested primarily in a Peruvian connection, his research has shown conclusively that the Colombian cartel alone is large enough to place it among the Fortune 500 corporations. Cocaine production in Peru and Bolivia in 1995 represented about 90 percent of the world's cocaine base; the remaining 10 percent was produced in Columbia (*Journal of Inter-American and World Affairs, 1997*). Cocaine is Latin America's second largest export, accounting for 3–4 percent of the GDP of Peru and Bolivia, and up to 8 percent of that of Columbia. The cocaine industry employs close to half a million people in the Andean region alone. Columbian coca cultivation rose 11 percent in 2000.

Former Peruvian President Alan Garcia once described cocaine as Latin America's "only successful multinational." It can be and has been analyzed in traditional business categories, with its own entrepreneurs, chemists, laboratories, employment agencies, small organizations, distribution systems, market giants, growth phases, and so forth. Cocaine's profit margins have narrowed in some markets, while expanding in others. It often seeks new markets in order to expand its product line. For example, in the mid-1980s "crack," a potent form of smoked cocaine, was moved heavily into new markets in Europe. Between the mid-1960s and the late 1990s the demand for cocaine grew dramatically (weathering some up and down markets) because of successful supply and marketing. Middlemen in Miami and Los Angeles were established to increase already abundant profits. Heavy investments were made in airplanes, efficient modes of production, training managers, and regular schedules of distribution. In the late 1980s there was a downturn in cocaine consumption after the deaths of two prominent athletes. In the early 1990s the market recovered slightly before slipping again in the mid-1990s. However, cocaine remains an enormously powerful industry in many countries.

Roberto sees the cocaine industry as not being subject to taxes, tariffs, or government regulations other than those pertaining to its illegality. It is a pure form of the free market

This case was prepared by Tom L. Beauchamp and updated by Jeff Greene and Sasha Lyutse; it relies in part on accounts in *The Wall Street Journal* and *The Economist.*

in which supply and demand control transactions. This fact about the business appeals to Roberto, as it seems perfectly suited to his libertarian views. He is well aware that there are severe problems of coercion and violence in some parts of the industry, but he is certain that the wealthy clientele whom he would supply in Los Angeles would neither abuse the drug nor redistribute it to others who might be harmed. Roberto is confident that his Peruvian associates are honorable and that he can escape problems of violence, coercion, and abusive marketing. However, he has just read a newspaper story that cocaine-use emergencies—especially those involving cocaine-induced heart attacks—have tripled in the last five years. It is only this fact that has given him pause before deciding to enter the cocaine business. He views these health emergencies as unfortunate but not unfair outcomes of the business. Therefore, it is his humanity and not his theory of justice that gives him pause.

### Questions

1. Would a libertarian—such as Roberto—say that the cocaine business is not unfair so long as no coercion is involved and the system is a pure function of supply and demand?
2. Does justice demand that cocaine be outlawed, or is this not a matter of justice at all? Are questions of justice even meaningful when the activity is beyond the boundaries of law?
3. Is the distinction Roberto draws between what is unfortunate and what is unfair relevant to a decision about whether an activity is just?

## CASE 6. *Covering the Costs of Health Care*

Medicare and Medicaid were passed into law in the United States to provide coverage for health care costs in populations that could not afford adequate coverage, especially the elderly, poor, and disabled. Then, as now, health care technology produced by major corporations was rapidly being developed and costs were skyrocketing. In 1994, $140 billion was spent in Medicare. Current trends show little letup in this explosion of costs. In 1994 Medicare and Medicaid comprised 16.4 percent of the total federal budget. By 2006 this figure is expected to balloon to approximately 10 percent higher (around 26.4 percent). For U.S. corporations and individuals, health care has become a burdensome expense.

With over 40 million Americans uninsured, health care costs have been under intense study by many politicians and agencies. In an effort to limit future increases in physician costs, the Omnibus Budget Reconciliation Act of 1989 created a Medicare Fee Schedule that affected 34.7 million U.S. citizens. This schedule attempts to redistribute payments across specialties in medicine and geographic areas of the country. The legislation required that this restructuring be phased in over a five-year period from 1992 to 1996, but affected very few parties needing coverage. In passing the legislation, members of Congress agreed that Medicare's former payment policies fueled unacceptable increases in expenditure for health care services. Neither the old legislation nor the new covers the kind of catastrophic illness that can wipe out a family's assets and put a family in lifetime debt.

This case was prepared by Tom L. Beauchamp and Jeff Greene.

It has been demonstrated that there is substantial variation across the United States in payment rates for services. Urban, specialist, and in-patient services are typically much higher than rural, generalist, and ambulatory services. Surgeons make more money than those in other specialties. It has been widely agreed that these differentials are independent of quality of services, depending more on urban location, the high costs of specialists, and the like. A large supply of physicians in a single location does not stimulate competition and drive prices down; instead, higher fees for physician services tend to be the norm. Social scientists who have studied the changes made in the Omnibus Budget Reconciliation Act of 1989 and their impact throughout the 1990s predict that large redistributions of Medicare payments among specialties will occur, thus changing longstanding patterns in physicians' salaries.

When Bill Clinton came into office, he promised major reforms in the health care system. The Clinton plan, headed by first lady Hillary Clinton, attempted to steer the nation toward serious health care reform. The goal was to eliminate waste and inflated prices, and to give health care access to all—so-called universal access. However, with many of the economic consequences falling on the business community, the Clinton plan met strong criticism. Private interests spent over $300 million, and Republicans fought hard to kill the bill—and they succeeded.

Many believed that the Clinton plan did not adequately handle the primary reason for continued increases in health care costs, namely advances in technology that push the growth of costs in the health care industry much higher than costs in the rest of the economy. Consider a typical case, involving a man named Toney Kincard. For 10 years he was tortured by over 600 seizures a week. Kincard was unable to carry on a conversation, eat dinner with his family, or even shower unsupervised. Despite thousands of dollars spent in drug therapy, he lost both his job and his driver's license. In 1989 he became the second person to try a new product, the Vogus Nerve Stimulator. Since his $50,000 outlay to receive this product, he has been seizure-free and says, "The stimulator was the best thing that happened to my life. It was worth everything it cost."

There is little doubt that such expensive technology is invaluable for improving the lives of many people. However, these products will continue to drive up the price of health care for everyone. Experts believe that advances in molecular biology and genetic therapy, among many other technologies, will continue in the twenty-first century to propel the cost of health care well beyond what government or private insurance can cover. President George W. Bush continued in his adminstration to take the line—directly opposed to that of Clinton—that government should not increase its commitment to health care coverage. Bush saw the issues as fundamentally ones of the free market.

## Questions

1. Is a nation obligated to provide quality health care for the elderly or any other person who otherwise could not afford care? Is the obligation unrelated to the ability to pay?
2. Should health care be distributed purely on a free-market basis? Should everyone have access to even the highest priced procedures?
3. Is Medicare justifiable on either utilitarian or egalitarian premises of justice? Could a libertarian possibly support Medicare?
4. Would a communitarian approve of Medicare even if he or she did not consider the system sufficiently comprehensive? Are libertarians and communitarians necessarily in opposition on the question of state-supported systems of health care coverage?

## Suggested Supplementary Readings


*Concepts and Principles of Justice*

BEAUCHAMP, TOM L. *Philosophical Ethics.* 3rd ed. New York: McGraw-Hill, 2001. Chaps. 8–9.

DEGEORGE, RICHARD T. "International Business Ethics." *Business Ethics Quarterly,* 4 (1994): 1–9.

FEINBERG, JOEL. "Justice and Personal Desert." In *Nomos 6: Justice,* edited by Carl J. Friedrich and John W. Chapman. New York: Atherton Press, 1963.

KIPNIS, KENNETH, and DIANA T. MEYERS. *Economic Justice.* Totowa, NJ: Rowman and Allanheld, 1985.

KYMLICKA, WILL, Ed. *Justice in Political Philosophy: Schools of Thought in Politics.* Two vols. Brookfield, VT: Ashgate, 1992.

MILLER, RICHARD. *Moral Differences: Truth, Justice, and Conscience in a World of Conflict.* Princeton: Princeton University Press, 1992.

SEN, AMARTYA. "Economics, Business Principles and Moral Sentiments." *Business Ethics Quarterly,* 7 (1997): 5–15.

STERBA, JAMES P. *Justice for Here and Now.* New York: Cambridge University Press, 1998.

*Egalitarian Theories*

ARNESON, RICHARD J., "Egalitarianism and Responsibility." *Journal of Ethics* 3 (1999): 225–47.

BARRY, BRIAN. *Theories of Justice.* Berkeley: University of California Press, 1989.

CHRISTMAN, JOHN P. *The Myth of Property: Toward an Egalitarian Theory of Ownership.* New York: Oxford University Press, 1994.

COHEN, G. A. "Where the Action Is: in the Site of Distributive Justice." *Philosophy and Public Affairs,* 26 (1997): 3–30.

———. "Self-Ownership, Freedom, and Equality," *Canadian Journal of Philosophy* (2002): 36–67.

DANIELS, NORMAN. *Justice and Justification: Reflective Equilibrium in Theory and Practice.* New York: Cambridge University Press, 1997.

———. Ed. *Reading Rawls: Critical Studies of a Theory of Justice.* New York: Basic Books, 1975.

DANIELS, NORMAN, DONALD W. LIGHT, and RONALD L. CAPLAN. *Benchmarks of Fairness for Health Care Reform.* New York: Oxford University Press, 1996.

NAGEL, THOMAS. "Equality." In *Mortal Questions.* Cambridge, England: Cambridge University Press, 1979.

OKIN, SUSAN. *Justice, Gender, and the Family.* New York: Basic Books, 1989.

POGGE, THOMAS W. "An Egalitarian Law of Peoples." *Philosophy and Public Affairs,* 23 (Summer 1994): 195–224.

POGGE, THOMAS W. *Realizing Rawls.* Ithaca, NY: Cornell University Press, 1991.

POJMAN, LOUIS, and ROBERT WESTMORELAND, Eds. *Equality: Selected Readings.* New York: Oxford University Press, 1997.

POWERS, MADISON, and FADEN, RUTH. "Inequalities in Health, Inequalities in Health Care: Four Generations of Discussion about Justice and Cost-Effectiveness Analysis." *Kennedy Institute of Ethics Journal,* 10 (June 2000), 109–27.

ROEMER, JOHN E. "Egalitarianism Against the Veil of Ignorance." *Journal of Philosophy,* 99 (April 2002): 167–84.

ROEMER, JOHN E. *Theories of Distributive Justice.* Cambridge, MA: Harvard University Press, 1996.

SEN, AMARTYA. *Economic Inequality.* Oxford: Clarendon Press, 1997.

STARK, ANDREW. "Beyond Choice: Rethinking the Post-Rawlsian Debate Over Egalitarian Justice." *Political Theory: An International Journal of Political Philosophy,* 30 (Fall 2002): 36–67.

*Libertarian Theories*

BOAZ, DAVID. *The Libertarian Reader: Classic and Contemporary Readings.* New York: The Free Press, 1997.

ENGELHARDT, H. TRISTRAM, JR. *The Foundations of Bioethics.* 2nd ed. New York: Oxford University Press, 1996.

EPSTEIN, RICHARD. *Mortal Peril: Our Inalienable Right to Health Care?* Reading, MA: Addison-Wesley, 1997.

FRIED, BARBARA. "Wilt Chamberlain Revisited: Nozick's 'Justice in Transfer' and the Problem of Market-Based Distribution." *Philosophy and Public Affairs,* 24 (1995): 226–45.

FRIEDMAN, MILTON. *Capitalism and Freedom.* Chicago: University of Chicago Press, 1962.

HAYEK, FRIEDRICH. *The Constitution of Liberty.* Chicago: University of Chicago Press, 1960.

———. *Individualism and Economic Order.* Chicago: University of Chicago Press, 1948.

———. *The Mirage of Social Justice.* Vol. 2 (*Law, Legislation, and Liberty*). Chicago: University of Chicago Press, 1976.

MACK, ERIC. "Libertarianism Untamed." *Journal of Social Philosophy* (Winter 1991): 64–72.

———. "Self-Ownership and the Right of Property." *Monist* (October 1990): 519–43.

MACHAN, TIBOR R., and DOUGLAS B. RASMUSSEN, Eds. *Liberty for the Twenty-First Century: Contemporary Libertarian Thought.* Lanham, MD: Rowman and Littlefield, 1995.

PAUL JEFFREY, Ed. *Reading Nozick.* Totowa, NJ: Rowman and Littlefield, 1981.

PERRY, STEPHEN R. "Libertarianism, Entitlement, and Responsibility." *Philosophy and Public Affairs,* 26 (1997): 351–96.

*Utilitarian Theories*

ALLISON, LINCOLN, Ed. *The Utilitarian Response: Essays in the Contemporary Viability of Utilitarian Political Philosophy.* London: Sage, 1990.

FREY, R. G., Ed. *Utility and Rights.* Minneapolis: University of Minnesota Press, 1984.

GOLDMAN, ALAN H. "Business Ethics: Profits, Utilities, and Moral Rights." *Philosophy and Public Affairs,* 9 (1980): 260–86.

GOOLD, SUSAN D. "Allocating Health Care: Cost-Utility Analysis, Informed Democratic Decision Making, or the Veil of Ignorance?" *Journal of Health Politics, Policy, and Law,* 21 (1996), 69–98.

GRIFFIN, JAMES. "Modern Utilitarianism." *Revue Internationale de Philosophie,* 36 (1982): 331–75.

———. *Well-Being: Its Meaning, Measurement, and Importance.* Oxford, England: Clarendon Press, 1986.

HARDIN, RUSSELL. *Morality within the Limits of Reason.* Chicago: University of Chicago Press, 1988.

HARSANYI, JOHN C. "Equality, Responsibility, and Justice as Seen from a Utilitarian Perspective." *Theory and Decision,* 31 (1991): 141–58.

———. "Rule Utilitarianism, Equality, and Justice." *Social Philosophy and Policy,* 2 (1985): 115–27.

SEN, AMARTYA, and BERNARD WILLIAMS, Eds. *Utilitarianism and Beyond.* Cambridge, England: Cambridge University Press, 1982.

*Communitarian Theories*

AVINERI, SHLOMO, and AVNER DE-SHALIT, Eds. *Communitarianism and Individualism.* Oxford, England: Oxford University Press, 1992.

BELL, DANIEL A. *Communitarianism and Its Critics.* Oxford, England: Clarendon Press, 1993.

BUCHANAN, ALLEN. "Assessing the Communitarian Critique of Liberalism." *Ethics,* 99 (1989).

FREEDEN, MICHAEL. "Human Rights and Welfare: A Communitarian View." *Ethics,* 100 (1990).

GUTMANN, AMY. "Communitarian Critics of Liberalism." *Philosophy and Public Affairs,* 14 (1985).

KYMLICKA, WILL. "Communitarianism, Liberalism and Superliberalism." *Critical Review,* 8 (Spring 1994): 263–84.

———. *Liberalism, Community, and Culture.* Oxford, England: Clarendon Press, 1989.

MACINTYRE, ALASDAIR. *Whose Justice? Which Rationality?* Notre Dame, IN: Notre Dame University Press, 1988.

PAUL, JEFFREY, and FRED D. MILLER. "Communitarian and Liberal Theories of the Good." *Review of Metaphysics,* 43 (1990): 803–30.

RASMUSSEN, DAVID, Ed. *Universalism vs. Communitarianism: Contemporary Debates in Ethics.* Cambridge, MA: MIT Press, 1990.

ROSENBLUM, NANCY L., Ed. *Liberalism and the Moral Life.* Cambridge, MA: Harvard University Press, 1989.

SANDEL, MICHAEL J. *Democracy's Discontent: America in Search of a Public Philosophy.* Cambridge, MA: Harvard University Press, 1996.

WALZER, MICHAEL. "The Communitarian Critique of Liberalism." *Political Theory,* 18 (1990).

*Capitalism, International Markets, and Social Policy*

ANDERSON, ELIZABETH, "The Ethical Limitations of the Market," *Economics and Philosophy* (1990).

ARNESON, RICHARD J., "Is Socialism Dead? A Comment in Market Socialism and Basic Income Capitalism," *Ethics*, 102 (April 1992): 485–511.

ATTFIELD, ROBIN, and BARRY WILKINS, Eds. *International Justice and the Third World.* New York: Routledge, 1992.

BERGER, PETER. *The Capitalist Revolution.* New York: Basic Books, Inc., Publishers, 1986, Chap. 2.

BOWIE, NORMAN. "Fair Markets." *Journal of Business Ethics*, 7 (1988).

BUCHANAN, ALLEN. *Ethics, Efficiency and the Market.* Totowa, NJ: Rowman and Allanheld, 1985.

COPP, DAVID. "The Right to an Adequate Standard of Living: Justice, Autonomy, and the Basic Needs." *Social Philosophy and Policy*, 9 (Winter 1992): 231–61.

HEATH, EUGENE. *Morality and The Market: Ethics and Virtue in the Conduct of Business.* New York: McGraw-Hill, 2002.

JACKSON, KEVIN T. "Global Distributive Justice and the Corporate Duty to Aid." *Journal of Business Ethics*, 12 (1993): 547–52.

LUPER-FOY, STEVEN. "Justice and Natural Resources." *Environmental Values*, 1 (Spring 1992): 47–64.

———. *Problems of International Justice.* Boulder, CO: Westview Press, 1988.

PRATT, CORNELIUS B. "Multinational Corporate Social Policy Process for Ethical Responsibility in Sub-Saharan Africa." *Journal of Business Ethics*, 10 (July 1991): 527–41.

WERHANE, PATRICIA H. "Exporting Mental Models: Global Capitalism in the 21st Century," *Business Ethics Quarterly*, 10 (January 2000): 353–62.